The Taylor, *Economics,* Fifth Edition website provides a wealth of learning and review opportunities for students. Connect to the site via **college.hmco.com/pic/taylor5e** to review flashcards, take practice tests, see applications of economic concepts to current events, link to useful research sites, and explore topics in more depth.

Economics

About the Author

John B. Taylor is one of the field's most inspiring teachers. As the Raymond Professor of Economics at Stanford University, his distinctive instructional methods have made him a legend among introductory economics students and have won him both the Hoagland and Rhodes prizes for teaching excellence. As described by the *Wall Street Journal,* Taylor's "sober appearance . . . belies a somewhat zany teaching style." Few of his students forget how he first illustrated a shift of the demand curve (by dressing up as a California raisin and dancing to "Heard It Through the Grapevine"), or how he proved that the supply and demand model actually works (by having student buyers and sellers call out live bids to him in the classroom). It is this gift for clear explanations and memorable illustrations that makes his textbook so useful to students around the country.

Professor Taylor is also widely recognized for his research on the foundations of modern monetary theory and policy. One of his well-known research contributions is a rule—now widely called the Taylor Rule—used at central banks around the world. *U.S. News and World Report* wrote about his rule, "Amaze Your Friends! Predict the Fed's Next Move!" His latest research focuses on international monetary policy.

Taylor has had an active career in public service, recently completing a four-year stint as the head of the International Affairs division at the United States Treasury, where he had responsibility for currency policy, international debt, and oversight of the International Monetary Fund and the World Bank and worked closely with leaders and policymakers from countries throughout the world. He has also served as economic adviser to the governor of his state (California), to the U.S. Congressional Budget Office, and to the President of the United States and has served on several boards and as a consultant to private industry.

Professor Taylor began his career at Princeton, where he graduated with highest honors in economics. He then received his Ph.D. from Stanford and taught at Columbia, Yale, and Princeton before returning to Stanford.

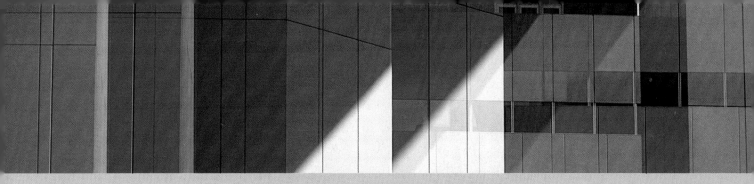

Economics

FIFTH EDITION

John B. Taylor

Houghton Mifflin Company
Boston   New York

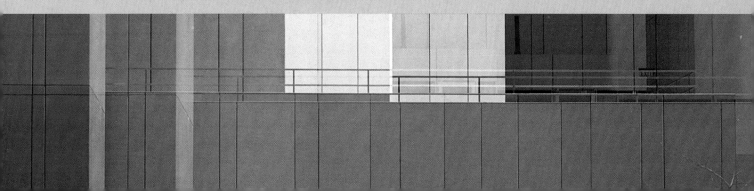

Publisher: George Hoffman
Senior Sponsoring Editor: Ann West
Development Editor: Jessica Carlisle
Editorial Associate: Alison McGonagle
Senior Project Editor: Carol Merrigan
Editorial Assistants: Eric Moore, Anthony D'Aries
Art and Design Manager: Gary Crespo
Composition Buyer: Chuck Dutton
Senior Photo Editor: Jennifer Meyer Dare
Manufacturing Buyer: Florence Cadran
Marketing Manager: Mike Schenk
Marketing Associate: Kathleen Mellon

Cover image: © Harold Burch, Harold Burch Design, NYC

Printed in the U.S.A.

Library of Congress Control Number: 2005937209

Instructor's Exam Copy:
ISBN 13: 978-0-618-73244-9
ISBN 10: 0-618-73244-6

For orders, use Student Text ISBNs:
ISBN 13: 978-0-618-64085-0
ISBN 10: 0-618-64085-1

1 2 3 4 5 6 7 8 9-VH-09 08 07 06

Brief Contents

Contents

| PART 2 | **Principles of Microeconomics** 110 |

PART 3 | **The Economics of the Firm**

Chapter 16 Physical Capital and Financial Markets 424

PART 5   Principles of Macroeconomics 456

Chapter 17   Macroeconomics: The Big Picture 458

Chapter 25   Using the Economic Fluctuations Model   656

PART 7   # Trade and Global Markets 720

Preface

My goal in writing this book has been to present modern economics in a form that is intuitive, relevant, and memorable to students who have had no prior exposure to the subject. I have been gratified by the positive responses to the first four editions that I've received from economists who teach introductory economics. But most rewarding for me have been the kind thank-yous from students—frequently by email from colleges around the country—for the clarity of the presentation and for the one-on-one teacher-student focus of the writing. When I write, I often imagine that I am talking with one of these students in my office.

Standing on the Shoulders of Giants

When I took the introductory economics course in college in the 1960s, I found both the course and the textbook (Paul Samuelson's) fascinating. People called 1960s-vintage economics the "new economics," because many new ideas, including those put forth by John Maynard Keynes, were being applied for the first time in public policy. But during the 1970s, the 1980s, the 1990s, and the early 2000s, economics underwent another tremendous wave of change. Now, at the beginning of the twenty-first century, economics places much greater emphasis on incentives, expectations, long-run fundamentals, individual experiences, institutions, and the importance of stable, predictable economic policies. These new ideas are of great relevance to real-world economic policy and confirm to students that economic ideas do indeed affect people's lives.

The world economy has also changed radically in recent years. Following two back-to-back record-breaking expansions, the U.S. economy went into a short recession in 2001—one of the shortest recessions on record. This is still a challenging time for the world economy, and yet there are many reasons to be optimistic. Market economies are now the preferred choice of virtually all countries around the world. The two most populous countries of the world, India and China, have opened up their economies and are experiencing rapid economic growth. Billions of people are linked together through international trade in this "new economy." With these changes, economics is now more fascinating and more relevant than ever.

In revising the fourth edition, I wanted to give these changes a prominent, clearly explained place within the basic tradition of economics upon which they stand. I emphasize the central ideas of economics: that people make purposeful choices with scarce resources and interact with other people when they make these choices. I have added more examples that resonate with today's students to make these choices clear. I demonstrate how a market economy works and explain why markets are efficient when incentives are right and inefficient when incentives are wrong. I stress long-run fundamentals, but I discuss real-world public policy issues where the short run matters, too. Big policy questions that are being debated by economists and other policymakers today—such as the arguments for and against universal health-care coverage or how social security should be reformed—receive special attention in new Point-Counterpoint boxes, which end each major text part.

I believe that the fifth edition has achieved the right mix of old and new. I know from experience that its "newness" and the knowledge that the ideas are actually used in practice make economics more interesting to students, thereby making learning economics easier.

Changes to the Fifth Edition

Many of this text's adopters have commented on how much they and their students enjoy reading the book and appreciate the graphs with their yellow "conversation boxes," the real-world examples, and the modern approach to economic policy. With this revision, I have attempted to strengthen these features by replacing and adding new examples where appropriate, to reflect the latest trends and policy decision points in the world's economy. I have also updated and replaced several of the case studies and have revised or replaced many chapter-opening vignettes to keep the "drama" alive. In addition, I've added many new examples of economic concepts covered in the "Economics in Action" and "Reading the News About . . ." boxes, which now include topics as diverse as elasticities for cars and movies, supply shifts caused by natural disasters, and recent Fed decisions. There are seven new Point-Counterpoint boxes, one at the end of each text part. These essays summarize the economic debates over current policy issues, giving students an opportunity to apply what they have learned in the previous chapters. By considering the opposing sides on such questions as, "Do individuals always make rational decisions?" or "Is outsourcing bad for the United States?" students are encouraged to weigh in with their opinions—backed by clear economic arguments.

Content Changes

A detailed account of the chapter-by-chapter changes in the text can be found in the Transition Guide available in the Instructor's Resource Manual or on the book's web site. Here are just a few highlights:

- In Chapter 2, data on U.S. health-care spending over the last 15 years have been updated through 2004, revealing that spending on health care has increased faster than the U.S. economy in recent years. The data here are used to show how economics explains economic events—and how it can be used to try to predict events in the future and/or make recommendations for policy.

- Chapter 3 contains many new real-life examples to illustrate the determinants of demand and supply. It also features a new Case Study that looks closely at gasoline price increases in 2004 and 2005, and a new "Reading the News About . . ." box focused on oil price increases. Material on elasticity that was formerly included at the end of this chapter has been moved to Chapter 4.

- Chapter 4, "Elasticity and Its Uses," now provides a self-contained examination of elasticity and all relevant applications, including a new section on cross-price elasticity.

- Chapter 6, "The Supply Curve and the Behavior of Firms," begins with a new opening vignette about the entrepreneur who first began producing patriotic ribbon magnets for cars.

- In Chapter 11, "Product Differentiation, Monopolistic Competition, and Oligopoly," *convenience* has been added to the discussion of sources of product differentiation, and a new "Reading the News About . . ." box looks at video rentals as an example of oligopoly.

- Tax rate data and examples have been updated in Chapter 14, "Taxes, Transfers, and Income Distribution."

- The revised macroeconomics chapters continue to improve on the new approach to teaching modern macroeconomics that was introduced with the first edition. That approach starts with long-run fundamentals about unemployment, economic growth, and the composition of spending. It stresses that the United States is part of the world economy. It shows how the Fed's decisions about the interest rate are intended both to keep inflation under control and to prevent or mitigate recessions. The 2001 recession has provided some interesting new data to explore in this regard, and key economic data have been updated throughout these chapters.

- Chapter 17, "Macroeconomics: The Big Picture," updates the macroeconomic impact of September 11 and the discussion of the 2001 recession and rising unemployment with new data and figures.

- In Chapter 18, "Measuring the Product, Income, and Spending of Nations," the discussion of savings for different entities (individual and national) has been simplified, with less focus on the $S - I = X$ equation.

- A new "Reading the News About . . ." box in Chapter 26, "Fiscal Policy," shifts the focus from budget surpluses back to budget deficits, reflecting the recent reversal of the government's budget situation from deficit to surplus and back again. The discussion of international trade in Chapter 30, "International Trade Policy," has been updated to include current trade policies, and a case study on tariff policy has been added.

- Chapter 31 is now titled "Transition Economies," reflecting increased emphasis on the process of transition (and results) for formerly command economies moving to market systems.

A Brief Tour

Economics is designed for a two-term course. Recognizing that teachers use a great variety of sequences and syllabi, the text allows for alternative plans of coverage. Furthermore, the text is also available in two self-contained volumes, *Principles of Microeconomics* and *Principles of Macroeconomics*.

The text provides a complete, self-contained analysis of competitive markets in the first seven chapters (Parts 1 and 2), before going on to develop more difficult concepts, such as long-run versus short-run cost curves or monopolistic competition. This approach enables the student to learn, appreciate, and use important concepts such as efficiency and deadweight loss early in the course.

The basic workings of markets and the reasons they improve people's lives are the subjects of Part 1. Chapter 1 outlines the unifying themes of economics: scarcity, choice, and economic interaction. The role of prices, the inherent international aspect of economics, the importance of property rights and incentives, and the difference between central planning and markets are some of the key ideas in this chapter. Chapter 2 introduces the field of economics through a case study showing how economists observe and explain economic puzzles. Chapters 3 and 4 cover the basic supply and demand model and elasticity. Here, the goal is to show how to use the supply and demand model to make sense of the world—and to learn how to "think like an economist." The concept of elasticity is now wholly contained in Chapter 4. A trio of chapters—5, 6, and 7—explains why competitive markets are efficient, perhaps the most important idea in economics. The parallel exposition of utility maximization (Chapter 5) and profit maximization (Chapter 6) culminates in a detailed description of why competitive markets are efficient (Chapter 7). The inclusion of interesting results from experimental economics plays a dual role: to illustrate how well models work, and to make the discussion of these important topics less abstract.

A modern market economy is not static; rather, it grows and changes over time as firms add new and better machines and as people add to their skills and training. Chapters 8 and 9 describe how firms and markets grow and change over time. Chapters 10 and 11 demonstrate how economists model the behavior of firms that are not perfectly competitive, such as monopolies. The models of dynamic behavior and imperfect competition developed here are used to explain the rise and fall of real-world firms and industries. Chapter 12 reviews the policy implications.

Chapter 13 considers labor markets. Chapters 14 and 15 are devoted to the role of government in the economy. Tax policy, welfare reform, environmental policy, and the role of government in producing public goods are analyzed. Different countries have taken widely different approaches to the economy. The policy of some countries has been to directly intervene in virtually every economic decision; other countries have followed more hands-off policies. The problem of government failure is analyzed using models of government behavior. Chapter 16 discusses capital markets.

The study of macroeconomics begins with Chapter 17. This chapter is an overview of the facts, emphasizing that macroeconomics is concerned with the growth and fluctuations in the economy as a whole. Chapter 18 shows how GDP and other variables are measured.

Chapter 19 starts with the first macro model to determine the long-run shares of GDP. Chapter 20 gives an analysis of how the level of unemployment in the economy as a whole is determined. Labor, capital, and technology are then presented in Chapter 21 as the fundamental determinants of the economy's growth path. One clear advantage of this approach is that it allows students to focus first on issues about which there is general agreement among economists. Moreover, this ordering helps students better understand short-term economic fluctuations. Similarly, the long-run treatment of money, presented in Chapter 22, sets the stage for the discussion of economic fluctuations.

As shown in the five chapters of Part 6 (Chapters 23 through 27), the economy does fluctuate as it grows over time. Declines in production and increases in unemployment (characteristics of recessions) have not vanished from the landscape as long-term growth issues have come to the fore. Part 6 delves into the causes of these fluctuations and proposes an analysis of why they end. It begins by explaining why shifts in aggregate demand may cause the economy to fluctuate and ends by showing that price adjustment plays a significant role in the end of recessions.

Countries have tried a variety of approaches to deal with economic growth and economic fluctuations. Part 7 (Chapters 28 through 31) examines these approaches to policy, about which there are many differing opinions. I have tried to explain these as clearly and as objectively as I can; there are also areas of agreement, which are stressed.

Pedagogical Features

The following pedagogical features are designed to help students learn economics.

Examples within the text. Illustrations of real-world situations help explain economic ideas and models. I have attempted to include a wide variety of brief examples and longer case studies throughout the text. Examples include the use of health-care statistics in Chapter 2, the case study on the demand and supply of gasoline in Chapter 3, and the case study on milk price supports in Chapter 7. Many other examples are simply woven into the text.

Boxed examples to give real-life perspectives. "Reading the News About . . ." boxes—many of them new to this edition—explain how to decipher recent news stories about economic activities and policy; "Economics in Action" boxes examine the contributions of the great economists, such as Adam Smith, or notable current events. Many of these current events boxes have also been revised or replaced in this edition.

Stimulating vignettes at the beginning of each chapter. Examples of opening vignettes include the opportunity costs of college for Tiger Woods in Chapter 1 and the work of health-care economist Mark McClellan in Chapter 2. Chapter 6 begins with the story of the entrepreneur who began the car magnet ribbon craze in 2004.

Functional use of full color. Color is used to distinguish between curves and to show how the curves shift dynamically over time. An example of the effective use of multiple colors can be found in the equilibrium price and equilibrium quantity figure in Chapter 3 (Figure 3.8).

Complete captions and small conversation boxes in graphs. The captions and small yellow-shaded conversation boxes make many of the figures completely self-contained. In some graphs, sequential numbering of these conversation boxes stresses the dynamic nature of the curves. Again, Figure 3.8 provides a good example.

Conversation boxes in text margins. These appear when an additional explanation or reminder might help students grasp a new concept more easily.

Use of photos and cartoons to illustrate abstract ideas. Special care has gone into the search for and selection of photos and cartoons to illustrate difficult economic ideas, such as inelastic supply curves or opportunity costs. Each text photo or photo spread has a short title and caption to explain its relevance to the text discussion.

Key term definitions. Definitions of key terms appear in the margins and in the alphabetized glossary at the end of the book. The key terms are listed at the end of every chapter and appendix.

Brief reviews at the end of each major section. These reviews summarize the key points in abbreviated form as the chapter evolves; they are useful for preliminary skim reading as well as for review.

Questions for review at the end of every chapter. These are tests of recall and require only short answers; they can be used for oral review or as a quick self-check.

Problems. An essential tool in learning economics, the problems have been carefully selected, revised, and tested for this edition. An ample supply of these appears at the end of every chapter and appendix. Some of the problems ask the reader to work out examples that are slightly different from the ones in the text; others require a more critical thinking approach. A second set of problems that parallels those in the text is included in the accompanying test bank and on the instructor's HMClassPrep with HMTesting CD. This problem set is also available to instructors via the Online Teaching Center.

Enhanced Teaching and Learning Package for Students and Instructors

The highly effective teaching and learning package prepared to accompany this text has been completely revised, updated, and expanded to provide a full range of support for students and instructors. It includes several new options for instructors who wish to take full advantage of the online environment in managing their courses. Students, too, will derive great benefit from the newly revised online tutorials and quizzing that will help walk them through the main concepts from each chapter.

Student Resources

Micro and Macro Study Guides. Revised and updated by David Papell of the University of Houston, Wm. Stewart Mounts, Jr., of Mercer University, and John Solow of the University of Iowa, these study guides provide a wonderful learning opportunity that many students will value. Each chapter contains an overview, an informal chapter review, and a section called "Zeroing In," which harnesses students' intuition to explain the chapter's most important concepts. The study guides also provide ample means for practice in using the economic ideas and graphs introduced in each text chapter and address a variety of learning needs through graph-based questions and problems as well as multiple-choice practice tests. A section called "Working It Out" provides worked problems that take the student step by step through the analytical process needed for real-world applications of the core concepts covered in the chapter. These are followed by practice problems that require students to use the same analytical tools on their own. Detailed answers are provided for all review and practice questions. End-of-part quizzes offer students yet another chance to test their retention of material before taking in-class exams.

Online Study Center The Taylor *Economics* Online Study Center (found at college.hmco.com/pic/taylor5e) provides an extended learning environment for students where materials are carefully developed to complement and supplement each chapter. Students will find key economic links as well as numerous opportunities to test their mastery of chapter content—including glossary terms and flash cards; brief, objective-type quizzes; and more extended Web-based assignments developed by John Kane of SUNY, Oswego, and John Min of Northern Virginia Community College.

Your Guide to an A. Students who purchase the text package that includes a passkey for accompanying course management or the "Your Guide to an 'A' Passkey" will receive an additional set of resources developed to reinforce chapter concepts for a variety of learning styles. Included here are step-by-step online tutorials with interactive graphs, audio chapter reviews for downloading, and additional ACE practice quizzes. In addition, the "Your Guide to an 'A' Passkey" includes access to SmarThinking[R] Online Tutoring Service. This live tutoring service allows students to interact online with an experienced SmarThinking e-structor (online tutor) between 9:00 P.M. and 1:00 A.M. EST every Sunday through Thursday. SmarThinking provides state-of-the-art communication tools, such as chat technology and virtual whiteboards designed for easy rendering of economic formulas and graphs, to help students absorb key concepts and learn to think economically.

Instructor Resources

Micro and Macro Test Banks. A reliable test bank is the most important resource for efficient and effective teaching and learning. The Micro and Macro Test Banks for the fifth edition have been revised and prepared by Jim Lee of Texas A & M, Corpus Christi, and Stuart Glosser of the University of Wisconsin—Whitewater. They contain more than 5,000 test questions—including multiple-choice, true/false, short answer, and problems—many of which are based on graphs. The questions are coded for correct answer, question type, level of difficulty, and text topic. The test banks also include a set of parallel problems that match the end-of-chapter problems from the text and are conveniently available in both printed and computerized form.

HMClassPrep with HMTesting CD-ROM. Organized by chapter for easy reference and class planning, this all-in-one instructor CD contains a wealth of resources, including lecture outlines, teaching objectives and tips, solutions to text problems, a set of parallel problems and solutions, and discussion ideas. Two sets of PowerPoint slides are also contained on this CD, as are *all the questions* found in the Macro and Micro Test Banks. HMTesting software (powered by Diploma™) provides instructors with all the tools they need to create, customize, and deliver multiple types of tests. Instructors can import questions directly from the test bank, create their own questions, or edit existing questions, all within Diploma's powerful electronic platform. The program prints graphs and tables in addition to the text part of each question. Instructors can scramble the questions and answer choices, edit questions, add their own questions to the pool, and customize their exams in various other ways. HMTesting provides a complete testing solution, including classroom administration and online testing features in addition to test generation. The program is available in Windows and Mac versions.

Instructor's Resource Manual. Prepared and revised by John Taylor and Wm. Stewart Mounts, Jr., of Mercer University, the Instructor's Resource Manual provides both first-time and experienced instructors with a variety of additional resources for use with the text. Each chapter contains a brief overview, teaching objectives, key terms from the text, a section that orients instructors to the text's unique approach, and a suggested lecture outline with teaching tips that provide additional examples not found in the text as well as hints for teaching more difficult material. Discussion topics and solutions to end-of-chapter text problems are also provided.

PowerPoint Slides. Two complete sets of downloadable PowerPoint slides are available to adopters of the text on the HMClassPrep with HMTesting CD-ROM and from the Online Teaching Center. To gain access to the web site's instructor resources, obtain a user name and password from your Houghton Mifflin sales representative.

Overhead Transparencies. Overhead transparencies for key figures from the text are available to adopters of *Economics, Principles of Microeconomics,* and *Principles of Macroeconomics.*

Course Management Resources

One of the most challenging aspects of teaching a Principles course is providing students with ample opportunity for practice and review. The Eduspace® online learning tool pairs the widely recognized resources of Blackboard® with quality, text-specific content from Houghton Mifflin. Auto-graded homework exercises from the text come ready to use for online assignments and grading. Students will find a wealth of chapter review material as well, including tutorials with interactive graphs developed for each chapter. Students who need more individualized, one-on-one tutorial help will have access to the SmarThinking Online Tutoring Service (described earlier). The content found on the Eduspace online learning tool is also available on Blackboard course cartridges and WebCT® ePacks for instructors who wish to use these systems to create distance-learning or hybrid courses. This textbook is available in eBook format for quick access.

Online Teaching Center. The Taylor *Economics* Online Teaching Center (found at college.hmco.com/pic/taylor5e) provides guided Web activities that relate to the key concepts of each chapter of the textbook. These include, among other materials, Internet Assignments (with solutions) prepared by John Kane of SUNY, Oswego, and Economics W.I.R.E.D. Web links, developed by John S. Min of Northern Virginia Community College. The W.I.R.E.D. links are accompanied by brief tips to the instructor on how the material might best be used in the classroom as well as discussion questions or exercises for assessing student learning. In addition, the instructor web site contains all the instructor materials found in the Instructor's Resource Manual and a complete set of parallel questions (and solutions) matching the end-of-chapter problems from the text.

Acknowledgments

Completing a project like this is a team effort. I have always been fortunate to work with some very talented economists at Stanford—colleagues and students—who have provided me with many ideas and feedback through each edition. But in the case of the fifth edition, I must acknowledge with very special gratitude the substantial contribution of Akila Weerapana, of Wellesley College. Akila first demonstrated his extraordinary research and teaching skills even before completing his Ph.D. at Stanford, when he provided a great deal of useful feedback on this book. After receiving his Ph.D., Akila joined the faculty at Wellesley College, where he has taught the Principles course for many semesters and further established his reputation for teaching excellence, and where, in 2002, he received the Anna and Samuel Pinanski Teaching Award. Akila's research in monetary economics and international macro-economics has been published in journals ranging from the *Journal of Economic Education* to the *European Journal of Political Economy*. His ability to get complex topics across to his students is clearly reflected in many of the changes of this revision. And the enthusiasm for bringing policy implications alive that Akila shares with me is also reflected in his enormous contributions to the new Point-Counterpoint boxes in this fifth edition.

I would also like to thank Janet Gerson, who has contributed to this revision a number of terrific examples from real life—found and developed over many years of teaching the Principles course at the University of Michigan. I am grateful to Jan for sharing these interesting and motivating illustrations with me and giving more students the opportunity to benefit from her insights about the usefulness of economic analysis in our daily lives.

Many other college teachers have taken the time to write with questions or comments about the text and ideas for improvement that have come from their own teaching. I would like to thank in particular David H. Reiley, University of Arizona, for taking the time to provide me with his suggestions for improvements in several chapters. David's analytical skills and dedication to teaching have been evident in the thoughtful comments he has sent to me. I would also like to especially mention the in-depth reviews I received from Samiran Banerjee, Georgia Institute of Technology; Brian Boike, Boston University; David Gleicher, Adelphi University; Abbas Grammy, California State University; Gregory Green, Idaho State University; Jongsung Kim, Bryant University; Fredric Menz, Clarkson University; John Neri, University of Maryland; Edd Noell, Westmont College; Olugbenga Onafowora, Susquehanna University; Sanela Porca, University of South Carolina; and Della Lee Sue, Marist College. These instructors provided comments and suggestions that were critical to the development of the fifth edition.

Special thanks goes to Erik Craft, University of Richmond, who carried out the final accuracy review for this edition. I am most appreciative of Erik's thorough and careful review of text and art—and unparalleled scent for potential discrepancies!

I am grateful to the authors of the fifth edition supplements, including Wm. Stewart Mounts, Jr., David Papell, Cliff Sowell, Jim Lee, and Stuart Glosser. Their careful attention to text changes both small and large has resulted in ancillaries that match the text in content and spirit. Many thanks also to Eugenio D. Suarez, who reviewed much of this work.

Finally, I would like to thank the excellent team of professionals at Houghton Mifflin who have labored over this fifth edition, including Ann West, Jessica Carlisle, Carol Merrigan, and Alison McGonagle.

Reviewers

This book would not exist without the help of all the reviewers and readers who have provided suggestions incorporated into each revision.

Mark D. Agee
Pennsylvania State University, Altoona

James Alm
University of Colorado at Boulder

Lee J. Alston
University of Illinois

Christine Amsler
Michigan State University

Lisa Anderson
College of William and Mary

Dean Baim
Pepperdine University

R. J. Ballman, Jr.
Augustana College

Samiran Banerjee
Georgia Institute of Technology

Raymond S. Barnstone
Northeastern University and Lesley College

Laurie J. Bates
Bryant College

Kari Battaglia
University of North Texas

Klaus G. Becker
Texas Tech University

Valerie R. Bencivenga
Cornell University

Sidney M. Blummer
California Polytechnic University

William M. Boal
Drake University

Brian Boike
Boston University

Roger Bowles
University of Bath

Paula Bracy
University of Toledo

Jozell Brister
Abilene Christian University

Robert Brown
Texas Technical University

Robert Buchele
Smith College

Mark L. Burkey
North Carolina A&T State University

Michael R. Butler
Texas Christian University

Richard Call
American River College

Leonard Carlson
Emory University

Michael J. Carter
University of Massachusetts, Lowell

William E. Chapel
University of Mississippi

Chiuping Chen
American River College

Kenneth Chinn
Southeastern Oklahoma State University

Stephen L. Cobb
University of North Texas

Mike Cohick
Collin County Community College

Kathy L. Combs
California State University, Los Angeles

Joyce Cooper
Boston University

Erik D. Craft
University of Richmond

Steven Craig
University of Houston

Sarah Culver
University of Alabama, Birmingham

Ward S. Curran
Trinity College

Joseph Daniels
Marquette University

Audrey Davidson
University of Louisville

Gregg Davis
Marshall University

Gregory E. DeFreitas
Hofstra University

David N. DeJong
University of Pittsburgh

David Denslow
University of Florida

Enrica Detragiache
Johns Hopkins University

Michael Devereux
University of British Columbia

Michael Dowd
University of Toledo

Douglas Downing
Seattle Pacific University

Dean Dudley
United States Military Academy

Mary E. Edwards
St. Cloud State University

Ken Farr
Georgia College

David Figlio
University of Oregon

Gerald Friedman
University of Massachusetts, Amherst

Edwin T. Fujii
University of Hawaii

Charles Geiss
University of Missouri

Janet Gerson
University of Michigan

J. Robert Gillette
University of Kentucky

Donna Ginther
Southern Methodist College

David Gleicher
Adelphi University

Mark Glick
University of Utah

Stuart M. Glosser
University of Wisconsin, Whitewater

Abbas Grammy
California State University

Phil Graves
University of Colorado, Boulder

Gregory Green
Idaho State University

Paul W. Grimes
Mississippi State University

Lorna S. Gross
Worcester State College

Shoshana Grossbard-Shechtman
San Diego State University

Robin Hahnel
American University

Alan Haight
Bowling Green State University

David R. Hakes
University of Northern Iowa

Greg Hamilton
Marist College

David Hansen
Linfield College

Mehdi Haririan
Bloomsburg University

Richard Harper
University of West Florida

Mitchell Harwitz
State University of New York, Buffalo

Mary Ann Hendryson
Western Washington University

James B. Herendeen
University of Texas, El Paso

Pershing J. Hill
University of Alaska, Anchorage

Denise Hixson
Midlands Technical College

Gail Mitchell Hoyt
University of Richmond

Jim Hvidding
Kutztown University

Beth Ingram
University of Iowa

Murat F. Iyigun
University of Colorado, Boulder

Joyce Jacobsen
Wesleyan University

Syed Jafri
Tarleton State University

David Jaques
California Polytech University, Pomona

Allan Jenkins
University of Nebraska

David Johnson
Wilfred Laurier University

Charles W. Johnston
University of Michigan, Flint

Nake Kamrany
University of Southern California

John Kane
State University of New York, Oswego

Manfred Keil
Claremont McKenna College

Kristen Keith
University of Alaska

Elizabeth Kelly
University of Wisconsin—Madison

Jongsung Kim
Bryant University

John Klein
Georgia State University

Harry T. Kolendrianos
Danville Community College

Margaret Landman
Bridgewater State College

Philip J. Lane
Fairfield University

William Lang
Rutgers University

William D. Lastrapes
University of Georgia

Jim Lee
Texas A & M University

Lawrence A. Leger
Loughborough University

David Li
University of Michigan

Susan Linz
Michigan State University

John K. Lodewijks
University of New South Wales

R. Ashley Lyman
University of Idaho

Bridget Lyons
Sacred Heart University

Craig MacPhee
University of Nebraska, Lincoln

Michael Magura
University of Toledo

Robert A. Margo
Vanderbilt University

John D. Mason
Gordon College

Robert McAuliffe
Babson College

Henry N. McCarl
University of Alabama, Birmingham

Laurence C. McCulloch
Ohio State University

Rob Roy McGregor
University of North Carolina, Charlotte

Richard McIntyre
University of Rhode Island

Mark McLeod
Virginia Tech

Gaminie Meepagala
Howard University

Frederick Menz
Clarkson University

Micke Meurs
American University

Khan A. Mohabbat
Northern Illinois University

Douglas W. Morgan
University of California, Santa Barbara

Norma Morgan
Curry College

Peter Morgan
State University of New York at Buffalo

Wm. Stewart Mounts, Jr.
Mercer University

Vai-Lam Mui
University of Southern California

David C. Murphy
Boston College

Andrew Narwold
University of San Diego

Ronald C. Necoechea
Ball State University

John Neri
University of Maryland

Rebecca Neumann
University of Colorado at Boulder

Edd Noell
Westmont College

Hong V. Nguyen
University of Scranton

Lou Noyd
Northern Kentucky University

Rachel Nugent
Pacific Lutheran University

Anthony Patrick O'Brien
Lehigh University

William C. O'Connor
Western Montana College

Olugbenga Onafowora
Susquehanna University

Eliot S. Orton
New Mexico State University

Jan Palmer
Ohio University

David Papell
University of Houston

Walter Park
American University

Charles Parker
Wayne State College

A. Cristina Cunha Parsons
Trinity College, Washington D.C.

James Payne
Eastern Kentucky University

David Petersen
American River College, Sacramento

E. Charles Pflanz
Scottsdale Community College

William A. Phillips
University of Southern Maine

Charles Plott
California Institute of Technology

Sanela Porca
University of South Carolina

Lidija Polutnik
Babson College

David L. Prychitko
State University of New York, Oswego

Salim Rashid
University of Illinois, Urbana-Champaign

Margaret A. Ray
Mary Washington College

Geoffrey Renshaw
University of Warwick

John Ridpath
York University

Greg Rose
Sacramento City College

B. Peter Rosendorff
University of Southern California

Robert J. Rossana
Wayne State University

Marina Rosser
James Madison University

Kartic C. Roy
University of Queensland

Daniel Rubenson
Southern Oregon State College

Jeffrey Rubin
Rutgers University

Robert S. Rycroft
Mary Washington College

Jonathan Sandy
University of San Diego

Gary Saxonhouse
University of Michigan

Edward Scahill
University of Scranton

James Byron Schlomach
Texas A&M University

Torsten Schmidt
University of New Hampshire

Thomas J. Shea
Springfield College

William J. Simeone
Providence College

Michael Smitka
Washington & Lee University

Ronald Soligo
Rice University

John L. Solow
University of Iowa

Clifford Sowell
Berea College

Michael Spagat
Brown University

David Spencer
Brigham Young University

Sarah L. Stafford
College of William and Mary

J. R. Stanfield
Colorado State University

Ann B. Sternlicht
University of Richmond

Richard Stevenson
Liverpool University

James Stodder
Rensselaer Polytechnic Institute

Leslie S. Stratton
University of Arizona

Robert Stuart
Rutgers University

Della Lee Sue
Marist College

Dave Surdam
Loyola University, Chicago

James Swoffard
University of South Alabama

Bette Lewis Tokar
Holy Family College

Paul Turner
University of Leeds

Lee J. Vanscyoc
University of Wisconsin, Oshkosh

Gerald R. Visgilio
Connecticut College

Manhar Vyas
University of Pittsburgh

Shaianne T.O. Warner
Ithaca College

William V. Weber
Eastern Illinois University

Akila Weerapana
Wellesley College

Karl Wesolowski
Salem State College

Joseph Wesson
State University of New York, Potsdam

Geoff Whittam
University of Glasgow

Kenneth P. Wickman
State University of New York, Cortland

Catherine Winnett
University of Bath

Jennifer P. Wissink
Cornell University

Simon Wren-Lewis
University of Strathclyde

Peter R. Wyman
Spokane Falls Community College

Yung Y. Yang
California State University, Sacramento

PART 1

Introduction to Economics

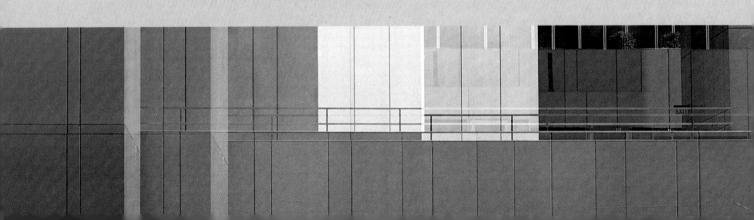

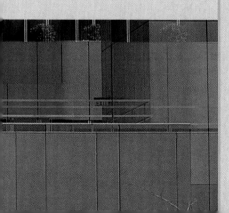

CHAPTER 1

The Central Idea

This is a true story. In the spring of 1996, a 19-year-old college sophomore, who had just finished taking introductory economics, was faced with a *choice*: to continue college for an additional two years or to devote full time to a job. The job was being a professional golfer on the Pro Tour—a job for which the sophomore was uniquely qualified, having won three U.S. amateur titles. Doing both college and the Pro Tour was not an option because time is *scarce*: With only 24 hours in the day, he simply did not have time to do both. For this sophomore, completing college had a great cost: not only the two years of college expenses, but also the forgone tournament winnings and advertising endorsements that a successful pro golf career would bring. The golfer—his name is Tiger Woods—made a choice. He became a pro. By the fall of 1996 he was selected Sportsman of the Year by *Sports Illustrated*. In 1997 he stunned the golfing world with a record-setting win of the venerable Masters Tournament, and with his second Masters victory in 2001, Woods became the first player to hold all four major professional championships at the same time. He won the Masters again in 2005, by which time he had earned over $50 million in prizes worldwide, and much more in advertising and endorsements.

Tiger Woods would not have had the same opportunity had he not been able to *interact with people*. Golf fans who enjoyed watching him play golf interacted with him: They paid to see him play. Executives who ran companies like Nike and American Express interacted with him: They paid him for his endorsement. And Tiger's family, teachers, and friends interacted with him: They conveyed basic skills, enhanced his confidence, and helped him remain cool under pressure. Tiger gained from these interactions with people—and the people gained, too.

This true story illustrates the idea that lies at the center of economics: that people make *purposeful choices* with *scarce* resources, and *interact* with other people when they make these choices. More than anything else, **economics** is the study of how people deal with scarcity.

Scarcity is a situation in which people's resources are limited. People always face a scarcity of something—frequently, as in Tiger Woods's case, time. Scarcity implies that people must make a **choice** to forgo, or give up, one thing in favor of another: to work full time or go to school, to take economics or biology this term, to work or stay at home with the children.

Economic interaction between people occurs every time they trade or exchange goods or services with each other. For example, a college student buys education services from a college in exchange for tuition. A teenager sells labor services to Taco Bell in exchange for cash. Within a family, one spouse may agree to cook every day in exchange for the other spouse's doing the dishes every day.

As these examples indicate, economic interactions can occur either within an *organization* or *group*, such as a family, or in a *market*. A **market** is simply an arrangement by which buyers and sellers can interact and exchange goods and services with each other. Examples of interactions in markets are the buying and selling of a college education and the buying and selling of the labor services of Taco Bell workers. There are many, many other markets, from the New York stock market to a local flea market.

The purpose of this book is to introduce you to the field of economics and to help you understand the economic challenges and opportunities you face as an individual in the economy. The goal is not to peek passively at economics but to learn to think like an economist.

The first step toward this goal is for you to get an intuitive feel for how pervasive scarcity, choice, and economic interaction are in the real world—and to learn some of the powerful implications of this basic fact of economic life. That is the purpose of this chapter.

economics: the study of how people deal with scarcity.

scarcity: the situation in which the quantity of resources is insufficient to meet all wants.

choice: a selection among alternative goods, services, or actions.

economic interaction: exchanges of goods and services between people.

market: an arrangement by which economic exchanges between people take place.

The choice was to continue college or join the Pro Tour. What would you have done?

Scarcity and Choice for Individuals

It is easy to find everyday examples of how people make purposeful choices when they are confronted with a scarcity of time or resources. A choice that may be on your

Economics in Action

Gains from Trade on the Internet

The Internet has created many new opportunities for gains from trade. Internet auction sites like eBay allow sellers a way to offer their goods for sale and buyers a way to make bids on sale items. The gains are similar to those of Maria and Adam as they trade sunglasses for hats. Hundreds of different types of sunglasses and baseball hats (and millions of other things) can be bought and sold on eBay—5,566 types of sunglasses and 913 types of baseball hats were for sale at last count.

If you—like Maria—want to sell a pair of sunglasses and buy a hat, you can simply go to *www.ebay.com*, offer a pair of sunglasses to sell, and search for the hat you would like to buy. The computer screen will show photos of some of the sunglasses and baseball hats offered.

Whereas many Internet-related businesses started in the mid-1990s have contracted or disappeared completely in the tech implosion of recent years, eBay has remained hugely successful—perhaps because it is so simple. It provides information and a means of communicating transactions—a sort of virtual flea market. Today there are nearly 50 million registered users, with millions of sales transacted in a single day.

How well do you think the simple example of Maria and Adam illustrates the real-world gains from trade by people using eBay to buy and sell things?

The founder (left) and the chief executive (right) of eBay offer new ways to gain from trade.

mind when you study economics is how much time to spend on it versus other activities. If you spend all your time on economics, you may get 100 on the final exam, but that might mean you get a zero in biology. If you spend all your time on biology, then you may get 100 in biology and a zero in economics. Most people resolve the choice by *balancing* out their time to get a decent grade in both subjects. If you are premed, then biology will probably get more time. If you are interested in business, then more time on economics might be appropriate.

Now let us apply this basic principle to two fundamental economic problems: individual choices about what to *consume* and *produce*. For each type of economic problem, we first show how scarcity forces one to make a choice, then show how people gain from interacting with other people.

Consumer Decisions

Consider Maria, who is going for a hike in a park on a sunny day. Maria would love to wear a hat (baseball style with her school logo) and sunglasses on the hike, but she has brought neither with her. Maria has brought $20 with her, however, and there is a store in the park that is having a "two for one" sale. She can buy two hats for $20 or two pairs of sunglasses for $20. Her scarcity of funds causes her to make a choice. The $20 limit on her spending is an example of a *budget constraint*, because she is limited to spending no more than this amount. Her choice will depend on her tastes. Let us assume that when she is forced by scarcity to make a choice, she will choose the sunglasses. She would prefer to buy one hat and one pair of sunglasses, but that is not possible.

opportunity cost: the value of the next-best forgone alternative that was not chosen because something else was chosen.

▪ **Opportunity Cost.**   Maria's decision is an example of an economic problem that all people face: A budget constraint forces them to make a choice between different items that they want. Such choices create opportunity costs. The **opportunity cost** of a choice is the value of the forgone alternative that was not chosen. The opportunity cost of the hats is the loss from not being able to wear the sunglasses. An opportunity cost occurs every time there is a choice. For example, the opportunity cost of going to an 8 A.M. class rather than sleeping in is the sleep you lose when you get up early. The opportunity cost of Tiger Woods's staying in college was millions of dollars in prize money.

In many cases involving choice and scarcity, there are many more than two things to choose from. If you choose vanilla ice cream out of a list of many possible flavors, then the opportunity cost is the loss from not being able to consume the *next-best* flavor, perhaps strawberry. In general, when there are more than two items, the opportunity cost is the value of the next-best alternative.

Now, suppose Maria is not the only hiker. Also in the park is Adam, who also has $20 to spend. Adam also loves both hats and sunglasses, but he likes hats more than sunglasses. When forced to make a choice, he buys the hats. His decision is shaped by scarcity just as Maria's is: Scarcity comes from the budget constraint; he must make a choice, and there is an opportunity cost for each choice. [or Resource]

gains from trade: improvements in income, production, or satisfaction owing to the exchange of goods or services.

▪ **Gains from Trade: A Better Allocation.**   Now suppose that Adam and Maria meet each other in the park. Let's consider the possibility of economic interaction between them. Maria has two pairs of sunglasses and Adam has two hats, so Maria and Adam can trade with each other. Maria can trade one of her pairs of sunglasses for one of Adam's hats, as shown in Figure 1.1. Through such a trade, both Maria and Adam can improve their situation. There are **gains from trade** because the trade reallocates goods between the two individuals in a way they both prefer. Trade occurs because Maria is willing to exchange one pair of sunglasses for one hat, and Adam is willing to exchange one hat for one pair of sunglasses. Because trade is mutually advantageous for both Maria and Adam, they will voluntarily engage in it if they are able to. In fact, if they do not gain from the trade, then neither will bother to make the trade.

This trade is an example of an economic interaction in which a reallocation of goods through trade makes both people better off. There is no change in the total quantity of goods produced. The number of hats and sunglasses has remained the same. Trade simply reallocates existing goods.

The trade between Maria and Adam is typical of many economic interactions we will study in this book. Thinking like an economist in this example means recognizing that a voluntary exchange of goods between people must make them better off. Many economic exchanges are like this, even though they are more complicated than the exchange of hats and sunglasses.

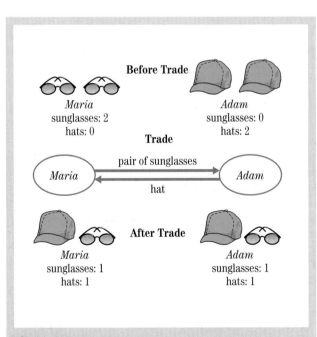

**Figure 1.1
Gains from Trade Through a Better Allocation of Goods**
Without trade, Maria has more pairs of sunglasses than she would like, and Adam has more hats than he would like. By trading a hat for a pair of sunglasses, they both gain.

Producer Decisions

Now consider two producers—Emily, a poet, and Johann, a printer. Both face scarcity and must make choices. Because of differences in training, abilities, or inclination, Emily is much better at writing poetry than Johann, but Johann is much better at printing greeting cards than Emily. Suppose that Emily and Johann cannot interact with each other (perhaps they live on different islands and cannot communicate).

If Emily writes poetry full time, she can produce 10 poems in a day; but if she wants to make and sell greeting cards with her poems in them, she must spend some time printing cards and thereby spend less time writing poems. However, Emily is not very good at printing cards; it takes her so much time to do so that if she prints one card, she has time to write only 1 poem rather than 10 poems during the day.

If Johann prints full time, he can produce 10 different greeting cards in a day. However, if he wants to sell greeting cards, he must write poems to put inside them. Johann is so poor at writing poems that if he writes only 1 poem a day, his production of greeting cards drops from 10 to 1 per day.

Following is a summary of the choices Emily and Johann face because of a scarcity of time and resources.

	Emily, the Poet		**Johann, the Printer**	
	Write Full Time	*Write and Print*	*Print Full Time*	*Write and Print*
Cards	0	1	10	1
Poems	10	1	0	1

If Emily and Johann cannot interact, then each can produce only 1 greeting card with a poem on the inside in a day. Alternatively, Emily could produce 10 poems without the cards and Johann could produce 10 cards without the poems, but then neither would earn anything. We therefore assume that when confronted with this choice, both Emily and Johann will each choose to produce 1 greeting card with a poem inside. In total, they produce 2 greeting cards.

■ **Gains from Trade: Greater Production.**   Now consider the possibility of economic interaction. Suppose that Emily and Johann can trade. Johann could sell his printing services to Emily, agreeing to print her poems on nice greeting cards. Then Emily could sell the greeting cards to people. Under this arrangement, Emily could spend all day writing poetry, and Johann could spend all day printing. In total, they could produce 10 different greeting cards together, expending the same time and effort it took to produce 2 greeting cards when they could not trade.

Note that in this example the interaction took place in a market: Johann sold his print jobs to Emily. Another approach would be for Emily and Johann to go into business together, forming a firm, Dickinson and Gutenberg Greetings, Inc. Then their economic interaction would occur within the firm, without buying or selling in the market.

Whether in a market or within a firm, the gains from trade in this example are huge. By trading, Emily and Johann can increase their production of greeting cards by five times, from 2 cards to 10 cards.

■ **Specialization, Division of Labor, and Comparative Advantage.**   This example illustrates another way in which economic interaction improves people's lives. Economic interaction allows for *specialization*: people concentrating on what

division of labor: the division of production into various parts in which different groups of workers specialize.

they are good at. Emily specializes in poetry, and Johann specializes in printing. The specialization creates a division of labor. A **division of labor** occurs when some workers specialize in one task while others specialize in another task. They divide the overall production into parts, with some workers concentrating on one part (printing) and other workers concentrating on another part (writing).

The poetry/printing example of Emily and Johann also illustrates another economic concept, **comparative advantage.** In general, a person or group of people has a comparative advantage in producing one good relative to another good if that person or group can produce that good with comparatively less time, effort, or resources than another person or group can produce that good. For example, compared with Johann, Emily has a comparative advantage in writing relative to printing. And compared with Emily, Johann has a comparative advantage in printing relative to writing. As this example shows, production can be increased if people specialize in the skill in which they have a comparative advantage[1]—that is, if Emily specializes in writing and Johann in printing.

comparative advantage: a situation in which a person or group can produce one good at a lower opportunity cost than another person or group.

International Trade

Thus far, we have said nothing about where Emily and Johann live or work. They could reside in the same country, but they could also reside in different countries. Emily could live in the United States; Johann, in Germany. If this is so, when Emily purchases Johann's printing service, **international trade** will take place because the trade is between people in two different countries. Similarly, Maria could live in Detroit, Michigan, and Adam in Windsor, Ontario. If this is so, their trade will also be international.

international trade: the exchange of goods and services between people or firms in different nations.

The gains from international trade are thus of the same kind as the gains from trade within a country. By trading, people can better satisfy their preferences for goods (as in the case of Maria and Adam), or they can better utilize their comparative advantage (as in the case of Emily and Johann). In either situation, there is a gain to both participants from trade.

REVIEW

- All individuals face scarcity in one form or another. Scarcity forces people to make choices. When there is choice, there is also an opportunity cost of not doing one thing because another thing has been chosen.

- People benefit from economic interactions—trading goods and services—with other people.

- Gains from trade occur because goods and services can be allocated in ways that are more satisfactory to people.

- Gains from trade also occur because trade permits specialization through the division of labor. People should specialize in the production of goods in which they have a comparative advantage.

---

1. Other examples are explored in the chapter "The Gains from International Trade," where you can see that comparative advantage can also occur when one person is absolutely better at both activities.

Scarcity and Choice for the Economy as a Whole

Just as individuals face scarcity and choice, so does the economy as a whole. The total amount of resources in an economy—workers, land, machinery, factories—is limited. Thus, the economy cannot produce all the health care, crime prevention, education, or entertainment that people want. A choice must be made. Let us first consider how to represent scarcity and choice in the whole economy and then consider alternative ways to make the choices.

Production Possibilities

Table 1.1
Production Possibilities

	Movies	Computers
A	0	25,000
B	100	24,000
C	200	22,000
D	300	18,000
E	400	13,000
F	500	0

production possibilities: alternative combinations of production of various goods that are possible, given the economy's resources.

To simplify things, let us suppose that production in the economy can be divided into two broad categories. Suppose the economy can produce either computers (mainframes, PCs, hand calculators) or movies (thrillers, love stories, mysteries, musicals). The choice between computers and movies is symbolic of one of the most fundamental choices individuals in any society must face: how much to invest in order to produce more or better goods in the future versus how much to consume in the present. Computers help people produce more or better goods. Movies are a form of consumption. Other pairs of goods could also be used in our example. Another popular example is guns versus butter, representing defense goods versus nondefense goods.

With a scarcity of resources such as labor and capital, there is a choice between producing some goods, such as computers, versus other goods, such as movies. If the economy produces more of one, then it must produce less of the other. Table 1.1 gives an example of the alternative choices, or the **production possibilities,** for computers and movies. Observe that there are six different choices, some with more computers and fewer movies, others with fewer computers and more movies.

Table 1.1 tells us what happens as available resources in the economy are moved from movie production to computer production or vice versa. If resources move from producing movies to producing computers, then fewer movies are produced. For example, if all resources are used to produce computers, then 25,000 computers and zero movies can be produced, according to the table. If all resources are used to produce movies, then no computers can be produced. These are two extremes, of course. If 100 movies are produced, then we produce 24,000 computers rather than 25,000 computers. If 200 movies are produced, then computer production must fall to 22,000.

Increasing Opportunity Costs

The production possibilities in Table 1.1 illustrate the concept of opportunity cost for the economy as a whole. The opportunity cost of producing more movies is the value of the forgone computers. For example, the opportunity cost of producing 200 movies rather than 100 movies is 2,000 computers.

An important economic idea about opportunity costs is demonstrated in Table 1.1. Observe that movie production increases as we move down the table. As we move from row to row, movie production increases by the same number: 100 movies. The decline in computer production between the first and second rows—from 25,000 to 24,000 computers—is 1,000 computers. The decline between the second and third rows—from 24,000 to 22,000 computers—is 2,000 computers. Thus, the decline in computer production gets greater as we produce more movies. As we

ECONOMICS IN ACTION

Teaching Jobs and Graduate School Applications—Two Sides of the Same Coin

Dozens of new teachers join schools in Silicon Valley, California. Applications to MBA programs at Chicago and MIT soar. Do these two seemingly unrelated events have anything in common? Actually, they do. Behind them we find the same economic phenomenon at work: opportunity costs.

For years, California and other parts of the United States have experienced teacher shortages. During the economic boom of the 1990s, college graduates who might have been interested in teaching had better-paying alternatives in the private sector. In 2000, a teaching job in Silicon Valley paid an average salary of $50,000, while a job in the computer industry paid an average of $80,000, not counting possible gains from stock options—at least a $30,000 differential.

At the same time, college graduates who were considering advancing their education faced a similar decision: "Should I get an MBA and improve my career and future salaries, or should I accept an immediate, high-paying job at a start-up or consulting firm?"

As the recession hit the United States in 2001, many workers were laid off, and others saw their salaries reduced. The U.S. unemployment rate grew from 4.7 percent in January 2001 to 5.6 percent in January 2002, and in Santa Clara County—the heart of Silicon Valley—the increase in the unemployment rate was more dramatic: from 1.7 percent to 7.7 percent. Hewlett-Packard, for example, laid off 6,000 workers—almost 7 percent of its work force—while one of its spinoffs, Agilent, reduced salaries 10 percent for all its 48,000 employees in 2001.

With lower salaries and fewer jobs in the private sector, the opportunity cost of teaching and studying fell. Business schools reported a barrage of applications, with increases of between 50 and 100 percent over the previous year. School districts witnessed a sharp decrease in the number of vacancies available, with many new teachers willing to undergo months of training and substantial pay cuts relative to their old high-tech jobs.

Think of the options you will be facing when you graduate. Given the jobs and salaries currently available, what career do you think you would like to pursue? What would your opportunity cost be?

---

move from 400 movies to 500 movies, we lose 13,000 computers. In other words, the opportunity cost, in terms of computers, of producing more movies increases as we produce more movies. Each extra movie requires a loss of more and more computers. What we have just described is called **increasing opportunity costs,** with emphasis on the word *increasing*.

Why do opportunity costs increase? You can think about it in the following way. Some of the available resources are better suited for movie production than for computer production, and vice versa. Workers who are good at building computers might not be so good at acting, for example, or moviemaking may require an area with a dry, sunny climate. As more and more resources go into making movies, we are forced to take resources that are much better at computer making and use them for moviemaking. Thus, more and more computer production must be lost to increase the production of movies by the same amount. Adding specialized computer designers to a movie cast would be very costly in terms of lost computers, and it might add little to movie production.

increasing opportunity cost: a situation in which producing more of one good requires giving up an increasing amount of production of another good.

The Production Possibilities Curve

Figure 1.2 is a graphical representation of the production possibilities in Table 1.1 that nicely illustrates increasing opportunity costs. We put movies on the horizontal axis and computers on the vertical axis of the figure. Each pair of numbers in a row of the table becomes a point on the graph. For example, point *A* on the graph is from row A of the table. Point *B* is from row B, and so on.

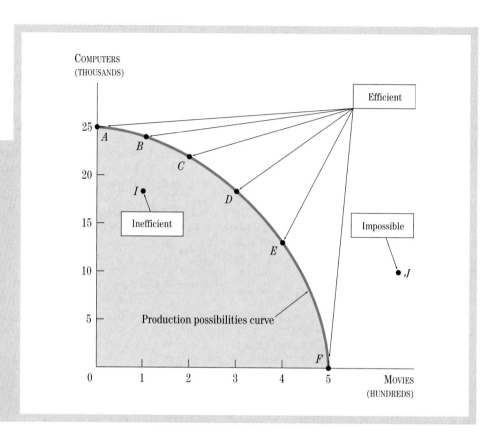

Figure 1.2
The Production Possibilities Curve
Each point on the curve shows the maximum amount of computers that can be produced when a given amount of movies is produced. The points with letters are the same as those in Table 1.1 and are connected by smooth lines. Points in the shaded area inside the curve are inefficient. Points outside the curve are impossible. For the efficient points on the curve, the more movies that are produced, the fewer computers that are produced. The curve is bowed out because of increasing opportunity costs.

production possibilities curve: a curve showing the maximum combinations of production of two goods that are possible, given the economy's resources.

When we connect the points in Figure 1.2, we obtain the **production possibilities curve.** It shows the maximum number of computers that can be produced for each quantity of movies produced. Note that the curve in Figure 1.2 slopes downward and is bowed out from the origin. That the curve is bowed out indicates that the opportunity cost of producing movies increases as more movies are produced. As resources move from computer making to moviemaking, each additional movie means a greater loss of computer production.

■ **Inefficient, Efficient, or Impossible?**   The production possibilities curve shows the effects of scarcity and choice in the economy as a whole. Three situations can be distinguished in Figure 1.2, depending on whether production is in the shaded area, on the curve, or outside the curve.

First, imagine production at point *I*. This point, with 100 movies and 18,000 computers, is inside the curve. But the production possibilities curve tells us that it is possible with the same amount of resources to produce more computers, more movies, or both. For some reason, the economy is not working well at point *I*. For example, instead of using movie film, people may be taking still photos and then sticking them together with tape to make the movie. Points inside the curve, like point *I*, are *inefficient* because the economy could produce a larger number of movies, as at point *D*, or a larger number of computers, as at point *B*. Points inside the production possibilities curve are possible, but they are inefficient.

Second, consider points on the production possibilities curve. These points are *efficient*. They represent the maximum amount that can be produced with available resources. The only way to raise production of one good is to lower production of the other good. Thus, points on the curve show a *tradeoff* between one good and another.

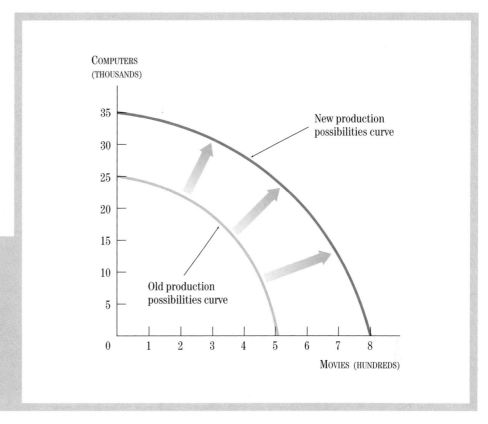

Figure 1.3
Shifts in the Production Possibilities Curve
The production possibilities curve shifts out as the economy grows. The maximum amounts of movies and computers that can be produced increase. Improvements in technology, more machines, or more labor permit the economy to produce more.

Third, consider points to the right and above the production possibilities curve, like point *J* in Figure 1.2. These points are *impossible*. The economy does not have the resources to produce those quantities.

■ **Shifts in the Production Possibilities Curve.**   The production possibilities curve is not immovable. It can *shift* out or in. For example, the curve is shown to shift out in Figure 1.3. More resources—more workers, for example—shift the production possibilities curve out. A technological innovation that allowed one to edit movies faster would also shift the curve outward. So would more cameras, lights, and studios. When the production possibilities curve shifts out, the economy grows because more goods and services can be produced. The production possibilities curve need not shift outward by the same amount in all directions. There can be more movement up than to the right, for example.

As the production possibilities curve shifts out, impossibilities are converted into possibilities. Some of what was impossible for the U.S. economy in 1970 is possible now. Some of what is impossible now will be possible in 2020. Hence, the economists' notion of possibilities is a temporary one. When we say that a certain combination of computers and movies is impossible, we do not mean "forever impossible," we only mean "currently impossible."

■ **Scarcity, Choice, and Economic Progress.**   However, the conversion of impossibilities into possibilities is also an economic problem of choice and scarcity: If we invest less now—in machines, in education, in children, in technology—and consume more now, then we will have less available in the future. If we take computers and movies as symbolic of investment and consumption, then choosing more

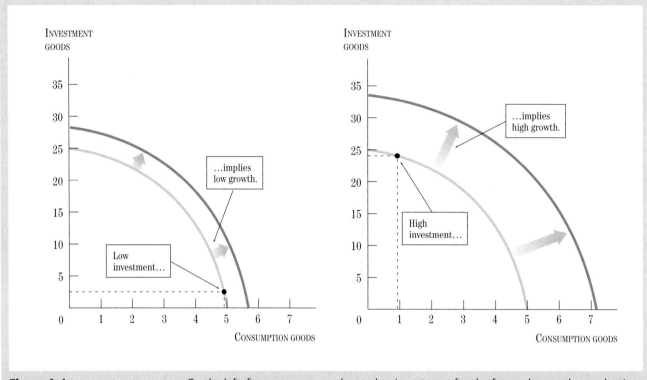

Figure 1.4
Shifts in the Production Possibilities Curve Depend on Choices

On the left, few resources are devoted to investment for the future; hence, the production possibilities curve shifts only a little over time. On the right, more resources are devoted to investment and less to consumption; hence, the production possibilities curve shifts out by a larger amount over time.

investment will result in a larger outward shift of the production possibilities curve, as illustrated in Figure 1.4. More investment enables the economy to produce more in the future.

The production possibilities curve represents a *tradeoff,* but it does not mean that some people win only if others lose. First, it is not necessary for someone to lose in order for the production possibilities curve to shift out. When the curve shifts out, the production of both items increases. Although some people may fare better than others as the production possibilities curve is pushed out, no one necessarily loses. In principle, everyone can gain. Second, if the economy is at an inefficient point (like point *I* in Figure 1.2), then production of both goods can be increased with no tradeoff. In general, therefore, the economy is more like a win-win situation, where everyone can achieve a gain.

REVIEW
- The production possibilities curve represents the choices open to a whole economy when it is confronted by a scarcity of resources. As more of one item is produced, less of another item must be produced. The opportunity cost of producing more of one item is the reduced production of another item.

- The production possibilities curve is bowed out because of increasing opportunity costs.

- Points inside the curve are inefficient. Points on the curve are efficient. Points outside the curve are impossible.

- The production possibilities curve shifts out as resources increase.

- Outward shifts of the production possibilities curve or moves from inefficient to efficient points are the reasons why the economy is not a zero-sum game, despite the existence of scarcity and choice.

Market Economies and the Price System

The Three Fundamental Economic Questions
Any economic system has to answer three questions: What goods and services should be produced—cars, televisions, or something else? How should these goods or services be produced—in what type of factory, and with how much equipment and labor? And for whom should these goods be produced?

The production possibilities curve enables us to discuss key questions about the economy.

Three Questions

There are three essential questions or problems that every economy must find a way to solve, whether it is a small island economy or a large economy like the United States.

- *What* is to be produced: movies, computers, guns, butter, greeting cards, Rollerblades, health care, or something else? In other words, where on the production possibilities curve should an economy be?

What?

How?

For Whom?

- *How* are these goods to be produced? In other words, how can an economy use the available resources so that it is not at an inefficient point inside the production possibilities curve?

- *For whom* are the goods to be produced? We know from the hat/sunglasses example that the allocation of goods in an economy affects people's well-being. An economy in which Maria could not trade her sunglasses for a hat would not work as well as one in which such trades and reallocations are possible. Moreover, an economy in which some people get everything and others get virtually nothing is also not working well.

market economy: an economy characterized by freely determined prices and the free exchange of goods and services in markets.

Broadly speaking, the **market economy** and the **command economy** are two alternative approaches to answering these questions. In a market economy, most decisions about what, how, and for whom to produce are made by individual consumers, firms, governments, and other organizations interacting in markets. In a command, or centrally planned, economy, most decisions about what, how, and for whom to produce are made by those who control the government, which, through a central plan, commands and controls what people do.

command economy: an economy in which the government determines prices and production; also called a centrally planned economy.

Command economies are much less common today than they were in the midtwentieth century, when nearly half the world's population, including the residents of Eastern Europe, the Soviet Union, and China, lived in centrally planned economies. After many decades of struggling to make this system work, leaders of the command economies gradually grew disillusioned with the high degree of inefficiency resulting from the planned approach—which required that the state, or central planners, make critical detailed production decisions—which often resulted in shortages or surplus of products and, as a by-product, in political unrest. In recent years, most command economies have been engaged in the complex process of converting from a command to a market system, with varying degrees of success. This is partly due to the fact that these economies had none or few of the social, legal, or political fixtures critical to the market system. China has probably been the most successful of these economies at making the transition, developing a model that the Chinese term *market socialism*. Beginning in the 1970s, elements of both the command and market economies coexisted in China; in the mid 1990s, market mechanisms grew more dominant. While its political system is still highly centralized, many people credit China's rapid economic growth in recent years to its decentralized economic system.

Key Elements of a Market Economy

Let's take a closer look at some of the ingredients critical to a market economy.

freely determined price: a price that is determined by the individuals and firms interacting in markets.

■ **Freely Determined Prices.** In a market economy, most prices—such as the price of computers—are freely determined by individuals and firms interacting in markets. These **freely determined prices** are an essential characteristic of a market economy. In a command economy, most prices are set by government, and this leads to inefficiencies in the economy. For example, in the Soviet Union, the price of bread was set so low that farmers fed bread to the cows. Feeding bread to livestock is an enormous waste of resources. Livestock could eat plain grain. By feeding the cows bread, farmers added the cost of the labor to bake the bread and the fuel to heat the bread ovens to the cost of livestock feed. This is inefficient, like point *I* in Figure 1.2.

In practice, not all prices in market economies are freely determined. For example, some cities control the price of rental apartments. We will look at these exceptions later. But the vast majority of prices are free to vary.

property rights: rights over the use, sale, and proceeds from a good or resource.

incentive: a device that motivates people to take action, usually so as to increase economic efficiency.

market failure: any situation in which the market does not lead to an efficient economic outcome and in which there is a potential role for government.

government failure: a situation in which the government makes things worse than the market, even though there may be market failure.

◼ **Property Rights and Incentives.** Property rights are another key element of a market economy. **Property rights** give individuals the legal authority to keep or sell property, whether land or other resources. Property rights are needed for a market economy because they give people the ability to buy and sell goods. Without property rights, people could take whatever they wanted without paying. People would have to devote time and resources to protecting their earnings or goods.

Moreover, by giving people the rights to the earnings from their work, as well as letting them suffer some of the consequences or losses from their mistakes, property rights provide **incentives.** For example, if an inventor could not get the property rights to an invention, then the incentive to produce the invention would be low or even nonexistent. Hence there would be few inventions, and we would all be worse off. If there were no property rights, people would not have incentives to specialize and reap the gains from the division of labor. Any extra earnings from specialization could be taken away.

◼ **Freedom to Trade at Home and Abroad.** Economic interaction is a way to improve economic outcomes, as the examples in this chapter indicate. Allowing people to interact freely is thus another necessary ingredient of a market economy. Freedom to trade can be extended beyond national borders to other economies.

International trade increases the opportunities to gain from trade. This is especially important in small countries, where it is impossible to produce everything. But the gains from exchange and comparative advantage also exist for larger countries.

◼ **A Role for Government.** Just because prices are freely determined and people are free to trade in a market economy does not mean that there is no role for government. For example, in virtually all market economies, the government provides defense and police protection. The government also helps establish property rights. But how far beyond that should it go? Should the government also address the "for whom" question by providing a safety net—a mechanism to deal with the individuals in the economy who are poor, who go bankrupt, who remain unemployed? Most would say yes, but what should the government's role be? Economics provides an analytical framework to answer such questions. In certain circumstances—called **market failure**—the market economy does not provide good enough answers to the "what, how, and for whom" questions, and the government has a role to play in improving on the market. However, the government, even in the case of market failure, may do worse than the market, in which case economists say there is **government failure.**

◼ **The Role of Private Organizations.** It is an interesting feature of market economies that many economic interactions between people take place in organizations—firms, families, charitable organizations—rather than in markets. Some economic interactions that take place in organizations could take place in the market. In some circumstances, the same type of interaction takes place in a firm and in a market simultaneously. For example, many large firms employ lawyers as part of their permanent staff. Other firms simply purchase the services of such lawyers in the market; if the firm wants to sue someone or is being sued by someone, it hires an outside lawyer to represent it.

Economic interactions in firms differ from those in the market. Staff lawyers inside large firms are usually paid annual salaries that do not depend directly on the number of hours worked or their success in the lawsuits. In contrast, outside lawyers are paid an hourly fee and a contingency fee based on the number of hours worked and how successful they are.

Economic interactions can take place in a marketplace, between two friends, on the Internet, or even on the radio, as this article attests. All you need is someone who wants to sell something and someone else who wants to buy. Tradio helps potential buyers and sellers learn about each other in a virtual market, realizing gains from trade that would not be possible without the exchange of information. Even though radio stations do not charge buyers and sellers, you will notice that tradio is not just a public service. Tradio is very low-cost programming that attracts a large audience and many paid ads from local businesses—a win-win situation for individual buyers and sellers, radio stations, and local businesses. Gains from trade in action!

Who Needs eBay? For Towns Across U.S., Tradio Is Real Deal

By Reid J. Epstein, Staff Reporter
THE WALL STREET JOURNAL
September 11, 2002

GLASGOW, Mont.—It was a little after nine one recent morning, and local residents were already on the line to Lori Mason's radio show.

One caller wanted to unload a riding lawnmower ($500). Another tried to sell an irrigation pump ($100), and four offered up washing machines, including one that "leaks a little bit" ($10). Others still were looking to buy eight bales of straw, fresh dill and a large dog house.

When one young woman phoned in to put her '79 GMC pickup on the block, the 54-year-old Ms. Mason not only recognized her voice but urged her to loosen up.

"Oh, sorry," said the caller, 23-year-old day-care provider Jamie Seyfert. "We're willing to trade for guns, jet skis or anything fun."

This is the sound of "tradio" (pronounced TRADE-ee-o), a kind of on-air swap meet that has been a fixture of small-town stations from Florida to Alaska for decades. Far from being rendered obsolete by the Internet, many tradio shows are doing surprisingly well these days. They are the top moneymakers for some stations, often commanding a premium from local advertisers. And the format may be pushing into bigger markets. In April, WCCO in Minneapolis introduced "The WCCO Great Garage Sale" and saw its ratings jump 29% in the time slot.

Three-Stoplight Town

Here in Glasgow, a three-stoplight railroad town of 3,253 people on the lonely plains of northeastern Montana, the half-hour show is simulcast three mornings a week from the second-floor studio of locally owned stations KLTZ and KLAN. Virtually everyone in town, from the mayor to the editor of the weekly paper, has bought or sold something on the show.

Here's how it works: Callers announce they're selling something—a gas heater that "would be good in your garage, your huntin' shack or whatever," a "very large collection of Fiestaware dishes in all the new colors" or some "very friendly young goats"—and leave their phone number. Anyone interested calls the seller, and the transaction is negotiated face-to-face.

Internet Connection

While it may sound archaic in the age of eBay, the tradio format seems to be benefiting from the buzz generated by the popular Web auction site. Some tradio shows are using the Internet to their advantage—allowing listeners to submit items for sale via e-mail and posting items called into the show on their Web sites.

The tradio format first took hold in the early 1950s when powerful nationwide radio networks cut back on programming. To fill the void, small-town stations began broadcasting obituaries, birthdays and anniversaries. An appliance-store owner in Seguin is believed by many in the industry to have started the first tradio show. He began buying air time to read notices of items for sale that customers had posted on a bulletin board inside his store.

In small towns that don't have daily newspapers—the closest daily to Glasgow is the *Herald* in Williston, N.D., 144 miles away—tradio takes the place of classifieds and, perhaps more important, gossip. When Ms. Mason heard a caller say he was selling his $100 irrigation pump, she exclaimed, "You're on the new water line!" and quizzed him about the difference that had made in his water supply.

Another big attraction is the price. A classified ad in the weekly *Glasgow Courier* costs $5.25 per column inch, while calls to "Tradio" are free. And eBay, which exacts a sliding fee based on the price of the item sold, also requires a hookup to the Internet.

Alicia Sibley, a 24-year-old hay farmer, is a regular listener to the Glasgow show. She was driving her tractor a few weeks ago when she heard a caller offering to sell a 6-foot freezer. She phoned the seller—who had bought the freezer to stock up on frozen foods for fear of a catastrophe at the turn of the millennium—and made a deal for $200. "It's a real nice one, too," Ms. Sibley said. "I saved around $200."

Incentives within an organization are as important as incentives in markets. If the lawyers on a firm's legal staff get to keep some of the damages the firm wins in a lawsuit, they will have more incentive to do a good job. Some firms even try to create marketlike competition between departments or workers in order to give more incentives.

Why do some economic interactions occur in markets and others in organizations? Ronald Coase of the University of Chicago won the Nobel Prize for showing that organizations such as firms are created to reduce market *transaction costs*, the costs of buying and selling, which include finding a buyer or a seller and reaching agreement on a price. When market transaction costs are high, we see more transactions taking place within organizations. For example, a firm might have a legal staff rather than outside lawyers because searching for a good lawyer every time there is a lawsuit is too costly. In a crisis, a good lawyer may not be available.

The Price System

The previous discussion indicates that in market economies, freely determined prices are essential for determining what is produced, how, and for whom. For this reason, a market economy is said to use *the price system* to solve these problems. In this section, we show that prices do a surprising amount of work: (1) Prices serve as *signals* about what should be produced and consumed when there are changes in tastes or changes in technology, (2) prices provide *incentives* to people to alter their production or consumption, and (3) prices affect the *distribution of income*, or who gets what in the economy.

Let's use an example. Suppose that there is a sudden new trend for college students to ride bicycles more and drive cars less. How do prices help people in the economy decide what to do in response to this new trend?

■ **Signals.** First, consider how the information about the change in tastes is signaled to the producers of bicycles and cars. As students buy more bicycles, the price of bicycles rises. A higher price will signal that it is more profitable for firms to produce more bicycles. In addition, some bicycle components, like lightweight metal, will also increase in price. Increased lightweight metal prices signal that production of lightweight metal should increase. As the price of metal rises, wages for metalworkers may increase. Thus, prices are a signal all the way from the consumer to the metalworkers that more bicycles should be produced. This is what is meant by the expression "prices are a signal."

It is important to note that no single individual knows the information that is transmitted by prices. Any economy is characterized by limited information, where people cannot know the exact reasons why prices for certain goods rise or fall. Hence, it is rather amazing that prices can signal this information.

■ **Incentives.** Now let's use this example to consider how prices provide incentives. A higher price for bicycles will increase the incentives for firms to produce bicycles. Because they receive more for each bicycle, they produce more. If there is a large price increase that is not merely temporary, new firms may enter the bicycle business. In contrast, the reduced prices for cars signal to car producers that production should decrease.

■ **Distribution.** How do prices affect the distribution of income? On the one hand, workers who find the production of the good they make increasing because of the higher demand for bicycles will earn more. On the other hand, income will be reduced for those who make cars or who have to pay more for bicycles. Local delivery services that use bicycles will see their costs increase.

REVIEW

- The market economy and the command economy are two alternative systems for addressing the questions any economy must face: what to produce, how to produce, and for whom to produce.

- A market economy is characterized by several key elements, such as freely determined prices, property rights, and freedom to trade at home and abroad.

- For a market economy to work well, markets should be competitive and the government should play a role.

- Prices are signals, they provide incentives, and they affect the distribution of income.

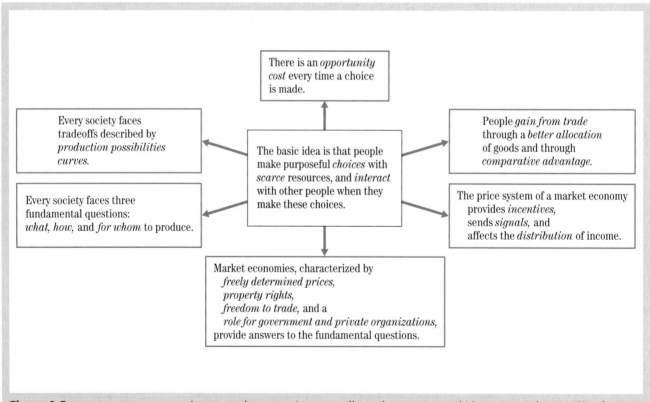

**Figure 1.5
From One Central Idea, Many
Powerful Ideas Follow**

As you study economics, you will see the same central idea again and again. This figure illustrates how many powerful economic ideas are connected to the one in the center.

Conclusion

One basic idea lies at the center of economics: People make purposeful choices with scarce resources, and interact with other people when they make these choices.

This introductory chapter illustrates this idea, starting with Tiger Woods's decision to leave school and continuing with simple examples of people making choices about what to consume or produce.

From this central idea, many other powerful ideas follow, as summarized visually in Figure 1.5. There is an *opportunity cost* every time a choice is made. People *gain from trade*, both through a *better allocation* of goods and through *comparative advantage*. Every society faces tradeoffs described by *production possibilities curves*. Every society faces three fundamental questions: *what, how,* and *for whom* to produce. Market economies—characterized by *freely determined prices, property rights, freedom to trade,* and *a role for both government and private organizations*—give an answer to these three questions. The price system of a market economy works by providing *incentives*, sending *signals*, and affecting the *distribution* of income.

You will see this central idea again and again as you study economics.

KEY POINTS

1. Everyone faces a scarcity of something, usually time or resources.
2. Scarcity leads to choice, and choice leads to opportunity costs.
3. Trade leads to gains because it allows goods and services to be reallocated in a way that improves people's well-being.
4. Trade also leads to gains because it permits people to specialize in what they are relatively good at.
5. The production possibilities curve summarizes the tradeoffs in the whole economy due to scarcity. Economic production is efficient if the economy is on the production possibilities curve.
6. The three basic questions that any economy must face are what, how, and for whom production should take place.
7. A well-functioning market system involves freely determined prices, property rights, freedom to trade, and a role for government and private organizations.
8. If prices are set at the wrong levels by government, waste and inefficiency—such as feeding bread to livestock—will result.
9. Prices transmit signals, provide incentives, and affect the distribution of income.

KEY TERMS

economics
scarcity
choice
economic interaction
market
opportunity cost
gains from trade
division of labor
comparative advantage
international trade
production possibilities
increasing opportunity cost
production possibilities curve
market economy
command economy
freely determined prices
property rights
incentives
market failure
government failure

QUESTIONS FOR REVIEW

1. How do scarcity, choice, and economic interaction fit into the basic idea at the center of economics?
2. Why does scarcity imply a choice among alternatives?
3. Why does choice create opportunity costs?
4. What is the difference between economic interaction in markets and in organizations?
5. Why is there a gain from trade even if total production of goods and services does not change?

6. How can specialization lead to a gain from trade?

7. What is the principle of increasing opportunity costs?

8. What are the key ingredients of a market economy?

9. What are the three basic questions that any economic system must address?

10. What are the three roles of prices?

PROBLEMS

1. Suppose that you are president of the student government, and you have $10,000 for guest speakers for the year. Spike Lee costs $10,000 per appearance. Former economic advisers to the government charge $1,000 per lecture. Hence, you cannot have both Spike Lee and the former economic advisers. Explain the economic problem of choice and scarcity in this case. What issues would you consider in arriving at a decision?

2. Compare the opportunity cost of one more year of school versus working for one year for (1) a high school graduate, (2) a college graduate, and (3) a medical school graduate.

3. Allison will graduate from high school next June. She has ranked her three possible postgraduation plans in the following order: (1) work for two years at a consulting job in her home town paying $20,000 per year, (2) attend a local community college for two years, spending $5,000 per year on tuition and expenses, and (3) travel around the world tutoring a rock star's child for pay of $5,000 per year. What is the opportunity cost of her choice?

4. Suppose you have two salt shakers and a friend of yours has two pepper shakers. Explain how you can both gain from trade. Is this a gain from trade through *better allocation* or *greater production*? Suppose now that your friend lives in another country, whose government does not allow trade between your countries. Who would lose as a result of this trade barrier?

5. Suppose Tina and Julia can produce jars of salsa and computer-designed advertisements in the following combinations in a given week:

Tina		Julia	
Salsa	*Ads*	*Salsa*	*Ads*
50	0	25	0
40	1	20	1
30	2	15	2
20	3	10	3
10	4	5	4
0	5	0	5

a. If Tina and Julia are each currently producing 2 advertisements per week, how many jars of salsa are they producing? What is the total production of salsa and advertisements between them?

b. Is there a possibility for increasing production? Why or why not?

c. Suppose Julia completely specializes in producing advertisements and Tina completely specializes in producing salsa. What will be the total production of advertisements and salsa?

6. Suppose you must divide your time between studying for your math final and writing a final paper for your English class. The fraction of time you spend studying math and its relation to your grade in the two classes is given in the table below.

Fraction of Time Spent on Math	Math Grade	English Grade
0	0	97
20	45	92
40	65	85
60	75	70
80	82	50
100	88	0

a. Draw a tradeoff curve for the math grade versus the English grade.

b. What is the opportunity cost of increasing the time spent on math from 80 to 100 percent? What is the opportunity cost of increasing the time spent on math from 60 to 80 percent?

c. Are there increasing opportunity costs from spending more time on math? Explain.

d. What can you do to get a 92 in both subjects? Explain.

7. A small country produces only two goods, cars and computers. Given its limited resources, this country has the following production possibilities:

Cars	Computers
0	200
25	180
50	130
75	70
100	0

a. Draw the production possibilities curve.

b. Suppose car production uses mainly machines and computer production uses mainly labor. Show what happens to the curve when the number of machines increases but labor remains unchanged.

8. After World War II and until the 1980s, the Japanese economy grew very rapidly, and its citizens now enjoy a high standard of living. How would you explain the fast Japanese growth in terms of tradeoffs and decisions made by individuals and societies?

9. Tracy tells Huey that he can improve his economics grades without sacrificing fun activities or grades in other courses. Can you imagine ways in which this might be possible? What does that imply about the initial situation?

   If Huey is taking just two courses and he can improve his economics grade without hurting his math grade, how could you represent this situation graphically?

10. Compare two countries. In one country, the government sets prices and never adjusts them. In the other country, the government adjusts prices daily, endeavoring to allocate resources to consumers to satisfy their tastes. Is either of these a market economy? Why or why not?

11. Suppose decreased production of oil in the Middle East causes the price of oil to rise all over the world. Explain how this change in the price signals information to U.S. producers, provides incentives to U.S. producers, and affects the distribution of income.

12. "When you look at the economies in the United States, Europe, or Japan, you see most of the ingredients of a market economy. For example, consider bicycles. Prices in the bicycle market are free to vary; people have property rights to the bicycles they buy; many people sell bicycles; many bicycles sold in the United States, Europe, and Japan come from other countries; the government regulates bicycle use (no bicycles on the freeways, for example); and bicycle production takes place within firms with many workers." Replace bicycles with another good or service of your choosing in this quotation and comment on whether the quotation is still true.

CHAPTER 2

Observing and Explaining the Economy

Mark McClellan is a lot like Tiger Woods. He trained long and hard before he became a professional, and he now excels in his field. But Mark is not an expert at driving and putting golf balls. Rather, he is an expert at observing and explaining economic trends in the biggest industry in America.

After college, Mark went on to earn a Ph.D. in economics. He also went to medical school, completed an internship and residency in a hospital, and became a practicing medical doctor. Why would an economist become a doctor? Because the biggest industry in America is not automobiles, oil, or construction—but health care. Mark concluded that to observe and explain the health-care industry, he needed to be an expert in economics as well as medicine. And all of the training has paid off. As a health-care economist, Mark has demonstrated, among other things, that doctors sometimes provide treatments of little actual value to their patients and that it is the fear of malpractice suits that motivates doctors to do so. His economic expertise and insights on health-care policy have earned him a place, first, in 2001 and 2002, as one of the three members of President Bush's Council of Economic Advisers, then, from 2002 to 2004, as Commissioner of the Food and Drug Administration, and most recently as Administrator of the Centers for Medicare and Medicaid Services.

The purpose of this chapter is to give you a broad overview of economics by looking at the kinds of things economists such as Mark McClellan actually do. Economics is a way of thinking. It entails accurately *describing* economic events, *explaining* why the events occur, *predicting* under what circumstances such events might take place in the future, and *recommending* appropriate courses of action. To make use of economics, you will want to learn to do the describing, the explaining, and even the predicting and recommending yourself—that is, to reason and think like an economist. By making use of economics in this way, you can better understand the economic challenges and opportunities you face, and thereby make improvements in your own life or the lives of those around you.

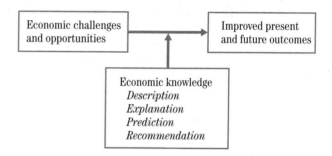

Just as physicists try to explain the existence of black holes in outer space or biologists try to explain why dinosaurs became extinct, economists try to explain puzzling observations and facts about the economy. Many observations come from everyday life. Are there some economic observations—from your own experience, from recent news stories, or from your history or political science courses—that you find puzzling? Some of your questions might be like these:

- Why is college tuition so high?
- Why have the wages of college graduates increased much more rapidly than the wages of high school dropouts since the 1970s?
- Why are there 17 different types of Colgate toothpaste now, while there were only two types 30 years ago?
- Why is the average income of people in the United States about 35 times higher than that of people in China?
- Why is unemployment much higher in Europe than in the United States?
- Why has health-care spending increased faster than the rest of the U.S. economy?
- Why has the price of health care increased more than most other prices?

All these questions are based on observations about the economy. Some, like the question about college tuition, are fairly obvious and are based on casual observation. But in order to answer such questions, economists, like physicists or biologists, need to systematically document and quantify their observations and look for patterns. If we can establish the date when dinosaurs became extinct, then we may be able to test our hunch that a cataclysmic event such as an asteroid hitting the earth caused their extinction. To illustrate how economists document and quantify their observations, let us briefly focus on the last two of the preceding questions, the ones concerning health care and the economy. This will also give us an opportunity to introduce some key indicators used to measure the economy.

Health-Care Spending in America

Health-care spending and prices are more than a curiosity. The more a society spends on health care, the less it can spend on other things, as we know from the production possibilities curve of Chapter 1. Concerns about health-care spending have led to major proposals for changing the way health care is provided and paid for in the United States. Health care *is* a major political issue. People who are dissatisfied with their own health care want the right to sue their health-care providers. Debates about the addition of a prescription drug benefit to Medicare—a government health-care program for the elderly—raged during the period leading up to the 2004 presidential and congressional elections. But let's focus on our first observation and question.

> **Observation 1:** Health-care spending has increased faster than the rest of the U.S. economy since 1990.

How has health-care spending changed relative to the rest of the economy? To determine this, we need a measure of health-care spending and a measure of the size of the overall economy.

Spending as a Share of GDP

gross domestic product (GDP): a measure of the value of all the goods and services newly produced in an economy during a specified period of time.

The most comprehensive available measure of the size of an economy is the **gross domestic product (GDP).** For the United States, GDP is the total value of all products made in the United States during a specified period of time, such as a year. GDP includes all newly made goods, such as cars, trucks, shoes, airplanes, houses, and telephones; it also includes services, such as education, rock concerts, and health care. To measure the total value of all products made in the economy, economists add up the dollars that people spend on the products.

How large is GDP in the United States? In 2004, it was $11,735 billion, or about $11.7 trillion. We can compute GDP for any year. The question about health-care spending and the size of the economy requires that we look at the U.S. economy since 1990. In 1990, GDP was $5,803 billion. Column (1) of Table 2.1 provides a history of GDP since 1990.

Graphs are frequently a more helpful way to present data like those shown in Table 2.1. Figure 2.1 plots the data on GDP from column (1) of Table 2.1. The vertical axis is measured in billions of dollars; the horizontal axis is measured in years. For example, the point at the extreme lower left in Figure 2.1 represents GDP of $5,803 billion (on the vertical axis) in the year 1990 (on the horizontal axis). The points are connected by a line, which helps us visualize the steady growth of GDP during this period.

Now let us consider health-care spending, which includes payments for hospital services, lab tests, nursing homes, visits to the doctor or dentist, drugs, hearing aids, and eyeglasses. If we add up all spending on health care, we get $1,392 billion in 2004.

Table 2.1
GDP and Health-Care Spending, 1990–2004

Year	(1) GDP	(2) Health-Care Spending	(3) Health-Care Share of GDP (percent)
1990	5,803	556	9.6
1991	5,996	609	10.2
1992	6,338	672	10.6
1993	6,657	715	10.7
1994	7,073	753	10.6
1995	7,398	798	10.8
1996	7,817	833	10.7
1997	8,304	873	10.5
1998	8,747	921	10.5
1999	9,268	961	10.4
2000	9,817	1,027	10.5
2001	10,128	1,114	11.0
2002	10,487	1,210	11.5
2003	11,004	1,301	11.8
2004	11,735	1,392	11.9

Note: GDP and health-care spending are measured in billions of dollars.
Source: The source of all data in this section is the U.S. Department of
Commerce National Income and Product Accounts.

100 times column 2
divided by column 1

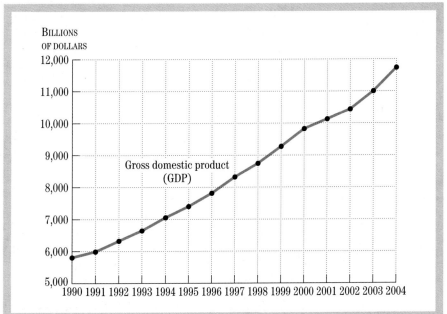

Figure 2.1
Gross Domestic Product (GDP) in the United States, 1990–2004
GDP is the total dollar value of newly produced goods and services. It can be measured by adding up what people spend on everything, from health care to cars. For
each year from 1990 to 2004, GDP is plotted; the line connects all the points.

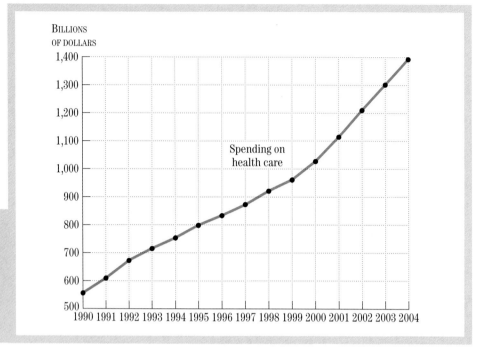

Figure 2.2
Spending on Health Care in the United States, 1990–2004
Health-care spending is the dollar value of payments for hospitals, doctors, dentists, nursing homes, drugs, and other items that provide medical care. Health care is one part of GDP.

This amount is more than three times as large as the entire automobile industry, including cars, trucks, and parts. Health care is the biggest industry in the United States.

Health-care spending since 1990 is listed in column (2) of Table 2.1 and is plotted in Figure 2.2. Figures 2.1 and 2.2 show that both GDP and health-care spending have grown since 1990. One way to assess the growth of health-care spending compared to spending on all goods and services is to look at health-care spending as a share, or percentage, of GDP. For example, in 2000, health-care spending was $1,027 billion, and GDP was $9,817 billion. Thus, the share (in percentage terms) of GDP going to health care was:

$$\frac{\text{Health-care spending}}{\text{GDP}} \times 100 = \frac{\text{health-care spending}}{\text{as a share of GDP}}$$

$$\frac{1,027}{9,817} \times 100 = 10.5 \text{ percent}$$

Observation 2: The price of health care has risen compared with the price of other goods and services in the economy.

Column (3) of Table 2.1 gives the results of this calculation for all years from 1990 to 2004. Again, it is helpful to plot the shares, as in Figure 2.3. Observe how health-care spending rose as a percentage of GDP—or relative to the size of the economy—in the early 1990s, slowed down a little in the late 1990s, but then increased again in the 2000s. We have now quantified the observation about rising health-care spending. Now let us go on to consider the second question about health care and see whether the price of health care has risen compared with the price of other goods and services in the economy.

The Relative Price

relative price: the price of a particular good compared to the price of other things.

To see whether the price of health care has increased more or less rapidly than other things, we look at the relative price of health care. The **relative price** is a measure of health-care prices compared with the average prices of all goods and services, computed by dividing the health-care price by the average price of all goods and services:

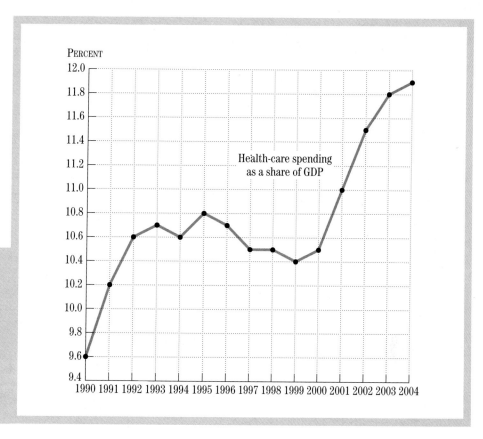

Figure 2.3
Health-Care Spending as a Share of GDP
Each point on the graph is the ratio of spending on health care from Figure 2.2 to GDP from Figure 2.1, expressed as a percentage. For example, in 2000, health-care spending was $1,027 billion and GDP was $9,817 billion. The ratio is 1,027/9,817 = .105, or 10.5 percent.

$$\frac{\text{Relative price}}{\text{of health care}} = \frac{\text{health-care price}}{\text{average price of all goods and services}}$$

The relative price of health care is shown in Table 2.2 and plotted in Figure 2.4. Observe that the relative price of health care has risen since 1990. In other words, the price of health care has increased relative to the average of all other prices.

Correlations Between Economic Variables

So far, we have focused on two economic variables to quantify our observations about health care in the United States. These variables are (1) health-care spending's share of GDP and (2) the relative price of health care. An **economic variable** is any economic measure that can vary over a range of values. Are these two economic variables correlated? Are there interesting patterns?

economic variable: any economic measure that can vary over a range of values.

Figure 2.5 is useful for determining whether the relative price of health care and health care's share of GDP have been correlated. Each point in the figure corresponds to a relative price and a health-care share taken from Table 2.2 and from the last column of Table 2.1. The relative price is on the vertical axis, and health care as a share of GDP is on the horizontal axis.

The points in Figure 2.5 trace out some patterns. As the relative price of health care increased from 1990 to 1993, so did spending on health care as a share of GDP. Two variables are *correlated* if they tend to move up or down at the same time. There is a *positive correlation* if the two variables move in the same direction: When one goes up, the other goes up. Health-care spending as a share of GDP and the relative price of health care were positively correlated from 1990 to 1993 and from 2001 to 2004.

Table 2.2
Relative Price of Health Care

Year	Relative Health-Care Price
1990	0.887
1991	0.908
1992	0.936
1993	0.958
1994	0.977
1995	0.993
1996	1.000
1997	1.008
1998	1.022
1999	1.032
2000	1.039
2001	1.051
2002	1.060
2003	1.077
2004	1.087

Note: The relative price is a ratio of the price of health care to the average price of all goods and services. The ratio is set to 1 in 1996. This year is arbitrary: Using another year would not change the patterns of the relative prices.

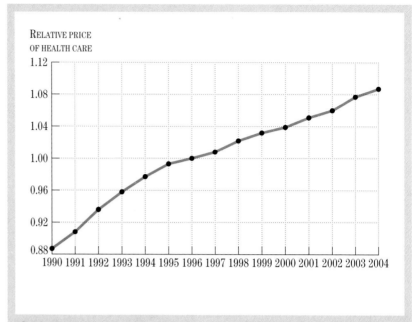

Figure 2.4
Relative Price of Health Care
Health-care prices rose more rapidly than other prices in the 1990s. Hence, the relative price of health care has increased; the increase was especially rapid in the early 1990s and the early 2000s.

Two variables are negatively correlated if they tend to move in opposite directions. From 1995 to 2000, a higher relative price of health care was associated with lower spending shares; thus, there was a *negative correlation* during those years.

■ **Correlation versus Causation.**   Just because there is a correlation between two variables does not mean that one caused the other. There is a difference between *causation* and *correlation*. *Correlation* means that one event is usually observed to occur along with another. For example, high readings on a thermometer occur when it is hot outside. *Causation* means that one event brings about another event. But correlation does not imply causation. For example, the high reading on the thermometer does not cause the hot weather, even though the high reading and the hot weather are correlated. In this example, we know that the causation is the other way around: Hot weather causes the reading on the thermometer to be high.

More to the point for economics, if you looked only at the correlation in Figure 2.5 from 1990 to 1993, you might be tempted to say that the higher price of health care caused health-care spending to rise. But that correlation does not permit us to make such a conclusion about causation. We need to know more about the effects of the price of health care on health-care spending and about what determines the price before we can make statements about causality. In fact, between 1995 and 1999, spending on health care fell as a share of GDP as the relative price rose. One would have been proven wrong if one had argued that a higher price of health care would increase health-care spending.

controlled experiments:
empirical tests of theories in a controlled setting in which particular effects can be isolated.

■ **The Lack of Controlled Experiments in Economics.**   In many sciences—certainly psychology, medicine, and biology—investigators perform **controlled experiments** to determine whether one event causes another event. An example of a

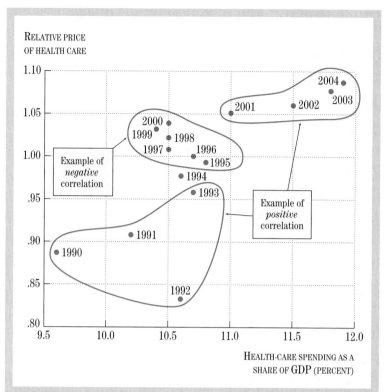

RELATIVE PRICE
OF HEALTH CARE

Example of
negative
correlation

Example of
positive
correlation

HEALTH-CARE SPENDING AS A
SHARE OF GDP (PERCENT)

Figure 2.5
Relative Price of Health Care versus Health-Care
Spending Share
The figure plots pairs of points: the relative price of health care on the
vertical axis and health-care spending as a share of GDP on the horizontal axis. The observations come from Table 2.2 and the last column
of Table 2.1.

experimental economics: a
branch of economics that uses
laboratory experiments to analyze
economic behavior.

controlled experiment is the clinical trial of new
drugs. New drugs are tested by trying them out
on two groups of individuals. One group gets
the drug; the other group gets a placebo (a pill
without the drug). If the experiment results in a
significantly greater number of people being
cured among the group taking the drug than
among the control group not taking the drug,
investigators conclude that the drug causes the
cure.

Unfortunately, such controlled experiments are rare in economics. In the case of
health-care prices and health-care spending,
we cannot go back and repeat the years from
1990 to 2004 with a different health-care price
and see what happens. True, we could look at
other countries' experience, or we could look at
the experience of different states within the
United States. Economists use such comparisons to help determine causation. For example, we could look at one state in which the
price of medical care increased and one in
which it did not. We could then look at the
health-care spending in each state to see if
higher prices caused health-care spending to
increase. But, unfortunately, no two countries
or states are alike in all respects. Thus, attempting to control for other factors is not as easy as
in the case of clinical trials.

In recent years, economists have adapted
some methods of experimental science and
have begun to conduct economic experiments
in laboratory settings that are similar to the real
world. The experiments can be repeated, and various effects can be controlled for.
Experimental economics is a growing area of economics. The findings of experimental economics have affected economists' understanding of how the economy
works. Experiments in economics also provide an excellent way to *learn* how the
economy works, much as experiments in science courses can help one learn about
gravity or the structure of plant cells. But because it is difficult to replicate real-world
settings exactly in such experiments, they have not yet been applied as widely as the
clinical or laboratory experiments in other sciences.

■ **Faulty Data.** Economic data are not always accurate. People sometimes do not
understand the survey questions, are too busy to fill them out carefully, or do not
have the correct information. Hospitals reporting data on health-care prices, for
example, may not take into account changes in the quality of health care. When people purchase medical care, the quality of the service provided can vary widely over
time and from doctor to doctor.

If the quality of health care is improving, then the higher relative prices we have
observed might partly reflect better service rather than an increase in the price of the
same service. The actual increase in the price of health care might have been less
rapid if we measured the improved quality, such as reduced chances of serious stroke
or depression because of better drugs.

REVIEW

- Economists endeavor to explain facts and observations about the economy, but it is not always easy to establish what the facts are. To establish patterns, it is sometimes necessary to carefully organize information and present it in tables or graphs.

- GDP is a measure of all the goods and services produced in a country during a period of time.

- Correlation does not imply causation. Because controlled experiments are rare in economics, establishing causation is more difficult in economics than in other sciences.

- Recent advances in experimental economics are improving this situation.

- Economic observations are not always accurate. For example, the quality of a service such as medical care can be difficult to measure.

The Circular Flow Diagram: People Interacting in Markets

circular flow diagram: a diagram illustrating the flow of funds through the economy as people buy and sell in markets.

Behind the health-care and GDP observations in the figures and tables we've just examined are real people who purchase and produce health care and other services and goods in the economy. Any explanation of spending trends must be based on the choices these people make and how they interact with each other. In order to organize our thinking about who these people are and how they interact in the economy, a diagram is helpful. It is called the **circular flow diagram** and is shown in Figure 2.6. The circular flow diagram shows how funds flow through the economy as people buy and sell things. Notice the arrows pointing in a circular pattern (that's how the diagram gets its name). To understand how the diagram works, we need to discuss the boxes that the arrows point into and out of.

When using a circular flow diagram, economists place the things that people buy and sell into three groups: (1) *goods and services*, such as flu shots or medical physicals; (2) *labor*, such as the work of nurses and doctors; and (3) *capital*, such as the x-ray machines or the hospital beds that are needed to provide health care. In general, the term *capital* refers to the equipment and structures used to produce goods and services. Corresponding to each of these three groups is a market in which items in the group are bought and sold: (1) *the goods and services market*, (2) *the labor market*, and (3) *the capital market*. These three markets are shown by the blue boxes in the middle part of Figure 2.6, with the light blue boxes giving examples from the health-care industry.

Now consider the *households* and the *firms* in the circular flow diagram. A household is an individual or group of individuals occupying a set of living quarters. For example, a household could be a group of college graduates sharing an apartment, a divorced person living alone, a family with four children, or a single retiree. A firm is a producer of goods and services. For example, a firm in the health-care industry could be a local hospital or a large health maintenance organization. Of course, there are many other types of producers in the economy: General Motors produces cars, the University of Texas produces educational services, the U.S. government produces defense services, and so on. The circular flow diagram puts all producers into the "firm" category.

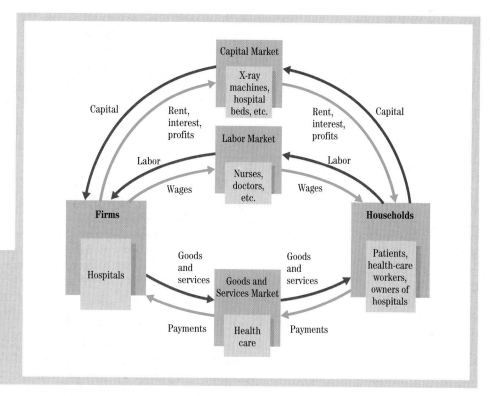

Figure 2.6
A Circular Flow Diagram
This diagram shows how funds flow through the economy from households to firms and back again. Buying and selling take place in the goods and services markets, the labor market, and the capital market.

The households and firms are shown in the blue boxes on the right and left, respectively, of the circular flow diagram, with the light blue boxes again giving examples from the health-care industry. The households are shown doing three things in the circular flow diagram:

- Households buy goods and services; for example, an older person gets a flu shot at the doctor's office.

- Households sell their labor services to firms in the labor market; for example, a nurse works for an HMO and receives wages in return.

- Households supply capital to firms in the capital market; for example, a young couple may rent out the first floor of their house as a doctor's office and receive rent in return. Households also supply capital by owning shares in firms (and receiving part of the profits) or making loans to firms (and receiving interest).

Note that in each of these cases, firms are on the other side of the market from households. Thus the firms are also shown doing three things: They sell goods and services to households, they buy labor services from households, and they buy capital from households.

The arrows in the circular flow diagram show the results of all this buying and selling. The counterclockwise (red) arrows show the movement of goods and services, labor, and capital. The clockwise (green) arrows show the flow of funds used to pay for these items: payments for goods and services, wages for labor, and rent, interest, and profit for capital. Funds flow through the economy from households to firms and back again.

The circular flow diagram is a useful visual device for keeping track of the people in the economy and the markets in which they interact. If we are going to understand the workings of any part of the economy—including health care—we must think about these households and firms as they interact in the markets. That is where economic theory or models come into play.

REVIEW • The circular flow diagram is useful for showing how households and firms interact in markets and how funds flow through the economy.

Economic Models

economic model: an explanation of how the economy or part of the economy works.

In order to explain economic facts and observations, one needs an economic theory, or a *model*. An **economic model** is an explanation of how the economy or a part of the economy works. In practice, most economists use the terms *theory* and *model* interchangeably, although sometimes the term *theory* suggests a general explanation and the term *model* suggests a more specific explanation. The term *law* is also typically used interchangeably with the terms *model* and *theory* in economics.

What Are Economic Models?

Economic models are always abstractions, or simplifications, of the real world. They take very complicated phenomena, such as the behavior of people, firms, and governments, and simplify them, in much the same way as a model of a building used by architects is an abstraction, or simplification, of the actual building. Some models can be very detailed; others are just broad abstractions. Be sure to remember that the model and the phenomenon being explained by the model are different.

Do not be critical of economic models just because they are simplifications. In every science, models are simplifications of reality. Models are successful if they explain reality reasonably well. In fact, if they were not simplifications, they would be hard to use effectively. Economic models differ from those in the physical sciences because they endeavor to explain human behavior, which is complex and often unpredictable. It is for this reason that the brilliant physicist Max Planck said that economics was harder than physics.

Economic models can be described with words, with numerical tables, with graphs, or with algebra. To use economics, it is important to be able to work with these different descriptions. Figures 2.7 and 2.8 show how models can be illustrated with graphs. By looking at graphs, we can see quickly whether the model has an inverse or a direct relationship. If a model says that one variable varies inversely with the other, this means that if the first variable rises, then the second falls. If a model says that one variable varies directly with another, this means that if one variable rises, the other also rises. In economics, the expression "is positively related to" is frequently used in place of the phrase "varies directly with," which is more common in other sciences. Similarly, the expression "is negatively related to" is frequently used in place of "varies inversely with."

positively related: a situation in which an increase in one variable is associated with an increase in another variable; also called *directly related.*

negatively related: a situation in which an increase in one variable is associated with a decrease in another variable; also called *inversely related.*

In Figure 2.7, two variables—perhaps a relative price variable and a spending variable—are shown to be **positively related.** In other words, when variable 1 increases from *A* to *B*, variable 2 increases from *C* to *D* by the specific amount given by the curve. Likewise, when variable 1 decreases from *B* to *A*, variable 2 decreases from *D* to *C*. In Figure 2.8, a model with two variables that are **negatively related** is shown. Here, when variable 1 increases from *A* to *B*, variable 2 decreases from *D* to *C*. Likewise, when variable 1 decreases from *B* to *A*, variable 2 increases from *C* to *D*. Models have *constants* as well as variables. The constants in the models in Figures 2.7 and 2.8 are the positions and shapes of the curves.

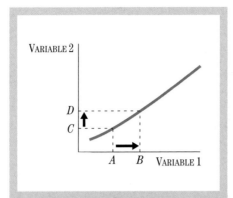

Figure 2.7
A Model with Two Positively Related Variables
The upward-sloping line shows how the variables are related. When one variable increases from *A* to *B*, the other variable increases from *C* to *D*. If one variable declines from *B* to *A*, the other variable declines from *D* to *C*. We say that variable 1 is positively related to variable 2, or that variable 1 varies directly with variable 2.

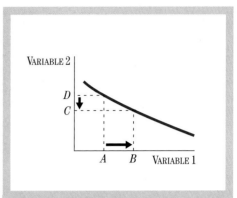

Figure 2.8
A Model with Two Negatively Related Variables
When one variable increases from *A* to *B*, the other variable decreases from *D* to *C*. Likewise, when one variable decreases from *B* to *A*, the other variable increases from *C* to *D*. We say that variable 1 is negatively related to variable 2, or that variable 1 varies inversely with variable 2.

As you study economic models in this book, you will begin to see that they have a common approach to human behavior. Economic models describe how people deal with scarcity, or with situations where they would like to have more, or do more, than their resources will allow. Scarcity requires that people *choose* between one thing and another. For example, in developing a model of health-care spending, an economist would examine how people with a limited amount of income would choose between more health care and less of something else. Or the economist might examine how a health maintenance organization would decide whether to hire more nurses and fewer doctors in producing a given amount of health care in the community. In modeling the behavior of consumers and firms, economists assume that people make purposeful choices to improve their well-being when confronting such scarcity. More than anything else, the problem of scarcity provides a broad and common core to the field of economics.

■ **An Example: A Model with Two Variables.** Figure 2.9 shows a model describing how doctors employed in a health maintenance organization provide physical examinations. The model states that the more doctors who are employed at the HMO, the more physical exams can be given. The model is represented in four different ways: (1) with words, (2) with a numerical table, (3) with a graph, and (4) with algebra.

On the lower right of Figure 2.9, we have the verbal description: more doctors, more physical exams, but additional doctors increase the number of exams by smaller amounts, presumably because the diagnostic facilities at the HMO are limited; for example, there are only so many rooms available for physical exams.

On the upper left, we have a table with numbers showing how the number of examinations depends on the number of doctors. Exactly how many examinations are given by each number of doctors is shown in the table. Clearly this table is much more specific than the verbal description. Be sure to distinguish between the meaning of a table that presents a model (like the table in Figure 2.9) and a table that

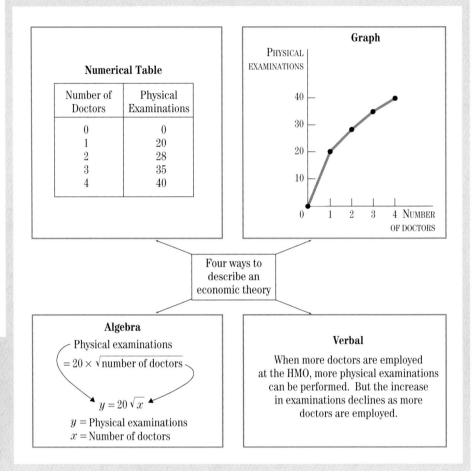

Numerical Table

Number of Doctors	Physical Examinations
0	0
1	20
2	28
3	35
4	40

Graph

Algebra

Physical examinations
$= 20 \times \sqrt{\text{number of doctors}}$

$y = 20 \sqrt{x}$

$y =$ Physical examinations
$x =$ Number of doctors

Verbal

When more doctors are employed at the HMO, more physical examinations can be performed. But the increase in examinations declines as more doctors are employed.

Four ways to describe an economic theory

Figure 2.9
Economic Models in Four Ways
Each way has advantages and disadvantages; this book focuses mostly on verbal descriptions, graphs, and numerical tables, but occasionally some algebra will be used to help explain things.

presents data (like Table 2.1). They look similar, but one is a model of the real world and the other represents observations about the real world.

On the upper right, we have a curve showing the relationship between doctors and physical examinations. The curve shows how many exams each number of doctors can perform. The points on the curve are plotted from the information in the table. The vertical axis has the number of examinations; the horizontal axis has the number of doctors. The points are connected with a line to help visualize the curve.

Finally, in the lower left we show the doctor-examination relationship in algebraic form. In this case, the number of exams is equal to the square root of the number of doctors times 20. If we use the symbol y for the number of exams and x for the number of doctors, the model looks a lot like the equations in an algebra course.

All four ways of representing models have advantages and disadvantages. The advantage of the verbal representation is that we usually communicate with people in words, and if we want our economic models to have any use, we need to communicate with people who have not studied economics. However, the verbal representation is not as precise as the other three. In addition to verbal analysis, in this book we will focus on tabular and graphical representations rather than on algebraic descriptions.

■ **Prediction and the *Ceteris Paribus* Assumption.**   Prediction is one of the most important uses of models. For example, using the model in Figure 2.8, we can predict that if variable 1 rises from *A* to *B*, then variable 2 will fall from *D* to *C*. Using the model for physical exams at an HMO, we might predict that having more doctors at the HMO will increase the number of physicals that can be given. Economists use models to predict variables ranging from GDP next year to the price of medical care in the year 2007.

ceteris paribus: "all other things being equal"; refers to holding all other variables constant or keeping all other things the same when one variable is changed.

In order to use models for prediction, economists use the assumption of ***ceteris paribus,*** which means "all other things being equal." For example, the prediction that variable 2 will fall from *D* to *C* assumes that the curve in Figure 2.8 does not shift: The position of the curve when variable 1 is at *A* is *equal* to the position of the curve when variable 1 is at *B*. If other things were not equal—if the curve shifted—then we could not predict that variable 2 would fall from *D* to *C* when variable 1 rose from *A* to *B*. Similarly, predicting that more doctors can produce more physical exams assumes that there is no power outage that would cause the diagnostic equipment to stop operating.

Microeconomic Models versus Macroeconomic Models

There are two main branches of economics: microeconomics and macroeconomics; thus, there are both microeconomic and macroeconomic models.

microeconomics: the branch of economics that examines individual decision-making at firms and households and the way they interact in specific industries and markets.

macroeconomics: the branch of economics that examines the workings and problems of the economy as a whole—GDP growth and unemployment.

Microeconomics studies the behavior of individual firms and households or specific markets like the health-care market or the college graduate market. It looks at variables such as the price of a college education or the reason for increased wages of college graduates. Microeconomic models explain why the price of gasoline varies from station to station and why there are discount airfares.

Macroeconomics focuses on the whole economy—the whole national economy or even the whole world economy. It tries to explain the changes in GDP over time rather than the changes in a part of GDP like health-care spending. It looks at questions such as what causes the GDP to grow and why many more workers are unemployed in Europe than in the United States.

The Use of Existing Models

Because economics has been around for a long time, there are many existing models that can be applied to explain observations or make predictions that are useful to decision-makers. Much of what economists do in practice, whether in government or business or universities, is use models that are already in existence.

The models are used in many different types of applications, from determining the effects of discrimination in the workplace to evaluating the gains from lower health-care prices. Frequently the models are applied in new and clever ways.

The Development of New Models

Like models in other sciences, economic models change and new models are developed. Many of the models in this book are very different from the models in books published 40 years ago. New economic models evolve because some new observations cannot be explained by existing models.

The process of the development of new models or theories in economics proceeds much like that in any other science. First one develops a *hypothesis*, or a hunch, to explain a puzzling observation. Then one tests the hypothesis by seeing if its predictions of other observations are good. If the hypothesis passes this test, then it becomes accepted. In practice, however, this is at best a rough description of the process of scientific discovery in economics. Existing models are constantly being reexamined and tested. Some economists specialize in testing models; others specialize in developing them. There is an ongoing process of creating and testing of models in economics.

REVIEW
- Economists use economic models to explain economic observations. Economic models are similar to models in other sciences. They are abstractions, or simplifications, of reality, and they have variables and constants. But economic models are different from models in the physical sciences because they must deal with human behavior. Models can be represented verbally, with numerical tables, with graphs, and with algebra.

- New economic models are developed in part because existing models cannot explain facts or observations.

The Impact of Economics on Public Policy

capitalism an economic system based on a market economy in which capital is individually owned, and production and employment decisions are decentralized.

socialism an economic system in which the government owns and controls all the capital and makes decisions about prices and quantities as part of a central plan.

mixed economy: a market economy in which the government plays a very large role.

positive economics: economic analysis that explains what happens in the economy and why, without making recommendations about economic policy.

Ever since the birth of economics as a field—around 1776, when Adam Smith published the *Wealth of Nations*—economists have been concerned about and motivated by a desire to improve the economic policy of governments. In fact, economics was originally called *political economy*. Much of the *Wealth of Nations* is about what the government should or should not do to affect the domestic and international economy.

Adam Smith argued for a system of *laissez faire*—little government control—where the role of the government is mainly to promote competition, provide for national defense, and reduce restrictions on the exchange of goods and services. One hundred years later, Karl Marx brought a new perspective to Smith's (and other classical economists') view of political economy, arguing against the laissez-faire approach. His analysis of market economies, or **capitalism,** centered on the contradictions that he saw arising out of such a system, particularly the conflict between the owners of production and laborers. He argued that these contradictions would result in the inevitable collapse of capitalism and the emergence of a new economic system, called **socialism,** in which government would essentially own and control all production. While Marx actually wrote very little about what a socialist or communist economy would look like, the centrally planned economies that arose in the Soviet Union, Eastern Europe, and China in the twentieth century can be traced to Marx's ideas. Most countries today have rejected the command economy and have moved toward market economies, but the debate about the role of government continues. In many modern market economies, the government plays a large role, and for this reason, such economies are sometimes called **mixed economies.** How great should the role of government be in a market economy? Should the government provide health-care services? Should it try to break up large firms?

Positive versus Normative Economics

In debating the role of government in the economy, economists distinguish between positive and normative economics. **Positive economics** is about what is; **normative economics** is about what should be. For example, positive economics endeavors to explain why health-care spending slowed down in the mid-1990s.

normative economics: economic analysis that makes recommendations about economic policy.

Council of Economic Advisers: a three-member group of economists appointed by the president of the United States to analyze the economy and make recommendations about economic policy.

Normative economics aims to develop and recommend policies that might prevent health-care spending from rising rapidly in the future. In general, normative economics is concerned with making recommendations about what the government should do—whether it should control the price of electricity or health care, for example. Economists who advise governments spend much of their time doing normative economics. In the United States, the president's **Council of Economic Advisers** has legal responsibility for advising the president about which economic policies are good and which are bad.

Positive economics can also be used to explain *why* governments do what they do. For example, why did the U.S. government control airfares and then stop? Why were tax rates cut in the 1980s, increased in the 1990s, then cut again in the 2000s? Positive analysis of government policy requires a mixture of both political science and economic science, with a focus on what motivates voters and the politicians they elect.

Economics as a Science versus a Partisan Policy Tool

Although economics, like any other science, is based on facts and theories, it is not always used in a purely scientific way.

In political campaigns, economists put forth arguments in favor of one candidate, emphasizing the good side of their candidate and de-emphasizing the bad side. In a court of law, one economist may help a defendant—making the best case possible—and another economist may help the plaintiff—again, making the best case possible. In other words, economics is not always used objectively. A good reason to learn economics for yourself is to see through fallacious arguments.

But economics is not the only science that is used in these two entirely different modes. For example, there is currently a great controversy about the use of biology and chemistry to make estimates of the costs and benefits of different environmental policies. This is a politically controversial subject, and some on both sides of the controversy have been accused of using science in nonobjective ways.

Economics Is Not the Only Factor in Policy Issues

Although economics can be very useful in policy decisions, it is frequently not the only factor. For example, national security sometimes calls for a recommendation on a policy issue different from one based on a purely economic point of view. Although most economists recommend free exchange of goods between countries, the U.S. government restricted exports of high-technology goods such as computers during the cold war because defense specialists worried that the technology could help the military in the Soviet Union, and this was viewed as more important than the economic argument. There are still heavy restrictions on trade in nuclear fuels for fear of the proliferation of nuclear weapons.

Disagreement Between Economists

Watching economists debate issues on television or reading their opinions in a newspaper or magazine certainly gives the impression that they rarely agree. There are major controversies in economics, and we will examine them in this book. But when people survey economists' beliefs, they find a surprising amount of agreement.

Why, then, the popular impression of disagreement? Because there are many economists, and one can always find some economist with a different viewpoint. When people sue other people in court and economics is an issue, it is always

ECONOMICS IN ACTION

Science or Persuasion?

In a recent court case, a grocery store chain, Lucky Stores, was sued for discriminating against female workers. The case illustrates how economics can be used in a partisan as well as a scientific way.

Economists were called as expert witnesses for both sides. Labor economist John Pencavel testified for the plaintiffs, the women who brought the suit. He found that women at Lucky earned between 76 and 82 percent of what Lucky's male workers earned. Pencavel found that women were regularly placed in jobs that paid less than jobs given male coworkers, although there was no significant difference between them in terms of education and experience. There was little difference in the wages of the male and female workers within each type of job, but some jobs paid more than others, and women happened to be assigned to the lower-paying jobs.

Joan Haworth, another labor economist, was an expert witness for the defendant, Lucky Stores. She reported survey evidence showing that Lucky's assignment of women and men to different jobs reflected differences in the work preferences of men and women. Thus, Lucky justified its job assignments by arguing that there was a gender difference in attitudes toward work. Lucky argued that its employment policies were based on observed differences in the career aspirations of male and female employees. For example, one manager at Lucky testified that women were more interested in cash register work and men were more interested in floor work.

After weighing the facts and economic arguments, the judge decided the case in favor of the plaintiffs.

You be the judge. Would you have been persuaded by the economic argument used by Lucky Stores or by the defendants?

Although male and female employees received equal pay for equal work, the judge concluded that Lucky's employment policies involved discrimination. The judge wrote: "The court finds defendant's explanation that the statistical disparities between men and women at Lucky are caused by differences in the work interests of men and women to be unpersuasive."

The decision is a landmark because of the economic analysis that showed that discrimination could exist even if men and women were being paid the same wage for equal work. Of course, not all sex discrimination cases are decided in favor of the plaintiffs. But whoever wins a given case, economics is almost always a key consideration in the judge's decision.

possible to find economists who will testify for each side, even if 99 percent of economists would agree with one side. Similarly, television interviews or news shows want to give both sides of public policy issues. Thus, even if 99 percent of economists agree with one side, it is possible to find at least one on the other side.

Economists are human beings with varying moral beliefs and different backgrounds and political views that are frequently unrelated to economic models. For example, an economist who is very concerned about the importation of drugs into the United States might appear to be more willing to condone a restriction on coffee exports from Brazil and other coffee-exporting countries, which might give Colombia a higher price for its coffee to offset a loss in revenue from cocaine. Another economist, who felt less strongly about drug imports, might argue strongly against such a restriction on coffee. But if they were asked about restrictions on trade in the abstract, both economists would probably argue for government policies that prevent them.

- Economic theory can be used to make better economic decisions. Improving government policy decisions has long been a purpose of economics.
- The most basic economic policy questions concern the general role of government in a market economy.

Conclusion: A Reader's Guide

In Chapter 1, we explored the central idea of economics: scarcity, choice, and economic interaction. In this chapter, we discussed how economists observe economic phenomena and use economic models to explain these phenomena. It is now time to move on and learn more about the models and application of the central idea. As you study economic models in the following chapters, it will be useful to keep three points in mind. They are implied by the ideas raised in this chapter.

First, *economics—more than other subjects—requires a mixture of verbal and quantitative skills.* Frequently, those who come to economics with a good background in physical science and mathematics find the mix of formal models with more informal verbal descriptions of markets and institutions unusual and perhaps a little difficult. If you are one of these people, you might wish for a more cut-and-dried, or mathematical, approach.

In contrast, those who are good at history or philosophy may find the emphasis on formal models and graphs difficult and might even prefer a more historical approach that looked more at watershed events and famous individuals and less at formal models of how many individuals behave. If you are one of these people, you might wish that economic models were less abstract.

In reality, however, economics is a mixture of formal modeling, historical analysis, and philosophy. If you are very good at math and you think the symbols and graphs of elementary economics are too simple, think of Max Planck's comment about economics and focus on the complexity of the economic phenomena that these simple models and graphs are explaining. Then when you are asked an open-ended question about government policy that does not have a simple yes or no answer, you will not be caught off guard. Or if your advantage is in history or philosophy, you should spend more time honing your skills at using models and graphs. Then when you are asked to solve a cut-and-dried economic problem with an exact answer requiring graphical analysis, you will not be caught off guard.

Second, *economics is about more than the stock market.* When your friends or relatives hear that you are taking economics, they may ask you for advice about what stock to buy. Economists' friends and relatives are always asking them for such advice. But economics alone offers no predictions about the success of particular companies. Rather, economics gives you some tools you can use to obtain information about companies and to analyze them yourself—perhaps eventually to become an investment adviser.

Economics will also help you answer questions about whether to invest in the stock market or in a bank or how many stocks to buy. But the scope of economics is much, much broader than the stock market or banks, as the questions at the start of the chapter indicate. In fact, the scope of economics is even wider than these examples. Economists use their models, or theories, to study environmental pollution, crime, discrimination, and who should have the right to sue whom.

Third, and perhaps most important, *the study of economics is an intellectually fascinating adventure in its own right.* Yes, economics is highly relevant, and it affects people's lives. But once you learn how economic models work, you will find that they are actually fun to use. And they would be just as much fun if they were not so relevant. Every now and then, just after you have learned about a new economic model, put the book down and think of the economic model independent of its message or relevance to society—try to enjoy it the way you would a good movie. In this way, too, you will be learning to think like an economist.

KEY POINTS

1. Economics is a way of thinking that requires observation (describing economic events), building and using economic models to explain economic events and predict future events, and recommending courses of action for government—and business—based on these observations and models.

2. Economic models are abstractions, or simplifications, of reality and attempt to explain human behavior as expressed by economic measures.

3. Economic models, like models in other sciences, can be described with words, with tables, with graphs, or with mathematics. All four ways are important and complement one another.

4. The circular flow diagram shows the major players in the economy and how they interact in markets.

5. A plot showing that two variables are correlated during a period of time does not mean that one causes the other.

6. Faulty data and the lack of controlled experiments sometimes make economic observations difficult to interpret.

7. Sometimes new facts require that economists develop new models.

8. Decisions about the role of government in areas from airfares to health care are influenced by economic analysis.

9. Improving economic policy has been a goal of economists since the time of Adam Smith.

KEY TERMS

gross domestic product (GDP)
relative price
economic variable
controlled experiments

experimental economics
circular flow diagram
economic model
positively related
negatively related

ceteris paribus
microeconomics
macroeconomics
capitalism
socialism

mixed economy
positive economics
normative economics
Council of Economic
  Advisers

QUESTIONS FOR REVIEW

1. Why do economists need to document and quantify observations about the economy?

2. What is the most comprehensive available measure of the size of an economy?

3. What is meant by a relative price?

4. Why doesn't correlation imply causation?

5. What do the arrows in the circular flow diagram indicate?

6. How do economic models differ from the economic phenomena they explain?

7. Why are controlled experiments rare in economics?

8. How do economists use the *ceteris paribus* assumption?

9. What is the difference between macroeconomics and microeconomics?

10. What is the difference between positive and normative economics?

PROBLEMS

1. Which of the following items are microeconomic, and which are macroeconomic?
   a. The number of people with jobs in the United States
   b. A tax on sport utility vehicles
   c. Prices of sunglasses
   d. GDP

2. Identify whether the following policy statements are positive or normative. Explain.
   a. "The price of Internet stocks is too high."
   b. "The government should control the price of health care."
   c. "Increases in consumer spending improved the economy last year."
   d. "The government should break up Microsoft."

3. Interpret the data on spending on clothing in the table below by filling in the blanks.
   a. What has happened to clothing spending as a share of GDP over this 30-year period?
   b. What has happened to the relative price of clothing over this period, and how could it be related to the clothing spending share?
   c. Draw a graph showing the relationship between clothing spending as a share of GDP and the relative price of clothing.

Year	GDP (billions of dollars)	Spending on Clothing	Clothing Spending as a Share of GDP (%)	Relative Clothing Price
1970	1,039.7	47.8		1.88
1980	2,795.6		3.84	1.43
1990		204.1	3.52	1.17
2000	9,817.0	319.1		0.89

4. Draw a diagram like Figure 2.6 for the market for air travel and give examples of capital, labor, and firms in that market. Show that there is a complete circular flow of funds and goods in the economy as a whole.

5. Why is it typical for economists to make the *ceteris paribus* assumption when making predictions?

6. Consider an economic model of web page production. Show how to represent this model graphically, algebraically, and verbally, as in Figure 2.9.

Number of Programmers	Web Pages
0	0
1	10
4	20
9	30
16	40

7. What is the difference between the price of a good and its relative price? Which information is more useful if you are interested in analyzing the change in spending on that good?

8. Indicate whether you expect positive or negative correlation for the following pairs of variables. What is required in order to show causation?
   a. Sunrise and crowing roosters
   b. Price of theater tickets and number of theatergoers
   c. Purchases of candy and purchases of Valentine's Day cards

Reading, Understanding, and Creating Graphs

Whether you follow the stock market, the health-care market, or the whole economy, graphs are needed to understand what is going on. That is why the financial pages of newspapers contain so many graphs. Knowing how to read, understand, and even create your own graphs is part of learning to "think like an economist." Graphs help us see correlations, or patterns in economic observations. Graphs are also useful for understanding economic models. They help us see how variables in the model behave. They help us describe assumptions about what firms and consumers do.

Computer software to create graphs is now widely available. A graphing program with many examples is provided with the software that accompanies this text. To understand how helpful graphs can be, you might want to create a few of your own graphs using the time-series data in the "Explore" section of the software. Here we provide an overview of basic graphing techniques.

Visualizing Observations with Graphs

Most economic graphs are drawn in two dimensions, like the surface of this page, and are constructed using a Cartesian coordinate system. The idea of Cartesian coordinates is that pairs of observations on variables can be represented in a plane by designating one axis for one variable and the other axis for the other variable. Each point, or coordinate, on the plane corresponds to a pair of observations.

Time-Series Graphs

In many instances, we want to see how a variable changes over time. Consider the federal debt held by the public—all the outstanding borrowing of the federal government that has not yet been paid back. Table 2A.1 shows observations of the U.S. federal debt. The observations are for every 10 years. The observations in Table 2A.1 are graphed in Figure 2A.1. The graph in Figure 2A.1 is called a **time-series graph** because it plots a series—that is, several values of the variable—over time.

Observe the scales on the horizontal and vertical axes in Figure 2A.1. The seven years are put on the horizontal axis, spread evenly from the year 1950 to the year 2010. The last year is a forecast. For the vertical axis, one needs to decide on a scale. The range of variation for the debt in Table 2A.1 is very wide—from a minimum of $219 billion

Table 2A.1 U.S. Federal Government Debt	
Year	Debt (billions of dollars)
1950	219
1960	237
1970	283
1980	712
1990	2,412
2000	3,410
2010 (Projected)	5,949

Source: Congressional Budget Office.

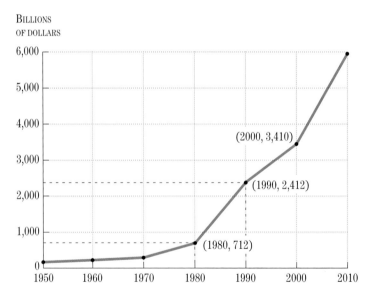

Figure 2A.1
U.S. Federal Debt
Each point corresponds to a pair of observations—the year and the debt—from Table 2A.1.

Figure 2A.2
Stretching the Debt Story in Two Ways
The points in both graphs are identical to those in Figure 2A.1, but by stretching or shrinking the scales the problem can be made to look either less dramatic or more dramatic.

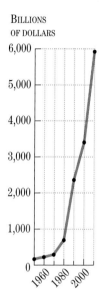

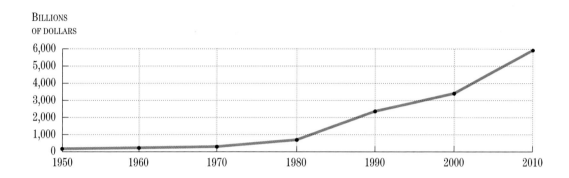

to a maximum of $5,949 billion. Thus, the range on the vertical axis—from $0 to $6,000 billion in Figure 2A.1—must be wide enough to contain all these points.

Now observe how each pair of points from Table 2A.1 is plotted in Figure 2A.1. The point for the pair of observations for the year 1950 and the debt of $219 billion is found by going over to 1950 on the horizontal axis, then going up to $219 billion and putting a dot there. The point for 1960 and $237 billion and all the other points are found in the same way. In order to better visualize the points, they can be connected with lines. These lines are not part of the observations; they are only a convenience to help in eyeballing the observations. The points for 1980, 1990, and 2000 are labeled with the pairs of observations corresponding to Table 2A.1, but in general there is no need to put in such labels.

One could choose scales different from those in Figure 2A.1, and if you plotted your own graph from Table 2A.1 without looking at Figure 2A.1, your scales would probably be different. The scales determine how much movement there is in a time-series graph. For example, Figure 2A.2 shows two ways to stretch the scales to make the increase and decrease in the debt look more or less dramatic. So as not to be fooled by graphs, therefore, it is important to look at the scales and think about what they mean.

As an alternative to time-series graphs with dots connected by a line, the observations can be shown on a bar graph, as in Figure 2A.3. Some people prefer the visual look of a bar graph, but, as is clear from a comparison of Figures 2A.1 and 2A.3, they provide the same information.

The debt as a percentage of GDP is given in Table 2A.2 and graphed in Figure 2A.4. Note that this figure

makes the debt look very different from the way it looks in the first one. As a percentage of GDP, the debt fell from the end of World War II (when it was very large because of the war debt) until around 1980. It increased during the 1980s and declined in the 1990s, but has started to increase again in the 2000s.

Sometimes the data to be graphed have no observations close to 0, in which case including 0 on the vertical

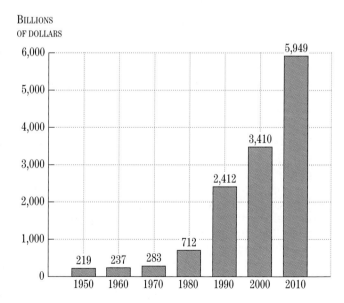

Figure 2A.3
U.S. Federal Debt in Bars
The observations are identical to those in Figure 2A.1.

Table 2A.2
U.S. Federal Debt as a Percentage of GDP

Year	Debt (percent of GDP)
1950	82.5
1960	46.8
1970	28.2
1980	25.7
1990	42.3
2000	35.9
2010 (Projected)	37.8

Source: U.S. Department of Commerce and Table 2A.1.

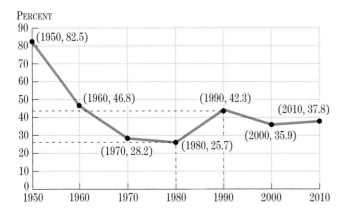

Figure 2A.4
U.S. Federal Debt as a Percentage of GDP
Each point corresponds to a pair of observations from Table 2A.2.

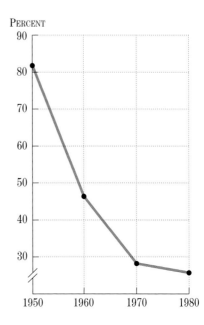

Figure 2A.5
A Look at Debt as a Percentage of GDP from 1950 to 1980
(*Note:* To alert the reader that the bottom part of the axis is not shown, a break point is sometimes used, as shown here.)

axis would leave some wasted space at the bottom of the graph. To eliminate this space and have more room to see the graph itself, we can start the range near the minimum value and end it near the maximum value. This is done in Figure 2A.5, where the debt as a percentage of GDP is shown *up to 1980*. Note, however, that cutting off the bottom of the scale could be misleading to people who do not look at the axis. In particular, 0 percent is no longer at the point where the horizontal and vertical axes intersect. To warn people about the missing part of the scale, a little cut is sometimes put on the axis, as is done in Figure 2A.5, but you have to look carefully at the scale.

Time-Series Graphs Showing Two or More Variables

So far, we have shown how a graph can be used to show observations on one variable over time. What if we want to see how two or more variables change over time

together? Suppose, for example, we want to look at how observations on debt as a percentage of GDP compare with the interest rate the government must pay on its debt. (The interest rate for 2010 is, of course, a forecast.) The two variables are shown in Table 2A.3.

The two sets of observations can easily be placed on the same time-series graph. In other words, we can plot the observations on the debt percentage and connect the dots and then plot the interest rate observations and connect the dots. If the scales of measurement of the two

Table 2A.3
Interest Rate and Federal Debt as a Percentage of GDP

Year	Debt (percent of GDP)	Interest Rate (percent)
1950	82.5	1.2
1960	46.8	2.9
1970	28.2	6.5
1980	25.7	11.5
1990	42.3	7.5
2000	35.9	5.5
2010 (Projected)	37.8	5.5

Source: Federal Reserve Board and Table 2A.2.

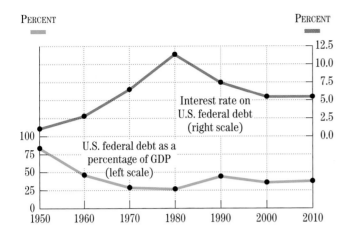

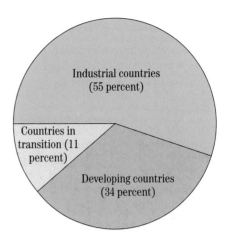

Figure 2A.6
Comparing Two Time Series with a Dual Scale
When two variables have different scales, a dual scale is useful. Here the interest rate and the debt as a percentage of GDP are plotted from Table 2A.3.

Figure 2A.8
Pie Chart Showing the Shares of the World's GDP
The pie chart shows how the world's GDP is divided up into that produced by (1) the industrial countries, such as the United States, Germany, and Japan; (2) the developing countries, such as India, China, and Nigeria; and (3) countries in transition from communism to capitalism, such as Russia and Poland.

variables are much different, then it may be hard to see both, however. For example, the interest rate ranges between 1 and 12 percent; it would not be very visible on a graph going all the way from 0 to 100 percent, a range that is fine for the debt percentage. In this situation, a **dual scale** can be used, as shown in Figure 2A.6. One scale is put on the left-hand vertical axis, and the other scale is put on the right-hand vertical axis. With a dual-scale diagram, it is very important to be aware of

the two scales. In Figure 2A.6 we emphasize the different axes by the color line segment at the top of each vertical axis. The color line segment corresponds to the color of the curve plotted using that scale.

Scatter Plots

Finally, two variables can be usefully compared with a **scatter plot.** The Cartesian coordinate method is used, as in the time-series graph; however, we do not put the year on one of the axes. Instead, the horizontal axis is used for one of the variables and the vertical axis for the other variable. We do this for the debt percentage and the interest rate in Figure 2A.7. The interest rate is on the vertical axis, and the debt percentage is on the horizontal axis. For example, the point at the upper left is 26.8 percent for the debt as a percentage of GDP and 11.5 percent for the interest rate.

Pie Charts

Time-series graphs, bar graphs, and scatter plots are not the only visual ways to observe economic data. For example, the *pie chart* in Figure 2A.8 is useful for comparing percentage shares for a small number of different groups or a small number of time periods. In this example, the pie chart is a visual representation of how the industrial countries produce more than half of the world's GDP, while the developing countries produce 34 percent and the former communist countries in Eastern Europe and the former Soviet Union, now in transition toward market economies, produce about 11 percent.

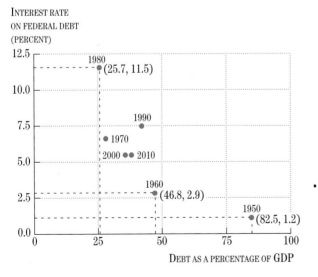

Figure 2A.7
Scatter Plot
Interest rate and debt as a percentage of GDP are shown.

Visualizing Models with Graphs

Graphs can also represent models. Like graphs showing observations, graphs showing models are usually restricted to curves in two dimensions.

Slopes of Curves

Does a curve slope up or down? How steep is it? These questions are important in economics, as in other sciences. The **slope** of a curve tells us how much the variable on the vertical axis changes when we change the variable on the horizontal axis by one unit.

The slope is computed as follows:

$$\text{Slope} = \frac{\text{change in variable on vertical axis}}{\text{change in variable on horizontal axis}}$$

In most algebra courses, the vertical axis is usually called the y-axis and the horizontal axis is called the x-axis. Thus, the slope is sometime described as

$$\text{Slope} = \frac{\text{change in } y}{\text{change in } x} = \frac{\Delta y}{\Delta x}$$

where the Greek letter Δ (delta) means "change in." In other words, the slope is the ratio of the "rise" (vertical change) to the "run" (horizontal change).

Figure 2A.9 shows how to compute the slope. In this case, the slope declines as the variable on the x-axis increases.

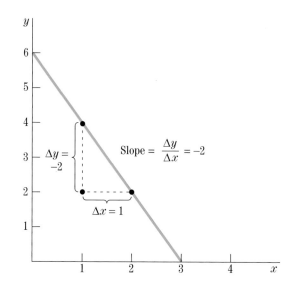

Figure 2A.10
A Relationship with a Negative Slope
Here the slope is negative: $(\Delta y)/(\Delta x) = -2$. As x increases, y falls. The line slopes down from left to right. In this case, y and x are inversely, or negatively, related.

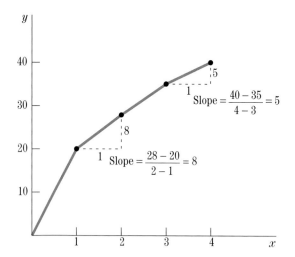

Figure 2A.9
Measuring the Slope
The slope between two points is given by the change along the vertical axis divided by the change along the horizontal axis. In this example, the slope declines as x increases. Since the curve slopes up from left to right, it has a positive slope.

Observe that *the steeper the curve, the larger the slope*. When the curve gets very flat, the slope gets close to zero. Curves can either be upward-sloping or downward-sloping. If the curve slopes up from left to right, as in Figure 2A.9, it has a **positive slope,** and we say that the two variables are positively related. If the curve slopes down from left to right, it has a **negative slope,** and we say that the two variables are negatively related. Figure 2A.10 shows a case where the slope is negative. When x increases by 1 unit ($\Delta x = 1$), y declines by 2 units ($\Delta y = -2$). Thus, the slope equals -2; it is negative. Observe how the curve slopes down from left to right.

If the curve is a straight line, then the slope is a constant. Curves that are straight lines—as in Figure 2A.10—are called **linear.** But economic relationships do not need to be linear, as the example in Figure 2A.9 makes clear. Figure 2A.11 shows six different examples of curves and indicates how they are described.

Graphs of Models with More than Two Variables

In most cases, economic models involve more than two variables. For example, the number of physical examinations could depend on the number of nurses as well as the number of doctors. Or the amount of lemonade demanded might depend on the weather as well as on the price.

Economists have devised several methods for representing models with more than two variables with two-

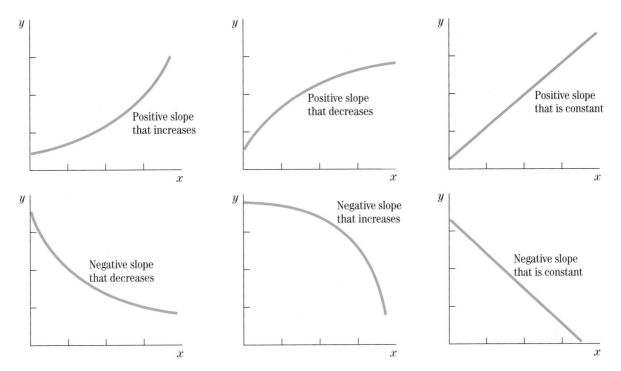

Figure 2A.11
Six Types of Relationships
In the top row, the variables are positively related. In the bottom row, they are negatively related.

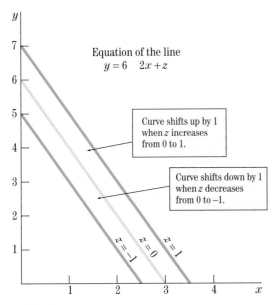

Figure 2A.12
A Third Variable Shifts the Curve
In order to represent models with three variables (x, y, and z) on a two-dimensional graph, economists distinguish between movements along the curve (when x and y change, holding z unchanged) and shifts of the curve (when z changes).

dimensional graphs. Suppose, for example, that the relationship between y and x in Figure 2A.10 depends on a third variable z. For a given value of x, larger values of z lead to larger values of y. This example is graphed in Figure 2A.12. As in Figure 2A.10, when x increases, y falls. This is a **movement along the curve.** But what if z changes? We represent this as a **shift of the curve.** An increase in z shifts the curve up; a decrease in z shifts the curve down.

Thus, by distinguishing between shifts of and movements along a curve, economists represent models with more than two variables in only two dimensions. Only two variables (x and y) are shown explicitly on the graph, and when the third (z) is fixed, changes in x and y are movements along the curve. When z changes, the curve shifts. The distinction between "movements along" and "shifts of" curves comes up many times in economics.

Key Terms and Definitions

Cartesian coordinate system: a graphing system in which ordered pairs of numbers are represented on a plane by the distances from a point to two perpendicular lines, called axes.

time-series graph: a graph that plots a variable over time, usually with time on the horizontal axis.

dual scale: a graph that uses time on the horizontal axis and different scales on the left and right vertical axes to compare the movements of two variables over time.

scatter plot: a graph in which points in a Cartesian coordinate system represent the values of two variables.

slope: a characteristic of a curve that is defined as the change in the variable on the vertical axis divided by the change in the variable on the horizontal axis.

positive slope: a slope of a curve that is greater than zero, representing a positive or direct relationship between two variables.

negative slope: a slope of a curve that is less than zero, representing a negative or inverse relationship between two variables.

linear: a situation in which a curve is straight, with a constant slope.

movement along the curve: a situation in which a change in the variable on one axis causes a change in the variable on the other axis, but the position of the curve is maintained.

shift of the curve: a change in the position of a curve, usually caused by a change in a variable not represented on either axis.

Questions for Review

1. What is the difference between a scatter plot and a time-series graph?
2. Why are dual scales sometimes necessary?
3. What is the advantage of graphs over verbal representations of models?
4. What does a curve with a negative slope look like?
5. What is the difference between a shift in a curve and a movement along a curve?

Problems

1. The table below presents data on the debt and the debt to GDP ratio predicted by the Congressional Budget Office for the United States for each year through 2015.
   a. Construct a time-series plot of the ratio of government debt to GDP.
   b. Construct a time-series plot of the debt.
   c. Construct a scatter plot of the debt ratio and the debt.

Year	Debt	Debt to GDP Ratio
2005	4,656	38.1
2006	4,965	38.5
2007	5,246	38.6
2008	5,506	38.5
2009	5,737	38.2
2010	5,949	37.8
2011	6,054	36.7
2012	6,004	34.8
2013	5,941	33.0
2014	5,847	31.1
2015	5,726	29.1

Source: Congressional Budget Office.

2. The following table presents data on U.S. turkey production and prices.

Year	Turkey Production (billions of pounds)	Price per Pound
1995	5.07	0.99
1996	5.40	1.02
1997	5.41	0.98
1998	5.22	0.95
1999	5.23	0.98
2000	5.33	0.99

   a. Construct a time-series plot of turkey production in the United States.
   b. Construct a time-series plot of the price of turkey per pound.
   c. Construct a scatter plot of turkey production and turkey prices.

3. The following table shows the number of physical examinations given by doctors at an HMO with three different-size clinics: small, medium, and large. The larger the clinic, the more patients the doctors can handle.

Exams per Small Clinic	Exams per Medium Clinic	Exams per Large Clinic	Number of Doctors
0	0	0	0
20	30	35	1
28	42	49	2
35	53	62	3
40	60	70	4

   a. Show the relationship between doctors and physical exams given with *three* curves, where the number of doctors is on the horizontal axis and the number of examinations is on the vertical axis.
   b. Describe how the three relationships compare with one another.
   c. Is a change in the number of doctors a shift of or a movement along the curve?
   d. Is a change in the size of the clinic a shift of or a movement along the curve?

The Supply and Demand Model

It's pretty much the same thing every March. Four college basketball teams win a place in the top round of the national tournament, the Final Four. Each college lets students at the college buy a limited number of tickets for about $100 a seat. Then, when the students get to the city where the Final Four is being played, they find people on the street willing to pay staggering amounts of money for those tickets—as much as $5,000. And it is always tempting to sell the tickets and watch the game on TV. Some, of course, do sell. But how are these prices on the street market (and, increasingly, through ticket brokers on the Internet) determined? How are prices in general determined? What causes the price of health care to rise? What causes the price of computers to fall? What determines the price at which people buy or sell gasoline, electronic goods, printing services, or foreign currencies? The purpose of this chapter is to show how to find the answers to such questions.

To do so, we need to construct a model—a simplified description of how a market works. The model economists use to explain how prices are determined in a market is called the *supply and demand model*. This model describes how particular markets—such as the health-care market or the computer market—work. It consists of three elements: *demand*, describing the behavior of consumers in the market; *supply*, describing the behavior of firms in the market; and *market equilibrium*, connecting supply and demand and describing how consumers and firms interact in the market.

Supply and Demand in the Final Four
The model of supply and demand can explain how $500 tickets to the NCAA Final Four are sold well before the first college basketball game of the season. It also explains more routine buyer and seller interactions, describing the behavior of sellers and buyers and how they connect in markets.

Economists like to compare the supply and demand model to a pair of scissors. Demand is one blade of the scissors. Supply is the other. Either blade alone is incomplete and virtually useless; but when the two blades of a pair of scissors are connected to form the scissors, they become an amazingly useful, yet simple, tool. So it is with the supply and demand model.

In this chapter, we first describe each of the three elements of the model. We then show how to use the model to answer a host of questions about price determination in a market economy. The news story excerpted in the "Reading the News About . . ." box on page 52 illustrates how supply and demand works in a real (world oil) market. Think about the issues considered there as you learn the elements of the model. The Case Study near the end of this chapter takes a closer look at how supply and demand works in a related real world market—the gasoline market.

Demand

demand: a relationship between **price** and **quantity demanded.**

price: the amount of money or other goods that one must pay to obtain a particular good.

quantity demanded: the quantity of a good that people want to buy at a given price during a specific time period.

To an economist, the term *demand*—whether the demand for health care or the demand for computers—has a very specific meaning. **Demand** is a relationship between two economic variables: (1) *the price of a particular good* and (2) *the quantity of the good consumers are willing to buy at that price during a specific time period,* all other things being equal. For short, we call the first variable the **price** and the second variable the **quantity demanded.** The phrase *all other things being equal,* or *ceteris paribus,* is appended to the definition of demand because the quantity consumers are willing to buy depends on many other things besides the price of the good; we want to hold these other things constant, or equal, while we examine the relationship between price and quantity demanded.

Demand can be represented with a numerical table or a graph. In either case, demand describes how much of a good consumers will purchase at each price. Consider the demand for bicycles in the United States. An example of the demand for bicycles is shown in Table 3.1. Several prices for a typical bicycle are listed in the first

Table 3.1			
Demand Schedule for Bicycles (millions of bicycles per year)			
Price	**Quantity Demanded**	**Price**	**Quantity Demanded**
$140	18	$240	5
$160	14	$260	3
$180	11	$289	2
$200	9	$300	1
$220	7		

Economists use the supply and demand model both to explain past observations and to better understand what would happen to prices in a particular market under different scenarios. The hypothetical example of a bicycle market has been useful for explaining general features of the supply and demand model. But now we want to show how the model can be applied to real-world situations. To illustrate the applicability of the supply-demand model, we look in detail at a specific market—the market for gasoline in the United States. Those of you who own cars are keenly aware of the impact of recent price fluctuations in this market.

Bush Touts Energy Technologies To Satisfy Global, U.S. Demand

By John D. McKinnon and
John J. Fialka
Staff Reporters
WALL STREET JOURNAL
APRIL 28, 2005

President Bush sought to dispel growing worries about energy costs, saying new technologies promise eventually to end U.S. dependence on pricey foreign oil and help meet soaring global energy demands in places like China and India.

In an upbeat speech to a generally friendly audience of small-business owners, Mr. Bush outlined a series of measures he plans to expand U.S. energy capacity, from promoting new nuclear power-plant construction to building new oil refineries on old military bases. He also wants to encourage use of new and alternative fuels, including cleaner-burning diesel soon to come on the market, and promote a range of new conservation technologies.

Mr. Bush also said his administration will push for more use of clean-coal and nuclear technologies to answer growing energy needs in fast-growing economies in Asia. That rising demand is contributing substantially to current high prices for oil and gasoline, but Mr.

Bush said the trend is on the way to being reversed.

"Our country is on the doorstep of incredible technological advances that will make energy more abundant and more affordable for our citizens," the president said. "By harnessing the power of technology, we're going to be able to grow our economy, protect our environment, and achieve greater energy independence. That's why I'm so optimistic about our future here in America."

Mr. Bush and his aides have been at pains for several days to show that current high gasoline prices are only part of an energy picture that is actually brighter than critics say—and will improve further if Congress finally passes Mr. Bush's long-delayed energy proposals.

Earlier this week, Mr. Bush invited Saudi Crown Prince Abdullah to his ranch in Texas to highlight that country's plans to expand its oil-producing capacity. Erosion of the Saudis' capacity cushion has been a big reason for the recent spike in the crude oil prices.

Yesterday's speech was aimed at filling in the rest of the picture.

Democratic leaders were predictably skeptical it would have much short-term impact. Sen. John Kerry (D., Mass.) said

the Republicans' energy plans "won't help the families, truckers, farmers and small businesses suffering from skyrocketing gas prices today."

David Hamilton, a spokesman for the Sierra Club, asserted that the president's speech was a continuation of administration policies that "help industry, step on state's rights and thumb a nose at sound science."

Business groups were more enthusiastic. Allen Schaeffer, executive director of the Diesel Technology Forum, says Mr. Bush's plans for a new tax credit to encourage consumers to buy clean-diesel cars will help auto makers reach the decision that the U.S. market has more potential than previously thought. Mr. Schaeffer noted that tax incentives in Western Europe have convinced 42% of new-car buyers to buy diesels. By contrast, only 3.3% of new cars and light trucks in the U.S. are diesel powered, and most of them are pickup trucks.

John Rice, president and CEO of GE Energy, which is building clean-coal and nuclear plants, said the new initiatives represent a big opportunity for his company, both domestically and abroad. "The president understands clearly that all of us have to be in the game in these new technologies in order for them to be effective and have an impact," he said.

The need reduce demand

The need to increase supply

Source: Republished with permission of the *Wall Street Journal*, from John C. McKinnon and John J. Fialka, "Bush Touts Energy Technologies to Satisfy Global, US Demand," April 28, 2005, conveyed via Copyright Clearance Center, Inc.

column of the table, ranging from $140 to $300. Of course, there are many kinds of bicycles—mountain bikes, racing bikes, children's bikes, and inexpensive one-speed bikes with cruiser brakes—so you need to think about the price of an average, or typical, bike.

Listed in the second column of Table 3.1 is the quantity demanded (in millions of bicycles) each year in the United States at the price in the first column. This is the total demand in the bicycle market. For example, at a price of $180 per bicycle, consumers would buy 11 million bicycles. That is, the quantity demanded would be 11 million bicycles each year in the United States, according to Table 3.1.

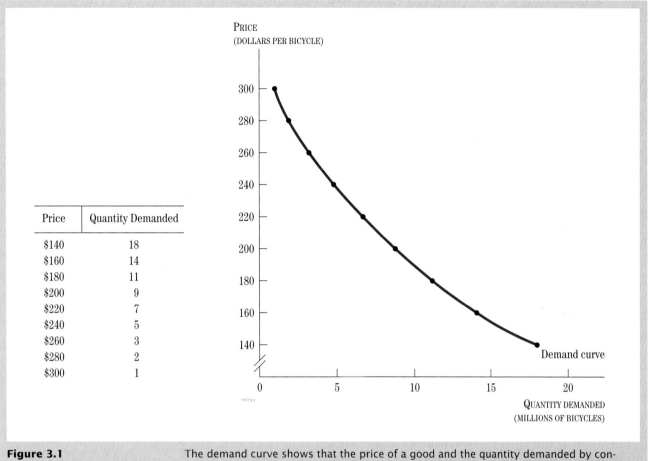

Price	Quantity Demanded
$140	18
$160	14
$180	11
$200	9
$220	7
$240	5
$260	3
$280	2
$300	1

**Figure 3.1
The Demand Curve**

The demand curve shows that the price of a good and the quantity demanded by consumers are negatively related. The curve slopes down. For each price, the demand curve gives the quantity demanded, or the quantity that consumers are willing to buy at that price. The points along the demand curve for bicycles shown here are the same as the pairs of numbers in Table 3.1.

Observe that as the price rises, the quantity demanded by consumers goes down. If the price goes up from $180 to $200 per bicycle, for example, the quantity demanded goes down from 11 million to 9 million bicycles. On the other hand, if the price goes down, the quantity demanded goes up. If the price falls from $180 to $160, for example, the quantity demanded rises from 11 million to 14 million bicycles.

demand schedule: a tabular presentation of demand showing the price and quantity demanded for a particular good, all else being equal.

law of demand: the tendency for the quantity demanded of a good in a market to decline as its price rises.

The relationship between price and quantity demanded in Table 3.1 is called a **demand schedule.** This relationship is an example of the law of demand. The **law of demand** says that the higher the price, the lower the quantity demanded in the market; and the lower the price, the higher the quantity demanded in the market. In other words, the law of demand says that the price and the quantity demanded are negatively related, all other things being equal.

The Demand Curve

Figure 3.1 represents demand graphically. It is a graph with the price of the good on the vertical axis and the quantity demanded of the good on the horizontal axis. It shows the demand for bicycles given in Table 3.1. Each of the nine rows in Table 3.1

demand curve: a graph of demand showing the downward-sloping relationship between price and quantity demanded.

corresponds to one of the nine points in Figure 3.1. For example, the point at the lower right part of the graph corresponds to the first row of the table, when the price is $140 and the quantity demanded is 18 million bicycles. The resulting curve showing all the combinations of price and quantity demanded is the **demand curve.** It slopes downward from left to right because the quantity demanded is negatively related to the price. To remember that the *d*emand curve slopes *d*ownward, think of the *d* in *demand*.

Why does the demand curve slope downward? The demand curve tells us the quantity demanded by all consumers. Consumers must make choices with scarce resources. They must choose between bicycles and other goods. If the price of bicycles falls, then some consumers who previously found the price of bicycles too high may decide to buy a bicycle. The lower price of bicycles gives them an incentive to buy bicycles rather than other goods. It is important to remember that when economists draw a demand curve, they hold constant the price of other goods: running shoes, in-line skates, motor scooters, and so on. When the price of bicycles falls, bicycles become more attractive to people in comparison with these other goods. As a result, the quantity demanded rises when the price falls. Conversely, when the price of bicycles rises, some people may decide to buy in-line skates or motor scooters instead of bicycles. As a result, the quantity demanded declines when the price rises.

There's plenty of evidence in the real world that demand curves are downward-sloping. In June of 2004, vehicle sales at General Motors were slowing. In July, General Motors increased the cash-back offer on most of its trucks and cars. You might (correctly) speculate that this reduction in the price of vehicles was intended to increase vehicle sales. The policy implications of a downward-sloping demand curve frequently sound like common sense. Suggestions on how to reduce student drinking on college campuses include raising the price of alcohol. The idea, of course, is that students would buy less alcohol if it were more expensive.

Shifts in Demand

Now, price is not the only thing that affects the quantity of a good that people buy. The weather, people's concerns about the environment, or the availability of bike lanes on roads can influence people's decisions to purchase bicycles, for example. The quantity of bicycles bought might increase if a climate change brought on an extended period of dry weather. Because people would enjoy riding their bicycles more in dry weather, more bicycles would be purchased at any given price. Or perhaps a health trend might lead people to get exercise by riding bicycles rather than driving their cars. This would also lead to more purchases of bicycles.

The demand curve is drawn assuming that all other things are equal, except the price of the good. A change in any one of these other things, previously assumed to be equal, will shift the demand curve. An increase in demand shifts the demand curve to the right. A decrease in demand shifts the demand curve to the left. This is illustrated in Figure 3.2. The lightly shaded curve labeled "old demand curve" is the same as the demand curve in Figure 3.1. The arrow shows how this curve has shifted to the right to the more darkly shaded curve labeled "new demand curve." Thus, Figure 3.2 shows the demand curve for bicycles shifting to the right. When the demand curve shifts to the right, more bicycles are purchased than before at any given price. For example, before the shift in demand, a $200 price led to 9 million bicycles purchased. But when the demand curve shifts to the right because of drier weather, that same price leads to 13 million bicycles purchased. The demand curve would shift to the left if a climate change to wetter weather reduced people's purchases of bicycles at any given price.

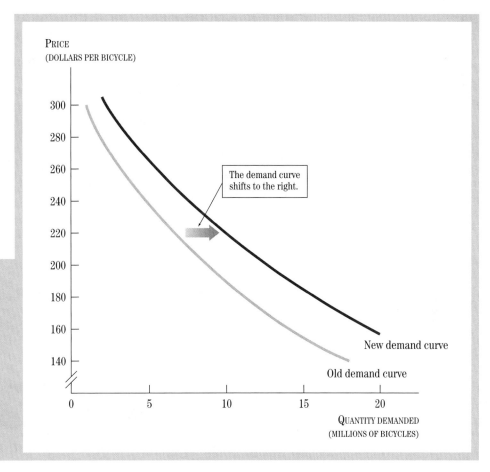

Figure 3.2
A Shift in the Demand Curve
The demand curve shows how the quantity demanded of a good is related to the price of the good, all other things being equal. A change in one of these other things—the weather or people's tastes, for example— will shift the demand curve, as shown in the graph. In this case, the demand for bicycles increases; the demand curve for bicycles shifts to the right.

There are many reasons the demand curve may shift. Most of them can be attributed to one of several sources: *consumers' preferences, consumers' information, consumers' incomes, the number of consumers in the market, consumers' expectations of future prices,* and *the price of related goods.* Let us briefly consider each source of shifts in demand.

■ **Consumers' Preferences.** In general, a change in people's tastes or preferences for a product compared to other products will change the amount of the product they purchase at any given price. After September 11, 2001, changes in consumers' preferences shifted the demand for many goods. Examples include an increase in the demand for stuffed animals as adults searched for comfort, an increase in New York City in the demand for shoes that are easy to walk in, and an increase in the demand for cell phones by people who wanted more access to communication.

■ **Consumers' Information.** A change in information relating to a product can also cause the demand curve to shift. For example, when people learned about the dangers of smoking, the demand for cigarettes declined. Immediately after the mass recall of Firestone tires in 2000, there was a decrease in demand for Firestone tires, which became evident when the sales of Firestone tires fell by 40 percent.

i.e. mp3 downloads for CDs or cassettes

normal good: a good for which demand increases when income rises and decreases when income falls.

inferior good: a good for which demand decreases when income rises and increases when income falls.

■ **Consumers' Incomes.**   If people's incomes change, then their purchases of goods usually change. An increase in income increases the demand for most goods. A decline in income reduces the demand for these goods. Goods for which demand increases when income rises and decreases when income falls are called **normal goods** by economists. For example, when the U.S. stock market boomed in the late 1990s, demand for jewelry increased as a result of the increase in consumers' wealth. The economic slowdown in 2001 caused a decrease in demand for snowplow service. Jewelry and snowplow service are therefore examples of normal goods.

However, the demand for some goods may decline when income increases. Such goods are called **inferior goods** by economists. The demand for inferior goods declines when people's income increases because they can afford more attractive goods. During the late 1990s U.S. stock market boom, demand for Christmas candy decreased. The economic slowdown in 2001 caused an increase in demand for snow shovels. This tells you that Christmas candy and snow shovels are inferior goods. Jewelry is more attractive to consumers than candy, and snowplow service is more attractive to consumers than snow shovels.

Notice that whether goods are normal or inferior, the demand for them usually shifts when consumers' incomes change. In 2001, as a result of the economic slowdown, lipstick sales increased. Does this tell you that lipstick is a normal or an inferior good? Since demand increased as a result of a decrease in consumers' incomes, lipstick is an inferior good. One explanation is that women were suddenly more careful with their money and bought lipstick because of its low price, even though other more expensive items were more attractive.

■ **Number of Consumers in the Market.**   Demand is a relationship between price and the quantity demanded by _all_ consumers in the market. If the number of consumers increases, then demand will increase. If the number of consumers falls, then demand will decrease. For example, the number of teenagers in the U.S. population expanded sharply in the late 1990s. This increased the demand for _Seventeen_ magazine, for Rollerblades, for Clearasil, and for other goods that teenagers tend to buy. As the baby-boom generation in the United States ages, the demand for home hair coloring kits and luxury skin care products (for men as well as for women) is increasing.

■ **Consumers' Expectations of the Future Price.**   If people expect the price of a good to increase, they will want to buy it before the price increases. Conversely, if people expect the price to decline, they will purchase less and wait for the decline. One sees this effect of expectations of future price changes often. "We'd better buy before the price goes up" is a common reason for purchasing items during a clearance sale. Or, "Let's put off buying that big-screen TV until the postholiday sales."

In general, it is difficult to forecast the future, but sometimes consumers know quite a bit about whether the price of a good will rise or fall, and they react accordingly. Thus, demand increases if people expect the _future_ price of the good to rise. And demand decreases if people expect the _future_ price of the good to fall.

In 1995, President Clinton threatened a 100 percent tariff (tax) on some luxury cars produced in Japan. This resulted in an immediate increase in demand for these cars, since buyers were afraid they would become too expensive after the tariff was imposed.

substitute: a good that has many of the same characteristics as and can be used in place of another good.

■ **Prices of Closely Related Goods.**   A change in the price of a closely related good can increase or decrease demand for another good, depending on whether the good is a substitute or a complement. A **substitute** is a good that provides some of

Substitutes and complements
Music CDs and downloaded music are examples of substitutes; they share similar characteristics. You would expect, therefore, that a rise in the price of CDs would result in an increase in the sale of down-loaded music- and vice versa. SUVs and gasoline are examples of complements; they tend to be consumed together. With an increase in gasoline prices in 2004 and 2005, consumers were less eager to purchase SUVs, and their sales declined.

complement: a good that is usually consumed or used together with another good.

the same uses or enjoyment as another good. Butter and margarine are substitutes. In general, the demand for a good will increase if the price of a substitute for the good rises, and the demand for a good will decrease if the price of a substitute falls. Sales of CDs and downloaded music are substitutes. You would therefore expect an increase in the price of downloaded music to increase the demand for CDs. This may help explain why the recording industry filed lawsuits against users of online file-sharing software in 2003.

A **complement** is a good that tends to be consumed together with another good. Gasoline and SUVs are complements. The increase in gasoline prices in 2004 and 2005 led to a decrease in demand for SUVs.

Movements Along versus Shifts of the Demand Curve

We have shown that the demand curve can shift, and we have given many possible reasons for such shifts. In using demand curves, it is very important to distinguish *shifts* of the demand curve from *movements along* the demand curve. This distinction is illustrated in Figure 3.3.

A *movement along* the demand curve occurs when the quantity demanded changes as a result of a *change in the price of the good*. For example, if the price of bicycles rises, causing the quantity demanded by consumers to fall, then there is a movement along the demand curve. A movement along the demand curve for bicycles occurs when the quantity demanded changes from point *A* to point *B* or from point *A* to point *C* in Figure 3.3. At point *A*, the price is $200 and the quantity demanded is 9 million. At point *B*, the price is $220 and the quantity demanded is 7 million. If the quantity changes because the price changes, economists say that there is a *change in the quantity demanded*.

A *shift* of the demand curve, on the other hand, occurs if there is a change due to *any source except the price*. When the demand curve shifts, economists say that there is a *change in demand*. Remember, the term *demand* refers to the entire curve or schedule relating price and quantity demanded, while the term *quantity demanded* refers to a single point on the demand curve. You should be able to tell whether any economic event causes (1) a change in demand or (2) a change in the quantity demanded; or, equivalently, (1) a shift in the demand curve or (2) a movement along the demand curve.

Here's an example to test your understanding of demand shifts and movement along the demand curve. Disney's theme park attendance was lower in 2001 than in

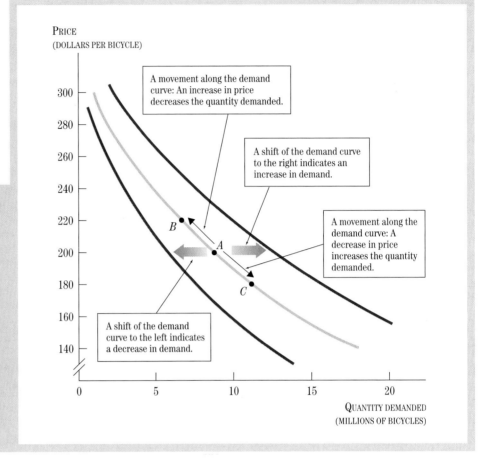

Figure 3.3
Shifts of versus Movements Along the Demand Curve
A *shift* of the demand curve occurs when there is a change in something (other than the good's own price) that affects the quantity of a good that consumers are willing to buy. An increase in demand is a shift to the right of the demand curve. A decrease in demand is a shift to the left of the demand curve. A *movement along* the demand curve occurs when the price of the good changes, causing the quantity demanded to change, as, for example, from point *A* to point *B* or *C*.

previous years as a result of the weak economy. Because of the fall in attendance, Disney lowered the adult admission price at its California Adventure park. Is this describing a *change in demand* or a *change in the quantity demanded* in the market for theme parks? The decrease in attendance caused by the weak economy in 2001 describes a decrease in demand. Going to a theme park is therefore a normal good. When Disney lowered its admission price, it was in anticipation of an increase in quantity demanded—the park management anticipated more attendance at a lower price. The decrease in price and resulting increase in quantity demanded describe movement along the demand curve.

REVIEW

- Demand is a relationship between the price of a good and the quantity people will buy at each price, all other things being equal. The demand curve slopes down. The price and the quantity demanded are negatively related.

- When the price of a good changes, the quantity demanded changes and we have a movement along the demand curve.

- When something other than the price changes and affects demand, there is a shift in the demand curve, or, simply, a change in demand.

Supply

supply: a relationship between **price** and **quantity supplied.**

quantity supplied: the quantity of a good that firms are willing to sell at a given price.

Price	Quantity Supplied
$140	1
$160	4
$180	7
$200	9
$220	11
$240	13
$260	15
$280	16
$300	17

Table 3.2 Supply Schedule for Bicycles (millions of bicycles per year)

supply schedule: a tabular presentation of supply showing the price and quantity supplied of a particular good, all else being equal.

law of supply: the tendency for the quantity supplied of a good in a market to increase as its price rises.

supply curve: a graph of supply showing the upward-sloping relationship between price and quantity supplied.

Whereas demand refers to the behavior of consumers, supply refers to the behavior of firms. The term *supply*—whether it is the supply of health care or the supply of computers—has a very specific meaning for economists. **Supply** is a relationship between two variables: (1) *the price of a particular good* and (2) *the quantity of the good firms are willing to sell at that price*, all other things being the same. For short, we call the first variable the **price** and the second variable the **quantity supplied.**

Supply can be represented with a numerical table or a graph. An example of the supply of bicycles is shown in Table 3.2. Listed in the first column of Table 3.2 is the price of bicycles; the range of prices is the same as for the demand schedule in Table 3.1. The second column lists the quantity supplied (in millions of bicycles) in the entire market by bicycle-producing firms at each price. For example, at a price of $180, the quantity supplied is 7 million bicycles. Observe that as the price increases, the quantity supplied increases, and that as the price decreases, the quantity supplied decreases. For example, if the price rises from $180 to $200, the quantity supplied increases from 7 to 9 million bicycles. The relationship between price and quantity supplied in Table 3.2 is a **supply schedule.** This relationship is an example of the law of supply. The **law of supply** says that the higher the price, the higher the quantity supplied, and the lower the price, the lower the quantity supplied. In other words, the law of supply says that the price and the quantity supplied are positively related.

The Supply Curve

We can represent the supply schedule in Table 3.2 graphically by plotting the price and quantity supplied on a graph, as shown in Figure 3.4. The scales of each axis in Figure 3.4 are exactly the same as those in Figure 3.1, except that Figure 3.4 shows the quantity supplied, whereas Figure 3.1 shows the quantity demanded. Each pair of numbers in Table 3.2 is plotted as a point in Figure 3.4. The resulting curve showing all the combinations of prices and quantities supplied is the **supply curve.** Note that the curve slopes upward: $280 represents a high price, and there the quantity supplied is high—16 million bicycles. If the price is down at $160 a bicycle, then firms are willing to sell only 4 million bicycles.

Why does the supply curve slope upward? Imagine yourself running a firm that produces and sells bicycles. If the price of the bicycles goes up, from $180 to $280, then you can earn $100 more for each bicycle you produce and sell. Given your production costs, if you earn more from each bicycle, you will have a greater incentive to produce and sell more bicycles. If producing more bicycles increases the costs of producing each bicycle, perhaps because you must pay the bike assembly workers a higher wage for working overtime, the higher price will give you the incentive to incur these costs. Other bicycle firms will be thinking the same way. Thus, firms are willing to sell more bicycles as the price rises. Conversely, the incentive for firms to sell bicycles will decline as the price falls. Basically, that is why there is a positive relationship between price and quantity supplied.

When formulating economic policy, it is important to remember this supply relationship. When the price of a good increases, it leads to an increase in the quantity supplied. U.S. agricultural policy guarantees farmers a specific price on certain crops. The U.S. government pays these farmers if the price the crops sell for is too low. In response to this guaranteed higher price, U.S. farmers grow more crops than U.S. consumers buy. This excess production of crops decreases crop prices in international markets. Therefore, U.S. agricultural policy continues to be discussed in international trade talks.

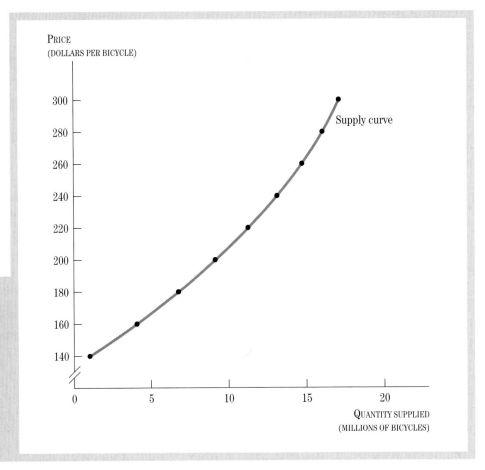

Figure 3.4
The Supply Curve
The supply curve shows that the price and the quantity supplied by firms in the market are positively related. The curve slopes up. For each price on the vertical axis, the supply curve shows the quantity that firms are willing to sell along the horizontal axis. The points along the supply curve for bicycles match the pairs of numbers in Table 3.2.

Shifts in Supply

The supply curve is drawn on the assumption that all other things are equal, except the price of the good. If any one of these other things changes, then the supply curve shifts. For example, suppose a new machine is invented that makes it less costly for firms to produce bicycles; then firms would have more incentive at any given price to produce and sell more bicycles. Supply would increase; the supply curve would shift to the right.

Figure 3.5 shows how the supply curve for bicycles would shift to the right because of a new cost-reducing machine. The supply curve would shift to the left if there were a decrease in supply. Supply would decrease, for example, if bicycle-producing firms suddenly found that their existing machines became too hot and had to be oiled with an expensive lubricant each time a bicycle was produced. This would raise costs, lower supply, and shift the supply curve to the left.

Many things can cause the supply curve to shift. Most of these can be categorized by the source of the change in supply: *technology, the price of goods used in production, the number of firms in the market, expectations of future prices,* and *government taxes, subsidies, and regulations.* Let us briefly consider the sources of shifts in supply.

■ **Technology.**   Anything that changes the amount a firm can produce with a given amount of inputs to production can be considered a change in technology. A

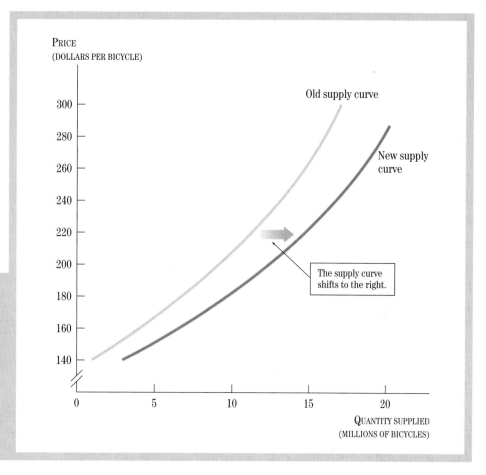

PRICE
(DOLLARS PER BICYCLE)

Old supply curve

New supply
curve

The supply curve
shifts to the right.

QUANTITY SUPPLIED
(MILLIONS OF BICYCLES)

Figure 3.5
A Shift in the Supply Curve
The supply curve is a relationship between the quantity supplied of a good and the price of the good, all other things being equal. A change in one of these other things (other than the good's price) will shift the supply curve, as shown in the graph. In this case, the supply of bicycles increases; the supply curve for bicycles shifts to the right.

2002 study reported the number of labor hours needed to produce an automobile. DaimlerChrysler needed 44 hours per vehicle, while Nissan needed only 29 hours per vehicle. Suppose auto producers initially all needed 44 hours to produce a vehicle and changed their production technology to need instead only 29 hours per vehicle. This improvement in technology would correspond to an increase in supply, a shift in the supply curve to the right. Another way of viewing an increase in supply is that producers are willing to sell any given quantity at a lower price than before. This makes sense, since production costs are lower with the improvement in technology.

Droughts, earthquakes, and terrorists' bombing of factories also affect the amount that can be produced with given inputs. A drought that reduces the amount of wheat that can be produced on a farm in the Midwest and a freeze that reduces the number of oranges yielded by trees in Florida orchards are examples. Because such events change the amount that can be produced with a given amount of inputs, they are similar to changes in technology, though these examples reduce rather than increase supply. In these cases, the supply curve shifts to the left.

■ **The Price of Goods Used in Production.** If the prices of the inputs to production—raw materials, labor, and capital—increase, then it becomes more costly to produce goods, and firms will produce less at any given price; the supply curve will shift to the left. When McDonald's requested in 2000 that its egg suppliers treat their hens more humanely, the egg suppliers were concerned that this would cause the supply of eggs to decrease. That is, to produce any given quantity of eggs, the price they sold for would have to be higher. An increase in production costs causes supply to decrease, and a decrease in production costs causes supply to increase.

■ **The Number of Firms in the Market.** Remember that the supply curve refers to *all* the firms producing the product. If the number of firms increases, then more goods will be produced at each price; supply increases, and the supply curve shifts to the right.

The same rule applies to the supply of labor. In 2001, a shortage of substitute teachers in many school districts around the country grew to crisis proportions. In response, some school districts decided to lower the requirements for substitute teachers. This, they hoped, would encourage more people to work as substitute teachers at any wage, causing the supply of substitute teachers to increase.

A decline in the number of firms would shift the supply curve to the left. For example, the number of drive-in movie theaters has declined sharply over the last 30 years; hence the supply curve has shifted to the left.

■ **Expectations of Future Prices.** If firms expect the price of the good they produce to rise in the future, then they will hold off selling at least part of their production until the price rises. For example, farmers in the United States who anticipate an increase in wheat prices because of political turbulence in Russia may decide to store more wheat in silos and sell it later, after the price rises. Thus, expectations of *future* price increases tend to reduce supply. Conversely, expectations of *future* price decreases tend to increase supply.

■ **Government Taxes, Subsidies, and Regulations.** The government has the ability to affect the supply of particular goods produced by firms. For example, the government imposes taxes on firms to pay for such government services as education, police, and national defense. These taxes increase firms' costs and reduce supply. The supply curve shifts to the left when a tax on what firms sell in the market increases.

The government also makes payments—subsidies—to firms to encourage the firms to produce certain goods. Such subsidies have the opposite effect of taxes on supply. An increase in subsidies reduces firms' costs and increases the supply. For example, the state of Arizona for a brief time subsidized SUVs that run on both propane and gasoline. Compare this to the U. S. government's imposition of a tax on cigarettes and on alcohol. We interpret the cigarette tax as a decrease in the supply of cigarettes and the hybrid SUV subsidy as an increase in the supply of hybrid SUVs.

Governments also regulate firms. In some cases, such regulations can change the firms' costs of production and thereby affect supply. For example, when the government requires that firms install safety features on their products, the cost of producing the products rises, and thus supply declines.

Movements Along versus Shifts of the Supply Curve

Figure 3.6 compares *shifts* of the supply curve with *movements along* the supply curve. A *movement along* the supply curve occurs when a change in price causes a change in the quantity supplied. Economists then say that there is a *change in the quantity supplied*, as, for example, when the quantity supplied changes from point *D* to point *F* or from point *D* to point *E* in Figure 3.6.

A *shift* of the supply curve occurs if there is a change due to *any source except the price*. When the supply curve shifts, economists say that there is a *change in supply*.

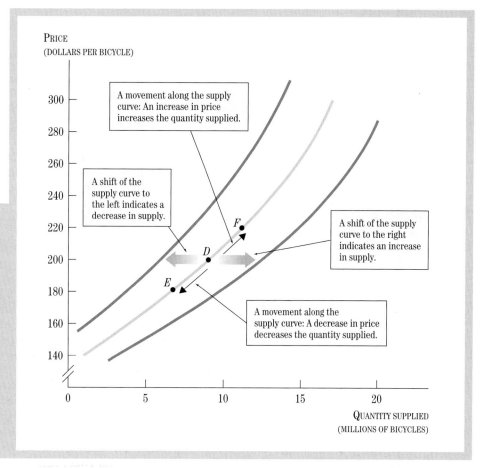

Figure 3.6
Shifts of versus Movements Along the Supply Curve
A *shift* of the supply curve occurs when there is a change in something (other than the price) that affects the amount of a good that firms are willing to supply. An increase in supply is a shift to the right of the supply curve. A decrease in supply is a shift to the left of the supply curve. A movement along the supply curve occurs when the price of the good changes, causing the quantity supplied by firms to change—for example, from point *D* to point *E* or *F*.

The term *supply* refers to the entire supply curve. The term *quantity supplied* refers to a point on the supply curve. As we will soon see, it is important to be able to tell whether a change in something causes (1) a change in supply or (2) a change in the quantity supplied; or, equivalently, (1) a shift in the supply curve or (2) a movement along the supply curve.

Here's an example to test your ability to distinguish between movement along a supply curve and a shift in the supply curve. You will recall that U.S. agricultural policy guarantees farmers a specific price on certain crops. The U.S. government pays these farmers if the price their crops sell for is too low. An economist suggested that the government should instead pay farmers to not plant some of their fields. Which policy is describing a *change in supply* and which is describing a *change in the quantity supplied* in the market for corn?

A policy that pay farmers to leave cornfields unplanted describes a decrease in supply. The amount of corn supplied will be lower at any price. When the U.S. government guarantees the price of corn, this describes an increase in the quantity supplied—more corn will be grown in anticipation of the higher price. The increase in price leading to an increase in quantity supplied corresponds to movement along the supply curve. You can imagine that these policies would lead to differences in the amount of corn grown in the United States and in the price of corn.

REVIEW
- Supply is a positive relationship between the price of a good and the quantity supplied of the good by firms. The supply curve slopes upward because higher prices give firms more incentive to produce and sell more.

- When the quantity supplied changes because of a change in price, we have a movement along the supply curve. Other factors—such as technology, the number of firms, and expectations—affect supply. When these determinants change, the supply curve shifts.

Market Equilibrium: Combining Supply and Demand

Thus far, as summarized in Figure 3.7, we have examined consumers' demand for goods in a market and firms' supply of goods in a market. Now we put supply and demand together to complete the supply and demand model. When consumers buy goods and firms sell goods, they interact in a market, and a price is determined. Recall that a market does not need to be located at one place; the U.S. bicycle market consists of all the bicycle firms that sell bicycles and all the consumers who buy bicycles.

Although it may sound amazing, no single person or firm determines the price in the market. Instead, the market determines the price. As buyers and sellers interact, prices may go up for a while and then go down. Alfred Marshall, the economist who did the most to develop the supply and demand model in the late nineteenth century, called this process the "higgling and bargaining" of the market. The assumption underlying the supply and demand model is that, in the give and take of the marketplace, prices adjust until they settle down at a level where the quantity supplied by firms equals the quantity demanded by consumers. Let's see how.

Table 3.3
Finding the Market Equilibrium

Price	Quantity Demanded	Quantity Supplied	Shortage, Surplus, or Equilibrium	Price Rises or Falls
$140	18	1	Shortage = 17	Price rises
$160	14	4	Shortage = 10	Price rises
$180	11	7	Shortage = 4	Price rises
$200	9	9	Equilibrium	No change
$220	7	11	Surplus = 4	Price falls
$240	5	13	Surplus = 8	Price falls
$260	3	15	Surplus = 12	Price falls
$280	2	16	Surplus = 14	Price falls
$300	1	17	Surplus = 16	Price falls

Quantity supplied equals quantity demanded. (→ $200 row)

SUPPLY

Supply describes firms.

The supply curve looks like this:

DEMAND

Demand describes consumers.

The demand curve looks like th

Law of Supply

Price and quantity supplied are positively related.

Law of Demand

Price and quantity demanded are negatively related.

Movements along supply curve occur

when price rises and quantity supplied rises or when price falls and quantity supplied falls.

Movements along demand curve occur

when price rises and quantity demanded falls or when price falls and quantity demanded rises.

Shifts in supply are due to:

Technology (new inventions)

Number of firms in market

Price of goods used in production (inputs such as fertilizer, labor)

Expectations of future prices (firms will sell less now if prices are expected to rise; for example, farmers may store goods to sell next year)

Government taxes, subsidies, regulations (commodity taxes, agricultural subsidies, safety regulations)

Shifts in demand are due to:

Preferences (nice weather or fitness craze changes tastes)

Number of consumers in market

Consumers' information (about smoking, or faulty products, for example)

Consumers' income (normal goods versus inferior goods)

Expectations of future prices (consumers will buy more now if prices are expected to rise in the future)

Price of related goods (both substitutes, like butter and margarine, and complements, like gasoline and SUVs)

Figure 3.7
Overview of Supply and Demand

Determination of the Market Price

To determine the market price, we combine the demand relationship between the price and the quantity demanded with the supply relationship between the price and the quantity supplied. We can do this using either a table or a diagram. First consider Table 3.3, which combines the demand schedule from Table 3.1 with the supply schedule from Table 3.2. The price is in the first column, the quantity demanded by consumers is in the second column, and the quantity supplied by firms is in the third column. Observe that the quantity consumers are willing to buy is shown to decline with the price, while the quantity firms are willing to sell is shown to increase with the price. In order to determine the price in the market, consider each of the prices in Table 3.3.

■ **Finding the Market Price.**   Pick a price in Table 3.3, any price. Suppose the price you choose is $160. Then the quantity demanded by consumers (14 million bicycles) is greater than the quantity supplied by firms (4 million bicycles). In other words, there is a shortage of $14 - 4 = 10$ million bicycles. A **shortage,** or **excess demand,** is a situation in which the quantity demanded is greater than the quantity supplied. With a shortage of bicycles, the price will quickly rise above $160; firms will charge higher prices, and consumers who are willing to pay more than $160 for a bicycle will pay higher prices to firms. Thus, $160 cannot last as the market price. Observe that as the price rises above $160, the quantity demanded falls and the quantity supplied rises. Thus, as the price rises, the shortage begins to decrease. If you choose any price below $200, the same thing will happen: There will be a shortage, and the price will rise. The shortage disappears only when the price rises to $200, as shown in Table 3.3.

Now pick a price above $200. Suppose you pick $260. Then the quantity demanded by consumers (3 million bicycles) is less than the quantity supplied by firms (15 million bicycles). In other words, there is a surplus of 12 million bicycles. A **surplus,** or **excess supply,** is a situation in which the quantity supplied is greater than the quantity demanded. With a surplus of bicycles, the price will fall: Firms that are willing to sell bicycles for less than $260 will offer to sell to consumers at lower prices. Thus, $260 cannot be the market price either. Observe that as the price falls below $260, the quantity demanded rises and the quantity supplied falls. Thus, the surplus decreases. If you choose any price above $200, the same thing will happen: There will be a surplus, and the price will fall. The surplus disappears only when the price falls to $200.

Thus, we have shown that for any price below $200, there is a shortage, and the price rises; while for any price above $200, there is a surplus, and the price falls. What if the market price is $200? Then the quantity supplied equals the quantity demanded; there is neither a shortage nor a surplus, and there is no reason for the price to rise or fall. This price of $200 is therefore the most likely market price. It is called the **equilibrium price** because at this price the quantity supplied equals the quantity demanded, and there is no tendency for the price to change. There is no other price for which quantity supplied equals quantity demanded. If you look at all the other prices, you will see that there is either a shortage or a surplus, and thus there is a tendency for the price to either rise or fall.

The quantity bought and sold at the equilibrium price is 9 million bicycles. This is the **equilibrium quantity.** When the price equals the equilibrium price and the quantity bought and sold equals the equilibrium quantity, we say that there is a **market equilibrium.**

Our discussion of the determination of the equilibrium price shows how the market price coordinates the buying and selling decisions of many firms and consumers. We see that the price serves a *rationing function.* That is, the price alleviates shortages: A higher price reduces the quantity demanded or increases the quantity supplied when necessary to eliminate a shortage. Similarly, a lower price increases the quantity demanded or decreases the quantity supplied when there is a surplus. Thus, both shortages and surpluses are eliminated by the forces of supply and demand.

■ **Two Predictions.**   By combining supply and demand, we have completed the supply and demand model. The model can be applied to many markets, not just the example of the bicycle market. One prediction of the supply and demand model is that *the price in the market will be the price for which the quantity supplied equals the quantity demanded.* Thus, the model provides an answer to the question of what

shortage (excess demand): the situation in which quantity demanded is greater than quantity supplied.

surplus (excess supply):   the situation in which quantity supplied is greater than quantity demanded.

equilibrium price: the price at which quantity supplied equals quantity demanded.

equilibrium quantity: the quantity traded at the equilibrium price.

market equilibrium: the situation in which the price is equal to the equilibrium price and the quantity traded equals the equilibrium quantity.

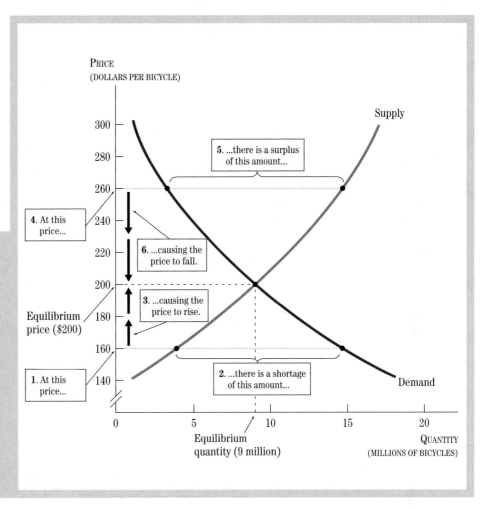

**Figure 3.8
Equilibrium Price and
Equilibrium Quantity**
When buyers and sellers interact in the market, the equilibrium price is at the point of intersection of the supply curve and the demand curve. At this point, the quantity supplied equals the quantity demanded. The equilibrium quantity is also determined at that point. At a higher price, the quantity demanded will be less than the quantity supplied; there will be a surplus. At a lower price, the quantity demanded will be greater than the quantity supplied; there will be a shortage.

determines the price in the market. Another prediction of the model is that *the quantity bought and sold in the market is the quantity for which the quantity supplied equals the quantity demanded.*

Finding the Equilibrium with a Supply and Demand Diagram

The equilibrium price and quantity in a market can also be found with the help of a graph. Figure 3.8 combines the demand curve from Figure 3.1 and the supply curve from Figure 3.4 in the same diagram. Observe that the downward-sloping demand curve intersects the upward-sloping supply curve at a single point. At that point of intersection, the quantity supplied equals the quantity demanded. Hence, the *equilibrium price occurs at the intersection of the supply curve and the demand curve.* The equilibrium price of $200 is shown in Figure 3.8. At that price, the quantity demanded is 9 million bicycles, and the quantity supplied is 9 million bicycles. This is the equilibrium quantity.

If the price were lower than this equilibrium price, say, $160, then the quantity demanded would be greater than the quantity supplied. There would be a shortage, and the price would begin to rise, as shown in the graph. The increase in gasoline prices in 2004 and 2005 led to an increase in demand for hybrid automobiles. With a shortage of hybrid vehicles and long waiting lists, some automobile sellers increased the price of the hybrids. When there is a shortage, the quantity demanded is greater than the quantity supplied, and there is pressure on the price to increase.

On the other hand, if the price were above the equilibrium price, say, $260, then there would be a surplus, as shown in the graph, and the price would begin to fall. After September 11, 2001, a large number of vacationers cancelled vacation plans that involved air travel. Caribbean hotels facing this decrease in demand began to offer big discounts. When there is a surplus, the quantity supplied is greater than the quantity demanded, and there is pressure on the price to fall.

Thus, the market price will tend to move toward the equilibrium price at the intersection of the supply curve and the demand curve. We can calculate exactly what the equilibrium price is on Figure 3.8 by drawing a line over to the vertical axis. And we can calculate the equilibrium quantity by drawing a line down to the horizontal axis.

A Change in the Market

In order to use the supply and demand model to explain or predict changes in prices, we need to consider what happens to the equilibrium price when there is a change in supply or demand. We first consider a change in demand and then a change in supply.

■ **Effects of a Change in Demand.** Figure 3.9 shows the effects of a shift in the demand curve for bicycles. Suppose that a shift occurs because of a fitness craze that increases the demand for bicycles. The demand curve shifts to the right, as shown in graph (a) in Figure 3.9. The demand curve before the shift and the demand curve after the shift are labeled the "old demand curve" and the "new demand curve," respectively.

If you look at the graph, you can see that something must happen to the equilibrium price when the demand curve shifts. The equilibrium price is determined at the intersection of the supply curve and the demand curve. With the new demand curve, there is a new intersection and, therefore, a new equilibrium price. The equilibrium price is no longer $200 in Figure 3.9(a); it is up to $220 per bicycle. Thus, the supply and demand model predicts that the price in the market will rise if there is an increase in demand. Note also that there is a change in the equilibrium quantity of bicycles. The quantity of bicycles sold and bought has increased from 9 million to 11 million. Thus, the equilibrium quantity has increased along with the equilibrium price. The supply and demand model predicts that an increase in demand will raise both the price and the quantity sold in the market.

We can use the same method to find out what happens if demand decreases, as shown in graph (b) in Figure 3.9. In this case, the demand curve shifts to the left. At the new intersection of the supply and demand curves, the equilibrium price is lower, and the quantity sold is also lower. Thus, the supply and demand model predicts that a decrease in demand will both lower the price and lower the quantity sold in the market.

Note in these examples that when the demand curve shifts, it leads to a movement along the supply curve. First, the demand curve shifts to the right or to the left. Then there is movement along the supply curve because the change in the price affects the quantity of bicycles firms will sell.

■ **Effects of a Change in Supply.** Figure 3.10 shows what happens when there is a change in the market that shifts the supply curve. In graph (a) of Figure 3.10 we

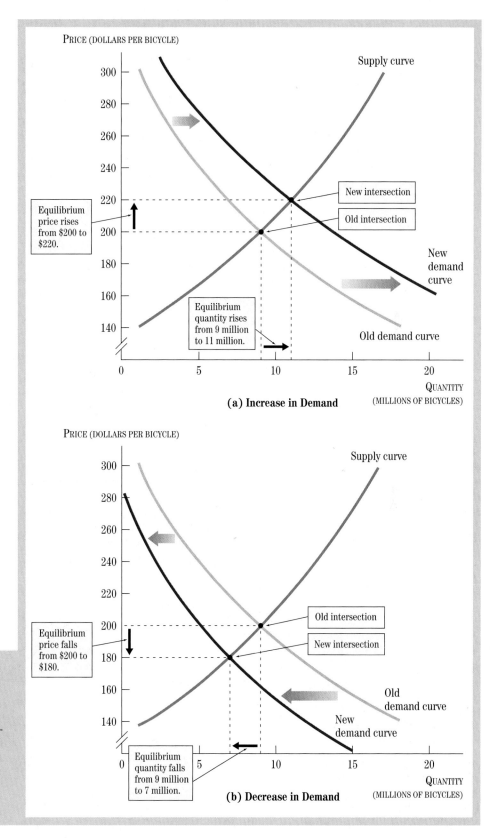

Figure 3.9
Effects of a Shift in Demand
When demand increases, as in graph (a), the demand curve shifts to the right. The equilibrium price rises, and the equilibrium quantity also rises. When demand decreases, as in graph (b), the demand curve shifts to the left. The equilibrium price falls, and the equilibrium quantity also falls.

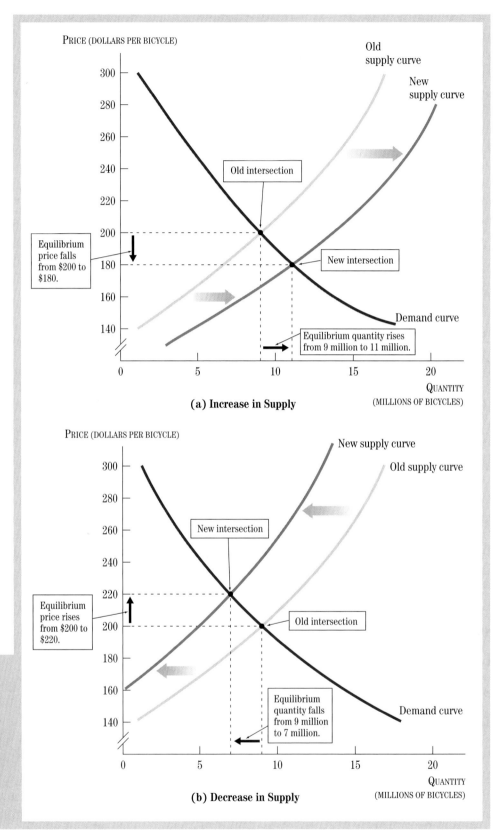

(a) Increase in Supply

(b) Decrease in Supply

Figure 3.10
Effects of a Shift in Supply
When supply increases, as in graph (a), the supply curve shifts to the right; the equilibrium price falls, and the equilibrium quantity rises. When supply decreases, as in graph (b), the supply curve shifts to the left; the equilibrium price rises, and the equilibrium quantity falls.

Table 3.4
Effects of Shifts in Demand and Supply Curves

Shift	Effect on Equilibrium Price	Effect on Equilibrium Quantity
Increase in demand	Up	Up
Decrease in demand	Down	Down
Increase in supply	Down	Up
Decrease in supply	Up	Down

show the effect of an increase in supply, and in graph (b) we show the effect of a decrease in supply.

When the supply curve of bicycles shifts to the right, there is a new equilibrium price, which is lower than the old equilibrium price. In addition, the equilibrium quantity rises. Thus, the supply and demand model predicts that an increase in the supply of bicycles—perhaps because of better technology in bicycle production—will lower the price and raise the quantity of bicycles sold.

When the supply curve of bicycles shifts to the left, the equilibrium price rises, as shown in graph (b) of Figure 3.10, and the equilibrium quantity falls. Thus, the model predicts that anything that reduces supply will raise the price of bicycles and lower the quantity of bicycles produced.

Table 3.4 summarizes the results of this analysis of shifts in the supply and demand curves.

■ **When Both Curves Shift.** The supply and demand model is easiest to use when something shifts either demand or supply but not both. However, in reality, it is possible for something or several different things to simultaneously shift both supply and demand. To predict whether the price or the quantity rises or falls in such cases, we need to know whether demand or supply shifts by a larger amount. Dealing with the possibility of simultaneous shifts in demand and supply curves is important in practice, as we show in the next section.

REVIEW
- When firms and consumers interact in a market, a price is determined by the market.

- The supply and demand model predicts that the price is found at the intersection of the supply and demand curves. This price is called the equilibrium price.

- At this price, the quantity supplied equals the quantity demanded, and there is no tendency for the price to change.

- A shift in the demand curve or the supply curve will change the equilibrium price and the equilibrium quantity. By considering changes in supply or demand, the model can be used to explain or predict price changes.

Using the Supply and Demand Model to Analyze Real-World Issues

In April 2005, President Bush held a press conference to discuss issues that he felt were of critical importance to the American people. One of these issues was the high price of gasoline. How does the high price of gasoline affect you? Perhaps when gasoline gets more expensive, you cut back on driving, or maybe you ask your parents for more money to buy gasoline, or perhaps you just have less money to spend on other things because you are spending more on gasoline. President Bush recognized this impact by asserting, "Millions of American families and small businesses are hurting because of higher gasoline prices."

Why does the price of gasoline go up? How does the high price of gasoline affect the American people and American businesses? What can policymakers do to lower the price of gasoline? The model of supply and demand gives us a tool to model the market for gasoline, to examine the causes of the high price, to comment on the impact on the American people and American businesses, and to focus on what policymakers can do to lower the price of gasoline.

In his April 2005 press conference, President Bush explained the reason for the high price of gasoline. "Over the past decade, America's energy consumption has been growing about 40 times faster than our energy production." A closer analysis of

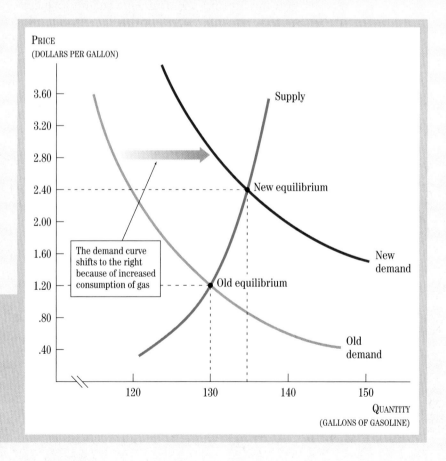

Figure 3.11
Effect of an Increase in Demand on the Supply of Gasoline
You can see here that when demand for gasoline increases, the demand curve shifts to the right. The equilibrium price rises, as does the equilibrium quantity.

the market for gasoline using the model of supply and demand helps us understand the causes of this imbalance in demand and supply. Demand for gasoline has been increasing as more Americans drive gas-guzzling SUVs and Americans drive more miles. Supply of gasoline has been decreasing as a result of a reduction in U.S. refining capacity. Stricter environmental regulations for refining gasoline and the increasing price of oil both lead to an increase in production costs for gasoline. The supply of gasoline decreases as a result of an increase in production costs—that is, a higher price is needed to sell any quantity.

We use a supply and demand model to analyze these changes. As shown in Figure 3.11, increased consumption causes a shift of the demand curve to the right. The quantity demanded is greater than the quantity supplied at the current price, causing the price to rise. When there is an increase in demand and at the same time a decrease in supply, as shown in Figure 3.12, the equilibrium price rises again.

How does the high price of gasoline hurt American businesses and the American people? Here are a few examples. When Wal-Mart's earnings were lower than expected in May 2005, Wal-Mart blamed the low earnings partially on high gasoline prices. Wal-Mart speculated that its customers had less money to spend because of the high price of gasoline. With SUV sales falling in 2005, American auto producers lowered SUV prices to increase their sales. The decrease in sales of SUVs was attributed partially to the high price of gasoline. Think about how your behavior changes when the price of gasoline increases.

What policymakers do to lower the price of gasoline? President Bush stressed in his press conference that Congress needs to pass an energy bill to address the high price of energy. President Bush stated, "You can't wave a magic wand. I wish I could."

**Figure 3.12
Combined Effect of a Simultaneous Increase in Demand and Decrease in Supply of Gasoline**
When demand for gasoline increases and, at the same time, the supply of gasoline *decreases* because of decreased refining capacity, the supply curve will shift to the left; again, the equilibrium price increases, but this time the equilibrium quantity decreases, although not back to the original quantity. In this situation, the increase in demand is larger than the decrease in supply.

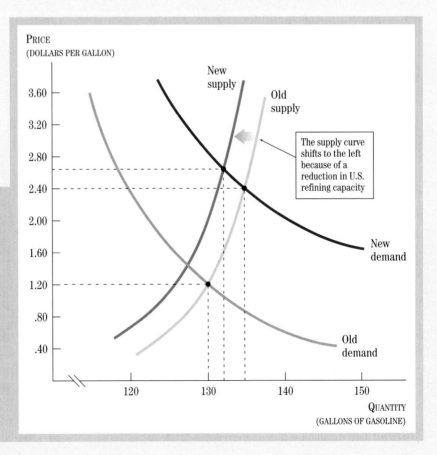

A magic wand won't work, but the model of supply and demand can predict what will. We'll discuss some of the policies proposed for the energy bill and see that these policies can be modeled as either a decrease in the demand for gasoline, an increase in the supply of gasoline, a decrease in the demand for oil, or an increase in the supply of oil.

President Bush described the essential ingredients of a successful energy policy—it must use new technologies for energy conservation; it must promote the development of new sources of energy; and it must help China and India, both countries with rapidly increasing demand for energy, conserve energy. New technologies for conservation of energy and developing new sources of energy would reduce the demand for oil and for gasoline. This decrease in demand for oil would lead to a decrease in the equilibrium price of oil. Since oil is a major input in the production of gasoline, a decrease in the price of oil corresponds to an increase in the supply of gasoline. Both the decrease in the demand for gasoline and the increase in the supply of gasoline lead to a reduction in the equilibrium price of gasoline. Indeed, this energy policy would help relieve the distress to the American people and businesses caused by the high price of gasoline.

An energy policy that focuses on new technologies for conservation and new sources of energy cannot lead to a quick change in the price of gasoline. President Bush pointed this out, noting that the best way to get the price of gasoline to fall soon would be to encourage oil-producing nations to increase their supply of oil. An increase in the supply of oil would decrease the price of oil, leading to an increase in the supply of gasoline and a reduction in the price of gasoline.

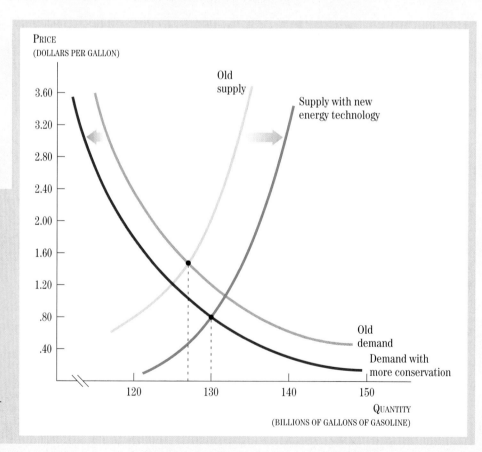

Figure 3.13
Predicted Effects of Energy Policy
The supply and demand model can also be used to predict what would happen with a successful energy policy that promoted the development of new sources of energy and energy conservation. Here, demand decreases slightly due to the effects of energy conservation, and supply increases due to the development of new technology for energy development. When demand decreases and supply increases, the equilibrium price goes down and the equilibrium quantity increases.

Figure 3.13 illustrates the gasoline market with a simultaneous decrease in demand and increase in supply. Both the decrease in the demand for gasoline and the increase in the supply of gasoline would lead to a decrease in the equilibrium price of gasoline. This is a prediction that policymakers could easily make. What if they wanted to also predict the change in the consumption of gasoline resulting from this energy bill? A decrease in demand would decrease equilibrium consumption, while an increase in supply would increase equilibrium consumption. Policymakers therefore could not predict whether gasoline consumption would rise or fall without knowing whether demand or supply would shift by a larger amount. Figure 3.13 shows a resulting increase in the consumption of gasoline because the supply increase is greater in magnitude than the demand decrease. Draw a graph yourself, but make the demand decrease larger than the supply increase. You will see a resulting decrease in the consumption of gasoline. If policymakers want an energy bill that reduces the price of gasoline and reduces the quantity of gasoline consumed, they need to be sure that conservation efforts are the primary focus of the plan.

REVIEW

- The supply and demand model can be used in practical applications to explain price changes in many markets. It can also be used to predict what will happen to prices when certain actions—such as introducing a new energy policy—are taken.

- In applying the model, economists consider shifts of the supply curve or the demand curve. In the case study of gasoline prices, both the supply curve and the demand curve shifted.

Interference with Market Prices

Thus far, we have used the supply and demand model in situations in which the price is freely determined without government control. But many times throughout history, and around the world today, governments have attempted to control market prices. The usual reason is that government leaders have not been happy with the outcome of the market, or they were pressured by groups who would benefit from price controls.

price control: a government law or regulation that sets or limits the price to be charged for a particular good.

Price controls were used widely by the U.S. government during World War II and again in the early 1970s. Price controls now exist in certain housing markets, agriculture markets, and labor markets in the United States. What are the effects of this government interference in the market? The supply and demand model can help answer this question.

Price Ceilings and Price Floors

price ceiling: a government price control that sets the maximum allowable price for a good.

In general there are two broad types of government price controls. Controls can stipulate a **price ceiling,** or a maximum price at which a good can be bought and sold. For example, the United States government controlled oil prices in the early 1970s, stipulating that firms could not charge more than a stated maximum price of $5.25 per barrel of crude oil; the equilibrium price was well over $10 per barrel at this time. Some cities in the United States have price controls on rental apartments. Landlords

rent control: a government price control that sets the maximum allowable rent on a house or apartment.

price floor: a government price control that sets the minimum allowable price for a good.

minimum wage: a wage per hour below which it is illegal to pay workers.

are not permitted to charge a rent higher than the maximum stipulated by the **rent control** law in these cities. Price ceilings are imposed by governments because of complaints that the market price is too high. The purpose is to help the consumers who must pay the prices. For example, rent controls exist in order to help people who must pay rent. However, as we will see, price controls have harmful side effects that can end up hurting those consumers the law is apparently trying to help.

Government price controls can also stipulate a **price floor,** or a minimum price. Price floors are imposed by governments in order to help the suppliers of goods and services. For example, the U.S. government requires that the price of sugar not fall below a certain amount in the United States. In the labor market, the U.S. government requires that firms pay workers a wage of at least a given level, called the **minimum wage.**

Shortages and Related Problems Resulting from Price Ceilings

If the government prevents firms from charging more than a certain amount for their products, then a shortage is likely to result, as illustrated in Figure 3.14. When the maximum price remains below the equilibrium price for the market, there is a persistent shortage; sellers are unwilling to supply as much as buyers want to buy. This is illustrated for the general case of any good in the top graph in Figure 3.14 and for the specific case of rent control in the bottom graph.

▓ **Dealing with Persistent Shortages.**   Because higher prices are not allowed, the shortage must be dealt with in other ways. Sometimes the government issues a limited amount of ration coupons to people to alleviate the shortage; this was done in World War II. The law required that people present these ration coupons at stores in order to buy goods. Thus, the total quantity demanded could not be greater than the amount of ration coupons. Alternatively, if there are no ration coupons, then the shortage might result in long waiting lines. In the past, in centrally planned economies, long lines for bread were frequently observed because of price controls on bread. Sometimes black markets develop, in which people buy and sell goods outside the watch of the government and charge whatever price they want. This typically happens in command economies. Black markets are also common in less-developed countries today when the governments in these countries impose price controls.

Another effect of price ceilings is a reduction in the quality of the good sold. By lowering the quality of the good, the producer can reduce the costs of producing it. Low-quality housing frequently results from rent control. By lowering the quality of the apartments—perhaps being slow to paint the walls or repair the elevator—landlords make the apartments shoddy and unattractive.

▓ **Making Things Worse.**   Although the stated purpose of price ceilings is to help people who have to pay high prices, the preceding examples indicate how they can make things worse. Issuing ration coupons raises difficult problems about who gets the coupons. In the case of a price ceiling on gasoline, for example, should the government give more coupons to those who commute by car than to those who do not? More generally, who is to decide who deserves the coupons? Rationing by waiting in line is also a poor outcome. People waiting in line could be doing more enjoyable or more useful things. Similarly, black markets, being illegal, encourage people to go

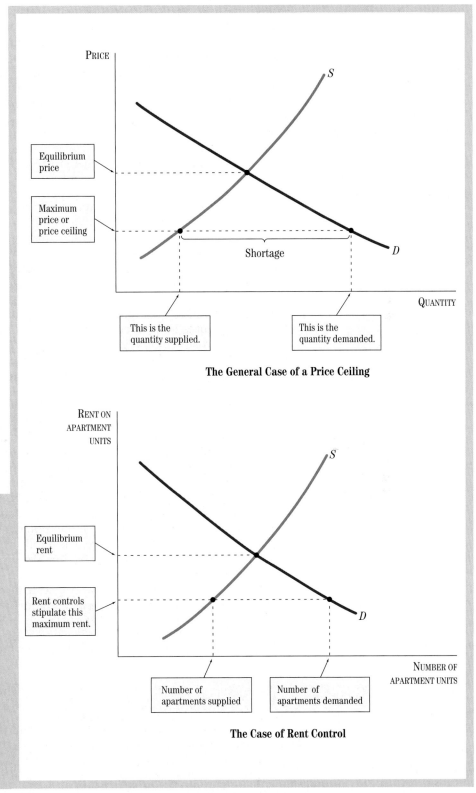

The General Case of a Price Ceiling

The Case of Rent Control

Figure 3.14
Effects of a Maximum Price Law
The top diagram shows the general case when the government prevents the market price from rising above a particular maximum price, or sets a price ceiling below the equilibrium price. The lower diagram shows a particular example of a price ceiling, rent controls on apartment units. The supply and demand model predicts that there will be a shortage. The shortage occurs because the quantity supplied is less than consumers are willing to buy at that price. The shortage leads to rationing, black markets, or lower product quality.

outside the law; people thereby lose their rights to protection in the case of theft or fraud. Lowering the quality of the good is also a bad way to alleviate the problem of a high price. This simply eliminates the higher-quality good from production; consumers and producers lose.

Paradoxically, price ceilings frequently end up hurting those they try to help. Many people who benefit from controls, for example, are not poor at all. If rent controls reduce the supply of apartments, they make less housing available for everyone.

Surpluses and Related Problems Resulting from Price Floors

If the government imposes a price floor, then a surplus will occur, as shown in Figure 3.15. With the price above the equilibrium price, suppliers of goods and services want to sell more than people are willing to buy. Hence, there is a surplus. This is illustrated for the general case of any good in the top graph of Figure 3.15 and for the specific case of the minimum wage in the bottom graph.

How is this surplus dealt with in actual markets? In markets for farm products, the government usually has to buy the surplus and, perhaps, put it in storage; but buying farm products above the equilibrium price costs taxpayers money, and the higher price raises costs to consumers. For this reason, economists argue against price floors on agricultural goods. As an alternative, the government sometimes reduces the supply by telling firms to plant fewer acres or to destroy crops, or by restricting the amount that can come from abroad. In the United States, the federal government uses acreage restrictions in the case of wheat and other grains; it also uses import restrictions in the case of sugar. But government requirements that land be kept idle or crops destroyed are particularly repugnant to most people.

As we will see in more detail later in this book, the supply and demand model can also be applied to labor markets. In that case, the price is the price of labor, or the wage. What does the supply and demand model predict about the effects of a minimum wage? In the case of labor markets, a minimum wage can cause unemployment. If the equilibrium wage is below the minimum wage, then some workers would be willing to work for less than the minimum wage. But employers are not permitted to pay them less than the minimum wage. Therefore, there is an oversupply of workers at the minimum wage. The number of workers demanded is less than the number of workers willing to work; thus, the supply and demand model predicts that the minimum wage causes unemployment.

The minimum wage would have no effect if the equilibrium wage were above the minimum wage. The supply and demand model predicts that the minimum wage affects workers whose wages would be below the minimum. Thus, a minimum wage would be most likely to increase unemployment for teenage workers with very few skills if their wages would otherwise be below the minimum.

REVIEW
- Price ceilings cause persistent shortages, which, in turn, cause rationing, black markets, and a reduced quality of goods and services.

- Price floors cause persistent surpluses and unemployment, according to the supply and demand model. In the case of price floors on agricultural products, the surpluses are bought by the government and put in storage. In the case of the minimum wage, the surpluses mean more unemployment for those who can get jobs only at a wage below the minimum wage.

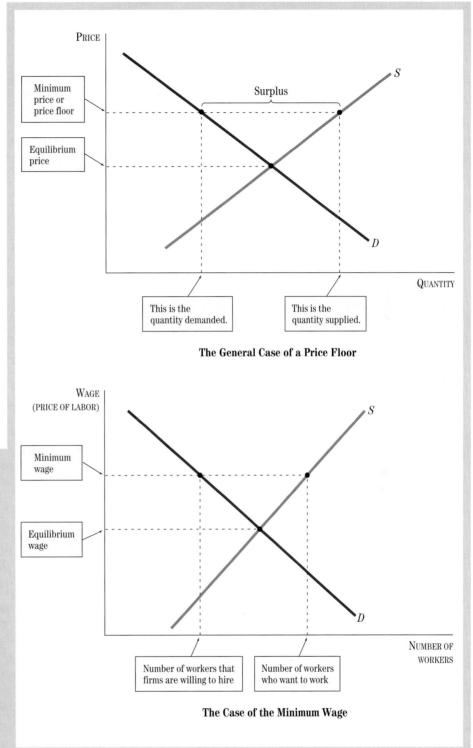

Figure 3.15
Effects of a Minimum Price Law
The top diagram shows the general case when the government prevents the market price from falling below a particular minimum price, or sets a price floor above the equilibrium price. The lower diagram shows a particular example when the price of labor—the wage—cannot fall below the minimum wage. The supply and demand model predicts that sellers are willing to sell a greater quantity than buyers are willing to buy at that price. Thus, there is a surplus of the good or, in the case of labor, unemployment for some of those who would be hired only at a lower wage.

PRICE

Minimum price or price floor

Equilibrium price

Surplus

S

D

This is the quantity demanded.

This is the quantity supplied.

QUANTITY

The General Case of a Price Floor

WAGE
(PRICE OF LABOR)

Minimum wage

Equilibrium wage

S

D

Number of workers that firms are willing to hire

Number of workers who want to work

NUMBER OF WORKERS

The Case of the Minimum Wage

Conclusion

This chapter has shown how prices are determined in markets where buyers and sellers interact freely. The supply and demand model is used to describe how prices are determined in such markets. It is probably the most frequently used model in economics and has been in existence for over a hundred years in pretty much the same form as economists use it now. You will come to appreciate it more and more as you study economics.

A key feature of the model is that the price is found by the intersection of the supply and demand curves. To apply the model in practice, we need to look for factors that shift either the supply curve or the demand curve. In the most successful applications of the supply and demand model, the factors that affect supply and demand can be separated.

In later chapters we will see more about how the supply and demand model is implied by the central economic idea that people make purposeful choices with scarce resources and interact with other people as they make these choices. By doing so, we will be able to take a closer look at the three basic questions: what, how, and for whom to produce.

KEY POINTS

1. Demand is a negative relationship between the price of a good and the quantity demanded by consumers. It can be shown graphically by a downward-sloping demand curve.

2. A movement along the demand curve occurs when a higher price reduces the quantity demanded or a lower price increases the quantity demanded.

3. A shift of the demand curve occurs when something besides the price causes the quantity people are willing to buy to change.

4. Supply is a positive relationship between the price of a good and the quantity supplied by firms. It can be shown graphically by an upward-sloping supply curve.

5. A movement along the supply curve occurs when a higher price increases the quantity supplied or a lower price decreases the quantity supplied.

6. A shift of the supply curve occurs when something besides the price causes the quantity firms are willing to sell to change.

7. The equilibrium price and equilibrium quantity are determined by the intersection of the supply curve and the demand curve, where the quantity supplied equals the quantity demanded.

8. By shifting either the supply curve or the demand curve, observations on prices can be explained and predictions about prices can be made.

9. Price ceilings cause shortages, with the quantity supplied less than the quantity demanded. Shortages lead to rationing or black markets.

10. Price floors cause surpluses, with the quantity supplied greater than the quantity demanded.

KEY TERMS

demand
price
quantity demanded
demand schedule
law of demand
demand curve
normal good

inferior good
substitute
complement
supply
quantity supplied
supply schedule
law of supply

supply curve
shortage (excess demand)
surplus (excess supply)
equilibrium price
equilibrium quantity
market equilibrium
price control

price ceiling
rent control
price floor
minimum wage

QUESTIONS FOR REVIEW

1. Why does the demand curve slope downward?
2. Why does the supply curve slope upward?
3. What is the difference between a shift in the demand curve and a movement along the demand curve?
4. What are four things that cause a demand curve to shift?
5. What are four things that cause a supply curve to shift?
6. What is the difference between a shift in the supply curve and a movement along the supply curve?
7. What are the equilibrium price and equilibrium quantity?
8. What happens to the equilibrium price if the supply curve shifts to the right and the demand curve does not shift?
9. What happens to the equilibrium price if the demand curve shifts to the right and the supply curve does not shift?
10. Do price ceilings cause shortages or surpluses? What about price floors? Explain.

PROBLEMS

1. Consider the following supply and demand model of the world tea market (in billions of pounds).

Price per Pound	Quantity Supplied	Quantity Demanded
$.38	1,500	525
$.37	1,000	600
$.36	700	700
$.35	600	900
$.34	550	1,200

   a. Is there a shortage or a surplus when the price is $.38? What about $.34?
   b. What are the equilibrium price and the equilibrium quantity?
   c. Graph the supply curve and the demand curve.
   d. Show how the equilibrium price and quantity can be found on the graph.
   e. If there is a shortage or surplus at a price of $.38, calculate its size in billions of pounds and show it on the graph.

2. Consider the supply and demand model in problem 1. Suppose that there is a drought in Sri Lanka that reduces the supply of tea by 400 billion pounds at every price. Suppose demand does not change.
   a. Write down in a table the new supply schedule for tea.
   b. Find the new equilibrium price and the new equilibrium quantity. Explain how the market adjusts to the new equilibrium.

   c. Did the equilibrium quantity change by more or less than the change in supply?
   d. Graph the new supply curve along with the old supply curve and the demand curve.
   e. Show the change in the equilibrium price and the equilibrium quantity on the graph.

3. Use the supply and demand model to explain what happens to the equilibrium price and the equilibrium quantity for frozen yogurt in the following cases:
   a. There is a large expansion in the number of firms producing frozen yogurt.
   b. It is widely publicized in the press that frozen yogurt isn't as healthful as was previously thought.
   c. There is a sudden increase in the price of milk, which is used to produce frozen yogurt.
   d. Frozen yogurt suddenly becomes popular because a movie idol promotes it in television commercials.

4. For each of the following markets, indicate whether the stated change causes a shift in the supply curve, a shift in the demand curve, a movement along the supply curve, and/or a movement along the demand curve.
   a. The housing market: Consumers' incomes fall.
   b. The tea market: The price of sugar goes down.
   c. The coffee market: There is a freeze in Brazil that severely damages the coffee crop.
   d. The fast food market: The number of fast food restaurants in an area decreases.
   e. The peanut market in the U.S. Southeast: A drought lowers supply.

5. Draw a supply and demand diagram to indicate the market for prescription drugs in the United States, with the equilibrium price and quantity labeled. Suppose the government imposes a strict ceiling on the price of prescription drugs sold in the United States. Show what happens in this market if the ceiling is less than the equilibrium price. How would the pharmaceutical firms that develop such drugs in their research laboratories respond?

6. Consider the market for automatic teller machine services in a city. The price is the fee for a cash withdrawal.
   a. Sketch the demand curve and the supply curve for ATM transactions.
   b. How is the equilibrium price determined?
   c. If the town council imposes a ban on ATM fees, equivalent to a price ceiling in this market, what happens to quantity supplied and quantity demanded?
   d. Economists frequently argue against price controls because of the incentives they give to suppliers. Explain why this interference in the market may provide bad incentives.

7. In 1991 the price of milk fell 30 percent. Senator Leahy of Vermont, a big milk-producing state, supported a law in the U.S. Congress to put a floor on the price. The floor was $13.09 per hundred pounds of milk. The market price was $11.47.
   a. Draw a supply and demand diagram. Explain the effects of the legislation. Would the legislation cause a surplus or a shortage?
   b. The dairy farmers supported the legislation, and consumer groups opposed it. Why?

8. Why is it necessary for people to stand in line for days before the sale of tickets to concerts by the most famous performers? Is the price mechanism working properly? Why are scalpers present on these occasions?

9. Assuming that either supply or demand, but not both, changes, indicate the direction and change in either supply or demand that must have occurred to produce the following:
   a. A decrease in the price and quantity of apples
   b. A decrease in the price of bananas with an increase in the quantity of bananas
   c. An increase in the price and quantity of cars
   d. An increase in the quantity of computers with a decrease in the price

10. Using the demand and supply diagrams (one for each market), show what short-run changes in price and quantity would be expected in the following markets if worries about air safety cause travelers to shy away from air travel. Each graph should contain the original and new demand and supply curves, and the original and new equilibrium prices and quantities. For each market, write one sentence explaining why each curve shifts or does not shift.
    a. The market for air travel
    b. The market for rail travel
    c. The market for hotel rooms in Hawaii

11. Determine which of the following four sentences use the terminology of the supply and demand model correctly.
    a. "The price of bicycles rose, and therefore the demand for bicycles went down."
    b. "The demand for bicycles increased, and therefore the price went up."
    c. "The price of bicycles fell, decreasing the supply of bicycles."
    d. "The supply of bicycles increased, and therefore the price of bicycles fell."

12. a. Suppose you find out that an increase in the price of first-class postage leads to an increase in the demand for overnight delivery service and a decrease in the demand for envelopes. For which good is postage a complement, and for which is it a substitute?
    b. Suppose someone told you that an increase in the price of gasoline caused a decrease in the demand for public transportation by train. Is this what you would predict? Why or why not?
    c. Suppose an economic forecasting group has determined that an increase in the price of orange juice has no effect on the demand for soft drinks. What can you conclude from this information?

13. Suppose a decrease in consumers' incomes causes a decrease in the demand for chicken and an increase in the demand for potatoes. Which good is inferior and which is normal? How will the equilibrium price and quantity change for each good?

14. a. Straight-line demand and supply curves can be represented by linear algebraic equations. Given the following algebraic expressions for supply and demand, calculate the equilibrium price and quantity by solving the two equations for P and Q.

   Supply: $Q = 5 + 2P$
   Demand: $Q = 9 - 2P$

   b. For the equations defined in part (a), show that when you substitute the equilibrium price into either the supply or the demand equation, you get the same equilibrium quantity.
   c. Suppose that the demand curve shifts as a result of an increase in consumers' incomes. The new demand equation is $Q = 13 - 2P$. Calculate the new equilibrium price and quantity.

CHAPTER 4

Elasticity and Its Uses

When oil prices rose to over $55 a barrel in April 2005—nearly 50 percent higher than the year before—it was "*déja vu* all over again." Oil prices had been rising steadily since 2000 and had also risen sharply several times before—in 1990, in 1980, and in the early 1970s. Each time the story was similar: Oil-producing countries cut back the supply of oil, and the price of oil rose. In 1990 the supply was cut because Iraq invaded Kuwait and destroyed its oil fields. In 2000 the supply was cut when the producing countries got together to raise the price. But this time, the story was somewhat different. There were no critical cuts in supply from any of the major oil-exporting countries. Instead, the world's oil producers were just not able to keep up with the continually increasing demand for oil from around the world, an increase fueled in large part by a significantly increasing demand from China. Because oil is a key input to many products, from the gasoline that people put in their cars and trucks to the asphalt they drive them on, higher oil prices have a serious impact on many people.

The supply and demand model tells us that a reduction in oil supply or an increase in oil demand will increase the price of oil. But by how much? For example, would the price of oil be expected to nearly double when Iraq's military actions removed 7 percent of the world's oil supply? And how much would the price fall if the U.S. government persuaded the oil-producing countries in April 2005 to increase production by 4 percent?

There is an elegant, but remarkably useful, economic concept called *elasticity* that economists use when they work with the supply and demand model. In economics, elasticity is a measure of how sensitive one variable is to another. In the case of the supply and demand model, elasticity measures how sensitive the quantity of a good that people demand, or that firms supply, is to the price of the good. In this chapter we show how the concept of elasticity can be used to answer the questions raised above about oil supply and price and many other questions. We first show why elasticity is important and provide a formula to show how elasticity is calculated. We then show how it is used in many different ways and demonstrate how to work with and talk about elasticity.

Elasticity of Demand

Defining the Price Elasticity of Demand

The price elasticity of demand is a measure of the sensitivity of the *quantity demanded* of a good to the *price* of the good. "Price elasticity of demand" is sometimes shortened to "elasticity of demand," the "demand elasticity," or even simply "elasticity" when the meaning is clear from the context. The price elasticity of demand always refers to a particular demand curve or demand schedule, such as the world demand for oil or the U.S. demand for bicycles. For a particular demand curve, all other things besides the price of the good being equal, these relationships hold: As the price increases, the quantity demanded by consumers declines; as the price decreases, the quantity demanded by consumers increases. The price elasticity of demand is a measure of *how much* the quantity demanded changes when the price changes.

For example, when economists report that the price elasticity of demand for contact lenses is high, they mean that the quantity of contact lenses demanded by people changes by a large amount when the price changes. Or if they report that the price elasticity of demand for bread is low, they mean that the quantity of bread demanded changes by only a small amount when the price of bread changes.

price elasticity of demand: the percentage change in the quantity demanded of a good divided by the percentage change in the price of that good.

We can define the price elasticity of demand clearly with a formula: **Price elasticity of demand** is the percentage change in quantity demanded divided by the percentage change in the price. That is,

$$\text{Price elasticity of demand} = \frac{\text{percentage change in quantity demanded}}{\text{percentage change in the price}}$$

We emphasize that the price elasticity of demand refers to a particular demand curve; thus, the numerator of this formula is the percentage change in quantity demanded when the price changes by the percentage amount shown in the denominator. All the other factors that affect demand are held constant when we compute the price elasticity of demand.

For example, the price elasticity of demand for gasoline is about .2. Thus, if the price of gasoline increases by 10 percent, the quantity of gasoline demanded will fall by 2 percent (.2 × 10). The price elasticity of demand for alcoholic beverages is about 1.5; thus, if the price of alcoholic beverages rises by 10 percent, the quantity demanded will fall by 15 percent (1.5 × 10). As you can see from these examples, elasticity is a way to determine by how much the *quantity demanded* changes when the price changes.

The Size of the Elasticity: High versus Low

There are two graphs in Figure 4.1, each showing a different possible demand curve for oil in the world. We want to show why it is important to know which of these two demand curves is correct, or at least which one gives a better description of economic behavior in the oil market. Each graph has the price of oil on the vertical axis (in dollars per barrel) and the quantity of oil demanded on the horizontal axis (in millions of barrels of oil a day).

Both of the demand curves pass through the same point *A*, where the price of oil is $20 per barrel and the quantity demanded is 60 million barrels per day. But observe

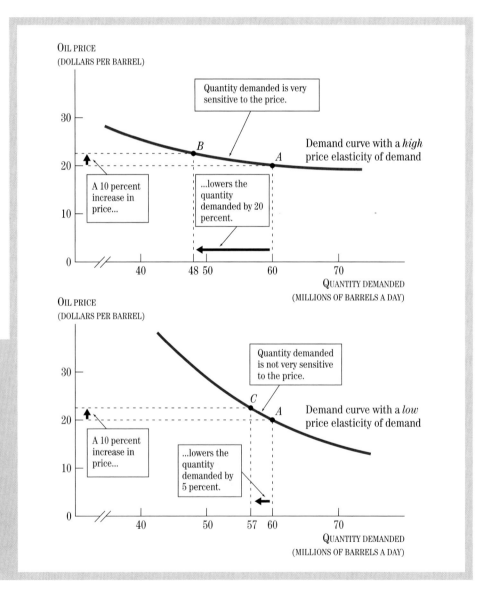

Figure 4.1
Comparing Different Sizes of the Price Elasticity of Demand
Both sets of axes have exactly the same scale. In the top graph, the quantity demanded is very sensitive to the price; the elasticity is high. In the bottom graph, the quantity demanded is not very sensitive to the price; the elasticity is low. Thus, the same increase in price ($2, or 10 percent) reduces the quantity demanded much more when the elasticity is high (top graph) than when it is low (bottom graph).

How Policymakers Use Price Elasticity of Demand to Discourage Underage Drinking

Policymakers use information about the price of elasticity of demand in many ways. Take the government's efforts to reduce underage drinking. In a 2003 study on underage drinking, the National Academy of Sciences recommended that one way to reduce underage drinking would be to increase the tax on alcohol. To implement this policy effectively, it would be important for policymakers to know which demand curve most accurately represents the demand for alcohol by underage drinkers. The amount that a tax would reduce the quantity of alcohol consumed by underage drinkers depends on their price elasticity of demand.

Recall that a new tax is modeled as a decrease in supply. You can see how this works by drawing this supply shift and a demand curve with high price elasticity of demand and then drawing the same supply shift and a demand curve with a low price elasticity of demand, as in Figure 4.2. Alcohol consumption responds more to the tax when the price elasticity of demand is high. If the price elasticity of demand for alcohol by underage drinkers is low (that is, if the quantity of alcohol demanded by underage drinkers changes by only a small amount when the price of alcohol changes), then a new tax on alcohol must be large to accomplish the goal of a reduction in underage drinking. If the price elasticity of demand for alcohol by underage drinkers is high (that is, if the quantity of alcohol demanded by underage drinkers changes by a large amount when the price of alcohol changes), then the tax might not need to be very big to accomplish the policymakers' goal. Which do you think is more likely?

that the two different curves show different degrees of sensitivity of the quantity demanded to the price. In the top graph, where the demand curve is relatively flat, the quantity demanded of oil is very sensitive to the price; in other words, the demand curve has a high elasticity. For example, consider a change from point A to point B: When the price rises by $2, from $20 to $22, or by 10 percent ($2/$20 = .10, or 10 percent), the quantity demanded falls by 12 million, from 60 million to 48 million barrels a day, or by 20 percent (12/60 = .20 or 20 percent).

On the other hand, in the bottom graph, the quantity demanded is not very sensitive to the price; in other words, the demand curve has a low elasticity. It is relatively steep. When the price rises by $2, or 10 percent, from point A to point C, the quantity demanded falls by 3 million barrels, or only 5 percent. Thus, the sensitivity of the quantity to the price, or the size of the elasticity, is what distinguishes these two graphs.

The Impact of a Change in Supply on the Price of Oil

Now consider what happens when there is a decline in supply in the world oil market. In Figure 4.2 we combine the supply curve for oil with the two possible demand curves for oil from Figure 4.1. Initially the oil market is in equilibrium in Figure 4.2; in both graphs, the quantity demanded equals the quantity supplied. The equilibrium price is $20 per barrel and the equilibrium quantity is 60 million barrels a day, just like at point A in Figure 4.1. A reduction in the supply of oil—perhaps because of the invasion of Kuwait by Iraq in 1990, or perhaps because of the reduction in production by Iraq in 2000—is also shown. The exact same leftward shift in supply is shown in the top and bottom graphs of Figure 4.2.

Now, observe how the equilibrium price changes in the two graphs. Recall that this change is our prediction—using the supply and demand model—of what would happen to the price of oil if the supply declined. There is a huge difference in the size of the predicted price increase in the two graphs. In the top graph, the oil price increases only a little. If the elasticity is very high, then only a small increase in the

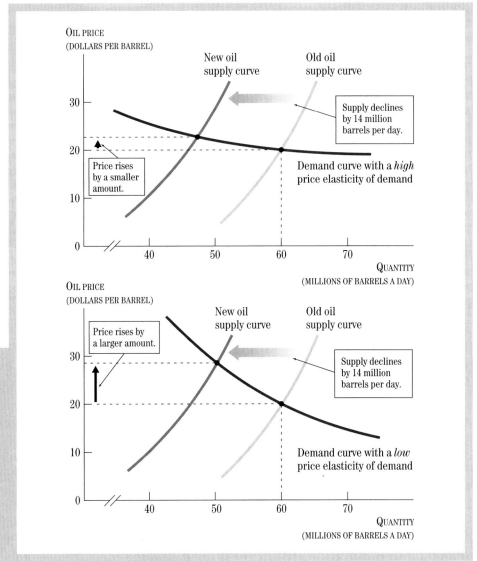

Figure 4.2
The Importance of the Size of the Price Elasticity of Demand
The impact on the oil price of a reduction in oil supply is shown for two different demand curves. The reduction in supply is the same for both graphs. When the price elasticity of demand is high (top graph), there is only a small increase in the price. When the price elasticity of demand is low (bottom graph), the price rises by much more.

price is enough to get people to reduce their use of oil and thereby bring the quantity demanded down to a lower quantity supplied. On the other hand, in the bottom diagram, the price rises by much more. Here the elasticity is very low, and so a large increase in price is needed to get people to reduce their use of oil and bring the quantity demanded down to the quantity supplied.

Thus, in order to determine how much the price will rise in response to a shift in oil supply, we need to know how sensitive the quantity demanded is to the price, or the size of the elasticity of demand.

REVIEW ▪ The price elasticity of demand is a number that tells us how sensitive the quantity demanded is to the price. It is defined as the percentage change in the quantity demanded divided by the percentage change in the price.

ECONOMICS IN ACTION

Predicting the Size of a Price Increase

Economists used a numerical value of elasticity to predict the size of the oil price rise caused by the Iraqi invasion of Kuwait in 1990. Here are the steps they took:

- First, they determined—after looking at historical studies of oil prices and quantities—that the price elasticity of the demand for oil was .1. In other words, $e_d = .1$.

- Second, they calculated—after consulting with oil producers—that the invasion of Kuwait would reduce the world oil supply by 7 percent. They assumed that this 7 percent would also be the percentage decline in the quantity of oil demanded because other sources of oil could not increase in a short period of time. In other words, $\Delta Q_d/Q_d = .07$, or 7 percent.

- Third, they plugged these numbers into the formula for elasticity to calculate that the oil price would rise by 70 percent. Here is the exact calculation behind this step: Rearrange the definition of elasticity, $e_d = (\Delta Q_d/Q_d)/(\Delta P/P)$, to put the percentage change

in the price on the left. That is, $\Delta P/P = (\Delta Q_d/Q_d)/e_d$. Now plug in $\Delta Q_d/Q_d = .07$ and $e_d = .1$ to get $.07/(.1) = .70$, or 70 percent.

The 70 percent price rise predicted might seem large. In fact, the actual rise in the price of oil in 1990 was large, even larger than 70 percent: The price of oil rose from $17 per barrel in July 1990 to $36 in October 1990, or about 112 percent. (The larger-than-predicted price increase may have been due to worries that Iraq would also invade Saudi Arabia and reduce the oil supply even further.)

This type of calculation—showing that a huge oil price increase could be caused by the 7 percent reduction in oil supply—was a factor in the decision by the United States and its allies to send troops to the Middle East to halt the Iraqi invasion of Saudi Arabia and to eventually force Iraq out of Kuwait.

Could you use the same type of reasoning to determine how much the price of oil would *fall* if oil producers *increased* supply? Suppose the increase was 4 percent.

Working with Demand Elasticities

Having demonstrated the practical importance of elasticity, let us examine the concept in more detail and show how to use it. Some symbols will be helpful.

If we let the symbol e_d represent the price elasticity of demand, then we can write the definition as

$$e_d = \frac{\Delta Q_d}{Q_d} \div \frac{\Delta P}{P} = \frac{\Delta Q_d/Q_d}{\Delta P/P}$$

where Q_d is the quantity demanded, P is the price, and Δ means "change in." In other words, the elasticity of demand equals the "percentage change in the quantity demanded" divided by the "percentage change in the price." Observe that to compute the percentage change in the numerator and the denominator, we need to divide the change in the variable (ΔP or ΔQ_d) by the variable (P or Q_d).

Because the quantity demanded is negatively related to the price along a demand curve, the elasticity of demand is a negative number: When $\Delta P/P$ is positive, $\Delta Q_d/Q_d$ is negative. But when economists write or talk about elasticity, they usually ignore the negative sign and report the absolute value of the number. Because the demand curve always slopes downward, this nearly universal convention need not cause any confusion, as long as you remember it.

It is easy to do back-of-the-envelope computations of price elasticity of demand. When the price of Australian wine fell 8.5 percent in 2004, the quantity sold increased 11 percent. The price elasticity of demand for Australian wine is 11/8.5 = 1.3. At the University of Michigan, when student season ticket prices for hockey games rose 48 percent in 1998, student purchases of season tickets fell 41.1 percent. The price elasticity of demand for season hockey tickets is 41.1/48 = 0.86. Notice that measured in percentage changes, the demand for Australian wine is responsive to changes in the price, and the demand for hockey season tickets is not very responsive to changes in the price. Is this what you'd expect?

The Advantage of a Unit-Free Measure

unit-free measure: a measure that does not depend on a unit of measurement.

An attractive feature of the price elasticity of demand is that it does not depend on the units of measurement of the quantity demanded—whether barrels of oil or pounds of peanuts. It is a **unit-free measure** because it uses *percentage changes* in price and quantity demanded. Thus, it provides a way to compare the price sensitivity of the demand for many different goods. It even allows us to compare the price sensitivity of less expensive goods—like rice—with that of more expensive goods—like steak.

For example, suppose that when the price of rice rises from 50 cents to 60 cents per pound, the quantity demanded falls from 20 tons to 19 tons: That is a decline of 1 ton for a 10 *cent* price increase.

In contrast, suppose that when the price of steak rises by $1, from $5 to $6 per pound, the quantity demanded falls by 1 ton, from 20 tons to 19 tons of steak. That would be a decline of 1 ton for a 1 *dollar* price increase.

Using these numbers, the price sensitivity of the demand for steak and the demand for rice might appear to be very different: 10 cents to get a ton of reduced purchases versus $1 to get a ton of reduced purchases. Yet the elasticities are the same. The percentage change in price is 20 percent in each case ($1/$5 = $.10/$.50 = .20, or 20 percent), and the percentage change in quantity is 5 percent in each case: 1 ton of rice/20 tons of rice = 1 ton of steak/20 tons of steak = .05, or 5 percent. Hence, the elasticity is 5/20 = 1/4 in both cases.

Elasticity allows us to compare the price sensitivity of different goods by looking at ratios of percentage changes regardless of the units for measuring either price or quantity. With millions of different goods and hundreds of different units of measurement, this is indeed a major advantage.

Elasticity versus Slope

The *elasticity of the demand curve* is not the same as the *slope of the demand curve.* The slope of the demand curve is defined as the change in price divided by the change in quantity demanded: $\Delta P/\Delta Q$. The slope is not unit-free; it depends on how the price and quantity are measured. Thus, it is not a good measure of price sensitivity when we compare different goods.

To illustrate the difference between slope and elasticity, we show in Figure 4.3 a demand curve for rice and a demand curve for steak. The two demand curves have different slopes because the prices are so different. In fact, the slope of the steak demand curve is 10 times greater than the slope of the rice demand curve. Yet the elasticity is the same for the change from *A* to *B* for both demand curves.

After looking at Figure 4.1, you might be tempted to say that demand curves that are very steep have a low elasticity, and demand curves that are very flat have a high elasticity. However, because the slope and the elasticity are such different concepts, we must be careful not to simply look at a steep curve and say that it has a high elasticity. Moreover, as we show shortly, a curve with a constant slope has a different elasticity at every point on the curve!

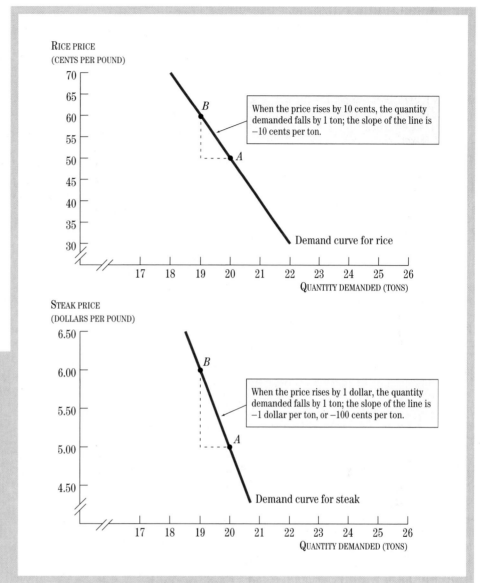

Figure 4.3
Different Slopes and Same Elasticities
The slope of the steak demand curve in the bottom graph is greater than the slope of the rice demand curve in the top graph. The price elasticity of demand for rice and steak from point *A* to point *B* is the same, however. From point *A* to point *B*, the price rises by 20 percent and the quantity demanded decreases by 5 percent. Thus, the elasticity is 1/4 for both rice and steak at these points.

Talking About Elasticities

Economists classify demand curves by the size of the price elasticities of demand, and they have developed a very precise terminology for doing so.

■ **Elastic versus Inelastic Demand.** Goods for which the price elasticity is greater than 1 have an **elastic demand.** For example, the quantity of foreign travel demanded decreases by more than 1 percent when the price rises by 1 percent because many people tend to travel at home rather than abroad when the price of foreign travel rises.

Goods for which the price elasticity of demand is less than 1 have an **inelastic demand.** For example, the quantity of eggs demanded decreases by less

elastic demand: demand for which the price elasticity is greater than 1.

inelastic demand: demand for which the price elasticity is less than 1.

than 1 percent when the price of eggs rises by 1 percent because many people do not want to substitute other things for eggs at breakfast.

■ Perfectly Elastic versus Perfectly Inelastic Demand. A demand curve that is vertical is called **perfectly inelastic.** Figure 4.4 shows a perfectly inelastic demand curve. The elasticity is zero because when the price changes, the quantity demanded does not change at all. No matter what the price, the same quantity is demanded. People who need insulin have a perfectly inelastic demand for insulin. As long as there are no substitutes for insulin, they will pay whatever they have to in order to get the insulin.

A demand curve that is horizontal is called **perfectly elastic.** Figure 4.4 also shows a perfectly elastic demand curve. The elasticity is infinite. The perfectly flat demand curve is sometimes hard to imagine because it entails infinitely large movements of quantity for tiny changes in price. In order to better visualize this case, you can imagine that the curve is tilted ever so slightly. The infinity case is extreme and is used to approximate demand curves with very high elasticities.

Table 4.1 summarizes the terminology about elasticities.

perfectly inelastic demand: demand for which the price elasticity is zero, indicating no response to a change in price and therefore a vertical demand curve.

perfectly elastic demand: demand for which the price elasticity is infinite, indicating an infinite response to a change in the price and therefore a horizontal demand curve.

Calculating the Elasticity with a Midpoint Formula

To calculate the elasticity, we need to find the percentage change in the quantity demanded and divide it by the percentage change in the price. As we have already illustrated with examples, to get the percentage change in the price or quantity, we need to divide the change in price (ΔP) by the price (P) or the change in quantity demanded (ΔQ_d) by the quantity demanded (Q_d). But when price and quantity demanded change, there is a question about what to use for P and Q_d. Should we use the old price and old quantity demanded before the change, or should we use the new price and new quantity demanded after the change?

The most common convention economists use is a compromise between these two alternatives. They take the *average,* or the *midpoint,* of the old and new quantities demanded and the old and new prices. That is, they compute the elasticity using the following formula, called the *midpoint formula:*

$$\frac{\text{Price elasticity}}{\text{of demand}} = \frac{\text{change in quantity}}{\text{average of old and new quantities}} \div$$

$$\frac{\text{change in price}}{\text{average of old and new prices}}$$

For example, if we use the midpoint formula to calculate the price elasticity of demand for oil when the price changes from \$20 to

Figure 4.4
Perfectly Elastic and Perfectly Inelastic Demand
A perfectly inelastic demand curve is a vertical line at a certain quantity; the quantity demanded is completely insensitive to the price: Whatever happens to the price, the quantity demanded does not change. A perfectly elastic demand curve is a flat line at a certain price; an increase in price reduces the quantity demanded to zero; a small decrease in price raises the quantity demanded by a huge (literally infinite) amount.

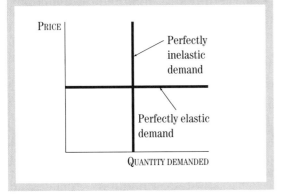

Table 4.1
Terminology for Price Elasticity of Demand

Term	Value of Price Elasticity of Demand (e_d)
Perfectly inelastic	0 (vertical demand curve)
Inelastic	Less than 1
Elastic	Greater than 1
Perfectly elastic	Infinity (horizontal demand curve)

Creating and Advancing Elasticity

Alfred Marshall created the powerful unit-free concept called elasticity, for which other economists are eternally grateful. The great economist John Maynard Keynes said, "I do not think Marshall did economists any greater service." Marshall defined elasticity in a remarkable book, *Principles of Economics*, published exactly 100 years before the economists used elasticity to predict the oil price increase when Iraq invaded Kuwait. Here is how Marshall put it:

> The elasticity of demand in a market is great or small according as the amount demanded increases much or little for a given fall in price, and diminishes much or little for a given rise in price.

Marshall's *Principles of Economics* had an enormous impact on economic thinking and thus on economic policy. More than anyone else, Marshall showed how to use the supply and demand model to analyze real-world problems. "Economics in Action" could have been his motto. Many economists credit Marshall with developing the *style* of economic reasoning that is routinely followed in applied economics work today. Marshall taught economists how to think like economists.

Marshall was born south of London to a family that was not particularly well-off; his father was a dominat-ing figure and forbade Alfred to study mathematics, which Marshall loved but his father did not understand. Rather than go to Oxford, where his father wanted him to go, Marshall went to Cambridge.

Marshall did not decide to become an economist until after college. The reason for his choice? He said he saw economics as a way to help the poor and unfortunate in society. Marshall was the greatest economist of the neoclassical school of the late nineteenth and early twentieth centuries. The neoclassical school maintained most of the principles of the classical school founded by Adam Smith, but improved on them with the supply and demand model and its underlying foundation.

Marshall's simple, yet broad, definition of economics has itself become a classic. To Marshall,

> Political Economy or Economics is a study of mankind in the ordinary business of life; it examines that part of individual and social action which is most closely connected with the attainment and with the use of the material requisites of wellbeing.

Based on your study of economics so far, do you think Marshall's definition is a good one?

$22 and the quantity demanded changes from 60 million to 48 million barrels a day, we get

$$\frac{60 - 48}{(60 + 48)/2} \div \frac{\$20 - \$22}{(\$20 + \$22)/2} = .2222 \div (-.0952) = -2.33$$

That is, the price elasticity of demand is 2.33 using the midpoint formula. In this case, this is close to the value of 2 we obtained by using the old price ($20) rather than the average, $21 = ($20 + $22)/2, and the old quantity demanded (60) rather than the average quantity, 54 = (60 + 48)/2.

Revenue and the Price Elasticity of Demand

When people purchase 60 million barrels of oil at $20 a barrel, they must pay a total of $1,200 million ($20 × 60 million). This is a payment to the oil producers and is the producers' revenue. In general, revenue is the price (P) times the quantity (Q), or $P \times Q$.

■ **The Two Effects of Price on Revenue.** Because revenue is defined as price times quantity, an increase or a decrease in the price has an effect on revenue. However, there are two opposite effects. Consider an increase in the price. An increase in the price raises the payment per unit but also reduces the number of units. In other words, when the price increases, people pay more for each item, and

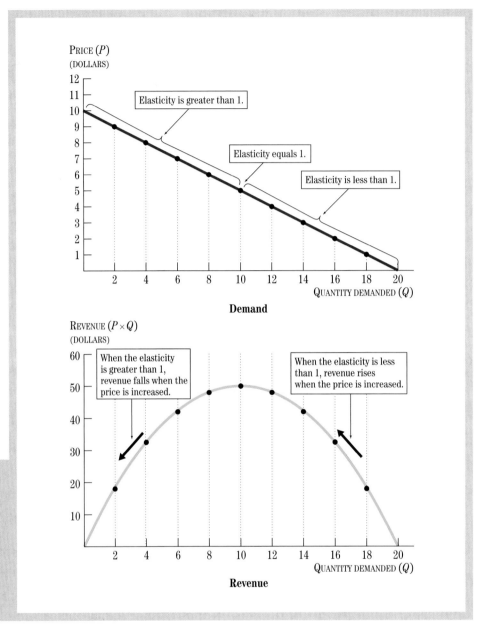

Figure 4.5
Revenue and Elasticity of a Straight-Line Demand Curve
Along the straight-line demand curve at the top, the price elasticity ranges from above 1 (to the left) to below 1 (to the right). When the price elasticity is greater than 1, an increase in the price will reduce revenue, as shown in the lower panel.

this increases revenue; but they buy fewer items, and this decrease in the quantity demanded reduces revenue. The elasticity determines which of these two opposite effects dominates.

Figure 4.5 illustrates how the price elasticity determines the effect of a price change on revenue for the special case of a demand curve that is a straight line. Look first at the demand curve shown in the top panel of Figure 4.5. Observe that the elasticity is greater than 1 on the left part of the demand curve and less than 1 on the right part of the demand curve.

Now look at the lower panel in Figure 4.5; it shows how revenue is related to price in the case of this same straight-line demand curve. Observe how revenue changes as the price increases. When the price elasticity is greater than 1—in the region on the left—an increase in the price will lower revenue. For example, an increase in the price

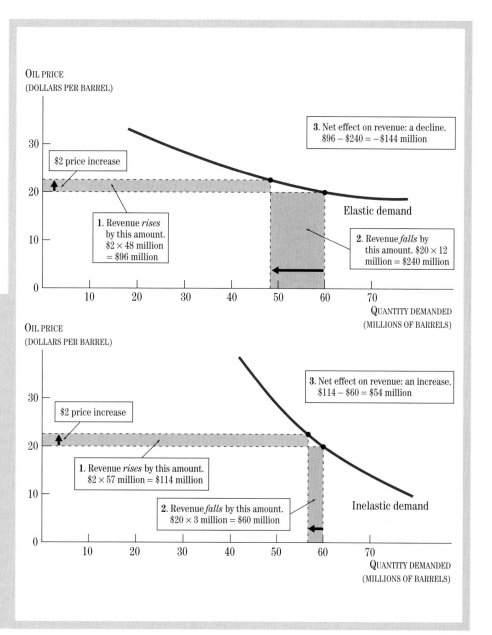

Figure 4.6
Effects of an Increase in the Price of Oil on Revenue
These graphs are replicas of the demand curves for oil shown in Figure 4.1, with the scale changed to show the change in revenue when the price of oil is increased. An increase in the price has two effects on revenue, as shown by the gray- and pink-shaded rectangles. The increase in revenue (gray rectangle) is due to the higher price. The decrease in revenue (pink rectangle) is due to the decline in the quantity demanded as the price is increased. In the top graph, where elasticity is greater than 1, the net effect is a decline in revenue; in the bottom graph, where elasticity is less than 1, the net effect is an increase in revenue.

from $8 per unit to $9 per unit reduces the quantity demanded from 4 units to 2 units and revenue falls from $32 to $18; the gain in revenue from the higher price per unit is offset by the loss in revenue from the decline in the number of units sold. However, when the price elasticity is less than 1—in the region on the right—an increase in the price will raise revenue. For example, an increase in the price from $1 to $2 per unit reduces the quantity demanded from 18 units to 16 units and revenue rises from $18 to $32; in this case, the loss in revenue from the decline in the number of units sold is not large enough to offset the gain in revenue from the higher price per unit.

Another illustration of the relationship between elasticity and revenue changes is found in Figure 4.6, which is a replica of Figure 4.1 with the scales changed to better illustrate the effects on revenue. We now know that the elasticity in the top graph is greater than 1 and the elasticity in the bottom graph is less than 1. We can

Table 4.2
Revenue and the Price Elasticity of Demand

Elasticity Is	Effect of a Price Increase on Revenue	Effect of a Price Decrease on Revenue
Less than 1 (< 1)	Revenue increases	Revenue decreases
Equal to 1 (= 1)	No change in revenue	No change in revenue
Greater than 1 (> 1)	Revenue decreases	Revenue increases

see that the same price increase leads to a large decline in the quantity demanded when the elasticity is large and to a small decline in the quantity demanded when the elasticity is small. The two effects of a price increase are illustrated in the graphs. Revenue falls when the price is increased in the top graph and rises when the price is increased in the bottom graph.

Table 4.2 summarizes the relationship between revenue and the price elasticity of demand. Observe that an increase in price will raise revenue if the elasticity is less than 1 and will lower revenue if the elasticity is greater than 1.

Businesses need to know the price elasticity of demand for their products. The most recent U.S. recession led to a decrease in demand for business air travel. In 2003, United Airlines announced 40 percent cuts in some one-way business fares. Would more businesspeople decide to fly with lower fares? If so, would the increase in customers lead to an increase or a decrease in United Airlines' revenue? The answer depends on the price elasticity of demand for business air travel.

The recent increase in the use of wireless phones and prepaid phone cards has resulted in a decrease in the demand for pay phones. In 2001, because of this decrease in demand, SBC Communications Inc. increased the price of a pay phone call. Could this increase in price lead to an increase in revenue? The answer depends on the price elasticity of demand for pay phone calls. Notice that an increase in price could increase revenue, but a decrease in price could also increase revenue, depending on the price elasticity of demand.

If demand for business air travel is price elastic and demand for pay phones is price inelastic, then both United Airlines and SBC changed prices to increase revenue— United Airlines cutting business fares to increase revenue with price-elastic demand, and SBC increasing the price of using a pay phone call to increase revenue with price-inelastic demand. The next section discusses the determinants of price elasticity of demand. You should judge as you read this chapter whether demand for business air travel and demand for pay phone calls are likely to be price elastic or price inelastic.

What Determines the Size of the Price Elasticity of Demand?

Table 4.3 shows price elasticities of demand for several different goods and services. The price elasticity for jewelry, for example, is 2.6. This means that for each percentage increase in the price of jewelry, the quantity demanded will fall by 2.6 percent. Compared with other elasticities, this is large. On the other hand, the price elasticity of eggs is very small. For each percentage increase in the price of eggs, the quantity of eggs demanded falls by only 0.1 percent.

Why do these elasticities differ in size? Several factors determine a good's elasticity.

Table 4.3
Estimated Price Elasticities of Demand

Type of Good or Service	Price Elasticity
Jewelry	2.6
Eggs	0.1
Telephone (first line)	0.1
Telephone (second line)	0.4
Foreign travel	1.2
Cigarettes (18–24)	0.6
Cigarettes (25–39)	0.4
Cigarettes (40–older)	0.1
Gasoline (short run)	0.2
Gasoline (long run)	0.7

Price Elasticity of Cell Phone Service in the Desert
There's probably not much of a substitute available for long-distance communication in the desert, which would make the price elasticity of the cell phone used here quite low. Do you think the caller in this picture would be equally insensitive to an increase of $0.10 per minute in the price of her calls if she were seated in her apartment in Chicago?

■ **The Degree of Substitutability.**   A key factor is whether there are good substitutes for the item in question. Can people easily find a substitute when the price goes up? If the answer is yes, then the price elasticity will be high. Foreign travel has a high elasticity because there is a reasonably good substitute: domestic travel.

On the other hand, the low price elasticity for eggs can be explained by the lack of good substitutes. As many fans of eggs know, these items are unique; synthetic eggs are not good substitutes. Hence, the price elasticity of eggs is small. People will continue to buy them even if the price rises a lot.

The degree of substitutability depends in part on whether a good is a necessity or a luxury. There are no good substitutes for a refrigerator if you want to easily preserve food for more than a few hours. However, a fancy refrigerator with an exterior that blends in with the rest of your kitchen is more of a luxury and is likely to have a higher price elasticity.

■ **Big-Ticket versus Little-Ticket Items.**   If a good represents a large fraction of people's income, then the price elasticity will be high. If the price of foreign travel doubles, many people will not be able to afford to travel abroad. On the other hand, if the good represents a small fraction of income, the elasticity will be low. For example, if the price of eggs doubles, most people will still be able to afford to buy as many eggs as before the price rise.

■ **Temporary versus Permanent Price Changes.**   If a change in price is known to be temporary, the price elasticity of demand will tend to be high because many people can easily shift their purchases either later or earlier. For example, suppose a sewing machine store announces a discount price to last only one day. Then people will shift their purchase of the sewing machine they were thinking about buying to the sale day.

On the other hand, if the price cut is permanent, the price elasticity will be smaller. People who expect the price decrease to be permanent will not find it advantageous to buy sooner rather than later.

■ **Differences in Preferences.**   Various groups of consumers may have different levels of elasticity. For example, young cigarette smokers, whose habit of smoking may not be entrenched, are more sensitive to changes in prices than older smokers. Table 4.3 shows how the price elasticity of demand for cigarettes for young adults between 18 and 24 years old is much higher than the very low price elasticity for people older than 40.

■ **Long-Run versus Short-Run Elasticity.**   Frequently the price elasticity of demand is low immediately after a price change but then increases after a period of time has passed. In order to analyze these changes, economists distinguish between the *short run* and the *long run*. The short run is simply a period of time before people have made all their adjustments or changed their habits; the long run is a period of time long enough for people to make such adjustments or change their habits.

Many personal adjustments to a change in prices take a long time. For example, when the price of gas increases, people can reduce the quantity demanded in the short run only by driving less and using other forms of transportation more, or by reducing the heating in their homes. This may be inconvenient or impossible. In the long run, however, when it comes time to buy a new car or a new heating system, they can buy a more fuel-efficient one, or one that uses an alternative energy source. Thus, the quantity of gas demanded falls by larger amounts in the long run than in the short run (Table 4.3).

***What is the Price Elasticity of Demand for
Star Wars Movies?***
*For these fans, the prospect of attending the May
2005 opening of* Star Wars: Episode III—Revenge
of the Sith *is price inelastic (i.e., they will pay
almost anything for a ticket to this opening); but
for moviegoers in general, the answer to that question may say a lot about the future of the movie
industry. If purchases of movie tickets fall off as the
price of a general admission ticket goes up, and at
the same time revenue from ticket sales increases,
then demand for movie tickets is price inelastic.*

Habits that are difficult to break also cause differences between
short-run and long-run elasticity. Even a large increase in the price of
tobacco may have a small effect on the quantity purchased because
people cannot break the smoking habit quickly. But after a period of
time, the high price of cigarettes may encourage them to break the
habit, while discouraging potential new users. Thus, the long-run elasticity for tobacco is higher than the short-run elasticity.

Here are a few examples to test your understanding of the determinants of the price elasticity of demand. The movie industry reported
that its summer 2004 revenue was 3 percent higher than the previous
year. A closer analysis reveals that ticket sales were down 1 percent.
How could ticket revenue increase at the same time that the number of
tickets sold decreased? The ticket price must have increased. Demand
for movies must also be price inelastic, so that the reduction in ticket
sales was more than offset by the increase in the price of the movie
tickets. Does this make sense for the movie industry? It is plausible that
some people feel they *must see* the newest release and that the cost of
the movie is a little-ticket item for many people who go to the movies.
This would make the price elasticity of demand low and demand plausibly price inelastic.

General Motors Corporation reported that in 2002 its revenue rose by
5.4 percent. At the same time, General Motors offered large discounts to
customers purchasing cars. How could revenue increase while the price
of cars was going down? It must be that more cars were sold at the lower
price and that demand for these cars is price elastic. The reduction in
price was therefore offset by the increase in cars sold, and revenue
increased. Does this make sense for General Motors cars? It is plausible that customers
feel there are close substitutes and that this is a big-ticket purchase for many customers.
This would make the price elasticity of demand high and demand plausibly price elastic.

Income Elasticity and Cross-Price Elasticity of Demand

Recall that the price elasticity of demand refers to movements along the demand
curve. We emphasized in Chapter 3 the difference between a shift in the demand
curve and a movement along the demand curve. A *shift* in the demand curve occurs
when there is a change in the quantity people are willing to buy due to a change in
anything except the price—for example, a change in income.

The concept of elasticity can be applied to changes in the quantity consumers are
willing to buy caused by changes in income. This elasticity must be distinguished from
the price elasticity of demand. The **income elasticity of demand** is the percentage
change in the quantity of a good demanded at any given price divided by a percentage
change in income. That is,

$$\text{Income elasticity of demand} = \frac{\text{percentage change in quantity demanded}}{\text{percentage change in income}}$$

income elasticity of demand:
the percentage change in quantity
demanded of a good divided by
the percentage change in income.

For example, if incomes rise by 10 percent and, as a result, people purchase 15 percent
more health care at a given price, the income elasticity of health care is 1.5. Table 4.4
lists income elasticities of demand for several different goods and services.

As discussed in Chapter 3, the demand for most goods increases when people's
incomes increase. If you have more income, your demand for movies will probably
increase at each price. Recall that a normal good is a good or service whose demand
increases as income increases. But not every good is a normal good; if the demand

**Table 4.4
Estimated Income
Elasticities of Demand**

Type of Good or Service	Income Elasticity
Food	0.58
Clothing/footwear	0.88
Transport	1.18
Medical Care	1.35
Recreation	1.42

for a good declines when income increases, the good is called an inferior good. The income elasticity of demand for an inferior good is negative and is reported as a negative number by economists.

Another type of elasticity relating to shifts in the demand curve is the **cross-price elasticity of demand,** which is defined as the percentage change in the quantity demanded divided by the percentage change in the price of another good. For example, an increase in the price of Rollerblades would *increase* the quantity demanded of bicycles at every price as people shifted away from Rollerblading to bicycle riding. Rollerblades are a substitute for bicycles. A cross-price elasticity can also go in the other direction. An increase in the price of bicycle helmets may *reduce* the demand for bicycles. Bicycle helmets and bicycles are complements. For a complement, the cross-price elasticity of demand is negative.

cross-price elasticity of demand: the percentage change in the quantity demanded of one good divided by the percentage change in the price of another good.

REVIEW

- The price elasticity of demand is a unit-free number that is different from the slope of the demand curve.

- The elasticity helps determine how large a price increase will occur as a result of a shift in supply, and how much revenue will change when the price rises.

- Horizontal demand curves have infinite price elasticity. Vertical demand curves have zero price elasticity. Most products have a price elasticity between these two extremes.

- The size of the price elasticity of demand depends on the availability of substitutes for the item, whether the item represents a large fraction of income, and whether the price change is temporary or permanent.

- Whereas the price elasticity of demand refers to movements along the demand curve, the income elasticity of demand refers to shifts in the demand curve caused by changes in income. Most goods are normal and have a positive income elasticity of demand. Inferior goods have a negative income elasticity of demand. The cross-price elasticity of demand also relates to shifts in the demand curve, in this case, a change in the price of a complement or substitute good.

Elasticity of Supply

Knowing how sensitive the quantity supplied is to a change in price is just as important as knowing how sensitive the quantity demanded is. The price elasticity of supply measures this sensitivity. "Price elasticity of supply" is sometimes shortened to "supply elasticity" or "elasticity of supply." Supply describes the behavior of firms that produce goods. A high price elasticity of supply means that firms raise their production by a large amount if the price increases. A low price elasticity of supply means that firms raise their production only a little if the price increases.

The **price elasticity of supply** is defined as the percentage change in the quantity supplied divided by the percentage change in the price. That is,

price elasticity of supply: the percentage change in quantity supplied divided by the percentage change in price.

$$\text{Price elasticity of supply} = \frac{\text{percentage change in quantity supplied}}{\text{percentage change in the price}}$$

The price elasticity of supply refers to a particular supply curve, such as the supply curve for gasoline or video games. All other things that affect supply are held constant when we compute the price elasticity of supply. For example, suppose the price elasticity of supply for video games is .5. Then, if the price of video games rises by 10 percent, the quantity of video games supplied will increase by 5 percent (.5 × 10).

Working with Supply Elasticities

All the attractive features of the price elasticity of demand also apply to the price elasticity of supply. To see this, let us first take a look at the definition of the price elasticity of supply using symbols. If we let the symbol e_s be the price elasticity of supply, then it can be written as

$$e_s = \frac{\Delta Q_s}{Q_s} \div \frac{\Delta P}{P} = \frac{\Delta Q_s / Q_s}{\Delta P / P}$$

where Q_s is the quantity supplied and P is the price. In other words, the price elasticity of supply is the percentage change in the quantity supplied divided by the percentage change in price. Observe the similarity of this expression to the analogous expression for the price elasticity of demand on page 89: The only difference is the use of quantity supplied (Q_s) rather than quantity demanded (Q_d). This means that the concepts and terminology for supply elasticity are very similar to those for demand elasticity. For example, if you go to Table 4.1 and replace "Demand" with "Supply," you have the terminology of price elasticity of supply. Moreover, like the price elasticity of demand, the price elasticity of supply is a unit-free measure, and the elasticity of supply and the slope of the supply curve are not the same thing.

Because of this similarity, our discussion of supply elasticity can be very brief. It is useful to consider the extreme cases of perfectly elastic supply and perfectly

Perfectly Inelastic Supply
The paintings of Leonardo Da Vinci provide an example of a good with a perfectly inelastic supply. The supply curve is vertical because no matter how high the price, no more Mona Lisas can be produced. However, what about the demand to see the Mona Lisa? Is it perfectly inelastic? Will raising the price of admission charged by the Louvre Museum in Paris reduce the number of people coming to see the painting?

inelastic supply, and then to go through an example illustrating the importance of knowing the size of the price elasticity of supply.

perfectly elastic supply: supply for which the price elasticity is infinite, indicating an infinite response of quantity supplied to a change in price and thereby a horizontal supply curve.

perfectly inelastic supply: supply for which the price elasticity is zero, indicating no response of quantity supplied to a change in price and thereby a vertical supply curve.

■ **Perfectly Elastic and Perfectly Inelastic Supply.**   As in the case of demand, there can be **perfectly elastic supply** or **perfectly inelastic supply,** as shown in Figure 4.7. The vertical supply curve is perfectly inelastic; it has zero elasticity. Such supply curves are not unusual. For example, there is only one *Mona Lisa*. A higher price cannot bring about a higher quantity supplied, not even one more *Mona Lisa*. But the supply of most goods is not vertical. Higher prices will encourage coffee producers to use more fertilizer, hire more workers, and eventually plant more coffee trees. Thus the quantity supplied increases when the price rises.

The horizontal supply curve is perfectly elastic. In this case, the price does not change at all. It is the same regardless of the quantity supplied. It is easier to understand the horizontal supply curve if you view it as an approximation to a supply curve that is *nearly* horizontal, one with a very high elasticity. Then only a small increase in price brings forth a huge increase in the quantity supplied by firms.

■ **Why the Size of the Price Elasticity of Supply Is Important.**   Now let us look at the importance of knowing the size of the supply elasticity even if it is not at one of these two extremes. Figure 4.8 shows two different supply curves for coffee. The horizontal axis shows the quantity of coffee supplied around the world in billions of pounds; the vertical axis shows the price in dollars per pound of coffee. For the supply curve in the top graph, the quantity supplied is very sensitive to the price;

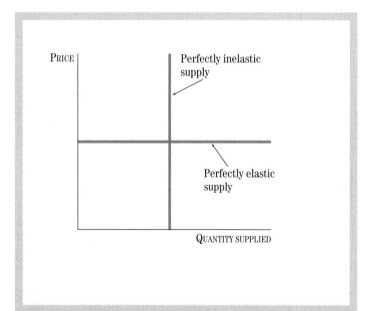

Figure 4.7
Perfectly Elastic and Perfectly Inelastic Supply
When the quantity supplied is completely unresponsive to the price, the supply curve is vertical and the price elasticity of supply is zero; this case is called perfectly inelastic supply. When the quantity supplied responds by large amounts to a price change, the supply curve is horizontal; economists then say supply is perfectly elastic.

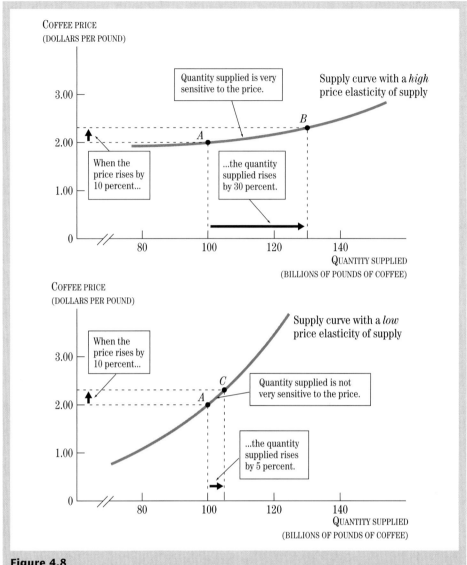

Figure 4.8
Comparing Different Sizes of the Price Elasticities of Supply
In the top graph, the quantity supplied is much more sensitive to price than in the bottom graph. The price elasticity of supply is greater between points *A* and *B* at the top than between points *A* and *C* at the bottom.

the price elasticity of supply is high. For the supply curve in the bottom graph, the price elasticity of supply is much lower.

The price elasticity of supply is important for finding out the response of price to shifts in demand. This is shown in Figure 4.9, where the demand for coffee declines, perhaps because of concerns about the effect of the caffeine in coffee or because of a decrease in the price of caffeine-free substitutes for coffee. In any case, if the price elasticity of supply is high, as in the top graph, the price does not change as much as when the price elasticity of supply is low, as in the bottom graph. With a high price elasticity, a small change in price is enough to get firms to bring the quantity supplied down to the lower quantity demanded.

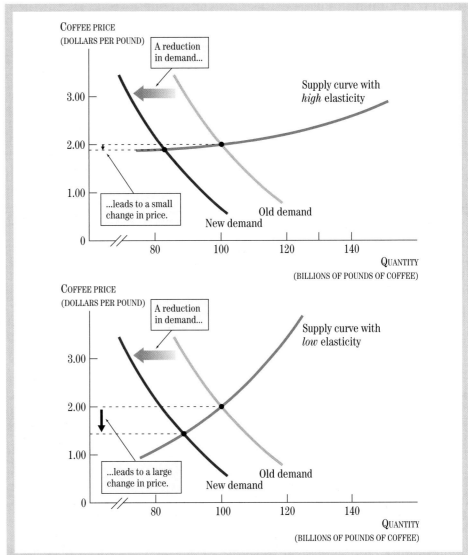

Figure 4.9
Importance of Knowing the Size of the Price Elasticity of Supply
When demand changes, the price will also change. If the price elasticity of supply is high, there will be a small change in price. If the price elasticity of supply is low, there will be a large change in price.

REVIEW
- The price elasticity of supply is a number that tells us how sensitive the quantity supplied is to the price. It is defined as the percentage change in the quantity supplied divided by the percentage change in the price.

- The attractive features of the price elasticity of demand are also true for the price elasticity of supply. Its size does not depend on the units of measurement of either price or quantity.

- The price elasticity of supply is useful for determining how much prices will change when there is a change in demand.

Conclusion

In this chapter, we have seen that *how much* the equilibrium price and quantity change in response to changes in supply or demand depends on the size of the elasticity of the supply and demand curves. Armed with these elasticities, we can predict what will happen to prices after a change in the supply of a good. We can also predict what will happen to prices after a change in demand. And we can predict whether revenue will increase or decrease when prices, fees, or taxes are cut or raised.

Distinguishing between movements along and shifts of the curves, knowing the importance of the elasticity, and describing in words what happens when the intersection of the curves changes are all important parts of thinking like an economist.

KEY POINTS

1. Elasticity is a measure of the sensitivity of one economic variable to another. For example, the price elasticity of demand measures how much the quantity demanded changes when the price changes.

2. The price elasticity of demand is the percentage change in the quantity demanded divided by the percentage change in price. It refers to changes in price and quantity demanded along the demand curve, all other things being equal.

3. Elasticity is a unit-free measure.

4. Demand is elastic if the price elasticity of demand is greater than 1 and inelastic if the price elasticity of demand is less than 1.

5. When the elasticity is greater than 1, an increase in the price reduces the quantity demanded by a percentage greater than the percentage increase in the price, thereby reducing revenue. When the elasticity is less than 1, an increase in the price reduces the quantity demanded by a percentage less than the percentage increase in the price, thereby increasing revenue.

6. The elasticity of demand for a good depends on whether the good has close substitutes, whether its value is a large or small fraction of total income, and the time period of the change.

7. If a good has a low price elasticity of demand, then a change in supply will cause a big change in price. Conversely, if a good has a high price elasticity of demand, then a change in supply will cause a small change in price.

8. Whereas the price elasticity of demand refers to movements along the demand curve, the income elasticity of demand refers to shifts in the demand curve caused by changes in income, and the cross-price elasticity of demand refers to shifts in the demand curve caused by changes in the price of other goods. Most goods are normal and have a positive income elasticity of demand. Inferior goods have a negative income elasticity of demand.

9. The price elasticity of supply is defined as the percentage change in the quantity supplied divided by the percentage change in the price.

10. If a good has a low price elasticity of supply, then a change in demand will cause a big change in price. Conversely, if a good has a high price elasticity of supply, then a change in demand will cause a small change in price.

KEY TERMS

price elasticity of demand	perfectly inelastic demand	income elasticity of demand	price elasticity of supply
unit-free measure	perfectly elastic demand	cross-price elasticity of demand	perfectly elastic supply
elastic demand			perfectly inelastic supply
inelastic demand			

QUESTIONS FOR REVIEW

1. Why is the price elasticity of demand a unit-free measure of the sensitivity of the quantity demanded to a price change?

2. What factors determine whether the price elasticity of demand is high or low?

3. What is the difference between the price elasticity of demand and the income elasticity of demand?

4. Why is the price elasticity of demand useful for finding the size of the price change that occurs when supply shifts?

5. What is the difference between elastic and inelastic demand?

6. For what values of the price elasticity of demand do increases in the price increase revenue?

7. What is the slope of a perfectly elastic supply curve?

8. Why is the price elasticity of demand lower in the short run than in the long run?

9. What is the income elasticity of demand?

10. If the price elasticity of demand for textbooks is 2 and the price of textbooks increases by 10 percent, by how much does the quantity demanded fall?

PROBLEMS

1. Using the price elasticities of demand in Table 4.3, determine
   a. which items have an elastic demand and which have an inelastic demand
   b. which items have a *perfectly* elastic demand and which have a *perfectly* inelastic demand
   c. the effect on the quantity demanded of a price decrease of 20 percent
   d. the effect on the price of a shift in supply that reduces the quantity demanded by 10 percent (compare the equilibrium after the supply shift with the equilibrium before the supply shift)
   e. for which items revenues will increase when the price increases

2. The price of parking in a downtown parking garage affects the number of people who want to park there. The manager notices that as the hourly parking fee is raised, total revenue falls. Why is this true? Assuming a linear demand curve, what is the elasticity of demand for parking when total revenue begins to fall? To maximize total revenue, at what elasticity will the manager set the price?

3. What does it mean for the supply curve to be perfectly inelastic? How does revenue change as the demand curve shifts?

4. Compare a market in which supply and demand are very (but not perfectly) inelastic to one in which supply and demand are very (but not perfectly) elastic. Suppose the government decides to impose a price floor $1 above the equilibrium price in each of these markets. Compare, diagrammatically, the surpluses that result. In which market is the surplus larger?

5. Calculate the price elasticity of demand for the following goods:
   a. The price of movie theater tickets goes up by 10 percent, causing the quantity demanded to go down by 4 percent.
   b. Computer prices fall by 20 percent, causing the quantity demanded to increase by 15 percent.

c. The price of apples rises by 5 percent, causing the quantity demanded to fall by 5 percent.
   d. The price of ice cream falls by 6 percent, causing the quantity demanded to rise by 10 percent.

6. Use the following data for a demand curve.

Price	Quantity
11	10
10	20
9	30
8	40
7	50
6	60
5	70
4	80
3	90

   a. Use the midpoint formula to calculate the elasticity between a price of $10 and $11.
   b. Use the midpoint formula to calculate the elasticity between $3 and $4.
   c. Since this is a linear demand curve, why does the elasticity change?
   d. At what point is price times quantity maximized? What is the elasticity at that point?

7. Use the following data to calculate the price elasticity of supply for the price between $7 and $8 and the price between $3 and $4. Use the midpoint formula. How does supply elasticity change as you move up the supply curve?

Price	Quantity Supplied
2	10
3	20
4	30
5	40
6	50
7	60
8	70
9	80

8. Suppose that the demand for cigarettes is perfectly inelastic. If the government imposes a tax per pack of cigarettes, by how much will cigarette consumption fall? Show this in a diagram.

9. Given the following income elasticities of demand, would you classify the following goods as normal or inferior goods?
   a. Potatoes: elasticity = 0.5
   b. Pinto beans: elasticity = −0.1
   c. Bottled water: elasticity = 1.1
   d. Video cameras: elasticity = 1.4

10. Calculate the cross-price elasticity for the following goods. Are they substitutes or complements?
    a. The price of movie theater tickets goes up by 10 percent, causing the quantity demanded for video rentals to go up by 4 percent.
    b. The price of computers falls by 20 percent, causing the quantity demanded of software to increase by 15 percent.
    c. The price of apples falls by 5 percent, causing the quantity demanded of pears to fall by 5 percent.
    d. The price of ice cream falls by 6 percent, causing the quantity demanded of frozen yogurt to fall by 1 percent.

11. The following data on world coffee production from 1985 to 1987 come from the *CRB Commodity Year Book*.

	Production (millions of bags)	Price (dollars/pound)
1985	96	1.42
1986	80	2.01
1987	103	1.09

    a. Plot the observations on a scatter diagram with price on the vertical axis and production on the horizontal axis.
    b. Assume that production equals the quantity demanded around the world and that the coffee demand curve did not change between 1985 and 1987. First, calculate the price elasticity of demand for 1985 to 1986 using the midpoint formula. Next, calculate the same elasticities from 1986 to 1987. Would you say the demand for coffee is elastic or inelastic?
    c. If the two calculations in part (b) differ by much, explain why.

12. In 1992, the federal government placed a tax of 10 percent on goods like luxury automobiles and yachts. The boat-manufacturing industry had huge declines in orders for boats and laid off many workers, whereas the reaction in the auto industry was much milder. (The tax on yachts was subsequently removed.) Explain this situation using two supply and demand diagrams. Compare the elasticity of demand for luxury autos with that for yachts based on the experience with the luxury tax.

POINT COUNTERPOINT

The Issue:
Should the United States Adopt Universal Health-Care Coverage?

Everyone is concerned about the rising cost of health care in the United States. According to one study by the Kaiser Family Foundation,[1] more than 60 percent of nonelderly Americans rely on employer-provided health insurance plans to cover the cost of health care. The same study reports that the premiums for family coverage under these plans have increased (in nominal terms) by 59 percent since 2000; over the same period, nominal wages increased by only 12.3 percent. Health-care costs have also caused financial strain for Medicare (the federal health insurance program primarily targeted at people 65 years of age and above) and Medicaid (a joint federal and state program targeted at people with low incomes and limited resources), the two largest government-funded health-care programs. The Congressional Budget Office forecasts that over the next 30 years, Medicare costs will triple as a percentage of GDP, while Medicaid costs will double.[2]

As the price of health care has risen, many Americans have found access to adequate health care increasingly difficult to obtain. The Census Bureau estimates that almost 40 million Americans are uninsured. These rising trends in both the cost of health care and the number of uninsured has led to a resurgence of interest in adopting a system of universal health-care coverage in the United States. Under such a system, every individual would have access to health insurance regardless of his or her ability to pay for that coverage. Universal health-care systems are currently in use in Canada, the United Kingdom, and other Western European nations.

The debate over whether the United States should adopt universal health insurance centers on a few key issues: the cost of running such a system, the quality of the health care supplied by such a system, and the impact of the system on existing stakeholders in the current health-care system: patients, health-care providers, insurers, and pharmaceutical companies.[3]

POINT In Favor of a System of Universal Health-Care Coverage

The Institute of Medicine, a branch of the National Academy of Sciences, has supported the creation of a uni-

versal system of health-care coverage, beginning as early as 2010.[4] The Institute of Medicine argues that a universal system of health-care coverage will provide several important benefits to society.

- Universal health-care coverage will reduce the substantial income and health-related risks faced by individuals who are uninsured under the current system. This lack of insurance can occur for a variety of reasons: working for smaller employers, premiums that are unaffordable for many working-class families, and the high cost of non-employment-based private health insurance.
- Gaps in health-care coverage can be very expensive. Many Americans are unemployed for short periods of time (when they switch jobs, for example) and often go without insurance for a period of several months. During these periods, they are unlikely to seek treatment for medical conditions, resulting in worsening health and higher costs when they eventually gain access to health insurance.
- There are substantial costs to society, both hidden and transparent, from having a large pool of uninsured workers. Lack of access to basic health care can result in more public health problems, greater use of emergency rooms to treat basic health problems, shorter life spans, and less productive workers.

The American Medical Students Association (AMSA), which identifies itself as "the oldest and largest independent association of physicians-in-training in the United States," also strongly advocates adopting a system of universal health-care coverage in the United States.[5] It argues that universal health-care coverage would not cost more than what we are spending now; in fact, it would result in substantially reduced overhead, as it would eliminate much of the paperwork now required for reimbursement. The association also contends that a single-payer universal health plan would ration services based on medical necessity rather than for profit-related reasons, which is essentially what happens now.

1 Kaiser Family Foundation, "Employer Health Benefits 2004 Annual Survey," Available at http://www.kff.org/insurance/7148/upload/2004-Employer-Health-Benefits-Survey-Summary-of-Findings.pdf.
2 Congressional Budget Office, "Long Term Budget Outlook," October 2000. Available at http://www.cbo.gov/showdoc.cfm?index=2517&sequence=0.
3 An excellent discussion of the prospects for universal health-care coverage in the United States can be found in Uwe E. Reinhardt, "Is There Hope for the Uninsured?" Health Insurance Forum, Aug. 27, 2003. Available at http://content.healthaffairs.org/cgi/content/full/hlthaff.w3.376v1/DC1.
4 Institute of Medicine of the National Academies, "Insuring America's Health: Principles and Recommendations," Jan. 14, 2004. Available at http://www.iom.edu/report.asp?id=17632.

COUNTERPOINT Against a System of Universal Health-Care Coverage

Most of the arguments against changing to a system of universal health care are not against universal health coverage per se, but instead focus on the proposed ways in which the government would pay for the increased coverage. The AMSA recommends that the federal government adopt one of three methods:[6]

1. The federal government would require employers to provide health insurance for their workers, with the government providing coverage for those not employed.
2. The federal government would require all individuals to obtain private insurance coverage, with the government providing tax credits to help individuals pay for the cost of insurance.
3. The federal government would establish a single-payer system that would eliminate insurance premiums and enrollment qualifications, with the cost of such a program being covered by increased taxes.

Under the first two methods, the government would simply supplement the existing system of health-care coverage in the United States by requiring either that more employers provide insurance for their workers or that more uninsured people buy private health insurance; the government would then provide the funds needed (in the form of tax credits and transfer payments) for firms or individuals to bear the costs of this increased access. Many employers, particularly small businesses, balk at the cost of providing insurance for more employees and argue that the government does not provide enough resources to help them bear these costs. For example, in November of 2004, California business interests led a campaign against Proposition 72, which would have implemented a plan in which employers would have to provide health insurance for their workers, with the state providing assistance to lower-income employees to enable them to buy such insurance and giving tax credits to small firms that had fewer than 50 workers. The California Chamber of Commerce co-chaired the campaign against Proposition 72, arguing that the proposed expansion of coverage would force firms to cut wages, lay off workers, or cease operations in California.[7]

The other alternative, then, is for the United States to move away from the current employment-based private health insurance system toward a single-payer system such as the ones used in countries like Canada and the United Kingdom. Under a single-payer system, all individuals have access to health care, with the costs of that care being paid for by the government. In turn, the government funds these higher expenditures by raising taxes. Because the government is the single payer, it can control the costs of providing health care to a greater degree than under the existing system.

The Cato Institute has been one of the leading organizations arguing that the United States should not move to a single-payer health-care system. Like many libertarian groups, Cato primarily objects to the enhanced role of the government in a Canadian-style health-care system; in other words, it objects to the "single-payer" aspect rather than the "universal" aspect of a universal single-payer health-care system. A 2005 policy brief makes the following arguments against a universal health-care system.[8]

- Single-payer systems make access to health care more unequal: instead of everyone waiting to be treated according to need, the wealthy would find ways to "jump the queue" and obtain treatment.
- There would be less incentive for firms to develop new pharmaceuticals and new medical devices or to conduct research on new medical procedures that can save patients' lives because of the tight control of medical costs. Patients would suffer in the long run.
- The long waiting times that result from rationing health care worsen the quality of life and endanger the health of patients. In many countries with single-payer systems, there are long waiting times for non-emergency medical treatments.
- Physician compensation would be reduced under a single-payer system of health care, providing less incentive for people to enter the medical profession.
- The evidence on the overhead costs of running Medicare suggests that cost savings from switching to a single-payer system may be small to nonexistent.

Using Your Economics

1. What incentives can the government provide to ensure that new, effective medicines and technologies are developed under a single-payer system?
2. More than a dozen states have already initiated discussions about legislation related to the provision of universal health care. Will a universal health-care system be more effective if it is implemented at the federal level or at the state level?

5 American Medical Students Association, "Myths and Facts About Single-Payer Universal Health Care." Available at http://www.amsa.org/hp/myths.cfm.
6 Ibid.
7 California Chamber of Commerce, "California Chamber Urges a 'No' Vote on Proposition 72," Aug. 5, 2004. Available at http://www.calchamber.com/headlines/index.cfm?navid=374&action=detail&id=380.
8 John C. Goodman, "Health Care in a Free Society," CATO Policy Analysis #532. Available at http://www.cato.org/pubs/pas/pa532.pdf.

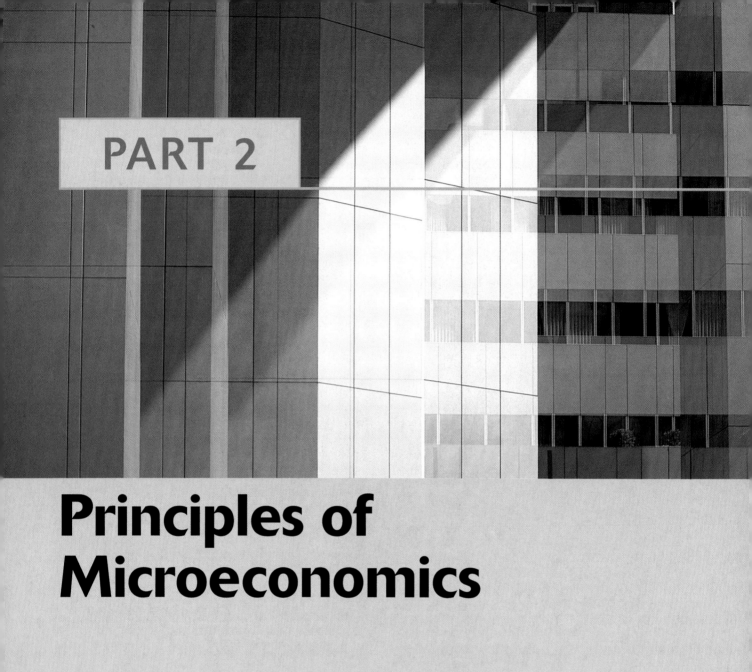

Principles of
Microeconomics

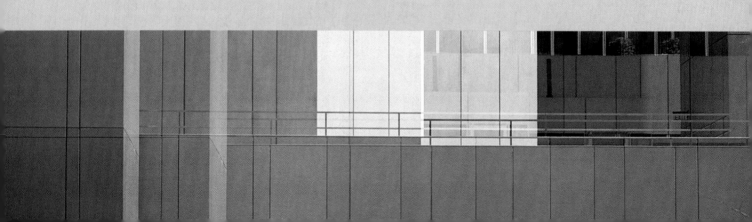

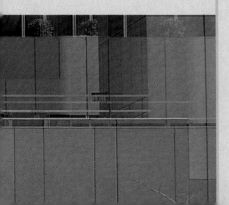

111

CHAPTER 5

The Demand Curve and the Behavior of Consumers

This is a true story about a college professor who loves to teach introductory economics. The professor is younger than most college professors, but is hard of hearing and wears hearing aids in both ears. The professor teaches one of those large lecture courses, and most students aren't even aware that the professor wears the hearing aids.

In the middle of one of the lectures—in order to illustrate an important point about demand curves—the professor simultaneously brings one hand to one ear and the other hand to the other ear and suddenly pulls out both hearing aids, saying, "I can't hear a thing. If it were not for these hearing aids I wouldn't be here. I couldn't be a teacher. Do you know how much benefit I get from these hearing aids? Certainly more than from my car and maybe even more than from my house. If I had to give you a dollar amount, I would say that the benefit to me is about $60,000. Without the hearing aids, I would probably earn less, and I know my life would not be as enjoyable. Of course, I had to buy these hearing aids, and they are not very cheap. They cost me $500. But, you know, they cost me a lot less than they benefit me. The difference between $60,000 and $500 is $59,500, a huge amount. That difference is a measure of what the hearing aid market delivers to me over and above what I had to pay for the hearing aids. Most

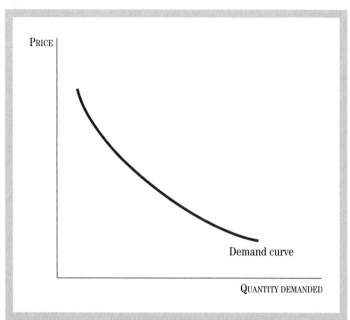

Figure 5.1
A Typical Demand Curve
Demand curves typically slope downward. In this chapter, we examine the behavior of the consumers who underlie the demand curve.

people would call that a good deal, but because I am an economics professor I call it a *consumer surplus.*"

In this chapter we show how and why the demand curve for any good—whether hearing aids, MP3 players, grapes, or bananas—can be used to measure the "good deal" or the "consumer surplus" that markets deliver to people.

Figure 5.1 shows a typical demand curve, with price on the vertical axis and quantity demanded on the horizontal axis. The demand curve is for an entire market, which might consist of millions of consumers. In this chapter we look under the surface of the demand curve and examine the behavior of these consumers. This examination has two purposes. The first is to see exactly what determines the slope and position of the demand curve—why it slopes downward and why changes in people's preferences or income cause it to shift.

The second purpose of examining the behavior of consumers is to see how well a market economy actually works. When we study the interactions of people in markets, it is the foundation of demand curves—people's preferences and choices—that we are investigating, not the demand curves themselves. Consumers do not go to the market with a demand curve; they go with certain preferences and objectives. One of the most important conclusions of the study of economics is that, under certain circumstances, a market economy works better than alternative systems to produce and allocate goods and resources. In order to understand that conclusion—to question it, to criticize it, to prove it, to defend it—we must look at the consumer behavior beneath the demand curve.

Our examination of consumer behavior in this chapter involves constructing a model. The main assumption of the model is that people make purposeful choices with limited resources to increase their satisfaction and better their lives. To make this assumption operational, economists have developed the idea of *utility*, which represents people's preferences for different items (products, jobs, leisure time) among a set of alternatives. We first define utility and then show how economists use utility to derive the slope and position of the demand curve.

Utility and Consumer Preferences

Every person has tastes and preferences for some goods relative to other goods. The millions of people who underlie a typical demand curve do not all have the same tastes and preferences, of course. Some people like Brussels sprouts; some people hate Brussels sprouts. We first focus on individual consumers and then show how the behavior of the millions of individuals adds up.

utility: a numerical indicator of a person's preferences in which higher levels of utility indicate a greater preference.

Utility is a numerical indicator of a person's preference for some goods compared to others. If one prefers some activity, such as eating a pizza and drinking two Cokes, to some other activity, such as eating two pizzas and drinking one Coke, then the utility from "one pizza and two Cokes" is greater than the utility from "two pizzas and one Coke." In general, if activity A is preferred to alternative B, then the utility from A is greater than the utility from B.

Be careful not to confuse the economist's definition of utility with the everyday meaning. If you look up *utility* in the dictionary, you will probably see the word *usefulness*, but to an economist, higher *utility* does not mean greater "usefulness"; it simply means that the item is preferred to another item. Watching "The Academy Awards" or "The NCAA Final Four" might give you more utility than attending a review session for your economics course, even though it is certainly not as useful for studying for the final.

A Consumer's Utility Depends on the Consumption of Goods

Let us consider an example of utility. Grapes are a product with which we have a lot of experience. They have been around for more than 4,000 years (at least since 2400 B.C. in ancient Egypt), and, in one form or another, they are still consumed around the world. Bananas are another popular fruit, also consumed around the world. Let us use grapes and bananas for our example of utility.

Figure 5.2 shows an example of the utility that one individual might get from consuming different amounts of grapes and bananas. Because every person is different, Figure 5.2 is just an example. You might imagine that the person is you, standing in front of a bin of fresh grapes and bananas in a grocery store, deciding how many pounds to buy. Or it could be the person in the picture at an open-air market who has some cash and is deciding how many pounds of grapes and bananas to buy with the cash.

Observe how Figure 5.2 is organized. The number of pounds of grapes is listed vertically on the left outside the box, from 0 up to 5 pounds. The number of pounds of bananas is listed horizontally below the box, from 0 over to 5 pounds. The entries inside the box show the utility from consuming different combinations of grapes and bananas.

To find the utility, first go to the row corresponding to the number of pounds of grapes and then go to the column corresponding to the number of pounds of bananas. The box at the intersection of the row and column shows the utility for the consumption of that specific combination of grapes and bananas. For example, if the individual consumes 2 pounds of grapes and 1 pound of bananas, then the utility is 20.

Note that this individual gets more utility from 2 pounds of grapes and 1 pound of bananas (utility = 20) than from 1 pound of grapes and 1 pound of bananas (utility = 16), which seems reasonable. In other

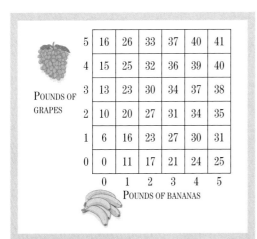

Figure 5.2
Example of Utility from Grapes and Bananas
The numbers inside the box give the utility from consuming the amounts of grapes and the amounts of bananas shown outside the box. For example, utility from 4 pounds of grapes and 3 pounds of bananas is 36. Combinations of grapes and bananas with higher utility are preferred to combinations with lower utility.

"If we buy two at full price, we can buy another six we don't want at half price."

words, 1 additional pound of grapes increases utility by 4 (from 16 to 20). This increase in utility is called marginal utility. In general, *marginal utility* is the increase in utility from consuming an additional unit of a good.

Utility Indicates Preference

We can now show exactly how utility is a numerical indicator of a person's preference for one good compared with another. Recall that when utility from one activity is greater than utility from an alternative, the activity is preferred to the alternative. According to Figure 5.2, the consumer prefers a combination of 4 pounds of grapes and 1 pound of bananas to a combination of 1 pound of grapes and 2 pounds of bananas because the utility of the former (25) is greater than the utility of the latter (23). Other combinations can be ranked similarly. In some cases there are ties; for example, the consumer is *indifferent* as to 2 pounds of grapes and 3 pounds of bananas versus 1 pound of grapes and 5 pounds of bananas because the utility of both is 31.

By ranking different combinations of goods in this way, we can see that a consumer's utility describes the consumer's preference for one good compared with another. Of all possible combinations, the one with the highest (maximum) utility is the one that is preferred to all the others. Thus, by maximizing utility, the consumer can be said to be making decisions that lead to the most preferred outcome from the viewpoint of the consumer. In this way, utility maximization implements the assumption that people make purposeful choices to increase their satisfaction.

An important fact about utility as exemplified in Figure 5.2 is that the units used to measure it do not matter. For example, suppose we multiply the utilities from grapes and from bananas in Figure 5.2 by 2, and then reexamine what utility implies about preferences. Rather than 23 units of utility, we would have 46 units of utility from 1 pound of grapes and 2 pounds of bananas. But rather than this combination, the consumer would still prefer 4 pounds of grapes and 1 pound of bananas, which would have a utility of $2 \times 25 = 50$. In fact, you can multiply utility by any positive number—even a billion or a billionth—and still get the same ordering of one combination compared to another.

The fact that the description of people's preferences does not depend on the units we use to measure utility is very important, because in reality economists have no way to measure utility. That is why Figure 5.2 does not give units. In particular, no one can say that one person's utility is higher or lower than another person's utility. The utilities of different people cannot be compared. An important feature of economists' use of utility is that it does not require or imply that the utilities of different people can be compared. Only the preference of a particular person for one type of good in comparison with another type of good is represented by utility.

REVIEW
- Utility is a numerical indicator of a person's preferences for different goods. For each combination of goods, there is a numerical value of utility.

- Combinations of goods with a higher utility are preferred to combinations of goods with a lower utility.

- The units by which utility is measured do not affect the preference for one combination compared with another.

The Budget Constraint and Utility Maximization

We have now shown how a consumer's preferences can be described by utility. Maximizing utility is an assumption equivalent to making purposeful choices to improve one's satisfaction. Now let us introduce the limits on the consumer's choice and explain how utility maximization works.

The Budget Constraint

Consumers are limited in how much they can spend when they choose between grapes or bananas or other goods. For example, suppose that the individual choosing between grapes and bananas is limited to spending a total of $8. That is, total spending on grapes plus bananas must be less than or equal to $8. This limit on total spending is called the **budget constraint.** In general, a budget constraint tells us that total expenditures on all goods and services must be less than a certain amount, perhaps the person's income for the year. The budget constraint is what limits the consumer's choices.

budget constraint: an income limitation on a person's expenditure on goods and services.

How much a consumer can spend and still remain within the budget constraint depends on the prices of the goods. For the example of grapes and bananas, if the consumer buys 1 pound of grapes at $2 and 2 pounds of bananas at $1, then expenditures are $4, well within the budget constraint of $8. But if 5 pounds of each were purchased at these prices, expenditures would be $15, a sum outside the budget constraint and, therefore, not possible.

Modeling a Consumer's Choice
This consumer, with a limited amount to spend, makes a choice that maximizes her utility. The combination of grapes and bananas that she prefers to other possible combinations of grapes and bananas must have a higher utility for her than the other combinations have.

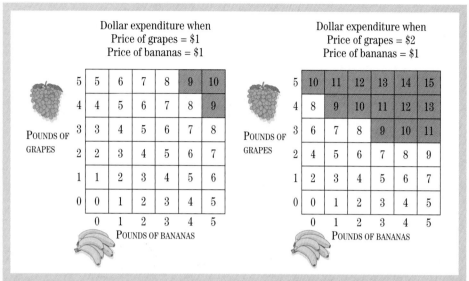

Figure 5.3
The Budget Constraint and Expenditures at Two Different Prices
The numbers inside the box give the total dollar expenditures on different combinations of grapes and bananas. For example, in the left box, where the price of both bananas and grapes is $1 per pound, the total dollar expenditure would be $7 for 4 pounds of grapes and 3 pounds of bananas. If the price of grapes were $2 per pound and the price of bananas were $1 per pound, as in the right box, that same combination would cost $11. The numbers in the red-shaded area are greater than the $8 budget constraint.

Figure 5.3 shows expenditures on grapes and bananas for two different situations. In both situations the price of bananas is $1; but in the situation in the left-hand box the price of grapes is $1, while in the right-hand box the price of grapes is $2. All the combinations of grapes and bananas from Figure 5.2 are shown in Figure 5.3. Several of the combinations are not within the $8 budget constraint; these are in the red-shaded area. Observe that when the price of grapes rises from $1 to $2, more combinations are outside the budget constraint and fewer are within the budget constraint. In general, a higher price for a good reduces consumption opportunities for the individual.

Maximizing Utility Subject to the Budget Constraint

utility maximization: an assumption that people try to achieve the highest level of utility given their budget constraint.

Given the utility in Figure 5.2 and the budget constraint in Figure 5.3, we can now show what happens when the individual maximizes utility subject to the budget constraint. **Utility maximization** means that people choose the highest possible level of utility given their budget constraint. In Figure 5.4, we show utility, from Figure 5.2, but now we shade in red the combinations for which expenditures are greater than the $8 budget constraint from Figure 5.3. The budget constraint means that you can't go in the red area.

Suppose first that the price of grapes is $1 per pound and the price of bananas is $1 per pound. By looking at the box on the left, you can find the highest level of utility achievable by the consumer with an $8 budget constraint. It is 39 units of utility from 4 pounds of grapes and 4 pounds of bananas. These values are shown in blue boldface type. This is the most preferred combination that the individual can buy

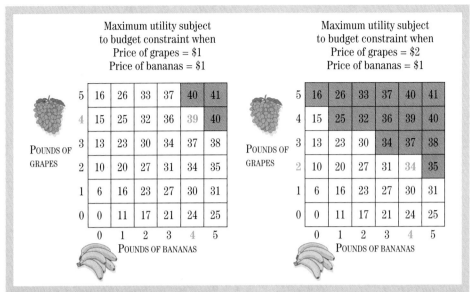

Figure 5.4
Maximizing Utility Subject to the Budget Constraint at Two Different Prices
The red-shaded areas are the same as the red-shaded areas in Figure 5.3 and therefore represent combinations for which total expenditures would be greater than the $8 budget constraint. They are not possible choices. The bold number is the maximum level of utility for which spending is less than or equal to $8. In the left box, the maximum utility of 39 represents a choice of 4 pounds of grapes and 4 pounds of bananas. In the right box, with the higher price of grapes, the maximum utility is 34, corresponding to 2 pounds of grapes and 4 pounds of bananas. Hence, a higher price of grapes leads to a lower quantity of grapes demanded.

and still remain within the budget constraint. Thus, utility maximization predicts that the consumer will purchase 4 pounds of grapes and 4 pounds of bananas at these prices. There is no other combination that will yield greater utility and still be within the $8 budget constraint.

■ **Effect of a Change in Price: A Movement Along a Demand Curve.**   Now suppose that the price of grapes rises from $1 to $2 per pound with the price of bananas staying the same. The options for expenditures in this case are shown in the box on the right in Figure 5.4. You can see the combination—2 pounds of grapes and 4 pounds of bananas—for which the maximum utility (34) is reached.

Now observe something very important: The quantity of grapes demanded at the higher price of grapes is less than the quantity demanded at the lower price of grapes. When the price of grapes is $1 per pound, 4 pounds of grapes are purchased; at the price of $2 per pound, 2 pounds of grapes are purchased. Thus, we have shown that the assumption that people maximize utility subject to a budget constraint implies that a higher price leads to a reduced quantity demanded. In other words, as shown in the margin, we have derived two points on a demand curve for the consumer. When the price goes up, the quantity demanded goes down; when the price goes down, the quantity demanded goes up. These are *movements along* a demand curve, as shown in the small graph in the margin, which indicates the two prices and the quantity demanded at each price; a line is drawn through the points to illustrate the downward-sloping demand curve.

Price of Grapes	Quantity of Grapes Demanded by the Consumer
$1	4 pounds
$2	2 pounds

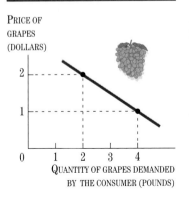

Price of Grapes	Quantity of Grapes Demanded by the Consumer
$1	2 pounds
$2	1 pound

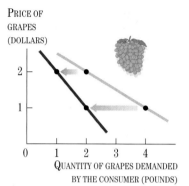

PRICE OF
GRAPES
(DOLLARS)

QUANTITY OF GRAPES DEMANDED
BY THE CONSUMER (POUNDS)

■ Effect of a Change in Income: A Shift in the Demand Curve.

Now consider the effect of a change in the individual's income on the quantity of grapes that the individual will purchase. Suppose that the individual now has $5 to spend rather than $8; in other words, there is a $3 reduction in the individual's income. What will happen to the quantity of grapes demanded by the consumer? If the price is again $1 per pound of grapes and $1 per pound of bananas, then the boxes on the left of Figures 5.3 and 5.4 apply. (You might want to shade in the additional area of these two boxes that represents combinations of grapes and bananas that are not feasible with only $5 to spend.) If expenditures are limited to $5, then the maximum utility (31) occurs when 2 pounds of grapes and 3 pounds of bananas are purchased. Recall that with $8 to spend, the consumer was willing to buy 4 pounds of grapes. Thus, at a price of grapes of $1 per pound, the decrease in income leads to a reduction in the amount of grapes the consumer is willing to buy.

We can also calculate the effects of the income change at a different set of prices. If the price is $2 for grapes and $1 for bananas, then the boxes on the right of Figures 5.3 and 5.4 apply. (Again, you might want to shade in the additional area of these two boxes that represents combinations of grapes and bananas that are not feasible with only $5 to spend.) With a limit of $5 to spend, the maximum utility (27) occurs when 1 pound of grapes and 3 pounds of bananas are purchased. The decrease in income leads to a decrease in the amount of grapes the consumer will purchase at each price of grapes. Thus, as shown in the margin, we have derived another demand curve corresponding to the decreased amount of income. Observe that the demand curve with the lower amount of income ($5) is shifted to the left compared with the demand curve with the higher amount of income ($8). Thus, we have shown explicitly that a change in income will *shift* the consumer's demand curve.

■ Income and Substitution Effects of a Price Change.

Using the concepts of utility and the budget constraint, economists distinguish between two separate reasons why an increase in the price leads to a decrease in the quantity demanded. These are (1) the income effect and (2) the substitution effect.

The Income Effect of a Change in the Price We noted how an increase in the price reduces the number of options available to the consumer. When the price of grapes rises from $1 to $2 per pound, choices such as 4 pounds of grapes and 4 pounds of bananas are no longer within the budget constraint, although they were within the budget constraint at a grape price of $1 per pound. A total of fourteen options are outside the budget constraint (in the red-shaded area of the right tables of Figures 5.3 and 5.4) when the price of grapes is $2, whereas only three are outside the budget constraint (in the red-shaded area of the left tables of Figures 5.3 and 5.4) when the price is $1. This reduction in the options when the price rises is similar to what would happen if the consumer suddenly had less income to spend on both goods without any change in prices. Let's show this effect in the context of the banana and grape example.

Originally we observed a price of grapes and bananas of $1 per pound, and $8 of available income, with an optimal quantity of 4 pounds of grapes and 4 pounds of bananas, and 39 units of utility. After the increase in the price of grapes to $2 per pound, the consumer now purchases 2 pounds of grapes and 4 pounds of bananas, with a lower level of utility of 34 units. Now imagine that we want to achieve the same lower level of utility (34 units) in a different way, by keeping the original prices constant while lowering the available income. If prices are still $1 per pound for grapes and bananas, Figure 5.5 shows that a budget constraint of $6 eliminates 10 combinations of grapes and bananas, and the consumer buys 3 pounds of grapes and 3 pounds of bananas to maximize the utility level at 34 units. (Note that in this

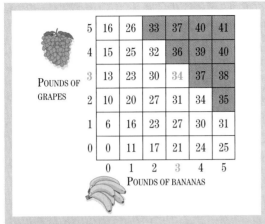

Figure 5.5
Income Effect
The red-shaded area represents combinations that are not feasible for a price per pound of $1 for both grapes and bananas, and an available income of $6. The consumer may choose to buy 3 pounds of grapes and 3 pounds of bananas, showing the effect of a reduction of income on the quantity consumed.

income effect: the amount by which the quantity demanded falls because of the decline in real income from a price increase.

substitution effect: the amount by which quantity demanded falls when the price rises, exclusive of the income effect.

particular example, 2 pounds of grapes and 4 pounds of bananas also yield 34 units of utility and the consumer is indifferent between two combinations of goods. For a more general analysis, read the appendix to this chapter.) The decrease from 4 pounds of grapes to 3 pounds of grapes measures the income effect.

The **income effect** is the amount by which quantity demanded falls because of the decline in real income from the price increase. Of course, a reduction in the grape price will have the opposite effect: It will increase the real income the consumer has to spend on both goods and in particular on grapes. The income effect is a general phenomenon that applies to all normal goods; for example, when the price of gasoline rises, people will spend less on gasoline in part because their real income has declined. With less real income, they will spend less on most goods and services.

The Substitution Effect of a Change in the Price An increase in the price of grapes with no change in the price of other goods causes an increase in the relative price of grapes. Because grapes become relatively more expensive, people will switch their purchases away from grapes toward other goods even if there is no income effect. The **substitution effect** is the amount by which the quantity demanded falls when the price rises, exclusive of the income effect.

In the grape-banana example, the increase in price from $1 to $2, with $8 of available income, makes the combination of 3 pounds of grapes and 3 pounds of bananas of Figure 5.5 unavailable too. The feasible combination that maximizes utility is 2 pounds of grapes and 4 pounds of bananas, with a utility of 34 units. The total reduction in grape consumption of 2 pounds can be split, in this example, into 1 pound (from 4 to 3 pounds) due to the income effect and 1 pound (from 3 to 2 pounds) due to the substitution effect. The income effect reduces both grape and banana consumption, while the substitution effect just reduces the quantity demanded of the good with the increasing price, as illustrated in the table and graph below. The exact size of the income and substitution effects differs from example to example. In some cases the income effect is larger than the substitution effect; in other cases the substitution effect is larger.

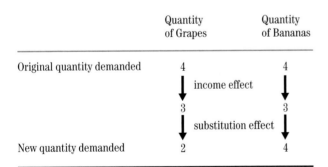

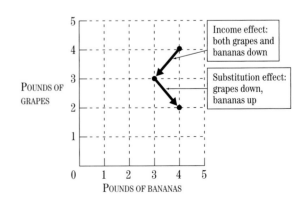

Visualizing the Income and Substitution Effects
Plotting the quantities from the above table in a graph with one good on the vertical axis and another on the horizontal axis helps in visualizing the income and substitution effects.

- The demand curve can be derived from the assumption that people maximize utility subject to a budget constraint.

- A change in the price of a good changes the number of combinations within the budget constraint and thus changes the utility-maximizing quantity demanded. This represents a movement along the demand curve.

- A change in income also changes the budget constraint and thus also changes the utility-maximizing quantity demanded. This represents a shift of the demand curve.

- The total effect of a change in the price on the quantity demanded can be divided into two parts—an income effect and a substitution effect.

Willingness to Pay and the Demand Curve

The choice between one good (grapes) and another good (bananas) in the previous section is useful for showing how to derive a demand curve from the basic idea that consumers maximize utility subject to a budget constraint. Now we want to use the demand curve to determine how well markets work for consumers. This requires moving beyond the simple choice between one good and another good and considering the choice between one good and all possible other goods.

Measuring Willingness to Pay and Marginal Benefit

Table 5.1
Willingness to Pay (Benefit) and Marginal Benefit

Quantity of X	Willingness to Pay for X (Benefit from X)	Marginal Benefit from X
0	$0.00	—
1	$5.00	$5.00
2	$8.00	$3.00
3	$9.50	$1.50
4	$10.50	$1.00
5	$11.00	$.50

The connecting lines emphasize how marginal benefit is the *change* in benefit (or willingness to pay) as one more unit of a good is consumed.

marginal benefit: the increase in the benefit from, or the willingness to pay for, one more unit of a good.

Suppose we asked a person who is consuming a zero amount of good X, "How much money would you be willing to pay for one unit of X?" Because the money that the person would pay can be used to buy all goods, not just one good, the question implicitly asks the person to compare X with all other goods. In general, the answer to this question would depend on how much utility would increase with one unit of X and on how much utility would decrease because less would be spent on other goods, given the budget constraint. In other words, the answer would depend on the person's preferences for X and all other goods as represented by utility.

Suppose that the answer is $5. Let us assume that the answer to the question gives us the true measure of the consumer's preferences. Then, once we get an answer to the first question, we could ask, "How much would you be willing to pay for two units of X?" Suppose the answer is, "I would be willing to pay $8." We could then continue to ask the consumer about more and more units of X. We summarize the hypothetical answers in Table 5.1. The column labeled "Willingness to Pay for X" tabulates the answers to the question.

Assuming that the answers to the questions are true, willingness to pay measures how much the consumer would *benefit* from different amounts of X. **Marginal benefit** from X is the increase in benefit from, or the willingness to pay for, one more unit of a good. As a person consumes more and more of a good, the marginal benefit from additional amounts is likely to diminish. Imagine you are very hungry, there is no food in the house, and you are craving pizza. At this point you might be willing to pay $5.00 for a big, hot slice of pizza. Now suppose you already have that slice of pizza, but you're still a little hungry. You might be willing to pay $3.00 for an additional slice. The more pizza you have, the less you are willing to pay for even more pizza. Observe that the marginal benefit in Table 5.1 diminishes as more is consumed.

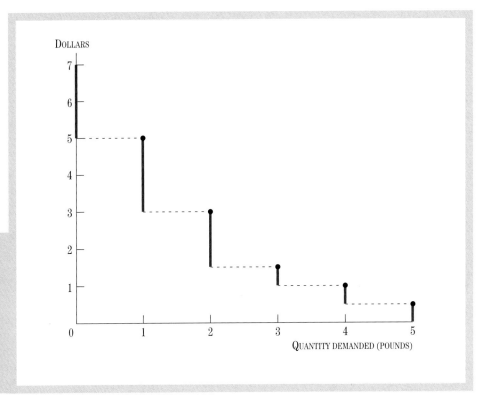

Figure 5.6
Derivation of the Individual Demand Curve
The dots are exactly the same as the marginal benefit in Table 5.1. At each dot, price equals marginal benefit. The vertical lines indicate how much is demanded at each price if the consumer is restricted to purchasing whole pounds.

Graphical Derivation of the Individual Demand Curve

A demand curve can be derived from the information about willingness to pay (benefit) and marginal benefit of X for the person described in Table 5.1. Suppose that X is raisins (rice, salt, tea, orange juice, CDs, movies, or any other good will serve just as well as an example). Suppose that the person has $10 to spend on raisins and other goods. We want to ask how many pounds of raisins the person would buy at different prices. We imagine different hypothetical prices for raisins, from astronomical levels like $7 a pound to bargain basement levels like $.50 a pound.

To proceed graphically, we first plot the marginal benefit from Table 5.1 in Figure 5.6. Focus first on the black dots in Figure 5.6. The lines will be explained in the next few paragraphs. The horizontal axis in Figure 5.6 measures the quantity of raisins. On the vertical axis we want to indicate the price as well as the marginal benefit, so we measure the scale of the vertical axis in dollars. The black dots in Figure 5.6 represent the marginal benefit an individual gets from consuming different amounts of raisins.

How many pounds of raisins would this person consume at different prices for raisins? First, suppose that the price is very high—$7 a pound. Draw an arrow pointing to this $7 price in Figure 5.6. We are going to derive a demand curve for this individual by gradually lowering the price from this high value and seeing how many pounds would be purchased at each price. As the price declines, you can slide your arrow down the vertical axis. For each price, we ask the same question: How many pounds would the person buy? To make things simple at the start, assume that the person buys only whole pounds of raisins. You might want to imagine that the raisins come in 1-pound cellophane packages. We consider fractions of pounds later.

Suppose, then, that the price is $7 a pound. The marginal benefit from 1 pound of raisins is $5. Thus, the price is greater than the marginal benefit. Would the person buy a pound of raisins at this price? Because the price the person would have to pay is greater than the marginal benefit, *the answer would be no;* the person would not buy a pound of raisins at a price of $7. If the minimum amount of raisins that can be purchased is 1 pound, then the person will buy no pounds at a price of $7 per pound. We have shown, therefore, that the quantity demanded of raisins is *zero* when the price is $7.

Now start to lower the price. As long as the price is more than $5, the person will not buy any raisins. Hence, the quantity demanded at all prices higher than $5 is zero. We indicate this by the red line on the vertical axis above the $5 mark.

Now watch what happens when the price drops to $5. The marginal benefit from a pound of raisins is $5 and the price is $5, so the marginal benefit of the pound of raisins is sufficient to cover the price. Now the person gets sufficient marginal benefit to buy 1 pound of raisins. Strictly speaking, the price would have to be a little less than $5, perhaps $4.99, for the person to get more by purchasing 1 rather than 0 pounds of raisins. At a price of $5, the person will be indifferent between 1 pound and 0 pounds. At a price of $4.99, the person would buy, but at a price of $5.01, the person would not buy. The price of $5 is right in between. However, let us assume that the person buys 1 pound rather than 0 pounds when the price is $5. This is indicated in Figure 5.6 by showing that the quantity demanded is given by the black dot at 1 pound when the price equals $5.

Continue lowering the price, slipping the arrow down the axis. The quantity demanded will stay at 1 pound as long as the price remains above the marginal benefit of buying another pound of raisins, or $3. We therefore extend the red line downward at 1 pound as the price falls from $5 down to $3. Consider, for example, a price of $4. The person has already decided that 1 pound will be bought; the question is whether a second pound of raisins is worthwhile. Another pound has a marginal benefit of $3 (willingness to pay goes from $5 to $8 as the quantity increases from 1 to 2 pounds). The person has to pay $4, which is more than the marginal benefit. Hence, *the quantity demanded stays at 1 pound when the price is $4.* However, when the price falls to $3, another pound is purchased. That is, when the price is $3, the quantity demanded is 2 pounds, which is shown graphically by the black dot at 2 pounds.

Now suppose the price falls below $3, perhaps to $2. Is a third pound purchased? The marginal benefit of a third pound is $1.50; is it worth it to buy a third pound at $2 per pound? No. The quantity demanded stays at 2 pounds when the price is between $3 and $1.50, which we denote by extending the red line downward from the black dot at 2 pounds. This story can be continued. As the price continues to fall, more pounds of raisins are demanded.

By considering various prices from over $5 to under $.50, we have traced out an **individual demand curve** that slopes downward. As the price is lowered, more raisins are purchased. The demand curve is downward-sloping because of diminishing marginal benefit. At each black dot in the diagram, price equals the marginal benefit.

The jagged shape of the demand curve in Figure 5.6 may look strange. It is due to the assumption that only 1-pound packages of raisins are considered by the consumer. In the case of raisins, it is usually possible to buy fractions of a pound, and if the marginal benefits of the fractions are between the values for the whole pounds, then the demand curve will be a smooth line, as shown in Figure 5.7. Then price will equal marginal benefit not only at the black dots but also on the lines connecting the dots. If you are unsure of this, imagine creating a new Table 5.1 and Figure 5.6 with *ounces* of raisins. There will be a point at each ounce, and with 16 ounces per pound, there will be so many points that the curve will be as smooth as Figure 5.7.

Check the answer. To check that zero is the correct answer, suppose that the person did buy 1 pound of raisins for $7. Then the person would have $3 left over ($10 − $7 = $3), and with the benefit of 1 pound of raisins being $5, that would be a total of $8 (since $3 + $5 = $8). Because $8 is less than the original $10, by buying 1 pound of raisins the person would be worse off than by buying no raisins.

Check the answer. To check that 1 pound is the correct answer, look at how well off the person is after a decision to buy 1 pound compared with a decision to buy 2 pounds. If the person buys 1 pound at $4, then the person has $6 left over ($10 − $4 = $6), and with the benefit (willingness to pay) being $5 for that pound, the person would be well off in the amount of $11 (since $6 + $5 = $11). Now, if the person buys 2 pounds at $4 per pound, then the person has $2 left over ($10 − $8 = $2), and with the benefit (willingness to pay) being $8 for the 2 pounds, the person has the equivalent of $10 (since $2 + $8 = $10). Because $11 is greater than $10, the person is better off buying 1 pound than buying 2 pounds.

individual demand curve: a curve showing the relationship between quantity demanded of a good by an individual and the price of the good.

Our study of utility maximization in this chapter assumes that people try to maximize their utility, a numerical value representing a person's tastes and preferences, given a certain budget constraint. While we are often faced with similar cut-and-dried choices in real life (should I get the soda or the iced tea?), our choices more often reflect a variety of preferences that are hard to quantify and place a specific value on. As a result, our decision-making in real life may not always seem completely "rational." We may make economic decisions that will give us a short-term gain but a long-term loss. We may give our money away—because charitable giving may make us feel beneficent or because it seems like the right thing to do.

In the article that follows, you'll read about the work going on in the area of behavioral economics, or neuroeconomics, which looks more closely at the ways people make decisions and how they go about "satisfying their preferences."

Mind games

From the *Economist*, print edition
January 13, 2005

Can studying the human brain revolutionise economics?

ALTHOUGH Plato compared the human soul to a chariot pulled by the two horses of reason and emotion, modern economics has mostly been a one-horse show. It has been obsessed with reason. In decisions from how much to produce to whether to save and invest, humans have been assumed to be coolly rational calculators of their own self-interest. Over the past few years, however, evidence from psychology has persuaded many economists that reason does not always have its way. Now, judging from a series of presentations at the American Economic Association meetings in Philadelphia last weekend, a burgeoning new field dubbed "neuroeconomics" seems poised to provide fresh insights on how the two horses together produce economic behaviour.

The current bout of research is made possible by the arrival of new technologies such as functional magnetic-resonance imaging, which allows second-by-second observation of brain activity. At several American universities, economists and their collaborators in the neurosciences have been placing human subjects in such brain scanners and asking them to perform a variety of economic tasks and games.

For example, the idea that humans compute the "expected value" of future events is central to many economic models. Whether people will invest in shares or buy insurance depends on how they estimate the odds of future events weighted by the gains and losses in each case. Your pension, for example, might have a very low expected value if there is a large probability that bonds and shares will plunge just before you retire.

Brian Knutson, of Stanford University, carried out one recent brain-scan experiment to understand how humans compute such things. Subjects were asked to perform a task, in this case pressing a button during a short interval in which a certain shape was flashed on to a screen. In some trials, the subjects could win up to $5 if successful, while in others they would have to defend against a $5 loss. Before presenting the target, the researchers signalled to subjects which kind of trial they were in.

Brain activity in certain neural systems seemed to reveal a strong correlation with the amount of money at stake. Moreover, the prospects of gains and losses activated different parts of the brain. Traditional economists had long thought—or assumed—that the prospect of a $1,000 gain could compensate you for an equally likely loss of the same size. In subsequent trials, subjects were given another signal: one that provided an estimate of the odds of success. That allowed the researchers to identify the regions of the brain used for recognising an amount of money and for estimating the probability of winning (or losing) it. Having identified these regions, the hope is that future work can measure how the brain performs in situations such as share selection, gambling or deciding to participate in a pension scheme.

David Laibson, an economist at Harvard University, thinks that such experiments underscore the big role that expectations play in a person's well-being. Economists have usually assumed that people's well-being, or "utility", depends on their level of consumption, but it might be that changes in consumption, especially unexpected downward ones, as in these experiments, can be especially unpleasant.

Mr. Laibson's own work tries to solve a different riddle: why people seem to apply vastly different discount rates to immediate and short-term rewards compared with rewards occurring well into the future. People tend much to prefer, say, $100 now to $115 next week, but they are indifferent between $100 a year from now and $115 in a year and a week. In one recent experiment, noted in our science section on October 30th, Mr. Laibson and others found that the brain's response to short-term riches (in this case, gift certificates of $15 or $20) occurs largely in the limbic system, a region that governs emotion. By contrast, the prospect of rewards farther into the future triggers the prefrontal cortex, which is often associated with reason and calculation. Thus, choosing immediate economic gratification, by spending excessively on credit cards or not saving enough even though you "know better", could be a sign that the limbic system is in charge. Government policies, such as forced savings or "cooling off" periods for buying property or cars, may be one remedy.

And then there is trust and deception. Colin Camerer, of the California Institute of Technology, has conducted experiments in which brain-scanned participants play strategic games with anonymous partners. When players are doing the best that they can to "win" the game by anticipating their opponents' moves, their brains tend to show a high degree of co-ordination between the "thinking" and the "feeling" regions. Economic equilibrium, by this measure, is an identifiable "state of mind".

Don't let it go to your head

Some neuroeconomists claim that such brain-scanning experiments are the start of a revolution in economics. No longer will economists rely on crude statistical models of how people behave in response to a policy change, such as an interest-rate rise or a tax increase. Instead, they will be able to peer directly into the brain to predict behaviour.

One day, perhaps; but much work remains. Identifying the parts of the brain that control economic actions is one thing. Harder tasks include determining how neural systems work together to create behaviour, and how wide is the variation in brain patterns between different people. Then there are age-old questions of free will: is your failure to save for old age simply a lifestyle choice, or is it down to faulty brain circuits? Neuroeconomics is already providing fascinating conclusions. But Plato's chariot will remain an alluring explanation for a while yet.

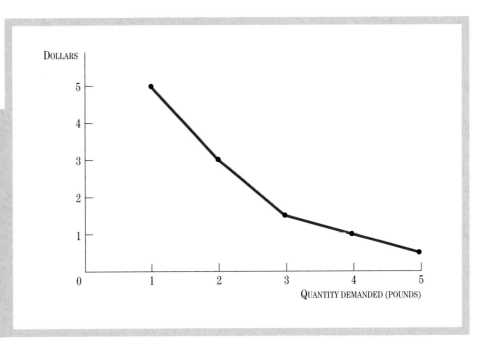

Figure 5.7
A Smooth Individual Demand Curve
If the consumer can buy fractions of a pound and if the marginal benefits of these fractions are between the whole-pound amounts, the demand curve becomes a smooth line, as in the figure, rather than the series of steps in Figure 5.5. In some cases, such as the demand for cars, we cannot consider fractions, and so these individual demand curves will look like steps.

The Price Equals Marginal Benefit Rule

We have discovered an important principle of consumer behavior. If the consumer can adjust consumption of a good in small increments—such as fractions of a pound—then the consumer will buy an amount for which the *price equals marginal benefit*. This condition can be applied to any good—apples, peanuts, comic books, the number of movies you see each year—not just raisins.

The price equals marginal benefit rule can explain a number of otherwise puzzling observations. For example, consider Adam Smith's diamond-water paradox. As Smith put it, "Nothing is more useful than water: but it will purchase scarce any thing; scarce any thing can be had in exchange for it. A diamond, on the contrary, has scarce any value in use; but a very great quantity of other goods may frequently be had in exchange for it."[1] Why are diamonds expensive and water cheap even though diamonds are less "useful" to the world's population than water?

The price equals marginal benefit rule helps explain the paradox. The price of diamonds will be high if the marginal benefit of diamonds is high. The price of water will be low if the marginal benefit of water is low. As we saw earlier, the marginal benefit of something declines the more people consume of it. Thus, water has relatively low marginal benefit because with water being so plentiful, people consume much of it every day. The marginal benefit is low even though the total benefit from water consumption in the world is very high. On the other hand, diamonds have a high marginal benefit because with diamonds being so scarce, people consume relatively little of them. The marginal benefit of diamonds is high even though the total benefit of diamonds may be low. Thus, the price equals marginal benefit rule explains the diamond-water paradox.

---

1. Adam Smith, *Wealth of Nations* (New York: Modern Library Edition, 1994), pp. 31–32.

The Market Demand Curve

market demand curve: the horizontal summation of all the individual demand curves for a good; also simply called the demand curve.

Thus far, we have graphically derived the *individual* demand curve. Now we consider the **market demand curve,** which is the sum of the individual demand curves. Figure 5.8 shows how we do the summing up. The figure shows the demand curves for raisins for two individuals, Ann and Pete. To get the market demand curve, add up, for each given price, the total amount demanded by both Pete and Ann. For example, at a price of $5, Pete's demand is 1 pound and Ann's demand is 1 pound. The market demand is then 2 pounds. When the price is $3 a pound, the demand is 2 pounds for Pete and 2 pounds for Ann, or 4 pounds for the market as a whole. Obviously, the market for raisins consists of more than just Pete and Ann. To get the whole market, you would have to sum up the demands for millions of people.

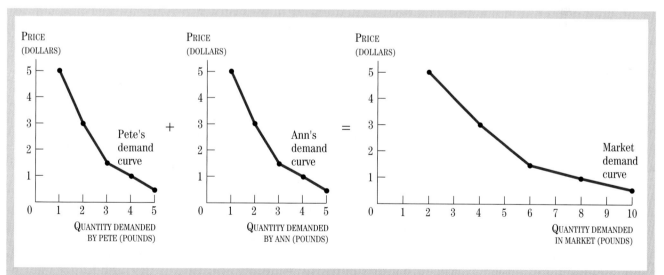

Figure 5.8 Derivation of the Market Demand Curve

The market demand curve is the sum of the demand curves of many individuals. The figure shows this for only two individuals with the same preferences. As more individuals with a diversity of tastes are added, the market demand curve becomes smoother and looks more like Figure 5.1.

Different Types of Individuals

In Figure 5.8, Pete's and Ann's demand curves are the same. They do not have to be. In fact, it is most likely that Ann and Pete have different preferences. Pete could be a peanut fan and be willing to pay less for raisins than Ann. It is incorrect to assume that everyone will be willing to pay the same amount for any good. There are all kinds of people in the world with different preferences. But you can still add up the demands of all these people at any given price to get the market demand curve. As you add up many individual demand curves for different types of people, the market demand curve gets smoother, even when the product cannot be bought in fractions of a unit. For example, the market demand curve for cars is smooth even though most individuals buy either zero, one, or perhaps two cars. When you add the demand curves for millions of people, the market demand curve for cars looks like the market demand curve (Figure 5.1) that we typically draw—smooth and downward-sloping. To confirm your understanding of the market demand curve, make sure you work through problems 5 and 7 at the end of the chapter.

REVIEW

- The market demand curve is derived from individual demand curves. At each price we add up how much is demanded by all individuals; the total is the market demand at that price.

- Even if the individual demand curves are not smooth, the market demand curve will be smooth because people have different tastes and preferences and prefer different benefits.

Consumer Surplus

consumer surplus: the difference between what a person is willing to pay for an additional unit of a good—the marginal benefit—and the market price of the good; for the market as a whole, it is the sum of all the individual consumer surpluses, or the area below the market demand curve and above the market price.

In many cases, people are willing to pay more for an item consumed than they have to pay for it. You might be willing to pay five times the $8 admission price to see your favorite movie. But like everyone else in line, you pay only $8, even though it is worth $40 to you. The difference between the $40 and the $8 is called *consumer surplus.*

In general, **consumer surplus** is the difference between the willingness to pay for an additional item (say, $40 for a movie)—its marginal benefit—and the price paid for it (say, $8 for a movie). Suppose the price of raisins is $4 per pound. Then the consumer in our previous example purchases 1 pound and the marginal benefit of that pound is $5. In that situation, the consumer gets a consumer surplus because the marginal benefit of the raisins to the consumer is $5 but the price paid is only $4. Consumer surplus is the difference, or $1. If the price were $3.50, then the consumer surplus would be greater, or $1.50.

Suppose the price falls further, so that two items are purchased. Consumer surplus is then defined as the sum of the differences between the marginal benefit of each item and the price paid for the item. For example, if the price per pound of raisins is $2, as in Figure 5.9, then 2 pounds of raisins will be purchased and the consumer surplus will be $5 − $2 = $3 for the first pound plus $3 − $2 = $1 for the second pound, for a total of $4. That is, the consumer surplus is $4.

Figure 5.9 shows graphically how consumer surplus is the area between the demand curve and the line indicating the price. In Figure 5.9, the total shaded area is equal to 4, consisting of two rectangular blocks, one with an area of 3 and the other

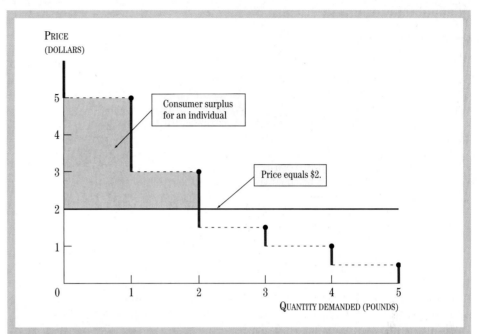

Figure 5.9
Consumer Surplus for an Individual
The consumer surplus is the difference between the marginal benefit a person gets from consuming a good and the price. It is given by the area between the demand curve and the price.

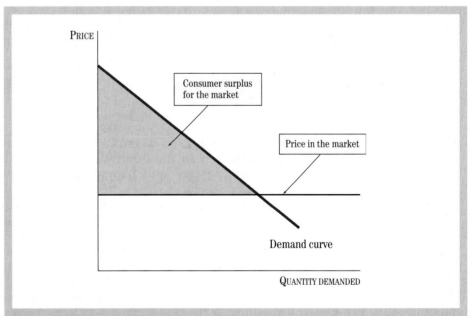

Figure 5.10
Consumer Surplus for the Market
The sum of the consumer surplus for all individuals in the market is the area between the demand curve and the price.

ECONOMICS IN ACTION

Building Roads and Bridges with Consumer Surplus

You may be surprised to learn that the concept of consumer surplus was not invented by an economist but by an engineer. Jules Dupuit was a civil engineer living in France in the mid-1800s. He wanted to demonstrate that the value of the roads and bridges he was building was much more than what people were willing to pay to use them. Consumer surplus was his idea of a demonstration. If a person paid a toll to cross a bridge, then the price of the toll could be as much of an underestimate of the benefit as the price of hearing aids is to the professor of economics in the introduction to this chapter. Thus, his consumer surplus argument helped persuade people to build more bridges and roads.

Dupuit offered a visual description of consumer surplus: "If society is paying 500 million for the services rendered by the road, that only proves one thing—that [the benefit from the road] is at least 500 million. But it may be a hundred times or a thousand times greater. . . . If you take the [500 million] as the figure . . . you are acting like a man who, wishing to measure the height of a wall in the dark and finding that he cannot reach the top with this raised arm says: 'This wall is two meters high, for if it were not, my hand would reach above it.' In daylight and equipped with a ladder . . . our alleged two-meter wall is fifty meters high."*

Do you think Dupuit's walls are a good analogy? In Dupuit's vision, how many "meters high" is consumer surplus?

*English translation of Jules Dupuit, "De la Mesure de l'Utilité des Travaux Publics," translated and reprinted in K. J. Arrow and T. Skitovsky, eds., *Readings in Welfare Economics* (Homewood, Ill.: Irwin, 1969).

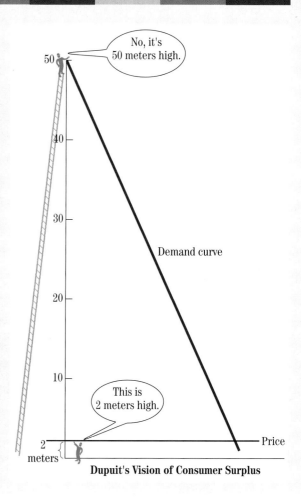

Dupuit's Vision of Consumer Surplus

with an area of 1. The area is the extra amount that the consumer is getting because the market price is lower than what the consumer is willing to pay.

Consumer surplus for the entire market is the sum of the consumer surpluses of all individuals who have purchased goods in the market. In Figure 5.10, consumer surplus is the area between the market demand curve and the market price line.

Consumer surplus has many uses in economics. It is used to measure how well the market system works. We will show in Chapter 7 that the market system maximizes consumer surplus under certain circumstances. Consumer surplus can also be used to measure the gains to consumers from an innovation. For example, if a new production technique lowers the price of raisins, then the consumer surplus will increase: The area between the demand curve and the market price line increases. This increase is a measure of how much the new technique is worth to society.

Consumer surplus is also used to evaluate the benefits of government policies, such as building a new bridge or creating a new wilderness area. These policies will increase or decrease consumer surplus, and their value to society can be estimated using the concept of consumer surplus.

REVIEW
- Consumer surplus is the area between the demand curve and the market price line. It is a measure of how much the consumer gains from buying goods in the market.
- The consumer surplus for the market is the sum of the individual consumer surpluses.
- Consumer surplus is an important tool for measuring the performance of an economic system or for assessing the impact of alternative government policies.

Conclusion

This chapter is the first of three that looks at the individual behavior that underlies the economist's demand and supply curves. This chapter focused on consumers, Chapter 6 looks at firms, and Chapter 7 looks at the interaction of consumers and firms in markets. The payoffs in terms of understanding how and how well markets work will not be fully realized until we have completed all three chapters, but we have already derived a number of useful results.

We showed that the idea that people make purposeful choices with limited resources can be made operational with utility. We showed that utility maximization implies that a higher price reduces the quantity demanded.

By looking at consumers' willingness to pay, we showed that each consumer's demand curve for a good is given by the good's marginal benefit and that consumer surplus is the area under the demand curve and above the price.

KEY POINTS

1. The idea of utility maximization subject to a budget constraint implements the assumption that people make purposeful choices with limited resources.
2. Utility indicates the preferences people have for one activity compared with other activities.
3. The budget constraint shows the limit on how much a person can spend.
4. Economists assume—at least as an approximation—that people maximize their utility. To do so, people act as if they adjust their consumption to get to the highest level of utility.
5. Utility maximization implies that a higher price reduces the quantity demanded.
6. A person's demand curve can be derived from that person's utility.
7. Market demand curves are derived from individual demand curves.
8. Consumer surplus is the area between the demand curve and the market price line. Because a demand curve can be derived from willingness to pay and marginal benefits, consumer surplus is a measure of how much benefit a consumer gains from buying a product.

KEY TERMS

utility
budget constraint
utility maximization
income effect
substitution effect
marginal benefit
individual demand curve
market demand curve
consumer surplus

QUESTIONS FOR REVIEW

1. What is the relationship between utility and preferences?
2. Why don't the units by which utility is measured matter?
3. What is the relationship between utility maximization subject to a budget constraint and purposeful choice with limited resources?
4. Why does an increase in the price of a good reduce the number of combinations of goods a person can buy?
5. Why does a reduction in income lead to a reduction in the quantity demanded at each price?
6. Why are market demand curves usually smoother than individual demand curves?
7. What is the area below the demand curve and above the price?

PROBLEMS

1. Using the example of utility in Figure 5.2, find the quantity of each good the consumer will purchase in the cases shown in the table below.

Case	Budget	Price of Grapes	Price of Bananas
A	$7	$1	$1
B	$6	$2	$1
C	$8	$1	$2

2. Analyze the following data for Masa's utility from consumption of books and coffee.

QUANTITY OF BOOKS					
4	50	75	81	83	84
3	46	70	76	78	79
2	40	60	66	68	69
1	30	40	46	48	49
0	0	10	16	18	19
	0	1	2	3	4

QUANTITY OF COFFEE

a. Determine how much of each good Masa will consume if he has $20 and if the price of books is $10 and the price of coffee is $3.
b. Suppose the price of coffee goes up to $5. How much coffee will Masa consume now? Why does the amount change?

3. Using the information from problem 2, multiply the utility received from books and coffee by 10. Will your answers to 2(a) and 2(b) change? Explain.

4. The following table shows Carl's willingness to pay for clothing.

Quantity of Clothing	Willingness to Pay
1	$35
2	$60
3	$80
4	$97
5	$112
6	$126

a. Calculate Carl's marginal benefit from clothing.
b. Draw Carl's individual demand curve for clothing.
c. Suppose the price of one item of clothing is $17. How much would Carl consume, and what is his consumer surplus? Show your answer graphically as well as numerically.

5. The table below shows Andrew's willingness to pay for clothing.
a. Draw Andrew's individual demand curve next to Carl's, and then add them together horizontally to derive a market demand curve.
b. If the current market price of clothing is $20, how many items of clothing will each buy? Show this in the diagram.

Quantity of Clothing	Willingness to Pay
1	$70
2	$105
3	$130
4	$150
5	$167
6	$182

6. Consider the example of willingness to pay for *X* (raisins) in Table 5.1. Assume that the price is $.75 and that the person has $10 to spend. Compute the sum of the benefit (willingness to pay) and what the person has left over after paying for different amounts of raisins from 0 to 5 pounds. How many pounds of raisins will maximize the sum of the benefit plus the dollars left over? How does the answer compare to that using the price equals marginal benefit condition?

7. The following table shows Margaret's and Dennis's willingness to pay for cookies.

Quantity of Cookies	Margaret	Dennis
1	$7	$15
2	$13	$25
3	$18	$34
4	$21	$42
5	$23	$45

a. Calculate the marginal benefits for both people.

b. Derive Margaret's and Dennis's individual demand curves for cookies. Derive the market demand curve if only Margaret and Dennis are in the market.

c. Suppose that the price of cookies is $4.50. How many cookies will Margaret and Dennis buy? Calculate their consumer surplus. Draw a diagram like Figure 5.8 to show the area representing consumer surplus.

d. Show the consumer surplus for the whole market using the market demand curve. Draw a diagram like Figure 5.9.

8. Suppose that the willingness to pay for hearing aids by the economics professor mentioned in the introduction to this chapter was $60,000 for 1 pair, $60,400 for two pairs, $60,600 for three pairs, and $60,700 for four pairs. Draw the professor's demand curve for hearing aids. If the price of a pair of hearing aids is $500, how many pairs would the professor buy? What is the professor's consumer surplus? Show the consumer surplus in a diagram. Now suppose that a technological breakthrough reduces the price of hearing aids to $150 a pair. How many pairs will the professor buy now? What is the new consumer surplus?

Consumer Theory with Indifference Curves

Chapter 5 derives the demand curve from the assumption that consumers maximize utility subject to a budget constraint. Here we give a graphical illustration of that derivation.

Consider a single consumer deciding how much of two items to buy. Let one of the items be X and the other be Y. We first show that the consumer's budget constraint can be represented by a budget line, and then we show that the consumer's preferences can be represented by indifference curves.

The Budget Line

Suppose that the consumer has $20 to spend on X and Y, and suppose that the price of X is $2 per unit and the price of Y is $4 per unit. How much of X and Y can the consumer buy? If the consumer spends all $20 on Y, then 5 units of Y and no units of X are consumed. If the consumer buys 4 units of Y at $4 per unit, then $16 will be spent on Y and the remaining $4 can be spent buying 2 units of X. These and several other amounts of X and Y that can be bought with $20 are shown in the following table.

Units of Y	Units of X	Expenditures
5	0	5 × $4 + 0 × $2 = $20
4	2	4 × $4 + 2 × $2 = $20
3	4	3 × $4 + 4 × $2 = $20
2	6	2 × $4 + 6 × $2 = $20
1	8	1 × $4 + 8 × $2 = $20
0	10	0 × $4 + 10 × $2 = $20

These combinations represent the maximum amounts that can be purchased with $20. Note that the amounts are inversely related; as more is spent on X, less must be spent on Y. This inverse relationship is shown graphically in Figure 5A.1. We put units of Y on the vertical axis and units of X on the horizontal axis, and then plot the pairs of points from the table. The points are then connected. The points trace a downward-sloping line starting at the upper left at $X = 0$ and $Y = 5$ and ending on the right with $X = 10$ and $Y = 0$. All the other combinations of X and Y in the table, such as $X = 4$ and $Y = 3$, are shown on the line. If it is possible to consume fractions of X and Y, then all the points on the line between the plotted points can also be purchased with the $20.

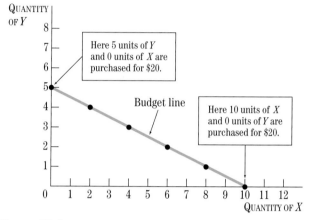

Figure 5A.1
Budget Line for a Consumer
The line shows how much a consumer with $20 can consume of quantity X at a price of $2 per unit and quantity Y at $4 per unit. If $20 is spent on Y and nothing on X, then 5 units of Y can be purchased, as shown on the vertical axis. If $20 is spent on X and nothing on Y, then 10 units of X can be purchased, as shown on the vertical axis. Other combinations are shown on the line.

(For example, 2.5 units of Y and 5 units of X would cost $20: 2.5 × $4 + 5 × $2 = $20.) Because all these pairs of X and Y on this line can be purchased with a $20 budget, we call it the **budget line.** The consumer is constrained to buy combinations of X and Y that are either on or below the budget line. Amounts of X and Y consumed below the budget line cost less than $20. Points above the line require more than $20 and are not feasible.

The budget line will shift out if the consumer has more to spend, as shown in Figure 5A.2. For example, if the consumer has $24 rather than $20, then the budget line will shift up by 1 unit because the extra $4 permits the consumer to buy 1 more unit of Y. Alternatively, we could say that the budget line shifts to the right by 2 units in this case because the consumer can buy 2 more units of X with $4 more.

The steepness of the budget line depends on the prices of X and Y. In particular, the slope of the budget line is equal to -1 times the ratio of the price of X to the price of Y. That is, slope $= -(P_X/P_Y)$, which is $-\frac{1}{2}$ in this example. Why is the slope determined by the price ratio? Recall that the slope is the change in Y divided by the change in X. Along the budget line, as X is increased by 1 unit, Y must fall by $\frac{1}{2}$ unit: Buying 1 more unit of X costs

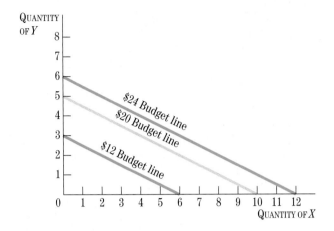

Figure 5A.2
Effect of a Change in Income on the Budget Line
If the consumer has more to spend, then the budget line is farther out. If the consumer has less to spend, then the budget line is farther in. Here a higher and a lower budget line are compared with the $20 budget line in Figure 5A.1.

$2 and requires buying ½ unit less of Y. Thus, the slope is −½.

In order to derive the demand curve for X, we need to find out what happens when the price of X changes. What happens to the budget line when the price of X increases from $2 to $4, for example? The budget line twists down, as shown in Figure 5A.3. The intuitive rationale for the twist is that the slope steepens to $-(P_X/P_Y) = -\$4/\$4 = -1$, and the position of $X = 0$ and $Y = 5$ on the vertical axis does not change, because 5 units of Y can still be

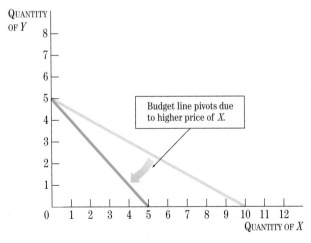

Figure 5A.3
Effect of a Higher Price of X on the Budget Line
The budget line pivots if the price of X changes. Here the price of X rises from $2 to $4 and the budget line twists down.

purchased. You can show this by creating a new table with pairs of X and Y that can be purchased with $20 at the new price and then plotting the points.

To summarize, we have shown how a budget line represents the budget constraint for the consumer; now we show how to represent the consumer's preferences.

The Indifference Curve

Utility is an indicator of how a consumer prefers one combination of items in comparison with another. If the level of utility is the same for two combinations of X and Y, then the consumer is *indifferent* between the two combinations. Suppose that the utility is the same for the combinations of X and Y that appear below.

Units of Y	Units of X
6	1
4	2
2	6
1	12

The consumer is indifferent among these combinations. Observe that these amounts are inversely related. As consumption of Y declines, the consumer must be compensated with more X if the level of utility is not to decline.

We can plot these different amounts on the same type of graph we used for the budget line, as shown in Figure 5A.4. The consumer is indifferent among all four points. We have connected the points with a curve to

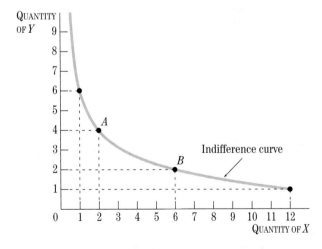

Figure 5A.4
An Indifference Curve for a Consumer
The consumer is indifferent between A and B or any other point on an indifference curve. For example, the consumer is indifferent between consuming 4 units of Y and 2 of X or 2 units of Y and 6 of X.

represent other combinations of X and Y about which the consumer is indifferent. The curve is called an **indifference curve** because the consumer is indifferent among all points on the curve. The indifference curve slopes downward from left to right.

The slope of the indifference curve can be found from the marginal utility, X and Y. **Marginal utility** is *the increase in utility from consuming an additional unit of a good.* For example, look back at Figure 5.2 and consider the marginal utility of increasing consumption of grapes by 1 additional pound, from 3 pounds to 4 pounds. You will see that utility increases by 2 when grape consumption increases from 3 pounds to 4 pounds. Thus, the marginal utility of grapes is 2 at the amount of consumption. Let MU_X be the marginal utility of X and let MU_Y be the marginal utility of Y.

The slope of the indifference curve is equal to negative 1 times the ratio of the marginal utility of X to the marginal utility of Y; that is, slope = $-(MU_X/MU_Y)$. The reason is that utility is the same for all points on an indifference curve. In other words, the decline in utility as X falls $(-MU_X \times \Delta X)$ must equal the increase in utility as Y rises $(MU_Y \times \Delta Y)$. Thus, $(MU_X \times \Delta X) = -(-MU_Y \times \Delta Y)$, or $-MU_X/MU_Y = \Delta Y/\Delta X$, which is the slope of the indifference curve.

Note that the indifference curve is bowed in toward the origin. That is, the indifference curve is steep when a small amount of X is consumed and flat when a large amount of X is consumed. This curvature is due to the declining marginal rate of substitution. When the consumer is consuming only a little bit of X, a large amount of Y is required as compensation for a reduction in X. As X increases, less of Y is required as compensation.

The ratio of marginal utilities MU_X/MU_Y is called the **marginal rate of substitution;** it gives the number of units of one good (Y) for which the consumer is willing to trade one unit of the other good (X) and have the same amount of utility—or be indifferent. For example, if the marginal rate of substitution is 4, then the consumer is willing to trade 4 units of Y for 1 unit of X with utility remaining the same.

We can represent higher levels of utility or more preferred combinations of X and Y by higher indifference curves, as shown in Figure 5A.5. Any point on a higher indifference curve is preferred to any point on a lower indifference curve.

Getting to the Highest Indifference Curve Given the Budget Line

Now we can combine the budget line and the indifference curves on the same diagram to illustrate the model of consumer behavior. Utility maximization subject to the budget constraint means getting to the highest possible indifference curve without going above the budget line. The process is shown in Figure 5A.6. The budget line

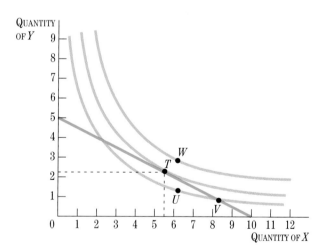

Figure 5A.5
Higher and Lower Indifference Curves
Amounts of X and Y on indifference curves that are higher are preferred to amounts on indifference curves that are lower. Of the three combinations C, D, and E, the combination at D is the least preferred and the combination at C is the most preferred.

Figure 5A.6
The Best Choice for the Consumer
When the budget line is tangent to the indifference curve, the consumer cannot do any better. The point of tangency is at point T. Compare this with the other points. Point U is not the best point because it is inside the budget line. Point V is not the best point because there are other points on the budget line that are preferred. Point W is preferred to point T, but it is not feasible.

from Figure 5A.1 and the indifference curves from Figure 5A.5 are shown in the diagram. The consumer cannot go beyond the budget line, and any point inside the budget line is inferior to points on the budget line. Thus the combination of X and Y with the highest utility must be on the budget line. The highest indifference curve with points on the budget line is the one that just touches—is tangent to—the budget line. This occurs at point T in Figure 5A.6. The **tangency point** is the highest level of utility the consumer can achieve subject to the budget constraint. It is the combination of X and Y that the consumer chooses. Figure 5A.6 shows that, in this example, the consumer buys $2^1/_4$ units of Y and $5^1/_2$ units of X.

The Utility-Maximizing Rule

Observe that at the tangency point, the slope of the budget line is equal to the slope of the indifference curve. That is, $P_X/P_Y = MU_X/MU_Y$. In other words, the ratio of the price of two goods equals the ratio of the marginal utility of the two goods as long as the consumer is maximizing utility. This equality between the price ratio and the ratio of the marginal utilities, or the marginal rate of substitution, is called the *utility-maximizing rule.*

Effect of a Price Change on the Quantity Demanded

Now suppose that the price of X increases; then the budget line twists down, as shown in the lower panel of Figure 5A.7. With the new budget line, the old consumer choice of $2^1/_4$ units of X and $5^1/_2$ units of Y is no longer feasible: Point T is outside the new budget line. The highest level of utility the consumer can now achieve is at point S in the lower panel of Figure 5A.7. At point S, the quantity of X has declined. Thus, a higher price of X has reduced the quantity of X demanded.

In the top graph in Figure 5A.7, we show the relationship between the price of X and the quantity of X demanded. The price of X is put on the vertical axis, and the quantity of X demanded is put on the horizontal axis. The lower quantity demanded at the higher price shows the negative slope of the demand curve.

Effect of an Income Change on Demand

We can also examine what happens when the consumer's income changes but the price remains constant. This is illustrated in Figure 5A.8, where income declines. The lower income leads to less consumption of both X and Y. In this case, both X and Y are normal goods because consumption goes down when income goes down. If the consumption of X increased as the budget curve shifted in, then X would be an inferior good.

Graphical Illustration of Income Effect and Substitution Effect

The effect of a change in the price on the quantity demanded can be divided into an income effect and a substitution effect. These two effects can be represented graphically as shown in Figure 5A.9.

As in Figure 5A.7, there is a twist in the budget line due to the higher price of X. But now we draw in another budget line—the dashed line in Figure 5A.8—corresponding to a lower level of income due to the higher price of X, but without twisting the line. This budget line has the same slope as the original line. Thus the dashed budget line shows the reduction in income due to the price increase of X but keeps the relative price of X to Y the same as it was before the price of X increased. The

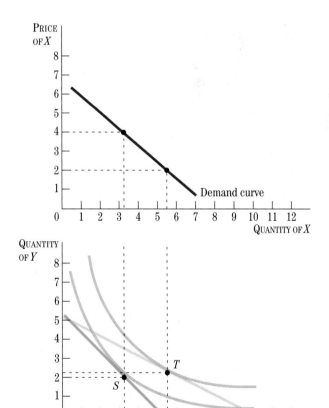

Figure 5A.7
An Increase in the Price of X
If the price of X rises, the budget line pivots down and the consumer's choice changes from point T to point S in the lower panel. The quantity of X consumed goes down. The price of X and the quantity of X are plotted in the top panel, showing the negative relationship between price and quantity demanded.

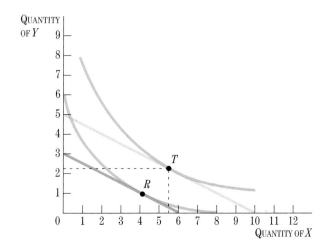

Figure 5A.8
A Decrease in Income
If the consumer's income falls, there is a new point at which utility is maximized: The consumer moves from point *T* to point *R*. In this case, consumption of both *X* and *Y* declines. Neither good is an inferior good in this example.

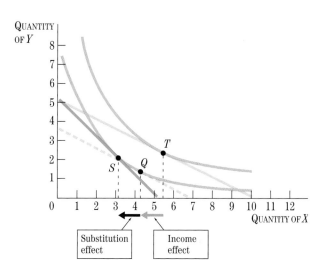

Figure 5A.9
Illustration of Income Effect and Substitution Effect of a Price Change
The dashed budget line has the same slope as the original line and leads to the income effect. The rest of the decline in the quantity of *X* is the substitution effect.

dashed line can be used to find the income effect without the substitution effect because it has the same slope as the original budget line.

   Observe that the tangency of this dashed budget line with the indifference curve at *Q* gives a lower level of consumption of *X* compared with the original point *T*. The decline of consumption from *T* to *Q* is the income effect. The remaining decline from *Q* to *S* is the substitution effect.

Key Points

1. The budget line represents the consumer's budget constraint in a diagram with the quantity consumed of each of two goods on the axes.

2. The budget line is downward-sloping, with the slope equal to negative 1 times the ratio of the price of the good on the horizontal axis to the price of the good on the vertical axis.

3. A higher price of the good on the horizontal axis twists the budget line down.

4. An indifference curve shows the combinations of goods among which the consumer is indifferent.

5. Combinations of goods on higher indifference curves are preferred to combinations of goods on lower indifference curves.

6. The model of consumer behavior assumes that the consumer tries to get to the highest possible indifference curve without going beyond the budget line.

7. The consumer chooses the combination at the tangency of the budget line and the indifference curve.

8. A higher price of a good lowers the quantity demanded, according to the indifference curve and budget line diagram.

Key Terms and Definitions

budget line: a line showing the maximum combinations of two goods that it is possible for a consumer to buy, given a budget constraint and the market prices of the two goods.

indifference curve: a curve showing the combinations of two goods that leave the consumer with the same level of utility.

marginal utility: the increase in utility when consumption of a good increases by one unit.

marginal rate of substitution: the amount of one good for which the consumer is willing to trade one unit of another good and still have the same utility.

tangency point: the only point in common for two curves; the point where the two curves just touch.

Questions for Review

1. Why does the budget line slope downward?

2. What determines the slope of the budget line?

3. Why does the indifference curve slope downward?

4. Why does the consumer choose a point where the indifference curve is tangent to the budget line?

Problems

1. Draw a diagram like Figure 5A.7. Assume that income is $20, the price of good X is $2, and the price of good Y is $4.
   a. Show what happens to the budget line if the price of X falls from $2 to $1.60. What is the maximum amount of X that can be purchased?
   b. Illustrate the new point of consumer choice (by drawing the appropriate indifference curve).
   c. Show the demand curve for the consumer.

2. Darnell has $30 to spend on either muffins, which cost $3 each, or cartons of orange juice, which cost $1.50 each.
   a. Graph Darnell's budget line for muffins and orange juice. What is the maximum quantity of orange juice that Darnell can buy with $30?
   b. Suppose the price of orange juice increases to $2 per carton. Show the change in the budget line.
   c. Draw indifference curves to show the change in consumption of orange juice, assuming that orange juice is a normal good.

3. Suppose the consumer in Figure 5A.7 has $24 to spend rather than $20. Draw two diagrams—one in which X is a normal good and one in which X is an inferior good.

4. Sarah has $20 to spend on slices of pizza and cans of diet cola. Pizza costs $1 per slice, and diet cola costs $.50 per can.
   a. Graph Sarah's budget line for pizza and diet cola.
   b. Suppose Sarah's total budget for pizza and diet cola increases to $25. How does her budget line shift?
   c. Draw a set of indifference curves for the situation in which pizza is a normal good, and one for the situation in which pizza is an inferior good.

5. Suppose the consumer is consuming at a point on the budget line that is not tangent to an indifference curve. Explain why utility is not being maximized at this point.

CHAPTER 6

The Supply Curve and the Behavior of Firms

Americans love their bumper stickers. They buy tens of thousands of them every year to proclaim their loyalty to movements, political candidates, schools, or a particular way of life. But some people who would like to express their views on their car might hesitate before applying a sticker that could be hard to remove later on. So when yellow-ribbon car magnets proclaiming support for U.S. troops in Iraq showed up in stores in 2003, many people eagerly bought them, paying far more for the magnets (around $5 each) than the pennies it cost to produce them—creating, in economic terminology, a *producer surplus*. Dwain Gullion, who began the whole craze with the casual production of 1,000 magnets he intended to sell at his Christian bookstore, had to gear up production fast. By the summer of 2004, Gullion's new company, Magnet America, was shipping more than 100,000 magnets a week and employing more than 100 contract workers. Other firms quickly got into the act, and soon Gullion had some hard decisions to make about his business.

In this chapter, we look at the behavior of firms such as Magnet America. The behavior of firms can be described by supply curves like the one shown in Figure 6.1. The supply curve tells us how much all the firms in the market—not just a single firm like Magnet America—would produce at each price.

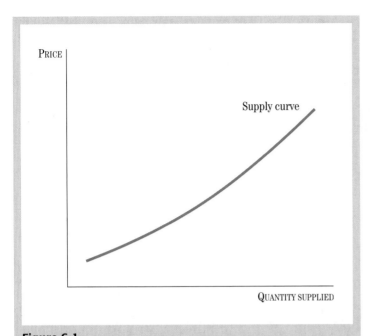

Figure 6.1
A Typical Supply Curve for a Market
Supply curves typically slope upward. In this chapter, we look at the factors that motivate firms in the market to increase the quantity supplied as the price rises.

As with our study of the consumers who underlie the demand curve in Chapter 5, there are two important reasons to study the firms that underlie the supply curve. First, we want to show why the supply curve has the slope and position it does. Such information enables us to assess how a change in technology or trends or a new government policy affects the supply curve. Second, we want to show how and why a supply curve can be used to measure the "producer surplus" of firms.

This chapter on supply parallels Chapter 5, on demand, and we will exploit that parallel to make our analysis easier. Recall from Chapter 1 that the central idea of economics is that *people make purposeful choices with scarce resources and interact with other people when they make these choices*. In Chapter 5, we looked at consumers making purposeful choices with scarce resources by assuming that they maximize utility subject to a budget constraint. In this chapter, we look at firms making purposeful choices with scarce resources by assuming that they maximize profits subject to a production function (see Figure 6.2). In Chapter 7, we consider the interaction of consumers and firms in markets as they make these choices.

Basic Economic Principle	When Applied to the Behavior of Consumers	When Applied to the Behavior of Firms
People…	*Consumers…*	*Firms…*
make purposeful choices…	maximize utility…	maximize profits…
with scarce resources.	subject to a budget constraint relating expenditure to income.	subject to a production function relating output to input.

Figure 6.2
Applying the Central Idea of Economics
People make purposeful choices with scarce resources and interact with other people when they make these choices. In Chapter 5, the people were the consumers. In this chapter, they are the firms. In Chapter 7, the consumers and the firms interact with each other.

The new terms introduced in this chapter have analogies with terms introduced in Chapter 5. For example, we will explicitly define producer surplus and compare it to consumer surplus. We will derive a supply curve for an individual firm, which will tell us the quantity of a good the firm would supply at different prices. The supply curve for an individual firm is analogous to the demand curve for an individual consumer, which tells us the quantity of a good the individual consumer demands at different prices.

Definition of a Firm

firm: an organization that produces goods or services.

We start by looking at the behavior of a single firm. A **firm**, by definition, is an organization that produces goods or services. Just as no two consumers are exactly alike, no two firms are exactly alike. A firm can be a small family farm in the country or a grocery store in the city. Bakeries, restaurants, auto dealers, and bicycle shops are all examples of firms that are usually relatively small. Other firms—such as General Motors—are very large, producing many different products in large volume.

The terms *firm, company*, and *business* are used interchangeably. A firm may include several *establishments*, which are separate physical locations, such as an office, a factory, or a store, where work is done. For example, the U.S.-based grocery chain Kroger is a firm with over 2,000 establishments—more than 1,000 supermarkets and more than 1,000 convenience stores, including 208 Kwik-Starts and 105 Mini-Marts. Of course, many small firms have only one establishment.

In the United States, about 80 percent of all firms are *sole proprietorships*, with one owner, or *partnerships*, with only a few owners, who usually manage the firm. Most of these are very small when compared with corporations like General Motors. A *corporation* is unlike a sole proprietorship or partnership in that the managers are usually somewhat removed from the owners. For example, most people who own shares of General Motors never even meet the managers of the firm. This separation of managers and owners means that the managers must be given an incentive to keep the owners' interests in mind. A common incentive is to have managers share in the profits of the firm.

You might expect that the decisions made by the managers of a firm are more complicated—and consequently more difficult to understand—than the decisions made by consumers. Of course, many more people have had the experience of being a consumer than have had the experience of managing a firm. But if you can picture yourself as the owner/manager of your own firm, you will see that the economics of a firm's decision about how much to sell is analogous to the economics of a consumer's decision about how much to buy.

Your Own Firm: A Pumpkin Patch

Imagine that you are the owner and manager of a firm that grows pumpkins on a pumpkin patch; the patch has good soil and gets plenty of rain. Your firm is one of many specializing in growing and selling pumpkins—in other words, there are many other firms with which you must compete. During the spring and summer you grow the pumpkins, and in the fall you sell them. As owner and manager of the firm, you must pay rent at the start of each growing season to the landlord who owns the pumpkin patch. During the season, you hire workers to tend the patch. The more workers tending the pumpkins, the more pumpkins you can grow on the patch.

Your firm is typical of many small firms and has features that apply to larger firms as well. Your firm is one with a single product (pumpkins) and two factors of production—land (the patch) and labor (the workers). One of the factors of production, land, cannot be changed during the season because the rent was paid in advance; this makes land a *fixed factor*. The other factor, labor, can be varied during the season, because you can choose to hire more or fewer workers; this makes labor a *variable factor*.

Your Firm as a Price-Taker in a Competitive Market

Keep your firm in mind as you go through this chapter. It will be referred to often. Our aim is to determine the supply curve for a firm like your firm. *A supply curve for a single firm tells us the quantity of a good that that firm will produce at different prices.* To find the supply curve, we imagine that the firm looks at the price of the good it is selling and then decides how much to produce. For example, a baker considers the price of a loaf of bread prevailing in the market when deciding how many loaves of bread to produce. Because the firm takes the price in the market as a given when it makes a decision about production, we say that the firm is a **price-taker.** We assume that your pumpkin firm is a price-taker. This means that you decide how much to produce and sell after looking at the price of pumpkins in the market.

price-taker: any firm that takes the market price as given; this firm cannot affect the market price because the market is competitive.

This description of a firm as a price-taker may seem odd to you. After all, if the firm doesn't set the price, then who does? Of course, in some sense, each firm does. If you go to a bakery for a loaf of bread, a price tag states the price of the loaf, so the baker is clearly determining the price. But this is not the way economists look at it; there is a subtlety here in the way economists describe the market. When there are many bakers selling bread, in an important sense, the individual bakers do not have the ability to affect the price by much. If one baker charges $3 for a loaf of bread, and all the other bakers in the community charge $1.50 for the same loaf, no one will buy bread from the first baker. People will not even go to the store if they know the price is that high. They will go to other bakeries, where bread sells for $1.50 a loaf. Although in principle an individual firm has the ability to set any price it wants, in reality a firm cannot charge a price far from the price that prevails in the market without soon losing all its customers.

competitive market: a market in which no firm has the power to affect the market price of a good.

A market in which a single firm cannot affect the market price is called a **competitive market.** The market for fresh bread, with many bakeries in any reasonably sized community, is competitive. Because many firms are producing pumpkins along with your pumpkin firm, the pumpkin market is also competitive. A competitive market requires that there be at least several firms competing with one another. Exactly how many firms are required to make a market competitive is difficult to say without studying the market carefully—as we do in later chapters. If a market is competitive, so that firms are price-takers, then we can derive a supply curve by asking, "How much bread would the baker produce if the price of bread were $1 a loaf? $1.50 a loaf? $2 a loaf?" and so on. Or, in the case of your pumpkin firm, "How many pumpkins would the pumpkin firm produce if the price of pumpkins were $35 a crate? $70 a crate?" and so on.

Other Types of Markets

Not all markets are as competitive as the fresh bread market or the pumpkin market, and part of our job later in the book is to study these markets. The exact opposite of a competitive market is where there is only one firm, in which case the firm is called a *monopoly*. Strictly speaking, a monopoly does not have a supply curve because the monopoly does not take the price as given. Instead, the monopoly can dictate the price (it is a *price-maker*). The question "How much does the monopoly produce at a given price?" has no meaning because the monopoly need not take the price as given. We consider monopolies in Chapter 10. For now we focus on the price-taking firms in a competitive market.

This subtlety about firms taking prices as given does not seem to arise in the case of the consumer. In deriving the demand curve in Chapter 5, we assumed that the individual consumer could not affect the price. This seems natural because we do not usually see buyers setting the price for bread or other commodities. As long as there are at least several buyers and several sellers in the market, we can assume that the price is taken as given by both buyers and sellers. In Chapter 7, when we study the interaction of buyers and sellers in markets, we will show how the market price is determined.

REVIEW
- There are a great variety of sizes and types of firms.
- A market is competitive if no single firm can affect the market price.
- In a competitive market with many firms, each firm is a price-taker.
- The supply curve of a firm describes how the quantity produced depends on the price.

The Firm's Profits

profits: total revenue received from selling the product minus the total costs of producing the product.

Profits for any firm—a bakery producing bread or a farm producing pumpkins—are defined as the *total revenue* received from selling the product minus the *total costs* of producing the product. That is,

Profits = total revenue − total costs

When profits are negative—total revenue is less than total costs—the firm runs a *loss*. When profits are zero—total revenue is equal to total costs—the firm is *breaking even*.

We assume that the firm *maximizes* profits. That is, the firm decides on the quantity of production that will make profits as high as possible. To see how this is done, we must examine how profits depend on the quantity produced. To do this, we must consider how total revenue and total costs—the two determinants of profits—depend on the quantity produced. We consider first total revenue and then total costs.

Total Revenue

total revenue: the price per unit times the quantity the firm sells.

Total revenue is the total number of dollars the firm receives from people who buy its product. Total revenue can be computed by multiplying the price of each unit sold by the quantity sold. That is,

$$\text{Total revenue} = \text{price} \times \text{quantity}$$
$$= P \times Q$$

Table 6.1
Total Revenue from Pumpkin Production at Three Prices

Quantity Produced (crates)	Total Revenue		
	Price = $35/crate	*Price = $70/crate*	*Price = $100/crate*
0	0	0	0
1	35	70	100
2	70	140	200
3	105	210	300
4	140	280	400
5	175	350	500

where we use the letter P to stand for price and Q to stand for quantity. Because we are looking at an individual firm and a particular product, P is the price of the particular product the individual firm is selling, and Q is the number of items the firm sells. There are a variety of ways to measure the quantity sold: numbers of crates of pumpkins, slices of pizza, loaves of bread, quarts of milk, kilowatts of electricity, and so on. In the United States, pounds and tons are usually used to measure items like coal, grapes, wheat, and sugar, but kilos would do as well.

Note that total revenue depends both on the price of the item being sold and on the number of items sold. For example, if the price of bread is $1.50 per loaf and 100 loaves are sold, then total revenue is $150. If the price rises to $2 a loaf and 200 loaves are sold, then total revenue is $400. The more items sold at a given price, the higher total revenue is. Thus, the firm can increase total revenue by producing and selling more goods.

Table 6.1 shows how total revenue increases with the quantity produced for your firm producing pumpkins. Each row of the table shows the total revenue the firm receives from selling varying amounts of pumpkins. Each column showing total revenue corresponds to a different price: $35 per crate, $70 per crate, and $100 per crate. For example, when the firm can get $70 per crate, it receives $280 for selling 4 crates.

Production and Costs

total costs: the sum of variable costs and fixed costs.

Now that we have seen how total revenue depends on the quantity produced, let's examine how total costs depend on the quantity produced. **Total costs** are what the firm has to incur in order to produce the product. For your pumpkin firm, total costs include the workers' salaries and the rent on the land. To see how total costs depend on the quantity produced, we must look at what happens to the quantity of labor and land used by the firm when the quantity produced increases or decreases.

Reminder: In Chapter 1, we saw that costs include *opportunity costs*. Thus, total costs for your pumpkin firm would include the opportunity cost of any time you spent operating the firm rather than doing something else, like studying for an exam. To emphasize that opportunity costs are included in total costs when computing profits, economists sometimes use the term *economic profits* rather than simply profits.

■ **The Time Period.** We look at the firm's production decisions over a short period of time—such as one growing season—rather than over a long period of time—such as several growing seasons. Because we focus on the short run, we assume that only the labor input to production can be varied. Our analysis of the firm in this chapter is called a *short-run* analysis because the time is too short to change the other factors of production, such as land; only labor can be changed. We make this assumption simply because it is easier to examine the firm's decisions when only one factor of production can be changed. It is a simplifying assumption that we will modify. In Chapter 8 we take up the *long run*, in which other factors of production—such as the size of the pumpkin patch—can change as well as labor.

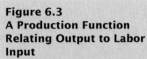

Figure 6.3
A Production Function Relating Output to Labor Input
As more workers are employed, production increases. But the increase in production added by each additional hour of work declines as more workers are hired because the land the workers have to work with does not increase. Thus, there is a decreasing marginal product of labor, or diminishing returns to labor.

production function: a relationship that shows the quantity of output for any given amount of input.

marginal product of labor: the change in production due to a one-unit increase in labor input.

diminishing returns to labor: a situation in which the increase in output due to a unit increase in labor declines with increasing labor input; a decreasing marginal product of labor.

◼ **The Production Function.** Figure 6.3 plots the relationship between pumpkin production and labor input. The number of hours of work is on the horizontal axis, and the quantity produced is on the vertical axis. Each point in Figure 6.3 shows the number of hours of work and the quantity of pumpkins produced: To produce 3 crates requires 10 hours of work; to produce 5 crates requires 30 hours of work. Clearly, more pumpkin production requires more labor input. The graph in Figure 6.3 is called the firm's **production function** because it tells us how much is produced for each amount of labor input. This production function is for a given size of pumpkin patch.

The **marginal product of labor** is defined as the increase in production that comes from an additional unit of labor. Figure 6.3 shows that the marginal product of labor *declines* as labor input increases. Because of the curvature of the production function, the same increase in hours of work leads to a smaller increase in production when labor input is large than when labor input is small.

Another term for the phenomenon of declining marginal product of labor is **diminishing returns to labor.** In your pumpkin firm, diminishing returns to labor occur as additional workers are employed. As more and more workers are employed on a given amount of land, each additional worker adds less and less additional output. Diminishing returns is a general phenomenon that occurs when some inputs to production—such as land or machines—are fixed. Because the size of your pumpkin patch is fixed, additional workers must eventually add less to production. Otherwise a single plot of land could produce all the world's pumpkins by employing huge numbers of workers. Thus, the return to each additional worker declines. Diminishing returns to labor occur in nonagricultural examples as well. Employing more and more workers at a single McDonald's will increase the amount of fast food produced by less and less.

◼ **Costs.** Table 6.2 shows how total costs depend on the quantity of pumpkins produced at your pumpkin firm. The first column shows the quantity of pumpkins

Table 6.2
Example of Costs for a Single Firm

Quantity Produced (crates)	Hours of Labor Input	Variable Costs at $10 Wage (dollars)	Fixed Costs (dollars)	Total Costs (dollars)
0	0	0	50	50
1	2	20	50	70
2	5	50	50	100
3	10	100	50	150
4	18	180	50	230
5	30	300	50	350

produced. The second column shows the labor input required to produce that quantity of pumpkins, using the production function from Figure 6.3. The other columns show how total costs are determined.

The first row shows how much it costs if you decide to produce zero pumpkins. We assume that you have to pay $50 up front for rent on the patch even if you decide to produce no pumpkins. These payments are considered *fixed costs* because they must be paid no matter how many pumpkins are produced. By definition, **fixed costs** are the part of total costs that do not depend on how much is produced.

fixed costs: costs of production that do not depend on the quantity of production.

The next row of Table 6.2 shows the costs of producing 1 crate of pumpkins. The additional costs of producing 1 crate compared to zero crates are $20. That is payment for 2 hours of work at $10 per hour. The $20 in payments are **variable costs**

variable costs: costs of production that vary with the quantity of production.

because they vary according to how much is produced. These costs are variable because more workers are hired as more is produced. Variable costs and fixed costs together constitute all the costs of producing the product and must be subtracted from revenue to get profits. Hence, *the sum of fixed costs and variable costs equals total costs*, as shown in the last column of Table 6.2.

The third row of Table 6.2 shows the costs of producing 2 crates of pumpkins. Clearly 2 crates are more costly to produce than 1 crate because more workers are needed. Variable costs, with 5 hours of work at $10 per hour, rise to $50. As more pumpkins are harvested, more workers must be hired, and the total costs increase. The remaining rows of Table 6.2 show what happens to costs as the quantity produced increases further.

Diminishing Returns to Labor
Adding the second worker to this machine in a French vineyard increased the quantity of grapes produced by much less than the first worker did. Adding a third worker to the machine would increase the quantity of grapes produced by even less than adding the second worker did. Thus, this is an example of a decreasing marginal product of labor, or diminishing returns to labor.

Table 6.3
Total Costs and Marginal Cost

Quantity Produced (crates)	Total Costs (dollars)	Marginal Cost (dollars)
0	50	—
1	70	20
2	100	30
3	150	50
4	230	80
5	350	120

The connecting lines emphasize how marginal cost is the change in total costs as the quantity produced increases by one unit.

marginal cost: the change in total costs due to a one-unit change in quantity produced.

Marginal cost is defined as the increase in total costs associated with an additional unit of production. Table 6.3 shows how marginal cost is calculated for the example in Table 6.2. For example, the marginal cost of increasing production from 1 crate to 2 crates is $30 ($100 − $70 = $30), and the marginal cost of increasing production from 2 crates to 3 crates is $50 ($150 − $100 = $50).

Notice how marginal cost increases as production increases. Marginal cost is greater when we go from 2 to 3 crates ($50) than when we go from 1 to 2 crates ($30). The pattern of *increasing marginal cost* is apparent throughout the range of production in Table 6.3.

Observe that *increasing marginal cost is due to the diminishing marginal product of labor:* The marginal cost of going from 2 crates to 3 crates is greater than that of going from 1 crate to 2 crates because more worker hours are required to raise production from 2 crates to 3 crates than are required to raise production from 1 crate to 2 crates.

Increasing marginal cost is a general phenomenon that occurs in many production processes. It is essential for deriving the supply curve. In fact, as we will see, increasing marginal cost is the whole reason that the supply curve for an individual firm slopes upward.

There are exceptions to the principle of increasing marginal cost. One important exception is that marginal cost need not be increasing over the entire range of production. For example, there might be a decrease in marginal cost at very low levels of production. If a team of at least two workers is needed to harvest pumpkins, for example, then the marginal product of a second worker might be greater than the marginal product of a first worker. One worker might add very little, whereas the second might add a lot. But diminishing returns to labor and increasing marginal cost eventually set in as more workers are hired and more pumpkins are produced.

This chapter assumes that marginal cost increases over the whole range of production. This is a common assumption used by economists and is a good approximation except for very low levels of production. In Chapter 8, we will see what happens when marginal cost declines at low levels of production.

■ **Graphical Representation of Total Costs and Marginal Cost.**   A better understanding of how a firm's total costs depend on production can be obtained by representing the total costs graphically. Figure 6.4 plots the pairs of numbers for total costs and quantity produced from the first two columns of Table 6.3. Dollars are on the vertical axis, and the quantity of pumpkins produced is on the horizontal axis. Note how the total costs curve bends up: As marginal cost increases, the curve gets

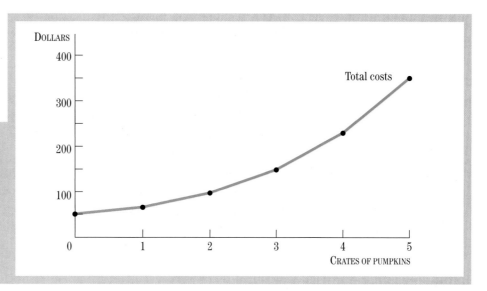

**Figure 6.4
Total Costs**
In order to produce goods, a firm incurs costs. For example, more workers must be paid to produce more goods. As more goods are produced, the firm's total costs rise, as shown here. At higher levels of production, costs increase by larger amounts for each additional item produced.

steeper, or the slope increases. The marginal cost is the slope of the total costs curve. The increasing slope is a visual way to show the increasing marginal cost.

Figure 6.5 shows the relationship between marginal cost and number of crates of pumpkins produced. The points in Figure 6.5 correspond to the pairs of numbers in the first and third columns of Table 6.3. Note that the marginal cost curve slopes upward, illustrating how marginal cost increases. The firm's objective to maximize

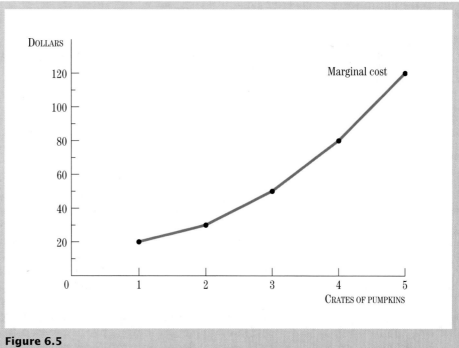

**Figure 6.5
Marginal Cost**
The change in total costs as more units of the good are produced is called marginal cost. Marginal cost increases as more units are produced, as illustrated here.

profits, coupled with the shape of the marginal cost curve, determines the upward-sloping supply curve, as we explain in the next section.

REVIEW
- Profits are defined as the difference between total revenue and total costs.
- Profits depend on the quantity produced because both total revenue and total costs depend on the quantity produced.
- Total revenue is defined as the price (P) times the quantity (Q) produced and sold. Total revenue increases as the quantity produced increases.
- Total costs increase with the quantity produced because it takes more inputs—such as workers—to produce more output.
- Marginal cost increases as more is produced because of diminishing returns to labor. As labor is increased with a fixed amount of capital, the increase in output from each additional unit of labor declines.

Profit Maximization and the Individual Firm's Supply Curve

profit maximization: an assumption that firms try to achieve the highest possible level of profits—total revenue minus total costs—given their production function.

To derive the firm's supply curve, we assume that the firm chooses a quantity of production that maximizes profits. This is the assumption of **profit maximization.** Now that we have seen how profits depend on the quantity produced, we can proceed to show how the firm chooses a quantity to maximize profits.

An Initial Approach to Derive the Supply Curve

Continuing with our pumpkin firm, we create a table that uses total revenue and total costs to calculate profits. Because total revenue depends on the price, we need a separate panel for each of three possible prices.

■ **A Profit Table.**   Table 6.4 shows profits for your pumpkin firm. Total revenue, shown in the third column, increases with the number of pumpkins sold. Because total revenue depends on the price, we need a separate panel showing profits for each price. Table 6.4 has three panels, one for each of three possible prices. (The prices are the same as in Table 6.1.) Suppose the price of pumpkins is $35 a crate. Then if you sell 1 crate, the revenue is $35; if you sell 2 crates, the revenue is $70, and so on. Total revenue equals the price ($35) times the number of crates sold. Clearly, if no pumpkins are sold, the total revenue will be zero. Panels II and III show total revenue for two higher prices—$70 per crate and $100 per crate. For each total price, revenue increases as more is produced and sold.

Table 6.4 also shows how total costs increase with production. This is the same information already presented in Table 6.2. We repeat it here so that total costs can easily be compared with total revenue to calculate profits. Note how total costs, like total revenue, increase with production, from $50 for no pumpkins to $350 for 5 crates of pumpkins. The range of total costs is the same for all these panels because total costs do not depend on the price.

Table 6.4
Profit Tables Showing Total Costs and Total Revenue at Different Prices

PANEL I
If price equals $35 per crate, then production equals 2 crates.

Crates	Total Costs	Total Revenue	Profits
0	50	0	−50
1	70	35	−35
2	100	70	−30
3	150	105	−45
4	230	140	−90
5	350	175	−175

PANEL II
If price equals $70 per crate, then production equals 3 crates.

Crates	Total Costs	Total Revenue	Profits
0	50	0	−50
1	70	70	0
2	100	140	40
3	150	210	60
4	230	280	50
5	350	350	0

PANEL III
If price equals $100 per crate, then production equals 4 crates.

Crates	Total Costs	Total Revenue	Profits
0	50	0	−50
1	70	100	30
2	100	200	100
3	150	300	150
4	230	400	170
5	350	500	150

The last column of Table 6.4 shows profits: Total revenue minus total costs. Consider the $35 per crate price in panel I first. When no pumpkins are produced, profits are −$50. You lose $50 because $50 is paid for the land and total revenue is zero. If you produce 1 crate, the loss is $35; in other words, profits are −$35; the total cost of producing 1 crate ($70) minus the revenue from 1 crate ($35) equals −$35. For 2 crates, profits are still negative. Total revenue is $70 while total costs are $100, leaving a loss of $30. Three crates of pumpkins yield a loss of $45.

A glance down the last column in panel I shows that profits are negative at all production levels. In this case, any production at all may seem fruitless. But remember that you already paid $50 for the use of the pumpkin patch. Hence, it is best to produce 2 crates and cut your losses to $30. You still lose, but not as much as by producing only zero or 1 crate. This may seem strange because profits are negative.

But the profit-maximizing level of production is 2 crates. The maximum of profits would be −$30. Stated differently, the minimum loss would be $30.

The same type of profit-maximizing exercise with a different price is illustrated in panel II of Table 6.4. Here the price of pumpkins is $70, and so the total revenue is higher. If you sell nothing, then total revenue is zero and the loss is $50. If you sell 1 crate, total revenue is $70 and profits are zero. But if you sell 2 crates, total costs are $100 and total revenue is $140. Finally, some positive profit can be seen. But profits can be increased further: The profit-maximizing level of production is 3 crates.

Panel III shows profits for a higher price, $100 a crate. At this price, you would produce 4 crates. Profits would be $170. More or less production would lower profits.

In these three cases, you maximize profits by adjusting the quantity supplied. As the price rises from $35 to $70 to $100, the profit-maximizing quantity of pumpkins supplied goes from 2 crates to 3 crates to 4 crates. Thus, the price and the quantity supplied are positively related. This is the positively sloped supply curve.

■ **A Profit Graph.**   The relationship between profits and production for your pumpkin firm given in Table 6.4 can be illustrated with a graph that compares total costs and total revenue. This is done in Figure 6.6. The curved line in the top graph of

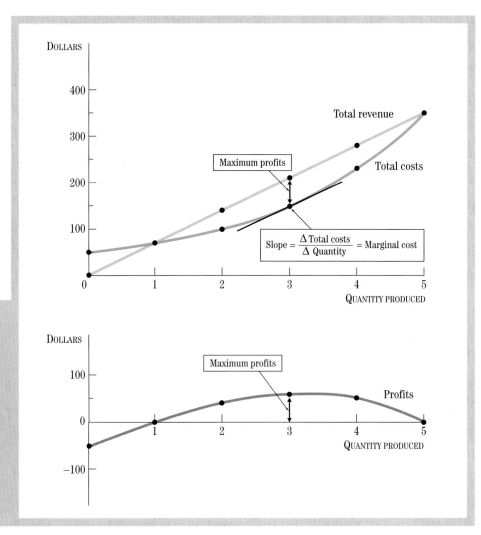

Figure 6.6
An Initial Approach to Profit Maximization
The top panel shows total costs and total revenue for a price of $70 per crate of pumpkins. Profits are the gap between total revenue and total costs. At the profit-maximizing point, the slope of the total costs curve equals the slope of the total revenue line. Hence, price equals marginal cost. The bottom panel shows explicitly how profits first increase and then decrease as production increases.

Figure 6.6 is the total costs curve. It corresponds to the total costs listed in Table 6.4 and is the same as the total costs curve in Figure 6.4. The upward-sloping straight line shows what total revenue would be for a price of $70 per crate. This line corresponds to the total revenue column in panel II of Table 6.4.

Profits are given by the gap between the total revenue line and the total costs curve. The gap—profits—is plotted in the lower panel of Figure 6.6. Note how profits first increase and then decrease as more is produced. The profit-maximizing firm chooses the quantity to produce that leads to the biggest gap, or the biggest level of profits. That quantity is 3 crates of pumpkins.

The Marginal Approach to Derive the Supply Curve

Economists use a different approach to analyzing profit maximization and deriving the supply curve. Once you know this approach, you will find it easier and faster than using total revenue, total costs, and total profits.

Continuing with our pumpkin firm, we first plot the marginal cost from Table 6.3 in Figure 6.7. Focus for now on the black dots in Figure 6.7; we derive the lines in the next few paragraphs. Each dot in Figure 6.7 represents the marginal cost of producing pumpkins at a different level of production. Figure 6.7 summarizes all that we need to know in order to find the quantity that a profit-maximizing firm will produce.

■ **Finding the Quantity Supplied at Different Prices.**   Suppose the price of pumpkins is $10 a crate. Mark this point on the vertical axis of the diagram in Figure 6.7 with an arrow. We are going to derive the supply curve for your pumpkin firm by gradually raising the price from the low $10 value and determining how much you would produce at each price. At $10, the price is less than the marginal cost of producing 1 unit, which is $20, according to Figure 6.7. Would it make sense to produce pumpkins at this price? No, because producing 1 crate of pumpkins has a marginal cost of $20. The *additional* revenue that comes from producing one more

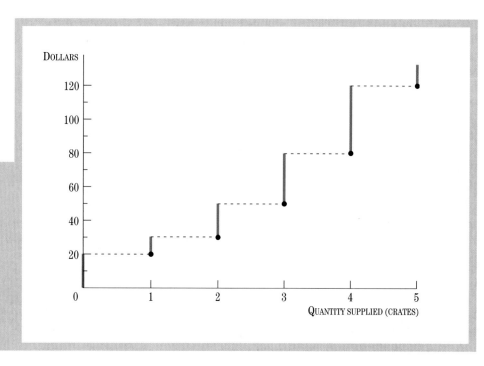

**Figure 6.7
Derivation of the Individual Firm's Supply Curve**
The dots represent the marginal cost from Table 6.3. At each dot, price equals marginal cost. These dots and the thick vertical lines indicate the quantity the firm is willing to supply at each price. Along the vertical lines, the firm produces the quantity that keeps marginal cost closest to price without exceeding it.

marginal revenue: the change in total revenue due to a one-unit increase in quantity sold.

crate is $10. The additional, or extra, revenue that results from producing and selling one more unit of output is called **marginal revenue.** Because laying out $20 and getting back $10 reduces profits, you would not bother to produce any pumpkins. In other words, the marginal cost of increasing production from 0 to 1 crate would be greater than the marginal revenue from selling 1 crate. Producing nothing would be the profit-maximizing thing to do.

Suppose the price of pumpkins rises. Move your arrow up the vertical axis of Figure 6.7. As long as the price is below $20, there is no production. Thus, the amount supplied at prices from $0 to $20 is given by the thick line at the bottom of the vertical axis, where quantity supplied equals zero.

Suppose the price rises to $20. Now the price equals the marginal cost, and the additional, or marginal, revenue from selling a crate of pumpkins will just cover the marginal cost of producing the crate. You now have sufficient incentive to produce some pumpkins. Strictly speaking, the price would have to be a little bit greater than $20 (say, $20.01) for you to earn more by producing 1 crate rather than 0 crates. At a price of exactly $20, you might be indifferent between 0 crates and 1 crate. At a price of $19.99, you would definitely produce nothing. At a price of $20.01, you would definitely produce 1 crate. The price of $20 is right between, but let's assume that you produce 1 crate rather than 0 crates at a price of $20. We indicate this in Figure 6.7 by showing that the quantity supplied is given by the black dot at 1 crate and $20.

Now consider further increases in the price. At prices above $20 up to $30, you would produce 1 crate because the price received for producing an extra crate is less than the marginal cost of $30. However, at a price of $30, the quantity supplied increases to 2 crates because price just equals the marginal cost of increasing production from 1 to 2 crates. A supply curve is now beginning to take shape. You can complete the curve by continuing to raise the price and watching what happens.

To shorten the story, let us move toward the other end of the scale. Suppose the price of pumpkins is $100. At $100, the price is greater than the marginal cost of producing the fourth crate, which is $80. Suppose you are producing 4 crates of pumpkins. Would it make sense to produce another crate? No, because increasing production from 4 crates to 5 crates has a marginal cost of $120. The marginal revenue that comes from producing one more crate is $100. Because laying out $120 and getting back $100 is a losing proposition, you would not do it. Production would stay at 4 crates. If production went up to 5 crates, profits would go down because the marginal cost of producing the fifth crate is greater than the marginal revenue. Producing 5 crates would not be a profit-maximizing thing to do.

What happens if the price rises to $110? At $110 the marginal cost is still less than the price, so it still makes sense to produce 4 crates. What if the price rises to $120? Then the price just equals the marginal cost at 5 crates, and you would produce 5 crates. When the price rises to the marginal cost at five units, then production increases to five units.

We have traced out the complete *individual* supply curve for your firm using Figure 6.7 with the assumption of profit maximization and the concept of marginal cost. The supply curve in Figure 6.7 is steplike; it consists of small vertical segments shooting up from the dots. Strictly speaking, it is only at the dots that price equals marginal cost. On the vertical segments above the dots, the price is actually greater than the marginal cost of production, but the price is not great enough to move on to a higher level of production.

In reality, however, for most products it is possible to divide production into smaller units—half crates, quarter crates, even a single pumpkin. As we do so, the jaggedness of the diagram disappears, as shown in Figure 6.8. It is the simple numerical example with production limited to whole-crate amounts that leads to steps in the supply curve. In reality, the diagram would consist of hundreds of dots rather

Green Pricing and Incentives

Profit maximization shows explicitly *why firms respond to incentives*. When the price of a good rises, a firm can increase its profits by producing more of that good. So the firm responds by producing more. The importance of incentives for firms has not gone unnoticed by practical people who have learned some economics. For example, the environmental group Friends of the Earth was looking for an "energetic person" to take a job as an "economics incentives associate" with responsibility for looking for "incentives for environmental protection."

Environmental protection is an area with fascinating and rapidly growing opportunities to use economic incentives. One of the new ideas is *green pricing*, used to encourage electric power firms to produce electricity using renewable resources, such as solar power or wind power. The goal is to reduce global warming and pollution caused when electricity is produced with coal or oil rather than with the sun or the wind.

Green-pricing programs have already been tried in many cities and states. The programs are very similar. Here is how the program works in Traverse City, Michigan. People agree to pay Traverse City Power and Light (the firm that produces electricity) an extra $7.50 per month (on average) if they can be sure that their electric power is produced with a wind turbine, rather than with a nonrenewable resource. This higher price is enough to cover the higher marginal cost of using wind power and thus gives Traverse City Power and Light the incentive to produce more electricity with wind power. Thus, a higher price for wind-produced electricity leads to a larger amount of wind-produced electricity. Price incentives work once again.

While green-pricing programs focus on firms' incentives (as in this chapter), the analysis in Chapter 5 suggests that such programs will have to focus more on consumers' incentives. People cannot actually tell the difference between wind-produced electricity and coal-produced electricity (both work just as well to power a VCR or a reading light), so they have no incentive to pay the extra amount. They have to volunteer. Perhaps concern for the environment will help get a sizable group of volunteers; Traverse City was considering producing stickers that people could put in their window to

show that "they gave." But critics of green pricing argue that such efforts will never be large enough to have any noticeable effect on global warming or pollution. What do you predict? Will green-pricing programs continue to be small, or could they develop into a large program with a significant effect? Answering that question might be your first assignment if you accepted that job as "economics incentive associate."

than five dots. With hundreds of dots, the vertical segments would be too small to see and the firm's supply curve would be a smooth line. Price would equal marginal cost at every single point.

■ **The Price Equals Marginal Cost Rule.** In deriving the supply curve with Figure 6.7, we have discovered the key condition for profit maximization for a firm in

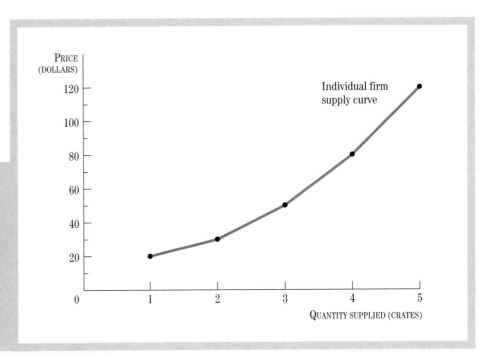

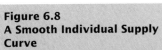

Figure 6.8
A Smooth Individual Supply Curve
If the firm can adjust its production by small amounts, the supply curve becomes a smooth line, as in this figure, rather than a series of steps, as in Figure 6.7. In some cases, such as the building of an airport, a dam, or a suspension bridge, fractions are not possible, and the supply curves will still have steps.

a competitive market: *The firm will choose its quantity such that price equals marginal cost.* You can see that from Figure 6.7. When the price is $80, the firm chooses a level of production for which the marginal cost equals $80 and produces 4 crates.

The price equals marginal cost rule for a competitive firm is a special case of a more general profit-maximization rule that we used, without calling it a rule, in our derivation of the supply curve. This more general rule is that *the firm will choose a quantity to produce so that marginal revenue equals marginal cost.* This more general rule makes intuitive sense for any profit-maximizing firm, whether it is a competitive firm or a monopoly. If the marginal revenue from producing an additional quantity of output is greater than the marginal cost, then the firm should produce that quantity; by doing so, it will increase total revenue by more than it increases total costs, and therefore it will increase profits. However, if the marginal revenue from an additional quantity is less than the marginal cost, then the firm should not produce that quantity. The firm maximizes profits by choosing the quantity of production for which marginal revenue equals marginal cost. Why is the price equals marginal cost rule a special case of the marginal revenue equals marginal cost rule? Because *for the case of a price-taking firm in a competitive market, the marginal revenue is equal to the price.* For example, as we showed above, if the price of pumpkins is $10 per crate, then the marginal, or additional, revenue from producing 1 crate of pumpkins is $10. Later, in Chapter 10, we will show that for a *monopoly*, the marginal revenue does not equal the price, so that even though marginal revenue equals marginal cost, the price does not equal marginal cost.

A Comparison of the Two Approaches to Profit Maximization

We have now considered two different approaches to profit maximization. One approach looks at the explicit relationship between profits and production. The other approach compares the price to the marginal cost. Both approaches give the same answer. How do the approaches compare?

In Table 6.4 we looked at several prices, and we derived the profit-maximizing level of production by looking at profits for different levels of production at these prices. To do so, we had to create a new table for each price. This is quite time-consuming. In contrast, with the marginal cost approach, we only had to look at marginal cost for each unit of production and compare it with the price. Thus, the price equals marginal cost approach is considerably easier. Moreover, because marginal cost increases as the number of items produced increases, the price equals marginal cost approach tells us why the supply curve slopes upward. It is for these two reasons that economists usually use the price equals marginal cost approach.

REVIEW
- Profit-maximizing firms respond to higher prices by increasing the quantity they are willing to produce. Their response is the supply curve.
- The supply curve can be derived by comparing price and marginal cost. A profit-maximizing firm will produce a quantity that equates price and marginal cost.
- The upward-sloping marginal cost curve implies an upward-sloping supply curve.
- The supply curve can also be derived by looking at the relationship between profits and production. The profit-maximizing quantity is the same as that determined by the price equals marginal cost approach.

The Market Supply Curve

The *market* supply curve can be obtained by adding up the supply curves of all the *individual* firms in the market. Figure 6.9 gives an example in which there are two individual firm supply curves for pumpkins: One curve corresponds to your pumpkin firm, and the other, which is identical to yours, corresponds to the firm of your competitor, Fred, who is growing pumpkins on the other side of town. You and Fred have the same marginal cost for pumpkin growing, so your supply curves are exactly the same. You will both choose to produce the same number of pumpkins if the price is the same.

If only you and Fred are in the market, the market supply curve is the sum of just your two supplies. You get the market curve by adding in the horizontal direction, as shown in Figure 6.9. For example, if the price is $30, the quantity supplied by Fred will be 2 crates, and the quantity you supply will be 2 crates; thus the quantity supplied in the market at $30 is 4 crates. If the price rises to $50, Fred will produce 3 crates and you will also produce 3 crates; thus the quantity supplied in the market rises to 6 crates.

In reality, of course, there are more than two firms in a competitive market, and the individual supply curves for different firms in the market are usually different. But the concept of deriving the market supply curve is the same whether there are only 2 firms or 2,000 firms, and whether they are all the same or are all different. After adding up the individual supply curves for all the firms in the market, we arrive at a market supply curve like Figure 6.1. Thus, we have fulfilled one of the objectives of this chapter—deriving the market supply curve.

If there are many different firms in the market, the market supply curve can be much smoother than the individual supply curves. For example, a novelist may be

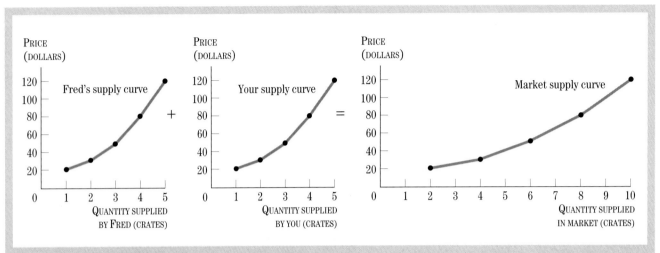

Figure 6.9
Derivation of the Market Supply Curve
The market supply curve is the sum of the individual firms' supply curves for all the firms in the market. The figure shows how the supply curves of two firms—Fred's and yours—sum to a market supply curve.

able to write only one novel a year. If a publisher offers a price to write the novel that is above the marginal cost of producing the novel, then the novelist will write the novel. Otherwise, the novel will not be written. But the market for novels in any one year consists of many authors with many different marginal costs. As the price of novels rises, more and more authors will decide to write novels, and the market supply curve for novels will look very smooth.

The Slope of the Supply Curve

We have shown that the slope and position of the individual firms' supply curves depend on the marginal cost at the different firms. If marginal cost rises very sharply with more production, then the supply curve will be very steep. If marginal cost increases more gradually, then the supply curve will be flatter.

Because the market supply curve is the sum of the individual firms' supply curves, its slope will also depend on marginal cost. The market supply curve can get very steep at high levels of production because marginal cost gets very high when production is high.

Shifts in the Supply Curve

Because the supply curve for the individual firm is given by its marginal cost, anything that decreases marginal cost will shift down the individual supply curves and therefore the market supply curve. For example, a new technology might reduce the marginal cost at every level of production. If this happens, then the market supply curve will shift down by the amount that marginal cost declines. Observe that a downward shift of a supply curve is equivalent to a rightward shift. Similarly, an increase in marginal cost—perhaps because of a disease affecting the pumpkins, so that more labor is required for each crate of pumpkins—would shift the supply curve upward or to the left (see Figure 6.10).

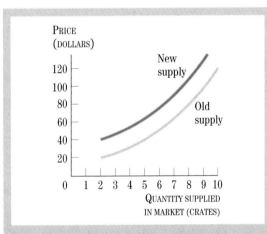

Figure 6.10
Shifts in the Market Supply Curve
An increase in marginal cost would shift the supply curve upward or to the left.

- The market supply curve is derived by adding up the individual supply curves of all the firms in the market.

- When the price rises, the individual firms in the market increase the quantity supplied. Hence, the market supply curve is upward-sloping.

- The slope of the supply curve depends on how sharply marginal cost increases.

- Anything that raises or lowers marginal cost will shift the market supply curve.

Producer Surplus

producer surplus: the difference between the price received by a firm for an additional item sold and the marginal cost of the item's production; for the market as a whole, it is the sum of all the individual firms' producer surpluses, or the area above the market supply curve and below the market price.

A firm would not produce and sell an item if it could not get a price at least as high as the marginal cost of producing that item. The **producer surplus** is the difference between the marginal cost of an item and the price received for it. For example, your marginal cost of washing cars on the weekend might be $4 per car. If the car-washing price in your area is $9 per car and this is the price you receive, then your producer surplus would be $5 per car. Or suppose, in your pumpkin firm, that the price of pumpkins is $25. Then you get $25 for producing 1 crate and incur $20 in marginal cost. The difference, $5, is your producer surplus. If the price of pumpkins is $35, you produce 2 crates and your producer surplus is $15 ($35 − $20) for the first crate plus $5 ($35 − $30) for the second crate, for a total of $20 producer surplus.

A Graphical Representation of Producer Surplus

The producer surplus can be represented graphically as the area above the individual firm supply curve and below the price line, as illustrated in Figure 6.11. The producer

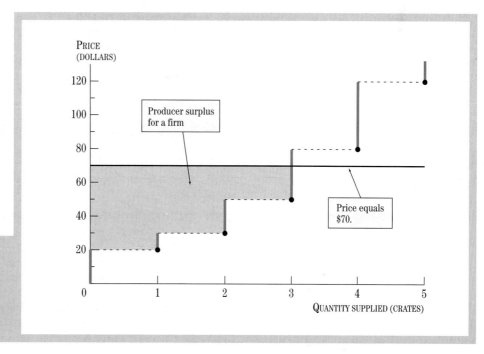

Figure 6.11
Producer Surplus for an Individual Firm
As shown here, for an individual firm, the producer surplus is the area between the price line and the supply curve.

Marginal cost is defined as the increase in total costs associated with each additional unit of production. Anything that decreases marginal cost will shift the supply curve down (or to the right), and anything that increases marginal cost will shift the supply curve up (or to the left). Reading the article below about how U.S. firms have adjusted to the effects of the tsunami, can you identify the firms that are likely to see a shift in their supply curve in response to increased marginal costs—and those that are likely not to experience such a shift?

After Tsunami, US Firms Adjust

by Diane E. Lewis
Global Staff
January 6, 2005

US companies whose goods are made in Southeast Asia are shifting production and changing distribution routes in order to limit the commercial impact of the deadly earthquake and tsunami.

Clothing retailer Gap Inc., with more than 700 manufacturing contractors worldwide, sought to minimize disruptions by transferring shipments bound for an Indian port to another site in the country.

"There were problems in southern India," said spokeswoman Kris Marubio. "Roads leading to the major thoroughfare were impacted. So we moved them to other ports in India. We did this over the past few days."

Although Southeast Asia has become a hub for apparel and footwear manufacturers, big US companies have so many contractors that they can readily shift production from one country to another without affecting retail prices, analysts say.

Gourmet coffee roasters, however, don't have that luxury. The natural disaster could limit the supply of coffee grown on the island of Sumatra and drive up already high prices.

Chuck Coffman, president of Armeno Coffee in Northborough, said Sumatran coffee has risen to about $3 per pound, almost double what he had been paying last year. He sells 17 varieties of Indonesian coffee, including Sumatran coffee made from the Arabica bean, prized among gourmands.

But this week, Coffman learned that future supplies could be jeopardized by lack of workers and bad roads.

"No one knows what will happen," said Coffman. "What we are fearing is that the crop will mature, but there will not be enough workers to pick it, and they may not be able to get it down from the mountains."

surplus is analogous to the consumer surplus, the area below the demand curve and above the price line, derived in Chapter 5.

The producer surplus in the whole market can be obtained by adding up the producer surplus for all producers or by looking at the area above the market supply curve and below the price. This is illustrated in Figure 6.12.

Before the natural disaster, the price of Sumatran coffee had risen 25 cents a pound last year because of concerns over limited supply. Now consumers will be paying more for Sumatran coffee.

"Potentially, I think there will be a higher acceptance for the higher price by the consumer," said Thomas Fricke, chief executive and cofounder of organic coffee producer ForesTrade, which gets 60 to 70 percent of its coffee from the Aceh region, one of the hardest-hit areas.

Consumers "have the perception that people in Indonesia are having a difficult time and may be willing to accommodate higher prices, regardless whether the impact warrants it or not," he said.

Consumers could also see tuna and other fish prices increase. The tsunami destroyed fishing fleets in Indonesia, India, and Thailand, said John Connelly, president of the National Fisheries Institute in Washington, D.C. "Fishing fleets have been decimated, and that could impact the tuna we get," he said, adding that Thailand is a major exporter of tuna to the United States.

UPS, the global package delivery service, dealt with the disaster by implementing a plan to get relief and commercial goods into parts of Indonesia with smaller aircraft.

"Commerce is pretty much at a standstill in some areas because there is so much congestion due to the aid relief in the airport and ports," said spokesman John Flick. "Before the tsunami, when we flew to Jakarta, we used one aircraft. Now, Jakarta has been taken out of the equation. We're going directly to the smaller islands, and going directly to smaller aircraft to move goods."

While many apparel and footwear factories may have escaped damage, distribution problems could arise, analysts say. Footwear companies like Reebok and Nike, which produce a good portion of their shoes in the region, could face some obstacles if they rely on trucks to transport goods along roads uprooted by the earthquake, or use ports glutted with goods from relief efforts.

"The biggest impact may be that some of the trucks that move product from the factory to ports will not be available," said Madison Riley, a principal and national service director for consulting firm Kurt Salmon & Associates Inc.

"Future distribution could be impacted somewhat," he said. "But I don't see prices going up. Instead, if products are delayed retailers might cancel some of it and wholesalers could be stuck with it. But there could be a greater opportunity for lower-cost products."

At Reebok, where about 40 percent of its shoes are made in Thailand and Indonesia, there were no disruptions to the firm's **supply chain** or production, said spokesman Denise Kaigler.

Nike said one of its apparel contractors in Sri Lanka appears to have been damaged by the tsunami, but that would not affect overall production. Five percent of the firm's global apparel production is located in the region, said Caitlin Morrs, Nike's senior manager of global issues management.

As of October, Nike had 42 contractors in Indonesia, including nine footwear producers, 29 apparel makers, and five producers of athletic equipment such as yoga mats and golf bags, she said. Most were based in Jakarta, where there is no damage.

Source: Diane Lewis, "After Tsunami, US Firms Adjust," *Boston Globe*, January 6, 2005. Copyright 2005 by the *Boston Globe*. Reproduced with permission of the *Boston Globe* in the format textbook, conveyed via Copyright Clearance Center, Inc.

The applications of producer surplus are similar to those of consumer surplus. Producer surplus provides a measure of how much a producer gains from the market. The sum of producer surplus plus consumer surplus is a comprehensive measure of how well a market economy works, as we will see in Chapter 7.

What Is the Difference Between Profits and Producer Surplus?

Profits and producer surplus are not the same thing. Profits are the difference between total revenue and total costs, while the producer surplus measures the difference between the price and the marginal cost of every unit. How can we compare these two measures?

Suppose the price of pumpkins is $70 per crate; then you are willing to produce 3 crates of pumpkins. Total revenue is $210 and total costs are $150; thus, you are making a $60 profit. (See panel II of Table 6.4.) How much is your producer surplus when 3 crates are sold at $70? As just defined,

$$\text{Producer surplus} = (P - MC_1) + (P - MC_2) + (P - MC_3)$$
$$= (\$70 - \$20) + (\$70 - \$30) + (\$70 - \$50) = \$110$$

where MC_1 is the marginal cost of the first crate, MC_2 is the marginal cost of the second crate, and MC_3 is the marginal cost of the third crate. Thus, profits are $60 and producer surplus is $110.

Notice that there is a difference of $50 between profits and producer surplus. That number happens to be equal to the fixed costs of the firm. Thus, producer surplus equals profit plus fixed costs. Try the same method for different prices and quantities sold, and you will arrive at the same result: Producer surplus always equals profits plus fixed costs. We now show that this is no coincidence.

Consider Table 6.5. The first four columns of Table 6.5 are already familiar from the earlier tables. The fifth column shows the sum of the marginal costs for all that is produced. For example, the sum of marginal costs when production is 3 crates is $20 plus $30 plus $50 equals $100. The last column shows the difference between total costs and fixed costs—that is, variable costs. Notice that the last two columns are equal.

Thus, as we sum up marginal costs for any quantity Q produced, we count all costs except fixed costs. In other words,

Sum of marginal costs = total costs − fixed costs = variable costs

When the producer sells a quantity Q, we can say that

$$\text{Producer surplus} = (P - MC_1) + (P - MC_2) + (P - MC_3) + \cdots + (P - MC_Q)$$

The number of terms in this sum is Q. For the example above, $Q = 3$ and there were Q terms in the sum. Thus, we can translate this definition of producer surplus into the price (P) of the good times the quantity (Q) sold minus the sum of the marginal costs of all units. That is,

$$\text{Producer surplus} = (P \times Q) - \text{sum of marginal costs}$$

As we now know, $P \times Q$ is the total revenue, and the sum of marginal costs equals the difference between total costs and fixed costs. Substituting these relationships into the preceding gives

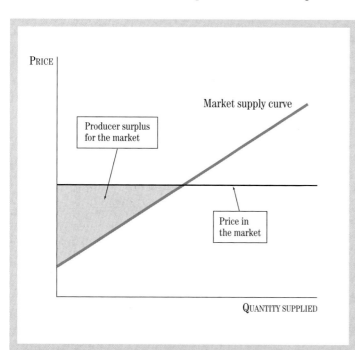

Figure 6.12
Producer Surplus for the Market
If we add up producer surplus for every firm, we get the producer surplus for the whole market. This is given by the area between the price and the market supply curve.

Table 6.5
Summing Up Marginal Costs

Crates of Pumpkins	Fixed Costs	Total Costs	Marginal Cost	Sum of Marginal Costs	Total Costs Less Fixed Costs
1	50	70	20	20	20
2	50	100	30	50	50
3	50	150	50	100	100
4	50	230	80	180	180
5	50	350	120	300	300

Producer surplus = total revenue − (total costs − fixed costs)

Finally, since profits equal total revenue minus total costs, we obtain the relationship between producer surplus and profits:

Producer surplus = profits + fixed costs

REVIEW

- Producer surplus is the price a firm receives for selling a unit of a product minus the marginal cost of producing that unit.

- The producer surplus for a firm is the area below the price line and above the firm's supply curve.

- For all the firms in a market, the producer surplus is the area below the price line and above the market supply curve.

- Producer surplus is different from profits. Producer surplus is greater than profits by the amount of fixed costs.

Conclusion

In this chapter, we have derived the supply curve in a competitive market by looking at the behavior of firms. We assumed that a firm decides how much to produce by maximizing profits. The firm makes this decision taking prices as given and considering its production function, which relates the number of hours of work at the firm to the output of the firm. The production function enters the firm's profit calculations through its effects on the firm's costs. Because the production function has diminishing returns to labor, the firm faces increasing marginal cost. From the firm's marginal cost, we can quickly find the firm's supply curve. Profit maximization implies that the firm will produce the quantity where price equals marginal cost.

The connection between marginal cost and the supply curve is fundamental to understanding how markets work. We will make use of this connection many times throughout this book, especially when we consider public policy issues, such as the efficiency of markets, taxation, and regulation of firms. When economists see or draw a supply curve, they are usually thinking about the marginal cost of the firms that underlie the supply curve. The supply curve and the marginal cost curve are virtually synonymous for economists.

The price equals marginal cost rule for a profit-maximizing firm is fundamental for understanding how well markets work. When, in Chapter 7, we combine this rule with the analogous rule that the price equals the marginal benefit of a good for a consumer, we will discover an attractive feature of competitive markets.

We have examined firm behavior in this chapter and consumer behavior in Chapter 5, and the next step in our analysis of markets is to examine the interaction of these firms and consumers. That is the subject of Chapter 7.

KEY POINTS

1. A firm is an organization that uses inputs to produce goods or services.
2. In competitive markets, firms are price-takers.
3. The foundations of supply are found in the profit-maximizing behavior of firms.
4. Profits are defined as total revenue minus total costs.
5. The production function shows how production increases with more labor; the marginal product of labor declines as more labor is added and capital is not changed.
6. Marginal cost increases as more is produced because of diminishing returns to labor.
7. A price-taking firm produces up to the point where price equals marginal cost, which is the key rule for profit maximization.
8. The reason the supply curve slopes upward is that marginal cost is increasing. A higher price enables the firm to produce at higher levels of marginal cost.
9. We can also determine the profit-maximizing quantity of production by looking at how profits depend on production and finding the highest level of profits.
10. The market supply curve is obtained by adding up the individual supply curves. The market supply curve can be smooth even if the individual supply curves are not.
11. Producer surplus is the area above either the individual or the market supply curve and below the price line.
12. Producer surplus and profit are not the same thing. Producer surplus equals profits plus fixed costs.

KEY TERMS

firm
price-taker
competitive market
profits
total revenue
total costs
production function
marginal product of labor
diminishing returns to labor
fixed costs
variable costs
marginal cost
profit maximization
marginal revenue
producer surplus

QUESTIONS FOR REVIEW

1. What is a firm?
2. What is the difference between a corporation and a sole proprietorship?
3. Why do total costs increase as more is produced?
4. Why does marginal cost increase as more is produced?
5. What is the relationship between an individual supply curve and marginal cost?
6. Why does profit maximization imply that price equals marginal cost?
7. Why would a firm never choose to produce at a point where the price of an item is less than the marginal cost of the item?
8. What does it mean to say that firms are price-takers?
9. When does it make sense to assume that firms are price-takers?
10. How is the market supply curve derived from individual supply curves?
11. Why might the market supply curve be smoother than the individual supply curves?
12. What is producer surplus?

PROBLEMS

1. The table at the top of the next page shows the total costs of producing strawberries on a small plot of land.

Pounds of Strawberries	Total Costs (dollars)
0	10
1	11
2	14
3	18
4	25
5	34

a. Calculate the marginal cost schedule.
b. Draw the farmer's supply curve.
c. Suppose the price of 1 pound of strawberries is $4. How much would this farmer produce? Show graphically the area of producer surplus. What are profits?
d. Suppose the price of strawberries goes up to $7 per pound. How much will the farmer produce now? What are profits now?

2. Consider the example of the cost of pumpkins in Table 6.4. Compute the total revenue, total costs, and profits when the price of a crate of pumpkins is $60. How many crates of pumpkins will maximize profits? Now find the profit-maximizing quantity by using the marginal cost approach. How do your answers compare? Which approach did you find easier?

3. Consider the following information:

Daily Production and Costs at Jill's Bread Bakers

Quantity Produced (dozens of loaves)	Total Costs (dollars)
0	20
1	22
2	26
3	32
4	40
5	50
6	62
7	76

a. Calculate the marginal cost for Jill's bread production.
b. Draw the supply curve for this firm.
c. Jill can sell as many loaves as she wants in the market at a price of $12 for a dozen loaves. How many loaves will she sell each day? Use your diagram to show how much producer surplus she receives.

4. Suppose you are able to mow lawns at $12 per hour. The only cost to you is the opportunity cost of your time. For the first 3 hours, the opportunity cost of your time is $9 per hour. But after 3 hours, the opportunity cost of your time rises to $15 per hour because of other

commitments. Draw the marginal cost to you of mowing lawns. Draw in the price you receive for mowing lawns. For how long will you mow lawns? Calculate your producer surplus.

5. Suppose a price-taking firm has the following total costs schedule:

Quantity	Total Costs
0	20
1	30
2	42
3	55
4	75
5	100
6	130

a. Calculate marginal cost. If the price in the market is $20, how many units will the firm produce?
b. Suppose the price in the market falls to $12 per unit. How many units of output will this firm produce in order to maximize profits?
c. Suppose there is an improvement in technology that shifts total costs down by $8 at every level of production. How much will the firm produce and what will profits be at a price of $20 and at a price of $12?

6. Consider the following information about a firm:

Quantity	Total Costs	Total Revenue
0	500	0
1	700	500
2	1,100	1,000
3	1,500	1,500
4	2,300	2,000
5	3,500	2,500

On the same diagram, plot the total revenues and total costs curves for this firm. What are the maximum profits that this firm can earn? Show this level of profits in the diagram. Do the slopes of the two curves appear to be the same at the maximum profit level?

7. Using the information in problem 6, find the fixed costs and the producer surplus when the firm produces the profit-maximizing quantity. Show that this amount of producer surplus equals profits plus fixed costs.

8. Does the assumption that firms are price-takers seem less valid than the assumption that consumers are price-takers? Explain why. Suppose that there are 50 firms and 50 consumers in the market. Would both assumptions be equally accurate in that case?

CHAPTER 7

The Interaction of People in Markets

This is an old but true story, going back to before the field of economics even existed. It is about an absent-minded philosophy professor who was interested in human interaction. He was particularly fascinated by how the economy, consisting of the interaction of millions of people pursuing their own interests, worked. He did not have much to go on; there were no economics professors at his school or at any other school. So, although he was a gifted teacher, he quit his teaching job at the university and traveled; he interviewed businesspeople; he visited factories; he talked to workers; he watched ships come and go; he studied the economies of other countries and of other times. He did everything he could to find about the economy. Amazingly, not only was he able to pull all this material together into a coherent view, he also managed to get it down on paper for other people to read, learn, and enjoy. By doing so, he invented the field of economics. His view of the economy is still dominant today.

The professor's name was Adam Smith, and the book he wrote, called *Wealth of Nations*, was first published in 1776. His deepest insight, among many deep insights, is called the **invisible hand** theorem, still most often stated using his words: "It is not from the benevolence of the butcher, the brewer, or the baker that we expect our dinner, but from their regard to their own interest." And whether it is the butcher, the brewer, or the baker, he is "led by an invisible hand to promote an end which was no part of his intention. . . . By pursuing his own interest he frequently promotes that of the society more effectually than when

Corporate leaders gather in a field outside Darien, Connecticut, where one of them claims to have seen the invisible hand of the marketplace.

he really intends to promote it." In other words, without any formal coordination, firms (butchers, brewers, bakers, and many others) that are pursuing their own interests interact with consumers who are also pursuing their own interests, and somehow everyone ends up producing and consuming a quantity that is efficient.

The main goal of this chapter is to state clearly and prove the invisible hand theorem. The theorem is not always true, and we want to be clear about the circumstances in which it is true. We first need to explain what is meant by *efficient* (the modern term for Smith's "effectual"), and then show why and under what circumstances the quantity produced and consumed is efficient. We also show how to measure the economic loss from producing more or less than the efficient quantity.

Chapters 5 and 6 have paved the way for our goal in this chapter. In Chapter 5 we studied consumers. We can say that consumers are pursuing their own interests, because they maximize their utility. In Chapter 6 we studied firms. We can say that firms are pursuing their own interests, because they maximize profits. Now we study the interactions of firms and consumers in competitive markets. Figure 7.1 is a schematic illustration of the model we use to explain this interaction and thereby explain the invisible hand theorem. The model, called the **competitive equilibrium model,** is an embellishment of the supply and demand model discussed in Chapter 3, but now with the behavior of consumers and firms explicit.

invisible hand: the idea that the free interaction of people in a market economy leads to a desirable social outcome; the term was coined by Adam Smith.

competitive equilibrium model: a model that assumes utility maximization on the part of consumers and profit maximization on the part of firms, along with competitive markets and freely determined prices.

Individual Consumers and Firms in a Market

In our analysis of economic interaction, it is very important to think about what individual consumers and firms are doing. Consider an example of consumers and producers of the same commodity: long-stemmed roses. Maria and Ken are two of many potential rose consumers who are deciding how many roses to buy. Both are willing to pay a certain amount for roses, but not necessarily the same amount. Hugo and Mimi are two of many rose producers who are deciding how many roses to produce in their gardens. Both have marginal costs for producing roses, but not necessarily the same marginal costs.

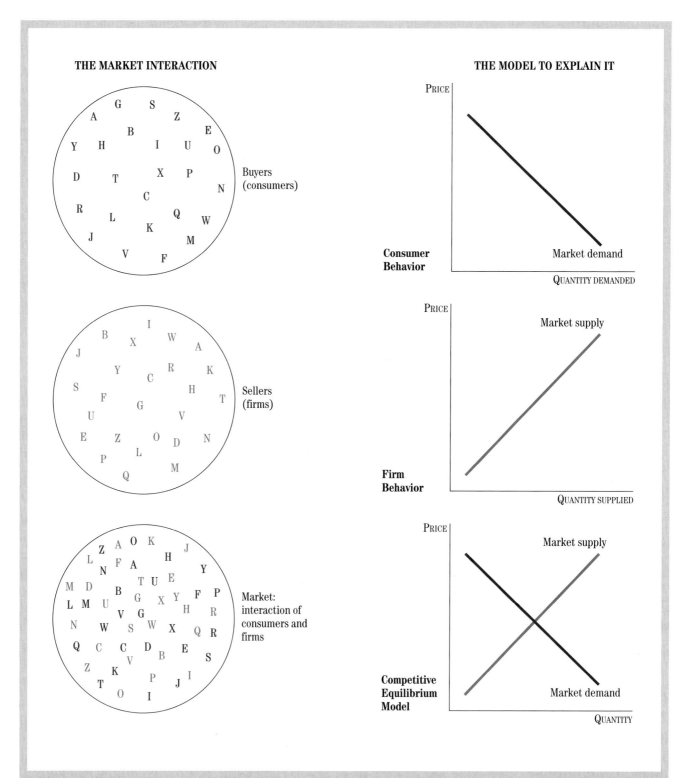

THE MARKET INTERACTION

THE MODEL TO EXPLAIN IT

Buyers (consumers)

Consumer Behavior

Sellers (firms)

Firm Behavior

Market: interaction of consumers and firms

Competitive Equilibrium Model

Figure 7.1
The Market Interaction and the Model to Explain It

In this chapter, we explain how individual buyers and sellers interact in a market (on the left) by combining the behavior of consumers (Chapter 5) with the behavior of firms (Chapter 6) to get a model of competitive equilibrium (Chapter 7).

The Hard Way to Process Information, Coordinate, and Motivate

The rose decisions of Maria, Ken, Hugo, Mimi, and all the others in the market clearly interact with one another. For example, an increase in Hugo's marginal costs—perhaps because of an extra rose-processing expense to ward off a new insect—will probably reduce the amount of roses he decides to produce; either this means less rose consumption for Ken, Maria, and other consumers, or it means more rose production for Mimi and other producers. Similarly, if Ken decides to purchase more roses, someone else must decide to decrease consumption or increase production. How are all these decisions worked out? What *information* is needed in order to determine whether it is better for Mimi's garden to produce more or for Hugo's garden to produce more? What *coordinates* a change in consumption or production by one person with an offsetting change in consumption or production by other people? What *motivates* some people to consume less and others to produce more if one person decides to consume more?

Suppose you had to work this out. To make your job easier, suppose that Maria, Ken, Hugo, and Mimi were the whole world as far as roses go. If you and they were all in one place together, you might imagine conducting their consumption and production activities the way the leader of a marching band would conduct the band members. You raise your baton toward Maria to signal more consumption; you shake your head at Ken to signal less consumption; you point your finger at Hugo to signal more production; you turn your back on Mimi to signal no change in production; you blow your whistle to signal when to begin consuming and producing.

To provide motivation, you might change your facial expression when you look at Maria; a frown or perhaps a smile may help to motivate her to purchase more roses. Your choice of which finger to point at Hugo may affect his motivation, and the shrill of your whistle might serve to motivate them all to do what you say.

To do your job right, you will also need to have information about rose production for Mimi's and Hugo's gardens. For example, to know whether it is appropriate to point your finger at Hugo and turn your back on Mimi, you need to know which garden has lower marginal costs of rose production.

If this is not already beginning to sound ridiculously impossible, remember that if you had this job in the real world, you would have to coordinate, motivate, and know intimately millions of consumers and producers. This is an amazingly complex job even for this single, relatively simple commodity.

The Easy Way to Process Information, Coordinate, and Motivate

Fortunately, you do not need to worry about being called upon to perform such an impossible task. There is a remarkable device that does the information processing, coordinating, and motivating for us. No one person invented this device; it evolved slowly over thousands of years and is probably still evolving. It is called *the market* (in this case, the long-stemmed-rose market). Of course, like many markets, the rose market does not take place in any one location. It consists of all the florists, street carts, and farmers' markets where roses are sold and all the gardens and greenhouses where roses are grown, whether in the United States, Europe, Latin America, Africa, Australia, or Asia. Fortunately, a market can serve as an information-processing, coordinating, and motivating device even if it does not take place at any one location. Buyers and sellers never have to see one another.

How does the market work? What will be the total quantity of roses consumed? Who will consume what amount? What will be the total quantity of roses produced?

One-Stop Shopping for Processing Information, Coordinating, and Motivating: The Market
This New York City flower vendor represents just one piece of the huge and multifaceted market for flowers that exists throughout the world.

Which garden will produce what amount? Let us see how economists answer these questions about how people interact in a market.

The Competitive Equilibrium Model

Economists use the *individual* demand curves and the *individual* supply curves derived in Chapters 5 and 6 to describe what happens to consumers and firms when they interact in a market.

Recall that each of the individual demand curves depends on the marginal benefit—the willingness to pay for additional consumption—the individual gets from consuming the goods. Together these marginal benefits create a market demand curve for roses. The demand curve shows how much consumers in total are willing to buy at each price.

Recall also that individual supply curves depend on the marginal costs of the firms. Together their marginal costs create a market supply curve for roses. The supply curve shows the total quantity supplied by all firms at each price.

The resulting market demand and supply curves are shown in the center of Figure 7.2, flanked by Maria's and Ken's individual demand curves and by Hugo's and Mimi's individual supply curves. Note that we have used the same units for the quantity supplied and the quantity demanded in Figure 7.2; the price (*P*, measured in dollars per rose) is on the vertical axis, and the quantity (*Q*, the number of roses) is on the horizontal axis. We continue to assume that Maria, Ken, Hugo, and Mimi are the whole market so that we can show the market in one diagram. A competitive market would typically require more buyers and sellers.

We have seen supply and demand curves like those in the center of Figure 7.2 before in Chapter 3. But now—after Chapters 5 and 6—we know much more about what the demand and supply curves mean. Individual consumer behavior and individual firm behavior are now seen as underlying the supply and demand model. To emphasize that the supply and demand model incorporates utility-maximizing consumers and profit-maximizing firms in competitive markets, we refer to it as the

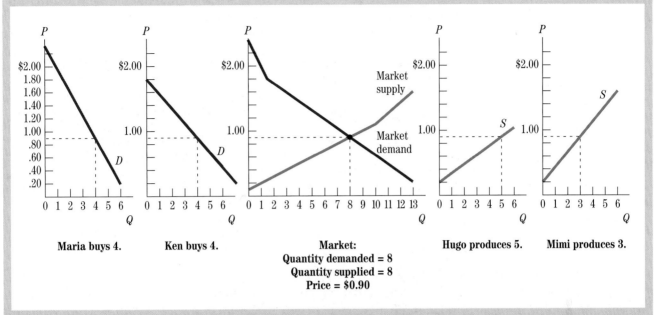

Maria buys 4.   **Ken buys 4.**

Market:
Quantity demanded = 8
Quantity supplied = 8
Price = $0.90

Hugo produces 5.   **Mimi produces 3.**

Figure 7.2
Price and Quantity
Determination

The market demand curve is the sum of the individual demand curves of the consumers in the market. The market supply curve is the sum of the individual supply curves for the producers. When quantity demanded equals quantity supplied, the two curves intersect. The equilibrium price and quantity will be given by this intersection. The individual firm and consumer decisions can then be read off the individual supply and demand curves at those prices.

competitive equilibrium model. The competitive equilibrium model, as we have said, is simply the supply and demand model with the behavior of consumers and firms made explicit. Because the competitive equilibrium model has more to it than the supply and demand model, we can do more with it.

■ **Individual Production and Consumption Decisions.** A key prediction of the competitive equilibrium model is that a price will emerge from the interaction of people in the market such that the quantity supplied *equals* the quantity demanded. This is the *equilibrium price.* Graphically, the price is given at the point of intersection of the market supply curve and the market demand curve; here the quantity supplied in the market equals the quantity demanded in the market. For the example shown in Figure 7.2, the equilibrium price is $.90 a rose.

Once we have determined the price in this way, the supply and demand curves tell us how much in total will be consumed and produced at that price. We look at the market demand curve and see how much is demanded at that price, and we look at the market supply curve and see how much is supplied at that price. Because the curves intersect at the market price, the quantity demanded and the quantity supplied are the same. They are at the point on the horizontal axis directly below the intersection. In Figure 7.2, the quantity bought and sold is 8 roses.

Thus far, we have not done anything more with the competitive equilibrium model than we did with the supply and demand model. But now, armed with the price, we can go to the individual demand curves to see how much Maria and Ken will buy. Look to the left in Figure 7.2 to find the quantity demanded by Maria and by Ken when the price is $.90 a rose. They each buy 4 roses. Maria and Ken are motivated to buy this amount—without any central coordinator—because, at $.90 a rose,

equilibrium price: the price at which quantity supplied equals quantity demanded. (Ch. 3)

they maximize their respective utilities by consuming this amount. Observe that Maria and Ken do not have the same individual demand curves. Nevertheless, the quantity demanded by each can still be determined from their demand curves, as shown in Figure 7.2.

The individual supply curves tell us how much Hugo and Mimi will produce. Look to the right in Figure 7.2 to see how much Hugo and Mimi produce when the price is $.90 a rose. Hugo produces 5 roses, and Mimi produces 3 roses. Hugo and Mimi are motivated to produce this amount—again without any central coordinator—because, at $.90 a rose, they maximize their profits by producing this amount.

In sum, the competitive equilibrium model, which includes the behavior of the consumers and the firms, predicts the price, the quantity consumed by each person, and the quantity produced by each firm. It also predicts a certain marginal benefit of consumption for each consumer and a certain marginal cost for each producer. Hence, the model provides answers to all the questions posed earlier.

■ **Adjustment to the Equilibrium Price.** As can be seen from Figure 7.2, if the price is higher than the predicted market price at the intersection of the supply curve and the demand curve, then the quantity supplied is greater than the quantity demanded; we say that there is a *surplus*. When there is a surplus, the price will fall, resulting in demand increasing and supply decreasing until the surplus disappears. However, if the price is lower than the predicted market price, then the quantity demanded is greater than the quantity supplied; we say that there is a *shortage*. When there is a shortage, the price will rise, resulting in demand decreasing and supply increasing until the shortage disappears. At this low price, the marginal benefit is greater than the marginal cost, and the price will rise until the shortage disappears. Thus, if the price falls when there is a surplus and rises when there is a shortage, the price will converge to the equilibrium price.

surplus (excess supply): the situation in which quantity supplied is greater than quantity demanded. (Ch. 3)

shortage (excess demand): the situation in which quantity demanded is greater than quantity supplied. (Ch. 3)

REVIEW

- Centrally coordinating and motivating the thousands of consumers and producers of any good would be an amazingly complex task requiring a vast amount of information.

- The market is a device that provides information and coordinates and motivates consumers and producers in a decentralized way. The market does this job in a way that no one individual can.

- Economists describe the interactions of people in the market through the competitive equilibrium model. According to the model, the equilibrium price and total quantity are given by the intersection of the market supply and demand curves; individual decisions about consumption and production are given through the individual demand and supply curves, which are based on utility maximization and profit maximization.

A Double-Auction Market

How well does the competitive equilibrium model work in explaining the actual interaction of individual firms and consumers? Economists answer this question by observing markets in which one can see exactly what all the buyers and sellers do. Because it is difficult, if not impossible, to observe all the participants in actual markets, it is necessary to set up experimental markets for this purpose. An experimental market is much like a real-world market except that one can observe all the actions of the participants. In this section we describe such a market and compare it to the model.

Market Participants and Their Incentives

A simple kind of market in which several buyers and several sellers interact is the **double-auction market.** In a double-auction market, *both* buyers and sellers call out prices. Buyers bid a certain price for items they want to buy, and sellers ask a certain price for items they want to sell. Four or five buyers and four or five sellers are enough to make the market work, but many more can also participate.

Many real-world markets are like double-auction markets. For example, the New York Stock Exchange and the commodity exchanges in Chicago are double-auction markets. In Chicago, traders in trading pits call out whether they want to buy and sell.

As soon as the market opens, buyers can bid and sellers can ask certain prices. A transaction takes place any time a buyer accepts a price a seller asks or a seller accepts a price a buyer bids.

In order to make this experimental market work like markets in the real world, the buyers and sellers must be given some objectives and take their actions seriously. Each buyer is given a marginal benefit schedule. Each seller is given a marginal cost schedule. A small sheet of paper describing these marginal benefits or marginal costs is given to each of the buyers and sellers who participate in the market. An example of both a seller's marginal cost sheet and a buyer's marginal benefit sheet is shown in Table 7.1.

■ **Buyers Earn a Consumer Surplus.** During each trading period, buyers may purchase any number of items but can bid for only one unit at a time. For each item successfully purchased, the buyer receives the amount listed on the sheet under the column marked "marginal benefit." Thus, the buyer's personal gain on each item purchased is the difference between the marginal benefit of that item and the amount paid for it. Notice that a motivated buyer will want to get the lowest price possible. Other buyers will be competing to do the same thing. It would not be wise for a buyer to buy an item for more than the marginal benefit because that would result in a loss.

For example, suppose you have the buyer's sheet shown in Table 7.1 and you buy two items. The marginal benefit from the first item is $25, and the marginal benefit from the second item is $20. If you pay $15 for the first item and $10 for the second item, then your total gain is ($25 − $15) + ($20 − $10) = $20. Observe that each of the terms in this sum is the marginal benefit minus the price, or the *consumer surplus*.

■ **Sellers Earn a Producer Surplus.** During each trading period, sellers are free to sell any number of items but can ask a price for only one item at a time. Each item sold costs the amount listed on the sheet under the column marked "marginal cost." The seller's personal gain on each item sold is the difference between the price the item sold for and the marginal cost of the item. Notice that a seller is motivated to get the highest price but is competing with other sellers who may be asking lower prices. It would not be wise for a seller to accept a price lower than the marginal cost, because that would result in a loss.

For example, suppose you have the seller's sheet shown in Table 7.1 and you sell two items. The marginal cost of the first item is $1, and the marginal cost of the second item is $6. If you sell the first item for $15 and the second item for $10, your gain is ($15 − $1) + ($10 − $6) = $18. Observe that each of the terms in this sum is the price minus the marginal cost, or the *producer surplus*.

double-auction market: a market in which several buyers and several sellers state prices at which they are willing to buy or sell a good.

Table 7.1
Marginal Benefit and Marginal Cost for a Double-Auction Market

Example Buyer Sheet

Number of Items	Marginal Benefit (dollars)
1	25
2	20
3	15
4	10
5	5

Example Seller Sheet

Number of Items	Marginal Cost (dollars)
1	1
2	6
3	11
4	16
5	21

consumer surplus: the difference between what a person is willing to pay for an additional unit of a good—the marginal benefit—and the market price of the good. (Ch. 5)

Be sure to distinguish between *market surplus* and *consumer surplus* or *producer surplus*.

producer surplus: the difference between the price received by a firm for an additional item sold and the marginal cost of the item's production. (Ch. 6)

Predictions of the Competitive Equilibrium Model

Observe that the stage is now set for a market. Buyers are motivated; sellers are motivated. Buyers and sellers can hear or see all the bids and asks. Now what would you predict would happen in this market? Does the outcome depend on the personalities, culture, or intelligence of the buyers and sellers? Does the competitive equilibrium model of consumers (buyers) and firms (sellers) predict the outcome?

■ **Constructing the Model.**   Figures 7.3, 7.4, and 7.5 show the competitive equilibrium model that corresponds to this market. The marginal benefits for the buyers and marginal costs for the sellers are used to construct the individual demand curves and the individual supply curves. At the bottom of Figure 7.3 are the marginal benefit sheets of the buyers. Each buyer has one sheet. The graph above each sheet is the individual demand curve derived from the sheet, using the methods of Chapter 5. The market demand curve appears on the right. It is the sum of the individual demand curves. Figure 7.4 shows comparable information for the sellers. There are

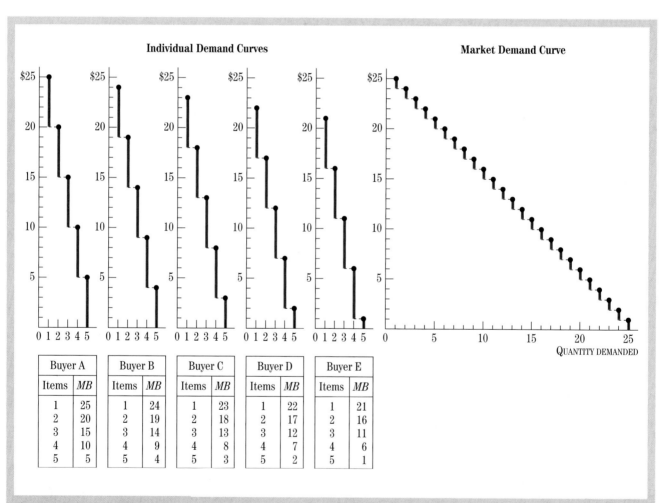

Figure 7.3
Modeling the Demand Side of the Double-Auction Market

There are five buyers in the market. The marginal benefits (*MB*) for each buyer are shown on that buyer's sheet. The corresponding individual demand curve is above the sheet. The market demand curve is shown on the right. It is the sum of all the items demanded at each price.

marginal costs and upward-sloping individual supply curves. The market supply curve is on the right. It is the sum of the individual supply curves.

Figure 7.5 shows the prediction of the competitive equilibrium model about the price and the quantity that will come out of this market. The demand curve of Figure 7.3 is combined with the supply curve of Figure 7.4. The two curves intersect at a price of $13 and a quantity of 13 items. In other words, the model predicts that when these 10 people interact in the market, the sellers will sell a total of 13 units, the buyers will buy a total of 13 units, and the market price will be $13. Is the prediction correct?

■ **Results.** This experimental market has been tried many times, and similar results have occurred each time. First, after one or two trading periods, the price will settle down to about $13. Sometimes it will be $12 or $14, but rarely does it deviate much from $13. Second, after one or two trading periods, the quantity traded will be very close to 13 units. Again, sometimes it will be slightly more or slightly less.

In other words, the model as shown in Figure 7.5 comes very close to predicting the outcome of the double-auction market. Of course, if you gave different marginal

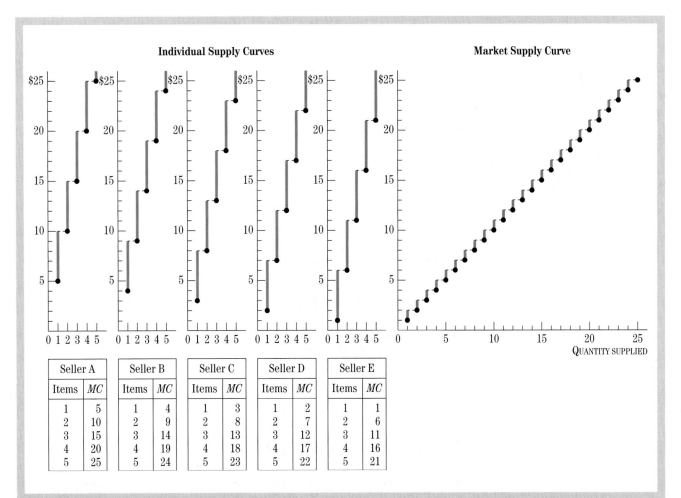

Seller A		Seller B		Seller C		Seller D		Seller E	
Items	MC	Items	MC	Items	MC	Items	MC	Items	MC
1	5	1	4	1	3	1	2	1	1
2	10	2	9	2	8	2	7	2	6
3	15	3	14	3	13	3	12	3	11
4	20	4	19	4	18	4	17	4	16
5	25	5	24	5	23	5	22	5	21

Figure 7.4
Modeling the Supply Side of the Double-Auction Market

There are five sellers in the market. The marginal costs (MC) for each seller are shown on that seller's sheet. The corresponding individual supply curve is shown above each sheet. The market supply curve is shown on the right. It is the sum of all items supplied at each price.

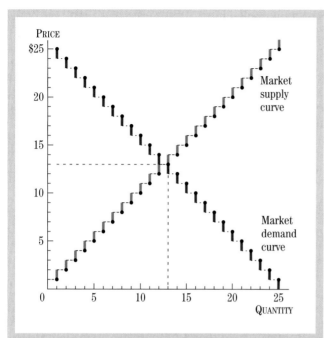

Figure 7.5
Predicted Price and Quantity in the Double-Auction Market
The competitive equilibrium model predicts that the price and quantity traded will be at the intersection of the market supply and demand curves, as shown in the figure. The market demand curve is from Figure 7.3, and the market supply curve is from Figure 7.4. The predicted market price is $13, and the predicted quantity traded is 13 units.

benefits and marginal costs to the buyers and sellers, you would have different supply and demand curves and therefore would get different answers, but the answers would be very close to those predicted by the model. Even though no one individual sets the price—the buyers and sellers are calling out prices in intense competition—the price settles down to the price predicted by the model.

Experimental economists such as Vernon Smith at the University of Arizona and Charles Plott of the California Institute of Technology have found that the model works surprisingly well in predicting the outcome of these experiments, even with a very small number of participants. The finding that the model predicts so well for a very small number of buyers and sellers has been called a "scientific mystery" by Vernon Smith.[1]

Surprise or not, the double-auction market demonstrates both how a market works and how a model works at predicting the outcome of the market. In the next few sections of this chapter, we use this model to measure the gains from trading in the market system. That the model works well in such experiments gives us more confidence in using it for these purposes.

To be sure, even though experiments are set up to mimic the operation of actual markets, they are still done in a laboratory setting. Market participants in the real world may be more or less sophisticated than those in the experiments, and the rules—if there are any—may be more complex in the real world. Thus, even though the experimental confirmation of the model is reassuring, we must remember that it is a model, not reality.

REVIEW

- Experimental markets can be used to test economic models and to demonstrate how markets work.

- The double-auction market is a good type of market for testing the predictions of the competitive equilibrium model.

- The competitive equilibrium model works remarkably well. The price and quantity sold in the double-auction market are usually very close to those predicted by the model.

Are Competitive Markets Efficient?

We have shown how to use the competitive equilibrium model to explain *how* a market works. Now let's use the competitive equilibrium model to see *how well* the market works. Are the quantities produced and consumed in the market efficient?

---

1. Vernon L. Smith, "Microeconomic Systems as an Experimental Science," *American Economic Review,* Vol. 72, 1982.

The Meaning of Efficient

In general, an inefficient outcome is one that wastes scarce resources, and an efficient outcome is one that does not waste scarce resources. Extremely inefficient economic outcomes are easy to spot. Constructing 275 million new video rental stores each year in the United States (or approximately one store per person) would obviously be wasteful. The workers building the new stores could be building other things that people wanted. If the U.S. economy produced such an outcome, everyone would say it was inefficient; shifting production to fewer video rental stores would clearly make many people better off.

An equally inefficient situation would occur if only one new video rental store a year was built; at that rate it would take more than 2,000 years to build the number of Blockbuster video rental stores that now exist in the United States. In such a situation, shifting production toward more video rental stores would clearly make many people better off.

Both these situations are inefficient because a change in production could make people better off. We might, therefore, define an efficient outcome as one that is so good that there is no change that would make people better off.

■ **The Need for a More Precise Definition.**   However, because the economy consists of many different people, we need to be more careful in defining efficiency. For every economic outcome, it is possible to make someone better off at the expense of someone else. If someone takes a long-stemmed rose from Maria and gives it to Ken, then Ken is better off but Maria is worse off. More generally, the possibility of transferring a good from one person to another, thereby making someone better off at the expense of someone else, is not an indication that an economic situation is inefficient or wasteful.

However, if there were a situation in which it was possible to change consumption or production in a way that would make someone better off without hurting someone else, then that situation would be inefficient. In such a situation, resources are being wasted, because someone, perhaps many people, could have a better life without someone else being harmed.

Based on such considerations, economists have developed the following definition of efficiency: An outcome is **Pareto efficient** if it is not possible to make someone better off without hurting someone else. Economists use the term *Pareto* to distinguish this definition of efficiency from other meanings, but the word *efficient* by itself is used when the meaning is clear from the context. Italian economist Vilfredo Pareto is the person who developed this concept of efficiency. Unless we say otherwise, when we use the term *efficient* in this chapter, we mean efficient in the sense of Pareto. If a market is not efficient in the sense of Pareto, then there is something wrong with the market.

Pareto efficient: a situation in which it is not possible to make someone better off without making someone else worse off.

■ **Three Conditions for Efficient Outcomes.**   There are three conditions that must hold if a market outcome is to be efficient in the sense of Pareto efficient.

First, *the marginal benefit* (MB) *must equal the marginal cost* (MC) *of the last item produced.* Why is this condition needed for efficiency? Suppose it did not hold. If the marginal cost is greater than the marginal benefit, then too much is being produced. In the example of producing 275 million video rental stores a year, the marginal cost of producing the 275 millionth video rental store is much greater than the marginal benefit. Reducing production (by a lot) would be appropriate. If the marginal cost is less than the marginal benefit of the product, then too little is being produced. In the example of producing only one video rental store a year, the marginal cost is certainly much less than the marginal benefit; more production would be appropriate. Only when marginal benefit is equal to marginal cost is the economic outcome efficient. This must occur for all goods from video rental stores to roses.

First efficiency condition: $MB = MC$ for last item produced.

One way to better appreciate this condition is to imagine that you grow your own roses in your own garden. Clearly you would never produce more roses if the marginal cost to you was greater than the marginal benefit to you. But you would produce more roses if your marginal benefit from more roses was greater than your marginal cost. Only when marginal benefit equals marginal cost would you stop producing and consuming more.

The second condition for efficiency relates to the production of goods at different firms. It is that *the marginal cost of a good should be equal for every producer.* Again, if this were not the case, then production could be increased without cost. For example, if Hugo's rose garden could produce an extra dozen roses at a marginal cost of $10 and Mimi's rose garden could produce an extra dozen roses at a marginal cost of $50, then it would make sense for Hugo's garden to increase production and for Mimi's garden to decrease production. Mimi could take the $50 she saved by producing less and have more than enough to pay Hugo's costs of producing an extra dozen. Only when the marginal costs are the same is there no way to increase production without cost. Note that it is not necessary for Hugo and Mimi or any other producer to be the same or even to have the same total costs; all that we require for efficiency is that the *marginal* costs be the same.

The third condition for efficiency relates to the allocation of goods to different consumers. It is that *the marginal benefit of consuming the same good should be equal for all consumers.* If the marginal benefits were not equal, then there could be a gain for some people with no loss for anyone else. For example, suppose Ken's marginal benefit from roses was $3 and Maria's was $1; then if Maria sold roses to Ken for $2, both would be better off. But if their marginal benefits were the same, then no improvement for one without harming the other would be possible.

In sum, there are three conditions for efficiency: (1) the marginal benefit equals the marginal cost for the last item produced; (2) the marginal cost of producing each good is equal for all producers; and (3) the marginal benefit from consuming each good is equal for all consumers.

> **Second efficiency condition:** Every producer's *MC* is the same.

> **Third efficiency condition:** Every consumer's *MB* is the same.

Is the Market Efficient?

Given the three conditions for efficiency, can we say that the market is efficient? The competitive equilibrium model provides us with a quick answer to that question.

According to the model of consumer behavior in Chapter 5, an individual consumer chooses a quantity of a good such that *price equals marginal benefit*—that is, $P = MB$. This equality holds for every consumer at every point on the market demand curve. Remember that the marginal benefit is the willingness to pay dollars to consume an additional amount of a good. According to the model of firm behavior in Chapter 6, a firm produces a quantity of a good such that *price equals marginal cost.* That is, $P = MC$. This equality holds for every firm at every point on the market supply curve. At a point of intersection of the supply curve and the demand curve, both of these conditions must hold because the point of intersection is on both the supply curve and the demand curve and the price P is the same. That is, $P = MB$ and $P = MC$ simultaneously. This implies that at the quantity produced by the market, *marginal benefit equals marginal cost.* That is, $MB = MC$. This is true of every good.

Thus we have proved that a competitive market satisfies the first condition of efficiency. The marginal cost of producing roses, grapes, bread, peanuts, or automobiles is equal to the marginal benefit that people get from consuming them. This occurs without any person coordinating consumers and producers. Producing more or less of the item will only lead to a violation of this key equality between marginal cost and marginal benefit.

> Here's the reason in a nutshell why the first condition is satisfied:
>
> At a market equilibrium:
>
> $P = MB$ and $P = MC$
>
> Thus since $P = P$, we must have
>
> $MC = MB$

Here's the reason in a nutshell why the second condition is satisfied:

$$\text{Hugo's } MC = P$$
$$\text{Mimi's } MC = P$$

Thus

$$\text{Hugo's } MC = \text{Mimi's } MC$$

Here's the reason in a nutshell why the third condition is satisfied:

$$\text{Maria's } MB = P \text{ and}$$
$$\text{Ken's } MB = P$$

Thus

$$\text{Maria's } MB = \text{Ken's } MB$$

first theorem of welfare economics: the conclusion that a competitive market results in an efficient outcome; sometimes called the "invisible hand theorem"; the definition of efficiency used in the theorem is Pareto efficiency.

To better appreciate the result, again imagine that you grow your own roses in your own garden. Clearly, you would never grow more roses if the marginal benefit to you was less than your marginal cost. What is striking is that when you do not grow your own roses or even when you do not know anything about growing roses, the marginal benefit of more roses to you will be equal to the marginal cost of producing more roses.

The result is illustrated in Figure 7.6. At the market equilibrium quantity (point *E*), the marginal cost (the point on the supply curve) is equal to the marginal benefit (the point on the demand curve). At any other point, either marginal benefit will be greater than marginal cost or marginal benefit will be less than marginal cost.

The other two criteria for efficiency also hold in a competitive market. To see this, it will help to look back at Figure 7.2. Observe that in a market equilibrium, the marginal cost for the producers is the same, because *they all face the same price;* along each of their individual supply curves, all producers—Hugo, Mimi, and others—set marginal cost equal to the price. Similarly, in a market equilibrium, *all consumers*—Maria, Ken, and others—*face the same market price.* Hence, their marginal benefits are all equal, because on each of their individual demand curves the marginal benefit equals the price. Thus, it is not possible to make one person better off without hurting someone else. In a competitive market, the marginal benefits are equal. Thus, there is no improvement for one that does not hurt someone else.

In sum, for each good produced in a competitive market, (1) the marginal benefit equals the marginal cost of the last item produced, (2) the marginal cost is equal for all producers in the market, and (3) the marginal benefit is equal for all consumers in the market. Thus, we can say that the competitive market is Pareto efficient.

The proposition that competitive markets are efficient is one of the most important in economics, so much so that when it is proven with the mathematics necessary to keep track of many different goods and time periods, it is called the **first theorem of welfare economics.** The word *theorem* reflects the mathematics used in the advanced proof of the idea. The word *welfare* means that the theorem is

Figure 7.6
The Efficiency of the Market: Marginal Benefit Equals Marginal Cost
Only at quantity *E* is the marginal benefit of an extra unit equal to the marginal cost of an extra unit. Point *D* is not efficient because the marginal benefit of an extra unit is greater than the marginal cost of producing it. Part *F* is also not efficient because the marginal cost of producing an extra unit is greater than the marginal benefit.

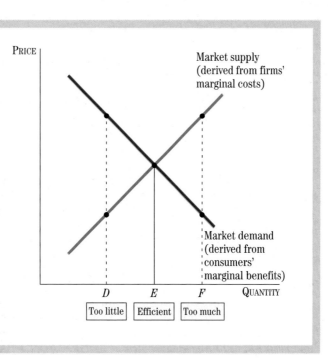

Ticket scalping—selling a ticket to an event at a higher price than its face value—is a fascinating subject, illustrating how the workings of free markets intertwine with the complexity of human emotion. A common view of scalping is expressed in this comment written in an MIT newspaper by a student who had just bought an extra ticket to his own graduation from a scalper: "There is no disputing the fact that we live in a capitalist society where the laws of supply and demand apply to many transactions, but are we not an academic community of concerned individuals? Graduation tickets were not meant to be sold to the highest bidder, like the scalpers who peddle tickets to the latest rock concert or playoff sporting event." (*The Tech*, 5/27/94, p 4.)

Musicians (and possibly some sports teams) might agree more with the MIT student than he suspects. The Internet has generated an exceedingly efficient way of supplying tickets to people who demand them. But, as described in the article below, many musical acts view this type of sale as detrimental to their livelihood in the long run. Losing control of the sale may prevent a type of interaction (between fan and musical performer) that many bands would prefer to encourage. Why do you think bands want to get back control of their tickets sales and remove the middleman from this economic interaction?

A Guide to Tickets
Where Have All the Good Seats Gone?

by Steve Morse, *Boston Globe* Staff
May 1, 2005

Tired of scalpers marking up ticket prices and frustrated with high service fees from brokers, many music acts are taking more control of their ticketing as a way to connect with fans.

The biggest trend is for bands to offer tickets through their online fan club sites, with some charging annual membership fees. U2 charges $40, the Dave Matthews Band charges $35, and Madonna charges about $38.

The intent is to get tickets into the hands of diehard fans before the tickets go on sale to everyone else. Typically, bands hold Internet "presales" to club members a week or two before a public sale, which is usually handled by broker Ticketmaster.

But for fans, the clubs certainly don't guarantee tickets. Nor cheap tickets either. Last year Madonna's fan site offered $700 VIP seats. But bands for the most part offer lower service fees and throw in discounts on merchandise and other sweeteners to promote artist-to-fan interaction without a middleman.

One concern is that some scalpers just join the fan clubs, which was a problem with a recent U2.com presale. But bands are making vigorous attempts to cross-check names, credit card numbers, and e-mail and postal addresses to weed out violators who may be buying tickets in bulk, as well as work with online auction site eBay to identify culprits.

"You can't always make everyone happy, but we do the best job we can," says Coran Capshaw, who manages the Dave Matthews Band and heads Musictoday.com, which handles fan sites for Madonna, Kenny Chesney, Britney Spears, and other top-name acts.

Musictoday.com operates out of Charlottesville, Va., and employs 200 people who coordinate the ticketing and the discounted merchandise and other privileges (from CD samplers to special magazines) that come with the memberships. Tens of thousands of fans have joined

about the overall well-being of people in the economy (the word *welfare* is synonymous with "well-being," not with a transfer payment to a poor person). The word *first* is used to distinguish this theorem from the second theorem of welfare economics, which states the converse of the first: Any Pareto efficient outcome can be obtained via a competitive market.

Efficiency and Income Inequality

income inequality: disparity in levels of income among individuals in the economy.

Efficiency is a very important goal of an economic system, but it is not the only goal. Another goal is that no one, or at least as few people as possible, falls into dire economic circumstances. For example, reducing **income inequality** to an amount that makes poverty a rare occurrence is also a desirable goal in most economic systems.

the Matthews band's fan site called "Warehouse," says Capshaw, who declined to be more specific.

Capshaw says his role model was the Grateful Dead, who pioneered direct-mail marketing. The Dead would take up to 50 percent of a venue's seats and distribute customized souvenir tickets.

Most bands can now only get 8 to 10 percent of a show's tickets because they run up against tight contracts between Ticketmaster and the venues. In the touring business, concert sites such as the Tweeter Center and Bank of America Pavilion make agreements with Ticketmaster to sell tickets and charge customers a fee for that service. Ticketmaster then shares part of the service fees with the music promoter and the venue, but not the bands.

Acts that have lobbied to control their tickets for years, such as the Dave Matthews Band and String Cheese Incident, can get a higher percentage of a show's tickets. When Ticketmaster tried to cut back String Cheese's allotment in 2003, the band filed an antitrust suit against the ticketing agency. The suit was settled out of court for undisclosed terms, and String Cheese now says it is pleased with its current share.

John Pleasants, chief executive of Ticketmaster, said ticket presales have gained in popularity the last five years, in part because bands are trying to develop new revenue streams through their fan clubs. Pleasants said Ticketmaster runs the presales for many bands.

"Artists are the people who are at the top of the value chain," Pleasants said. "These are the people who create the content and there is no question that, as a generalization, these folks are looking to get more compensation for what they do, as opposed to less, and so they will look for opportunities like fan clubs or extra merchandise sales."

Some venue promoters dislike fan club sites. A Clear Channel Entertainment executive says a fan club presale can hurt the subsequent public sale of tickets because many nonmembers will assume the best seats are already taken. For that reason, Clear Channel in Boston, the executive adds, makes sure that many good tickets are still held for the public sale.

Lower service fees are another key reason fan club sites have flourished. The jam band String Cheese Incident tacks on an average fee of $4 per ticket, but that's often less than half of what Ticketmaster might charge.

"Hopefully by lowering the fees, the fans can afford to see more music," said String Cheese manager Mike Luba.

His group first started selling tickets out of a candle shop run by bassist Keith Moseley's brother, Kevin, a decade ago in Durango, Colo. That evolved into SCI Ticketing and is now called Baselineticketing.com, which has since signed up more than 20 acts, from punk superstars Green Day to Boston breakout band the Dresden Dolls. Most of Baselineticketing.com's acts do not charge membership fees because they are opposed to a "two-tiered process" that allows wealthier fans to have an advantage over those of more modest means.

"Still, you might rather pay $40 for a membership than pay scalpers for tickets," said Bob Grossweiner, a senior editor with liveDaily.com, an online magazine about the music industry.

Dashed expectations can anger fans, as U2 learned when the presale for the first leg of its American tour went awry. Many members didn't get tickets, fans complained, and the band apologized.

"We weren't expecting the amount of members who joined," said Sebastian Clayton, brother of U2 bassist Adam Clayton, who runs the site. He said the system was overwhelmed when tickets became available in January.

"We were left in the lurch and weren't able to fill everyone's order," said Sebastian. He said the problem was fixed after U2 tacked on another leg to its tour.

Fan club sites can be big business. Take U2.com. With 100,000 members paying a $40 annual fee, that amounts to $4 million of revenue.

"It's capitalists outfoxing other capitalists," Grossweiner says.

It is important to emphasize that efficiency and income equality are not the same thing. An allocation of bread between Hugo and Mimi is efficient if their marginal benefit of bread is the same and if the marginal benefits equal the marginal cost of bread. Then there is no mutually advantageous trade of bread between Hugo and Mimi that will make one better off without hurting the other.

However, suppose that Hugo has a low income, earning only $7,000 per year, and that Mimi has a high income, earning $70,000 per year. Suppose a severe drought raises the price of wheat and thus the price of bread. If the price of bread in the market gets very high, say, $3 a loaf, then Hugo will be able to buy few loaves of bread and may go hungry, especially if he has a family. In this case, the economy gets good marks on efficiency grounds but fails miserably on income inequality grounds.

To remedy the situation, a common suggestion is to put price controls on bread. For example, to help Hugo and others like him, a law might be passed requiring that bread prices not exceed $.50 a loaf. Although this may help the income inequality problem, it will cause great inefficiency because it interferes with the market. At $.50 a loaf, bread producers will not produce very much, and Mimi will probably start buying bread to feed the birds, wasting scarce resources.

A better solution to the income inequality problem is to transfer income to Hugo and other low-income people from Mimi and other high-income people. With a transfer of income—say, through a tax and an income-support payment to the poor—the market would be able to function and the gross inefficiencies caused by price controls on bread would not occur. Even at the high price of bread, Hugo will be able to eat, perhaps buying some rice or a bread substitute, and the bread, which is so expensive to produce, will not be wasted on the birds. We will see that such transfers have advantages and disadvantages. Compared to price controls, their main advantage is that they allow the market to operate efficiently.

The temptation to deal with income inequality problems in ways that interfere with the efficiency of the market is great in all societies. Price ceilings (rent controls) on rental apartments in some U.S. cities, which we examined in Chapter 3, are one example. But this interference wastes economic resources.

REVIEW
- Economic inefficiency implies a waste of resources. A Pareto efficient outcome is one in which no person's situation can be improved without hurting someone else. A key criterion for Pareto efficiency is that production and consumption be such that the marginal benefit of a good equals its marginal cost.

- One of the most desirable features of competitive markets is that at the equilibrium level of production, marginal benefit equals marginal cost. On the demand curve, marginal benefit equals the market price. On the supply curve, marginal cost equals the market price. Because the quantity demanded equals the quantity supplied in equilibrium, together these imply that marginal benefit equals marginal cost.

- Thus competitive markets are efficient. Any change in consumption or production that makes one person better off must make someone else worse off.

- Efficiency is not the same thing as income equality. An efficient outcome can coexist with an unequal outcome.

Measuring Waste from Inefficiency

We know from Chapters 5 and 6 that consumer surplus and producer surplus are measures of how much consumers and producers gain from buying and selling in a market. The larger these two surpluses are, the better off people are.

Maximizing the Sum of Producer Plus Consumer Surplus

An attractive feature of competitive markets is that they maximize the sum of consumer and producer surplus. Producer and consumer surplus are shown in the market supply and market demand diagram in Figure 7.7. Recall that the producer

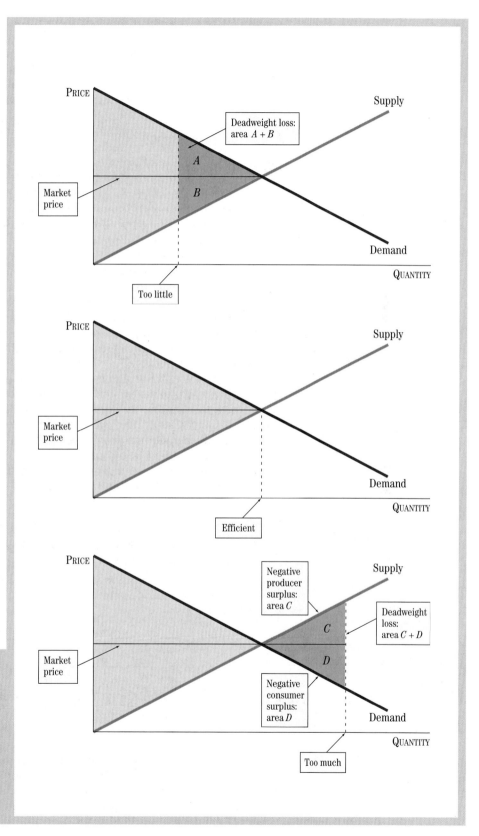

Another way to think about the lightly shaded areas in the graphs: The sum of consumer surplus plus producer surplus is the triangular area between the demand curve and the supply curve—shown by the lightly shaded area in the middle graph of Figure 7.7. The graph shows another way to think about this sum: The sum of consumer surplus plus producer surplus equals the marginal benefit minus the marginal cost of all the items produced.

Figure 7.7
Measuring Economic Loss
When production is less or more than the market equilibrium amount, the economic loss is measured by the loss of consumer surplus plus producer surplus. In the top diagram, the quantity produced is too small. In the bottom diagram, it is too large. In the middle diagram, it is efficient.

surplus for all producers is the area above the supply curve and below the market price line. The consumer surplus for all consumers is the area below the demand curve and above the market price line. Both the consumer surplus and the producer surplus are shown in Figure 7.7. The lightly shaded gray area is the sum of consumer surplus plus producer surplus. The equilibrium quantity is at the intersection of the two curves. At this point, consumer surplus plus producer surplus is maximized.

Deadweight Loss

Figure 7.7 also shows what happens to consumer surplus plus producer surplus when the efficient level of production does not occur. The top panel of Figure 7.7 shows a situation in which the quantity produced is lower than the market equilibrium quantity. Clearly, the sum of consumer and producer surplus is lower. By producing a smaller quantity, we lose the amount of the consumer and producer surplus in the darkly shaded triangular area $A + B$. The bottom panel of Figure 7.7 shows the opposite situation, in which the quantity produced is too high. In this case, we have to subtract the triangular area $C + D$ from the lightly shaded area on the left because price is greater than marginal benefit and lower than marginal cost, which means that consumer surplus and producer surplus are negative in the area $C + D$. In both the top and bottom panels of the figure, these darkly shaded triangles are a loss to society from producing more or less than the efficient amount. Economists call the loss in this darkly shaded area the **deadweight loss.** It is a measure of the waste from inefficient production.

deadweight loss: the loss in producer and consumer surplus due to an inefficient level of production.

Deadweight loss is not simply a theoretical curiosity with a gruesome name; it is used by economists to measure the size of the waste to society of deviations from the competitive equilibrium. By calculating deadweight loss, economists can estimate the benefits and costs of many government programs. When you hear or read that the cost of U.S. agricultural programs is billions of dollars or that the benefit of a world-trade agreement is trillions of dollars, it is the increase or decrease in deadweight loss that is being referred to. In order to compute the deadweight loss, all we need is the demand curve and the supply curve.

REVIEW
- Competitive markets maximize producer surplus plus consumer surplus.
- If the quantity produced is either greater or less than the market equilibrium amount, the sum of consumer surplus plus producer surplus is less than at the market equilibrium. The decline in consumer plus producer surplus measures the waste from producing the wrong amount. It is called deadweight loss.

CASE STUDY

Price Controls and Deadweight Loss in the Milk Industry

Since the 1930s, the federal government has intervened in the milk market (and other agricultural markets) in order to stabilize farm prices and provide some income protection for U.S. farmers. The government has used a combination of complex regulations that include government purchases and subsequent disposal of dairy products, import restrictions, export subsidies, and pricing mechanisms depending on the

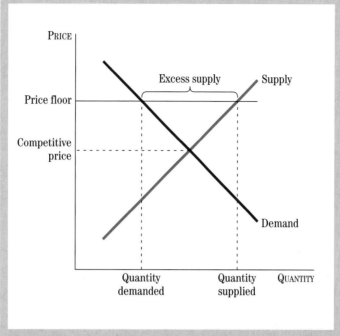

Figure 7.8
Price and Quantity Effects of a Price Floor
If the price floor is set higher than the competitive market price, the quantity demanded by consumers decreases and the quantity supplied by firms increases, creating excess supply.

location and purpose of the production of milk. We can see how price controls lead to deadweight loss by looking more closely at one of these programs.

The Food and Agriculture Act of 1977 was aimed at sustaining higher prices received by dairy farmers. Figure 7.8 shows a stylized representation of the milk market with a price floor. As we know, the competitive market price occurs when the quantity demanded equals the quantity supplied, but the higher price floor mandated by the government reduced the quantity demanded and gave farmers an incentive to produce more milk, causing excess supply. To support the price floor, the government purchased the excess supply of milk in the form of dry milk, butter, and cheese. Of course, there was a cost to this program: close to $2 billion a year in net government expenditures in the early 1980s. In the late 1980s and early 1990s, in an effort to reduce the excess supply of milk while keeping prices high, the federal government taxed farmers who increased their milk production.

Figure 7.9 shows the reduction in consumer surplus, the increase in producer surplus, and the excess supply of milk that is purchased by the government. In 1994 economists Peter Helmberger and Yu-Hui Chen estimated what would happen if the government deregulated the milk market. In the short run, they found that consumer surplus would increase by $3.9 billion a year, producer surplus would decrease by $4 billion, and net government expenditures would decrease by $600 million, eliminating a deadweight loss of $500 million a year. As you can see, the price floor is more expensive than directly transferring money from consumers to farmers, as explained in the Efficiency and Income Inequality section.

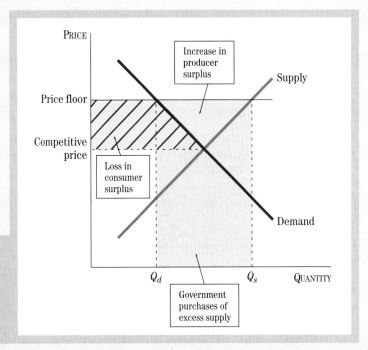

Figure 7.9
A Costly Price Floor Program
Each unit of excess supply has to be purchased by the government at a price higher than the competitive market price, making this a very costly program.

The Federal Agricultural Improvement and Reform (FAIR) Act of 1996 mandated the elimination of the price support program by the end of 1999. However, the dairy subsidies were soon reinstated by the farm bill signed by President Bush in May 2002, which increased total agricultural subsidies from $100 billion to close to $200 billion a year. The current system of dairy subsidies chose the market price of drinking milk in Boston as the standard for the rest of the country. When that price falls below $16.94 per hundred pounds, all U.S. dairy farmers receive a governmental subsidy of 45 percent of the difference between the Boston market price and $16.94. What do you think will be the effects of this legislation on the milk market?

REVIEW
- Price floors hurt consumers and usually benefit producers. The net effect is a loss to society.
- Agricultural subsidies in the United States were doubled in 2002.

The Deadweight Loss from Taxation

Another important application of deadweight loss is in estimating the impact of a tax. To see how, let's examine the impact of a tax on a commodity like gasoline. We will see that the tax shifts the supply curve, leads to a reduction in the quantity produced, and reduces the sum of producer surplus plus consumer surplus.

A Tax Paid by a Producer Shifts the Supply Curve

A tax on sales is a payment that must be made to the government by the seller of a product. The tax may be a percentage of the dollar value spent on the products sold, in which case it is called an *ad valorem tax*. A 6 percent state tax on retail purchases is an ad valorem tax. Or it may be proportional to the number of items sold, in which case the tax is called a *specific tax*. A tax on gasoline of $.50 per gallon is an example of a specific tax.

Because the tax payment is made by the producer or the seller to the government, the immediate impact of the tax is to add to the marginal cost of producing the product. Hence, the immediate impact of the tax will be to shift the supply curve. For example, suppose each producer of gasoline has to send a certain amount, say, $.50 per gallon produced and sold, to the government. Then $.50 must be added to the marginal cost per gallon for each producer.

The resulting shift of the supply curve is shown in Figure 7.10. The vertical distance between the old and the new supply curves is the size of the sales tax in dollars. The supply curve shifts up by this amount because this is how much is added to the marginal costs of the producer. (Observe that this upward shift can just as accurately be called a leftward shift because the new supply curve is above and to the left of the old curve. Saying that the supply curve shifts up may seem confusing because when we say "up," we seem to be meaning "more supply." But the "up" is along the vertical axis, which has the price on it. The upward, or leftward, movement of the supply curve is in the direction of less supply, not more supply.)

A New Equilibrium Price and Quantity

What does the competitive equilibrium model imply about the change in the price and the quantity produced? Observe that there is a new intersection of the supply curve and the demand curve. Thus, the price rises to a new, higher level, and the quantity produced declines.

The price increase, as shown in Figure 7.10, is not as large as the increase in the tax. The vertical distance between the old and the new supply curves is the amount of the tax, but the price increases by less than this distance. Thus the producers are not able to "pass on" the entire tax to the consumers in the form of higher prices. If the tax increase is $.50, then the price increase is less than $.50, perhaps $.40. The producers have been forced by the market—by the movement along the demand curve—to reduce their production, and by doing so they have absorbed some of the tax increase.

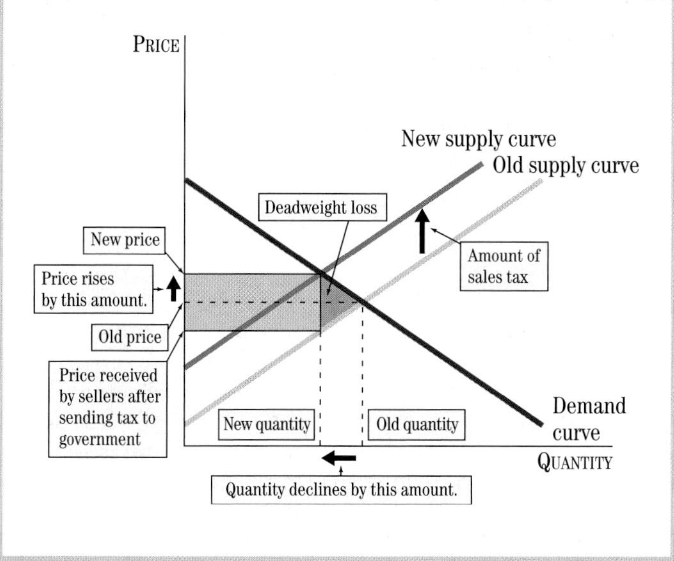

Deadweight Loss and Tax Revenue

Now consider what happens to consumer surplus and producer surplus with the sales tax. Because the total quantity produced is lower, there is a loss in consumer surplus and producer surplus. The right part of the triangle of consumer plus producer surplus has been cut off, and this is a measure of the deadweight loss to society, as shown in Figure 7.10. This loss occurs despite the fact that the tax revenue going to the government is used for financing government activity. The deadweight loss is incurred because there is a movement of production away from the efficient level. Taxes may be necessary to

Figure 7.10
Deadweight Loss from a Tax
In this graph the dark triangle represents the deadweight loss and the blue rectangle the amount of tax revenue that goes to the government. The sales tax, which is collected and paid to the government by the seller, adds to the marginal cost of each item the producer sells. Hence, the supply curve shifts up. The price rises, but by less than the tax increase.

ECONOMICS IN ACTION

Tax Prediction Passes Economists' Test

The competitive equilibrium model gives a remarkably precise prediction that an increase in a tax on gasoline will increase the price of gasoline, but by no more than the tax increase. This model is also very useful because it predicts that gasoline stations will pass on some but not all of the tax to consumers. The same is true for any other good. If there is a tax on long-stemmed roses, producers such as Hugo and Mimi will have to send the tax payment to the government, but they will find that the price they get for roses will increase as a partial offset. Consumers such as Ken and Maria will have to pay more for roses, but their price increase will be less than the amount of the tax.

But how accurate is the prediction? Economists have tested the prediction with experimental double-auction markets and found that it passes the test. Here is how the test works: Add a fixed amount—say, $6—to the marginal cost sheets of sellers in the double auction. Replacing the original sellers' sheets in Figure 7.4 with new sheets in which marginal cost is $6 higher would show the impact of a $6 tax.

The effect of such a change on the market supply curve is shown on the graph. It shifts up by exactly $6. According to the competitive equilibrium model, the price should rise by $3 and production should fall by 3 units. The price increase should be less than the tax increase, with about half the increase passed on to the buyers, according to the model.

Economists who run such experimental markets find that in this case, the price rises to about $16 and the quantity falls to 10 units, compared with $13 and 13 units without the tax, much as predicted by the

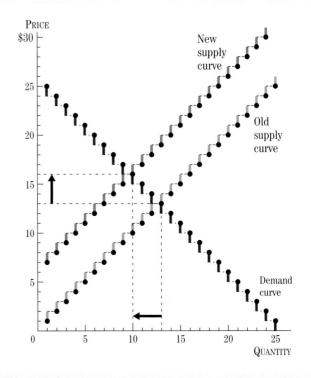

model. This occurs even if the buyers know nothing about the tax. The interaction of only a few sellers and buyers in the market with very limited information results in the outcome predicted by the competitive equilibrium model.

finance the government, but they cause a deadweight loss to society. In Chapter 14, where we study the effects of different types of taxes, we will show that the deadweight loss depends on the price elasticity of supply and demand.

Figure 7.10 also tells us how much tax revenue goes to the government in the case of a specific tax. The tax revenue is the tax times the number of items sold. If the tax is $1 and 100 items are sold, the tax revenue is $100. This amount is shown by the blue rectangle. Some of what was producer surplus and consumer surplus thus goes to the government. Another portion, the deadweight loss, is no longer available. No one gets it.

REVIEW
- The impact of a tax on the economy can be analyzed using consumer surplus and producer surplus.

- Taxes are necessary to finance government expenditures, but they lower the production of the item being taxed.

- The loss to society from the decline in production is measured by the reduction in consumer surplus and producer surplus, the deadweight loss due to the tax.

Informational Efficiency

We have shown that a competitive market works well in that the outcome is Pareto efficient. For every good, the sum of consumer surplus and producer surplus is maximized. These are important and attractive characteristics of a competitive market.

Another important and attractive characteristic of a competitive market is that the market processes information very efficiently. For example, in the double-auction market, the price reflects the marginal benefit for every buyer and the marginal cost for every seller. If a government official were asked to set the price in a real market, there would be no way that such information could be obtained, especially with millions of buyers and sellers. In other words, the market seems to be informationally efficient. Pareto efficiency is different from this *informational efficiency*.

In the 1930s and 1940s, as the government of the Soviet Union tried to centrally plan production in the entire economy, economists became more interested in the informational efficiency of markets. One of the most outspoken critics of central planning, and a strong advocate of the market system, was Friedrich Hayek, who emphasized the importance of the informational efficiencies of the market. In Hayek's view, a major disadvantage of central planning—where the government sets all the prices and the quantities—is that it is informationally inefficient.

If you had all the information about all the buyers and sellers in the double-auction market, you could set the price to achieve a Pareto efficient outcome. To see Hayek's point, it is perhaps enough to observe such experimental markets and see that without private information about every buyer and seller, you or any

Coordination Without a Market
Although prices provide a valuable coordination role in a market economy, some activities are better coordinated without the market. It would not be efficient to coordinate each of the hand and foot movements of these 100 skydivers with prices.

government official would not know where to set the price. Complicate this with millions of buyers, millions of different products, and rapidly changing tastes and technology, and you can quickly comprehend Hayek's arguments. However, economists do not have results as neat as the first theorem of welfare economics to prove Hayek's point. The reason is that in some situations, the market would be unwieldy, and it is difficult to describe these situations with any generality.

Consider the example of coordinating the members of a marching band consisting of several different instruments and several different players. Suppose you were asked how to coordinate the members of a marching band through a price system in a market! You might set a price for playing loud versus soft and then vary the price according to how loud you wanted the band to play. But using the price system to conduct a real band would be an impossible task. It would be better to conduct the marching band without prices and without a market, just as all marching bands in the world are conducted. Coordinating millions of producers and consumers of roses by a central conductor is just as difficult as coordinating the members of a marching band by a price system. Rose production and consumption is handled well by the market and poorly by a central conductor. On the other hand, a marching band is handled poorly by the market and well by a central conductor.

Two obvious difficulties arise in using a market system to coordinate activities like a marching band. First, prices will not bring about a sufficiently precise or speedy response. It is essential that the flute and the sax start playing at the same moment; a one-second delay will turn music into noise. It is better to tell the musicians to play this note at this volume at this time. Second, it is possible for the conductor to get information about each band member. A band leader knows which band member is capable of doing what.

In most situations in which the informational advantage of the price system and the market is not large and in which great precision in coordination is required, organizations spring up. Musicians form a band, a community forms a police force, and so on.

REVIEW
- The market has the ability to process information efficiently. Market experiments demonstrate informational efficiency. The lack of informational efficiency is a key reason why central planning does not work well in complex and changing environments.

- For some activities, however, the market has few informational advantages. A production process in which exact timing is essential will be poorly coordinated through prices. In almost all these situations, firms or organizations form and replace market transactions.

Conclusion

Adam Smith's idea of the "invisible hand" is perhaps the most important discovery in economics: Individuals, by freely pursuing their own interests in a market economy, are led as if by an invisible hand to an outcome that is best overall. The first theorem of welfare economics is the modern statement of Adam Smith's famous principle; in tribute to Smith's seminal idea, we call it the "invisible hand theorem," although the theorem was not actually proved by economists until the mid-twentieth century. Understanding why, and under what circumstances, the invisible hand theorem is true is an important part of thinking like an economist.

Understanding the theorem has required an investment in economic model building: The behavior of consumers and the behavior of firms were combined into a competitive equilibrium model describing how consumers and firms interact in markets. This model is an embellishment of the supply and demand model we used in Chapters 3 and 4. Experimental markets demonstrate that the model works well in predicting actual outcomes.

Building the competitive equilibrium model has had payoffs beyond understanding this most important theorem in economics. Armed with the ideas of consumer surplus and producer surplus, we can now measure the costs of deviations from the competitive market equilibrium. Such measures are used by economists to assess the costs and benefits of government programs that interfere, for bad or good, with the market outcomes. Starting with Chapter 10, we will see that deviations from the competitive market equilibrium are caused by monopolies and other factors. But first we will look more closely at how costs and production within individual firms and competitive industries change over time. We do this in Chapters 8 and 9.

KEY POINTS

1. The interaction of producers and consumers or buyers and sellers in a market can be explained by the competitive equilibrium model.

2. Processing information and coordinating and motivating millions of consumption and production decisions is difficult, but the market is a device that can do the job remarkably well.

3. The competitive equilibrium model keeps track of the individual decisions of consumers and producers.

4. Even with only a few sellers and buyers, experimental markets appear to be well explained by the competitive equilibrium model.

5. An outcome is Pareto efficient if it is not possible to change production or consumption in a way that will make one person better off without hurting someone else.

6. A competitive market is Pareto efficient.

7. In a competitive market, marginal benefit equals marginal cost for the last item produced, and the sum of producer surplus and consumer surplus is maximized.

8. Deviations from the Pareto efficient outcome create a loss to society called deadweight loss.

9. Deadweight loss is caused by a tax that reduces the quantity produced.

10. The market system is also informationally efficient. However, there are no general theorems that prove the informational efficiency of the market.

KEY TERMS

invisible hand
competitive equilibrium
  model

double-auction market
Pareto efficient

first theorem of welfare
  economics

income inequality
deadweight loss

QUESTIONS FOR REVIEW

1. What are the information-processing, coordination, and motivation functions that arise when buyers and sellers interact?

2. Why is it difficult for one person or group of persons to perform the functions listed in question 1?

3. How does the market perform these functions?

4. How does the competitive equilibrium model explain the decisions of consumers and producers?

5. What is a double-auction market?

6. Do experimental double-auction markets validate the competitive equilibrium model?

7. What is the meaning of Pareto efficiency, and how does it differ from informational efficiency?

8. Why must marginal benefit equal marginal cost for Pareto efficiency?

9. Why is the sum of consumer surplus and producer surplus maximized in the market?

10. What is deadweight loss, and how do taxes cause it?

PROBLEMS

1. Suppose poor weather results in major damage to the coffee crop, resulting in lower supply.
   a. Draw a supply and demand diagram to show what will happen to the equilibrium price and quantity of coffee in the United States. Assume that the demand curve does not shift.
   b. Suppose the U.S. government observes that the price of coffee is increasing rapidly and imposes a price ceiling equal to the original equilibrium price. What effect does the price ceiling have on the quantity supplied and demanded of coffee? As a result of the price ceiling, how much coffee will actually be bought and sold?
   c. How are consumer and producer surplus affected by the price ceiling?

2. In 1975, 18 million calculators were produced and sold at an average price of $60. In 1983, 31 million calculators were produced and sold at an average price of $30. Assume that the demand curve for calculators did not shift between 1975 and 1983.
   a. Sketch market demand and market supply curves for calculators in 1975 and in 1983 to illustrate the change in price and quantity. Mark the 1975 and 1983 prices and quantities on the axes.
   b. Describe an event that could have led to the changes you just illustrated.
   c. Show the gain to consumers from this event on your sketch.

3. Consider the following supply and demand schedule:

Price	Supply	Demand
$.25	2	14
$.50	6	12
$.75	10	10
$1.00	14	8
$1.25	18	6
$1.50	22	4
$1.75	26	2

   a. Sketch the market supply and demand curves. Show the equilibrium quantity, price, producer surplus, and consumer surplus.
   b. Describe what would happen to the price of this product if a tax of $.75 per unit sold were enacted by the government. Show your answer graphically.
   c. Show the deadweight loss due to the tax on your diagram.

4. Calculate the consumer surplus using the market demand curve in Figure 7.3. Assume that the market price is $10. Show that you get the same answer by adding up the consumer surplus for all five buyers. How much does consumer surplus increase for the market as a whole and for each individual when the market price falls to $5?

5. Calculate the producer surplus using the market supply curve in Figure 7.4. Assume that the market price is $10. Show that you get the same answer by adding up the producer surplus for all five sellers. How much does producer surplus increase for the market as a whole and for each seller when the market price rises to $15?

6. Suppose that in a competitive market there are three buyers (Linda, Sue, and Pete) with the marginal benefit (*MB*) schedules below. If the price is $8, what will be the consumer surplus for each person? What is the consumer surplus for the market as a whole?

Quantity	MB—Linda	MB—Sue	MB—Pete
1	15	14	13
2	12	11	10
3	9	8	7
4	6	5	4
5	3	2	1

7. Suppose that in a competitive market there are three sellers (Max, Scott, and Karen) with the marginal cost (*MC*) schedules shown below. If the price is $8, what will be the producer surplus for each person? What is the producer surplus for the market as a whole?

Quantity	MC—Max	MC—Scott	MC—Karen
1	3	2	1
2	6	5	4
3	9	8	7
4	12	11	10
5	15	14	13

8. Suppose that in the market from the previous two questions the government imposes a $4 sales tax, which causes the equilibrium price to go up to $10. Draw a graph showing the original supply curve, the new supply curve, and the demand curve. Use this graph to show:
   a. The deadweight loss resulting from the $4 tax based on the original price and quantity.
   b. The amount of revenue collected by the government.
   c. The effect the tax has on producer and consumer surplus.

9. For which of the following items—milk, wine, coffee, bread, gasoline, 100 percent wool sweaters, sports cars, VCRs—do you think the deadweight loss of a sales tax would be the largest? The smallest? Explain.

10. What would the competitive equilibrium model predict about the quantity sold if people were not allowed to bid or ask more than $4 for any good in the market described in problems 4 and 5? What if they were not allowed to bid or ask less than $12? Illustrate your answers in a graph and show the deadweight loss in each case.

11. Firm A and firm B both produce the same product with the following total costs:

Firm A		Firm B	
Quantity Produced	*Total Costs*	*Quantity Produced*	*Total Costs*
0	5	0	2
1	6	1	5
2	8	2	9
3	11	3	14
4	15	4	20

Consider a situation in which 4 units are produced: Firm A produces 2 units, and firm B produces 2 units. Explain why this situation is not Pareto efficient. Could such a situation occur in a competitive market if both firms maximized profits? How could production be changed at the two firms in order to produce the 4 items at lower cost? Suppose the price is $3. How much would each firm produce?

The Issue:
Do Individuals Always Make Rational Decisions?

In 2002, the Bank of Sweden Prize in Economic Sciences, better known as the Nobel Prize in Economics, was awarded to Daniel Kahneman of Princeton University and Vernon Smith of George Mason University.[1] The two winners were, as one would expect, considered to be intellectual giants in the field of economics. But what made the 2002 award somewhat unusual was that Professor Kahneman was a psychologist by training; he majored in psychology as an undergraduate at the Hebrew University in Jerusalem and received a Ph.D. in psychology from Berkeley. Rumor has it that Professor Kahneman never took a single course in economics!

Traditionally, economists have assumed that individual behavior can best be described as rational decision-making based on self-interest. A simplistic definition of what it means to be "rational" is that individuals use all available information to maximize their well-being given the constraints that they face. The contribution of Professor Kahneman and his collaborators is to think of individuals as human beings, who process all available information, but do so in a world in which emotion, memory, and fear also play a significant role. Using this approach, we can better understand some anomalies of individual decision-making that have puzzled economists over the years. Some of the puzzles that Kahneman's work has helped resolve include why people seemed to be willing to draw sweeping conclusions from very small samples of data;[2] why individuals who prefer a sure gain of $1,000 over a 10 percent chance of winning $10,000 seem to prefer a 10 percent chance of losing $10,000 over a sure loss of $1,000;[3] why the framing of a question may significantly affect the solution that people come up with;[4] and why some people seem to be averse to losses to such an extent that they turn down potentially lucrative opportunities because of fear of a low-probability outcome of a loss. By showing how to incorporate such traits into the decision-making process of individuals, Professor Kahneman and his colleague, the late Amos Tversky, opened up many new areas of research.

One of the areas of research that this new "behavioral economics" has had a substantial impact on is finance. One of the most well-established ideas in finance is that the stock market is "efficient," in that market participants process all available information so quickly that the prices of stocks are an accurate reflection of what is currently known about the underlying companies. The implications of efficient markets are very powerful—especially the idea that the future behavior of stock prices can't be predicted, since all the information available to make predictions has already been incorporated into stock prices today. Even though efficient market theory is a compelling description of how markets work, researchers have always found anomalies that could not be easily explained. The ideas developed in behavioral economics were used to understand these anomalies. In essence, the flaws, biases, and quirks of individuals affect their decisions to buy or sell (or not participate) in the stock market, resulting in bubbles, collapses, and, most importantly, opportunities for the discerning observer to predict future stock prices. How convincingly do the ideas of behavioral economics challenge efficient market theory? Read the arguments below and make up your own mind.

Financial Markets Are Not Always Efficient POINT

Robert Shiller, an economist and author of the well-known book *Irrational Exuberance,* believes that fluctuations in the stock market are not always driven by good information. His own research shows that stock prices are far too volatile to be explained by economic fundamentals (such as the company's earnings, the industry's health, or the growth of the overall economy) alone. Therefore, Shiller believes that researchers need to seek alternative explanations and that incorporating human psychology is one of the most promising avenues of research.[5] He identifies some important contributions to

1 You can read about the Nobel Prize awarded in 2002 to Vernon Smith and Daniel Kahneman online at http://nobelprize.org/economics/laureates/2002/public.html.
2 For instance, if three out of four stocks recommended by a friend increased in price, that friend would be considered to be a talented stock picker.
3 In other words, people behave differently when faced with losses than when faced with gains.
4 Facing a hypothetical epidemic that threatened the lives of 600 people, public health professionals, when asked to choose either a policy that would save 200 lives for sure or a policy that would have a one-third chance of saving 600 lives but a two-thirds chance of failing completely,

would choose the former. However, when the question was phrased differently, so that they had to choose between a policy that would result in 400 deaths for sure and a policy that would have a one-third chance of resulting in 0 deaths but a two-thirds chance of resulting in 600 deaths, they would choose the latter. Notice that only the phrasing is different, the choices are identical.
5 For a thorough overview, see Robert Shiller, "From Efficient Markets to Behavioral Finance," Cowles Foundation Discussion Paper No. 1385, October 2002. Available at http://cowles.econ.yale.edu/P/cd/d13b/d1385.pdf.

our understanding of financial markets made by behavioral finance:

- Psychology leads to feedback effects that drive stock bubbles. When stock prices go up and people hear that their friends and colleagues have done well in the stock market, they themselves may enter the market, seeking high returns. This increased demand, in turn, drives prices higher, leading to more gains and more people entering the market because they have heard about these gains. This leads to an asset bubble, as happened in the dot-com industry in the late 1990s. A similar effect can lead to financial panics.

- Because people extrapolate from small samples, they tend to overemphasize the importance of recent performance. So, for example, stocks that have done very well over the last six-month period will do substantially better over the next year than stocks that did very badly over the last six-month period. Why? Because individuals rush to buy the stocks that seem to be "winners" and dump the ones that seem to be "losers." When the same stocks are examined over longer periods of time, there is no obvious sign that the ones that were deemed to be "winners" were in fact better than the ones deemed to be "losers."

- In efficient market theory, the irrational optimists and pessimists are countered by the smart investors, so that when people irrationally drive stock prices up, the smart investors sell and pocket gains, while when prices are driven irrationally down, the smart investors step up and buy stocks on the cheap. But smart investors may not be able to do this on a large enough scale if there are a lot of irrational optimists and pessimists around. Because of loss aversion, the potential for suffering large losses when faced with a particularly large and determined group of irrational investors may weigh heavily on the minds of the smart investors.

- The importance of framing has also had an enormous impact in the area of finance. When employees are offered a plan that requires them to contribute, say, 10 percent of their income to a retirement account, but allows them the option of contributing a smaller amount, people are more likely to choose to contribute 10 percent. If a similar group were offered a retirement plan that does not specify a contribution, they would choose to contribute less than 10 percent.

COUNTERPOINT

Market Efficiency Survives the Challenge from Behavioral Finance

Even though behavioral finance has flourished as an area of research interest in recent years, it is by no means immune from criticism. The primary criticism found in a survey of the field by the Wharton School of Business at the University of Pennsylvania is that while various researchers have been able to use specific findings of behavioral economics to explain certain anomalies, the conclusions that they reach sometimes contradict each other. For example, sometimes individuals rush to sell stocks when they fall in value because they have heard of other friends who have lost a lot of money, yet some theories predict that individuals are slow to sell stocks that have gone down in value.

One of the strongest critics of behavioral finance is Eugene Fama, probably the leading exponent of the theory of efficient markets. Fama claims that most anomalies are short term and that markets are in fact efficient in the long run.[6] Fama argues that market efficiency does not claim that there are no anomalies (unexpected underreactions or overreactions to information), but instead suggests that underreactions are just as likely to occur as overreactions.

Fama also does not agree that some of these so-called anomalies are in fact anomalies. For example, one of the best-known anomalies is the poor long-term performance of initial public offerings (IPOs). Even though IPOs are often announced with great fanfare and see substantial price increases on the first day or two, studies have shown that buying an IPO results in a return that is substantially lower than from buying a non-IPO share of a company of similar size. However, when different criteria are used for selecting a company to compare the IPO with, the IPO no longer seems to perform worse.

Using Your Economics

1. If you were offered (a) a 50 percent chance of winning $1 million or (b) a guaranteed $500,000, which option would you take? If you were kidnapped for ransom and offered (a) you will be released if you pay $500,000 or (b) you will be released if you toss a coin and it comes up heads, but if it comes up tails, the price of your freedom goes up to $1 million, which would you take?

2. Behavioral economists believe that certain changes in probability affect individuals' behavior more than other changes. For example, if the likelihood of some event occurring changes from 38 percent to 39 percent, individuals are unlikely to respond as much as they would have if the likelihood had changed from 99 percent to 100 percent or from 0 percent to 1 percent. Can you think of some examples when this would be true?

6 Eugene Fama, "Market Efficiency, Long-Term Returns and Behavioral Finance," *Journal of Financial Economics*, 49(3), 1998.

PART 3

The Economics of the Firm

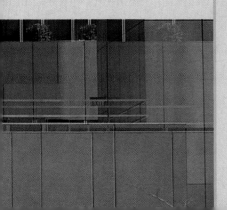

CHAPTER 8

Costs and the Changes at Firms over Time

O n a cold Saturday morning in December 1999, a wrenching story appeared on the front page of a California newspaper. It began:

> The end came at precisely 11:46 a.m. Friday. After 82 years, after four generations of toil and take-home pay, with deep roots tapping into two centuries, the end came without frill or fanfare. . . . There were tears. There were handshakes. . . . "Listen. There's a silence. It's like a hush has fallen over the place," said Bob Armstrong, the superintendent of the plant, which has been cranking out cans since the United States entered World War II in 1941.[1]

The story was an account of a firm—a cannery—shutting down its production facilities. Many firms, such as this cannery, shut down each year in the United States. But many more firms start up, so that the number of firms in existence continues to increase year after year. In the United States, about 700,000 firms

---

1. Geoffrey Tomb, "As the Final Harvest Ends, a Tech Torture Begins," *San Jose Mercury News*, December 18, 1999, p. 1.

Small businesses make up the largest share of businesses in the United States, employing, on average, half of all private sector employees. There are nearly 23 million small businesses in the United States, and they are opening and closing at a fairly steady rate. At least two-thirds of small businesses survive the first two years; about fifty percent are still open after four years. Small businesses close for a variety of reasons, including lack of adequate capital, but some businesses simply run their course. This storefront sign announces the 2002 closing of Florence Huie's laundry business in Derby, Connecticut—a business Ms. Huie started with her husband in 1960.

start up each year. Many firms are successful and will expand, but others may have to downsize and eventually shut down.

The purpose of this chapter is to develop a model for analyzing such changes at firms over time. To do so, we will extend the model of firm behavior developed in Chapter 6.

Costs, as we will see, are of vital importance to a firm's decision to start up, expand, or shut down. We will look carefully at firms' costs in this chapter. Some of the most rapidly growing firms in the United States have prospered because of new technologies that cut costs. For example, Wal-Mart—a rapidly expanding firm in the 1990s—developed a system whereby salesclerks electronically scan a bar code on each item purchased and automatically transmit the information back to the manufacturer, who can then immediately begin producing more of that item. This reduced costs.

Costs determine how large firms should be. Differences in the costs of manufacturing cement and haircuts, for example, mean that cement firms are usually large and barbershops are usually small. Costs also determine how firms should expand. For example, when firms choose between expanding their manufacturing facilities in the United States and acquiring another company abroad, they take into account the costs of labor and transportation as well as the effects of government policy toward firms.

Costs are such a crucial determinant of firm behavior that economists can capture the whole essence of a firm with a graph of its costs. By looking at such a graph, economists can determine the profitability of a firm and whether it should shut down or expand. This chapter shows how.

Finding Average Cost at an Individual Firm

In this section, we show how to find the average cost of production at a hypothetical transportation firm called On-the-Move. We will see that *average cost* plays an important role in the firm's decisions. To understand average cost, we must first review the ideas of total costs, fixed costs, variable costs, and marginal cost and show how these are related to the firm's production function.

Total Costs, Fixed Costs, Variable Costs, and Marginal Cost

total costs: the sum of variable costs and fixed costs. (Ch. 6)

fixed costs: costs of production that do not depend on the quantity of production. (Ch. 6)

variable costs: costs of production that vary with the quantity of production. (Ch. 6)

Total costs (*TC*) are the sum of all costs incurred by a firm in producing goods or services. The more that is produced, the larger are total costs. Recall from Chapter 6 that *fixed costs* (*FC*) and *variable costs* (*VC*) are the two key components of total costs.

Fixed costs are the part of total costs that do not vary with the amount produced in the short run; fixed costs include the cost of the factories, land, machines, and all other things that do not change when production changes in the short run. *Variable costs* are the part of total costs that vary in the short run as production changes. Variable costs include wage payments for workers, gasoline for trucks, fertilizer for crops, and all other things that change when the amount produced changes. By definition, total costs equal fixed costs plus variable costs; or, in symbols, $TC = FC + VC$.

short run: the period of time during which it is not possible to change all inputs to production; only some inputs, such as labor, can be changed.

long run: the minimum period of time during which all inputs to production can be changed.

■ **The Short Run and the Long Run.** Distinguishing the short run from the long run is the key to distinguishing fixed costs from variable costs. The *short run* and the *long run* are two broad categories into which economists parcel time. The **short run** is the period of time during which it is not possible to change all the inputs to production; only some inputs, such as labor, can be changed in the short run. The short run is too short, for example, to build a new factory or apartment building, to lay a fiber-optic cable, to launch a new communications satellite, or to get out of a lease on a storefront. The **long run,** in contrast, is long enough that all inputs, including capital, can be changed. Hence, the cost of each of the items that cannot be changed in the short run—factories, buildings, satellites—is fixed in the short run but can be changed in the long run.

Economists frequently use *capital* as an example of a factor that does not change in the short run and use *labor* as an example of a factor that can change in the short run. In fact, salaries paid to certain types of workers who have special skills and knowledge about the firm are better viewed as being fixed costs, and rents on certain capital items such as laptop computers or sewing machines are better viewed as being variable costs. Nevertheless, in the examples in this chapter, we refer to the cost of labor as the main variable cost and the cost of capital as the main fixed cost.

■ **Costs for On-the-Move.** Table 8.1 illustrates these definitions with cost data for On-the-Move. The firm, located in Houston, Texas, specializes in the strenuous but delicate job of moving pianos from one part of Houston to another. We use these hypothetical data rather than actual data to keep the example simple, but it is important to realize that the same analysis can be applied to data from any firm. Roadway Express, an actual moving firm that started in Houston with 16 trucks and has since gone nationwide, is a more complex example illustrating the same point. Table 8.1 lists the total costs, fixed costs, and variable costs for different levels of output at On-the-Move. Observe that fixed costs do not change but variable costs increase with output.

Table 8.1
Finding Average and Marginal Cost for On-the-Move
(costs measured in dollars per day)

Quantity (pianos moved per day) (Q)	Total Costs (TC)	Fixed Costs (FC)	Variable Costs (VC)	Average Total Cost (ATC)	Average Fixed Cost (AFC)	Average Variable Cost (AVC)	Marginal Cost (MC)
0	300	300	0	—	—	—	—
1	450	300	150	450	300	150	150
2	570	300	270	285	150	135	120
3	670	300	370	223	100	123	100
4	780	300	480	195	75	120	110
5	900	300	600	180	60	120	120
6	1,040	300	740	173	50	123	140
7	1,200	300	900	171	43	128	160
8	1,390	300	1,090	174	38	136	190
9	1,640	300	1,340	182	33	149	250
10	1,960	300	1,660	196	30	166	320
11	2,460	300	2,160	223	27	196	500

$$TC = FC + VC$$

$$ATC = \frac{TC}{Q}$$

$$AFC = \frac{FC}{Q}$$

$$AVC = \frac{VC}{Q}$$

$$\frac{\text{Change in } TC}{\text{Change in } Q}$$

The pictographs in Figure 8.1 show that fixed costs do not change in the short run at On-the-Move. Fixed costs, or the cost for four trucks and two terminals where the trucks are parked, are $300 per day regardless of how many pianos are moved during the day. Figure 8.1 also shows that variable costs increase with the amount produced. They increase from $600 to $1,660 as the number of pianos delivered per day rises from 5 to 10. Variable costs are shown in Figure 8.1 to rise because additional workers are hired to carry the goods and to drive and service the trucks. Thus, total costs rise from $900 to $1,960 as the number of pianos delivered rises from 5 to 10.

Figure 8.2 shows the same type of information as Figure 8.1 in graph form. Pairs of numbers on total costs and quantity from Table 8.1 are plotted in Figure 8.2. Connecting these dots results in the total costs curve. You can see how the total costs of moving the pianos steadily increase with the number of pianos moved. Fixed costs are shown to be unchanged at all levels of output. Figure 8.2 shows variable costs by the distance between the total costs curve and the fixed costs curve.

marginal cost: the change in total costs due to a one-unit change in quantity produced. (Ch. 6)

■ **Marginal Cost.** Table 8.1 also shows how the *marginal cost* of On-the-Move depends on the quantity of services produced (the number of pianos moved). Recall from Chapter 6 that marginal cost is the change in total costs due to a one-unit change in the quantity produced. For example, the marginal cost of increasing production from 5 moves to 6 moves a day is $140, or the change in total costs ($1,040 − $900 = $140) divided by the change in production (6 − 5 = 1). The last column of Table 8.1 shows the marginal cost for each additional piano moved by On-the-Move, from the first to the eleventh piano.

Observe that in Table 8.1, marginal cost declines at low levels of production and then begins to increase again. Marginal cost reaches a minimum of $100 when production increases from 2 to 3 units of output. Recall that in the examples in Chapter 6

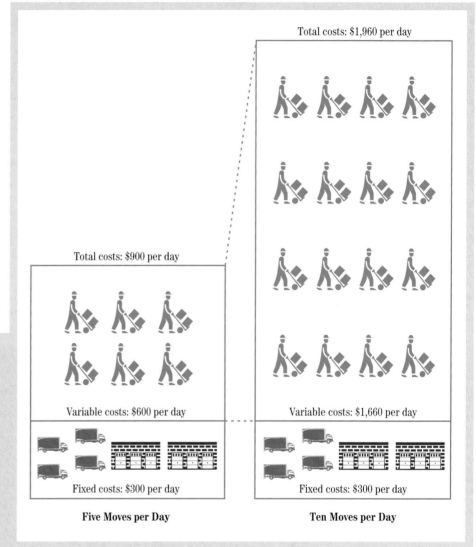

Figure 8.1
Fixed Costs versus Variable Costs
Fixed costs remain constant as the output of the firm increases in the short run. In the example of On-the-Move, fixed costs are the daily rental or interest costs for trucks and terminals under long-term lease or owned by the firm. Variable costs change with the level of output. In the case of On-the-Move, more workers must be hired to move more pianos.

(Table 6.4), marginal cost increased throughout the whole range of production. In the example of On-the-Move, marginal cost declines over part of the range of production. We will explain the reason for the difference, but first we need to define average cost.

Average Cost

average total cost (*ATC*):
total costs of production divided by the quantity produced (also called cost per unit).

average variable cost (*AVC*):
variable costs divided by the quantity produced.

average fixed cost (*AFC*):
fixed costs divided by the quantity produced.

Average total cost (*ATC*) is defined as total costs (*TC*) of production divided by the quantity (*Q*) produced. In symbols, *ATC* = *TC*/*Q*. For example, if the total costs of producing 4 items are $3,000, then the average total cost is $750 ($3,000/4). Another name for average total cost is *cost per unit*. We can also define average cost for fixed and variable costs. Thus, **average variable cost (*AVC*)** is defined as variable costs divided by the quantity produced: *AVC* = *VC*/*Q*. **Average fixed cost (*AFC*)** is defined as fixed costs divided by the quantity produced: *AFC* = *FC*/*Q*. Of the three averages,

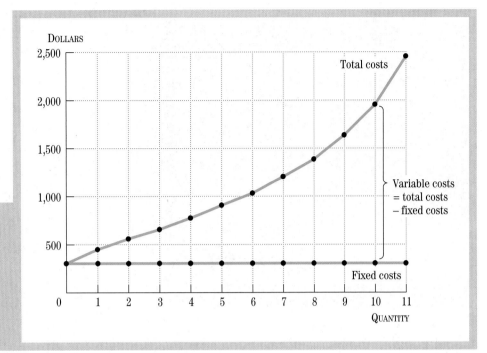

Figure 8.2
Total Costs Minus Fixed Costs Equal Variable Costs
The two lines on the diagram show total costs and fixed costs for On-the-Move. Variable costs are the difference between the two lines. Variable costs rise with production, but fixed costs are constant.

we will use average total cost most frequently; the other two averages are important for knowing whether to shut down a firm or keep it open when it is losing money.

Average total cost for On-the-Move is shown in Table 8.1. For example, total costs for 2 pianos moved ($Q = 2$) are $570; dividing $570 by 2 gives an average total cost of $285. For 3 pianos moved ($Q = 3$), total costs are $670; dividing by 3 gives $223 for average total cost. Notice that average total cost declines as production increases from low levels. Then average total cost starts to increase. In the example, average total cost starts to increase at 8 units: $1,390 divided by 8 is $174, and $1,200 divided by 7 is $171. That average total cost first decreases and then increases as production rises is a common pattern for most firms.

Average variable cost is also illustrated in Table 8.1. For 2 pianos moved ($Q = 2$), for example, average variable cost is $270 divided by 2, or $135. You can see that average variable cost, in this example, first declines and then increases throughout the rest of the range of production.

Finally, observe in Table 8.1 that average fixed cost gets smaller as production rises. Because average fixed cost is calculated by dividing fixed costs by the quantity produced, average fixed cost must decline as the quantity produced rises.

Costs Depend on the Firm's Production Function

The cost information in Table 8.1 is determined by how much *input* of labor and capital it takes to produce *output* and by the price of capital and labor. First consider some illustrative calculations of costs as the firm increases production from Q equals zero to 1 and then to 2.

■ **Varying Labor Input but Not Capital Input in the Short Run.**   According to Table 8.1, it costs On-the-Move $300 a day for capital, which is 4 trucks and 2 terminals. Let's assume that the $300 consists of $25 per day for each of the 4 trucks and

Inputs and the Production Function
Labor (the two workers) and capital (the truck) are inputs to production (moving the piano).

$100 per day for each of the 2 terminals ($25 × 4 + $100 × 2 = $300). These are the fixed costs that will be incurred even if zero pianos are moved. If the trucks and terminals were leased for one year, then the fixed costs would include the rental payment on the lease. If the trucks and the terminals were purchased on credit by On-the-Move, then the fixed costs would include interest payments on the loans. If the trucks and the terminals were bought outright, then the fixed costs would include the opportunity cost—the forgone interest payments—of the funds used to buy the trucks and the terminals.

To move pianos, however, On-the-Move needs labor. To move 1 piano, it might be enough to have 1 driver, 1 mechanic to service the truck, and another worker to help carry and load the piano. The example assumes that the cost of labor input is $150, which might consist of 15 hours of work at $10 per hour; perhaps 5 hours of work for each of the 3 workers. As production increases from $Q = 0$ to $Q = 1$, variable costs increase from zero to $150 and total costs increase from $300 to $450. Thus, the marginal cost of moving 1 piano rather than zero pianos is $150.

To move to a higher level of production, On-the-Move requires more workers. According to Table 8.1, if production rises from 1 piano moved to 2 pianos moved, then total costs increase from $450 to $570; marginal cost is $120. With wages of $10 an hour, this marginal cost would be the cost of 12 more hours of work—perhaps another driver and loader each working 5 hours a day plus increasing the hours of the mechanic by 2. As we observed already, marginal cost *declines* as production increases from 1 to 2 units of output. Now we are beginning to see why. Marginal cost decreases because labor input rises by less when increasing production from 1 to 2 units than it does when increasing production from zero to 1 unit. The reason has to do with the nature of the firm's production; perhaps the mechanic can service two trucks in less than twice the time it takes to service one truck (5 hours for one, 7 hours for two). Although these calculations illustrate how costs depend on the inputs to production, to see what is going on throughout the whole range of production, we need to look at the firm's production function.

production function: a relationship that shows the quantity of output for any given amount of input. (Ch. 6)

▪ **The Production Function.**   Table 8.2 shows the number of hours of work required to move different numbers of pianos at On-the-Move. It is On-the-Move's short-run *production function,* showing how much output can be produced for each amount of labor input. To calculate the variable costs at On-the-Move, using the information in Table 8.2, continue to assume that the wage is $10 per hour. Then to move 1 piano takes 15 hours of work; at $10 per hour, variable costs are $150. To move 10 pianos takes 166 hours of work; at $10 per hour, variable costs are $1,660. Similar calculations for all levels of output are shown in the third column of Table 8.2. Note that the variable costs in Table 8.2 are the same as those in Table 8.1. Thus, we have shown explicitly how the firm's costs depend on its production function.

Recall from Chapter 6 that the *marginal product of labor* is the change in production that can be obtained with an additional unit of labor. Decreasing marginal product of labor is called *diminishing returns to labor*. Increasing marginal product of labor is called *increasing returns to labor*.

Table 8.2
Using the Production Function to Compute Variable Costs

Quantity (pianos moved)	Hours of Work	Labor Costs at $10 Wage (variable costs)
0	0	0
1	15	150
2	27	270
3	37	370
4	48	480
5	60	600
6	74	740
7	90	900
8	109	1,090
9	134	1,340
10	166	1,660
11	216	2,160

Observe that increasing marginal product of labor exists at low levels of production; for example, it takes only 10 hours of labor to increase production [by 1 unit] from 2 to 3 units, whereas it takes 12 hours of labor to increase production [by 1 unit] from 1 to 2 units. At higher levels of production, decreasing marginal product of labor exists.

The marginal product of labor is illustrated in Figure 8.3, which shows a graph of the production function from Table 8.2. Figure 8.3 shows how, for low levels of labor input, the marginal product of labor increases: Output increases by more from a given change in labor input as labor input increases. At low levels of production, increasing marginal product of labor is a possibility because the firm's capital can be better utilized: During an oil change, for example, the mechanic can work on another truck as oil drains from the first truck. At high levels of labor input, marginal product starts to decline; diminishing returns set in. The same increase in labor input results in smaller and smaller increases in output.

Table 8.2 shows increasing marginal product of labor up to 3 units of output produced. Then diminishing returns begin. This pattern of increasing marginal product of labor up to 3 units of output and then decreasing marginal product is what causes the pattern of decreasing marginal cost up to 3 units of output produced followed by increasing marginal cost. More generally, if the marginal product of labor is increasing, then marginal cost is decreasing, and vice versa. With more and more workers required to produce a given amount of output, the marginal cost of producing that amount will increase. To summarize:

Increasing marginal product of labor → Decreasing marginal cost

Decreasing marginal product of labor → Increasing marginal cost

Be sure to distinguish between the marginal product of labor and the average product of labor. The **average product of labor** is the quantity produced, or *total product*, divided by the amount of labor input. Thus, the average product of labor is Q/L, where Q is total product and L is labor input. On the other hand, the marginal product of labor is $\Delta Q/\Delta L$, where ΔQ is the change in the quantity produced and ΔL is the change in labor input.

average product of labor: the quantity produced divided by the amount of labor input.

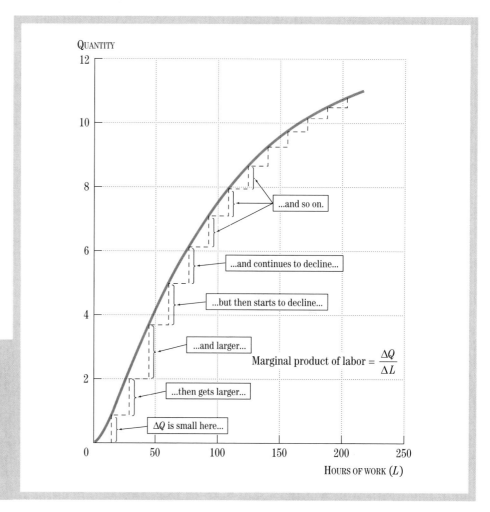

Figure 8.3
On-the-Move's Production Function
The curve shows the production function in which more labor input gives more output. Capital (trucks and terminals) is not changed. Observe that the marginal product of labor first increases and then decreases with more labor input.

Labels within the figure:
- QUANTITY (y-axis)
- HOURS OF WORK (L) (x-axis)
- ΔQ is small here...
- ...then gets larger...
- ...and larger...
- ...but then starts to decline...
- ...and continues to decline...
- ...and so on.
- Marginal product of labor $= \dfrac{\Delta Q}{\Delta L}$

REVIEW

- The short run is the period of time in which it is not possible to change all inputs to production; only some inputs, such as labor, can be changed. The long run is the period of time in which the firm can vary all inputs to production, including capital.

- Fixed costs are constant in the short run for all levels of production. Variable costs increase in the short run as more is produced. Total costs are fixed costs plus variable costs.

- Useful information about a firm comes from looking at average cost, or cost per unit. There are three types of average cost:

  1. Average total cost is defined as total costs divided by quantity, or $ATC = TC/Q$.
  2. Average variable cost is defined as variable costs divided by quantity, or $AVC = VC/Q$.
  3. Average fixed cost is defined as fixed costs divided by quantity, or $AFC = FC/Q$.

- Costs depend on the firm's production function. When marginal product of labor is decreasing, marginal cost is increasing.

Average Cost Curves

The information about average cost in Table 8.1 can be turned into an informative graph, as shown in Figure 8.4. The vertical axis of Figure 8.4 shows the dollar cost, and the horizontal axis shows the quantity produced. The pairs of points from Table 8.1 are plotted as dots in Figure 8.4, and the dots have been connected to help visualize the curves. Although the curves use exactly the same information as in Table 8.1, they are more useful. The curves are called the *marginal cost curve*, the *average total cost curve*, and the *average variable cost curve*. We label the curves *MC*, *ATC*, and *AVC*, respectively.

It is very clear from Figure 8.4 that marginal cost first decreases and then increases, as observed in Table 8.1. We now know the reason: The marginal product of each additional worker increases at lower levels of production and then decreases at higher levels of production, as shown in Figure 8.3.

Figure 8.4 also makes it very clear that average total cost first declines and then increases. In other words, the average total cost curve is *U-shaped*.

The relative positions of the average total cost curve and the marginal cost curve in Figure 8.4 are important and will come up repeatedly. Observe that when the marginal cost curve is below the average total cost curve, average total cost is declining. For example, when production rises from $Q = 1$ to $Q = 2$ in Figure 8.4, marginal cost is less than average total cost and average total cost declines. However, look at the right-hand side of Figure 8.4, where marginal cost is greater than average total cost; then average total cost increases. For example, a marginal cost of $320 is greater than the average total cost of $182, and average total cost goes up to $196. This is a general and important result: *When marginal cost is less than average total cost, then average total cost is declining; when marginal cost is greater than average total cost, then average total cost is increasing.*

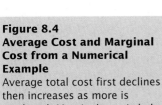

Figure 8.4
Average Cost and Marginal Cost from a Numerical Example
Average total cost first declines then increases as more is produced. Marginal cost is below average total cost when average total cost is falling and above average total cost when average total cost is rising. This relationship also holds between average variable cost and marginal cost. These cost curves are plotted from the data given in Table 8.1.

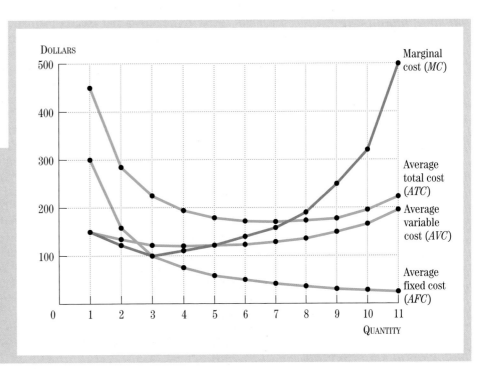

This result also holds for average variable cost: If marginal cost is greater than average variable cost, then average variable cost is increasing; if marginal cost is less than average variable cost, then average variable cost is decreasing. These relationships between the two average cost curves and the marginal cost curve are essential to the analysis that follows.

Marginal versus Average in the Classroom

The reason for the relationship between marginal cost and average total cost or average variable cost can be seen with an analogy. Consider another example of averages, say, average grades on the midterm exam in an economics class. Suppose that the average grade of people in the classroom the day after an exam is 64. Now imagine that another person, who has a midterm grade of 100, enters the classroom. We know that 100 is greater than the average grade of 64. In other words, the "marginal grade" of 100 is greater than the average grade; when the person with the grade of 100 enters the room, the average grade in the classroom increases. Now suppose that a different person who has never attended any lectures and has a midterm grade of zero comes in. The "marginal grade" of zero is less than the average grade of 64; hence, the average grade declines. This is a property of averaging and applies to grades, heights, weights, and so on, as well as to costs. When you bring someone into a group whose grade is less than the group's average, then the average declines. A below-average contribution causes the average to fall; on the other hand, an above-average contribution causes the average to rise. The relationships between marginal cost and average total cost or average variable cost say nothing more than this.

Generic Cost Curves

The relationship between marginal and average allows us to sketch a *generic* cost curve diagram, the general properties of which characterize virtually all firms, not just On-the-Move. Such a diagram is shown in Figure 8.5. Again, the vertical axis is the dollar cost and the horizontal axis is the quantity, but in a generic picture, we do not scale the axes because they apply to any firm, whether in textiles, moving, or electronics. Note that the marginal cost curve cuts both the average variable cost curve and the average total cost curve at their minimum points. To the left of the point where the curves cross, marginal cost is less than average total cost, and so average total cost declines. As the marginal cost curve passes through the minimum, average total cost begins to increase. Try drawing your own diagram. If the marginal cost curve does not go through the lowest point of both the average total cost curve and the average variable cost curve, you have made an error.

There is another important relationship in Figure 8.5. The distance between the average total cost curve and the average variable cost curve gets smaller as production increases because fixed costs are a smaller and smaller proportion of total costs as production increases. Recall that fixed costs are the difference between total costs and variable costs. Thus, the gap between average total cost and average variable cost is average fixed cost, or fixed costs divided by quantity, FC/Q. Since fixed costs (FC) do not change, the ratio FC/Q declines as Q increases. The distance between the average total cost curve and the average variable cost curve is this distance FC/Q, which declines as quantity increases. Hence, the distance between the ATC curve and the AVC curve grows smaller as you move to the right in the diagram. Any picture you draw should show this relationship.

Observe that the marginal cost curve in the generic picture of Figure 8.5 has a region of declining marginal cost at low production levels. The graph allows for the

It's helpful to use the following checklist when you draw this graph:

1. Make sure the marginal cost curve cuts through the average total cost curve and the average variable cost curve at their minimum points, and understand the reason for this.

2. Make sure the distance between average total cost and average variable cost gets smaller as you increase the amount of production.

3. Put a small dip on the left-hand side of the marginal cost curve before the upward slope begins. This makes your curve look more interesting and allows for the possibility of decreasing marginal cost at very low levels of production.

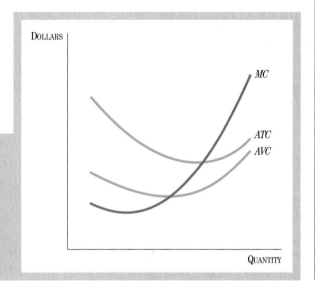

Figure 8.5
Generic Sketch of Average Cost and Marginal Cost
Every firm can be described by cost curves of the type drawn here. Compare these generic curves with the specific curves in Figure 8.4. Check these curves against the checklist in the margin.

possibility that at low production levels, the marginal product of labor increases and, therefore, marginal cost declines. This was true for On-the-Move, which had increasing marginal product of labor up to 3 pianos moved, and we allow for it in the generic case.

You may have noticed that for the cost curves for On-the-Move in Figure 8.4, the marginal cost curve and the average variable cost curve touch at 1 unit of output. This occurs because the marginal cost of producing 1 rather than zero units of output must equal the variable cost of producing 1 unit, as shown in Table 8.1. Thus, if the generic cost curve were drawn all the way over to 1 unit of output on the left of Figure 8.5, the marginal cost and the average variable cost curve would start at the same point. Because we do not usually draw generic cost curves that go all the way over to the vertical axis, we do not usually show them starting at the same point.

REVIEW

- The marginal cost curve and the average cost curves are closely related. The marginal cost (*MC*) curve cuts through both the average total cost (*ATC*) curve and the average variable cost (*AVC*) curve at their lowest points.

- Another important property of a cost curve diagram is that the gap between average total cost and average variable cost gets smaller as more is produced.

- The relationships between marginal cost and the two average cost curves are represented by the following general rule: When marginal cost is less than average total cost (or average variable cost), then average total cost (or average variable cost) is declining; when marginal cost is greater than average total cost (or average variable cost), then average total cost (or average variable cost) is increasing.

Costs and Production: The Short Run

As we saw in Chapter 6, a competitive firm takes the market price as given. If it is maximizing profits, it will choose a quantity to produce in the short run such that its marginal cost equals the market price ($P = MC$). The resulting level of production for a competitive firm with the cost curves in Figure 8.5 is shown in Figure 8.6. The quantity produced is determined by the intersection of the marginal cost (MC) curve and the market price line (P). We draw a dashed vertical line to mark the quantity (Q) produced. But when the firm produces this quantity, are its profits positive, or is the firm running a loss? If it is running a loss, should it shut down in the short run? To answer these questions, we need to use the cost curves to find the firm's profits.

The Profit or Loss Rectangle

Profits equal total revenue minus total costs. To calculate profits with the average cost diagram, we need to represent total revenue and total costs on the average cost diagram.

■ **The Total Revenue Area.** Figure 8.6 shows a particular market price P and the corresponding level of production Q chosen by the firm. The total revenue that the firm gets from selling quantity Q is price P times quantity Q. Figure 8.7 shows that this total revenue can be represented by the area of a rectangle with width Q and height P. This rectangle is shown by the shaded area in Figure 8.7. Because the width

Figure 8.6
Price Equals Marginal Cost
If a firm is maximizing profits, then it chooses a quantity (Q) such that price equals marginal cost. Thus, the quantity is determined by the intersection of the market price line and the marginal cost curve, as shown on the diagram. In this picture the *ATC* and *AVC* curves are a sideshow, but they enter the main act in Figure 8.7, when we look at the firm's level of profits.

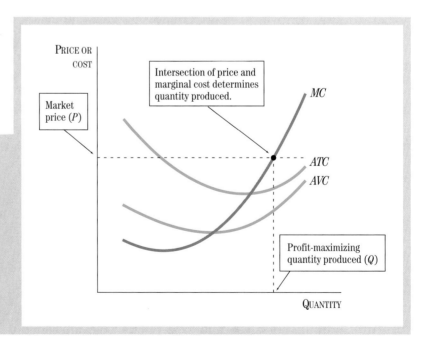

of this rectangle is the quantity produced Q and the height of this rectangle is the market price P, the area is $P \times Q$, or total revenue.

■ **The Total Costs Area.** Total costs can also be represented in Figure 8.7. First, observe the dashed vertical line in Figure 8.7 marking the profit-maximizing quan-tity produced. Next, observe the point where the average total cost curve intersects this dashed vertical line. This point tells us what the firm's average total cost is when it produces the profit-maximizing quantity. The area of the rectangle with the hash marks shows the firm's total costs. Why? Remember that average total cost is defined as total costs divided by quantity. If we take average total cost and multiply by quantity, we get total costs: $ATC \times Q = TC$. The quantity produced (Q) is the width of the rectangle, and average total cost (ATC) is the height of the rectangle. Hence, total costs are given by the area of the rectangle with the hash marks.

■ **Profits or Losses.** Since profits are total revenue less total costs, we compute profits by looking at the difference between the two rectangles. The difference is itself a rectangle, shown by the part of the revenue rectangle that rises above the total costs rectangle. *Profits are positive* because total revenue is greater than total costs in Figure 8.7. But profits can also be negative, as shown in Figure 8.8.

Suppose that the market price is at a point where the intersection of the marginal cost curve and the market price line gives a quantity of production for which average total cost is *above* the price. This situation is shown in Figure 8.8. At this lower price, we still have the necessary condition for profit maximization. The firm will produce the quantity that equates price and marginal cost, as shown by the intersection of the price line and the marginal cost curve.

Figure 8.7
Showing Profits on the Cost Curve Diagram
The price and quantity produced are the same as those in Figure 8.6. The area of the shaded rectangle is total revenue. We use the *ATC* curve to find total costs in order to compute profits. First we mark where the *ATC* curve intersects the dashed vertical line showing the quantity produced. The area of the rectangle with the hash marks is total costs because the total costs (*TC*) equal average total cost (*ATC*) times quantity produced, $TC = ATC \times Q$. The part of the shaded rectangle rising above the hash-marked area is profits.

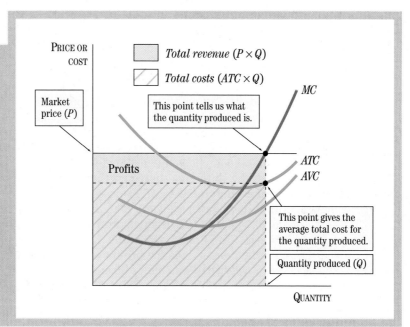

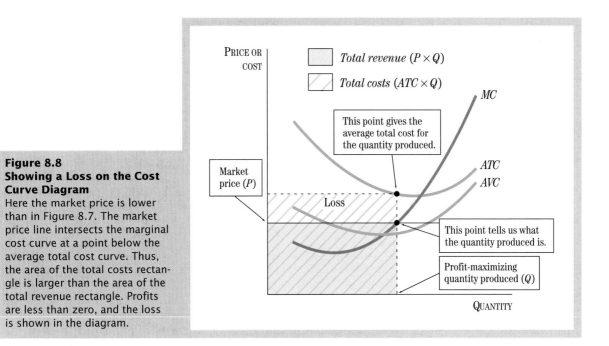

Figure 8.8
Showing a Loss on the Cost Curve Diagram
Here the market price is lower than in Figure 8.7. The market price line intersects the marginal cost curve at a point below the average total cost curve. Thus, the area of the total costs rectangle is larger than the area of the total revenue rectangle. Profits are less than zero, and the loss is shown in the diagram.

The amount of total revenue at this price is again price times quantity ($P \times Q$), or the shaded rectangle.

Total costs are average total cost times the quantity produced, that is, $ATC \times Q$, or the area of the rectangle with the hash marks.

The difference between total revenue and total costs is profit, but in this case *profits are negative*, or there is a loss. Total revenue is less than total costs, as shown by the cost rectangle's extending above the revenue rectangle. The extent of cost overhang is the loss.

The Breakeven Point

breakeven point: the point at which price equals the minimum of average total cost.

Now draw the market price line through the point where the marginal cost curve intersects the average total cost curve. Recall that this is the minimum point on the average total cost curve. This situation is shown in the middle panel of Figure 8.9. At that price, the firm chooses a quantity for which average total cost equals the price, so that the total revenue rectangle and the total cost rectangle are exactly the same. Thus, the difference between their areas is zero. At that price, the firm is at a **breakeven point:** $P = ATC$, and economic profits are zero. The firm earns positive profits if the price is greater than the breakeven point ($P > ATC$), as shown in the left panel. The firm has negative profits (a loss) if the price is lower than the breakeven point ($P < ATC$), as shown in the right panel of Figure 8.9.

The case of negative profits raises the question of why the firm does not shut down. Every day we hear of businesses losing money. In 1993, for example, Adidas, the running shoe company, lost $100 million, but it did not shut down. Why does a firm with negative profits stay in business? The reason is that if the firm shut down, losses would be even larger. In the short run, the fixed costs have to be paid. By continuing operations, the firm can minimize its losses. Let's examine this more carefully and determine when exactly the firm should shut down.

You can use some algebra to check the result that a firm should stop producing when the price is less than average variable cost: $P < AVC$. Note that

Profits = total revenue – total costs

Because total costs equal variable costs plus fixed costs, we can replace total costs to get

Profits = $P \times Q - (VC + FC)$

Now, since

$VC = AVC \times Q$, we have

Profits = $P \times Q - AVC \times Q - FC$

Rearranging this gives

Profits = $(P - AVC) \times Q - FC$

If $P < AVC$, the first term in this expression is negative unless $Q = 0$. Thus, if $P < AVC$, the best your firm can do is set $Q = 0$. This eliminates the negative drain on profits in the first term in the last expression. You minimize your loss by setting $Q = 0$.

The Shutdown Point

The firm should shut down if the price falls below the minimum point of the average variable cost curve and is not expected to rise again. In this case, the market price equals marginal cost at a quantity where total revenue ($P \times Q$) is smaller than the variable costs ($AVC \times Q$) of producing at that point.

When total revenue is less than variable costs, it makes sense to stop producing. For example, if the price of moving pianos is so low that the revenue from moving the pianos is less than the workers are paid to move the pianos, it is best not to move any pianos. It is better to shut down production. The fixed costs for the trucks and the garage would have been paid, but with the price so low, revenues cannot cover the payment to the workers.

The right panel of Figure 8.10 shows the case where the price is below average variable cost ($P < AVC$) and the firm should shut down. However, if the price is above average variable cost ($P > AVC$), as shown in the left panel of Figure 8.10, the firm should not shut down, even if the price is below average total cost and profits are negative. Because total revenue is greater than variable costs, shutting down would eliminate this extra revenue. It is better to keep producing in the short run. We assume that the firm must pay the fixed costs, as it is obligated for them over the short run. For example, Adidas did not shut down in 1993 because it had to pay fixed costs in the short run; with the price of running shoes greater than the average variable cost of producing them, the losses were less than if it had shut down.

Economists have developed the concept of sunk cost, which may help you understand and remember why a firm like Adidas would continue to operate in the short run even though it was reporting losses. A *sunk cost* is a cost that you have committed to pay and that you cannot recover. For example, if a firm signs a year's lease for factory space, it must make rental payments until the lease is up, whether the

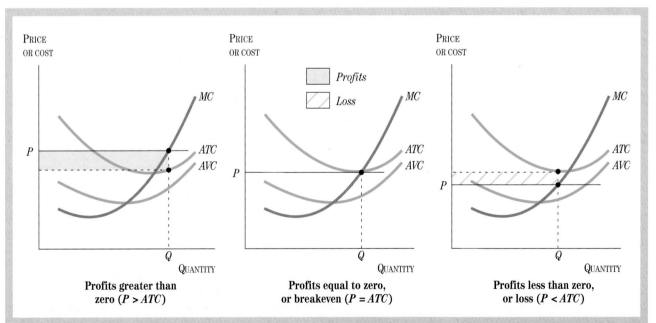

Profits greater than zero ($P > ATC$)

Profits equal to zero, or breakeven ($P = ATC$)

Profits less than zero, or loss ($P < ATC$)

Figure 8.9
The Breakeven Point

When profits are zero, we are at the breakeven point, as shown in the middle panel. In this case, the market price line intersects the marginal cost curve exactly where it crosses the average total cost curve. The left panel shows a higher market price, and profits are greater than zero. The right panel shows a lower market price, and profits are less than zero—there is a loss. The cost curves are exactly the same in each diagram.

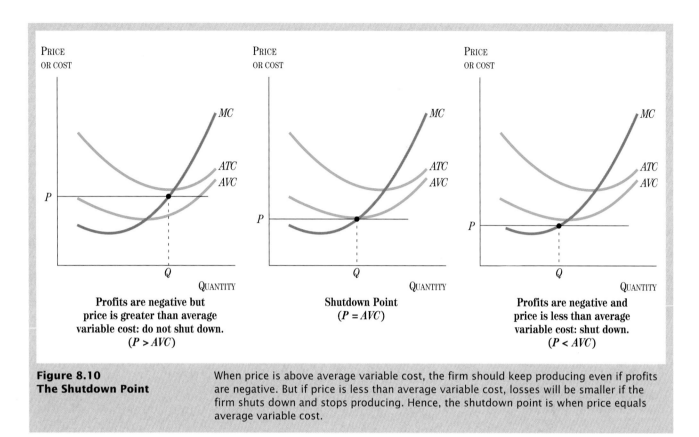

Profits are negative but
price is greater than average
variable cost: do not shut down.
(*P* > *AVC*)

Shutdown Point
(*P* = *AVC*)

Profits are negative and
price is less than average
variable cost: shut down.
(*P* < *AVC*)

Figure 8.10
The Shutdown Point

When price is above average variable cost, the firm should keep producing even if profits
are negative. But if price is less than average variable cost, losses will be smaller if the
firm shuts down and stops producing. Hence, the shutdown point is when price equals
average variable cost.

shutdown point: the point at
which price equals the minimum
of average variable cost.

Two different points:
Shutdown point
  P = minimum *AVC*
Breakeven point
  P = minimum *ATC*

space is used or not. The rental payments are an example of a sunk cost. In the short
run, fixed costs—such as lease payments—are sunk costs to a firm. The firm cannot
recover these costs by shutting down. All Adidas could do in the short run was reduce
its losses, and it did so by continuing to produce (assuming that the revenue from
each pair of shoes was greater than the variable cost of producing them). The important thing about a sunk cost is that once you commit to it, there is nothing you can do
about it, so you might as well ignore it in your decisions. If you paid for season tickets
to the opera and then lost your taste for opera, there is no reason to go to the opera
and be miserable.

Now, observe that the middle panel of Figure 8.10 shows the case where price
exactly equals the minimum point of the average variable cost curve. In this case,
price equals marginal cost at a quantity where total revenue equals variable costs
and price equals average variable cost (*P* = *AVC*). This is called the **shutdown point.**
If the price falls below the shutdown point, the firm should shut down. If the price is
above the shutdown point, the firm should continue producing.

In thinking about the shutdown point, the time period is important. We are
looking at the firm during the short run, when it is obligated to pay its fixed costs and
cannot alter its capital. The question for On-the-Move is what to do when it has
already committed to paying for the trucks and terminals, but the price of moving
pianos falls to such a low level that it does not cover variable costs. The shutdown
rule says to stop in that situation. However, if profits are negative and the price is
greater than average variable cost, then it is best to keep producing.

The shutdown point can be incorporated into the firm's supply curve. Recall
that the supply curve of a single firm tells us the quantity of a good that the firm will

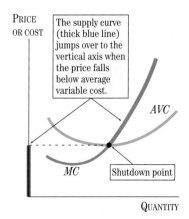

PRICE OR COST

The supply curve (thick blue line) jumps over to the vertical axis when the price falls below average variable cost.

AVC

MC   Shutdown point

QUANTITY

produce at different prices. As long as the price is above average variable cost, the firm will produce a quantity such that marginal cost equals the price. Thus, for prices above average variable cost, the marginal cost curve is the firm's supply curve, as shown in the figure in the margin. However, if the price falls below average variable cost, then the firm will shut down; in other words, the quantity produced will equal zero ($Q = 0$). Thus, for prices below average variable cost, the supply curve jumps over to the vertical axis, where $Q = 0$, as shown in the figure in the margin.

Be sure that you understand the difference between these two points: the shutdown point and the breakeven point. The shutdown point is where price equals the minimum average variable cost (Figure 8.10). The breakeven point is where price equals the minimum average total cost (Figure 8.9). If the price is between average total cost and average variable cost, then the firm is not breaking even; it is losing money. However, it does not make sense to shut down if the price is above the shutdown point.

REVIEW

- Profits can be represented as a rectangle on the cost curve diagram. So can losses. The profit or loss rectangle is the difference between the revenue rectangle and the loss rectangle.

- At the breakeven point, profits are zero. When $P < AVC$, profits are maximized by shutting down.

Costs and Production: The Long Run

Thus far, we have focused our analysis on the short run. By definition, the short run is the period of time during which it is not possible for firms to adjust certain inputs to production. But what happens in the long run, when it *is* possible for firms to make such adjustments? For example, what happens to On-the-Move when it opens new terminals or takes out a lease on a fleet of new trucks? To answer this question, we need to show how the firm can adjust its fixed costs as well as its variable costs in the long run. All costs can be adjusted in the long run.

The Effect of Capital Expansion on Total Costs

First, consider what happens to fixed costs when the firm increases its capital. Suppose On-the-Move increases the size of its fleet from 4 trucks to 8 trucks and raises the number of terminals from 2 to 4. Then its fixed costs would increase because more rent would have to be paid for 4 terminals and 8 trucks than for 2 terminals and 4 trucks. To obtain the increase in fixed costs, we need to use the price of capital. Again, suppose trucks cost $25 per day and a terminal costs $100 per day. Then 4 trucks and 2 terminals would cost $300 and 8 trucks and 4 terminals would cost $600. Fixed costs would rise from $300 to $600.

Second, consider what happens to variable costs when the firm increases its capital. An increase in capital increases the amount that each additional worker can produce. For example, according to Table 8.2, 166 worker-hours were required for On-the-Move to move 10 pianos when there were 4 trucks and 2 terminals. With more capital (8 trucks and 4 terminals), it will take fewer hours of work to move the pianos. Assume, for example, that it takes only 120 worker-hours to deliver 10 pianos. In this scenario, with the wage equal to $10 per hour, the variable cost of moving 10 pianos falls from $1,660 to $1,200. In other words, variable costs decline as the firm expands its capital.

Now consider total costs. With fixed costs larger and variable costs smaller as a result of the increase in capital, what is the effect on total costs, which are the sum of fixed costs and variable costs? After the expansion, total costs will be higher at very low levels of output, where fixed costs dominate, but will be lower at high levels of output, where variable costs dominate. Figure 8.11 illustrates this using the total cost curve. Figure 8.11 is essentially the same as Figure 8.2 except that the green curves show the old costs before the expansion of capital and the purple curves show the new costs with the additional capital. The diagram shows that the new fixed costs are higher and the new variable costs are lower. The new total cost curve (TC_2) is twisted relative to the old total cost curve (TC_1). The new total cost curve is above the old total cost curve at low levels of output and below the old total cost curve at high levels of output.

Table 8.3 provides the numerical information about the costs that appear in Figure 8.11. To see the effect of the firm's expansion on its costs, compare the fixed costs, variable costs, and total costs in Table 8.3 with those in Table 8.1. Observe that fixed costs are higher: $600 rather than $300. Variable costs are lower throughout the range of production. As a result, total costs are higher in Table 8.3 than in Table 8.1 for production of less than 8 units, and lower in Table 8.3 than in Table 8.1 for production of 8 units or more.

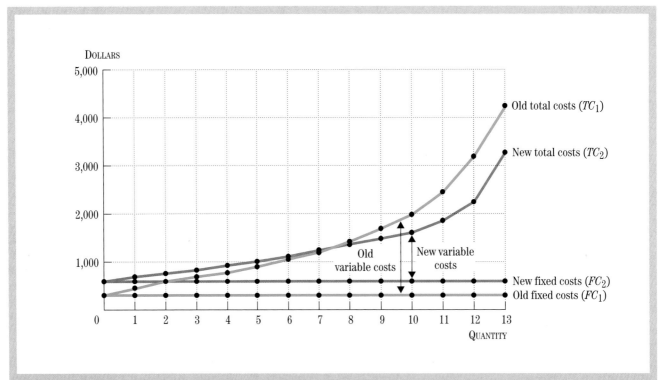

Figure 8.11
Shifts in Total Costs as a Firm Increases Its Capital in the Long Run

When a firm increases its capital, its fixed costs increase; as shown in the diagram, fixed costs rise from FC_1 to FC_2. However, its variable costs decrease, which is also shown. Thus, the new total cost curve (TC_2) will be above the old total cost curve (TC_1) for low-level output and below the old total cost curve (TC_1) for high-level output.

Table 8.3
Costs with More Capital (Compared with Table 8.1, fixed costs are higher and variable costs are lower in this table because capital is higher than in Table 8.1. Costs are measured in dollars.)

Quantity	Total Costs	Fixed Costs	Variable Costs	Average Total Cost
0	600	600	0	—
1	690	600	90	690
2	770	600	170	385
3	840	600	240	280
4	920	600	320	230
5	1,010	600	410	202
6	1,110	600	510	185
7	1,220	600	620	174
8	1,340	600	740	168
9	1,470	600	870	163
10	1,610	600	1,010	161
11	1,880	600	1,280	171
12	2,300	600	1,700	192

Effects of a Capital Expansion on Average Total Cost

Our analysis of the effects of the firm's capital expansion on total costs can be used to derive the effects on average total cost. Remember, average total cost (ATC) is total costs (TC) divided by the quantity (Q). Thus, if total costs increase at a given quantity of output, so will average total cost. And if total costs decrease at a given level of output, so will average total cost.

This is illustrated in Figure 8.12. An average total cost curve, labeled ATC_1, corresponding to average total cost in Table 8.1 is plotted. Another average total cost curve, labeled ATC_2, corresponding to average total cost in Table 8.3 is also plotted. The new average total cost curve (ATC_2) is above the old average total cost curve (ATC_1) at low levels of output and below the old average total cost curve (ATC_1) at higher levels of output. Average total cost is higher for production of less than 8 units and lower for production of 8 units or more. This is precisely what is shown for total costs in Figure 8.11.

The Long-Run *ATC* Curve

Now that we have seen what happens at On-the-Move when capital is expanded by a certain amount, we can see what happens when capital increases by even larger amounts. For example, suppose On-the-Move expands throughout Houston and even beyond Houston by expanding the size of its fleet of trucks and the number of terminals to park and service the trucks.

Figure 8.13 shows four different average total cost curves. Each of the average total cost curves corresponds to increased capital expansion at On-the-Move. The first two of these, ATC_1 and ATC_2, are the average total cost curves from Figure 8.12. Note that the second curve (ATC_2) is above the first (ATC_1) at low levels of output and below the first at high levels of output. The third and fourth curves are for even more trucks and terminals. The third average total cost curve (ATC_3) is above the second

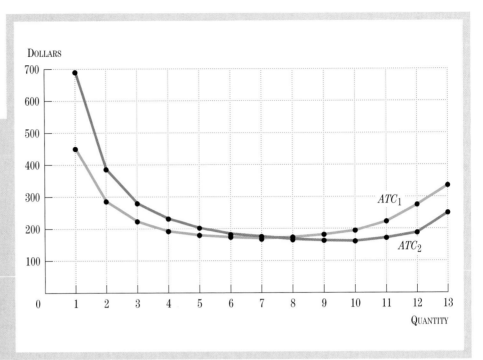

Figure 8.12
Shifts in Average Total Cost Curves When a Firm Expands Its Capital
The effects on average total cost follow directly from the effects on total costs in Figure 8.11. Here ATC_1 is the average total cost curve with a lower amount of capital, and ATC_2 is the average total cost curve with a higher amount of capital. To the left, at lower levels of output, higher fixed costs raise average total cost; to the right, at higher levels of output, lower variable costs tend to lower average total cost.

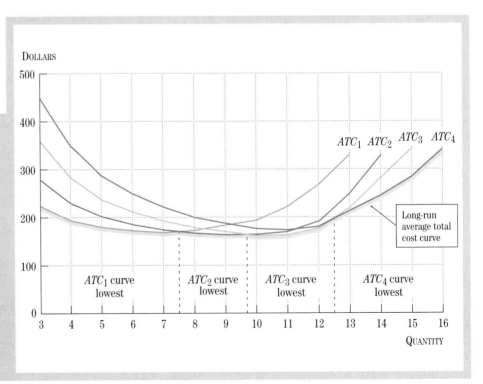

Figure 8.13
Long-Run versus Short-Run Average Total Cost
In the short run, it is not possible to change certain inputs, like the size of the factory or the number of machines. In the long run, these can be changed. For example, in the long run, On-the-Move can build more terminals around town. This means that the ATC curve shifts. The diagram shows four different ATC curves for On-the-Move; each new ATC curve represents more terminals, buildings, and machines than the ATC curve to its left. The long-run average total cost curve is shown by the thicker light green line.

(ATC_2) at lower levels of output and below the second (ATC_2) at higher levels of output. The same is true of the fourth compared to the third.

The thick light green curve tracing out the bottoms of the four average total cost curves gives the lowest average total cost at any quantity produced. For example, at 11 pianos moved, the lowest average total cost is $164. This occurs on the average total cost curve ATC_3. This thick line tells us what average total cost is when the firm can expand (or contract) its capital; in other words, this is the average total cost curve for the long run. For this reason, we call the curve that traces out the points on the lowest average total cost curves the **long-run average total cost curve.** The other average total cost curve that we have been discussing is called the *short-run average total cost curve*, or simply the average total cost curve.

The long-run average total cost curve is one way in which economists study the behavior of a firm over time. Frequently economists will simply draw a generic long-run average total cost curve without the short-run curves. Whether the long-run average total cost curve slopes up or down, and over what range, is crucial for understanding the nature of a firm, the industry in which it operates, and the role of government.

The lack of smoothness in the long-run average total cost curve may seem strange. It occurs in Figure 8.13 because we have drawn only four short-run average total cost curves. If it is possible to expand capital in smaller amounts, then the curve will look smoother. For example, between the first and second short-run average total cost curves (ATC_1 and ATC_2) in Figure 8.13, there might be an average total cost curve for 6 trucks and 3 terminals. When we put in more and more short-run average total cost curves, the long-run average total cost curve gets smoother and smoother. But it still simply traces out the points of lowest cost for each level of output.

Capital Expansion and Production in the Long Run

How does a firm like On-the-Move decide whether to expand or contract its capital in the long run? How much does it produce in the long run? The decision is similar to the short-run decision about whether to hire more workers to move more pianos. Again, the firm sets the quantity produced to maximize profits. But now the quantity produced and profits can be affected by changes in capital as well as labor. At any level of capital and labor input, we can compute profits. For each level of capital, there is a short-run average total cost curve. Profits can be computed from this average total cost curve as described in Figure 8.7. Hence, for any level of capital, profits can be computed by the firm.

If the firm can increase its profits by expanding its capital and its output, then we predict that it will do so. If we find that the firm can increase its profits by reducing its capital and its output, then we predict that it will do so. In other words, the firm adjusts the amount of capital to maximize profits.

The Mix of Capital and Labor

In the long run, the firm adjusts both its capital and its labor. Both inputs are variable in the long run. What determines the mix of labor and capital when both are variable? The relative price of labor compared to capital will be the deciding factor.

In deriving the cost curves for On-the-Move, we assumed that the cost of labor was $10 per hour and that the cost of capital, consisting of trucks and terminals, was $25 a day for trucks and $100 a day for terminals. If the cost of labor was higher, say, $20 per hour, then On-the-Move would have the incentive to rent more trucks rather than hire more workers, at least to the extent that this was feasible.

long-run average total cost curve: the curve that traces out the short-run average total cost curves, showing the lowest average total cost for each quantity produced as the firm expands in the long run.

ECONOMICS IN ACTION

Expanding (and Shrinking) a Firm over Time

The first general-merchandise "five and dime" store was opened by Woolworth in 1879. By building new stores and merging with other firms over time, Woolworth expanded greatly in size. By 1919 it had 1,081 stores in the United States, France, England, and Germany. Through the development of discount stores (Woolco) and specialty stores (including the Lady Foot Locker shown here), this firm continued to expand. In 1999 the company dropped the name Woolworth and became Venator. The newly named firm sold many of its non-footwear businesses and eventually was renamed Foot Locker, Inc., in November 2001. By 2005, Foot Locker had over 4,000 specialty stores in Australia, Europe, New Zealand, and North America.

However, if the cost of capital rose relative to that of labor, then the firm would have the incentive to hire more workers. In general, the firm will use more capital relative to labor if the cost of capital declines relative to that of labor. And conversely, the firm will use less capital relative to labor if the cost of capital rises relative to that of labor.

REVIEW

- In the long run, the firm can expand by increasing its capital. Fixed costs increase and variable costs decline at each level of production as the firm expands its capital. Thus, total costs, and average total cost, are higher at low levels of production and lower at high levels of production.

- The long-run average total cost curve traces out the points on the lowest short-run average total cost curve for each level of production.

Economies of Scale

The long-run average total cost curve describes a situation in which the firm can expand all its inputs—both its capital and its labor. When all inputs increase, we say that the *scale* of the firm increases. For example, if the number of workers at the firm

220

doubles, the number of trucks doubles, the number of terminals doubles, and so on, then we say that the scale of the firm doubles. Thus, the long-run average total cost curve describes what happens to a firm's average total cost when its scale increases. There is some specialized terminology about different shapes of the long-run average total cost curve.

We say that there are **economies of scale,** or *increasing returns to scale*, if long-run average total cost falls as the scale of the firm increases. We say that there are **diseconomies of scale,** or *decreasing returns to scale*, if long-run average total cost rises as the scale of the firm increases. The situation in the middle, where long-run average total cost neither rises nor falls, is called **constant returns to scale.** Figure 8.14 illustrates these three possible shapes for the long-run average total cost curve.

economies of scale: a situation in which long-run average total cost declines as the output of a firm increases.

diseconomies of scale: a situation in which long-run average total cost increases as the output of a firm increases.

constant returns to scale: a situation in which long-run average total cost is constant as the output of a firm changes.

Determining Whether a Firm Has Economies or Diseconomies of Scale

Whether there are increasing, decreasing, or constant returns to scale depends on the type of firm and the type of product. Consider a firm like On-the-Move. One can imagine that there would be economies of scale as the firm expanded the number of terminals around the city of Houston; with more terminals, trucks could be serviced at many different locations and would not have to be driven so far at the end of the day or towed so far in the event of a breakdown. With a larger work force, On-the-Move could have workers who *specialize* in moving different types of pianos or who specialize in servicing different parts of the trucks. Some might specialize in moves to high-rise buildings. In other words, as the scale of a firm increases, the work can be divided into different tasks and some members of the labor force can specialize in each task.

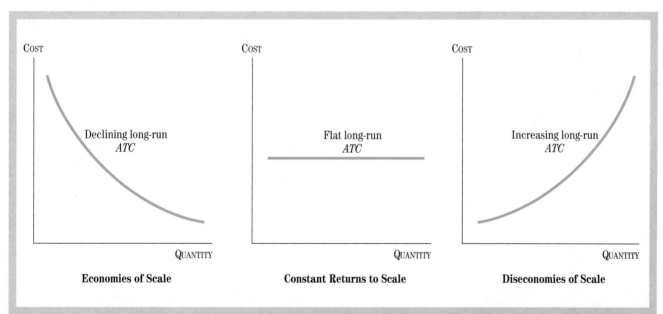

Figure 8.14
Economies and Diseconomies of Scale

If the long-run average total cost curve slopes downward, we say there are economies of scale. If the long-run average total cost curve slopes upward, we say there are diseconomies of scale. If the long-run average total cost curve is flat, we say there are constant returns to scale, as shown in the middle panel.

Gulliver and Economies of Scale
Like a firm expanding all its inputs—capital and labor—Gulliver found that he was bigger in all dimensions—arms and legs and head—than the Lilliputians. When economists consider economies of scale, they think of all the firm's inputs increasing, not just one. But when they consider diminishing returns to labor, they think of only one input (labor) increasing, which would be like Gulliver's finding that only his arms were bigger than the Lilliputians', with everything else the same size.

Is there a limit to economies of scale? What about expanding beyond Houston to Galveston, Dallas, Tulsa, Mexico City, or even Lima, Peru? In the case of piano moving, returns to scale would probably begin to decline at some point. The extra administrative costs of organizing a large interstate or worldwide piano-moving firm would probably raise average total cost. Thus, one could imagine that the long-run average total cost curve for On-the-Move would first decline and then increase as the firm grows in size.

Although no two firms are alike, the long-run average total cost curve for most firms probably declines at low levels of output, then remains flat, and finally begins to increase at high levels of output. As a firm gets very large, administrative expenses, as well as coordination and incentive problems, will begin to raise average total cost. The smallest scale of production for which long-run average total cost is at a minimum is called the **minimum efficient scale.** A typical long-run average cost curve and its minimum efficient scale are shown in Figure 8.15.

Mergers and Economies of Scope

An increase or decrease in the scale of a firm through capital expansion or contraction—as described in the previous two sections—is one kind of change in the firm over time. Firms can also change over time in other ways. They can grow through mergers between one firm and another firm. If the product lines of the two firms are similar, then such mergers may be a way to reduce costs. That is one reason why large oil companies, such as Exxon and Mobil, merged in the 1990s. Mergers are also a common way for firms to combine different skills or resources to develop new products. For example, America Online, an Internet firm, and Time Warner, a large firm producing movies, magazines, and CDs, merged in 2001. By bringing together distribution resources with content resources, this merger was intended to widen the scope of both firms and help them develop new products. The results did not turn out as expected, however, and in 2003 Time Warner dropped AOL from its corporate name in an effort to demonstrate that the company still valued its "core" assets—magazines, books, cable (HBO, CNN), and movies. Combining different types of firms

minimum efficient scale: the smallest scale of production for which long-run average total cost is at a minimum.

Figure 8.15
Typical Shape of the Long-Run Average Total Cost Curve
For many types of firms, the long-run *ATC* curve slopes down at low levels of output, then reaches a flat area, and finally begins to slope up at high levels. The minimum efficient scale is shown.

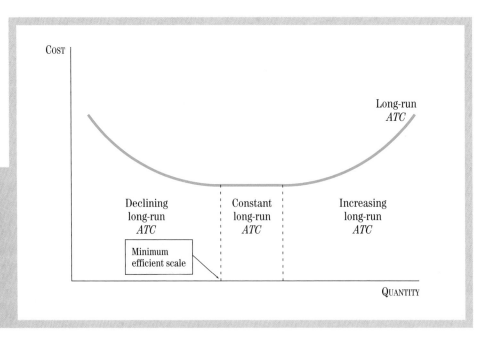

Table 8.4
Recent Big Mergers

Names Before Merger		Name After Merger	Primary Industry
Exxon	Mobil	ExxonMobil	Oil
BP	Amoco	BP Amoco (now BP)	Oil
J.P. Morgan	Chase Manhattan	J.P. Morgan Chase	Banking
Bank of America	Fleet Boston Financial	Bank of America Corp.	Banking
Chrysler	Daimler-Benz	DaimlerChrysler	Motor vehicles
WorldCom	MCI Communications	MCI WorldCom (now WorldCom)	Telecommuni-cations
Walt Disney	Capital Cities/ABC	Walt Disney	Entertainment
America Online	Netscape	America Online	Internet
America Online	Time Warner	AOL Time Warner	Internet + entertainment

Most of these mergers are in the same industry and illustrate economies of scale except for the last, which may be due to expected economies of scope.

to reduce costs or create new products is sometimes called *economies of scope*. Table 8.4 lists some of the big mergers of recent years. Observe that most of those listed involve similar products.

When two firms merge into one firm, each of the original firms may become a division within the new firm. A merger of one firm with another means that the coordination of production moves from the market to within the organization. For example, the merger of the U.S. firm Chrysler with the German firm Daimler-Benz meant that the cars were produced in two divisions of the same firm.

REVIEW

- Economies of scale are nothing more than a downward-sloping long-run average total cost curve. Economies of scale may occur because of the specialization that the division of labor in larger firms permits.

- Although economies of scale probably exist over some regions of production, the evidence indicates that as firms grow very large, diseconomies of scale set in.

- Firms sometimes expand by merging with other firms. Many big mergers occurred in the 1990s.

Conclusion

In this chapter we have developed a model for studying why firms shut down, expand, or contract. This long-term analysis of changes at firms over time is an extension of the analysis of a firm's short-run behavior in Chapter 6.

A centerpiece of the model is a graph (Figure 8.5) that shows the firm's average total cost and average variable cost. Using this graph, we can determine whether a firm will shut down in the short run. Using additional average total cost curves corresponding to alternative levels of capital, we can also determine whether the firm will expand or contract.

ECONOMICS IN ACTION

Economist Finds Economies of Scale at Pin Factory

One way to get an intuitive feel for economies of scale is to visit a factory and watch people in action. If you look carefully, you can actually see economies of scale. Here is a short but wonderfully vivid description of workers at a pin-making factory. An economist wrote the description after a visit to the factory, and it illustrates how economists think. The workers are producing pins from metal wire.

> One man draws out the wire, another straightens it, a third cuts it, a fourth points it, a fifth grinds it at the top for receiving the head; to make the head requires two or three distinct operations; to put it on is a peculiar business, to whiten the pins is another . . . [T]en men only . . . could make upwards of forty eight thousand pins in a day. Each person, therefore, . . . might be considered as making four thousand eight hundred pins in a day.
>
> But if they had each wrought separately and independently they certainly could not each of them have made twenty, perhaps, not one pin in a day.
>
> That is certainly not the two hundred and fortieth, perhaps not the four thousand eight hundredth part of what they are at present capable of producing.

This story of the pin factory is not new. In what century do you think the economist watched this firm in action? And who do you think the economist was? (*Hint:* It was written up in a book called *Wealth of Nations*.) Whatever the answer, the story is as relevant now as it was when the account was written.

A more modern example of economies of scale involves Wal-Mart, the retail company founded by Sam Walton in 1962, now selling $217.8 billion and employing over 1,300,000 employees. How did Wal-Mart grow to be the largest U.S. company in revenues in just forty years?

One of the keys to Wal-Mart's success is the use of economies of scale. With over 3,000 stores in the United States and over 1,000 additional stores in nine other countries, Wal-Mart uses central distribution points, a streamlined supply chain closely coordinated with its suppliers, lower inventories, centrally coordinated marketing, and its enormous buying power to lower its costs. Wal-Mart's focus on economies of scale, increased productivity, and cost reduction allowed it to charge lower prices and increase its market share from 9% in 1987 to 27% in 1995. As an example of Wal-Mart's advantage over other general-merchandise retailers, its productivity measured by real sales per employee was 36% higher than its closest competitor in 1999. As a matter of fact, the economies of scale of the retail industry—particularly Wal-Mart—contributed greatly to the increase in U.S. productivity in the 1990s.

What similarities and differences do you see between Wal-Mart and the pin factory? What aspects other than economies of scale would you consider when measuring Wal-Mart's success and its impact on the economy?

The economist looks at what each worker does, and estimates that production each day at this ten-person firm equals 48,000 pins, or 4,800 per worker.

Now the economist imagines production at a much smaller firm consisting of one worker. Daily production is estimated at between 1 and 20 pins per worker.

Thus *production per worker* at the small firm is only 1/240 or 1/4,800 as much as at the large firm. That is big economies of scale.

By looking at a firm's long-run average total cost curve (Figure 8.15), we can tell whether a firm has economies of scale. We will use the average total cost curve extensively in the next several chapters of this book.

KEY POINTS

1. Firms start up, expand, contract, or shut down when conditions in the economy change.

2. The short run and the long run are two broad categories into which economists categorize time periods. The short run is the period of time during which it is not possible for the firm to change all the inputs to production; only some inputs, such as labor, can be changed. The long run is the minimum period of time in which the firm can vary all inputs to production, including capital.

3. Average total cost, or cost per unit, is widely used by economists, accountants, and investors to assess a firm's cost behavior.

4. When the market price equals the minimum of average total cost, the firm breaks even. At higher prices, profits are positive. At lower prices, profits are negative.

5. When the market price equals the minimum of average variable cost, the firm is just at the point of shutting down. If the price is below average variable cost, the firm should shut down.

6. The long-run average total cost curve describes how a firm's costs behave when the firm expands its capital.

7. If long-run average total cost declines, then there are economies of scale. For many firms, there is a range over which the long-run average total cost curve is flat, and we say that there are constant returns to scale. When firms get very large, diseconomies of scale set in.

8. Firms can expand by merging with other firms. Such mergers are motivated by either economies of scale or economies of scope.

KEY TERMS

short run	average fixed cost (*AFC*)	long-run average total cost curve	diseconomies of scale
long run	average product of labor	economies of scale	constant returns to scale
average total cost (*ATC*)	breakeven point		minimum efficient scale
average variable cost (*AVC*)	shutdown point		

QUESTIONS FOR REVIEW

1. What is the difference between average total cost and average variable cost?

2. Why does the marginal cost curve cut through the average total cost curve exactly at the minimum of the average total cost curve?

3. Why are total revenue, total costs, and profits given by areas of rectangles in the cost curve diagram?

4. What is the difference between the breakeven point and the shutdown point?

5. Why do average total cost curves shift as the firm expands, and how does the shift relate to economies of scale?

6. Why might a merger lower average total cost?

7. What is the minimum efficient scale of a firm?

PROBLEMS

1. Draw the typical average total cost, average variable cost, and marginal cost curves for a profit-maximizing, price-taking firm.
   a. Show the case where price equals average total cost.
   b. Show the rectangles that represent fixed costs and variable costs. What happens to the size of these areas as the market price increases? Show this in your diagram.

2. Consider the age of the people in a restaurant. Suppose the first person you notice is 40 years old and the second and third are 33 and 27, respectively.
   a. Graph the average and marginal age of the three people in the restaurant, placing age on the vertical axis and quantity of people on the horizontal axis in the same order in which you notice them.
   b. What do you notice about the relationship between marginal and average age?
   c. Suppose the fourth person entering the restaurant is 41 years old. What happens to the average age?

3. Fill out the table below, and then answer the following questions.

Q	TC	FC	VC	ATC	AVC	MC
0	8					
1	12					
2	14					
3	20					
4	30					
5	50					

a. Suppose the firm is a price-taker. If the price is $15 per unit, will this firm be earning economic profits? How much? What quantity will it produce?
b. What is the breakeven price? the shutdown price?

4. Suppose the firm in problem 3 can buy an additional machine that causes its minimum short-run average total cost to become $10. Does this expansion involve economies or diseconomies of scale? Sketch this situation in a diagram.

5. Plot the following data on quantity of production and long-run average total cost for a firm. Show the areas of economies and diseconomies of scale and constant returns to scale. What is the minimum efficient scale?

Quantity	Long-Run ATC
1	33
2	27
3	25
4	25
5	30
6	38
7	50

6. Suppose the average total cost curves for a firm for three different amounts of capital are as follows:

Quantity	ATC_1	ATC_2	ATC_3
1	40	50	60
2	30	35	40
3	20	25	30
4	30	15	25
5	40	30	20
6	50	40	30

a. Plot the three average total cost curves in the same diagram.
b. Determine the long-run average total cost curve and show it in the same diagram as in part (a).

7. Fill out the table below for a competitive firm that can sell its product for $13 a unit.
a. What quantity will this firm produce? Why?
b. At that quantity level, what profits or losses will this firm make?
c. Is this market in long-run equilibrium? Why or why not?
d. In the short run, at what price would this firm break even? At what price would the firm shut down? Explain briefly.

8. Suppose you paid $20 at the start of the term for a four-month subscription to the *Economist* magazine. Then, after one week, you find out that reading the magazine will not help you get a better grade in your economics course and that you do not enjoy reading it. Your parents advise you to read the magazine anyway because you paid for it. Is this good advice? Write a letter to your parents explaining the concept of sunk costs and relate it to their advice.

Problem 7

Quantity	Total Cost	Fixed Cost	Variable Cost	Average Total Cost	Average Variable Cost	Marginal Cost	Total Revenue	Marginal Revenue	Profit
0									
1				$27.00		$9.00			
2				$16.00					
3					$5.00				
4					$5.50				
5					$8.40				

Producer Theory with Isoquants

In this chapter we looked at how firms adjust their labor and capital inputs when the cost of these inputs changes over time. Here we give a graphical illustration of a firm's choice between labor and capital. The graphs are similar to the budget lines and indifference curves used to describe consumer choice in the appendix to Chapter 5. We use these graphs to show exactly how a firm's choice between labor and capital depends on the relative price of labor and capital.

Combining Capital and Labor

Consider an example of a firm with two inputs to production: capital and labor. Table 8A.1 shows the possible combinations of inputs available to the firm. For example, if the firm has 2 units of capital and uses 24 hours of labor, it can produce 3 units of output. The hypothetical numbers in Table 8A.1 could represent a wide variety of firms producing different types of products, but observe that we have chosen the units in the table to be the same as those for the firm shown in Table 8.2. (To make a comparison between Table 8A.1 and Table 8.2, you can think of a "unit" of capital as corresponding to 4 trucks and 2 terminals with a cost of $300; 2 units of capital is 8 trucks and 4 terminals at a cost of $600.) Table 8A.1 could refer to a firm with any type of capital (computers, machine tools, telephones, or pizza ovens). To allow for all these possibilities, we refer to capital as a "unit" of capital.

The information in Table 8A.1 can be represented graphically, as shown in Figure 8A.1. Each column is plotted with labor input on the horizontal axis and the quantity produced on the vertical axis. Each column represents the production function for a given level of capital. Note that higher levels of capital increase the amount that can be produced with a given amount of labor. In

Table 8A.1
Production with Four Levels of Capital

| Quantity Produced | Labor Input (hours) | | | |
	With 1 Unit of Capital	With 2 Units of Capital	With 3 Units of Capital	With 4 Units of Capital
0	0	0	0	0
1	15	9	6	5
2	27	17	12	10
3	37	24	17	13
4	48	32	22	18
5	60	41	29	23
6	74	51	36	29
7	90	62	43	35
8	109	74	52	41
9	134	87	61	49
10	166	101	71	57
11	216	128	90	72
12	290	170	119	95
13	400	270	189	151
14	—	400	300	220
15	—	—	425	300
16	—	—	—	430

Note: The column showing labor input with 1 unit of capital corresponds to the production function for On-the-Move discussed in Chapter 8 (see Table 8.2). The omitted entries in the table represent quantities of production that cannot be achieved without more capital.

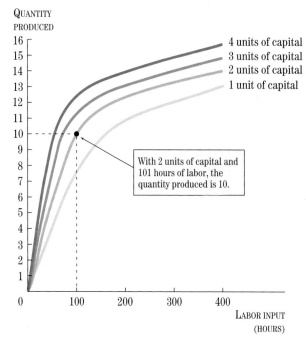

Figure 8A.1
The Production Function with Four Levels of Capital
As the amount of labor input increases, so does the amount of output. Each curve corresponds to a different level of capital. Higher curves represent higher levels of capital. The points on these four curves are obtained from the four columns of Table 8A.1.

227

other words, as we add more capital, the relationship between labor and output shifts up.

The information in Table 8A.1 and Figure 8A.1 can be displayed in another graph, Figure 8A.2, which provides a visual picture of how labor and capital jointly help a firm produce its product. Figure 8A.2 puts capital on the vertical axis and labor on the horizontal axis. We represent the quantity produced in Figure 8A.2 by writing a number in a circle equal to the amount produced with each amount of labor and capital. For example, with 1 unit of capital and 60 hours of labor, the firm can produce 5 units of output, according to Table 8A.1. Thus, we write the number 5 at the point in Figure 8A.2 that represents labor input equal to 60 and capital input equal to 1.

Isoquants

Observe in Figure 8A.2 that the same amount of output can be produced using different combinations of capital and labor. We illustrate this in the figure by connecting the circles with the same quantity by a curved line. Each curve gives the combinations of labor and capital that produce the same quantity of output. The curves in Figure 8A.2 are called *isoquants*, where "iso" means "the same" and "quant" stands for "quantity produced." Thus, an **isoquant** is a curve that shows all the possible combinations of labor and capital that result in the same quantity of production. Isoquants convey a lot of information visually. Higher isoquants—those up and to the right—represent higher levels of output. Each isoquant slopes down because as capital input declines, labor input must increase if the quantity produced is to remain the same. The slope of the isoquants tells us how much labor must be substituted for capital (or vice versa) to leave production unchanged. Thus, the isoquants are good for studying how firms substitute one input for another when the prices of the inputs change. The slope of the isoquant is called the **rate of technical substitution,** because it tells us how much capital needs to be substituted for labor to give the same amount of production when labor is reduced by one unit.

Remember that the points in Figure 8A.2 do not display any information that is not in Table 8A.1 or Figure

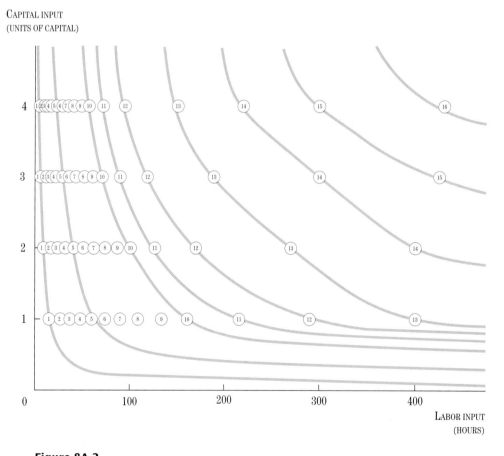

Figure 8A.2
Isoquants
Each circled number gives the quantity produced for the amounts of labor and capital on the axes at that point. The lines connecting equal quantities are called *isoquants*.

8A.1. The same information appears in a different and convenient way.

Isocost Lines

A firm's total costs can also be shown on a diagram like Figure 8A.2. In considering the choice between capital and labor, the firm needs to consider the price of both. Suppose that labor costs $10 per hour and capital costs $300 per unit. Then if the firm uses 1 unit of capital and 150 hours of labor, its total costs will be $1 \times \$300 + 150 \times \$10 = \$1,800$. For the same total costs, the firm can pay for other combinations of labor and capital. For example, 2 units of capital and 120 hours of labor also cost $1,800. Other combinations are as follows:

Hours of Labor	Units of Capital	Total Costs
180	0	$180 \times \$10 + 0 \times \$300 = \$1,800$
150	1	$150 \times \$10 + 1 \times \$300 = \$1,800$
120	2	$120 \times \$10 + 2 \times \$300 = \$1,800$
90	3	$90 \times \$10 + 3 \times \$300 = \$1,800$
60	4	$60 \times \$10 + 4 \times \$300 = \$1,800$
30	5	$30 \times \$10 + 5 \times \$300 = \$1,800$
0	6	$0 \times \$10 + 6 \times \$300 = \$1,800$

In other words, the $1,800 can be spent on any of these combinations of labor and capital. With $1,800, the firm can use 6 units of capital, but that would not permit the firm to hire any workers.

These different combinations of labor and capital that have total costs of $1,800 are plotted in Figure 8A.3. Each combination of labor and capital in the table is plotted, and the points are connected by a line. The line is called an **isocost line.** An isocost line shows the combinations of capital and labor that have the same total costs.

The position of the isocost line depends on the amount of total costs. Higher total costs are represented by higher isocost lines. This is shown in Figure 8A.4. Observe that the isocost line for total costs of $2,100 is above the one for total costs of $1,800.

The slope of the isocost line depends on the ratio of the price of labor to the price of capital. In particular, the slope equals -1 times the ratio of the price of labor to the price of capital. This is illustrated in Figure 8A.5 for the case where total costs equal $1,800. If the price of labor falls from $10 to $6, then the isocost line gets flatter. Thus, if the hourly wage were $6 instead of $10, the firm

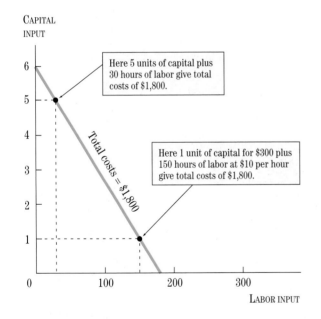

Figure 8A.3
An Isocost Line
Each isocost line shows all the combinations of labor and capital that give the same total costs. In this case, the price of capital is $300 per unit and the price of labor is $10 per hour. Total costs are $1,800. For example, if 1 unit of capital and 150 hours of labor are employed, total costs are $1,800 = (1 \times \$300) + (150 \times \$10)$.

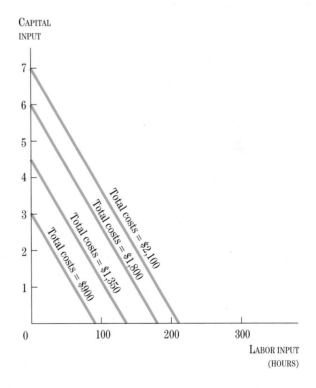

Figure 8A.4
Several Isocost Lines with Different Total Costs
Isocost lines with higher total costs are above and to the right of those with lower total costs. All the isocost lines in this diagram have a capital cost of $300 per unit and a labor cost of $10 per hour.

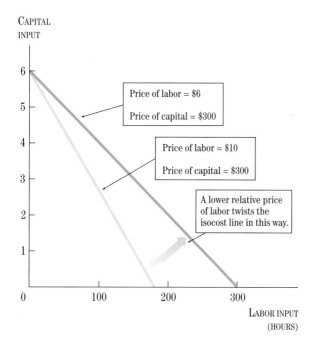

Figure 8A.5
Effect of a Change in Relative Prices on the Isocost Line
When the price of labor falls relative to the price of capital, the isocost line gets flatter, as in this diagram. In this case, the price of labor falls from $10 per hour to $6 per hour while the price of capital remains at $300 per unit. Total costs remain equal to $1,800 in this case.

would be able to pay for 250 hours of work and 1 unit of capital, compared with only 150 hours and 1 unit of capital, and still have total costs of $1,800. Thus, as the price of labor (the wage) falls relative to the price of capital, the isocost line gets flatter.

Minimizing Costs for a Given Quantity

The isoquant and isocost lines can be used to determine the least-cost combination of capital and labor for any given quantity of production. Figure 8A.6 shows how. In Figure 8A.6 we show three isocost lines, along with an isoquant representing 11 units of output. For the isocost lines, the price of labor is $10 and the price of capital is $300. The point where the isocost line just touches the isoquant is a *tangency point*. It is labeled *A*.

Point *A* is where the firm minimizes the cost of producing 11 units of output. To see this, suppose you are at point *A* and you move to the left and up along the same isoquant to point *B*. This means that the firm increases capital and decreases hours of labor, keeping the quantity produced constant at 11 units; that is, the firm substitutes capital for labor. But such a substitution increases the firm's costs, as shown in the figure. The payment for

the extra capital will be greater than the saving from the reduced labor. Thus, moving along the isoquant from *A* to *B* would increase the total costs to the firm.

A similar reasoning applies to moving from point *A* to point *C*. The firm uses fewer labor hours and less capital at point *C*, so that total costs are lower than at point *A*. But at point *C* the firm does not have enough inputs to produce 11 units of output. Thus, point *A* is the lowest-cost point at which the firm can produce 11 units of output. It is the point at which the lowest isocost line is touching the isoquant.

The Cost Minimization Rule

The rate of technical substitution of capital for labor and the ratio of the price of labor to the price of capital are equal at point *A*, because the slopes of the isoquant and of the isocost line are equal at point *A*. If the firm is minimizing its costs, then the rate of technical substitution must equal the input price ratio. The equality between the rate of technical substitution and the input price ratio is called the *cost minimization rule*.

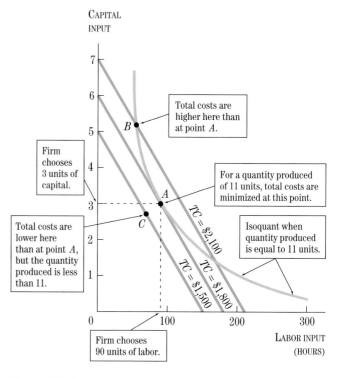

Figure 8A.6
Choosing Capital and Labor to Minimize Total Costs
The diagram illustrates how a firm chooses a mix of labor and capital to minimize total costs for a given level of output. Here the given level of output is 11 units, as shown by the single isoquant. Total costs are minimized by choosing the combination of labor and capital given by the tangency (point *A*) between the isocost line and the isoquant. For any other point on the isoquant, the quantity would be the same but total costs would be higher.

Observe that isoquants are analogous to the indifference curves and the isocost lines are analogous to the budget line described in the appendix to Chapter 5. The cost minimization rule for a firm is much like the utility maximizing rule for a consumer.

A Change in the Relative Price of Labor

Now we show how isoquants and isocost lines can be used to predict how a firm will adjust its mix of inputs when there is a change in input prices. For example, suppose that the hourly wage falls from $10 to $6 and the price of capital rises from $300 to $600. That is, labor becomes cheaper relative to capital. Originally, the ratio of the price of labor to capital was 10/300 = .033; now it is 6/600 = .010. This is a big reduction, and we would expect the firm to adjust by changing capital and labor input. Figure 8A.7 shows how the firm would adjust the mix of capital and labor for a given quantity of output. Figure 8A.7 keeps the isoquant fixed but includes a new isocost line that reflects the lower relative price of labor and is tangent to the isoquant. Since the new isocost line is flatter, the point of tangency with the given isoquant no longer occurs at point A, where 3 units of capital are combined with 90 hours of labor. Now tangency occurs at point D, where there is a combination of 2 units of capital

and 130 hours of labor. In other words, the firm has substituted labor for capital when the relative price of labor fell. At the new point D, the firm would use 1 less unit of capital and 40 more hours of labor.

In summary, common sense tells us that the firm will hire more labor and use less capital when the price of labor falls relative to the price of capital. The isoquants and isocost lines confirm this and tell us by exactly how much.

Key Terms and Definitions

isoquant: a curve showing all the possible combinations of two inputs that yield the same quantity of output.

rate of technical substitution: the rate at which one input must be substituted for another input to maintain the same production; it is the slope of the isoquant.

isocost line: a line showing the combinations of two inputs that result in the same total costs.

Questions for Review

1. Why does the isoquant slope downward?
2. Why does the isocost line slope downward?
3. What determines the slope of the isocost line?
4. Why does the firm minimize cost for a given level of output by choosing capital and labor at the point where the isocost line is tangent to the isoquant?

Problems

1. Graph the isocost line associated with a wage of $10 per hour and a price of capital of $50 for total costs of $200, $240, and $300. Suppose the wage rises to $15 and the price of capital stays at $50. Show how the isocost line moves if total costs are $300.

2. Sketch a typical isocost line and isoquant where the firm has chosen the combination of capital and labor that minimizes total costs for a given quantity of output. Now suppose the price of capital rises and the wage does not change. What must the firm do to maintain the same level of output as before the increase in the price of capital and still minimize costs? Will it substitute away from capital?

3. Draw a diagram with an isocost line and an isoquant next to a diagram with a budget line and an indifference curve from the appendix to Chapter 5. List the similarities and differences. How are the isocost and budget lines analogous to each other? How are the isoquant and the indifference curve analogous to each other? What is the importance of the tangency point in each case?

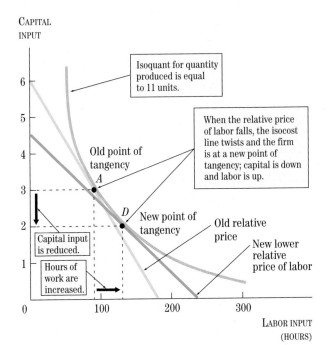

Figure 8A.7
Effect of a Lower Price of Labor Relative to Capital
The dark green isocost line has a lower price of labor relative to capital than the light green line. Hence, the amount of capital used by the firm decreases from 3 units to 2 units, and the amount of labor rises from 90 hours to 130 hours.

CHAPTER 9

The Rise and Fall of Industries

Fred Smith's college term paper led to the birth of a new industry. In the paper, he described his idea for a new product: reliable overnight mail service. Although he got only a C on the paper, Fred Smith pursued his idea. He became an entrepreneur. After college, in 1973, he started a business firm that guaranteed next-day delivery of a letter or a package virtually anywhere in the United States. The firm, Federal Express, was successful, very successful; its sales reached $1 billion by 1982, $4 billion by 1988, $8 billion by 1992, and over $29 billion by 2005.

Seeing high profits at Federal Express, many other firms entered the express delivery industry. In the late 1970s, United Parcel Service (UPS) entered; in the early 1980s, the U.S. Postal Service entered; many small local firms you've probably never heard of also got into the act. The entire industry expanded along with Federal Express.

The express delivery industry is an example of an industry on the rise. Many other examples of fast-growing industries exist in the annals of economic history. Estée Lauder founded a cosmetic firm 50 years ago; it grew along with the cosmetics industry as a whole.

Kemmons Wilson started the motel franchising industry when he saw the potential demand for clean, reliable rooms for travelers and opened his first Holiday Inn in Memphis in 1952; by 1968, there were 1,000 Holiday Inns, and now the industry includes other motel firms such as Days Inn and Motel 6.

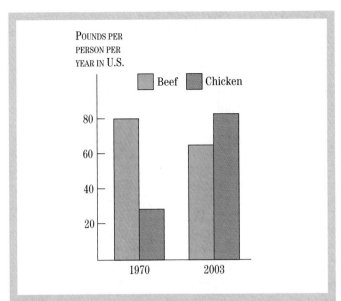

Figure 9.1
Taste Shifts and the Rise and Fall of Different Industries
Changes in tastes cause some industries to grow and others to contract. Concerns about fat in the diet may have been one reason that consumer tastes shifted from beef to chicken in the United States. In any case, the chicken industry has flourished and the beef industry has suffered as a result of the taste shift. Can you think of any other reasons why the per capita consumption of chicken increased in this period? Given your knowledge of supply and demand, how would you test your hypothesis?

Of course, industries do not always grow. The U.S. beef industry has declined as the U.S. chicken industry has risen. The mainframe computer industry has declined as the personal computer industry has risen.

The causes of the rise and fall of industries can be traced to new ideas such as overnight delivery, to new cost-reducing technologies such as the Internet, or to changes in consumer tastes, such as a shift in preference toward foods with less fat. This latter shift, for example, is one reason behind the rise of the chicken industry and the fall of the beef industry, as shown in Figure 9.1. In 2003 and 2004, the widespread popularity of low-carb diets, which favor reducing the intake of foods like bread and pasta in favor of high-protein foods like meat and cheese, caused some concern among bread producers and retailers and prompted several major U.S. food companies to produce low-carb versions of many products. Other companies entered the market with low-carb specialty products. Some industries have recurring ups and downs. The oil tanker shipping industry, for example, regularly expands when oil demand increases and declines when oil demand falls.

In this chapter, we develop a model to explain the behavior of whole industries over time. We examine how economic forces cause industries to adjust to new technologies and to shifts in consumer tastes. Our analysis assumes that the firms are operating in competitive markets. The initial forces causing an industry to rise or fall are described by shifts in a cost curve or a demand curve. Changes in the industry then occur as firms either enter or exit the industry. The central task of this chapter is to show how an industry grows or contracts as firms enter or exit the industry. Do profits fall or rise? Do the prices consumers pay increase or decrease? Before addressing these questions, we provide a brief definition of industries and some examples of different industry types.

Markets and Industries

industry: a group of firms producing a similar product.

An **industry** is a group of firms producing a similar product. The cosmetics industry, for example, refers to the firms producing cosmetics. The term *market* is sometimes used instead of industry. For example, the phrases "the firms in the cosmetics industry" and "the firms in the cosmetics market" mean the same thing. But the term *market* can also refer to the consumers who buy the goods and to the interaction of the producers and the consumers. Both firms and consumers are in the cosmetics market, but only firms are in the cosmetics industry.

Manufacturing is the making of goods by mechanical or chemical processes. In economics, the word *industry* is much broader than manufacturing. Firms in an industry can produce *services* such as overnight delivery or overnight accommodations as well as manufactured goods.

Many industries are global. Firms in the United States sell or produce many of their goods in other countries. U.S. firms compete with firms in Japan, Europe, and elsewhere. The aspirin industry has been a global industry for 100 years. Reduced transportation and communication costs in recent years have made most other industries global. Until competition from Europe and Japan intensified 30 years ago, the automobile industry in the United States consisted mainly of three firms—General Motors, Ford, and Chrysler. Now the industry is truly global, with Honda, Toyota, Hyundai, and Nissan selling cars in the United States, and Ford and General Motors selling cars throughout the world.

The Long-Run Competitive Equilibrium Model of an Industry

The model we develop to explain the behavior of industries assumes that firms in the industry maximize profits and that they are competitive. As in the competitive equilibrium model of Chapter 7, individual firms are price-takers; that is, they cannot affect the price. But in order to explain how the industry changes over time, in this chapter we add something new to the competitive equilibrium model: Over time, some firms will enter an industry and other firms will exit an industry. Because the entry and exit of firms takes time, we call this model the **long-run competitive equilibrium model.**

long-run competitive equilibrium model: a model of firms in an industry in which free entry and exit produce an equilibrium such that price equals the minimum of average total cost.

When we use the long-run competitive equilibrium model to explain the behavior of an actual industry, we do not necessarily mean that the industry itself exactly conforms to the assumptions of the model. A model is a means of explaining events in real-world industries; it is not the real world itself. In fact, some industries are very competitive and some are not very competitive. But the model can work well as an approximation in many industries. In Chapters 10 and 11 we will develop alternative models of industry behavior that describe monopoly and the gray area between monopoly and competitive markets. But for this chapter, we focus on the competitive model. This model was one of the first developed by economists to explain the dynamic behavior of an industry; it has wide applicability, and it works well. Moreover, understanding the model will make it easier to understand the alternative models developed in later chapters.

Setting Up the Model with Graphs

The assumption that a competitive firm cannot affect the price is illustrated in Figure 9.2. The left graph views the market from the perspective of a single typical firm in an industry. The price is on the vertical axis, and the quantity produced by the single firm is on the horizontal axis. The market demand curve for the goods produced by

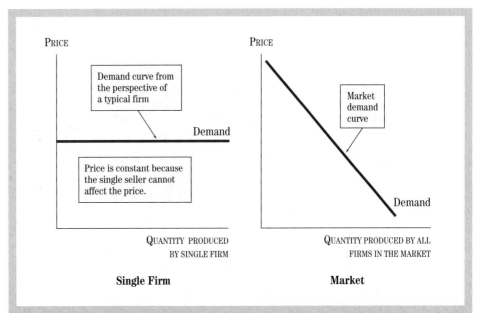

Figure 9.2
How a Competitive Firm Sees Demand in the Market
A competitive market is, by definition, one in which a single firm cannot affect the price. The firm takes the market price as given. Hence, the firm sees a flat demand curve, as shown in the graph on the left. Nevertheless, if all firms change production, the market price changes, as shown in the graph on the right. The two graphs are not alternatives. In a competitive market, they hold simultaneously. (In the graph on the right, a given length along the horizontal axis represents a much greater quantity than the same length in the graph on the left.)

the firms in the industry is shown in the right graph of Figure 9.2. The price is also on the vertical axis of the graph on the right, but the horizontal axis measures the *whole market or industry* production. Because the single firm cannot affect the price, the price, which represents the given market or industry price, is shown by a flat line drawn in the left graph. Notice that even though the single firm takes the price as given, the market demand curve is downward-sloping because it refers to the whole market. If the price in the market rises, then the quantity demanded of the product will fall. If the market price increases, then the quantity demanded will decline.

free entry and exit: movement of firms into and out of an industry that is not blocked by regulation, other firms, or any other barriers.

■ **Entry and Exit.** The new characteristic of competitive markets stressed in this chapter is the **free entry and exit** of firms in an industry. The question firms face is whether to *enter* an industry if they are not already in it, or whether to *exit* from an industry they are in. The decisions are based on profits—total revenue less total costs. If profits are positive, there is incentive to enter the industry. If profits are negative, there is incentive to exit the industry. When profits are equal to zero, there is no incentive for either entry or exit.

When firms enter or exit an industry, the entire market or industry supply curve is affected. Recall that the market or industry supply curve is the sum of all the individual firms' supply curves. With more firms supplying goods, the total quantity of goods supplied increases at every price. Thus, more firms in the industry means that the market supply curve shifts to the right; fewer firms in the industry means that the market supply curve shifts to the left.

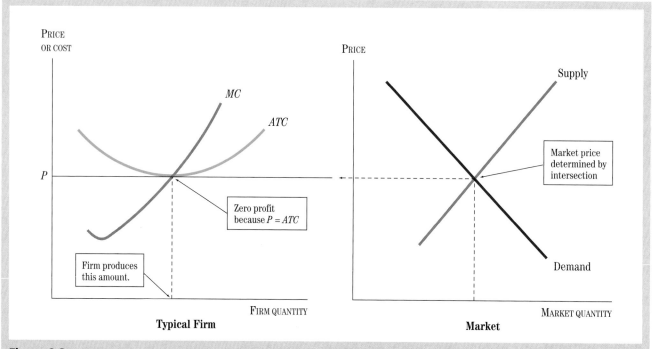

Figure 9.3
Long-Run Equilibrium in a Competitive Market
The left graph shows the typical firm's cost curves and the market price. The right graph shows the market supply and demand curves. The price is the same in both graphs because there is a single price in the market. The price is at a level where profits are zero because price equals average total cost.

long-run equilibrium: a situation in which entry into and exit from an industry are complete and economic profits are zero, with price (P) equal to average total cost (ATC).

■ **Long-Run Equilibrium.**   Figure 9.3 is a two-part diagram that shows the profit-maximizing behavior of a typical firm along with the market supply and demand curves. This diagram is generic; it could be drawn to correspond to the numerical specifications of the grape industry or any other industry. In the left graph are the cost curves of the typical firm in the industry with their typical positions: Marginal cost cuts through the average total cost curve at its lowest point. We did not draw in the average variable cost curve in order to keep the diagram from getting too cluttered.

The price line represents the current market price in the industry, for example, the price of a ton of grapes. Because the price line just touches the average total cost curve, we know from Chapter 8 that profits are zero. There is no incentive for firms to either enter or exit the industry. A situation in which profits are zero and there is no incentive to enter or exit—as shown in Figure 9.3—is called a **long-run equilibrium.**

The market supply and demand curves are to the right of the cost curve diagram in Figure 9.3. The horizontal axis for the market supply and demand curves has a much different scale from that for the individual supply curves. An inch in the right-hand diagram represents much more production than an inch in the left-hand diagram because the diagram on the right is the sum of all the production of all the firms in the market. The market demand curve is downward-sloping: The higher the price, the less the quantity demanded. The intersection of the market supply curve and the market demand curve determines the market price.

The left and right graphs of Figure 9.3 are drawn with the same market price, and this price links the two graphs together. The price touches the bottom of the average total cost curve on the left graph, and this is the price that is at the intersection of the market supply and demand curves. The graphs are set up this way. They are meant to represent a situation of long-run equilibrium: The quantity demanded equals the quantity supplied in the market *and* profits are zero.

An Increase in Demand

Suppose there is a shift in demand—for example, suppose the demand for Zinfandel grapes increases. We show this increase in demand in the top right graph of Figure 9.4; the market demand curve shifts out from D to D'.

■ **Short-Run Effects.**   Focus first on the top part of Figure 9.4, representing the short run. With the shift in the demand curve, we move up along the supply curve to a new intersection of the market supply curve and the market demand curve at a higher price. An increase in demand causes a rise in the market price.

Now note in the top left graph that we have moved the price line up from P to P'. Profit-maximizing firms that are already in the industry will produce more because the market price is higher. This is seen in the top left graph of Figure 9.4; the higher price intersects the marginal cost curve at a higher quantity of production. As production increases, marginal cost rises until it equals the new price.

Note also—and this is crucial—that at this higher price and higher level of production, the typical firm is now earning profits, as shown by the shaded rectangle in the top left graph. Price is above average total cost, and so profits have risen above zero. We have gone from a situation in which profits were zero for firms in the industry to a situation in which profits are positive. Thus, we have moved away from a long-run equilibrium because of the disturbance that shifted the market demand curve. This shift has created a situation in the market in which there is a profit opportunity, encouraging new firms to enter the industry.

■ **Toward a New Long-Run Equilibrium.**   Now focus on the two graphs in the bottom part of Figure 9.4, representing the long run. They show what happens as new firms enter the industry. In the lower right-hand graph, the supply curve for the whole industry or market shifts to the right from S to S'. Why? Because the market supply curve is the sum of the individual supply curves, and now there are firms entering the industry and adding to supply.

The rightward shift in the supply curve causes a reduction in the price below P', where it was in the short run. The price will continue adjusting until the price line just touches the bottom of the average total cost curve, where average total cost equals marginal cost. At this point, profits will again be zero and the industry will be in long-run equilibrium. Of course, this adjustment to a new long-run equilibrium takes time. It takes time for firms to decide whether or not to go into business, and it takes time to set up a firm once a decision is made.

The new long-run equilibrium for the typical firm is shown in the lower left graph. It may take several years for an industry to move from the top of Figure 9.4 to the bottom. In fact, it would be more accurate to draw several rows of diagrams between the top and the bottom, showing how the process occurs gradually over time. These additional rows could show more and more firms entering the industry with the price falling until eventually profits are zero again and the incentive to enter the market disappears. The market supply curve will shift to the right until the price comes back to the point where average total cost is at a minimum, where profits are zero, and where no firms will enter or exit the industry.

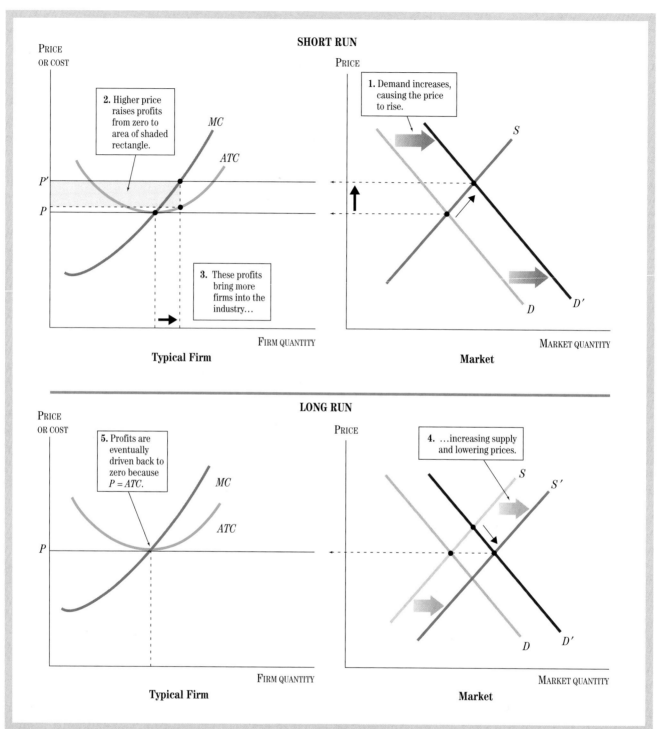

Figure 9.4
The Rise of an Industry after a Shift in Demand
The diagrams at the top show the short run. A shift in the demand curve to the right causes the price to rise from *P* to *P'*; each firm produces more, and profits rise. Higher profits cause firms to enter the industry. The diagrams at the bottom show the long run. As firms enter, the market supply curve shifts to the right, and the price falls back to *P*. New entry does not stop until profits return to zero in the long run.

■ **Economic Profits versus Accounting Profits.**   It is important at this point to emphasize that the economist's definition of profits is different from an accountant's definition. When you read about the profits of General Motors in the newspaper, it is the accountant's definition that is being reported. There is nothing wrong with the accountant's definition of profits, but it is different from the economist's definition. When an accountant calculates profits for a firm, the total costs do not include the opportunity cost of the owner's time or the owner's funds. Such opportunity costs are *implicit:* The wage that the owner could get elsewhere and the interest that could be earned on the funds if they were invested elsewhere are not explicitly paid, and the accountant therefore ignores them. When computing **accounting profits,** such implicit opportunity costs are *not* included in total costs. When computing **economic profits**—the measure of profits economists use—implicit opportunity costs are included in total costs. Economic profits are equal to accounting profits less any opportunity costs the accountants did not include when measuring total costs.

accounting profits: total revenue minus total costs, where total costs exclude the implicit opportunity costs; this is the definition of profits usually reported by firms.

economic profits: total revenue minus total costs, where total costs include opportunity costs, whether implicit or explicit.

For example, suppose accounting profits for a bakery are $40,000 a year. Suppose the owner of the bakery could earn $35,000 a year working as a manager at a video rental store. Suppose also that the owner could sell the bakery business for $50,000 and invest the money in a bank, where it would earn interest at 6 percent per year, or $3,000. Then the opportunity cost—which the accountant would not include in total costs—is $38,000 ($35,000 plus $3,000). To get economic profits, we have to subtract this opportunity cost from accounting profits. Thus, economic profits would be only $2,000.

Economic profits are used by economists because they measure the incentive the owner of the firm has to stay in business versus doing something else. In this case, with $2,000 in economic profits, the owner has an incentive to stay in the business. But if the owner could earn $39,000 managing a video rental store, then economic profits for the bakery would be −$2,000 (40,000 − 39,000 − 3,000), and the owner would have an incentive to run the video store. Even though accounting profits at the bakery were $40,000, the owner would have an incentive to go to work elsewhere because economic profits would be −$2,000. Thus, economic profits are a better measure of incentives than accounting profits, and this is why economists focus on economic profits. When we refer to profits in this book, we mean economic profits because we are interested in the incentives firms have to either enter or exit an industry.

normal profits: the amount of accounting profits when economic profits are equal to zero.

Observe that if the bakery owner could earn exactly $37,000 at the video rental store, then economic profits at the bakery would be zero. Then the owner would be indifferent on economic considerations alone between staying in the bakery business or going to work for the video rental company. The term **normal profits** refers to the amount of accounting profits that exist when economic profits are equal to zero. In this last case, normal profits would be $40,000.

■ **The Equilibrium Number of Firms.**   The long-run equilibrium model predicts that there will be a certain number of firms in the industry. The equilibrium number of firms will be such that there is no incentive for more firms to enter the industry or for others to leave. But how many firms is this? If the minimum point on the average cost curve of the typical firm represents production at a very small scale, then there will be many firms. That is, many firms will each produce a very small amount. If the minimum point represents production at a large scale, then there will be fewer firms; that is, a few firms will each produce a large amount.

To see this, consider the hypothetical case where all firms are identical. For example, if the minimum point on the average total cost curve for each firm in the grape industry occurs at 10,000 tons and the size of the whole market is 100,000 tons, then the model predicts 10 firms in the industry. If the quantity where average total cost is at a minimum is 1,000 tons, then there will be 100 firms. If in the latter case the demand for grapes increases and brings about a new long-run equilibrium of 130,000 tons, then the number of firms in the industry will rise from 100 to 130.

■ **Entry Combined with Individual Firm Expansion.** Thus far, we have described the growth of an industry in terms of the increase in the number of firms. In the short run, immediately after a change in demand, there is no entry or exit; then entry takes place and the industry moves toward a new equilibrium in the long run. Recall from Chapter 8 that something else can occur in the long run but not in the short run: In the short run, a firm cannot expand its size by investing in new capital, but in the long run it can expand.

In reality, industries usually grow by a combination of the expansion of existing firms and the entry of new firms. For example, this was what happened in the expedited package express industry, which grew both because UPS and other firms entered and because Federal Express expanded.

The expansion of an existing firm can occur under one of two conditions. First, the original size of the firm may be smaller than the minimum efficient scale, so the firm may be able to lower its average costs while producing more units. Second, a change in technology or in the prices of inputs may change the cost function of the firm, pushing the minimum efficient scale to a larger number of units. Note that if the firm is already producing at the minimum long-run average total cost, then an increase in demand will not affect the size of the firm, and you will observe only entry of new firms into the industry.

A Decrease in Demand

The long-run competitive equilibrium model can also be used to explain the decline of an industry. Suppose there is a shift in the demand curve from D to D', as illustrated in the top right graph in Figure 9.5. This causes the market price to fall. The lower market price (P') causes existing firms to cut back on production in the short run: As production decreases, marginal cost falls until it equals the new lower price for each firm. However, the firms are now running losses. As shown in the top left graph of Figure 9.5, profits drop below zero.

With profits less than zero, firms now have an incentive to leave the industry. As they leave, the market supply curve shifts to the left from S to S' as shown in the bottom right graph of Figure 9.5. This causes the price to rise again. The end of the process is a new long-run equilibrium, as shown in the bottom left graph of Figure 9.5. In the long run, fewer firms are in the industry, total production in the industry is lower, and profits are back to zero.

Shifts in Cost Curves

Our analysis of the rise and fall of an industry thus far has centered around shifts in demand. But new technologies and ideas for new products that reduce costs can also cause an industry to change. The long-run competitive equilibrium model can also be used to explain these changes, as shown in Figure 9.6.

The case of cost-reducing technologies—as when Wal-Mart introduced checkout counter scanners—can be handled by shifting down the average total cost curve along with the marginal cost curve, as shown in Figure 9.6. This will lead to a situation of positive profits because average total cost falls below the original market price P. If other firms already in the industry adopt similar cost-cutting strategies, the market price will fall to P', but profits will still be positive, as shown in Figure 9.6. With positive profits, other firms will have incentives to enter the industry with similar

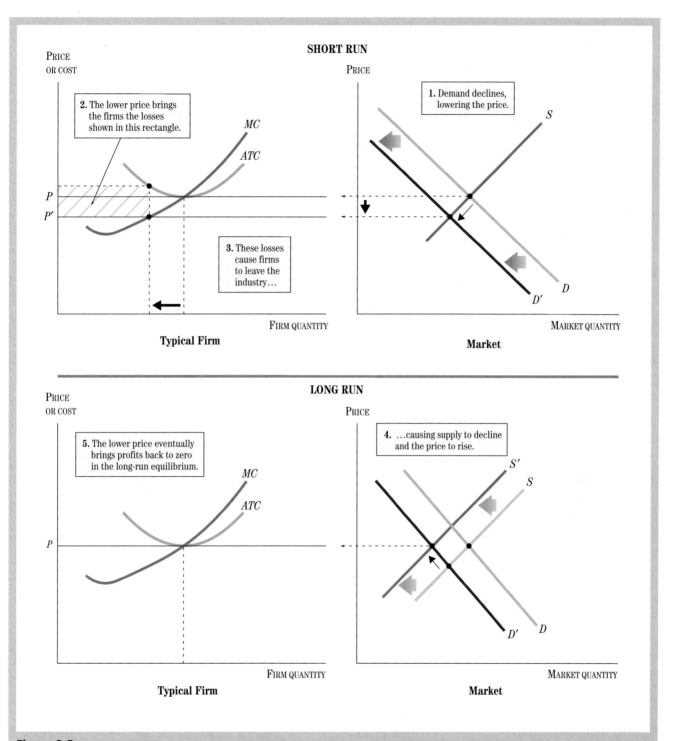

Figure 9.5
The Decline of an Industry after a Shift in Demand
In the short run, a reduction in demand lowers the price from *P* to *P'* and causes losses. Firms leave the industry, causing prices to rise back to *P*. In the long run, profits return to zero, the number of firms in the industry has declined, and the total quantity produced in the industry has fallen.

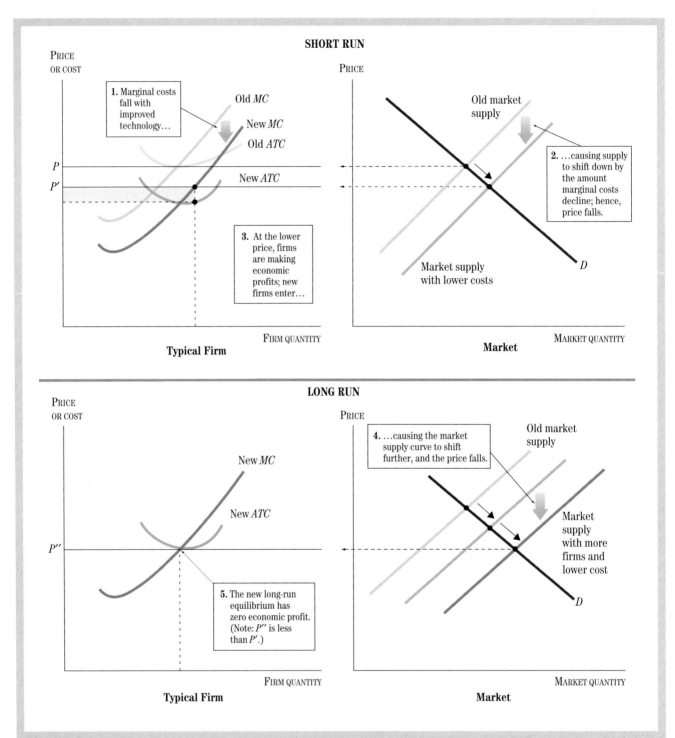

Figure 9.6
Effect of a Reduction in Costs
A new technology reduces costs and shifts the typical firm's *ATC* and *MC* curves down. The market supply curve shifts down by the same amount as the shift in marginal cost if other firms in the industry adopt the new technology right away. But because there are economic profits, new firms have incentives to enter the industry. As shown in the lower left graph, in the long run, profits return to zero.

Digital Cameras and the Future of Silver Halide Film

The long-run competitive equilibrium model is useful not only for explaining what happened to an industry in the past, but also for predicting what will happen to an industry in the future. Such predictions can help guide investment or career decisions.

The photographic film industry provides an interesting example of an industry undergoing change based on other industry changes. Photographic film, called silver halide film, was developed over 100 years ago and can give extremely high resolution and detail. The same technology is used for x-ray pictures, where detailed views are needed to detect hairline fractures and the like. This amazing film technology has brought enjoyment and better health to many millions of people.

But in recent years, digital cameras have begun to outsell cameras that use film. With a digital camera, you can take snapshots and load the images directly into a desktop computer. You can enlarge the images yourself, or have fun coloring your hair purple and e-mailing the image to your mother or father. Digital cameras are different from analog cameras in a very important way: *Digital cameras do not use film.* The more people use digital cameras, the less film they will buy. Thus, we can predict that the demand for photographic film and developing services will decline in the future as digital cameras improve and become cheaper. The demand curve will shift to the left, profits will decline, and firms will exit the industry. Figure 9.5 tells the story.

But is that the whole story? Film sales and film developing services may be declining rapidly, but many people still want to print their favorite images. And while some of the prints will be made on home inkjet printers, there is still a large demand for printing from retailers due to the high cost and amount of time it takes to make a print at home. These prints, whether they come from film or a digital image, are produced on silver halide–based photo-

graphic paper. Not only is the demand for photographic paper and printing services likely to grow, but the Silver Institute estimates that silver usage for these products will rise from 46.0 million troy ounces in 2000 to 60.1 million troy ounces in 2008.[1]

Naturally, other things could change. If the cost of printing high-quality photographs at home declines, fewer people might go outside to have their photos printed. And who knows what shifts another new entry into this market—the camera phone—might bring? Regardless of what happens, the economic model can help us determine the impact of changing technology and demand on industries in the economy.

---

[1]Don Franz, "The Global Silver Halide Photographic Market," *Silver News*, First Quarter 2004, www.silverinstitute.org.

Will digital cameras continue to shift the demand curve for film?

technologies. As the market supply curve shifts out after more firms enter the industry, the price falls further to P'', and eventually competition brings economic profits back to zero.

If new entrants drive economic profits to zero in the long run, then what incentives do firms have to develop cost-cutting technologies? The answer is that the economic profits in the short run can be substantial. Wal-Mart may have made hundreds of millions of dollars in economic profits before the competition eroded them. Hence, Wal-Mart benefited for a while from cost-cutting innovations. No idea will generate economic profits forever in a competitive market, but the short-run profits can still provide plenty of incentive.

REVIEW

- Entry and exit of firms in search of profit opportunities play a key role in the long-run competitive equilibrium model. The decision to enter or exit an industry is determined by profit potential. Positive economic profits will attract new firms. Negative economic profits will cause firms to exit the industry. In long-run equilibrium, economic profits are zero.

- The market supply curve shifts as firms enter or exit the industry. With more firms, the market supply curve shifts to the right. With fewer firms, the market supply curve shifts to the left.

- The model can be used to explain the rise and fall of many different industries, whether due to shifts in demand or to shifts in cost curves.

CASE STUDY

How Does the Model Explain the Facts?

For the purposes of using the long-run competitive equilibrium model in practice, economists usually need to narrow their focus.

Consider, for example, changes in the grape industry. The grape industry includes many different types of products. Some grape types are used to make raisins, other grapes are grown to be table grapes, and many different types of grapes are used for wine. Even within each of these categories, there are particular styles of grapes.

A good case study is the Zinfandel grape. This is one grape that is still largely confined to the United States, so we do not need to consider developments throughout the world. It is used to produce a particular type of wine, also called Zinfandel. Figure 9.7 shows the rise and fall in the price of Zinfandel grapes. The price more than tripled between 1985 and 1988. Then, nearly as sharply, the price declined from 1989 to 1991.

Figure 9.8 shows what happened to production in the Zinfandel grape industry during this period. The industry grew rapidly from 1985 to 1988. New vineyard acreage entering the industry each year more than tripled. In 1988, industry growth slowed and the number of acres of new vineyards declined sharply. By 1991, growth was close to zero, with only a handful of new vineyards entering.

How can we explain this huge rise and subsequent slowdown of the Zinfandel grape industry? The most likely explanation centers around the discovery of a new product. In the mid-1980s, it was discovered that Zinfandel grapes could be used to produce a new type of wine called "white Zinfandel," which proved to be very popular. Previously the grape had been used only to produce a heavy red wine that was less popular. This discovery greatly increased the demand for the Zinfandel grape.

According to the competitive equilibrium model, the increase in demand would be represented as a shift of the demand curve to the right, exactly as shown in Figure

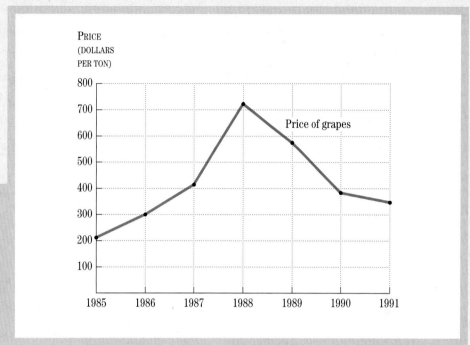

Figure 9.7
The Price of Grapes, 1985–1991
The price of Zinfandel grapes rose in the late 1980s because tastes shifted in favor of white wine made from these grapes. The higher price raised profits at Zinfandel vineyards and the number of vineyard acres increased as a result, as shown in Figure 9.8.

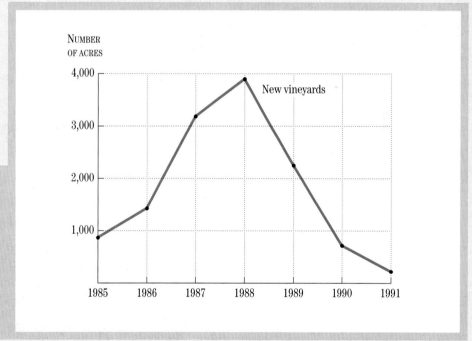

Figure 9.8
New Vineyards in the Grape Market, 1985–1991
As profits from growing Zinfandel grapes rose, the number of vineyards increased. The resulting increase in supply eventually lowered the price, which lowered profits, and the number of new vineyards declined. It takes several years for a new vineyard to start producing grapes.

9.4. The model would predict a rise in the price of grapes, and that is exactly what happened. The price rose from 1985 to 1988 after the demand curve shifted, as shown in Figure 9.7. With the higher price, the profits from Zinfandel grape production would increase; thus, the model predicts the entry of new firms. In fact, as shown in Figure 9.8, Zinfandel vineyard acreage did increase sharply in this same time period.

The following article discusses fluctuations in the California grape industry. It shows how a positive demand shock, in this case resulting from the discovery of potential health benefits of drinking wine, leads to improved profits for domestic wine producers, in turn leading more firms to enter into production. Over time, the increase in supply drove prices down and moved the wine industry toward long-run equilibrium. Recently, however, increases in wine imports from countries like South Africa, Chile, and Australia, as well as competition from other types of alcoholic beverages, have reduced the demand for domestic wine, causing prices to drop as the industry again moves toward long-run competitive equilibrium.

"What We Have Is Insufficient Demand for Wine Grape Supplies"

westernfarmpress.com
Feb. 4, 2003 12:00 PM, Harry Cline

California's wine grape industry is not going to heck in an oak barrel or a stainless steel tank.

"What we have is insufficient demand for the existing supplies," pronounced wine industry expert Barry Bedwell in explaining the current economic plight of California wine grapes in his best impersonation of actor Strother Martin. As you recall, Martin was immortalized for his famous line, "What we have here is a failure to communicate" from the movie Cool Hand Luke.

Bedwell, California wine broker coordinator for Joseph W. Ciatti Co. and Jon Fredrikson of Gomberg, Fredrikson and Associates avoided the G (glut) word like a glass of bad White Grenache when they reported on the status of the industry to a rapt crowd of more than 1,000 at the 9th annual United Wine and Grape Symposium recently in Sacramento, Calif.

Fredrikson and Bedwell are two of the most respected wine industry analysts. Bedwell's opening comment about "insufficient demand" was calculated to net a laugh from the audience, and it did.

According to the model, in the long run, the increased supply from the new entrants to the industry should lower the price. As shown in Figure 9.7, the price did fall after 1988.

Again according to the model, the lower price should reduce profit opportunities, and the number of new entrants should decline. Sure enough, the data show that the number of new entrants peaked in 1988 and then declined.

At the end of this process, the price had returned to near the original price and the number of new entrants was close to zero. Apparently a new equilibrium was reached. Overall, the facts during this episode of change in the industry seem to be explained quite well by the model.

REVIEW
- To apply the long-run competitive equilibrium model, economists focus on a single industry with a clear shift in demand or supply.
- Case studies like that of the Zinfandel grape industry show that the model works.

However, it has not been a laughing matter for most wine grape growers and many wineries over at least the past two years as acreage coming into production has soared, creating an oversupply in many varietals and sending prices plummeting; imports taking an increasingly bigger share of the U.S. wine market and wine finding tough going in getting shelf space from beers and spirits.

No Wine Glut

However, there is no California wine glut, Bedwell said. There are oversupplies of some varietals like Cabernet Sauvignon, Pinot Noir and perhaps Syrah. However, supply and demand are getting closer to balances for Chardonnay, red Zinfandel, Sauvignon Blanc, Merlot and White Zinfandel.

The California wine industry is in a "down cycle," not in wine glut, according to Bedwell, after experiencing a decade of phenomenal growth following the 1991 French Paradox. That broadcast heralded the health benefits of moderate wine drinking. Sales have increased by 75 million cases since then.

"What I think Jon and I were trying to do in our industry assessments is counter the overwhelming negative publicity of the wine industry over the past few months that is ignoring the cyclical aspects of this industry," said Bedwell.

"This is a remarkably strong, $1.5 billion a year industry," Bedwell said.

"Is there an oversupply of wine grapes? Absolutely," said Bedwell, who said the value of wine grapes dropped $200 million last year and likely will drop another 7 percent to 10 percent this season as the industry works off oversupplies.

"The California situation is not a glut," echoed Fredrikson. "A glut is the wine lake in Europe where growers are producing wine that is not intended for sale as wine but to be used as gasohol as part of a social program."

Bedwell said the California wine industry has become notorious for overreacting. When things are good, new plantings quickly catch up with grape and wine demand and an oversupply situation is created, even with growing wine sales. When things go bad, growers become too aggressive with bulldozers in taking out vineyards.

- An increase in demand caused the price of Zinfandel grapes to rise. Grape-producing firms saw a profit opportunity and entered the industry, transforming existing land into vineyards. The supply of grapes began to increase. As a result, the price started to come back down again.

Minimum Costs per Unit and the Efficient Allocation of Capital

If firms can enter or exit a competitive industry, as assumed in this model, then there are several other attractive features of the competitive market that we can add to those discussed in Chapter 7.

Average Total Cost Is Minimized

In the long-run equilibrium, average total cost is as low as technology will permit. You can see this in Figures 9.3, 9.4, 9.5, and 9.6. In each case, the typical firm produces a quantity at which average total cost is at the *minimum point* of the firm's average total cost curve. This amount of production must occur in the long-run equilibrium because profits are zero. For profits to be zero, price must equal average total cost ($P = ATC$). The only place where $P = MC$ and $P = ATC$ is at the lowest point on the ATC curve. At this point, costs per unit are at a minimum.

In the long run, firms can expand or contract as well as enter or exit an industry. As they expand or contract, their costs are described by the long-run ATC curve. Thus, in the long-run competitive equilibrium, firms operate at the lowest point of the long-run average total cost curve.

That average total cost is at a minimum is an attractive feature of a competitive market where firms are free to enter and exit. It means that goods are produced at the lowest cost, with the price consumers pay equal to that lowest cost. If firms could not enter and exit, this attractive feature would be lost.

Efficient Allocation of Capital among Industries

An efficient allocation of capital among industries is also achieved by entry and exit in competitive markets. Entry of firms into the Zinfandel grape industry, for example, means that more capital has gone into that industry, where it can better satisfy consumer tastes, and less capital has gone into some other industry.

In the case of a declining industry, capital moves out of the industry to other industries, where it is more efficiently used. For example, capital moved away from the beef industry toward the chicken industry when the former contracted and the latter expanded in recent years. Thus, the long-run competitive equilibrium has another attractive property: Capital is allocated to its most efficient use. Again, this property is due to the free entry and exit of firms. If entry and exit were limited or if the market were not competitive for some other reason, this advantage would be lost.

REVIEW
- In a long-run competitive equilibrium, firms operate at the minimum point on their long-run average total cost curves and capital is allocated efficiently across different industries.

- Minimum-cost production is a benefit to society of the competitive market with free entry and exit.

External Economies and Diseconomies of Scale

In Chapter 8 we introduced the concept of economies and diseconomies of scale for a firm. A firm whose long-run average total cost declines as the firm expands has economies of scale. If long-run average total cost rises as the firm expands, there are diseconomies of scale. Economies and diseconomies of scale may exist for whole industries as well as for firms, as we now show.

External Diseconomies of Scale

When the number of firms in the Zinfandel grape industry increases, the demand for water for irrigation in grape-growing regions also increases, and this may raise the price of water in these regions. If it does, then the cost of producing grapes increases. With the marginal cost of each grape producer increasing, the supply curve for each firm and for the industry or the market shifts up and to the left. Even though no single firm's decision affects the price of water for irrigation, the expansion of the industry does.

This is shown in the market supply and demand curves in Figure 9.9. Suppose there is a shift in the demand curve from D_1 to D_2. As the industry expands, more firms enter the industry and the supply curve shifts to the right from S_1 to S_2. Because the marginal cost at each firm rises as the industry expands, the supply curve does not shift to the right by as much as the demand curve shifts. Thus, the intersection of the demand curve D_2 and the supply curve S_2 occurs at a higher price than the intersection of S_1 and D_1.

We could consider a further shift in demand to D_3, leading to a shift in supply to S_3. This would result in yet another long-run equilibrium at a higher price because average total cost is higher. Observe that as successive market demand curves intersect successive market supply curves, the price rises and quantity rises; an upward-sloping **long-run industry supply curve** is traced out. We call the phenomenon of an upward-sloping long-run industry supply curve **external diseconomies of scale.** The word *external* indicates that cost increases are external to the firm, due, for example, to a higher price for inputs (such as water) to production. In contrast, the diseconomies of scale considered in Chapter 8 were internal to the firm, due, for example, to increased costs of managing a larger firm; they can be called *internal diseconomies of scale* to distinguish them from the external case.

long-run industry supply curve: a curve traced out by the intersections of demand curves shifting to the right and the corresponding short-run supply curves.

external diseconomies of scale: a situation in which growth in an industry causes average total cost for the individual firm to rise because of some factor external to the firm; it corresponds to an upward-sloping long-run industry supply curve.

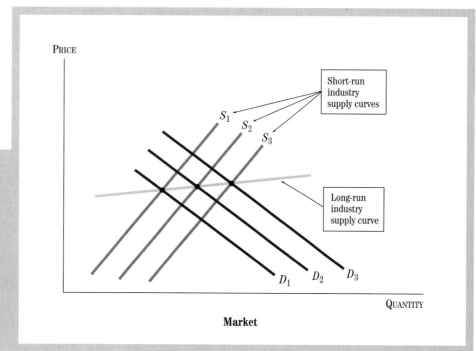

Figure 9.9
External Diseconomies of Scale
As demand increases and more firms enter the industry, each firm's costs increase, perhaps because the prices of inputs to production rise. The higher costs tend to limit the shift of the market supply curve to the right when new firms enter. The long-run industry supply curve slopes up, a phenomenon that is called external diseconomies of scale.

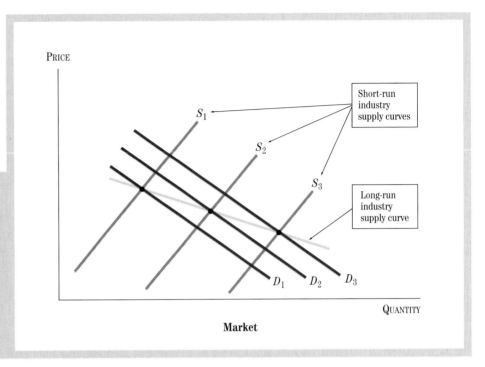

Figure 9.10
External Economies of Scale
As demand expands and more firms enter the industry, each firm's costs decline, which causes the supply curve to shift to the right by even more than it would as a result of the increase in the number of firms. The long-run industry supply curve is thus downward-sloping, a phenomenon that is called external economies of scale.

External Economies of Scale

external economies of scale: a situation in which growth in an industry causes average total cost for the individual firm to fall because of some factor external to the firm; it corresponds to a downward-sloping long-run industry supply curve.

External economies of scale are also possible. For example, the expansion of the Zinfandel grape industry might make it worthwhile for students at agricultural schools to become specialists in Zinfandel grapes. With a smaller industry, such specialization would not have been worthwhile. The expertise that comes from that specialization could reduce the cost of grape production by more than the cost of hiring the specialist. Then as the industry expands, both the average total cost and the marginal cost for individual firms may decline.

The case of external economies of scale is shown in Figure 9.10. Again, suppose there is a shift in the demand curve from D_1 to D_2. When the industry expands, the market supply curve shifts out from S_1 to S_2, or by *more* than the increase in demand, so that the price falls. The reason the market supply curve shifts more than the market demand curve is that marginal cost at each firm has declined as the number of firms in the industry has increased. This larger shift in supply compared to demand is shown in Figure 9.10. Thus, the price falls as the industry expands.

With additional shifts in demand from D_2 to D_3, the market demand curves intersect with successive market supply curves at lower prices, resulting in a long-run industry supply curve that is downward-sloping. Again, the word *external* is used to distinguish these economies that occur outside the firm from those that are internal to the firm.

Our example of the reason why external economies occur is that a larger industry allows for opportunities for *specialization*—grape-growing specialists who then provide services to the industry. There are other such examples. The expansion of the personal computer industry made it worthwhile for many small specialized firms servicing personal computer manufacturers to emerge. With a smaller-scale industry, this would not have been possible.

Note the difference between internal and external economies of scale. The expansion of a single firm can generate internal economies of scale with the number

Internal economies or diseconomies of scale occur when a *single firm* expands (Chapter 8). *External* economies or diseconomies of scale occur when an *industry* expands (Chapter 9).

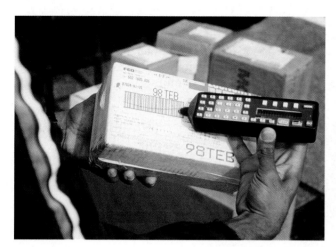

External Economies of Scale
As an industry expands in size, firms in other industries have incentives to develop new products to service the industry. These new products reduce average total cost in the industry, thereby giving rise to economies of scale, as illustrated by the development of special electronic scanners for use by the expanding express delivery service industry (left). The new ideas may in turn be used to reduce costs in other industries, as illustrated by the use of electronic scanners for self-service checkout in the retail food industry (right).

of firms in the industry fixed because individuals within the firm can specialize. The expansion of an industry can generate external economies of scale even if the size of each firm in the industry does not increase. As an industry expands, firms might even split up into several specialized firms, each concentrating on one part of the specialized work.

The Standard Assumption: A Flat Long-Run Industry Supply Curve

In the examples used in the previous sections of this chapter, there were neither external economies of scale nor external diseconomies of scale. To convince yourself of this, look back to the graphs in the lower right-hand panels of Figures 9.4 and 9.5. You will see that the market price in the long-run equilibrium after the shift in demand is the same as before the shift in demand. If you draw a line between the intersection points of the supply and demand curves in those graphs, you will get a flat line. Thus, the long-run industry curve will be perfectly horizontal, in contrast to the upward slope in Figure 9.9 and the downward slope in Figure 9.10. The intersections of the shifting demand and supply curves trace out neither an upward-sloping long-run industry supply curve—the case of external diseconomies of scale—nor a downward-sloping long-run industry supply curve—the case of external economies of scale. The assumption of a flat long-run industry supply curve is the standard one economists use to study industries where neither type of external scale effect is known to occur.

External and Internal Economies of Scale Together

In practice, it is possible for external and internal economies of scale to occur at the same time in one industry. When an industry grows in scale through the addition of new firms, it is common for the typical firm in the industry to expand its scale.

Federal Express has grown in size at the same time that more firms have entered the industry. Through its larger size, Federal Express has achieved internal economies of scale (for example, by spreading the costs of its computer tracking system over more deliveries), and the larger industry as a whole has benefited from external economies of scale (as illustrated by the scanners shown in the photo).

REVIEW

- External diseconomies of scale occur when an expansion of an industry raises costs at individual firms, perhaps because of a rise in input prices.

- External economies of scale arise when expansion of an industry lowers costs at individual firms in the industry. Opportunities for specialization for individuals and firms serving the industry are one reason for external economies of scale.

Conclusion

In this chapter, we have addressed one of the most pervasive and perplexing realities of a market economy: the changes that occur when whole industries rise or fall over time. As consumer tastes change and new ideas are discovered, such changes are an ever-present phenomenon in modern economies around the world.

The model we have developed in this chapter to explain such changes extends the competitive equilibrium model we developed in Chapters 5, 6, 7, and 8 to allow for the entry or exit of firms into or out of an industry. Because such entry or exit usually takes time, we emphasize that this modification applies to the long run. Profits motivate firms to enter or exit an industry. Profits draw firms into the industry over time, whereas losses cause firms to leave. As firms enter, the industry expands. As firms leave, the industry declines. In the long-run equilibrium, profit opportunities have disappeared, and entry or exit stops.

In Chapters 10 and 11, we begin to leave the realm of the competitive market. We will develop models of the behavior of monopolies and other firms for which the assumption of a competitive market is not accurate. In the process, we will see that many of the results we have obtained with competitive markets in this chapter are no longer true.

However, many of the ideas and concepts developed in this and the previous few chapters on the competitive model will be used in these chapters. The cost curve diagram will reappear in the model of monopoly in Chapter 10; the idea of entry and exit will reappear in Chapter 11.

As we consider these new models and new results, we will use the models of this chapter as a basis of comparison. A central question will be: "How different are the results from those of the long-run competitive equilibrium model?" Keep that question in mind as you proceed to the following chapters.

KEY POINTS

1. Economic history is filled with stories about the rise and fall of industries. Industries grow rapidly when cost-reducing technologies are discovered or demand increases. They decline when demand decreases.

2. Because of reduced transportation and communication costs, most industries today are global.

3. The economists' competitive equilibrium model assumes that firms are price-takers.

4. The long-run competitive equilibrium model also assumes that firms enter or exit an industry until economic profits are driven to zero.

5. The long-run competitive equilibrium model can be used to explain many facts about the rise and fall of industries over time.

6. In the long run, the competitive equilibrium model implies that after entry and exit have taken place, average total costs are minimized and capital is allocated efficiently among industries.

7. Industries may exhibit either external economies of scale, when the long-run industry supply curve slopes down, or external diseconomies of scale, when the long-run industry supply curve slopes up.

KEY TERMS

industry

long-run competitive equilibrium model

free entry and exit

long-run equilibrium

accounting profits

economic profits

normal profits

long-run industry supply curve

external diseconomies of scale

external economies of scale

QUESTIONS FOR REVIEW

1. What are three possible sources of the rise of industries? Of the fall of industries?

2. What is the difference between economic profits and accounting profits?

3. Why do firms enter an industry? Why do they exit?

4. Why does the market supply curve shift to the right when there are positive profits in an industry?

5. Why is "zero profits" a condition of long-run equilibrium?

6. What does the demand curve look like to a single firm in a competitive industry?

7. Why are average total costs minimized in a long-run competitive equilibrium?

8. What are external economies of scale? How do they differ from internal economies of scale?

9. How does the long-run/short-run distinction differ when applied to a firm versus an industry?

PROBLEMS

1. Suppose corn farmers in the United States can be represented by a competitive industry with no economies or diseconomies of scale. Describe how this industry would adjust to an increase in demand for corn. Explain your answer graphically, showing the cost curves for the typical farmer as well as the market supply and demand curves. Distinguish between the short run and the long run.

2. Suppose the government gives a subsidy to textile firms, paying each firm a specific amount per unit of production. What will happen to output and the number of firms in the short run and the long run?

3. Sketch a diagram showing the costs and price of the typical price-taking firm in long-run equilibrium. Suppose a technology is invented that reduces average total cost and marginal cost. Draw this new situation. Describe how the industry adjusts. How will the long-run equilibrium price change? What happens to the number of firms in the industry?

4. Suppose the government imposes a sales tax on a good sold by firms in a competitive industry. Describe what happens to the price of the good in the short run and in the long run when firms are free to enter and exit. What happens to the number of firms in the industry and to total production in the industry?

5. Consider a typical carpet-cleaning firm that currently faces $24 in fixed costs and an $8 hourly wage for workers. The price it gets for each office cleaned in a large office building is $48 at the present long-run equilibrium. The production function of the firm is shown in the following table:

Number of Offices Cleaned	Hours of Work
0	0
1	5
2	9
3	15
4	22
5	30

a. Find marginal costs and average total costs for the typical firm.

b. How many offices are cleaned by the typical firm in long-run equilibrium?

c. Suppose there is an increase in demand. Describe the process that leads to a new long-run equilibrium. What is the new price in the long-run equilibrium? What is the quantity produced by the typical firm? Draw the market demand and supply curves before and after the shift. (Assume that the hourly wage remains at $8 per hour.)

d. Now assume that the increased number of cleaning firms causes a rise in the hourly wage from $8 to $9. How would your answer differ from that for part (c)? In particular, compare the equilibrium price and the market demand and supply curves.

6. Compare and contrast economic profits, accounting profits, and normal profits.

7. Many young children drink from sippy cups—plastic cups with a spout that prevents the liquid contents from spilling. Recently pediatric dentists have attacked the use of sippy cups, saying that they may contribute to the formation of cavities.

a. Graphically show the competitive market for sippy cups before and after this news is released to the public. What would you predict will happen to equilibrium price and quantity in the short run?

b. Now graphically show the long-term equilibrium of the sippy cup market. Which curves shift? Why? Compare the long-term equilibrium price and quantity with its original counterparts.

8. What is the difference between the short run and the long run for a firm (as described in Chapter 8) and the short run and the long run for an industry (as described in this chapter)?

9. What is the incentive for one firm in a competitive industry to pursue cost-cutting measures? What will happen in the long run?

10. This problem combines changes in capital at each firm over the long run with entry and exit of firms into or out of an industry in the long run. Given the data in the table for a typical firm in a competitive industry (with identical firms), sketch the two short-run average total cost curves (ATC_1 and ATC_2) and the two marginal cost curves (MC_1 and MC_2).

a. Suppose the price is $9 per unit. How much will the firm produce, and with what level of capital?

b. Suppose the firm is currently producing with 2 units of capital. If the price falls to $7 per unit, will the firm contract when it is able to change its capital? Why?

c. What is the long-run industry equilibrium price and quantity for the typical firm? If there is a market demand of 4,000 units at that price, how many of these identical firms will there be in the industry?

d. Why might the firm operate with 2 units of capital in the short run if the long-run equilibrium implies 1 unit of capital?

Quantity	Costs with 1 Unit of Capital		Costs with 2 Units of Capital	
	ATC_1	MC_1	ATC_2	MC_2
1	7.0	5	10.0	6
2	5.5	4	7.5	5
3	4.7	3	6.3	4
4	4.5	4	5.5	3
5	4.6	5	5.0	3
6	4.8	6	4.8	4
7	5.1	7	4.9	5
8	5.5	8	5.0	6
9	5.9	9	5.2	7
10	6.3	10	5.5	8
11	6.7	11	5.8	9
12	7.2	12	6.2	10

CHAPTER 10

Monopoly

Sending the board game Monopoly to prospective customers at the start of the 1990s was how Advanced Micro Devices called attention to Intel's monopoly. Both Advanced Micro Devices and Intel produce the central processor—the brains—of personal computers. Intel had a monopoly because it was the sole producer of the 386 computer chip, the most popular central processor for personal computers in the early 1990s. Intel's researchers had invented the chip. The company created the monopoly legally by obtaining patents and copyrights from the government that gave it the sole right to produce the chip. No other firm could compete with Intel unless Intel gave permission, and Intel did not want to give permission to Advanced Micro Devices. As frequently happens, however, Advanced Micro Devices designed its own 386 chip, a clone of Intel's that did not infringe on Intel's patents. By 1991, Advanced Micro Devices was ready to compete with Intel and used the Monopoly game to help launch its product. But by the time it had done so, Intel had invented a more advanced chip—the 486—and created yet another monopoly. Nevertheless, Advanced Micro Devices soon got into the new act, developing chips that virtually replicated Intel's 486. Today the story continues with yet newer and faster processors and memory devices.

When one firm, like Intel, is the sole producer of a good, it is by definition a monopoly in the market for that good. An important feature of today's economy is that monopolies, as in the computer chip example, frequently do not last very long. Rapid changes in technology can make patents and copyrights useless well before their life is over.

Nevertheless, some monopolies still last a long time. De Beers is one of the most famous examples of a monopoly. It controls 80 percent of the world's diamond supply and, therefore, is virtually a monopoly. It has maintained its monopoly position since 1929.

Monopolies operate very differently from firms in competitive markets. The biggest difference is that monopolies have the power to set the price in their markets. They use this power to charge higher prices than competitive firms would.

The aim of this chapter is to develop a model of monopoly that can be used to explain this behavior and thereby help us understand how real-world monopolies operate. The model explains how a monopoly decides what price to charge its customers and what quantity to sell. It shows that monopolies cause a loss to society when compared with firms providing goods in competitive markets; the model also provides a way to measure that loss. We also use the model to explain some puzzling pricing behavior, such as why some airlines charge a lower fare to travelers who stay over on a Saturday night.

Monopolies and the reasons for their existence raise important public policy questions about the role of government in the economy. For example, the loss that monopolies cause to society creates a potential role for government: It may step in to reduce this loss.

A Model of Monopoly

monopoly: one firm in an industry selling a product for which there are no close substitutes.

barriers to entry: anything that prevents firms from entering a market.

market power: a firm's power to set its price without losing its entire share of the market.

price-maker: a firm that has the power to set its price, rather than taking the price set by the market.

A **monopoly** occurs when there is only one firm in an industry selling a product for which there are no close substitutes. Thus, implicit in the definition of monopoly are **barriers to entry**—other firms are not free to enter the industry. For example, The Diamond Trading Company creates barriers to entry by maintaining exclusive rights to the diamonds in most of the world's diamond mines.

The economist's model of a monopoly assumes that the monopoly will choose a level of output that maximizes profits. In this respect, the model of a monopoly is like that of a competitive firm. If increasing production will increase a monopoly's profits, then the monopoly will raise production, just as a competitive firm would. If cutting production will increase a monopoly's profits, then the monopoly will cut its production, just as a competitive firm would.

The difference between a monopoly and a competitive firm is not what motivates them, but rather how their actions affect the market price. The most important difference is that a monopoly has **market power.** That is, a monopoly has the power to set the price in the market, whereas a competitor does not. This is why a monopoly is called a **price-maker** rather than a *price-taker*, the term used to refer to a competitive firm.

The monopoly power of the salt industry has been illustrated throughout history. Salt monopolies have contributed to the rise of several state powers—from governments in ancient China to medieval Europe, where Venice's control of the salt monopoly helped finance their navy and allowed them to dominate world trade.

Getting an Intuitive Feel for the Market Power of a Monopoly

We can demonstrate the monopoly's power to affect the price in the market by looking at either what happens when the monopoly changes its price or what happens when the monopoly changes the quantity it produces. We consider the price decision first.

■ **There Is No One to Undercut the Monopolist's Price.**   When there are several sellers competing with one another in a competitive market, one seller can try to sell at a higher price, but no one will buy at that price because there is always another seller nearby who will undercut that price. If a seller charges a higher price, everyone will ignore that seller; there is no effect on the market price.

The monopoly's situation is quite different. Instead of there being several sellers, there is only one seller. If the single seller sets a high price, it has no need to worry about being undercut by other sellers. There are no other sellers. Thus, the single seller—the monopoly—has the power to set a high price. True, the buyers will probably buy less at the higher price—that is, as the price rises, the quantity demanded declines—but because there are no other sellers, they will probably buy something from the lone seller.

■ **The Impact of Quantity Decisions on the Price.**   Another way to see this important difference between a monopoly and a competitor is to examine what happens to the price when a firm changes the quantity it produces. Suppose that there are 100 firms competing in the bagel-baking market in a large city, each producing about the same quantity of bagels each day. Suppose that one of the firms—Bageloaf—decides to cut its production in half. Although this is a huge cut for one firm, it is a small cut compared to the whole market—only one-half a percent. *Thus the market price will rise very little.* Moreover, if this little price increase affects the behavior of the other 99 firms at all, it will motivate them to increase their production slightly. As they increase the quantity they supply, they partially offset the cut in supply by Bageloaf, and so the change in market price will be even smaller. Thus, by any measure, the overall impact on the price from the change in Bageloaf's production is negligible. Bageloaf has essentially no power to affect the price of bagels in the city.

But now suppose that Bageloaf and the 99 other firms are taken over by Bagelopoly, which then becomes the only bagel bakery in the city. Now, if Bagelopoly cuts production in half, the total quantity of bagels supplied to the whole market is cut in half, and *this will have a big effect on the price in the market.*

If Bagelopoly cut its production even further, the price would rise further. However, if Bagelopoly increased the quantity it produced, the price of bagels would fall. Thus, Bagelopoly has immense power to affect the price. Even if Bagelopoly does not know exactly what the price elasticity of demand for bagels is, it can adjust the quantity it will produce either up or down in order to change the price.

■ **Showing Market Power with a Graph.**   Figure 10.1 contrasts the market power of a monopoly with that of a competitive firm. The right-hand graph shows that the competitive firm views the market price as essentially out of its control. The market price is shown by the flat line and is thus the same regardless of how much the firm produces. If the competitive firm tried to charge a higher price, nobody would buy because there would be many competitors charging a lower price; so, effectively, the competitive firm cannot charge a higher price.

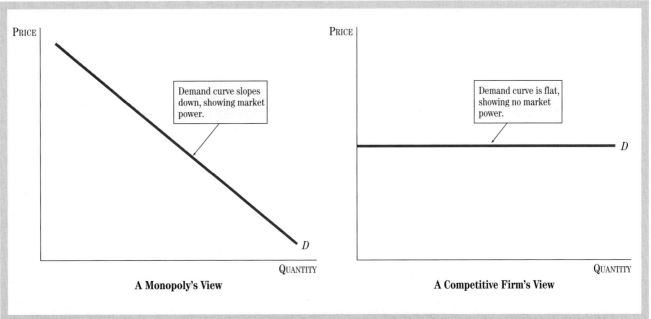

Figure 10.1
How the Market Power of a Monopoly and a Competitive Firm Differ

A monopoly is the only firm in the market. Thus, the market demand curve and the demand curve of the monopoly are the same. By raising the price, the monopoly sells less. In contrast, the competitive firm has no impact on the market price. If the competitive firm charges a higher price, its sales will drop to zero.

To a monopoly, on the other hand, things look quite different. Because the monopoly is the sole producer of the product, it represents the entire market. The monopoly—shown in the left-hand graph—sees a downward-sloping market demand curve for its product. *The downward-sloping demand curve seen by the monopoly is the same as the market demand curve.* If the monopoly charges a higher price, the quantity demanded declines along the demand curve. With a higher price, fewer people buy the item, but with no competitors to undercut that higher price, there is still some demand for the product.

The difference in the market power of a monopoly and a competitive firm—illustrated by the slope of the demand curve each faces—causes the difference in the behavior of the two types of firms.

The Effects of a Monopoly's Decision on Revenues

Now that we have seen how the monopoly can affect the price in its market by changing the quantity it produces, let's see how its revenues are affected by the quantity it produces.

Table 10.1 gives a specific numerical example of a monopoly. Depending on the units for measuring the quantity Q, the monopoly could be producing computer chips or diamonds.

The two columns on the left represent the market demand curve, showing that there is a negative relationship between the price and the quantity sold: As the quantity sold rises from 3 to 4, for example, the price falls from $130 to $120 per unit.

The third column of Table 10.1 shows what happens to the monopoly's total revenue, or price times quantity, as the quantity of output increases. Observe that at the beginning, when the monopoly increases the quantity produced, total revenue rises:

Table 10.1
Revenue, Costs, and Profits for a Monopoly (price, revenue, and cost measured in dollars)

Market Demand

Quantity Produced and Sold (Q)	Price (P)	Total Revenue (TR)	Marginal Revenue (MR)	Total Costs (TC)	Marginal Cost (MC)	Profits
0	160	0	—	70	—	−70
1	150	150	150	79	9	71
2	140	280	130	84	5	196
3	130	390	110	94	10	296
4	120	480	90	114	20	366
5	110	550	70	148	34	402
6	100	600	50	196	48	404
7	90	630	30	261	65	369
8	80	640	10	351	90	289
9	70	630	−10	481	130	149
10	60	600	−30	656	175	−56

$TR = P \times Q$

$\dfrac{\text{Change in } TR}{\text{Change in } Q}$

$\dfrac{\text{Change in } TC}{\text{Change in } Q}$

$TR - TC$

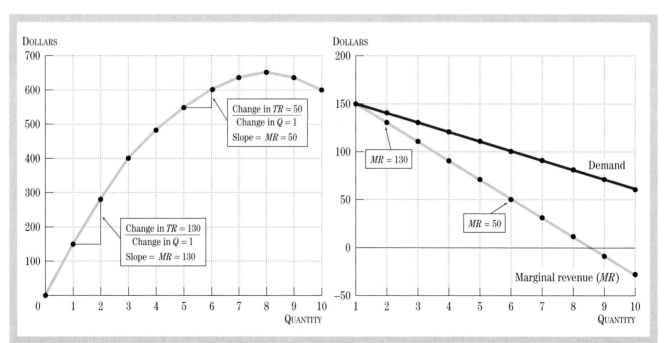

Figure 10.2
Total Revenue, Marginal Revenue, and Demand

The graph on the left plots total revenue for each level of output for Table 10.1. Total revenue first rises and then declines as the quantity of output increases. Marginal revenue is the change in total revenue for each additional increase in the quantity of output and is shown by the yellow curve at the right. Observe that the marginal revenue curve lies below the demand curve at each level of output except Q = 1.

When zero units are sold, total revenue is clearly zero; when 1 unit is sold, total revenue is $1 \times \$150$, or $150; when 2 units are sold, total revenue is $2 \times \$140$, or $280; and so on. However, as the quantity sold increases, total revenue rises by smaller and smaller amounts and eventually starts to fall. In Table 10.1, total revenue reaches a peak of $640 at 8 units sold and then starts to decline.

The left-hand graph in Figure 10.2 shows how total revenue changes with the quantity of output for the example in Table 10.1. It shows that total revenue reaches a maximum. Although a monopolist has the power to influence the price, this does not mean that it can get as high a level of total revenue as it wants. Why does total revenue increase by smaller and smaller amounts and then decline as production increases? Because in order to sell more output, the monopolist must lower the price in order to get people to buy the increased output. As it raises output, it must lower the price more and more, and this causes the increase in total revenue to get smaller. As the price falls to very low levels, revenue actually declines.

■ **Declining Marginal Revenue.** In order to determine the quantity the monopolist produces to maximize profits, we must measure marginal revenue. *Marginal revenue*, introduced in Chapter 6, is the change in total revenue from one more unit of output sold. For example, if total revenue increases from $480 to $550 as output rises by 1 unit, marginal revenue is $70 ($550 − $480 = $70). Marginal revenue for the monopolist in Table 10.1 is shown in the fourth column, next to total revenue. In addition, marginal revenue is plotted in the right-hand graph of Figure 10.2, where it is labeled *MR*.

An important relationship between marginal revenue and price, shown in Table 10.1 and Figure 10.2, is that *marginal revenue declines as the quantity of output rises*. This is just another way to say that the changes in total revenue get smaller and smaller as output increases, as we already noted.

■ **Marginal Revenue Is Less than the Price.** Another important relationship between marginal revenue and price is that for every level of output, *marginal revenue is less than the price* (except at the first unit of output, where it equals the price). To observe this, compare the price (P) and marginal revenue (MR) in Table 10.1 or in the right-hand panel of Figure 10.2.

Note that the red line in Figure 10.2 showing the price and the quantity of output demanded is simply the demand curve facing the monopolist. Thus, another way to say that marginal revenue is less than the price at a given level of output is to say that the *marginal revenue curve lies below the demand curve*.

Why is the marginal revenue curve below the demand curve? When the monopolist increases output by one unit, there are two effects on total revenue: (1) a positive effect, which equals the price P times the additional unit sold, and (2) a negative effect, which equals the reduction in the price on all items previously sold times the number of such items sold. For example, as the monopolist in Table 10.1 increases production from 4 to 5 units and the price falls from $120 to $110, marginal revenue is $70; this $70 is equal to the increased revenue from the extra unit produced, or $110, less the decreased revenue from the reduction in the price, or $40 ($10 times the 4 units previously produced). Marginal revenue ($MR = \$70$) is thus less than the price ($P = \$110$). The two effects on marginal revenue are shown in the graph in the margin when quantity increases from 3 to 4. Other numerical examples are shown in the table on page 262. Because the second effect—the reduction in revenue due to the lower price on the items previously produced—is subtracted from the first, the price is always greater than the marginal revenue.

■ **Marginal Revenue Can Be Negative.** Note that marginal revenue is negative when output is 9 or 10 units in the example. Then total revenue *falls* as additional

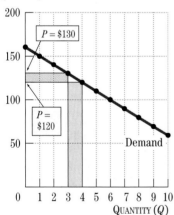

PRICE (*P*)
(DOLLARS)

Graph Showing the Two Effects on Marginal Revenue
When the monopoly raises output from 3 units to 4 units, revenue increases; that is, marginal revenue is greater than zero. There is a positive effect (blue rectangle) because one more item is sold and a negative effect (red rectangle) because prices on previously sold items fall. Here the positive effect (area of blue rectangle is $120) is greater than the negative effect (area of red rectangle is $30), so marginal revenue is $90.

units are produced. It would be crazy for a monopolist to produce so much that its marginal revenue was negative.

Marginal revenue is negative when the price elasticity of demand is less than 1. To see this, some algebra is helpful. Note from the examples in the table below that the following equation holds.

$$MR = (P \times \Delta Q) - (\Delta P \times Q)$$

If $MR < 0$, then

$$P \times \Delta Q < \Delta P \times Q$$

which implies that

$$\frac{(\Delta Q/Q)}{(\Delta P/P)} < 1$$

or, in words, that the price elasticity of demand is less than 1. Thus, we conclude that a monopoly would never produce a level of output where the price elasticity of demand is less than 1.

Quantity Sold	Marginal Revenue (MR)		Price × (Change in Quantity) $P \times (\Delta Q)$		(Change in Price) × (Previous Quantity Sold) $(\Delta P) \times (Q)$
1	150	=	$150 × 1	−	$10 × 0
2	130	=	$140 × 1	−	$10 × 1
3	110	=	$130 × 1	−	$10 × 2
4	90	=	$120 × 1	−	$10 × 3
5	70	=	$110 × 1	−	$10 × 4
6	50	=	$100 × 1	−	$10 × 5
7	30	=	$90 × 1	−	$10 × 6
8	10	=	$80 × 1	−	$10 × 7
9	−10	=	$70 × 1	−	$10 × 8
10	−30	=	$60 × 1	−	$10 × 9

average revenue: total revenue divided by quantity.

■ **Average Revenue.** We can also use average revenue to show that marginal revenue is less than the price. **Average revenue** is defined as total revenue divided by the quantity of output; that is, $AR = TR/Q$. Because total revenue (TR) equals price times quantity ($P \times Q$), we can write average revenue (AR) as ($P \times Q$)/Q or, simply, the price P. In other words, the demand curve—which shows price at each level of output— also shows average revenue for each level of output.

Now recall from Chapter 8 that when the average of anything (costs, grades, heights, or revenues) declines, the marginal must be less than the average. Thus, because average revenues decline (that is, the demand curve slopes down), the marginal revenue curve must lie below the demand curve.

Finding Output to Maximize Profits at the Monopoly

Now that we have seen how a monopoly's revenues depend on the quantity it produces, let's see how its profits depend on the quantity it produces. Once we identify the relationship between profit and the quantity the monopoly will produce, we can determine the level of output that maximizes the monopoly's profits. To determine profits, we must look at the costs of the monopoly and then subtract total costs from total revenue.

Observe that the last three columns of Table 10.1 on page 260 show the costs and profits for the example monopoly. There are no new concepts about a monopoly's costs compared to a competitive firm's costs, so we can use the cost measures we developed in Chapters 7 to 9. The most important concepts are that total costs increase as more is produced and that marginal cost also increases, at least for high levels of output.

■ **Comparing Total Revenue and Total Costs.** The difference between total revenue and total costs is profits. Observe in Table 10.1 that as the quantity produced increases, both the total revenue from selling the product and the total costs of producing the product increase. However, at some level of production, total costs start to increase more than revenue increases, so that eventually profits must reach a maximum.

A quick glance at the profits column in Table 10.1 will show that this maximum level of profits is $404 and is reached when the monopoly produces 6 units of output. The price the monopoly must charge so that people will buy 6 units of output is $100, according to the second column of Table 10.1.

To help you visualize how profits change with quantity produced and to find the maximum level of profits, Figure 10.3 plots total costs, total revenue, and profits from Table 10.1. Profits are shown as the gap between total costs and total revenue. The gap reaches a maximum when output *Q* equals 6.

■ **Equating Marginal Cost and Marginal Revenue.** There is an alternative, more intuitive approach to finding the level of production that maximizes a monopolist's profits. This approach looks at marginal revenue and marginal cost and employs a rule that economists use extensively.

Consider producing different levels of output, starting with 1 unit and then rising unit by unit. Compare the marginal revenue from selling each additional unit of output with the marginal cost of producing it. If the marginal revenue is greater than

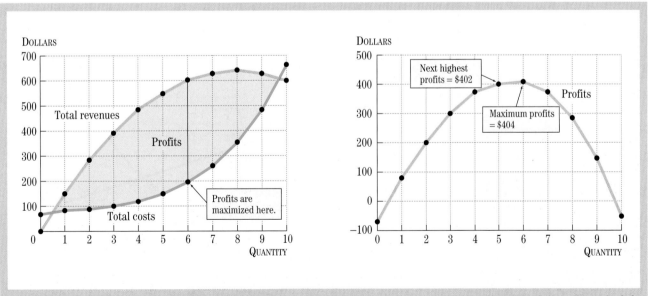

Figure 10.3
Finding a Quantity of Output to Maximize Profits

Profits are shown as the gap between total revenue and total costs in the graph on the left and are plotted on the graph on the right. Profits are at a maximum when the quantity of output is 6.

the marginal cost of the additional unit, then profits will increase if the unit is produced. Thus, the unit should be produced, because total revenue rises by more than total costs. For example, in Table 10.1, the marginal revenue from producing 1 unit of output is $150 and the marginal cost is $9. Thus, at least 1 unit should be produced. What about 2 units? Then marginal revenue equals $130 and marginal cost equals $5, so it makes sense to produce 2 units. Continuing this way, the monopolist should increase its output as long as marginal revenue is greater than marginal cost. But because marginal revenue is decreasing and eventually marginal cost is increasing, at some level of output marginal revenue will drop below marginal cost. The monopolist should not produce at that level. For example, in Table 10.1, the marginal revenue from selling 7 units of output is less than the marginal cost of producing it. Thus, the monopolist should not produce 7 units; instead, 6 units of production, with $MR = 50$ and $MC = 48$, is the profit-maximization level; this is the highest level of output for which marginal revenue is greater than marginal cost. Note that this level of output is exactly what we obtain by looking at the gap between total revenue and total costs.

Thus, *the monopolist should produce up to the level of production where marginal cost equals marginal revenue (MC = MR)*. If the level of production cannot be adjusted so exactly that marginal revenue is precisely equal to marginal cost, then the firm should produce at the highest level of output for which marginal revenue exceeds marginal cost, as in Table 10.1. In most cases, the monopoly will be able to adjust its output by smaller fractional amounts (for example, pounds of diamonds rather than tons of diamonds), and therefore marginal revenue will equal marginal cost.

A picture of how this marginal revenue equals marginal cost rule works is shown in Figure 10.4. The marginal revenue curve is plotted, along with the marginal cost curve. As the quantity produced increases above very low levels, the marginal cost

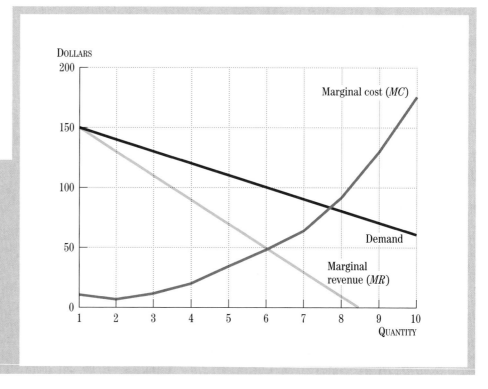

Figure 10.4
Marginal Revenue and Marginal Cost
The profit-maximizing monopoly will produce up to the point where marginal revenue equals marginal cost, as shown in the diagram. If fractional units cannot be produced, then the monopoly will produce at the highest level of output for which marginal revenue is greater than marginal cost. These curves are drawn for the monopoly in Table 10.1.

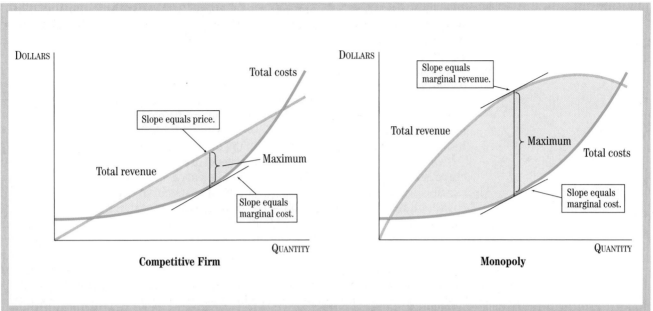

Figure 10.5
Profit Maximization for a Monopoly and a Competitive Firm

Total revenue for a competitive firm rises steadily with the amount sold; total revenue for a monopoly first rises and then falls. However, both the monopolist and the competitor maximize profits by making the gap between the total costs curve and the total revenue curve as large as possible or by setting the slope of the total revenue curve equal to the slope of the total costs curve. Thus, marginal revenue equals marginal cost. For the competitive firm, marginal revenue equals the price.

curve slopes up and the marginal revenue curve slopes down. Marginal revenue equals marginal cost at the level of output where the two curves intersect.

$MC = MR$ at a Monopoly versus $MC = P$ at a Competitive Firm

It is useful to compare the $MC = MR$ rule for the monopolist with the $MC = P$ rule for the competitive firm that we derived in Chapter 6.

■ **Marginal Revenue Equals the Price for a Price-Taker.** For a competitive firm, total revenue is equal to the quantity sold (Q) multiplied by the market price (P), but the competitive firm cannot affect the price. Thus, when the quantity sold is increased by one unit, revenue is increased by the price. In other words, for a competitive firm, marginal revenue equals the price; to say that a competitive firm sets its marginal cost equal to marginal revenue is to say that it sets its marginal cost equal to the price. Thus, the $MC = MR$ rule applies to both monopolies and competitive firms that maximize profits.

■ **A Graphical Comparison.** Figure 10.5 is a visual comparison of the two rules. A monopoly is shown on the right graph of Figure 10.5. This is the kind of graph we drew in Figure 10.3 except that it applies to any firm, so we do not show the units. A competitive firm is shown in the left graph of Figure 10.5. This is exactly like the graph showing a competitive firm in Figure 6.8. The scale on these two figures might be quite different; only the shapes are important for this comparison.

Look carefully at the shape of the total revenue curve for the monopoly and contrast it with the total revenue curve for the competitive firm. The total revenue curve for the monopoly starts to turn down at higher levels of output, whereas the total revenue curve for the competitive firm keeps rising in a straight line.

To illustrate the maximization of profits, we have put the same total costs curve on both graphs in Figure 10.5. Both types of firms maximize profits by setting production so that the gap between the total revenue curve and the total costs curve is as large as possible. That level of output, the profit-maximizing level, is shown for both firms. Higher or lower levels of output will reduce profits, as shown by the gaps between total revenue and total costs in the diagrams.

Observe that at the profit-maximizing level of output, the slope of the total costs curve is equal to the slope of the total revenue curve. Those of you who know some calculus will notice that the slope of the total costs curve is the derivative of total costs with respect to production—that is, the marginal cost. Similarly, the slope of the total revenue curve is the marginal revenue—the increase in total revenue when output increases. Thus, we have another way of seeing that marginal revenue equals marginal cost for profit maximization.

For the competitive firm, marginal revenue is the price, which implies the condition of profit maximization at a competitive firm derived in Chapter 6: Marginal cost equals price. However, for the monopolist, marginal revenue and price are not the same thing.

REVIEW

- When one firm is the sole producer of a product with no close substitutes, it is a monopoly. Most monopolies do not last forever. They come and go as technology changes. Barriers to the entry of new firms are needed to maintain a monopoly.

- A monopoly is like a competitive firm in that it tries to maximize profits. But unlike a competitive firm, a monopoly has market power; it can affect the market price. The demand curve the monopoly faces is the same as the market demand curve.

- Marginal revenue is the change in total revenue as output increases by one unit. Marginal revenue is less than the price at each level of output (except the first). If a firm maximizes profits, then marginal revenue equals marginal cost ($MR = MC$).

- For a competitive firm, marginal revenue equals marginal cost equals price ($MR = MC = P$).

- For a monopoly, marginal revenue also equals marginal cost, but marginal revenue does not equal the price. Hence, for the monopolist, price is not necessarily equal to marginal cost.

The Generic Diagram of a Monopoly and Its Profits

Look at Figure 10.6, which combines the monopoly's demand and marginal revenue curves with its average total cost curve and marginal cost curve. This diagram is the workhorse of the model of a monopoly, just as Figure 8.6 on page 210 is the workhorse of the model of a competitive firm. As with the diagram for a competitive firm,

Figure 10.6
The Generic Diagram for a Monopoly
The marginal revenue and demand curves are superimposed on the monopoly's cost curves. The monopoly's production, price, and profits can be seen on the same diagram. Quantity is given by the intersection of the marginal revenue curve and the marginal cost curve. Price is given by the demand curve at the point corresponding to the quantity produced, and average total cost is given by the *ATC* curve at that quantity. Monopoly profits are given by the rectangle that is the difference between total revenue and total costs.

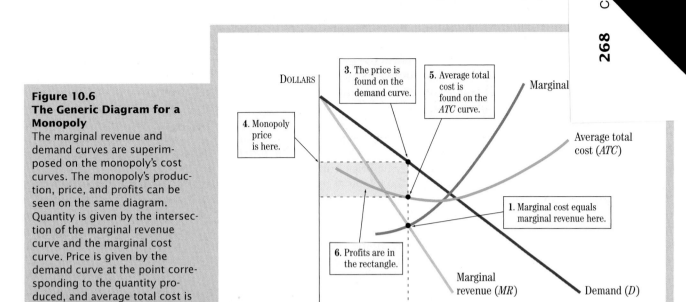

you should be able to draw it in your sleep. It is a generic diagram that applies to any monopolist, not just the one in Table 10.1, so we do not put scales on the axes.

Observe that Figure 10.6 shows four curves: a downward-sloping demand curve (*D*), a marginal revenue curve (*MR*), an average total cost curve (*ATC*), and a marginal cost curve (*MC*). The position of these curves is very important. First, the marginal cost curve cuts through the average total cost curve at the lowest point on the average total cost curve. Second, the marginal revenue curve is below the demand curve over the entire range of production (except at the vertical axis near 1, where they are equal).

We have already given the reasons for these two relationships (in Chapter 8 and in the previous section of this chapter), but it would be a good idea for you to practice sketching your own diagram like Figure 10.6 to make sure the positions of your curves meet these requirements.[1]

Determining Monopoly Output and Price on the Diagram

In Figure 10.6 we show how to calculate the monopoly output and price. First, find the point of intersection of the marginal revenue curve and the marginal cost curve. Second, draw a dashed vertical line through this point and look down the dashed line at the horizontal axis to see what the quantity produced is. Producing a larger quantity would lower marginal revenue below marginal cost. Producing a smaller

---

1. When sketching diagrams, it is useful to know that when the demand curve is a straight line, the marginal revenue curve is always twice as steep as the demand curve and, if extended, would cut the horizontal axis exactly halfway between zero and the point where the demand curve would cut the horizontal axis.

quantity would raise marginal revenue above marginal cost. The quantity shown is the profit-maximizing level. It is the amount the monopolist produces.

What price will the monopolist charge? We again use Figure 10.6, but be careful: Unlike the quantity, the monopolist's price is *not* determined by the intersection of the marginal revenue curve and the marginal cost curve. The price has to be such that the quantity demanded is equal to the quantity that the monopolist decides to produce. To find the price, we need to look at the demand curve in Figure 10.6. The demand curve gives the relationship between price and quantity demanded. It tells how much the monopolist will charge for its product in order to sell the amount produced.

To calculate the price, extend the dashed vertical line upward from the point of intersection of the marginal cost curve and the marginal revenue curve until it intersects the demand curve. At the intersection of the demand curve and the vertical line, we find the price that will generate a quantity demanded equal to the quantity produced. Now draw a horizontal line over to the left from the point of intersection to mark the price on the vertical axis. This is the monopoly's price, about which we will have more to say later.

Determining the Monopoly's Profits

Profits can also be shown on the diagram in Figure 10.6. Profits are given by the difference between the area of two rectangles, a total revenue rectangle and a total costs rectangle. Total revenue is price times quantity and is thus equal to the area of the rectangle with height equal to the monopoly price and length equal to the quantity produced. Total costs are average total cost times quantity and are thus equal to the area of the rectangle with height equal to *ATC* and length equal to the quantity produced. Profits are then equal to the green-shaded area that is the difference between these two rectangles.

It is possible for a monopoly to have negative profits, or losses, as shown in Figure 10.7. In this case, the price is below average total cost, and therefore total

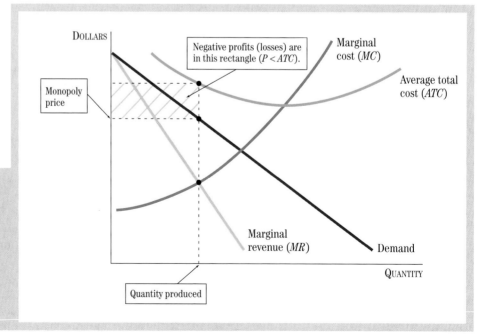

Figure 10.7
A Monopoly with Negative Profits
If a monopoly finds that average total cost is greater than the price at which marginal revenue equals marginal cost, then it runs losses. If price is also less than average variable cost, then the monopoly should shut down, just like a competitive firm.

revenue is less than total costs. Like a competitive firm, a monopolist with negative profits will shut down if the price is less than average variable cost. It will eventually exit the market if negative profits persist.

REVIEW
- A monopolist's profit-maximizing output and price can be determined graphically. The diagram shows four curves: the marginal revenue curve, the demand curve, the marginal cost curve, and the average total cost curve. The marginal revenue curve is always below the demand curve.

- The monopoly's production is determined at the point where marginal revenue equals marginal cost.

- The monopoly's price is determined from the demand curve at the point where the quantity produced equals the quantity demanded.

- The monopoly's profits are determined by subtracting the total costs rectangle from the total revenue rectangle. The total revenue rectangle is given by the price times the quantity produced. The total costs rectangle is given by the average total cost times the quantity produced.

Competition, Monopoly, and Deadweight Loss

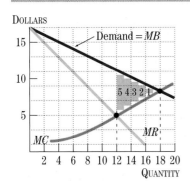

Numerical Example of Dead-weight Loss Calculation
The monopoly shown in the diagram above produces only 12 items, but a competitive industry would produce 18 items. For the 13th through 17th items, which are not produced by the monopoly, the marginal benefit is greater than the marginal cost by the amounts $5, $4, $3, $2, and $1, respectively, as shown by the areas between the demand curve and the supply curve for the competitive industry. Hence, the deadweight loss caused by the monopoly is the sum $5 + $4 + $3 + $2 + $1 = $15.

Are monopolies harmful to society? Do they reduce consumer surplus? Can we measure these effects? To answer these questions, economists compare the price and output of a monopoly with those of a competitive industry. First, observe in Figure 10.6 or Figure 10.7 that the monopoly does not operate at the minimum point on the average total cost curve even in the long run. Recall that firms in a competitive industry do operate at the lowest point on the average total cost curve in the long run.

To go further in our comparison, we use Figure 10.8, which is a repeat of Figure 10.6, except that the average total cost curve is removed to reduce the clutter. All the other curves are the same.

Comparison with Competition

Suppose that instead of there being only one firm in the market, there are now many competitive firms. For example, suppose Bagelopoly—a single firm producing bagels in a large city—is broken down into 100 different bagel bakeries like Bageloaf. The production point for the monopolistic firm and its price before the breakup are marked as "monopoly quantity" and "monopoly price" in Figure 10.8. What are production and price after the breakup?

The market supply curve for the new competitive industry would be Bagelopoly's old marginal cost curve because this is the sum of the marginal cost curves of all the newly created firms in the industry. Equilibrium in the competitive industry is where this market supply curve crosses the market demand curve. The amount of production at that point is marked by "competitive quantity" in Figure 10.8. The price at that equilibrium is marked by "competitive price" on the vertical axis.

Compare the quantity and price for the monopolist and the competitive industry. It is clear from the diagram in the margin that the quantity produced by the monopolist is less than the quantity produced by the competitive industry. It is also

**Figure 10.8
Deadweight Loss from
Monopoly**
The monopolist's output and
price are determined as in Figure
10.6. To get the competitive
price, we imagine that competitive firms make up an industry
supply curve that is the same as
the monopolist's marginal cost
curve. The competitive price and
quantity are given by the
intersection of the supply curve
and the demand curve. The
monopoly quantity is lower than
the competitive quantity. The
monopoly price is higher than
the competitive price. The
deadweight loss is the reduction
in consumer plus producer surplus due to the lower level of
production by the monopolist.

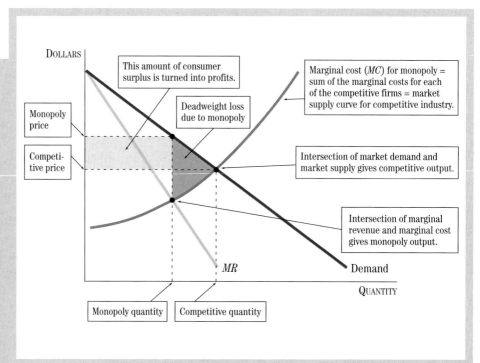

clear that the monopoly will charge a higher price than will emerge from a competitive industry. In sum, the monopoly produces less and charges a higher price than
the competitive industry would.

This is a very important result. The monopoly exploits its market power by
holding back on quantity produced and causing the price to rise compared with the
competitive equilibrium. This is always the case. Convince yourself by drawing
different diagrams. For example, when De Beers exercises its market power, it
holds back production of diamonds, thereby raising the price and earning economic
profits.

Note that even though the monopoly has the power to do so, it does not increase
its price without limit. When the price is set very high, marginal cost rises above marginal revenue. That behavior is not profit-maximizing.

Deadweight Loss from Monopoly

The economic harm caused by a monopoly occurs because it produces less than a
competitive industry would. How harmful, then, is a monopoly?

■ **Consumer Surplus and Producer Surplus Again.** Economists measure the
harm caused by monopolies by the decline in the sum of consumer surplus plus
producer surplus. Recall that *consumer surplus* is the area above the market price
line and below the demand curve, the demand curve being a measure of consumers'
marginal benefit from consuming the good. The *producer surplus* is the area above
the marginal cost curve and below the market price line. Consumer surplus plus
producer surplus is thus the area between the demand curve and the marginal cost
curve. It measures the sum of the marginal benefits to consumers of the good less the

sum of the marginal costs to the producers of the good. A competitive market will maximize the sum of consumer plus producer surplus.

With a lower quantity produced by a monopoly, however, the sum of consumer surplus and producer surplus is reduced, as shown in Figure 10.8. This reduction in consumer plus producer surplus is called the *deadweight loss due to monopoly*. It is a quantitative measure of the harm a monopoly causes the economy. A numerical example is given in the margin.

How large is the deadweight loss in the U.S. economy? Using the method illustrated in Figure 10.8, empirical economists estimate that the loss is between .5 and 2 percent of GDP, or between $60 billion and $240 billion per year. Of course, the deadweight loss is a larger percentage of production in industries where monopolies are a greater presence.

Figure 10.8 also shows that the monopoly takes, in the form of profits, some of the consumer surplus that would have gone to the consumers in competitive markets. Consumer surplus is now the area below the demand curve and above the monopoly price, which is higher than the competitive price. However, this transfer of consumer surplus to the monopoly is not a deadweight loss, because what the consumers lose, the monopoly gains. This transfer affects the distribution of income, but it is not a net loss to society.

■ **Meaningful Comparisons.**   In any given application, one needs to be careful that the comparison of monopoly and competition makes sense. Some industries cannot be broken up into many competitive firms the way bagel bakeries can. Having 100 water companies serving one local area, for example, would be very costly. The choice for society is not between a monopolistic water industry and a competitive water industry. Although we might try to affect the monopoly's decisions by government actions, we should not try to break up water services within each community.

History provides many other examples. Western settlers in the United States during the nineteenth century had a larger consumer surplus from the monopolist railroads—in spite of the monopolists' profits—than they did from competitive wagon trains. Modern-day users of the information highway—computers and telecommunications—reap a larger consumer surplus from Intel's computer chips, even if they are produced monopolistically, than they would from a competitive abacus industry.

The Monopoly Price Is Greater than Marginal Cost

Another way to think about the loss to society from monopoly is to observe the difference between price and marginal cost. Figure 10.8, for example, shows that the monopoly price is well above the marginal cost at the quantity where the monopoly chooses to produce.

■ **Marginal Benefit Is More than Marginal Cost.**   Because consumers will consume up to the point where the marginal benefit of a good equals its price, the excessive price means that the marginal benefit of a good is greater than the marginal cost. This is inefficient because producing more of the good would increase benefits to consumers by more than the cost of producing it.

The size of the difference between price and marginal cost depends on the elasticity of the monopoly's demand curve. If the demand curve is highly elastic (close to a competitive firm's view as shown in Figure 10.1), then the difference between price and marginal cost is small.

price-cost margin: the difference between price and marginal cost divided by the price. This index is an indicator of market power, where an index of 0 indicates no market power and a higher price-cost margin indicates greater market power.

■ **The Price-Cost Margin.** A common measure of the difference between price and marginal cost is the **price-cost margin.** It is defined as

$$\frac{\text{Price minus marginal cost}}{\text{Price}}$$

For example, if the price is \$4 and the marginal cost is \$2, the price-cost margin is $(4 - 2)/4 = .5$. The price-cost margin for a competitive firm is zero because price equals marginal cost.

Economists use a rule of thumb to show how the price-cost margin depends on the price elasticity of demand. The rule of thumb is shown in the equation below.

$$\text{Price-cost margin} = \frac{1}{\text{price elasticity of demand}}$$

For example, when the elasticity of demand is 2, the price-cost margin is .5. The flat demand curve has an infinite elasticity, in which case the price-cost margin is zero; in other words, price equals marginal cost.

REVIEW

- A monopoly creates a deadweight loss because it restricts output below what the competitive market would produce. The cost is measured by the deadweight loss, which is the reduction in the sum of consumer plus producer surplus.

- Sometimes the comparison between monopoly and competition is only hypothetical because it would either be impossible or make no sense to break up the monopoly into competitive firms.

- Another way to measure the impact of a monopoly is by the difference between price and marginal cost. Monopolies always charge a price higher than marginal cost. The difference—summarized in the price-cost margin—depends inversely on the elasticity of demand.

Why Monopolies Exist

Given this demonstration that monopolies lead to high prices and a deadweight loss to society, you may be wondering why monopolies exist. In this section, we consider three reasons for the existence of monopolies.

Natural Monopolies

The nature of production is a key factor in determining the number of firms in the industry. If big firms are needed in order to produce at low cost, it may be natural for a few firms or only one firm to exist. In particular, *economies of scale*—a declining long-run average total cost curve over some range of production—can lead to a monopoly. Recall from Chapter 8 that the *minimum efficient scale* of a firm is the minimum size of the firm for which average total costs are lowest. If the minimum efficient scale is only a small fraction of the size of the market, then there will be many firms.

natural monopoly: a single firm in an industry in which average total cost is declining over the entire range of production and the minimum efficient scale is larger than the size of the market.

For example, suppose the minimum efficient scale for beauty salons in a city is a size that serves 30 customers a day at each salon. Suppose the quantity of hair stylings demanded in the city is 300 per day. We can then expect there will be 10 beauty salons (300/30 = 10) in the city. But if the minimum efficient scale is larger (for example, 60 customers per day), then the number of firms in the industry will be smaller (for example, 300/60 = 5 salons). At the extreme case where the minimum efficient scale of the firm is as large as or larger than the size of the market (for example, 300 per day), there will probably be only one firm (300/300 = 1), which will be a monopoly.

A water company in a small town, for example, has a minimum efficient scale larger than the number of houses and businesses in the town. There are huge fixed costs to lay pipe down the street, but each house connection has a relatively low cost, so average total cost declines as more houses are connected. Other industries that usually have a very large minimum efficient scale are electricity and local telephone service. In each of these industries, average total cost is lowest if one firm delivers the service. **Natural monopolies** exist when average total cost is declining and the minimum efficient scale is larger than the size of the market.

The prices charged by many natural monopolies are regulated by government. The purpose of the regulation is to keep the price below the monopoly price and closer to the competitive price. Such regulation can thereby reduce the deadweight loss of the monopoly. Alternative methods of regulating natural monopolies are discussed in Chapter 12. Water companies and electric companies are regulated by government.

A change in technology that changes the minimum efficient scale of firms can radically alter the number of firms in the industry. For example, AT&T used to be viewed as a natural monopoly in long-distance telephone service. Because laying copper wire across the United States required a huge cost, it made little sense to have more than one firm. The U.S. government regulated the prices that AT&T charged its customers, endeavoring to keep the price of calls below the monopoly price and closer to the competitive price. But when the technology for transmitting signals by microwave developed, it became easier for other firms also to provide services. Thus, MCI and Sprint, as well as AT&T, could provide services at least as cheaply as one firm. Because of this technological change, the government decided to end the AT&T monopoly by allowing MCI and Sprint to compete with AT&T. Nationwide telephone service is no longer a monopoly.

Patents and Copyrights

Another way monopolies arise is through the granting of patents and copyrights by the government. Intel's patent was the source of its monopoly on its computer chips. The U.S. Constitution and the laws of many other countries require that government grant patents to inventors. If a firm registers an invention with the U.S. government, it can be granted a monopoly in the production of that item for 20 years. In other words, the government prohibits other firms from producing the good without the permission of the patent holder. Patents are given for many inventions, including the discovery of new drugs. Pharmaceutical companies hold patents on many of their products, giving them a monopoly to produce and sell these products. Copyrights on computer software, chips, movies, and books also give firms the sole right to market the products. Thus, patents and copyrights can create monopolies.

The award of monopoly rights through patents and copyrights serves a useful purpose. It can stimulate innovation by rewarding the inventor. In other words, the chance to get a patent or copyright gives the inventor more incentive to devote time and resources to invent new products or to take a risk and try out new ideas.

Pharmaceutical companies, for example, argue that their patents on drugs are a reward for inventing the drugs. The higher prices and deadweight loss caused by the patent can be viewed as the cost of the new ideas and products. By passing laws to control drug prices, government could lower the prices of drugs to today's sick people. This would be popular, but doing so would reduce the incentive for the firms to invent new drugs. Society—and, in particular, people in future years—could suffer a loss. When patents expire, we usually see a major shift toward competition. In general, when assessing the deadweight loss due to monopoly, one must consider the benefits of the research and the new products that monopoly profits may create.

As technology has advanced, patents and copyrights have had to become increasingly complex in order to prevent firms from getting around them. Nevertheless, patent and copyright protection does not always work in maintaining the monopoly. Many times potential competing firms get around copyrights on computer software and chips by "reverse engineering," in which specialists look carefully at how each part of a product works, starting with the final output. Elaborate mechanisms have been developed, such as "clean rooms," in which one group of scientists and programmers tells another group what each subfunction of the invention does but does not tell them how it is done. The other group then tries to invent an alternative way to perform the task. Because they cannot see how it is done, they avoid violating the copyright.

Licenses

Sometimes the government creates a monopoly by giving or selling to one firm a license to produce the product. The U.S. Postal Service is a government-sponsored monopoly. A law makes it illegal to use a firm other than the U.S. Postal Service for first-class mail. However, even this monopoly is diminishing with competition from overnight mail services and fax technology.

National parks sometimes grant or sell to single firms licenses to provide food and lodging services. The Curry Company, for example, was granted a monopoly to provide services in Yosemite National Park. For a long time the Pennsylvania Turnpike—a toll road running the width of the state—licensed a monopoly to Howard Johnson Company to provide food for travelers on the long stretches of the road. In recent years, seeing the advantage of competition, the turnpike authorities have allowed several different fast-food chains to get licenses.

Attempts to Monopolize and Erect Barriers to Entry

Adam Smith warned that firms would try to create monopolies in order to raise their prices. One of the reasons Smith favored free trade between countries was that it would reduce the ability of firms in one country to form a monopoly; if they did form a monopoly and there were no restrictions on trade serving as barriers to entry for firms in other countries, then foreign firms would break the monopoly.

History shows us many examples of firms attempting to monopolize an industry by merging with other firms and then erecting barriers to entry. De Beers is one example of such a strategy apparently being successful on a global level. In the last part of the nineteenth century, several large firms were viewed as monopolies. Standard Oil, started by John D. Rockefeller in the 1880s, is a well-known example. The firm had control of most of the oil-refining capacity in the United States. Thus, Standard Oil was close to having a monopoly in oil refining. However, the federal government forced Standard Oil to break up into smaller firms. We will consider other examples of the government's breaking up monopolies or preventing them from forming in Chapter 12.

Barriers to entry allow a monopoly to persist, so for a firm to maintain a monopoly, it needs barriers to entry. The box "Reading the News About Barriers to Entry in the Microprocessor Industry" discusses a recent suit that has been brought by Advanced Micro Devices against Intel for erecting barriers to entry.

Barriers to entry can also be created by professional certification. For example, economists have argued that the medical and legal professions in the United States erect barriers to the entry of new doctors and lawyers by having tough standards for admittance to medical school or to the bar and by restricting the types of services that can be performed by nurses or paralegals. Doctors' and lawyers' fees might be lower if there were lower barriers to entry and, therefore, more competition.

Simply observing that a firm has no competitors is not enough to prove that there are barriers to entry. Sometimes the threat of potential entry into a market may be enough to get a monopolist to act like a competitive firm. For example, the possibility of a new bookstore's opening up off campus may put pressure on the campus bookstore to keep its prices low. When other firms, such as off-campus bookstores, can potentially and easily enter the market, they create what economists call a **contestable market.** In general, the threat of competition in contestable markets can induce monopolists to act like competitors.

contestable market: a market in which the threat of competition is enough to encourage firms to act like competitors.

REVIEW

- Economies of scale, patents, copyrights, and licenses are some of the reasons monopolies exist.
- Natural monopolies are frequently regulated by government.
- Many large monopolies in the United States, such as Standard Oil and AT&T, have been broken apart by government action.

Price Discrimination

price discrimination: a situation in which different groups of consumers are charged different prices for the same good.

In the model of monopoly we have studied in this chapter, the monopolists charge a single price for the good they sell. In some cases, however, firms charge different people different prices for the same item. This is called **price discrimination.** Price discrimination is common and is likely to become more common in the future as firms become more sophisticated in their price setting. Everyday examples include senior citizen discounts at movie theaters and discounts on airline tickets for Saturday-night stayovers.

Some price discrimination is less noticeable because it occurs in geographically separated markets. Charging different prices in foreign markets and domestic markets is common. For example, Japanese cameras are less expensive in the United States than in Japan. In contrast, the price of luxury German cars in the United States is frequently higher than in Germany.

Volume or quantity discounts are another form of price discrimination. Higher prices are sometimes charged to customers who buy smaller amounts of an item. For example, electric utility firms sometimes charge more per kilowatt-hour to customers who use only a little electricity.

What makes a monopoly a monopoly? Intel may be the world's largest chip maker, but other companies have competed in the microprocessor chip market ever since Advanced Micro Devices won a series of legal battles in the 1990s that allowed it to make chips with its own designs. Now AMD argues that Intel, which can no longer rely on patents and copyrights to protect its monopoly, is using illegal tactics to win back its monopoly on this market. AMD claims that Intel's use of marketing subsidies to win sales, heavy discounts, and threatened retaliation against Intel customers for using AMD products amount to unfair barriers to entry. What do you think?

AMD Files Broad Suit Against Intel
Antitrust Case Argues Steps Were Set to Keep Monopoly Over Global Chip Market

By DON CLARK
Staff Reporter of THE WALL STREET JOURNAL
June 28, 2005

Advanced Micro Devices Inc. has filed a broad antitrust suit against Intel Corp., accusing its giant rival of using illegal inducements and coercion to dissuade companies from buying AMD's computer chips.

The suit, filed late yesterday in federal court in Delaware, alleges that Intel has engaged in a "relentless" global campaign to maintain a monopoly over microprocessors that serve as the electronic brains in most computers. AMD alleges that Intel used improper subsidies to win sales, and threatened retaliation against firms for using or selling AMD products.

Tom Beerman, an Intel spokesman, said it hadn't seen the suit, and said only "we believe our sales practices are both fair and consistent with federal antitrust law," he said.

The case pits a struggling challenger against the world's largest chip maker, in what promises to be a protracted and pivotal fight. Although launched by a company rather than the government, the case could have large-scale repercussions in the industry. So far Intel has faced less antitrust scrutiny than its software partner, Microsoft Corp., which was the subject of a major antitrust prosecution by the Justice Department, but it matches Microsoft's influence in setting technology standards and grabbing a huge share of computer-industry profits.

AMD's 48-page complaint, which follows a recent antitrust ruling against Intel in Japan, may prompt a debate on Intel marketing subsidies that have become a mainstay for computer makers with thin profit margins. If a court rules against such practices, dominant companies could lose an important tool to command customer loyalty.

The case could illuminate confidential dealings between Intel and other industry players. AMD's complaint lists examples of what it characterizes as bribes, threats or intimidation by Intel involving 12 computer makers, nine distributors and 17 retailers. Customers cited include International Business Machines Corp., Hewlett-Packard Co., Dell Inc., Sony Corp., Toshiba Corp. and Gateway Inc.

Consumers with Different Price Elasticities of Demand

Why is there price discrimination? Figure 10.9 shows a diagram of a monopoly that gives one explanation. Suppose the good being sold is airline travel between two remote islands, and suppose there is only one airline between the two islands. The two graphs in Figure 10.9 represent demand curves with different elasticities. On the

The allegations are based largely on discussions between AMD and customers. To document Intel's alleged behavior, AMD plans to seek subpoenas to obtain private email from those companies, and risk alienating industry executives by asking them to testify on its behalf.

"They need to sustain their complaint by customer testimony," said Eleanor Fox, a professor at the New York University School of Law, who isn't involved in the case. "Customers may not be so friendly to the idea."

Hector Ruiz, AMD's chief executive, said it has consulted with many Intel customers and partners, whom he expects to help in the litigation. "To a person, they are going to be glad that we put this on the table, though they may not come out and say so," he said.

Intel, of Santa Clara, Calif., commands more than 80% of the unit sales and 90% of the revenues in the market for x86 microprocessors, named for a set of instructions that help define what software a chip uses. AMD, based in nearby Sunnyvale, estimates that its share of x86 unit sales peaked in 2001 at 20.8% but ebbed to 15.8% by 2004.

AMD originally made chips using designs from Intel. That arrangement collapsed in the mid-1980s, setting off a series of legal battles that were settled in 1995. The agreement gave AMD rights to make x86 chips with original designs.

AMD's complaint alleges that, once it began making headway with new products in 1999, Intel fought back with illegal tactics. One focus is a variety of rebate that AMD says Intel distributes at the end of the quarter to customers who buy nearly all their chips from the company.

Because Intel chips have become a standard feature for many personal-computer models, Intel wins more than half of many companies' chip purchases, the AMD complaint states. In competing for the remainder, Intel can offer 8% to 10% discounts over all the chips they sell a company—an advantage AMD can counter only with prohibitive price cuts in bidding for a minority chunk of the business, AMD said.

"The last thing AMD fears is price competition," says Thomas McCoy, AMD's vice president of legal affairs and chief administrative officer. But Intel's rebates amount to "dictating to the industry how many AMD-based computers it can sell," he said.

Related issues were raised in March by Japan's Fair Trade Commission, which alleged that Intel violated antitrust laws by using rebates and marketing funds to dissuade five Japanese PC makers from buying from AMD and Transmeta Corp. The deals required the firms to buy 90% or 100% of their chips from Intel, or to limit specific lines of PCs to Intel chips, the Japanese agency said.

Intel chose not to contest that ruling.

Ms. Fox, the antitrust expert, predicted the case will turn on whether Intel can show that its marketing practices benefit consumers, often a powerful argument in antitrust cases. But one court ruling could help AMD, she noted.

In 2003 the U.S. Court of Appeals for the Third Circuit sided with LePage's Inc. in an antitrust case against 3M Co. over private-label transparent tape. The judges ruled against 3M's "bundled rebates," which offered incentives to customers who purchased 3M product lines in addition to its tape. Charles Diamond, an attorney for AMD at O'Melveny & Myers LLP, said its allegations are very similar to LePage's, noting that the same appeals court could be the final arbiter of AMD's case.

The case could go to trial in late 2006, Mr. McCoy said.

left is the demand for vacation air travel. Vacationers are frequently more price sensitive than businesspeople. They can be more flexible with their time; they can take a boat rather than the plane; they can stay home and paint the house. Hence, for vacationers, the price elasticity of demand is high. Business travelers, however, do not have much choice. As shown on the graph to the right, they are less sensitive to price.

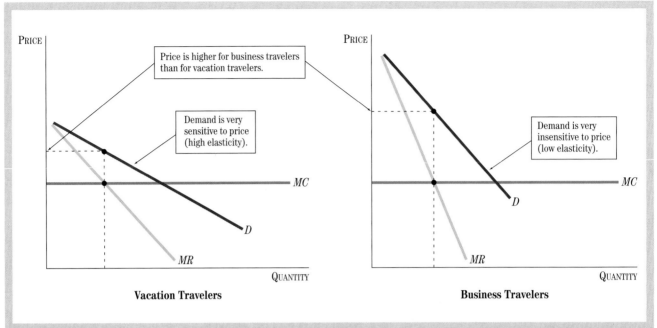

PRICE

Price is higher for business travelers than for vacation travelers.

Demand is very sensitive to price (high elasticity).

MC

D

MR

QUANTITY

Vacation Travelers

PRICE

Demand is very insensitive to price (low elasticity).

MC

D

MR

QUANTITY

Business Travelers

**Figure 10.9
Price Discrimination
Targeted at Different
Groups**

The monopolist has two groups of potential buyers for its travel services. For convenience, we assume the marginal cost curve is flat. The group on the left has a high price elasticity of demand. The group on the right has a low price elasticity of demand. If the monopolist can discriminate between the buyers, then it is optimal to charge a lower price to the high-elasticity group and a higher price to the low-elasticity group.

An important business meeting may require a businessperson to fly to the other island with little advance notice. For business travel, the price elasticity of demand is low. Difference between price elasticities is a key reason for price discrimination.

In Figure 10.9, notice that both groups have downward-sloping demand curves and downward-sloping marginal revenue curves. For simplicity, marginal cost is constant and is shown with a straight line.

Figure 10.9 predicts that business travelers will be charged a higher price than vacationers. Why? Marginal revenue equals marginal cost at a higher price for business travelers than for vacationers. The model of monopoly predicts that the firm will charge a higher price to those with a lower elasticity and a lower price to those with a higher elasticity.

In fact, this is the type of price discrimination we see with airlines. But how can the airlines distinguish a business traveler from a vacation traveler? Clothing will not work: A business traveler could easily change from a suit to an aloha shirt and shorts to get the low fare. One device used by some airlines is the Saturday-night stayover. Business travelers prefer to work and travel during the week. They value being home with family or friends on a Saturday night. Vacationers frequently do not mind extending their travel by a day or two to include a Saturday night, and they may want to vacation over the weekend. Hence, there is a strong correlation between vacation travelers and those who do not mind staying over a Saturday night. A good way to price-discriminate, therefore, is to charge a lower price to people who stay in their destination on a Saturday night and to charge a higher price to those who are unwilling to do so.

"Would it bother you to hear how little I paid for this flight?"

Price discrimination based on different price elasticity of demand requires that the firm be able to prevent people who buy at a lower price from selling the item to other people. Thus, price discrimination is much more common in services than in manufactured goods.

Quantity Discounts

Another important form of price discrimination involves setting prices according to how much is purchased. If a business makes 100 telephone calls a day, it probably has to pay a higher fee per call than if it makes 1,000 a day. Telephone monopolies can increase their profits by such a price scheme, as shown in Figure 10.10.

The single-price monopoly is shown in the bottom graph of Figure 10.10. Two ways in which the monopoly can make higher profits by charging different prices are shown in the top two panels. In both cases, there is no difference in the price elasticity of demand for different consumers. To make it easy, assume that all consumers are identical. The demand curve is the sum of the marginal benefits of all the consumers in the market.

On the upper left, the firm sets a higher price for the first few items a consumer buys and a lower price for the remaining items. Frequent flier miles on airlines are an example of this kind of pricing. If you fly more than a certain number of miles, you get a free ticket. Thus, the per mile fare for 20,000 miles is less than the fare for 10,000 miles. As the diagram shows, profits for the firm are higher in such a situation. In the example at the left, the higher price is the fare without the discount.

On the upper right, we see how profits can be increased if the firm gives even deeper discounts to high-volume purchasers. As long as the high-volume purchasers cannot sell the product to the low-volume purchasers, there are extra profits to be made.

The upper right graph in Figure 10.10 illustrates an important benefit of price discrimination: It can reduce deadweight loss. With price discrimination, a monopoly actually produces more. For example, those who get a lower price because of frequent flier discounts may actually end up buying more. The result is that the airline has more flights. As already noted, the deadweight loss from a monopolist occurs because production is too low. If price discrimination allows more production, then it reduces deadweight loss.

Monopolies versus Other Firms with Market Power

The preceding examples of price discrimination involved monopolies, but price discrimination also occurs in firms that are not monopolies. United, American, and Delta all offer different fares to customers based on different price elasticities when they fly the same routes. We will see in Chapter 11 that firms can have some monopoly power—face downward-sloping demand as shown in Figures 10.9 and 10.10—even if they are not monopolies. For example, firms in industries in which one firm's products are slightly different from other firms' products have market power. The preceding explanation of price discrimination can, therefore, apply to such firms.

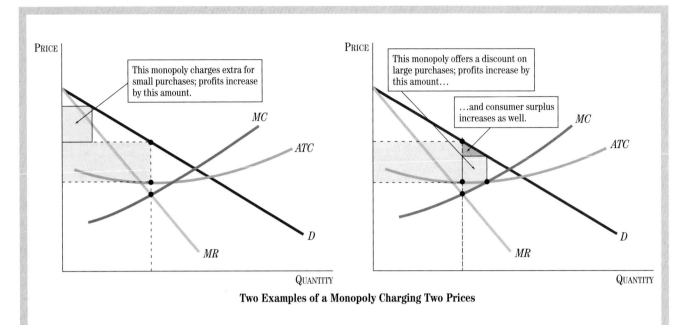

Two Examples of a Monopoly Charging Two Prices

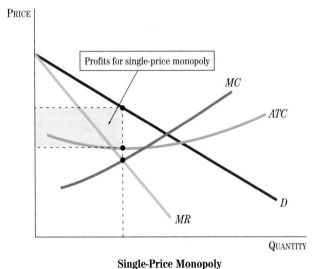

Single-Price Monopoly

**Figure 10.10
Price Discrimination Through
Quantity Discounts or
Premiums**

The standard single-price monopoly is shown at the bottom. If the monopoly can charge a higher price to customers who buy only a little, profits can increase, as shown on the upper left. If the monopoly can give a discount to people who purchase a lot, it can also increase profits, as shown on the upper right. In this case, production increases.

REVIEW

- Because a monopolist has market power, it can charge different prices to different consumers as long as it can prevent the consumers from reselling the good.

- Price discrimination explains telephone pricing as well as the complicated airfares on airlines.

- Deadweight loss is reduced by price discrimination.

Conclusion

The model of a monopoly that we developed in this chapter centers on a key diagram, Figure 10.6 on page 267. Learning how to work with this diagram of a monopoly is very important. In fact, economists use this same diagram to describe any firm that has some market power, not just monopolies, as we show in Chapter 11. Before proceeding, it is a good idea to practice sketching this generic diagram of a monopoly and finding output, price, and profits for different positions of the curve.

From the point of view of economic efficiency, the economic performance of monopolies is not nearly as good as that of competitive industries. Output is too low, marginal benefits are not equal to marginal costs, and consumer surplus plus producer surplus is diminished. But when assessing these losses, the fact that the expectation of monopoly profits—even if temporary—is the inducement for firms to do research and develop new products must also be considered.

Nevertheless, the deadweight loss caused by monopolies provides a potential opportunity for government to intervene in the economy. In fact, the U.S. government actively intervenes in the economy either to prevent monopolies from forming or to regulate monopolies when it is not appropriate to break them apart. We look further into government prevention or regulation of monopolies in Chapter 12.

KEY POINTS

1. A monopoly occurs when only one firm sells a product for which there are no close substitutes. The world diamond market is nearly a monopoly. Many local markets for water, sewage, electricity, and telephones are monopolies.

2. A monopolist possesses market power in the sense that it can lower the market price by producing more or raise the market price by producing less.

3. The model of a monopoly assumes that the monopoly tries to maximize profits and that it faces a downward-sloping demand curve.

4. A monopoly's total revenue increases and then decreases as it increases production.

5. A monopoly chooses a quantity such that marginal revenue equals marginal cost.

6. A monopoly produces a smaller quantity and charges a higher price than a competitive industry; the lower production causes a deadweight loss.

7. It is frequently not possible to create a competitive industry out of a monopoly, in which case the comparison between monopoly and competition is hypothetical.

8. Monopolies exist because of economies of scale that make the minimum efficient size of the firm larger than the market, and because of barriers to entry, including government patents and licenses.

9. Many monopolies are short-lived; technological change can rapidly change a firm from a monopoly to a competitive firm, as exemplified by the long-distance telephone market.

10. A price-discriminating monopoly charges different prices to different customers depending on how elastic their demand is.

KEY TERMS

monopoly	price-maker	price-cost margin	contestable market
barriers to entry	average revenue	natural monopoly	price discrimination
market power			

QUESTIONS FOR REVIEW

1. What is a monopoly?

2. What market power does a monopoly have?

3. How does a monopoly choose its profit-maximizing output and price?

4. Why does marginal revenue decline as more is produced by a monopoly?

5. Why is the marginal revenue curve below the demand curve for a monopoly but not for a competitive firm?

6. Why does a monopolist produce less than a competitive industry?

7. What forces tend to cause monopolies?

8. What is the deadweight loss from a monopoly?

9. What is price discrimination?

10. How does price discrimination reduce deadweight loss?

PROBLEMS

1. Suppose the price elasticity of demand for a drug is 1.25.
   a. Suppose only one monopolist firm produces the drug. If the monopolist cuts production by 15 percent, by what percentage does the price rise?
   b. Now suppose that the market is competitive, with 100 firms each supplying 1 percent of the market. If one of the competitive firms cuts its own production by 15 percent and the other 99 firms do not change production, by what percentage does the price rise?
   c. Will this decision by this one firm have any effect on the other firms in the industry? Explain.

2. The following table gives the total cost and total revenue schedule for a monopolist.

Quantity	Total Cost (in dollars)	Total Revenue (in dollars)
0	144	0
1	160	90
2	170	160
3	194	210
4	222	240
5	260	250
6	315	240
7	375	210

   a. Calculate the marginal revenue and marginal cost, and sketch the demand curve.
   b. Determine the profit-maximizing price and quantity, and calculate the resulting profit.

3. The following table gives the round-trip airfares from Los Angeles to New York offered by United Airlines.

Price	Advance Purchase	Minimum Stay	Cancellation Penalty
$ 418	14 days	Overnight on Saturday	100%
$ 683	3 days	Overnight on Saturday	100%
$1,900	None required	None required	None

Explain why United might want to charge different prices for the same route. Why are there minimum-stay requirements and cancellation penalties?

4. Sketch the diagram for a monopoly with an upward-sloping marginal cost curve that is earning economic profits. Suppose the government imposes a tax on each item the monopoly sells. Draw the diagram corresponding to this situation. How does this tax affect the monopoly's production and price? Show what happens to the area of deadweight loss.

5. Children, students, and senior citizens frequently are eligible for discounted tickets to movies. Is this an example of price discrimination? Explain the conditions necessary for price discrimination to occur and draw the graphs to describe this situation.

6. Why is it that firms need market power in order to price-discriminate? What other circumstances are required in order for a firm to price-discriminate? Give an example of a firm or industry that price-discriminates and explain how it is possible in that case.

7. Fill in the missing data on a monopolist in the following table:

Quantity of Output	Price	Total Revenue	Marginal Revenue	Marginal Cost	Average Total Cost
1	11				18.00
2	10				11.00
3	9				7.67
4	8				6.75
5	7				6.60
6	6				7.00
7	5				8.00

   a. At what quantity will the monopolist produce in order to maximize profits? What will be the price at this level of output? What will be the profits?
   b. What quantity maximizes total revenue? What is the elasticity of demand at that point? Why is this not the profit-maximizing quantity?

8. What is the price-cost margin for the typical competitive firm? What is the price-cost margin (at the profit-maximizing quantity) for the monopoly described in problem 7?

9. Calculate the deadweight loss of the monopoly described in the table on the facing page.

Problem 9

Quantity	Price	Total Revenue	Marginal Revenue	Total Cost	Marginal Cost	Profit
0	320	0	—	140	—	−140
2	305	610	305	158	9	452
4	290	1,160	275	168	5	992
6	275	1,650	245	188	10	1,462
8	260	2,080	215	228	20	1,852
10	245	2,450	185	296	34	2,154
12	230	2,760	155	392	48	2,368
14	215	3,010	125	522	65	2,488
16	200	3,200	95	702	90	2,498
18	185	3,330	65	962	130	2,368
20	170	3,400	35	1,312	175	2,088
22	155	3,410	5	1,762	225	1,648
24	140	3,360	−25	2,322	280	1,038

10. The first table below shows the marginal benefit schedule for the three buyers in a market. The second table below shows the marginal cost schedules for the three sellers in the market.

Quantity	MB— Linda	MB— Sue	MB— Pete
1	15	14	13
2	12	11	10
3	9	8	7
4	6	5	4
5	3	2	1

Quantity	MC— Max	MC— Scott	MC— Karen
1	3	2	1
2	6	5	4
3	9	8	7
4	12	11	10
5	15	14	13

Suppose the three sellers in the market merge to form a monopoly. The buyers continue to act independently. Assume that the marginal cost is the sum of the marginal costs of the three original sellers.
a. Compute the marginal revenue for the monopoly and plot it.
b. What output and what price do you predict the monopoly will choose?
c. What is the price-cost margin?
d. Show the loss of consumer surplus due to the monopoly.
e. Show the deadweight loss due to the monopoly.

11. Suppose you are an economic adviser to the president, and the president asks you to prepare an economic analysis of Monopoly, Inc., a firm that sells a patented device used in high-definition television sets. You have the following information about Monopoly, Inc.

Quantity (millions)	Price	Marginal Cost
1	10	4
2	9	5
3	8	6
4	7	7
5	6	8
6	5	9
7	4	10
8	3	11
9	2	12
10	1	13

a. Given the data in the table, graphically show all the elements necessary to represent the monopolist's profit maximization. *Note:* You do not need to draw the average total cost curve.
b. What level of output does Monopoly, Inc., produce? What price does it sell this output at?
c. Does Monopoly, Inc., produce at the socially optimal level? Why or why not? Show any inefficiency on your graph.
d. Because of Monopoly, Inc.'s strong political lobby, the president is considering subsidizing the monopoly's production. As an economist, however, you are not concerned with politics, but want to ensure that this policy would not make the economy any worse off. Devise a subsidy whereby you could both satisfy the president's political needs and improve the efficiency of the economy. Why does your plan improve economic efficiency?

CHAPTER 11

Product Differentiation, Monopolistic Competition, and Oligopoly

When John Johnson launched his magazine business in 1942, he differentiated his products from existing products in a way that was valued by millions of African Americans. As a result, the new product lines, the magazines *Ebony* and *Jet*, were huge successes. Johnson became a multimillionaire, and his firm became the second largest black-owned firm in the United States. Similarly, when Liz Claiborne started her new clothing firm in 1976, she differentiated her products from existing products in a way that was valued by millions of American women. She offered stylish yet affordable clothes for working women, and she too was successful: By 1991, Liz Claiborne, Inc., was the largest producer of women's clothing in the world. Such stories of people finding ways to differentiate their products from existing products are told thousands of times a year, although not everyone is as successful as John Johnson and Liz Claiborne.

John Johnson's magazines and Liz Claiborne's suits and dresses were different in a way that was valued by consumers. Because their products were different from the products made by the many other firms in their industries—

magazine publishing and women's clothing, respectively—they each had market power in the sense that they could charge a higher price for their products and not lose all their customers. Thus, neither Johnson Publishing nor Liz Claiborne, Inc., was just another firm entering a competitive industry in which every firm sold the same product. But Johnson Publishing and Liz Claiborne, Inc., were not monopolies either; there were other firms in their industries, and they could not prevent entry into the industries by even more firms. As is typical of many firms, they seemed to be hybrids between a competitive firm and a monopoly.

In this chapter, we develop a model that is widely used by economists to explain the behavior of such firms. It is called *the model of monopolistic competition*. **Monopolistic competition** occurs in an industry with many firms and free entry, where the product of each firm is slightly differentiated from the product of every other firm. We contrast the predictions of this model with those of the models of competition and monopoly developed in previous chapters.

monopolistic competition: a market structure characterized by many firms selling differentiated products in an industry in which there is free entry and exit.

We also develop a *model of oligopoly* in this chapter, because product differentiation is not the only reason many firms seem to fall between the models of monopoly and competition. In an **oligopoly,** there are very few firms in the industry. Because there are very few firms, each firm has market power. The actions of any one firm can significantly affect the market price.

oligopoly: an industry characterized by few firms selling the same product with limited entry of other firms.

The firms' behavior is strategic in the sense that each needs to anticipate what the others will do and develop a strategy to respond. Such situations, whether in games or in industry, are very complex. Neither the model of a competitive industry, where no one firm can affect the price, nor the model of monopoly, where one firm completely dominates the market, adequately describes such a situation. Hence, there is a need for a model of oligopoly to explain situations in which a few firms produce goods and services and engage in strategic behavior: thinking about, anticipating, and reacting to the other firms' moves.

Figure 11.1 compares the models of monopolistic competition, oligopoly, monopoly, and competition. Over time, an industry can change from being a monopoly to monopolistic competition, to oligopoly, to competition, and back again, as a result of changes in the number of firms or the degree of product differentiation.

In order to emphasize the distinction between the models of competition and monopolistic competition or between the models of monopoly and monopolistic competition, the terms *pure competition* and *pure monopoly* are sometimes used. In this book, we simply use the terms *competition* and *monopoly*.

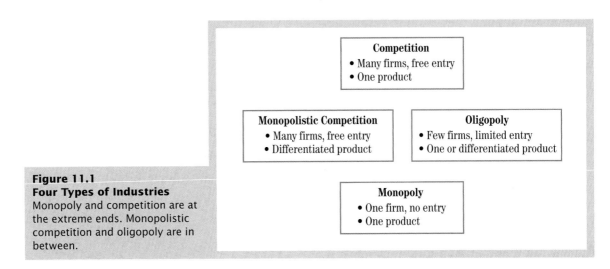

Figure 11.1
Four Types of Industries
Monopoly and competition are at the extreme ends. Monopolistic competition and oligopoly are in between.

Product Differentiation

product differentiation: the effort by firms to produce goods that are slightly different from other types of goods.

The effort by firms to fashion products that are different from other firms' products in ways that people value is called **product differentiation.** Product differentiation is pervasive in market economies. It leads to a great variety of consumer goods and capital goods. Goods for which there is no product differentiation, such as aluminum ingots or gold bullion, are called *homogeneous products*, meaning that they are all exactly the same.

Variety of Goods in a Market Economy

Product differentiation is obvious from a casual examination of the wide variety of goods in a modern market economy. Table 11.1 gives an indication of this wide vari-

Table 11.1
Variety: An Illustration of Product Differentiation

Item	Number of Different Types	Item	Number of Different Types
Automobile models	260	National soft drink brands	87
Automobile styles	1,212		
SUV models	38	Bottled water brands	50
SUV styles	192	Milk types	19
Personal computer models	400	Colgate toothpastes	17
		Mouthwashes	66
Movie releases	458	Dental flosses	64
Magazine titles	790	Over-the-counter	
New book titles	77,446	pain relievers	141
Amusement parks	1,174	Levis jeans styles	70
TV screen sizes	15	Running shoe styles	285
Frito-Lay chip varieties	78	Women's hosiery styles	90
Breakfast cereals	340	Contact lens types	36

Source: 1998 Annual Report, Federal Reserve Bank of Dallas.

Product Differentiation versus Homogeneous Product
Even bottled water has become a highly differentiated product, more like breakfast cereal and soft drinks than like gold bullion, a homogeneous product for which there is no product differentiation.

ety. If you like to run, you have a choice of 285 different types of running shoes. You can choose among 340 different types of cereals for breakfast and wear 70 different types of Levis jeans.

The wide variety of products in a market economy contrasts starkly with the absence of such variety that existed in the once centrally planned economies of Eastern Europe and the Soviet Union. Stores in Moscow or Warsaw would typically have only one type of each product—one type of wrench, for example—produced according to the specifications of the central planners. There was even relatively little variety in food and clothing. One of the first results of market economic reform in these countries has been an increase in the variety of goods available.

Product differentiation is a major activity of both existing firms and potential new firms. Business schools teach managers that product differentiation ranks with cost cutting as one of the two basic ways in which a firm can improve its performance. An entrepreneur can enter an existing industry either by finding a cheaper way to produce an existing product or by introducing a product that is differentiated from existing products in a way that will appeal to consumers.

Product differentiation usually means something less than inventing an entirely new product. Aspirin was an entirely new product when it was invented; wrapping aspirin in a special coating to make it easier to swallow is product differentiation. Coke, when it was invented in 1886, was a new product, whereas Pepsi, RC Cola, Jolt Cola, Yes Cola, and Mr. Cola, which followed over the years, are differentiated products.

Product differentiation also exists for capital goods—the machines and equipment used by firms to produce their products. The large earthmoving equipment produced by Caterpillar is different from that produced by other firms, such as Komatsu of Japan. One difference is the extensive spare parts and repair service that go along with Caterpillar equipment. Bulldozers and road graders frequently break down and need quick repairs; by stationing parts distributorships and knowledgeable mechanics all over the world, Caterpillar can offer quick repairs in the event of costly breakdowns. In other words, the products are differentiated on the basis of service and a worldwide network.

Puzzles Explained by Product Differentiation

Product differentiation explains certain facts about a market economy that could be puzzling if all goods were homogeneous.

intraindustry trade: trade between countries in goods from the same or similar industries.

interindustry trade: trade between countries in goods from different industries.

■ **Intraindustry Trade.** Differentiated products lead to trade between countries of goods from the *same industry*, called **intraindustry trade.** Trade between countries of goods from *different industries*, called **interindustry trade,** can be explained by comparative advantage. Bananas are traded for wheat because one of these goods is grown better in warm climates and the other is grown better in cooler climates. But why should intraindustry trade take place? Why should the United States both buy beer from Canada and sell beer to Canada? Beer is produced in many different countries, but a beer company in one country will differentiate its beer from that of a beer company in another country. In order for people to benefit from the variety of beer, we might see beer produced in the United States (for example, Budweiser) being exported to Canada and, at the same time, see beer produced in Canada (for example, Molson) being exported to the United States. If all beer were exactly the same (a homogeneous commodity), such trade within the beer industry would make little sense, but it is easily understood when products are differentiated.

■ **Advertising.** Product differentiation also provides one explanation of why there appears to be so much advertising—the attempt by firms to tell consumers what is good about their products. If all products were homogeneous, then advertising would make little sense: A bar of gold bullion is a bar of gold bullion, no matter who sells it. But if a firm has a newly differentiated product in which it has invested millions of dollars, then it needs to advertise it to prospective customers. You can have the greatest product in the world, but it will not sell if no one knows about it. Advertising is a way to provide information to consumers about how products differ.

Economists have debated the role of advertising in the economy for many years. Many have worried about the waste associated with advertising. It is hard to see how catchy phrases like "It's the right one, baby" are providing useful information about Diet Pepsi to consumers. One explanation is that the purpose of the advertising in these cases is to get people to try the product. If they like it, they will buy more; if they do not like it, they will not—but without the ad they might not ever try it. Whatever the reason, advertising will not sell an inferior product—at least, not for long. For example, despite heavy advertising, Federal Express failed miserably with Zapmail— a product that guaranteed delivery of high-quality faxes of documents around the country within hours—because of the superiority of inexpensive fax machines that even small businesses could buy.

Others say that advertising is wasteful partly because it is used to create a *perception* of product differentiation rather than genuine differences between products. For example, suppose Coke and Pepsi are homogeneous products (to some people's tastes, they are identical). Then advertising simply has the purpose of creating a perception in people's minds that the products are different. If this is the case, product differentiation may be providing a false benefit, and the advertising used to promote it is a waste of people's time and effort.

■ **Consumer Information Services.** The existence of magazines such as *Consumer Reports* is explained by product differentiation. These magazines would be of little use to consumers if all products were alike.

Such services may also help consumers sort through exaggerated claims in advertising or help them get a better perception of what the real differences between products are. It is hard to sell an expensive product that ends up last on a consumer-rating list, even with the most creative advertising.

How Are Products Differentiated?

Altering a product's *physical characteristics*—the sharpness of the knife, the calorie content of the sports drink, the mix of cotton and polyester in the shirt, and so on—is the most common method of product differentiation. However, as the example of Caterpillar shows, products can be differentiated on features other than the physical characteristics. Related features such as low installation costs, fast delivery, large inventory, and money-back guarantees also serve to differentiate products.

Location is another important way in which products are differentiated. A Blockbuster Video or a McDonald's down the block is a very different product for you from a Blockbuster Video or a McDonald's 100 miles away. Yet only the location differentiates the product.

Time is yet another way to differentiate products. An airline service with only one daily departure from Chicago to Dallas is different from a service with 12 departures a day. Adding more flights of exactly the same type of air service is a way to differentiate the product. A 24-hour supermarket provides a different service from one that is open only during the day.

Convenience is increasingly being used by firms to differentiate products. How could peanut butter and jelly sandwiches, a standard for lunch, be more convenient? You can buy frozen peanut butter and jelly sandwiches on white bread. You can buy individually wrapped "slices" of peanut butter and jelly. How could a cup of coffee be more convenient? You could try coffee sold in a self-heating can that is hot exactly when you're ready to drink it.

The Optimal Amount of Product Differentiation at a Firm

Product differentiation is costly. Developing a new variety of spot remover that will remove mustard from wool (no existing product is any good at this) would require chemical research, marketing research, and sales effort. Opening another Lenscrafters (there are already hundreds in the United States) requires constructing a new store and equipping it with eyeglass equipment, trained personnel, and inventory.

But product differentiation can bring in additional revenue for a firm. The new spot remover will be valued by ice skaters and football fans who want to keep warm with woolen blankets or scarves but who also like mustard on their hot dogs. The people in the neighborhood where the new Lenscrafters opens will value it because they do not have to drive or walk as far.

The assumption of profit maximization implies that firms will undertake an activity if it increases profits. Thus, firms will attempt to differentiate their products if the additional revenue from product differentiation is greater than the additional costs. This is exactly the advice given to managers in business school courses. "Create the largest gap between buyer value . . . and the cost of uniqueness" is the way Harvard Business School professor Michael Porter puts it in his book *Competitive Advantage*.[1] If the additional revenue is greater than the additional cost, then business firms will undertake a product-differentiation activity.

---

1. Michael Porter, *Competitive Advantage* (New York: Free Press, 1985), p. 153.

ECONOMICS IN ACTION

What's the Future of Product Differentiation?

How many types of running shoes do you think will be available for people to buy 10 years from now? There are now about 285 different types, but the number has grown tremendously in the last 25 years—there were only 5 types in the 1970s. This large increase in product differentiation is not unique to running shoes; it has occurred in virtually all markets. Colgate now produces 17 different types of toothpaste, compared with only 2 types in the 1970s. But will this rapid increase in product differentiation continue?

To determine whether an economic trend will continue, we first need to explain the trend. According to the theory of the optimal amount of product differentiation at a firm (see Figure 11.2 on page 291), a possible explanation for the increase in product differentiation is a reduction in its cost. Shifting the curve showing the "additional cost of product differentiation" down in Figure 11.2 would lead to more differentiated products. In fact, there is evidence that the cost of product differentiation has been reduced; computerized machines used to produce shoes make it easier to change the settings and alter the shape, thickness, or treads of rubber soles.

So the model explains the recent trends very well, and if the costs of product differentiation continue to fall in the future, we can expect a greater variety of products.

There is already evidence that computer technology is continuing to lower the cost of product differentiation. For example, a company called Footmaxx uses computers to determine a person's individual foot shape and gait characteristics. As the customer walks on a sensitive pad, the foot shape and pressure are captured many times throughout the gait cycle, and the data are fed into a computer, which prescribes a custom orthotic insole, designed to fit the foot exactly and correct the individual's gait. Nike's iD division has been letting sneakerheads design their own shoes online for several years; in May 2005, it went one step further by inviting sneaker fans to use their cell phones to customize a pair of shoes that was displayed on a 22-story screen in the middle of Times Square in New York City. After a minute-long session designing their shoe, the consumer could then download the design as wallpaper for his or her mobile phone or go online and buy the newly designed sneakers. The interactive experience combined both design and technology innovations. Other companies are following suit. Converse recently launched its own "Design Your Own" service on its web site.

In principle, it will be possible to choose a shoe that is unique to the individual—not only in style and color, but also in the shape of the foot and the characteristics of the gait. One can imagine more than a thousand types of running shoes—perhaps millions, one for every runner! Similar ideas are being developed for clothing, where a person's body is scanned by a laser and a shirt comes out exactly in the person's size.

Of course, these projections for the future require the *ceteris paribus* assumption that other things will remain the same. How important do you think that assumption is in this case? In particular, do you think consumers might change their behavior in response to such an explosion of product types?

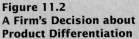

**Figure 11.2
A Firm's Decision about
Product Differentiation**
Determining how much product differentiation a firm should undertake is a matter of equating the additional revenue from and additional cost of another differentiated product. (Note that these "additional cost" and "additional revenue" curves are analogous to marginal cost and marginal revenue curves except that they depend on the amount of product *differentiation* rather than the *quantity* of a particular product.)

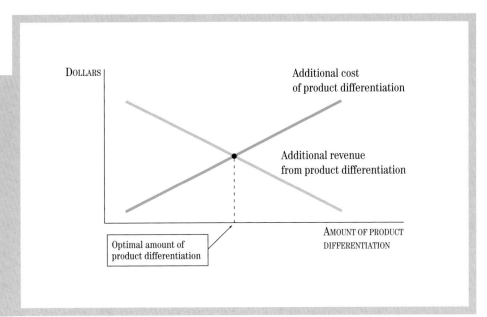

For a given firm, therefore, there is an *optimal* amount of product differentiation that balances out the additional revenue and the additional cost of the product differentiation. This is illustrated in Figure 11.2, which shows the amount of product differentiation chosen by a firm. For a company that owns and operates a haunted house, the horizontal axis is the amount of gore and scary features in the haunted house. The additional revenue from adding more gore and scary features to a haunted house is shown by the downward-sloping line. While more gore and scary features attract additional customers, the additional revenue from increasing the amount of gore and scary features declines because there are only so many people who would consider visiting a haunted house in a given area. It is therefore increasingly difficult to attract additional customers. The additional cost of adding more gore and scary features to a haunted house is shown by the upward-sloping line. This additional cost increases because the cheapest effects that could be included for differentiation would be added first. The optimal amount of gore and scary features for a haunted-house operator is at the point where the additional revenue from more gore and scary features is just equal to the additional cost. Beyond that point, more gore and scary features would reduce profits, since the additional cost would exceed the additional revenue.

This is far from a trivial analysis for haunted-house owners. Theme parks are increasingly interested in attracting Halloween traffic, and more gore and scary features attract more customers. In some theme parks, Halloween is the largest event all year.

Using this analysis in practice is difficult because the revenue gains from product differentiation depend on what other firms do. The amount of additional revenue generated by additional gore and scary features in a haunted house depends on how much gore and how many scary features are included in other nearby haunted houses.

Monopolistic Competition

The model of monopolistic competition, first developed by Edward Chamberlin of Harvard University in the 1930s, is designed to describe the behavior of firms operating in differentiated product markets. Monopolistic competition gets its name from the fact that it is a hybrid of monopoly and competition. Recall that monopoly has one seller facing a downward-sloping market demand curve with barriers to the entry of other firms. Competition has many sellers, each facing a horizontal demand curve with no barriers to entry and exit. Monopolistic competition, like competition, has many firms with free entry and exit, but, as in monopoly, each firm faces a downward-sloping demand curve for its product.

The monopolistically competitive firm's demand curve slopes downward because of product differentiation. When a monopolistically competitive firm raises its price, the quantity demanded of its product goes down but does not plummet to zero, as in the case of a competitive firm. For example, if Nike raises the price of its running shoes, it will lose some sales to Reebok, but it will still sell a considerable number of running shoes because some people prefer Nike shoes to other brands. Nike running shoes and Reebok running shoes are differentiated products to many consumers. On the other hand, a competitive firm selling a product like wheat, which is a much more homogeneous product, can expect to lose virtually all its customers to another firm if it raises its price above the market price.

As we will see, free entry and exit is an important property of monopolistic competition. Because of it, firms can come into the market if there is a profit to be made or leave the market if they are running losses.

A Typical Monopolistic Competitor

Figure 11.3 illustrates the key features of the model of monopolistic competition. Each graph in Figure 11.3 shows a typical monopolistically competitive firm. At first glance, the graphs look exactly like the graph for a monopoly, introduced in Chapter 10. They should, because both monopolistic and monopolistically competitive firms face downward-sloping demand curves. However, the demand curve facing a monopolistically competitive firm has a different interpretation because there are other firms in the industry. The demand curve is not the market demand curve; rather, it is the demand curve that is *specific* to a particular firm. When new firms enter the industry—for example, when L.A. Gear enters with Nike and Reebok—the

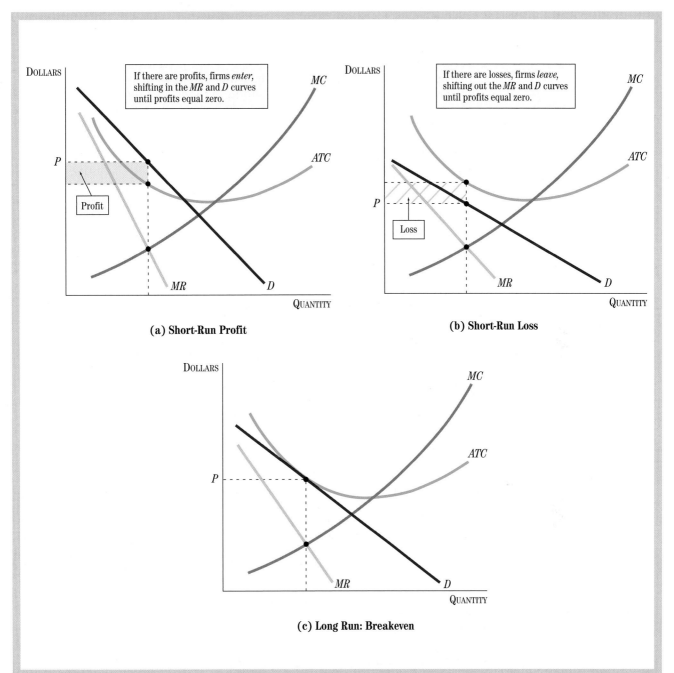

(a) Short-Run Profit

If there are profits, firms enter, shifting in the MR and D curves until profits equal zero.

(b) Short-Run Loss

If there are losses, firms leave, shifting out the MR and D curves until profits equal zero.

(c) Long Run: Breakeven

Figure 11.3
Monopolistic Competition

Each graph shows a typical firm in a monopolistically competitive industry. Firms enter the industry if there are profits, as in graph (a). This will shift the demand and marginal revenue curves to the left for the typical firm because some buyers will switch to the new firms. Firms leave if there are losses, as in graph (b). This will shift the demand and marginal revenue curves to the right because the firms that stay in the industry get more buyers. In the long run, profits are driven to zero, as in graph (c).

demand curves specific to both Nike and Reebok shift to the left. When firms leave, the demand curves of the remaining firms shift to the right. The reason is that new firms take some of the quantity demanded away from existing firms, and when some firms exit, there is a greater quantity demanded for the remaining firms.

The difference between the graphs for a monopolist and a monopolistic competitor shows up when we move from the short run to the long run; that is, when firms enter and exit. This is illustrated in Figure 11.3. Note that the three graphs in the figure have exactly the same average total cost curve. The graphs differ from one another in that the location of the demand and marginal revenue curves relative to the average total cost curve is different in each. Graphs (a) and (b) represent the short run. Graph (c) represents the long run, after the entry and exit of firms in the industry.

Observe that the demand curve in graph (c) is drawn so that it just touches the average total cost curve. At this point, the profit-maximizing price equals average total cost. Thus, total revenue is equal to total costs, and profits are zero. On the other hand, in graphs (a) and (b), the demand curve is drawn so that there is either a positive profit or a negative profit (loss) because price is either greater than or less than average total cost.

▦ The Short Run: Just Like a Monopoly.

Consider the short-run situation, before firms either enter or exit the industry. The monopolistic competitor's profit-maximization decision is like that of the monopoly. To maximize profits, it sets its quantity where marginal revenue equals marginal cost. Because the monopolistically competitive firm faces a downward-sloping demand curve, its profit-maximizing price and quantity balance the increased revenue from a higher price with the lost customers brought on by the higher price. The marginal-revenue-equals-marginal-cost condition achieves this balance. The profit-maximizing quantity of production is shown by the dashed vertical lines in graphs (a) and (b) of Figure 11.3.

For example, ForEyes, Lenscrafters, and Pearle Vision are monopolistic competitors in many shopping areas in the United States. Each local eyeglass store has an optometrist, but each offers slightly different services. At a shopping area with several of these eyeglass stores, if one of them raises prices slightly, then fewer people will purchase glasses there. Some people will walk all the way to the other end of the mall to the store with the lower-priced glasses. Others, however, will be happy to stay with the store that raised its prices because they like the service and the location. These outlets are not monopolists, but the downward slope of their demand curves makes their pricing decision much like that of monopolists. The slope of the demand curve for a monopolistic competitor may be different from that for a monopolist, but the qualitative relationship between demand, revenue, and costs—and the firm's decisions in setting quantity and price—is the same.

▦ Entry and Exit: Just Like Competition.

Now consider entry and exit, which can take place over time. In the model of long-run competitive equilibrium in Chapter 9, we showed that if there were economic profits to be made, new firms would enter the industry. If firms were running losses, then firms would exit the industry. Only when economic profits were zero would the industry be in long-run equilibrium, with no tendency for firms either to enter or to exit.

In monopolistic competition, the entry and exit decisions are driven by the same considerations. If profits are positive, as in graph (a) of Figure 11.3, firms have incentive to enter the industry. Consider the market for hair products. Suave products are similar in appearance and function to other more expensive brands. If another producer has a top-selling shampoo, Suave will enter the market, selling a similar shampoo. If profits are negative, as shown in graph (b) of Figure 11.3, firms have incentive to exit the industry. Caribou Coffee, formerly located near the University of Michigan in Ann Arbor, closed because its costs exceeded its revenue. Demand for coffee was not high enough to support the number of coffee shops near campus.

As we move from the short run to the long run, the demand curve for each of the old firms will tend to shift to the point at which the demand curve and the average total cost curve are tangent—that is, the point where the two curves just touch and have the same slope. Entry into the industry will shift the demand curve of each existing firm to the left, and exit will shift the demand curve of each remaining firm to the right.

We now know why the demand and marginal revenue curves shift in this way. With new firms entering the market, the existing firms will be sharing their sales with the new firms. If Suave sells a new brand of shampoo similar to Pantene shampoo, then some consumers who had been buying Pantene will instead buy Suave's similar new shampoo. The demand for Pantene and other shampoos will therefore decline due to the availability of Suave's new product. Thus, the existing firms will see their demand curves shift to the left—each one will find it sells less at each price. The differences in the positions of the demand (and marginal revenue) curves in the short run and long run illustrate this shift. This shift in the demand curve occurs because new firms in the market are taking some of the demand, not because consumers have shifted their tastes away from the product. The shift in the demand curve causes each firm's profits to decline, and eventually profits decline to zero. (Recall that these are economic profits, not accounting profits, and are therefore a good measure of the incentive for firms to enter the industry.)

The case of negative profits and exit is similar. If demand is such that firms are running a loss, then some firms will exit the industry, causing the demand curve facing the remaining firms to shift to the right, until the losses (negative economic profits) are driven to zero. When Caribou Coffee closed in Ann Arbor, University of Michigan students bought coffee at other nearby coffee shops instead, increasing the demand for coffee at these nearby shops. This is illustrated by comparing graph (b) of Figure 11.3, where there are losses in the short run, with graph (c), where there are zero profits.

The Long-Run Monopolistically Competitive Equilibrium

There are two differences between monopolistically competitive firms and competitive firms in the long run. To see these differences, consider Figure 11.4, which replicates graph (c) of Figure 11.3, showing the position of the typical monopolistic competitor in long-run equilibrium, after entry and exit have taken place.

First, observe that price is greater than marginal cost for a monopolistically competitive firm. This was also true for the monopoly; it means that the market is not as efficient as a competitive market. Production is too low because the marginal benefit of additional production is greater than the marginal cost. Because each firm has some market power, it restricts output slightly and gets a higher price. The sum of producer plus consumer surplus is reduced relative to that in a competitive market. In other words, there is a loss of efficiency—a deadweight loss.

Second, as shown in Figure 11.4, the quantity produced is not at the minimum point on the average total cost curve, as it was for the competitive industry. That is, the quantity that the monopolistic competitor produces is at a higher-cost point than the quantity the perfect competitor would produce. Thus, monopolistically competitive firms operate in a situation of **excess costs.** If each firm expanded production and lowered its price, average total cost would decline. Each firm operates with some **excess capacity** in the sense that it could increase output and reduce average total cost. The firms choose not to do so because they have some market power to keep their prices a little higher and their output a little lower than that. Their market power comes from the downward-sloping demand curve they face. For

excess costs: costs of production that are higher than the minimum average total cost.

excess capacity: a situation in which a firm produces below the level that gives the minimum average total cost.

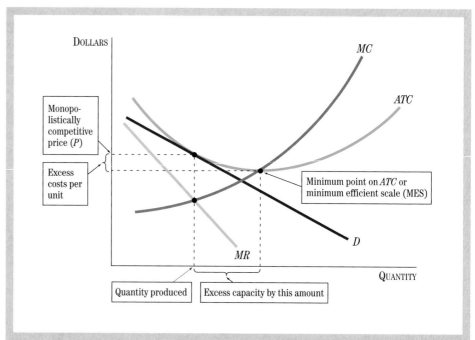

Figure 11.4
Excess Costs per Unit and Excess Capacity with Monopolistic Competition
In the long run, profits are zero for a monopolistically competitive firm, but the firm does not produce the quantity that minimizes average total cost. If the firm increases production, costs per unit will decline. In this sense, the firm operates at less than full capacity; it has excess capacity.

example, each coffee shop charges a little more and sells slightly fewer cups of coffee than it would in a perfectly competitive market.

■ **Comparing Monopoly, Competition, and Monopolistic Competition.**
Table 11.2 compares the different effects of competition, monopoly, and monopolistic competition.

A competitive firm will produce the quantity that equates price and marginal cost. A competitive market is efficient in that consumer surplus plus producer surplus is maximized and there is no deadweight loss. Average total cost is minimized.

In monopoly, price is greater than marginal cost. A monopoly is inefficient because consumer surplus plus producer surplus is not maximized, so there is deadweight loss. Moreover, average total cost is not minimized. Economic profits remain positive because firms cannot enter the market.

Table 11.2

Type of Model	Price	Deadweight Loss?	Average Total Cost Minimized?	Profit in Long Run?
Competition	$P = MC$	No	Yes	No
Monopolistic competition	$P > MC$	Yes	No	No
Monopoly	$P > MC$	Yes	No	Yes

In monopolistic competition, price is also greater than marginal cost. Thus, consumer surplus plus producer surplus is not maximized and there is deadweight loss; average total cost is not minimized. However, profits are zero in the long-run equilibrium because of entry and exit. Monopolistic competition does not result in as efficient an outcome as competition. Monopolistic competition, as well as monopoly, is inefficient.

■ **Product Variety versus Deadweight Loss.** When comparing monopolistic competition with competition, we must recognize—as with the comparison of monopoly and competition in the last chapter—that replacing monopolistic competition with competition may be an impossibility or require a loss to society. Remember that product differentiation is the key reason for monopolistic competition. We showed in the previous section that the variety of products that comes from product differentiation is usually something that consumers value. Some people like having both Pepsi and Coke. Roads and airports are better because of the different capabilities of earthmoving equipment sold by Caterpillar and Komatsu. Thus, eliminating monopolistic competition by having a single competitive product, whether Coksi or Catematsu, even if it were possible, would probably reduce consumer surplus by more than the gain that would come from competition over monopolistic competition.

More generally, product differentiation may be of sufficient value to consumers that it makes sense to have monopolistically competitive firms despite the deadweight loss. Or, to state it somewhat differently, the deadweight loss from monopolistic competition is part of the price consumers pay for the variety or the diversity of products.

REVIEW
- The model of monopolistic competition is a hybrid of competition and monopoly. Entry and exit are possible, as in competition, but firms see a downward-sloping demand curve, as in monopoly, although there are many firms.

- The analysis of monopolistic competition in the short run is much like that of monopoly, but entry and exit lead to zero economic profits in the long run.

- Monopolistic competitors produce less than competitive firms and charge prices higher than marginal costs. Thus, there is a deadweight loss from monopolistic competition. In the long run, monopolistic competition produces less than the quantity that would minimize average total cost.

- The deadweight loss and excess costs can be viewed as the price of product variety.

Oligopoly

Thus far, we have seen two situations in which firms have market power: monopoly and monopolistic competition. But those are not the only two. When there are *very few* producers in an industry—a situation termed *oligopoly*—each firm can have an influence on the market price even if the goods are homogeneous. For example, if Saudi Arabia—one of the major producers of crude oil in the world and a member of the Organization of Petroleum Exporting Countries (OPEC)—decides to cut its production of crude oil, a relatively homogeneous commodity, it can have a significant effect on the world price of oil. However, the effect on the price will depend on what other producers do. If the other producing countries—Iran, Kuwait, and so on—increase their production to offset the Saudi cuts, then the price will not change by much. Thus, Saudi Arabia, either through formal discussion with other oil-producing countries in OPEC or by guessing, must take account of what the other producers will do.

Such situations are not unusual. The managers of a firm in an industry with only a few other firms know that their firm has market power. But they also know that the other firms in the industry have market power too. If the managers of a firm make the right assessment about how other firms will react to any course of action they take, then their firm will profit. This awareness and consideration of the market power and the reactions of other firms in the industry is called **strategic behavior.** Strategic behavior also may exist when there is product differentiation, as in monopolistically competitive industries, but to study and explain strategic behavior, it is simpler to focus on oligopolies producing homogeneous products.

A common approach to the study of strategic behavior of firms is the use of **game theory,** an area of applied mathematics that studies games of strategy like poker or chess. Game theory has many applications in economics and the other behavioral sciences. Because oligopoly behavior has many of the features of games of strategy, game theory provides a precise framework to better understand oligopolies.

An Overview of Game Theory

Game theory, like the basic economic theory of the firm and consumer (described in Chapters 5 and 6 of this book), makes the assumption that people make purposeful choices with limited resources. More precisely, game theory assumes that the players in a game try to maximize their payoffs—the amount they win or lose in the game. Depending on the application, a payoff might be measured by utility, if the player is a person, or by profits, if the player is a firm.

However, game theory endeavors to go beyond basic economic theory in that each player takes explicit account of the actions of each and every other player. It asks questions like: "What should Mary do if Deborah sees her and raises her by $10?" The aims of game theory are to analyze the choices facing each player and to design utility-maximizing actions, or strategies, that respond to every action of the other players.

An important example in game theory is the game called **prisoner's dilemma,** illustrated in Figure 11.5. The game is between Ann and Pete, two prisoners who have been arrested for a crime that they committed. The **payoff matrix** shown in Figure 11.5 has two rows and two columns. The two columns for Ann show her options, which are labeled at the top "confess" and "remain silent." The two rows for Pete show his options; these are also labeled "confess" and "remain silent." Inside the boxes, we see what happens to Ann and Pete for each option, confess or remain silent. The top right of each box shows what happens to Ann. The bottom left of each box shows what happens to Pete.

The police already have enough information to get a conviction for a lesser crime, for which Ann and Pete would each get a 3-year jail sentence. Thus, if both Ann and Pete remain silent, they are sent to jail for 3 years each, as shown in the lower right-hand corner of the table.

But Ann and Pete each have the option of confessing to the more serious crime that they committed. If Ann confesses and Pete does not, she gets a reward. If Pete confesses and Ann does not, he gets a reward. The reward is a reduced penalty: The jail sentence is only 1 year—not as severe as the 3 years it would be if the prosecutor

strategic behavior: firm behavior that takes into account the market power and reactions of other firms in the industry.

game theory: a branch of applied mathematics with many uses in economics, including the analysis of the interaction of firms that take each other's actions into account.

prisoner's dilemma: a game in which individual incentives lead to a nonoptimal (noncooperative) outcome. If the players can credibly commit to cooperate, then they achieve the best (cooperative) outcome.

payoff matrix: a table containing strategies and payoffs for two players in a game.

Figure 11.5
Two Prisoners Facing a Prisoner's Dilemma
Pete and Ann are in separate jail cells, held for a crime they *did* commit. The punishment for each—in years in jail—is given in the appropriate box and depends on whether they both confess or they both remain silent or one confesses while the other remains silent. The top right of each box shows Ann's punishment; the bottom left of each box shows Pete's punishment.

had no confession. However, the penalty for being convicted of the more serious crime in the absence of a confession is 7 years. Thus, if Ann confesses and Pete does not, he gets a 7-year sentence. If both confess, they each get a 5-year sentence.

What should Pete and Ann do? The answer depends on their judgment about what the other person will do. And this is the point of the example. Ann can either confess or remain silent. The consequences of her action depend on what Pete does. If Ann confesses and Pete confesses, she gets 5 years. If Ann confesses and Pete remains silent, Ann gets 1 year. If Ann remains silent and Pete remains silent, she gets 3 years. Finally, if Ann remains silent and Pete confesses, she gets 7 years. Pete is in the same situation that Ann is.

Think about a strategy for Ann. Ann is better off confessing, regardless of what Pete does. If Ann confesses and Pete confesses, Ann gets 5 years rather than 7 years. If Ann confesses and Pete remains silent, then Ann gets 1 year rather than 3 years. Hence, there is a great incentive for Ann to confess because she does better in either case.

Pete is in the same situation. He can compare what his sentence would be whether Ann confesses or remains silent. In this case, Pete is better off confessing regardless of whether Ann confesses or remains silent.

What this reasoning suggests is that both Ann and Pete will confess. If they both had remained silent, they would have gone to jail for only 3 years, but the apparently sensible strategy is to confess and go to jail for 5 years. This is the prisoner's dilemma. The case where both remain silent is called the **cooperative outcome** of the game because to achieve this, they would somehow have to agree in advance not to confess and then keep their word. The case where both confess is called the **noncooperative outcome** of the game because Pete and Ann follow an "everyone for himself or herself" strategy. Note that the cooperative outcome is preferred to the noncooperative outcome by both Pete and Ann, yet both choose the option that results in the noncooperative outcome.

The mathematician and Nobel laureate in economics John Nash defined the noncooperative equilibrium—which economists call a **Nash equilibrium**—as a set of strategies from which no player would like to deviate unilaterally—that is, no player would see an increase in his or her payoff by changing his or her strategy while the other players keep their strategies constant.

cooperative outcome: an equilibrium in a game where the players agree to cooperate.

noncooperative outcome: an equilibrium in a game where the players cannot agree to cooperate and instead follow their individual incentives.

Nash equilibrium: a set of strategies from which no player would like to deviate unilaterally.

Applying Game Theory

How do we apply game theory to the strategy of firms in an oligopoly? To make the application easier, focus on the case where there are only two firms. This is a particular type of oligopoly called *duopoly*. Let's first introduce an example of how to analyze a simple duopoly with game theory, and then we can generalize to more complex problems.

A Duopoly Game

The town of Pumpkinville announces that on October 10 it will hold a farmer's market where folks can buy giant pumpkins to carve in time for Halloween. Jack and Jill are the only two producers of giant pumpkins in Pumpkinville—Jack has a farm 5 miles east of town, while his competitor, Jill, has a farm 5 miles west of town. Back in April, Jack and Jill planted the seeds, and they cared for the pumpkins during the summer. Today is October 9. Jack and Jill each have 60 giant pumpkins ready to harvest, and they have to decide how many pumpkins they should harvest and transport to the market. The farmers are profit maximizers, and they take their costs and revenues into account. All the costs until today (seeds, fertilizer, water, labor, and so on) are sunk, cannot be altered, and should not affect the decision of whether to send the pumpkins to market or let them rot on the ground. The only relevant cost is the $1 per pumpkin for harvest and transportation.

Jack and Jill also know that the townsfolk love their pumpkins, but they are not willing to pay *any* price. The market demand for giant pumpkins is Price = $241 − $2 × Quantity, where the quantity is the sum of what Jack and Jill independently and simultaneously bring to the market on October 10. For example, if Jack decides to harvest and transport 60 pumpkins, while Jill decides to send only 30, then the total quantity supplied to the market will be 90, and the market price for giant pumpkins will be $61 (241 − 2 × 90). As you can see, Jack's decision will influence the price that Jill receives for her pumpkins, and vice versa. This situation is perfect for game theoretic analysis.

To simplify our analysis, let's assume that Jack's and Jill's strategies are limited to three actions: They can bring either 30, 40, or 60 pumpkins to the market. With the information on cost, prices, and available strategies, Jack and Jill can build the payoff matrix in Figure 11.6.

The first step is to build the skeleton of the matrix. We know there are two players—Jack and Jill—and three possible actions—30, 40, or 60 pumpkins. Thus, we build a three-by-three matrix with a total of nine blank boxes, one for each combination of Jack's and Jill's actions—the boxes are numbered for easy reference. Each of these boxes will be filled with the profits that Jack and Jill obtain given their actions. For example, in box 1 both Jack and Jill choose to harvest and transport only 30 pumpkins to the market. Let's calculate Jack's payoffs first. Total revenue will be the price of a pumpkin times the number of pumpkins sold by Jack. For this first box, Jack sells 30 pumpkins, while the market quantity is 60 pumpkins (30 from Jill's farm and 30 from Jack's), so the price is $121 (241 − 2 × 60) and total revenue is $3,630 ($121 times 30 pumpkins). Jack's relevant cost is $30 ($1 times 30 pumpkins). We subtract $30 from $3,630, and we get a payoff of $3,600 for Jack, which we write on the bottom left corner of the first box. The calculation for Jill is similar, and it also yields $3,600 (top right corner of the first box). The rest of the payoff matrix in Figure 11.6 is calculated in a similar way.

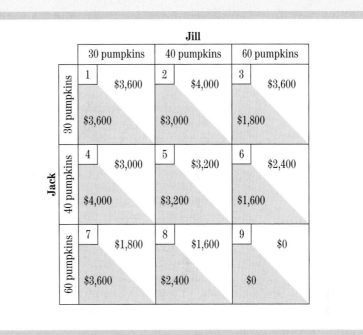

Figure 11.6
Payoff Matrix for Jack and Jill
The payoff matrix contains the profits for Jack and Jill for every possible combination of their actions. For example, in box 6, Jack sends 40 pumpkins to the market, while Jill delivers 60; the market quantity will be 100, and the price will be $41 (241 − 2 × 100). Jack's revenue will be $1,640 (40 × $41) and his cost will be $40 ($1 per pumpkin), and thus his payoff is $1,600 ($1,640 − $40). Jill receives the same price per pumpkin, but since she sold 60, her revenue will be higher ($2,460), with costs of $60 and a payoff of $2,400.

Jack and Jill are aware of the nine possible outcomes, and the question is how each of them is going to choose a quantity to deliver to the farmer's market. Remember that today is October 9, and that the farmers have only one shot at this decision. Once they harvest their pumpkins and bring them to the market on October 10, it will be too late to change their choices. So Jack and Jill engage in a mental exercise, trying to figure out what each other will do.

Put yourself in Jill's shoes. She can easily see that her maximum payoff of $4,000 happens when she sends 40 pumpkins to the market while Jack sends only 30. However, Jill knows that Jack is a profit maximizer too, and if Jill sells 40 pumpkins, then Jack can increase his payoff from $3,000 to $3,200 by selling 40 instead of 30 pumpkins. So box 2 cannot be a solution to Jill's and Jack's problem, and neither can box 4. Jill may soon realize that box 1 provides the highest combined payoff ($7,200), and she may wonder whether that might be a feasible solution. However, if Jill chooses to sell 30 pumpkins, once again Jack will have the incentive to increase his production and sell 40 pumpkins, leaving Jill with a lower profit. Jill has the same incentive to sell 40 pumpkins, so box 1 does not work either.

At this point you can guess that we are looking for a combination of strategies from which neither player would like to deviate unilaterally—that is, a Nash equilibrium. In box 5, we find that neither Jack nor Jill wants to produce more or less pumpkins, given the production of their competitor. When Jack and Jill sell 40 pumpkins each, for a payoff of $3,200 each, we have the only Nash equilibrium of the game—check all remaining boxes yourself—and economics and game theory predict that that will be the outcome of the duopoly when the firms are choosing quantities.

■ **Competition in Quantities versus Competition in Prices.**   In this example, Jack's and Jill's decision variable is the number of pumpkins. Price is left to be determined by the market demand, given the total number of pumpkins. This model of oligopoly is called *Cournot competition* in honor of the French economist Augustin Cournot, who created the original version of this model in 1838 (Cournot did not use game theory and the concept of Nash equilibrium, which was not invented until 1950).

Instead of competing in quantities, oligopolists can also compete in prices; this is called *Bertrand competition* for the French mathematician who reworked Cournot's model in terms of prices in 1883.

■ **Comparison with Monopoly and Perfect Competition.** Figure 11.7 shows the demand and marginal cost curves for pumpkins. The intersection of demand and marginal cost represents the competitive equilibrium, where Jack and Jill each supply 60 pumpkins at a price of $1 and obtain zero profits. The maximum combined payoff is the monopoly solution, which occurs when each farmer sells 30 pumpkins at a price of $121 per pumpkin. The Cournot solution lies between the monopoly and competitive equilibria in terms of price, quantity, and profit.

We do not analyze the Bertrand model in this book, but it may be interesting to note that it predicts that oligopolists will charge the same price and sell the same number of units as competitive firms would.

explicit collusion: open cooperation of firms to make mutually beneficial pricing or production decisions.

■ **Collusion.** The firms know that their combined profits can be maximized if they act together as a monopolist. There are three ways in which firms might act together. The first is by **explicit collusion,** in which the managers communicate with

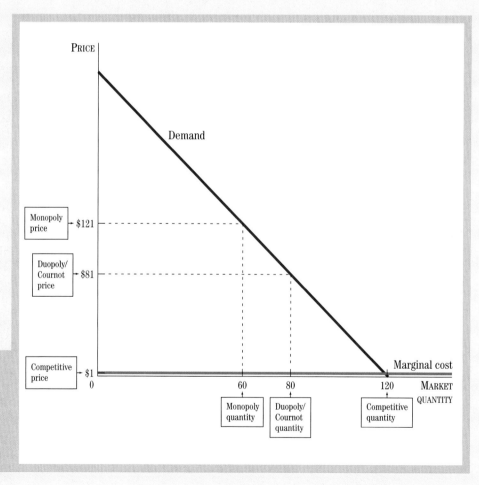

**Figure 11.7
Comparison of Monopoly, Duopoly, and Competitive Equilibria**
Prices and quantities for a Cournot duopoly lie between the equilibria for a monopoly and a competitive market.

each other and agree to fix prices or cut back on production. Although explicit collusion is illegal, it still happens. In the 1980s and 1990s, several firms in Florida and Texas were found guilty of agreeing to fix prices for milk sold to schools. In 1998, the firm Ucar International was found guilty of conspiring with other firms to fix prices and squelch competition in the market for graphite electrodes, a component of steelmaking furnaces. The governments of many countries that produce oil routinely collude to cut back production and raise prices. A group of producers that coordinates its pricing and production decisions is called a **cartel.**

Second, there might be **tacit collusion,** where there is no explicit communication between firms, but firms keep prices high by regularly following the behavior of one firm in the industry. The dominant firm is sometimes called a **price leader.**

Third, the firms could merge, but that also might be illegal in the United States, as we discuss in Chapter 12.

■ Incentives to Defect.   Notice that the duopoly situation has some similarities to the prisoner's dilemma. Just as there is an incentive for Pete and Ann to confess, there is an incentive for Jill and Jack to deviate from producing 30 pumpkins each, the solution that would give them the maximum combined payoff, as if they were behaving as one monopolist. In oligopoly, game theory predicts that unless there is a way to bind each firm to cooperation, there is a tendency to defect. Since the defection results in a lower than monopoly price, consumers gain from the defection, and deadweight loss is reduced.

cartel: a group of producers in the same industry who coordinate pricing and production decisions.

tacit collusion: implicit or unstated cooperation of firms to make mutually beneficial pricing or production decisions.

price leader: the price-setting firm in a collusive industry in which other firms follow the leader.

Incentives to Cooperate: Repeated Games

Although the prisoner's dilemma and the Cournot duopoly suggest that there is a tendency to the noncooperative outcome, there is a difference between the situation of the prisoners Ann and Pete and the farmers Jack and Jill. Firms will presumably have future opportunities to interact. Pumpkinville's farmer's market will probably be open next year and for many years. If the same game is to be played year after year—a repeated game—then the firms might be able to build up a reputation for not defecting.

Experimental economists have conducted experiments in which two people play the same prisoner's dilemma game over and over again. (The people in the experiments are given small monetary rewards rather than jail penalties!) These experiments indicate that people frequently end up using strategies that lead to a cooperative outcome. A typical strategy people use is called "tit-for-tat." Using a tit-for-tat strategy, one player regularly matches, *in the next game*, the actions of the other player *in the current game*. For example, Pete's tit-for-tat strategy would be to confess the next time the game is played if Ann confesses in the current game, and not to confess the next time the game is played if Ann does not confess in the current game. A tit-for-tat strategy gives the other player incentive to follow the cooperative action—not confess—and thereby leads to a cooperative outcome. There are several other strategies that players can use to support a specific outcome in a repeated game.

Secret Defections

The incentive for one firm to defect from an agreement will depend on how likely it is that other firms will detect the defection. In the pumpkin example, it is impossible for Jack to increase his production without Jill's knowing it. This makes defection less likely. If one firm can secretly increase production or cut prices, enforcing the agreement will be more difficult. This is the problem with the world coffee cartel; it is

The online video rental market, dominated by Netflix since its inception in 1999, has been challenged in recent years by the entry of Blockbuster and Wal-Mart. But as the article below implies, the exit of Wal-Mart might change this market situation. What do you think Mr. Squali, the analyst quoted in the article, means when he says that with the segment now a duopoly, "there is a chance for a price improvement and an end to the price bloodbath"?

Wal-Mart Ends Online Video Rentals and Promotes Netflix

By SAUL HANSELL (NYTimes)
May 20, 2005

Wal-Mart, which dominates so much of the retail world, is retreating from one of its more ambitious online ventures, a DVD rental service meant to compete in the market pioneered by Netflix. Instead, Wal-Mart said yesterday it had struck a deal to refer its online video rental customers to Netflix.

The withdrawal is another sign that Wal-Mart's power in brick-and-mortar retailing does not extend easily into the online world. Walmart.com, which sells more than a million individual items, has not proved to be a major threat to online leaders like Amazon.com. In contrast with its stores, Wal-Mart's online operation has not offered significantly lower prices than its rivals.

John Fleming, the company's executive vice president and chief marketing officer, who also oversees Walmart.com, said in a phone interview that the video rental service no longer fits into Wal-Mart's Internet strategy.

"The real big opportunity for us is in businesses that have the potential to integrate with our stores," he said.

In particular, he said that DVD sales on Walmart.com were growing rapidly, drawing strength from Wal-Mart's dominance of the overall DVD sales market. It accounts for about one-third of the DVD's sold in the United States.

Netflix and Wal-Mart declined to discuss the financial terms of the arrangement, but Netflix said it would not have a material effect on its financial results for the year.

Analysts said that Netflix would probably pay a bounty to Wal-Mart for each customer that converted to its service, much as it does with many other business partners. In addition, Netflix will promote Wal-Mart's DVD sales on its site, although analysts said this promotion would probably have little impact.

In the past, Netflix has had similar arrangements with Amazon.com and Best Buy, but those generated few sales.

Wal-Mart entered the online rental market in June 2003, and by March 31 of this year, it had attracted just under 300,000 customers, according to Majestic Research, a New York investment analysis firm.

easy to ship coffee around the world or cut prices without being detected. Crude oil shipments are more easily seen, but a member of OPEC could try to sell oil secretly to China. This might go on for a long time without detection. The impact of such secret defections is much like the situation in boxes 2 and 4 in Figure 11.6. Profits to the defector increase, and profits to the other producers decrease.

Netflix, by contrast, said it had three million subscribers on March 31. And Blockbuster, the dominant rental store chain, which entered the online rental market last August, had 820,000 subscribers, according to Majestic.

Blockbuster appears to have been able to gain traction against Netflix through a combination of low pricing, aggressive promotion and links with its video rental stores.

Blockbuster responded yesterday to the news of Wal-Mart's retreat by offering former Wal-Mart and Netflix customers a two-month free trial of its rental service.

Netflix appears to remain in the lead, analysts said, because its brand is so associated with online rentals and because it has more distribution centers, providing faster deliveries for customers.

All of the rental services allow users to rent a set number of DVD's at a time. As soon as customers mail back one DVD, they can receive another one from a list they enter on a Web site. Blockbuster, however, also gives its customers two free rentals a month from its stores, and Majestic Research has found that 60 percent of Blockbuster users download the free in-store rental coupon each month.

The competition among the rivals has led to a price war. Netflix initially offered the most popular version of its service—which allows three DVD's to be rented at one time—in 1999 for $19.99 a month, raising that price to $21.99 in early 2004. Wal-Mart's three-DVD plan had been $18.76 a month. But last November, when Blockbuster lowered its price to $17.49 a month, Netflix dropped its price to $17.99, and Wal-Mart to $17.36. In January, Blockbuster lowered its price again, to $14.99.

Netflix did not lower prices, but it started promoting a two-DVD plan for $14.99.

Both Blockbuster and Netflix plan to grow rapidly. Netflix said it hoped to end the year at approximately four million subscribers. Blockbuster said it hoped to have two million subscribers by the end of March 2006.

This war has been expensive for all sides. The average revenue per user a month at Netflix has dropped to $18.92 in the first quarter of 2005, from $22.51 in the third quarter of 2004, according to Youssef Squali, an analyst with Jefferies & Company, who does not own Netflix shares.

Blockbuster said it would invest $120 million in marketing and operations for the online rental service this year, in addition to the $50 million it spent last year. The service could break even next year, it said. Mr. Squali said that Wal-Mart's departure from the market could encourage both companies to raise prices. He pointed to the investor revolt at Blockbuster, which resulted in the election of the financier Carl C. Icahn to its board, as a sign the company might rethink its spending on the online rental market.

"Since the segment has become a duopoly," Mr. Squali said, "there is a chance for a price improvement and an end to the price bloodbath."

Shane Evangelist, general manager of Blockbuster online, said that for now his orders from the board remain the same.

"We are going to grow the business as fast as possible," he said.

For a long time, Japanese construction firms operated a now well-known collusion scheme called *dango*. All firms submitted high-priced bids to the government and took turns offering slightly lower bids. Ironically, and unfortunately for consumers, making the bids public made it harder for any firm to defect because firms in the agreement would know at once which firm had lowered its prices.

> **REVIEW**
> - Game theory provides a framework for studying strategic behavior in an oligopoly. Games, including the prisoner's dilemma, describe the strategies firms can use when they have the options of charging a monopoly price or a lower price.
> - Game theory illustrates why firms in an oligopoly will be tempted to defect from any agreement.
> - To the extent that a firm colludes, either explicitly or tacitly, it reduces economic efficiency by raising price above marginal cost.

Conclusion

In this chapter, we have explored two different types of models—monopolistic competition and oligopoly—that lie in the complex terrain between competition and monopoly. The models were motivated by the need to explain how real-world firms—Johnson Publications, Liz Claiborne, Nike, PepsiCo, the members of OPEC, and the members of the coffee cartel—operate in markets with differentiated products or with a small number of other firms.

In the models introduced in this chapter, firms have market power in that they can affect the price of the good in their market. Market power enables a firm to charge a price higher than marginal cost. It is a source of deadweight loss. Observations of the behavior of actual firms show a wide variation in market power among firms.

The ideas about monopolistic competition and oligopoly discussed in this chapter are used by economists in government and businesses. Economists working in the U.S. Department of Justice use them to determine whether the government should intervene in certain industries, as we will explore in Chapter 12. Consultants to business use them to help firms decide how to differentiate their products from those of other firms.

Having concluded our discussion of the four basic types of models of markets in this chapter, it is useful to remember the important distinction between *models* and the *facts* the models endeavor to explain or predict. None of the assumptions of these models—such as homogeneous products or free entry—hold exactly in reality. For example, when contrasted with the monopolistic competition model of this chapter, the model of competition, with its assumption of homogeneous goods, might seem not to apply to very many markets at all. Very few goods are exactly homogeneous. But when economists apply their models, they realize that these models are approximations of reality. How close an approximation comes to reality depends much on the application. The model of competition can be helpful in explaining the behavior of firms in industries that are approximately competitive, just as the model of monopoly can be helpful in explaining the behavior of firms in industries that are approximately monopolistic. Now we have a richer set of models that apply to situations far removed from competition or monopoly.

KEY POINTS

1. Firms that can differentiate their product and act strategically are in industries that fall between competition and monopoly.

2. Product differentiation—the effort by firms to create different products of value to consumers—is pervasive in a modern market economy. It helps explain intraindustry trade, advertising, and information services.

3. Monopolistic competition arises because of product differentiation. With monopolistic competition, firms have market power, but exit from and entry into the industry lead to a situation of zero profits in the long run.

4. With monopolistic competition, the firm sets the quantity produced so that price exceeds marginal cost. As a result, there is a deadweight loss, and average total cost is not minimized.

5. The deadweight loss and excess costs of monopolistic competition are part of the price paid for product variety.

6. Strategic behavior occurs in industries with a small number of firms because each firm has market power to affect the price, and each firm cannot ignore the response of other firms to its own actions.

7. Game theory suggests that noncooperative outcomes are likely, implying that collusive behavior will frequently break down, unless firms acquire a reputation for not defecting and secret defections can be prevented.

KEY TERMS

monopolistic competition	excess costs	payoff matrix	cartel
oligopoly	excess capacity	cooperative outcome	tacit collusion
product differentiation	strategic behavior	noncooperative outcome	price leader
intraindustry trade	game theory	Nash equilibrium	
interindustry trade	prisoner's dilemma	explicit collusion	

QUESTIONS FOR REVIEW

1. What is product differentiation?

2. What factors are relevant to the determination of optimal product differentiation?

3. Why is product differentiation an important reason for monopolistic competition?

4. What are two key differences between monopolistic competition and monopoly?

5. Why don't monopolistic competitors keep their average total cost at a minimum?

6. Why is the noncooperative outcome of a prisoner's dilemma game likely?

7. Why is duopoly like a prisoner's dilemma?

8. What is the difference between explicit and tacit collusion?

9. Why are secret defections a problem for cartels?

10. What are two alternative ways to assess the market power of firms in an industry?

PROBLEMS

1. Match the following characteristics with the appropriate models of firm behavior and explain the long-run efficiency (or inefficiency) of each.
   a. Many firms, differentiated product, free entry
   b. Patents, licenses, or barriers to entry; one firm
   c. Many firms, homogeneous product, free entry
   d. Few firms, strategic behavior

2. Consider Al's gasoline station, which sells Texaco at a busy intersection along with three other stations selling Shell, Conoco, and Chevron.
   a. Draw the marginal cost, average total cost, demand, and marginal revenue for Al's station, assuming that the profit-maximizing price is greater than average total cost. Show Al's profits.
   b. Explain what would happen in this situation to bring about a long-run equilibrium. Would more stations open, or would some leave?

3. Suppose the government places a sales tax on firms in a monopolistically competitive industry. Draw a diagram showing the short-run impact and the adjustment to the new long-run industry equilibrium. What happens to the equilibrium price and number of firms in the industry?

4. Compare the long-run equilibrium of a competitive firm with that of a monopolistically competitive firm with the same cost structure. Why is the long-run price different in these two models? Does the monopolistically competitive firm operate at a minimum cost? Draw a diagram and explain.

5. Suppose monopolistically competitive firms in the software industry make a technological improvement that shifts down average total cost but does not affect marginal cost. What will happen to the equilibrium number of firms, the quantity produced, and the long-run price of software?

6. Suppose there are 10 monopolistically competitive restaurants in your town with identical costs. Given the following information, calculate the short-run price and quantity produced by each of the firms.

Each Firm's Demand		Each Firm's Costs	
Quantity	Price	Average Total Cost	Marginal Cost
1	10.00	13	—
2	8.00	9	5
3	6.00	8	6
4	4.00	9	12
5	2.00	10	14

a. Would the price rise or fall at the typical firm in the long run? Explain.
b. What would be the level of production if this industry were a competitive industry?
c. If there is free entry and exit in both monopolistic competition and competition, why is there a difference in the quantity the typical firm produces?

7. Which of the following conditions will tend to induce collusion among sellers in a market?
a. The transactions are publicly announced.
b. There are few sellers.
c. Some sellers have lower costs than other sellers.
d. The market is open for only one year.
e. The sellers cannot meet one another.

8. Two firms, Faster and Quicker, are the only two producers of sports cars on an island that has no contact with the outside world. The firms collude and agree to share the market equally. If neither firm cheats on the agreement, each firm makes $3 million in economic profits. If only one firm cheats, the cheater can increase its economic profit to $4.5 million, while the firm that abides by the agreement incurs an economic loss of $1 million. If both firms cheat, they earn zero economic profit. Neither firm has any way of policing the actions of the other.
a. What is the payoff matrix of the game that is played just once?
b. What is the equilibrium if the game is played only once? Explain.
c. What do you think will happen if the game can be played many times? Why?
d. What do you think will happen if a third firm comes into the market? Will it be harder or easier to achieve cooperation among the three firms? Why?

9. Store A and Store B are the only two flower shops in a small town. The demand for a dozen roses is $P = 25 - Q$. Neither Store A nor Store B has any fixed costs, whereas the marginal cost of Store A is constant at $3, and the marginal cost of Store B is constant at $5. Each seller can sell either 5 dozen or 10 dozen roses, and they meet only once in this market.
a. Create the payoff matrix. Show your calculations and explain verbally as necessary.
b. Find the Nash equilibrium or equilibria. Explain verbally.
c. If there are multiple equilibria, which equilibrium do you think is most likely to occur and why?

CHAPTER 12

Antitrust Policy and Regulation

When Microsoft came to dominate the personal computer software industry in the 1990s, the U.S. Department of Justice charged the company with using monopoly power to restrict competition, and Microsoft's founder, Bill Gates, was called before a federal judge to defend the company against the charges. The media compared Bill Gates's Microsoft monopoly with John D. Rockefeller's Standard Oil monopoly of the 1890s. When two office superstores, Staples and Office Depot, wanted to merge, the U.S. Federal Trade Commission objected and eventually succeeded in stopping the merger. When a new wireless communications device, the personal communications server, was developed, another government agency, the Federal Communications Commission, determined in advance the very structure of the new market—how many firms there would be in each region and whether or not existing cellular phone companies could compete.

These events represent just a few of the thousands of ways in which the government intervenes in the operations of firms. The intent of the government in many of these cases is to promote competition, which we know is an essential ingredient of market efficiency. Recall that the models of monopoly and monopolistic competition in Chapters 10 and 11 show that when firms have market power, they raise prices above marginal cost, reduce the quantity produced, and create a deadweight loss to society. In such cases, the government may be able to intervene to reduce the deadweight loss and increase economic efficiency.

This chapter uses the models developed in Chapters 10 and 11 to explain the different ways the government can promote competition and regulate firms with market power. We consider two broad types of policy: (1) antitrust policy, which is concerned with preventing anticompetitive practices like price fixing and with limiting firms' market power by preventing mergers or breaking up existing firms, and (2) regulatory policy, in which the government requires firms that have a natural monopoly to set prices at prescribed levels.

Antitrust Policy

antitrust policy: government actions designed to promote competition among firms in the economy; also called competition policy or antimonopoly policy.

Antitrust policy refers to the actions the government takes to promote competition among firms in the economy. Antitrust policy includes challenging and breaking up existing firms with significant market power, preventing mergers that would increase monopoly power significantly, prohibiting price fixing, and limiting anticompetitive arrangements between firms and their suppliers.

Attacking Existing Monopoly Power

Antitrust policy began in the United States just over 100 years ago in response to a massive wave of mergers and consolidations. Similar merger movements occurred in Europe at about the same time. These mergers were made possible by rapid innovations in transportation, communication, and management techniques. Railroads and telegraph lines expanded across the country, allowing large firms to place manufacturing facilities and sales offices in many different population centers. It was during this period that the Standard Oil Company grew rapidly, acquiring about 100 firms and gaining about 90 percent of U.S. oil refinery capacity. Similarly, the United States Steel Corporation was formed in 1901 by merging many smaller steel companies. It captured about 65 percent of the steel ingot market. These large firms were called *trusts*.

Sherman Antitrust Act: a law passed in 1890 in the United States to reduce anticompetitive behavior; Section 1 makes price fixing illegal, and Section 2 makes attempts to monopolize illegal.

The **Sherman Antitrust Act** of 1890 was passed in an effort to prevent these large companies from using their monopoly power. Section 2 of the act focused on the large existing firms. It stated, "Every person who shall monopolize, or attempt to monopolize . . . any part of the trade or commerce among the several states, or with foreign nations, shall be deemed guilty of a felony."

■ **A Brief History: From Standard Oil to Microsoft.** It was on the basis of the Sherman Antitrust Act that Theodore Roosevelt's administration took action to break apart Standard Oil. After 10 years of litigation, the Supreme Court ruled in 1911 that Standard Oil monopolized the oil-refining industry illegally. To remedy the problem, the courts ordered that Standard Oil be broken into a number of separate entities. Standard Oil of New York became Mobil; Standard Oil of California became Chevron; Standard Oil of Indiana became Amoco; Standard Oil of New Jersey became Exxon. Competition among these companies was slow to develop, since their shares were still controlled by Rockefeller. But as the shares were distributed to heirs and then sold, the companies began to compete against each other. Now the oil-refining companies have much less monopoly power. In fact, with the greater degree of competition, the Clinton administration began to allow some of these firms to merge, although not into one single oil-refining firm. For example, on November 30, 1999, Exxon and Mobil merged to form a new firm called Exxon Mobil.

rule of reason: an evolving standard by which antitrust cases are decided, requiring not only the existence of monopoly power but also the intent to restrict trade.

Soon after its success in splitting apart Standard Oil, the U.S. government took successful action under the Sherman Act against the tobacco trust, splitting up the American Tobacco Company into sixteen different companies. It also broke up several monopolies in railroads, food processing, and chemicals. However, the government was not successful in using the Sherman Act against United States Steel. As part of the Standard Oil decision, the Supreme Court developed a **rule of reason** that required not only that a firm have monopoly power but also that it intend to use that power against other firms in a way that would restrict competition. Monopoly *per se*, in and of itself, was not enough, according to the Supreme Court in 1911. Since most competitors and customers of United States Steel said that the company's actions did not restrain competition, the Supreme Court, applying its rule of reason, decided in 1920 that United States Steel was not guilty under the Sherman Act.

Twenty-five years later, a 1945 Supreme Court decision that found Alcoa Aluminum guilty of monopolization refined the rule of reason to make it easier to prove guilt. Although a monopoly per se was still not enough, the intent to willingly acquire and maintain a monopoly—easier to prove than an intent to restrict competition—was enough to establish guilt.

In 1969 the U.S. government brought antitrust action against IBM because of its dominance in the mainframe computer market. After a number of years of litigation, the government dropped the case. One reason was rapid change in the computer market. Mainframes were facing competition from smaller computers. Firms such as Digital Equipment and Apple Computer were competing with IBM by 1982, when the government withdrew its case. Looking at the competition picture more broadly and recognizing that it had already spent millions, the government decided that antitrust action was no longer warranted.

The U.S. government took action against AT&T in the 1970s. It argued that AT&T, as the only significant supplier of telephone service in the nation, was restraining trade. As a result of that antitrust action, AT&T was broken apart and had to compete with MCI and Sprint in providing long-distance telephone service nationwide. This increase in competition lowered the cost of long-distance calls.

The most recent big case was brought against Microsoft. After several antitrust-related investigations, negotiations, and lawsuits in the 1990s, a federal judge found that Microsoft had monopoly power and used it to harm its competitors and consumers, and ordered the firm's breakup in June 2000. However, that order was reversed in 2001, and the federal government reached an agreement whereby Microsoft would provide over a billion dollars in computer software and services and cash to public schools. Several state governments opposed the agreement, seeking stronger penalties on Microsoft.

predatory pricing: action on the part of one firm to set a price below its shutdown point in order to drive its competitors out of business.

■ **Predatory Pricing.** Attempts by firms to monopolize by predatory pricing have also been challenged by the government and by other firms, though breakup is not usually the intended remedy. **Predatory pricing** refers to the attempt by a firm to charge a price below its shutdown point in order to drive its competitors out of business, after which it then forms a monopoly.

A 1986 Supreme Court decision, *Matsushita v. Zenith*, has made predatory pricing harder to prove. Matsushita and several other Japanese companies were accused by Zenith of predatory pricing of televisions in the U.S. market. After five years of litigation and appeals, the Court decided that there was not sufficient evidence for predatory pricing. The Court argued that the Japanese firms' share of the U.S. market was too small compared to Zenith's to make monopolization plausible. Moreover, the low price of the Japanese televisions seemed to be based on low production costs. Thus, the Court's majority opinion stated that this predatory pricing case appeared to make "no economic sense."

"This town isn't big enough for both of us— let's merge."

Predatory pricing is difficult to distinguish from vigorous competition, which is essential to a well-functioning market economy. For example, Wal-Mart has been accused of predatory pricing by smaller retailers, who find it is hard to compete with Wal-Mart's low prices. Yet, in many of these cases, it is likely that Wal-Mart is more efficient. Its lower prices are due to lower costs. In 1993, Northwest Airlines sued American Airlines for predatory pricing in Texas but lost. The jury decided that although American Airlines was charging prices below its shutdown point, it was not attempting to monopolize the market.

Merger Policy

There were thirty-three breakups of firms ordered by the courts from 1890 to 1981, including those of Standard Oil and AT&T. However, there have been no breakups since the AT&T breakup in 1981. There has been a decline in the frequency of government-forced breakups in recent years, which may be due to greater international competition or to the effectiveness of merger policy, which we now consider. For firms to occupy a huge share of the market, they must either grow internally or merge with other firms. A merger policy that prevents mergers that create firms with huge market power reduces the need to break up firms.

Clayton Antitrust Act: a law passed in 1914 in the United States aimed at preventing monopolies from forming through mergers.

Federal Trade Commission (FTC): the government agency established to help enforce antitrust legislation in the United States; it shares this responsibility with the Antitrust Division of the Justice Department.

Antitrust Division of the Justice Department: the division of the Justice Department in the United States that enforces antitrust legislation, along with the Federal Trade Commission.

Herfindahl-Hirschman index (HHI): an index ranging in value from 0 to 10,000 indicating the concentration in an industry; it is calculated by summing the squares of the market shares of all the firms in the industry.

■ **The Legislation, the Antitrust Division, and the FTC.** The Sherman Antitrust Act dealt with monopolies that were already in existence. The **Clayton Antitrust Act** of 1914 aimed to prevent the creation of monopolies and now provides the legal basis for preventing mergers that would significantly reduce competition. The **Federal Trade Commission (FTC)** was set up in 1914 to help enforce these acts along with the Justice Department.

To this day, the **Antitrust Division of the Justice Department** and the FTC have dual responsibility for competition policy in the United States. The Justice Department has more investigative power and can bring criminal charges, but for the most part, there is a dual responsibility.

■ **Economic Analysis.** How does the government decide whether a merger by firms reduces competition in the market? The economists and lawyers in the Justice Department and the FTC provide much of the analysis. They focus on the market power of the firm. The more concentrated the firms in an industry, the more likely it is that the firms have significant market power. Concentration is usually measured by the Herfindahl-Hirschman index.

■ **The "Herf."** The **Herfindahl-Hirschman index (HHI)** is used so frequently to analyze mergers that it has a nickname: the "Herf." The HHI is defined as the sum of the squares of the market shares of all the firms in the industry. The more concentrated the industry, the larger the shares and, therefore, the larger the HHI. For example, if there is one firm, the HHI is $(100)^2 = 10,000$, the maximum value. If there are two firms, each with a 50 percent share, the HHI is $(50)^2 + (50)^2 = 5,000$. If there are 10 firms with equal shares, the HHI is 1,000. Values of the HHI for several hypothetical examples of firm shares in particular industries are listed in Table 12.1.

Observe that the HHI tends to be lower when there are more firms in the industry and when the shares of each firm are more equal. Even when the number of firms in the industry is very large, the HHI can be large if one or two firms have a large

Table 12.1
Examples of the HHI in Different Industries

Industry Example	Number of Firms	Shares (percent)	HHI
A	3	42,42,16	3,784
B	4	42,42,8,8	3,656
C	5	42,42,8,4,4	3,624

share. For example, an industry with 20 firms in which one firm has 81 percent of the market and the others each have 1 percent has a very large HHI of 6,580, even greater than that of a two-firm industry with equal shares.

According to the *merger guidelines* put forth by the Justice Department and the FTC, mergers in industries with a postmerger HHI *above 1,800* will likely be challenged if the HHI rises by 50 points or more. When the HHI is *below 1,000*, a challenge is unlikely. *Between 1,000 and 1,800*, a challenge will likely occur if the HHI rises by 100 points or more.

Some examples are found in Table 12.1. Suppose that the two smallest firms in industry C in Table 12.1 merge and the industry thereby takes the form of industry B. Then the HHI rises by 32, from 3,624 to 3,656. Hence it is unlikely that the government would challenge this merger. In contrast, suppose that the two smallest firms in industry B merge. Then the HHI increases by 128 and the government would be likely to challenge the merger.

The HHI is used because it indicates how likely it is that firms in the industry after the merger will have enough market power to raise prices well above marginal cost, reduce the quantity produced, and cause economic inefficiency. For example, when the FTC blocked the merger of Office Depot and Staples in 1997, it stated that the "post-merger HHIs average over 3000" and that "increases in HHIs are on average over 800 points."[1]

The FTC or Justice Department looks at other things in addition to concentration measures. Ease of entry of new firms into the industry is an important factor, as is the potential contestability of the market by other firms. Recall the idea of *contestable markets* discussed in Chapter 10: Even if firms are highly concentrated in an industry, potential entry by other firms provides competitive pressure on the industry. Thus, an industry with a high degree of concentration may, in fact, be acting competitively because of the threat of new firms coming into the business.

contestable market: a market in which the threat of competition is enough to encourage firms to act like competitors. (Ch. 10)

market definition: demarcation of a geographic region and a category of goods or services in which firms compete.

■ **Market Definition.**   When measuring concentration in a market, the market definition is very important. **Market definition** is a description of the types of goods and services included in the market and the geographic area of the market. Table 12.2 shows the range of possibilities for market definition when considering the merger of soft drink producers. Should the market definition be narrow (carbonated soft drinks) or broad (all nonalcoholic beverages)? The market definition makes a big difference for concentration measures. In 1986 the FTC blocked a merger between Coca-Cola and Dr. Pepper, which would have increased the HHI by 341 in the carbonated soft drink market. In contrast, the HHI would have increased by only 74 if bottled water, powdered soft drinks, tea, juices, and coffee were also included in the market, along with carbonated soft drinks.

---

1. Public Brief to D.C. District Court on *FTC* v. *Staples and Office Depot*, April 7, 1997.

Table 12.2
Different Market Definitions in the Beverage Industry

						Milk
					Tea	Tea
				Coffee	Coffee	Coffee
			Juice drinks	Juice drinks	Juice drinks	Juice drinks
		Bottled water	Bottled water	Bottled water	Bottled water	Bottled water
	Powdered soft drinks	Powdered soft drinks	Powdered soft drinks	Powdered soft drinks	Powdered soft drinks	Powdered soft drinks
Carbonated soft drinks	Carbonated soft drinks	Carbonated soft drinks	Carbonated soft drinks	Carbonated soft drinks	Carbonated soft drinks	Carbonated soft drinks
Narrow Market Definition			**Medium Market Definition**			**Broad Market Definition**

Defining the geographic area of a market is also a key aspect of defining the market for a good or service. In an integrated world economy, a significant amount of competition comes from firms in other countries. For example, in the automobile industry in the United States, there have been only three major producers. This is a highly concentrated industry. However, intense competition coming from Japanese, Korean, German, and other automobile companies increases the amount of competition. The rationale for challenging a merger is mitigated substantially by international competition.

■ **Horizontal versus Vertical Mergers.**   Merger policy also distinguishes between **horizontal mergers,** in which two firms selling the same good or the same type of good merge, and **vertical mergers,** in which a firm merges with its supplier, as, for example, when a clothing manufacturer merges with a retail clothing store chain. The merger guidelines refer to horizontal mergers. Virtually all economists agree that horizontal mergers have the potential to increase market power, all else the same.

There is considerable disagreement among economists about the effects of vertical mergers, however. A vertical merger will seldom reduce competition if there are firms competing at each level of production. However, some feel that a vertical merger may aid in reducing competition at the retail store level.

horizontal merger: a combining of two firms that sell the same good or the same type of good.

vertical merger: a combining of two firms, one of which supplies goods to the other.

Price Fixing

In addition to breaking up firms and preventing firms with a great amount of market power from merging, antitrust policy looks for specific forms of conspiracy to restrict competition among firms. For example, when two or more firms conspire to fix prices, they engage in an illegal anticompetitive practice. **Price fixing** is a serious, frequently criminal, offense. Section 1 of the Sherman Antitrust Act makes price fixing illegal *per se.*

price fixing: the situation in which firms conspire to set prices for goods sold in the same market.

Staples and Office Depot announced plans to merge in 1996. At the time of the announcement, the two firms teamed up to place a full-page advertisement in major newspapers around the country. In huge print the ad stated:

> **Something Special Will Happen When**
> **the Two Low Price Leaders Combine ...**
> **LOWER PRICES**
> **On Office Products Every Day!**

The ad then went on to explain how the proposed merger would lower prices by reducing costs through economies of scale. Through this ad, the companies were making their own news, trying to influence public opinion and thereby get approval for the merger from the Federal Trade Commission (FTC).

But the FTC did not believe the ads. The economists at the FTC immediately found that the HHI would increase by large amounts if one defined the market as "office superstores" and excluded stores such as Wal-Mart that also sold office supplies. The FTC also found that prices for paper, ballpoint pens, envelopes, and so on, were higher, not lower, in areas with only one store than in areas where Office Depot and Staples competed. So, the FTC asked a federal judge to prevent the merger. The FTC claimed that "the proposed merger would violate Section 7 of the Clayton Act."

Economists served as expert witnesses on both sides of the issue, arguing about whether to define the market narrowly or broadly and about whether prices would be lower or higher with the merger. The judge was not convinced by the two companies, by their expert witnesses, or by the ads. The judge ruled to stop the merger. On the question of market definition, the judge argued in his opinion that "No one entering a Wal-Mart would mistake it for an office superstore. No one entering Staples or Office Depot would mistakenly think he or she was in Best Buy or CompUSA. You certainly know an office superstore when you see one." If you were the judge, would you have included Wal-Mart and those other firms in the definition of the office supply market? Would you be skeptical about such ads if you saw them in the newspaper now?

Laws against price fixing are enforced by bringing lawsuits against the alleged price fixers. Suits are brought both directly by the Justice Department and by individual firms that are harmed by price fixing. The number of private suits greatly exceeds the number of government suits. Individual firms can collect **treble damages** (a provision included in the Clayton Act)—three times the actual damages. The treble damage penalty aims to deter price fixing.

treble damages: penalties awarded to the injured party equal to three times the value of the injury.

One of the most famous price-fixing cases in U.S. history occurred in the 1950s and involved Westinghouse and General Electric. Through an elaborate system of secret codes and secret meeting places, the executives of these two firms agreed together to set the price of electrical generators and other equipment they were selling in the same market. Through this agreement, they set the price well above competitive levels, but they were discovered and found guilty of price fixing. Treble damages amounting to about $500 million were awarded, and criminal sentences were handed down; some executives went to prison.

A more recent price-fixing case involved the production of food additives. The large agricultural firm Archer-Daniels-Midland (ADM) was sued by the Justice Department for fixing prices with other international producers. In 1996, as part of the settlement in this case, ADM paid over $100 million in fines.

Table 12.3
Price-Cost Margins in Several Industries

Industry	Price-Cost Margin
Food processing	.50
Coffee roasting	.04
Rubber	.05
Textiles	.07
Electrical machinery	.20
Tobacco	.65
Retail gasoline	.10
Standard automobiles	.10
Luxury automobiles	.34

Source: T. F. Bresnahan, "Empirical Studies of Industries with Market Power," *Handbook of Industrial Organization*, Vol. II, ed. R. Schmalensee and R. D. Willig (Amsterdam: Elsevier Science Publishers, 1989).

■ **Price-Cost Margins.** A way of measuring market power is the *price-cost margin*. The greater the price (P) is above the marginal cost (MC), the more market power firms have. Table 12.3 gives some estimates of the price-cost margin $[(P - MC)/P]$ for firms in several different industries. The higher the price-cost margin, the more market power firms in the industry have. Observe in Table 12.3 that the price-cost margin is very small for coffee roasting, rubber, textiles, retail gasoline, and standard automobiles. The firms in these markets apparently have little market power. In contrast, the price-cost margin is very high for food processing and tobacco.

An interesting example is Anheuser-Busch, the producer of Budweiser beer. Before the introduction of Lite Beer by Miller, Anheuser-Busch had considerable market power; the price-cost margin was .3. After Lite Beer was introduced, the firm lost market power. The price-cost margin dropped to .03. Evidently Lite Beer made Miller a more visible player in the beer market and thus increased competition in the market in the sense that Anheuser-Busch's market power declined.

Vertical Restraints

exclusive territories: the regions over which a manufacturer limits the distribution or selling of its products to one retailer or wholesaler.

exclusive dealing: a condition of a contract by which a manufacturer does not allow a retailer to sell goods made by a competing manufacturer.

resale price maintenance: the situation in which a producer sets a list price and does not allow the retailer to offer a discount to consumers.

The price-fixing arrangements just described are an effort to restrict trade in one horizontal market, such as the electrical machinery market or the market for food additives. Such restraints of trade clearly raise prices, reduce the quantity produced, and cause deadweight loss. But there are also efforts by firms to restrain trade vertically. For example, **exclusive territories** occur when a manufacturer of a product gives certain retailers or wholesalers exclusive rights to sell the product in a given area. This practice is common in soft drink and beer distribution. **Exclusive dealing** is the practice by which a manufacturer does not allow a retailer to sell goods made by a competitor. **Resale price maintenance** is the practice of a manufacturer's setting a list price for a good and then forbidding the retailer to offer a discount.

Do vertical restraints reduce economic efficiency? There is considerable agreement among economists that manufacturers cannot increase their own market power by restraints on the firms to which they supply goods. A manufacturer's requiring that a retailer take a certain action does not give the manufacturer a greater ability to raise prices over competitors without losing sales. In addition, in some circumstances such restraints may actually increase economic efficiency.

Consider resale price maintenance, for example. Suppose that low-price discount stores compete with high-price retail stores that provide services to customers. If a discount store could offer the same product with little or no service, then people could go to the higher-price store, look the product over, get some useful advice from knowledgeable salespeople, and then buy at the discount store. Soon such services would disappear. Resale price maintenance can thus be viewed as a means of preserving such service by preventing the discount store from charging a lower price.

If a producer and retailer are vertically integrated into one firm, then clearly they coordinate the price decisions. For example, the Gap sells its own products in its retail outlets, and it obviously sets the retail price. Outlawing resale price maintenance would mean that firms that were not vertically integrated could not do the same thing as the Gap does. Why should Levi Strauss not be permitted to set the price of Levis sold at retail stores that compete with the Gap?

However, some argue that resale price maintenance is a way to reduce competition at the retail level. They see retailers having competitive pressure to keep prices low as more important than the possible loss of some retail customer services.

In sum, there is more controversy among economists about the effect of vertical restraints than about horizontal restraints.

REVIEW
- Breaking up monopolies, preventing mergers that would create too much market power, and enforcing laws against price fixing are the main government actions that constitute antitrust policy.
- Section 1 of the Sherman Antitrust Act outlaws price fixing.
- Section 2 of the Sherman Antitrust Act allows the government to break up firms with monopoly power.
- The Clayton Antitrust Act provides the legal basis for merger policy.
- All these policies aim to increase competition and thus improve the efficiency of a market economy.
- There is more controversy about the effects of vertical mergers and vertical restraints than about horizontal mergers and horizontal restraints.

Regulating Natural Monopolies

The goal of antitrust policy is to increase competition and improve the efficiency of markets. Under some circumstances, however, antitrust policy against a monopoly is not necessarily in the interest of efficiency. In the provision of certain goods, such as water, it is inefficient for more than one company to deliver the product to households. To provide its services, a water company must dig up the streets, lay the water pipes, and maintain them. It would be inefficient to have two companies supply water because that would require two sets of pipes and would be a duplication of resources. Another example is electricity. It makes no sense to have two electric utility firms supply the same neighborhood with two sets of wires. A single supplier of electricity is more efficient.

Economies of Scale and Natural Monopolies

natural monopoly: a single firm in an industry in which average total cost is declining over the entire range of production and the minimum efficient scale is larger than the size of the market. (Ch. 10)

Water and electricity are examples of *natural monopolies,* industries in which one firm can supply the entire market at a lower cost than two firms can. Recall from the discussion in Chapter 10 that the key characteristic of a natural monopoly is a declining average total cost curve. Average total cost declines as more is produced because fixed costs are very large compared to variable costs. Once the main line is laid for the water supply, it is relatively easy to hook up another house. Similarly, with electricity, once the main lines are installed, it is relatively easy to run wires into a house. A large initial outlay is necessary to lay the main water pipes or main electrical lines, but thereafter the cost is relatively low. The more houses that are hooked up, the less the average total cost is. Recall that when the long-run average total cost curve declines, there are *economies of scale.*

economies of scale: a situation in which long-run average total cost declines as the output of a firm increases. (Ch. 8)

Figure 12.1 shows graphically why one firm can always produce more cheaply than two or more firms when the average total cost curve is downward-sloping. The figure shows quantity produced on the horizontal axis and dollars on the vertical axis; a downward-sloping average total cost curve is plotted. If two firms divide up the market (for example, if two water companies supply water to the neighborhood), then the average total cost is higher than if one firm produces for the entire market. It

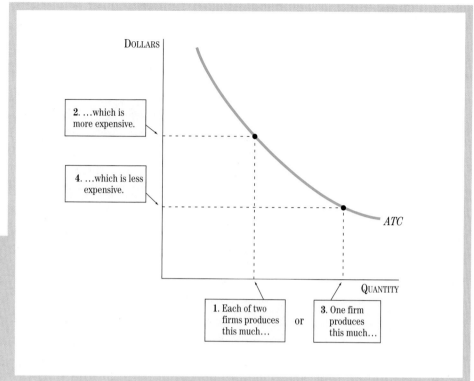

**Figure 12.1
Natural Monopoly: Declining
Average Total Cost**
If two firms supply the market,
dividing total production
between them, costs are higher
than if one firm supplies the market. The costs would be even
greater if more than two firms
split up the market.

2. ...which is
more expensive.

4. ...which is less
expensive.

ATC

DOLLARS

QUANTITY

1. Each of two
firms produces
this much...

or

3. One firm
produces
this much...

is more costly for two or more firms to produce a given quantity in the case of a
declining average total cost curve than for one firm.

Alternative Methods of Regulation

What is the best government policy toward a natural monopoly? Having one firm in
an industry lowers the cost of production, but there will be inefficiencies associated
with a monopoly: Price will be higher than marginal cost, and there will be a
deadweight loss. To get both the advantages of one firm producing *and* a lower price,
the government can regulate the firm.

The monopoly price and quantity of a natural monopoly with declining average
total cost are illustrated in Figure 12.2. The monopoly quantity occurs where marginal revenue equals marginal cost, the profit-maximizing point for the monopolist.
The monopoly price is above marginal cost. If the firm's price was regulated, then the
government could require the firm to set a lower price, thereby raising output and
eliminating some of the deadweight loss associated with the monopoly. There are
three ways for the government to regulate the price: marginal cost pricing, average
total cost pricing, and incentive regulation.

■ **Marginal Cost Pricing.** We know that there is no deadweight loss with competition because firms choose a quantity of output such that marginal cost is equal to
price. Hence, one possibility is for the government to require the monopoly to set its
price equal to marginal cost. This method is called **marginal cost pricing.** However,
with declining average total cost, the marginal cost is lower than average total cost.
This is shown in Figure 12.2 for the case where marginal cost is constant. Thus, if
price were equal to marginal cost, *the price would be less than average total cost*, and

marginal cost pricing: a regulatory method that stipulates that
the firm charge a price that equals
marginal cost.

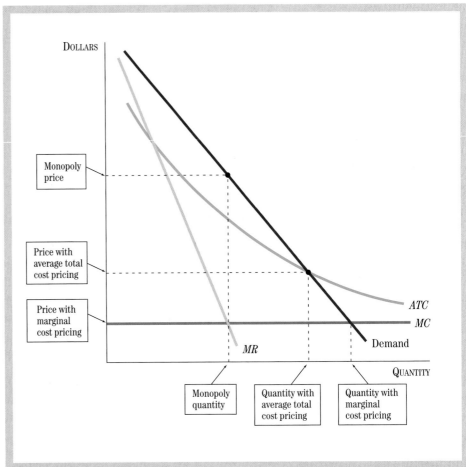

Figure 12.2
Monopoly Price versus Alternative Regulatory Schemes
Two alternatives, marginal cost pricing and average total cost pricing, are compared with the monopoly price. Marginal cost pricing gives the greatest quantity supplied, but since price is less than average total cost, the firm earns negative profits. Average total cost pricing results in a larger quantity supplied, and the firm earns zero economic profits.

the monopoly's profits would be negative (a loss). There would be no incentive for any firm to come into the market.

For example, if the regulators of an electrical utility use a pricing rule with price equal to marginal cost, there will be no incentive for the electrical utility to build a plant or produce electricity. Although the idea of mimicking a competitive firm by setting price equal to marginal cost might sound reasonable, it fails to work in practice.

■ **Average Total Cost Pricing.**   Another method of regulation would have the firm set the price equal to average total cost. This is called **average total cost pricing** or, sometimes, cost-of-service pricing. It is also illustrated in Figure 12.2. When price is equal to average total cost, we know that economic profits will be equal to zero. With the economic profits equal to zero, there will be enough to pay the managers and the investors in the firm their opportunity costs. Although price is still above

average total cost pricing: a regulatory method that stipulates that the firm charge a price that equals average total cost.

California Electricity Crisis

Electricity has long been considered a natural monopoly, subject to federal regulation. In the United States, the Federal Power Act of 1935 led to the creation of a group of geographically contained "vertical" monopolies over the generation, distribution, and sale of power in each company's region. But in the 1990s, deregulation legislation allowed for market competition among power generators (though not among electricity distributors). In 2000 and 2001, California energy suppliers falsified price data and trading records to manipulate the Californian market and illegally increase the price of electricity and natural gas. The energy shortages forced California to ration electricity and use selective power outages. Some people believe that deregulation may have been partly responsible for California's electricity crisis, whereas others believe that the way partial deregulation was implemented—that is, the new set of rules and incentives in the market—were partially responsible for the crisis.

View down San Francisco's Market Street at the end of day 14 of a stage-three State of California power alert, in late January 2001.

marginal cost, it is less than the monopoly price; the deadweight loss will be smaller and more electricity will be produced compared with the monopoly.

But there are some serious problems with average total cost pricing. Suppose the firm knows that whatever its average total cost is, it will be allowed to charge a price equal to average total cost. In that situation, there is no incentive to reduce costs. Sloppy work or less innovative management could increase costs. With the regulatory scheme in which the price equals average total cost, the price would rise to cover any increase in cost. Inefficiencies could occur with no penalty whatsoever. This approach provides neither an incentive to reduce costs nor a penalty for increasing costs at the regulated firm.

■ Incentive Regulation.   The third regulation method endeavors to deal with the problem that average total cost pricing provides too little incentive to keep costs low. The method is called **incentive regulation.** It is a relatively new idea, but it is quickly spreading, and most predict that it is the way of the future. The method projects a regulated price out over a number of years. That price can be based on an estimate of average total cost. The regulated firm is told that the projected price will not be revised upward or downward for a number of years. If the regulated firm achieves an average total cost lower than the price, it will be able to keep the profits, or perhaps pass on some of the profits to a worker who came up with the idea for the innovation. Similarly, if sloppy management causes average total cost to rise, then profits will fall because the regulatory agency will not revise the price.

Thus, under incentive regulation, the regulated price is only imperfectly related to average total cost. The firm has a profit incentive to reduce costs. If a firm does poorly, it pays the penalty in terms of lower profits or losses.

Under incentive regulation, the incentives can be adjusted. For example, the California Public Utility Commission (the regulators of utility firms in California) has

incentive regulation: a regulatory method that sets prices for several years ahead and then allows the firm to keep any additional profits or suffer any losses over that period of time.

321

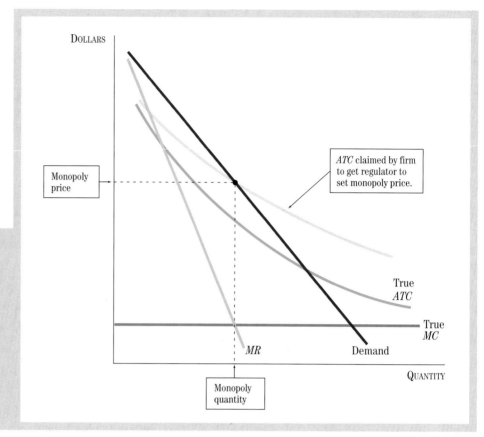

Figure 12.3
Asymmetric Information and Regulation
If a regulator uses average total cost pricing but does not have complete information about costs at the firm, the firm could give misleading information about its costs in order to get a higher price from the regulator. In an extreme case, shown in this figure, the firm could say its costs were so high that it could get the monopoly price.

incentive schemes by which electrical utility firms and their customers share equally in the benefits of reduced costs and in the penalties from increased costs. This reduces the incentive to the firm in comparison to the case where the benefits and penalties are not shared.

Incentive regulation is sometimes made difficult by *asymmetric information*; that is, when one of the parties has access to more or better information. In this case, the regulated firm has more information than the regulator about its equipment, technology, and workers. Thus, the firm can mislead the regulator and say that its average total cost is higher than it actually is in order to get a higher price, as shown in Figure 12.3.

REVIEW

- In the case of a natural monopoly, one firm can produce at a lower average total cost than two or more firms, but a monopoly causes deadweight loss.

- If government regulates the monopoly through marginal cost pricing, the firm will run losses.

- Average total cost pricing leads to increased costs because it doesn't provide incentives to keep costs down.

- Incentive regulation is becoming the preferred method of regulation.

To Regulate or Not to Regulate

Our analysis thus far suggests that the government should regulate firms' prices in situations where natural monopolies exist. In practice, this requires deciding when a natural monopoly exists, which is frequently difficult.

There are many examples in American history of the government's regulating a firm's prices even when it is far-fetched to think about the firm as a natural monopoly. For example, for a long period of time, trucking was regulated by the federal government. Trucking regulation grew out of railroad regulation, which was originally justified when railroads were the only rapid form of transportation and thus were natural monopolies. Under trucking regulation, the federal government put a floor on the price that trucking companies could charge when shipping goods interstate. Federal regulation of trucking was disbanded in the early 1980s. Studies have shown that trucking rates fell as a result.

Borderline Cases

Clearly, trucking is not a natural monopoly. The trucking industry is at the opposite end of the spectrum from water or electrical utility companies, which are almost always regulated.

But there are many borderline cases that are more controversial. Many of these arise in high-technology industries such as telecommunications and computing. An important example is cable television. In 1992, there was considerable debate about whether the federal government should regulate cable television. On first thought, it may appear that cable television is no different from electricity or water. Once a cable television company lays the cable down in a neighborhood, there is a fairly small cost to connect each individual house to it. On the other hand, there are alternatives to cable television for many homes. For example, over-the-air television channels do provide some competition to cable television. If one lives in an area where there are few over-the-air channels, there is little competition. However, if there are six, seven, or eight over-the-air channels, then there is more competition.

Competition for Cable?
Satellites provide consumers another way of accessing television broadcasts, not only in remote areas such as this ranch, but also in highly populated areas where the additional competition keeps cable prices down and quality up.

Until 1992, the Federal Communications Commission (FCC), the federal agency that regulates the telecommunications industry, measured competition by the number of over-the-air channels. At first, the commission decided that three over-the-air channels represented effective competition. It did not regulate cable television companies in areas where there were more than three over-the-air channels. Later on, when it noticed that prices of cable television were rising and consumers were complaining, the FCC raised the limit to six over-the-air channels. In 1992, Congress passed a law saying that it did not matter how many channels there were; the law required the FCC to regulate cable television firms in any case.

Over-the-air channels are not the only competition for cable television. People can use satellite dishes, which provide access to numerous channels at a price competitive with cable. Eventually, it may be possible to use the telephone wires to transmit television signals, in which case the telephone companies could compete with the cable television companies.

High-tech industries change quickly, and it is difficult for government regulators to keep up with the changes. Inflexible regulatory rules could slow innovation. In fact, upon taking over as chairman of the FCC in 2005, some of the first statements Kevin Martin made were about his plans to loosen rules so that neither phone nor cable companies would be required to share their Internet connections with competitors like America Online. He argued that these legacy regulations discouraged companies from investing in high-speed Internet service.

Regulators as Captives of Industry

Government and government agencies are run by people who have their own motivations, such as being reelected or increasing their influence. Thus, despite the economic advice about what government regulatory agencies should do, the agencies may end up doing something else. In fact, regulators have sometimes ended up helping the industry at the expense of the consumer. The railroad industry is an example. Originally, regulation of railroads was set up to reduce prices below the monopoly price. But as competition to the railroads from trucks and eventually airlines increased, the industry continued to be regulated. Eventually, the regulators were helping the industry; they kept prices from falling to prevent railroad firms from failing. And by regulating trucking prices, they kept trucking firms from competing with the railroads. The Teamsters Union, which represents truck drivers, was one of the strongest supporters of regulation because it knew that the regulations were keeping trucking prices high. In a sense, the regulators became captives of both the firms and the workers in the industry.

An economist, George Stigler, won the Nobel Prize for showing how regulatory agencies could become captive to the industry and therefore tend to thwart competition. The concern that regulators will become captives is one reason some economists worry about allowing the government to regulate a new industry, like cable television. Eventually, the government may try to protect the cable television operators in order to prevent them from failing. The government might limit competition in the future from satellite dishes or from the telephone company.

The Deregulation Movement

deregulation movement:
begun in the late 1970s, the drive to reduce the government regulations controlling prices and entry in many industries.

Starting in the late 1970s under Jimmy Carter and continuing in the 1980s under Ronald Reagan, the **deregulation movement**—the lifting of price regulations—radically changed several key industries. The list of initiatives that constitute this deregulation movement is impressive. For example, air cargo was deregulated in 1977, air travel was deregulated in 1978, satellite transmissions were deregulated in 1979, trucking was deregulated in 1980, cable television was deregulated in 1980 (although regulation was reimposed in 1992), crude oil prices and refined petroleum products were deregulated in 1981, and radio was deregulated in 1981. There was also deregulation of prices in the financial industry. Prior to the 1980s, the price—that is, the interest rate on deposits—was controlled by the financial regulators. Regulation of brokerage fees was also eliminated.

This deregulation of prices reduced deadweight loss. Airline prices have declined for many travelers. It is now cheaper to ship goods by truck or by rail. Economists have estimated the size of this reduction in deadweight loss by calculating the increase in the area between the demand curve and the marginal cost curve as the quantity produced increased.

Some people complain about deregulation. Business travelers complain that they have to pay more for air travel, although vacation travelers can pay less. Deregulation of the airline industry led to widespread fears that large airlines would dominate the industry because of their market power at the hubs. However, the large airlines are now so cost-heavy that smaller regional airlines have made significant headway in attracting even business travelers with their low-cost flights. Boston-based business travelers, for example, might be willing to suffer the inconvenience of traveling to Providence to take a cheaper Southwest Airlines flight rather than fly out of Boston on one of the large carriers.

REVIEW

- In many cases it is clear that a natural monopoly exists and thus price regulation is needed. However, in certain industries like cable television, there is controversy about the need for regulation.

- There has frequently been price regulation where there is no natural monopoly, as in trucking.

- The deregulation movement began in the late 1970s and continued into the 1980s. It was in response to economic analysis that showed that it is harmful to regulate the prices of firms that are not natural monopolies.

- Trucking, airline, and railroad transportation prices are lower as a result of this deregulation. As with most economic changes, not everyone benefited. Business travelers saw the costs of some services increase.

Conclusion

This chapter analyzed a key role of government in a market economy: maintaining competitive markets through antitrust policy or the regulation of firms. By reducing the deadweight loss due to monopoly, the government can reduce market failure and improve people's lives.

However, this analysis must be placed in the context of what in reality motivates government policymakers. The example of regulators becoming captives of industry reminds us that having an analysis of what should be done is very different from getting it done. Government failure is a problem that must be confronted just like market failure. Reducing government failure requires designing the institutions of government to give government decision-makers the proper incentives.

KEY POINTS

1. The government has an important role to play in maintaining competition in a market economy.

2. Part of antitrust policy is breaking apart firms with significant market power, although this technique is now used infrequently. Section 2 of the Sherman Antitrust Act provides the legal authority for challenging existing monopolies.

3. A more frequently used part of antitrust policy is preventing mergers that would cause significant market power. In the United States, the government must approve mergers.

4. Concentration measures such as the HHI are used to decide whether a merger should take place.

5. Price fixing is a serious antitrust offense in the United States, and the laws against it are enforced by allowing private firms to sue, providing for treble damages, and allowing the government to ask for criminal penalties.

6. In the case of natural monopolies, the government can either run the firm or regulate a private firm. In the United States, the latter route is usually taken.

7. Regulatory agencies have been using incentive regulation more frequently in order to give firms incentives to hold costs down.

8. The deregulation movement has consisted mainly of removing price regulations from firms that are not natural monopolies, such as trucking and airlines.

9. Overall the deregulation movement has significantly lowered costs to consumers, but it is controversial because services have been cut back in certain areas.

KEY TERMS

antitrust policy
Sherman Antitrust Act
rule of reason
predatory pricing
Clayton Antitrust Act

Federal Trade Commission (FTC)
Antitrust Division of the Justice Department
Herfindahl-Hirschman index (HHI)
market definition

horizontal merger
vertical merger
price fixing
treble damages
exclusive territories
exclusive dealing

resale price maintenance
marginal cost pricing
average total cost pricing
incentive regulation
deregulation movement

QUESTIONS FOR REVIEW

1. What historical development gave the impetus to the original antitrust legislation in the United States?

2. What is the difference between Section 1 and Section 2 of the Sherman Antitrust Act?

3. What is the difference between the rule of reason and the per se rule in the case of monopolization and in the case of price fixing?

4. What law gives the government the right to prevent mergers that would increase market power?

5. Why is the market definition crucial when calculating the HHI index in the case of mergers?

6. Why is marginal cost pricing a faulty pricing rule for regulatory agencies?

7. How does incentive regulation improve on average cost pricing?

8. Why is there more controversy about regulating cable television than about regulating water companies?

PROBLEMS

1. Which legislation—Section 1 of the Sherman Act, Section 2 of the Sherman Act, or the Clayton Act—gives the government the authority to take action in each of the following areas: prosecuting price fixing, preventing proposed mergers, breaking up existing monopolies, suing for predatory pricing?

2. Why is it better to break up monopolies that are not natural monopolies rather than regulate them, even if it is possible to regulate them?

3. In reflecting on a recent term of service, a former head of the Antitrust Division said, "I was convinced that a little bit of efficiency outweighs a whole lot of market power." Evaluate this statement by considering two sources of efficiency: decreasing average total cost and research and development. Describe how these should be balanced against the deadweight loss from market power.

4. Compare the following two hypothetical cases of price fixing.
   a. General Motors, Ford, and Chrysler are found to be coordinating their prices for Chevy Blazers, Ford Broncos, and Jeep Cherokees.

b. General Motors is coordinating with Chevy dealers around the country to set the price for Chevy Blazers.

Which is more likely to raise prices and cause a deadweight loss? Explain.

5. The following table shows the market shares of firms in three different industries.

Industry	Number of Firms	Shares	HHI
1	100	Each firm with 1 percent	
2	15	10 firms with 5 percent	
		5 firms with 10 percent	
3	3	1 firm with 60 percent	
		2 firms with 20 percent	

a. Complete the above table by calculating the Herfindahl-Hirschman index.
b. Will the FTC try to prevent a significant merger in industry 2? In industry 3? Why?

6. Use the merger guidelines to decide whether the following changes in industry C in Table 12.1 would be permitted.
a. The three small firms merge into one firm.
b. One of the firms with 4 percent share merges with the firm with 8 percent share.

7. If economies of scale are important, is it possible for consumers to be better off if the government allows more mergers?

8. In some states, regulatory authorities are beginning to allow some competition among electric power companies. What must the regulators think about the nature of this industry? What other industries have gone through this transformation? What are the benefits of deregulation?

9. Sketch a graph of a natural monopoly with declining average total cost and constant marginal cost.
a. Show how the monopoly causes a deadweight loss, with price not equal to marginal cost.
b. Describe the pros and cons of three alternative ways to regulate the monopoly and reduce deadweight loss: marginal cost pricing, average total cost pricing, and incentive regulation.

10. The demand schedule and total costs for a natural monopoly are given in the following table.

Price	Quantity	Total Costs
16	6	80
15	7	85
14	8	90
13	9	95
12	10	100
11	11	105
10	12	110
9	13	115
8	14	120
7	15	125
6	16	130
5	17	135
4	18	140

a. Why is this firm a natural monopoly? What will the monopoly price be? Calculate profits.
b. Suppose the government sees that this is a natural monopoly and decides to regulate it. If the regulators use average total cost pricing, what will the price and quantity be? What should profits be when the regulators are using average total cost pricing?
c. If the regulators use marginal cost pricing, what will the price and quantity be? Why is this policy difficult for regulators to pursue in practice? What are profits in this situation?
d. Why might the government want to use incentive regulation?

11. Historically, local telephone companies have been natural monopolies, but cellular phones are now offering services that are a substitute for wire connections.
a. If traditional phone companies are under incentive regulation, how would the introduction of cellular phones affect them? Show it graphically.
b. What should the regulatory agency do?

12. Some people argue that coal mines are natural monopolies. In fact, until recently, all coal mines in Great Britain were owned by the government. What conditions in the industry do you need to check in order to tell whether the industry is a natural monopoly?

The Issue:
Are Mergers Good for the Economy?

The announcement of a potential merger between two large companies can send a shiver of anticipation rippling through the economy. Some of the anticipation is positive: The complicated financial and legal transactions involved imply a lot of work for investment bankers and lawyers, the shareholders of one or both companies may anticipate a sharp rise in the value of their holdings, and consumers expect new and exciting products to emerge from the combined firm. But some of the anticipation will also be negative: Competitors will be concerned about how the increased market power of the merged firm will affect their business, employees of the firms being merged will worry that they will lose their jobs once the new firm begins eliminating duplicate positions, consumers will worry that the new firm will raise prices, and government antitrust regulators will worry about the impact of the merger on the degree of competition in the industry. Almost every merger that takes place in the economy will therefore have a constituency of supporters and a constituency of opponents.

Some of the biggest mergers that have taken place recently involve companies that you may be familiar with: AOL and Time Warner (combined market value $112 billion), Exxon and Mobil ($86 billion), Gillette and Procter & Gamble ($57 billion). While all mergers take place in anticipation that the sum will be greater than the parts, not all are successful. The best way to understand the opportunities and concerns that arise when two firms decide to merge is to look at a specific example. The merger between Fleet and Bank of America (a deal valued at $50 billion) took place in April of 2004, concluding a process that began in October of 2003 when Bank of America announced its intention to buy Fleet. Shareholders of Fleet had to agree to the deal, and since the merger involved two banking companies, the Federal Reserve had to approve it before the two banks could join together. Over the next year, the new company (now called Bank of America) consolidated the two businesses and transformed Fleet bank branches into Bank of America branches. An article in *Forbes* magazine that appeared around the time that Bank of America announced its intention to buy Fleet discussed how the decision to merge came about and what changes the merger would bring about.[1]

The combined bank would have $933 billion in assets, making it the third largest in the world. The combined customer deposits of Fleet and Bank of America accounted for almost 10 percent of cash held by U.S. individuals and firms! Because of the geographic strengths of the respective banks, there was limited overlap in terms of dealing with consumers. The challenge for the companies was deciding where to consolidate and where to expand. The two companies predicted that they would be able to reduce costs by $1.5 billion by coordinating their operations in credit cards, mutual funds, and trading.

As with all mergers, there were groups that were very enthusiastic about the Fleet/Bank of America merger and others who were extremely concerned about its potential negative impact.

The Bank of America/Fleet Merger Is Good for the Economy POINT

Outside of Fleet and Bank of America's stockholders, no other entity's approval of the merger mattered more than the Federal Reserve's. In a detailed order issued on March 8, 2004, the Federal Reserve described why it thought the Fleet/Bank of America merger should be allowed to go ahead.[2] The Fed provides 60 days' notice for "interested parties" to submit their opinions on issues regarding the merger. Public meetings were held in San Francisco and Boston, and the Fed heard testimony from 180 interested parties and received written comments from more than 2,000 individuals and organizations. A large number of commenters supported the merger and commended the community development efforts of Fleet and Bank of America. But a large number of commenters opposed the proposed merger on the grounds that it would reduce lending to small businesses and in low- and middle-income areas, that it would reduce competition and increase industry concentration, and that job losses would result from branch closings and the elimination of Fleet's corporate headquarters in Boston. After considering how the merger would affect the HHIs[3] in the New York and Florida markets, the Fed concluded that the merger would not result in monopoly power.

1 Ari Weinberg, "Bank of America Expands Its Fleet," Forbes.com, Oct. 27, 2003. Available online at http://www.forbes.com/2003/10/27/cx_aw_1027bofa.html.

2 If you are feeling particularly inspired, you can read the entire report online at http://www.federalreserve.gov/boarddocs/press/orders/2004/20040308/attachment.pdf.

3 A discussion of HHIs can be found in the chapter on antitrust regulation in this textbook.

Congress also held hearings on the merger. In testimony before the House Committee on Financial Services, Anne Finucane, president of Northeast Bank of America, discussed the effects of the merger on employment and communities:[4] She concluded that:

- The impact of mergers on jobs depends critically on the type of merger. In an "in-market" merger, where two banks doing business in the same market join together, consolidation affects headquarters, back-office, and support operations as well as bank branches. But in "out-of-market" mergers, such as the proposed Fleet/Bank of America merger, only headquarters and back-office operations are affected. In fact, only two branches in Florida were closed as a result of the merger.
- The merged entity has cut almost 3,000 jobs in New England, but it plans to hire more employees, so that the overall reduction is around 1,800 jobs.
- Bank of America honored and exceeded all goals it had set for community lending in previous mergers. The same was true for Fleet when it merged with Bank Boston in 1999. The new entity could thus be trusted to be serious about fulfilling its pledge of $750 billion over 10 years.

COUNTERPOINT The Bank of America/Fleet Merger Is Bad for the (Regional) Economy

There were many groups that strongly disapproved of the Bank of America merger on various grounds. Some of the strongest opposition came from the New England/Mid-Atlantic region, where politicians worried about the employment impact of layoffs and community advocates worried about what would happen to lending to local communities when a strong regional bank was replaced by a bank with a more national/international focus. Andrea Nuciforo, Jr., chair of the Massachusetts State Senate Committee on Banks and Banking, presented some of his concerns to Congress at the House Financial Services Committee hearings.[5]

- The history of bank mergers in Massachusetts has been one in which promises are made that jobs will not be cut, only to be followed by layoffs and replacements of full-time workers with part-time workers. When Fleet merged with Bank Boston in 1999, almost 4,000 jobs were cut. The *Boston Globe* reported that Bank of America intended to cut 12,500 jobs nationwide, including almost 850 in Massachusetts.

- While bank mergers are bad for many low-level employees who are laid off, they tend to be very lucrative for bank executives. This is true even for those executives who leave. Fleet's CEO received $20 million when Bank Boston and Fleet merged, the president of Fleet would get $17 million in the Bank of America merger, and two executives who left the company after the merger each received $20 to $25 million in severance packages.
- The approval system for bank mergers does not hold banks accountable. Six months after promising to maintain employment levels in the merger hearings held before the Fed, Bank of America laid off workers and converted full-time positions to part-time ones.

Chris Cole, the regulatory counsel for the Independent Community Bankers of America (ICBA), a trade association representing community banks and smaller thrift institutions, also gave testimony before the House committee about the impact of bank mergers on smaller banks and bank competition.[6] ICBA is concerned about the concentration of banking in America and the effect that this concentration has on bank competition, consumers, small businesses, and communities. In his testimony, Cole reported that there is little evidence that mergers have benefited consumers through economies of scale. Large bank mergers often seem to result in higher prices to consumers. Fees charged to consumers by banks with a multistate presence tend to be significantly higher than the fees charged by banks with a single-state presence.

The ICBA recommended that large national banks like Bank of America be examined in the two years following the merger to see if they are indeed honoring their pledges and to compare their actual community spending with Fleet National Bank's programs prior to the merger.

Using Your Economics

1. How different do you think the merger of two large national banks is from the merger of a large national bank with a small community bank in terms of the issues discussed above?
2. What (not necessarily bank-related) merger did you read about most recently in the newspaper? Was that a horizontal merger (two similar companies joining together) or a vertical merger (a company merging with a supplier)? Who would benefit from that merger and why? Who would lose from that merger and why?

4 As with most nonclassified House committee hearings these days, you can find the testimony online at http://financialservices.house.gov/media/pdf/121404af.pdf.

5 State Senator Nuciforo's testimony is available online at http://financialservices.house.gov/media/pdf/121404an.pdf.

6 Mr. Cole's testimony can be read online at http://www.icba.org/advocacy/testimonydetail.cfm?ItemNumber=537&sn.ItemNumber=1699.

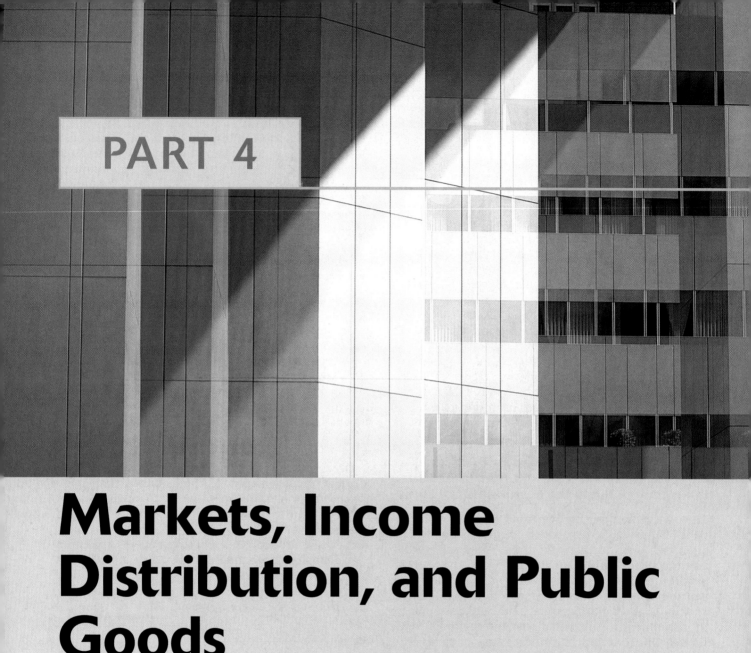

Markets, Income Distribution, and Public Goods

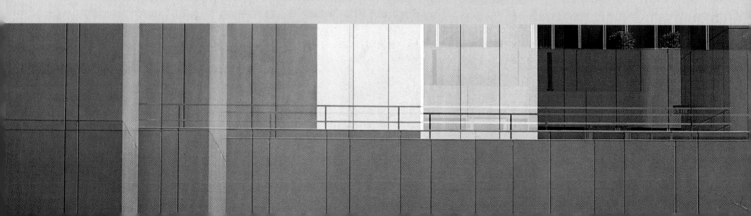

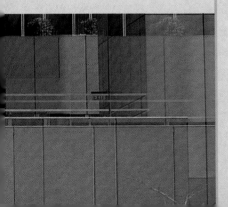

CHAPTER 13

Labor Markets

What occupation will offer the best jobs in the future? What college major will provide the best chance of getting one of those jobs? Will women's earnings catch up to or exceed men's earnings in the future?

All these questions pertain to labor markets. Labor markets are the most pervasive markets in the world, touching many more people directly than stock markets do. For most people, income from the stock market is a small fraction of the wages and salaries earned in the labor market. It is not surprising, therefore, that many beginning economics students ask their teachers more questions about labor markets, such as the ones in the first paragraph, than they do about stock markets, even though many originally choose to take economics to learn more about the stock market.

In analyzing labor markets, economists stress their similarity to other markets; this enables economists to use the standard supply and demand model. To see the analogy, consider Figure 13.1, which illustrates a typical *labor market*. It shows a typical labor supply curve and typical labor demand curve. On the vertical axis is the price of labor, or the wage. On the horizontal axis is the quantity of labor, either the number of workers or the number of hours worked. People work at many different types of jobs—physical therapists, accountants, mechanics, teachers, Web developers, judges, professional athletes—and there is a labor market for each type. The labor market diagram in Figure 13.1 could refer to any one of these particular types of labor. The first thing to remember

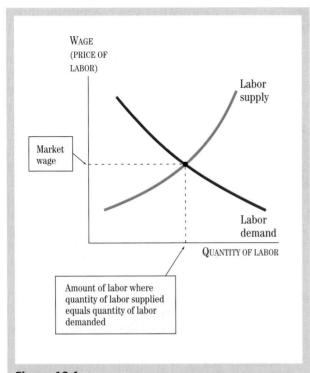

Figure 13.1
Labor Demand Curve and Labor Supply Curve
The basic economic approach to the labor market is to make an analogy with other markets. Labor is what is bought or sold on the labor market. The demand curve shows how much labor firms are willing to buy at a particular wage. The supply curve shows how much labor workers are willing to sell at a particular wage.

about the labor demand curve and the labor supply curve is that firms demand labor and people supply it. Labor—like other factors of production—is demanded by firms because it can be used to produce goods and services; the labor demand curve tells us the quantity of labor demanded by firms at each wage. The labor supply curve tells us the quantity of labor supplied by workers at each wage.

Note that the labor demand curve slopes downward and the labor supply curve slopes upward, just like other demand and supply curves. Thus, a higher wage reduces the quantity of labor demanded by firms, and a higher wage increases the quantity of labor supplied by people. Note also that the curves intersect at a particular wage and a particular quantity of labor. As with any other market, this intersection predicts the quantity of something (in this case, labor) and its price (in this case, the wage).

In this chapter, we show how the labor demand and supply model rests on the central economic idea that people make purposeful choices with limited resources and interact with other people when they make these choices. We will see that the model can be used to explain interesting facts about the labor market. We start by reviewing these facts, and we then explain why wages change over time and why there are gaps between the wages of skilled and unskilled workers, between the wages of women and men, and between the wages of union and nonunion workers. Even some of the problems caused by discrimination can be better understood using the standard tools of supply and demand.

Wage Trends

Are wages in the United States increasing? Are they increasing more rapidly or more slowly than in the recent past? In this section, we look at recent wage trends. First, we define exactly what is meant by the wage and show how it is measured.

Measuring Workers' Pay

When examining data on workers' pay, we must be specific about (1) what is included in the measure of pay, (2) whether inflation may be distorting the measure, and (3) the interval of time over which workers receive pay.

fringe benefits: compensation that a worker receives excluding direct money payments for time worked: insurance, retirement benefits, vacation time, and maternity and sick leave.

■ **Pay Includes Fringe Benefits.**   Pay for work includes not only the direct payment to a worker—whether in the form of a paycheck, currency in a pay envelope, or a deposit in the worker's bank account—but also **fringe benefits.** Fringe benefits may consist of many different items: health or life insurance, when the employer buys part or all of the insurance for the employee; retirement benefits, where the employer puts aside funds for the employee's retirement; paid time off such as vacations and sick or maternity leave; and discounts on the company's products.

In recent years, fringe benefits have become an increasingly larger share of total compensation in the United States and many other countries. In the United States, fringe benefits are now about 29 percent of total pay. In 1960, fringe benefits were only about 8 percent of total pay.

wage: the price of labor defined over a period of time worked.

The term *wage* sometimes refers to the part of the payment for work that excludes fringe benefits. For example, a minimum wage of $5.15 per hour does not usually include fringe benefits. But in most economics textbooks, the term **wage** refers to the *total* amount a firm pays workers, *including* fringe benefits. This book uses the usual textbook terminology. Thus, the wage is the price of labor.

real wage: the wage or price of labor adjusted for inflation; in contrast, the nominal wage has not been adjusted for inflation.

■ **Adjusting for Inflation: Real Wages versus Nominal Wages.**   When comparing wages in different years, it is necessary to adjust for inflation, the general increase in prices over time. The **real wage** is a measure of the wage that has been adjusted for changes in inflation. The real wage is computed by dividing the stated wage by a measure of the price of the goods and services. The most commonly used measure for this purpose is the consumer price index (CPI), which gives the price of a fixed collection, or market basket, of goods and services each year compared to some base year. For example, the CPI increased from about 1.00 in the 1994 base year to 1.27 in 2004. This means that the same goods and services that cost $100 in 1983 cost $127 in 2004. Suppose the hourly wage for a truck driver increased from $10 to $19 from 1994 to 2004, or by 90 percent; then the real wage increased from $10 (= $10/1.00) to $14.96 (= $19/1.27), or an increase of about 50 percent. Thus, because of the increase in prices, the real wage gain for the truck driver was less than the 90 percent stated wage gain would suggest. The term *nominal wage* is used to emphasize that the wage has not been corrected for inflation. The real wage is the best way to compare wages in different years.

■ **The Time Interval: Hourly versus Weekly Measures of Pay.**   It is also important to distinguish between *hourly* and *weekly* measures of workers' pay. Weekly earnings are the total amount a worker earns during a week. Clearly, weekly earnings will be less for part-time work than for full-time work (usually 40 hours per week) if hourly earnings are the same.

Because part-time work has increased and the average number of hours per week has declined in the last 30 years in the United States, weekly earnings for the average worker have increased less rapidly than hourly earnings.

Wage Trends

Having described how to measure wage trends, let's now look at what has happened to wages in the United States in recent years. Figure 13.2 shows average real hourly wages in the United States. In 2004, the average wage was about $22.23 per hour, *including* a total of about $6.48 in fringe benefits.

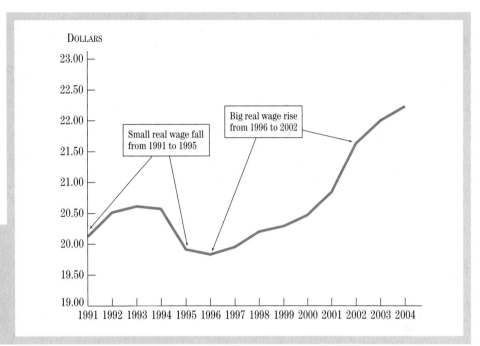

Figure 13.2
The Average Hourly Real Wage
In the United States, average real hourly wages (including fringe benefits) started to grow more rapidly in the mid-1990s. (Wages are in 1999 dollars.)

What is most noticeable in Figure 13.2 is that workers' pay began to rise more rapidly in the mid-1990s, after stagnating for several years. From 1996 to 2002, real wages rose by an average of 1.9 percent per year, a rate more than 6 times greater than the .3 percent average in the earlier years of the decade. Later in this chapter we will provide an economic explanation for this remarkable development and examine whether or not it will continue.

Figure 13.2 shows the average wage for all workers. What about the dispersion, or distribution, of wages across the population? Casual observation reveals large differences between the earnings of some people or groups and others. Sports celebrities and corporate executives are paid in the millions, many times the average wage in the United States. Workers with higher skills are paid more than workers with lower skills. College graduates earn more on average than those with a high school education or less. But there are other types of wage dispersions. For example, women on average earn less than men.

The distribution of wages across workers has also changed substantially in recent years. One development that has received much attention from economists is that the pay gap between skilled and less skilled workers has increased. In the mid-1970s, college graduates earned about 45 percent more than high school graduates. In the 1990s, this was up to about 65 percent.

Another change is in the wage difference between women and men, which, though still wide, has been narrowing in recent years. In the mid-1970s, women on average earned less than 60 cents for each dollar men earned. By the late 1990s, the gap had closed to around 76 cents.

What causes these changes? Can the economists' model of labor markets explain them? After developing the model in the next section, we will endeavor to answer these questions.

Labor Demand

labor market: the market in which individuals supply their labor time to firms in exchange for wages and salaries.

labor demand: the relationship between the quantity of labor demanded by firms and the wage.

labor supply: the relationship between the quantity of labor supplied by individuals and the wage.

derived demand: demand for an input derived from the demand for the product produced with that input.

The **labor market** consists of firms that have a demand for labor and people who supply the labor. In this section, we look at **labor demand,** the relationship between the quantity of labor demanded by firms and the wage. In the next section, we look at **labor supply,** the relationship between the quantity of labor supplied by people and the wage. We start with a single firm's demand for labor and then sum up all the firms that are in the labor market to get the market demand for labor.

In deriving a firm's labor demand, economists assume that the firm's decision about how many workers to employ, like its decision about how much of a good or service to produce, is based on profit maximization. The demand for labor is a **derived demand;** that is, it is derived from the goods or services that the firm produces with the labor. The firm sells these goods and services to consumers in product markets, which are distinct from the labor market. Labor and other factors of production are not directly demanded by consumers; the goods and services labor produces are what is demanded by consumers. Thus, the demand for labor derives from these goods and services.

A Firm's Employment Decision

Recall how the idea of profit maximization was applied to a firm's decision about the quantity to produce: If producing another ton of steel will increase a steel firm's profits—that is, if the marginal revenue from producing a ton is greater than the marginal cost of producing the ton—then the firm will produce that ton of output. However, if producing another ton of steel reduces the firm's profits, then the firm will not produce that ton.

The idea of profit maximization is applied in a very similar way to a firm's decision about how many workers to employ: If employing another worker increases the firm's profits, then the firm will employ that worker. If employing another worker reduces the firm's profits, then the firm will not employ the worker.

We have already seen that a firm produces a quantity that equates marginal revenue to marginal cost ($MR = MC$). The firm satisfies an analogous condition in deciding how much labor to employ, as we discuss next.

■ **From Marginal Product to Marginal Revenue Product.** To determine a firm's demand curve for labor, we must examine how the firm uses labor to produce

Table 13.1
Labor Input and Marginal Revenue Product at a Competitive Firm

Workers Employed Each Week (L)	Quantity Produced (Q)	Marginal Product of Labor (MP)	Price of Output (dollars) (P)	Total Revenue (dollars) (TR)	Marginal Revenue Product of Labor (dollars) (MRP)
0	0	—	100	0	—
1	17	17	100	1,700	1,700
2	31	14	100	3,100	1,400
3	42	11	100	4,200	1,100
4	51	9	100	5,100	900
5	58	7	100	5,800	700
6	63	5	100	6,300	500
7	66	3	100	6,600	300
8	68	2	100	6,800	200
9	69	1	100	6,900	100

$\dfrac{\text{Change in } Q}{\text{Change in } L}$ | P does not depend on Q. | $P \times Q$ | $\dfrac{\text{Change in } TR}{\text{Change in } L}$ or $P \times MP$

its output of goods and services. We start by assuming that the firm sells its output in a *competitive market*; that is, the firm is a *price-taker*. We also assume that the firm takes the wage as given in the labor market; in other words, the firm is hiring such a small proportion of the workers in the labor market that it cannot affect the market wage for those workers. Table 13.1 gives an example of such a competitive firm. It shows the weekly production and labor input of a firm called Getajob, which produces professional-looking job résumés in a college town. To produce a résumé, workers at Getajob talk to each of their clients—usually college seniors—give advice on what should go into the résumé, and then produce the résumé.

The first two columns of Table 13.1 show how Getajob can increase its production of résumés each week by employing more workers. This is the *production function* for the firm; it assumes that the firm has a certain amount of capital—word-processing equipment, a small office near the campus, and so on. We assume that labor is the only variable input to production in the short run, so that the cost of increasing the production of résumés depends only on the additional cost of employing more workers. Observe that the *marginal product (MP) of labor*—which we defined in Chapter 6 as the change in the quantity produced when one additional unit of labor is employed—declines as more workers are employed. In other words, there is a diminishing marginal product of labor, or diminishing return to labor: As more workers are hired with office space and equipment fixed, each additional worker adds less and less to production. For example, the first worker employed can produce 17 résumés a week, but if there are already 8 workers at Getajob, hiring a ninth worker will increase production by only 1 résumé.

Suppose that the market price for producing this type of résumé service is $100 per résumé, as shown in the fourth column of Table 13.1. Because Getajob is assumed to be a *competitive firm*, it cannot affect this price. Then, the total revenue of the firm for each amount of labor employed can be computed by multiplying the

marginal product of labor: the change in production due to a one-unit increase in labor input. (Ch. 6)

marginal revenue product of labor: the change in total revenue due to a one-unit increase in labor input.

> **Wait.** Before you read any further, make sure you can explain the difference between marginal product (*MP*) and marginal revenue product (*MRP*).

price (*P*) times the quantity produced (*Q*) with each amount of labor (*L*). This is shown in the next-to-last column. For example, total revenue with *L* = 3 workers employed is *P* = $100 times *Q* = 42, or $4,200.

The last column of Table 13.1 shows the **marginal revenue product (*MRP*) of labor.** *The marginal revenue product of labor is defined as the change in total revenue when one additional unit of labor is employed.* For example, the marginal revenue product of labor from hiring a third worker is the total revenue with 3 workers ($4,200) minus the total revenue with 2 workers ($3,100), or $4,200 − $3,100 = $1,100. The marginal revenue product of labor is used to find the demand curve for labor, as we will soon see.

What is the difference between the marginal product (*MP*) and the marginal revenue product (*MRP*)? The marginal product is the increase in the *quantity produced* when labor is increased by one unit. The marginal revenue product is the increase in *total revenue* when labor is increased by one unit. For a *competitive firm* taking the market price as given, the marginal revenue product (*MRP*) can be calculated by multiplying the marginal product (*MP*) by the price of output (*P*). For example, the marginal product when the third worker is hired is 11 résumés; thus, the additional revenue that the third worker will generate for the firm is $100 per résumé times 11, or $1,100.

Observe in Table 13.1 that the marginal revenue product of labor declines as more workers are employed. This is because the marginal product of labor declines.

■ The Marginal Revenue Product of Labor Equals the Wage (*MRP* = *W*).

Now we are almost ready to derive the firm's demand curve for labor. Suppose first that the wage for workers with the type of skills Getajob needs in order to produce résumés is $600 per week (for example, $15 per hour for 40 hours). Then, hiring 1 worker certainly makes sense because the marginal revenue product of labor is $1,700, or much greater than the $600 wage cost of hiring the worker. How about 2 workers? The marginal revenue product from employing a second worker is $1,400, still greater than $600, so it makes sense to hire a second worker. Continuing this way, we see that the *firm will hire a total of 5 workers when the wage is $600 per week*, because hiring a sixth worker would result in a marginal revenue product of only $500, less than the $600 per week wage.

Thus, if a firm maximizes profits, it will hire the largest number of workers for which the marginal revenue product of labor is greater than the wage; if fractional units of labor input (for example, hours rather than weeks of work) are possible, then the firm will keep hiring workers until the marginal revenue product of labor exactly equals the wage. Thus, we have derived a key rule of profit maximization: Firms will hire workers up to the point where the *marginal revenue product of labor equals the wage.*

The rule that the marginal revenue product of labor equals the wage can be written in symbols as *MRP* = *W*.

Looking for Work
These day workers are job hunting for construction clean-up work at a downtown street corner in Austin, Texas. The workers signal their availability by showing up at the street corner; labor contractors will come by and hire the number of workers they need that day.

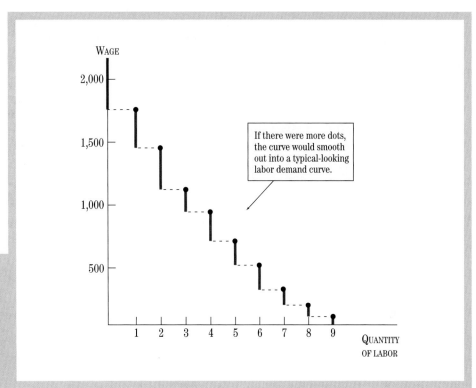

Figure 13.3
Determining a Firm's Demand Curve for Labor
The black dots are exactly the same as the marginal revenue product of labor in Table 13.1. The red line indicates the quantity of labor demanded at each wage.

The Firm's Derived Demand for Labor

Now, to find the demand curve for labor, we need to determine how many workers the firm will hire at *different* wages. We know that Getajob will hire 5 workers if the wage is $600 per week. What if the wage is $800 per week? Then the firm will hire only 4 workers; the marginal revenue product of the fifth worker ($700) is now less than the wage ($800), so the firm will not be maximizing its profits if it hires 5 workers. Thus we have shown that a higher wage reduces the quantity of labor demanded by the firm. What if the wage is lower than $600? Suppose the wage is $250 a week, for example. Then the firm will hire 7 workers. Thus, a lower wage increases the quantity of labor demanded by the firm.

Figure 13.3 shows how to determine the entire demand curve for labor. It shows the wage on the vertical axis and the quantity of labor on the horizontal axis. The plotted points are the marginal revenue products from Table 13.1. To find the demand curve, we ask how much labor the firm would employ at each wage. Starting with a high wage, we reduce the wage gradually, asking at each wage how much labor the firm would employ. At a weekly wage of $2,000, the marginal revenue product is less than the wage, so it does not make sense to hire any workers. Therefore, the quantity demanded is zero at wages above $2,000. At a weekly wage of $1,500, it makes sense to hire one worker, and so on. As the wage is gradually lowered, the quantity of labor demanded rises, as shown by the red line in Figure 13.3. The step-like downward-sloping curve is the labor demand curve. There would be more black dots and the curve would be very smooth if we measured work in fractions of a week rather than in whole weeks.

Table 13.2
Labor Input and Marginal Revenue Product for a Firm with Power to Affect the Market Price

Workers Employed Each Week (L)	Quantity Produced (Q)	Marginal Product of Labor (dollars) (MP)	Price of Output (dollars) (P)	Total Revenue (dollars) (TR)	Marginal Revenue Product of Labor (dollars) (MRP)
0	0	—	100	0	—
1	17	17	92	1,564	1,564
2	31	14	85	2,635	1,071
3	42	11	79	3,318	683
4	51	9	75	3,825	507
5	58	7	71	4,118	293
6	63	5	69	4,347	229
7	66	3	67	4,422	75
8	68	2	66	4,488	66
9	69	1	65	4,485	−3

$$\frac{\text{Change in } Q}{\text{Change in } L}$$

P declines with Q.

$P \times Q$

$$\frac{\text{Change in } TR}{\text{Change in } L}$$

Observe in Figure 13.3 that a firm's demand curve for labor is completely determined by the firm's marginal revenue product of labor. We have shown why the demand curve for labor is downward-sloping: because the marginal revenue product of labor curve is downward-sloping. A higher wage will reduce the quantity of labor demanded, and a lower wage will increase the quantity of labor demanded; these are *movements along* the downward-sloping labor demand curve. We also can explain why a firm's labor demand curve would *shift*. For example, if the price (P) of the good (résumés) rises—perhaps because the demand curve for résumés shifts outward—then the marginal revenue product of labor ($MRP = P \times MP$) will rise and the demand curve for labor will shift outward. Similarly, a rise in the marginal product of labor (MP) will shift the labor demand curve outward. On the other hand, a decline in the price (P) or a decline in the marginal product (MP) will shift the labor demand curve to the left.

■ **What If the Firm Has Market Power?** This approach to deriving the demand curve for labor works equally well for the case of a firm that is not a price-taker but is instead a monopoly or a monopolistic competitor. Table 13.2 shows an example of such a firm. The key difference between the firm in Table 13.1 and the firm in Table 13.2 is in the column for the price. Rather than facing a constant price for its output and thus a horizontal demand curve, this firm faces a downward-sloping demand curve: It can increase the quantity of résumés demanded by lowering its price. For example, if Getajob's résumés are slightly differentiated from those of other résumé producers in town, then the demand curve that Getajob faces when selling résumés may be downward-sloping.

Once we observe that the price and output are inversely related, we can continue just as we did with the competitive firm. Again, total revenue is equal to the price times the quantity, and marginal revenue product is the change in total revenue as 1 more worker is hired. Again, the marginal revenue product declines as more workers are hired, as shown in the last column of Table 13.2. However, now the marginal

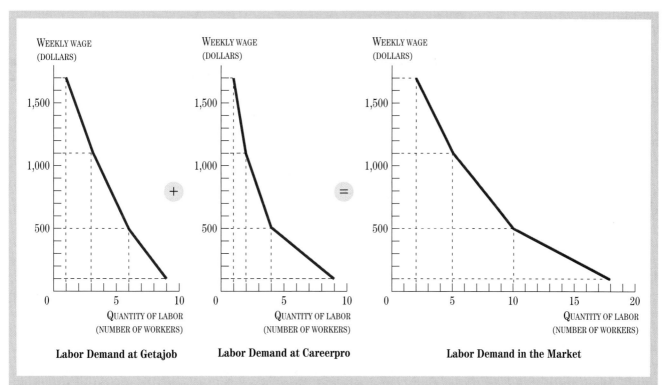

**Figure 13.4
Summing Firms' Demands to
Get the Labor Market Demand
Curve**

The labor demand curve in the market is obtained by summing the quantities of labor demanded by all the firms at each wage.

revenue product declines more sharply as more workers are employed, and it even turns negative. The reason is that as more workers are hired and more output is produced and sold, the price of output must fall. This cuts into revenue, even though output increases, because the lower price on items previously sold reduces revenue. But the principle of labor demand is the same: Firms hire up to the point where the marginal revenue product of labor equals the wage. The marginal revenue product determines the labor demand curve.

In the case of a firm with market power, the simple relationship $MRP = P \times MP$ no longer holds, however, because the firm does not take the market price as given. Instead, we replace the price (P) by the more general marginal revenue (MR) in that relationship. This implies that the marginal revenue product is equal to the marginal revenue (MR) times the marginal product (MP). The relationship $MRP = MR \times MP$ holds for all firms, whether they have market power or not. Only for a competitive firm is $MR = P$.

■ **Market Demand for Labor.** To get the demand for labor in the market as a whole, we must add up the labor demand curves for all the firms demanding workers in the labor market. At each wage, we sum the total quantity of labor demanded by all firms in the market; this is illustrated in Figure 13.4 for the case of two firms producing résumés. The two curves on the left are labor demand curves for two résumé-producing firms, Getajob and Careerpro. (The curves are smoothed out compared with Figure 13.3 so that they are easier to see.) The process of summing individual

Table 13.3
Marginal Cost and the Production Decision at Getajob

Workers Employed Each Week (L)	Quantity Produced (Q)	Variable Costs (dollars) (VC)	Marginal Cost (dollars) (MC)
0	0	0	0
1	17	600	35
2	31	1,200	43
3	42	1,800	55
4	51	2,400	67
5	58	3,000	86
6	63	3,600	120
7	66	4,200	200
8	68	4,800	300
9	69	5,400	600

$600 wage × L

Change in VC / Change in Q

firms' demands for labor to get the market demand is analogous to summing individual demand curves for goods to get the market demand curve for goods. At each wage, we sum the labor demand at all the firms to get the market demand.

A Comparison of $MRP = W$ with $MC = P$

Note that a firm's decision to employ workers is closely tied to its decision about how much to produce. We have emphasized the former decision here and the latter decision in earlier chapters. To draw attention to this connection, we show in Table 13.3 the marginal cost when the wage is $600. Marginal cost is equal to the change in variable costs divided by the change in quantity produced. Variable costs are the wage times the amount of labor employed.

Now, consider the quantity of output the firm would produce if it compared price and marginal cost as discussed in earlier chapters. If the price of output is $100, the firm will produce 58 résumés, the highest level of output for which price is greater than marginal cost. This is exactly what we found using the $MRP = W$ rule, because 58 units of output requires 5 workers. Recall that employing 5 workers is the profit-maximizing labor choice when the wage is $600.

If the profit-maximizing firm could produce fractional units, then it would set marginal cost exactly equal to price ($MC = P$). The resulting production decision would be exactly the same as that implied by the rule that the marginal revenue product of labor equals the wage.

REVIEW

- The demand for labor is a relationship between the quantity of labor a firm will employ and the wage.

- The demand for labor is a derived demand because it is derived from the goods and services produced by labor. When the quantity of labor is the decision variable, the firm maximizes profits by setting the marginal revenue product of labor equal to the wage.

- When the wage rises, the quantity of labor demanded by firms declines. When the wage falls, the quantity of labor demanded increases. These are movements along the labor demand curve.

- When the price of a commodity produced by a particular type of labor rises, the demand curve for that type of labor shifts outward.

Labor Supply

We now focus on *labor supply*. The market labor supply curve is the sum of many people's individual labor supply curves. The decision about whether to work and how much to work depends very much on individual circumstances.

Work versus Two Alternatives: Home Work and Leisure

Consider a person deciding how much to work—either how many hours a week or how many weeks a year. As with any economic decision, we need to consider the alternative to work. Economists have traditionally called the alternative *leisure*, although many of the activities that make up the alternative to work are not normally thought of as leisure. These activities include "home work," like painting the house or caring for children at home, as well as pure leisure time, such as simply talking to friends on the telephone, going bowling, or hiking in the country. The price of leisure is the opportunity cost of not working, that is, the wage. If a person's marginal benefit from more leisure is greater than the wage, then the person will choose more leisure. The decision to consume more leisure is thus like the decision to consume more of any other good. This may seem strange, but the analogy works quite well in practice.

■ **Effects of Wage Changes: Income and Substitution Effects.** Like the decision to consume a commodity, the decision to work can be analyzed with the concepts of the *substitution effect* and the *income effect*.

The *substitution effect* says that the higher the wage, the more attractive work will seem compared to its alternatives: home work or leisure. A higher wage makes work more rewarding compared to the alternatives. Think about your own work opportunities. You may have many nonwork choices, including studying, sleeping, and watching TV. Although you enjoy these activities, suppose that the wage paid for part-time student employment triples. Then you might decide to work an extra hour each day. The sacrifice—less time to study, sleep, watch TV, and so on—will be worth the higher wage. The inducement to work a little more because of the higher wage is the substitution effect. The quantity of labor supplied tends to increase when the wage rises because of the substitution effect.

The *income effect*, as in the demand for goods, reflects the effect of the price change on your real income. For example, if the wage for student employment triples, and you are already working, you might think that you can work less. With a higher wage, you can earn the same amount by working less. You may even have more money to do things other than work. Note that the income effect works in the opposite direction from the substitution effect: The quantity of labor supplied tends to decrease, rather than increase, when the wage rises because of the income effect.

■ **The Shape of Supply Curves.** Because the substitution effect and the income effect work in opposite directions, the labor supply curve can slope either upward or downward. The supply curve slopes upward if the substitution effect dominates but slopes downward if the income effect dominates. Several possibilities for labor supply curves are illustrated in Figure 13.5.

Moreover, the same supply curve may slope upward for some range of wages and downward for another range. For example, at high wage levels—when people earn enough to take long vacations—the income effect may dominate. At lower wages, the substitution effect may be dominant. This would then result in a **backward-bending labor supply curve,** as shown in Figure 13.6.

This derivation of the labor supply curve may seem unrealistic. After all, the workweek is 40 hours for many jobs; you may not have much choice about the number of hours per week. In fact, the sensitivity of the quantity of labor supplied to the wage is probably small for many workers. But economists have shown that the effect is large for some workers, and therefore it is useful to distinguish one worker's supply curve from another's.

In a family with two adults and children, for example, one of the adults may already have a job and the other may be choosing between working at home and working outside the home. This decision may be very sensitive to the wage and perhaps the cost of child care or of consuming more prepared meals. In fact, the increased number of women working outside the home may be due to the increased opportunities and wages for women. The increase in the wage induces workers to work more in the labor market. Economists have observed a fairly strong wage effect on the amount women work, as illustrated in the Reading the News About box on page 345.

One also needs to distinguish between the effects of a temporary change in the wage and a more permanent change. Empirical studies show that the quantity of labor supplied rises more in response to a temporary increase in the wage than to

backward-bending labor supply curve: the situation in which the income effect outweighs the substitution effect of an increase in the wage at higher levels of income, causing the labor supply curve to bend back and take on a negative slope.

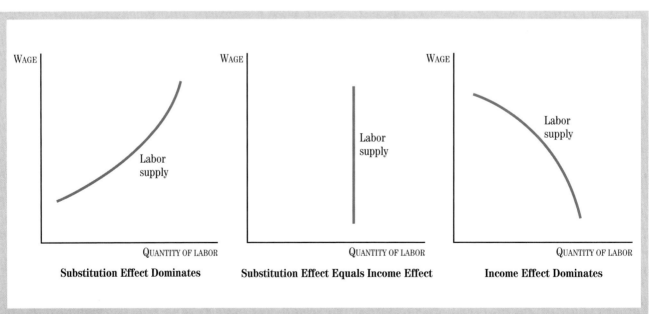

Substitution Effect Dominates   Substitution Effect Equals Income Effect   Income Effect Dominates

Figure 13.5
Three Labor Supply Curves

The three curves differ in the relative strength of the income and substitution effects. The labor supply curve on the left slopes upward because the substitution effect is stronger than the income effect. For the curve on the right, the income effect is stronger than the substitution effect. For the vertical curve in the middle, the two effects are the same.

As more and more families have two potential workers, the decision about labor supply has become a household decision. The following newspaper article from the *San Jose Mercury News* (February 14, 1993) tells a story that pairs the human side of the decision with the economic side. According to the calculations in the table, the net earnings from work—after taxes and all other expenses—may be very small in some cases.

Does It Pay to Stay Home?

By Mark Schwanhausser
Mercury News staff writer

For Yolanda Achanzar, going to work was like listening to an old-fashioned cash register ring. She'd drop off her two toddlers with a sitter (*ka-ching*: $29 a day). She'd commute to the office in her Mercury Villager (*ka-ching*: $8). She'd dig into her purse for breakfast and lunch (*ka-ching*: $10). And she'd dress up for work (*ka-ching*: $5 a day, $8.50 if she snagged her hose, $12.50 if you include the dry-cleaning bills). "If you add all that up," she said, "it's just not worth it, vs. the time you could have spent with your children, loving them, rearing them, nurturing them."

And so, although she loved her job and co-workers, although her $25,000 paycheck accounted for nearly 40 percent of her family's total income, she chucked her job Friday to stay home with 27-month-old Marissa and 14-month-old Jordan. She felt she simply couldn't afford her job any longer.

Achanzar and her husband, Gil, are among the millions of American parents who agonize trying to discover the proper mix for a family's financial welfare, the children's care and the parents' careers. For them, money is an issue—and something has to give.

For many parents, the decision starts with a bottom-line analysis of dollars in and dollars out. But next comes the long-term equation that consists of nothing but variables. How much is it worth to stay home with the kids? What lifestyle will we have?

Many parents finally decide it doesn't pay to have two incomes any longer, once they account for the cost of child care and other work-related expenses. Here are budget comparisons for two hypothetical couples trying to decide if the lower-paid spouse should stay home with their one child—and the fiscal impact the decision will have on their current standard of living.

	Both spouses work	One stays home	Both spouses work	One stays home
Income				
Spouse A	$35,600	$35,600	$67,000	$67,000
Spouse B	24,000	0	35,000	0
Total	**59,600**	**35,600**	**102,000**	**67,000**
Taxes[1]				
Taxable income	46,700	22,700	89,100	54,100
Federal	7,949	2,929	19,900	10,091
State	1,938	383	5,866	2,564
Social Security	4,559	2,723	7,091	4,413
Total taxes	**14,446**	**6,035**	**32,857**	**17,068**
Work expenses[2]				
Child care	5,000	0	10,000	0
Transportation	1,500	0	2,250	0
Meals	1,250	0	2,000	0
Wardrobe	900	0	1,200	0
Dry cleaning	360	0	500	0
Total expenses	**9,010**	**0**	**15,950**	**0**
Total income	59,600	35,600	102,000	67,000
Total taxes	14,446	6,035	32,857	17,068
Total expenses	9,010	0	15,950	0
Left to spend	**$36,144**	**$29,565**	**$53,193**	**$49,932**
Decreases in spendable cash		**$6,579**		**$3,261**
Percentage change		**18%**		**6%**

[1]Includes $480 federal child-care credit and variable state credit.
[2]Work expenses are for the lower-paid spouse only. Although that spouse's work expenses would be erased by staying home, bills at home would rise and should be included in a full-cost analysis.

Source: San Jose Mercury News, February 14, 1993

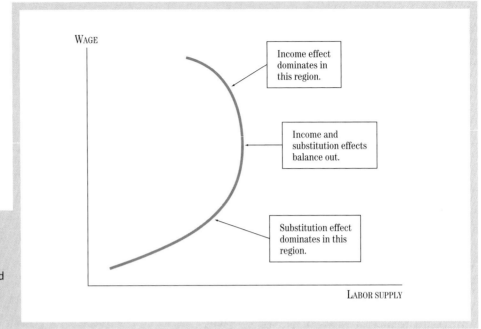

Figure 13.6
Backward-Bending Labor
Supply Curve
A person may have a labor supply curve that is positively sloped
for a low wage, is steeper for a
higher wage, and then bends
backward for a still higher wage.

a permanent increase. What's the explanation? Consider an example. If you have a
special one-time opportunity tomorrow to earn $100 an hour rather than your usual
$6 an hour, you are likely to put off some leisure for one day; the substitution effect
dominates. But if you are lucky enough to land a lifetime job at $100 an hour rather
than $6 an hour, you may decide to work fewer hours and have more leisure time; the
income effect dominates.

This difference between temporary and permanent changes helps explain the
dramatic decline in the average hours worked per week in the United States as wages
have risen over the last century. These are more permanent changes, for which the
income effect dominates.

Work versus Another Alternative: Getting Human Capital

The skills of a worker depend in part on how much schooling and training the
worker has. The decision to obtain these skills—to finish high school and attend a
community college or obtain a four-year college degree—is much like the choice
between work and leisure. In fact, an important decision for many young people is
whether to go to work or to finish high school; if they have finished high school, the
choice is whether to go to work or to go to college.

Economists view the education and training that raise skills and productivity as
a form of *investment*, a decision to spend funds or time on something now because it
pays off in the future. Continuing the analogy, an investment in a college education
raises the amount of **human capital**—a person's knowledge and skills—in the same
way that the investment in a factory or machine by a business firm raises physical
capital. Figure 13.7 demonstrates the kind of difference this investment can make.

The decision to invest in human capital can be approached like any other economic choice. Suppose the decision is whether Angela should go to college or get a

human capital: a person's
accumulated knowledge and
skills.

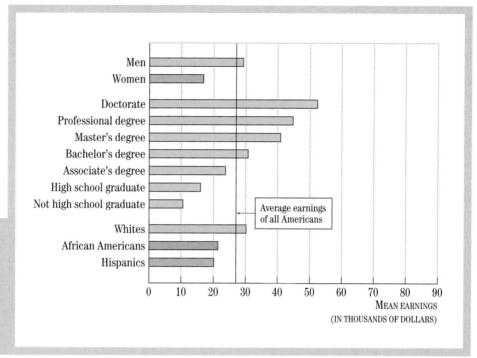

Figure 13.7
Higher Education and Economic Success
According to this chart, education pays off in terms of earnings, with doctorate degree holders earning the most, followed by workers with professional and master's degrees.

job. If she does not go to college, she saves on tuition and can begin earning an income right away. If she goes to college, she pays tuition and forgoes the opportunity to earn income at a full-time job. However, if Angela is like most people, college will improve her skills and land her a better job at higher pay. The returns on college education are the extra pay. Angela ought to go to college—invest in human capital—if the returns are greater than the cost.

on-the-job training: the building of the skills of a firm's employees while they work for the firm.

People can increase their skills at work as well as in school. In fact, **on-the-job training** is one of the most important ways in which workers' productivity increases. On-the-job training can be either *firm-specific*, where the skills are useful only at one firm, or *general-purpose*, where the skills are transferable to other jobs.

REVIEW

- The labor supply curve can be viewed as the outcome of an individual's choice between work and some other activity, whether home work, schooling, or leisure.

- There is both a substitution effect and an income effect on the labor supply. The substitution effect is the increased attractiveness of work relative to its alternative as the wage rises. The income effect is the increased attractiveness of leisure because there is more to spend when the wage rises. In some situations the income effect dominates. In other situations the substitution effect dominates.

- Human capital is the knowledge and skills that a person accumulates from going to school and receiving on-the-job training. The return on human capital has increased in recent years.

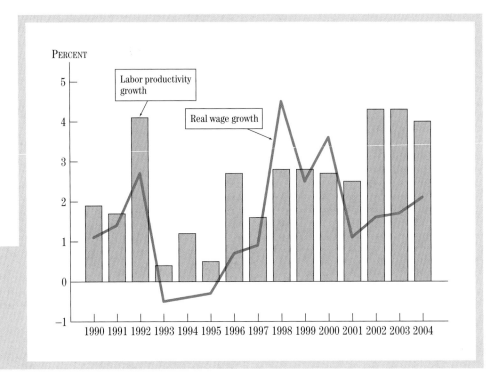

Figure 13.8
Labor Productivity Growth and Real Wage Growth
Labor productivity growth is closely related to the growth of real wages, much as would be predicted by the labor supply and demand model.

Explaining Wage Differences

When we combine the labor demand and labor supply curves derived in the previous two sections, we get the model of the labor market summarized in Figure 13.1. The model predicts that the wage in the labor market will be at the intersection of the supply and demand curves. The point of intersection, where the quantity of labor supplied equals the quantity of labor demanded, is the **labor market equilibrium.**

labor market equilibrium: the situation in which the quantity of labor supplied equals the quantity of labor demanded.

Labor Productivity

The model of the labor market predicts that the wage equals the marginal revenue product. If the marginal product of labor employed at a firm increases, then the model predicts that the wage will rise. Suppose the marginal product of labor rises for the economy as a whole; then wages should also rise. Is this what occurs in reality?

■ **The Wage Boom and Labor Productivity Boom.** In Figure 13.8, the line graph shows the percentage by which real wages have increased each year since 1990, using the wage data we examined earlier in this chapter. Note that wages rose rapidly starting in 1996. The bars in Figure 13.8 show output per hour of work in the same period. Output per hour of work is called **labor productivity** and is a good indication of trends in the marginal product of labor on average in the United States. The labor market model predicts that wages in the United States should increase when labor productivity increases. Do they?

labor productivity: output per hour of work.

Figure 13.8 shows a strong correlation between labor productivity and the real wage. Note that the change in the labor productivity trend occurred in the mid-

Does Productivity or Compensating Differentials Explain the Academic Wage Gap?

People with Ph.D.'s who teach or do research at colleges and universities are paid 10 percent less than people with Ph.D.'s who work for government and 20 percent less than people with Ph.D.'s who work for business firms. Why does the academic wage gap exist?

There are two possibilities: (1) People with Ph.D.'s who work in business and government are more skilled and more productive, or (2) people with Ph.D.'s who work in business and government are paid a compensating wage differential because the job is less pleasant. (They don't have the pleasure of teaching students or the flexible academic hours.)

How can we tell which is the right explanation? Looking at what happens to people with Ph.D.'s when they move provides an answer. If their wages increase when they move to a nonacademic job, then compensating wage differentials rather than productivity differences is the correct explanation.

The following table shows the average salary increases between 1985 and 1987 of people with Ph.D.'s who either (1) did not move, (2) moved to another college or university, or (3) moved to business or government. The salary increases are largest for those who left academia. For example, the average salary increase for engineering Ph.D.'s nearly doubled when they moved from academia to work in a business firm or government. This indicates that the differences are due not to skill but to compensating wage differentials.

This is one of the rare cases in which economists have actually been able to obtain data that distinguish compensating wage differentials from productivity or other explanations for wage differences. But if the case is representative, compensating wage differentials may play a big part in wage dispersion.

Largest increase for every type of Ph.D.

Increase in Salary (dollars)

	Did Not Move	Moved to Another College	Left Academia
Physical science	7,303	10,216	15,330
Mathematical science	6,523	9,716	15,727
Environmental science	6,292	4,688	11,333
Life science	5,870	6,710	8,115
Psychology	5,920	6,559	10,371
Social science	5,796	7,687	12,485
Engineering	7,294	6,724	14,025
Humanities	5,042	5,380	8,204

Source: Adapted from Albert Rees, "The Salaries of Ph.D.'s in Academia and Elsewhere," *Journal of Economic Perspectives*, Winter 1993. Reprinted with permission.

1990s, at almost the same time as the change in the trend of real wage growth. The close empirical association between wages and labor productivity that is evident in this chart suggests that labor productivity is a key explanation of wage changes over time.

■ **Wage Dispersion and Productivity.** Can labor productivity also explain wage differences between people? If the marginal product of labor increases with additional skills from investment in human capital, then, on average, wages for people with a college education should be higher than those for people without a college education. Hence, productivity differences are an explanation for the wage gap between workers who do not receive education beyond high school and those who are college educated.

Although human capital differences undoubtedly explain some of the dispersion of wages, some people have argued that the greater productivity of college-educated workers is due not to the skills learned in college but to the fact that colleges screen applicants. For example, people who are not highly motivated or who have difficulty communicating have trouble getting into college. Hence, college graduates would earn higher wages even if they learned nothing in college. If this is so, a college degree *signals* to employers that the graduate is likely to be a productive worker.

Unfortunately, it is difficult to distinguish the skill-enhancing from the signaling effects of college. Certainly your grades and your major in college affect the kind of job you get and how much you earn, suggesting that more than signaling is important to employers. In reality, signaling and human capital both probably have a role to play in explaining the higher wages of college graduates.

Whether it is signaling or human capital that explains the higher wages of college graduates, labor productivity differences are still the underlying explanation for the wage differences. However, labor productivity does not explain everything about wages. Consider now some other factors.

Compensating Wage Differentials

Not all jobs that require workers with the same level of skill and productivity are alike. Some jobs are more pleasant, less stressful, or safer than other jobs. For example, the skills necessary to be a deep-sea salvage diver and a lifeguard are similar—good at swimming, good judgment, and good health. But the risks—such as decompression sickness—for a deep-sea diver are greater and the opportunity for social interaction is less. If the pay for both jobs were the same, say, $10 per hour, most people would prefer the lifeguard job.

High Wages for High Work
Compensating wage differentials are illustrated by the relatively high wages paid to someone for performing risky jobs such as window washing on a skyscraper.

But this situation could not last. With many lifeguard applicants, the beach authorities would be unlikely to raise the wage above $10 and might even try to cut the wage if budget cuts occurred. With few applicants, the deep-sea salvage companies would have to raise the wage. After a while, it would not be surprising to see the wage for lifeguards at $9 per hour and the wage for deep-sea divers at $12 per hour; these wages would be labor market equilibrium wages in the supply and demand model for lifeguards and deep-sea divers. Thus, we would be in a situation where the skills of the workers were identical but their wages were much different. The higher-risk job pays a higher wage than the lower-risk job.

Situations in which wages differ because of the characteristics of the job are widespread. Hazardous duty pay is common in the military. Wage data show that night-shift workers in manufacturing plants are paid wages that are about 3 percent higher on average than those of daytime workers, presumably to compensate for the inconvenience.

compensating wage differential: a difference in wages for people with similar skills based on some characteristic of the job, such as riskiness, discomfort, or convenience of the time schedule.

Such differences in wages are called **compensating wage differentials.** They are an important source of differences in wages that are not based on marginal product. With compensating differentials, workers may seek out riskier jobs in order to be paid more.

Discrimination

As noted earlier, the gap in earnings between women and men has been narrowing in recent years. Women now make close to 80 percent of the wages of men, whereas 50 years ago, women earned only about 50 percent of the wages of men. The gap is also closing for blacks and whites, although not quite as quickly. In the 1950s, the ratio of wages of blacks to that of whites was about 60 percent; it has narrowed to about 70 percent since then. Wage differences between white and minority workers and between men and women are an indication of discrimination if the wage differences cannot be explained by differences in marginal product or other factors unrelated to race or gender.

■ **Wage Differences for Workers with the Same Marginal Products.** Some, but not all, of these differences may be attributed to differences in human capital. The wage gaps between blacks and whites and between men and women with comparable education and job experience are smaller than the ratios in the preceding paragraph. But a gap still exists.

Discrimination on the basis of race or gender prejudice can explain such differences. This is shown in Figure 13.9. *Discrimination* can be defined in the supply and demand model as not hiring women or minority workers even though their marginal product is just as high as that of other workers, or paying a lower wage to such workers even though their marginal product is equal to that of other workers. Either way, discrimination can be interpreted as a leftward shift of the labor demand curve for women or minority workers. As shown in Figure 13.9, this reduces the wages and employment for those discriminated against.

■ **Competitive Markets and Discrimination.** An important implication of this supply and demand interpretation of the effects of discrimination is that competition among firms may reduce it. This is an advantage of competitive markets that should be added to the advantages already mentioned. Why might competition reduce discrimination? Because firms in competitive markets that discriminate will lose out to firms that do not. Much like firms that do not keep their costs as low as other firms, they will eventually be driven out of the industry.

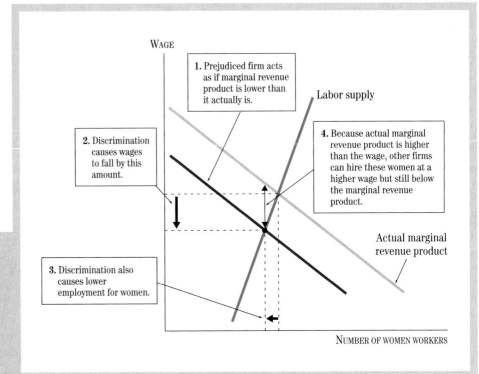

WAGE

1. Prejudiced firm acts as if marginal revenue product is lower than it actually is.

Labor supply

2. Discrimination causes wages to fall by this amount.

4. Because actual marginal revenue product is higher than the wage, other firms can hire these women at a higher wage but still below the marginal revenue product.

Actual marginal revenue product

3. Discrimination also causes lower employment for women.

NUMBER OF WOMEN WORKERS

Figure 13.9
Discrimination in the Labor Market
Firms that discriminate against women pay them a wage that is less than their marginal product. But this gives other firms an opportunity to recruit workers from prejudiced firms by paying higher wages.

If markets are competitive, then firms that discriminate against women or minorities will pay them a wage lower than their marginal revenue product, as shown in Figure 13.9. In this situation, any profit-maximizing firm will see that it can raise its profits by paying these workers a little more—but still less than their marginal revenue product—and hiring them away from firms that discriminate. As long as the discriminating firms pay less than the marginal product of labor, other firms can hire the workers and raise profits. Remember that a firm will increase profits if the wage is less than the marginal revenue product. But eventually competition for workers will raise wages until the wages are equal to the marginal products of labor.

This description of events relies on a market's being competitive. If firms have monopoly power or entry is limited, so that economic profits are not driven to zero, then discrimination can continue to exist. That discrimination effects on wages do persist may be a sign that there is market power and barriers to entry. In any case, there are laws against discrimination that give those who are discriminated against for race, gender, or other reasons the right to sue those who are discriminating.

Some laws have been proposed requiring that employers pay the same wage to workers with comparable skills. Such proposals are called *comparable worth proposals*. The intent of such proposals is to bring the wages of different groups into line. However, such laws might force wages to be the same in situations where wages are different for reasons other than discrimination, such as compensating wage differentials. This would lead to shortages or surpluses, much as price ceilings or price floors in any market do. In the lifeguard/deep-sea diver example, a law requiring employers to pay lifeguards and deep-sea divers the same wage would cause a surplus of lifeguards and a shortage of deep-sea divers. For example, suppose that with comparable worth legislation, the wage for both lifeguards and deep-sea divers was $10 per hour. Because the labor market equilibrium wage for lifeguards, $9 per hour, is less

Hopeful parents

than $10 per hour, there would be a surplus of lifeguards: More people would be willing to be lifeguards than employers would be willing to hire. And because the labor market equilibrium wage for deep-sea divers, $12 per hour, is greater than $10, there would be a shortage of deep-sea divers: Firms would be willing to hire more deep-sea divers than the number of deep-sea divers willing to dive for the $10 per hour wage.

Minimum Wage Laws

Another example in which the government stipulates a wage that employers must pay is *minimum wage legislation*, which is common in many countries. The minimum wage sets a floor for the price of labor. Because wages differ due to skills, the impact of the minimum wage depends on the skills of the workers. Figure 13.10 shows what the supply and demand model predicts about the impact of the minimum wage on skilled and unskilled workers. A labor market for unskilled workers is shown on the left; the minimum wage is shown to be above the labor market equilibrium wage. There is thus a surplus, or unemployment: The quantity of labor demanded by firms at the minimum wage is less than the quantity of labor workers are willing to supply at that wage. A labor market for skilled workers is shown on the right: The minimum wage is shown to be below the market equilibrium wage for skilled workers. Thus

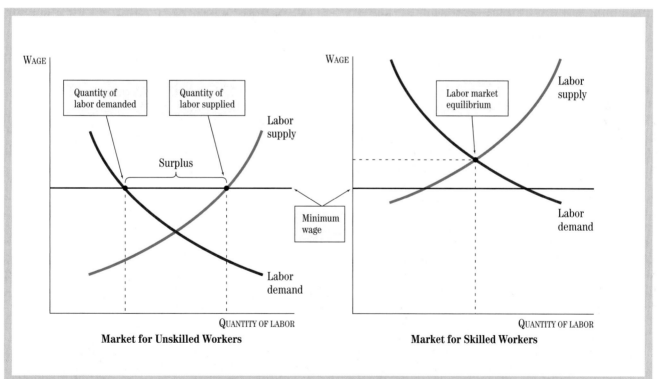

Figure 13.10
Effects of a Minimum Wage

If there are government restrictions on wages that hold them above the labor market equilibrium, then a surplus (unemployment) will arise. Unemployment is more likely for unskilled workers because the equilibrium wage is lower.

a minimum wage at the level shown in the graph would not cause unemployment among skilled workers.

Therefore, the labor supply and demand model predicts that the minimum wage is a cause of unemployment among less skilled or less experienced workers, and thereby ends up hurting some of the least well off in society. This is why many economists are concerned about the impact of minimum wage legislation.

In interpreting this result, remember that the supply and demand model is a *model* of reality, not reality itself. Although the model explains much about wages, its predictions about minimum wage laws should be verified like the predictions of any other economic model. In fact, labor economists have been trying to check the predictions of the model for the minimum wage for many years. Some, such as Jacob Mincer of Columbia University, have provided evidence that the predicted minimum wage impact is verified in real-world labor markets. Others, such as David Card of the University of California at Berkeley and Alan Krueger of Princeton University, have examined the effects of different minimum wage laws on different states on low-skilled fast-food workers and have not found evidence of the predicted impact on unemployment. David Neumark of Michigan State University and William Wascher of the Federal Reserve have disputed Card's and Krueger's data and found that the minimum wage enacted in those same states did have a negative effect on employment. Because of this controversy, testing the supply and demand model of labor has been a hot topic for the past twenty years.

REVIEW

- Labor productivity differences are an explanation for some of the differences in wages.

- Compensating wage differentials occur because some jobs are more attractive than others. They are another source of wage disparity.

- Discrimination reduces the wages of those who are discriminated against below their marginal revenue product.

- Data suggest that the wage effects of discrimination continue to exist but have declined in recent years. The female–male wage gap and the black–white wage gap have declined but are still significant.

- Competition can be a force against the effects of discrimination.

Wage Payments and Incentives

The agreement to buy or sell labor is frequently a long-term one. Job-specific training and the difficulty of changing jobs make quick turnover costly for both firms and workers. Thus employers and workers need to have an understanding of what will happen in the future, when, for example, the marginal product of labor at the firm increases or decreases.

Most workers would prefer a certain wage to an uncertain one; such workers will prefer a fixed wage that does not change every time the marginal revenue product changes. Long-term arrangements of this kind are quite common. A worker—a person working at Getajob, for example—is hired at a given weekly wage. If marginal revenue product declines because of a week of stormy winter weather with frequent power outages, Getajob will not reduce the weekly wage. On the other hand, when a crowd of college seniors arrives at the shop in May, the Getajob workers will have to work harder—their marginal revenue product will rise—but they will not be paid a higher wage. Thus, the weekly wage does not change with the actual week-to-week changes in the marginal revenue product of the worker. The wage reflects marginal revenue product over a longer period. Most workers in the United States are paid in this way.

Piece-Rate Wages

piece-rate system: a system by which workers are paid a specific amount per unit they produce.

An alternative wage payment arrangement endeavors to match productivity with the wage much more closely. Such contracts are used when the weekly or hourly wage does not provide sufficient *incentive* or where the manager cannot observe the worker carefully. Under a **piece-rate system,** the specific amount workers are paid depends on how much they produce. Thus, if their marginal product drops off, for whatever reason, they are paid less. Piece rates are common in the apparel and agriculture industries.

Consider California lettuce growers, for example. The growers hire crews of workers to cut and pack the lettuce. A typical crew consists of two cutters and one packer, who split their earnings equally. The crew is paid a piece rate, about $1.20 for a box of lettuce that might contain two dozen heads. A three-person crew can pick and pack about 75 boxes an hour. Thus, each worker can earn about $30 an hour. But if they slack off, their wages decline rapidly.

On the same lettuce farms, the growers may pay other workers on an hourly or weekly basis. The workers who wash the lettuce are paid an hourly wage. Truck drivers and the workers who carry the boxes to the trucks are also paid by the hour.

Why the difference? Piece rates are used when incentives are important and it is difficult to monitor the workers. This would apply to small crews of lettuce workers out in the fields but not to workers washing lettuce at the main building. Another reason is that some jobs, like washing lettuce or driving a truck, require particular care and safety. Workers might drive the truck too fast or wash the lettuce carelessly under a piece-rate system.

Deferred Wage Payments

deferred payment contract: an agreement between a worker and an employer whereby the worker is paid less than the marginal revenue product when young, and subsequently paid more than the marginal revenue product when old.

Yet another payment arrangement occurs when a firm pays workers less than their marginal revenue product when they are young and more than their marginal revenue product at a later time as a reward for working hard. Lawyers and accountants frequently work hard at their firms when they are young; if they do well, they make partner and are then paid much more than their marginal revenue product when they are older. Such contracts are called **deferred payment contracts.**

Generous retirement plans are another form of deferred payment contract. A reward for staying at the firm and working hard is a nice retirement package.

REVIEW
- Many labor market transactions are long term.

- Most employees receive a fixed hourly or weekly wage, even though their marginal revenue product fluctuates.

- Piece-rate contracts adjust the payment directly according to actual marginal product; they are a way to increase incentives to be more productive.

- Deferred compensation is another form of payment that aims at improving incentives and worker motivation.

Labor Unions

labor union: a coalition of workers, organized to improve the wages and working conditions of the members.

industrial union: a union organized within a given industry, whose members come from a variety of occupations.

craft union: a union organized to represent a single occupation, whose members come from a variety of industries.

The model of labor supply and demand can also help us understand the impact of labor unions. **Labor unions** such as the United Auto Workers or the United Farm Workers are organizations with the stated aim of improving the wages and working conditions of their members. There are two types of unions: **Industrial unions** represent most of the workers in an industry—such as the rubber workers, farm workers, or steelworkers—regardless of their occupation; **craft unions** represent workers in a single occupation or group of occupations, such as printers or dockworkers. In the 1930s and 1940s, there were disputes between those organizing craft unions and industrial unions. John L. Lewis, a labor union leader, argued that craft unions were not suitable for large numbers of unskilled workers. Hence, he and other union leaders split in 1936 from the American Federation of Labor (AFL), a group representing many labor unions, and formed the Congress of Industrial Organizations (CIO). It was not until 1955 that the AFL and CIO resolved their disputes and merged; one of the reasons for their resolution was that union membership was beginning to decline.

But the decline continued. In 2005, there was a split within AFL-CIO. Three large unions representing service workers, truck drivers, and food and commercial workers withdrew from the AFL-CIO expressing their unhappiness over the decline of union membership. About 12.5 percent of the U.S. labor force is currently unionized, down from about 25 percent in the mid-1950s. The fraction is much higher in other countries.

Unions negotiate with firms on behalf of their members in a collective bargaining process. Federal law, including the National Labor Relations Act (1935), gives workers the right to organize into unions and bargain with employers. The National Labor Relations Board has been set up to make sure that firms do not illegally prevent workers from organizing and to monitor union elections of leaders.

In studying unions, it is important to distinguish between the union leaders who speak for the union members and the union members themselves. Like politicians, union leaders must be elected, and as with politicians, we can sometimes better understand the actions of union leaders by assuming that they are motivated by the desire to be elected or reelected.

The Collective Voice of Union Workers
The lockout of dock workers in West Coast ports in the fall of 2002 paralyzed billions of dollars' worth of cargo going in and out of the United States. At the heart of the conflict was the introduction of new technology that would eliminate 200 to 600 jobs.

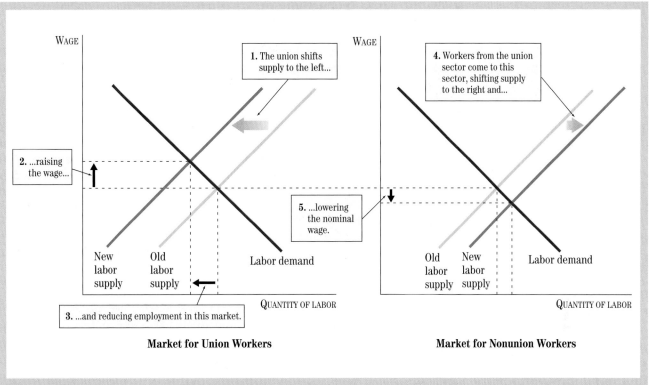

Figure 13.11 box contents:

1. The union shifts supply to the left...

2. ...raising the wage...

3. ...and reducing employment in this market.

4. Workers from the union sector come to this sector, shifting supply to the right and...

5. ...lowering the nominal wage.

WAGE   WAGE

New labor supply   Old labor supply   Labor demand

QUANTITY OF LABOR

Old labor supply   New labor supply   Labor demand

QUANTITY OF LABOR

Market for Union Workers   **Market for Nonunion Workers**

**Figure 13.11
The Effect of Unions on
Wages**

According to one view of labor unions, the union wage is increased relative to nonunion wages as a result of restricting the supply of workers. The supply in the union sector is reduced, but the supply in the nonunion sector is increased.

Union/Nonunion Wage Differentials

Studies of the wages of union workers and nonunion workers have shown that union wages are about 15 percent higher than nonunion wages, even when workers' skills are the same. There are two different explanations of how unions raise wages.

■ **The Restricted Supply Explanation.** One theory is that unions raise wages by restricting supply. By restricting membership, for example, they shift the labor supply curve to the left, raising wages, just as a monopolist raises the price of the good it sells by restricting supply. But when a union restricts supply, workers outside the union in another industry get paid less.

This effect of unions is illustrated in Figure 13.11. The graph on the right is one industry; the graph on the left is another industry. Suppose both industries require workers of the same skill level. Imagine the situation before the union is formed. Then the wages for the workers on the left and on the right in Figure 13.11 would be the same.

Now suppose a union organizes the industry on the left. Wages rise in the industry on the left, but the quantity of labor demanded in the industry falls. The workers in the industry on the left who become unemployed will probably move to the industry on the right. As they do so, the labor supply curve in the right-hand graph of Figure 13.11 shifts and the wage in that industry declines. Thus, a wage gap between the similarly skilled union and nonunion workers is created.

■ **The Increased Productivity Explanation.** Another theory, which was developed extensively in the book *What Do Unions Do?* by Richard Freeman and James Medoff of Harvard University, is that labor unions raise the wages of workers by increasing their marginal product. They do this by providing a channel of communication with management, motivating workers, and providing a democratic means of resolving disputes.

A worker who has a dispute with the management of a firm or who sees the opportunity to get a higher wage at another firm could, in principle, move. But such moves can have huge costs: The firm may have invested in job-specific training and the worker might like the area where the firm is located. In situations where exit from a firm is costly, people find other ways to improve their situation without exiting. The economist Albert Hirschman, in a famous book called *Exit, Voice, and Loyalty,* has called this alternative "voice." Rather than exit or quit, the worker may try to show the firm that a raise is deserved. Or the worker can discuss with the employer how conditions can be changed. The choice between exit and voice arises in many contexts: Should you transfer to a new college or tell the dean how the teaching might be improved? Should parents send their children to a private school or work to improve the local public school?

In many situations, exercising your voice requires collective action. If you alone complain to the dean, nothing much will happen, but if you organize a "students against lousy teaching" group, you may see some changes. Those who emphasize this collective-voice role of labor unions argue that unions provide a means through which workers improve their productivity. This explains why the wages of union workers are higher than those of nonunion workers with the same skills and training.

Monopsony and Bilateral Monopoly

The analysis of labor unions in Figure 13.11 stresses the market power of unions as *sellers* of their members' labor in the labor market: By restricting supply, the union can raise the price of its members' wages, much as a monopolist or a group of oligopolists with market power can raise the price of the goods they sell.

However, the *buyers* in the labor market—that is, the firms that purchase the labor—may also have market power to affect the wage, contrary to the assumption we have made throughout this chapter that firms do not have such market power in the labor market. **Monopsony** is a situation in which there is only one buyer. By reducing its demand, a monopsony can reduce the price in the market; it moves down along the supply curve, with both quantity and price lower.

monopsony: a situation in which there is a single buyer of a particular good or service in a given market.

bilateral monopoly: the situation in which there is one buyer and one seller in a market.

The situation in which there is only one seller (a monopoly) and one buyer (a monopsony) in a market is called a **bilateral monopoly.** A labor market with one labor union deciding the labor supply and one firm deciding the labor demand is an example of a bilateral monopoly.

In fact, there are few examples of monopsony; for most types of workers—sales clerks, accountants, engineers—there are typically many potential employers. Exceptions are found in small towns, where, for example, there may be only one auto repair shop. Then, if auto mechanics do not want to move, the auto repair shop is effectively the only employer. Another exception is found in professional sports leagues, where team owners form agreements with one another restricting workers' (that is, the players') mobility between teams. Such restrictions have been loosened significantly in recent years but still exist. If players had more freedom to move between teams, the teams' monopsony power would be reduced. Indeed, the loosening of restrictions that has already occurred has led to huge increases in players' salaries.

The outcome of a bilateral monopoly is difficult to predict. Compared to a situation where a monopsony faces competitive sellers, however, the bilateral monopoly can lead to a more efficient outcome. A firm with a monopsony facing many competitive sellers would buy *less* than a group of competitive buyers, in order to drive down the wage. By banding together, the sellers can confront this monopsony power with their own monopoly power. For example, they could refuse to work for less than the competitive wage. If their refusal is credible, they could take away the incentive for the monopsony to reduce labor demand because doing so would not reduce the wage.

REVIEW
- About 14 percent of U.S. workers belong to either industrial or craft unions.
- Workers who belong to unions are paid about 15 percent more on average than workers with the same skills who are not in unions. There are two conflicting explanations about why.
- One explanation is that labor unions improve productivity by improving worker motivation and providing workers with a collective voice.
- Another view is that labor unions raise productivity by restricting supply, much as a monopolist would, rather than by increasing productivity.

Conclusion and Some Advice

In this chapter, we have shown that the labor supply and demand model is a powerful tool with many applications. In fact, the model may apply to you, so consider carefully what it implies.

First, increasing your own labor productivity is a good way to increase your earnings. Many of the large differences in wages across individuals and across time are due to differences in productivity. Productivity is enhanced by increases in human capital, whether obtained in school or on the job. Such human capital will also prove useful if your firm shuts down and you need to find another job.

Second, if you are choosing between two occupations that you like equally well, choose the one that is less popular with other students of your generation and for which it looks like demand will be increasing. Both the supply and the demand for labor affect the wage, and if the supply is expected to grow more rapidly than the demand in the occupation you are training for, wages will not be as high as in the occupation for which labor is in relatively short supply.

Third, be sure to think about the wage you receive or the raises you get in real terms, not nominal terms, and make sure you are aware of fringe benefits offered or not offered.

Fourth, think about your job in a longer-term perspective. Partly for incentive reasons, some jobs pay little at the start, with the promise of higher payments later.

KEY POINTS

1. Wage growth in the United States, which is defined by the real hourly average pay (including fringe benefits), has been increasing at a faster rate since the mid-1990s. Wage dispersion has also increased.

2. The demand for labor is a derived demand that comes from the profit-maximizing decisions of firms. Firms adjust their employment to make the marginal revenue product of labor equal to the wage. For a competitive firm, the marginal product equals the wage divided by the price.

3. The supply curve for labor can be explained by looking at the choices of individuals or households. A person will work more hours if the wage is greater than the marginal benefit of more leisure.

4. The substitution effect and the income effect work in opposite directions, so that the labor supply curve can be either upward-sloping, vertical, downward-sloping, or backward-bending.

5. Long-term movements in wages are closely correlated with changes in labor productivity. Labor productivity differences also explain some of the differences in wages paid to different people.

6. Productivity does not explain everything. Compensating wage differentials and discrimination are other reasons wages differ.

7. When worker incentives or motivation are a problem, piece rates and deferred compensation can be used as alternative forms of payment arrangements.

8. Union workers earn more than nonunion workers who have the same skills. This occurs either because unions increase labor productivity or because they restrict the supply of workers in an industry.

KEY TERMS

fringe benefits

wage

real wage

labor market

labor demand

labor supply

derived demand

marginal revenue product of labor

backward-bending labor supply curve

human capital

on-the-job training

labor market equilibrium

labor productivity

compensating wage differential

piece-rate system

deferred payment contract

labor union

industrial union

craft union

monopsony

bilateral monopoly

QUESTIONS FOR REVIEW

1. Are fringe benefits a significant part of average pay in the United States?

2. Why is labor demand a derived demand?

3. What is the marginal revenue product, and why must it equal the wage if a firm is maximizing profits?

4. Why is the demand for labor downward-sloping?

5. Why do the substitution effect and the income effect on labor supply work in opposite directions?

6. How can compensating wage differentials explain why workers with the same skills are paid different amounts?

7. Why does discrimination against women and minorities reduce their wage, and why does competition reduce the effects of discrimination?

8. Why are piece rates sometimes used instead of weekly wages?

9. What is the difference between the two main views of labor unions?

PROBLEMS

1. Marcelo farms corn on 500 acres in a competitive industry, receiving $3 per bushel. The relationship between the number of workers Marcelo hires and production of corn is shown in the next column.

Number of Workers	Corn Production (bushels per year)
1	30,000
2	43,000
3	51,000
4	55,000
5	57,000
6	58,000

a. Calculate the marginal product and marginal revenue product of labor for Marcelo's farm.

b. If the wage for farm workers is $8,000 per year, how many workers will Marcelo hire? Explain.

c. Suppose the yearly wage for farm workers is $8,000, the fixed rent is $30,000 per year, and there are no other costs. Calculate Marcelo's profits or losses. Will there be entry or exit from this industry?

2. Real wages in the United States are higher than in Guatemala. Using the supply and demand model for labor, explain why a difference in marginal product might explain this. Name one factor that may cause this difference in marginal product and explain its effect.

3. Draw a typical supply and demand for labor diagram to represent the market for doctors. Suppose a government regulation does not allow the wage rate for this profession to go as high as the market-determined wage rate. Depict this in your diagram. Will there be a shortage or surplus of doctors at that wage rate?

4. Use the definition of the demand for labor as the marginal revenue product to argue that the increasing wage dispersion between skilled and unskilled workers could come from (1) increases in the relative productivity of skilled workers and (2) increases in the demand for the products produced by skilled workers.

5. Given your answer to problem 4, what policies can the government pursue to correct this wage dispersion by affecting labor demand? What kinds of policies would the government pursue if it wanted to affect the supply of labor to correct excessive wage dispersion?

6. College professors are frequently paid less than others with equivalent skills working outside academia. Use the idea of compensating differentials to explain why professors' wages are relatively low.

7. A toy manufacturing company is considering hiring sales representatives to market its new toys to retail stores. Under what circumstances should it pay a commission for every order of toys promoted by its sales representatives, and under what circumstances should it pay the sales representatives an hourly wage?

8. Analyze the labor supply schedules for Joshua and Scott below.

Wage	Hours Worked by Scott	Hours Worked by Joshua
$5	5	0
$8	10	8
$12	20	15
$15	30	25
$18	40	35
$20	45	33
$25	50	30

a. Draw the labor supply schedules for Joshua and Scott.
b. How does Scott's marginal benefit from more leisure compare with Joshua's?
c. At what point does the income effect begin to outweigh the substitution effect for Joshua? Explain.

9. A competitive firm has the production function shown in the table below. Calculate the marginal product of labor and draw the marginal revenue product schedule when the market price of the good this firm produces equals $10 per ton.

Quantity of Labor	Tons of Output
1	10
2	18
3	25
4	30
5	34
6	37
7	38

a. If the wage is $40, how many workers will the firm hire? Explain the reasoning behind the firm's decision.
b. If the price of the product this firm produces goes up to $15 per ton, how many workers will the firm hire? (Assume the market wage stays the same.) Why does it make sense for the firm to hire more workers?

10. Suppose a firm with some market power faces a downward-sloping demand curve for the product it produces. Given the following information on demand, complete the table below and draw the resulting demand curve for labor. If the hourly wage is $30, how many workers will this firm hire?

11. The government of Firmland wants to favor firms, and it is considering implementing a maximum wage. As an economic adviser to the government of Firmland, explain (verbally and graphically) the consequences of the maximum wage in the competitive labor market. Make sure your explanation includes the gains or losses to firms, workers, and the people of Firmland as a whole.

Problem 10	Quantity of Labor	Quantity of Output	Marginal Product of Labor	Price of Output	Total Revenue	Marginal Revenue	Marginal Revenue Product of Labor
	10	100		9			
	20	180		8			
	30	240		7			
	40	280		6			
	50	300		5			
	60	310		4			

CHAPTER 14

Taxes, Transfers, and Income Distribution

I n 1996, President Clinton signed one of the most significant and controversial pieces of legislation of his eight years in office, promising to "end welfare as we know it." The bill allowed state governments to limit the period of time during which a poor mother with children could receive welfare payments without working. The result of the bill was that millions of poor people in the United States left the welfare rolls. The legislation was popular because it removed people from welfare and placed many in jobs. But it was severely criticized because it seemed too harsh.

There is a wide range of individual opinion about the causes of income inequality and what government should do about it. Many feel compassion and a moral obligation to help the very poor. Others feel it is unfair that some people make more in one day than others do in an entire year. Others see nothing unfair about a very unequal income distribution as long as there is equality of opportunity. Still others worry that a very unequal distribution of income can cause social unrest and deter a society from other goals, including an efficient economy.

Throughout the twentieth century all the world's democracies have chosen to set up government-run redistribution systems aimed at either reducing income inequality or helping the poor. Taxes and transfers lie at the heart of any government redistribution system. By taxing individuals who are relatively well off and making transfer payments to those who are relatively less well off, the aim is to make income distribution less unequal.

The purpose of this chapter is to provide an economic analysis of taxes and transfers. We begin the chapter with an analysis of the tax system, which is used to pay not only for transfer payments to the poor but also for government spending of all types—military, police, road building, schools. We then go on to consider transfers, such as welfare payments to the poor and social security payments to the elderly. Finally, we examine the actual distribution of income and discuss how it has been affected by the tax and transfer system in the United States.

This is an exciting time to study tax and income distribution policy. We are now observing some of the effects of the major welfare legislation enacted in the late 1990s. Passionate debates rage about whether taxes should be decreased or whether the rich should pay more or less in taxes. A major issue in the 2000 presidential election was whether tax rates should be reduced, and when he was elected, President Bush did put forward a tax cut that was passed by Congress— the Economic Growth and Tax Relief Reconciliation Act of 2001. What effects does lowering tax rates have on the economic behavior of people? How does it affect income distribution?

This chapter endeavors to provide you with some economic principles that will help you form and defend your opinions about these controversial matters.

The Tax System

We first consider the several different types of taxes used in the United States. Then we review the effects of these taxes and consider some proposals for reforming the tax system.

The major types of taxes that exist in the United States are the *personal income tax* on people's total income, the *payroll tax* on wage and salary income, the *corporate income tax* on corporate profit income, *excise/sales taxes* on goods and services purchased, *estate* and *gift taxes* on inheritances and gifts from one person to another, and *tariffs*, which are taxes on goods imported into the country. In addition, many local governments raise revenue through *property taxes*.

As shown in Figure 14.1, the personal income tax and the payroll tax are by far the largest sources of tax revenue for the federal government. Together they account for nearly 85 percent of federal tax revenue. Hence, we focus most of our attention on these two taxes in the following discussion.

The Personal Income Tax

personal income tax: a tax on all forms of income an individual or household receives.

The **personal income tax** is a tax on all the income an individual or household receives, including wage and salary income, interest and dividend income, income

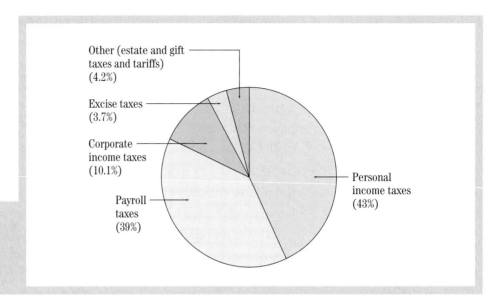

Figure 14.1
Taxes Paid to the Federal Government
Nearly 85 percent of federal taxes comes from the personal income tax and the payroll tax.

from a small business, rents on property, royalties, and capital gains. (A *capital gain* is the increase in the value of an asset like a corporate stock. When the asset is sold, the capital gain—equal to the difference between the original purchase price and the selling price of the asset—is treated as income and is taxed.) The personal income tax was introduced in 1917 in the United States, soon after the ratification of the Sixteenth Amendment to the U.S. Constitution, which authorized income taxes. Most states have now joined the federal government and have enacted a personal income tax; we focus our attention on the personal income tax collected by the federal government.

■ **Computing the Personal Income Tax.** To explain the economic effects of the personal income tax, we must examine how people actually compute their own tax. The amount of tax a household owes depends on the tax rate and the amount of taxable income. **Taxable income** is defined as a household's income minus certain exemptions and deductions. An *exemption* is a dollar amount that can be subtracted for each person in the household. *Deductions* are other items—such as interest payments on a home mortgage, charitable contributions, and moving expenses—that can be subtracted.

taxable income: a household's income minus exemptions and deductions.

Consider, for example, the Lee family, which has four members: a wife, a husband, and two children. Suppose the Lees can subtract $3,100 as a personal exemption for each of the four people in the family, for a total of $12,400, and are entitled to a deduction of $9,700. Thus, they can subtract a total of $22,100 ($12,400 + $9,700) from their income. Suppose that the husband and wife together earn a total income of $75,000. Then their taxable income is $52,900 ($75,000 − $22,100).

Now let us see how we combine taxable income with the tax rate to compute the tax. Figure 14.2 shows two different tax rate schedules that appeared in a recent IRS 1040 form. The tax rate schedule labeled "Schedule X" in the figure is for a taxpayer who is single; the tax rate schedule labeled "Schedule Y-1" is for two married taxpayers who are paying their taxes together. The first two columns give a range for taxable income, or the "amount on Form 1040, line 37." The next two columns tell how to compute the tax. The percentages in the tax rate schedule are the tax rates.

Look first at Schedule Y-1; the 10 percent tax rate in the schedule applies to all taxable income up to $14,300, at which point any additional income up to $58,100 is taxed at 15 percent. Any additional income over $58,100 but less than $117,250 is taxed at 25 percent, and so on for tax rates of 28 percent, 33 percent, and 35 percent. Each of the rows in these schedules corresponds to a different tax rate; the range of taxable income in each row is called a **tax bracket.**

As an example, let us compute the Lees' tax. Recall that their taxable income is $52,900. They are married and filing jointly, so we look at Schedule Y-1. We go to the second line because $52,900 is between $14,300 and $58,100. In other words, the Lees are in the 15 percent tax bracket. We find that they must pay $1,430 plus 15 percent of the amount their income is over $14,300—that is, plus .15 × ($52,900 − $14,300) = $5,790. Thus, the amount of tax they must pay is $1,430 + $5,790 = $7,220.

Now consider what happens when the Lees' income changes. Suppose that one of the Lees decides to earn more income by working more hours and the Lees' income rises by $2,800. Thus, their taxable income rises from $52,900 to $55,700. Now what is their tax? Again looking at Schedule Y-1, we see that the tax is $1,430 plus .15 × ($55,700 − $14,300) = $6,210. Thus, the Lees' tax has increased from $7,220 to

tax bracket: a range of taxable income that is taxed at the same rate.

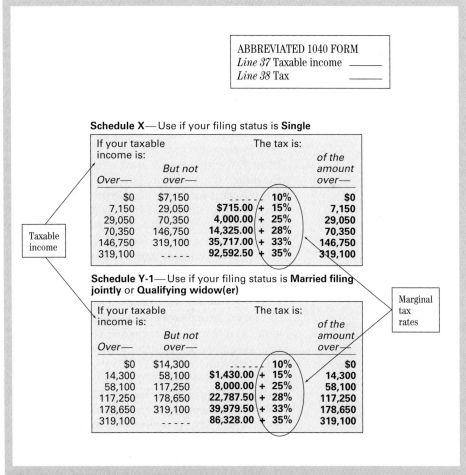

Figure 14.2
Two Tax Rate Schedules from the 1040 Form
The tables show how to compute the tax for each amount of taxable income. Observe how the marginal rates rise from one tax bracket to the next.

$7,640, or $420, as their income rose by $2,800. Observe that the tax rose by exactly 15 percent of the increase in income.

■ The Marginal Tax Rate.   The amount by which taxes change when one's income changes is the **marginal tax rate.** It is defined as the change in taxes divided by the change in income. In examining how the Lees compute their tax, we have discovered that their marginal tax rate is 15 percent. In other words, when their income increased, their taxes rose by 15 percent of the increase in income. As long as they stay within the 15 percent tax bracket, their marginal tax rate is 15 percent.

> **marginal tax rate:** the change in total tax divided by the change in income.

Observe that the marginal tax rate depends on one's income. The marginal rate varies from 10 percent for low incomes up to 35 percent for very high incomes. Suppose that one of the Lees did not work and that their taxable income was $12,900 rather than $52,900. Then they would be in the 10 percent bracket and their marginal tax rate would be 10 percent.

> **average tax rate:** the total tax paid divided by the total taxable income.

In contrast to the marginal tax rate, the **average tax rate** is the total tax paid divided by the total taxable income. For example, the Lees' average tax rate before we considered changes in their income was $\frac{\$7,220}{\$52,900} = .136$, or 13.6 percent, lower than the 15 percent marginal tax rate. In other words, the Lees pay 13.6 percent of their total taxable income in taxes but must pay 15 percent of any additional income in taxes. The average tax rate is less than the marginal tax rate because the Lees pay only 10 percent on the first $14,300 of taxable income.

Economists feel that the marginal rate is important for assessing the effects of taxes on individual behavior. Their reasoning can be illustrated with the Lees again. Suppose that the Lees' marginal tax rate was 10 percent rather than 15 percent. Then, if one of the Lees decided to work an additional half day a week, the family would be able to keep 90 cents for each extra dollar earned, sending 10 cents to the government. But with a marginal tax rate of 15 percent, the Lees could keep only 85 cents on the dollar. If the marginal tax rate for the Lees was 35 percent, then they could keep only 65 cents for each dollar earned. To take the example to an even greater extreme, suppose the marginal rate was 91 percent, which was the highest marginal rate before President Kennedy proposed reducing tax rates. Then, for each extra dollar earned, one could keep only 9 cents! Clearly, the marginal tax rate is going to influence people's choices about how much to work if they have a choice. The marginal tax rate has a significant effect on what people gain from working additional hours. This is why economists stress the marginal tax rate rather than the average tax rate when they look at the impact of the personal income tax on people's behavior.

Figure 14.3 provides a visual perspective on marginal tax rates. It plots the marginal tax rate from IRS Schedule Y-1 in Figure 14.2; the marginal tax rate is on the vertical axis, and taxable income is on the horizontal axis. Observe how the marginal tax rate rises with income.

> **progressive tax:** a tax for which the amount of an individual's taxes rises as a proportion of income as the person's income increases.
>
> **regressive tax:** a tax for which the amount of an individual's taxes falls as a proportion of income as the person's income increases.
>
> **proportional tax:** a tax for which the amount of an individual's taxes as a percentage of income is constant as the person's income rises.

*A tax is **progressive** if the amount of the tax as a percentage of income rises as income increases.* If the marginal tax rate rises with income—in which case people with higher incomes pay a larger percentage of their income in taxes—then the tax is progressive. *A tax is **regressive** if the amount of the tax as a percentage of income falls as income rises.* An income tax would be regressive if the marginal tax rate declined as income rose, or if people with high incomes could use deductions or other schemes to reduce the tax they paid to a smaller percentage of income than people with lower incomes paid. *A tax is **proportional** if the amount of the tax as a percentage of income is constant as income rises.*

■ Zero Tax on Low Incomes.   In assessing how progressive the income tax is, one needs to remember that the taxes are based on taxable income, which is less

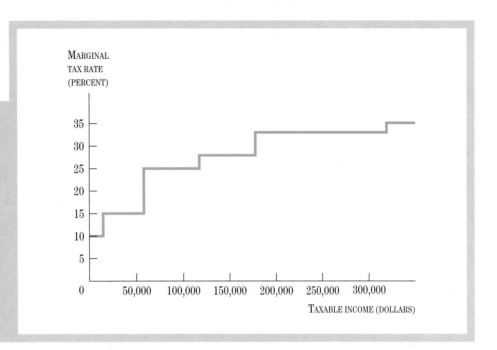

Figure 14.3
Marginal Tax Rates
As an example, the marginal tax rates from the IRS tax rate schedule Y-1 are plotted. The marginal tax rate is the change in the amount of tax paid for an extra dollar earned. The marginal tax rate increases with income. Each step takes the taxpayer to a higher tax bracket. Thus, higher-income people have a higher marginal tax rate than lower-income people. Under a flat tax, the marginal tax rate would be constant for all taxable income levels.

than the income a household actually receives. Taxable income can be zero even if a household's income is greater than zero. For example, if the Lee family earned only $22,100 for the year, then their taxable income would be zero, because $22,100 equals the sum of their exemptions and deductions. Thus, they would not have to pay any personal income tax on incomes up to $22,100, according to the tax rate schedule. In general, the personal income tax is zero for household incomes up to the sum of the exemptions and deductions.

flat tax: a tax system in which there is a constant marginal tax rate for all levels of taxable income.

A **flat tax** occurs when the marginal tax rates are constant for all levels of taxable income, in which case the line in Figure 14.3 would become flat. Even a flat rate tax system would have a degree of progressivity: The tax paid would rise as a percentage of income from zero (for workers below the sum of exemptions and deductions) to a positive amount as income rises.

The Payroll Tax

payroll tax: a tax on the wages and salaries of individuals.

The **payroll tax** is a tax on the wages and salaries of individuals; the payroll tax goes to finance social security benefits, Medicare, and Unemployment insurance.

Payroll taxes are submitted to the government by employers. For example, the Lees' employers must submit 15.3 percent of the Lees' wage and salary income to the federal government. Thus, the payroll tax on the Lees' wage and salary income of $75,000 would be $11,475 (that is, .153 × $75,000), more than the total that the Lees would pay in personal income taxes!

The tax law says that half of the 15.3 percent payroll tax is to be paid by the worker and half is to be paid by the employer. Thus, the Lees would be notified of only half of the payroll tax, or $5,737.50, even though their employer sent $11,475 to the government. If a person is self-employed—a business consultant, say, or a free-lance editor—then the person pays the full 15.3 percent, because a self-employed person is both the employee and the employer. One of the most important things to understand about the payroll tax is that, as we will soon prove, its economic effects

Repeal of the federal estate tax has been a topic of frequent debate since it was included as part of the Bush tax cuts enacted in 2001. Under this legislation, the estate tax is to be gradually phased out until it is completely gone in 2010, but unless further measures are taken to repeal the tax permanently, the estate tax will return in 2011 under sunset provisions of that law. As with most tax policy, the estate tax issue is not simple or clear-cut, and it has, in fact, generated a great deal of heat, as described in the article below.

White House Watch: Ann McFeatters / Send in the spin

The 'death tax' debate is alive and kicking in the Senate

Sunday, August 14, 2005

WASHINGTON—Once again, we are about to be hit with an emotional barrage of misleading "information" about the nation's urgent need to deal with the federal estate tax, which President Bush dubs the "death tax" and demands "must be repealed forever."

In an essay for The Wall Street Journal, Senate Majority Leader Bill Frist of Tennessee, one of the wealthiest members of the Senate, insists the "death tax is the cruelest, most unfair tax our government imposes." He said that in the first week after Labor Day he will call for a Senate vote to repeal it. "There will be no more hiding on the issue of permanent death-tax repeal," he warned.

The House voted April 13 to permanently repeal the estate tax. So Frist's vow sets up another all-out fight in the Senate. Republicans want to act now on repeal, even if they're defeated in their attempt, so they can use it as an issue against Democrats in next year's congressional elections. For their part, many Democrats intend to filibuster and charge Republicans with kowtowing to the rich.

The 2001 tax cut orchestrated by Bush gradually phases out the estate tax until it is gone completely in 2010. But in 2011, it comes back with a vengeance unless Congress permanently repeals the tax or lifts the amount exempted or otherwise changes the law.

So, what's the deal? Would the nation be better off without the grim-sounding "death tax"?

Those who shout "yes!" argue that the tax is duplicative because in some cases federal income taxes already have been imposed on assets accumulated. However, at the time of death, capital gains tax usually has not been paid on the vast block of stocks or bonds or property that have risen substantially in value.

do not depend on who is legally required to pay what share of the tax; only the total 15.3 percent matters.

Other Taxes

corporate income tax: a tax on the accounting profits of corporations.

All other federal taxes together amount to less than one-fifth of total revenue. **Corporate income taxes** are taxes on the accounting profits of corporations. Currently the corporate tax rate ranges from 15 percent to 38 percent, depending on the level of earnings.

Supporters of repeal say estate taxes are unfair to farm families and small businesses. But the Tax Policy Center estimates that last year estate taxes were paid on only 440 farms and small businesses out of the thousands of farms and small businesses left to heirs, and that taxes paid averaged less than 20 percent of the value of the estate. Also, there are special rules for estates with farms and businesses that reduce taxes owed.

Those who shout "no!" to repeal say the number of families actually subject to the estate tax is minuscule. The Congressional Research Service notes IRS figures that show that of the 2.4 million people who die in this country each year, only 1.3 percent of their estates owe any estate tax.

The "no" side makes the point that billions of dollars lost to the government by repeal would either mean cuts in federal programs or higher taxes elsewhere. The Congressional Budget Office estimates lost revenue from repealing the estate tax would be $380 billion over 10 years.

In a little-noticed irony, millions of American who pay no estate tax now could be hit with heavy new capital gains taxes on inheritances, depending on what Congress does. And the complications of determining how much capital gains would be due on property held for years by someone now deceased would be mind-boggling. Nobody in his or her right mind would want to be executor of a will.

The astonishing thing is that this would be so arduous, even for tax lawyers, and taxes could be so much higher that there would be a huge uproar at the same time Bush is promising, as he did this past week, to "develop a simpler [tax] code that's a fairer code and one that encourages economic growth."

Without any doubt, the coming debate will be mean and confusing. The argument of the American Conservative Union, for repeal, is: "Everything you have worked hard for your entire life, everything you wanted to leave to your children and grandchildren to keep your legacy alive, will again be taxed. And this time the tax rate will be that of a loan shark." FactCheck.org, which calls itself a nonpartisan, nonprofit, consumer advocate for voters and takes no stand on repeal, says nothing in that statement is true.

Supporters of keeping the estate tax argue that the true beneficiaries of repeal would be America's wealthiest families, those with many millions of dollars and flanks of lawyers able to figure out how to set up new tax shelters such as family limited partnerships and avoid capital gains taxes. Calling repeal the "Paris Hilton Relief Act," they claim the estate tax is one of the fairest, most progressive taxes, and that repeal would lower contributions to charity by 6 percent. But that's a highly debatable claim.

There is little doubt that the inordinately complex estate tax, at the least, needs an overhaul with higher exemptions. A million dollars ain't what it used to be.

But the vitriolic, misleading, partisan debate in the Senate we're about to have to endure will not do anyone any good.

excise tax: a tax paid on the value of goods at the time of purchase.

sales tax: a type of excise tax that applies to total expenditures on a broad group of goods.

Excise taxes are taxes on goods that are paid when the goods are purchased. The federal government taxes several specific items, including gasoline, tobacco, beer, wine, and hard liquor. A **sales tax** is a type of excise tax that applies to total expenditures on a broad group of goods. For example, if your expenditures on many different goods at a retail store total $100 and the sales tax rate is 5 percent, then you pay $5 in sales tax. There is no national sales tax in the United States, but sales taxes are a major source of revenue for many state and local governments.

Finally, the federal government raises revenue by imposing tariffs on goods as they enter the United States. Until the Sixteenth Amendment was ratified and the

property tax: a tax on the value of property owned.

personal income tax was introduced, tariffs were the major source of revenue for the U.S. government. Now revenue from tariffs is a minor portion of total revenue.

Local governments rely heavily on **property taxes**—taxes on residential homes and business real estate—to raise revenue. Recall that income taxes—both personal and corporate—are also used at the state level.

The Effects of Taxes

The purpose of most of the taxes just described is to raise revenue, but the taxes have effects on people's behavior. To examine these effects, let us start with a tax we looked at before in Chapter 7: a tax on a good or service.

■ **The Effect of a Tax on a Good.** Recall that a tax on a good adds the amount of the tax to the marginal cost of the seller of the good. For example, a tax of $1 on a gallon of gasoline will add $1 to the marginal cost of each gallon. An increase in tax therefore shifts the supply curve up by the amount of the tax, a result shown in Figure 7.10 on page 187. Once the supply curve shifts, the ultimate impact on price and quantity will depend on the price elasticities of supply and demand.

The four panels of Figure 14.4 are designed to enable us to show how the price elasticity of demand and the price elasticity of supply determine the impact of the tax. In each of the four panels of the figure, the supply curve shifts up due to a tax of the same amount, shown by the blue arrow to the left of each vertical axis. And in each of the four panels, the equilibrium price rises and the equilibrium quantity falls. The equilibrium quantity falls because people reduce the quantity demanded of the good as its price rises because of the tax. The decline in the equilibrium quantity creates a loss of consumer surplus plus producer surplus, which we have called the deadweight loss from the tax. The size of the deadweight loss and the relative size of the impact on the price and the quantity are different in each panel of Figure 14.4 because the supply curve and the demand curve have different price elasticities.

One key point illustrated in Figure 14.4 is that *when the price elasticity of demand or the price elasticity of supply is very low, the deadweight loss from the tax is small.* This is shown in the two graphs in the left part of Figure 14.4, which have either a low elasticity of demand (top left) or a low elasticity of supply (bottom left). In either case, the deadweight loss is small compared with that in the graphs at the right, which have higher elasticities.

The intuitive reason why low elasticities result in small deadweight losses is that the quantity of the good does not change very much when the price changes. Recall that a low price elasticity of demand means that quantity demanded is not very sensitive to a change in the price, as, for example, in the case of a good like salt, which has few substitutes. A low elasticity of supply means that there is only a small change in the quantity supplied when the price changes. Thus, in the case of low elasticities, there is only a small difference between the efficient quantity of production and the quantity of production with the tax. There is little loss of efficiency. On the other hand, *when the price elasticity of demand or the price elasticity of supply is very high, the deadweight loss from the tax will be relatively large.* Here changes in price have big effects on either the quantity demanded or the quantity supplied, and the deadweight loss is large.

The price elasticities of supply and demand also affect how much the price changes in response to a tax. If the price rises by a large amount, then the tax is passed on to buyers in higher prices, and the burden of the tax falls more on buyers. If the price rises little or not at all, then the seller absorbs the burden of the tax, and most of the tax is not passed on to buyers. **Tax incidence** refers to who actually bears

tax incidence: the allocation of the burden of the tax between buyer and seller.

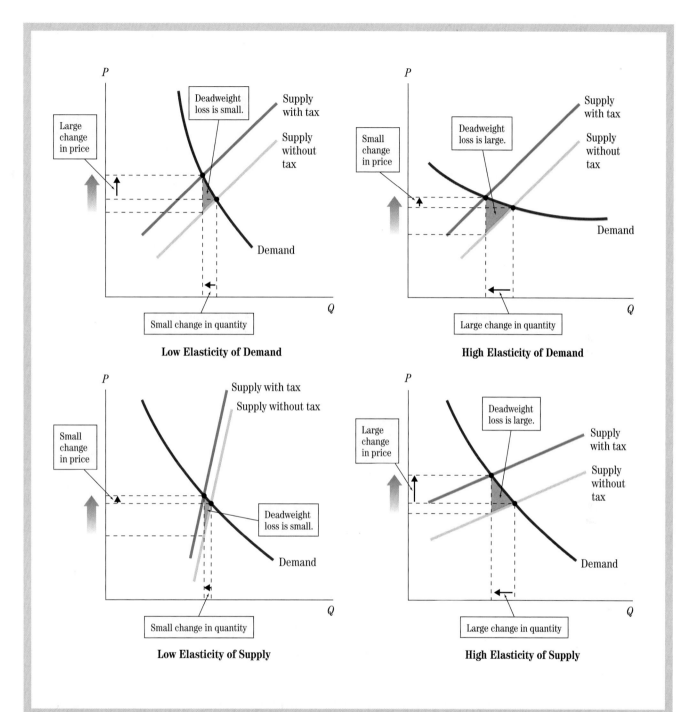

Figure 14.4
How Elasticities Determine the Effects of Taxes

1) *Deadweight loss effects:* When price elasticities are low, as in the left graphs, the deadweight loss is small and the change in equilibrium quantity is small. When price elasticities are high, as in the right graphs, the deadweight loss is large and the change in equilibrium quantity is large. 2) *Tax incidence and price effects:* When the price elasticity of demand is low or the price elasticity of supply is high, the tax is largely passed on to the consumer in higher prices. In contrast, when the price elasticity of demand is high or the price elasticity of supply is low, the burden of the tax falls on the producer because there is little price change.

the burden of the tax, the buyers or the sellers. By comparing the graphs in Figure 14.4, we see that *the smaller the price elasticity of demand and the larger the price elasticity of supply, the greater the rise in the price.* Comparing the upper two graphs of Figure 14.4, we see that the price rise is larger on the left, where the elasticity of demand is lower. The price elasticity of demand for cigarettes is very low. In 2004, the state of Michigan increased its tax on a pack of cigarettes by 75 cents, from $1.25 to $2.00. State policymakers predicted that the tax increase would raise $295 million per year in revenue and would cause people to stop smoking. They estimated that practically doubling the state's tax on cigarettes would cause cigarette sales to go down by 14 percent. Since demand for cigarettes is price inelastic, we can predict that the tax will largely be passed on to cigarette consumers, who will pay higher prices for cigarettes. The sellers can pass on the higher price to consumers when the elasticity of demand is low.

Comparing the lower two graphs of Figure 14.4, we see that the price rise is smaller on the left, where the elasticity of supply is lower. Thus, taxing a good like land, which has a low elasticity of supply, will not affect the price very much. The suppliers of the land bear the burden of the tax.

■ **Effects of the Personal Income Tax.** We can apply our analysis of a tax on gasoline or salt to any other tax, including the personal income tax. The personal income tax is a tax on *labor* income (wages and salaries) as well as on *capital* income (interest, dividends, small business profits). However, labor income is by far the larger share of most people's income: For all 1040 forms filed, wages and salaries are over 75 percent of total income. Thus, we first focus on the personal income tax as a tax on labor income.

The analysis of the personal income tax is illustrated in Figure 14.5. Because the personal income tax is a tax on labor income, we need a model of the labor market to examine the effects of the tax. Figure 14.5 shows a labor demand curve and a labor supply curve. The wage paid to the worker is on the vertical axis, and the quantity of labor is on the horizontal axis. Figure 14.5 shows that the personal income tax shifts up the labor supply curve. The size of the upward shift depends on the marginal tax rate. For example, if a person were to supply more time working, the income received from work would be reduced by the marginal tax. If the person was in the 15 percent bracket, the income received from working would be 85 cents for each extra dollar earned working. Thus, to supply exactly the same quantity as without the tax, people require a higher wage. Because the wage paid to the worker is on the vertical axis, the labor supply curve shifts up to show this.

As the labor supply curve shifts up, the equilibrium quantity of labor declines. Thus, we predict that an income tax will reduce the amount of work. The reduced amount of work will cause a deadweight loss just like that caused by the tax on a commodity. The size of the decline in hours of work will depend on the labor supply and labor demand elasticities. The higher the labor supply elasticity, the greater the reduction in the quantity of labor supplied in response to the personal income tax.

Economists disagree about the size of the labor supply elasticity. One thing that is sure is that the elasticity is different for different people. For example, the labor supply elasticity appears to be quite high for second earners in a two-person family such as the Lees. If elasticity is high, a high marginal tax rate can reduce hours of work and thereby income. But if the labor supply curve has a low elasticity, there is little effect on hours of work.

■ **The Effect of a Payroll Tax.** We can use the same type of labor market diagram to analyze a payroll tax, as shown in Figure 14.6. Clearly, the payroll tax is a tax on labor in that it applies to wages and salaries. However, in the case of the payroll

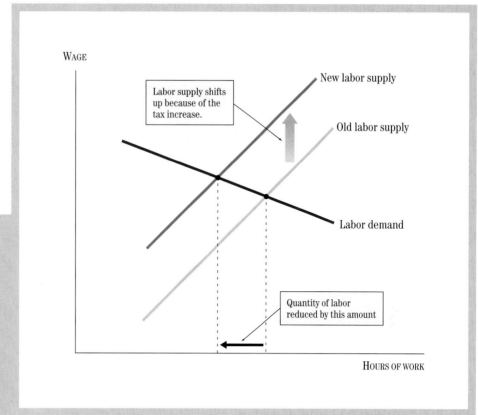

Figure 14.5
Effects of a Higher Income Tax on Labor Supply
An income tax shifts the labor supply curve up by the amount of the tax on each extra hour of work because the worker must pay part of wage income to the government and thus receives less for each hour of work. Thus, the quantity of labor supplied declines. The decline in hours worked would be small if the supply curve had a low elasticity.

tax, we need to consider that the tax is paid by both the employer and the employee, as required by law. Figure 14.6 handles the two cases.

Suppose that the wage before the tax is $10 per hour and that the payroll tax is 10 percent, or $1 per hour. The case where the tax is paid by the employee is shown on the right of Figure 14.6. This picture looks much like Figure 14.5. The labor supply curve shifts up by the amount of the tax ($1) because the worker now has to pay a tax to the government for each hour worked. In other words, the worker will supply the same amount of work when the wage is $11 and the tax is $1 as when the wage is $10 and the tax is zero.

When the labor supply curve shifts up, we see in the right-hand panel of Figure 14.6 that the equilibrium quantity of labor employed declines. Observe that the wage paid by the employer rises because the reduced supply requires a reduction in the quantity of labor demanded, which is brought about by a higher wage. However, the "after-tax wage"—the wage less the tax—declines because the tax increases by more than the wage increases.

The case where the tax is paid by the employer is shown in the left graph of Figure 14.6. In this case, the labor demand curve shifts down by the amount of the tax ($1) because the firm has to pay an additional $1 for each hour of work. When the labor demand curve shifts down, the equilibrium quantity of labor employed declines and the wage falls. Observe that the impact of the payroll tax is the same in both cases: There is a new equilibrium in the labor market with a lower wage and a lower quantity of labor.

Thus, a payroll tax has both an employment-reduction effect and a wage-reduction effect. As with any tax, the size of the quantity change and the price (wage)

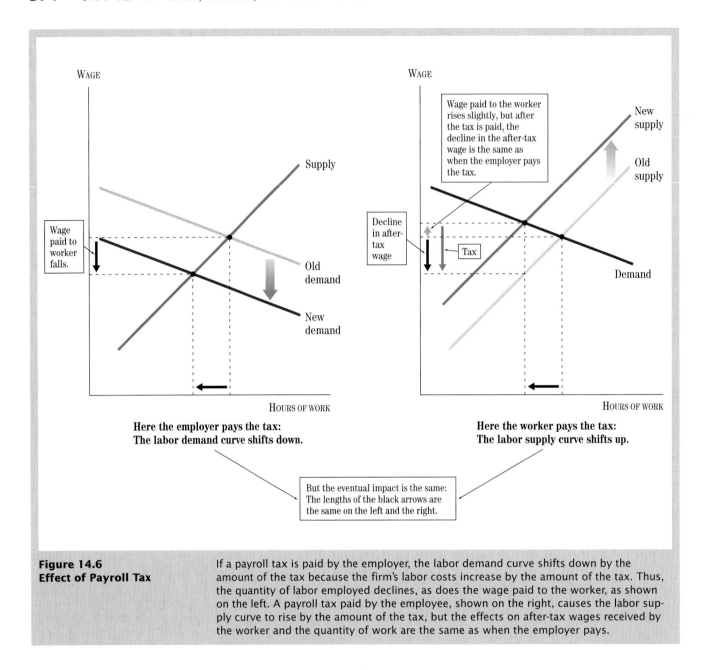

Figure 14.6
Effect of Payroll Tax

If a payroll tax is paid by the employer, the labor demand curve shifts down by the amount of the tax because the firm's labor costs increase by the amount of the tax. Thus, the quantity of labor employed declines, as does the wage paid to the worker, as shown on the left. A payroll tax paid by the employee, shown on the right, causes the labor supply curve to rise by the amount of the tax, but the effects on after-tax wages received by the worker and the quantity of work are the same as when the employer pays.

change depends on the supply and demand elasticities. For example, if the labor supply elasticity is low, there will be a small reduction in employment, but the wage will fall by a large amount. However, if the labor supply elasticity is high, there will be a large employment effect, but the wage effect will be small.

tax revenue: the tax rate times the amount subject to tax.

■ **The Possibility of a Perverse Effect on Tax Revenue.**   Tax revenue received by the government is equal to the tax rate times the amount that is subject to the tax. For example, in the case of a gasoline tax, the tax revenue is the tax per gallon times the number of gallons sold. As the tax rate increases, the amount subject to the tax will fall because the higher price due to the tax reduces the quantity

Table 14.1
Tax Rates and Tax Revenue: An Example

Tax Revenues	Tax Rate	Wage	Hours Worked
$10,000	.50	$10/hour	2,000
$11,250	.75	$10/hour	1,500
$ 4,500	.90	$10/hour	500

demanded. If the quantity demanded falls sharply enough, then tax revenue could actually fall when the tax rate is increased.

The same possibility arises in the case of taxes on labor, either the payroll tax or the personal income tax. In the case of the payroll tax or the personal income tax for a worker, tax revenue is equal to the tax rate times the wage and salary income. As the tax rate rises, the amount of income subject to tax may fall if labor supply declines. Thus, in principle, it is possible that a higher tax rate could result in reduced tax revenue. For example, consider the high marginal tax rates shown in Table 14.1: 50 percent, 75 percent, and 90 percent. If labor supply declines with a higher tax rate, as assumed in the table, then tax revenue first increases as the tax rate goes from 50 to 75 percent but then declines as the tax rate goes from 75 to 90 percent.

The general relationship between tax rates and tax revenue is illustrated in Figure 14.7. As in the example of Table 14.1, tax revenue first rises and then falls as the tax rate increases. Figure 14.7 can apply to any tax on anything. At the two extremes of zero percent tax rate and 100 percent tax rate, tax revenue is zero. What happens between these two extremes depends on the elasticities. This relationship between the tax rate and tax revenue, now frequently called the Laffer curve after the economist Arthur Laffer, who made it popular in the 1980s, has long been known to economists. It implies that if the tax rate is so high that we are on the downward-sloping part of the curve, then reducing the tax rate may increase tax revenue. However, there is great debate among economists about the tax rate at which the curve bends around (40 percent? 50 percent? 90 percent?) and how it applies in different situations.

Other factors influencing tax revenue when taxes get very high are tax avoidance and tax evasion. *Tax avoidance* means finding legal ways to reduce taxes, such as buying a home rather than renting in order to have a deduction for interest payments on a mortgage. *Tax evasion* is an illegal means of reducing one's tax. For example, at high tax rates, people have incentives to evade the tax by not reporting income. Workers are tempted not to report tips. Or people resort to barter, which is difficult for the government to track down. For example, an employer may "pay" a little extra to a truck driver by allowing free use of the truck on weekends for fishing trips.

Tax Policy and the Tradeoff Between Efficiency and Equality

We have observed in our analysis of each tax that the equilibrium quantity of the item taxed declines when the tax rate rises. This is where the inefficiency of the tax comes from. If the tax rate is very high, or the elasticities are very high, the inefficiency can be so severe that it could thwart one of the purposes of raising the taxes: to provide income support in order to raise the well-being of the

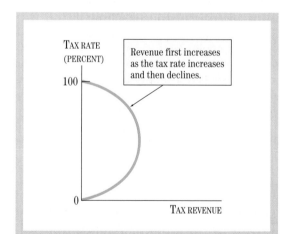

Figure 14.7
The Tax Rate and Tax Revenue
As the tax rate increases from low levels, tax revenue rises. At some point, however, the high tax rate reduces the quantity of the item that is taxed and encourages so much tax avoidance that the amount of tax revenue declines. This curve is frequently called the *Laffer curve*. The particular tax rate at which the curve bends depends on the price elasticity of the item being taxed and is a subject of great debate among economists.

"And do you promise to love, honor, and cherish each other, and pay the United States government more taxes as a married couple than you would have paid if you had just continued living together?"

ability-to-pay principle: the view that those with greater income should pay more in taxes than those with less income.

least well-off in the society. Why? Because the reduction in the quantity of labor supplied or goods produced could be so great that there would be less total income in the society. Thus, there would be less going to the poor even if they received a larger share of total income. In other words, there is a *tradeoff between equality and efficiency*. If one raises taxes too high for the purpose of making the income distribution more equal, the total amount of income may decline. In that event, there will be less available to redistribute.

Given these considerations, how should the tax system—the combination of all the taxes in society—be designed or improved?

First, in order to reduce deadweight loss to a minimum, the ideal tax system should tax items with small price elasticities of supply and demand rather than items with large elasticities. We know that the deadweight loss is small when elasticities are small. The optimal tax system would have tax rates inversely related to the elasticities.

Second, the ideal tax system would try to keep the marginal tax rates low and the amount that is subject to tax high. For example, we saw that deductions reduce the amount subject to personal income tax by lowering taxable income. Some deductions are put in the tax system to encourage certain activities: A deduction for research expenses may encourage firms to fund research, for example. However, the more deductions there are, the higher the tax rate has to be in order to get the same tax revenue. If people were not allowed to exclude so many items from income, a lower marginal tax rate could generate the same amount of revenue. And a lower marginal tax rate has the advantage of reducing the inefficiency of the tax.

Most tax reform efforts have involved trying to reduce the number of deductions while lowering marginal tax rates. This was the idea behind the tax reform efforts in the 1960s under President Kennedy and in the 1980s under President Reagan. In the early 2000s the marginal tax rates on all taxpayers were reduced substantially.

Third, the ideal tax system should be as simple and as fair as possible. If a tax system is not simple, then valuable resources—people's time, computers, and so on— must be devoted to paying and processing taxes. The tax system is seen as unfair if it is regressive. Another view of fairness frequently used is the **ability-to-pay principle;** this view is that those with greater income should pay more in taxes than those with less income. The tax system is also viewed as unfair if people with the same incomes are taxed at different rates. For example, in the U.S. tax system, a married couple making more than $120,000 a year pays a higher tax than an unmarried couple with exactly the same income. This is viewed by some as unfair.

REVIEW
- Taxes are used to make transfer payments to individuals as well as to build roads and provide for education and national defense.

- Taxes cause inefficiencies in the form of reduced economic activity and deadweight loss.

- There is a tradeoff between efficiency and equality; raising taxes to reduce inequality may increase economic inefficiency and thereby reduce the amount of total income.

- To minimize the inefficiencies, items with low elasticities should be taxed more than items with high elasticities.

- In the case of taxes on labor income—a payroll tax or the income tax for most people—the amount of work declines as the tax is increased.

Transfer Payments

transfer payment: a grant of funds from the government to an individual.

means-tested transfer: a transfer payment that depends on the income of the recipient.

social insurance transfer: a transfer payment, such as social security, that does not depend on the income of the recipient.

family support programs: transfer programs through which the federal government makes grants to states to give cash to certain low-income families.

Medicaid: a health insurance program designed primarily for families with low incomes.

supplemental security income (SSI): a means-tested transfer program designed primarily to help the poor who are disabled or blind.

A **transfer payment** is a payment from the government to an individual that is not in exchange for a good or service. Transfer payments can be either in cash or in kind. In-kind payments include vouchers to buy food or housing.

There are two types of government transfer payments in the United States: **means-tested transfers,** which depend on the income (the means) of the recipient and focus on helping poor people, and **social insurance transfers,** which do not depend on the income of the recipient. We will discuss each type of transfer, starting with the means-tested transfer programs.

Means-Tested Transfer Programs

Means-tested transfer payments are made to millions of people in the United States each year. The major programs are listed in Table 14.2.

The 1996 federal welfare law (called the Personal Responsibility and Work Opportunity Reconciliation Act, or PRWORA) replaced Aid to Families with Dependent Children (AFDC)—a transfer program providing cash payments to poor families with children. Usually, AFDC has simply been called "welfare." Under the new **family support programs,** the federal government provides grants to states, which then decide which poor families are eligible. In contrast, under AFDC the federal government stipulated eligibility requirements.

Medicaid is a health insurance program that is designed primarily to pay for health care for people with low incomes. Under the new welfare law, Medicaid eligibility is based substantially on the rules for eligibility from the former AFDC program, although it is no longer linked automatically to AFDC. Once income increases to a certain level, Medicaid support stops, so that the family must find another means of obtaining health insurance. **Supplemental security income (SSI)** is a program designed to help the neediest elderly as well as poor people who are disabled or blind. About 6.6 million people receive SSI assistance, including 4.6 million disabled and 2 million aged people.

Table 14.2
Means-Tested Transfer Programs in the United States (Each of these federal programs requires that the recipient's income or assets be below a certain amount in order to receive payment.)

Family Support Programs (Welfare)	Payments to poor families with children as determined by each state
Medicaid	Health insurance primarily for welfare recipients
SSI (Supplemental Security Income)	Payments to poor people who are old, disabled, or blind
Food Stamp Program	Coupons for low-income people to buy food
Head Start	Preschool education for low-income children
Housing Assistance	Rental subsidies and aid for construction

food stamp program: a government program that provides people with low incomes with coupons (food stamps) that they can use to buy food.

Head Start: a government transfer program that provides day care and nursery school training for poor children.

housing assistance programs: government programs that provide subsidies either to low-income families to rent housing or to contractors to build low-income housing.

earned income tax credit (EITC): a part of the personal income tax through which people with low income who work receive a payment from the government or a rebate on their taxes.

The **food stamp program** is a major means-tested transfer program; it makes payments to about 17 million people each year. Like Medicaid, food stamps are an in-kind payment. People are not supposed to use the coupons to buy anything but food. This is a popular program because the intent of the money is to provide nutrition and because the program is fairly inexpensive to run. The National School Lunch Program is similar to food stamps in that it aims to provide food to lower-income children. It provides school lunches for about 27 million children.

Head Start, another in-kind program, provides for preschool assistance to poor children to help them get a good start in school. It also is a popular program because there is evidence that it improves the performance, at least temporarily, of preschool children as they enter elementary school.

Housing assistance programs provide rental subsidies to people who cannot afford to buy a home. The programs sometimes provide aid to business firms that construct low-income housing. Many complain about waste and poor incentives in the housing programs and argue that these programs are in need of reform.

The Earned Income Tax Credit (EITC)

Another program aimed at helping the poor in the United States is the **earned income tax credit (EITC).** It is like a means-tested transfer payment in that people receive a payment from the government if their income is below a certain amount. However, it is actually part of the personal income tax (the form to obtain the payment is sent to people by the IRS along with the 1040 form).

The program provides assistance to about 18 million families. The EITC is for working people whose income is below a certain level, either because their wage is very low or because they work part time. They get a refundable credit that raises their take-home pay. For example, consider the four-person Lee family again. We know that if they earn less than $22,100, they pay no income tax. However, if the Lees earn between $0 and $10,750 in wages and salary and have no other income, then the EITC will pay 40 cents for each dollar they earn up to a maximum of $4,300 per year. To make sure that the EITC does not make payments to high-income people, the payments decline if the Lees make more than $15,050. For each dollar they earn above $15,050, they lose 22 cents of their $4,300 until the benefits run out (when their income reaches $35,458 with more than one qualifying child).

Observe that the EITC raises the incentive to work for incomes up to $10,750 and reduces the incentive to work for incomes greater than $15,050 and less than $35,458. With the EITC, the marginal tax rate is effectively *negative* 40 percent for income below $10,750; that is, you *get* 40 cents rather than *pay* 40 cents for each dollar you earn. But the EITC adds 22 percent to the marginal tax rate for incomes over $15,050 up to $35,458.

Incentive Effects

The previous sections describe a variety of government programs that aim to transfer funds to the poor. As we will see, evidence suggests that these programs do have an impact in reducing income inequality. However, some people feel that the programs may create a disincentive to work, since welfare payments are reduced when income from work rises.

The top panel of Figure 14.8 illustrates the first disincentive problem. The total income of an individual is plotted against the number of hours worked. Total income consists of wage income from work plus a welfare payment. The more steeply sloped

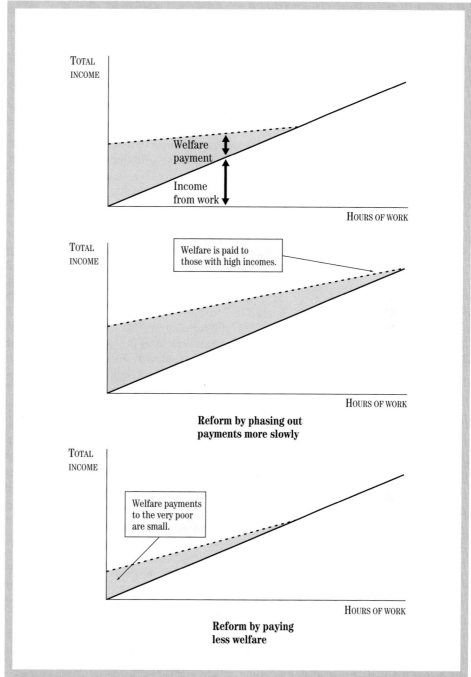

Figure 14.8
Welfare Reform to Improve Work Incentives
The top graph shows how welfare reduces the marginal earnings from working more hours because welfare payments are phased out. There are two basic approaches to reform: phasing out the payments more slowly (as in the middle graph) or lowering the welfare payment (as in the lower graph). Both have advantages and disadvantages.

solid black line shows the individual's wage income from work: The more hours worked, the more wage income the individual receives. This line intercepts the horizontal axis at zero income, so if there is no work and there is no welfare or charity, the person is in a state of extreme poverty.

The individual's total income is shown by the less steeply sloped dashed line in the top graph of Figure 14.8. It intercepts the vertical axis at an amount equal to the welfare payment the individual gets when he or she is not working at all. As the individual begins to work, the need for welfare declines, and so the welfare payment declines. Observe that the amount of the welfare payment, which is represented by the shaded gap between the steep line and the less steep line, diminishes as the hours of work increase, and finally, after a certain number of hours worked, the welfare payment disappears.

Because the welfare payment is reduced when the individual's income from work rises, it creates a disincentive. The flatter the dashed line, the greater the disincentive. For example, if someone decides to work 10 hours a week for a total of $50 per week, but the welfare payment is reduced by $30 per week, then effectively the marginal tax rate is 60 percent, high enough to discourage work.

Welfare reform endeavors to change the welfare system in order to reduce this disincentive. Looking at Figure 14.8, we see that there are two ways to make the dashed line steeper and thereby provide more incentive to work. One way is to reduce the amount of welfare paid at the zero income amount. Graphically, this is shown in the lower graph of Figure 14.8. This twists the dashed line because the intercept on the vertical axis is lower but the intersection of the dashed line and the solid line is at the same number of hours of work as in the top graph. This will increase the slope of the dashed line and therefore provide more incentive to work. But the problem with this approach is that poor people get less welfare: The poverty rate could rise.

A second way to make the dashed line steeper is to raise the place at which it intersects the black solid line, as in the middle graph of Figure 14.8. But that might mean making welfare payments to people who do not need them at all, people who earn $50,000 or $60,000 annually.

The welfare reform act signed into law by President Clinton in 1996 leaves the decision as to which welfare reform approach to take up to the states. Thus, the states have gone off in different directions, some cutting welfare checks and others raising the amount that can be earned before welfare is reduced. Some states have taken other approaches to get around the disincentive difficulty. Florida, Tennessee, and Texas require adult welfare recipients to go to work immediately. Twenty-four states require that people work after two years on welfare. Other states require that a single parent finish high school in order to get the full welfare payment. These proposals are aimed at increasing the incentive to get off welfare and go to work. Have they worked? Supporters say emphatically, yes—welfare rolls have been dramatically reduced. Critics argue that many of those previous recipients of welfare are still struggling—they may be working, but they are not earning enough to raise themselves out of poverty. These critics contend that many of these people will have trouble keeping jobs unless they have adequate support services, such as health insurance and child care.

social security: the system through which individuals make payments to the government when they work and receive payments from the government when they retire or become disabled.

Social Insurance Programs

Many transfer payments in the United States are not means-tested. The largest of these are social security, Medicare, and unemployment insurance. **Social security** is

Medicare: a government health insurance program for the elderly.

unemployment insurance: a program that makes payments to people who lose their jobs.

the system through which payments from the government are made to individuals when they retire or become disabled. **Medicare** is a health insurance program for older people. **Unemployment insurance** pays money to individuals who are laid off from work.

Social security, Medicare, and unemployment insurance are called *social insurance* because they make payments to anyone—rich or poor—under certain specific circumstances. Social security provides benefits when a worker becomes disabled or retires. Medicare provides payments when an older person requires medical care, and unemployment compensation is paid to workers when they are laid off from a job.

But these programs have features that make them much more than insurance programs. The programs have effects on income distribution because they transfer income between different groups. Consider social security and Medicare. Payroll taxes from workers pay for these programs. But the payroll taxes paid by an individual are only loosely related to the funds paid out to the same individual. In reality, each year the funds paid in by the workers are paid out to the current older people. In other words, social security is more like a transfer program from young people to older people than an insurance program.

However, because the social insurance programs are not means-tested, they also transfer income to middle-income and even wealthy individuals. In other words, they are not well targeted at the lower-income groups. For this reason, many people have suggested that these programs be means-tested. In fact, recent legislation has effectively reduced social security benefits to higher-income older people by requiring that a major part of the benefits be included in taxable income; social security benefits were formerly excluded from taxable income.

Mandated Benefits

mandated benefits: benefits that a firm is required by law to provide to its employees.

Mandated benefits occur when a firm is required by the government to provide a benefit for its workers. For example, a federal law requires firms to give unpaid leave to employees to care for a newborn baby or a sick relative. Such benefits are a cost to the firm (for example, the cost of finding and training a replacement or providing health insurance to the worker on leave). But, of course, they are a benefit to the worker. Another example of a mandated benefit is a proposal that would require firms to pay a portion of the health insurance costs of their workers.

The effects of mandated benefits can be analyzed using the supply and demand for labor diagram, much as we analyzed the effects of a payroll tax. As shown in Figure 14.9, the labor demand curve shifts down, as it did in Figure 14.6 for the employer-paid payroll tax, because the mandated benefits are a cost to the firm. But the mandated benefits provide a benefit to the workers, which shifts the labor supply curve down. The labor supply curve will probably not shift down as much as the labor demand curve because the worker probably will not value the benefit quite as much as its cost to the firm.

In any case, the new equilibrium in Figure 14.9 shows that the wage paid to the worker will fall by nearly the amount of the mandated benefit. In other words, despite the fact that the employer is "paying" for the mandated benefit, it is the worker who mainly pays. There will also be a reduction in employment.

If the workers value the benefit exactly as much as it costs the firm, then the wage will fall by the full amount of the benefit. In this case, employment will not fall at all.

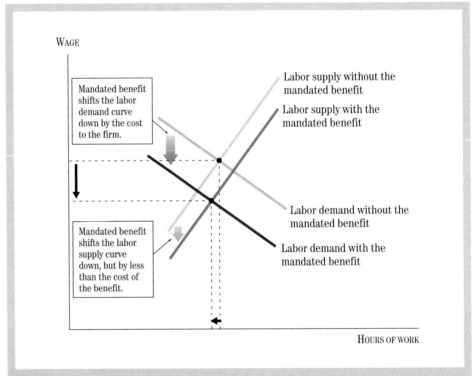

Figure 14.9
Effect of a Mandated Benefit
A mandated benefit is a cost to the firm; it shifts down the demand curve for labor just as a payroll tax does. But in the case of a mandated benefit, the labor supply curve shifts down too. Hence, the wage paid to the worker falls, as does employment.

REVIEW

- There are two major types of transfer payments. Means-tested payments—family support, Medicaid, food stamps—depend on the income of the recipient. Social insurance—social security, unemployment compensation, and Medicare—does not depend on the income of the recipient.

- Means-tested transfer payments create disincentives. The purpose of welfare reform is to reduce those disincentives.

- Under welfare reform, states are trying different methods to reduce disincentives, including work requirements and time limits on payment of benefits to welfare recipients.

The Distribution of Income in the United States

What does the distribution of income in the United States actually look like? What effect does the tax and transfer system described in the previous two sections have on income distribution? Does the United States have a less equal income distribution than other countries? What has been happening to income distribution over time? To answer these questions, we need a quantitative measure of income distribution.

The Personal Distribution of Income

Current Population Survey: a monthly survey of a sample of U.S. households done by the U.S. Census Bureau; it measures employment, unemployment, the labor force, and other characteristics of the U.S. population.

Data about people's income in the United States are collected by the Census Bureau in a monthly survey of about 70,000 households called the **Current Population Survey.** Using the information on the income of households in this survey, an estimate of the distribution of income for the entire country is made.

Economists and statisticians usually study the income distribution of families or households rather than individuals. A *family* is defined by the Census Bureau as a group of two or more people related by birth, marriage, or adoption who live in the same housing unit. A *household* consists of all related family members and unrelated individuals who live in the same housing unit. Because the members of a family or a household typically share their income, it is usually more sensible to consider families or households rather than individuals. One would not say that a young child who earns nothing is poor if the child's mother or father earns $100,000 a year. In a family without children in which one spouse works and the other remains at home, one would not say that the working spouse is rich and the nonworking spouse is poor.

Because there are so many people in the population, it is necessary to have a simple way to summarize the income data. One way to do this is to arrange the population into a small number of groups ranging from the poorest to the richest. Most typically, the population is divided into fifths, called **quintiles,** with the same percentage of families or households in each quintile. For example, in Table 14.3, the 76 million families in the United States are divided into five quintiles, with 15.2 million families in each quintile. The first row shows the poorest 20 percent—the bottom quintile. The next several rows show the higher-income quintiles, with the last row showing the 20 percent with the highest incomes.

quintiles: divisions or groupings of one-fifth of a population ordered by income, wealth, or some other statistic.

The second and third columns of Table 14.3 show how much income is earned by families in each of the five groups. The bottom 20 percent of families have incomes below $24,000, the families in the next quintile have incomes greater than $24,000 but less than $41,440, and so on. Note that the lower limit for families in the top 20 percent is $94,469. The lower limit for the top 5 percent (not shown in the table) is $164,323.

Inequality can be better measured by considering the total income in each quintile as a percentage of the total income in the country. Table 14.4 provides this information. The second column in Table 14.4 shows the income received by families in each quintile as a percentage of total income in the United States.

Table 14.3
Range of Annual Family Incomes for Five Quintiles

Quintile	Income Greater Than	Income Less Than
Bottom 20 percent	0	$24,000
Second 20 percent	$24,000	$41,440
Third 20 percent	$41,440	$63,000
Fourth 20 percent	$63,000	$94,469
Top 20 percent	$94,469	—

Source: Statistical Abstract of the United States, 2004, Table 672.

Table 14.4
Distribution of Family Income by Quintile

Quintile	Percentage of Income	Cumulative Percentage of Income
Bottom 20 percent	4.2	4.2
Second 20 percent	9.7	13.9
Third 20 percent	15.5	29.4
Fourth 20 percent	23.0	52.4
Top 20 percent	47.6	100.0

Source: Statistical Abstract of the United States, 2004, Table 670.

A quick look at Table 14.4 shows that the distribution of income is far from equal. Those in the lower 20 percent earn only 4.2 percent of total income. On the other hand, those in the top 20 percent earn 47.6 percent of total income. Thus, the amount of income earned by the rich is a large multiple of the amount of income earned by the poor.

These percentages are summed up in the third column of Table 14.4. This cumulative percentage shows that the bottom 20 percent earn 4.2 percent of the income, the bottom 40 percent earn 13.9 percent of the income, the bottom 60 percent earn 29.4 percent of the income, and the bottom 80 percent earn 52.4 percent of the income. The top 5 percent, not shown in Table 14.4, earn 20.8 percent of the aggregate income.

The Lorenz Curve and Gini Coefficient

The data in Table 14.4 can be presented in a useful graphical form. Figure 14.10 shows the cumulative percentage of income from the third column of Table 14.4 on the vertical axis and the percentage representing each quintile from the first column on the horizontal axis. The five dots in the figure are the five pairs of observations from the table. For example, point *A* at the lower left corresponds to the 4.2 percent of income earned by the lowest 20 percent of people. Point *B* corresponds to the 13.9 percent of income earned by the lowest 40 percent of people. The other points are plotted the same way. The uppermost point is where 100 percent of the income is earned by 100 percent of the people.

If we connect these five points, we get a curve that is bowed out. This curve is called the **Lorenz curve.** To measure how bowed out the curve is, we draw the solid black 45-degree line. The 45-degree line is a line of perfect equality. On that line, the lowest 20 percent earn exactly 20 percent of the income, the lowest 40 percent earn exactly 40 percent of the income, and so on. Every household earns exactly the same amount.

The degree to which the Lorenz curve is bowed out from the 45-degree line provides a visual gauge of the inequality of income. The more bowed out the line is, the more unequal is the income distribution. The box on page 386 shows how the Lorenz curve in the United States compares with that in some other countries and with the world as a whole.

The most unequal distribution possible would occur when only one person earns all the income. In that case, the curve could be so bowed out from the

Lorenz curve: a curve showing the relation between the cumulative percentage of the population and the proportion of total income earned by each cumulative percentage. It measures income inequality.

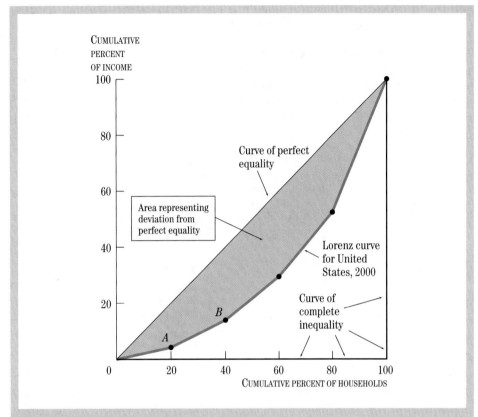

Figure 14.10
The Lorenz Curve for the United States
Each point on the Lorenz curve gives the percentage of income received by a percentage of households. The plotted points are for the United States. Point *A* shows that 4.2 percent of income is received by the lowest 20 percent of families. Point *B* shows that 13.9 percent of income is received by the lowest 40 percent of families. These two points and the others in the figure come from Table 14.4. In addition, the 45-degree line shows perfect equality, and the solid lines along the horizontal and right-hand vertical axes show perfect inequality. The shaded area between the 45-degree line and the Lorenz curve is a measure of inequality. The ratio of this area to the area of the triangle below the 45-degree line is the Gini coefficient. The Gini coefficient for 2000 is .462.

Gini coefficient: an index of income inequality ranging between 0 (for perfect equality) and 1 (for absolute inequality); it is defined as the ratio of the area between the Lorenz curve and the perfect equality line to the area between the lines of perfect equality and perfect inequality.

45-degree line that it would consist of a straight line on the horizontal axis up to 100 and then a vertical line. For example, 99.9 percent of the households would earn zero percent of the income. Only when the richest person is included do we get 100 percent of the income.

The **Gini coefficient** is a useful numerical measure of how bowed out the Lorenz curve is. It is defined as the ratio of the area of the gap between the 45-degree line and the Lorenz curve to the area between the lines of perfect equality and perfect inequality. The Gini coefficient can range between 0 and 1. It has a value of zero if the area between the diagonal line and the Lorenz curve is zero. Thus, when the Gini coefficient is zero, we have perfect equality. The Gini coefficient would be 1 if only one person earned all the income in the economy.

ECONOMICS IN ACTION

Income Distribution Around the World

Lorenz curves can be calculated for different countries or groups of countries. For most European countries, the Lorenz curve is closer to equality than it is for the United States. Canada, Australia, and the United Kingdom have Lorenz curves very similar to that of the United States.

However, income distribution varies much more when we look beyond the developed countries. As the figure shows, Bangladesh, a very poor country, has a more equal income distribution than the United States. Brazil, a middle-income country that is also much poorer than the United States, has a much less equal income distribution. Among individual countries, Bangladesh and Brazil are close to the extremes: 60 percent of the population receives 40 percent of the income in Bangladesh and 19 percent of the income in Brazil, compared to 29.8 percent in the United States.

Income distribution for the world as a whole is far more unequal than that for any one country because the very poor in some countries are combined with the very rich in other countries. For example, when West Germany united with East Germany to form one country, the income distribution became more unequal for the unified country as a whole than it had been for either country before unification. The Lorenz curve for the world as a whole—as illustrated in the figure—shows far greater inequality than the curve for any one country: 60 percent of the world's population receives only 5 percent of the income.

Note: World curve computed from population data for low-, lower-middle-, upper-middle-, and high-income countries.

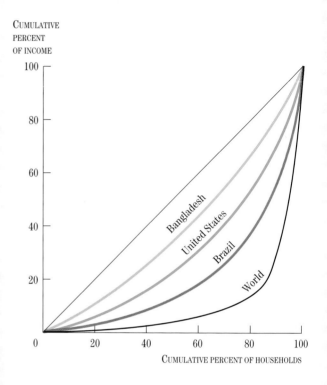

Figure 14.11 shows how the Gini coefficient has changed in the United States over the last 50 years. The Gini coefficient has varied within a narrow range, from .32 to .46. The most notable feature of the trend in the Gini coefficient in Figure 14.11 is the decline after World War II until around 1970 and the subsequent increase. It is clear that in recent years income inequality has increased. Higher earnings of skilled and educated workers relative to the less skilled and less educated may partly explain this change in income distribution. But the reason for these changes in income inequality is still a major unsettled question for economists.

It is important to note, however, that an increase in income inequality, as in Figure 14.11, does not necessarily mean that the rich got richer and the poor got poorer. For example, if one looks at average income in each quintile, one finds an increase for all groups from the 1970s to the 1990s, even after adjusting for inflation. However, average income in the top quintile increased by a larger percentage amount than average income in the bottom quintile.

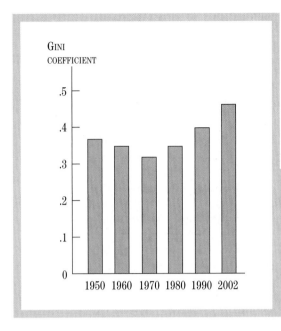

GINI
COEFFICIENT

Figure 14.11
Changes in Income Inequality:
The U.S. Gini Coefficient
The Gini coefficient is large when
there is more inequality, as measured by the Lorenz curve in Figure
14.10. Thus, by this measure,
inequality fell in the United States
from 1950 to 1970 but increased
from 1970 to 2002.

■ **Income Mobility and Longer-Term Income Inequality.** In interpreting
income distribution statistics, it is important to recognize that the quintiles do not
refer to the same people as the years go by. People move from quintile to quintile.
People who are in the top quintile in one year may be in the bottom quintile the next
year. And people who are in the bottom quintile one year may be in the top quintile
the next year. In its 2003 Survey of Income and Program Participation, the U.S.
Census Bureau reported that 38 percent of those households in the lowest income
quintile in 1996 were in a higher income quintile in 1999.

Distinguishing between income in any one year and income over several years is
important. In a typical life span, people usually earn less when they are young than
when they are middle-aged. As they grow older and become more experienced, their
wages and salaries increase. When people retire, their income usually declines again.
Thus, even if everyone had the exact same lifetime income, one would see inequality
in the income distribution every year. Middle-aged people would be relatively rich,
while young and old people would be relatively poor.

More generally, many people seem to move around the income distribution
from year to year. Some undergo hardship, such as a layoff or a permanent loss of job
because of a change in the economy. Even if they are eventually rehired, in the short
run they fall to the lower end of the income distribution when they are unemployed.
On the other hand, some people do well and move quickly to the top of the income
distribution.

How significant is income mobility? Economic research shows that about two-
thirds of the people in any one quintile move to another over a 10-year period. About
half of those in the top quintile move to a lower quintile, and about half of those in
the bottom quintile move to a higher quintile. This degree of mobility has not
changed in the last 20 years.

■ **Changing Composition of Households.** The formation or splitting up of
households can also affect the distribution of income. For example, if two individuals

who were living separately form a household, the household income doubles. Households splitting apart can also alter the income distribution drastically. If one adult leaves the family, perhaps because of divorce or desertion, and the other one stays home with the children, the income of the household declines substantially. In 2003, 28 percent of families with single mothers were found to be living below the poverty line, as compared to a rate of 10 percent for all families.

It appears that the splitting apart of households has had an impact on income distribution in the United States. According to some estimates, if household composition had not changed in the United States in the last 20 years, there would have been only half as great an increase in inequality as measured by the Gini coefficient.

■ **Distribution of Income versus Distribution of Wealth.** Another factor to keep in mind when interpreting data on the income distribution is the distinction between *income* and *wealth*. Your annual income is what you earn each year. Your wealth, or your net worth, is all you own minus what you owe others. Wealth changes over a person's lifetime even more than income does as people save for retirement. For example, a young person who has just graduated may have little wealth or, with a college loan still to pay off, may have negative net worth. However, by saving a bit each year—perhaps through a retirement plan at work—the person gradually accumulates wealth. By the time retirement age is reached, the person may have a sizable retirement fund, and thus be relatively wealthy.

A survey of about 3,000 families in the United States in 2001 found that the top 10 percent of households held about 72 percent of the net worth in the United States. Although such surveys are not as accurate as the regular monthly surveys of 60,000 households on which our information about income distribution is based, it is clear that the distribution of wealth is less equal than the distribution of income. About one-third of the net worth in this survey was in the form of net worth held in small businesses.

The Poor and the Poverty Rate

Many believe the main purpose of government redistribution of income is to help the poor. For this reason, the term *social safety net* is sometimes used for an income redistribution system; the idea is that these programs try to prevent those who were born poor or who have become poor from falling too far down in income and therefore in nutrition, health, and general well-being.

Poverty can be observed virtually everywhere. The poor are visible in the blighted sections of cities and in remote rural areas. Almost everyone has seen the serious problems of the homeless in cities of the United States. CNN has brought the agony of poverty around the world to our TV screens.

poverty rate: the percentage of people living below the poverty line.

poverty line: an estimate of the minimum amount of annual income required for a family to avoid severe economic hardship.

To gauge the success or failure of government policies to alleviate poverty, economists have developed quantitative measures of poverty. The **poverty rate** is the percentage of people who live in poverty. To calculate the poverty rate, one needs to define what it means to live in poverty. In the United States, poverty is usually quantitatively defined by a **poverty line,** an estimate of the minimal amount of annual income a family needs in order to avoid severe economic hardship. The poverty line in the United States is based on a survey showing that families spend, on average, one-third of their income on food. The poverty line is thus obtained by multiplying by 3 the Department of Agriculture's estimate of the amount of money needed to purchase a low-cost nutritionally adequate amount of food. In addition, adjustments are made for the size of the family. Table 14.5 shows the poverty line for several different family sizes. Since the 1960s, when it was first developed, the poverty line has been increased to adjust for inflation.

Table 14.5
The Poverty Line in the United States, 2004

Family Size	Poverty Line
Unrelated individuals	$ 9,827
Two persons	$12,649
Three persons	$14,776
Four persons	$19,484
Seven persons	$31,096

Source: U.S. Census Bureau.

Using the poverty line and data on the income distribution, one can determine the number of people who live in poverty and the poverty rate. The overall poverty rates in the United States have varied over the last 50 years. The overall poverty rate for families declined sharply from 18 percent in 1960 to 10 percent in 1970, but has remained relatively constant since 1970. In 2004 the poverty rate for families was 10 percent, while the poverty rate for all individuals was 12.7 percent, or 37 million people.

There are important trends in poverty for different groups in the population. For example, the percentage of children who live in poverty rose in the 1970s, 1980s, and early 1990s. During the same time period, the poverty rate for the elderly has declined, and this has held down the overall poverty rate. In 1993, when child poverty was at a peak, 22.7 percent of children were living in poverty; at the same time, the poverty rate for the elderly was 12.2 percent. The dramatic decline in the poverty rate for the elderly (from 24.6 percent in 1970), is largely attributed to the change in Social Security benefits during that time period—along with better retirement benefits.

The increase in poverty for children is troublesome, and it is difficult to explain. Some of it may have to do with the increase in single-headed households with children, which are usually poorer than two-adult households. Poverty rates in households with a single head and at least one child have ranged between 35 and 40 percent in the last 20 years—three times the overall poverty rate. However, since 1993, the poverty rate for children has made some progress, declining from 22.7 percent to 16.2 percent in 2000. Since then, it has risen slightly to 17.8 percent in 2004.

Effects of Taxes and Transfers on Income Distribution and Poverty

We have seen that two goals of the tax and transfer system are to redistribute income and reduce poverty. How successful is this redistribution effort? Estimates by the U.S. Census Bureau indicate that the tax and transfer system reduces the poverty rate by about 10 percentage points: Without the tax and transfer system, the Census Bureau estimates that the poverty rate would be 20 percent rather than 10 percent. Those in the second quintile have their average income increased by an average of about $4,000 as a result of the tax and transfer system. Those in the uppermost part of the income distribution have their average income reduced by about $22,000 as a result of the tax and transfer system.

To be sure, these estimates ignore any of the incentive effects mentioned earlier, such as the reduced work incentives that might result from the tax and transfer system. And they ignore any possible response of private efforts to redistribute income—such as charities—that might occur as a result of changes in the government's role.

REVIEW

- The distribution of income can be measured by the percentage of income earned by quintiles of households or families. The Lorenz curve and the Gini coefficient are computed from this distribution.

- The poverty rate is a quantitative measure of the amount of poverty in the United States.

- The distribution of income has become more unequal in the United States since the early 1970s. The change is partly due to a growing dispersion of wages between unskilled workers with little education and highly skilled workers with more education.

- Over the last three decades, the poverty rate among children has increased while the poverty rate for the elderly has declined.

- Estimates indicate that the tax and transfer system currently makes the poverty rate lower than it would otherwise be.

- Nevertheless, the increase in poverty among children has raised serious concerns about the tax and transfer system in the United States.

Conclusion

In a democracy, the amount of government redistribution of income is decided by the people and their representatives. A majority seem to want some redistribution of income, but there is debate about how much the government should do.

Why doesn't a democracy lead to much more redistribution? After all, 60 percent of the people, according to Table 14.4, receive only 30 percent of the income. Since 60 percent of the voting population is enough to win an election, this 60 percent could vote to redistribute income much further. Why hasn't it?

There are probably a number of reasons. First, there is the tradeoff between equality and efficiency stressed in this chapter. People realize that taking away incentives to work will reduce the size of the pie for everyone.

Another reason is that most of us believe that people should be rewarded for their work. Just as we can think of a fair income distribution, we can think about a fair reward system. If some students want to work hard in high school so that they can attend college, why shouldn't they get the additional income that comes from that?

There is also the connection between personal freedom and economic freedom. Government involvement in income distribution means government involvement in people's lives. Those who cherish the idea of personal freedom worry about a system that takes a large amount of income from people who work.

Finally, much income redistribution occurs through the private sector—private charities and churches. The distribution of food and the provision of health care have long been supported by nongovernment organizations. In times of floods or earthquakes, it is common for people to volunteer to help those in distress. Private charity has certain advantages over government. Individuals become more personally involved if they perform a public service, whether volunteering at a soup kitchen or tutoring at an elementary school. But incentives for redistribution through private charity may be too small. People may give less to a charitable organization if they believe others are not giving. Thus, the private sector may not be sufficient.

KEY POINTS

1. The government in modern democracies plays a major role in trying to help the poor and provide a more equal income distribution.

2. Taxes are needed to pay for transfers and other government spending. In the United States, the personal income tax and the payroll tax are by far the most significant sources of tax revenue at the federal level. Sales taxes and property taxes play a significant role at the local level.

3. Taxes cause inefficiencies, as measured by deadweight loss, because taxes reduce the amount of the economic activity being taxed—whether it is the production of a good or the labor of workers.

4. The incidence of a tax depends on the price elasticity of supply and demand. The deadweight loss from taxes on goods with low price elasticities is relatively small.

5. Transfer payments are classified into means-tested programs—such as welfare and food stamps—and social insurance programs—such as social security and unemployment insurance.

6. Transfer payments can cause inefficiency as a result of disincentives to work or the incentive for families to split up.

7. There is a tradeoff between equality and efficiency. Tax reform and welfare reform try to improve incentives and reduce inefficiency.

8. The distribution of income has grown more unequal in recent years.

9. Poverty among children has increased, while poverty among the elderly has declined in recent years.

10. The tax and transfer system has reduced income inequality and lowered poverty rates, but there is much room for improvement and reform.

KEY TERMS

personal income tax
taxable income
tax bracket
marginal tax rate
average tax rate
progressive tax
regressive tax
proportional tax
flat tax
payroll tax
corporate income tax

excise tax
sales tax
property tax
tax incidence
tax revenue
ability-to-pay principle
transfer payment
means-tested transfer
social insurance transfer
family support programs
Medicaid

supplemental security income (SSI)
food stamp program
Head Start
housing assistance programs
earned income tax credit (EITC)
social security
Medicare
unemployment insurance

mandated benefits
Current Population Survey
quintiles
Lorenz curve
Gini coefficient
poverty rate
poverty line

QUESTIONS FOR REVIEW

1. What are the two largest sources of tax revenue for the federal government?

2. What is the difference between income and taxable income?

3. Why is there a deadweight loss from the personal income tax?

4. Why are the effects of a payroll tax the same whether the employer or the worker pays it?

5. Why is deadweight loss from a payroll tax small when the elasticity of labor supply is small?

6. What is the difference between a marginal tax rate and an average tax rate? Why is the former more important for incentives?

7. What causes the tradeoff between equality and efficiency?

8. In what way do both welfare reform and tax reform focus on incentives?

9. What was the primary goal of the welfare reform law passed in 1996?

10. How is the distribution of income measured by the Lorenz curve and the Gini coefficient?

11. Why are income mobility and lifetime income important for interpreting the income distribution statistics?

PROBLEMS

1. The following table gives the income distribution in Brazil and in Australia. Draw the Lorenz curve for each. Which country has the larger Gini coefficient?

Quintile	Percent of Income in Brazil	Percent of Income in Australia
Bottom 20 percent	2.4	4.4
Second 20 percent	5.7	11.1
Third 20 percent	10.7	17.5
Fourth 20 percent	18.6	24.8
Top 20 percent	62.6	42.2

2. Suppose the government decides to increase the payroll tax paid by employers. If the labor supply curve has a low elasticity, what will happen to the workers' wages? Who actually bears the burden of the tax, the workers or the firms? Would it be different if the labor supply had a high elasticity?

3. The table on the next page gives hours worked and the welfare payment received.
   a. Calculate the missing data in the table, given that the hourly wage is $5 and total income is the sum of the wage payment and the welfare payment.

Hours Worked	Wage Payment	Welfare Payment	Total Income
0		10,000	
500		8,000	
1,000		6,000	
1,500		4,000	
2,000		2,000	

    b. Draw a graph that shows how much total income a worker earns with and without this welfare program. Put the number of hours worked on the horizontal axis and total income on the vertical axis.

    c. What is the increase in total income for each additional hour worked without any welfare program? Compare it with the increase in total income for each additional hour worked under the welfare program.

    d. How could the welfare program be changed to increase the incentive to work without reducing total income for a full-time worker (40 hours per week, 50 weeks per year, $5 per hour) below $12,000, which is already below the poverty line for a family of four?

4. Suppose that the labor demand curve is perfectly flat. What is the impact on a typical worker's hourly wage if the government increases the payroll tax paid by employers by 10 percent of the wage? Show what happens in a labor supply and labor demand graph like Figure 14.6. Why does the slope of the labor supply curve not affect your answer?

5. Given the data in the table below, draw the Lorenz curve before and after the proposed tax. Is this tax progressive or regressive?

Quintile	Percent of Income Without Tax	Percent of Income with Tax
Bottom 20 percent	6	7
Second 20 percent	9	12
Third 20 percent	18	20
Fourth 20 percent	25	25
Top 20 percent	42	36

6. The Family Leave Act is a federal law that requires employers to give unpaid leave to employees to care for a newborn or a sick relative. Show how the Family Leave Act affects the supply and demand for labor. According to this model, what will happen to wages and employment compared to the prelaw situation?

7. Many states do not tax food items because that kind of tax is considered regressive. Explain. California tried to impose a "snack" tax—one applying only to what the legislators thought was junk food. Suppose snack food has a higher elasticity of demand than nonsnack food. Draw a supply and demand diagram to explain which tax—on snack food or nonsnack food—will cause the price to rise more. Which will have a greater deadweight loss?

8. Some economists argue that we should use more progressive taxes, while others claim that we should adopt a flat tax. List some reasons for and against using progressive taxes.

9. Suppose the government is trying to decide between putting a sales tax on luxuries, which usually have very high demand elasticities, or on gasoline. Which tax will have a bigger effect on the market price? Which tax will cause the quantity traded in the market to decline more? Draw a diagram to explain.

10. Suppose Fred, a bookkeeper, had taxable income of $21,000 last year. His doctor, Celia, had taxable income of $140,000 last year. Use the tax rate schedule in Figure 14.2 to figure out how much each owes in income taxes. What are their marginal tax rates? What are their average tax rates? (Assume that both are single.)

11. Analyze the distribution of income, using the household incomes in the following table. Rank the families by income. Compute the percentage of total income going to the poorest 20 percent of the families, the second 20 percent, and the richest 20 percent. Draw a Lorenz curve for the income distribution of these 10 families. Is their distribution more equal or less equal than that of the population of the United States as a whole?

Family	Income
Jones	$ 12,000
Pavlov	$100,000
Cohen	$ 24,000
Baker	$ 87,000
Dixon	$ 66,000
Sun	$ 72,000
Tanaka	$ 18,000
Bernardo	$ 45,000
Smith	$ 28,000
Lopez	$ 33,000

CHAPTER 15

Public Goods, Externalities, and Government Behavior

Economists who have worked at the President's Council of Economic Advisers in Washington are frequently asked what they did there. One answer—given recently by an economist who worked on President Kennedy's Council way back in the early 1960s—is timeless; it still applies today, and it will undoubtedly apply in the future. The economist was Robert Solow,[1] who later won a Nobel Prize in economics.

Solow put it this way: "On any given day in the executive branch, there are more meetings than Heinz has varieties. At a very large proportion of these meetings, the representative of some agency or some interest will be trying to sell a harebrained economic proposal. I am exaggerating a little. Not every one of these ideas is crazy. Most of them are just bad: either impractical, inefficient, excessively costly, likely to be accompanied by undesirable side effects, or just misguided—unlikely to accomplish their stated purpose. Someone has to knock those proposals down. . . . That is where the Council's comparative advantage lies." Solow emphasized that he had good people and good arguments to work with, but that "does not mean that we won all the battles; we lost at least as many

---

1. Robert M. Solow, "It Ain't the Things You Don't Know That Hurt You, It's the Things You Know That Ain't So," *American Economic Review*, May 1997, pp. 107–108.

as we won. The race is not always won by the best arguments, not in political life anyway. But we always felt we had a chance and we kept trying."

The purpose of this chapter is to examine two important concepts—public goods and externalities—that economists on the President's Council and elsewhere use to determine whether a proposal for government action is bad or good. We also show how cost-benefit analysis can be used to help determine the correct course of action. Finally, we examine different models of government behavior to understand why "in political life" the best economic arguments do not always win. We will see that politicians are influenced by incentives as much as anyone else.

Public Goods

Table 15.1
Types of Goods and Services Produced by Government in the United States

Type of Good or Service	Employment as a Percent of Total Government
Education	45
Health and hospitals	10
National defense (civilian)	5
Police protection	5
Postal service	4
Highways	3
Judicial and legal	2
Parks and recreation	2
Fire protection	2
Sanitation, sewage	1
All other	21

public good: a good or service that has two characteristics: non-rivalry in consumption and nonexcludability.

nonrivalry: the situation in which increased consumption of a good by one person does not decrease the amount available for consumption by others.

Table 15.1 shows the range of goods and services produced by all governments in the United States: the federal government, 50 state governments, and 87,453 local governments (counties, cities, towns, and school districts). Education is by far the largest in terms of employment, followed by health and hospital services, national defense, police, the postal service, and highways. (The figures for national defense include only civilian workers; if Table 15.1 included those serving in the armed forces, national defense would be second on the list.) The other categories, from the judicial and legal system (federal, state, and county courts) to parks and recreation, are each significant but small relative to the total.

Observe also the types of goods and services that are not on the list because they are produced by the private sector. Manufacturing, mining, retail trade, wholesale trade, hotel services, and motion picture production are some of the items largely left to the private sector. Note also that for all the goods and services on the list in Table 15.1, the private sector provides at least some of the production. There are 6 million workers in the private health-care sector, for example, compared to 2 million in government health care. The private sector is also involved in mail delivery, education, garbage collection, and even fire protection (volunteer fire departments).

Nonrivalry and Nonexcludability

Why is it necessary for governments to produce *any* goods and services? The concept of a public good helps us answer the question. A **public good** is a good or service that has two characteristics: *nonrivalry in consumption* and *nonexcludability*.

Nonrivalry in consumption means that more consumption of a good by one person does not imply less consumption of it by another person. For example, if you breathe more clean air by jogging rather than watching television, there is no less clean air for others to breathe. Or when a new baby is born, the baby immediately benefits from national defense without anyone else having to give up the benefits of national defense. Once a country's national defense—the military personnel, the strategic alliances, the missile defense system—is in place, the whole nation enjoys the security simultaneously; the total benefit is the sum of the benefits of every person. Clean air and national defense are examples of goods with nonrivalry. In contrast, for most goods, there is rivalry in consumption. For example, if you consume

In the wake of Hurricane Katrina
A Chinook helicopter drops sand
bags to plug a canal levee break in
the Gentilly neighborhood of New
Orleans, Louisiana on September
11, 2005. Levees are a public good,
having characteristics of both non-
rivalry and non-excludability.

more french fries, then either someone else must consume fewer french fries or more french fries must be produced. But for a good with nonrivalry in consumption, everybody can consume more if they want to. There is a collective aspect to the good.

nonexcludability: the situation in which no one can be excluded from consuming a good.

Nonexcludability means that one cannot exclude people from consuming the good. For example, people cannot be excluded from the benefits of national defense. In contrast, most goods have the characteristic of excludability. If you do not pay for the french fries that you ordered at the drive-through window, the server will not give them to you.

A public good is a good or service that has nonrivalry in consumption and nonexcludability. In contrast, a *private* good has excludability and rivalry.

Free Riders: A Difficulty for the Private Sector

free-rider problem: a problem arising in the case of public goods because those who do not contribute to the costs of providing the public good cannot be excluded from the benefits of the good.

Goods that have nonrivalry in consumption and nonexcludability create a **free-rider problem:** People can enjoy the good or service without reducing others' enjoyment even if they do not pay. To understand this concept, imagine that you bought a huge bus for the purpose of transporting students around town and collecting a little money for your service. But suppose the bus had a broken rear door that allowed people to get on and off without paying and without interfering with other people's travel. In that situation, you would have free riders. If you could not fix the door or do something else to exclude the free riders, you would not be in the transportation business long, because without fares, you would have losses.

National defense is like the huge bus with the broken rear door. You cannot exclude people from enjoying it, even if they do not pay, and one person's security does not reduce the security of others. It is clear that a private firm will have difficulty producing and selling national defense to the people of a country. For this reason, a collective action of government to provide this defense, requiring that people pay for it with taxes, is necessary. Similar actions are taken with other public goods such as police protection, fire protection, and the judicial system. That clean air has the property of a public good explains why government is involved in its "production." In this case, the government might help produce clean air by prohibiting the burning of

The Classic Lighthouse Example
How can the free-rider problem be avoided without government providing the service?

user fee: a fee charged for the use of a good normally provided by the government.

leaves or the using of backyard barbecues. We will return to the government's role in air quality when we discuss the concept of externality.

Information also has the features of a public good. Everyone can benefit from information that a hurricane is on the way; there is no rivalry in consuming this information. Information about the state of the economy can also benefit everyone. For this reason, such information has been largely supplied by governments. In the United States, the Department of Commerce collects and distributes information about the economy, and the U.S. Weather Service collects information about the weather.

Avoiding Free-Rider Problems

Not all public goods are provided by the government. When they are not, some other means of dealing with the free-rider problem is needed. A classic example used by economists to explore the nature of public goods is the lighthouse that warns ships of nearby rocks and prevents them from running aground. A lighthouse has the feature of nonrivalry. If one ship enjoys the benefit of the light and goes safely by, this does not mean that another ship cannot go by. There is no rivalry in the consumption of the light provided by the lighthouse. Similarly, it is impossible to exclude ships from using the lighthouse because any ship can benefit from the light it projects.

However, lighthouse services are not always provided by the government. Early lighthouses were built by associations of shippers, who charged fees to the ships in nearby ports. This system worked well because the fees could be collected from most shippers as they entered nearby ports. The free-rider problem was avoided, so general tax revenue to pay for the lighthouse was not needed.

When the users of a government-provided service are charged for its use (some excludability is needed), the charge is called a **user fee.** In recent years, user fees have become more common in many government-provided services, including the national parks. The aim is to target the payments more closely to the users of the goods and services.

Although police services are almost always provided by government, there are many examples of security services provided by private firms. For example, a business firm may hire a guard to watch its premises. In these cases, the service is focused at a particular group, and excludability is possible, and so the free-rider problem can be avoided.

New Technology

Modern technology is constantly changing the degree to which there is nonrivalry and nonexcludability for particular goods. When radio and television were invented, it became clear that once a radio or television program was broadcast, it was possible for anyone to tune in to the broadcast. A radio or television broadcast has both characteristics of a public good. But private firms have provided the vast majority of radio and television broadcasting services in the United States. The free-rider problem was partially avoided by using advertising to pay for the service. Paying directly would be impossible because of the inability to exclude individuals who do not pay.

More recently, technology is changing the public good features of television. Cable TV and the ability to scramble signals for those who use satellites to obtain their television signals have reduced the problem of nonexcludability. If one does not pay a cable television bill, the service can be turned off. If one does not pay the satellite fee, the signals can be scrambled so that reception is impossible. Thus, it is now common to see cable television stations delivering specialized programming to small audiences that pay extra for the special service.

Public Goods and Actual Government Production

If we look at the types of goods produced by government in Table 15.1, we see many public goods, such as national defense, police protection, and the judicial and legal system. However, many of the goods in the list do not have features of public goods. Postal delivery, for example, is a service that has both rivalry in consumption and excludability. If you do not put a stamp on your letter, it is not delivered, and there is certainly rivalry in the consumption of a postal delivery worker's time. In principle, education also is characterized by rivalry in consumption and excludability. For a given-sized school, additional students reduce the education of other students, and it is technologically possible to exclude people. Although there are other reasons why the government might be involved in the production of these goods, it is important to note that the production of a good by the government does not make that good a public good. In centrally planned economies, the government produces virtually everything, private goods as well as public goods. The economist's definition of a public good is specific and is useful for determining when the government should produce something and when it is better left to the market.

Cost-Benefit Analysis

Suppose it is decided that a good or service is a public good and that if it is to be produced at all, government should provide it. Should the good be produced? How much of the good should be produced? Such decisions are ultimately made by voters and elected officials after much political debate. Some economic analysis of the costs and benefits of the goods and services should inform the participants in this debate. Balancing the costs and benefits of a good or service is called **cost-benefit analysis.**

cost-benefit analysis: an appraisal of a project based on the costs and benefits derived from it.

■ **Marginal Cost and Marginal Benefit.** To determine the quantity of a government-provided service that should be produced, the marginal cost and marginal benefit of the service should be considered. In the case of police services, for example, a decision about whether to increase the size of the police force should consider both the marginal benefit to the people in the city—the reduction in the loss of life and property caused by crime, the increased enjoyment from a secure environment, and safer schools—and the marginal cost—the increased payroll for the police. If the marginal benefit of more police is greater than the marginal cost of more police, then the police force should be increased. The optimal size of the police force should be such that the marginal cost of more police is equal to the marginal benefit of more police.

Measuring the costs of producing government-provided services is not difficult because government workers' wages and materials used in production have explicit dollar values.

But measuring the benefits of government-provided services is much more difficult. How do we measure how much people value greater security in their community? How do we value a reduction in violence at schools or a reduced murder rate? Public opinion polls in which people are asked how much they would be willing to pay are a possibility. For example, people can be asked in surveys how much they would be willing to pay for more police in an area. Such estimates of willingness to pay are called **contingent valuations** because they give the value contingent on the public good's existing and the person's having to pay for it. Some economists think that contingent valuation is not reliable if people do not actually have to pay for the good or service. People may not give a good estimate of their true willingness to pay.

contingent valuation: an estimation of the willingness to pay for a project on the part of consumers who may benefit from the project.

Externalities: From the Environment to Education

externality: the situation in which the costs of producing or the benefits of consuming a good spill over onto those who are not producing or consuming the good.

We have seen that the existence of public goods provides an economic rationale for government involvement in the production of certain goods and services. Another rationale for government involvement in production is a market failure known as an externality. An **externality** occurs when the costs of producing a good or the benefits from consuming a good spill over to individuals who are not producing or consuming the good. The production of goods that cause pollution is the classic example of an externality. For example, when a coal-fired electric utility plant produces energy, it emits smoke that contains carbon dioxide, sulfur dioxide, and other pollutants into the air. These pollutants can make life miserable for people breathing the air and cause serious health concerns. Similarly, automobiles emit pollutants and reduce the quality of life for people in areas where cars are driven. Those who drive cars add a cost to others. These are examples of **negative externalities** because they have a negative effect—a cost—on the well-being of others. A **positive externality** occurs when a positive effect—a benefit—from producing or consuming a good spills over to others. For example, you might benefit if your neighbor plants a beautiful garden that is visible from your house or apartment. Let us first look at the effects of negative externalities and then consider positive externalities.

negative externality: the situation in which costs spill over onto someone not involved in producing or consuming the good.

positive externality: the situation in which benefits spill over onto someone not involved in producing or consuming the good.

Negative Externalities

In the case of negative externalities, a competitive market does not generate the efficient amount of production. The quantity produced is greater than the efficient quantity. For example, too much air-polluting electrical energy may be produced. The reason is that producers do not take into account the external costs when they calculate their costs of production. If they did take these costs into account, they would produce less.

The reason why competitive markets are not efficient in the case of negative externalities can be illustrated using the supply and demand curves. For example, consider an example of a negative externality due to pollution caused by the

Oil Spill: A Negative Externality
The oil spilled into the ocean by this sinking oil tanker is an example of a negative externality: The production of goods or services (transportation of oil) by a firm raises costs or reduces benefits to people (the oil spill).

marginal private cost: the marginal cost of production as viewed by the private firm or individual.

marginal social cost: the marginal cost of production as viewed by society as a whole.

production of electricity. A negative externality occurs because the production of electricity raises pollution costs to other firms or individuals. The electrical utility plant pollutes the air and adds costs greater than the costs perceived by the electrical utility. The externality makes the marginal cost as perceived by the private firm, which we now call the **marginal private cost,** less than the true marginal cost that is incurred by society, which we call the **marginal social cost.** Marginal social cost is the sum of the firm's marginal private cost and the increase in external costs to society as more is produced. The marginal external cost is the change in external costs as more is produced. That is,

Marginal social cost = marginal private cost + marginal external cost

We illustrate this in Figure 15.1 by drawing a marginal private cost curve below the marginal social cost curve. We use the term *marginal private cost* to refer to what we have thus far called marginal cost in order to distinguish it from marginal social cost. Recall that adding up all the marginal (private) cost curves for the firms in a market gives the market supply curve, as labeled in the diagram.

Figure 15.1 also shows the marginal benefit to consumers from using the product, in this case electrical energy. This is the market demand curve for electricity. According to the supply and demand model, the interaction of firms and consumers in the market will result in a situation in which the marginal cost of production—the marginal private cost—equals marginal benefit. This situation occurs at the market equilibrium, where the quantity supplied equals the quantity demanded. The resulting quantity produced is indicated by point *B* in Figure 15.1.

However, at this amount of production, the marginal benefit of production is less than the marginal *social* cost of production. Marginal benefit equals marginal private cost but is less than marginal social cost. Only at point *A* in the figure is marginal benefit equal to marginal social cost. Thus, point *A* represents the efficient level of production. Because of the externality, too much is produced. Firms produce too much because they do not incur the external costs. There is a deadweight loss, as shown in Figure 15.1. Consumer surplus plus producer surplus is not maximized.

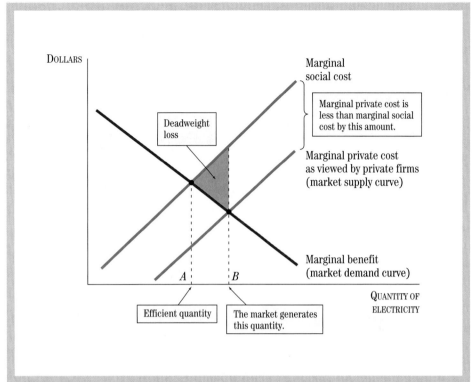

Figure 15.1
Illustration of a Typical Negative Externality
Because production of the good creates costs external to the firm (for example, pollution), the marginal social cost is greater than the marginal private cost to the firm. Thus, the equilibrium quantity that emerges from a competitive market is too large: Marginal benefit is less than marginal social cost.

Positive Externalities

A positive externality occurs when the activity of one person makes another person better off, either reducing costs or increasing benefits. Let us examine what happens when a positive externality raises social benefits above private benefits. For example, increased earnings are a benefit from attending high school, college, graduate school, or continuing education. But the education also benefits society. The greater education that these individuals receive is spread to others. Going to school and learning to read and write makes people better citizens. Learning about hygiene and becoming health conscious puts less of a burden on the public health system.

Another example of a good with a positive externality is research. Firms that engage in research get some of the benefits of that research through the products that they can sell—maybe novel products. But in many cases the research spreads, and other people can take advantage of it as well. Research that spills over to other industries or other individuals is an externality. The benefit from the research expenditures goes beyond the individual; it creates inefficiencies just as negative externalities do.

To show how positive externalities affect the quantity produced in a competitive market, we need to look at the supply and demand curves. The externality makes the marginal benefit as perceived by the consumer, which we now call the **marginal private benefit,** less than the true benefit to society, which we call the **marginal social benefit.** With a positive externality, the marginal social benefit is greater than the

marginal private benefit: the marginal benefit from consumption of a good as viewed by a private individual.

marginal social benefit: the marginal benefit from consumption of a good from the viewpoint of society as a whole.

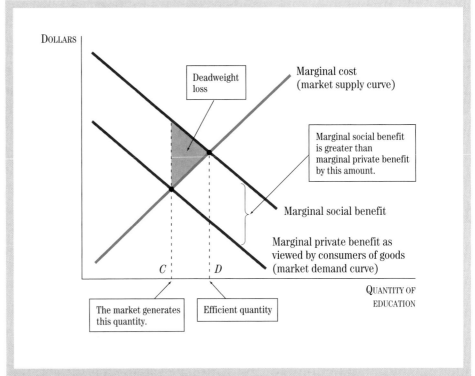

Figure 15.2
Illustration of a Typical Positive Externality
Because consumption of the good (for example, education) gives benefits to others, the marginal social benefit is greater than the marginal private benefit. Hence, the equilibrium quantity that emerges from a competitive market is too low.

marginal private benefit because there is a marginal external benefit from more consumption. That is,

Marginal social benefit = marginal private benefit + marginal external benefit

Figure 15.2 shows the impact of this difference between marginal social benefit and marginal private benefit. Suppose that Figure 15.2 refers to the market for education. Then the quantity of education is on the horizontal axis. The marginal social benefit curve is above the marginal private benefit curve in the figure. The marginal private benefit curve for consumers is the market demand curve. Consider the equilibrium quantity at point *C*, where the quantity supplied equals the quantity demanded in Figure 15.2. The market results in a quantity produced that is less than the efficient quantity, which occurs when the marginal *social* benefit equals the marginal cost, as shown at point *D*. The quantity generated by the market is at a point where the marginal social benefit is greater than the marginal cost. Production and consumption of education are inefficient; the quantity of education is too low. Again, there is a deadweight loss due to externality, as shown in Figure 15.2.

Externalities Spread Across Borders

Externalities are sometimes international problems. Sulfur dioxide emissions from electrical utility plants are an externality whose international effects have received much attention. The sulfur dioxide travels high into the air and is then dispersed by winds across long distances. Rainfall then brings the sulfur dioxide back to earth in the form of acid rain, which lands on forests and lakes hundreds of miles away. In some cases, the acid rain occurs in countries different from the country in which the sulfur dioxide was first emitted. In North America, acid rain that results from burning fuel in the Midwest industrial centers may fall in Canada or upstate New York.

Global warming is another example of an externality with international dimension. When too much carbon dioxide accumulates in the earth's atmosphere, it prevents the sun's warmth from escaping out of the atmosphere, causing a greenhouse effect. Global warming is caused by the emission of carbon dioxide by firms and individuals but has effects all over the world.

REVIEW
- Externalities occur when the benefits or costs of producing and consuming spill over to others. Externalities cause the marginal private cost to be different from the marginal social cost, or the marginal private benefit to be different from the marginal social benefit.

- Externalities are a cause of market failure. Production of goods with negative externalities is more than the efficient amount. Production of goods with positive externalities is less than the efficient amount.

- Many externalities are global, occurring across borders, as when pollution emitted in one country has negative effects in other countries.

Remedies for Externalities

As the previous section shows, competitive markets do not generate an efficient level of production when externalities exist. What are some of the ways in which a society can alleviate problems caused by these externalities? In some cases, the solution has been for government to produce the good or service. In practice, elementary education is provided by governments all over the world with requirements that children attend school through a certain age. Education is by far the government-produced good or service with the most employment in the United States. But in most cases where externalities are present, production is left to the private sector, and government endeavors to influence the quantity produced. In fact, much of college education and some K–12 education is provided by the private sector in the United States.

How can production in the private sector be influenced by government so as to lead to a more efficient level of production of goods and services in the economy? We will see that the answer involves changing behavior so that the externalities are taken into account internally by firms and consumers. In other words, the challenge is to **internalize** the externalities.

internalize: the process of providing incentives so that externalities are taken into account internally by firms or consumers.

There are four alternative ways to bring about a more efficient level of production in the case of externalities. The first one discussed here, private remedies, does not require direct government intervention. The other three—command and control, taxes or subsidies, and tradable permits—do.

Private Remedies: Agreements Between the Affected Parties

private remedy: a procedure that eliminates or internalizes externalities without government action other than defining property rights.

In some cases, people, through **private remedies,** can eliminate externalities themselves without government assistance. A Nobel Prize winner in economics, Ronald Coase of the University of Chicago, pointed out this possibility in a paper published in 1960.

Consider the following simple example. Suppose that the externality relates to the production of two products: health care and candy. Suppose that a hospital is built next door to a large candy factory. Making candy requires noisy pounding and vibrating machinery. Unfortunately, the walls of the new hospital are thin. The loud candy machinery can be heard in the hospital. Thus, there is an externality that we might call noise pollution. It has a cost. It makes the hospital less effective; for example, it is difficult for the doctors to hear their patients' hearts through the stethoscopes.

What can be done? The city mayor could adopt a rule prohibiting loud noise near the hospital, but that would severely impinge on the candy making in the city. Or, because the hospital was built after the candy factory, the mayor could say, "Too bad, doctors; candy is important too." Alternatively, it might be better for the candy workers and doctors to work this externality out themselves. The supervisor of the candy workers could negotiate with the doctors. Perhaps the candy workers could agree to use the loud machines only during the afternoon, during which the doctors would take an extended break. Or perhaps a thick wall could be built between the buildings.

Thus, it is possible to resolve the externality by negotiation between the two parties affected. The privately negotiated alternatives seem more efficient than the mayor's rulings because the production of both candy and health care continues. Note that in these alternatives, both parties alter their behavior. For example, the doctors take a break, and the candy factory limits loud noise to the afternoon. Thus, the parties find a solution in which the polluter does not make all the adjustments, as would be the case if the mayor adopted a "no loud noise" rule.

property rights: rights over the use, sale, and proceeds from a good or resource. (Ch. 1)

■ **The Importance of Assigning Property Rights.**   For a negotiation like this to work, however, it is essential that property rights be well defined. *Property rights* determine who has the right to pollute or infringe on whom. Who, for example, is being infringed on in the case of the noise pollution? Does the candy factory have the right to use loud machinery, or does the hospital have the right to peace and quiet? The mayor's ruling could establish who has the property right, but more likely the case would be taken to a court and the court would decide. After many such cases, precedent would establish who has the property rights in future cases.

The property rights will determine who actually pays for the adjustment that remedies the externality. If the candy factory has the right, then the workers can demand some compensation (perhaps free health-care services) from the hospital for limiting their noise in the afternoon. If the hospital has the right, then perhaps the doctors can get compensated with free candy during the break. The **Coase theorem** states that no matter who is assigned the property rights, the negotiations will lead to an efficient outcome as described in the candy/health-care example. The assignment of the property rights determines who makes the compensation.

Coase theorem: the idea that private negotiations between people will lead to an efficient resolution of externalities regardless of who has the property rights as long as the property rights are defined.

transaction costs: the costs of buying or selling in a market, including search, bargaining, and writing contracts.

■ **Transaction Costs.**   Even if property rights are well defined, for a private agreement like this to occur, transaction costs associated with the agreement must be small compared to the costs of the externality itself. **Transaction costs** are the time and effort needed to reach an agreement. As Coase put it, "in order to carry out a market transaction, it is necessary to discover who it is that one wishes to deal with, to inform people that one wishes to deal and on what terms, to conduct negotiations leading up to a bargain, to draw up the contract, to undertake the inspection needed to make sure that the terms of the contract are being observed, and so on. These operations are often extremely costly."[2] Real-world negotiations are clearly time-consuming, requiring skilled and expensive lawyers in many cases. If these negotiation costs are large, then the private parties may not be able to reach an agreement. If the negotiation in the health-care/candy example took many years and had to be repeated many times, then it might be better to adopt a simple "no loud noise" rule.

■ **The Free-Rider Problem Again.** Free-rider problems can also prevent a private agreement from taking place. For example, a free-rider problem might occur if the hospital was very large, say, 400 doctors. Suppose that the candy workers have the right to noise pollute, so that they require a payment in the form of health care. The hospital would need contributions from the doctors to provide the care. Thus, if each doctor worked in the hospital an extra day a year, this might be sufficient.

However, any one of the 400 doctors could refuse to work the extra day. Some of the doctors could say that they have other job opportunities where they do not have to work an extra day. In other words, doctors who did not pay could free-ride: work at the hospital and still benefit from the agreement. Because of this free-rider problem, the hospital might find it hard to provide health care to the candy workers, and a private settlement might be impossible.

Thus, in the case where the transaction costs are high or free-rider problems exist, a private remedy may not be feasible. Then the role of government comes into play, much as it did in the case of public goods, where the free-rider problem was significant. Again as Coase put it, "Instead of instituting a legal system of rights which can be modified by transactions on the market, the government may impose regulations which state what people must or must not do and which have to be obeyed."[3]

Command and Control Remedies

command and control: the regulations and restrictions that the government uses to correct market imperfections.

When private remedies for externalities are either too costly or not feasible because of free-rider problems, there is a role for government. One form of government intervention to solve the problem of externalities is the placement of restrictions or regulations on individuals or firms, often referred to as **command and control.** Such restrictions could make it illegal to pollute more than a certain amount. Firms that polluted more than that amount could then be fined. For example, in the United States, the corporate average fleet efficiency (CAFE) standards require that the fleet of cars produced by automobile manufacturers each year achieve a stated number of miles per gallon on the average. Another example is a government requirement that electrical utilities put "scrubbers" in their smokestacks to remove certain pollutants from the smoke they emit. In this case, the government regulates the technology that the firms use. Reducing pollution by regulating what firms or individuals produce is a classic example of command and control. Through commands, the government controls what the private sector does. In principle, the externalities are made internal to the firm by requiring that the firm act as if it took the external costs into account.

---

2. Ronald Coase, "The Problem of Social Cost," *Journal of Law and Economics*, October 1960, Vol. 3, p. 15.

3. Ronald Coase, "The Problem of Social Cost," *Journal of Law and Economics*, October 1960, Vol. 3, p. 17.

Command and control methods are used widely by agencies such as the Environmental Protection Agency (EPA), which has responsibility for federal environmental policy in the United States. There are many disadvantages to command and control in the environmental area, however, and economists have criticized such methods. The most significant disadvantage is that command and control does not allow firms to find other, cheaper ways to reduce pollution. Command and control ignores the incentives firms might have to discover cheaper technologies. For example, under command and control, electrical utilities have to install a scrubber even if there is a better, cheaper alternative. New machinery without a scrubber might be more efficient than installing a scrubber. Similarly, developing alternative fuels or simply raising the price of gasoline might be a cheaper way to reduce pollution than the CAFE standards.

Taxes and Subsidies

Because of these disadvantages, economists recommend alternatives to command and control techniques to reduce pollution or to reduce the inefficiencies due to other externalities. Taxes and subsidies are one such alternative. How do they work?

Goods that have negative externalities are taxed. When there are many drivers in a city, roads become congested, leading to traffic backups and delays. Each driver contributes to the congestion, imposing external costs on the other drivers. In 2003, a new tax, called a congestion charge, was imposed on vehicles that drive in central London during the day. The idea was to reduce congestion in central London by making it more expensive to drive there. Cameras mounted above the roads check vehicle registration numbers to make sure that the tax has been paid. This tax internalizes the externality by making drivers pay for the external congestion costs through the tax. If the demand for days of driving in central London is downward-sloping, the tax will reduce driving in central London, reduce the external costs imposed on drivers, and create government revenue.

If a good has a positive externality, too little of it is consumed in a competitive economy. A subsidy can be used to increase consumption of the good. In 2000, the state of Arizona gave a $20,000 subsidy to people who bought an SUV that runs on both gasoline and propane. The idea was to give an incentive for people to buy vehicles that pollute less. The pollution reduction would then benefit all Arizona residents. This subsidy internalizes the externality by making the consumer feel the extra benefits through the subsidy. Do you think Arizona residents responded to the change in the price of these SUVs? As you probably guessed, they did; so many Arizona residents took advantage of the subsidy that an emergency session of the state legislature was convened to curtail the program.

Unlike command and control, taxes and subsidies allow firms or people to respond to price or cost changes. With changes in technology, a firm might find it could afford to pollute even less than would be allowed under a command and control guideline.

The way that taxes can be used to reduce pollution is illustrated graphically in Figure 15.3, which uses the same curves as Figure 15.1. Recall that the marginal social cost of production is greater than the marginal private cost, as viewed from the private firm, because the good pollutes. We know that taxes raise the marginal cost to the individual firm. They thereby shift up

Big Brother Is Watching Your Car!
Closed circuit television cameras loom above traffic in central London to monitor the license plates of the estimated 250,000 cars entering the city each day. Drivers pay a "congestion charge" to drive in central London, making it more expensive to drive there, with the ultimate goal of reducing traffic backups.

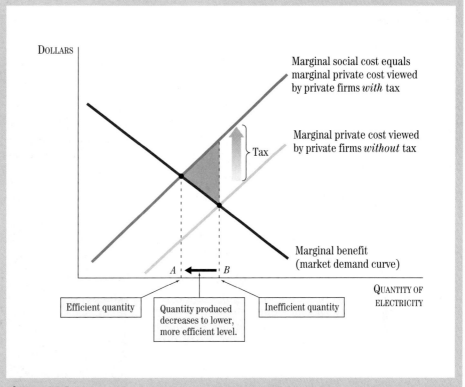

DOLLARS

Marginal social cost equals
marginal private cost viewed
by private firms *with* tax

Marginal private cost viewed
by private firms *without* tax

} Tax

Marginal benefit
(market demand curve)

A   *B*

QUANTITY OF
ELECTRICITY

Efficient quantity

Quantity produced
decreases to lower,
more efficient level.

Inefficient quantity

Figure 15.3
Using Taxes in the Case of a Negative Externality
A tax equal to the difference between the marginal private cost and the marginal social
cost in Figure 15.1 shifts the supply curve up. This reduces the equilibrium quantity produced to the lower, more efficient level.

the market supply curve and lead to a market equilibrium with a smaller quantity
produced. If the tax is chosen to exactly equal the difference between the marginal
social cost and the marginal private cost, then the quantity produced will decline
from the inefficient quantity shown at point *B* to the efficient quantity shown at point
A in Figure 15.3.

There are many examples of taxes being used at least in part to reduce pollution.
Gasoline taxes are widely viewed as being good for the environment because they
reduce gasoline consumption, which pollutes the air. In the United States there is an
average tax of 46 cents on each gallon of gasoline. The big advantage of taxes or subsidies compared with command and control is that the market is still being used. For
example, if there is a shift in demand, the firm can adjust its technique of production
as the price changes. But with command and control, adjustment must wait until the
government changes its commands or controls.

In the case of positive externalities, subsidies rather than taxes can be used to
increase production and bring marginal social benefits into line with marginal
costs. For example, in Figure 15.4, which uses the same curve as Figure 15.2, a subsidy to encourage education, a good with a positive externality, is illustrated. In
this case, a subsidy to students raises the marginal benefit of education (as perceived by them) up to the marginal social benefit. As a result, the quantity of education rises from the inefficient level (*C*) to the efficient level (*D*), as illustrated in
Figure 15.4.

ECONOMICS IN ACTION

Externalities from Biodiversity

Biodiversity—the rich variety of plant and animal life in the world—has been recognized as important to maintaining the world's ecosystem. Any species may hold unique benefits for pharmaceutical and medical research. Many important pharmaceutical products throughout history—from aspirin to life-saving drugs—have been discovered in the natural environment and then modified or improved by researchers. Preserving biodiversity is important for future discoveries and applications.

One of the great sources of biodiversity is the rain forests of South America. However, these rain forests are being cut and burned to make room for farms.

Observe that there is an externality here. Those governments or individuals who own the rain forests may suffer little from cutting them down and losing the biodiversity. The benefit of the biodiversity is external to them, spread around the world and, indeed, to future generations, who must forgo the opportunity for better drugs that the variety of plant and animal life might bring. This externality is global, not restricted to any one country. Thus, resolving it is even more difficult than in the case of a single country with one government.

This externality is now being reduced by private remedies—negotiations between affected parties. In some cases, pharmaceutical companies have offered the owners of the rain forests an opportunity to share in some of the patent and copyright royalties from the discovery of new drugs. In exchange for not cutting down the forests, the owners of the forests can share in any royalties from drugs derived from plant and animal life from the forests. If such royalties are available, then by cutting down the forests the owners forgo the royalties; this raises the cost of cutting and burning and effectively internalizes the externality.

It is not yet clear whether the incentive will be great enough to slow the cutting and burning of the forests, or whether an international agreement among

A benefit of this tropical rain forest may be a life-saving drug. Why is it an external benefit? How can it be internalized?

governments around the world is feasible. In fact, the difficulty of coordinating international government action in these cases may be the reason why interested private parties are looking for ways to resolve the externality themselves.

In addition to subsidizing education, the government subsidizes research, another good with a positive externality, by providing research grants to private firms and individuals. The National Science Foundation supports basic research, and the National Institutes of Health support medical research. In supporting research with a limited budget, it is important for the government to place more emphasis on research that has big externalities. Many view basic research as having larger positive externalities than applied research. The ideas in basic research, such as that on the structure of the atom, affect many parts of the economy. Applied research, such as that on a new lightweight metal for a bike, has more limited use, and the firm can prevent others from using it. Products developed through applied research can be

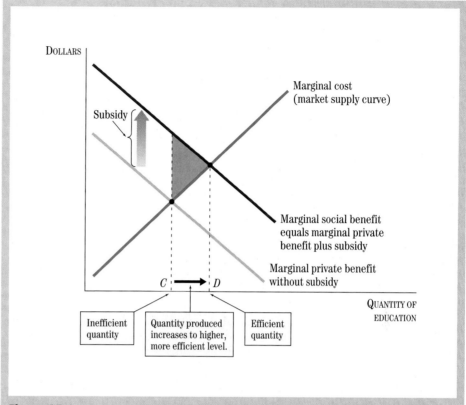

Figure 15.4
Using Subsidies in the Case of a Positive Externality
A subsidy equal to the difference between the marginal social benefit and the marginal private benefit of education or research shifts the demand curve up. This increases the equilibrium quantity produced to the higher, more efficient level and eliminates the deadweight loss due to the externality.

sold for profit. This suggests that more government funds should go toward basic research than toward applied research. In fact, the federal government in the United States does spend more to subsidize basic research than applied research.

■ **Emission Taxes.** A more direct way to use taxes to deal with pollution externalities is to tax the firm based on the amount of pollution emitted. For example, an electrical utility could be charged fees depending on how many particles of sulfur dioxide it emits, rather than on how much electricity it produces. Such charges are called **emission taxes.** They are much like taxes on the amount of the product sold, but they focus directly on the amount of pollution.

Emission taxes have an advantage over taxes on production in that the firm can use technology to change the amount of pollution associated with its production. Thus, rather than producing less electricity, the firm can reduce the amount of pollution associated with a given amount of electricity if it can find a cheaper way to do so. Emission taxes have an even greater advantage over command and control than a tax on the product has.

emission tax: a charge made to firms that pollute the environment based on the quantity of pollution they emit.

■ **Why Is Command and Control Used More Than Taxes?** There is one feature of command and control that many people like: The total amount of pollution can be better controlled than with a tax. This may explain why command and control is used more than taxes. Suppose, for example, that a tax is used to equate marginal social cost with marginal benefit, as in Figure 15.3. Now suppose there is a sudden reduction in the private cost of producing electricity. The private marginal cost curve will shift down and, with the tax unchanged, production (and pollution) will increase. A regulation that stipulates a certain quantity to produce would not have this problem. The total amount of pollution would be fixed. Fortunately, in recent years, a new idea in pollution control has emerged that has both this advantage of command and control and the flexibility of the market. This new idea is tradable permits.

Tradable Permits

tradable permit: a governmentally granted license to pollute that can be bought and sold.

Tradable permits use the market to help achieve the standards set by the government. Rather than force a firm to meet a certain standard, the government issues each firm a permit that allows the firm to emit a certain limited amount of pollutants into the atmosphere. Firms have an incentive to lower their emissions because they can sell the permit if they do not use it. Firms that can lower their emissions cheaply will choose to do so and benefit by selling their permits to other firms for which reducing the pollution is more costly. Tradable permits not only allow the market system to work, they give firms incentive to find the least costly form of pollution control.

■ **Control over Firms as a Group Rather Than Individual Firms.** Tradable permits are ideal in certain circumstances. For example, they work well in the case of acid rain, which falls over a wider area than that of the individual polluting firm. With acid rain, it is the total amount of pollution from all firms in the country or the region that matters most. To reduce the total amount of pollution, the government issues a number of permits specifying permissible levels of pollution. Once these permits are issued, those firms that can reduce the emissions in the most cost-efficient manner will sell their permits to other firms. They can raise profits by reducing pollution themselves and selling their permits to other firms with less efficient pollution-control methods. The total amount of pollution in the economy is equal to the total amount of permits issued and, therefore, is controlled perfectly.

Tradable permits are a new idea but are likely to be an increasingly common way to reduce pollution in the future. A tradable permit program called RECLAIM is being used in Los Angeles. Under the 1990 Clean Air Act, tradable permits can be used on a national basis.

Tradable permits could also work in global warming. The amount of global warming depends on the total amount of carbon dioxide emissions in the world's atmosphere. It does not matter whether a firm in Los Angeles or in Shanghai emits the carbon dioxide. Tradable permits could control the total amount of pollution. The permits would let firms or individuals decide on the most cost-effective way for them to reduce the total amount of pollution.

■ **Assigning and Defining Property Rights.** Tradable permits illustrate how important property rights are for resolving externalities. The role of government in this case is to create a market by defining certain rights to pollute and then allowing firms to buy and sell these rights. Once rights are assigned, the market can work and achieve efficiency.

Balancing the Costs and Benefits of Reducing Externalities

As with public goods, it is important to use a cost-benefit analysis when considering externalities. There are benefits to reducing pollution, but there are costs also. The costs of reducing pollution in the United States are about $120 billion per year, or about 2 percent of GDP. This percentage is expected to rise over time. These costs should be compared to the benefits associated with pollution control on a case-by-case basis.

For example, the Environmental Protection Agency introduced a new rule for stricter standards on the amount of sulfur allowed in diesel fuel in 2000. Environmentalists were concerned that diesel exhaust is causing accelerated cancer rates, but trucking companies that use diesel fuel were concerned about the effect of the stricter standards on the price of their fuel. The Environmental Protection Agency estimated that the new, stricter standards would prevent 8,300 deaths and 360,000 asthma attacks, while increasing the price of diesel fuel by four to five cents per gallon. The oil industry reported that implementation of the stricter standards would cost $8 billion.

The stricter standards save lives and reduce suffering for hundreds of thousands of people. These benefits should be compared to the cost of the stricter standards to determine environmental policy. Why was this rule change so hotly debated? You may have noticed that the citizens who avoid cancer and breathing problems benefit from the stricter standards, while the cost is borne by the oil producers and trucking companies.

■ **Environmental Policy Is Debated**   The following two examples illustrate recent environmental policy debates, with a proposed change in an environmental rule, the reported benefits and costs of reducing the externality, and the actual outcome in each case. Imagine that you are in charge of determining U.S. environmental policy. Think about the benefits and the costs of the stricter regulation, and the tradeoff between costs and benefits. Would you decide that a new, stricter regulation should be in place to reduce the externality?

In the first example, the cost of reducing the externality was judged to be too high compared to the benefits. In the 2000 campaign for the presidency, George W. Bush supported the regulation of carbon dioxide emissions. Bush called carbon dioxide a pollutant that contributes to global warming. Environmental groups supported the regulation of carbon dioxide emissions and were enthusiastic about Bush's concern about global warming. In 2001, President Bush changed his mind about regulating carbon dioxide emissions. A study by the Energy Department showed that this regulation would result in nearly a quadrupling of the cost of producing electricity from coal, causing large price increases for both electricity and natural gas. President Bush stated that the impact on utility prices made the cost of regulating carbon dioxide emissions too high.

In this second example, the benefits from reducing the externality were judged to be worthwhile compared to the costs. Three days before leaving office, President Clinton lowered the standard for arsenic in drinking water by 80 percent. In March 2001, the Environmental Protection Agency rescinded the new, stricter standard and debated its merits. Scientific studies show that higher levels of arsenic in drinking water lead to higher risks of fatal cancer, heart disease, and diabetes. Arsenic is a by-product in mining, is used as a wood preservative for lumber, and occurs naturally in water in some areas. The cost of the stricter standard for arsenic in drinking water was estimated to be billions of dollars. In this case, the Bush administration

Economics has become a vital tool of environmentalists working to preserve the natural environment. Many have found that applying economic reasoning to issues that were once argued only on moral or ethical grounds can be a very effective way to persuade businesses and governments to consider environmental issues—and ultimately achieve the environmentalists' goals.

Green Groups See Potent Tool In Economics

By JESSICA E. VASCELLARO
Staff Reporter of THE WALL STREET JOURNAL
August 23, 2005

Many economists dream of getting high-paying jobs on Wall Street, at prestigious think tanks and universities or at powerful government agencies like the Federal Reserve.

But a growing number are choosing to use their skills not to track inflation or interest rates but to rescue rivers and trees. These are the "green economists," more formally known as environmental economists, who use economic arguments and systems to persuade companies to clean up pollution and to help conserve natural areas.

Working at dozens of advocacy groups and a myriad of state and federal environmental agencies, they are helping to formulate the intellectual framework behind approaches to protecting endangered species, reducing pollution and preventing climate change. They also are becoming a link between left-leaning advocacy groups and the public and private sectors.

"In the past, many advocacy groups interpreted economics as how to make a profit or maximize income," says Lawrence Goulder, a professor of environmental and resource economics at Stanford University in Stanford, Calif. "More economists are realizing that it offers a framework for resource allocation where resources are not only labor and capital but natural resources as well."

Environmental economists are on the payroll of government agencies (the Environmental Protection Agency had about 164 on staff in 2004, up 36% from 1995) and groups like the Wilderness Society, a Washington-based conservation group, which has four of them to work on projects such as assessing the economic impact of building off-road driving trails. Environmental Defense, also based in Washington, was one of the first environmental-advocacy groups to hire economists and now has about eight, who do such things as develop market incentives to address environmental problems like climate change and water shortages.

"There used to be this idea that we shouldn't have to monetize the environment because it is invaluable," says Caroline Alkire, who in 1991 joined the Wilderness Society, an advocacy group in Washington, D.C., as one of the group's first economists. "But if we are going to engage in debate on the Hill about drilling in the Arctic we need to be able to combat the financial arguments. We have to play that card or we are going to lose."

decided to impose the stricter standard, convinced that the health benefits were worth the cost.

Some people are concerned that a cost-benefit analysis will reduce spending on the environment too much. They argue that there is no tradeoff between costs and benefits. Environmental regulations can benefit rather than cost the economy, they argue, because requiring individuals to reduce pollution creates a demand for pollution-reducing devices and creates jobs in the pollution-reducing industry. But unless the pollution-reducing equipment is creating a benefit to society greater than

The field of environmental economics began to take form in the 1960s when academics started to apply the tools of economics to the nascent green movement. The discipline grew more popular throughout the 1980s when the Environmental Protection Agency adopted a system of tradable permits for phasing out leaded gasoline. It wasn't until the 1990 amendment to the Clean Air Act, however, that most environmentalists started to take economics seriously.

The amendment implemented a system of tradable allowances for acid rain, a program pushed by Environmental Defense. Under the law, plants that can reduce their emissions more cost-effectively may sell their allowances to more heavy polluters. Today, the program has exceeded its goal of reducing the amount of acid rain to half its 1980 level and is celebrated as evidence that markets can help achieve environmental goals.

Its success has convinced its former critics, who at the time contended that environmental regulation was a matter of ethics, not economics, and favored installing expensive acid rain removal technology in all power plants instead.

Greenpeace, the international environmental giant, was one of the leading opponents of the 1990 amendment. But Kert Davies, research director for Greenpeace USA, said its success and the lack of any significant action on climate policy throughout early 1990s brought the organization around to the concept. "We now believe that [tradable permits] are the most straightforward system of reducing emissions and creating the incentives necessary for massive reductions."

Organizations are also applying economic reasoning toward saving wildlife. In response to arguments that undeveloped land hurts economic growth, Defenders of Wildlife founded a conservation-economics program in 1999 and recently oversaw a study of how much tourists would be willing to pay to visit a red-wolf reservation and educational center in Columbia, N.C. The finding that the center's $2 million price tag would be paid by tourism revenue in five to 10 years is helping raise money for the center and being used by advocacy groups attempting to reintroduce the population in the area.

Environmentalists have also come to recognize that if they can couch their arguments in economic terms, not only governments but also corporations are more likely to listen. Since 2001, the San Francisco-based Rainforest Action Network has persuaded J.P. Morgan Chase & Co., Citigroup Inc. and Bank of America Corp. to account for the cost of pollution in their loan-underwriting processes and, in some cases, to avoid investing in industrial logging companies.

"Companies are looking for certainty and stability," says Michael Brune, executive director of the Rainforest Action Network. "They can do that by investing in sustainable energy, where they don't run the risk of lawsuits or federal regulation or the reputation of being associated with environmentally controversial projects."

the benefits of other goods, shifting more resources to pollution abatement will not be an efficient allocation of society's resources.

Many people argue that the surest way to reduce pollution around the world is to make sure the less-developed economies of the world increase their level of income. This will give them more resources to spend on pollution control; in fact, poor countries will not spend much on reducing pollution until the problems of poverty and hunger are reduced. Environmental degradation in Eastern Europe was severe when these economies were centrally planned. It is likely that the environment will improve when they have more resources to spend on it.

REVIEW

- There are four basic ways to improve the efficiency of markets in the case of externalities: private remedies, command and control, taxes and subsidies, and tradable permits. The latter three involve direct government intervention and are needed when high transaction costs or free-rider problems rule private remedies out.

- Taxes and subsidies, as well as tradable permits, endeavor to use the market to help internalize the externality.

- Tradable permits require that the government define and assign property rights. Once the rights are defined and assigned, the market can allocate the resources to reduce pollution efficiently.

Models of Government Behavior

The previous two sections have outlined what government should do to correct market failure due to public goods and externalities. Regardless of the reason market failure occurs, the outcome is similar: Production may be too little or too much, and producer surplus plus consumer surplus is not maximized. The result is deadweight loss, and the role of government is to change the level of production or employment so as to increase producer surplus plus consumer surplus. Using economics to explain the role of government in this way is considered a *normative* analysis of government policy. Normative economics is the study of what *should be* done. But there is another way to look at government policy. It falls into the area of *positive* rather than normative economics and looks at what governments *actually do* rather than what they should do.

One of the reasons for studying what governments actually do is that frequently the normative recommendations are not followed, or government performs its role poorly. **Government failure** occurs when the government fails to improve on the market or even makes things worse. Sometimes government fails, and sometimes it succeeds. One objective of positive analysis of government is to understand why there is success and failure in different situations.

government failure: the situation where the government fails to improve on the market or even makes things worse.

Public Choice Models

Government itself is run by people. Government behavior depends on the actions of voters, politicians, civil servants, and political appointees from judges to Cabinet officials. The work of government also depends on the large number of people who work in political campaigns, who are active in political parties, who lobby, and who participate in grassroots campaigns, from letter writing to e-mail messages to political protests. Government organizations exist at the state and local levels as well as at the federal level. What motivates the behavior of all these people?

The motivations of politicians and government workers are complex and varied. But the central idea of economics that people make purposeful choices with limited resources should apply to politics and government, as well as to consumers and firms. Many people enter politics for genuine patriotic reasons and are motivated by a desire to improve the well-being of people in their city, state, or country, or even the world. Their motivations may be deeper than watching out for their own best interests, narrowly defined. For example, Alexander Hamilton, the first chief economic spokesman for the United States as the first secretary of the treasury, worked hard to put the newly formed country on a firm economic foundation by having the federal government assume the debts of the states after the Revolutionary War.

But the desire to get elected, or to get votes on issues after being elected, is also part of the motivation of all politicians. Alexander Hamilton would not have done his job if he had not made one of the great political deals of all time, trading his vote on one issue for votes on another. In order to get the votes of the representatives from Virginia and Maryland for the federal government to assume the debts of the states, he agreed to vote to place the capital of the new country along the banks of the Potomac River between Maryland and Virginia, instead of selecting New York City.

Economic models of government behavior are called **public choice models.** They start from the premise that politicians are motivated by increasing their chances of getting themselves or the members of their party elected or reelected. And without explicit incentives to the contrary, government workers are presumed to be motivated by increasing their power or prestige, through increasing the size of their department or by getting promoted. By understanding this self-interest motivation, we can learn much about government, including the reasons for government failure and the reasons for government success.

public choice models: models of government behavior that assume that those in government take actions to maximize their own well-being, such as getting reelected.

Economic Policy Decisions Through Voting

Let us first examine how voting is used to make economic policy decisions in a political environment. We will use the assumption of public choice models: that getting elected is the primary motivation of politicians.

Table 15.2
Alternative Levels of National Defense Spending

National Defense as a Share of GDP

1 percent	Japan's maximum
2 percent	U.S. in 1940
3 percent	U.S. in 2000
4 percent	Post–cold war
10 percent	U.S. in 1960
39 percent	U.S. in 1944

■ **Single Issues with Unanimity.** Let us start with the easiest case: There is only one economic policy decision to be made, and all the voters agree on what it should be. For example, suppose that the issue is spending on national defense, a public good where the government has a key role to play according to the normative economic analysis discussed earlier.

Suppose the specific issue is how much to spend on national defense now that the cold war is over. Some alternatives are shown in Table 15.2.

Suppose that everyone agrees that a level of national defense of around 4 percent of GDP in the United States is appropriate for the post–cold war period, in the absence of major world political changes such as the events of September 11. In reality, of course, opinions differ greatly about the appropriate level. But suppose that after looking at history or making international comparisons or listening to experts on defense and world politics, everyone agrees that 4 percent of GDP is the right amount to spend.

Under these circumstances, when there is only one issue on which all voters agree, voting will lead to the action that everyone prefers, that is, 4 percent, even if politicians are motivated by nothing other than getting elected. Suppose that one politician or political party runs for election on a plank of 39 percent defense spending and that the other argues in favor of 2 percent; clearly, the party with 2 percent will win because it is much closer to the people's views. But then the other politician or party will see the need to move toward the consensus and will run on a 5 percent spending platform; if the other party stays at 2 percent, then the higher-spending party will win. But clearly the other party will then try to get closer to 4 percent, and eventually 4 percent will be the winner.

This example shows that the political system yields the preferred outcome. Of course, after being elected, the politician might break the promise made during the campaign. But if such a change cannot be justified on the basis of a change in circumstances, that politician may have difficulty getting reelected.

■ **The Median Voter Theorem.** What if people have different views? Suppose there is no unanimity about a 4 percent share of GDP for defense. Instead, the country consists of people with many different opinions. Some want more than 4 percent; some want less than 4 percent. Suppose that about half of the people want more than 4 percent and half want less than 4 percent; in other words, 4 percent is the desire of the *median* voter.

If there is only one issue, there will be convergence of the positions of the politicians or the parties toward the median voter's belief. For example, if one party or politician calls for 7 percent spending and the other party calls for 4 percent, then the party calling for 4 percent will attract more voters. Clearly, more than half of the voters are closer to 4 percent than to 7 percent. The **median voter theorem** predicts that the politicians who run on what the median voter wants will be elected. The views of the people at the extremes will not matter at all.

■ **Convergence of Positions in a Two-Party System.** An interesting corollary to the median voter theorem is that political parties or politicians will gravitate toward the center of opinion—toward the median voter. For example, in the case of national defense, it makes no sense for any politician to run on a 39 percent recommendation. The parties will gravitate toward the median voter. This **convergence of positions** may explain the tendency for Democrats and Republicans to take similar positions on many issues.

■ **Voting Paradoxes.** When there are many different issues—defense, taxes, welfare, health-care reform—and people have different opinions and views about each issue, the outcome of voting becomes more complicated. Certain decision-making problems arise. The example of the **voting paradox** illustrates some of these problems.

Suppose three voters have different preferences on three different economic policy options—A, B, and C. Ali likes A best, B second best, and C the least; Betty likes B best, C second best, and A the least; and Camilla likes C best, A second best, and B the least. The three policy options could be three different levels of defense spending (high, medium, and low) or three different pollution control plans (emission taxes, tradable permits, and command and control). Table 15.3 shows the three voters and their different preferences on each option.

median voter theorem: a theorem stating that the median or middle of political preferences will be reflected in government decisions.

convergence of positions: the concentration of the stances of political parties around the center of citizens' opinions.

voting paradox: a situation where voting patterns will not consistently reflect citizens' preferences because of multiple issues on which people vote.

Table 15.3
Preferences That Generate a Voting Paradox

Ranking	Ali	Betty	Camilla
First	A	B	C
Second	B	C	A
Third	C	A	B

In voting on one option versus another, we get:
On A versus B: A wins 2 to 1
On B versus C: B wins 2 to 1
On A versus C: C wins 2 to 1

Paradox because A wins over B and B wins over C, yet C wins over A

Consider three different elections held at different points in time, each with one issue paired up against another. First, there is an election on A versus B, then on B versus C, and then on C versus A. The voting is by simple majority: The issue with the most votes wins. When the vote is on the alternatives A versus B, we see that A wins 2 to 1. That is, both Ali and Camilla like A better than B and vote for it, while only Betty likes B better than A and votes for B. When the vote is on B versus C, we see that B wins 2 to 1. Finally (this vote might be called for by a frustrated Camilla, who sees an opportunity), there is a vote on C versus A, and we see that now C wins 2 to 1. Although it looked like A was a winner over C—because A was preferred to B and B was preferred to C—we see that in the third vote, C is preferred to A; this is the paradox.

The voting paradox suggests that there might be instability in economic policies. Depending on how the votes were put together, the policy could shift from high defense to medium defense to low defense, or from one pollution control system to another, then to another, and then back again. Or taxes could be cut, then raised, and then raised again. All these changes could happen with nothing else in the world having changed. We could even imagine shifting between different economic systems involving different amounts of government intervention—from communism to capitalism to socialism to communism and back again!

This particular voting paradox has been known for two hundred years, but it is only relatively recently that we have come to know that the problem is not unique to this example. Kenneth Arrow showed that this type of paradox is common to any voting scheme. That no democratic voting scheme can avoid inefficiencies of the type described in the voting paradox is called the **Arrow impossibility theorem.**

The voting paradox suggests a certain inherent degree of instability in decisions made by government. Clearly, shifting between different tax systems frequently is a source of uncertainty and inefficiency. The voting paradox may be a reason for government failure in cases where the government takes on some activity such as correcting a market failure.

Arrow impossibility theorem: a theorem that says that no democratic voting scheme can avoid a voting paradox.

Special Interest Groups

The voting paradox is one reason for government failure. Special interest groups are another. It is not unusual for special interest groups to spend time and financial resources to influence legislation. They want policies that are good for them, even if the policies are not necessarily good for the country as a whole. For example, look at the farming industry, which has a great deal of government intervention. What is the explanation for the intervention? If you look back at the reasons for government intervention—income distribution, public goods, externalities—you will see that they do not apply to the farm sector. Food does not fit the definition of a public good, and many farmers who benefit from the intervention have higher incomes than other people in the society who do not benefit from such intervention. One can thus view the government regulation of agricultural markets as a form of government failure.

■ **Concentrated Benefits and Diffuse Costs.** One explanation for government failure in such situations is that special interest groups can have powerful effects on legislation that harms or benefits a small group of people a great deal but affects almost everyone else only a little. For example, the federal subsidy to the sugar growers in the United States costs taxpayers and consumers somewhere between $800 million and $2.5 billion per year, or about $3.20 to $10 per person per year. However, the gain from the subsidy amounts to about $136,000 per sugar

ECONOMICS IN ACTION

Advising the Government to Auction Off the Spectrum

The U.S. government is responsible for distributing rights to use the radio-frequency spectrum in the United States. Each section, or band, of the spectrum is like a piece of property. Just as a farmer needs a piece of land to grow crops, a telecommunications firm needs a piece of the airwaves to send signals. And just as a piece of land has a price, so does a piece of the airwaves.

For many years, the U.S. government gave away the rights to use the spectrum in an arbitrary and inefficient manner. It was a classic example of elected officials and bureaucrats gaining influence or prestige by choosing who would get the rights. Economists had long recommended that government sell—auction off—the spectrum rather than give it away. They used models of government behavior to show why the traditional approach was inefficient and why it persisted. Finally, in 1993, Congress passed a bill giving the Federal Communications Commission (FCC) the authority to auction off the spectrum.

Auctioning off the airwaves is different from auctioning off art, however, because the value of a piece of the spectrum to firms depends on whether they also have adjacent parts of the spectrum—either adjacent geographically (like Florida and Georgia) or adjacent in frequency (with nearly the same megahertz number).

Because spectrum auctions were different, economists were called in to help design the spectrum auc-

The first FCC auction.

tion. The auction design chosen by the FCC was a novel one. In most auctions, goods are auctioned off *sequentially*—first one piece of art, then the next, and so on. In contrast, following the advice of economists, bands of spectrum were auctioned off *simultaneously* by the FCC. In other words, firms could bid on several bands at the same time. It would be as if ten works of art were auctioned off at the same time, with buyers able to offer different bids on each piece of art. Thus, if the bids on one piece were too high, a buyer could change the bid on another piece before the final sale was made. This simultaneous procedure dealt with the distinct characteristics of the spectrum, namely, that many buyers wanted adjacent bands rather than a single band.

Because such a simultaneous auction had never taken place before, economic experiments were used to try it out. For example, Charles Plott of the California Institute of Technology conducted experiments on simultaneous auction proposals made by Paul Milgrom and Robert Wilson of Stanford University. Partly because the proposal worked well in the experiments, the FCC decided to use this approach. The auction process has been heralded as a great success, and the FCC is expected to continue auctioning the use of the spectrum. The Congressional Budget Office estimates that the revenue from these auctions in 2003–2005 will be around $24 billion.

---

grower. Thus, the small cost is hardly enough to lead each consumer to spend time fighting Congress. However, the payments are certainly worth the sugar growers' effort to travel to Washington and to contribute to some political campaigns. When the costs are spread over millions of users and the benefits are concentrated on only a few, it is hard to eliminate government programs. Those who benefit have much more incentive to lobby and work hard for or against certain candidates. Thus, the process of obtaining funds for election or getting support from the powerful interest groups can have large effects on policy.

▓ **Wasteful Lobbying.**   There is another economic harm from special interest lobbying. It is the waste of time and resources that the lobbying entails. Lobbyists are usually highly talented and skilled people, and millions of dollars in resources are spent on lobbying for legislation or other government actions.

In many less-developed countries—where special interest lobbying is more prevalent than in the United States—such activity consumes a significant amount of scarce resources.

Incentive Problems in Government

In any large government, many of the services are provided by civil servants rather than politicians and political appointees. In fact, it was to avoid the scandals of the spoils system—in which politicians would reward those who helped in a political campaign with jobs—that the civil service system set rules to protect against firing and established examinations and other criteria for qualifying workers for jobs.

But what motivates government managers and workers? Profit maximization as in the case of business firms is not a factor. Perhaps increasing the size of the agency or the department of government is the goal of managers. But simply increasing the size of an agency is not likely to result in an efficient delivery of services. Profit motives and competition with other firms give private firms an incentive to keep costs down and look for innovative production techniques and new products. But these incentives do not automatically arise in government. For this reason, it is likely that a government service, whether a public good or a regulation, will not be provided as efficiently as a good provided by the private sector. This is another possible reason for government failure.

Better Government Through Market-Based Incentives

In recent years, there has been an effort to use incentives to improve the efficiency of government. Many of these ideas were summarized in a popular 1992 book, *Reinventing Government: How the Entrepreneurial Spirit Is Transforming the Public Sector*, by David Osborne and Ted Gaebler, which lent its name to the "reinventing government" movement of the 1990s.

Admitting that "cynicism about government runs deep within the American soul" and that "our government is in deep trouble today," the authors give hundreds of examples of how the "entrepreneurial spirit" can be used to make police services, sanitation, and schools more efficient. In many cases, efficiency can be improved by having government workers rewarded for providing high-quality service with higher pay or other benefits. In other words, marketlike incentives would be used to encourage greater government efficiency.

A big part of improving government can come through providing competition. Vouchers—including food stamps, housing vouchers, college tuition grants, elementary school grants—have been suggested by economists as a way to add competition and improve government efficiency. For example, Osborne and Gaebler contrast two different systems of government support for World War II veterans: (1) the GI bill, which gave veterans vouchers to go to any college, private or public, and (2) the Veterans Administration hospitals, where the government itself provides medical service. They conclude that the first system worked much better, and by analogy should be used in other cases where vouchers or government-produced services are the choices.

REVIEW

- Public choice models of government behavior assume that politicians and government workers endeavor to improve their own well-being, much as models of firms and consumer behavior assume firms and consumers do.

- In cases where there is consensus among voters, voting will bring about the consensus government policy. When there is no consensus, the median voter theorem shows that the center of opinion is what matters for decisions. However, the voting paradox points out that in more complex decisions with many options, the decisions can be unstable, leading to government failure.

- Other causes for government failure include special interest groups and poor incentives in government.

- Economic models of government behavior suggest ways to reduce the likelihood of government failure and increase government efficiency.

- Incentives and competition have been suggested as ways to improve the operation of government.

Conclusion

In this chapter, we have explored market failure due to public goods and to externalities. A competitive market provides too little in the way of public goods such as national defense and too little in the way of goods for which there are positive externalities, such as education and research. A competitive market results in too much production of goods for which there are negative externalities, such as goods that pollute the environment.

Most of the remedies for market failure involve the action of government. The provision of public goods by the government should require a careful cost-benefit analysis to make sure that the benefits are greater than the cost of producing a public good. The opportunities for private parties to work out externalities may be limited by transaction costs and free-rider problems. But there are ways in which the market system can aid the government, as in the case of tradable permits. In these cases, the main role of the government is to define and assign property rights.

It is very important, however, to develop models of government behavior and to recognize the possibility of government failure. In reality, political considerations enter into the production of public goods. A member of Congress from one part of the country might push for a public works project in his or her local district in order to be reelected. Moreover, the externality argument emphasized in this chapter is frequently abused as a political device, providing justification for wasteful expenditures. Thus, finding ways to improve decision-making in government, such as through market-based incentives, is needed if government is to play its role in providing remedies for market failures.

KEY POINTS

1. Public goods are defined by two key characteristics, non-rivalry and nonexcludability. National defense and police services are examples of public goods.

2. The existence of public goods provides a role for government because competitive markets frequently have difficulty producing such goods in the efficient amount.

3. Cost-benefit analysis is a technique to decide how much of a public good should be produced. Measuring benefits and deciding how to discount the future are difficult in the case of public goods.

4. Externalities occur when the costs or benefits of a good spill over to other parts of the economy. They create another potential role for government.

5. Goods may have a positive externality or a negative externality.

6. Externalities can sometimes be internalized in the private sector without government. But in many cases, externalities require some government action.

7. Taxes and subsidies or tradable permits are preferred to command and control because the market can still transmit information and provide incentives.

8. Models of government behavior are based on the economic assumption that people try to improve their well-being. In the case of politicians, this usually means taking actions to improve their chances of being elected or reelected.

9. The median voter theorem and the voting paradox are some of the results of the analysis of voting; the latter suggests a reason for government failure.

10. Special interest groups and poor incentives are some of the other reasons for government failure.

11. Marketlike incentives and competition are ways suggested by economists to reduce government failure.

KEY TERMS

public good	externality	internalize	public choice models
nonrivalry	negative externality	private remedy	median voter theorem
nonexcludability	positive externality	Coase theorem	convergence of positions
free-rider problem	marginal private cost	transaction cost	voting paradox
user fee	marginal social cost	command and control	Arrow impossibility
cost-benefit analysis	marginal private benefit	emission tax	theorem
contingent valuation	marginal social benefit	tradable permit	

QUESTIONS FOR REVIEW

1. What types of goods are produced or supplied by the government at the federal, state, and local levels?

2. Why do nonexcludability and nonrivalry make production by private firms in a market difficult?

3. Why is it difficult to measure the benefits of public goods when deciding how much to produce?

4. What is the use of cost-benefit analysis in the case of public goods?

5. What is the difference between a positive externality and a negative externality?

6. Why are private remedies for externalities not always feasible?

7. What is the advantage of emission taxes over command and control?

8. How do subsidies for education remedy a market failure?

9. What is the difference between the median voter theorem and the voting paradox?

10. What are the similarities and differences between market failure and government failure?

PROBLEMS

1. The following table shows the marginal benefit per year (in dollars) to all the households in a small community from the hiring of additional firefighters. The table also shows the marginal cost per year (in dollars) of hiring additional firefighters per year.

Number of Firefighters	Marginal Benefit	Marginal Cost
1	1,000,000	34,000
2	500,000	35,000
3	300,000	36,000
4	100,000	37,000
5	70,000	38,000
6	50,000	39,000
7	40,000	40,000
8	30,000	41,000
9	20,000	42,000
10	10,000	44,000

a. Is the service provided by the additional firefighters a public good?

b. Why might the marginal benefit from an additional firefighter decline with the number of firefighters?

c. Plot the marginal benefit and the marginal cost in a graph, with the number of firefighters on the horizontal axis.

d. What is the optimal amount of this public good (in terms of the number of firefighters)? Illustrate your answer on the graph in part (c).

e. Is this marginal benefit schedule the same as the town's demand curve for firefighters?

2. Suppose that there are only three households in the town in problem 1 and that each one of them has the marginal benefit (in dollars) from additional firefighters described in the following table:

Number of Firefighters	Household A	Household B	Household C
1	500,000	300,000	200,000
2	300,000	100,000	100,000
3	200,000	50,000	50,000
4	50,000	30,000	20,000
5	36,000	20,000	14,000
6	25,000	15,000	10,000
7	20,000	14,000	6,000
8	15,000	13,000	2,000
9	10,000	9,000	1,000
10	5,000	4,500	500

a. Add up the marginal benefits of the three households for each number of firefighters. Check that your addition gives the same marginal benefit for all the households in the town as given in problem 1.

b. Plot each of the three marginal benefit schedules and the marginal benefit schedule for the whole town on the same graph, with the number of firefighters on the horizontal axis. (You will need a big vertical scale.) What is the relationship between the three household curves and the curve for the whole town?

3. Suppose there is a neighborhood crime watch in which people volunteer to patrol the street where you live. If you do not participate in the patrol, but your neighborhood is safer because of the crime watch, are you a free rider? Why? What can your neighbors do to eliminate the free-rider problem?

4. Public education is not a public good, but it has external effects. Explain.

5. Group projects—for example, when students are assigned to work together on the same term paper—can lead to a free-rider problem. Why? What are some methods that teachers use to alleviate this free-rider problem?

6. Suppose that people value the continued existence of dolphins in the Pacific Ocean, but that tuna-fishing fleets kill large numbers of these mammals. Draw a graph showing the externality. Describe two alternative approaches to remedy the externality.

7. Alice's neighbors across the street want her to help them tend the flower garden in front of their house. Why is the flower garden an externality to Alice? What does this mean about the quantity of flowers that will be planted in the neighborhood? If Alice is planning to sell her house soon, will she be more or less likely to help her neighbors? Why?

8. Property rights over the world's oceans are not well defined. Recently, experts have noted that stocks of fish are declining as the seas' resources are overused.

a. Explain, in economic terms, why this might have happened.

b. Commercial fishing firms all over the world are complaining about the decline in their industry. The response of many governments has been to subsidize the fleets in their countries. Explain why this is an example of government failure.

9. In an attempt to set user fees, a state surveyed a sample of households about willingness to pay for camping in a particular state forest. The following table shows the results of this survey:

Price per Visit (in dollars)	Number of Visits (households per year)
50	0
45	1
40	2
35	4
30	6
25	10
20	20
15	100
10	160
8	200
7	400
6	600
5	1,000
4	2,000
3	6,000
2	8,000
1	10,000
0	20,000

a. What would the consumer surplus be each year if the price were $10 per visit?

b. To improve the camping facilities in this forest, the state is considering charging a fee of $5 per visit. Based on a cost-benefit analysis, what should the state take into consideration before improving the facilities?

10. List one specific example of a market failure and one of a government failure. What does the government do in the case of this market failure? Is the government successful? How might the market be used to reduce this

government failure? Is the government trying to correct this problem? What advice would you give to the government?

11. Cite one issue on which Republicans and Democrats have a convergence of positions and one on which the parties' positions are quite different. Why is there a difference between the issues you have selected?

12. Use the median voter theorem to explain why the admission of a group of extreme right-wing students to a college in place of a more moderate group of right-wing students will not affect the election of the class president.

13. Use the set of preferences for Ali, Betty, and Camilla, shown in the table in the next column, to show that the paradox of voting does not always occur.

	Ali	Betty	Camilla
First	A	B	C
Second	B	A	A
Third	C	C	B

How does this example differ from the one in Table 15.3?

14. After September 11, the media paid closer attention to the potential use of shipped cargo containers to smuggle weapons and terrorists into the United States.
    a. Discuss why there may be a negative externality associated with the use of shipping containers.
    b. Graphically show the market for ship transportation of cargo. Make sure you include all the relevant aspects of this market, given your answer to part (a). Explain verbally as necessary.
    c. Graphically show any deadweight loss that occurs in this market.
    d. Discuss potential ways of reducing or eliminating deadweight loss in this market and the advantages and disadvantages of these remedies, including their impact on other markets.

CHAPTER 16

Physical Capital and Financial Markets

Winning a million dollars on *Who Wants to Be a Millionaire?* seems pretty easy. All the contestants need to do is answer a selection of multiple-choice questions. You can even call a friend for help. In reality, it is hard. First you have to be chosen from among 250,000 people who want to be on the show, and then you need to reach the final one-on-one. The chances are really not in your favor.

But, don't despair—there are more certain ways to become a millionaire. "As any decent financial adviser will tell you, almost anyone can do it," according to the *Wall Street Journal*, "If a 25-year-old earning $30,000 invests 10% a year and realizes an annual return of 6%, he or she will accumulate about $1.1 million by age 65. . . . [W]hen you weigh the odds of even getting on to *Millionaire* against those of a steady investment plan," the investment plan looks like the much safer choice.

It's clear that one can do very well over the long term by investing in stocks and other assets. The gains can be even greater when stock prices rise rapidly, as they did in the 1980s and 1990s. But stock prices do not always rise so rapidly. In fact, stock prices did not rise much at all in the 1970s, and they fell sharply in the 1930s. More recently, the twenty-first century has not been kind to the stock market, as there was a 30 percent decrease in the Dow Jones stock index in less than six months in 2002, and a more than 70 percent decrease in the Nasdaq stock index in less than three years. Stock prices are volatile, and thus stocks can be very risky.

In this chapter, we extend our analysis of different types of markets to capital markets, which include not only the exciting stock market, but also other fast-moving markets such as the bond market, the foreign exchange market, and markets for physical capital, such as houses, office buildings, and oil tankers.

To examine capital markets, we will use some of the basic tools of economics, including the supply and demand model and the idea of marginal revenue product introduced in Chapter 13. However, because prices in capital markets are very volatile and uncertain, to study these markets we need to consider some new tools to handle risk and uncertainty.

We begin by defining physical and financial capital and describing how they are used by firms. We show that a firm's demand for physical capital can be analyzed in much the same way that we analyzed a firm's demand for labor in Chapter 13. We then go on to consider the specific markets for financial capital: stocks and bonds, examining the financial pages of the *Wall Street Journal* and other newspapers in the process.

Capital Market Terminology

Some basic terminology about physical and financial capital is useful in studying capital markets.

Physical Capital

Physical capital refers to all the machines, factories, oil tankers, office buildings, and other physical resources used in the production of goods or services. In previous chapters on the behavior of firms, we simply used the term *capital* when referring to "physical capital" because we were not contrasting it with financial capital. Firms combine physical capital with labor inputs to produce goods and services. Businesses obtain physical capital by either building it, buying it, or renting it. For example, McDonald's might hire a construction firm to build a new facility near a highway, buy an old Burger King and renovate it, or rent a storefront in a mall.

Residential housing—single-family homes, apartments, trailers—is also a form of physical capital. It provides productive services in the form of living space that people can enjoy year after year. Government-owned roads, schools, and military equipment are also physical capital. It is useful to think of government capital as helping to produce services, whether transportation services, educational services, or national security.

An important characteristic of physical capital is that it lasts for a number of years. However, it does not remain in new condition permanently. Rather, it depreciates each year. **Depreciation** is the gradual decline in the productive usefulness of

depreciation: the decrease in an asset's value over time; for capital, it is the amount by which physical capital wears out over a given period of time.

capital. Trucks, trailers, and even buildings wear out and must eventually be either replaced or refurbished.

Financial Capital: Debt and Equity

When a firm starts up or expands, it needs to obtain funds. These funds are an example of *financial capital*. A firm needs these funds in order to purchase, rent, or build physical capital. It may also need funds to pay workers for a while until the firm starts to earn a profit. Older existing firms also need to obtain funds in order to expand or to buy physical capital.

Firms can obtain financial capital in two different ways: by issuing debt and by issuing equity. Examples of debt are bank loans and bonds. Loans and bonds are a type of contract called a **debt contract** in which the lender agrees to provide funds today in exchange for a promise that the borrower will pay back the funds at a future date with interest. The amount of interest is determined by the *interest rate*. If the amount borrowed is $10,000 and is due in one year and the interest rate is 10 percent per year, then the borrower pays the lender $11,000 at the end of the year. The $11,000 includes the *principal* on the loan ($10,000) plus the *interest payment* ($1,000 = .1 times $10,000). Firms typically obtain loans from banks, but larger firms also issue *corporate bonds*.

Firms are not the only issuers of debt. Most people who buy a house get a *mortgage*, which is a loan of funds to purchase real estate. In addition, many people get loans from banks to buy cars and consumer appliances. The biggest single issuer of debt in the United States is the federal government. The federal government borrows funds by selling *government bonds*.

Firms also obtain financial capital by issuing *stock*, or shares of ownership in the firm. Shares of ownership are a type of contract called an **equity contract.** In contrast to a debt contract, where the payment by the firm (the interest payment) does not depend on the profits of the firm, in an equity contract the payment by the firm does depend on the firm's profits. Sometimes the payment is a *dividend*, but shareholders can also benefit if the firm increases in value and their shares are worth more when they are sold.

Once bonds or stocks have been issued, they can be exchanged or traded. There are highly organized financial markets for trading stocks and bonds. The government and corporate bond markets are located in New York City, London, Tokyo, and other large financial centers. The stock markets include the New York Stock Exchange, the American Stock Exchange, several regional stock exchanges in the United States, and many stock exchanges in other countries.

Having defined some key terms, we now proceed to discuss the different types of capital markets. We begin with markets for physical capital.

debt contract: a contract in which a lender agrees to provide funds today in exchange for a promise from the borrower, who will repay that amount plus interest at some point in the future.

equity contract: shares of ownership in a firm; payments to the owners of the shares depend on the firm's profits.

REVIEW

- Physical capital and financial capital are distinct but closely related. To expand their physical capital, firms need to raise financial capital in some way.

- Debt contracts, such as bonds or loans, specify interest payments that do not depend on the profits of the firm. Equity contracts, such as stocks, pay dividends or earn capital gains that do depend on the profits of the firm.

- The bonds or stocks that firms issue can be traded. Organized markets for trading bonds and stocks are found in all the world's financial centers.

Markets for Physical Capital

The demand for physical capital is a relationship between the quantity of capital demanded by firms and the price of this capital. The demand for capital is a *derived demand* in the same sense that the demand for labor is a derived demand; that is, the demand for capital derives from the goods and services that firms produce with capital. In this section we show that just as the quantity of labor the firm employs depends on the marginal revenue product of labor, the quantity of capital the firm employs depends on the marginal revenue product of capital.

Rental Markets

The firm's capital decision is best understood if we first assume that the firm *rents* capital in a competitive rental market. In fact, it is common for firms to rent capital; for many types of equipment, there is a rental market in which many rental firms specialize in renting the equipment to other firms. For example, a construction firm can rent a dump truck; a clothing store can rent a storefront at a mall; an airline can lease an airplane. The price in the rental market is called the **rental price of capital.** It is the amount a rental firm charges for the use of capital equipment for a specified period of time, such as a month.

Consider a hypothetical construction company, called Perma, deciding whether to rent a dump truck from a rental company called A-1 Rental. To show how much capital a firm like Perma would rent, we need to consider the effect of this capital on the firm's profits. The marginal revenue product of capital can be used to assess this effect on profits. The **marginal revenue product of capital** is defined as the change in total revenue as the firm increases its capital by one unit. We assume that the marginal revenue product of capital declines as more capital is employed at the firm. For example, suppose the marginal revenue product of capital is $3,000 as capital rises from zero trucks to 1 truck, $1,500 as capital rises from 1 truck to 2 trucks, and $500 as capital rises from 2 trucks to 3 trucks.

Suppose the rental price of a dump truck is $1,000 a month. This is what A-1 Rental charges, and all other rental firms in the area charge essentially the same price. Because the rental market is competitive, neither A-1 Rental nor Perma has enough market power to affect the rental price. How many dump trucks would

rental price of capital: the amount that a rental company charges for the use of capital equipment for a specified period of time.

marginal revenue product of capital: the change in total revenue due to a one-unit increase in capital.

A Rental Market
Capital used by firms is frequently rented, as illustrated by this advertisement for computer rentals. The rental price is determined by supply and demand in the rental market.

Perma use? With the marginal product of capital from 1 dump truck equal to $3,000 a month, the firm will employ at least 1 dump truck. In other words, if the firm's total revenue increases by $3,000 and the rental price for the truck is $1,000, then it makes sense to rent the dump truck. With the marginal revenue product of capital from a second dump truck equal to $1,500, the firm will employ a second dump truck; by doing so, it can increase its profits by $500. However, with the marginal revenue product of capital from a third dump truck equal to only $500, the firm will lower its profits by renting a third dump truck. Hence, if the rental price of the dump truck is $1,000, the firm will employ exactly 2 dump trucks. The firm rents the largest amount of capital for which the marginal revenue product of capital is greater than the rental price; if fractional units of capital were possible, then the firm would keep renting more capital until *the marginal revenue product of capital was exactly equal to the rental price.*

■ **The Demand Curve for Capital.**   To derive the demand curve for capital, we must determine the quantity of capital demanded by the firm as the rental price of capital changes. For example, if the rental price of dump trucks declines to $400, then the quantity of dump trucks demanded by the firm will increase; a third dump truck will be rented because the price is now below the marginal revenue product of capital. In other words, as the rental price of capital falls, the quantity of capital demanded increases. Similarly, as the rental price of capital rises, the quantity of capital demanded decreases.

Figure 16.1 illustrates this general principle. It shows the marginal revenue product of capital for any firm. As more capital is employed, the marginal revenue product declines. For profit maximization, the firm will rent capital to the point where the marginal revenue product of capital equals the rental price. Thus, as we lower the rental price, the quantity of capital demanded increases. In other words, the demand curve for capital is downward-sloping.

Figure 16.1
Demand for Physical Capital by One Firm
A profit-maximizing firm chooses a quantity of capital that gives a marginal revenue product of capital equal to the rental price. Because the marginal revenue product of capital declines as more capital is used, a lower rental price of capital results in a larger quantity of capital demanded.

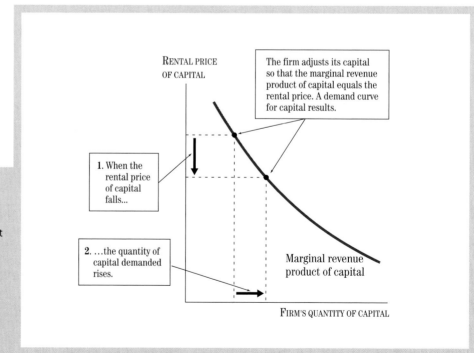

RENTAL PRICE OF CAPITAL

The firm adjusts its capital so that the marginal revenue product of capital equals the rental price. A demand curve for capital results.

1. When the rental price of capital falls...

2. ...the quantity of capital demanded rises.

Marginal revenue product of capital

FIRM'S QUANTITY OF CAPITAL

The demand curve for capital is determined by the marginal revenue product of capital. If the marginal revenue product changes, the demand curve for capital will shift. For example, if the marginal product of dump trucks rises, the demand for dump trucks by Perma will shift outward.

■ **Demand for Factors of Production in General.**   Observe how similar this description of the demand for capital is to the description of the demand for labor in Chapter 13, in which we showed that the marginal revenue product of labor equals the wage. Here we showed that the marginal revenue product of capital equals the rental price. This same principle applies to any factor of production for which the market in that factor is competitive. *For any input to production, a profit-maximizing firm will choose a quantity of that input such that the marginal revenue product equals the price of that input.*

■ **The Market Demand and Supply.**   The market demand for physical capital is found by adding up the demand for physical capital by many firms. Figure 16.2 shows such a market demand curve.

On the same diagram, we show the market supply curve. It is the sum of the supply curves for all the firms in the industry providing capital for rent, such as A-1 Rental. The equilibrium rental price and the equilibrium quantity of capital rented are shown in the diagram.

The supply and demand model for capital illustrated in Figure 16.2 can be used to predict the effects of tax changes or other changes in the capital market in much the same way as any other supply and demand model. For example, if the government places a tax on construction firms like Perma proportional to the quantity of trucks they rent, then the marginal revenue product of capital will decline and the demand curve for capital will shift down, or to the left. This will lower the equilibrium rental price received by A-1 and reduce the quantity of capital rented. Alternatively, a

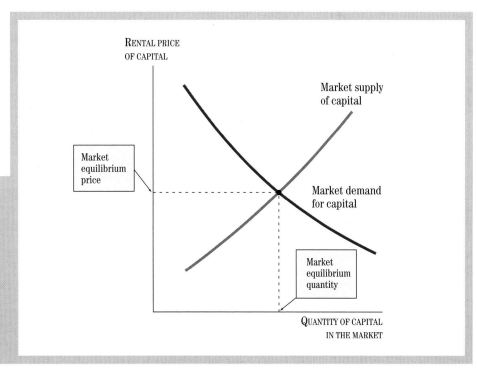

Figure 16.2
Market Supply and Demand for Physical Capital
The market demand for capital is the sum of the demands of the individual firms that use the equipment. The market supply is the sum of the supplies at the individual firms that provide the equipment. Market equilibrium occurs where the quantity of capital demanded equals the quantity of capital supplied.

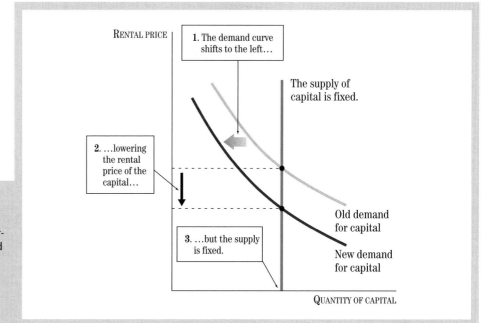

RENTAL PRICE

1. The demand curve shifts to the left...

The supply of capital is fixed.

2. ...lowering the rental price of the capital...

Old demand for capital

3. ...but the supply is fixed.

New demand for capital

QUANTITY OF CAPITAL

Figure 16.3
The Case of a Fixed Supply of Capital
When the supply of capital is perfectly inelastic, a shift in demand changes the rental price but not the quantity supplied. Marshall's stones are a hypothetical example of capital with a perfectly inelastic supply.

government subsidy on the rental of capital by construction firms would shift the demand curve for capital up, or to the right, and increase the quantity of capital rented.

■ **The Case of Fixed Supply: Economic Rents.** An important special case of a market for physical capital occurs when the supply is completely fixed. Alfred Marshall gave the following famous example of physical capital with a completely fixed supply: "Let us suppose that a meteoric shower of a few thousand large stones harder than diamonds fell all in one place, so that they were all picked up at once, and no amount of search could find any more. These stones, able to cut every material, would revolutionize many branches of industry . . . ."[1]

The important thing about Marshall's stones is that their supply cannot be increased or decreased regardless of the price of the stones. In other words, the supply curve for Marshall's stones is perfectly vertical, or perfectly inelastic, as shown in Figure 16.3.

Figure 16.3 shows what happens when there is a shift in demand for capital that is in fixed supply, such as Marshall's stones. A change in demand will change the price, but will not change the quantity. Demand completely determines the price in this case because the quantity supplied cannot change.

Economists have a special terminology for the price in this circumstance: **Economic rent** is the price of anything that has a fixed supply. Economic rent is also sometimes called *pure rent*. Economic rent is a significant concept in economics precisely because the quantity supplied does not depend on the price. Thus, a tax on economic rents would not change the amount supplied; it would not affect economic efficiency or cause a deadweight loss. For example, if the government passed a tax (even a 99.9 percent tax) on the rental payments charged by the lucky owners of Marshall's stones, there would be no change in the quantity of stones supplied.

economic rent: the price of something that has a fixed supply.

---

1. Alfred Marshall, *Principles of Economics*, 8th ed. (New York: MacMillan, 1920), p. 415.

Marshall's stones are of course a hypothetical example. In practice, certain types of land may come close to being an item in fixed supply, but it is always possible to improve land or clear land and thereby change its supply to some degree. The perfectly inelastic supply of Marshall's stones or the near perfectly inelastic supply of certain types of land is in sharp contrast to the higher elasticity of supply of most capital goods. The supply of dump trucks, apartment buildings, and other types of capital is sensitive to changes in the price. Increases in the price provide an incentive to increase the quantity supplied, and decreases in the price provide an incentive to decrease the quantity supplied. In reality, therefore, taxes on capital would be expected to change the quantity of capital supplied.

The Ownership of Physical Capital

Rental markets for capital are common, but they are not the only way in which firms obtain capital. The same construction firm that rents dump trucks might own the warehouse where it stores its building materials and the office where it keeps its books and meets prospective customers. Although there are legal and tax differences between renting and ownership, the economic principles are similar. In fact, even though owners of physical capital do not pay a rental price, economic considerations indicate that they pay an *implicit* rental price.

When a firm buys equipment, it must either use funds that it could have put in a bank, where they would earn interest, or borrow the funds. If it borrows the funds, the monthly interest payment on the loan is like a rental payment. If it uses its own funds, the interest it would have received at the bank is an opportunity cost and is considered to be similar to a rental payment. In addition to these payments, the firm that owns the equipment must factor in the wear and tear, or depreciation, on the equipment. The amount by which the firm's equipment deteriorates is also a cost.

implicit rental price: the cost of the funds used to buy the capital plus the depreciation of the capital over a given period of time.

In sum, the **implicit rental price** of capital for a year equals the interest payments for the year plus the amount of depreciation during the year. For example, suppose the interest rate is 10 percent, the purchase price of a dump truck is $40,000, and the dump truck depreciates $8,000 per year. Then the implicit rental price is $12,000 per year (.10 times $40,000, plus $8,000), or $1,000 a month, the same as the rental price in our dump truck example. It is important to note that the implicit rental price depends on the interest rate. The higher the interest rate, the higher the interest payments during the year, and thus the higher the implicit rental price. When the interest rate rises, the implicit rental price rises. When the interest rate falls, the implicit rental price falls.

The concept of the implicit rental price makes the firm's decision to buy a dump truck, or any other piece of capital, analogous to the decision to rent. The demand curve looks the same as that in Figure 16.1, except that it is the implicit rental price rather than the actual rental price that is on the vertical axis.

REVIEW
- The demand for physical capital at a firm is a derived demand.

- In a rental market when the rental price goes up, the quantity of capital demanded goes down because the marginal revenue product of capital curve slopes down.

- If capital is purchased rather than rented, then the rental price is replaced by the implicit rental price. The implicit rental price for a year is equal to the yearly interest payment on the loan to buy the equipment plus the amount of depreciation on the equipment during the year.

Stock and Bond Markets

Having seen how markets for physical capital work, let us turn to the examination of markets for financial capital: stocks and bonds. Stocks and bonds are also called securities. Once firms issue stocks or bonds, these securities can be traded on the financial markets. Their prices are determined by the actions of buyers and sellers, like prices in any other market.

Stock Prices and Rates of Return

return: the income received from the ownership of an asset; for a stock, the return is the dividend plus the capital gain.

capital gain: the increase in the value of an asset through an increase in its price.

capital loss: the decrease in the value of an asset through a decrease in its price.

> **Check the result.** The dividend was $.32. The closing price was $22.55. Dividing .32 by 22.55 gives .014 or 1.4 percent.

rate of return: the return on an asset stated as a percentage of the price of the asset.

dividend yield: the dividend stated as a percentage of the price of the stock.

earnings: the accounting profits of a firm.

price-earnings ratio: the price of a stock divided by its annual earnings per share.

The prices of the stocks of most large firms can be found in daily newspapers as shown in the box on the next page, which focuses on the listing for Hewlett-Packard stock. The annual **return** from holding a stock is defined as the *dividend* plus the *capital gain* during the year. The dividend is the amount the firm pays out to the owners of the stock each year. The **capital gain** during the year is the increase in the price of the stock during the year. A **capital loss** is a negative capital gain: a decrease in the price. The **rate of return** is the return stated as a percentage of the price of the stock.

The **dividend yield** is defined as the dividend stated as a percentage of the price. For example, the dividend for Hewlett-Packard in 2005 was $.32 per year. Given the stock price of $22.55, the dividend yield was 1.4 percent. The rate of return equals the percentage capital gain plus the dividend yield. For example, if the price of Hewlett-Packard stock went from $10 to $11 in a year, then the percentage capital gain would be $1 divided by $10, or 10 percent. Combined with a dividend yield of 1.4 percent, this would be a rate of return of 11.4 percent. In this example, the capital gain is a much bigger portion of the rate of return than the dividend; this is a defining characteristic of "growth stocks," of which Hewlett-Packard is an example.

Earnings is another word for the accounting profits of a firm. Firms do not pay out all of their profits as dividends; some of the profits are retained and invested in physical capital or research. Stock tables also list the **price-earnings ratio:** the price of the stock divided by the annual earnings per share. Observe in the box on the next page that the price-earnings ratio for Hewlett-Packard is 19. With the price of the stock at $22.55, this means that earnings for the year were $1.1868 per share ($22.55/$1.1868 = 19). A firm's earnings ultimately influence the return on the firm's stock, so the price-earnings ratio, or its inverse, which is 1/19, or 5.3 percent, for Hewlett-Packard, is closely watched.

Bond Prices and Rates of Return

Bond prices for both corporate and government bonds can also be found in the financial pages of the newspaper. The box "Reading the News About Bond Prices" on page 434 shows newspaper reports from two different dates on bonds issued by the U.S. government. These bond reports illustrate quite a bit about how bonds and bond markets work.

coupon: the fixed amount that a borrower agrees to pay to the bondholder each year.

maturity date: the date when the principal on a loan is to be paid back.

face value: the principal that will be paid back when a bond matures.

■ **Face Value, Maturity, Coupon, and Yield.** There are four key characteristics of a bond: *coupon, maturity date, face value,* and *yield.* The **coupon** is the fixed amount that the borrower agrees to pay the bondholder each year. The **maturity date** is the time when the coupon payments end and the principal is paid back. The **face value** is the amount of principal that will be paid back when the bond matures. Observe that the bond boldfaced in the box has a maturity date of November 2021 and a coupon equal to 8 percent of the face value of the bond. That is, 8 percent, or

Newspaper stock tables, such as this one from the *Wall Street Journal* (May 19, 2005), summarize information about firms and the stocks that they issue. The table here is part of a much bigger table called "New York Stock Exchange Composite Transactions," in which all stocks traded on the New York Stock Exchange are listed in alphabetical order. Other tables provide information about stocks traded on other stock exchanges, such as the American Stock Exchange or the Nasdaq, in exactly the same way.

To understand how to read this table, focus on one company, such as the computer firm Hewlett-Packard, which was started in a garage by David Packard and William Hewlett in the 1930s. A big part of the chief executive officer's job is to keep Hewlett-Packard's stock price strong, which means finding ways to continue to grow the earnings of the company. For example, in 2001, under former CEO Carly Fiorina's direction, Hewlett-Packard and Compaq decided to merge, with the intention of improving their joint position in a rapidly changing technology sector.

The information in the table pertains to a single day, May 15, 2005. As can be seen from the table, the price of Hewlett-Packard stock increased by 1 dollar to 22.55 on that day.

Key terms introduced in this chapter—such as dividend, dividend yield, and price-earnings ratio—are highlighted. To check your understanding, you can see if the *Wall Street Journal* has calculated the dividend yield correctly (as we have done for Hewlett-Packard in the margin on the opposite page) for one of the other firms in the table, such as Hershey, the maker of Hershey's Kisses. Or take a look at today's *Wall Street Journal* or focus on a stock on another stock exchange.

Ytd % Chg	52 weeks Hi	52 weeks Lo	Stock	Sym	Div	Yld %	PE	Vol 100s	Close	Net Chg
−7.2	15.55	9.93	Hercules	HPC		...	cc	4955	13.78	0.53
0.7	34	25.20	HeritageProp	n	2.10	6.5	35	1522	32.30	0.30
17.2	67.37	43.52	Hershey	HSY	.88	1.4	27	10555	65.10	0.22
−22.6	32.42	23.94	Hewitt	HEW n		...	22	3433	24.79	0.18
7.5	**22.26**	**16.08**	**HewlettPk**	**HPQ**	**.32**	**1.4**	**19**	**337216**	**22.55**	**1.00**
16.2	17.92	7.70	Hexcel	HXL		...	dd	2305	16.85	−0.25
8.3	33.10	22.08	Hibernia	HIB	.80	2.5	16	4931	31.95	0.35

Stock price percentage change for the calendar year to date	High and low price for previous year	Stock exchange symbol	Yearly dividend	Dividend as a percent of price	Price-earnings ratio	Number of shares traded (in hundreds)	Closing price of stock	Change in price from previous days
↓	↓	↓	↓	↓	↓	↓	↓	↓
Ytd % Chg	52 weeks Hi Lo	Sym	Div	Yld %	PE	Vol 100s	Close	Net Chg
7.5	22.26 16.08	HewlettPk HPQ	.32	1.4	19	337216	22.55	1.00

$80 a year on a bond with a face value of $1000, will be paid until 2021, and in November 2021, the $1000 face value will be paid back. (The coupon is called a "rate" because it is measured as a percentage of the face value.)

Once bonds have been issued by the government, they can be sold or bought in the bond market. In the bond market, there are bond traders who make a living buying and selling bonds. The bond traders will *bid* a certain price at which they will buy, and they will *ask* a certain price at which they will sell. The bid price is slightly lower than the ask price, which enables the bond traders to earn a profit by buying at a price that is slightly lower than the price at which they sell. For example, on August 23, 2005, the bid price on the bond in the box "Reading the News About Bond Prices" was $140^{16}/_{32}$, slightly lower than the ask price, which was $140^{17}/_{32}$. (Note that bond prices are rounded to the nearest thirty-second of a dollar.)

Once bonds have been issued by a firm or by a government, they are traded in bond markets. The prices of bonds in these markets are reported in the daily newspapers. Examples of such reports are given in the two tables below. The examples are part of larger tables in the *Wall Street Journal* called "Treasury Bonds, Notes and Bills," which list prices for many other government bonds issued by the U.S. Treasury. (Bonds have the longest maturities, followed by notes and then bills.)

The two tables refer to two different dates—August 2002 and August 2005—and come from two different issues of the paper. Observe that bonds with exactly the same coupon rate and maturity date are listed in the two tables. The two different dates enable you to see what happens to the price and the yield on these bonds over time.

Focus on the highlighted bond; it has a coupon rate of 8 percent and matures in November 2021. Thus, in November 2002, there were 19 years to maturity on this bond. Both the price that is *bid* for bonds by bond traders and the price that is *asked* for bonds by the traders are given in the table, but the bid and ask are very close to each other. (There is enough of a difference to give the traders some profit; note that the price asked by the trader is always greater than the price bid.)

Now look at what happened to the yield and the price between the two dates. In August 2002, the price was about $132, while in August 2005, it was about $140. Thus the price has risen. But the yield has declined, from 5.31 percent to 4.46 percent. This inverse relationship occurs for all the bonds listed in the tables and is necessarily true for all other bonds as well. Can you explain why?

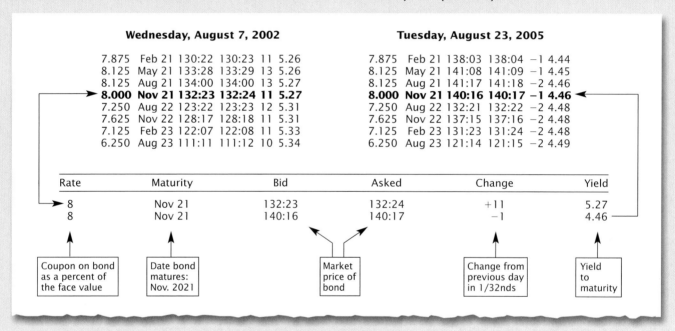

Wednesday, August 7, 2002

7.875	Feb 21	130:22	130:23	11	5.26
8.125	May 21	133:28	133:29	13	5.26
8.125	Aug 21	134:00	134:00	13	5.27
8.000	**Nov 21**	**132:23**	**132:24**	**11**	**5.27**
7.250	Aug 22	123:22	123:23	12	5.31
7.625	Nov 22	128:17	128:18	11	5.31
7.125	Feb 23	122:07	122:08	11	5.33
6.250	Aug 23	111:11	111:12	10	5.34

Tuesday, August 23, 2005

7.875	Feb 21	138:03	138:04	−1	4.44
8.125	May 21	141:08	141:09	−1	4.45
8.125	Aug 21	141:17	141:18	−2	4.46
8.000	**Nov 21**	**140:16**	**140:17**	**−1**	**4.46**
7.250	Aug 22	132:21	132:22	−2	4.48
7.625	Nov 22	137:15	137:16	−2	4.48
7.125	Feb 23	131:23	131:24	−2	4.48
6.250	Aug 23	121:14	121:15	−2	4.49

Rate	Maturity	Bid	Asked	Change	Yield
8	Nov 21	132:23	132:24	+11	5.27
8	Nov 21	140:16	140:17	−1	4.46

Coupon on bond as a percent of the face value	Date bond matures: Nov. 2021	Market price of bond	Change from previous day in 1/32nds	Yield to maturity

yield: the annual rate of return on a bond if the bond were held to maturity.

The **yield,** or yield to maturity, is defined as the annual rate of return on the bond if the bond were held to maturity. When people refer to the current interest rate on bonds, they are referring to the yield on the bond. Observe that the yield on the bold-faced bond maturing in November 2021 was 4.46 percent on August 23, 2005, somewhat below the 8 percent coupon.

■ **Bond Prices and Bond Yields.** There is an inverse, or negative, relationship between the yield and the price. To see this, look at the bonds in the two columns in the box. On August 23, 2005, the price of all the bonds listed is higher and the yield is lower than on August 7, 2002. Why is there an inverse relationship? Consider a simple example. Suppose you just bought a 1-year bond for $100 that says that the government will pay 5 percent of the face value, or $5, plus $100 at the end of the 1-year period. Now suppose that just after you bought the bond, interest rates on bank deposits suddenly jumped to 10 percent. Your bond says that you earn 5 percent per year, so if you hold it for the entire year, your rate of return is less than you could get on a bank deposit. Suddenly the bond looks much less attractive. You would probably want to sell it, but everyone else knows the bond is less attractive, also. You would not be able to get $100 for the bond. The price would decline until the rate of return on the bond just equaled the interest rate at the bank. For example, if the price fell to $95.45, then the payment of $105 at the end of the year would result in a 10 percent rate of return [that is, $.10 = (105 - 95.45)/95.45$]. In other words, the yield on the bond would rise until it equaled 10 percent rather than 5 percent.

Based on these considerations, there is a formula that gives the relationship between the price and the yield for bonds of any maturity. Let P be the price of the bond. Let R be the coupon. Let F be the face value. Let i be the yield. The formula relating to the price and the yield in the case of a 1-year bond is indicated in the first row of Table 16.1.

For a 1-year bond, a coupon payment of R is paid at the end of 1 year together with the face value of the bond. The price P is what you would be willing to pay *now*, *in the present*, for these future payments. It is the *present discounted value* of the coupon payment plus the face value at the end of the year. By looking at the formula in the first row of Table 16.1, you can see the negative relationship between the price (P) of the bond and the yield (i) on the bond. The higher the yield, the lower the price; and conversely, the lower the yield, the higher the price.

A 2-year-maturity bond is similar. You get R at the end of the first year and R plus the face value at the end of the second year. Now you want to divide the first-year payment by $1 + i$ and the second-year payment by $(1 + i)^2$. The formula still shows the inverse relationship between the yield and the price. A bond with a 3-year or longer maturity is similar. Computers do the calculation for the news reports, so even 30-year bond yields can easily be found from their price.

There is a convenient and simple approximation method for determining the price or yield on bonds with very long maturity dates. It says that the price is equal to the coupon divided by the yield: $P = R/i$. This is the easiest way to remember the inverse relationship between the price and the yield. It is a close approximation for long-term bonds like the 30-year bond.

Table 16.1
Bond Price Formula

One-year maturity: $P = \dfrac{R}{1+i} + \dfrac{F}{1+i}$

Two-year maturity: $P = \dfrac{R}{1+i} + \dfrac{R}{(1+i)^2} + \dfrac{F}{(1+i)^2}$

Three-year maturity: $P = \dfrac{R}{1+i} + \dfrac{R}{(1+i)^2} + \dfrac{R}{(1+i)^3} + \dfrac{F}{(1+i)^3}$

For very long term: $P = \dfrac{R}{i}$

P = price of bond
R = coupon
F = face value
i = yield

- Stocks and bonds are issued in order to obtain funds. Once issued, they are traded in stock and bond markets.
- The return from holding stock is the dividend plus the change in the price. The rate of return is equal to the return measured as a percentage of the price of the stock.
- The return from holding bonds is the coupon plus the change in the price of the bond. The rate of return measures this return as a percentage of the price of the bond.
- Bond yields and bond prices move in opposite directions.

Risk versus Return

The long-run average trend in stock prices has been up, but there have been significant declines from time to time, and the prices of individual stocks traded in the financial markets are very volatile. The price of a share of Hewlett-Packard, for example, declined from $31 to $20 a share in 2001, but the price of a share of Genesis Microchip rose from $9 to $66 during the same year—before dropping to $6 by August 2002. A change in price of 10 or 20 percent in one day is not uncommon. Because of such variability, buying stocks is a risky activity. The price of bonds can also change by a large amount. For example, from mid-1996 to mid-1997, the price of government bonds rose by nearly 20 percent, but from mid-1993 to mid-1994, the price of government bonds *fell* by nearly 20 percent! Thus, government bonds are also a risky investment.

In this section we show that the riskiness of stocks and bonds affects their return. To do so, we first examine how individuals behave when they face risk.

Behavior Under Uncertainty

Most people do not like uncertainty. They are *risk averse* in most of their activities. Given a choice between two jobs that pay the same wage, most people will be averse to choosing the riskier job where there is a good chance of being laid off. Similarly, given a choice between two investments that pay the same return, people will choose the less risky one.

Let us examine this idea of risk aversion further. To be more precise, suppose that Melissa has a choice between the two alternatives shown in Table 16.2. She must decide what to do with her life savings of $10,000 for the next year. At the end of the year, she plans to buy a house, and she will need some money for a down payment. She can put her $10,000 in a bank account, where the interest rate is 5 percent, or she can buy $10,000 worth of a stock that pays a dividend of 5 percent and will incur either a capital gain or a loss. In the bank, the value of her savings is safe, but if she buys the stock, there is a 50 percent chance that the price of the stock will fall by 30 percent and a 50 percent chance that the price of the stock will rise by 30 percent. In other words, the risky stock will leave Melissa with the possibility of a return of −$2,500 (a loss) or a return of $3,500 (a gain). (Here's the calculation: $10,000 × .05 − $10,000 × .30 = −$2,500 and $10,000 × .05 + $10,000 × .30 = $3,500.) The bank account leaves her with a guaranteed $500 return.

Table 16.2
Two Options: Different Risks, Same Expected Return

Low-Risk Option	High-Risk Option
A bank deposit with	*A corporate stock with*
5 percent interest	5 percent dividend and either a 30 percent price decline or a 30 percent price increase

expected return: the return on an uncertain investment calculated by weighting the gains or losses by the probability that they will occur.

If Melissa is a risk-averse person, she will choose the less risky of these two options. It is easy to see that Melissa might be miserable in the event of a loss, so she would want to avoid it completely and take the safe option. This example illustrates the fundamental difference between more risky and less risky investments. Because the prices of stocks fluctuate, they are riskier than bank accounts when held for short periods like a year.

Both the options in Table 16.2 have the same **expected return.** The expected return on an investment weighs the different gains or losses according to how probable they are. In the case of the safe bank account, there is a 100 percent chance that the return is $500, so the expected return is $500. In the case of the stock, the expected return would be $-$2,500 times the probability of this loss (1/2) plus $3,500 times the probability of this gain (also 1/2). Thus, the expected return is $500 ($-$2,500/2 + 3,500/2 = $-$1,250 + 1,750 = 500), the same as the return in the bank account.

The expected return is one way to measure how attractive an investment is. The word *expected* may appear misleading, since in the risky option $500 is not "expected" in the everyday use of the word. You do not expect $500; you expect either a loss of $2,500 or a gain of $3,500. If the term is confusing, think of the expected return as the average return that Melissa would get if she could take the second option year after year for many years. The losses of $2,500 and gains of $3,500 would average out to $500 per year after many years. (The term *expected return* has been carried over by economists and investment analysts from probability and statistics, where the term *expected value* is used to describe the mean, or the average, of a random variable.)

Although it is clear that Melissa would choose the less risky option of the two in Table 16.2, perhaps there is some compensation that Melissa would accept to offset her risk aversion. Although most people are averse to risk, they are willing to take on some risk if they are compensated for it. In the case of a risky financial investment, the compensation for higher risk could take the form of a higher expected return.

How could we make Melissa's expected return higher in the risky investment? Suppose Melissa had the choice between the same safe option as in Table 16.2 and a high-risk stock that paid a dividend of 20 percent. This new choice is shown in Table 16.3; the difference is that the risky stock now offers a dividend of 20 percent, much greater than the 5 percent in the first example and much greater than the 5 percent on the bank account. With the greater chance of a higher return on the stock, Melissa might be willing to buy the stock. Even in the worst situation, she loses just $1,000, which may still leave her with enough for the down payment on her new house. The expected return for the high-risk option is now $2,000, much greater than the $500 for the bank account (2,000 = $-$1,000/2 + 5,000/2 = $-$500 + 2,500).

In other words, Melissa would probably be willing to take on the risky investment. And if the 20 percent dividend in the example is not enough for her, some higher

Table 16.3	
Two Options: Different Risks, Different Expected Returns	
Low-Risk Option	**High-Risk Option**
A bank deposit with	*A corporate stock with*
5 percent interest	20 percent dividend and either a 30 percent price decline or a 30 percent price increase

Playing It Safe?
Most people are risk-averse when it come to large sums, but many are risk lovers when the stakes are low or when they can limit their potential losses—such as at casinos where people can choose to gamble a set amount or combine gambling with entertainment.

dividend (25 percent? 30 percent?) would be. This example illustrates the general point that risk-averse people are willing to take risks if they are paid for it.

Before we develop the implication of our analysis of individual behavior under uncertainty, we should pause to ask about the possibility that some people might be risk lovers rather than risk avoiders. The billions of dollars that are made in state lotteries in the United States and in private gambling casinos in Las Vegas, Atlantic City, and Monte Carlo indicate that some people enjoy risk. However, with few exceptions, most of the gambling on lotteries, slot machines, and even roulette wheels represents a small portion of the income or wealth of the gambler. Thus, you might be willing to spend $.50 or even $5 on lottery tickets or a slot machine for the chance of winning big, even if the odds are against you. Many people get enjoyment out of such wagers; but if the stakes are large compared to one's income or wealth, then few people want to play. For small sums, some people are risk lovers, but for large sums, virtually everybody becomes a risk avoider to some degree or another.

Risk and Rates of Return in Theory

What are the implications of our conclusion that investors will be willing to take risks if they are compensated with a higher return on the stock or bond? In the stock market, the prices of individual stocks are determined by the bidding of buyers and sellers. Suppose a stock, QED, had a price that gave it the same expected rate of return as a bank account. Now QED, being a common stock, clearly has more risk than a bank account because its price can change. Hence, no risk-averse investor will want to buy QED. Just as Melissa will prefer to put her funds in a bank account in the example of Table 16.2 rather than into the risky option, investors will put their funds in a bank rather than buy QED. People who own shares of QED will sell and put their funds into a bank. With everybody wanting to sell QED and no one wanting to buy it, the price of QED will start to fall.

Now, the price and the expected rate of return are inversely related—recall that for a stock the rate of return is the return divided by the price. Thus, if the price falls and the dividend does not change, the rate of return will rise. This fall in the price will drive up the expected rate of return on QED. As the expected rate of return increases, it will eventually reach a point where it is high enough to compensate risk-averse investors. In other words, when the expected rate of return rises far enough above the bank account rate to compensate people for holding the risk, the price fall will stop. We will have an equilibrium where the expected rate of return on the stock is higher than the interest rate on the safe bank account. The higher rate of return will be associated with the higher risk.

Now some stocks are more risky than others. For example, the risk on the stocks of small firms tends to be higher than the risk on the stocks of larger firms, because small firms tend to be those that are just starting up. Not having yet proved themselves, small firms have a higher risk. People like Melissa will sell the more risky, smaller company stocks until the expected rate of return on those stocks is high enough compared with the less risky stocks of larger companies.

In equilibrium, we therefore expect to see a positive relationship between risk and the expected rate of return on securities. Securities with higher risks will have higher returns than securities with lower risks. Figure 16.4 shows the resulting **equilibrium risk-return relationship.**

equilibrium risk-return relationship: the positive relationship between the risk and the expected rate of return on an asset, derived from the fact that, on average, risk-averse investors who take on more risk must be compensated with a higher return.

There is probably no more important lesson about capital markets than this relationship. Individual investors should know it well. It says that to get a higher rate of return *on average over the long run,* you have to accept a higher risk. Again, the market forces at work are the same as the ones that led to the compensating wage differentials in the labor market. In the labor market, the higher wage in some jobs is the price that workers accept to take on the greater risk, or, more generally, the less pleasant aspects of the job.

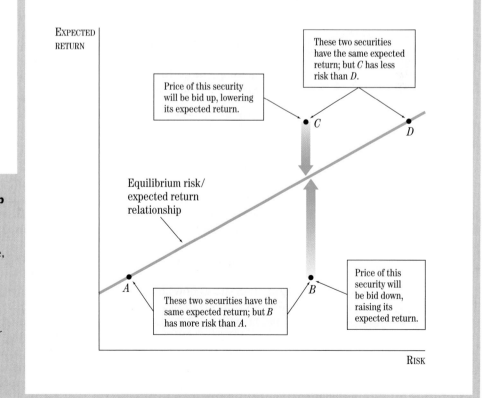

Figure 16.4
The Equilibrium Relationship Between Return and Risk
More risky securities tend to have higher returns on average over the long term. For example, bank deposits are low risk and have a low expected return. Corporate stocks are higher risk—their price fluctuates—but on average over the long term have a higher return. The higher return is like a compensating wage differential in the labor market. It compensates those who take on more risk.

Table 16.4
Average Rates of Return for Different Risks, 1926–2001

	Average Rate of Return per Year (percent)	Risk (average size of price fluctuations)
U.S. Treasury bills	3.8	3.2
Long-term corporate bonds	5.8	8.6
Large-company stocks	10.7	20.2
Small-company stocks	12.5	33.2

Note: These rates of return are not adjusted for inflation. The average rate of inflation was about 3 percent, which can be subtracted from each of the average returns to get the real return. The risk is the "standard deviation," a measure of volatility commonly used in probability and statistics.

Source: Data from Ibbotson Associates, *Stocks, Bonds, Bills and Inflation*, 2004 yearbook, Table 6–7.

Risk and Return in Reality

How well does this theoretical relationship work in reality? Very well. A tremendous amount of data over long periods of time on the financial markets support it. Table 16.4 presents data on the average return over 70 years for the four important types of securities we have mentioned in the theoretical discussion. The most risky of the four—the stocks of small firms—has the highest rate of return. Next highest in risk is the common stocks of large firms. The least risky—short-term Treasury bills that are as safe as bank deposits—has the smallest rate of return. Long-term bonds, where price changes can be large, have a rate of return greater than that of Treasury bills. Although the relative risks of these four types of securities may seem obvious, a measure of the differences in the sizes of their price volatility is shown in the second column and confirms the intuitive risk rankings.

In general, Table 16.4 is a striking confirmation of this fundamental result of financial markets that higher expected rates of return are associated with higher risk.

Diversification Reduces Risk

The familiar saying "Don't put all your eggs in one basket" is particularly relevant to stock markets. Rather than a basket of eggs, you have a portfolio of stocks. A *portfolio* is a collection of stocks. Putting your funds into a portfolio of two or more stocks, whose prices do not always move in the same direction, rather than one stock is called **portfolio diversification.** The risks from holding a single stock can be reduced significantly by putting half your funds in one stock and half in another. If one stock falls in price, the other stock may fall less, may not fall at all, or may even rise.

Holding two stocks in equal amounts is the most elementary form of diversification. With thousands of stocks to choose from, diversification is not limited to two. Figure 16.5 shows how sharply risk declines with diversification. By holding 10 different stocks rather than 1, you can reduce your risk to about 30 percent of what it would be with 1 stock. If you hold some international stocks, whose behavior will be even more different from that of any one U.S. stock, you can reduce the risk even further. Mutual fund companies provide a way for an investor with only limited funds to diversify by holding 500 or even 5,000 stocks along with other investors. Some mutual funds—called *index funds*—consist of all the stocks in an index like the Standard

portfolio diversification:
spreading the collection of assets owned in order to limit exposure to risk.

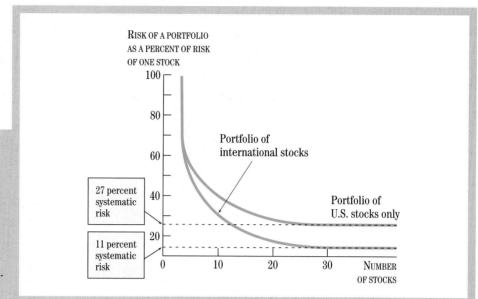

Figure 16.5
Risk Declines Sharply with Diversification
By holding more than one stock, the risk can be reduced. By holding 10 U.S. securities, the risk is reduced to 30 percent of the risk of holding one security. Diversifying internationally permits one to reduce risk further. (The risk is measured by the standard deviation.)

and Poor's (S&P) 500 Index, a weighted average of the stocks of 500 major companies. The Dow Jones Industrial Average of 30 companies, which draws headlines every time it passes through a 1,000-point mark, is less frequently used as an index for mutual funds because it has a smaller number of stocks.

systematic risk: the level of risk in asset markets that investors cannot reduce by diversification.

If you do not diversify, you are taking unneeded risks. But diversification cannot eliminate risk. A certain amount of risk cannot be diversified away. **Systematic risk** is what remains after diversification has reduced risk as much as it can. It is due to the ups and downs in the economy, which affect all stocks to some degree.

Efficient Market Theory

The shares of firms' stock on the market can be traded quickly at any time of day. For most large and medium-sized companies, some people are always willing to buy and sell. If people hear that Intel made a discovery that is expected to raise its profits, they rush to buy Intel stock. If people suddenly learn about a decline in a company's profits or losses, then people rush to sell that company's stock, as in the case of Genesis Microchip, described in the box on page 442. This rush to buy and sell changes prices instantaneously, so that the price adjusts rapidly to good news or bad news. The rapid adjustment means that there are rarely any unexploited profit opportunities for regular investors without inside information or a special ability to anticipate news, whether good or bad. The **efficient market hypothesis** is that there is an elimination of profit opportunities in financial markets as stock prices adjust quickly to new information. Rates of return greater than those due to the price of risk disappear soon after any good news about a stock appears.

efficient market hypothesis: the idea that markets adjust rapidly enough to eliminate profit opportunities immediately.

Many tests over the years have found the efficient market hypothesis to be a close approximation of security price determination. It has led to the growth in popularity of index funds, where investors do not pay advisers to tell them when to buy and sell stock. They simply invest in a fund that includes a large number of stocks.

The following excerpt from *The Daily Deal* (February 28, 2002) shows how fast prices adjust to new information in the stock market. As soon as Genesis Microchip—a company that designs, develops, and markets integrated circuits—revealed financial information that made the acquisition of another company not as profitable, its stock price dropped 41 percent in one day.

If you held Genesis stock and heard about the financial news and the drop in the price, you might have thought about selling the stock the next day. But that might not have been such a good idea, because the price already reflected the bad news.

Another type of news that affects stocks is new data about the state of the economy, collected and released by the U.S. government. Because of the impact of these data on markets, the government publishes a calendar that states in advance the date and exact time—precise to the minute—when inflation and unemployment statistics will be publicly released. The government distributes the news at the specified time to ensure that nobody has an unfair advantage.

Unexpected external factors can also affect the stock market. For example, the Dow Jones stock index dropped over 7 percent when the market reopened after September 11, 2001.

Strong Sales Make Sage Deal a Liability

The 41% slide in the share price of display chip maker Genesis Microchip Inc. on Feb. 27 proves that stellar financial performance is not always good for a company that just closed a major acquisition.

The Silicon Valley semiconductor company, which completed its $315 million purchase of smaller rival Sage Inc. on Feb. 20, told investors in a conference call Wednesday after the markets closed that the enlarged company will produce sales of $55 million in the first quarter of 2002, and $60 million in the second quarter.

Good news, it would seem, compared to pro forma projections before the merger closed last month. Yet the projections also revealed that Genesis so exceeded its own financial expectations in the last half of 2001 (while the Sage acquisition was still pending) that a deal which was supposed to be accretive to earnings was instead dilutive. The upshot: SoundView Technology Group Thursday reduced its earnings-per-share estimates for the upcoming fiscal year, which ends in March 2003, to $1.64 from $1.81 per share. "The company's definition of accretion will likely differ from what most investors expected," said SoundView analyst Scott Randall in the report.

Genesis' unexpectedly strong performance while the acquisition was pending—the San Jose, Calif.–based company reported 70% and 38% sequential revenue growth in the third and fourth periods of last year, respectively—clearly transformed the transaction from a financial enhancement, as it was billed when announced Sept. 28, to a drag on earnings, analysts said.

"Financially and in the near-term, Genesis would be better off if they wouldn't have done this deal," said Needham & Co. analyst Dan Scovel. Several other analysts downgraded Genesis stock Thursday morning. Trading in the shares was temporarily halted as the stock plummeted to a morning low of $24.35.

Genesis' recent strong performance also hurt it on another front. Its shares took an additional beating from news that the company would face a higher tax rate. During the Wednesday conference call, Genesis chief financial officer Peter Mangam said the company has revised its tax bracket from the 15% to 20% range upwards to 22% for the current fiscal year.

A major factor in this upward revision is Genesis having used up more tax credits than expected due to improved profitability in the second half of the fiscal year, Mangam said.

PRICE OF
GENESIS MICROCHIP STOCK
(IN DOLLARS)

- Risk-averse investors require compensation to hold risky assets. This compensation may take the form of a higher expected return.

- When buyers and sellers trade stocks or bonds in the market, a relationship between return and risk emerges: Higher risk is associated with higher returns.

- Diversification reduces risk, but not below a bare minimum called systematic risk.

- The efficient market hypothesis predicts that stock prices adjust to eliminate rates of return in excess of those required to compensate for systematic risk.

The Foreign Exchange Market

foreign exchange market: a market in which one currency (such as Japanese yen) can be exchanged for another currency (such as U.S. dollars).

exchange rate: the price of one currency in terms of another in the foreign exchange market. We express the exchange rate as the number of units of foreign currency that can be purchased with one unit of domestic currency.

The foreign exchange market is larger than the stock and bond markets combined. The **foreign exchange market** is where currencies of different countries are exchanged for one another. Foreign exchange traders—located at different financial centers around the world but linked together electronically—buy and sell an average of $1.5 trillion a day on this market. The prices on the foreign exchange market are the **exchange rates** between currencies, defined as the price of one currency in terms of another, for example, the number of yen per dollar.

Like any price, the exchange rate between two currencies depends on demand and supply. If the demand for dollars goes up, then the price for dollars in terms of foreign currency will rise. For example, if the demand for dollars goes up, the dollar may rise from about 107 yen per dollar to 138 yen per dollar. In practice, however, it is virtually impossible to determine the slopes and positions of supply and demand curves for foreign currency and use them to predict exchange rates. Thousands of currency traders are interested in obtaining foreign currency—not only to buy foreign goods, but also to hold foreign currency to speculate that its price might rise or fall. For example, you can exchange $1,000 for 100,000 yen if the exchange rate is 100 yen per dollar. Then if the dollar falls from 100 yen per dollar to 50 yen per dollar, you can trade your yen in for $2,000. That is a big rate of return. The supply and demand curves shift around by a large amount as expectations change. Exchange rate changes are difficult to predict and explain.

In fact, the foreign exchange market shares a very important similarity with stock and bond markets: *The exchange rate is greatly affected by people's expectations of rates of return from holding one currency compared with another.* The rate of return from holding one currency compared with another depends on the difference between the interest rates in each country and on whether the exchange rate is expected to appreciate or depreciate. When the rate of return changes, the exchange rate changes rapidly. For example, suppose that a high-ranking government official in Japan gives a speech with information that the yen is going to appreciate relative to the dollar; then people who heard the speech will buy yen anticipating a higher rate of return. But that buying will bid up the price of yen very quickly. A large sudden change in the exchange rate is observed. The story is much the same as when the president of a private corporation gives a speech announcing higher earnings at the corporation. People who hear the speech will buy that corporation's stock, expecting a higher rate of return, and the buying will bid up the price immediately. A large sudden change in the price of the stock is observed.

But exchange rates are also affected by other things in addition to rates of return. Because foreign currency is used to buy goods (such as cars) and services (such as vacations) in other countries, *the exchange rate is greatly affected by the price of goods and services in one country compared to another.* For example, if the average price of goods and services decreases in Japan compared to the United States—say, because of a deflation in Japan—then more Americans will want to buy Japanese goods and services. The demand for yen to buy Japanese goods and services will thus increase, causing the yen to appreciate in value.

In this section we look at these two influences on the foreign exchange market—the differences in rates of return and differences in the average price of goods and services. Because the average price of goods and services moves more slowly than rates of return, the effects of average price differences tend to be spread out over longer periods of time. We first look at this slower-moving, longer-term influence.

Differences in the Price of Goods and Services in Different Countries

purchasing power parity: the theory that exchange rates are determined in such a way that the prices of goods in different countries are the same when measured in the same currency.

To understand the influence of differences in the price of goods and services on the exchange rate, first suppose that the same exact good is sold in two countries and that transportation costs between countries are negligible compared to the price of the good. In this case, one would predict that the price of the good—after using the exchange rate to convert to the prices to the same currency—in the two countries should be the same. If the prices were not the same, then people could buy the good at the low-price location and sell it at the high-price location, making an easy profit. The principle that the prices of the same good in two locations should be equal in the absence of transportation costs is called the law of one price. The idea that the exchange rate between two countries is determined in such a way that the law of one price holds is called **purchasing power parity (PPP).**

Consider a good with a price that is much higher than its transportation cost—expensive vintage wine, for example. Suppose that in August 2002, the wine cost 1,500 dollars per case in the United States and 1,000 pounds per case in Britain. Then, according to purchasing power parity, the exchange rate should be 1.5 dollars per pound.

In fact, the exchange rate was 1.54 dollars per pound in August 2002, so in this example, purchasing power parity works quite well. If purchasing power parity did not hold closely for tradable goods, people would either buy wine in Britain and ship the wine to the United States in order to make a nice profit or vice versa. This would shift either supply or demand until purchasing power parity held. Hence, the exchange rate is such that the price of wine in the two countries is almost the same.

If goods are not so easily transported, then purchasing power parity does not always work as well. Suppose, for example, you tried to ship a McDonald's Big Mac purchased in the United States across the ocean. It would not be pleasant to eat. Even if you used an airplane, the Big Mac would be stale and decayed by the time it arrived at its destination. The transport costs in this case are prohibitive, and purchasing power parity does not always hold. Let us compare the price of a Big Mac in the United States with the price of a Big Mac in Europe. In April 2002, the average price of a Big Mac in the United States was about $2.49, while in Europe it was 2.67 euro. If the Big Macs were to cost exactly the same in the two locations, the exchange rate would have to be 1.072 euro per dollar. (To get this, divide 2.67 euro by 2.49 dollars to get 1.072 euro per dollar.) The actual exchange rate was 1.12 euro per dollar in April 2002. In this example, the Big Mac index implies that the dollar was overvalued against the

The table here is drawn from a larger table called "Currency Trading," published daily in the *Wall Street Journal*. The table shows the exchange rate (the price of foreign exchange) on the foreign exchange market on two days—the current day and the day before.

Observe that, for convenience, the exchange rate is stated in two equivalent ways: (1) the number of U.S. dollars for each unit of foreign currency, and (2) the number of foreign currency units for each U.S. dollar. One is the mathematical inverse of the other. For example, 111.05 yen per dollar is the same exchange rate as 1/(111.05) dollars per yen, or .009005 dollar per yen, as stated in the table for Thursday, August 4, 2005.

The exchange rate in the table is the price at which banks traded large amounts of foreign currency with other banks. If you went to a bank or to an automatic teller machine at an airport, you would get fewer units of foreign currency for each of your U.S. dollars, so that the banks can earn some profit on the service they provide to you.

Since 1999, the euro has replaced the German mark, the French franc, the Italian lira, and the currencies of other European countries that now form a single currency area.

Thursday, August 3, 2005
EXCHANGE RATES

The foreign exchange mid-range rates below apply to trading among banks in amounts of $1 million and more, as quoted at 4 p.m. Eastern time by Reuters and other sources. Retail transactions provide fewer units of foreign currency per dollar.

Country	U.S. $ equiv.		Currency per U.S. $		Country	U.S. $ equiv.		Currency per U.S. $	
	Wed	Tue	Wed	Tue		Wed	Tue	Wed	Tue
Argentina (Peso)-y	.3498	.3497	2.8588	2.8596	Mexico (Peso)				
Australia (Dollar)	.7722	.7656	1.2950	1.3062	Floating rate	.0945	.0943	10.5798	10.6067
Bahrain (Dinar)	2.6525	2.6525	.3770	.3770	New Zealand (Dollar)	.6913	.6876	1.4465	1.4543
Brazil (Real)	.4328	.4271	2.3105	2.3414	Norway (Krone)	.1571	.1553	6.3654	6.4392
Canada (Dollar)	.8219	.8222	1.2167	1.2162	Pakistan (Rupee)	.01677	.01676	59.630	59.666
Chile (Peso)	.001791	.001780	558.35	561.80	Peru (new Sol)	.3074	.3068	3.2531	3.2595
China (Yuan)-d	.1234	.1234	8.1051	8.1032	Philippines (Peso)	.01783	.01784	56.085	56.054
Colombia (Peso)	.0004332	.0004332	2308.40	2308.40	Poland (Zloty)	.3023	.2997	3.3080	3.3367
Czech. Rep. (Koruna)					Russia (Ruble)-a	.03510	.03500	28.490	28.571
Commercial rate	.04130	.04067	24.213	24.588	Saudi Arabia (Riyal)	.2667	.2667	3.7495	3.7495
Denmark (Krone)	.1654	.1634	6.0459	6.1200	Singapore (Dollar)	.6053	.6043	1.6521	1.6548
Ecuador (US Dollar)	1.0000	1.0000	1.0000	1.0000	Slovak Rep. (Koruna)	.03177	.03135	31.476	31.898
Egypt (Pound)-y	.1732	.1732	5.7750	5.7750	South Africa (Rand)	.1555	.1533	6.4309	6.5232
Hong Kong (Dollar)	.1286	.1287	7.7760	7.7700	South Korea (Won)	.0009847	.0009809	1015.54	1019.47
Hungary (Forint)	.005048	.004991	198.10	200.36	Sweden (Krona)	.1315	.1301	7.6046	7.6864
India (Rupee)	.02304	.02298	43.403	43.516	Switzerland (Franc)	.7929	.7832	1.2612	1.2768
Indonesia (Rupiah)	.0001026	.0001025	9747	9756	Taiwan (Dollar)	.03136	.03141	31.888	31.837
Israel (Shekel)	.2230	.2223	4.4843	4.4984	Thailand (Baht)	.02426	.02423	41.220	41.271
Japan (Yen)	.009005	.008974	111.05	111.43	Turkey (New Lira)	.7619	.7561	1.3125	1.3225
Jordan (Dinar)	1.4115	1.4121	.7085	.7082	U.K. (Pound)	1.7781	1.7703	.5624	.5649
Kuwait (Dinar)	3.4245	3.4240	.2920	.2921	United Arab (Dirham)	.2723	.2723	3.6724	3.6724
Lebanon (Pound)	.0006649	.0006651	1503.99	1503.53	Uruguay (Peso)				
Malaysia (Ringgit)-b	.2669	.2669	3.7467	3.7467	Financial	.04100	.04090	24.390	24.450
Malta (Lira)	2.8733	2.8407	.3480	.3520	Venezuela (Bolivar)	.000466	.000466	2145.92	2145.92
					SDR	1.4650	1.4604	.6826	.6847
					Euro	**1.2336**	**1.2195**	**.8106**	**.8200**

Special Drawing Rights (SDR) are based on exchange rates for the U.S., British, and Japanese currencies.
Source: International Monetary Fund.

Exchange rate stated two ways:
.009005 dollars per yen is the same exchange rate as 111.05 yen per dollar, because 1/(111.05) = .009005.

U.S. dollar decreased slightly from .8200 euro per dollar on Tuesday to .8106 euro per dollar on Wednesday.

euro in April 2002. However, by August 2002 the actual exchange rate was 1.03 euro per dollar—the dollar had depreciated so much that it was now undervalued against the euro, according to the Big Mac index.

To see how PPP is applied in practice, it is helpful to introduce some notation. Let P be the average price of goods in the United States and P^* the average price of goods in Japan. Then the purchasing power exchange rate (E) would be given by $E \times P = P^*$. For example, if the average price in the United States is $10 and the average price in Japan is 1,000 yen, then the purchasing power exchange rate is 100 yen per dollar, because $E \times P = (100 \times 10) = 1,000$ when $E = 100$. Now suppose that there is more inflation in the United States than in Japan, so that P rises to $20 and P^* stays constant; then, according to purchasing power parity, E must fall from 100 yen per dollar to 50 yen per dollar so that $E \times P = (50 \times 20)$ stays equal to P^*, which still equals 1,000 yen. Thus, an increase in prices in the United States will be matched by a depreciation of the dollar.

Such an association between changes in average prices and the change in the exchange rate is exactly what happens over long periods, as shown in Figure 16.6. This figure shows (1) the percent increase in average prices—or the *inflation rate*—in several large countries compared to that in the United States, and (2) the percent change in the exchange rates of those different countries' currencies with that of the United States. For example, over this period from 1975 to 1995, the inflation rate in Italy was higher than that in the United States. Over the same period of time, the dollar appreciated relative to the lira, the Italian currency. The United Kingdom also had a higher inflation rate than the United States, and the dollar appreciated relative to the pound. Japan and Germany, on the other hand, had inflation rates that were on average lower than that in the United States, and, as purchasing power parity would predict, the dollar depreciated relative to the yen and mark. Purchasing power parity works well in explaining exchange rates over this time span.

Over shorter periods of time, however, the purchasing power parity theory does not work very well. For example, in the mid-1980s, the U.S. dollar was much higher

**Figure 16.6
Purchasing Power Parity,
1970–2004**
As predicted by purchasing power parity, the U.S. dollar has appreciated against the currencies of countries with high inflation (Australia, Canada, Mexico, the United Kingdom) and depreciated against the currencies of countries with low inflation (Japan).

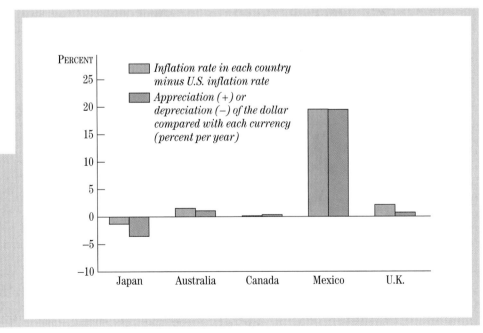

than could be explained by purchasing power parity. To explain such events, we need to look at another important factor affecting exchange rates: differences in rates of return.

Differences in Rates of Return

International investors operating in the global foreign exchange market decide where to place their funds in order to get the highest return. The capital they invest is highly mobile. The movement of funds around the world to receive the highest return creates a link between the rate of return and the exchange rate that can explain the departures from purchasing power parity.

For example, if the interest rate on bonds in the United States rises relative to interest rates abroad, then the U.S. dollar becomes more attractive to international investors. Or, if the dollar exchange rate is expected to rise, then dollars will be in greater demand. For an investor deciding whether to put funds in a bank in the United States or Japan, a rise in the U.S. interest rate compared to that of Japan makes the United States more attractive, and this raises the price of the dollar. Similarly, if the U.S. interest rate falls relative to Japan's, the dollar will depreciate relative to the yen as international investors move their funds from the United States to Japan.

Figure 16.7 shows how the exchange rate correlates with the interest rate differential in Japan. The rise of the dollar relative to other countries in the early 1980s and its subsequent decline in the late 1980s are highly correlated with the interest rate differential. In the early 1980s, interest rates in the United States rose relative to those in other countries, and then in the mid-1980s, interest rates in the United States declined relative to those in other countries.

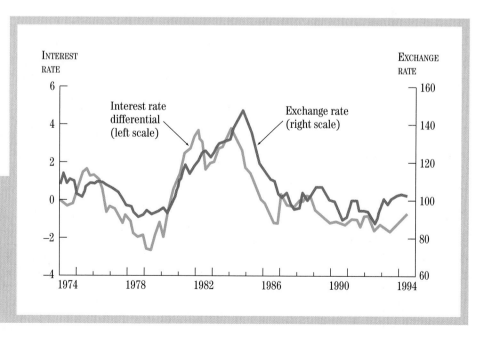

Figure 16.7
Links Between Rates of Return and the Exchange Rate
Note the correlation between the difference in interest rates between the United States and Japan (percent a year, green line) and the exchange rate (yen per dollar, blue line).

REVIEW
- The exchange rate is determined in the foreign exchange market, where different countries' currencies are bought and sold.

- Purchasing power parity is helpful in explaining exchange rates, but it does not explain everything.

- Another factor influencing exchange rates is the difference in rates of return between countries. When the interest rate in the United States rises relative to that in another country, the exchange rate rises. When news of an exchange rate appreciation spreads, people buy up the currency immediately.

- The relationship between rates of return and the exchange rate occurs because investors in the global foreign exchange market shift their funds in response to interest rate differentials.

Conclusion and Some Lessons

In this chapter we have seen how to employ some basic economic tools to analyze capital markets. In reviewing the lessons learned, it is helpful to see how they may apply to you personally.

First, by diversifying a portfolio of stocks, you can reduce risk substantially. Conversely, by holding an undiversified portfolio, you are needlessly incurring risk.

Second, be aware of the efficient market hypothesis that profit opportunity disappears quickly in financial markets. Instead of buying and selling securities frequently, investors may be better off investing in a mutual fund—like an index fund.

Third, if you do try to pick your own portfolio rather than use a mutual fund, concentrate on areas you are familiar with. If you go into a medical career, you may know more than even the best investors about the promise of a new medical device or drug.

Fourth, over the short run, holding corporate stocks is more risky than putting your funds in a bank account, but over the long term, the higher rate of return on stocks outweighs the risks for most people. However, if you need money in the short term—to pay next year's tuition, for example—stocks may not be worth the risk.

Fifth, exchange rates can fluctuate by large magnitudes and are very difficult to predict. If you are worried about a depreciation of the currency in a country you are about to travel to, then you can wait until the last minute to buy the currency, but speculating in foreign exchange is very risky.

KEY POINTS

1. Physical capital is a form of capital used to produce goods and services.

2. Financial capital, including the stocks and bonds traded on the exchanges, is used by firms to obtain funds to invest in physical capital.

3. A firm's demand for physical capital is a derived demand. A firm will use capital up to the point where the marginal revenue product of capital equals the rental price.

4. The supply and demand for capital determines the rental price or the implicit rental price.

5. Once stocks and bonds are issued by firms, the shares trade on financial markets.

6. The rate of return on stocks is equal to the dividend plus the change in the price as a percentage of the price. The rate of return on bonds is the coupon plus the change in the price as a percentage of the price.

7. Risk-averse investors will buy more risky stocks or bonds only if the expected rate of return is higher.

8. In market equilibrium, there is a positive relationship between risk and rate of return. If you want to get a higher rate of return, you have to accept higher risk. In any case, diversification reduces risk.

9. Purchasing power parity explains changes in exchange rates due to large changes in the price of goods and services in different countries.

10. The price of a country's currency rises when interest rates in that country rise compared to those in other countries.

KEY TERMS

depreciation

debt contract

equity contract

rental price of capital

marginal revenue product of capital

economic rent

implicit rental price

return

capital gain

capital loss

rate of return

dividend yield

earnings

price-earnings ratio

coupon

maturity date

face value

yield

expected return

equilibrium risk-return relationship

portfolio diversification

systematic risk

efficient market hypothesis

foreign exchange market

exchange rate

purchasing power parity

QUESTIONS FOR REVIEW

1. Why is the quantity of capital demanded negatively related to the rental price of capital?

2. What is economic rent, and what is its usefulness?

3. How does the implicit rental price of capital depend on the interest rate and depreciation?

4. What three interrelated profit-maximization rules connect a firm's labor, capital, and output decisions?

5. Why are the price and yield on bonds inversely related?

6. What is the rate of return on stocks? On bonds?

7. Why do stocks have higher rates of return than bank deposits over the long term?

8. What is the effect of diversification on risk?

9. Of what use is purchasing power parity as a theory of the price in foreign exchange markets?

10. Why does the difference between the interest rate in Japan and the United States matter for an American deciding how many Japanese yen to buy?

PROBLEMS

1. Which of the following are physical capital, and which are financial capital?
   a. A Toyota Camry at Avis Car Rental
   b. A loan you take out to start a newspaper business
   c. New desktop publishing equipment
   d. A bond issued by the U.S. government
   e. A pizza oven at Pizza Hut

2. Draw a market supply and demand for capital diagram to indicate what happens to the equilibrium rental price and quantity of capital as the marginal revenue product of capital increases. Explain.

3. Suppose that Marshall's stones were dropped all over the earth and finding them was difficult. Would the supply curve for capital still be perfectly inelastic? Would there be economic rent?

4. Suppose a company owns a computer that costs $5,000 and depreciates $1,000 per year. If the interest rate is 5 percent, what is the implicit rental price of the computer? Explain why the implicit rental price depends on the interest rate.

5. The U.S. government issues a 1-year bond with a face value of $1,000 and a zero coupon. If the market interest rate is 10 percent, what will the market price of the bond be? Now suppose you observe that the bond price falls by 5 percent. What happens to its yield?

6. You are considering the purchase of stocks of two firms: a biotechnology corporation and a supermarket chain. Because of the uncertainty in the biotechnology industry, you estimate that there is a 50-50 chance of your either earning an 80 percent return on your investment or losing 80 percent of your investment within a year. The food industry is more stable, so you estimate that you have a 50-50 chance of either earning 10 percent or losing 10 percent. Suppose that both stocks have equal expected returns. Which stock would you buy? Why? What do you think other investors would do? What would be the effect of these actions on the relative prices of the two stocks?

7. Suppose you have $10,000 and must choose between investing in your own human capital or investing in physical or financial capital. What factors will enter into your decision-making process? How much risk will be involved with each investment? What would you do? Why?

8. What is the expected return of the following stock market investment portfolio?

	Good Market	Bad Market	Disastrous Market
Probability	.50	.30	.20
Rate of return	.25	.10	−.25

   a. Would you choose this expected return or take a safe return of 7 percent from a savings deposit in your bank? Why?
   b. Suppose your teacher chooses the safe return from the bank. Is your teacher risk averse? How can you tell?

9. Graph the data on risk and expected return (in percent) for the following securities.

Asset	Expected Rate of Return	Risk
Bank deposit	3	0
U.S. Treasury bills	4	3
Goodcorp bonds	9	10
ABC stock	11	24
XYZ stock	13	24
Riskyco stock	16	39

Draw an equilibrium risk-return line through the points. Which two assets should have changes in their prices in the near future? In which direction will their prices change?

10. a. Suppose a 2-year bond has a 5 percent coupon and $1,000 face value, and the current market interest rate is 5 percent. What is the price of the bond?
   b. Now suppose that you believe that the interest rate will remain 5 percent this year, but next year will fall to 3 percent. How much are you willing to pay for the 2-year bond today? Why?

11. What are the benefits of buying a mutual fund? Is there any risk in this investment?

12. Suppose that the average price of goods in Europe rises from 100 in the year 2000 to 130 in the year 2010. Suppose that the average price of goods in the United States rises from 120 in the year 2000 to 140 in 2010. Suppose that the exchange rate in 2000 was 1 euro per dollar. If purchasing power parity held in 2000, what would purchasing power parity predict for the exchange rate in 2010?

Present Discounted Value

A dollar in the future is worth less than a dollar today. This principle underlies all economic decisions involving actions over time. Whether you put some dollars under the mattress to be spent next summer, whether you borrow money from a friend or family member to be paid back next year, or whether you are a sophisticated investor in stocks, bonds, or real estate, that same principle is essential to making good decisions. Here we explain why the principle is essential and derive a formula for determining exactly *how much* less a dollar in the future is worth than a dollar today. The formula is called the *present discounted value formula.*

Discounting the Future

First let's answer the question, why is the value of a dollar in the future less than the value of a dollar today? The simplest answer is that a dollar can earn interest over time. Suppose a person you trust completely to pay off a debt gives you an IOU promising to pay you $100 in one year; how much is that IOU worth to you today? How much would you be willing to pay for the IOU today? It would be less than $100, because you could put an amount less than $100 in a bank and get $100 at the end of a year. The exact amount depends on the interest rate. If the interest rate is 10 percent, the $100 should be worth $90.91 because, if you put $90.91 in a bank earning 10 percent per year, at the end of the year you will have exactly $100. That is, $90.91 plus interest payments of $9.09 ($90.91 times .1 rounded to the nearest penny) equals $100.

The process of translating a future payment into a value in the present is called **discounting.** The value in the present of a future payment is called the **present discounted value.** The interest rate used to do the discounting is called the **discount rate.** In the preceding example, a future payment of $100 has a present discounted value of $90.91, and the discount rate is 10 percent. If the discount rate were 20 percent, the present discounted value would be $83.33 (because if you put $83.33 in a bank for a year at a 20 percent interest rate, you would have, rounding to the nearest penny, $100 at the end of the year). The term *discount* is used because the value in the present is *less* than the future payment; in other words, the payment is "discounted," much as a $100 bicycle on sale might be "discounted" to $83.33.

Finding the Present Discounted Value

The previous examples suggest that there is a formula for calculating present value, and indeed there is. Let

the present discounted value be *PDV*

the discount rate be *i*

the future payment be *F*

The symbol *i* is measured as a decimal, but we speak of the discount rate in percentage terms; thus we would say "the discount rate is 10 percent" and write "$i = .1$."

Now, the present discounted value *PDV* is the amount for which, if you put it in a bank today at an interest rate *i*, you would get an amount in the future equal to the future payment *F*. For example, if the future date is one year from now, then if you put the amount *PDV* in a bank for one year, you would get *PDV* times $(1 + i)$ at the end of the year. Thus, the *PDV* should be such that

$$PDV \times (1 + i) = F$$

Now divide both sides by $(1 + i)$; you get

$$PDV = \frac{F}{(1 + i)}$$

which is the formula for the present discounted value in the case of a payment made one year in the future. That is,

$$\text{Present discounted value} = \frac{\text{payment in one year}}{(1 + \text{the discount rate})}$$

For example, if the payment in one year is $100 and the discount rate $i = .1$, then the present discounted value is $90.91 [$100/(1 + .1)], just as we reasoned previously.

To obtain the formula for the case where the payment is made more than one year in the future, we must recognize that the amount in the present can be put in a bank and earn interest at the discount rate for more than one year. For example, if the interest rate is 10 percent, we could get $100 at the end of 2 years by investing $82.64 today. That is, putting $82.64 in the bank would give $82.64 times (1.1) at the end of one year; keeping all this in the bank for another year would give $82.64 times (1.1) times (1.1), or $82.64 times 1.21, or $100.00, again rounding off. Thus, in the case of a future payment in 2 years, we would have

$$PDV = \frac{F}{(1 + i)^2}$$

Analogous reasoning implies that the present discounted value of a payment made N years in the future would be

$$PDV = \frac{F}{(1 + i)^N}$$

For example, the present discounted value of a $100 payment to be made 20 years in the future is $14.86 if the discount rate is 10 percent. In other words, if you put $14.86 in the bank today at an interest rate of 10 percent, you would have about $100 at the end of 20 years. What is the present discounted value of a $100 payment to be made 100 years in the future? The above formula tells us that the PDV is only $.00726, less than a penny! All of these examples indicate that the higher the discount rate or the further in the future the payment is to be received, the lower the present discounted value of a future payment.

In many cases, we need to find the present discounted value of a *series* of payments made in several different years. We can do this by combining the previous formulas. The present discounted value of payments F_1 made in 1 year and F_2 made in 2 years would be

$$PDV = \frac{F_1}{(1 + i)} + \frac{F_2}{(1 + i)^2}$$

For example, the present discounted value of $100 paid in one year and $100 paid in 2 years would be $90.91 plus $82.64, or $173.55. In general, the present discounted value of a series of future payments $F_1, F_2, \ldots, F_N$ over N years is

$$PDV = \frac{F_1}{(1 + i)} + \frac{F_2}{(1 + i)^2} + \cdots + \frac{F_N}{(1 + i)^N}$$

Key Points

1. A dollar to be paid in the future is worth less than a dollar today.

2. The present discounted value of a future payment is the amount you would have to put in a bank today to get that same payment in the future.

3. The higher the discount rate, the lower the present discounted value of a future payment.

Key Terms and Definitions

discounting: the process of translating a future payment into a value in the present.
present discounted value: the value in the present of future payments.
discount rate: an interest rate used to discount a future payment when computing present discounted value.

Questions for Review

1. Why is the present discounted value of a future payment of $1 less than $1?

2. What is the relationship between the discount rate and the interest rate?

3. What happens to the present discounted value of a future payment as the payment date stretches into the future?

4. Why is discounting important for decisions involving actions at different dates?

Problems

1. Find the present discounted value of
   a. $100 to be paid at the end of 3 years.
   b. $1,000 to be paid at the end of 1 year plus $1,000 to be paid at the end of 2 years.
   c. $10 to be paid at the end of 1 year, $10 at the end of 2 years, and $100 at the end of 3 years.

2. The Disney Company issued corporate bonds, sometimes called "Mickey Mouse" bonds, that simply promised to pay $1,000 in 100 years, with no payments of interest. What is the present discounted value of one of these bonds on the date issued if the interest rate is 10 percent? How about 5 percent?

3. Suppose you win $1,000,000 in a lottery and your winnings are scheduled to be paid as follows: $300,000 at the end of 1 year, $300,000 at the end of 2 years, and $400,000 at the end of 3 years. If the interest rate is 10 percent, what is the present discounted value of your winnings?

The Issue:
Should We Be Concerned About Income Inequality?

Live 8, a historic musical event, took place on July 2, 2005. Ten concerts were held on the same day in the United States, Canada, France, Germany, Italy, Japan, Russia, and the United Kingdom (collectively known as the G8), and in South Africa as well. The goal of the Live 8 concert organizers was to raise awareness of poverty in Africa among citizens of the G8 nations. In turn, these citizens would put pressure on their leaders to forgive the debts of, and increase aid to, African countries. Musically and politically, the concerts seemed to be a success. A week later, the leaders of the G8 nations pledged to increase African aid to $25 billion. Given that there are 700 million people who live in sub-Saharan Africa, the increase in aid worked out to approximately $40 per person.

For those of us who live in the developed world, $40 will do very little to improve our lives. But there is a staggering amount of income inequality across countries in the world. In sub-Saharan Africa, where the 700 million people have an average per capita income of less than $500, even $40 a person can make a difference. In the poorest African countries, like Sierra Leone and Niger, per capita income is only about $200.[1] Almost 60 percent of the population in these countries live on less than $1 a day. In contrast, per capita income in the United States is $37,500, which means that the average income of someone living in America is almost 200 times as large as the average income of someone living in Niger.

Income inequality is also present within countries, not just across countries. Even in a rich country like the United States, 12.7 percent of the population, or more than 35 million people, live on an income below the poverty line. Economist Paul Krugman argues[2] that the 13,000 richest families in the United States had as much income as the 20 million poorest families. The average family in the United States earns 1/300th of the income that one of those 13,000 richest families earns. Krugman also points out that over the past 30 years, the average annual salary in America increased by about 10 percent in real terms, but the average real compensation of CEOs increased almost 30-fold. To put it another way, the average CEO salary went from about 40 times the pay of an average worker to about 1,000 times the pay of an average worker.

Should we be concerned about this level of income inequality? Keep in mind that the question is not "Should we be concerned about poverty?" There is a subtle yet important difference between these two questions. Suppose you were asked if you would approve of implementing an economic policy that would increase per capita income in Niger by 50 percent (from $200 to $300). You would probably approve of such a policy. Now suppose you found out that implementing that policy would also double per capita income in the United States, from $37,500 to $75,000. This would imply that per capita income in the United States would now be 250 times per capita income in Niger instead of 200 times. Would that information change your approval of the policy? In the U.S. example, you should ask yourself if your approval of a policy that would increase the real wage of the typical worker by 10 percent would be tempered by the knowledge that the same policy would increase the CEO's compensation by 20 percent.

The critical question being raised here is whether you are concerned about income inequality per se, or whether you care about income inequality only because of your concern for the well-being of the poor.

Focus on Poverty, Not on Inequality

Martin Feldstein argues that the concern over rising income inequality is misplaced.[3] He does not believe that rising inequality per se warrants the creation of new redistributive policies that seek to reduce inequality. Instead, he argues, we should focus on reducing poverty and use redistributive policies only for alleviating poverty. Feldstein's reasoning can be summarized as follows:

- Economists use the Pareto principle to evaluate policies. If a policy makes someone better off without making others worse off, such a policy is generally thought of as being a good policy.[4] Therefore, changes that increase the earnings of high-income individuals without decreasing the earnings of lower-income individuals should be considered to be good policies.

1 You can find a variety of interesting cross-country data series in the World Bank's World Development Report. Available online at http://econ.worldbank.org/wdr/.
2 Paul Krugman, "For Richer," *New York Times Magazine,* Oct. 20, 2002. Available online at http://www.pkarchive.org/economy/ForRicher.html.
3 Martin Feldstein, "Reducing Poverty, Not Inequality," *Public Interest,* no. 137, Fall 1999. Available at http://www.nber.org/feldstein/pi99.html.
4 These are not the only good policies; policies that make some people worse off but others better off in a manner such that the gains outweigh the losses will also typically be regarded as being good policies.

- Applying the above principle to the changes that have taken place in the U.S. economy in recent years, the greater increase in the earnings of high-income individuals should not be a concern. These increases are driven by four factors: market forces rewarding individuals with advanced education; a rise in entrepreneurial activity resulting in a spurt of new business creation; the tendency of high-wage individuals like lawyers, doctors, and investment bankers to work long hours; and decreases in financial risk and the cost of capital that have translated into higher stock and bond prices, which are more likely to benefit the rich. None of these changes hurt the poor, even though they help the rich.
- Redistribution to alleviate poverty can easily be justified on the grounds that an extra $100 of income means less to a millionaire than it does to someone earning $10,000. However, that does not imply that we should prevent the millionaire from earning an extra $100 because that person still values the $100.
- Focusing on policies that can help the poor, such as improved education, better job training, and reducing incentives to stay on welfare instead of work, is the way to tackle "real and serious poverty" in the United States.
- Macroeconomists are concerned about the impact of inequality on economic growth. Work by Kristin Forbes, an economist at MIT, using data on income inequality gathered from a variety of countries, shows that in the short run, an increase in income inequality can actually lead to an increase in growth.[5]

COUNTERPOINT **Focus on Inequality, Not Just on Poverty**

Branko Milanovic, an economist at the World Bank, strongly disagrees with Martin Feldstein's view that we should care only about poverty alleviation, not inequality per se.[6] He argues that to be concerned only about poverty alleviation is to be internally intellectually inconsistent. Milanovic uses this example to make his point:

> Suppose a group of friends are in a room together and a benefactor (arbitrarily) gives $20,000 to one person and 25 cents to everyone else. Feldstein's argument would say that everyone is better off as a result and should therefore be happier. However, reality is likely to be very different. Many of the people who received

25 cents would think that they are worse off because someone else got $20,000. The reason for their feeling worse is that people compare themselves to their (perceived) peers. When a peer is treated better by society, individuals may feel as if they are being valued less by society. In other words, the income of others may enter into our own utility function, hence others doing better may affect our well-being.

Economist Nancy Birdsall points out that there has been a dramatic transformation in how economists think about inequality.[7] As recently as 1990, the World Bank's report on poverty made little or no mention of it, choosing instead to focus on poverty alleviation. Since then, Birdsall argues, many economists have changed their views about inequality. Inequality matters "not only because it affects growth or other economic variables but in and of itself." For one thing, Birdsall argues, recent research on the determinants of "happiness" has shown that people care about their relative standing (how their income compares to that of others in their community) and also about the expected change in their relative standing: They may be more willing to accept the fact that some people are better off than they are if they feel that in the future, they or their children can be the among the ones who are better off. In addition, inequality can undermine the political process. In countries where political institutions are weak, an unequal distribution of income and wealth can allow the better off to usurp the political process to maintain the status quo. This can lead to conflicts like civil war, which in turn adversely affect the economy.

Using Your Economics

1. Consider the Milanovic example about the group of friends in a room. How would you react if you were the recipient of the $20,000? How about if you were one of the recipients of the 25 cents? Would your responses be different if the recipient of the $20,000 had completed a task that everyone else had failed at?
2. The evidence suggests that income inequality in the United States has increased over the past few decades. What kind of policies should be recommended by someone concerned about rising inequality? How would those policies differ from the policies recommended by someone who is concerned only about poverty in the United States?

5 Kristin Forbes, "A Reassessment of the Relationship Between Inequality and Growth," *American Economic Review* 90(4), September 2000.
6 Branko Milanovic, "Why We All Do Care About Inequality (but Are Loath to Admit It)." Available at www.worldbank.org/research/inequality/pdf/feldstein.pdf.
7 Nancy Birdsall, "Why Global Inequality Matters," in Susan M. Collins and Carol Graham, eds., *Globalization, Poverty, and Inequality,* Brookings Institution Press 2004.

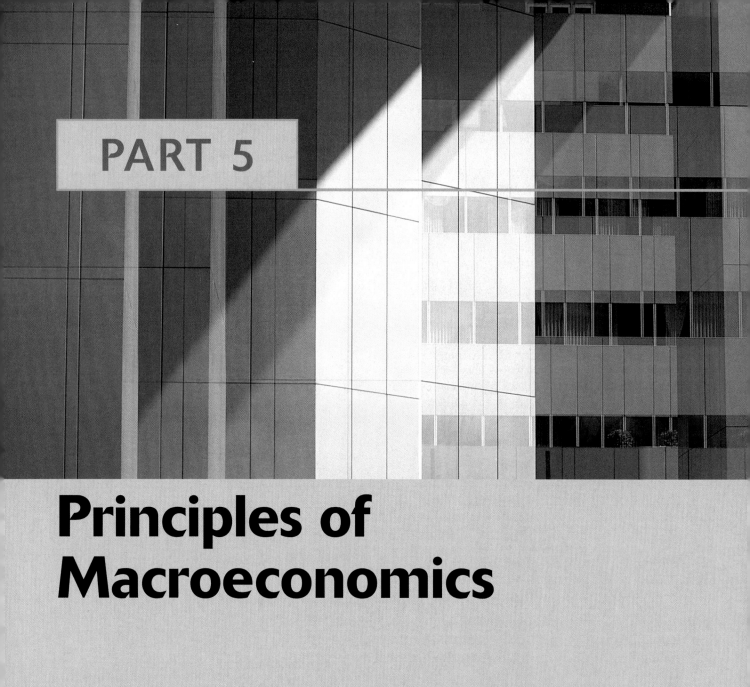

PART 5

Principles of Macroeconomics

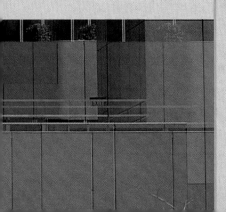

457

CHAPTER 17

Macroeconomics:
The Big Picture

An economic expansion is a period of continuous economic growth without a significant economic downturn. In 2001, a decade-long expansion, the longest in American history, came to an end. Throughout the decade, unemployment was low and falling, as is often the case in an expansion, and spending by consumers and investors was very robust.

An economic downturn that ends an expansion is known as a recession. During 2001, unemployment increased, as it often does in a recession, and spending by consumers and business firms fell. While the tragic events of September 11 contributed substantially to the economy's going into recession, all indications were that the economic slowdown had begun almost six months earlier. Once the signs of recession were evident, the president, members of Congress, and the Federal Reserve expressed their concern and moved quickly to implement policies that they claimed would help the economy return to a period of expansion.

According to the National Bureau of Economic Research, the recession lasted only eight months. The longest economic expansion on record seems to have been followed by one of the shortest recessions on record. Why was the expansion so long? What caused the economy to go into recession? Why was the recession so short-lived? Did the policy responses help the economy out of the recession? These are the types of questions that the study of macroeconomics helps us answer.

Macroeconomics is the study of the *whole market economy.* Like other parts of economics, macroeconomics uses the central idea that people make purposeful decisions with scarce resources. However, instead of focusing on the workings of one market—whether the market for peanuts or the market for bicycles—macroeconomics focuses on the economy as a whole. Macroeconomics looks at the big picture: Economic growth, recessions, unemployment, and inflation are among its subject matter. You should accordingly put on your "big picture glasses" when you study macroeconomics.

Macroeconomics is important to you and your future. For example, you will have a much better chance of finding a desirable job after you graduate from college during a period of economic expansion than during a period of recession. Strong economic growth can help alleviate poverty, free up resources to clean up the environment, and lead to a brighter future for your generation. By studying macroeconomics, you can better understand the changes that are taking place in the economy, better understand the role of good economic policies in driving economic growth and reducing unemployment, and become a more informed and educated citizen.

This chapter summarizes the overall workings of the economy, highlighting key facts to remember. It also provides a brief preview of the macroeconomic theory designed to explain these facts. The theory will be developed in later chapters.

Real GDP over Time

real gross domestic product (real GDP): a measure of the value of all the goods and services newly produced in a country during some period of time, adjusted for changes in prices over time.

economic growth: an upward trend in real GDP, reflecting expansion in the economy over time.

economic fluctuations: swings in real GDP that lead to deviations of the economy from its long-term growth trend.

Gross domestic product (GDP) is the economic variable of most interest to macroeconomists. GDP is the total value of all new goods and services produced in the economy during a specified period of time, usually a year or a quarter. The total value of goods and services can change either because the quantities of goods and services are changing or because their prices are changing. As a result, economists often prefer to use **real gross domestic product (real GDP)** as the measure of production; the adjective *real* means that we adjust the measure of production to account for changes in prices over time. Real GDP, also called *output* or *production,* is the most comprehensive measure of how well the economy is doing.

Figure 17.1 shows the changes in real GDP in recent years in the United States. When you look at real GDP over time, as in Figure 17.1, you notice two simultaneous patterns emerging. Over the long term, increases in real GDP demonstrate an upward trend, which economists call long-term **economic growth.** In the short term, there are **economic fluctuations**—more transient increases or decreases in real GDP. These short-term fluctuations in real GDP are also called *business cycles.* The difference between the long-term economic growth trend and the economic fluctuations can be better seen by drawing a relatively smooth line between the observations on real GDP. Such a smooth trend line is shown in Figure 17.1. Sometimes real GDP fluctuates above

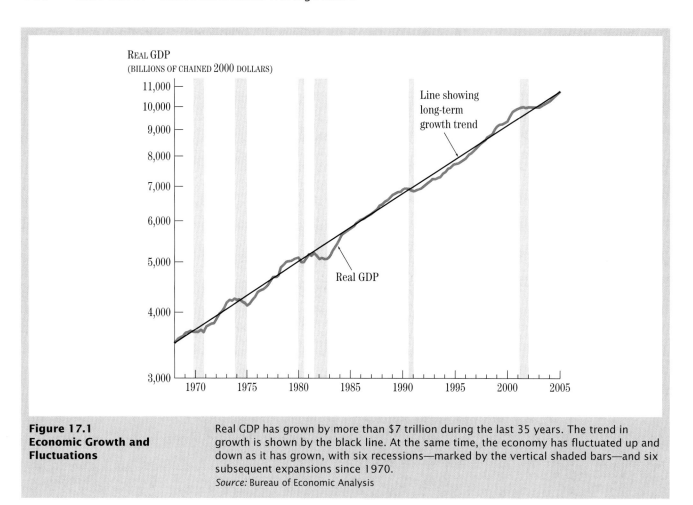

Figure 17.1
Economic Growth and
Fluctuations

Real GDP has grown by more than $7 trillion during the last 35 years. The trend in growth is shown by the black line. At the same time, the economy has fluctuated up and down as it has grown, with six recessions—marked by the vertical shaded bars—and six subsequent expansions since 1970.
Source: Bureau of Economic Analysis

the trend line, and sometimes it fluctuates below the trend line. In this section we look more closely at these two patterns: economic growth and economic fluctuations.

Economic Growth: The Relentless Uphill Climb

The large increase in real GDP shown in Figure 17.1 means that people in the United States now produce a much greater amount of goods and services each year than they did 35 years ago. Improvements in the economic well-being of individuals in any society cannot occur without such an increase in real GDP. To get a better measure of how individuals benefit from increases in real GDP, we consider average production per person, or *real GDP per capita*. Real GDP per capita is real GDP divided by the number of people in the economy. It is the total production of all food, clothes, cars, houses, CDs, concerts, education, computers, and so on, per person. When real GDP per capita is increasing, then the well-being—or the standard of living—of individuals in the economy, at least on average, is improving.

How much economic growth has there been during the last 35 years in the United States? The annual *economic growth rate*—the percentage increase in real GDP each year—provides a good measure. On the average, for the last 35 years, the annual economic growth rate has been about 3 percent. This may not sound like much, but it means that real GDP has almost tripled. The increase in production in the United States over the past 35 years is larger than what Japan and Germany together now produce. It is as if all the production of Japan and Germany—what is made by all the workers, machines, and technology in these countries—were annexed to the U.S. economy, as illustrated in Figure 17.2.

How much did real GDP *per capita* increase during this period? Because the U.S. population grew by about 90 million people during this period, the increase in real GDP per capita has been less dramatic than the increase in real GDP, but it is impressive nonetheless. The annual growth rate of real GDP per capita is the percentage increase in real GDP per capita each year. It has averaged about 2 percent per year. Again, this might not sound like much, but it has meant that real GDP per capita doubled from about $18,500 per person in 1969 to about $37,000 per person in 2004. That extra $18,500 per person represents increased opportunities for travel, TVs, housing, washing machines, aerobics classes, health care, antipollution devices for cars, and so on.

Over long spans of time, small differences in economic growth—even less than 1 percent per year—can transform societies. For example, economic growth in the southern states was only a fraction of a percent greater than in the North in the 100 years after the Civil War. Yet this enabled the South to rise from a real income per capita about half that of the North after the Civil War to one about the same as that of the North today. Economic growth is the reason that Italy has caught up with and even surpassed the United Kingdom in real GDP per capita; 100 years ago, Italy had a real GDP per capita about half that of the United Kingdom. Economic growth is also key to improvements in the less-developed countries in Africa, Asia, and Latin America. Because economic growth has been lagging in many of these countries, their real GDP per capita is considerably less than that of the United States.

Economic Fluctuations: Temporary Setbacks and Recoveries

Clearly, real GDP grows over time, but every now and then real GDP stops growing, falls, and then starts increasing rapidly again. These ups and downs in the economy—that is, economic fluctuations or business cycles—can be seen in Figure 17.1.

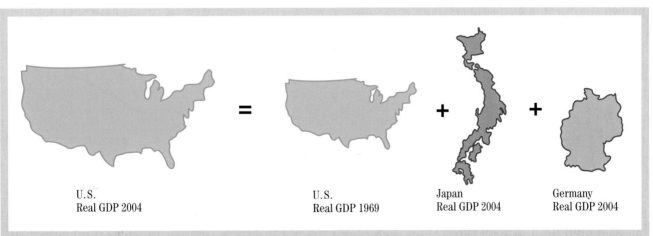

U.S.
Real GDP 2004

U.S.
Real GDP 1969

Japan
Real GDP 2004

Germany
Real GDP 2004

**Figure 17.2
Visualizing Economic
Growth**

Over the last 35 years, production in the U.S. economy has increased by more than the total current production of the Japanese and German economies combined. It is as if the United States had annexed Germany and Japan.

Recession   Expansion   Recession

recession: a decline in real GDP that lasts for at least six months.

peak: the highest point in real GDP before a recession.

trough: the lowest point of real GDP at the end of a recession.

expansion: the period between the trough of a recession and the next peak, consisting of a general rise in output and employment.

recovery: the early part of an economic expansion, immediately after the trough of the recession.

One of these business cycles, the one in 2001, is blown up for closer examination in Figure 17.3. No two business cycles are alike. Certain phases are common to all business cycles, however. These common phases are shown in the diagram in the margin. When real GDP falls, economists say that there is a **recession;** a rule of thumb says that the fall in real GDP must last for a half year or more before the decline is considered a recession. The highest point before the start of a recession is called the **peak.** The lowest point at the end of a recession is called the **trough,** a term that may cause you to imagine water accumulating at the bottom of one of the dips.

The period between recessions—from the trough to the next peak—is called an **expansion,** as shown for a typical fluctuation in the margin. The early part of an expansion is usually called a **recovery** because the economy is just recovering from the recession.

The peaks and troughs of the six recessions since the late 1960s are shown by vertical bars in Figure 17.1. The shaded areas represent the recessions. The areas between the shaded bars show the expansions. The dates of all peaks and troughs back to 1920 are shown in Table 17.1. The average length of each business cycle from peak to peak is five years, but it is clear from Table 17.1 that business cycles are not regularly occurring ups and downs, like sunup and sundown. Recessions occur irregularly. There were only 12 months between the back-to-back recessions of the early 1980s, while 58 months of uninterrupted growth occurred between the 1973–1975 recession and the 1980 recession. The recession phases of business cycles also vary in duration and depth. The 1980 recession, for example, was not nearly as long or as deep as the 1973–1975 recession.

The 1990–1991 recession was one of the shortest recessions in U.S. history, and it was followed by the longest expansion in U.S. history. Before that recession, almost uninterrupted economic growth had occurred for most of the 1980s—from the trough of the previous recession in November 1982 to a peak in July 1990.

Economists debate whether economic policies were responsible for the expansions of the 1980s and 1990s. We will examine these debates in later chapters. Another debate is the cause of the recession that began in 1990. The first month of the recession occurred just after Iraq invaded Kuwait, causing a disruption in the oil fields and a jump in world oil prices. Some argue that this jump in oil prices was a factor in the recession.

Figure 17.3
The Phases of Business Cycles
Although no two business cycles are alike, they have common features, including the *peak, recession,* and *trough,* shown here for the 2001 recession.
Source: Bureau of Economic Analysis

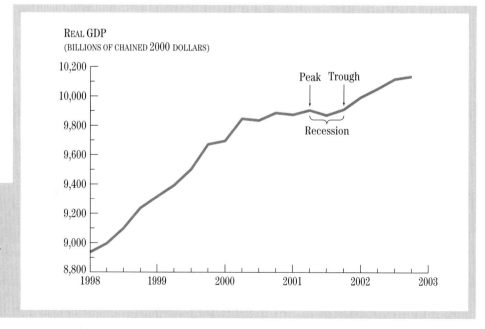

Table 17.1
Comparison of Recessions

Recession		Duration of Recession (months from peak to trough)	Decline in Real GDP (percent from peak to trough)	Duration of Next Expansion (months from trough to peak)
Peak	*Trough*			
Jan 1920–Jul 1921		18	8.7	22
May 1923–Jul 1924		14	4.1	27
Oct 1926–Nov 1927		13	2.0	21
Aug 1929–Mar 1933		43	32.6	50
May 1937–Jun 1938		13	18.2	80
Feb 1945–Oct 1945		8	11.0	37
Nov 1948–Oct 1949		11	1.5	45
Jul 1953–May 1954		10	3.2	39
Aug 1957–Apr 1958		8	3.3	24
Apr 1960–Feb 1961		10	1.2	106
Dec 1969–Nov 1970		11	1.0	36
Nov 1973–Mar 1975		16	4.9	58
Jan 1980–Jul 1980		6	2.5	12
Jul 1981–Nov 1982		16	3.0	92
Jul 1990–Mar 1991		8	1.4	120
Mar 2001–Nov 2001		8	0.0	37*

*As of December 2004.

Source: National Bureau of Economic Research.

■ **A Recession's Aftermath.**   The economy usually takes several years to return to normal after a recession. Thus, a period of bad economic times always follows a recession while the economy recovers. Remember that economists define recessions as periods in which real GDP is declining, not as periods in which real GDP is down. Despite the technical definition, many people still associate the word *recession* with bad economic times. For example, although the 2001 recession ended in November 2001, the unemployment rate kept rising for another year. Technically speaking, though, the recession was over in November 2001 when GDP began to grow again—well before the effects of an improving economy were felt by most people.

■ **Recessions versus Depressions.**   Recessions have been observed for as long as economists have tracked the economy. Some past recessions lasted so long and were so deep that they are called *depressions*. There is no formal definition of a depression. A depression is a huge recession.

Fortunately, we have not experienced a depression in the United States for a long time. Figure 17.4 shows the history of real GDP for about 100 years. The most noticeable decline in real GDP occurred in the 1929–1933 recession. Real GDP fell by 32.6 percent in this period. This decline in real GDP was so large that it was given its own designation by economists and historians—the *Great Depression*. The recessions of recent years have had much smaller declines.

Table 17.1 shows how much real GDP fell in each of the fifteen recessions since the 1920s. The 1920–1921 recession and the 1937–1938 recession were big enough to be classified as depressions, but both are small compared to the Great Depression. Real GDP also declined substantially after World War II, when war production declined.

Clearly, recent recessions have not been even remotely comparable in severity to the Great Depression or the other huge recessions of the 1920s and 1930s. The

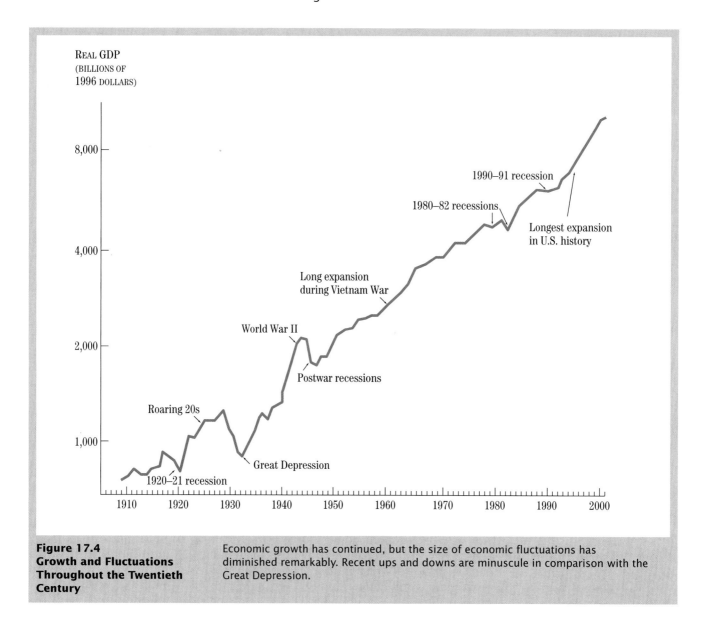

REAL GDP (BILLIONS OF 1996 DOLLARS)

**Figure 17.4
Growth and Fluctuations
Throughout the Twentieth
Century**

Economic growth has continued, but the size of economic fluctuations has diminished remarkably. Recent ups and downs are minuscule in comparison with the Great Depression.

1990–1991 recession, for example, had only one-twentieth the decline in real GDP that occurred during the Great Depression. But because any recession rivets attention on people's hardship and suffering, there is always a tendency to view a current recession as worse than all previous recessions. Some commentators reporting on the 1990–1991 recession wondered whether it should be compared with the Great Depression. For example, in September 1992, Louis Uchitelle of the *New York Times* wrote, "Technically, the recession is over, but spiritually, it continues. . . . The question is, what to call these hard times. What has been happening in America since 1989 seems momentous enough to enter history as a major economic event of the 20th century."[1]

---

1. Louis Uchitelle, "Even Words Fail in This Economy," *New York Times,* September 8, 1992, p. C2.

Unemployment, Inflation, and Interest Rates

As real GDP changes over time, so do other economic variables, such as unemployment, inflation, and interest rates. Looking at these other economic variables gives us a better understanding of the human story behind the changes in real GDP. They also provide additional information about the economy's performance—just as a person's pulse rate or cholesterol level gives information different from the body temperature. No one variable is sufficient.

Unemployment During Recessions

unemployment rate: the percentage of the labor force that is unemployed.

There are fluctuations in unemployment just as there are fluctuations in real GDP. The **unemployment rate** is the number of unemployed people as a percentage of the labor force; the labor force consists of those who are either working or looking for work. Every time the economy goes into a recession, the unemployment rate rises because people are laid off and new jobs are difficult to find. The individual stories behind the unemployment numbers frequently represent frustration and distress.

Figure 17.5 shows what happens to the unemployment rate as the economy goes through recessions and recoveries. The increase in the unemployment rate during a recession is eventually followed by a decline in unemployment during the recovery. Note, for example, how unemployment rose during the recessions of 1973–1975 and 1981–1982. Around the time of the 2001 recession, the unemployment rate rose from 4.3 percent to 5.6 percent.

Figure 17.5
The Unemployment Rate
The number of unemployed workers as a percentage of the labor force—the unemployment rate—increases during recessions because people are laid off and it is difficult to find work. Sometimes the unemployment rate continues to increase for a while after the recession is over, as in 1991 and 2001. But eventually unemployment declines during the economic recovery.
Source: Bureau of Labor Statistics

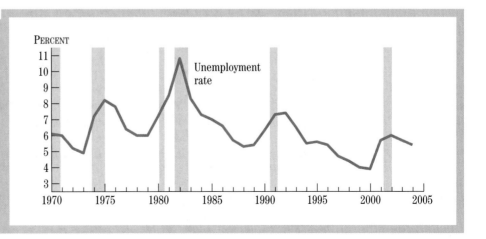

Figure 17.6 shows how high the unemployment rate got during the Great Depression. It rose to over 25 percent; one in four workers was out of work. Fortunately, recent increases in unemployment during recessions have been much smaller. The unemployment rate reached 10.4 percent in the early 1980s, the highest level since World War II.

Even though the most recent recession pales in comparison to the Great Depression, it still caused a lot of pain and hardship across the country. Figure 17.7 illustrates how rapidly unemployment rose, even in what most economists described as a mild recession. In the 12 months from March of 2001 to March of 2002, the unemployment rate increased by almost 1.5 percentage points. To put this number in more human terms, the number of unemployed workers across the country increased by about 2.1 million.

Inflation

inflation rate: the percentage increase in the overall price level over a given period of time, usually one year.

Just as output and unemployment have fluctuated over time, so has inflation. The **inflation rate** is the percentage increase in the average price of all goods and services from one year to the next. Figure 17.8 shows the inflation rate for the same 35-year period we have focused on in our examination of real GDP and unemployment. Clearly, a low and stable inflation rate has not been a feature of the United States during this period. There are several useful facts to note about the behavior of inflation.

First, inflation is closely correlated with the ups and downs in real GDP and employment: Inflation increased prior to every recession in the last 35 years and then subsided during and after every recession. We will want to explore whether this close correlation between the ups and downs in inflation and the ups and downs in the economy helps explain economic fluctuations.

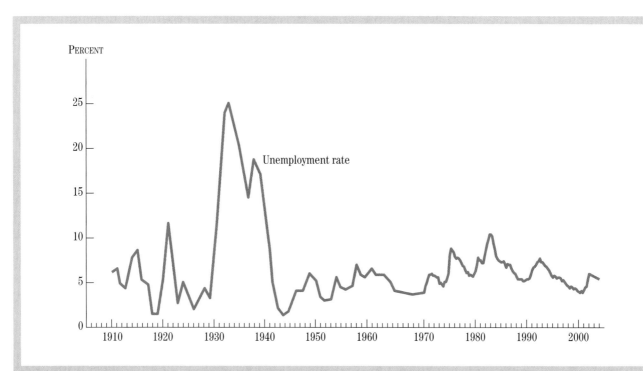

Figure 17.6
Unemployment During the Great Depression

The increase in unemployment in the United States during the Great Depression was huge compared with the increases in unemployment during more mild downturns in the economy. More than one in four workers were unemployed during the Great Depression.

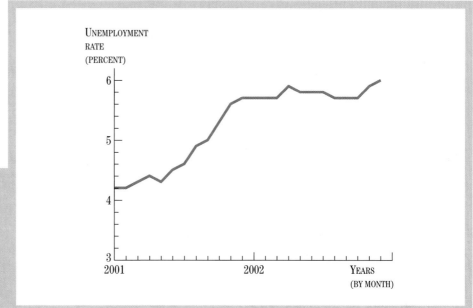

Figure 17.7
The Rapid Rise of Unemployment in 2001
When the economy moves from expansion into recession, unemployment can climb very rapidly over a period of a few months, as we saw at the end of the long expansion in 2001.
Source: Bureau of Labor Statistics

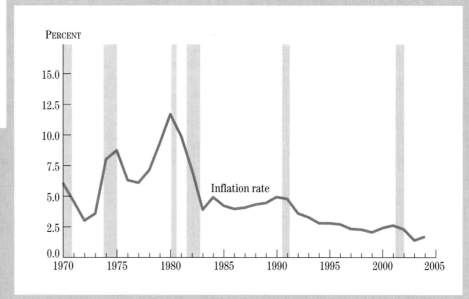

Figure 17.8
The Ups and Downs in Inflation
Inflation has increased before each recession and then declined during and immediately after each recession. In addition, a longer-term upward trend in inflation reached a peak in 1980. Since 1981, America has experienced a disinflation—a decline in the rate of inflation.

Second, there are longer-term trends in inflation. For example, inflation rose from a low point during the 1970s to a high point of double-digit inflation in 1980. This period of persistently high inflation until 1980 is called the *Great Inflation.* The Great Inflation ended in the early 1980s, when the inflation rate declined substantially. Such a decline in inflation is called *disinflation.* (When inflation is negative and the average price level falls, economists call it *deflation.*)

Third, judging by history, there is no reason to expect the inflation rate to be zero, even on average. The inflation rate averaged around 2 or 3 percent in the 1990s in the United States.

Why does inflation increase before recessions? Why does inflation fall during and after recessions? What caused the Great Inflation? Why is inflation not equal to zero

ECONOMICS IN ACTION

The Economic Impact of September 11

The tragic events of September 11, 2001, left a trail of human destruction that was hitherto almost unimaginable. In the days and months following September 11, people all over the United States tried to assess the human and economic toll of the events of that fateful day. The assessment that many macroeconomists were asked to make was to calculate the economic impact of the events of September 11. As the economist Paul Krugman, who is also a regular columnist for the *New York Times,* said in his Op-Ed column a few days after September 11, "It seems almost in bad taste to talk about dollars and cents after an act of mass murder. Nonetheless, we must ask about the economic aftershocks from Tuesday's horror." Macroeconomic theory can help us understand the long- and short-term economic impact of this and other such tragedies.

In the case of September 11, the most obvious short-term costs were the destruction of life and property in New York, Washington, D.C., and Pennsylvania; the disruption of financial markets, given that many large financial institutions were located in and around the World Trade Center; and the costs to airlines from disruptions in air travel in the days following the tragedy. However, the theory of economic fluctuations, presented in Chapters 23 and 24, tells us that spending shocks have feedback effects that aggravate the initial direct effects. In the case of New York, the disruption to the economy was substantially greater than the destruction of property and clean-up costs would indicate because of drastic cutbacks in tourism, which led to a sharp falloff in hotel stays, dining

out in restaurants, and shopping for expensive goods in Manhattan. The lack of spending by consumers led firms in the hotel, restaurant, and retail industries to lay off thousands of workers. According to a study done by the New York City Chamber of Commerce in September 2001, the cost in terms of reduced economic activity was expected to be almost $40 billion, and the cost in terms of employment was expected to be almost 25,000 jobs. Financial markets were severely disrupted in the short run: They were closed for the remainder of the week, and when they opened the following week, the Dow Jones Industrial Average fell from 9605.5 to 8920.7, a decline of about 7 percent. At the end of the first week of trading, the Dow had fallen to 8235.8, a decline of about 14 percent. The airline industry was hit hard: In the weeks following September 11, airlines announced plans to lay off tens of thousands of workers—20,000 apiece at American Airlines and United Airlines.

The theory of economic fluctuations states that when faced with an economic shock that reduces spending, policymakers can respond by putting into place specific measures designed not only to stop the fall in spending, but indeed to try to restore both confidence and spending by consumers and firms. The president promised $20 billion in federal aid to New York to help the city rebuild. As fears mounted that one or more airlines would have to go into bankruptcy, both Congress and the Senate sought to provide relief for the beleaguered airline industry by overwhelmingly approving a bill that provided $5 billion in federal funds and $10 billion in loan guarantees. The

even in more normal times, when the economy is neither in recession nor in boom? What can economic policy do to keep inflation low and stable? These are some of the questions and policy issues about inflation addressed by macroeconomics.

Interest Rates

interest rate: the amount received per dollar loaned per year, usually expressed as a percentage (e.g., 6 percent) of the loan.

The **interest rate** is the amount that lenders charge when they lend money, expressed as a percentage of the amount loaned. For example, if you borrow $100 for a year from a friend and the interest rate on the loan is 6 percent, then at the end of the year you must pay your friend back $6 in interest in addition to the $100 you borrowed. The interest rate is another key economic variable that is related to the growth and change in real GDP over time.

■ **Different Types of Interest Rates and Their Behavior.** There are many different interest rates in the economy: The *mortgage interest rate* is the rate on loans to buy a house; the *savings deposit interest rate* is the rate people get on their

response of monetary policymakers to the events of September 11 was equally swift: On September 17, the Federal Reserve cut interest rates from 3.5 percent to 3 percent, making it cheaper for firms and individuals to borrow money, and also announced its willingness to take steps to restore normalcy to financial markets. Help was offered not only by the government and the Federal Reserve; millions of people all over the United States contributed hundreds of millions of dollars to charities that helped the victims and their families make payments on their rent, school tuition, and health care, doing their part to keep the negative effects from deepening.

The theory of economic growth tells us that the long-term growth of an economy depends on its ability to produce goods and services, which in turn depends on the economy's stocks of labor, capital, and technology. While the destruction of life and property in New York and Washington, D.C., was substantial—"more than we can bear," in the words of Mayor Giuliani—the loss of labor and capital was small relative to the size of the entire U.S. population and the entire U.S. capital stock. In the same Op-Ed piece mentioned earlier, Paul Krugman speculated that the long-term effects would not be substantial: "Nobody has a dollar figure for the damage yet, but I would be surprised if the loss is more than 0.1 percent of U.S. wealth—comparable to the material effects of a major earthquake or hurricane." While such calculations may seem a little too cold-blooded at first glance, it is important that macroeconomists make such assessments so that we can develop a more complete understanding of the impacts of such tragedies, and also so that we can come up with appropriate policy responses to these events.

The prediction that the events of September 11 would not have a long-term effect seems to have been vindicated. In the weeks following September 11, the financial markets seemed to stabilize and then recover: By November 9 the Dow had reached the level it was at on September 10, and it ended the year almost 6 percent higher, at 10,021. GDP grew rapidly in the fourth quarter of 2001, and the unemployment rate seemed to stabilize and then improve as well.

The economy has recovered in the ensuing years. Between December of 2001 and December of 2004, GDP increased at an average annual growth rate of 3.4 percent, the unemployment rate declined from 5.7 percent to 5.2 percent, and the Dow increased from 10,021 to 10,785.

savings deposits at banks; the *Treasury bill rate* is the interest rate the government pays when it borrows money from people for a year or less; the *federal funds rate* is the interest rate banks charge each other on very short-term loans. Interest rates influence people's economic behavior. When interest rates rise, for example, it is more expensive to borrow funds to buy a house or a car, so many people postpone such purchases.

Figure 17.9 shows the behavior of a typical interest rate, the federal funds rate, during the last 35 years. First, note how closely the ups and downs in the interest rate are correlated with the ups and downs in the economy. Interest rates rise before each recession and then decline during and after each recession. Second, note that, as with the inflation rate, there are longer-term trends in the interest rate. The interest rate rose in the 1970s and early 1980s. Each fluctuation in interest rates during this period brought forth a higher peak in interest rates. Then, in the 1980s, the interest rate began a downward trend; each peak was lower than the previous peak. By the early 2000s, interest rates were lower than the levels of the early 1970s.

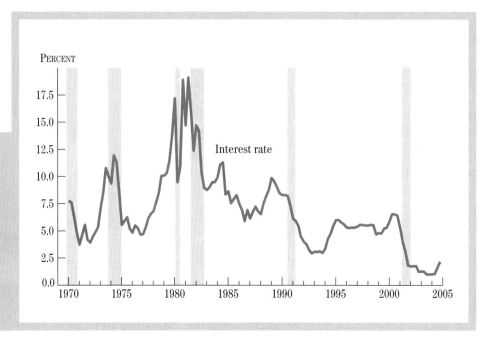

Figure 17.9
The Ups and Downs in Interest Rates
Interest rates generally rise just before a recession and then decline during and just after the recession. There was also a longer-term trend upward in interest rates in the 1970s and a downward trend after the 1980s. (The interest rate shown here is the federal funds interest rate.)
Source: Board of Governors of the Federal Reserve

real interest rate: the interest rate minus the expected rate of inflation; it adjusts the nominal interest rate for inflation.

nominal interest rate: the interest rate uncorrected for inflation.

■ **The Concept of the Real Interest Rate.**   As we will see, the trends and fluctuations in interest rates are intimately connected with the trends and fluctuations in inflation and real GDP. In fact, the long-term rise in interest rates in the 1960s and 1970s was partly due to the rise in the rate of inflation. When inflation rises, people who lend money will be paid back in funds that are worth less because the average price of goods rises more quickly. To compensate for this decline in the value of funds, lenders require a higher interest rate. For example, if the inflation rate is 20 percent and you lend someone $100 for a year at 6 percent, then you get back $106 at the end of the year. However, the *average* price of the goods you can buy with your $106 is now 20 percent higher. Thus, your 6 percent gain in interest has been offset by a 20 percent loss. It is as if you receive *negative* 14 percent interest: 6 percent interest less 20 percent inflation. The difference between the stated interest rate and the inflation rate is thus a better measure of the real interest rate. Economists define the **real interest rate** as the interest rate less the inflation rate people expect. The term **nominal interest rate** is used to refer to the interest rate on a loan, making no adjustment for inflation. For example, the real interest rate is 2 percent if the nominal interest rate is 5 percent and inflation is expected to be 3 percent (5 − 3 = 2). To keep the real interest rate from changing by a large amount as inflation rises, the nominal interest rate has to increase with inflation. Thus, the concept of the real interest rate helps us understand why inflation and interest rates have moved together. We will make much more use of the real interest rate in later chapters.

REVIEW
- The unemployment rate rises during recessions and falls during recoveries.
- Inflation and interest rates rise prior to recessions and then fall during and just after recessions.
- There was a long-term increase in interest rates and inflation in the 1970s. Interest rates and inflation were lower in the 1990s and into the 2000s.

Macroeconomic Theory and Policy

Because strong economic growth raises the living standards of people in an economy, and because increases in unemployment during recessions cause hardship, two goals of economic policy are to raise long-term growth and to reduce the size of short-term economic fluctuations. However, the facts—summarized above—about economic growth and fluctuations do not give economists a basis for making recommendations about economic policy. Before one can be confident about recommending a policy, one needs a coherent theory to explain the facts.

Macroeconomic theory is divided into two branches. *Economic growth theory* aims to explain the long-term upward rise of real GDP over time. *Economic fluctuations theory* tries to explain the short-term fluctuations in real GDP. Economic growth theory and economic fluctuations theory combine to form *macroeconomic theory,* which explains why the economy both grows and fluctuates over time.

The Theory of Long-Term Economic Growth

Economic growth theory starts by distinguishing the longer-term economic growth trend from the short-term fluctuations in the economy. This is not as easy as it may seem because the long-term growth trend itself may change.

It will be useful to give a name to the upward trend line in real GDP shown in Figure 17.1. We will call it **potential GDP.** Potential GDP represents the long-run tendency of the economy to grow. Real GDP fluctuates around potential GDP. No one knows exactly where potential GDP lies and exactly what its growth rate is, but any trend line that has the same long-term increase as real GDP and intersects real GDP in several places is probably a good estimate.

Note that potential GDP as defined here and as used by most macroeconomists is not the maximum amount of real GDP. As Figure 17.1 shows, sometimes real GDP goes above potential GDP. Thus, potential GDP is more like the average or normal level of real GDP.

Economic growth theory postulates that the potential GDP of an economy is given by its **aggregate supply.** *Aggregate* means total. Aggregate supply is all goods and services produced by all the firms in the economy using the available labor, capital, and technology. **Labor** is the total number of hours workers are available to work in producing real GDP. **Capital** is the total number of factories, cultivated plots of land, machines, computers, and other tools available for the workers to use to produce real GDP. **Technology** is all the available know-how—from organizational schemes to improved telecommunications to better computer programming skills—that workers and firms can use when they produce real GDP. Labor, capital, and technology jointly determine aggregate supply.

■ **The Production Function.** We can summarize the relationship between the three determinants and the aggregate supply of real GDP as

Real GDP = F(labor, capital, technology)

which we say in words as "real GDP is a function, F, of labor, capital, and technology." The function F means that there is some general relationship between these variables. For this relationship, we assume that higher capital, higher labor, and higher technology all mean higher real GDP; and lower capital, lower labor, and lower technology all mean less real GDP. We call this relationship the **production function** because it tells us how much production (real GDP) of goods and services can be obtained from a certain amount of labor, capital, and technology inputs. A higher long-term economic growth rate for the economy requires a higher growth rate for

potential GDP: the economy's long-term growth trend for real GDP, determined by the available supply of capital, labor, and technology. Real GDP fluctuates above and below potential GDP.

aggregate supply: the total value of all goods and services produced in the economy by the available supply of capital, labor, and technology (also called potential GDP).

labor: the number of hours people are available to work in producing goods and services.

capital: the factories, improvements to cultivated land, machinery and other tools, equipment, and structures used to produce goods and services.

technology: anything that raises the amount of output that can be produced with a given amount of labor and capital.

production function: the relationship that describes output as a function of labor, capital, and technology.

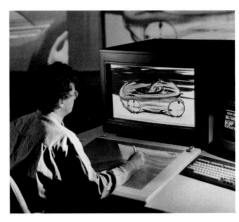

Aggregate Supply and the Production Function
The theory of economic growth is based on the production function, which is a model of how labor, capital, and technology jointly determine the aggregate supply of output in the economy. Here the workers at the automobile plant are part of the economy's **labor** *(left), the tools that the workers are using to assemble the cars are the economy's* **capital** *(middle), and computer programming skills are part of the economy's* **technology** *(right), which raises the value of output for a given amount of labor and capital.*

one or more of these three determinants. A lower long-term economic growth rate may be due to a slower growth rate for one or more of these three determinants.

The production function applies to the entire economy, but we also have production functions for individual firms in the economy. For example, consider the production of cars. The car factory and the machines in the factory are the capital. The workers who work in the factory are the labor. The assembly-line production method is the technology. The cars coming out of the factory are the output. The production function for the economy as a whole has real GDP as output, not just cars, and all available labor, capital, and technology as inputs, not just those producing cars.

The Role of Government Policy

Most governments have been interested in finding ways to increase economic growth. Economic policies that aim to increase long-term economic growth are sometimes called *supply-side policies* because they concentrate on increasing the growth of potential GDP, which is the aggregate supply of the economy.

■ **Fiscal Policy.**   Our preview of growth theory already tells us where policies to increase growth should focus: on increasing the available supply of labor, capital, and technology. The growth rate of capital depends on how much businesses invest in new capital each year. The amount that businesses choose to invest depends in part on the incentives they have to invest. We will see that the incentive to invest depends on the amount of taxing, spending, and borrowing by government. Hence, government policy can affect the incentive to invest and thereby stimulate long-term economic growth. Government policy concerning taxing, spending, and borrowing is called *fiscal policy.*

Labor supply also depends on incentives. In the case of labor, it is the incentive for firms to hire workers, for people to work harder or longer, for workers who are not in the labor force to come into the labor force, or for people to retire later in life. Again, government policy toward taxing, spending, and borrowing affects these incentives.

Finally, technology growth can also be affected by government policy if the government gives incentives for researchers to invent new technologies or provides funds for education so that workers can improve their skills and know-how.

■ **Monetary Policy.**   Keeping inflation low and stable is another part of government policy to stimulate long-term economic growth. We will see that the government has an important role to play in determining the inflation rate, especially over the long term, because the inflation rate in the long term depends on the growth rate of the money supply, which can be controlled by the government. Government policy concerning the money supply and the control of inflation is called *monetary policy*. The institution of government assigned to conduct monetary policy is the central bank. In the United States the central bank is the Federal Reserve System.

Why should low and stable inflation be part of an economic growth policy? An examination of inflation and economic growth in a number of countries indicates that inflation is negatively correlated with long-term economic growth. The reason for this negative correlation over the long term may be that inflation raises uncertainty and thereby reduces incentives to invest in capital or improve technology. The theory of economic growth tells us that lower capital growth and lower technological growth reduce economic growth.

The Theory of Economic Fluctuations

Our review of the performance of the economy showed some of the hardships that come from economic fluctuations, especially the recessions and unemployment. Can government economic policy improve economic performance by reducing the size of the fluctuations? To answer these questions, we need a theory to interpret the facts of economic fluctuations.

aggregate demand: the total demand for goods and services by consumers, businesses, government, and foreigners.

■ **Aggregate Demand and Economic Fluctuations.**   The theory of economic fluctuations emphasizes fluctuations in the demand for goods and services as the reason for the ups and downs in the economy. Because the focus is on the sum of the demand for all goods and services in the economy—not just the demand for peanuts or bicycles—we use the term *aggregate demand*. More precisely, **aggregate demand** is the sum of the demands from the four groups that contribute to demand in the whole economy: consumers, business firms, government, and foreigners.

According to this theory, the declines in real GDP below potential GDP during recessions are caused by declines in aggregate demand, and the increases in real GDP above potential GDP are caused by increases in aggregate demand. For example, the decrease in real GDP in the 1990–1991 recession may have been due to a decline in government demand. In fact, government military spending did decline sharply. Or the recession may have been due to a decline in demand by consumers as they learned about Iraq's invasion of Kuwait in August 1990, saw oil and gasoline prices rise, and worried about the threat of war.

Thus, a key assumption of the theory of economic fluctuations is that real GDP fluctuates around potential GDP. Why is this a good assumption? How do we know that the fluctuations in the economy are not due solely to fluctuations in potential GDP, that is, in the economy's aggregate supply? The rationale for the assumption is that most of the determinants of potential GDP usually change rather smoothly. Clearly, population grows relatively smoothly. We do not have a sudden drop in the U.S. population every few years, nor is there a huge migration of people from the United States during recessions. The same is true with factories and equipment in the economy. Unless there is a major war at home, we do not suddenly lose equipment or factories in the economy on a massive scale. Even disasters such as the deadly Gulf

Coast hurricanes of 2005 (Katrina and Rita), the 1994 earthquake in California, or the attacks of September 11, 2001, although devastating for those hit, take only a tiny fraction out of the potential GDP of the entire U.S. economy. Finally, technological know-how does not suddenly decline; we do not suddenly forget how to produce things. The steady upward movement of potential GDP thus represents gradual accumulations—growth of population, growth of capital, and growth of technology. However, although many economists place more emphasis on the role of aggregate demand in short-run economic fluctuations than on fluctuations in potential GDP, it is too extreme to insist that there are absolutely no fluctuations in potential GDP.

The Role of Macroeconomic Policy

Macroeconomic policy can have substantial effects on economic fluctuations. Many governments would like to implement policies that either help to avoid recessions or minimize the impact of recessions when they do occur. Monetary policymakers typically prefer to implement policies that minimize fluctuations in GDP. Policies used to influence economic fluctuations are sometimes called *demand-side policies* because they aim to influence aggregate demand in the economy.

■ **Fiscal Policy.** On the fiscal side, the primary tools that the government uses to influence demand are government purchases and taxes. If the economy shows signs of entering a recession, the government can try to increase demand by implementing tax cuts and/or spending increases. A good example was the tax cuts implemented by Congress in 2001 when the economy was showing signs of sliding into recession. Often these policies are intended to mitigate the negative impact on aggregate demand of other factors, such as a fall in consumer or investor confidence or a fall in our exports because of a recession in one of the countries that is among our major trading partners.

■ **Monetary Policy.** To keep inflation low and stable, the Federal Reserve will also implement policies that influence demand. The primary tools that the Federal Reserve uses to influence demand are changes in interest rates. If there are signs that inflation is on the rise because aggregate demand is growing faster than potential output, the Federal Reserve may step in and raise interest rates, which will slow down spending, as you will soon learn in Chapter 19. In addition to keeping inflation low and stable, the Federal Reserve is also concerned with minimizing the adverse impact of recessions. When the economy goes into recession, the Federal Reserve will try to increase demand by lowering interest rates. A good example of this type of behavior was seen in 2001 and 2002 when the Federal Reserve lowered interest rates twelve times—going from an interest rate of 6.5 percent to an interest rate of 1.25 percent.

REVIEW
- Economic growth theory concentrates on explaining the long-term upward path of the economy.
- Economic growth depends on three factors: the growth of capital, labor, and technology.
- Government policy can influence long-term economic growth by affecting these three factors. To raise long-term economic growth, government fiscal policies can provide incentives for investment in capital, for research and development of new technologies, for education, and for increased labor supply. A monetary policy of low and stable inflation can also have a positive effect on economic growth.

- Economic fluctuations theory assumes that fluctuations in GDP are due to fluctuations in aggregate demand.

- Monetary policy and fiscal policy can reduce the fluctuations in real GDP. Finding good policies is a major task of macroeconomics.

Conclusion

This chapter started with a brief review of the facts of economic growth and fluctuations. The key facts are that economic growth provides impressive gains in the well-being of individuals over the long term, that economic growth is temporarily interrupted by recessions, that unemployment rises in recessions, and that inflation and interest rates rise before recessions and decline during and after recessions. These are the facts on which macroeconomic theory is based and about which macroeconomic policy is concerned. Remembering these facts helps you understand theory and make judgments about government policy.

After showing how we measure real GDP and inflation in Chapter 18, we go on to look at explanations for the facts and proposals for macroeconomic policies in Chapters 19 through 27.

KEY POINTS

1. Macroeconomics is concerned with economic growth and fluctuations in the whole economy.

2. The U.S. economy and many other economies have grown dramatically in recent years.

3. Economists agree that economic growth occurs because of increases in labor, capital, and technological know-how.

4. Economic policies that provide incentives to increase capital and resources devoted to improving technology can raise productivity growth.

5. Economic fluctuations consist of recessions (when real GDP falls and unemployment increases) followed by recoveries (when real GDP rises rapidly and unemployment falls).

6. Recent recessions have been much less severe than the Great Depression of the 1930s, when real GDP fell by over 30 percent.

7. The unemployment rate is well above zero even when the economy is booming.

8. The most popular theory of economic fluctuations is that they occur because of fluctuations in aggregate demand.

9. Macroeconomic policies include monetary and fiscal policies that are aimed at keeping business cycles small and inflation low.

10. Economic growth theory and economic fluctuations theory combine to form macroeconomic theory, which explains why the economy grows and fluctuates over time.

KEY TERMS

real gross domestic product (real GDP)
economic growth
economic fluctuations
recession
peak

trough
expansion
recovery
unemployment rate
inflation rate
interest rate

real interest rate
nominal interest rate
potential GDP
aggregate supply
labor
capital

technology
production function
aggregate demand

QUESTIONS FOR REVIEW

1. What is the difference between economic growth and economic fluctuations?

2. Why do bad economic times continue after recessions end?

3. Why does unemployment rise in recessions?

4. How many recessions have there been since the Great Depression?

5. How do the 1990–1991 and the 2001 recessions compare?

6. What are the two broad branches of macroeconomic theory?

7. What are the three determinants of economic growth?

8. What is potential GDP?

9. What is aggregate demand?

10. What is the difference between monetary policy and fiscal policy?

PROBLEMS

1. The graph below shows a business cycle that occurred in the United States in the 1990s. Draw in potential GDP and show the peak, recession, trough, and recovery phases of this business cycle.

2. Suppose the U.S. economy is currently at the trough of a business cycle. What is the relationship between real and potential GDP? Is it likely that real GDP will stay in this relative position for a long period of time (say, 10 years)? Explain briefly.

3. Using the data from Canada and Britain shown in the table below, plot the unemployment rate on the vertical axis.

Rate of Unemployment (percent)

Year	Canada	Britain
1990	7.7	6.9
1991	9.8	8.8
1992	10.6	10.1
1993	10.8	10.5
1994	9.5	9.6
1995	8.6	8.7
1996	8.8	8.1
1997	8.4	7.0
1998	7.7	6.3
1999	7.0	6.0
2000	6.1	5.5

How do unemployment rates compare with the U.S. rate shown in text Figure 17.5?

4. Compare Figure 17.5, showing unemployment, with Figure 17.8, showing the inflation rate for the same period in the United States. Describe how unemployment and inflation are correlated over the long term and over the short term.

5. Suppose that you had savings deposited in an account at an interest rate of 5 percent and your father told you that he earned 10 percent interest 20 years ago. Which of you was getting the better return? Is that all the information you need? Suppose that the inflation rate in the

Problem 1

The Business Cycle Surrounding the 1990–91 Recession

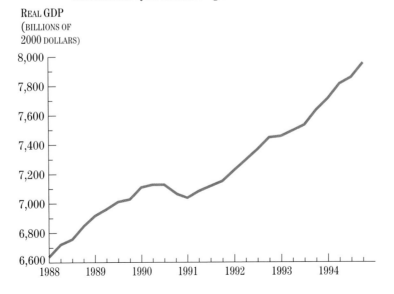

United States was 12 percent 20 years ago and is 3 percent now. Does this information change your answer? Be sure to use the concept of the real interest rate in your answer.

6. Suppose you have $1,000, which you can put in two different types of accounts at a bank. One account pays interest of 8 percent per year; the other pays interest at 2 percent per year plus the rate of inflation. Calculate the real return you will receive after 1 year if the inflation rate is 5 percent. Which account will you choose if you expect the rate of inflation to be 8 percent? Why?
7. Suppose people start retiring at a later age because of improved medical technology. How will this affect the economy's potential GDP? Why might the government want to encourage later retirement?
8. What factors can cause fluctuations in aggregate demand? Are these the same as the determinants of potential GDP? Why do economists think that changes in aggregate demand are the primary cause of short-term economic fluctuations?
9. What determines potential GDP? What factors could cause the growth rate of potential GDP to slow down? What economic policies can the government use to affect potential GDP?
10. The table below shows the amount of output that can be produced using different combinations of labor and capital in a hypothetical economy with a given type of technology. For example, 650 units of output are produced when 200 units of labor and 100 units of capital are combined. This table is an example of a production function.
    a. Hold capital constant at 100 while you increase labor. What happens to output?
    b. Now hold labor constant at 100 and raise the level of capital. What happens to output?
    c. Finally, what happens when you raise labor and capital by the same amount?

Capital \ Labor	*50*	*100*	*150*	*200*	*250*
50	200	324	432	528	618
100	246	400	532	650	760
150	278	452	600	734	858
200	304	492	654	800	936
250	324	526	700	856	1,000

The Miracle of Compound Growth

Compound growth explains why small differences in the annual economic growth rate make such huge differences in real GDP over time. Here we explain this compounding effect, show how to compute growth rates, and discuss alternative ways to plot growing variables over time.

How Compound Growth Works

Compound growth works just like compound interest on a savings account. Compound interest is defined as the "interest on the interest" you earned in earlier periods. For example, suppose you have a savings account in a bank that pays 6 percent per year in interest. That is, if you put $100 in the account, then after one year you will get $100 times .06, or $6 in interest. If you leave the original $100 plus the $6—that is, $106—in the bank for a second year, then at the end of the second year you will get $106 times .06, or $6.36 in interest. The $.36 is the "interest on the interest," that is, $6 times .06.

At the end of the second year, you have $100 + $6 + $6.36 = $112.36. If you leave that in the bank for a third year, you will get $6.74 in interest, of which $.74 is "interest on the interest" earned in the first two years. Note how the "interest on the interest" rises from $.36 in the second year to $.74 in the third year. Following the same calculations, the "interest on the interest" in the fourth year would be $1.15. After 13 years, the "interest on the interest" is greater than the $6 interest on the original $100! As a result of this compound interest, the size of your account grows rapidly. At the end of 20 years, it is $320.71; after 40 years, your $100 has grown to $1,028.57.

Compound growth applies the idea of compound interest to the economy. Consider, for example, a country in which real GDP is $100 billion and the growth rate is 6 percent per year. After one year, real GDP would increase by $100 billion times .06, or by $6 billion. Real GDP rises from $100 billion to $106 billion. In the second year, real GDP increases by $106 billion times .06, or by $6.36 billion. Real GDP rises from $106 billion to $112.36 billion. Table 17A.1 shows how, continuing this way, real GDP grows, rounding to the nearest $.1 billion.

Thus, in one person's lifetime, real GDP would increase by about 60 times.

Exponential Effects

A convenient way to compute these changes is to multiply the initial level by 1.06 year after year. For example,

Table 17A.1
Example of Compound Growth

	Real GDP (billions)		Real GDP (billions)
Year 0	$100.0	Year 20	$ 320.7
Year 1	$106.0	Year 30	$ 574.3
Year 2	$112.4	Year 40	$1,028.6
Year 3	$119.1	Year 50	$1,842.0
Year 4	$126.2	Year 60	$3,298.8
Year 5	$133.3	Year 70	$5,907.6
Year 10	$179.1		

the level of real GDP after one year is $100 billion times .06 plus $100 billion, or $100 billion times 1.06. After two years, it is $106 billion times 1.06, or $100 billion times $(1.06)^2$. Thus, for n years, we have

$$(\text{Initial level}) \times (1.06)^n = \text{level at end of } n \text{ years}$$

where the initial level could be $100 in a bank, the $100 billion level of real GDP, or anything else. For example, real GDP at the end of 70 years in the table shown earlier is $100 billion times $(1.06)^n = $100 billion times 59.076 = $5,907.6 billion, with $n = 70$. Here the growth rate (or the interest rate) is 6 percent. In general, we have

$$(\text{Initial level}) \times (1 + g)^n = \text{level at end of } n \text{ years}$$

where g is the annual growth rate, stated as a decimal; that is, 6 percent is .06. If you have a hand calculator with a key that does y^x, it is fairly easy to make these calculations, and if you try it you will see the power of compound growth. The term *exponential growth* is sometimes used because the number of years (n) appears as an exponent in the above expression.

When economists refer to average annual growth over time, they include this compounding effect. The growth rate is found by solving for g. That is, the growth rate, stated as a decimal fraction, between some initial level and a level n years later is given by

$$g = \left(\frac{\text{level at end of } n \text{ years}}{\text{initial level}}\right)^{1/n} - 1$$

For example, the average annual growth rate from year 0 to year 20 in the table is

$$g = \left(\frac{320.7}{100}\right)^{1/20} - 1$$

$$= (1.06) - 1$$

$$= .06$$

or 6 percent. Again, if your calculator has a key for y^x, you can make these calculations easily.

To get the annual growth rate for one year, you simply divide the level in the second year by the level in the first year and subtract 1 to get the growth rate.

Rule of 72

You can also find how long it takes something to increase by a certain percentage. For example, to calculate how many years it takes something that grows at rate g to dou-ble, you solve $(1 + g)^n = 2$ for n. The answer is approximately $n = .72/g$. In other words, if you divide 72 by the growth rate in percent, you get the number of years it takes to double the amount. This is called the *rule of 72*. If your bank account pays 7.2 percent interest, it will double in 10 years.

Plotting Growing Variables

You may have noticed that some time-series charts have vertical scales that shrink as the economic variable being plotted gets bigger. Look, for example, at the scale in Figures 17.1 and 17.4 for real GDP. This type of scale, which is called a *ratio scale* (or sometimes a proportional scale or logarithmic scale), is used by financial analysts

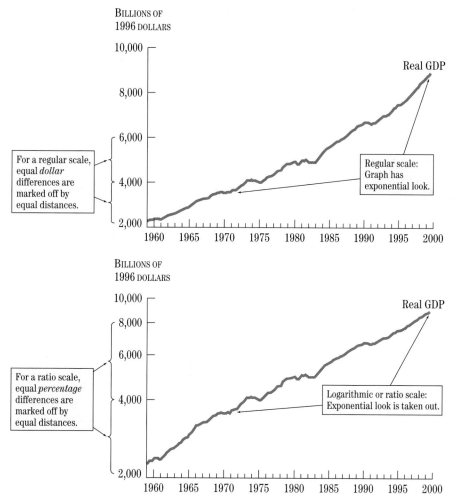

Figure 17A.1
Comparison of Two Different Scales: "Regular" versus "Ratio"

and economists to present variables that grow over time. The purpose of a ratio scale is to make equal percentage changes in the variable have the same vertical distance.

If you plot a variable that grows at a constant rate on a ratio scale, it looks like a straight line, even though it would look as if it were exploding on a standard scale. To show what ratio scales do, real GDP for the past 40 years is plotted in Figure 17A.1 using a regular scale and a ratio scale. Note how the fluctuations in real GDP in the 1960s look smaller on a regular scale compared with the ratio scale, and how the ratio scale tends to take out the exponential look. This difference is one reason to look carefully at the scales of graphs. (The reason that ratio scales are sometimes called logarithmic scales is that plotting the logarithm of a variable is the same as plotting the variable on a ratio scale.)

Key Points

1. Compound growth is similar to compound interest. Rather than applying the interest rate to the interest from earlier periods, one applies the growth rate to the growth from the previous period.

2. With compound growth, seemingly small differences in growth rates result in huge differences in real GDP.

3. When you see a diagram with the scale shrunk for the higher values, it is a logarithmic or ratio scale.

4. A ratio or logarithmic scale is more useful than a regular scale when a variable is growing over time.

Key Term and Definition

compound growth: applying the growth rate to growth from the previous period; similar to compound interest.

Questions for Review

1. What is the rule of 72?
2. What is a ratio scale?

Problems

1. Suppose that the annual rate of growth of GDP per capita is 2 percent. How much will real GDP per capita increase in 10 years? How much will it increase in 50 years? Answer the same questions for a growth rate of 1 percent.

2. Plot the data for the example economy in the table in this appendix on a graph at ten-year intervals from year 20 to year 60 on a *regular* scale. Now create a new graph with a *ratio* scale by first marking off 300, 600, 1,200, 2,400, and 4,800 at equal distances on the vertical axis. Plot the same data on this graph. Compare the two graphs.

CHAPTER 18

Measuring the Production, Income, and Spending of Nations

O n January 28, 2005, the Bureau of Economic Analysis (BEA), which releases the official government statistics on real GDP, announced in a press release that "real gross domestic product—the output of goods and services produced by labor and property located in the United States— increased at an annual rate of 3.1 percent in the fourth quarter of 2004." Exactly four weeks later, the BEA issued the following news release announcing the revision of the GDP figure released on January 28: "Real gross domestic product—the output of goods and services produced by labor and property located in the United States—increased at an annual rate of 3.8 percent in the fourth quarter of 2004." The difference between the two estimates was the equivalent of almost $20 billion! This example illustrates the complexity of measuring economic variables like real GDP. Choosing the appropriate policy measures for the economy requires having reliable data. In fact, top officials at the White House (including the president) find these data so important that they make sure they get them the night before they are released to the public.

Measuring the economy in a timely and accurate manner is also essential for people in financial markets and other lines of business. Bond and stock traders in New York, Tokyo, London, and everywhere else keep their eyes glued to their computer terminals when a new government statistic measuring the course of the economy is about to be released. By buying or selling quickly in response to the new information, they can make millions or avoid losing millions.

To economists, economic measurement is interesting in its own right, involving clever solutions to intriguing problems. One of the first Nobel Prizes in economics was given to Simon Kuznets for solving some of these measurement problems. Economics students cannot help but learn a little about how the economy works when they study how to measure it, just as geology students cannot help but learn a little about earthquakes when they study how the Richter scale measures them.

In this chapter, we examine how economists measure a nation's production, income, and spending. We stated in Chapter 17 that real gross domestic product (real GDP) is the most comprehensive measure we have of a country's production. But before we can measure real GDP, we must show how to measure GDP itself. In the process of describing the measurement of GDP, we will observe several key relationships and interpret what these relationships mean. We will focus on examples from the United States, but the same ideas apply to any country.

Measuring GDP

To use GDP as a measure of production, we must be precise about *what* is included in production, *where* production takes place, and *when* production takes place.

A Precise Definition of GDP

GDP is a measure of the value of all the goods and services newly produced in a country during some period of time. Let us dissect this definition to determine what is in GDP and what is not, as well as where and when GDP is produced.

- *What?* Only *newly produced* goods and services are included. That 10-year-old baby carriage sold in a garage sale is not in this year's GDP; it was included in GDP 10 years ago, when it was produced. Both *goods*—such as automobiles and new houses—and *services*—such as bus rides or a college education—are included in GDP.

- *Where?* Only goods and services produced *within the borders* of a country are included in GDP. Goods produced by Americans working in another country are not part of U.S. GDP; they are part of the other country's GDP. Goods and services produced by foreigners working in the United States are part of U.S. GDP.

- *When?* Only goods and services produced *during some specified period* of time are included in GDP. We always need to specify the period during which we are measuring GDP. For example, U.S. GDP in 2004 is the production during 2004. Production during a year is 365 times larger than production for a typical day.

Rounded off to the nearest billion, GDP, or total production, was $11,735 billion in the United States in 2004. Rounded off to the nearest trillion, GDP was $12 trillion. That is an average production of about $32 billion worth of goods and services a day for each of the 365 days during the year.

■ **Prices Determine the Importance of Goods and Services in GDP.** GDP is a single number, but it measures the production of many different things, from apples to oranges, from car insurance to life insurance, from audio CDs to DVDs. How can we add up such different products? Is a CD more important than a DVD? Each good is given a weight when we compute GDP, and that weight is its *price*. If the price of a DVD is greater than that of a CD, then the DVD will count more in GDP.

To see this, imagine that production consists entirely of CDs and DVDs. If a DVD costs $15 and a CD costs $10, then producing three DVDs will add $45 to GDP, and producing five CDs will add $50 to GDP. Thus, producing three DVDs plus five CDs adds $95 to GDP, as shown in Table 18.1.

Although this method of weighting by price might not appeal to you personally—you might like CDs more than DVDs—it is hard to imagine anything more workable. In a market system, prices tend to reflect the cost and value of the goods and services produced. One of the great problems of measuring GDP in centrally planned economies such as the Soviet Union was that the price of goods was set by the government; thus, the weight given each item may have had little to do with its cost or value to individuals. Without market prices, measuring GDP in the Soviet Union was difficult.

■ **Intermediate Goods versus Final Goods.** When measuring GDP, it is important not to count the same item more than once. Consider bicycle tires. When you buy a $150 bicycle, the tires are considered part of the bicycle. Suppose the tires are worth $20. It would be a mistake to count both the $20 value of the tires and the $150 value of the bicycle, for a total value of $170. That would count the tires twice, which is called double counting. When a tire is part of a new bicycle, it is an example of an **intermediate good.** Intermediate goods are part of **final goods,** which by definition are goods that undergo no further processing—in this case, the bicycle. *To avoid double counting, we never count intermediate goods; only final goods are part of the GDP.* If in a few years you buy a new $25 bicycle tire, then the tire will be a final good.

intermediate good: a good that undergoes further processing before it is sold to consumers.

final good: a new good that undergoes no further processing before it is sold to consumers.

■ **Three Ways to Measure GDP.** Economists measure GDP in three ways. All three give the same answer, but they refer to conceptually different activities in the economy and provide different ways to think about GDP. All three are reported in the national income and product accounts, the official U.S. government tabulation of GDP put together by economists and statisticians at the Department of Commerce.

Table 18.1
Adding Up Unlike Products: CDs and DVDs

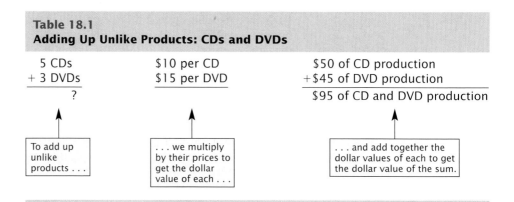

Table 18.2
Components of Spending in 2004 (billions of dollars)

Gross domestic product (GDP)	$11,735
Consumption	8,230
Investment	1,927
Government purchases	2,184
Net exports	−606

Source: U.S. Department of Commerce.

The first way measures the total amount that people *spend* on goods and services made in America. This is the *spending* approach. The second way measures the total income that is earned by all the workers and businesses that produce American goods and services. This is the *income* approach. In this approach, your income is a measure of what you produce. The third way measures the total of all the goods and services as they are *produced,* or as they are shipped out of the factory. This is the *production* approach. Note that each of the approaches considers the whole economy, and thus we frequently refer to them as aggregate spending, aggregate income, and aggregate production, where the word *aggregate* means total. Let us consider each of the three approaches in turn.

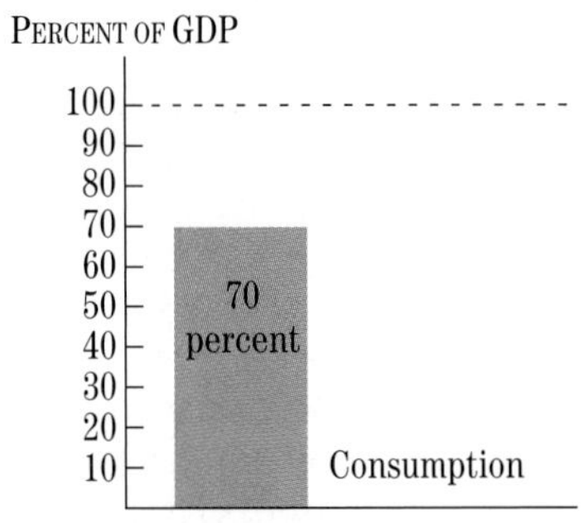

Figure 18.1
Consumption as a Share of GDP
Consumption is 70 percent of GDP in the United States.

The Spending Approach

Typically, total spending in the economy is divided into four components: *consumption, investment, government purchases,* and *net exports,* which equal exports minus imports. Each of the four components corresponds closely to one of four groups into which the economy is divided: consumers, businesses, governments, and foreigners. Before considering each component, look at Table 18.2, which shows how the $11,735 billion of GDP in the United States in 2004 was divided into the four categories.

consumption: purchases of final goods and services by individuals.

■ **Consumption.**   The first component, **consumption,** is purchases of final goods and services by individuals. Government statisticians, who collect the data in most countries, survey department stores, discount stores, car dealers, and other sellers to see how much consumers purchase each year ($8,230 billion in 2004, as given in Table 18.2). They count anything purchased by consumers as consumption. Consumption does not include spending by business or government. Consumer purchases may be big-ticket items such as a new convertible, an operation to remove a cancerous tumor, a new stereo, a weekend vacation, or college tuition, or smaller-ticket items such as an oil change, a medical checkup, a bus ride, or a driver's education class. Consumption is a whopping 70 percent of GDP in the United States (see Figure 18.1).

investment: purchases of final goods by firms plus purchases of newly produced residences by households.

■ **Investment.**   The second component, **investment,** consists of purchases of final goods by business firms and of newly produced residences by households. When a business such as a pizza delivery firm buys a new car, economists consider that purchase as part of investment rather than as consumption. The firm uses the car to make deliveries, which contributes to its production of delivered pizzas. Included in investment are all the new machines, new factories, and other tools used to produce goods and services. Purchases of intermediate goods that go directly into a manufactured product—such as a tire on a bicycle—are not counted as investment. These items are part of the finished product—the bicycle, in this case—purchased by consumers. We do not want to count such items twice.

The new machines, factories, and other tools that are part of investment in any year are sometimes called *business fixed investment;* this amounted to $1,221 billion in 2004. There are two other items that government statisticians include as part of investment: inventory investment and residential investment.

Inventory investment is defined as the change in *inventories,* which are the goods on store shelves, on showroom floors, or in warehouses that have not yet been sold or assembled into a final form for sale. For example, cars on the lot of a car dealer are part of inventories. When inventory investment is positive, then inventories are rising. When inventory investment is negative, then inventories are falling. For example, if a car dealer has an inventory of 20 cars on September 30, gets 15 new cars shipped from the factory during the month of October, and sells no cars during the month, then the dealer's inventory will be 35 cars on October 31. Inventory investment is positive 15 cars, and inventory rises from 20 cars to 35 cars. If 22 cars are then sold during the month of November and there are no shipments from the factory, the dealer's inventory will be 13 cars on November 30. Inventory investment is negative 22 cars, and inventory decreases from 35 cars to 13 cars.

Why is inventory investment included as a spending item when we compute GDP? The reason is that we want a measure of production. Consider the car example again. Car production rises by one car when a complete Jeep rolls out of the factory. But the Jeep is not usually instantaneously purchased by a consumer. First, the Jeep is shipped to a Jeep dealer, where it is put on the lot. If the government statisticians look at what consumers purchase, they will not count the Jeep because it has not been purchased yet. But if inventory investment is counted as part of investment spending, then the Jeep will get counted. That is why we include inventory investment in spending.

What happens when a consumer purchases the Jeep? Consumption will rise because the purchases of Jeeps have risen, and the car dealer's inventory goes down by one car. Thus, inventory investment is negative one car. Adding one Jeep consumed to negative one Jeep of inventory investment gives zero, which is just what we want because there is no change in production.

In 2004, inventory investment throughout the economy was $43 billion. Some firms subtracted inventories, but others added a greater amount. Inventory investment tends to fluctuate up and down and therefore plays a big role in the business cycle.

The other part of investment that is not business fixed investment is *residential investment,* the purchase of new houses and apartment buildings. About $663 billion worth of housing and apartments were constructed in 2004. Although much of this was purchased by consumers rather than businesses, it is included in investment because it produces services: shelter and, in some cases, a place to relax and enjoy life.

Combining the three parts of investment, we find that investment was $1,927 billion in 2004: $1,221 billion of business fixed investment, $663 billion of residential investment, and $43 billion of inventory investment. Investment was about 16 percent of GDP in 2004 (see Figure 18.2).

Note the special way the term *investment* is used in this discussion. To an economist, investment means the purchase of new factories, houses, or equipment. In everyday language, however, investment usually refers to an individual's putting away some funds for the future,

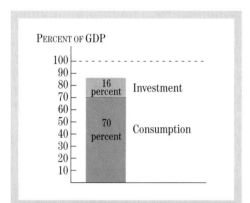

Figure 18.2
Investment and Consumption as a Share of GDP
Investment is a much smaller share of GDP than is consumption.

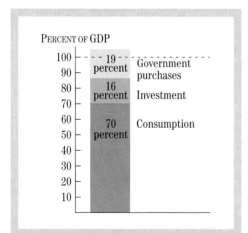

Figure 18.3
Government Purchases, Investment, and Consumption as a Share of GDP
Government purchases as a share of GDP are greater than investment and less than consumption. When the stacked bar goes above the 100 percent line, there are negative net exports (a trade deficit), as shown here. If the stacked bar stops below the 100 percent line, there is a trade surplus.

Distinguishing Between Stocks and Flows

The distinction between *stocks* and *flows* is one of the most useful concepts in economics. For example, it helps businesses understand the important difference between inventories and inventory investment (the change in inventories). The amount of inventories at a firm *at a particular date* is a *stock,* while the change in inventories *during a particular period* between two dates is a *flow.* To remember the distinction, notice that the expression "to take stock" means adding up all the inventories on the shelves. If a car dealer has 35 cars on the lot at the close of business on October 31, we say the stock of inventory is 35 cars. If the stock increases to 40 cars by the close of business on November 30, then the flow of inventory investment is 5 cars during the month of November.

The economist's distinction between stocks and flows can be illustrated by picturing water flowing into and out of a lake—for example, the Colorado River flowing into and out of Lake Powell behind Glen Canyon Dam. When more water flows in than flows out, the stock of water in Lake Powell rises. Similarly, a positive flow of inventory investment raises the stock of inventory at a firm. And just as the stock of water falls when more water flows out than flows in, negative inventory investment lowers the stock of inventory.

The distinction between stocks and flows is useful in other economic applications as well. The factories in America on December 31, 2004, are a stock. The number of factories built during 2004 is a flow. The funds in your checking account are a stock. The deposit you made last week is a flow.

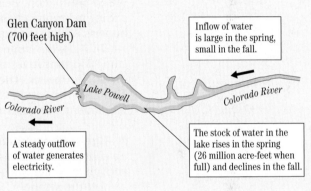

Glen Canyon Dam
(700 feet high)

Inflow of water is large in the spring, small in the fall.

Lake Powell

Colorado River

Colorado River

A steady outflow of water generates electricity.

The stock of water in the lake rises in the spring (26 million acre-feet when full) and declines in the fall.

perhaps in the stock market, such as "I'll invest in the stock market." Be sure to stay aware of this distinction.

government purchases: purchases by federal, state, and local governments of new goods and services.

■ **Government Purchases.** The third component of spending, **government purchases,** is spending by federal, state, and local governments on new goods and services. Most U.S. government purchases are for the military. At the state and local levels, education, roads, and police dominate government purchases. Government purchases of goods and services were equal to $2,184 billion in 2004 (see Figure 18.3).

Not all government outlays are included in government purchases. A government welfare payment or retirement payment to an individual is not a purchase of a good or service; it is a *transfer payment* of income from the government to an individual. Transfer payments do not represent new production of anything, unlike the purchase of a weapon or a new road or a new building. Because GDP measures the production of new goods and services, government outlays on transfer payments like social security, unemployment compensation, and welfare payments are excluded. Only purchases are counted because only these items represent something produced. Government *outlays* are purchases plus transfer payments.

487

net exports: the value of exports minus the value of imports.

exports: the total value of the goods and services that people in one country sell to people in other countries.

imports: the total value of the goods and services that people in one country buy from people in other countries.

trade balance: the value of exports minus the value of imports.

■ **Net Exports.** The final spending component is **net exports,** the difference between exports and imports. American **exports** are what Americans sell to foreigners, whether pharmaceuticals, computers, grain, or a vacation in Florida. American **imports** are what Americans buy from foreigners, whether cars, VCRs, shirts, or a vacation in France. Net exports are defined as exports minus imports. Net exports are a measure of how much more we sell to foreigners than we buy from foreigners. Another term for net exports is the **trade balance.** If net exports are positive, we have a trade surplus. If net exports are negative, we have a trade deficit. By these calculations, the United States had a trade deficit in 2004: $1,176 billion in exports and $1,782 billion in imports. Hence, net exports were a negative $606 billion, and appear in Table 18.2 as −$606 billion.

Why are net exports added in when computing GDP by the spending approach? There are two reasons. First, we included foreign goods in consumption and investment spending. For example, an imported Toyota purchased at a car dealer in the United States is included in consumption even though it is not produced in the United States. To measure what is produced in the United States, that Toyota must be deducted. Thus, imports must be subtracted to get a measure of total production in the economy. The second reason is that the exports Americans sell abroad are produced in the United States, but they are not counted in consumption or investment or government purchases in the United States. Thus, exports need to be added in to get a measure of production. Because, by definition, net exports are exports minus imports, adding net exports to spending is the same as adding in exports and subtracting out imports. Adding net exports to total spending kills two birds with one stone.

In 2004, the United States imported more than it exported, so the sum of consumption plus investment plus government purchases overstated what was produced in America. The sum of these three items exceeds GDP, as shown in Figure 18.3. In other words, GDP was $606 billion less than the sum of consumption plus investment plus government purchases.

■ **Algebraic Summary.** The notion that we can measure production by adding up consumption, investment, government purchases, and net exports is important enough to herald with some algebra.

Let the symbol C stand for consumption, I for investment, G for government spending, and X for net exports. Let Y stand for GDP because we use G for government purchases. We will use these symbols many times again. The idea that production equals spending can then be written as

> This is a key equation stating that production equals spending.

$$Y = C + I + G + X$$

This equation states, using algebraic symbols, that production, Y, equals spending: consumption, C, plus investment, I, plus government purchases, G, plus net exports, X (meaning exports minus imports). In 2004 the values of these items (in billions of dollars) were

$$11,735 = 8,230 + 1,927 + 2,184 + (-606)$$

This simple algebraic relationship plays a key role in later chapters.

The Income Approach

The income that people earn producing GDP in a country provides another measure of GDP. To see why, first consider a simple example of a single business firm.

Suppose you start a driver's education business. Your production and sales of driver's education services in your first year is $50,000; this is the amount you are paid in total by 500 people for the $100 service. To produce these services, you pay two driving teachers $20,000 each, or a total of $40,000, which is your total cost because the students use their own cars. Your profits are defined as the difference between sales and costs, or $50,000 − $40,000 = $10,000. Now, if you add the total amount of income earned in the production of your driver's education service—the amount earned by the two teachers plus the profits you earn—you get $20,000 + $20,000 + $10,000. This sum of incomes is exactly equal to $50,000, which is the same as the amount produced. Thus, by adding up the income of the people who produce the output of the firm, you get a measure of the output. The same idea is true for the country as a whole, which consists of many such businesses and workers.

To show how this works, we look at each of the income items in Table 18.3. We first describe each of these items and then show that when we add the items up, we get GDP.

labor income: the sum of wages, salaries, and fringe benefits paid to workers.

■ **Labor Income.** Economists classify wages, salaries, and fringe benefits paid to workers as **labor income,** or payments to people for their labor. *Wages* refers to payments to workers paid by the hour; *salaries* refers to payments to workers paid by the month or year; and *fringe benefits* refers to retirement, health, and other benefits paid by firms on behalf of workers. As shown in Table 18.3, labor income was $6,651 billion in 2004.

capital income: the sum of profits, rental payments, and interest payments.

■ **Capital Income.** Economists classify profits, rental payments, and interest payments as **capital income.** *Profits* include the profits of large corporations like General Motors or Exxon and also the income of small businesses and farms. The royalties an independent screenwriter receives from selling a movie script are also part of profits. *Rental payments* are income to persons who own buildings and rent them out. The rents they receive from their tenants are rental payments. *Interest payments* are income received from lending to business firms. Interest payments are included in capital income because they represent part of the income generated by the firms' production. Because many individuals pay interest (on mortgages, car loans, etc.) as well as receive interest (on deposits at a bank, etc.), interest payments are defined as the difference between receipts and payments. Table 18.3 shows that capital income was $2,799 billion in 2004, much less than labor income. Capital income is about 42 percent of labor income.

depreciation: the decrease in an asset's value over time; for capital, it is the amount by which physical capital wears out over a given period of time. (Ch. 16)

■ **Depreciation.** Depreciation is the amount by which factories and machines wear out each year. A remarkably large part of the investment that is part of GDP each year goes to replace worn-out factories and machines. Businesses need to replace depreciated equipment with investment in new equipment just to maintain productive capacity—the number of factories and machines available for use.

Table 18.3
Aggregate Income and GDP in 2004 (billions of dollars)

Aggregate income	
Labor income (wages, salaries, fringe benefits)	$6,651
Capital income (profits, interest, rents)	2,799
Depreciation	1,407
Indirect business taxes	890
Net income of foreigners	−44
Statistical discrepancy	32
Equals GDP	11,735

Source: U.S. Department of Commerce.

The difference between investment, the purchases of final goods by firms, and depreciation is called *net investment,* a measure of how much new investment there is each year after depreciation is subtracted. Net investment was $520 billion ($1,927 billion − $1,407 billion) in 2004. Sometimes the $1,927 billion of investment, including depreciation, is called *gross investment.* The reason for the term *gross* in gross domestic product is that it includes gross investment, not just net investment.

When profits and the other parts of capital income are reported to the government statisticians, depreciation has been subtracted out. But depreciation must be included as part of GDP because the new equipment that replaces old equipment must be produced by someone. Thus, when we use the income approach, it is necessary to add in depreciation if we are to have a measure of GDP.

■ **Indirect Business Taxes.** *Indirect business taxes* consist mainly of sales taxes sent directly by businesses to the government. For example, the price of gasoline at the pump includes a tax that people who buy gasoline pay as part of the price and that the gasoline station sends to the government. When we tabulate total production by adding up the value of what people spend, we use the prices businesses

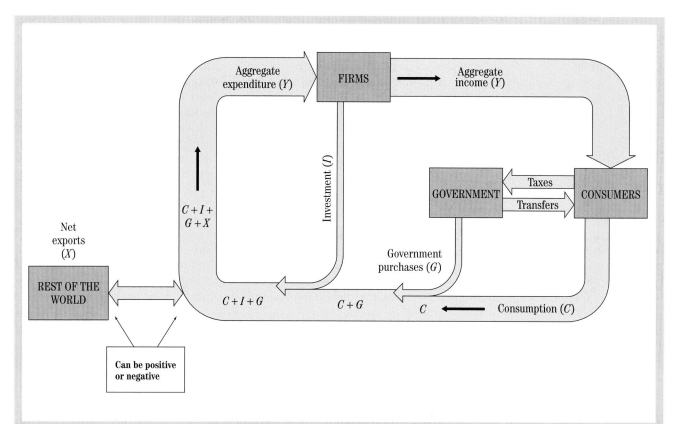

Figure 18.4
The Circular Flow of Income and Expenditure

This figure illustrates how aggregate expenditures equal aggregate income. Starting at the bottom right part of the figure, consumption (C) is joined by government purchases (G), investment (I), and net exports (X) to sum to aggregate expenditures (C + I + G + X) on the left. At the top of the figure, this aggregate spending is received by firms that produce the goods, and they pay out aggregate income (Y) to households in the form of wages and salaries as well as rents, interest, and profits. The government takes in taxes and makes transfer payments and government purchases.

charge for a specific good—such as gasoline. That price includes the sales tax that is sent to the government, but, like depreciation, the sales tax is not included in firms' profits. Thus, capital income does not include the sales taxes paid by businesses to the government. But those taxes are part of the income generated in producing GDP. We therefore must add sales taxes to capital and labor income.

▪ **Net Income of Foreigners.**   Foreigners produce part of the GDP in the United States. However, their income is not included in labor income or capital income. For example, the salary of a Canadian hockey player who plays for the Pittsburgh Penguins and keeps his official residence as Canada would not be included in U.S. labor income. But that income represents payment for services produced in the United States and so is part of U.S. GDP. We must add such income payments to foreigners for production in the United States because that production is part of GDP. Moreover, some of the U.S. labor and capital income is earned producing GDP in other countries, and to get a measure of income generated in producing U.S. GDP, we must subtract that out. For example, the salary of a U.S. baseball player who plays for the Toronto Blue Jays and keeps his official residence as the United States represents payment for services produced in Canada and so is not part of U.S. GDP. We must exclude such income payments for production in other countries. To account for both of these effects, we must add *net* income earned by foreigners in the United States—that is, the income earned by foreigners in the United States less what Americans earned abroad—to get GDP. In 2004, Americans earned more abroad ($406 billion) than foreigners earned in the United States ($362 billion); hence, in 2004, *net* income of foreigners was −$44 billion, as shown in Table 18.3.

Table 18.3 shows the effects of adding up these five items. The sum is close but not quite equal to GDP. The discrepancy reflects errors made in collecting data on income or spending. This discrepancy has a formal name: the *statistical discrepancy.* In percentage terms the amount is small, less than 1 percent of GDP, considering the different ways the data on income and spending are collected. If we add in the statistical discrepancy, then we have a measure of *aggregate income* that equals GDP. From now on we can use the same symbol (Y) to refer to GDP and to aggregate income, because GDP and aggregate income amount to the same thing.

The circular flow diagram in Figure 18.4 illustrates the link between aggregate income and aggregate spending. People earn income from producing goods and services, and they spend this income (Y) to buy goods and services (C, I, G, and X).

The Production Approach

The third measure of GDP adds up the production of each firm or industry in the economy. In order to make this method work, we must avoid the "double counting" problem discussed earlier. For example, if you try to compute GDP by adding new automobiles to new steel to new tires, you will count the steel and the tires that go into producing the new automobiles twice. Thus, when we measure GDP by production, it is necessary to count only the **value added** by each manufacturer. Value added is the value of a firm's production less the value of the intermediate goods used in production. In other words, it is the value the firm adds to the intermediate inputs to get the final output. An automobile manufacturer buys steel, tires, and other inputs and adds value by assembling the car. When we measure GDP by production, we count only the value added at each level of production. Figure 18.5 shows how adding up the value added for each firm involved in producing a cup of espresso in the economy will automatically avoid double counting and give a measure of the final value of the cup of espresso when it is purchased at a coffeehouse or cafe. The same is true for the economy as a whole.

value added: the value of a firm's production minus the value of the intermediate goods used in production.

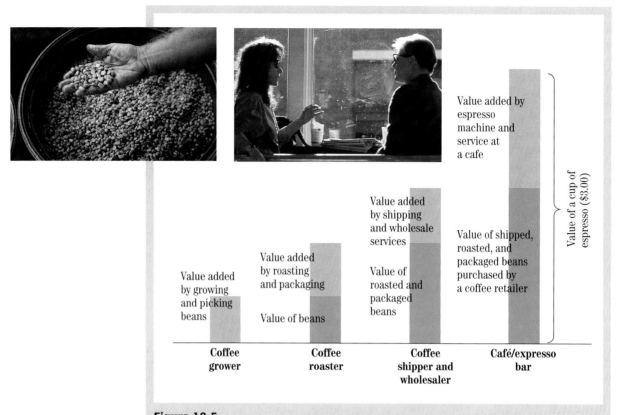

Figure 18.5
Value Added in Coffee: From Beans to Espresso
By adding up the value added at each stage of production, from coffee bean growing to espresso making, we get a measure of the value of a cup of espresso. Double counting is avoided. Using the same procedure for the whole economy permits us to compute GDP by adding up production.

REVIEW

- Adding up all the spending—consumption, investment, government purchases, and net exports—in the U.S. economy gives a measure of total production—gross domestic product (GDP). Inventory investment is treated as part of investment spending to ensure that we get a measure of production. Net exports are added to ensure that imported goods that are part of consumption are not counted as U.S. production and that U.S. exports are counted as U.S. production.

- The sum of labor income, capital income, depreciation, sales taxes, and net income paid to foreigners gives another way to measure GDP.

- GDP can also be measured by adding up production, but with this method we must be careful not to double count. By adding up only the value added by each firm or industry, we automatically prevent double counting. Value added is the difference between a firm's sales and its payments for intermediate inputs to production.

Savings

total amount of saving: a measure of the amount of resources a country has for investment, either in its own country or abroad.

Another important macroeconomic measure is the total amount of saving undertaken by an economy. The **total amount of saving** is a measure of the amount of resources that the country has available for investment, either in its own country or abroad. Countries with a high level of saving have a greater ability to undertake investment projects than countries with a low level of saving. It is important to keep in mind, however, that a country with a low level of saving can increase investment substantially if people and firms in other nations are willing to lend or invest their own savings in that country. The U.S. economy in the latter part of the 1990s was able to sustain a high level of investment even when U.S. saving was low. In this section, we will define the concept of national saving and show how it is calculated.

Individual Saving

For an individual, saving is defined as income less taxes and consumption. If you earn $25,000 in income during the year and pay taxes of $5,000 while spending $18,000 on consumption—food, rent, movies—by definition your saving for the year is $2,000 ($25,000 − $5,000 − $18,000). But if you instead spend $23,000 on food, rent, and movies for the year, then your saving is −$3,000; you will either have to take $3,000 out of the bank or borrow $3,000.

National Saving

national saving: aggregate income minus consumption minus government purchases.

For a country, saving is defined in a similar manner: by subtracting from a country's economy what is consumed. **National saving** is the sum of all saving in the economy. It is defined as income less consumption and government purchases. That is,

National saving = income − consumption − government purchases

Using the symbol S for national saving and the symbols already introduced for income (Y), consumption (C), and government purchases (G), we define national saving as

> Algebraic definition of national saving ➔

$$S = Y - C - G$$

Using the numbers from Table 18.2, national saving in 2004 was $1,321 billion ($11,735 billion − $8,230 billion − $2,184 billion).

The major component of national saving is private saving: the sum of all savings by individuals in the economy. Some people save a lot, some do not save at all, and some are *dissaving*—that is, they have negative saving. For example, when people retire, they usually consume a lot more than their income—they are dissaving. When people are middle-aged, their income is usually greater than their consumption—they are saving. Most young people either save very little or, if they are able to borrow, dissave. We define private saving as

Private saving = $Y - C - T$

For a country, however, there is also a government, and so we need to include government saving in our calculation of national saving. What do we mean by saving by the government? Most government purchases (about 85 percent) are of services that are like consumption—park services, police services, social services, and national defense services. The difference between the government's receipts from taxes and the government's expenditures, the budget surplus, is called government saving. When the surplus is negative, there is a budget deficit—the government is dissaving. We define government saving as

Government saving = $T - G$

Combining private and government saving, we see that

Private saving + government saving = $(Y - C - T) + (T - G) = (Y - C - G)$

Private saving + government saving = national savings

REVIEW
- For an individual, saving equals income minus consumption. For the United States, national saving is defined as income minus consumption minus government purchases. Government purchases are subtracted because many of them provide consumptionlike services.

Measuring Real GDP

Economists use GDP to assess how the economy is changing over time. For example, they might want to know how rapidly the production of goods and services has grown and what that implies about economic growth in the future. However, the dollar value of the goods and services in GDP is determined by the price of these goods and services. Thus, an increase in the prices of all goods and services will make measured GDP grow, even if there is no real increase in the amount of production in the economy. Suppose, for example, that the prices of all goods in the economy double and that the number of items produced of every good remains the same. Then the dollar value of these items will double even though physical production does not change. A $10,000 car will become a $20,000 car, a $10 CD will become a $20 CD, and so on. Thus, GDP will double as well. Clearly, GDP is not useful for comparing production at different dates when there are increases in all prices. Although the example of doubling all prices is extreme, we do know from Chapter 17 that there is a tendency for prices on the average to rise over time—a tendency that we have called inflation. Thus, when there is inflation, GDP becomes an unreliable measure of the changes in production over time.

real gross domestic product (real GDP): a measure of the value of all the goods and services newly produced in a country during some period of time, adjusted for changes in prices over time. (Ch. 17)

nominal GDP: gross domestic product without any correction for inflation; the same as GDP; the value of all the goods and services newly produced in a country during some period of time, usually a year.

Adjusting GDP for Inflation

Real GDP is a measure of production that corrects for inflation. To emphasize the difference between GDP and real GDP, we will define **nominal GDP** as what has previously been referred to as GDP.

■ **Computing Real GDP Growth Between Two Years.** To see how real GDP is calculated, consider an example. Suppose that total production consists entirely of the production of audio CDs and DVDs and that we want to compare this total production in two different years: 2003 and 2004.

	2003		**2004**	
	Price	*Quantity*	*Price*	*Quantity*
DVDs	$15	1,000	$20	1,200
CDs	$10	2,000	$15	2,200

Notice that the number of DVDs produced increases by 20 percent and the number of CDs produced increases by 10 percent from 2003 to 2004. Notice also that the price of DVDs is greater than the price of CDs, but both increase between the two years because of inflation. Nominal GDP is equal to the dollar amount spent on CDs plus the dollar amount spent on DVDs, or $35,000 in 2003 and $57,000 in 2004, a substantial 63 percent increase.

Nominal GDP in 2003 = $15 × 1,000 + $10 × 2,000 = $35,000

Nominal GDP in 2004 = $20 × 1,200 + $15 × 2,200 = $57,000

Clearly, nominal GDP is not a good measure of the increase in production: Nominal GDP increases by 63 percent, a much greater increase than the increase in either DVD production (20 percent) or CD production (10 percent). Thus, failing to correct for inflation gives a misleading estimate.

To calculate real GDP, we must use the *same* price for both years and, thereby, adjust for inflation. That is, the number of CDs and DVDs produced in the two years must be evaluated at the same prices. For example, production could be calculated in both years using 2003 prices. That is,

Using 2003 prices, production in 2003 = $15 × 1,000 + $10 × 2,000 = $35,000

Using 2003 prices, production in 2004 = $15 × 1,200 + $10 × 2,200 = $40,000

Keeping prices constant at 2003 levels, we see that the increase in production is from $35,000 in 2003 to $40,000 in 2004, an increase of 14.3 percent.

However, production can also be calculated in both years using 2004 prices. That is,

Using 2004 prices, production in 2003 = $20 × 1,000 + $15 × 2,000 = $50,000

Using 2004 prices, production in 2004 = $20 × 1,200 + $15 × 2,200 = $57,000

Keeping prices constant at 2004 levels, we see that the increase in production is from $50,000 in 2003 to $57,000 in 2004, an increase of 14.0 percent.

Observe that the percentage increase in production varies slightly (14.3 percent versus 14 percent) depending on whether 2003 or 2004 prices are used. Such differences are inevitable, because there is no reason to prefer the prices in one year to those of another year when controlling for inflation. Economists arrive at a single percentage by simply *averaging* the two percentages.[1] In this example, they would conclude that the *increase in real GDP from 2003 to 2004 is 14.15 percent*, the average of 14.3 percent and 14 percent.

This 14.15 percent increase in real GDP is much less than the 63 percent increase in nominal GDP and much closer to the actual increase in the number of CDs and tapes produced. By adjusting for inflation in this way, real GDP gives a better picture of the increase in actual production in the economy.

---

1. A "geometric" average is used. The geometric average of two numbers is the square root of the product of the two numbers.

■ **A Year-to-Year Chain.**   This example shows how the growth rate of real GDP between the two years 2003 and 2004 is calculated in the case of two goods. The same approach is used for any other two years and more than two goods. To correct for inflation across more than two years, economists simply do a series of these two-year corrections and then "chain" them together. Each year is a link in the chain. For example, if the growth rate from 2004 to 2005 is 12.15 percent, then chaining this together with the 14.15 percent from 2003 to 2004 would imply an average annual growth rate of 13.15 percent for the two years from 2003 to 2005. That is,

> Observe that 12.15 percent and 14.15 percent are *chained* together to get 13.15 percent average for two years.

By chaining other years together, link by link, the chain can be made as long as we want.

■ **From the 2000 Base Year to Other Years.**   To obtain real GDP in any one year, we start with a *base year* and then use the growth rates to compute GDP in another year. The base year is a year in which real GDP is set equal to nominal GDP. Currently, 2000 is the base year for government statistical calculations of GDP in the United States. Thus, real GDP in 2000 and nominal GDP in 2000 are the same: $9,817 billion.

To get real GDP in other years, economists start with the base year and use the real GDP growth rates to find GDP in any other year. Consider 2001. The growth rate of real GDP in 2001—calculated using the methods just described for the entire economy—was .75 percent. Thus, real GDP in 2001 was $9,891 billion, or .75 percent greater than $9,817 billion. The $9,891 billion is 2001 real GDP measured in 2000 dollars. To emphasize that this number is calculated by chaining years together with growth rates, government statisticians say that real GDP is measured in "chained 2000 dollars."

■ **Real GDP versus Nominal GDP over Time.**   Figure 18.6 compares real and nominal GDP from 1990 to 2004. Observe that for the 2000 base year, real GDP and nominal GDP are equal. However, by 2002, real GDP reached about $10.1 trillion, whereas nominal GDP was at $10.5 trillion. Thus, just as in the example, real GDP increased less than nominal GDP. For the years prior to 2000, real GDP is more than nominal GDP because 2000 prices were higher than prices in earlier years. From Figure 18.6 we can see that nominal GDP would give a very misleading picture of the U.S. economy.

The GDP Deflator

Nominal GDP grows faster than real GDP because of inflation. The greater the difference between nominal GDP growth and real GDP growth, the greater is the inflation. If there were a deflation, with prices falling, then nominal GDP would increase less than real GDP. Hence, a by-product of computing real GDP is a measure of the rate of inflation.

GDP deflator: nominal GDP divided by real GDP; it measures the level of prices of goods and services included in real GDP relative to a given base year.

price level: the average level of prices in the economy.

More precisely, if we divide nominal GDP by real GDP, we get the **GDP deflator,** a measure of the **price level,** which is the level of all the prices of the items in real GDP. That is,

$$\text{GDP deflator} = \frac{\text{nominal GDP}}{\text{real GDP}}$$

Here the GDP deflator is defined so that its value in the base year, such as 2000, is 1.00. (Sometimes it is scaled to equal 100 in the base year by multiplying by 100.)

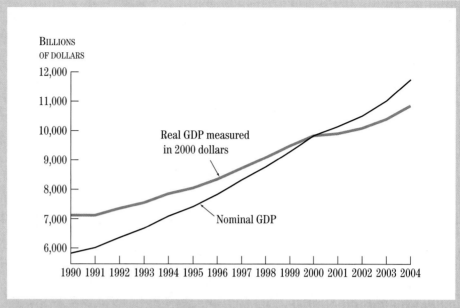

Figure 18.6
Real GDP versus Nominal GDP
Real GDP increases less than nominal GDP because real GDP takes out the effect of rising prices. The chart shows that for the 2000 base year, real GDP and nominal GDP are equal. Nominal GDP is below real GDP in earlier years because prices were generally lower before 2000.

The reason for the term *deflator* is that to get real GDP, we can deflate nominal GDP by dividing it by the GDP deflator. That is,

$$\text{Real GDP} = \frac{\text{nominal GDP}}{\text{GDP deflator}}$$

The percentage change in the GDP deflator from one year to the next is a measure of the rate of inflation.

Alternative Inflation Measures

consumer price index (CPI): a price index equal to the current price of a fixed market basket of consumer goods and services relative to a base year.

There are other measures of inflation. A frequently cited one is based on the **consumer price index (CPI),** which is the price of a fixed collection—a "market basket"—of consumer goods and services in a given year divided by the price of the same collection in some base year. For example, if the market basket consists of one DVD and two CDs, then the CPI for 2004 compared with the base year 2003 in the previous example would be

$$\frac{\$20 \times 1 + \$15 \times 2}{\$15 \times 1 + \$10 \times 2} = \frac{50}{35} = 1.43$$

The CPI inflation rate is the percent change in the CPI; it measures how fast the prices of the items in the basket increase in price.

The use of a fixed collection of goods and services in the CPI is one of the reasons economists think the CPI overstates inflation. When the price of goods rises, the

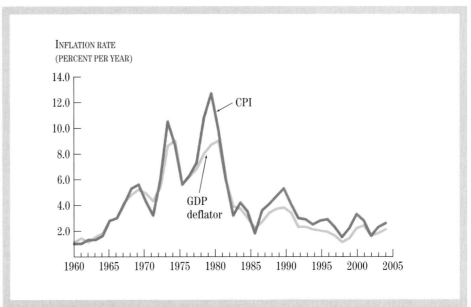

Figure 18.7
Comparison of Measures of Inflation
Measuring inflation with either the CPI or the GDP deflator shows the rise in inflation in the 1960s and 1970s and the lower inflation in the 1980s and 1990s. The CPI is more volatile: It bounces around more. (The inflation rate is based on yearly percent changes in the stated variable.)

quantity demanded should decline; when the price falls, the quantity demanded should rise. Thus, by not allowing the quantities to change when the price changes, the CPI puts too much weight on items with rising prices and too little weight on items with declining prices. The result is an overstatement of inflation.

During the 1990s, a group of economists appointed by the U.S. Senate and chaired by Michael Boskin of Stanford University found that the government, by adjusting expenditures according to this overstated CPI, was spending billions of dollars more than it would with a correct CPI. Hence, getting the economic statistics right makes a big difference.

Figure 18.7 shows how measures of inflation using the GDP deflator and the CPI compare. The general inflation movements are similar. The CPI is more volatile, however.

Yet another measure of inflation is the producer price index (PPI), which measures the prices of raw materials and intermediate goods as well as the prices of final goods sold by producers. Prices of raw materials—oil, wheat, copper—are sometimes watched carefully because they give early warning signs of increases in inflation.

REVIEW
- Real GDP corrects nominal GDP for inflation. Real GDP measures the production of goods and services in the dollars of a given base year, such as 2000.
- Real GDP is a better measure of changes in the physical amount of production in the economy than is nominal GDP.

- The GDP deflator is a measure of the price level in the economy. It is defined as the ratio of nominal GDP to real GDP. The percentage change in the GDP deflator from year to year is a measure of the inflation rate.

Shortcomings of the GDP Measure

Although GDP is the best measure of overall production we have, it is deficient in several ways. First, there are revisions to GDP that can change the assessment of the economy. Second, GDP omits some production. Third, the production of goods and services is only part of what affects the quality of life.

Revisions in GDP

Government statisticians obtain data on GDP from surveys of stores and businesses, and even from income tax data from the Internal Revenue Service. Not all of these data are collected quickly. Data on sales at stores and large firms come in within a month; exports and imports take several months. Some income tax data are reported only once a year. Information about small firms comes in even more slowly.

For this reason, the statistics on GDP are frequently revised as new data come in. For those who use the GDP data to make decisions, either in business or in government, faulty data on GDP, which are apparent only when the data are revised, can lead to mistakes. Revisions of GDP are inevitable and occur in all countries.

Omissions from GDP

Most of the production that is omitted from GDP either does not occur in a formal market or is difficult for government statisticians to measure. Examples are work done in the home, illegal commerce, and quality improvements in goods.

■ **Home Work and Production.** Much of the production that people do at home—making dinner or a sweater, changing the car oil or a baby's diapers, cutting the grass or the kids' hair—is productive activity, but it is not included in GDP because the transactions are not recorded in markets where statisticians measure spending. Such production would be included in GDP if people hired and paid someone else to do any of these things.

Note that some home production is included in GDP. If you run a mail order or telemarketing business out of your home and pay taxes on your income, then this production is likely to be counted in GDP.

■ **Leisure Activity.** Much leisure activity is not included in GDP even though it may be enjoyable. Going to the beach or hiking in the mountains more often and working less might be something you decide to do as your income increases. If people start taking Friday afternoons off, GDP will go down, but the level of well-being may increase. The consumption of leisure is omitted from GDP unless it involves a purchase in the market, such as a ticket to a movie or a ballgame.

■ **The Underground Economy.**   A large amount of production is not counted in GDP because it is purposely hidden from the view of the government. Illegal activity—growing marijuana in the California coastal range, selling pharmaceuticals not yet approved by the Food and Drug Administration—is excluded from GDP because no one wants to report this activity to the government. People who get cash payments—perhaps in the form of tips at hotels or restaurants—may not report them in order to avoid taxes, and these are not counted either. If people do not report interest on a loan to a friend or relative, this is also omitted from GDP.

The sum of all the missing items is referred to as the *underground economy*. Estimates of the size of the underground economy are understandably uncertain. They range from about 10 percent of GDP in the United States to about 25 percent in Italy to over 40 percent in Peru.

The underground economy makes GDP a less useful measure of the size of an economy, and we should be aware of it when we use GDP. But the underground economy does not render GDP a useless measure. It is unlikely that the underground economy grows much more or much less rapidly than the rest of the economy. Changes in laws can increase or decrease the incentives to produce outside the legal market economy, but these are unlikely to be large enough to change the estimated growth rates of GDP by much.

■ **Quality Improvements.**   Our measure of GDP sometimes misses improvements in the quality of goods and services. For example, a new model car may be more comfortable and absorb shocks better than the old model, but if the price is the same, it will not lead to an increase in GDP.

Other Measures of Well-Being

Even if real GDP did include the underground economy and all the improvements in goods and services, it would not serve as the only measure of well-being. There are many other important aspects of the well-being of individuals: a long and healthy life expectancy; a clean environment; a small chance of war, crime, or the death of a child. The production of goods and services in a country can affect these other things, and indeed be affected by them, but it is not a measure of them.

Consider what has happened to some other measures of well-being as real GDP per capita has grown. Life expectancy in the United States has increased from about 69 years in the 1950s to 76 years in the 1990s. This compares with a life expectancy of only 47 years in the early part of the last century. Infant mortality has also declined, from about 2.6 infant deaths per 100 live births in the mid-1950s to 0.9 in the mid-1990s. In the early part of the last century, infant mortality in the United States was 10 deaths for every 100 live births. The fraction of women who die in childbirth has also declined. So by some of these important measures, the quality of life has improved along with real GDP per capita.

But there are still serious problems and room for gains; as death rates from car accidents, heart disease, and stroke have decreased, death rates among young people from AIDS, suicide, and murder have been rising. Also of serious concern is the increasing percentage of children who live in poverty. Thus, the impressive gain in real GDP per capita has been correlated with both gains and losses in other measures of well-being.

A clean and safe environment is also a factor in the quality of life. But GDP itself does not provide an indication of whether pollution or many of the other measures of the quality of life are improving or getting worse.

Near the end of every month, stories about the latest GDP measurement for the United States appear in most newspapers around the country (and on web pages seen around the world). The stories are a response to the release of GDP data by economic statisticians at the U.S. Department of Commerce, where the national income and product accounts are tabulated.

The following story appeared in the *New York Times* on February 26, 2005. The discussion of GDP in this chapter should give you the information you need to understand the article and to judge whether the headline, the reporter's interpretation of the GDP data, and the economists' comments make sense. It reports strong GDP growth for the economy, as reflected in its headline and general tone.

There are several points to keep in mind when reading news stories about GDP.

First, the measures of GDP are reported for each of the four quarters of the year. There is a news story each month because the data are revised twice. In the first month after the end of the quarter, the first estimate of GDP is given. In the second and third months, the estimates are revised as new data about the economy are obtained; such a revision is reported in the following article. Sometimes you have to read carefully to know whether what you are reading is a first-time report or a revision.

Second, the GDP measure for a quarter of a year represents the aggregate production during the quarter, but the amount of production is stated at an *annual rate* to make the magnitude comparable to that of the annual GDP measure.

Third, the GDP measures for each quarter are *seasonally adjusted.* There is always more production in some seasons of the year than in other seasons, and these differences have little to do with where the economy is going. For example, in the fourth quarter (October–December), there is usually more production in anticipation of the holidays. Seasonal adjustments try to take out these fluctuations so that they do not show up in the reported measures of GDP.

Revised Data Paints Stronger Picture of Economy

Refers to growth rate of real GDP

Revision from initial release

Explanation for revision

WASHINGTON, Feb. 25—Economic momentum at the end of 2004 was stronger than previously thought, according to a government report on Friday that revised fourth-quarter output to reflect stronger exports and investment.

The Commerce Department said gross domestic product, the gauge of total goods and services production in the country, grew at a revised 3.8 percent annual rate in the final three months of last year instead of 3.1 percent reported a month ago. That was slightly stronger than the 3.7 percent rate that Wall Street economists had forecast and only a small decline from the third quarter's 4 percent pace.

Nearly half the revision came from a stronger trade performance, reflecting more robust exports than previously thought. Statistics Canada corrected a $1.4 billion error in underestimating United States exports to Canada during November, and later data also showed the trade deficit for December narrowed more than had been anticipated. Despite the revision, there was no change in the government's calculation that G.D.P. grew 4.4 percent in 2004, ahead of a 3 percent rise in 2003 and the strongest for any year since 1999, when it expanded 4.5 percent.

Also on Friday, a report from the National Association of Realtors, a trade group, said that sales of single-family homes eased 0.1 percent in January but still were running at healthy levels. Sales were at a seasonally adjusted annual rate of 6.8 million last month, the seventh-best rate on record as relatively low mortgage rates apparently continued to support the nation's housing markets.

The G.D.P. report indicated inflation was perking up in the fourth quarter. In addition, businesses kept up a brisk pace of new investment. Nonresidential investment climbed at a revised 14 percent rate instead of 10.3 percent reported a month ago and was ahead of the third quarter's 13 percent. Spending on new equipment and computer software increased 18 percent after growing 17.5 percent in the third quarter. But growth in consumer spending was revised down modestly to 4.2 percent from a previously reported 4.6 percent rise in the fourth quarter and was less vigorous than the third quarter's 5.1 percent gain.

Two economists at Merrill Lynch, Sheryl King and David Rosenberg, said in a commentary that they expected a strong first quarter but some gradual slowing in G.D.P. growth as stiffer credit costs begin to bite later in the year.

Outlook for next quarter

REVIEW
- Real GDP per capita is not without its shortcomings as an indicator of well-being in a society. Certain items are omitted—home production, leisure, the underground economy, and some quality improvements.
- There are other indicators of the quality of life, including vital statistics on mortality and the environment, that can be affected by GDP per capita but that are conceptually distinct and independently useful.

Conclusion

In this chapter, we have shown how to measure the size of an economy in terms of its GDP. In the process, we have explained that income, spending, and production in a country are all equal and that GDP can be adjusted to make comparisons over time.

In conclusion, it is important to recall that aggregate income (or production or spending), the subject of our study, tells us much about the quality of life of the people in a country, but it does not tell us everything. As the economist-philosopher John Stuart Mill said in his *Principles of Political Economy,* first published in 1848: "All know that it is one thing to be rich, another to be enlightened, brave or humane . . . those things, indeed, are all indirectly connected, and react upon one another."[2]

KEY POINTS

1. U.S. gross domestic product (GDP) is the total production of new goods and services in the United States during a particular period.
2. GDP can be measured by adding all spending on new goods and services in the United States. Changes in inventories and net exports must be added to spending.
3. GDP can also be measured by adding labor income, capital income, depreciation, indirect business taxes, and net income of foreigners. Except for a small statistical discrepancy, the income approach gives us the same answer as the spending approach.

4. Value added is a measure of a firm's production. Value added is defined as the difference between the value of the production sold and the cost of inputs to production. GDP can be measured by adding the value added of all firms in the economy.
5. National saving in the United States is defined as income less consumption less government purchases.
6. Real GDP is a measure of production adjusted for inflation. It is the best overall measure of changes in the production of goods and services over time.
7. GDP is not without its shortcomings. It does not include production in the underground economy or much work done in the home. And it is only one of many measures of well-being.

KEY TERMS

intermediate good	net exports	capital income	GDP deflator
final good	exports	value added	price level
consumption	imports	total amount of saving	consumer price index
investment	trade balance	national saving	(CPI)
government purchases	labor income	nominal GDP	

---

2. John Stuart Mill, *Principles of Political Economy* (New York: Bookseller, 1965), pp. 1–2.

QUESTIONS FOR REVIEW

1. Why do we add up total spending in order to compute GDP when GDP is supposed to be a measure of production?

2. Approximately what are the percentages of consumption, investment, government purchases, and net exports in GDP in the United States?

3. Why is the sum of all income equal to GDP?

4. What is national saving?

5. What is the significance of value added, and how does one measure it for a single item?

6. Why does national saving equal the sum of private and government saving?

7. Why are increases in nominal GDP not a good measure of economic growth?

8. Why is the production of meals in the home not included in GDP? Should it be?

9. Why is the purchase of a used car not included in GDP? Should it be?

10. Why do we add inventory investment to spending when computing GDP?

PROBLEMS

1. Determine whether each of the following would be included in GDP, and explain why or why not.
   a. You buy a used CD from a friend.
   b. You buy a new CD at a music shop.
   c. You cook your own dinner.
   d. You hire someone to cook your dinner.

2. Determine whether each of the following is consumption, investment, or neither. Explain your answer.
   a. A landscaping company buys a new four-wheel-drive vehicle to carry bushes and flowers.
   b. A doctor buys a new four-wheel-drive vehicle to use on vacation.
   c. A family puts a new kitchen in their house.
   d. The campus bookstore increases its inventory of textbooks.
   e. You buy toothpaste at the drugstore.
   f. The state government of Alaska buys four-wheel-drive vehicles for its game wardens.

3. Suppose that the Internet increases the size of the economy.
   a. How will this affect the accuracy of GDP as a measure of production?
   b. State two ways in which the Internet affects GDP as a measure of well-being.

4. In market economies, prices reflect the value people place on goods and services, and therefore it makes sense to use them as weights when calculating GDP. In centrally planned economies, however, prices are controlled by the government instead of by the market. Examine the following data for a centrally planned economy that subsequently frees prices:

Good	Quantity	Controlled Price	Market Price
Electricity	1,000	$ 2	$10
Gasoline	500	$20	$15

   a. Calculate GDP under the controlled prices and under market prices, assuming the quantities do not change. Did governmentally set prices mean an under- or overvaluation of production on the whole?
   b. How do people value each good in relation to the previously controlled prices?

5. Look at two scenarios for monthly inventories and sales for a company producing cereal. In both scenarios, the company's sales are the same.
   a. Calculate the inventory investment during each month and the resulting stock of inventory at the beginning of the following month for both scenarios.
   b. Does maintaining constant production lead to greater or lesser fluctuations in the stock of inventory? Explain.

SCENARIO A

Month	Start-of-the-Month Inventory Stock	Production	Sales	Inventory Investment
Jan.	50	50	45	
Feb.		50	55	
Mar.		50	80	
Apr.		50	50	
May		50	40	

SCENARIO B

Month	Start-of-the-Month Inventory Stock	Production	Sales	Inventory Investment
Jan.	50	45	45	
Feb.		55	55	
Mar.		80	80	
Apr.		50	50	
May		40	40	

6. Given the information in the table at the bottom of the page for three consecutive years in the U.S. economy, calculate the missing data.

7. Suppose there are only the following three goods in the economy.

Year	Good	Price	Quantity
2003	Tomatoes	$2.50	1,000
	Squash	$1.25	500
	Telephones	$100	10
2004	Tomatoes	$3.50	800
	Squash	$2.25	400
	Telephones	$100	14

a. Calculate nominal GDP for 2003 and 2004.
b. Calculate the percentage change in GDP from 2003 to 2004 using 2003 prices and using 2004 prices.
c. Calculate the percentage change in real GDP from 2003 to 2004 using your answers from (b).
d. What is the GDP deflator for 2004 if it equals 1.0 in 2003?

8. Use the following data for a South Dakota wheat farm.

Revenue	$1,000
Costs	
Wages and salaries	$700
Rent on land	$50
Rental fee for tractor	$100
Seed, fertilizer	$100
Pesticides, irrigation	$50

a. Calculate the value added by this farm.
b. Profits are revenue minus costs. Capital income consists of profits, rents, and interest. Show that value added equals capital income plus labor income paid by the farm.
c. Suppose that, because of flooding in Kansas, wheat prices increase suddenly and revenues rise to $1,100, but prices of intermediate inputs do not change. What happens to value added and profits in this case?

9. In 2001, national saving in Japan was 145 trillon yen. If the government had a 30-trillion-yen deficit, how much was saving by consumers and businesses in Japan? What if the government instead had a 30-trillion-yen surplus?

10. Suppose the data in the table on the next page describe the economic activity in a country for 2004. Given these data, calculate the following:
a. Inventory investment
b. Net exports
c. Gross domestic product
d. Statistical discrepancy
e. National saving

Verify that national saving equals investment plus net exports.

Problem 6

Year	Nominal GDP (in billions of U.S. dollars)	Real GDP (in billions of 2000 dollars)	GDP Deflator (2000 = 100)	Inflation (percent change in GDP deflator)	Real GDP per Capita (in 2000 dollars)	Population (in millions)
2000	9,817		100.0	2.2		283.7
2001		9,891		2.4		286.6
2002			104		37,450	289.5

Component of Spending	Value in Billions of Dollars
Consumption	140
Business fixed and residential investment	27
Inventory stock at the end of 2003	10
Inventory stock at the end of 2004	5
Depreciation	12
Government outlays	80
Government purchases	65
Total government tax receipts	60
Exports	21
Imports	17
Labor income	126
Capital income	70
Net income of foreigners	5
Indirect business taxes	28

CHAPTER 19

The Spending Allocation Model

I n 1994, economists working on the president's Council of Economic Advisors predicted that the administration's plan to reduce the share of government purchases in GDP would increase the share of investment in GDP. Their reasoning was that a reduction in the share of government purchases would lead to lower interest rates in the economy, which in turn would raise investment because "lower interest rates . . . are the way that the market accomplishes expenditure switching . . . away . . . from government purchases toward investment."[1]

The subsequent behavior of the economy confirms that the president's economic advisers were correct. Between 1994 and 1998, the share of investment in real GDP *increased* from 15 to 18 percent as the share of government purchases in real GDP *decreased* from 19 to 17 percent. How were the economic advisers able to make such a prediction? What type of economic model would predict that lowering the share of government purchases in GDP would result in lower interest rates, and, in turn, that lower interest rates would raise the share of investment purchases in GDP?

In this chapter, we will develop such an economic model, which we will call the *spending allocation model,* to determine how GDP is allocated among the major components of spending: consumption, investment, government purchases, and net exports. Because each share of spending must compete for the scarce resources in GDP, an increase in the share of one of the components will lead to a reduction in

---

1. *Economic Report of the President,* 1994, p. 83.

the share of another component. Our model shows that interest rates are a key factor that both influences and is influenced by spending. By explaining how interest rates are determined, our model helps us predict, just as the president's economic advisers predicted, how much of GDP goes to each of the four components: consumption, investment, government purchases, and net exports.

The spending allocation model has some very useful applications. We can use it not only to understand the macroeconomic implications of the reduction in government purchases in the early 1990s, but also to understand why the share of investment in GDP fell during the 1980s. However, when you read the description of the spending allocation model, keep in mind that this model applies more to the long run than to the short run. Therefore, it is most useful in thinking about economic developments that occur over a period of years instead of months. For example, the Council of Economic Advisors was very careful to note that the positive impact of the reduction of the share of government purchases on the share of investment would take several years to materialize.

The Spending Shares

We know that GDP is divided into four components: consumption, investment, government purchases, and net exports. Symbolically,

$$Y = C + I + G + X$$

where Y equals GDP, C equals consumption, I equals investment, G equals government purchases, and X equals net exports. This equation is the starting point for determining how large a share of GDP is allocated to each spending component.

Defining the Spending Shares

consumption share: the proportion of GDP that is used for consumption; equals consumption divided by GDP, or C/Y.

investment share: the proportion of GDP that is used for investment; equals investment divided by GDP, or I/Y. Sometimes called investment rate.

net exports share: the proportion of GDP that is equal to net exports; equals net exports divided by GDP, or X/Y.

government purchases share: the proportion of GDP that is used for government purchases; equals government purchases divided by GDP, or G/Y.

The **consumption share** of GDP is the proportion of GDP that is used for consumption. The consumption share of GDP is defined as consumption (C) divided by GDP, or C/Y. For example, if $C =$ \$6 trillion and $Y =$ \$10 trillion, then the consumption share is $C/Y = 0.6$, or 60 percent. We can define the other shares of GDP analogously: I/Y is the **investment share,** X/Y is the **net exports share,** and G/Y is the **government purchases share.** Sometimes the investment share is called the *investment rate.*

We can establish a simple relationship between the shares of spending in GDP by taking the equation $Y = C + I + G + X$ and dividing both sides by Y. This simple division gives us a relationship that says that the sum of the shares of spending in GDP must equal 1. Writing that algebraically yields

$$1 = \frac{C}{Y} + \frac{I}{Y} + \frac{G}{Y} + \frac{X}{Y}$$

If we use the shares that existed in 2004 (see Table 18.2), we get

$$1 = \frac{8,230}{11,735} + \frac{1,927}{11,735} + \frac{2,184}{11,735} + \frac{(-606)}{11,735}$$

$$= .7013 + .1642 + .1861 + (-.0516)$$

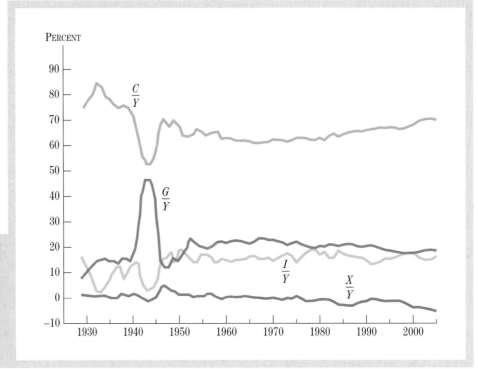

Figure 19.1
History of Spending Shares in GDP
The government purchases share rose sharply during World War II, and all three of the other shares declined. The government purchases share has been falling in recent years.

In other words, consumption accounted for 70.13 percent of GDP; investment for 16.42 percent of GDP; government purchases for 18.61 percent of GDP; and net exports, in deficit at negative $606 billion, for about negative 5.16 percent of GDP. The negative share for net exports occurs because Americans imported more than they exported in 2004. In this example, the sum of the four shares on the right equals 1, or, in percentage terms, 100 percent. And, of course, this must be true for any year.

Figure 19.1 shows the four shares of spending in GDP for the last 75 years in the United States. A huge temporary fluctuation in the shares of spending in GDP occurred in World War II, when government spending on the military rose sharply. Government purchases reached almost 50 percent of GDP, and the other three shares declined.

Clearly, the movements in government spending as a share of GDP are a factor in determining the investment share of GDP. Since World War II, the shares have been much steadier, but between 1990 and 2004, the government purchases share has decreased and the consumption and investment shares have gone up. The net exports share has been negative for the last 25 years, as the United States has run trade deficits. (Recall that when net exports are negative, there is a trade deficit.)

If One Share Goes Up, Another Must Go Down

The shares of spending equation demonstrates a simple but important point: A change in one of the shares implies a change in one or more of the other shares. That the shares must sum to 1 means that an increase in any of the shares must entail a reduction in one of the other shares. For example, an increase in the share of spending going to government purchases must result in a decrease in the share going to one or more of the other components of spending. Similarly, a decrease in the government purchases share must result in an increase in some other share, such as the investment share. One cannot have an increase in government purchases as a share of GDP (going from, say, 19 percent to 25 percent) without a decline in the share of either consumption or investment or net exports.

What determines how the shares of GDP are allocated? What is the mechanism through which a change in one share—such as the government share of GDP—brings about a change in one of the other shares? Does the investment share change? Or do the consumption and net exports shares change? To answer these questions, we need to consider the interest rate, which plays an important role in relating changes in one share to changes in another.

REVIEW
- Defining spending components as shares of GDP is a convenient way to describe how spending is allocated.

- Simple arithmetic tells us that the sum of all the shares of spending in GDP must equal 1.

- Thus, an increase in the share of GDP going to government purchases, for example, must be accompanied by a reduction in one or more of the other three shares—consumption, investment, or net exports.

The Effect of Interest Rates on Spending Shares

In this section, we show that the interest rate affects the three shares of spending by the private sector: consumption, investment, and net exports. Each private-sector spending component competes for a share of GDP along with government purchases, and the interest rate is a key factor in determining how the spending is allocated.

Consumption

The consumption share of GDP depends on people's decisions to consume, which are like any other choice with scarce resources, as defined in Chapter 1. If people raise their consumption relative to their income, then the consumption share of GDP will increase. Conversely, if people lower their consumption relative to their income, then the consumption share of GDP will decrease.

■ **Consumption and the Interest Rate.**   Keep in mind that people's decisions to consume more or less of their income today has implications for their consumption decisions tomorrow. Individuals who consume *more* today save *less*, and therefore have less to consume tomorrow. On the other hand, individuals who consume *less* today save *more*, and therefore have more to consume tomorrow. A person's choice between consuming today and consuming tomorrow depends on a relative price, just like any other economic decision. This relative price is the price of consumption today relative to the price of consumption tomorrow.

Changes in the interest rate will change the relative price. For instance, a higher interest rate will raise the price of consumption today relative to that of consumption tomorrow. Why? If the interest rate is higher, then any saving will deliver more funds in the future, which can then be used for future consumption (a larger home or more

college education, for example). Therefore, a higher interest rate, by raising the price of today's consumption, will result in lower consumption today. Conversely, a lower interest rate will reduce the price of consumption today relative to that of consumption tomorrow and bring about higher consumption today.

We can better illustrate this link between the interest rate and consumption with a numerical example. Suppose the interest rate increases from 2 percent to 6 percent. At an interest rate of 2 percent, putting $100 into a bank account will enable an individual to have $102 at the end of a year. However, at an interest rate of 6 percent, the same individual will be able to get $106 in a year by putting $100 in a bank account today. The increase in the interest rate from 2 percent to 6 percent raises the price of consuming $100 worth of goods today by $4. Even though this may seem like a small amount, keep in mind that small differences in interest rates can add up when you consider saving large sums of money to finance a college education or for retirement. So a higher interest rate gives people more incentive to consume less and save for the future, whereas a lower interest rate gives people more incentive to consume today instead of saving for the future. We can therefore conclude that consumption is negatively related to the interest rate.

What is true for individuals on average will also be true for the economy as a whole. Figure 19.2 shows how the consumption share is negatively related to the interest rate. For this example, when the interest rate is 4 percent, the share of consumption in GDP will be about 65 percent. If the interest rate increases to 8 percent, then the share declines to 64 percent. Alternatively, if the interest rate declines, the consumption share increases.

■ **Movements Along versus Shifts of the Consumption Share Line.** Observe that the relationship between the interest rate and consumption as a share of GDP in Figure 19.2 looks like a demand curve. Like a demand curve, it is downward-sloping. And like a demand curve, it shows the quantity consumers are willing to consume at each interest rate. The interest rate is like a price: A higher price—that is, a higher interest rate—reduces the amount of goods and services people will consume, and a lower price—that is, a lower interest rate—increases the amount they will consume. When an increase in the interest rate leads to a decline in consumption, we see a *movement along* the consumption share line, as shown in Figure 19.2.

As with a demand curve, it is important to distinguish such movements along the consumption share line from *shifts of* the consumption share line. The interest rate is not the only thing that affects consumption as a share of GDP. When a factor other than the interest rate changes the consumption share of

Figure 19.2
The Consumption Share and the Interest Rate
A higher interest rate lowers the amount of consumption relative to GDP. A higher interest rate discourages consumption and encourages saving.

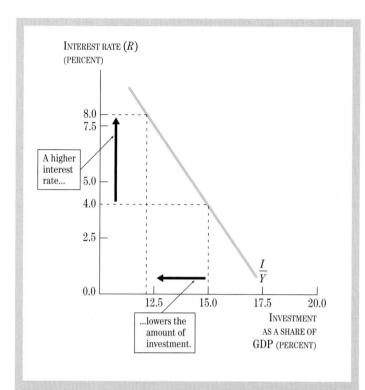

Figure 19.3
The Investment Share and the Interest Rate
A higher interest rate lowers the share of investment. The sensitivity of investment to the interest rate is greater than that of consumption to the interest rate, as shown in Figure 19.2.

GDP, there is a shift in the consumption share line in Figure 19.2. For example, an increase in taxes on consumption—such as a national sales tax—would reduce the quantity of goods people would consume relative to their income. In other words, an increase in taxes on consumption would shift the consumption share line in Figure 19.2 to the left: Less would be consumed relative to GDP at every interest rate. Conversely, a decrease in taxes on consumption would shift the consumption share line in Figure 19.2 to the right.

Investment

A similar relationship exists for investment and the interest rate. Figure 19.3 shows that there is a negative relationship between the interest rate and the investment share. For this example, when the interest rate rises from 4 percent to 8 percent, the investment share decreases from 15 percent to 12 percent. Economists have observed that investment is more sensitive to interest rates than consumption is. Therefore, the line for I/Y in Figure 19.3 is less steep than the line for C/Y in Figure 19.2.

Why does this negative relationship exist in the case of investment? When businesses decide to invest, they frequently have to borrow the funds to buy new machines and equipment or to build a new factory. Higher interest rates raise the cost of borrowing. Investment projects that would be undertaken at lower interest rates may be postponed or cancelled when interest rates rise because higher costs of borrowing discourage borrowing. Less borrowing means that fewer purchases of new equipment will be undertaken and fewer new factories built. On the other hand, when interest rates fall, the cost of borrowing falls as well, thus encouraging firms to purchase more equipment and build new factories. Note that this relationship holds even if firms use their own funds to finance their investment projects. Higher interest rates increase the opportunity cost of using their own funds for investment: Firms are tempted to leave their money in the bank earning a higher interest rate, instead of putting those funds into investment projects.

Recall that investment also includes the purchases of new houses. Most people need to take out loans (mortgages) to purchase houses. When the interest rate on mortgages rises, people purchase fewer or smaller houses; when the interest rate falls, people purchase more or larger houses.

The negative relationship between investment as a share of GDP and the interest rate has been observed in the economy for many years, and it makes sense: A higher interest rate discourages investment, and a lower interest rate encourages investment.

Observe that the relationship between the investment share of GDP and the interest rate in Figure 19.3 looks like a demand curve. It is downward-sloping. The interest rate is like the price: A higher interest rate decreases the amount of investment firms will do, and a lower interest rate increases the amount of investment firms will do.

Other factors besides the interest rate also affect investment; when these factors change, the investment share line in Figure 19.3 will *shift*. For example, an

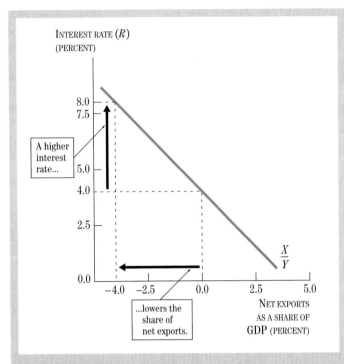

Figure 19.4
The Net Exports Share and the Interest Rate
A higher interest rate lowers the share of net exports because it tends to raise the exchange rate. The higher exchange rate lowers exports and raises imports, thereby lowering net exports. When net exports are negative, there is a trade deficit. When net exports are positive, there is a trade surplus.

investment tax credit, which lowers a firm's taxes if the firm buys new equipment, would increase the amount that firms would invest at each interest rate. An investment tax credit would shift the investment share line in Figure 19.3 to the right: The investment that firms are willing to do as a share of GDP at a given interest rate would rise. A change in firms' expectations of the future could also shift the investment share line; if firms feel that new computing or telecommunications equipment will lower their costs in the future, they will purchase the equipment, thereby increasing their investment at a given interest rate; the investment share line will shift to the right. Conversely, pessimism on the part of firms about the benefits of investment could shift the line to the left.

Net Exports

Net exports are also negatively related to the interest rate. As you can see in Figure 19.4, a negative relationship exists that is much like the relationship of consumption and investment to the interest rate. For this example, when the interest rate goes up from 4 percent to 8 percent, net exports go from zero to about −4 percent of GDP. Remember that when net exports are negative, there is a trade deficit.

The story behind this relationship is somewhat more involved than that for investment or for consumption. However, you may find the story more interesting because it includes the role of the foreign exchange rate—the price of foreign currency in terms of the domestic currency—in determining exports and imports, as well as the relationship between the interest rate and the exchange rate. In any case, it is important to grasp the key features. The story has three parts.

exchange rate: the price of one currency in terms of another in the foreign exchange market. We express the exchange rate as the number of units of foreign currency that can be purchased with one unit of domestic currency. (Ch. 16)

■ **The Interest Rate and the Exchange Rate.**   Let us start with the relationship between the interest rate and the *exchange rate*. International investors must decide whether to put their funds in assets denominated in dollars—such as an account at a U.S. bank in New York City—or in assets denominated in foreign currencies—such as an account at a Japanese bank in Tokyo. If interest rates rise in the United States, then international investors will put more funds in dollar-denominated assets. They can earn more by doing so. For example, suppose the interest rate paid on U.S. dollar deposits in New York rises and there is no change in the interest rate in Japan. Then international investors will shift their funds from Tokyo to New York in order to take advantage of the higher interest rate. As funds are shifted to the United States, the demand for dollars begins to increase. This increased demand puts upward pressure on the dollar exchange rate. The exchange rate will rise, which means that more foreign currency will be exchanged for one dollar in the foreign exchange market. In other words, the higher interest rate causes a higher level of the dollar exchange rate. For example, an increase in the interest rate in the United States might cause the dollar to increase from 100 yen per dollar to 120 yen per dollar. Conversely, a lower interest rate in the United States brings about a lower exchange rate for the dollar.

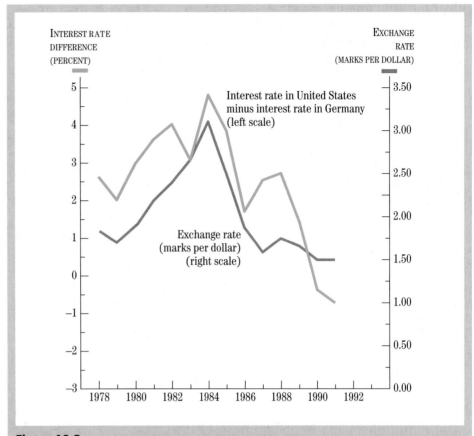

Figure 19.5
The Interest Rate and the Exchange Rate
The green line is the interest rate on U.S. Treasury bonds relative to the interest rate on German bonds (the difference between the two interest rates). As the U.S. interest rate rose compared to that in Germany, the value of the dollar rose relative to the German mark. The same type of relationship holds true for other currencies.

Thus, the interest rate and the exchange rate are positively related. Such a relationship is confirmed by observing interest rates and exchange rates in the market over several years. When the interest rate increases compared to interest rates abroad, the exchange rate rises. For example, Figure 19.5 shows that a large rise in the U.S. dollar relative to the German mark occurred in the mid-1980s when the U.S. interest rate rose sharply compared to the German interest rate.

■ **The Exchange Rate and Net Exports.**   A lower dollar exchange rate will make foreign goods imported into the United States less attractive to U.S. consumers because they will be more expensive. For example, at the end of 2004, the dollar exchange rate against the euro was relatively low at 0.75 euro (€) per dollar compared to the exchange rate three years earlier, at the end of 2001, which was €1.1 per dollar. In 2001, an American consumer could have bought a German-made Audi costing €36,000 for around $32,750 (36,000/1.1). In 2004, when the exchange rate was €0.75 per dollar, the Audi would be much more expensive; it would cost $48,000 (36,000/0.75). Thus, a lower exchange rate decreases the quantity demanded of imported goods.

In 2001, this man would have paid around €22,000 in Germany for a jeep that cost $20,000 in the United States. In 2004, the cost to Germans would have gone down to around €15,000 due to the lower exchange rate that year.

However, the lower exchange rate makes U.S. exports more attractive to foreign consumers. For example, a $20,000 Jeep Grand Cherokee would have cost €22,000 to a German consumer in 2001 but would cost only €15,000 in 2004.

We have shown that a lower exchange rate will raise exports and lower imports. Since net exports is the difference between exports and imports, a lower exchange rate must mean an increase in net exports. Conversely, a higher exchange rate will mean a decrease in net exports.

■ **Combining the Two Relationships.** Let us combine the two relationships. One relates the interest rate to the exchange rate, and the other relates the exchange rate to net exports. Combining the two, we get the following relationship between the interest rate and net exports:

Interest Rate		Exchange Rate		Net Exports
up	⟶	up	⟶	down
down	⟶	down	⟶	up

If the interest rate goes up, then the exchange rate goes up and net exports go down. Thus, a higher interest rate reduces net exports. The link is the exchange rate, which is increased by the higher interest rate and which, in turn, makes net exports fall. Of course, all of this works in reverse, too. If the interest rate goes down, then the exchange rate goes down and net exports go up. Thus, a lower interest rate increases net exports, because a lower interest rate means a lower exchange rate for the dollar, which stimulates U.S. exports and discourages imports.

By combining the relationships between the interest rate, the exchange rate, exports, and imports, we have derived the relationship between net exports as a share of GDP and the interest rate shown in Figure 19.4. Like the consumption share line and the investment share line, the net exports share line in the figure looks like a demand curve. It is downward-sloping. Changes in the interest rate lead to movements along the net exports line in Figure 19.4. Changes in other factors—such as a shift in foreign demand for U.S. products—may cause the line to shift.

Putting the Three Shares Together

We have shown that the consumption, investment, and net exports shares are all negatively related to the interest rate. The three diagrams—Figures 19.2, 19.3, and 19.4—summarize this key idea. Our next task is to determine the interest rate and, thereby, a particular value for each share. To determine the interest rate, we will require that the sum of these three shares equals what is left over after the government takes its share. This will ensure that all shares sum to 1.

REVIEW
- Consumption, investment, and net exports are negatively related to the interest rate.

- Higher interest rates raise the price of consumption this year relative to next year. This means that fewer goods will be consumed this year.

- Business firms invest less when interest rates rise because higher interest rates raise borrowing costs.

- Higher interest rates raise the exchange rate and thereby discourage exports and encourage imports, leading to a decline in net exports.

- Other factors besides the interest rate may affect consumption, investment, and net exports. When one of these factors changes, the relationship between the interest rate and consumption, investment, or net exports shifts.

Determining the Equilibrium Interest Rate

Because the interest rate affects each of the three shares (consumption, investment, and net exports), it also affects the *sum* of the three shares. This is shown by the downward-sloping line in diagram (d) of Figure 19.6. In diagram (d), an increase in the interest rate reduces the sum of the three shares of GDP.

Adding the Nongovernment Shares Graphically

Note carefully how Figure 19.6 is put together and how the downward-sloping line in diagram (d) is derived. We have taken the graphs from Figures 19.2, 19.3, and 19.4 and assembled them horizontally in diagrams (a), (b), and (c) of Figure 19.6. The downward-sloping red line in diagram (d) is the sum of the three downward-sloping lines in diagrams (a), (b), and (c). It is the nongovernment share of GDP, or NG/Y, where $NG = C + I + X$ and, as usual, Y is GDP. For example, when the interest rate is 4 percent, the line in diagram (d) shows that the nongovernment share—the sum of investment, consumption, and net exports as a share of GDP—is 80 percent; this is the sum of 65 percent for the consumption share, 15 percent for the investment

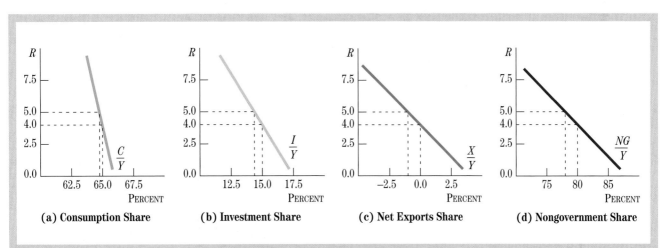

(a) Consumption Share   (b) Investment Share   (c) Net Exports Share   (d) Nongovernment Share

**Figure 19.6
Summing Up Consumption,
Investment, and Net Exports
Shares**

Diagrams (a), (b), and (c) are reproductions of Figures 19.2, 19.3, and 19.4. For each interest rate, the three shares are added together to get the sum of shares shown in diagram (d). For example, when the interest rate is 4 percent, we get 65 percent for consumption share, 15 percent for investment share, and 0 percent for net exports, summing to 80 percent. The sum of the three nongovernment shares (NG/Y) is negatively related to the interest rate (R).

share, and zero percent for the net exports share. Similarly, the other points in diagram (d) are obtained by adding up the three shares at other interest rate levels. For example, at an interest rate of 5 percent, we see that the sum of the share of consumption, investment, and net exports is down to about 78 percent.

The Share of GDP Available for Nongovernment Use

To determine the interest rate, we must consider the fourth share: government. The government share determines how much is available for nongovernment use, that is, for either consumption, investment, or net exports. For example, if the government share is 22 percent of GDP, then the sum of the consumption share, the investment share, and the net export share must equal 78 percent.

What brings this equality about? In a market economy, the government does not stipulate that consumption, investment, and net exports must equal 78 percent, or any other share of GDP. Instead, prices—in this case, the interest rate—adjust to provide individual consumers or firms with the incentive to make the necessary adjustments. Recall from Chapter 1 that the price in a market serves as both a signal and an incentive to individuals. In a market economy as a whole, the interest rate adjusts to ensure equality between (1) the sum of the investment, consumption, and net exports shares, and (2) the share of GDP available for investment, consumption, and net exports.

The Government's Share of GDP

We have determined that the interest rate has a negative effect on the consumption, investment, and net exports shares of GDP. What about the impact of interest rates on government purchases? We will assume that government purchases do not depend on the interest rate; instead, they are likely to be affected by the decisions made by elected representatives on behalf of the voters who elected them to office. So the share of government purchases will not be affected by fluctuations in interest rates.

Putting all these relationships together, we can conclude that the sum of the consumption, investment, and net exports shares must equal the share of GDP available after the government takes its share. In mathematical terms, we can describe this relationship as

$$\frac{NG}{Y} = 1 - \frac{G}{Y}$$

If consumption, investment, or net exports increases, then the nongovernment share will begin to rise above the share of GDP available after the government takes its share. This rise in spending will cause the interest rate in the economy to increase and bring consumption, investment, net exports, or all three back down so that the nongovernmental share once again equals the available share left by the government.

Finding the Equilibrium Interest Rate Graphically

Figure 19.7 illustrates how the interest rate brings about this equality. Look first at diagram (d). In diagram (d), the share of GDP available for nongovernment use is indicated by the vertical line. Since the government share of spending is assumed to depend not on the interest rate but rather on public decisions made by voters and politicians, the share of GDP available for nongovernment use is represented by a vertical line. In the case where government purchases are 22 percent of GDP, the vertical line is at 78 percent, as shown in Figure 19.7(d). If the government share were larger, we would draw the vertical line farther to the left, showing that the share available for nongovernment use was smaller.

The sum of the three nongovernment shares is shown by the downward-sloping line in Figure 19.7(d). This is the same line we derived in Figure 19.6(d). At the intersection of this downward-sloping line and the vertical line, the sum of investment, consumption, and net exports is equal to the share that is available for nongovernment use. For example, when the share available is 78 percent, we see in diagram (d) of Figure 19.7 that the point of intersection occurs when the interest rate is 5 percent. This is the **equilibrium interest rate,** the interest rate that makes the sum of the consumption, investment, and net exports shares equal to the share of GDP available. It is also the interest rate for which the sum of all shares of GDP equals 1.

equilibrium interest rate: the interest rate that equates the sum of the consumption, investment, and net exports shares to the share of GDP available for nongovernment use.

Once we determine the equilibrium interest rate, we can find the investment, consumption, and net exports shares. Each of these shares depends on the interest rate, as shown in diagrams (a), (b), and (c) of Figure 19.7. To determine each of the shares, simply draw a line across the three diagrams at the equilibrium interest rate. Then in diagram (a) we find the consumption share, in diagram (b) the investment share, and in diagram (c) the net exports share.

■ **Analogy with Supply and Demand.** Observe that the intersection of the two lines in diagram (d) of Figure 19.7 is much like the intersection of a demand curve and a supply curve. The red downward-sloping line—showing how the sum of investment, consumption, and net exports is negatively related to the interest rate—looks just like a demand curve. The blue vertical line—showing the share of GDP available for consumption, investment, and net exports—looks like a vertical supply curve. The intersection of the two curves determines the equilibrium price—in this case, the equilibrium interest rate in the economy as a whole. In the next section, we show how shifts in one or both of these two curves lead to a new

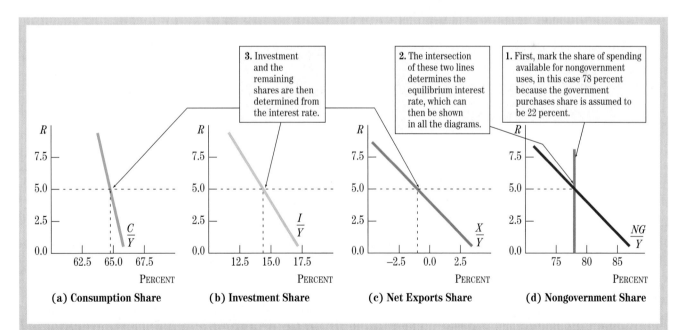

Figure 19.7
Determining the Equilibrium Interest Rate and the Shares of Spending

In this case, government purchases are assumed to be 22 percent of GDP. Mark the implied share available for nongovernment uses, 78 percent, in diagram (d). The equilibrium interest rate is determined at the intersection of the two lines in diagram (d). Given this interest rate, we can compute the consumption, investment, and net exports shares of spending in GDP using diagrams (a), (b), and (c).

equilibrium interest rate, much as shifts in supply and demand curves lead to a new equilibrium price.

■ **The Real Interest Rate in the Long Run.**   Having determined the equilibrium interest rate, it is important to mention once more that our analysis applies to the *long run*—perhaps three years or more—rather than to short-run economic fluctuations. It takes time for consumers and firms to completely respond to a change in interest rates.

Moreover, the interest rate in the analysis refers to the *real* interest rate, which, as defined in Chapter 17, is the interest rate on loans adjusted for inflation. The real interest rate is defined as the nominal interest rate less the expected inflation rate. If the inflation rate is low, there is little difference between the real interest rate and the nominal interest rate; but if inflation is high, there is a big difference, and the real interest rate is a much better measure of the incentives affecting consumers and firms. An interest rate of 50 percent would seem high but would actually be quite low—2 percent in real terms—if people expected inflation to be 48 percent.

Broadly speaking, the analysis in this section shows that the real interest rate in the long run is determined by balancing people's demands for consumption, investment, and net exports with the available supply of goods and services in the economy.

REVIEW
- The sum of the consumption, investment, and net exports shares of GDP is negatively related to the interest rate because each of the individual components is negatively related to the interest rate.

- The equilibrium interest rate is determined by the condition that the sum of the three nongovernment shares of GDP equals the share available to the private sector. Using the equilibrium interest rate, we can then find each of the nongovernment shares.

CASE STUDY

Shifts in Government Purchases and Consumption

Now let us show how the spending allocation model is used to predict the effects of actual changes in the economy. We focus on two shifts: a shift in government purchases and a shift in consumption. Thus, this case study has two separate parts.

A Shift in the Share of Government Purchases

What happens when government purchases increase or decrease as a share of GDP? We know as a matter of arithmetic that some other share must move in a direction opposite to that of the government share.

Suppose that the government share of GDP decreases by 2 percent, as happened in the 1990s as a result of a decrease in defense spending and other budget cuts. The effects of this change are shown in Figure 19.8. If government purchases as a share of GDP decrease by 2 percent, then we know that the share of GDP available for nongovernment use must *increase* by 2 percent. Thus, in diagram (d) of Figure 19.8, we shift the vertical line marking the available share to the right by 2 percentage points. As Figure 19.8(d) shows, there is now a new intersection of the two lines and a new, lower equilibrium interest rate. The decrease in the interest rate is the market mech-

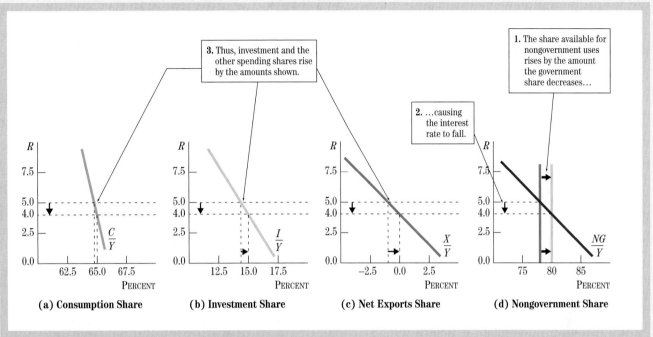

Figure 19.8
A Decrease in the Share of Government Purchases

If the government purchases share of GDP falls, then the share available for nongovernment uses must rise by the same amount. This causes a fall in interest rates, which increases consumption, investment, and net exports as a share of GDP.

anism that brings about an increase in consumption plus investment plus net exports as a share of GDP.

Diagram (d) of Figure 19.8, for example, shows that the new interest rate is 4 percent rather than 5 percent. That is, the interest rate has decreased by 1 percentage point.

To see the effect on consumption, investment, and net exports, we draw a horizontal line at 4 percent interest, as shown in Figure 19.8, and read off the implied shares. According to the diagram, the share of consumption increases, the share of investment increases, and the share of net exports increases. Thus, we have a prediction about consumption, investment, and net exports.

Table 19.1 shows how the analysis explains the effects of a reduction in government purchases in the 1990s. The government purchases share was reduced by 2.2 percent between 1989 and 1997, much as in Figure 19.8. During the same period, all of the other shares increased as a result of the decline in the interest rate. Although the precise magnitudes may not be exactly the same, the model explains the direction of movement very well.

The same process would work in reverse if we increased government purchases as a share of GDP. In Figure 19.8, the interest rates would have to rise. To find out the

Table 19.1
Change in Spending Shares: 1989–1997 (percent)

Consumption share	+1.0
Investment share	+0.8
Net exports share	+0.4
Government purchases share	**−2.2**

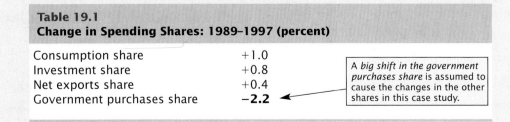

A *big shift in the government purchases share* is assumed to cause the changes in the other shares in this case study.

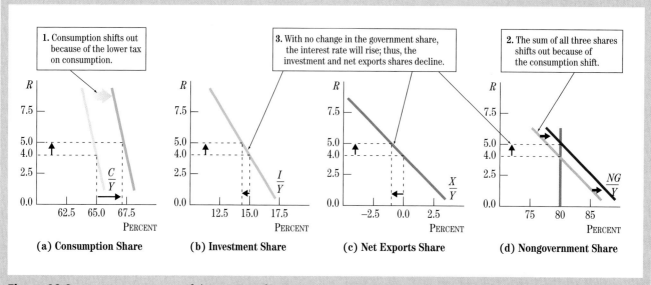

**Figure 19.9
A Shift in the Share of
Consumption**

If the amount of consumption relative to income rises at every interest rate—perhaps because of a tax change that reduces the tax on consumption—the interest rate will rise. Both investment and net exports decline.

effect on the other components of spending, we would draw a horizontal line at a higher interest rate. That would show us that investment, net exports, and consumption would fall as a share of GDP.

Sometimes a decline in investment due to an increase in government purchases is called **crowding out** because investment is "crowded out" by the government purchases. Thus, we have shown that an increase in government purchases as a share of GDP causes a crowding out of investment in the long run. However, because net exports and consumption also fall, the crowding out of investment is not as large as it would otherwise be.

crowding out: the decline in private investment owing to an increase in government purchases.

A Shift in Consumption

The second application of the model involves an increase in the amount people want to consume at every interest rate. This might occur because of a reduction in consumption taxes, which encourages them to consume more, relative to their income.

The impact of such a shift in the share of consumption is analyzed in Figure 19.9. The relationship between the interest rate and the consumption share shifts out in diagram (a); this causes the sum of the investment, consumption, and net exports shares to shift out, as shown by the shift in the line in diagram (d).

**Table 19.2
Change in Spending Shares: 1979–1989 (percent)**

Consumption share	**+3.3**
Investment share	−3.1
Net exports share	−0.5
Government purchases share	+0.3

A *big shift in the consumption share* is assumed to cause changes in the other shares in this case study.

The result is an increase in the equilibrium interest rate and a decline in the share of investment. However, because the share of net exports also declines, the impact on the share of investment is much less than if net exports had not changed. The action of foreigners reduces substantially the effect of the increased consumption on capital formation.

The overall prediction of the effects of such a shift is very close to what happened in the United States during the 1980s, as shown in Table 19.2. As the consumption share rose, the investment share and the net exports share fell. (The government purchases share was nearly unchanged.) According to most estimates, the real interest rate was higher in the 1980s than in the 1970s. Thus, the theory of investment put forth in this chapter explains the long-term trends in the shares of spending and interest rates under the assumption that there was a shift in the share of consumption.

REVIEW

- The impact on capital accumulation of a change in government spending can be analyzed by looking at what happens to the interest rate and each component of GDP.

- An increase in the government spending share reduces the share available for nongovernment use by exactly the same amount. This means that interest rates must rise. The rise in interest rates causes investment, consumption, and net exports to fall.

- An upward shift in the share of consumption causes the investment and net exports shares to fall and interest rates to rise.

The National Saving Rate

national saving rate: the proportion of GDP that is saved, neither consumed nor spent on government purchases; equals national saving (S) divided by GDP, or S/Y.

In Chapter 18, we defined national saving (S) as GDP minus consumption minus government purchases, or

$$S = Y - C - G$$

The ratio of national saving to GDP, or S/Y, is the **national saving rate.** For example, in 2004, national saving was $1,321 billion and GDP was $11,735 billion, so the national saving rate was $\frac{1,321}{11,735} = .1125$ or 11.25 percent. The spending allocation model has implications for the national saving rate. If we divide each term in the definition of national saving by Y, we can write the national saving rate as 1 minus the shares of consumption and government purchases in GDP. That is,

$$\frac{\text{National}}{\text{saving rate}} = 1 - \frac{\text{consumption}}{\text{share}} - \frac{\text{government}}{\text{purchases share}}$$

or

$$\frac{S}{Y} = 1 - \frac{C}{Y} - \frac{G}{Y}$$

This equation tells us that a change in the economy will affect the national saving rate through its effect on the consumption share and the government purchases share.

Note also that the equations tell us that the national saving rate depends on the interest rate. In particular, the national saving rate is positively related to the interest

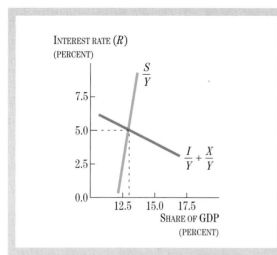

Figure 19.10
Determining the Interest Rate Using the Saving Rate Relationship
The saving rate (green line) depends positively on the interest rate. The sum (purple line) of the investment share and the net exports share depends negatively on the interest rate. The equilibrium interest rate is determined at the point where national saving equals investment plus net exports, or the intersection of the two lines.

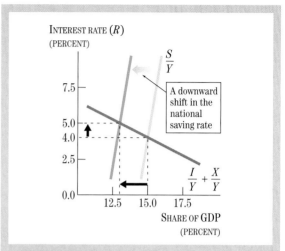

Figure 19.11
The Effect of a Downward Shift in the Saving Rate
The effect is the same as the shift upward in the consumption share illustrated in Figure 19.9. The lower national saving rate raises interest rates and lowers the investment share and the net exports share.

rate because the consumption share is negatively related to the interest rate. In other words, when the interest rate rises, the consumption share falls, implying that the saving rate rises.

Since

$$\frac{C}{Y} + \frac{I}{Y} + \frac{G}{Y} + \frac{X}{Y} = 1$$

we can use the above definition of the national saving rate to write

$$\frac{S}{Y} = \frac{I}{Y} + \frac{X}{Y}$$

or, in other words, the national saving rate equals the investment share plus the net exports share. Both sides of this equation depend on the interest rate, as shown in Figure 19.10. The upward-sloping line in Figure 19.10 shows the national saving rate. An increase in the interest rate causes the saving rate to rise. The downward-sloping line shows the sum of I/Y and X/Y; this sum is negatively related to the interest rate because both the investment share I/Y and the net exports share X/Y are negatively related to the interest rate.

At the intersection of the two lines in Figure 19.10, the national saving rate equals the investment share plus the net exports share. The intersection determines the equilibrium interest rate. The interest rate is exactly the same as that in Figure 19.7, which is based on exactly the same relationships.

Now let us look at the same shift in consumption share considered in the previous section, but with a focus on saving. An upward shift in the consumption share is equivalent to a downward shift in the saving rate. Thus, we shift the interest rate–saving rate relationship to the left in Figure 19.11, representing a downshift in the national saving rate. As shown in the figure, this leads to a higher interest rate and lower shares for investment and net exports. Hence, the predictions are the same as those of the previous analysis in Figure 19.9.

> **REVIEW**
> - The national saving rate is positively related to the interest rate. Equating the national saving rate and the sum of the investment and net exports shares is a way to determine the interest rate.
> - A downward shift in the national saving rate is equivalent to an upward shift in the consumption share.

Conclusion

In this chapter, we have developed a model that determines the equilibrium interest rate and explains how the shares of spending are allocated in the whole economy. The model can be used to analyze the impact of a change in government purchases or a shift in consumption or saving.

The model has introduced an important macroeconomic factor to consider when assessing the appropriate size of government. Private investment is affected by the size of government in the economy. Private investment is greater when government purchases are less.

On the other hand, government spending is needed to provide the roads, education, and legal system that help produce economic growth. But even when government spending does these good things, it reduces the share of GDP available for private investment. To the extent that consumption and net exports also shrink as government purchases increase, the effect on private investment is smaller.

Thus, there is a need for balance between government purchases and private investment. The mix will ultimately be determined in the political debate. This chapter provides some economic analysis that is useful in that debate.

KEY POINTS

1. Over the long term, consumption, investment, net exports, and government purchases compete for a share of GDP.

2. The four spending shares must sum to 1.

3. Higher interest rates raise the price of consumption and lead to a reduction of consumption as a share of GDP.

4. Higher interest rates also reduce investment.

5. Higher interest rates lower the share of net exports by causing the exchange rate to rise, which reduces exports and raises imports.

6. The equilibrium interest rate is found by equating the sum of the consumption, investment, and net exports shares to the share of GDP available for nongovernment use.

7. A decrease in the share of government purchases will lead to an increase in all the other shares of spending.

8. An increase in the share of government purchases crowds out the investment share in GDP by raising interest rates. Consumption and net exports shares also fall, crowding out the investment less severely.

KEY TERMS

consumption share
investment share
net exports share
government purchases share
equilibrium interest rate
crowding out
national saving rate

QUESTIONS FOR REVIEW

1. Why does an increase in the government share in GDP require a decrease in some other share?

2. What is the relationship between consumption and interest rates?

3. Why does investment fall when interest rates rise?

4. Why is there a relationship between the exchange rate and the interest rate?

5. How does the relationship between net exports and the exchange rate tie into the negative relationship between interest rates and net exports?

6. What determines the equilibrium interest rate?

7. What is crowding out?

8. In what sense does the theory in this chapter apply to the long run rather than to short-run economic fluctuations?

PROBLEMS

1. Suppose $C = 700$, $I = 200$, $G = 100$, and $X = 0$.
   a. What is GDP? Calculate each component's share of GDP.
   b. Suppose government spending increases to 150 and GDP does not change. What is government spending's share of GDP now? What is the new nongovernment share?
   c. Without doing any calculations, explain in general terms what happens to C/Y, X/Y, and I/Y after the government spending increase in (b). Describe the mechanism by which each of these changes happens.

2. Using the diagram below, find the equilibrium interest rate when the government share is 20 percent. What is the investment share? Show what happens to all the variables if there is an upward shift in the investment relation because of a new tax policy that encourages investment.

3. Describe the long-run impact of a decline in defense spending by 1 percent of GDP on interest rates and on consumption, investment, and net exports as a share of GDP. Consider two different cases:
   a. No other changes in policy accompany the defense cut.
   b. The funds saved from the defense cut are used to increase government expenditures on roads and bridges.

4. a. As government's share in GDP decreases, the nongovernment share increases. Depict this in a diagram. What happens to interest rates?
   b. As interest rates fall, what change is there in the exchange rate? What happens to net exports in this case? Does this match your earlier picture?
   c. Suppose net exports are very sensitive to changes in interest rates. Does that mean a relatively big or a relatively small change in net exports?

5. Many people believe that the U.S. saving rate is too low. Suppose all private citizens save at a higher rate. Show what happens in this case in the saving and investment diagram, where the S/Y curve shifts. Now show the same situation in the C/Y, I/Y, and X/Y diagrams. Which curve shifts? If government's share in GDP doesn't change, then what must happen to interest rates? Explain how this affects X/Y.

6. Draw two sets of diagrams like Figure 19.7 to depict two situations. In one set, draw investment and net exports as very sensitive to interest rates—that is, the I/Y and X/Y curves are very flat. In the other set, draw investment and net exports as insensitive to interest rates—that is, the I/Y and X/Y curves are nearly vertical. For the same increase in government's share in GDP, in which set of diagrams will interest rates rise more? Why?

7. The Tax Reform Act of 1986 eliminated the investment tax credit, thus increasing investment costs. Assuming that the government share of GDP is fixed, what effect should this have had on the interest rate and the shares of consumption and net exports in GDP?

Problem 2

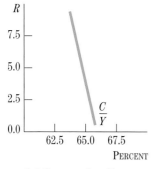

(a) Consumption Share

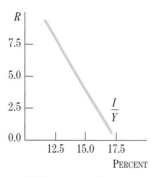

(b) Investment Share

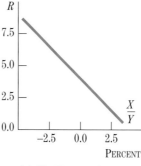

(c) Net Exports Share

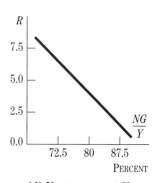

(d) Nongovernment Share

8. Suppose that there is a leftward shift in the C/Y line due to higher consumption taxes, but at the same time, the government increases its share of GDP to maintain the same interest rate. Describe graphically how this affects each of the shares of GDP. If the investment share is the only thing that affects growth in this system, what will happen to growth as a result of this government policy?

9. Suppose the following equations describe the relationship between shares of spending in GDP (Y) and the interest rate (R), measured in decimal fractions (that is, $R = .05$ means that the interest rate is 5 percent).

$$\frac{C}{Y} = .7 - .2(R - .05)$$

$$\frac{I}{Y} = .2 - .8(R - .05)$$

$$\frac{X}{Y} = 0 - .95(R - .05)$$

$$\frac{G}{Y} = .2$$

   a. Use algebra to determine the values of the interest rate and the shares of spending in GDP.
   b. Do the calculations again for a government share of 17 percent rather than 20 percent (that is, $G/Y = .17$).

10. Graph the relationships defined in problem 9a to scale in a four-part diagram like Figure 19.6. Use the diagram to analyze each of the following situations:

   a. Suppose there is an increase in the foreign demand for U.S. goods that changes the coefficient in the net exports share equation from 0 to .05. What happens to the interest rate and the consumption, investment, net exports, and government purchases shares in the United States?
   b. Determine how an increase in taxes that reduces the coefficient in the consumption share equation from .7 to .68 would affect the interest rate and the consumption, investment, net exports, and government purchases shares.
   c. Suppose firms are willing to invest 30 percent rather than 20 percent of GDP at an interest rate of 5 percent. How would this affect the interest rate and the shares of spending in GDP?

11. Derive and draw the national saving rate–interest rate relation (as in Figure 19.10) from the information on consumption, government spending, and net exports used in problem 9. In the same graph, draw investment plus net exports as a share of GDP. Determine the equilibrium level of saving and the interest rate using this graph.

CHAPTER 20

Unemployment and Employment

Jennifer, a 21-year-old college senior, was worried about her prospects of finding a job after graduating from college in 2005 because she had learned that in the previous year, the unemployment rate for young women in her age group was 9 percent. However, Jennifer was somewhat comforted by the thought that among college graduates like herself, the unemployment rate was only 2.5 percent. Jennifer was also interested in living and working in Spain for a few years to fully develop the Spanish language skills she had acquired in college. However, she had learned that the unemployment rate for young workers in Spain was 22 percent. She was particularly puzzled by this high unemployment rate because she had read that the Spanish economy, like the U.S. economy, was doing well.

Unemployment is the macroeconomic variable that affects people most personally. When the economy is booming and unemployment is low, it is easier for individuals to find jobs that are satisfying to them and that also pay well. In contrast, when the economy is in recession and unemployment is high, jobs are harder to find, and people will settle for jobs that do not closely match their skills and don't pay very much money. However, as Jennifer's story illustrates, unemployment rates often fluctuate for reasons that are unrelated to the state of the economy. Unemployment rates can, and do, vary among groups of individuals of different gender, age, race, and education. They also vary dramatically across countries, even to the extent that economies that are in recession may have lower unemployment rates than economies that are booming.

Why do unemployment rates differ so much among countries? Is it because of differences in education levels? Is it because of differences in attitudes toward work? Or is it because of differences in the economic policies implemented by the different countries' governments? This chapter will examine the nature and causes of unemployment and teach you how to use a simple model that can answer these questions and more. When you study the concepts in this chapter, keep in mind that unemployment has painful economic consequences. For those who experience it, there are the obvious hardships of income loss, loss of self-esteem, and an increasing toll on family life, along with the failure of young people who live in a world of persistent unemployment to acquire job skills that will help them become productive citizens in the future. Beyond these individual and family hardships, there are macroeconomic consequences of unemployment as well. When more workers are unemployed, the production of goods and services is less than it would be if more of those workers were employed. In other words, the economy is underutilizing its productive resources. It is essential for aspiring macroeconomists to learn more about unemployment and how to reduce it.

Unemployment and Other Labor Market Indicators

natural unemployment rate: the unemployment rate that exists when there is neither a recession nor a boom and real GDP is equal to potential GDP.

cyclical unemployment: unemployment due to a recession, when the rate of unemployment is above the natural rate of unemployment.

frictional unemployment: unemployment arising from normal turnover in the labor market, such as when people change occupations or locations, or are new entrants.

structural unemployment: unemployment due to structural problems such as poor skills, longer-term changes in demand, or insufficient work incentives.

In this section, we show how unemployment is defined and measured, and we discuss the various causes of unemployment.

Cyclical, Frictional, and Structural Unemployment

Recall from Chapter 17 that the unemployment rate rises when the economy goes into a recession and falls when the economy expands. For example, as shown in Figure 20.1, the unemployment rate fell in the mid- to late 1990s as the economy expanded rapidly and then rose when the economy went into a recession in 2001. Then the unemployment rate declined in the expansion of 2003 and 2004.

Economists use the term **natural unemployment rate** to refer to the unemployment rate that exists when the economy is not in a recession or a boom and real GDP is equal to potential GDP. The increase in unemployment above the natural rate during recessions is called **cyclical unemployment** because it is related to the short-term cyclical fluctuations in the economy. For example, the increase in the unemployment rate from 2001 to 2002 was cyclical. The natural unemployment rate is caused by a combination of **frictional unemployment** and **structural unemployment**. Frictional unemployment occurs when new workers enter the labor force and must look for work, or when workers change jobs for one reason or another and need some time to find another job. Most frictional unemployment is short-lived. In contrast, some workers are unemployed for a long time, six months or more; they may have trouble finding work because they have insufficient skills or because their skills

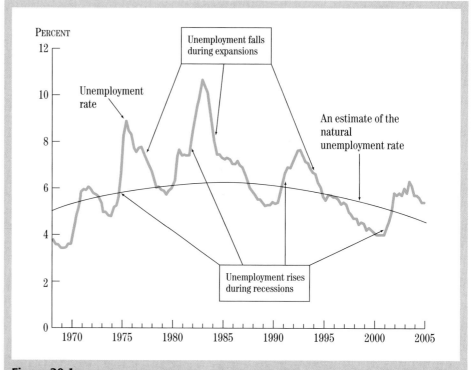

Figure 20.1
The Unemployment Rate
The unemployment rate fluctuates around the natural unemployment rate, rising during recessions and falling when the economy grows rapidly during expansions.

are no longer in demand as a result of a technological change or a shift in people's tastes toward new products. Such unemployment is called structural unemployment. The amount of frictional unemployment and structural unemployment in the economy is not constant, so the natural unemployment rate changes over time. But such changes are gradual and are not related to short-term economic fluctuations.

An estimate of the natural unemployment rate is shown in Figure 20.1. The natural rate of unemployment increased in the 1970s. One possible reason for the increase was the influx of young baby-boom workers into the labor force in the 1970s. Young people tend to have higher unemployment rates than older people. The natural unemployment rate declined in the 1990s as the labor force aged. It is important to remember that the natural unemployment rate is not a constant and that economists do not know its value precisely.

When economists use the term *natural* unemployment rate, they do not mean to say that this is "okay" or "just fine," as when your doctor tells you that having a higher temperature in the evening than in the morning is "natural." They simply mean that whenever the operation of the overall macroeconomy is close to normal in the sense that real GDP is near potential GDP, the unemployment rate hovers around this natural rate.

How Is Unemployment Measured?

To understand what the data on unemployment mean, one must understand how unemployment is measured. Each month, the U.S. Census Bureau surveys a sample

Current Population Survey: a monthly survey of a sample of U.S. households done by the U.S. Census Bureau; it measures employment, unemployment, the labor force, and other characteristics of the U.S. population. (Ch. 14)

labor force: all those who are either employed or unemployed.

working-age population: persons over 16 years of age who are not in an institution such as a jail or hospital.

of about 60,000 households in the United States. This survey is called the *Current Population Survey.* By asking the people in the survey a number of questions, the Census Bureau determines whether each person 16 years of age or over is employed or unemployed. The **labor force** consists of all people 16 years of age and over who are either employed or unemployed.

■ **Who Is Employed and Who Is Unemployed?** To be counted as unemployed, a person must be looking for work, but not have a job. To be counted as employed, a person must have a job, either a job outside the home—as in the case of a teaching job at a high school or a welding job at a factory—or a *paid* job inside the home—as in the case of a freelance editor or a telemarketer who works for pay at home. A person who has an *unpaid* job at home—for example, caring for children or working on the house—is not counted as employed. If a person is not counted as either unemployed or employed, then the person is not in the labor force. For example, a person who is working at home without pay and who is not looking for a paid job is considered not in the labor force.

Figure 20.2 illustrates the definitions of employment, unemployment, and the labor force. Using December 2004 as an example, it shows that out of a **working-age population** of 225.0 million, there were 140.2 million employed and 8.0 million unemployed; the remaining 76.8 million were of working age but were not in the labor force.

■ **The Labor Force and Discouraged Workers.** It is difficult to judge who should be counted as being in the labor force and who should not be counted. For example, consider two retired people. One decided to retire at age 65 and is now enjoying retirement in Florida. The other was laid off from a job at age 55 and, after looking for a job for two years, got discouraged and stopped looking, feeling forced into retirement. You may feel that the second person, but not the first, should be counted as unemployed. However, according to the official statistics, neither is unemployed; they are not in the labor force because they are not looking for work. In general, workers, such as the second retired worker, who have left the labor force after not being able to find a job are called *discouraged workers.*

Defining and measuring the labor force is the most difficult part of measuring the amount of unemployment. A recent change in the way the questions in the Current Population Survey were phrased revealed that many women who were working at home without pay were actually looking for a paid job; as a result of the change in the question, these women are now counted as unemployed rather than as out of the labor force.

■ **Part-Time Work.** A person is counted as employed in the Current Population Survey if he or she has worked at all during the week of the survey. Thus, part-time workers are counted as employed. The official definition of a *part-time worker* is one who works between 1 and 34 hours per week. About 18 percent of U.S. workers are employed part time.

There is a big difference between the percentage of men who work part time and the percentage of women who work part time. About 26 percent of women work part time, while only about 11 percent of men work part time. Women give personal choice rather than unavailability of full-time jobs as a reason for part-time work more frequently than men do. About 32 percent of employed women who have children under 3 work part time.

Because of part-time work, the average number of hours of work per worker each week is about 34 hours, less than the typical 40 hours a week.

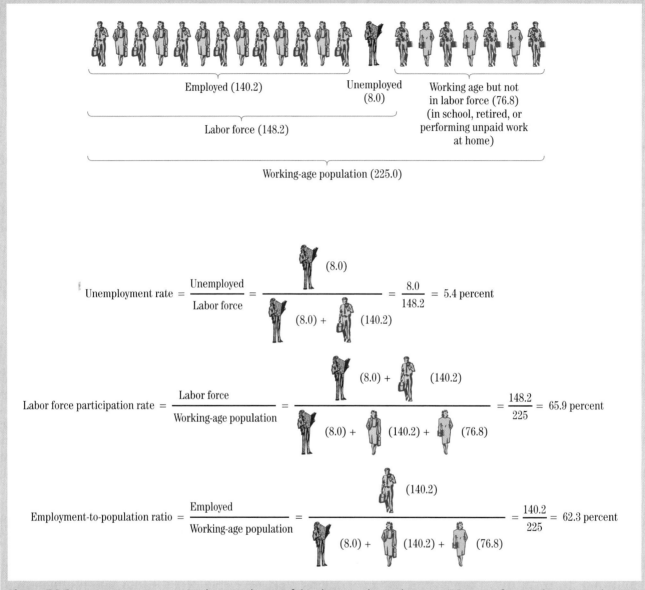

Figure 20.2
How to Find Labor Market
Indicators

As shown at the top of this diagram, the working-age (16 years of age and over) population is divided into three groups: employed, unemployed, and not in the labor force. Three key labor market indicators are then computed from these categories. For example, the unemployment rate is the number of people unemployed divided by the number of people in the labor force. (The numbers in parentheses are in millions and are the statistics for December 2004.)

unemployment rate: the percentage of the labor force that is unemployed. (Ch. 17)

labor force participation rate: the ratio (usually expressed as a percentage) of people in the labor force to the working-age population.

Comparing Three Key Indicators

Now let us examine the three key indicators of conditions in the labor market. These are

1. The *unemployment rate,* the percentage of the labor force that is unemployed

2. The **labor force participation rate,** the ratio of people in the labor force to the working-age population

employment-to-population ratio: the ratio (usually expressed as a percentage) of employed workers to the working-age population.

3. The **employment-to-population ratio,** the ratio of employed workers to the working-age population

Figure 20.2 gives an example of how each indicator is calculated. Both the unemployment rate and the labor force participation rate depend on the labor force, and therefore have the same measurement difficulties that the labor force does. Only the employment-to-population ratio does not depend on the labor force.

The labor force participation rate and the employment-to-population ratio have both had important longer-term upward trends. For example, the employment-to-population ratio has increased in the last 30 years from about 57 percent in 1974 to about 62 percent in 2004. The rising employment-to-population ratio indicates that the U.S. economy has created a lot of jobs over the past three decades. How does one explain this?

The rising percentage of women who are employed is a major factor, as shown in Figure 20.3. This increase is mainly due to more women entering the labor force, a trend that has been going on since the 1950s. In the early 1950s, about 32 percent of women were in the labor force, but now about 60 percent are. Possible explanations for this trend include reduced discrimination, increased opportunities and pay for women, the favorable experience of many women working for pay during World War II, and the women's movement, which emphasized the attractiveness of paid work outside the home.

Aggregate Hours of Labor Input

As we have seen, some people work part time. Others work full time; some work overtime. For these reasons, the number of people employed is not a good measure of the labor input to production in the economy. For example, consider two typists who both work half time; one works 4 hours in the morning, and the other works 4 hours in the afternoon, both 5 days a week. Together they work as much as one full-time typist; to say that the labor input of these two typists is twice as much as the labor input of one full-time typist would be an obvious mistake. Rather, their combined labor input is the same as that of one full-time typist: 40 hours a week.

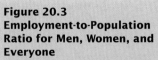

**Figure 20.3
Employment-to-Population
Ratio for Men, Women, and
Everyone**
The percentage of working-age women who are employed has increased steadily since the 1950s. The percentage of working-age men who are employed declined until the late 1970s, when it leveled off and started increasing.

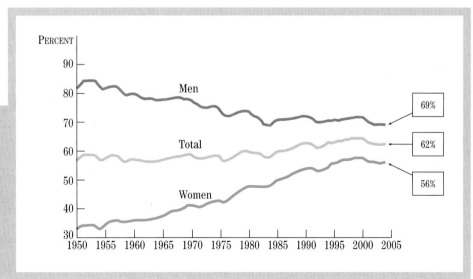

This example shows why economists consider the number of hours people work rather than the number of people who work when they measure labor input to production, whether it is typists at a firm or workers in the whole economy. Thus, the most comprehensive measure of labor input to the production of real GDP is the total number of hours worked by all workers, or **aggregate hours.** The number of aggregate hours of labor input depends on the number of hours of work for each person and the number of people working.

aggregate hours: the total number of hours worked by all workers in the economy in a given period of time.

The growth of aggregate labor hours in the United States is slowing down. It grew by about 1.7 percent per year in the 1970s and 1980s and is expected to grow by about 1.2 percent per year in the next ten years. The main reason for this slowdown is that the growth of the working-age population is slowing down.

REVIEW

- The unemployment rate in the United States fluctuates cyclically. The unemployment rate in the absence of cyclical increases or decreases is called the natural unemployment rate.

- Unemployment and employment in the United States are measured by the Current Population Survey.

- To be counted as unemployed, you have to be looking for work.

- The employment-to-population ratio rose in the 1980s and 1990s. More women have been entering the labor force since the early 1950s.

- Aggregate hours is the most comprehensive measure of labor input.

The Nature of Unemployment

Having examined the aggregate data, let us now look at the circumstances of people who are unemployed. There are many reasons for people to become unemployed, and people's experiences with unemployment vary widely.

Reasons People Are Unemployed

We can divide up the many reasons people become unemployed into four broad categories. People are unemployed because they have either lost their previous job (*job losers*), quit their previous job (*job leavers*), entered the labor force to look for work for the first time (*new entrants*), or re-entered the labor force after being out of it for a while (*re-entrants*). Figure 20.4 shows how the 5.4 percent unemployment rate in December 2004 was divided into these four categories.

■ **Job Losers.** Among the people who lost their jobs in a typical recent year was a vice president of a large bank in Chicago. When the vice president's financial services marketing department was eliminated, she lost her job. After three months of unemployment, which were spent searching for work and waiting for responses to her letters and telephone calls, the former vice president took a freelance job, using her banking expertise to advise clients. Within a year, she was making three times her former salary.

The vice president's unemployment experience, although surely trying for her at the time, had a happy ending. In fact, you might say that the labor market worked

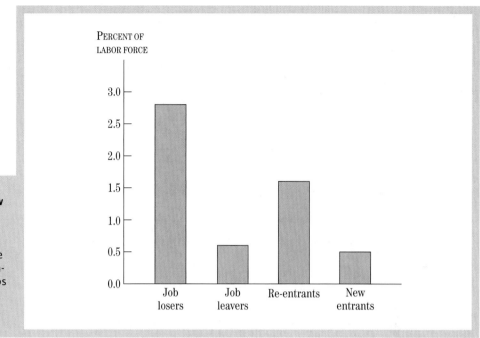

PERCENT OF
LABOR FORCE

Figure 20.4
Job Losers, Job Leavers, New Entrants, and Re-entrants (December 2004)
A significant part of the unemployment rate consists of people who lost their jobs. The rest consists of people who left their jobs to look for another job or who have just entered or re-entered the labor force.

pretty well. At least judging by her salary, she is more productive in her new job. Although one job was destroyed, another one—better, in this case—was created.

This transition from one job to another is part of the dynamism of any free market economy. The economist Joseph Schumpeter called this dynamism *creative destruction,* referring to the loss of whole business firms as well as jobs when new ideas and techniques replace the old. Creative destruction means that something better is created as something else is destroyed. In this case, a better job was created when another job was destroyed. On average, about 7 percent of jobs are destroyed each year by plant closings, bankruptcies, or downsizing of firms. In 2004, that would have amounted to about 10 million jobs destroyed. In an economy with growing employment, more jobs are created than are destroyed. In times of recession, however, when employment is likely to fall, more jobs are destroyed than are created. So the bank manager was "lucky" to have lost her job during a period when finding a comparable job was relatively easy.

Many people who lose their jobs are not as "lucky" as the woman in our story. Among the unemployed in recent years were middle-aged workers let go by "dot-com" firms after several years of employment. Finding a comparable job was difficult for such workers because most other such firms were also in financial difficulties, laying off workers instead of hiring them. The loss of such a job not only has disastrous effects on income, but can also have psychological effects. It may mean that a worker's children cannot go to college, or that the worker must sell his or her house. Unemployment compensation provides some relief—perhaps about $200 a week until it runs out. In many cases, though, this is well below what these workers were earning. Until they find a new job, they are obviously part of the millions of unemployed. Some may wait until a comparable job comes along; others may accept a lower-paying job. For example, one laid-off software programmer took a job as a lab instructor for one-fourth the pay.

People may lose their jobs even when the economy is not in a recession. On average, about half of all unemployed workers are unemployed because they lost their

Each month—usually on the first Friday of the month—the U.S. Department of Labor releases information about employment and unemployment in the previous month. The following is excerpted from the news release issued by the Bureau of Labor Statistics. You should be able to find the terms discussed in this article in the text.

Note that the unemployment rate was at 5.4 percent in February 2005. How does this compare with the unemployment rate in 1995 or in 1985? (See Figure 20.1.)

Employment Situation Summary

http://www.bls.gov/cps/

THE EMPLOYMENT SITUATION: February 2005

| The unemployment rate can rise even if employment increases. Why? |

Nonfarm payroll employment increased by 262,000 in February and the unemployment rate edged up to 5.4 percent, the Bureau of Labor Statistics of the U.S. Department of Labor reported today. Job growth occurred in both goods-producing and service-providing industries.

Unemployment (Household Survey Data)

| Summarizes the unemployment numbers |

In February, both the number of unemployed persons, 8.0 million, and the unemployment rate, 5.4 percent, returned to their December levels after dipping in January. The jobless rate had been either 5.4 or 5.5 percent during each of the last 6 months of 2004. In February, the unemployment rates for the major worker groups—adult men (4.9 percent), adult women (4.7 percent), teenagers (17.5 percent), whites (4.6 percent), blacks (10.9 percent), and Hispanics or Latinos (6.4 percent)—showed little change. The unemployment rate for Asians was 4.5 percent in February, not seasonally adjusted.

| Illustrates how unemployment rates vary by race & gender |

Total Employment and the Labor Force (Household Survey Data)

| Summarizes the employment numbers |

In February, total employment was about unchanged at 140.1 million, seasonally adjusted. The employment-population ratio—the proportion of the population age 16 and over with jobs—was little changed over the month at 62.3 percent. The rate has fluctuated between 62.1 and 62.5 percent for the past 2 years. In February, the civilian labor force was essentially unchanged at 148.1 million, and the participation rate held at 65.8 percent.

Over the year, the number of persons who held more than one job increased by 432,000 to 7.7 million, not seasonally adjusted. These multiple jobholders represented 5.5 percent of total employment in February, up from 5.3 percent a year earlier.

Persons Not in the Labor Force (Household Survey Data)

There were 1.7 million persons who were marginally attached to the labor force in February, little changed over the year. (Data are not seasonally adjusted.) These individuals wanted and were available to work and had looked for a job sometime in the prior 12 months. They were not counted as unemployed, however, because they did not actively search for work in the 4 weeks preceding the survey. Among the marginally attached, there were 485,000 discouraged workers who were not currently looking for work specifically because they believed no jobs were available for them.

Reasons People Are Unemployed
People are unemployed for different reasons: Some lost their job and are looking for another job (left), others quit their previous job and are still looking for a new job (middle), and still others just entered or re-entered the labor force and are unemployed while looking for work (right).

job vacancies: positions that firms are trying to fill, but for which they have yet to find suitable workers.

jobs for one reason or another. The economy is always in a state of flux, with some firms going out of business or shrinking and other firms starting up or expanding. Tastes change, new discoveries are made, and competition improves productivity and changes the relative fortunes of firms and workers.

Job vacancies are the jobs that firms are trying to fill. Job vacancies and unemployment exist simultaneously. Unfortunately, many job vacancies require different skills from those of unemployed workers, are in another part of the country, or are at lower wages than these workers' former salaries. Workers skilled at one job may be unemployed while firms cannot find workers with other skills.

The number of unemployed workers who have lost their jobs increases during recessions. It is more difficult to find a new job in a recession, when fewer firms are hiring.

■ **Job Leavers.** On average, American workers change jobs every three or four years. Many of these job changes occur when people are young: Young workers are finding out what they are good at or what they enjoy or are rapidly accumulating skills that give them greater opportunities. A small part of unemployment—less than one-fourth—consists of people who quit their previous job to look for another job. While they are looking for work, they are counted as unemployed.

There is very little increase in unemployment due to quits in recessions. Why? Two opposing forces net out to produce little change. In a recession, when unemployment is high, fewer workers quit their jobs because they fear being unemployed for a long period of time. This reduces quit unemployment; however, the lower number of job vacancies makes finding a job more difficult and raises unemployment.

■ **New Entrants and Re-entrants.** Figure 20.4 also shows that a large number of the unemployed workers have just entered the work force. If you do not have a job lined up before you graduate, there is a good chance that you will be unemployed for a period of time while you look for work following graduation. In fact, there is a huge increase in unemployment each June as millions of students enter the labor force for the first time. This is called *seasonal unemployment* because it occurs each graduation "season." In contrast, unemployment is relatively low around the holiday season, when many businesses hire extra employees. Government statisticians smooth

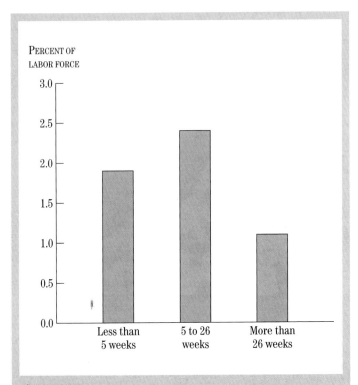

Figure 20.5
Unemployment by Duration (December 2004)
The overall unemployment rate was 5.4 percent in December 2004. About one-fifth of this unemployment was long term—more than 26 weeks. Long-term unemployment increases during recessions.

out this seasonal unemployment to help them see other trends in unemployment, so the newspaper reports on the unemployment rate rarely mention this phenomenon.

Some unemployed workers are re-entering the labor force. For example, a young person may decide to go back to school and then re-enter the labor force afterward. Others might choose to drop out of the labor force for several years to take care of small children at home—a job that is not counted in the unemployment statistics.

Some new entrants to the labor force find it very difficult to find a job. They remain unemployed for long periods of time. In fact, although the hardships of people who lose their jobs are severe, the hardships for many young people who seem to be endlessly looking for work are also severe.

The Duration of Unemployment

The hardships associated with unemployment depend on its duration. Figure 20.5 shows how the unemployment rate divides up according to how long the unemployed workers have been unemployed. A significant fraction of unemployment is very short term. A market economy with millions of people exercising free choice could not possibly function without some very short-term unemployment as people changed jobs or looked for new opportunities.

About one-fifth of unemployed workers are unemployed for more than six months—the truly long-term unemployed. Although the number of short-term unemployed does not vary much over the business cycle, the number of long-term unemployed increases dramatically in recessions.

Table 20.1
Unemployment Rates for Different Demographic Groups (percent of labor force for each group)

	1994	1999	2004
All persons	5.5	4.0	5.4
All females	5.5	4.1	5.2
All males	5.5	4.0	5.6
All whites	4.8	3.5	4.6
All blacks	9.9	7.8	10.8
All Hispanics	9.3	5.8	6.6
All females, 20 years and older	4.8	3.6	4.7
All males, 20 years and older	4.7	3.3	4.9
All teens, 16–19	17.0	13.4	17.6

Source: Bureau of Labor Statistics.

Unemployment for Different Groups

Regardless of how one interprets the numbers, certain groups of workers experience very long spells of unemployment and suffer great hardships as a result of the difficulty they have in finding work. Table 20.1 shows the unemployment rates for several different demographic groups in the United States in three time periods: 1994, and 2004, both periods when the economy had just emerged from recession, and 1999, when the economy was much stronger.

Unemployment is lowest for adult men and women. But unemployment is very high for teenagers. To some extent this is due to more frequent job changes and the period of time required to find work after graduating from school. But many teenagers who are looking for work have dropped out of school and therefore are unskilled and have little or no experience. Their unemployment rates are extremely high, especially those for young minorities. Thus, even when there is good news about the overall unemployment rate, the news may remain bleak for those with low skills and little experience. The overall unemployment rate does not capture the long-term hardships experienced by certain groups.

REVIEW

- People become unemployed when they lose their job, quit their job, or decide to enter or re-enter the labor force to look for a job. In a market economy, job loss occurs simultaneously with job creation.

- Being a new entrant is the least likely reason for a person to be unemployed. Losing a job and looking for work after some time out of the labor force are more likely reasons to be unemployed.

- Many unemployed people have been unemployed for a very short period of time. This frictional unemployment is probably not very harmful and is a necessary part of any market economy.

- On average, about one-fifth of unemployed people have been unemployed for six months or more. Long-term unemployment increases dramatically in recessions.

- Teenagers and minorities in the United States have very high unemployment rates, even in boom years.

Explaining Unemployment and Employment Trends

A good explanation of unemployment and employment trends is the supply and demand model of Chapter 3.

Labor Demand and Labor Supply

labor demand curve: a downward-sloping relationship showing the quantity of labor firms are willing to hire at each wage.

labor supply curve: the relationship showing the quantity of labor workers are willing to supply at each wage.

Figure 20.6 shows a labor demand curve and a labor supply curve. On the vertical axis is the price of labor (wage), and on the horizontal axis is the quantity of labor supplied or demanded. In a labor market, the **labor demand curve** describes the behavior of firms, indicating how much labor they would demand at a given wage. The **labor supply curve** describes the behavior of workers, showing how much labor they would supply at a given wage. The *wage,* usually measured in dollars per hour of

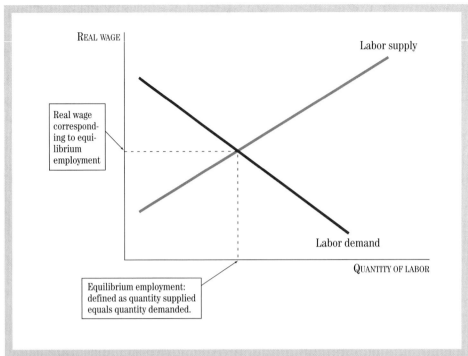

Figure 20.6
Labor Supply, Labor Demand, and Equilibrium Employment
The intersection of the labor supply curve and the labor demand curve determines equilibrium employment and the real wage.

real wage: the wage or price of labor adjusted for inflation; in contrast, the nominal wage has not been adjusted for inflation. (Ch. 13)

work, is the price of labor. To explain employment in the whole economy, it is best to think of the wage relative to the average price of goods. In other words, the wage on the vertical axis is the *real wage,* which we define as

$$\text{Real wage} = \frac{\text{wage}}{\text{price level}}$$

Firms consider the wages they must pay their workers in comparison with the price of the products they sell. The workers consider the wage in comparison with the price of the goods they buy. Thus, in the whole economy, it is the real wage that affects the quantity of labor supplied and demanded.

The labor demand curve slopes downward because the higher the real wage, the less labor firms demand. A lower real wage gives firms an incentive to hire more workers.

The labor supply curve slopes upward, showing that the higher the wage, the more labor workers are willing to supply. A higher real wage gives workers more incentive to work or to work longer hours.

As in any market, we would predict that the amount of labor traded—the number of workers employed—should be at the intersection of the labor demand curve and the labor supply curve, as shown in Figure 20.6. The intersection also determines the equilibrium real wage that brings the quantity supplied into equality with the quantity demanded.

Explaining Employment Trends

Our review of employment trends in the United States in recent decades showed that the employment-to-population ratio has been increasing. The labor supply and demand analysis provides an explanation for this increase.

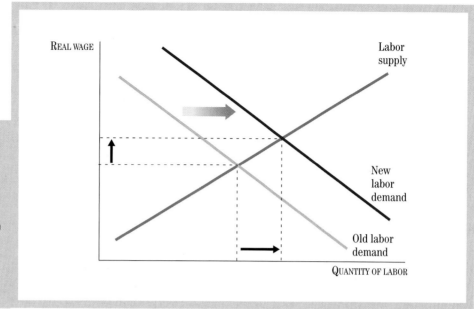

Figure 20.7
Explaining the Increase in the Employment-to-Population Ratio
One explanation for the rise in the employment-to-population ratio in recent decades is a shift in the labor demand curve, which would raise both the real wage and employment. For this purpose, interpret the horizontal axis as employment relative to the population.

Throughout the post–World War II period, real wages have been rising. Thus, we have a combination of an increased real wage and an increased proportion of the population working. This pattern is consistent with a shift in the labor demand curve and movement along the labor supply curve, as shown in Figure 20.7.

As described by the upward-sloping supply curve, the higher wages could be attracting more people into the work force. In fact, as wages have increased, there has been an especially large increase in the percentage of women in the work force. But what could have caused this movement along the supply curve? And why should it have been especially strong for women?

One possibility is that the growth of the service industries—medical, legal, retail trade, telecommunications, transportation—caused an especially large increase in the demand for labor. Economists have found that the labor supply of women is more sensitive to changes in the wage than the labor supply of men is. Thus, the increase in labor demand in service industries could explain the especially large rise in the employment-to-population ratio for women as well as the increase in the real wage.

Although labor supply and demand analysis can explain this phenomenon, other factors also may have played a role, such as laws prohibiting discrimination and the women's movement. The point here is to show that the supply and demand model fits the facts.

Many other employment trends can be explained by labor supply and labor demand analysis. The reduction in the labor force participation of older men because of earlier retirement, for example, can be explained by the increased retirement pay from private pensions and from social security, through which the government supports the elderly. Higher retirement payments make retirement more attractive compared to work and thus reduce labor supply.

Why Is the Unemployment Rate Always Greater Than Zero?

Despite its usefulness in explaining employment trends, the supply and demand model must be modified if it is to explain unemployment. Having read about unemployment in this chapter, do you see something wrong with the picture in

Figure 20.6? It seems inconsistent with the discussion of unemployment. With the quantity of labor supplied equal to the quantity of labor demanded, as in Figure 20.6, there seems to be no unemployment. The intersection of the supply and demand curves seems to predict a market situation that is contrary to the facts. Hence, in order to use the basic supply and demand analysis to explain why unemployment is greater than zero in the real world, we need to modify the story.

Economists have developed two different explanations that adapt the standard labor supply and demand analysis to account for unemployment. Though quite different, the explanations are complementary. In fact, it is essential for us to use both simultaneously if we are to understand unemployment. We will refer to the two explanations as **job rationing** and **job search.**

job rationing: a reason for unemployment in which the quantity of labor supplied is greater than the quantity demanded because the real wage is too high.

job search: a reason for unemployment in which uncertainty in the labor market and workers' limited information requires people to spend time searching for a job.

■ **Job Rationing.** The job-rationing story has two parts. One is an assumption that *the wage is higher than what would equate the quantity supplied with the quantity demanded.* There are several reasons why this might be the case, but first consider the consequences for the labor supply and demand diagram. Figure 20.8 shows the same labor supply and demand curves as Figure 20.6. However, in Figure 20.8, the wage is higher than the wage that would equate the quantity of labor supplied with the quantity of labor demanded. At this wage, the number of workers demanded by firms is smaller than the number of workers willing to supply their labor.

The other part of the job-rationing story tells us how to determine the number of workers who are unemployed. This part of the story assumes that the number of workers employed equals the number of workers demanded by business firms. When the wage is too high, firms hire a smaller number of workers, and workers supply whatever the firms demand. Figure 20.8 shows the resulting amount of employment at the given wage as point A on the labor demand curve. With employment equal to the number of workers demanded, we see that the number of workers willing to supply their labor is greater than the number of workers employed; the excess supply therefore results in unemployment. In the diagram, the amount of unemployment is measured in the horizontal direction.

Figure 20.8
Excess Supply of Labor and Unemployment
The supply and demand curves are exactly as in Figure 20.6. Here, however, the real wage is too high to bring the quantity supplied into equality with the quantity demanded. The number of workers employed is given by point A on the demand curve, where the real wage is above the equilibrium wage. At this higher real wage, the quantity supplied is greater than the quantity demanded—a situation we can think of as unemployment.

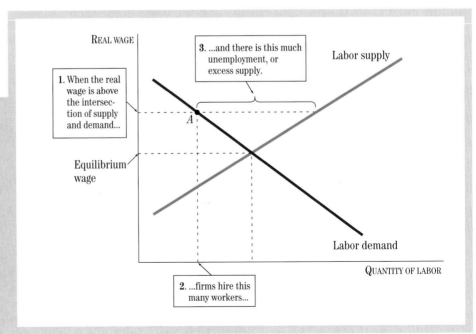

This is a situation in which workers would be willing to take a job at the wage that firms are paying, but there are not enough job offers at that wage. In effect, the available jobs are rationed—for example, by a first-come-first-served rule or by seniority. It is as if when enough workers have been hired, the firms close their hiring offices, and the remaining workers stay unemployed. If the wage were lower, then the firms would hire more workers, but the wage is not lower.

In most markets, a situation of excess supply brings about a reduction in the price—in this case, the wage. Thus, if this explanation of unemployment is to work in practice, there has to be a force at work that prevents the wage from falling. If the theory is to be helpful in explaining unemployment, then the force has to be permanently at work, not just in a recession. Why doesn't the wage fall when there is an excess supply of workers?

There are three explanations why the wage might be always too high to bring the quantity of labor demanded into balance with the quantity of labor supplied.

minimum wage: a wage per hour below which it is illegal to pay workers. (Ch. 3)

1. *Minimum wages.* Most countries have a legal *minimum wage,* or lowest possible wage, that employers can pay their employees. In the United States, in 2004 the minimum wage was $5.15 per hour. A minimum wage can cause unemployment to be higher than it otherwise would be, as shown on the diagram in Figure 20.8: Employers would move down and to the right along their labor demand curve and hire more workers if the wage were lower.

   One of the reasons teenage unemployment is high (as shown in Table 20.1) may be related to the minimum wage. Because many teenagers are unskilled, the wage firms would be willing to pay them is low. A minimum wage, therefore, may price them out of the market and cause them to be unemployed.

insider: a person who already works for a firm and has some influence over wage and hiring policy.

outsider: someone who is not working for a particular firm, making it difficult for him or her to get a job with that firm even though he or she is willing to work for a lower wage.

2. *Insiders versus outsiders.* Sometimes groups of workers—**insiders,** who have jobs—can prevent the wage from declining. If these workers have developed skills unique to the job, or if there is legislation preventing their firing without significant legal costs, then they have some power to keep wages up. Labor unions may help them keep the wage higher than it would otherwise be. One consequence of the higher wage is to prevent the firm from hiring unemployed workers—the **outsiders**—who would be willing to work at a lower wage. This is a common explanation for the very high unemployment in Europe, and the theory has been developed and applied to Europe by Swedish economist Assar Lindbeck and British economist Dennis Snower.

efficiency wage: a wage higher than that which would equate quantity supplied and quantity demanded, set by employers in order to increase worker efficiency—for example, by decreasing shirking by workers.

3. *Efficiency wages.* Firms may choose to pay workers an **efficiency wage**—an extra amount to encourage them to be more efficient. There are many reasons why workers' efficiency or productivity might increase with the wage. Turnover will be lower with a higher wage because there is less reason for workers to look for another job: They are unlikely to find a position paying more than their current wage. Lower turnover means lower training costs. Moreover, workers might not shirk as much with a higher wage. This is particularly important to the firm when jobs are difficult to monitor. With efficiency wages, workers who are working are paid more than the wage that equates the quantity supplied with the quantity demanded. When workers are paid efficiency wages, unemployment will be greater than zero.

■ **Job Search.** We now turn to the second explanation that modifies the standard labor supply and demand analysis. The labor market is constantly in a state of flux, with jobs being created and destroyed and people moving from one job to another. The demand for one type of work falls, and the demand for another type of work increases. Labor supply curves also shift.

In other words, the labor market is never truly in the state of rest conveyed by the fixed supply and demand curves in Figure 20.6. But how can we change the picture? Imagine labor demand and labor supply curves that constantly bounce around. The demand for labor, the supply of labor, and the wage will be different every period. Figure 20.6 will be in perpetual motion. Mathematicians use the adjective *stochastic* to describe this constant bouncing around. Economists apply the term *stochastic* to models of the labor market that are in perpetual motion. Rather than a fixed equilibrium of quantity and a fixed wage, there is a *stochastic equilibrium.* This stochastic equilibrium in the labor market is a way to characterize the constant job creation and job destruction that exist in the economy. People enter the work force, move from one job to another, lose their jobs, or drop out of the labor force. Wages change, inducing people to enter or re-enter the market. Figure 20.9 is a schematic representation of the flows of workers into and out of the labor market.

In a stochastic equilibrium, at any point in time people will be searching for a job. Many who do so will be unemployed for some time. They lost their job, quit their job, or came back to the job market after an absence from work. One of the reasons they remain unemployed for a while is that they find it to their advantage not to accept the first job that comes along. Rather, they wait for a possibly higher-paying job. While they wait, they are unemployed.

■ **Policies to Reduce the Natural Unemployment Rate.** Both the job-rationing model and the job-search model have implications for how public policy

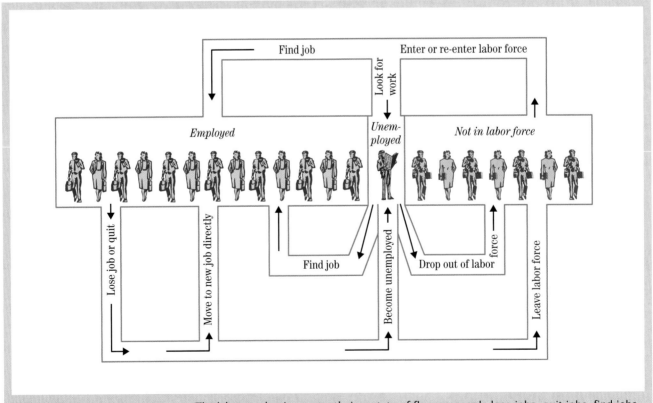

Figure 20.9
Labor Market Flows

The labor market is constantly in a state of flux, as people lose jobs, quit jobs, find jobs, and get in and out of the labor force. Most people pass through the unemployment box for a short period, but among the unemployed, some have not held jobs for a long time.

can reduce the natural rate of unemployment. We already mentioned how a very high minimum wage can increase unemployment. Conversely, a lower minimum wage for young workers could reduce unemployment. And if information about jobs is increased through job-placement centers or improved communication about the labor market, we would expect unemployment from job search to go down.

Unemployment compensation, paid to workers who have been laid off from their job, also affects job search. Unemployment compensation enables workers to spend more time looking for a job or to hold out for a higher-paying job. But in the United States, unemployment compensation does not last forever. In normal times it runs out after 26 weeks, and the evidence shows that many people stop searching and take a job just when their unemployment compensation runs out. Clearly, unemployment compensation not only helps mitigate the hardships associated with unemployment but allows people more time to search. But as a by-product, unemployment compensation increases unemployment.

REVIEW

- The supply and demand for labor is the starting point for explaining long-term employment trends. The intersection of supply and demand curves determines the amount of employment, and shifts in demand can explain why the employment-to-population ratio has increased.

- But the basic supply and demand theory needs to be modified to account for unemployment. Economists use two approaches, job rationing and job search, to explain why unemployment occurs.

- Job rationing occurs when the wage is too high. Unemployment can be interpreted as the difference between the quantity supplied and the quantity demanded at that high wage. Wages can be too high because of minimum-wage laws, insiders, or efficiency wages.

- Job search is another reason for unemployment. It takes time to find a job, and people have an incentive to wait for a good job.

CASE STUDY

Unemployment Among Young People Around the World

Unemployment rates for teenagers and young adults are generally much higher than for older workers because younger workers are less skilled and tend to change jobs more frequently.

But national unemployment rates vary greatly around the world. For example, Figure 20.10 shows the unemployment rate for young men and women in their early 20s in the United States and three other countries: Australia, France, and Spain. Observe that unemployment rates are higher for both men and women in Australia, and significantly higher in France and Spain, than in the United States. The United States has had lower unemployment rates for most demographic groups than many countries in the last 20 years, though the reverse was true in the 1960s and 1970s.

There is perhaps no more important macroeconomic problem than these high unemployment rates among young people. What factors cause the differences among the countries? Will the differences persist? Will Europe's unemployment problem improve? Will the United States' unemployment rate increase?

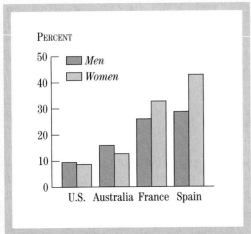

Figure 20.10
Unemployment Rates for Young Adults (ages 20–24)
Large, persistent differences are seen among different countries.

We can begin by ruling out the explanation that the differences are due to cyclical factors such as recessions. The differences in unemployment have persisted for many years through various ups and downs in the overall economy. Hence, the differences must reflect differences in the natural unemployment rate rather than cyclical differences in the countries.

Now, let's see whether the supply and demand model, augmented by rationing and job search, can explain the unemployment differences in Figure 20.10. According to the model, there are several possible explanations.

Differences in Unemployment Compensation for Young Adults

The story of job search tells us that a policy of more generous government compensation of unemployed workers leads to higher unemployment rates because unemployed workers can spend more time searching.

In fact, unemployment compensation for young adults is much greater in Australia and Spain than it is in the United States—amounting to only 10 percent of the average wage in the United States and as high as 40 percent in Australia and Spain. (Comparable data for France are not available.) Thus, this explanation of unemployment from job search theory appears to fit the facts.

Differences in Lifestyles

Suppose that for cultural or religious reasons it was more acceptable in some countries than in others for young adults to live with their parents. With their basic needs for food and shelter met, unemployed young people in these cultures might have less incentive to take any available job. Therefore, unemployment rates for young adults would tend to be higher in these countries.

Figure 20.11 shows the percentage of young adults living with their parents in the four countries in our case study. Observe from the graph that there is a strong correlation between this percentage and unemployment rates. Spain, which has the highest percentage of 20–24-year-olds living with their parents, has the highest unemployment rate in the case study. The United States is at the opposite end of the scale: lower unemployment and a lower percentage of young adults living at home.

The job-search theory again appears to be consistent with the data, but we need to worry about a reverse effect: It is possible that more young people live with their parents *because* they are unemployed.

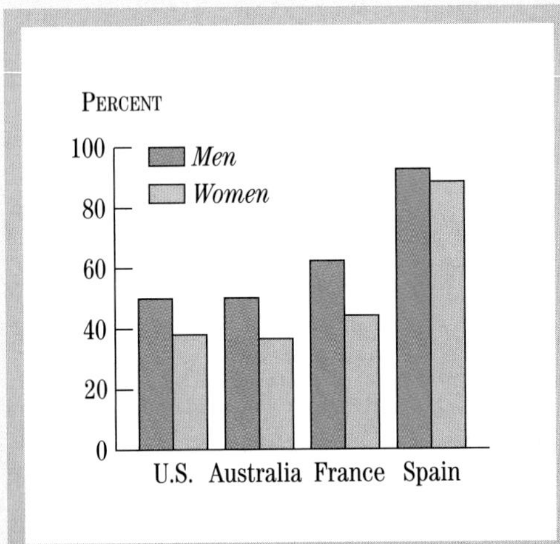

Figure 20.11
Percentage of 20–24-year-olds Still Living with Parents
Observe the close similarity with the unemployment rates for these countries in Figure 20.10.

Differences in the Minimum Wage

The supply and demand model predicts that higher minimum-wage laws would raise unemployment for younger people with low skills whose market wage was below the minimum. Minimum wages do differ across countries. Do they explain part of the differences in the unemployment rates for young people?

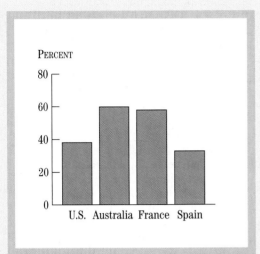

Figure 20.12
Minimum Wage as a Percentage of Average Wage
The minimum is lower in the United States than in France or Australia, but lowest in Spain.

Figure 20.12 shows the minimum wage as a percentage of the average wage in each of the four countries in our case study. The United States has a lower minimum wage than Australia and France, which suggests that this might be a reason for the lower unemployment rate in the United States.

Note that Spain also has a low minimum wage, even though it has the highest unemployment rates of the four countries. What could cause this apparent contradiction to the theory? One possibility is that the tradition of young adults living at home is so strong in Spain that it offsets the effect of the low minimum wage. In fact, lifestyle combined with the low minimum wage is a reasonable explanation for Spain's unemployment rates.

Differences in Taxes

Finally, let us consider differences in tax rates on wage income in the different countries. A higher tax rate on wages shifts the labor demand curve down, as shown in Figure 20.13, as firms find it more expensive to hire workers. Employment declines and unemployment increases.

Figure 20.14 gives the tax rates on wages for the four countries in the case study. The tax rate includes all forms of taxes on wages. Once again the theory that high taxes on labor can reduce labor demand and increase unemployment appears to be supported when one compares

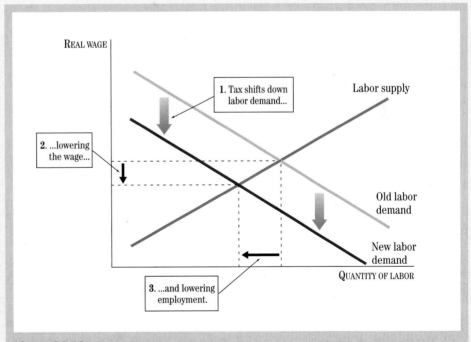

Figure 20.13
Effects of a Tax on Wages
A tax on labor lowers the labor demand curve by the amount of the tax because employers must pay more for workers. The new equilibrium has a lower wage and less employment.

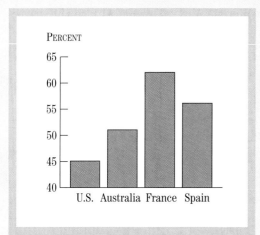

Figure 20.14
Tax Rates on Wages
The U.S. has a lower tax rate on wage income than the other three countries in the case study.

the United States, Australia, and France. And while the tax rates are higher in Spain than in Australia and the United States, they are lower than in France, meaning that some other factor, such as lifestyle differences, is needed to fully explain the very high unemployment in Spain compared to France.

Policy Implication and Forecast

In sum, the labor supply and demand model augmented with job rationing and job search provides a pretty good explanation for the international differences in unemployment rates. According to this analysis, the economic policies that would reduce unemployment among young adults in Europe include: allowing a lower minimum wage for young workers, reducing unemployment compensation, and reducing taxes (or even subsidizing employment). None of these policies would be implemented without cost to the workers, the firms that employ them, or the politicians who propose these policies. Therefore, we can predict that differences in unemployment rates in these countries will persist.

REVIEW
- Unemployment rates differ greatly across countries.
- At least in the case of young adults, the unemployment differences appear to be due to differences in unemployment compensation, lifestyle, minimum wages, and taxes.
- These explanations show the practical usefulness of the supply and demand model in understanding many, if not all, of the unemployment differences between countries.

Conclusion

Our analysis of employment and unemployment has put the spotlight on two different roles of labor. In one role, labor is simply an input to the production of real GDP. We showed that the amount of aggregate hours of all workers is the most comprehensive measure of labor input.

In its other role, labor is the people doing the work. The study of labor in this role looks at the problems people face when they lose their job, decide to enter the labor force, or take a part-time job. It also looks at the effects of minimum wages and unemployment compensation on unemployment, at the serious problems that high rates of unemployment seem to cause, and at the reasons why more women have entered the labor force in the past several decades.

KEY POINTS

1. Unemployment data are collected in the monthly Current Population Survey.

2. A person is unemployed if he or she is old enough to work and is looking for work, but does not have a job.

3. Unemployment is never zero in a market economy.

4. The employment-to-population ratio has risen in the United States during recent decades, and the average number of hours each worker works has declined.

5. Aggregate hours of work by all workers is the most comprehensive measure of labor input to production of real GDP.

6. People are unemployed for four reasons: They have lost their job, they have quit their job, they have entered the labor force for the first time, or they have re-entered the labor force.

7. The labor supply and demand model can be used to explain trends in employment in the economy.

8. Unemployment can be explained by both job rationing, in which the wage is too high to equate supply and demand, and job search, in which unemployed people look for work.

9. Economic policies, such as exemptions for teenagers from the minimum-wage laws, time limits on unemployment compensation, or the provision of information about job openings to reduce job-search time, can reduce the natural unemployment rate.

KEY TERMS

natural unemployment rate
cyclical unemployment
frictional unemployment
structural unemployment
labor force

working-age population
labor force participation rate
employment-to-population ratio

aggregate hours
job vacancies
labor demand curve
labor supply curve
job rationing

job search
insider
outsider
efficiency wage

QUESTIONS FOR REVIEW

1. How do economists define unemployment, and how do they measure how many people are unemployed?

2. How is the working-age population defined?

3. What is the definition of the labor force?

4. What has happened to the employment-to-population ratio for men and women since the 1950s?

5. What is the difference between frictional and structural unemployment?

6. Why isn't the unemployment rate equal to zero?

7. What fraction of unemployment is due to job loss, job quits, and new entrants and re-entrants?

8. What is the difference between unemployment due to job rationing and unemployment due to job search?

9. What three economic policies would reduce the natural rate of unemployment?

PROBLEMS

1. Which of the following people would be unemployed according to official statistics? Which ones would *you* define as unemployed? Why?
   a. A person who is home painting the house while seeking a permanent position as an electrician
   b. A full-time student

   c. A recent graduate who is looking for a job
   d. A parent who decides to stay home taking care of children full time
   e. A worker who quits his job because he thinks the pay is insufficient
   f. A teenager who gets discouraged looking for work and stops looking

2. The table below shows the demand for and supply of skilled labor at different hourly wages.

Demand for Labor		Supply of Labor	
Wage/Hour	*Quantity*	*Wage/Hour*	*Quantity*
$12	75	$12	47
14	68	14	54
16	61	16	61
18	54	18	68
20	47	20	75
22	40	22	82

   a. Draw the supply and demand curves for labor.
   b. What are the wage and quantity of labor at equilibrium?
   c. Suppose a law is passed forbidding employers to pay wages less than $20 per hour. What will the new quantity of labor in the market be? Who gains and who loses from this law?

3. a. Suppose the government decides to eliminate the minimum wage. What is likely to happen to the wages of unskilled workers in an area where the cost of living is very low? What is likely to happen to the wages of highly skilled computer programmers? Will this change in government policy reduce unemployment? Why or why not?

   b. Now suppose instead that the government changes unemployment benefits so that they end after two weeks. What is likely to happen to the unemployment rate? Will this change in government policy lead to an increase in labor productivity? Why or why not?

4. Job search and advertising are now on the Internet. Using e-mail, job applicants can submit résumés to prospective employers. One popular web site of this kind is www.hotjobs.com.

   a. How should this service affect the unemployment rate?

   b. Suppose everybody in the working-age population has access to hotjobs.com. Would you expect unemployment to be eliminated? Explain.

5. Suppose you own and run a bicycle repair shop with several employees. You decide to use your facilities at home to manage your business rather than hang around the bike shop while you do the books. You are surprised to discover that the productivity of your business falls. What happened? If you decide to keep your office at home, what will you have to do to increase the productivity of your business back to its previous level? If this same phenomenon is true of all businesses, then why may there be job rationing?

6. Use a supply and demand diagram to show the possible reduction in teenage unemployment from a lower minimum "training" wage for workers under 20 years of age. For what reasons might older unskilled workers complain about such a policy?

7. Use the theories of job rationing and job search to try to explain why the natural rate of unemployment in the United States is below that in France. What can the French government do to try to remedy this situation? Might these remedies be politically unpopular?

8. Suppose that the unemployment rate is 4 percent.

   a. If the working-age population is 205 million and the total labor force is 135 million, how many people are unemployed?

   b. What is the labor force participation rate?

   c. What is the employment-to-population ratio?

9. What effect would a decline in part-time employment have on average weekly hours per worker in the United States? If the employment-to-population ratio increases, what will happen to total hours of work in the United States?

10. Show that employment in the economy is equal to the working-age population times the labor force participation rate times (1 minus the unemployment rate) when both rates are measured as fractions. Use this equation to fill in the table below, which gives historical data for the United States. Calculate the 1950 employment-to-population ratio and compare it with the figures given in Figure 20.2. If the employment-to-population ratio for December 2004 had been the same as in 1950, what would total employment have been in December 2004?

11. The total employment in the economy is equal to the working-age population times (1 minus the unemployment rate) times the labor force participation rate.

   a. Using the data, fill in the table on the next page, showing how many employed people there were in the United States at the turn of each decade.

Problem 10

Year	Total Employment (millions)	Unemployment Rate (percent)	Labor Force Participation Rate (percent)	Working-Age Population (millions)
1950		5.2	59.7	106.2
1960	67.6	5.4	60.0	
1970	80.8		61.0	139.2

Source: U.S. Department of Labor.

b. Suppose the projection for the working-age population in the year 2020 for the United States is 265 million. If the unemployment rate and the labor force participation rate are the same in 2020 as they were in 2000, how much employment will there be?

c. Using the same projection of 265 million for the working-age population in 2020, calculate employment with an unemployment rate of 5 percent and a labor force participation rate of 60 percent. Do the same for a labor force participation rate of 70 percent. Which of these estimates do you think is more realistic? Why?

12. The age distribution of the population changes over time—in the United States, better health care and smaller family size in recent years means that there are increasingly larger proportions of people over age 16. At the same time, there is likely to be a decline in the labor force participation rate as baby boomers retire. Using the same method as in the previous question, calculate total employment and the employment-to-population ratio based on the scenario in the table below.

a. Describe what happens to total employment and the employment-to-population ratio in this scenario.

b. Is it possible that labor force participation would fall so much that total employment falls? How low would the labor force participation rate have to be in 2020 for total employment to be lower than in 2000?

Problem 11

Year	Total Employment (millions)	Unemployment Rate (percent)	Labor Force Participation Rate (percent)	Working-Age Population (millions)
1980		7.2	63.6	168.9
1990		6.3	66.4	190.0
2000		3.9	67.0	213.7

Source: U.S. Department of Labor.

Problem 12

Year	Unemployment Rate (percent)	Labor Force Participation Rate (percent)	Working-Age Population (millions)	Total Employment (millions)	Employment-to-Working-Age-Population Ratio
2000	3.9	67.0	214		
2010	5.0	64.0	240		
2020	5.0	62.0	265		

Source: U.S. Department of Labor.

CHAPTER 21

Productivity and Economic Growth

For most of human history, there was no economic growth. True, vast quantities of wealth were amassed by kings and queens through conquest and exploitation; coliseums, pyramids, and great walls were constructed by millions of slaves; and great works of art were produced by talented individuals of all continents. But output per hour of work—the productive power of labor that determines the well-being of most people—grew hardly at all for thousands of years. Except for the ruling classes, people lived in extreme poverty.

This situation changed dramatically around the eighteenth century. Figure 21.1 shows the growth rates of *output per hour of work,* or **productivity,** for different periods during the last 300 years. Observe that there was almost no growth in output per hour of work for most of the 1700s, much as in the thousands of years before. Then, in the late 1700s and early 1800s—the period historians call the Industrial Revolution—economic growth began to pick up. Growth accelerated in the early 1800s and then rose to historically unprecedented levels in the twentieth century.

The increase in economic growth during the last 200 years has taken the average person's income in the advanced countries to a level never dreamed of in antiquity, except by the richest emperors and empresses.

Why did the growth of real GDP per hour of work begin to increase and then take off in the eighteenth century? The purpose of this chapter is to develop a theory of economic growth that helps answer this and many other questions.

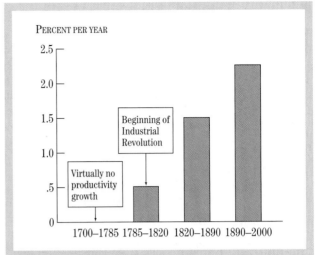

PERCENT PER YEAR

Figure 21.1
Productivity Growth During the Past 300 Years
Productivity is defined as output per hour of work. Productivity *growth* is defined as the percentage increase in productivity from one year to the next. The bars indicate the average productivity growth during the years stated.

The Role of Technology in Economic Growth
In today's highly automated world, the image (top) of women in long skirts packing fruit delicacies into glass jars in the mid to late 1800s seems quaint beside the image (bottom) of robotic arms in an assembly line at this modern-day car plant. Yet both represent huge leaps in industrial productivity at different periods of history. Capital and technology played critical roles in the development of each of these increasingly more efficient methods of production.

productivity: output per hour of work.

The theory of economic growth tells us that increases in labor can increase the growth of real GDP, but not the growth of real GDP per hour of work. To explain the growth of productivity, we must focus on the two other factors: capital and technology. Capital raises real GDP per hour of work by giving workers more tools and equipment to work with. Increasing the investment share of GDP will increase the growth of capital. However, as we will show in this chapter, capital alone is not sufficient to achieve the growth we have seen over the past 200 years. Technology—the knowledge and methods that underlie the production process—must also have played a big role.

Understanding the role of technology enables economists to better evaluate the advantages and disadvantages of various economic policies to improve economic growth. For example, should economic policies designed to stimulate economic growth focus more on capital or more on technology? Perhaps the most promising feature of the recent U.S. economy is an increase in productivity growth that began in the mid-1990s after nearly 25 years of relatively slow productivity growth. The right economic policies regarding technology might go a long way toward maintaining or even increasing this productivity growth rate.

551

Labor and Capital Without Technology

To prove that technology must have played a key role in the economic growth of the past two centuries, we consider a theory of economic growth that omits technology. We start with a simplified theory in which real GDP depends only on labor. That is, the amount of output in the economy can be described by the production function $Y = F(L)$, where Y is real GDP and L is labor input. When labor input increases, real GDP increases.

The proof that technology must have been a quantitatively important influence on economic growth goes as follows: First, we show that the theory with labor alone is too limited to explain growth. Second, we add capital and show that although the theory begins to look promising, it still fails to explain growth. The implication is that we need technology in order to grow.

The theory without capital is actually very close to the economic theory used by Thomas Robert Malthus to make pessimistic predictions about economic growth in his famous *Essay on the Principle of Population,* published in 1798. Let's see why the predictions were so pessimistic.

Labor Alone

First, consider the production of a single good. Imagine workers on a one-acre vineyard planting, maintaining, and harvesting grapes, and suppose that the only input that can be varied is labor. With more workers, the vineyard can produce more goods, but according to the simple story that output depends only on labor, the vineyard cannot increase capital because there is no capital. For example, the vineyard cannot buy wagons or wheelbarrows to haul fertilizer around. The only way the vineyard can increase output is by hiring more workers to haul the fertilizer.

Now, suppose all this is true for the economy as a whole. The firms in the economy can produce more output by hiring more workers, but they cannot increase capital. The situation is shown for the entire economy in Figure 21.2. On the vertical axis is output. On the horizontal axis is labor input. The curve shows that more labor can produce more output. The curve is a graphical plot of the aggregate production function $Y = F(L)$ for the whole economy.

diminishing returns: a situation in which successive increases in the use of an input, holding other inputs constant, will eventually cause a decline in the additional production derived from one more unit of that input.

■ **Diminishing Returns to Labor.** The slope of the curve in Figure 21.2 is important. The flattening out of the curve shows that there are **diminishing returns** to labor: The greater the number of workers used in producing output, the less the additional output that comes from each additional worker. Why? Consider production of a single good again, such as grapes at the vineyard. Increasing employment at the one-acre vineyard from one to two workers raises production more than increasing employment from 1,001 to 1,002 workers. A second worker could take charge of irrigation or inspect the vines for insects while the first worker harvested grapes. But with 1,001 workers on the vineyard, the 1,002nd worker could find little to do to raise production. Diminishing returns to labor exist because labor is the only input to production that we are changing. As more workers are employed on the same one-acre plot, the contribution that each additional worker makes goes down. Adding one worker when only one worker is employed can increase production by a large amount. But adding one worker when there are already 1,001 on the one-acre plot cannot add as much! For the same reasons, diminishing returns to labor exist for the whole economy.

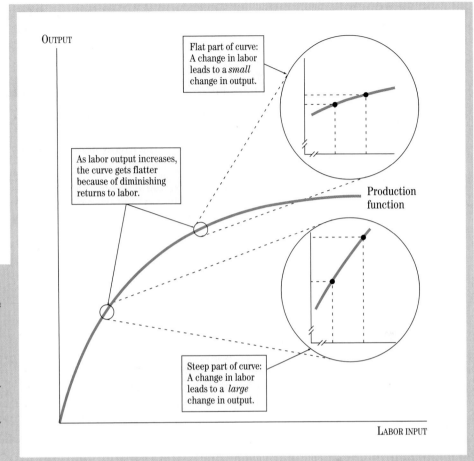

Figure 21.2
A Theory in Which Only Changes in Labor Can Change Output
The curve shows the production function $Y = F(L)$, where Y is output and L is labor input (hours of work). In this theory, capital and technology are out of the picture. With more labor working on a fixed supply of land, there are diminishing returns, as shown by the curvature of the production function.

When early economists, such as Malthus, wrote about economics in the late eighteenth and early nineteenth centuries, agriculture was a large part of the economy, employing more than 75 percent of all workers, compared with about 2 percent in the United States today. Farm product and gross domestic product were almost the same thing. Hence, agricultural examples such as the preceding one were very fitting. Although the amount of farmland could be increased somewhat by clearing more forests, the number of acres of land available for producing farm goods was limited, especially in England, where many early economists lived. It was not so unrealistic for them to think of labor as the only input to production that could be increased. Moreover, they saw only small improvements in farming methods in Europe for thousands of years, so they can be excused for underestimating the effects of capital and technology on output when they developed their economic theories.

Real GDP per worker was just beginning to grow rapidly as Malthus wrote (see Figure 21.1). As this growth continued, it gradually became clear that his dismal predictions that real GDP would gravitate toward the subsistence level of output were not coming true in England or in the other countries about which he wrote. The population was expanding, rather than stabilizing. Hence, Malthus turned out to be wrong.

To be sure, starvation has not disappeared from the planet. Population growth in the underdeveloped parts of the world has frequently faced limited food supplies, resulting in situations like those depicted by Malthus. But since the problems of less-developed countries have occurred alongside a remarkable fiftyfold increase in living standards in the advanced countries, history suggests that there are non-Malthusian explanations for the persistent poverty observed in many less-developed countries.

Labor and Capital Alone

Now let us add capital to the growth theory. The total amount of capital in the economy increases each year by the amount of net investment during the year. More precisely,

Capital at the end = net investment + capital at the end
of this year   during this year   of last year

> Recall that net investment is equal to gross investment less depreciation (p. 490). Depreciation is the amount of capital that wears out each year.

For example, if $10,000 billion is the value of all capital in the economy at the end of last year, then $100 billion of net investment during this year would raise the capital stock to $10,100 billion by the end of this year. This is a 1 percent increase in the capital stock.

With capital as an input to production, the production function becomes $Y = F(L, K)$, where K stands for capital. Output can be increased by using more capital, even if the amount of labor is not increased. Consider the vineyard example again. If a wheelbarrow is bought to haul the fertilizer around the vineyard, the vineyard can produce more grapes with the same number of workers. More capital at the vineyard increases output. The same is true for the economy as a whole. By increasing the amount of capital in the economy, more real GDP can be produced with the same number of workers.

Figure 21.3 illustrates how more capital raises output. The axes are the same as those in Figure 21.2, and the curve again shows that more output can be produced by more labor. But, in addition, Figure 21.3 shows that if we add capital to the econ-

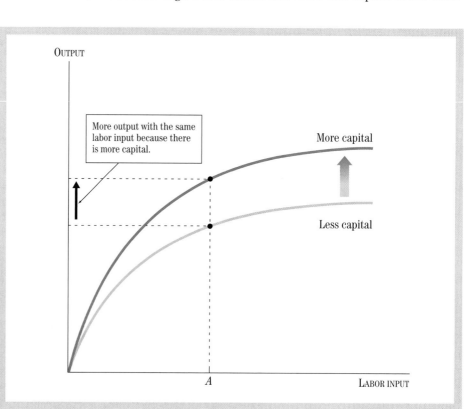

Figure 21.3
Capital Becomes a Factor of Production
The axes are just like those in Figure 21.2, but now if more capital is added to production, more output can be produced with the same labor input. For example, when labor input is at point *A*, more output can be produced with more capital.

More output with the same labor input because there is more capital.

More capital

Less capital

omy—by investing a certain amount each year—the relationship between output and labor shifts up: More capital provides more output at any level of labor input. To see this, pick a point on the horizontal axis, say, point *A,* to designate a certain amount of labor input. Then draw a vertical line up from this point, such as the dashed line shown. The vertical distance between the curve marked "less capital" and the curve marked "more capital" shows that additional capital raises production.

■ **Diminishing Returns to Capital.** However, the addition of capital to the theory does not solve everything. If labor has diminishing returns, why would not capital? Figure 21.4 shows that there are *diminishing returns to capital* too. Each additional amount of capital—another wheelbarrow or another hoe—results in a smaller addition to output. Hence, the gaps between the several production functions in Figure 21.4 get smaller and smaller as more capital is added. As more capital is added, there is less ability to increase output per worker. Compare adding one wheelbarrow to the vineyard when there is already one with adding one wheelbarrow when there are already fifty. Clearly, the fifty-first wheelbarrow would increase farm output by only a minuscule amount, certainly much less than the second wheelbarrow. With a one-acre vineyard, there would not even be much room for the fifty-first wheelbarrow!

Diminishing returns to capital also occur for the economy as a whole. Thus, adding more capital per worker cannot raise real GDP per worker above some limit, and even getting close to that limit will require an enormous amount of capital. Investment would have to be such a large share of GDP that there would be little left for anything else. Thus, even with capital, the model yields a very pessimistic conclusion—not as devastating as Malthus's prediction, but not nearly as optimistic as the

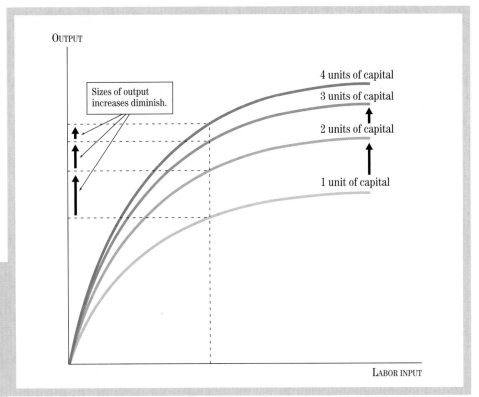

Figure 21.4
Capital Has Diminishing Returns Also
As capital per worker increases, each additional unit of capital produces less output. Thus, there is a limit to how much growth per worker additional capital per worker can bring.

fiftyfold (and still counting) gain in productivity that we have observed. Eventually, growth in output per hour of work would stop.

Thus, labor and capital alone cannot explain the phenomenal growth in either farm output or real GDP during the last 200 years.

REVIEW
- An economic growth theory with labor alone cannot account for the sustained increase in real GDP per hour of work that began in the late 1700s and continues today. Under such a theory, production would remain at subsistence levels.

- Adding capital to the theory can explain why real GDP can remain far above subsistence levels indefinitely, even with the population growing at a steady rate. However, it cannot explain the sustained *increases* in real GDP per hour of work that we have observed.

Technology: The Engine of Growth

We have seen that growth driven by increases in capital and labor, while important, is not sustainable. Diminishing returns imply that the additional output obtained by increasing these inputs becomes smaller and smaller, eventually leading to no further economic growth. In order for output to grow over the very long run, we need not just to add *more* inputs, but also to get more output from *existing* inputs. Technology is what enables us to get more output from a given quantity of inputs.

What Is Technology?

technology: anything that raises the amount of output that can be produced with a given amount of labor and capital. (Ch. 17)

Technology is very difficult to define, envision, and measure. A broad definition of **technology** is that it is anything that raises the amount of output that can be produced with a given amount of inputs (labor and capital). In essence, technology is the stock of knowledge or ideas that exist in an economy: the ideas that help produce goods and services such as baby food, wine, laser light shows, and satellite television; the ideas that help save lives, such as penicillin, vaccines, and heart transplants; and the ideas that help us travel all over the world and beyond, such as the jetliner and the space shuttle.

When we add technology to capital and labor, we have the modern theory of economic growth. The theory can be summarized by the now familiar aggregate production function

$$Y = F(L, K, T)$$

technological change: improvement in technology over time.

where T stands for technology. Increases in technology will therefore increase output. Such increases in technology are termed technological progress. Since technology is usually increasing over time, we sometimes use the term **technological change** instead of technological progress.

■ **Invention, Innovation, and Diffusion.** Technological change occurs when new ideas are developed into new products that increase production, such as the steel plow, the harvester, the combine, the automobile, radar, the telephone, the computer, the airplane, lasers, and fiber-optic cable. Economists distinguish between

Examples of Changes in Technology That Increased Output
Replacing horse-drawn tractors (on the left) with steam-powered tractors (in the center) is an example of a change in technology that increased output per worker. Another example is the introduction of computer technology for maintenance scheduling or ordering spare tractor parts on the Internet. What other advances in technology have increased farm output?

invention: a discovery of new knowledge.

innovation: application of new knowledge in a way that creates new products or significantly changes old ones.

diffusion: the spreading of an innovation throughout the economy.

an **invention,** which is the discovery of new knowledge or a new principle, such as electricity, and **innovation,** in which the new knowledge is brought into application with a new product, such as the electric light bulb. Economists also distinguish between the innovation itself and the **diffusion** of the innovation throughout the economy, a process that involves advertising, marketing, and spreading the innovation to new uses, such as the use of the electric light bulb to create night shifts in factories.

Thus, technology is much more than scientific knowledge. The discovery of DNA did not improve technology until it was applied to genetic engineering. The knowledge of mathematics made possible the invention and development of computers in the 1940s, a technology that has obviously improved productivity. Technology depends in part on scientific knowledge, and many people feel that science will become more and more important in future technological change.

The sewing machine is a good illustration of invention, innovation, and diffusion. In 1847, "17 machines capable of mechanically forming a stitch had been invented," according to Ross Thompson, an economic historian. But only one of these, Elias Howe's sewing machine, developed into a commercially successful innovation. A Boston machinist turned entrepreneur, Howe tried to sell his invention. As he did so, he and others found out how to modify the invention to make it more useful and attractive to potential buyers. Soon the invention turned into a popular innovation that was used widely. Wide diffusion of the innovation occurred as others produced household versions of the sewing machine, like the one marketed by the Singer Company. This story also illustrates that innovation and diffusion usually require the work of an entrepreneur who recognizes the potential of the invention.

■ **Organization and Specialization.** Technology also includes the way firms are organized. Better organization schemes can mean a smaller bureaucracy and more output per hour of work without the addition of capital. More efficient organization can improve the flow of information within a firm and thereby affect labor productivity. Better incentive programs that encourage workers to communicate their ideas to management, for example, increase productivity.

Henry Ford's idea of the assembly line greatly increased the productivity of workers. The assembly line enabled the car to come to the worker rather than having the worker go to the car. Thus, each worker could specialize in a certain type of activity; through specialization, productivity increased. The assembly line alone is estimated to have reduced the time it took a group of workers to produce a car from $12\frac{1}{2}$ hours to $\frac{1}{2}$ hour. Productivity increased, and so did wages.

New technology can affect how labor and capital are used at a firm. Economists distinguish between *labor-saving* and *capital-saving* technological change. *Labor-saving technological change* means that fewer workers are needed to produce the same amount of output; *capital-saving technological change* means that fewer machines are needed to produce the same amount of output. An example of a labor-saving technological change would be a steam-powered tractor replacing a horse-drawn plow, and later gasoline power replacing steam power, enabling the same worker to plow many more acres. An example of a capital-saving technological change is the night shift. Adding two crews of workers—one working in a steel mill from 4 P.M. to midnight and another working from midnight to 8 A.M.—makes the same steel-making furnaces three times as productive as when the working hours are only from 8 A.M. to 4 P.M.

Specialization of workers at a firm adds to productivity. Adam Smith emphasized the importance of specialization in his *Wealth of Nations;* his phrase *division of labor* refers to the way a manufacturing task could be divided up among a group of workers, each of whom would specialize in a part of the job.

Because specialization permits workers to repeat the same task many times, their productivity increases, as in the old adage "practice makes perfect." Each time the task is repeated, the worker becomes more proficient—a phenomenon economists call **learning by doing.** The commonsense principle of learning by doing is that the more one does something, the more one learns about how to do it. For example, as the number of airplanes produced of a particular type—say, a Boeing 777—increases, the workers become more and more skilled at producing that type of airplane. Careful studies of aircraft production have shown that productivity increases by 20 percent for each 100 percent increase in output of a particular type of plane. This relationship between learning and the amount of production is commonly called the "learning curve." Learning is a type of technological progress.

learning by doing: a situation in which workers become more proficient by doing a particular task many times.

■ **Human Capital.**   Many firms provide training courses for workers to increase their skills and their productivity. *On-the-job training* is a catchall term for any education, training, or skills a worker receives while at work.

Most workers receive much of their education and training before they begin working, whether in grade school, high school, college, or professional schools. Because increases in education and training can raise workers' productivity, such increases are considered another source of technological change.

The education and training of workers, called *human capital* by economists, is similar to physical capital—factories and equipment. In order to accumulate human capital—to become more educated or better trained—people must devote time and resources, much as a firm must devote resources to investment if physical capital is to increase.

human capital: a person's accumulated knowledge and skills. (Ch. 13)

The decision to invest in human capital is influenced by considerations similar to those that motivate a firm to invest in physical capital: the cost of the investment versus the expected return. For example, investing in a college education may require that one borrow the money for tuition; if the interest rate on the loan rises, then people will be less likely to invest in a college education. Thus, investment in education may be negatively related to the interest rate, much as physical investment is. This is one reason why, in order to encourage more education and thereby increase economic growth and productivity, the U.S. government provides low-interest loans to college students, making an investment in college more attractive. We will return to the government's role in education as part of its broader policy to increase economic growth later in the chapter.

The Production of Technology: The Invention Factory

Technology is sometimes discovered by chance by a lone inventor and sometimes by trial and error by an individual worker. A secretary who experiments with several different filing systems to reduce search time or with different locations for the computer, the printer, the telephone, and the photocopier is engaged in improving technology around the office. Frequently, technological progress is a continuous process in which a small adjustment here and a small adjustment there add up to major improvements over time.

But more and more technological change is the result of huge expenditures of research and development funds by industry and government. Thomas Edison's "invention factory" in Menlo Park, New Jersey, was one of the first examples of a large industrial laboratory devoted to the production of technology. It in turn influenced the development of many other labs, such as the David Sarnoff research lab of RCA. Merck & Co., a drug company, spends nearly $1 billion per year on research and development for the production of new technology.

Edison's Menlo Park laboratory had about 25 technicians working in three or four different buildings. In the six years from 1876 to 1882, the laboratory invented the light bulb, the phonograph, the telephone transmitter, and electrical generators. Each of these inventions turned out to be a successful innovation that was diffused widely. For each innovation, a *patent* was granted by the federal government. A patent indicates that the invention is original and gives the inventor the exclusive right to use it until the patent expires. In order to obtain a patent on the rights to an invention, an inventor must apply to the Patent and Trademark Office of the federal government. Patents give inventors an inducement to invent. The number of patents granted is an indicator of how much technological progress is going on. Edison obtained patents at a pace of about 67 a year at his lab.

Two Invention Factories: Past and Present
The amount of technology produced at Thomas Edison's invention factory (left) or at the research lab of a modern biotechnology firm like Cetus (right) can be explained by the laws of supply and demand. But how is technology different from most other goods? If one person uses more technology, is there just as much available for others to use?

Edison's invention factory required both labor and capital input, much like factories producing other commodities. The workers in such laboratories are highly skilled, with knowledge obtained through formal schooling or on-the-job training—human capital. A highly trained work force is an important prerequisite to the production of technology.

The supply of technology—the output of Edison's invention factory, for example—depends on the cost of producing the new technology, which must include the great risk that little or nothing will be invented, and the benefits from the new technology: how much Edison can charge for the rights to use his techniques for making light bulbs. Often inventive activity has changed as a result of shifts in the economy that change the costs and benefits. For example, increases in textile workers' wages stimulated the invention of textile machines, because such machines yielded greater profits by enabling the production of more output with fewer workers.

Special Features of the Technology Market

When viewed as a commodity that can be produced, technology has two special qualities that affect how much will be produced. The first is *nonrivalry*. This means that one person's use of the technology does not reduce the amount that another person can use. If one university uses the same book-filing system as another university, that does not reduce the quality of the first university's system. In contrast, most goods are rivals in consumption: If you drink a bottle of Coke, there is one fewer bottle of Coke around for other people to drink.

The second feature of technology is *nonexcludability*. This means that the inventor or the owner of the technology cannot exclude other people from using it. For example, the system software for Apple computers shows a series of logos and pull-down menus that can be moved around the screen with a mouse. The idea could easily be adapted for use in other software programs by other companies. In fact, the Windows program of Microsoft has features similar to those of the Apple software, but according to the court that ruled on Apple's complaint that Microsoft was illegally copying, the features were not so similar that Microsoft could not use them. Examples of rival, nonrival, excludable, and nonexcludable goods are given in Table 21.1.

As the example of Apple and Microsoft shows, the legal system and the enforcement of *intellectual property laws* determine in part the degree of nonexcludability. Intellectual property laws provide for trademarks and copyrights as well as patents. These laws help inventors exclude others from using their inventions without compensation. But it is impossible to exclude others from using much technology.

Thus, technology may *spill over* from one activity to another. If your economics teacher invents a new way to teach economics on a computer, it might spill over to your chemistry teacher, who sees how the technology can be applied to a different

Table 21.1
Classification of Goods and Services According to Rivalry and Excludability

	Rival	Nonrival
Excludable	Pencil CD player with headphones	Movie theater The opera
Nonexcludable	Swing in a public park Book in a public library	Fireworks on the Fourth of July Network television

subject. Sometimes spillovers occur because research personnel move from one firm to another. Henry Ford knew Thomas Edison and was stimulated to experiment on internal-combustion engines by Edison. Hence, Edison's research spilled over to another industry, but Edison would have found it very difficult to get compensation from Henry Ford even if he had wanted to.

Because inventors cannot be fully compensated for the benefits their ideas provide to others, they may produce too little technology. The private incentives to invent are less than the gain to society from the inventions. If the incentives were higher—say, through government subsidies to research and development—more inventions might be produced. Thus, there is a potential role for government in providing funds for research and development, both in industry and at universities. Before we consider this role, we must examine how to measure technological change in the economy as a whole.

REVIEW

- Technological change has a very broad definition. It is anything that increases production for a given level of labor and capital. Technological change has been an essential ingredient in the increase in the growth of real GDP per hour of work in the last 200 years.

- Technology can be improved by the education and training of workers—investment in human capital. Technology can also be improved through inventions produced in "invention factories" or industrial research laboratories, as well as by trial and error. In any case, the level of technology is determined by market forces.

- But technology exhibits nonrivalry in consumption and a high degree of nonexcludability. These are precisely the conditions in which there will be an underproduction of technology.

Measuring Technology

Both technology and capital cause productivity—real GDP per hour of work—to grow. Is it possible to determine how much productivity growth has been due to technology, as distinct from capital? Surprisingly, the answer is yes. A significant modern development in economics is the discovery and application of a technique to measure how important capital and technology each is for productivity growth in the economy. Robert Solow of MIT made the pioneering contribution and won the Nobel Prize for his innovation. In 1957 he published a paper that contained a simple mathematical formula. It is this formula—called the **growth accounting formula**—that enables economists to estimate the relative contributions of capital and technology.

growth accounting formula: an equation that states that the growth rate of productivity equals capital's share of income times the growth rate of capital per hour of work plus the growth rate of technology.

The Formula and Its Coefficient

The growth accounting formula is remarkably simple. It can be written as follows:

$$\text{Growth rate of productivity} = \frac{1}{3}\left(\begin{array}{c}\text{growth rate of capital} \\ \text{per hour of work}\end{array}\right) + \begin{array}{c}\text{growth rate} \\ \text{of technology}\end{array}$$

A Formula Goes to Washington

In 1957, when Robert Solow first published the growth accounting formula, it was of course a new idea. He therefore had to explain it in very simple terms if it was to have any impact. He presented the idea graphically, and it caught on quickly. By the early 1960s, he was being called to Washington to apply the ideas at President Kennedy's Council of Economic Advisers. The graphical approach is still used today. Here is how it works:

The growth accounting formula divides the growth of productivity into two sources: the growth of capital per hour of work and the growth of technological change. The figure on the left below explains this dissection graphically through the familiar distinction between shifts of and movements along the curves. The figure shows the relationship between productivity (Y/L) and capital per hour of work (K/L). More capital per hour leads to more output per hour, as shown by the purple curves in the figure. Technological change shifts the purple curve up because, by definition, technological change is anything that raises productivity for a given level of capital per hour of work.

The purple curves in the figure are much like a production function, except that productivity (Y/L), rather than output (Y), is what is being explained. Hence, we call each purple curve in the figure a *productivity curve.* The production function and the productivity curve are perfectly compatible with each other, but one focuses on output and the other on output per hour of work. Actual productivity increases in the economy are due to a combination of *movements along* the productivity

curve, because of more capital per hour, and *shifts of* the productivity curve, because of technological change. The purpose of the growth accounting formula is to determine how much of the increase is due to movement along the curve and how much is due to a shift of the curve. This is illustrated by two observations on productivity and capital per hour in two different years (year 1 and year 2). Observe how the increase in productivity from year 1 to year 2 is due partly to an upward shift of the productivity curve and partly to a movement along the curve.

This graphical approach can be applied in practice, as shown in the graph on the lower right. This graph focuses on the upper portion of three U.S. productivity curves corresponding to the three years 1955, 1975, and 1995 (the lower portions have been cut away for better visibility).

Observe on the vertical axis that productivity increased by a smaller percentage from 1975 to 1995 than it did from 1955 to 1975. Observe also that the curve shifted up by a much smaller amount from 1975 to 1995 than it did from 1955 to 1975. In fact, the decline in productivity growth from the earlier to the later period was almost entirely due to a smaller shift in the curve rather than to a smaller percentage increase in capital per hour of work. Once again, the role of technology is significant.

The case study later in this chapter shows that there has been an increase in productivity growth since 1995. Can you guess what it has mostly been due to?

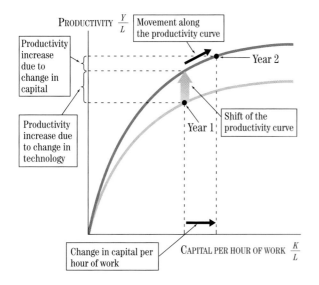

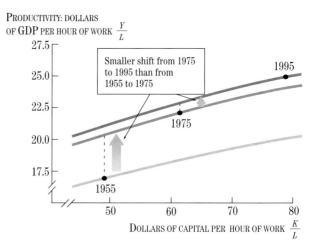

The two ingredients in the growth of productivity—the growth of *capital* and the growth of *technology*—are apparent in the formula. The growth accounting formula allows us to measure the importance of these two ingredients.

The growth accounting formula can be derived from the aggregate production function. The box on the next page contains a brief graphical explanation of the derivation.

It is important to know why the growth rate of capital per hour of work is multiplied by a coefficient that is less than one, or only 1/3 in the preceding formula. The simplest reason is that economists view the production function for the economy as one in which output rises by only 1/3 of the percentage by which capital increases. For example, a vineyard owner can estimate by what percent grape output will rise if the workers have more wheelbarrows to work with. If the number of wheelbarrows at the vineyard is increased by 100 percent and if the 1/3 coefficient applies to the vineyard, then grape production per hour of work will increase by 33 percent. In other words, this is a property of the grape production function. Statistical studies suggest that the 1/3 coefficient seems to apply to the production function for the economy as a whole.

Another reason for the 1/3 coefficient on capital growth relies on the basic principle of economics that inputs to production receive income according to their contribution to production. If you look back at Table 18.3, you will find that capital income (including depreciation) totaled $4,206 billion, which is about 1/3 of aggregate income ($11,735 billion). This provides statistical support for the 1/3 coefficient.

We should not give the impression, however, that economists know the coefficient on capital growth in the growth accounting formula with much precision. There is uncertainty about its size. It could be 1/4 or even 5/12. In any case, the growth accounting formula is a helpful rule of thumb to assist policymakers in deciding what emphasis to place on capital versus technology when developing programs to stimulate economic growth.

Using the Formula

Here is how the formula works. The growth rates of productivity and capital per hour of work are readily determined from available data sources in most countries. Using the formula, we can express the growth rate of technology.

$$\text{Growth rate of technology} = \text{growth rate of productivity} - \frac{1}{3}\left(\begin{array}{c}\text{growth rate of capital} \\ \text{per hour of work}\end{array}\right)$$

Thus, the growth rate of technology can be determined by subtracting 1/3 times the growth rate of capital per hour of work from the growth rate of real GDP per hour of work.

Consider an example. Suppose the growth rate of real GDP per hour of work is 2 percent per year. Suppose also that the growth rate of capital per hour of work is 3 percent per year. Then the growth rate of technology must be 1 percent per year: $2 - (1/3 \times 3) = 1$. Thus, one-half of the growth of productivity is due to technological change and one-half to growth of capital per hour of work.

REVIEW

- The growth accounting formula shows explicitly how productivity growth depends on the growth of capital per hour of work and on the growth of technology.

- Using the growth accounting formula along with data on productivity and capital, one can calculate the contribution of technology to economic growth.

Growth Accounting in Practice

Let us now examine what the growth accounting formula tells us about the importance of technology for economic growth.

The 1970s Productivity Growth Slowdown

Table 21.2 shows productivity growth in the United States for three different periods. It also shows the amount of this productivity growth that is due to the growth of capital and the growth of technology. The table was computed using the growth accounting formula.

If you compare the first two rows of the table, you can see that productivity growth slowed down in the 1970s, from 2.5 percent per year to only 1.2 percent per year. This slowdown was a major concern of policymakers during this period. At first, policymakers were slow to recognize it. When statisticians at the Bureau of Labor Statistics first reported the slowdown in the mid-1970s, many people thought that it was probably temporary and that productivity growth would soon rebound. Instead, productivity continued to grow slowly for nearly 20 years.

What was the reason for the slowdown? The growth accounting formula helps answer the question. According to the formula, both the growth of capital and the growth of technology slowed down. But the slowdown in the growth of technology was larger. Technology growth fell by .8 percentage point from the 1956–1975 period to the 1976–1995 period, while capital growth fell by .5 percentage point. This suggested that a greater focus on policies to stimulate technological change and education would be appropriate.

The 1990s Rebound and the New Economy

After remaining low for nearly a generation, productivity growth finally started to pick up again in the mid-1990s. The last row of Table 21.2 shows this rebound in productivity growth. In the second half of the 1990s and the first half of the 2000s, productivity growth rose to 2.9 percent—more than it was before the slowdown. Was capital or technology the main reason for the rebound? According to the growth accounting formula, technology growth surged from 1996 to 2003, contributing twice as much as capital.

Check the numbers in the table to make sure the formula was used correctly:

        2.5 = 1.1 + 1.4
        1.2 = .6 + .6
        2.9 = .9 + 2.0

So they check.

Table 21.2
Accounting for the 1970s Productivity Slowdown and the 1990s Productivity Rebound

Period	(1) Productivity Growth	(2) 1/3 Growth Rate of Capital per Hour of Work	(3) Technology Growth
1956–1975	2.5	1.1	1.4
1976–1995	1.2	.6	.6
1996–2003	2.9	.9	2.0

Source: Bureau of Labor Statistics, and Stephen Oliner and Daniel Sichel, "The Resurgence of Growth in the Late 1990s: Is Information Technology the Story?", Federal Reserve Board, 2000.

new economy: a term used to describe the period of high productivity growth, attributed largely to better computer and information technology.

This increase in productivity growth and the important role of technology in the late 1990s and early 2000s led people to call the U.S. economy the **new economy,** a term used to convey the idea that new technology—especially information technology such as faster computers, wireless phones, and the Internet—has enabled workers to be more productive, thereby raising productivity growth. That this technology growth is a big factor in the rebound is consistent with the term *the new economy.* But whatever one calls it, the higher productivity growth has already had an impact, from higher wage growth to more resources for both the public and private sectors to spend. See the box "Reading the News About the Productivity Growth Rebound" for some press reaction to this rebound in productivity.

Demise of the Soviet Union

Table 21.3 shows the application of the growth accounting formula to the former Soviet Union. It shows the high rates of productivity growth in the Soviet Union in the 1970s and the early 1980s. During that time, many Americans were still worried about the Soviet Union overtaking the United States, recalling former Soviet premier Nikita Khrushchev's highly publicized statement "We will bury you."

But as the table shows, most of that growth was due to increases in capital per worker and not to technological change. Such high rates of capital growth could not be maintained without a severe burden on the people. Eventually, the Soviet citizens complained about the high share of their output going to investment. They wanted the consumer goods that were being most visibly obtained in the market economies. One could have predicted problems and perhaps even the demise of the Soviet Union from an examination of the sources of growth.

Table 21.3
Growth Accounting in the Former Soviet Union

Period	(1) Productivity Growth	(2) 1/3 Growth Rate of Capital per Hour of Work	(3) Technology Growth
1971–1975	4.5	3.0	1.5
1976–1980	3.3	3.9	−.6
1981–1985	2.7	3.5	−.8

Source: A Study of the Soviet Economy, International Monetary Fund, The World Bank, Organization for Economic Cooperation and Development, and European Bank for Reconstruction and Development, 1999. Reprinted by permission.

REVIEW
- The productivity growth slowdown in the United States in the 1970s seems to have been due to a slowdown in both technology growth and capital growth, but technology played a larger role.
- Technology also played a larger role than capital in the rebound in productivity growth during the late 1990s and early 2000s.
- Applying the growth accounting formula to the former Soviet Union reveals that there was a serious problem of technological progress.

This article appeared in the *Financial Times* on February 13, 2002. It summarizes some data on the recent rapid productivity growth in the United States and emphasizes the importance of productivity growth for economic growth and higher living standards in the long run. The authors also identify the source of productivity growth: business investment spending by firms seeking to cut costs and increase their efficiency.

As you read the article, keep in mind that the 3.5 percent increase in productivity in the fourth quarter of 2001 is part of a sustained increase in productivity growth that began in 1995. The resurgence in productivity seems to have been strong enough even to withstand the onset of a recession after 10 years of growth.

Confounding the sceptics: Accelerating productivity is ushering in a period of solid US economic growth, argue John Lipsky and Jim Glassman

By Jim Glassman and John Lipsky

The striking news that US productivity increased at an annual rate of 3.5 per cent in the final quarter of 2001 will surely change the debate on the US economic and financial outlook. We now know that productivity grew by close to 2 per cent for last year as a whole. To put this result in perspective, remember that productivity fell in every previous US recession of the past 50 years.

Moreover, **productivity growth** will accelerate as the economy recovers, as is typical for this stage of the business cycle. Until the past decade, the expert consensus held that trend US **productivity growth** was no higher than 1–1.25 per cent a year. With productivity advancing at a faster pace than that even through a recession, what will the pessimists and sceptics, who declared the 1990s boom was little more than a new economy mirage, say now? The speed of productivity growth is critical to justifying our bullish assessment of US economic prospects. Productivity gains help to achieve stronger output growth and lower inflation. They will also underpin the value of US financial assets and the dollar. Moreover, optimism about productivity trends will encourage the Federal Reserve to adopt a patient attitude regarding the need for interest rate increases later this year.

Benefits of productivity growth

The practical importance of strong underlying productivity growth will be visible in the coming profits rebound. Still-to-be-published figures of the National Income Accounts will probably show that aggregate corporate profits turned the corner in last year's fourth quarter. This momentum shift has not yet been reflected clearly in analysts' estimates, which tend to focus on year-on-year earnings comparisons.

Faster productivity growth typically has been associated with faster income growth as well. Productivity surged between 1995 and 2000 at an average annual rate of about 2.6 per cent, spurred by a historic rise in business capital spending. At the same time, gross domestic product growth averaged about 4.1 per cent a year. Profits grew rapidly, reaching the highest share of GDP in three decades. Annual wage growth nonetheless averaged 2.1 per cent when adjusted for inflation, up from 0.6 per cent in the previous five-year period.

This performance was far more favourable than expert opinion had considered possible. A chorus of academics and analysts claimed the results were a statistical illusion caused by the internet mania; reality would be restored once the inevitable cyclical downturn arrived.

The surge in productivity in the 1990s

Closer consideration of the data has significantly undermined the curmudgeons' position, however. In particular, it turns out that only about 30 per cent of high-technology spending by businesses during 1995–2000 was accounted for by the communications and manufacturing sectors. The balance went to the service sector. One implication is that a significant portion of high-tech investment was used for cost reduction rather than for building excess new capacity, such as broadband networks.

Sources of productivity growth

The end-of-investment story is incomplete, too. In fact, US business capital spending remains impressively large. It is true that such spending has fallen by about Dollars 100bn, or about 1 per cent of GDP, since mid-2000—the sharpest drop for any 18-month period of the past 50 years. However, business spending on equipment and software still accounted for nearly 9 per cent of 2001 GDP, the fourth highest annual share in the past 50 years.

As profits improve, and businesses regain confidence, investment spending will rise. Based on forward-looking figures, we believe that business capital spending may begin to grow by this year's second quarter, much sooner than consensus expectations.

Technology Policy

The growth accounting formula tells us that if economic policy is to help maintain the higher productivity growth that began in the mid-1990s in the United States, it must provide incentives for, or remove disincentives to, technological progress. What policies might improve technological progress?

Policy to Encourage Investment in Human Capital

One policy is to improve education. A more highly trained work force is more productive. Better-educated workers are more able to make technological improvements. In other words, human capital can improve the production of technology. Hence, educational reform (higher standards, incentives for good teaching) and more funding would be ways to increase technological change. Some studies have shown that the U.S. educational system is falling behind other countries, especially in mathematics and science in the K–12 schools; hence, additional support seems warranted in order to increase economic growth.

Policy to Encourage Research and Innovation

Today, the United States and other advanced countries spend huge quantities on *research and development (R&D)*. Some of the research supports pure science, but much of it is applied research in engineering and medical technology. About 2.6 percent of U.S. GDP goes to research and development. The government provides much of its R&D funds through research grants and contracts to private firms and universities through the National Science Foundation and the National Institutes of Health and through its own research labs. But private firms are the users of most of the research funds.

The United States spends less on research and development as a share of GDP than other countries, but more in total. Total spending on research is a better measure of the usefulness of the spending than spending as a share of GDP if the benefits spill over to the whole economy.

During the cold war, much of U.S. research and development spending went for national defense. What should happen to those research dollars now that the cold war is over and overall defense spending has come down? Some argue that more civilian research should be supported. For many years the Defense Advanced Research Projects Agency (DARPA) funded research on computer networks and artificial intelligence. In 1993, the *D* in DARPA was dropped, signaling the new focus on civilian research.

Increased government support for research and development regardless of industry can be achieved through tax credits. A *tax credit for research* allows firms to deduct a certain fraction of their research expenditures from their taxes in order to reduce their tax bill. This increases the incentive to engage in research and development. Another way to increase the incentive for inventors and innovators is to give them a more certain claim to the property rights from their inventions. The government has a role here in defining and enforcing property rights through patent laws, trademarks, and copyrights.

Technology Embodied in New Capital

Although we have emphasized that capital and technology have two distinct effects on the growth rate of productivity, it is not always possible to separate them in practice. In order to take advantage of a new technology, it may be necessary to invest in new capital. Consider the Thompson Bagel Machine, invented by Dan Thompson, which can automatically roll and shape bagels. Before the machine was invented, bakers rolled and shaped the bagels by hand. According to Dan Thompson, who in 1993 was running the Thompson Bagel Machine Manufacturing Corporation, headquartered in Los Angeles, "You used to have two guys handshaping and boiling and baking who could turn out maybe 120 bagels an hour. With the machine and now the new ovens, I have one baker putting out 400 bagels an hour."[1] That is a productivity increase of over 500 percent! But the new technology is inseparable from the capital. In order to take advantage of the technology, bagel producers have to buy the machine and the new ovens to go with it.

Economists call this *embodied technological change* because it is embodied in the capital. An example of *disembodied technological change* would be the discovery of a new way to forecast the demand for bagels at the shop each morning so that fewer people would be disappointed on popular days and fewer bagels would be wasted on slack days. Taking advantage of this technology might not require any new capital.

The relationship between capital and technology has implications for technology policies. For example, policies that provide incentives for firms to invest might indirectly improve technology as they encourage investment in new, more productive equipment.

Is Government Intervention Appropriate?

Any time there is a question about whether government should intervene in the economy, such as with the technology policies just discussed, the operation of the private market should be examined carefully. For example, we noted that incentives for technology production may be too low without government intervention. Certainly some of the research a business firm undertakes can be kept secret from others. In such cases, the firm may have sufficient incentive to do the research. But many research results are hard to keep secret. In that case, there is a role for government intervention in subsidizing the research. In general, policies to increase economic growth should be given the test for whether government intervention in the economy is necessary: Is the private market providing the right incentives? If not, can the government do better without a large risk of government failure? If the answers are "no" and "yes," respectively, then government intervention is appropriate.

REVIEW
- Policy proposals to increase productivity growth by providing incentives to increase technology include educational reform, tax credits for research, increased funding for research, moving government support toward areas that have significant spillovers, and improving intellectual property laws to better define the property rights of inventors and extend them globally.

- Many technologies are embodied in new capital. Hence, policies to stimulate capital formation could also increase technology.

---

1. *The New York Times,* April 25, 1993.

Conclusion: Where Does Potential GDP Go from Here?

When we first examined the growth of the economy over time in Chapter 17, we noted the longer-term trend in real GDP. The long-run trend was called potential GDP. The growth of potential GDP depends on three factors: labor, capital, and technology, which we studied in this chapter.

To conclude our discussion of economic growth, let us see how economists combine forecasts of labor growth, capital growth, and technology growth to project potential GDP growth in the future. In March 2005, the Congressional Budget Office (CBO) forecast potential GDP growth of 2.9 percent per year from 2005 to 2015. The growth rate of potential GDP is the sum of the growth rate of total hours of work plus the growth rate of output per hour of work, or the productivity growth rate. The assumptions that underlie this forecast are a growth rate of total hours of .8 percent per year and a productivity growth rate of 2.1 percent per year.

A growth rate of 2.9 percent per year for potential GDP is quite reasonable, but the CBO warned that uncertainty about the roles of technology and capital and the sustainability of the recent increase in the growth rate of productivity make such a projection particularly uncertain in the future.

After discussing the monetary system in Chapter 22, we will turn to the study of fluctuations of real GDP around potential GDP.

KEY POINTS

1. The productivity growth rate—the percentage increase in output per hour of work—determines the economic well-being of people in the long run.

2. Malthus's pessimistic growth prediction was wrong because it omitted the effects of capital and, more importantly, technology.

3. Technology, along with labor and capital, determines economic growth. Technological progress explains much of the productivity growth wave that started in the late 1700s and enabled developed countries to get rich.

4. Technology as defined by economists is much broader than "high-tech" products or inventions. Technology includes such things as better organizational structure for a firm and better education for workers as well as innovations like fiber-optic cables.

5. As a commodity, technology has the special features of nonexcludability and nonrivalry.

6. Patent laws attempt to make technology more excludable and thereby increase the incentives to invest.

7. The growth accounting formula is itself a great invention that has enabled economists to better understand the role of technology in the economy.

8. Technology policy has the goal of offsetting disincentives to invest and innovate that exist in the private market.

9. Government support for education and research is a key part of a modern technology policy.

KEY TERMS

productivity
diminishing returns
technology
technological change
invention
innovation
diffusion
learning by doing
growth accounting formula
new economy

QUESTIONS FOR REVIEW

1. Why did Malthus's predictions turn out to be wrong for England?

2. What is the essential difference between economic growth in the last 200 years and in the 2,000 years before that?

3. Why are economists so sure that technology played a big role in economic growth during the last 200 years?

4. Why does technology include different ways to organize a business firm?

5. How is technology produced?

6. What is the importance of nonrivalry and nonexcludability for technology?

7. Of what practical use is the growth accounting formula?

8. What is wrong with a growth policy that focuses on capital formation but not on technology?

9. What do intellectual property rights have to do with economic growth?

10. What is the rationale for government intervention in the production of technology?

PROBLEMS

1. The following table shows how output (shaded) depends on capital and labor. Using the table, draw the production function $Y = F(L)$ when the capital stock (K) is 50 and when it is 100. What do you observe? Now draw the same curve when the capital stock is 150 and 200. Do you observe any difference in the resulting increase in output?

Labor

		50	100	150	200	250
Capital	**50**	200	324	432	528	618
	100	246	400	532	650	760
	150	278	452	600	734	858
	200	304	492	654	800	936
	250	324	526	700	856	1,000

2. Consider a country in which capital per hour of work from 1950 to 1973 grew by 3 percent per year and output per hour of work grew by about 3 percent per year. Suppose that from 1973 to 1991, capital per hour of work did not grow at all and output per hour of work grew by about 1 percent per year. How much of the slowdown in productivity (output per hour of work) growth was due to technological change? Explain. (Assume that the coefficient on capital in the growth accounting formula is 1/3.)

3. According to the spending allocation model in Chapter 19, a decrease in government spending results in, among other things, an increase in investment in the long run. Suppose the capital stock is $1 trillion and a fall in government spending causes a $50 billion rise in investment. Determine the effect of the change in government purchases on long-run output growth, using the growth accounting formula. (Assume that the coefficient on capital in the growth accounting formula is 1/3.)

4. The former Soviet Union had high rates of economic growth, especially in the 1950s and 1960s, but could not maintain them. Why? What does this tell us about the limitations of capital and of government?

5. a. Suppose that a country has no growth in technology, and that capital and labor hours are growing at the same rate. What is the growth rate of real GDP per hour of work? Explain.

   b. Suppose that capital in the country described in part (a) continues to grow at its previous rate, technology growth is still zero, but growth in labor hours falls to half its previous rate. What happens to growth in real GDP per hour of work?

6. If we estimate the share of capital in income incorrectly, it can affect our estimation of how large technological growth has been. Rework problem 2 assuming that capital's share is 1/4. Explain intuitively the difference in the importance of technology.

7. Identify each of the following as either a capital-saving or a labor-saving technological change:

   a. A gas station installs gasoline pumps that can be activated by a customer with a credit card.

   b. A university upgrades its phone system to include voicemail.

   c. A university reorganizes its departments in order to cut back on administrative costs.

8. Write a short memo explaining what government can do to increase economic growth in light of technology's special qualities.

9. Which of the following types of government spending are likely to help economic growth? Why?

   a. Military spending on advertising for recruits
   b. Military spending on laser research
   c. Funding for a nationwide computer network
   d. Subsidies for a national opera company
   e. Extra funding for educational programs

10. Many U.S. companies in the software, music, and movie industries have been asking the Chinese government to better enforce intellectual property rights. Discuss the impact of this enforcement on

   a. Chinese firms
   b. American firms
   c. Chinese consumers

Deriving the Growth Accounting Formula

The growth accounting formula states that

$$\begin{array}{c}\text{Growth rate of}\\ \text{productivity}\end{array} = \frac{1}{3}\left(\begin{array}{c}\text{growth rate}\\ \text{of capital}\\ \text{per hour}\\ \text{of work}\end{array}\right) + \begin{array}{c}\text{growth rate}\\ \text{of technology}\end{array}$$

To derive the formula, we start with the relationship between productivity (Y/L) and capital per hour of work (K/L) shown in Figure 21A.1. Because of diminishing returns to capital, the line is curved: As capital per hour of work increases, the increased productivity that comes from the additional capital per hour diminishes.

The curve in Figure 21A.1 is called a **productivity curve;** it can be represented in symbols as (Y/L) = $f(K/L)$, or productivity is a function of capital per hour of work.

An upward shift in the productivity curve due to an increase in technological change is shown in Figure 21A.2. For example, with capital per hour constant at point A in the figure, more technology leads to more productivity.

Productivity increases in the economy are due to a combination of *movements along* the productivity curve because of more capital per hour, and of *shifts of* the productivity curve because of technological change. The

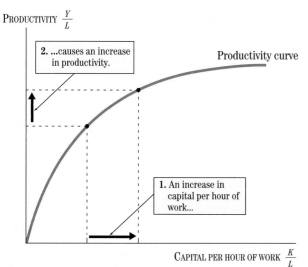

Figure 21A.1
Productivity Curve
Productivity, or output per hour of work, is shown to increase with the amount of capital that workers have, as measured by capital per hour of work. The productivity curve gets flatter as output per hour of work increases because of diminishing returns to capital.

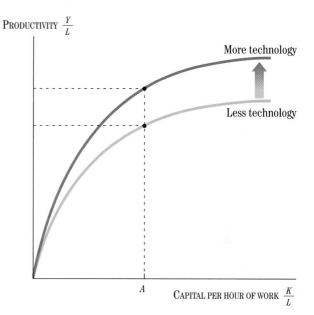

Figure 21A.2
A Shift in the Productivity Curve Due to Technology
An increase in technology permits an increase in productivity even if there is no change in capital per hour of work. For example, if capital per hour of work stays at A, productivity increases when the productivity curve shifts up.

growth accounting formula is derived by translating the *movements along* and the *shifts of* into two algebraic terms.

In Figure 21A.3, productivity and capital per hour in two different years (year 1 and year 2) are shown. These could be 2003 and 2004 or any other two years. In this example, the growth rate of productivity is given by the increase in productivity (C minus A) divided by the initial level of productivity (A), or ($C - A)/A$. (The definition of the growth rate of a variable is the change divided by the initial level.)

Observe in Figure 21A.3 how the increase in productivity can be divided into the part due to higher capital per hour of work (C minus B) and the part due to technology (B minus A). Thus, we have

$$\underbrace{(C-A)/A}_{\substack{\text{Growth rate of}\\ \text{productivity}}} = \underbrace{(C-B)/A}_{\substack{\text{term related to}\\ \text{capital per hour}}} + \underbrace{(B-A)/A}_{\substack{\text{growth rate}\\ \text{of technology}}}$$

which is already close to the growth accounting formula.

To finish the derivation, we need to examine the first term on the right. How does this term relate to capital per

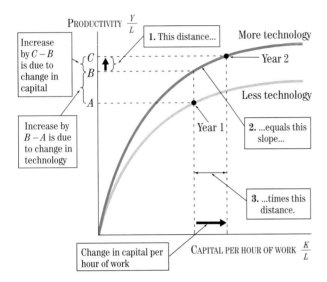

Figure 21A.3
Growth Accounting with Capital per Hour and Technology Increasing
Here a shift in the productivity curve and a movement along the productivity curve due to more capital per hour of work are combined. Productivity increases. The part of the increase due to capital and the part due to technological change are shown in the diagram.

hour of work? The numbered boxes in Figure 21A.3 show that $C - B$ equals the *change* in capital per hour of work $\Delta(K/L)$ times the *slope* of the productivity curve. (The slope times the change along the horizontal axis gives the changes along the vertical axis.) Let the symbol r be the slope, which measures how much additional capital increases output. Thus, $(C - B)/A$ is given by

$$\frac{\Delta(K/L)r}{Y/L} = \frac{\Delta(K/L)}{(K/L)}r(K/Y)$$

The expression on the right is obtained by multiplying the numerator and the denominator of the expression on the left by (K/Y). You might want to check the multiplication on your own. Now the term on the right is simply the growth rate of capital per hour times $r(K/Y)$. The amount of income paid to capital is r times K if capital is paid according to how much additional capital increases output. Aggregate income is given by Y. Thus, the term $r(K/Y)$ is the share of capital income in aggregate income. This share is approximately $1/3$. Thus, the expression $(C - B)/A$ is the growth rate of capital per hour of work times $1/3$. Thus, the growth accounting formula is derived.

Key Points

1. The productivity curve describes how more capital per hour of work increases productivity, or output per hour of work.

2. The productivity curve shifts up if there is an increase in technology.

3. The growth accounting formula is derived by dividing an increase in productivity into (1) a shift in the productivity curve due to more technology and (2) a movement along the productivity curve due to more capital per worker.

Key Term and Definition

productivity curve: a relationship stating the output per hour of work for each amount of capital per hour of work in the economy.

Questions for Review

1. What is the difference between the productivity curve and the production function?

2. What is the difference between a shift of the productivity curve and a movement along the curve?

3. Why does the share of capital income in total income appear in the growth accounting formula?

Problems

1. Consider the following relation between productivity and capital per hour for the economy.

Capital per Hour of Work (*K/L*)	Output per Hour of Work (*Y/L*)
$20	$40
$40	$80
$60	$110
$80	$130
$100	$140

   a. Plot the productivity curve.
   b. Suppose that in year 1, $K/L = 40$ and $Y/L = 80$, but in year 2, $K/L = 60$ and $Y/L = 110$. How much has technology contributed to the increase in productivity between the two years?
   c. Suppose that between year 2 and year 3, the productivity curve shifts up by $20 at each level of capital per hour of work. If $K/L = 80$ and $Y/L = 150$ in year 3, how many dollars did capital contribute to productivity growth between year 2 and year 3? How much was the contribution as a fraction of the growth rate of capital per worker?

2. Suppose the production function $Y = f(K, L)$ is such that Y equals the square root of the product (K times L). Plot the production function with Y on the vertical axis and L on the horizontal axis for the case where $K = 100$. Plot the productivity curve with Y/L on the vertical axis and K/L on the horizontal axis.

CHAPTER 22

Money and Inflation

I n 1896, William Jennings Bryan won the Democratic Party's nomination for president of the United States with the most riveting speech on an economic topic in American history. The speech was all about money. In a booming voice, he rallied the delegates at the national convention against a policy—called the *gold standard*—in which money was linked to the supply of gold. He roared, "We will answer their demands for a gold standard by saying to them: You shall not press down upon the brow of labor this crown of thorns. You shall not crucify mankind upon a cross of gold."

Bryan was against the gold standard because he wanted silver to be part of the monetary standard too. That way, both silver and gold could be made into coins. Bryan knew that if silver as well as gold was coined, there would be more money, and that more money would cause more inflation. He thought inflation would be a good thing. Bryan was right that more money would cause more inflation, but he lost the election. The voters apparently did not view inflation as a good thing. Instead of Bryan, they elected William McKinley, who supported the gold standard.

The purpose of this chapter is to examine the role of money in the economy. We first define money and show that commercial banks play a key role in providing money in a modern economy. We then examine how central banks—such as the Fed (the Federal Reserve) in the United States or the ECB (European Central Bank) in Europe—can control the supply of money. We also show why *excessive increases in the supply of money cause inflation*—a very important macroeconomic principle that was behind not only the 1896 election in the United States, but also many other political successes and failures around the world in the more than 100 years since then.

What Is Money?

In a broad sense, money performs three functions in the economy: It can serve as a medium of exchange, a unit of account, and a store of value. More details about the three functions are given below. Economists emphasize the medium of exchange dimension in defining money. They define **money** as the part of a person's wealth that can be readily used for transactions, such as buying a sandwich or a bicycle. This definition differs from the more typical usage, in which the term is used to describe someone's wealth or income—as when we say that "she makes a lot of money" or "he has a lot of money." To an economist, money does not include what a person earns in a year or the total assets that she has, but it does include the portion of that person's wealth—such as the notes and coins in her purse—that can be easily used for transactions.

money: that part of a person's wealth that can be readily used for transactions; money also serves as a store of value and a unit of account.

Three Functions of Money

medium of exchange: something that is generally accepted as a means of payment.

■ **Medium of Exchange.** Money serves as a **medium of exchange** in that it is an item that people are willing to accept as payment for what they are selling because they in turn can use it to pay for something else they want. For example, in ancient times, people received coins for their agricultural produce, such as grain, and then used these coins to buy clothing.

The use of coins was a great technological improvement over *barter,* in which goods are exchanged only for other goods. Under a barter system, there is no single medium of exchange. Thus, under a barter system, if you make shoes and want to buy apples, you have to find an apple seller who needs new shoes. The disadvantage of a barter system is that it requires a rare *coincidence of wants* in which the person who wants to consume what you want to sell (shoes, for example) has exactly what you want to consume (apples, for example).

store of value: something that will allow purchasing power to be carried from one period to the next.

■ **Store of Value.** Money also serves as a **store of value** from one period to another. For example, in ancient times, people could sell their produce in September for gold coins and then use the coins to buy staples in January. In other words, they could store their purchasing power from one season to another.

Coins are not the only thing that can serve as a store of value. For example, rice and corn can also be stored from one season to the next; therefore, they can also serve as a store of value. But if you are not a farmer with a large storage bin, coins are much more likely to be used as money.

unit of account: a standard unit in which prices can be quoted and values of goods can be compared.

■ **Unit of Account.** Money also serves a third function: providing a **unit of account.** The prices of goods are usually stated in units of money. For example, prices of shoes or apples in ancient Greece were stated in a certain number of tetradrachmas because people using these coins were familiar with that unit. Originally, units of money were determined by the weight of the metal. The British pound, for example, was originally a pound of silver. That terminology stuck even though, as we will see, modern money is unrelated to silver or any other metal.

To better understand the difference between the unit of account and the medium of exchange, it is helpful to find examples where they are based on different monies. For example, when inflation got very high in Argentina in the early 1990s, the prices of many goods were quoted in U.S. dollars rather than Argentine pesos, but people usually exchanged pesos when they bought or sold goods. Thus, the U.S. dollar was the unit of account, while the medium of exchange was still the peso. But such cases are the exception; the unit of account and the medium of exchange are usually the same money.

Commodity Money

Many items have been used for money throughout history. Salt, cattle, furs, tobacco, shells, and arrowheads have been used as money. Traces of their former use can still be found in our vocabulary. The word *salary* comes from the Latin word for salt, and the word *pecuniary* comes from the Latin word for cattle. In World War II prisoner-of-war camps, cigarettes were used for money. On the island of Yap in the Pacific Ocean, huge stones weighing several tons were used for money.

Throughout history, the most common form of money has been metallic coins, usually gold, silver, or bronze. Gold coins were used as early as the seventh century B.C. in Lydia (now western Turkey). The Chinese were issuing bronze coins with a hole in the middle in the fifth century B.C., and in the fourth century the Greeks issued silver coins called tetradrachmas that had the goddess Athena on one side and her sacred animal, the owl, on the other. All these examples of money are commodities and are therefore called *commodity money*. Metals proved to be the most common form of commodity money because they could be divided easily into smaller units, are very durable, and could be carried around.

When gold, silver, and other commodities were used as money, changes in the supply of these commodities would change their price relative to all other goods. An increase in the supply of gold, all else equal, would increase the number of gold coins that people were willing to pay in order to purchase other goods and services. In other

Stone Money of Yap Island, Micronesia

Silver Coins of Ancient Greece

words, the price of all other goods in the economy would rise relative to gold. Such an increase in the price of all goods in the economy is called inflation, as you may recall from the definitions of key economic concepts given in Chapter 18. Thus, increases in the supply of gold or any other commodity used as money would cause inflation. Whenever there were huge gold discoveries, the price of gold fell and there were increases in inflation in countries that used gold as money. Thus, inflation was determined largely by the supply of precious metals. This relationship between the supply of money and inflation, which seems so clear in the case of commodity money, has persisted into modern times, even though there are now many other forms of money.

From Coins to Paper Money to Deposits

Although coins and other commodity monies are improvements over barter, there are more efficient forms of money. Starting in the late eighteenth and early nineteenth centuries, *paper money* began to be used widely and supplemented or replaced coins as a form of money. Although there are a few examples of paper money being used earlier, it was at this time that it became generally recognized that paper money was easier to use and could save greatly on the use of precious metals.

Originally, the amount of paper currency was linked by law or convention to the supply of commodities. One reason for this link was the recognition that more money would cause inflation and that limiting the amount of paper money to the amount of some commodity like gold would limit the amount of paper money. Irving Fisher of Yale University, perhaps the most prolific and influential American economist of the early twentieth century, argued for linking paper money to commodities for precisely this reason. Many countries of the world linked their paper money to gold in the nineteenth and early twentieth centuries. They were on a *gold standard,* which meant that the price of gold in terms of paper money was fixed by the government. The government fixed the price by agreeing to buy and sell gold at that price. Today the United States and other countries have severed all links between their money and gold. They are no longer on the gold standard and apparently have no intention of returning. Governments now supply virtually all the coin and paper money—the two together are called **currency.**

currency: money in its physical form: coin and paper money.

checking deposit: an account at a financial institution on which checks can be written; also called checkable deposit.

Although paper money was much easier to make and to use than coins, it too has been surpassed by a more efficient form of money. Today many people have **checking deposits** at banks or other financial institutions. These are deposits of funds on which an individual can write a check to make payment for goods and services. The deposits serve as money because people can write checks on them. For example, when a student pays $100 for books with a check, the student's checking deposit at the bank goes down by $100, and the bookstore's checking deposit at the bank goes up by $100. Checking deposits are used in much the same way as when a student pays with a $100 bill, which is then placed in the store's cash register. The student's holding of money goes down by $100, and the store's goes up by $100. Deposits are used by many people as a partial replacement for coin or paper money. Writing checks to pay for goods has become more common than using currency.

Measures of the Money Supply

money supply: the sum of currency (coin and paper money) and deposits at banks.

Today economists define the **money supply** as the sum of currency (coin and paper money) and deposits at banks. But there are differences of opinion about what types of deposits should be included.

The narrowest measure of the money supply is called *M1.* The M1 measure consists mainly of currency plus checking deposits (travelers checks are also part of M1 but constitute less than 1 percent of total M1). The items in M1 have a great degree of

What makes something money? Economist and *New York Times* columnist Hal Varian's article below illustrates the "Medium of Exchange" function of money and the importance of social expectations about its value, arguing that paper currency can have value even without government backing.

ECONOMIC SCENE
Why Is That Dollar Bill in Your Pocket Worth Anything?

By HAL R. VARIAN

WHY is that dollar bill in your pocket worth anything? One answer is that it's valuable because it says it is. To the left of the portrait of George Washington, the dollar proclaims: "This note is legal tender for all debts, public and private."

Dollar bills are "fiat" money—they are valuable because the government in power says so. People can, however, write contracts that specify payment in other currencies. If a contract specifies payment in euros, dollars will not fulfill the contract, despite what is printed on them.

A more profound, and perhaps slightly unsettling, reason that a dollar has value is simply that lots of people are willing to accept it as payment. In this view, the value of a dollar comes not so much from government mandate as from social convention.

In the jargon of economists, the value of a dollar is a result of "network effects." Just as a fax machine is valuable to you only if lots of other people you correspond with also have fax machines, a currency is valuable to you only if a lot of people you transact with are willing to accept it as payment.

Indeed, one can have currencies that have no government backing. Gold has been used for centuries as a medium of exchange; cigarettes were used for payment in prisoner-of-war camps in World War II; and countless other goods, including cowrie shells and peacock feathers, have functioned as money throughout history. They were money because people were willing to accept them as payment for debts, public and private. Gold, cigarettes, cowrie shells and peacock feathers all have "use value" in addition to their "exchange value." These items were originally valued for their utility or their beauty, and they became used as currency. It is rare to see a purely paper currency functioning as money without the backing of some government or financial institution.

Rare, perhaps, but not unheard of. Mervyn A. King, governor of the Bank of England, cited an interesting example – the Iraqi dinar – in the Ely Lecture delivered at the recent American Economics Association meeting in San Diego. (Mr. King's speech can be downloaded from http://www.bankofenglandco.uk/speeches/speech208.pdf.)

Here is the story Mr. King told:

After the gulf war of 1991, Iraq was divided in two: the south ruled by Saddam Hussein, the north governed by the local Kurds. Mr. Hussein needed money to finance government spending, and in the time-honored tradition of dictators, created it himself.

The government could not import more of the bank notes then in use, because of United Nations sanctions, so Mr. Hussein ordered the local printing of a new currency. In May 1993, the

liquidity, which means that they can be quickly and easily used to purchase goods and services.

Many things that people would consider money, however, are not included in M1. For example, if you had no cash but you wanted to buy a birthday gift for a relative, you could withdraw cash from your savings deposit. A *savings deposit* is a deposit that pays interest and from which funds can normally be easily withdrawn at any time. In other words, a savings deposit is also liquid, but not quite as liquid as a checking deposit. Similarly, *time deposits*—which require the depositor to keep the money at the bank for a certain amount of time or else lose interest—are not as liquid as checking deposits, but it is possible to withdraw funds from them. Economists have created a broader measure of the money supply, called *M2,* that includes all that is in M1 plus savings deposits, time deposits, and certain accounts on which check writing is very limited. Still broader concepts of the money supply can be defined, but M1 and M2 are the most important ones. Table 22.1 shows the total amounts of different definitions of the money supply for the whole U.S. economy in December 2004.

Central Bank of Iraq announced that citizens had three weeks to exchange their old 25-dinar notes for the new "Saddam dinars," which bore his portrait.

During the next few years, so many Saddam dinars were printed in southern Iraq that they became virtually worthless. The face value of cash in circulation rose from 22 billion dinars in 1991 to 584 billion in four years, and inflation averaged about 250 percent a year over that period.

Residents of northern Iraq could not exchange their notes. The 25-dinar notes continued to circulate and became known as the "Swiss dinars," because they were printed with plates made in Switzerland.

The fact that the Swiss dinars continued to be used at all speaks to the power of social conventions. The Kurds in the north despised the Baghdad government, and would have much preferred to have their own currency. But there was no government in place powerful enough to mandate a currency change, so they kept using the old Swiss dinars by default.

The Swiss dinar was in fixed supply, while the Saddam dinar was flying off the printing presses, so it is not surprising that the Swiss dinar quickly became more valuable. By spring 2003, it took 300 Saddam dinars to buy one Swiss dinar.

The more interesting economic effect was the behavior of the Swiss dinar against the dollar. In fall 2002, as it became more and more likely that the United States would invade, the Swiss dinar became more and more valuable.

This appreciation was driven by expectations. If the Kurds had expected that they would once again fall under Saddam's sway, the Swiss dinar would have quickly become worthless. As this became less likely, and the belief that future governments would accept the Swiss dinar became more widespread, the local currency became more valuable. Of course, every exchange rate movement can be interpreted in two ways: in the north, the Kurdish regional government initially interpreted the rise in the Swiss dinar against the dollar as a fall in the value of the dollar.

The government soon realized, however, that since the dollar was stable against other currencies, the correct explanation was that recounted above: the increasing belief that the Swiss dinars would, in fact, be honored by future governments.

The government was right. On July 7, 2003, the American occupation administrator, L. Paul Bremer III, announced the creation of a new Iraqi dinar that would be exchanged for the two existing currencies at a rate that implied that one Swiss dinar would be worth 150 Saddam dinars.

Interestingly, the currency markets valued the Swiss dinars somewhat higher than the official 150 exchange rate, primarily because many counterfeit 10,000-dinar Saddam notes were in circulation.

This story illustrates that paper currency can take on a life of its own, even in the absence of government backing. At the same time, it is clear that government backing makes a significant contribution to the value of paper currency: the more likely it became that the Swiss dinars would be valued by a subsequent government, the more valuable they became.

Hal R. Varian is a professor of business, economics and information management at the University of California at Berkeley.

Source: The New York Times, January 15, 2004.

Only about one-half of the M1 definition of the money supply is currency, and only about one-tenth of the M2 definition is currency. There is disagreement among economists as to whether the more narrowly defined M1 or the more broadly defined M2 or something else is the best definition of the money supply. There is probably no best definition for all times and all purposes. For simplicity, in the rest of this chapter

Table 22.1
Measures of Money in the United States, December 2004 (billions of dollars)

Currency	697
M1: Currency plus checking deposits	1,362
M2: M1 plus time deposits, savings deposits, and other deposits on which check writing is limited or not allowed	6,417

Source: Federal Reserve Board.

we make no distinction between the Ms but simply refer to the money supply, *M,* as currency plus deposits.

REVIEW	
	▪ Commodity money—usually gold, silver, or bronze coins—originally served as the main type of money in most societies. Increases in the supply of these commodities would reduce their price relative to all other commodities and thereby cause inflation.
	▪ Later, paper currency and deposits at banks became forms of money.
	▪ There are three roles for money—as a medium of exchange, as a store of value, and as a unit of account.

The Fed, the Banks, and the Link from Reserves to Deposits

Federal Reserve System (the Fed): the central bank of the United States, which oversees the creation of money in the United States.

We have seen that increases in the supply of commodity money such as gold would increase inflation. So would the excessive printing of paper money (currency) by governments. But in today's world, money consists of both currency and deposits. Nevertheless, it is possible for governments—usually through a central bank—to control the supply of money. In the United States, the central bank is the **Federal Reserve System,** nicknamed the "Fed." To understand how the Fed can control the supply of money, we must first look at how the Fed can control the amount of deposits at banks.

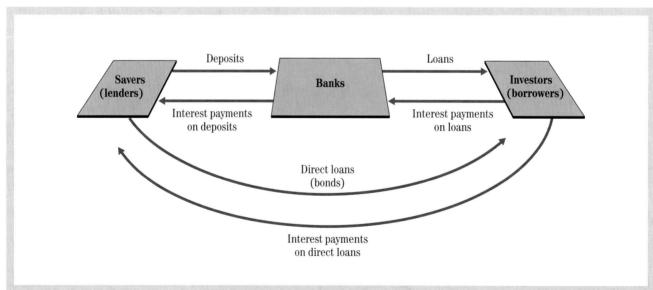

Figure 22.1
Channeling Funds from Savers to Investors

Savers, those whose income is greater than their consumption, can supply funds to investors in two ways: through banks (and other types of financial intermediaries) or by making direct loans, perhaps by buying bonds issued by a business firm. The banks earn profits by charging a higher interest on their loans than they pay on their deposits.

The Second (?) Most Powerful Person in America: Alan Greenspan

Alan Greenspan was appointed to the Board of Governors of the Federal Reserve System in August of 1987, to fill an unexpired term. He is scheduled to serve on the Board of Governors until early 2006. Dr. Greenspan has served as chairman of the Board of Governors ever since his initial appointment in 1987. The general public believes that Chairman Greenspan is the person most responsible for the long economic expansion of the 1990s, and his public reputation is unrivaled among policymakers. A good example of Alan Greenspan's lofty standing was the title chosen by Bob Woodward for Greenspan's biography: *Maestro*.

What, then, is the background of this man, considered by many to be the second (and by some the first!) most powerful man in America? According to the information provided by the Federal Reserve, Alan Greenspan was born on March 6, 1926, in New York City. He received a B.S. in economics (summa cum laude) in 1948, an M.A. in economics in 1950, and a Ph.D. in economics in 1977, all from New York University. It is interesting to note that Dr. Greenspan, unlike many academic economists, received his Ph.D. somewhat late in his career. In between his master's degree and his doctoral degree, Dr. Greenspan was chairman and president of Townsend-Greenspan & Co., Inc., an economic consulting firm in New York City. He used the experience he gained from his study of the economy, in particular through his understanding of

economic forecasting, to serve as chairman of the President's Council of Economic Advisers under President Ford. He also served a stint from 1981 to 1983 as chairman of the National Commission on Social Security Reform. Prior to joining the Fed, Dr. Greenspan acquired a wide variety of policy experience by serving as a member of President Reagan's Economic Policy Advisory Board, a senior adviser to the Brookings Panel on Economic Activity, and a consultant to the Congressional Budget Office.

So now you have a glimpse of what it takes to become the second most powerful person in America: a doctorate in economics, a thorough understanding of the economy, a wide background in policy, and the respect of everyone who comes into contact with you. A tall order indeed, but you can be comforted by the thought that introductory macroeconomics is the first step toward that goal.

---

bank: a firm that channels funds from savers to investors by accepting deposits and making loans.

A **bank**—such as Bank of America or Citibank—is a firm that channels funds from savers to investors by accepting deposits and making loans. Figure 22.1 illustrates this function of banks. Banks are a type of *financial intermediary* because they "intermediate" between savers and investors. Other examples of financial intermediaries are credit unions and savings and loan institutions. Banks are sometimes called *commercial banks* because many of their loans are to business firms engaged in commerce. Banks accept deposits from people who have funds and who want to earn interest and then lend the funds to other individuals who want to borrow and who are willing to pay interest. A bank earns profits by charging a higher interest rate to the borrowers than it pays to the depositors.

The Fed

The *central bank* of a country serves as a bank to other banks. In other words, commercial banks deposit funds at the central bank, and the central bank in turn makes loans to other commercial banks. We will see that the deposits of the commercial banks at the central bank are very important for controlling the money supply.

The Fed was established as the central bank for the United States in 1913 and now has over 25,000 employees spread all over the country.

■ **Board of Governors.**   At the core of the Fed is the *Federal Reserve Board,* or Board of Governors, consisting of seven people appointed to nonrenewable fourteen-year terms by the president of the United States and confirmed by the Senate. The Federal Reserve Board is located in Washington, D.C.

One of the governors is appointed by the president as chairman of the board; this appointment also requires Senate confirmation and can be renewed for additional terms. Alan Greenspan was appointed chairman by President Reagan in 1987 and reappointed by President Bush in 1991, by President Clinton in 1996 and in 2000, and by President George W. Bush in 2004.

Federal Open Market Committee (FOMC):   the committee, consisting of the seven members of the Board of Governors and the twelve presidents of the Fed district banks, that meets about eight times per year and makes decisions about the supply of money; only five of the presidents vote at any one time.

■ **The District Federal Reserve Banks.**   The Federal Reserve System includes not only the Federal Reserve Board in Washington but also twelve Federal Reserve Banks in different districts around the country (see Figure 22.2).

The term *Fed* refers to the whole Federal Reserve System, including the Board of Governors in Washington and the twelve district banks. Each district bank is headed by a president, who is chosen by commercial bankers and other people in the district and approved by the Board of Governors.

■ **The Federal Open Market Committee (FOMC).**   The Fed makes decisions about the supply of money through a committee called the **Federal Open Market Committee (FOMC).** The members of the FOMC are the seven governors and the

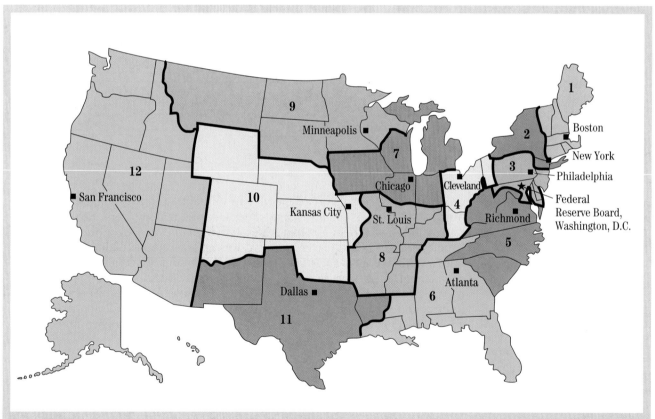

**Figure 22.2
The Twelve Districts of the Fed**

The country is divided into twelve districts, each with a district Federal Reserve Bank. Each district bank is headed by a president, who sits on the FOMC. Alaska and Hawaii are in District 12.

twelve district bank presidents, but only five of the presidents vote at any one time. Thus, there are twelve voting members of the FOMC at any one time. The FOMC meets in Washington about eight times a year to decide how to implement monetary policy. Figure 22.3 shows the relationship between the FOMC, the Board of Governors, and the district banks.

Even though the chair of the Fed has only one of the twelve votes on the FOMC, the position has considerably more power than this one vote might indicate. The chair also has executive authority over the operations of the whole Federal Reserve, sets the agenda at FOMC meetings, and represents the Fed in testimony before Congress. When journalists in the popular press write about the Fed, they usually talk as if the chair has almost complete power over Fed decisions. Some view the chair of the Fed as the second most powerful person in America, after the president of the United States.

Now that we have described the Fed, let us examine the operation of banks and how they, along with the Fed, create money.

The Banks

A commercial bank accepts deposits from individuals and makes loans to others. To understand how a bank functions, it is necessary to look at its balance sheet, which

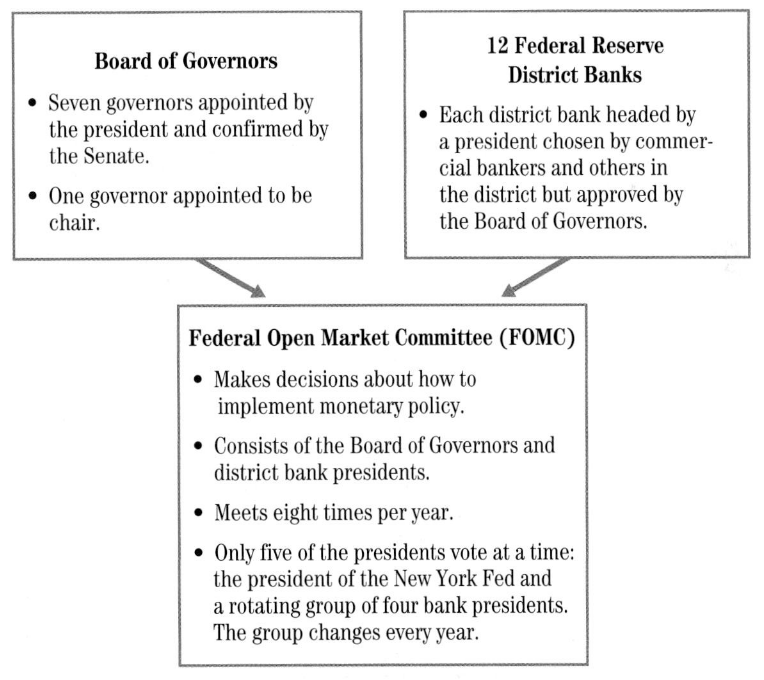

Board of Governors

- Seven governors appointed by the president and confirmed by the Senate.

- One governor appointed to be chair.

12 Federal Reserve District Banks

- Each district bank headed by a president chosen by commercial bankers and others in the district but approved by the Board of Governors.

Federal Open Market Committee (FOMC)

- Makes decisions about how to implement monetary policy.

- Consists of the Board of Governors and district bank presidents.

- Meets eight times per year.

- Only five of the presidents vote at a time: the president of the New York Fed and a rotating group of four bank presidents. The group changes every year.

Figure 22.3
The Structure of the Fed
Decisions about monetary policy are made by the FOMC, which consists of the Fed governors and district Fed presidents.

shows these deposits and loans. Table 22.2 is an example of a balance sheet for a bank, called BankOne.

asset: something of value owned by a person or a firm.

liability: something of value that a person or a firm owes to someone else.

The different items are divided into *assets* and *liabilities*. An **asset** is something of value owned by a person or a firm. A **liability** is something of value that a person or a firm owes, such as a debt, to someone else. Thus a bank's assets are anything the bank owns and any sum owed to the bank by someone else. A bank's liabilities are anything the bank owes to someone else. People's *deposits* at banks are the main liability of banks, as shown in Table 22.2. Certain assets, such as the bank's building and furniture, are not shown in this balance sheet because they do not change when the money supply changes. Also, when a bank starts up, the owners must put in some funds, called the bank's capital stock, that can be used in case the bank needs cash in an emergency. This asset is not shown in this balance sheet either.

reserves: deposits that commercial banks hold at the Fed.

Consider each of the assets shown in the balance sheet in Table 22.2. **Reserves** are deposits that commercial banks hold at the Fed, much as people hold deposits at commercial banks. Remember, the Fed is the bank for the commercial banks. Just as you can hold a deposit at a commercial bank, a commercial bank can hold a deposit at the Fed. Reserves are simply a name for these deposits by commercial banks at the Fed.

required reserve ratio: the fraction of a bank's deposits that it is required to hold at the Fed.

Under U.S. law, a commercial bank is required to hold reserves at the Fed equal to a fraction of the deposits people hold at the commercial bank; this fraction is called the **required reserve ratio.** Banks may in fact choose to hold a greater fraction of their deposits in the form of reserves at the Fed than they are required to. In reality, then, the ratio of reserves to deposits, known as the *reserve ratio,* may differ from the required reserve ratio: It can be larger, but it cannot be smaller. In the following example, we will assume that banks do not exercise this option, so that the reserve ratio is equal to the required reserve ratio. We will also assume that the required reserve ratio is 10 percent, which is very close to what it really is in the United States.

The two other assets of the bank are loans and bonds. *Loans* are made by banks to individuals or firms for a period of time; the banks earn interest on these loans. *Bonds* are promises of a firm or government to pay back a certain amount after a number of years. Bonds are issued by the U.S. government and by large corporations. Banks sometimes buy and hold such bonds, as BankOne has done in Table 22.2.

The Link from Reserves to Deposits

Because deposits at banks are a form of money, the Fed must be able to control the total amount of these deposits if it is to control the money supply. The link between the deposits at banks and the reserves at the Fed provides the key mechanism by which the Fed can exert control over the amount of deposits at the commercial banks. To see this, we first look at some examples to show how this link between reserves and deposits works in the whole economy. To make the story simpler for now, we assume that everyone uses deposits rather than currency for their money. (We will take up currency again in the next section.)

Table 22.2
Balance Sheet of BankOne (millions of dollars)

Assets		Liabilities		
Loans	70	Deposits	100	This is the initial situation. The ratio of reserves to deposits is .1.
Bonds	20			
Reserves	10			

■ **A Formula Linking Reserves to Deposits.**   To see how the Fed can change the amount of deposits in the economy, let us assume that the Fed increases the amount of reserves that banks hold at the Fed. The Fed can cause such an increase in reserves simply by buying something from a bank and paying for it by increasing that bank's reserves at the Fed. The Fed usually buys government bonds when it wants to increase reserves because banks have a lot of bonds.

On any given day, the Fed buys and sells billions of dollars of government bonds. When the Fed buys government bonds, it has to pay for them with something. It pays for them with bank reserves—the deposits banks have with the Fed. For example, if the Fed wants to buy bonds held by Citibank, it says, "We want $1 billion worth of bonds, and we will pay for them by increasing Citibank's account with us by $1 billion." This is an electronic transaction. Citibank's deposits at the Fed (reserves) have increased by $1 billion, and the Fed gets the bonds. They have exchanged bank reserves for the bonds. The buying or selling of bonds by the Federal Reserve is called an **open market operation.**

open market operation: the buying or selling of bonds by the central bank.

So let's assume that the Fed buys $10 million of government bonds from BankOne and pays for the bonds by increasing BankOne's reserves by $10 million. Thus reserves rise at banks in the economy. Now, with the reserve ratio the same (in this example equal to .1) for each bank in the economy, there is a formula linking reserves and deposits for the whole economy. It is given by

$$\text{Reserves} = (\text{reserve ratio}) \times \text{deposits}$$

where reserves and deposits refer to the amounts in the whole economy. If we divide both sides of this expression by the reserve ratio, we get

$$\text{Deposits} = \left(\frac{1}{\text{reserve ratio}}\right) \times \text{reserves}$$

Thus, any increase in reserves is multiplied by the inverse of the reserve ratio to get the increase in deposits. For example, if the $10 million change in reserves is multiplied by $(1/.1) = 10$, we get $100 million change in deposits.

One could have started the example by assuming that the Fed bought $10 million in government bonds from some person other than a bank. That person would deposit the check from the Fed in a bank, and in the end, the answer would be exactly the same: A $10 million increase in reserves leads to a $100 million increase in deposits.

One could also analyze the effects of a decrease in reserves using the same formula linking reserves and deposits. A decrease in reserves occurs when the Fed sells bonds. For example, a decrease in reserves of $10 million would lead to a decrease in deposits of $100 million.

■ **Bank-by-Bank Deposit Expansion.**   Now let's look at the details of what is going on in the banks. In our example, when the Fed buys bonds, BankOne's holdings of bonds decline by $10 million, from $20 million to $10 million, and BankOne's reserves at the Fed increase by $10 million, from $10 million to $20 million. The balance sheet would then look like Table 22.3, a change from Table 22.2. The key point is that there are now $10 million more reserves in the economy than before the Fed purchased the government bonds from BankOne. The reserves are held by BankOne, but they will not be held for long.

Recall that banks hold reserves equal to a certain fraction of their deposits, a fraction called the reserve ratio, which in this example we are assuming is 10 percent. But now, after the Fed's actions, BankOne has 20 percent of its deposits as reserves, or more than the required 10 percent. Because the reserves do not pay any interest, while loans and bonds do, the bank will have incentive to reduce its reserves and make more loans or buy more bonds.

Table 22.3
Balance Sheet of BankOne after Reserves Increase (millions of dollars)

Assets		Liabilities	
Loans	70	Deposits	100
Bonds	10		
Reserves	20		

> Note the effect of the Fed's purchase of bonds: Compared with Table 22.2, bonds are lower and reserves are higher in Table 22.3. The ratio of reserves to deposits is .2.

Suppose BankOne decreases its reserves by making more loans; with the reserve ratio of .1, the bank can loan $10 million. Suppose the bank loans $10 million to UNO, a small oil company, which uses the funds to buy an oil tanker from DOS, a shipbuilding firm. UNO pays DOS with a check from BankOne, and DOS deposits the check in its checking account at its own bank, BankTwo. Now BankTwo must ask BankOne for payment; BankOne will make the payment by lowering its reserve account at the Fed and increasing BankTwo's reserve account at the Fed by $10 million. BankOne's balance sheet at the end of these transactions is shown in Table 22.4.

Hence, after BankOne makes the loan and transfers its reserves to BankTwo, its reserves are back to 10 percent of its deposits. This is the end of the story for BankOne, but not for the economy as a whole because BankTwo now has $10 million more in reserves, and this is going to affect BankTwo's decisions. Let us see how.

Now BankTwo finds itself with $10 million in additional deposits and $10 million in additional reserves at the Fed. (Remember that deposits are a liability to BankTwo and the reserves are an asset; thus, assets and liabilities each have risen by $10 million.) However, BankTwo needs to hold only $1 million in reserves for the additional $10 million in deposits. Thus, BankTwo will want to make more loans until its reserves equal 10 percent of its deposits. It will lend out to other people an amount equal to 90 percent of the $10 million, or $9 million. In Table 22.5, the increase in deposits, loans, and reserves at BankTwo is shown in the first row. This is the end of the story for BankTwo, but not for the economy as a whole.

The people who get loans from BankTwo will use these loans to pay others. Thus, the funds will probably end up in yet another bank, called BankThree. Then, BankThree will find itself with $9 million in additional deposits and $9 million in additional reserves. BankThree will then lend 90 percent of the $9 million, or $8.1 million, as shown in the second row of Table 22.5. This process will continue from bank to bank. We begin to see that the initial increase in reserves is leading to a much bigger expansion of deposits. The whole process is shown in Table 22.5. Each row shows what happens at one of the banks. The sums of the columns show the change for the whole economy. If we sum the columns through the end of the process, we will see that deposits, and thus the money supply, increase by $100 million as a result

Table 22.4
Balance Sheet of BankOne after It Makes Loans

Assets		Liabilities	
Loans	80	Deposits	100
Bonds	10		
Reserves	10		

> By making more loans, the bank reduces the ratio of reserves to deposits back to .1.

Table 22.5
Deposit Expansion (millions of dollars)

	Deposits	Loans	Reserves
BankTwo	10.00	9.00	1.000
BankThree	9.00	8.10	0.900
BankFour	8.10	7.29	0.810
BankFive	7.29	6.56	0.729
BankSix	6.56	5.90	0.656
BankSeven	5.90	5.31	0.590
BankEight	5.31	4.78	0.531
BankNine	4.78	4.30	0.430
BankTen	4.30	3.87	0.387
.	.	.	.
.	.	.	.
.	.	.	.
Final Sum	100.00	90.00	10.000

The numbers in each column get smaller and smaller; if we add up the numbers for all the banks, even those beyond BankTen, we get the sum at the bottom.

of the $10 million increase in reserves. The increase in deposits is 10 times the actual increase in reserves—exactly what the formula predicted! In reality, the whole process takes a short period of time (days rather than weeks) because banks adjust their loans and reserves very quickly.

REVIEW
- Banks serve two important functions: They help channel funds from savers to investors, and their deposits can be used as money.
- Commercial banks hold deposits, called reserves, at the Fed.
- The Fed increases reserves by buying bonds and reduces reserves by selling bonds.
- The deposits at banks expand by a multiple of any increase in reserves. Thus, there is a link between reserves and deposits in the overall economy.

How the Fed Controls the Money Supply: Currency plus Deposits

We have now seen how the Fed can, through an increase in reserves, increase the amount of deposits or, through a decrease in reserves, reduce the amount of deposits. But the money supply includes currency as well as deposits. So let us now add currency to the story. With currency in the picture, there are now three things to keep track of: deposits, reserves, and currency. We will find it useful to introduce some shorthand notation to keep track of all three.

The Money Supply *(M)* and Bank Reserves *(BR)*

The supply of money is currency plus deposits. That is,

Money supply = currency + deposits

If we let *CU* stand for currency and *D* stand for deposits, then

$$M = CU + D$$

or, in words, the money supply equals currency plus deposits.

We already know that commercial banks hold a fraction of their deposits at the Fed. Let *BR* represent the reserves the commercial banks hold at the Fed, and let *rr* be the reserve ratio. Then the relationship between reserves and deposits described in the previous section can be written using symbols as

$$BR = rrD$$

or, in words, bank reserves equal the reserve ratio (*rr*) times deposits (*D*). For example, if banks are required to hold 10 percent of their deposits as reserves at the Fed, then *rr* = .1. Remember, reserves held at the central bank by the commercial banks are just like any other deposit, such as a checking deposit. For example, Citibank, a commercial bank headquartered in New York City, holds a large amount of reserves at the Fed.

Currency versus Deposits

Although currency and deposits are both part of the money supply, they have different characteristics. For some purposes, people prefer currency to checking deposits, and vice versa. These preferences determine how much currency and checking deposits there are in the economy. If you want to hold more currency in your wallet because you find it is more convenient than a checking deposit, you just go to the bank and reduce your checking deposit and carry around more currency. If you are worried about crime and do not want to have much currency in your wallet, then you go to the bank and deposit a larger amount in your checking account. Thus, people decide on the amount of currency versus deposits in the economy. In Japan, where crime is less prevalent than in many other countries, people use much more currency compared to checking accounts than in other countries. Even Japanese business executives who earn the equivalent of $120,000 a year frequently are paid monthly with the equivalent of $10,000 in cash.

currency to deposit ratio: the proportion of currency that people in the economy want to hold relative to their deposits; it equals currency divided by deposits.

In order to determine the amount of currency versus deposits in the economy as a whole, we assume that people want to hold currency equal to a certain fraction of their deposits. More precisely, we assume that there is a ratio called the **currency to deposit ratio** that at any time describes how much currency people want to hold compared to their deposits. If people are happy holding an amount of currency equal to 40 percent of their deposits, then the currency to deposit ratio is .4. If deposits equal $700 billion and the currency to deposit ratio is .4, then currency would equal $280 billion and the money supply would equal $980 billion. Different individuals will have different tastes, but on the average, there will be an overall ratio of currency to deposits in the economy. That ratio depends on people's behavior, on custom, and, as already mentioned, on security in the community.

The ratio also depends on technology; for example, credit cards have reduced the currency to deposit ratio. Note, however, that credit cards are not money any more than a driver's license used for identification when cashing a check is money. Credit cards make more use of checking deposits relative to currency because people usually pay their credit card bills with a check.

At any given point in time, we can take the currency to deposit ratio as a fairly stable number. If the currency to deposit ratio is k, then we can write

Currency = (currency to deposit ratio) × deposits
= k × deposits

Using the symbols we have already introduced, we can write this as

$CU = kD$

We now use this expression along with the previous two expressions for the money supply (M) and bank reserves (BR) to show how the Fed can control the money supply.

The Money Multiplier

We saw that the Fed can change the amount of bank reserves by buying and selling bonds. We also saw that when the Fed increases reserves, deposits expand. If currency held by people is equal to k times deposits, then currency will increase when deposits increase. Thus, by buying and selling bonds, the Fed can affect the supply of currency. The Fed can therefore control both currency and reserves. The sum of currency plus reserves is called the **monetary base** by economists. That is,

monetary base: currency plus reserves; the monetary base can be tightly controlled by the Fed.

Monetary base = currency + reserves

Because the Fed can control both currency and reserves, it can control the monetary base. If we let MB stand for the monetary base, then

$MB = CU + BR$

Table 22.6 shows the size of the monetary base in the U.S. economy in December 2004.

We now want to derive a link between the monetary base MB and the money supply M. That link can be used by the Fed to control the money supply. To derive the link, we will use some algebra and equations just like those the people at the Fed use. We can use the equation showing that the money supply equals currency plus deposits and the equation showing that currency is a certain fraction of deposits to get a relationship between the money supply and deposits. That is, substitute $CU = kD$ into the equation $M = CU + D$ to get $M = kD + D$, or

Follow the economic logic behind the algebra. The first equation links the *money supply* to deposits. The second equation links the *monetary base* to deposits. Thus the money supply and the monetary base must be linked together, as indicated by the third equation showing the money multiplier.

$M = (k + 1)D$

There is also the relationship that exists between bank reserves and deposits, $BR = rrD$, which together with $CU = kD$ can be substituted into the equation $MB = CU + BR$ to get $MB = kD + rrD$, or

$MB = (k + rr)D$

Now, to find the link between MB and M, divide M by MB and cancel out D to get

$$\frac{M}{MB} = \frac{(k+1)}{(k+rr)} \Rightarrow M = \frac{(k+1)}{(k+rr)}MB$$

We call this ratio, $(k + 1)/(k + rr)$, the money multiplier. For example, if the reserve ratio rr is .1 and the currency to deposit ratio k is .2, then the money multiplier is $(.2 + 1)/(.2 + .1) = 1.2/.3 = 4$. An increase in the monetary base MB of $100 million would increase the money supply M by $400 million. This large increase is the reason for the term *multiplier.* In general, the **money multiplier** is the number you multiply the monetary base by to get the money supply.

money multiplier: the multiple by which the money supply changes as a result of a change in the monetary base.

To see how the money multiplier works in practice, suppose the Fed buys bonds so as to increase the monetary base by $1 billion; according to the money multiplier, the money supply in the economy should increase by $4 billion. The actual increase

Table 22.6
The Monetary Base for the United States, December 2004 (billions of dollars)

Currency	697
Reserves	47
Monetary Base	744

Source: Federal Reserve Board.

in the money supply occurs through a bank-by-bank process just like that shown in Table 22.5, with currency now changing as well. With currency in the story, the total effect on the money supply of a change in the monetary base is smaller than in Table 22.5 because people do not put all their money in banks. This reduces the amount of deposit expansion. Note that if $k = 0$, the case without currency, the money multiplier is $(1/rr)$, just as in the formula relating deposits to reserves in the previous section. That is, with $k = 0$ and $CU = 0$, we have that deposits equal $1/r$ times reserves. With $rr = .1$, the money multiplier is 10. Thus, an increase in the monetary base of $10 million will increase money by $100 million, as in the previous section.

More important than the fact that the multiplier is greater than 1 is that it provides a link between the monetary base and the money supply in the economy. As long as the currency to deposit ratio and the reserve ratio do not change, the Fed can control the money supply by adjusting the monetary base.

REVIEW

- The monetary base is the sum of currency plus bank reserves. The Fed can change the money supply—currency plus deposits—by adjusting the monetary base. A change in the monetary base changes the money supply by a multiple of the increase in the monetary base. The multiple is called the money multiplier.

- The money multiplier depends on the reserve ratio and the currency to deposit ratio.

Money Growth and Inflation

Early in this chapter, in the section "Commodity Money," we showed that when gold, silver, or other commodities were the primary form of money, increases in the supply of money would cause inflation. Even though paper currency and deposits are now the main forms of money, the same principle holds today. That is, *all other things being equal,* an increase in the supply of money will cause inflation. In this section we examine this principle by looking at two important episodes of inflation during the twentieth century. Before we do so, we introduce a famous equation that can help us test the principle that an increase in the supply of money eventually causes inflation.

Consider first a simple example. Suppose that all of your transactions are in a video game arcade with food-vending machines and video game machines. You will need money in your pocket to carry out your transactions each day. If you use the vending and video game machines ten times a day, you will need ten times more money in your pocket than if you use the machines once a day. Hence, ten times more transactions means ten times more money. If the prices for vending machine items and minutes on a video game machine double, then you will need twice as much money for each day's activities, assuming that the higher price does not cure your habit. Hence, whether the value of transactions increases because the number of items purchased increases or because the price of each item increases, the amount of money used for transactions will rise.

What is true for you and the machines is true for the whole population and the whole economy. For the whole economy, real GDP is like the number of transactions with the machines, and the GDP deflator (a measure of the average price in the economy) is like the average price of the vending and game machines. Just as the amount of money you use for transactions in the game arcade is related to the number of transactions and the price of each transaction, so too is the supply of money in the economy related to real GDP and the GDP deflator.

The Quantity Equation of Money

quantity equation of money: the equation relating the price level and real GDP to the quantity of money and the velocity of money: The quantity of money times its velocity equals the price level times real GDP.

This relationship between money, real GDP, and the GDP deflator can be summarized by the **quantity equation of money,** which is written (as shown on page 000)

$$\text{Money supply} \times \text{velocity} = \text{GDP deflator} \times \text{real GDP}$$

or

$$MV = PY$$

where V is velocity, P is the GDP deflator, and Y is real GDP. For example, if the money supply was \$1,000 billion, real GDP was \$8,000 billion, and the GDP deflator was 1.1, then a value of 8.8 for velocity would satisfy the quantity equation ($1,000 \times 8.8 = 1.1 \times 8,000$).

velocity: a measure of how frequently money is turned over in the economy.

The term **velocity** measures how frequently money is turned over. It is the number of times a dollar is used on average each period to make purchases. To see this, suppose an automatic teller machine (ATM) is installed in the room with the vending machines and video games from the preceding example. Each morning you get cash from the ATM for your morning games, and each day at midday an employee takes the cash from the vending and game machines and restokes the ATM. You then replenish your cash from the ATM to pay for your afternoon use of the games and vending machines; you now need to carry only half as much currency in your pocket as before they installed the ATM, when you had to bring enough cash to last all day. From your perspective, therefore, the velocity of money doubles. Money turns over twice as fast. As this example shows, velocity in the economy depends on technology and, in particular, on how efficient we are at using money.

Now, let's use the quantity equation to show how an increase in the money supply is related to inflation. If you look carefully at the quantity equation of money, you can see that if velocity and real GDP are not affected by a change in money, then an increase in the money supply will increase the GDP deflator (the average level of prices in the economy). A higher percentage increase in money—that is, *higher money growth*—will lead to a higher percentage increase in prices—that is, *higher inflation*. Thus the quantity equation of money shows that higher rates of money growth lead to higher inflation, just as in the case of commodity money early in the chapter.

A restatement of the quantity equation using growth rates leads to a convenient relationship between money growth, inflation, real GDP growth, and velocity growth. In particular,

$$\text{Money growth} + \text{velocity growth} = \text{inflation} + \text{real GDP growth}$$

For example, if the money supply growth is 5 percent per year, velocity growth is 0 percent per year, and real GDP growth is 3 percent per year, then this equation says that inflation is 2 percent per year. (This growth rate form of the quantity equation follows directly from the quantity equation itself; in general, the rate of growth of a product of two terms is approximately equal to the sum of the growth rates of the two terms. Thus, the growth rate of M times V equals the growth rate of M plus the growth rate of V, and the growth rate of P times Y equals the growth rate of P plus the growth rate of Y.)

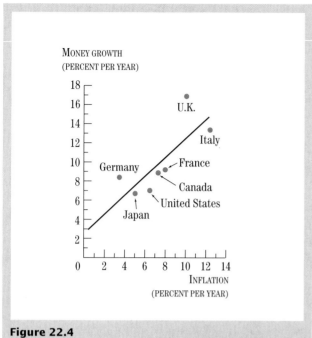

MONEY GROWTH
(PERCENT PER YEAR)

Figure 22.4
The Relation Between Money Growth and Inflation
As the data for these several countries show, higher
money growth is associated with higher inflation. The data
pertain to the period 1973–1991, when inflation differed
greatly among the countries.

The quantity equation tells us that along a long-run economic growth path in which real GDP growth is equal to potential GDP growth, an increase in money growth by a certain number of percentage points will result in the long run in an increase in inflation of the same number of percentage points unless there is a change in velocity growth. Thus, higher money growth will lead to higher inflation in the long run. If velocity growth remains at zero, as in the previous example, and real GDP growth remains at 3 percent per year, then an increase in money growth by 10 percentage points, from 5 to 15 percent, will increase inflation by 10 percentage points, from 2 to 12 percent.

Evidence

What evidence do we have that higher money growth leads to more inflation? The quantity equation tells us that we should look for evidence during periods when changes in real GDP and velocity were small compared to changes in money growth and inflation. During such periods, the change in money growth and inflation will be the dominant terms in the quantity equation.

■ **Worldwide Inflation in the 1970s and 1980s.**
Figure 22.4 shows such a period: the years from 1973 to 1991, when many economies had big inflations, some much bigger than others. Money growth is plotted on the vertical axis, and inflation on the horizontal axis. In Figure 22.4, each point represents a country. For countries with higher money growth, inflation was higher. Hence, the quantity equation works well during this period. During

100,000,000,000,000 German Mark Reichsbank Note, 1923

Hyperinflation and Too Much Money
So much money was printed during the period of German hyperinflation that it became cheaper to burn several million German marks to cook breakfast—as this woman was doing in 1923—than to buy kindling wood with the nearly worthless money.

the 1990s, inflation has been low in all these countries, so there has not been enough of a difference to test how well the equation works.

■ **Hyperinflations.**   Another, more dramatic type of evidence showing that high money growth can cause inflation is hyperinflation. A hyperinflation is simply a period of very high inflation. The inflation in Germany in 1923 is one of the most famous examples of a hyperinflation. Inflation rose to over 100 percent per week. The German government had incurred huge expenses during World War I, and huge demands for war reparations from the victors in World War I compounded the problem. Because the government could not raise enough taxes to pay its expenses, it started printing huge amounts of money, which caused the hyperinflation of 1923. Figure 22.5 shows the *weekly* increase in German prices. Shop owners closed their shops at lunchtime to change the prices. Workers were paid twice weekly. People would rush to the stores and buy everything they needed for the next few days. Firms also set up barter systems with their workers, exchanging consumer goods directly for labor.

As just stated, the hyperinflation was initially caused by the huge increase in money growth. However, once it started, everyone tried to get rid of cash as soon as possible, accelerating the inflationary process. Also, by the time the government received its tax revenue, it was not worth much because prices had risen sharply. So the government had to print even more money. In the last months of hyperinflation, more than 30 paper mills worked at full capacity to deliver paper currency. One hundred fifty printing firms had 2,000 presses running 24 hours a day to print German marks, and they could not keep up with the need for new notes. On November 15, 1923, an economic reform stabilized the inflation rate. By then, the German prices were 100 billion times higher than they had been before the hyperinflation.

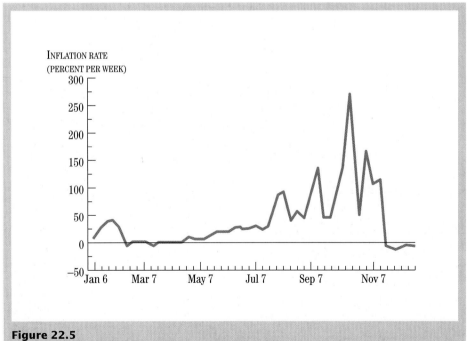

Figure 22.5
German Hyperinflation of 1923
The chart shows the weekly percent change in the price level in Germany in 1923. Inflation rose to truly astronomical levels for several months.

The German hyperinflation of 1923 was not a unique historical episode, and hyperinflation is not necessarily linked to war. There was hyperinflation in Brazil in the 1980s and in Argentina in the early 1990s. In the mid-1990s, high inflation in Russia was also caused by the creation of too much money. Money growth is the cause of all hyperinflations.

> **REVIEW**
> - The quantity equation of money says that the money supply times velocity equals real GDP times the GDP deflator.
> - Higher rates of money growth will eventually lead to higher inflation.
> - Evidence of the relation between money growth and inflation is found in the 1970s and 1980s in the United States and other large economies, as well as in hyperinflations in Germany in the 1920s and in Brazil, Argentina, and Russia more recently.

Conclusion

Money has fascinated economists for centuries. The famous quantity equation introduced in this chapter predates Adam Smith and was used by the economist-philosopher David Hume in the eighteenth century. Adam Smith placed money second only to the division of labor in the first chapters of the *Wealth of Nations*.

Although the role of money appears mysterious and has caused some great debates in economics and politics, the ideas presented in this chapter are not controversial. The three functions of money, the deposit expansion process, the money multiplier, the technical ability of the central bank to control the monetary base, and the fact that money is the cause of inflation in the long run are things many economists now agree on.

Many of the controversies about money pertain to the short-run fluctuations in the economy and revolve around the effects the Fed has on real GDP in the short run. After considering the reasons why real GDP may depart from potential GDP in the short run in Chapters 23 and 24, we will return to the effects the Fed has on short-run fluctuations in the economy.

KEY POINTS

1. Money has three roles: a medium of exchange, a store of value, and a unit of account.

2. Commodity money, ranging from salt to gold coins, has been used in place of barter for many centuries. Now paper money and deposits are also part of money.

3. Commercial banks are financial intermediaries; their deposits are part of the money supply.

4. Commercial banks hold reserves at the central bank.

5. The central bank changes reserves by buying and selling bonds.

6. The monetary base is currency plus reserves.

7. The central bank can control the monetary base by buying and selling bonds.

8. The money multiplier tells us how much the money supply changes when the monetary base changes.

9. The central bank in the United States is the Federal Reserve System (the Fed).

10. When stated in terms of growth rates, the quantity equation of money describes the relationship between money growth, real GDP growth, and inflation.

11. Higher money growth eventually leads to higher inflation.

KEY TERMS

money

medium of exchange

store of value

unit of account

currency

checking deposit

money supply

Federal Reserve System
  (the Fed)

bank

Federal Open Market
  Committee (FOMC)

asset

liability

reserves

required reserve ratio

open market operation

currency to deposit ratio

monetary base

money multiplier

quantity equation of
  money

velocity

QUESTIONS FOR REVIEW

1. What are the differences between the medium of exchange, store of value, and unit of account roles of money?

2. What are some examples of commodity money?

3. Why is it that currency is a part of money but that an expensive purse to put the currency in is not?

4. What is a bank?

5. What is the Fed, and how is the FOMC organized?

6. What happens to bank reserves when the Fed buys bonds?

7. What happens to the monetary base when the Fed buys bonds?

8. What is the money multiplier, and why does it depend on the required reserve ratio?

9. Why does higher money growth cause inflation?

10. What is the quantity equation of money?

PROBLEMS

1. Which of the following are money, and which are not?
   a. A credit card
   b. A dollar bill
   c. A check in your checkbook
   d. Funds in a checking account

2. State whether each of the following statements is true or false. Explain your answers in one or two sentences.
   a. The smaller the reserve ratio at banks, the larger the money multiplier.
   b. The Federal Reserve reduces reserves by buying government bonds.
   c. The same money is always used as both a unit of account and a medium of exchange at any one time in any one country.
   d. When commodity money is the only type of money, a decrease in the price of the commodity serving as money is inflation.

3. Credit cards are not included in the money supply, but currency and deposits at banks are included. Explain why credit cards are excluded. (*Hint:* Credit cards are a form of identification that allows you to borrow.)

4. Suppose the Fed buys a government bond for $10,000 from Citibank.
   a. For simplicity, suppose that $k = 0$: People hold no currency. If the required reserve ratio is 10 percent, how much of this initial $10,000 will Citibank lend out?
   b. Suppose the process of lending and depositing continues through the banking system until there is nothing left to lend. At that point, how much is the total increase in deposits created by the initial $10,000?
   c. How will the total increase in deposits change from part (b) if $k > 0$? Why?

5. Suppose that before the invention of the automatic teller machine, people held currency equal to 20 percent of their bank deposits. If the required reserve ratio is 20 percent, what is the money multiplier? Now suppose that after the invention of the ATM, people hold only 10 percent of the value of their deposits in currency. What is the money multiplier now? Explain how the change in the money multiplier occurs.

6. Suppose the Fed buys government bonds and the monetary base rises by $1 billion. If the required reserve ratio is .10 and the currency to deposit ratio is .5, by how much will the money supply change?

7. Assume that required reserves are 7 percent of deposits and that people hold no currency—all money is held in the form of checking deposits.
   a. Suppose that the Federal Reserve purchases $30,000 worth of government bonds from Ellen (a private citizen), and that Ellen deposits all of the proceeds from the sale into her checking account at Z Bank. Construct a balance sheet, with assets on the left and liabilities on the right, to show how Ellen's deposit creates new assets and liabilities for Z Bank.

b. How much of this new deposit can Z Bank lend out? Assume that it lends this amount to George, who then deposits the entire amount into his account at Y Bank. Show this on Y Bank's balance sheet.

c. Suppose George uses the loan to build an addition to his house. His contractor, Joe, deposits the money in his account at X Bank. How much is this deposit? How much in new excess reserves is created when he makes this new deposit?

d. The process of lending and relending creates money throughout the banking system. As a result of Ellen's deposit, how much money, in the form of deposits, has been created so far?

e. If this process resulting from Ellen's deposit continues forever, how much money will be created?

8. Consider the following table:

Year	Quantity of Money (billions of $)	Velocity	Real GDP (billions of $)	GDP Deflator
2002	1,217	8.62	10,075	
2003	1,299	8.47	10,381	
2004	1,367	8.58	10,842	

a. Fill in the missing data, using the quantity equation of money.

b. Why might velocity change in this way?

c. Calculate the inflation rate for 2003 and 2004.

d. If money growth had been 5 percent per year in 2003 and 2004, what would inflation have been, assuming real GDP and velocity as in the table?

The Issue:
Is Outsourcing Bad for the United States?

Outsourcing is a term that is used to describe a common business practice whereby some component or portion of one company's work is done by another company. Examples include a manufacturing firm buying component parts from a supplier, a bank hiring a software company to ensure that its electronic network is secure, and a magazine hiring freelance photographers to provide photographs to complement a news story. With the increased trend in globalization, the scope of outsourcing has expanded. These days, when you read about "outsourcing" in the popular media, you will often find the discussion to be about offshore outsourcing. Offshore outsourcing (referred to simply as outsourcing henceforth) occurs when some component or portion of a U.S.-based company's work is done by a foreign-based company. Everyone seems to agree that such outsourcing has increased over the last few years and that the growth trend is likely to continue over time. However, there is substantial disagreement about the extent and the impact of outsourcing.

Discussion about the extent of outsourcing centers on a few key studies, though even these numbers are under dispute. The most widely cited number comes from a report by Forrester Research, which estimates that 3.3 million U.S. jobs will be outsourced by 2015, an average of around 300,000 jobs a year.[1] Another widely cited study by the McKinsey Global Institute estimates that the entire developed world will have located 4.1 million service jobs in low-wage countries by 2008.[2]

In the last few years, the debate over the economic impact of outsourcing has moved squarely into the public spotlight. Passionate opinions about outsourcing abound in newspaper articles, magazine reports, television specials, and talk radio discussions. Many argue that outsourcing is harmful to the U.S. economy—that millions of jobs are being "shipped abroad," resulting in a weaker economy. Others argue that the job losses attributed to outsourcing are overstated, and that outsourcing can be a net benefit to the economy by allowing firms to produce goods and services more efficiently and cheaply. In an opinion poll conducted by Princeton Survey Research Associates, 68 percent of the respondents disagreed with

the claim that outsourcing is good for Americans.[3] This negative verdict stands in stark contrast to the opinions of many well-known international economists, who argue that outsourcing is simply the latest manifestation of international trade, an area where economic theory indicates that the benefits outweigh the costs.

Outsourcing Is Bad for the U.S. Economy   POINT

Robert Kuttner, the coeditor of the *American Prospect* and a columnist for *BusinessWeek,* emphatically disagrees with the notion that outsourcing is a trivial problem for the U.S. economy.[4] Kuttner's arguments are primarily based on the distribution of the costs and benefits of increased outsourcing and globalization. When a company is able to outsource work to another country where wages are lower, global wages will tend to converge. Decreased demand for the labor that is being outsourced implies that wages of U.S. workers in the outsourced sector will fall, while the increased demand for workers in India will cause their wages to rise. Workers in the United States will have to find comparable jobs in other sectors if they are to maintain their same standard of living, but they will find it difficult to do so. Kuttner worries that high-paying technology-sector jobs will end up being replaced by relatively low-paying service-sector jobs.

Kuttner also points out that the benefits of outsourcing, which come in the form of increased productivity, lower costs, and higher profits, are unlikely to go to the workers whose lives are disrupted. Instead, Kuttner argues, these benefits will mostly be captured by corporate insiders in the form of astronomical salaries and stock benefits, especially in industries where there isn't a strong union presence.

Proponents of the position that outsourcing is bad for the U.S. economy recently received support from economist Paul Samuelson, who won a Nobel Prize in 1970, partly for his seminal work on international trade.[5]

Samuelson presents a typical two-country, two-good international trade scenario similar to the one you studied in this textbook. He shows that there are gains from trade,

1   John C. McCarthy, "3.3 million U.S. Jobs to Go Offshore," Forrester Research Brief, November 11, 2002.
2   McKinsey Global Institute, "The Emerging Global Labor Market," June 2005.
3   *Newsweek* poll conducted by Princeton Survey Research Associates, February 19–20, 2004. Sample of 1,019 adults. The margin of error was ±3 percent.
4   Robert Kuttner, "The Problem with Outsourcing," *Boston Globe,* April 21, 2004.
5   Paul A. Samuelson, "When Ricardo and Mill Rebut and Confirm Arguments of Mainstream Economists Supporting Globalization," *Journal of Economic Perspectives,* vol. 18.3, Summer 2004. An interesting discussion of this paper by Arvind Panagariya, "Why the Recent Samuelson Paper is NOT about Offshore Outsourcing," is available online (http://www.columbia.edu/~ap2231/).

just as you have learned in this textbook. But he then goes on to extend the model to consider an increase in foreign productivity that is exactly large enough to result in neither the home country nor the foreign country having comparative advantage; this eliminates the need for trade.[6] If there is no trade, then all the benefits from trade that the home country had previously enjoyed from trade would be lost and it will be worse off. Samuelson uses this result to challenge what he terms as the mainstream economists' "oversimple complacencies" about outsourcing.

COUNTERPOINT Outsourcing Does Not Pose a Threat to the U.S. Economy

Jagdish Bhagwati, Arvind Panagariya, and T. N. Srinivasan argue that the job loss numbers associated with outsourcing are overstated. They point out that many workers who are laid off from one industry will shift into work in other industries. Even if the higher numbers for job losses attributed to outsourcing were valid, Bhagwati et al. emphasize that these numbers pale when considered in relation to the size of the overall labor market. In a typical recent year, the Forrester group's estimate of job loss is less than 1 percent of jobs in the affected industries. This year more than 30 million jobs will be destroyed in the U.S. economy. Any jobs lost because they are outsourced *from* the United States need to be weighed against jobs gained from other countries because they are outsourced *to* the United States. The authors present data showing that the United States runs a large trade surplus in services, indicating that we may well end up "providing" more service jobs to other countries than they "take away" from us.

Outsourcing, according to Bhagwati et al., is simply another form of international trade. Outsourcing allows companies to gain from trade by exploiting comparative advantage. By allowing relatively low-skilled service work—customer service, data entry, basic programming, reading X-rays—to be done in countries like India, companies are able to expand economic activity and hire more high-skilled service workers in the United States. And the perception that hundreds of millions of well-educated Chinese and Indian citizens are eagerly waiting to take jobs away from young Americans who are now studying in college is a far cry from reality. Only 6 percent

of 18- to 24-year-olds in India enroll in universities, and only a small fraction of these have the language and other skills needed to do the job of a U.S. worker.

Finally, the majority of service-sector jobs in the United States are in industries that can't be outsourced. Examples include catering, restaurant service jobs, home health care, and so on. Call centers, data entry, and customer service are the easiest types of jobs to outsource; we have to be careful not to extrapolate the increases in outsourcing to other industries.

The debate over outsourcing is also often conflated with the downward trend in manufacturing jobs in the United States. Political scientist Daniel Drezner points out that the decline in manufacturing jobs in the United States has much more to do with technological innovation than with outsourcing.[7] He points out that manufacturing jobs are declining worldwide, including in countries like China and Brazil. If the jobs were being outsourced from the United States, then we would expect to see manufacturing jobs increase in those countries.[8]

Economist Catherine Mann points out that dynamic changes driven by outsourcing can lead to increased productivity growth in the long run.[9] As an illustrative example, she points to the globalization of computer hardware that took place in the 1990s, almost a decade before the outsourcing of software and information services. The price of computer hardware is estimated to have dropped by 10 to 30 percent, making computers more affordable. This improved use of technology enhances productivity, economic activity, and welfare.

Using Your Economics

1. Bhagwati et al. pose the following question: "Are computer programmers [in the United States] earning $60,000 going to be bumped down to $15,000 jobs stocking shelves and bagging groceries at Wal-Mart?" Based on what you have learned about international trade and the discussion here, how would you answer?
2. Arguments about the threat posed by outsourcing often focus on the low relative wages of Indian workers compared to their U.S. counterparts. Why do you think the wages of Indian workers are so much lower than the wages of U.S. workers with similar skills? Do you see this disparity in wages persisting if the current trends in outsourcing continue?

6 In the two-good, two-country model that you are familiar with, neither country having comparative advantage is the special case where the two countries have *identical* relative efficiencies of producing each good.
7 Daniel W. Drezner, "The Outsourcing Bogeyman," *Foreign Affairs*, May/June 2004.
8 The impact of technological change on manufacturing employment would be seen most vividly if one were able to go back in time to visit an auto-manufacturing plant in Michigan or a steel mill in Pennsylvania and compare the relative use of capital and labor with their contemporary counterparts—a Toyota plant in Kentucky or a steel mill in Korea.
9 Catherine L. Mann, "Globalization of IT Services and White Collar Jobs: The Next Wave of Productivity Growth," Institute for International Economics, No. PB 03-11, December 2003. Available at http://www.iie.com/publications/pb/pb03-11.pdf.

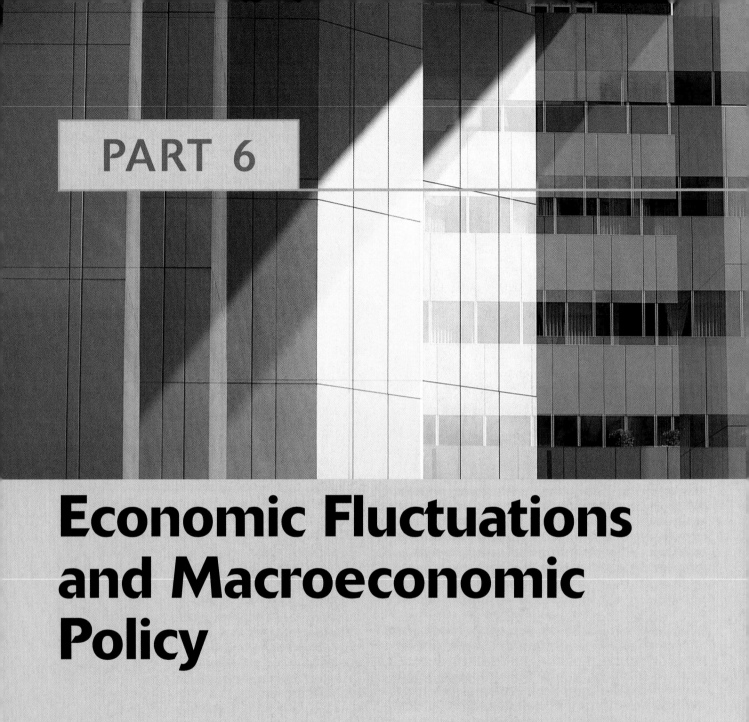

PART 6

Economic Fluctuations and Macroeconomic Policy

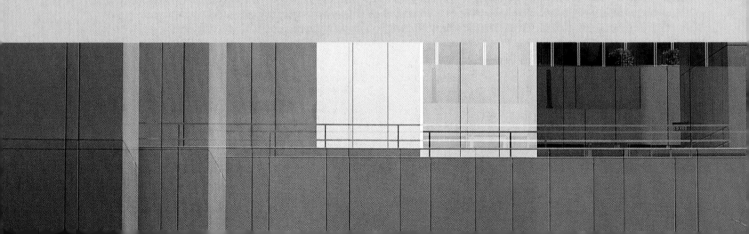

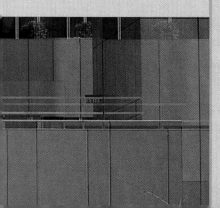

CHAPTER 23

The Nature and Causes of Economic Fluctuations

I n the early part of 2001, the record economic expansion that began all the way back in 1991 came to an end. A sharp fall in U.S. stock markets, particularly in the technology sector; falling consumer confidence; decisions by firms to cut back on investment spending; rapid increases in interest rates by the Federal Reserve in the year 2000; and rising oil prices are all potential explanations for the economic slowdown. The slowdown was considerably worsened by the tragic events of September 11, 2001, and the subsequent fall in spending and output.

By 2002, however, the economy was starting to show strong signs of recovery, encouraged by the actions of the government in cutting taxes and the Federal Reserve in lowering interest rates. The recovery gathered steam in 2003 as consumer spending on big-ticket items such as housing increased, with higher investment spending by firms following a few quarters later. By 2004, the economy was growing quite robustly again.

In this section, we take a closer look at economic fluctuations of the type that we saw in the early 2000s, as well as other episodes in U.S. history that have very different features. The goal is to improve our understanding of economic fluctuations, which are defined as departures of the economy from its long-term growth trend. These departures include recessions, which are periods in which

GDP declines sharply, moving the economy below its long-term trend, as well as booms, in which GDP rises rapidly, moving the economy above its long-term trend. Examples of recessions include the most recent slowdown of 2001, the sharp recession that hit the U.S. economy in the early 1980s, and the recessions that devasted the economies of Malaysia, Indonesia, and Korea in the late 1990s. Examples of booms include the long growth period between 1991 and 2001, in which the U.S. economy grew for over 120 consecutive months!

Studying economic fluctuations is vital because recessions bring unemployment and hardship to many people. While the importance of economic growth cannot be overstated, fluctuations around the growth trend are also vital for the livelihood of millions of people. John Maynard Keynes said it best in his book *A Tract on Monetary Reform:* "But this *long run* is a misleading guide to current affairs. *In the long run* we are all dead. Economists set themselves too easy, too useless a task if in tempestuous seasons they can only tell us that when the storm is long past the ocean is flat again." In less eloquent terms, the study of fluctuations is vital to understanding macroeconomics.

Economic fluctuations have been common for at least 200 years, but recessions have changed over time. One notable difference is that they have diminished in frequency and severity in the United States and many other countries, especially over the past two decades. A key purpose of studying economic fluctuations is to explain why this weakening of recessions has occurred and to determine whether economic policies are responsible for this trend.

After a decade of economic expansion, the U.S. economy went into recession in 2001. As shown in the magnified portion of Figure 23.1, real GDP was clearly above potential GDP in 1999 and 2000, but in mid-2001, real GDP began to fall. As the recession took hold, real GDP fell below potential GDP and continued to fall through the first quarter of 2001, when it reached its lowest point relative to potential GDP. A recovery then started that brought real GDP back to potential GDP by 2004.

Economic fluctuations occur simultaneously with long-term growth, as shown by the longer history in Figure 23.1. Real GDP has fluctuated around what might otherwise have been a steady upward-moving trend. Although no two economic fluctuations are alike—some are long, some are short; some are deep, some are shallow—they do have common features. Perhaps the most important one is that after a

"We figure it was HERE when the recession officially began."

departure of real GDP from potential GDP, the economy eventually returns to a more normal long-run growth path.

In this chapter, we look at the first steps the economy takes as it moves away from potential GDP. In other words, we examine the initial, or short-run, increase or decrease of real GDP above or below potential GDP. We will show that the first steps of real GDP away from potential GDP are caused by changes in aggregate

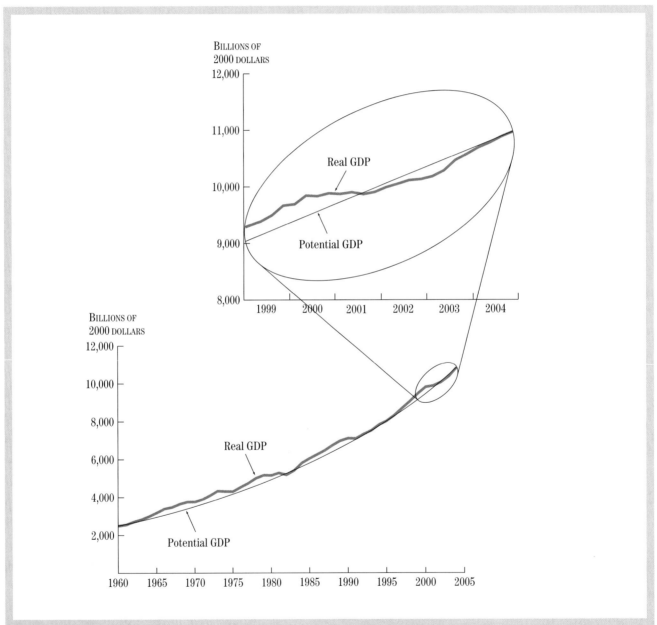

Figure 23.1
Narrowing the Focus on
Economic Fluctuations

The magnified economic fluctuations in this figure occurred as real GDP rose above potential GDP in the late 1990s and then fell below potential GDP as the economy went into a recession in 2001. By 2004, the economy had recovered.

demand. Aggregate demand is the total amount that consumers, businesses, government, and foreigners are willing to spend on all goods and services in the economy. In contrast, the growth of potential GDP is caused by increases in the available supply of inputs to production: labor, capital, and technology.

Changes in Aggregate Demand Lead to Changes in Production

Figure 23.2 illustrates the essential idea used to explain economic fluctuations: that increases or decreases in real GDP to levels above or below potential GDP occur largely because of increases or decreases in aggregate demand in the economy. Changes in aggregate demand occur when consumers, business firms, government, or foreigners expand or cut back their spending. Potential GDP in three years is represented by points *a*, *b*, and *c* in Figure 23.2. These three values of potential GDP are

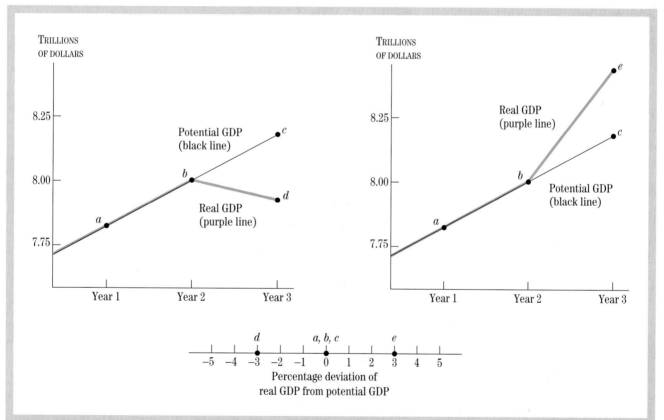

Figure 23.2
The First Step of an Economic Fluctuation

Potential GDP is shown by the black upward-sloping line in both diagrams. Points *a*, *b*, and *c* represent three different levels of potential GDP in three years. A downward departure of real GDP (shown in purple) from potential GDP is illustrated by point *d* on the left. Since real GDP falls, this is a recession. An upward departure of real GDP from potential GDP is illustrated by point *e* on the right. The departures are explained by changes in aggregate demand. The line at the bottom shows the percent deviation of real GDP from potential GDP.

part of the longer-term steady increase in potential GDP over time due to increases in the supply of labor and capital and improvements in technology. Potential GDP represents what firms would want to produce in "normal times," when the economy is neither in a recession nor in a boom. In normal times, real GDP is equal to potential GDP. Years 1 and 2 in Figure 23.2 are assumed to be normal years. However, year 3 is not a normal year. Point *d* in the left panel of the figure shows a recession because real GDP has declined from point *b*. Real GDP is below potential GDP at point *d*. Firms produce less and lay off workers. Unemployment rises. Eventually—this part of the story comes in later chapters—if demand stays low, firms begin to cut their prices, and real GDP moves back toward potential GDP. Thus, in recessions, changes in aggregate demand cause fluctuations in real GDP.

Point *e* in the right panel represents another departure of real GDP from potential GDP. In this case, real GDP rises above potential GDP. Firms produce more in response to the increase in aggregate demand; they employ more workers, and unemployment declines. Eventually—again, this part of the story comes in later chapters—if demand for their product stays high, firms raise their prices, and real GDP goes back down toward potential GDP.

Economists frequently measure the departures of real GDP from potential GDP in percentages rather than in dollar amounts. For example, if potential GDP is $8.0 trillion and real GDP is $8.4 trillion, then the percentage departure of real GDP from potential GDP is 5 percent: $(8.4 - 8.0)/8.0 = .05$. If real GDP were $7.6 trillion and potential GDP remained at $8.0 trillion, then the percentage departure would be -5 percent: $(7.6 - 8.0)/8.0 = -.05$. Percentages make it easier to compare economic fluctuations in different countries that have different sizes of real GDP. At the bottom of the two panels in Figure 23.2 is a horizontal line representing the size of the fluctuations in real GDP around potential GDP in year 1, year 2, and year 3. Points *d* and *e* in Figure 23.2 represent the first steps of an economic fluctuation.

potential GDP: the economy's long-term growth trend for real GDP determined by the available supply of capital, labor, and technology. Real GDP fluctuates above and below potential GDP. (Ch. 17)

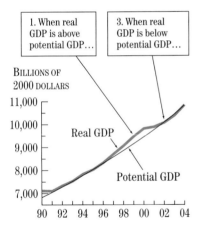

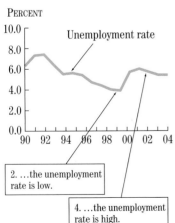

Production and Demand at Individual Firms

Why do firms produce more—bringing real GDP above *potential GDP*—when the demand for their products rises? Why do firms produce less—bringing real GDP below potential GDP—when the demand for their products falls? These questions have probably occupied more of economists' time than any other question in macroeconomics. Although more work still needs to be done, substantial improvements in economists' understanding of the issues have been made in the last 20 years.

■ **The Unemployment Rate and the Deviations of Real GDP from Potential GDP.**   First consider some simple facts about how firms operate. In normal times, when real GDP is equal to potential GDP, most firms operate with some excess capacity so that they can expand production without major bottlenecks. Small retail service businesses from taxi companies to dry cleaners can usually increase production when customer demand increases. Another taxi is added to a busy route and one of the drivers is asked to work overtime. One of the dry cleaning employees who has been working part time is happy to work full time. The same is true for large manufacturing firms. When asked what percent of capacity their production is in normal times, manufacturing firms typically answer about 80 percent. Thus, firms normally have room to expand production: Capacity utilization sometimes goes up to 90 percent or higher. If firms need more labor in order to expand production, they can ask workers to work overtime, call workers back from previous layoffs, or hire additional workers. *The unemployment rate drops below the natural unemployment rate when real GDP rises above potential GDP.*

In recessions, when demand declines, these same firms clearly have the capability to reduce production, and they do. In recessions, capacity utilization goes down

Production Decisions by Actual Firms
Individual firms—Mayflower moving services being just one example—raise production during booms when the demand for their goods or services rises, and lower production during recessions when the demand for their goods or services declines. These decisions by individual firms lead to fluctuations of real GDP above or below potential GDP.

to 70 percent or lower. Firms ask workers to stop working overtime, they move some workers to part time, or they lay off some workers. Some firms institute hiring freezes to make sure the personnel office does not keep hiring workers. *The unemployment rate rises above the natural unemployment rate when real GDP falls below potential GDP.* For example, the unemployment rate rose to more than 7 percent when the 1990–1991 recession brought real GDP below potential GDP. The relationship between the unemployment rate and the movements of real GDP relative to potential GDP is illustrated in the margin on page 606.

■ **Real-Life Examples of How Firms Respond to Demand.** Consider a typical service firm at the start of the 1990–1991 recession. Mayflower, the moving company named after the ship that moved the Pilgrims, found the demand for its moving and storage services growing rapidly in the boom of the late 1980s. The company expanded production by moving more households and, as a result, increased its employment from 6,800 workers in 1987 to 11,400 in 1989. In 1990, as the recession took hold, demand for Mayflower's services began to fall. The company reduced production—moved fewer households—and employment fell from 11,400 in 1989 to 10,900 in 1990, a decline of about 5 percent.

Consider the example of a construction firm at about the same time. As is typical in recessions, construction was hit hard in the 1990–1991 recession. Trammell Crow, the real estate construction company based in Dallas, Texas, found the demand for its construction services falling off dramatically in 1990. Hence, the firm produced fewer of these services. It built fewer shopping malls and convention centers. Total square feet under construction by Trammell Crow fell from 44 million in 1989 to 27 million in 1990. Employment at Trammell Crow also fell from the year 1989 to 1990. Employment had expanded rapidly during the 1988–1989 boom. Thus, Trammell Crow is another example showing how fluctuations in demand cause a change in production.

Could Economic Fluctuations Also Be Due to Changes in Potential GDP?

Recall from Chapter 17 that *potential GDP* depends on the economy's *aggregate supply*, which is determined by the available *capital, labor,* and *technology*. A drought or a flood would reduce supply.

real business cycle theory: a theory of macroeconomics that stresses that shifts in potential GDP are a primary cause of fluctuations in real GDP; the shifts in potential GDP are usually assumed to be caused by changes in technology.

Our discussion thus far of the production decisions of individual firms has shown why it is natural to identify fluctuations in real GDP with fluctuations in aggregate demand. To be sure, economic fluctuations also occur because of changes in potential GDP. For example, when agriculture was a much larger fraction of real GDP, droughts and floods had more noticeable effects on real GDP. Although agriculture is currently a very small fraction of total production, the possibility that increases or decreases in potential GDP may still play a large role in economic fluctuations is a topic currently being examined by economists. Economic theories that emphasize changes in potential GDP as a source of economic fluctuations are called **real business cycle theories.** Most frequently, changes in technology are assumed to be the reason for changes in potential GDP in real business cycle theories.

The factors that underlie potential GDP growth—population, capital, technological know-how—tend to evolve relatively smoothly. Population growth, for example, is much steadier than real GDP growth. We do not have a drop in the population every few years and a sudden spurt the next year. Slowdowns in population growth occur gradually over time as birthrates and death rates change. Similarly, although

In the aftermath of the tragic events of September 11, 2001, economists were called upon to analyze the potential effects on the U.S. economy. At the time, there were fears that the attacks could drive the economy into a longer recession, although many economists speculated that the effect would not be as long-lasting as had been feared. The following article, published almost a year after the attacks, summarized the impact of the tragedy on the economy. It concluded that while certain sectors, such as the airline industry, were still feeling the impacts of the attack, for most companies the bad news had come in the form of other negative events, such as the accounting scandals of 2002.

A Year After Sept. 11, Attacks' Economic Impact Lingers, but Effect Is Disparate

By ADAM GELLER, AP Business Writer

NEW YORK—A year ago, planted in front of televisions, numbed by endless images of the World Trade Center's destruction, consumers froze—and briefly forgot to consume. Investors stopped investing, and dumped stock. Travelers stopped traveling, at least by plane. Scores of companies slashed thousands of jobs, and economists warned that the combined effects could snowball.

But a year after terrorists attacked the trade center, the Pentagon—and by extension, the economy—the impact has not proven to be nearly as deep or as lasting as was feared. The economic consequences of Sept. 11 still linger, certainly. But the toll has proved disparate, inflicting the heaviest damage on sectors such as travel and tourism while leaving others unscathed. And it turns out events before and after have played a far larger role in shaping the economy than the attacks.

"I would say the impact has been less than we had initially thought in terms of economic contraction," said Gus Faucher, a senior economist with Economy.com, a research firm in West Chester, Pa. "It's a contributing factor to the weak economy, but it's not the primary factor."

Sizing up the impact of the attacks is complicated because the economy was already in a recession before last September. In the months since, it has been buffeted by other crises, including the collapse of Enron and a host of other corporate scandals, severe problems in the telecommunications industry, and the drop-off in the stock market. "Economically, the stock market setback may have had more of an impact than the terrorist attacks because it shaved some $7 trillion from our wealth," said Sung Won Sohn, an economist with Wells Fargo and Co.

Some of the expectations that shaped economic forecasts immediately after the attacks, particularly fears of a long war in Afghanistan with heavy American casualties, did not come to pass, said Ross DeVol, director of regional studies for the Millken Institute in Santa Barbara, Calif. The think tank early this year estimated the attacks would result in the elimination of 1.6 million jobs nationwide. But DeVol says now the number will probably be 1.2 million or less, most concentrated in industries like air travel and tourism, or in New York City.

The uneven impact means that assessments of the damage vary by vantage point. "The attacks certainly accelerated the action," said Terry Mercer, a technical illustrator for Boeing Corp., who's been unable to find work since the aerospace giant eliminated his job and 5,000 others from its Wichita, Kan., operations. "But everybody's feeling was that it (some cuts) was going to be coming anyway. We didn't have a lot of work even before the attacks."

The landscape looks very different to home builder Bob Simmons of McLean, Va., who said he was prepared for the worst last fall—but never had time to stop and wait for it. "For me, it's almost like a recap of last August except we have about 10 percent more sales," said Simmons, who builds homes in the suburbs of Washington, D.C.

Economists say the healthy housing market shows how a variety of factors helped mitigate the damage of Sept. 11. Consumers, told one of the best things they could for their nation was to shop, did just that. Record low interest rates kept families buying homes, and refinancing mortgages put cash in their pockets for other purchases. Detroit's zero-percent financing for new cars late last year captured consumers' attention. Government spending pumped additional money into the economy. "Who knows what the psychology was, but (the attack) was not as big a blow as we were expecting," said Economy.com's Faucher. "People still went out to dinner, they still went out to the mall to buy things and things just held up better than expected."

> September 11 was one of the many negative factors affecting the economy in 2001/2002.

> Even in bad times, some sectors continue to flourish.

individual factories or machines may be lost in a hurricane or flood, such losses do not happen in such a massive way across the whole country that they would show up as a recession or a boom in the whole economy. Thus, the amount of capital changes slowly over time. Even technological change does not seem capable of explaining most fluctuations. It is true that some inventions and innovations raise productivity substantially in certain sectors of the economy over short periods of time. The impact on the whole economy is more spread out and gradual, however. Moreover, people do not suddenly forget how to use a technology. There do not seem to be sudden decreases in technological know-how. For these reasons, potential GDP usually tends to grow relatively smoothly over time, compared to the fluctuations in aggregate demand.

REVIEW
- Economic fluctuations are largely a result of fluctuations in aggregate demand.
- When aggregate demand decreases, firms produce less; real GDP falls below potential GDP. Unemployment rises. When aggregate demand increases, firms first produce more; real GDP rises above potential GDP. Firms also hire more workers, and the unemployment rate falls.
- Short-run fluctuations in potential GDP also occur, but in reality most of the larger fluctuations in real GDP seem to be due to fluctuations of real GDP around a more steadily growing potential GDP.

Forecasting Real GDP

To illustrate how we use the idea that changes in aggregate demand lead to short-run fluctuations in real GDP, we will focus on an important macroeconomic task: short-term economic forecasting of real GDP about one year ahead. To *forecast* real GDP, economic forecasters divide aggregate demand into its four key components: consumption, investment, government purchases, and net exports. Remember that real GDP can be measured by adding together the four types of spending: what people *consume*, what firms *invest*, what *governments purchase*, and what *foreigners purchase* net of what they sell in the United States. In symbols, we have

$$Y = C + I + G + X$$

In other words, real GDP (Y) is the sum of consumption (C), investment (I), government purchases (G), and net exports (X).

A Forecast for Next Year

Suppose that it is December 2004 and a forecast of real GDP (Y) is being prepared for the year 2005. Using the preceding equation, a reasonable way to proceed would be to forecast consumption for the next year, then forecast investment, then forecast government purchases, and, finally, forecast net exports. When forecasting each item, the forecaster would consider a range of issues: Consumer confidence might affect consumption; business confidence might be a factor in investment; the mood of the country might be a factor in government purchases; and developments in foreign countries might affect the forecast for net exports. In any case, adding these four spending items together would give a forecast for real GDP for the year 2005. For

ECONOMICS IN ACTION

The Blue Chip Consensus Forecast

Short-term forecasting of real GDP—usually one year ahead—has become a major industry employing thousands of economists, statisticians, and computer programmers. Each month the *Blue Chip Economic Indicators* tabulates the forecasts of the top forecasters. A list of 54 different forecasters is given below. The average of all these forecasters is called the Blue Chip Consensus. If a government forecast differs much from this forecast, it is frequently criticized.

Consider, for example, the forecast for real GDP growth in the United States in 2004. The consensus forecast—the average of the economists surveyed in January 2004 by the Blue Chip Service—was that U.S. GDP growth would be 4.6 percent.

What did growth turn out to be in 2004? It turned out to be 4.4 percent. The forecasters were almost exactly right in their prediction! This isn't always the case, though. In 2001, when the economy was hit by unforeseeable negative shocks, the actual growth rate turned out to be 1.2 percent, whereas the prediction had been for a growth rate of 3.4 percent.

Blue Chip Forecasters

Banc of America Corp.	Ford Motor Company	National Assn. of Home Builders
Bank One	General Motors Corporation	National Association of Realtors
Bear Stearns & Co., Inc.	Genetski.com	National City Corporation
ClearView Economics	Georgia State University	Nomura Securities
Comerica	Goldman Sachs & Co.	Northern Trust Company
Conference Board	Huntington National Bank	Perna Associates
Credit Suisse First Boston	Inforum—Univ. of Maryland	Prudential Financial
DaimlerChrysler AG	JPMorgan Chase	Prudential Securities, Inc.
Daiwa Institute of Research America	Kellner Economic Advisers	SOM Economics, Inc.
Deutsche Banc Alex Brown	LaSalle National Bank	Standard & Poor's Corp.
DRI-WEFA	Loomis, Sayles & Company	Swiss Re
DuPont	Macroeconomic Advisers, LLC	Turning Points (Micrometrics)
Eaton Corporation	Merrill Lynch	U.S. Chamber of Commerce
Econoclast	Moody's Investors Service	U.S. Trust Co.
Eggert Economic Enterprises, Inc.	Morgan Stanley	UCLA Business Forecasting Proj.
Evans, Carroll & Associates	Mortgage Bankers Assn. of America	Wachovia Securities
Fannie Mae	Motorola, Inc.	Wayne Hummer Investments LLC
Federal Express Corp.	Naroff Economic Advisors	Wells Capital Management

example, one economist may forecast that $C = \$8,000$ billion, $I = \$1,500$ billion, $X = -\$500$ billion, and $G = \$2,000$ billion. Then that economist's forecast for real GDP is $11,000 billion. Forecasts are typically expressed as growth rates of real GDP from one year to the next. If real GDP in 2004 is $10,800, then the forecast would be for 1.9 percent growth for the year 2005.

Impact of a Change in Government Purchases

The preceding forecast is prepared by making one's best assumption about what is likely for government purchases and the other three components of spending. Another type of forecast—called a *conditional forecast*—describes what real GDP will be under alternative assumptions about the components of spending. For example, in the year 2005, the president of the United States might want an estimate of the effect of a proposal to change government purchases on the economy in 2006. A conditional forecast would be a forecast of real GDP conditional on this change in government purchases. A conditional forecast for real GDP can be made using similar methods. Let's see how.

Suppose the proposal is to cut federal government purchases by $100 billion in real terms in one year. What is the effect of such a change in government purchases on aggregate demand in the short run? If the government demands $100 billion less, then firms will produce $100 billion less. A forecast conditional on a $100 billion spending cut would be $100 billion less for real GDP, or $10,900 billion. Again, we just add up $8,000 billion, $1,500 billion, −$500 billion, and now $1,900 billion. Real GDP growth for the year is now forecast to be about 1.0 percent, conditional on the policy proposal.

The forecast is based on the equation $Y = C + I + G + X$ and the idea that changes in aggregate demand cause real GDP fluctuations. Although simple, it is specific and substantive. According to this method of forecasting, changes in aggregate demand are responsible for most of the short-run ups and downs in the economy. It is this explanation that most economic forecasters use when they forecast real GDP for one year ahead.

REVIEW

- The four components of spending can be added to make a forecast for real GDP. Making such a forecast is an important application of macroeconomics.

- Forecasts may be conditional on a particular event, such as a change in government purchases or a change in taxes.

The Response of Consumption to Income

In the forecasting example, we assumed that none of the other components— neither consumption, investment, nor net exports—change in response to the decline in government purchases. For example, consumption (C) was unchanged at $8,000 billion when we altered G in our conditional forecast. But these components of spending are likely to change. Thus, something important is missing from the procedure for forecasting real GDP. To improve the forecast, we must describe how the components of aggregate demand—consumption, investment, or net exports— might change in response to other developments in the economy. We will eventually consider the response of consumption, investment, and net exports to many factors, including interest rates, exchange rates, and income. However, bringing all these factors into consideration at once is complicated, and we must start with a *simplifying assumption*. Here the simplifying assumption is that consumption is the only component of expenditures that responds to income, and that income is the only influence on consumption. Consumption is a good place to begin because it is by far the largest component. Before we finish developing a complete theory of economic fluctuations, we will consider the other components and the other influences. Let us begin by examining why consumption may be affected by income.

The Consumption Function

consumption function: the positive relationship between consumption and income.

The **consumption function** describes how consumption depends on income. The notion of a consumption function originated with John Maynard Keynes, who wrote about it during the 1930s. Research on the consumption function has been intense ever since. For each individual, the consumption function says that the more income

Table 23.1
An Example of the Consumption Function (billions of dollars)

Consumption	Income
2,000	1,000
2,600	2,000
3,200	3,000
3,800	4,000
4,400	5,000
5,000	6,000
5,600	7,000
6,200	8,000
6,800	9,000
7,400	10,000
8,000	11,000
8,600	12,000
9,200	13,000
9,800	14,000

marginal propensity to consume (MPC): the slope of the consumption function, showing the change in consumption that is due to a given change in income.

one has, the more one consumes. For the national economy as a whole, it says that the more income Americans have, the more Americans consume. For the world economy as a whole, it says that the more income there is in the world, the more the people in the world consume. Table 23.1 gives a simple example of how consumption depends on income in the United States economy.

As you can see from the table, as income increases from $1,000 billion to $2,000 billion, consumption increases as well, from $2,000 billion to $2,600 billion, and as income increases from $3,000 billion to $4,000 billion, consumption increases from $3,200 billion to $3,800 billion. More income means more consumption, but the consumption function also tells us *how much* consumption increases when income increases. Each change in income of $1,000 billion causes an increase in consumption of $600 billion. The changes in consumption are smaller than the changes in income. Notice that, in this example, at very low levels of income, consumption is greater than income. If consumption were greater than income for a particular individual, that individual would have to borrow. At higher levels of income, when consumption is less than income, the individual would be able to save.

The consumption function is supposed to describe the behavior of individuals because the economy is made up of individuals. Consequently, it summarizes the behavior of all people in the economy with respect to consumption. The simple consumption function is not meant to be the complete explanation of consumption. Recall that it is based on a simplifying assumption.

■ **The Marginal Propensity to Consume.** A concept related to the consumption function is the **marginal propensity to consume,** or **MPC** for short. The marginal propensity to consume measures how much consumption changes for a given change in income. The term *marginal* refers to the additional amount of consumption that is due to a change in income. The term *propensity* refers to the inclination to consume. By definition,

$$\text{Marginal Propensity to Consume (MPC)} = \frac{\text{change in consumption}}{\text{change in income}}$$

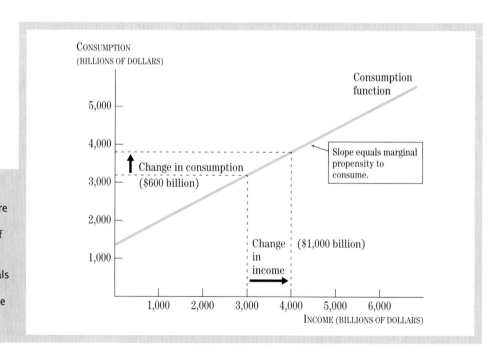

Figure 23.3
The Consumption Function
For the economy as a whole, more income leads to more consumption, as shown by the example of an upward-sloping consumption function in the figure. This represents the sum of all the individuals in the economy, many of whom consume more when their income rises. The graph is based on the numbers in Table 23.1.

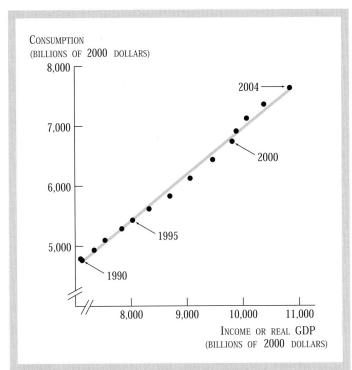

CONSUMPTION
(BILLIONS OF 2000 DOLLARS)

INCOME OR REAL GDP
(BILLIONS OF 2000 DOLLARS)

Figure 23.4
Consumption versus Aggregate Income
The graph shows the close relationship between consumption and aggregate income, or real GDP, in the U.S. economy. The points fall close to the straight line drawn in the diagram.

What is the MPC for the consumption function in Table 23.1? Observe that the change in consumption from row to row is 600. The change in income from row to row is 1,000; thus the MPC = 600/1,000 = .6. Although this is only a simple example, it turns out that the MPC for the U.S. economy is around that magnitude.

Figure 23.3 graphs the consumption function by putting income on the horizontal axis and consumption on the vertical axis. We get the upward-sloping line by plotting the pairs of observations on consumption and income in Table 23.1 and connecting them with a line. This line, which demonstrates that consumption rises with income, is the consumption function. Its slope is equal to the MPC. For this example, the MPC = .6. The graph shows that at low levels of income, consumption is greater than income, but at high levels of income, consumption is less than income.

■ **Which Measure of Income?** The consumption function is a straight-line relationship between consumption and income. Income in the relationship is sometimes measured by *aggregate income* (Y), which is also equal to real GDP, and sometimes by disposable income. *Disposable income* is the income that households receive in wages, dividends, and interest payments plus transfers they may get from the government minus any taxes they pay to the government. Disposable income is the preferred measure of income when one is interested in household consumption because this is what households have available to spend. But the consumption function for the whole economy for aggregate income and that for disposable income look similar because aggregate income and disposable income fluctuate and grow together. In the United States and most other countries, taxes and transfers are nearly proportional to aggregate income.

For the rest of this chapter, we will use aggregate income, or real GDP, as the measure of income in the consumption function. We put real GDP, or income (we drop the word *aggregate* in aggregate income), on the horizontal axis of the consumption function diagram, because real GDP and income are always equal. Figure 23.4 shows the actual relationship between consumption and income, or real GDP. Note, however, that when we consider an explicit change in taxes, we must take into account the difference between disposable income and income.

What about Interest Rates and Other Influences on Consumption?

Other factors besides income affect consumption. For example, you may recall from Chapter 19 that people's consumption is affected by the interest rate. Also, people's wealth—including their savings in a bank and their house—may affect their consumption. A person with a large amount of savings in a bank might consume a considerable amount even if the person's income in any one year is very low. Why have we not brought the interest rate or wealth into the picture here?

The answer is simple. To keep the analysis manageable at the start, we are putting the interest rate and other influences aside. We eventually return to consider the effects of interest rates and other factors on consumption. But during economic fluctuations, the effects of changes in income on consumption are most important, and we focus on these now.

REVIEW
- The consumption function describes the response of consumption to changes in income. The elementary consumption function ignores the effects of interest rates and wealth on consumption.

- The marginal propensity to consume (MPC) tells us *how much* consumption changes in response to a change in income.

- For the economy as a whole, the consumption function can be expressed in terms of aggregate income or disposable income. Aggregate income is always equal to real GDP.

Finding Real GDP When Consumption and Income Move Together

Now let us use the consumption function to get a better prediction of what happens to real GDP in the short run when government purchases change. In other words, we want to improve the conditional forecast of real GDP when there is a change in government purchases by taking the consumption function into account. Again, as in the earlier example of forecasting, let us assume that government spending will decline by $100 billion next year. Our goal is to find out what happens to real GDP in the short run.

Our first attempt at forecasting said that a reduction in government spending is going to reduce real GDP. But now we see that something else must happen, because consumption depends on income, and real GDP is equal to income. A reduction in government spending will reduce income. The consumption function tells us that a reduction in income must reduce consumption, which further reduces GDP.

Here is the chain of logic in brief:

1. A cut in government spending reduces real GDP.

2. Real GDP = income; thus income is reduced.

3. Consumption depends on income; thus consumption is reduced.

4. A reduction in consumption further reduces real GDP.

In sum, consumption will decline when we reduce government spending.

For example, when the government reduces defense spending, the firms that produce the defense goods find demand falling and produce less. Some of the defense workers are going to either work fewer hours a week or be laid off. Therefore, they will receive a reduced income or no income at all. In addition, the profits at the defense firms will decline; thus, the income of the owners of the firms will decline. With less income, the workers and the owners will spend less; that is, their consumption will decline. This is the connection between government spending and consumption that we are concerned about: The change in government purchases reduces defense workers' income, which results in less consumption.

ECONOMICS IN ACTION

Making *Time*'s Top 100

John Maynard Keynes was chosen by *Time* magazine as one of the 100 most influential people in the twentieth century. Keynes was the inventor of the marginal propensity to consume and of the broader idea emphasized in this chapter that a decline in aggregate demand could bring the economy below its potential.

Keynes was always active in bringing economics into practice. He gained notoriety in his thirties for a best-selling book called *The Economic Consequences of the Peace,* written in only two months during the summer of 1919. Keynes was an economic adviser to the British government, and he accompanied the prime minister to the Versailles peace conference in 1919 at the end of World War I. At that peace conference, the victors demanded heavy reparations from Germany, harming the German economy and thereby helping Hitler in his rise to power. In his 1919 book, Keynes predicted serious harm from the stiff reparations and ridiculed the heads of government at the conference, including his own prime minister, David Lloyd George, and the American president, Woodrow Wilson.

Keynes's most influential book, however, was *The General Theory of Employment, Interest and Money.* He wrote it in the midst of the Great Depression, providing an explanation for a worldwide tragedy that prevailing economic theory—with its microeconomic emphasis—hardly addressed. Much of the *General Theory* is difficult to read unless you are an economist, because as Keynes put it, his book is chiefly addressed to "my fellow economists." But Keynes's well-developed writing skills emerge in some of the less technical passages, especially those on speculation and expectations in financial markets. Keynes's ideas, such as the marginal propensity to consume and the importance of aggregate demand, spread rapidly and had a lasting influence: Referring to these ideas as the "Keynesian revolution" is no exaggeration.

Keynes appeared on the cover of *Time* magazine in 1965, when the influence of his economics was at its peak in Washington. However, in the 1970s, when inflation was rising and economic growth was slowing, Keynes's theory was criticized because it did not deal with inflation and with long-run economic growth. Moreover, by emphasizing aggregate demand so much,

Keynes's theory suggested to some policymakers that increases in government spending could increase real GDP almost without limit, regardless of supply constraints.

Keynes's *Tract on Monetary Reform,* written in 1923, focused more on inflation than did the *General Theory.* His earlier writings suggest that if he had lived longer, he might have explained the high inflation of the 1970s as effectively as he explained the Great Depression of the 1930s.

JOHN MAYNARD KEYNES, 1883–1946

Born: Cambridge, England, 1883

Education: Cambridge University, graduated 1906

Jobs: India Office, London, 1906–1909
Cambridge University, 1909–1915
British Treasury, 1915–1919
Cambridge University, 1919–1946

Major Publications: *The Economic Consequences of the Peace,* 1919; *A Tract on Monetary Reform,* 1923; *A Treatise on Money,* 1930; *The General Theory of Employment, Interest and Money,* 1936

Consider a specific case study. This type of logic was applied by economists to estimate the impact of closing Fort Ord, the military base near Monterey Bay in California, on the Monterey economy. When the estimates were made, the base employed 3,000 civilians and 14,000 military personnel. Payroll was $558 million. Thus, closing the base would reduce incomes by as much as $558 million as these workers were laid off or retired. Although some workers might quickly find jobs

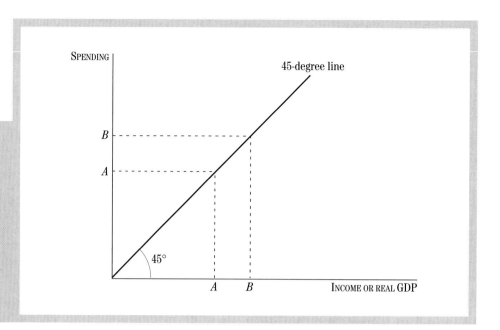

Figure 23.5
The 45-Degree Line
This simple line is a graphical representation of the income equals spending identity. The pairs of points on the 45-degree line have the same level of spending and income. For example, the level of spending at *A* is the same dollar amount as the level of income at *A*. Moreover, because income equals real GDP, we can put either income or real GDP on the horizontal axis.

elsewhere, there would be a decline in income that would result in a reduction in consumption by those workers. Using an MPC of .6, consumption would decline by $335 million (.6 times 558) if income was reduced by $558 million. This would tend to throw others in the Monterey area out of work as spending in retail and service stores declined. This would further reduce consumption, and so on. Although this case study refers to a small region of the entire country, the same logic applies to the economy as a whole.

The 45-Degree Line

We can use a convenient graph to calculate how much income and consumption change in the whole economy and thereby find out what happens to real GDP. In Figure 23.5 there is a line that shows graphically that income in the economy is equal to spending. That is, income (*Y*) equals spending (*C* + *I* + *G* + *X*). In Figure 23.5, income is on the horizontal axis and spending is on the vertical axis. All the points where spending equals income are on the upward-sloping line in Figure 23.5. The line has a slope of 1, or an angle of 45 degrees with the horizontal axis, because the distances from any point on the line to the horizontal axis and the vertical axis are equal. Along that line—which is called the **45-degree line**—spending and income are equal.

45-degree line: the line showing that expenditure equals aggregate income.

The Expenditure Line

expenditure line: the relation between the sum of the four components of spending (*C* + *I* + *G* + *X*) and aggregate income.

Figure 23.6 shows another relationship called the **expenditure line.** As in Figure 23.5, income, or real GDP, is on the horizontal axis, and spending is on the vertical axis. The top line in Figure 23.6 is the expenditure line. It is called the expenditure line because it shows how expenditure, or spending, depends on income. The four components that make up the expenditure line are consumption, investment, government purchases, and net exports. However, the expenditure line shows how these four components depend on income. It is this dependency of spending on income that is the defining characteristic of the expenditure line. Here is how the expenditure line is derived.

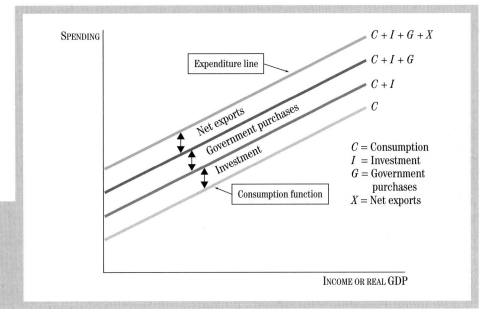

Figure 23.6
The Expenditure Line
By adding investment (*I*), government purchases (*G*), and net exports (*X*) to the consumption function, we build the expenditure line.

The consumption function is shown as the lowest line in Figure 23.6. It is simply the consumption function from Figure 23.3, which says that the higher income is, the more people want to consume. The next line above the consumption function in Figure 23.6 is parallel to the consumption function. This line represents the addition of investment to consumption at each level of income. It says that investment is so many billions of dollars in the U.S. economy, and the distance between the lines is this amount of investment. For example, if investment equals $800 billion, the distance between the consumption function and this next line is $800 billion.

The reason the line is parallel to the consumption line is that we are starting our explanation by saying that investment does not depend on income. This simplifying assumption means that investment is a constant number, and the distance between the lines is the same regardless of income. We just add the same amount at each point.

The next line in Figure 23.6 adds in a constant level of government purchases. This line is also parallel to the other lines because the increase at every level of income is the same. The distance between the lines represents a fixed level of government purchases, say, $2,000 billion, at every level of income.

Finally, to get the top line in Figure 23.6, we add in net exports. For simplicity, we assume that net exports do not depend on income, an assumption that we will change soon. Thus, the top line is parallel to all the other lines. The top line is the sum of *C* + *I* + *G* + *X*. It is the expenditure line. The most important thing to remember about the expenditure line is that it shows how the sum of the four components depends on income.

Before we can use the expenditure line, we must know what determines its slope and what causes it to shift.

■ **The Slope of the Expenditure Line.** Observe in Figure 23.6 that the expenditure line is parallel to the consumption function. Therefore, the slope of the expenditure line is the same as the slope of the consumption function. We already know that the slope of the consumption function is the MPC. Hence, the slope of the expenditure line is also equal to the MPC.

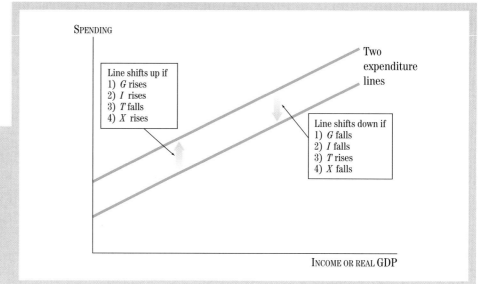

Figure 23.7
Shifts in the Expenditure Line
The expenditure line shifts down if (1) government purchases (*G*) fall, (2) investment (*I*) falls, (3) taxes (*T*) increase, or (4) net exports (*X*) fall. The expenditure line shifts up if (1) government purchases rise, (2) investment rises, (3) taxes are cut, or (4) net exports rise.

Because the MPC is less than 1, the aggregate expenditure line is flatter (the slope is smaller) than the 45-degree line, which has a slope of exactly 1. This fact will soon be used to find real GDP.

■ **Shifts in the Expenditure Line.** The expenditure line can shift for several reasons. Consider first what happens to the expenditure line if government purchases fall because of a cut in defense spending. As shown in Figure 23.7, the expenditure line shifts downward in a parallel fashion. The expenditure line is simply the sum *C* + *I* + *G* + *X*. Because *G* is less at all income levels, the line shifts down. The expenditure line is lowered because the distance between the consumption function and the other lines declines (see Figure 23.6). The reverse of this, an increase in government purchases, will cause the expenditure line to shift up.

What happens to the expenditure line if investment falls? Investment, remember, is the gap between the first and second lines in Figure 23.6. If investment declines (as might happen if businesses become pessimistic about the future and invest less), then the expenditure line shifts downward. With less investment, the gap between the lines shrinks. The reverse of this, an increase in investment, will cause the expenditure line to shift up, as shown in Figure 23.7.

A change in net exports, perhaps because of a change in the demand for U.S. exports to other countries, will also shift the expenditure line. A downward shift in net exports lowers the expenditure line, and an upward shift in net exports raises the expenditure line.

Finally, the expenditure line can also be shifted by changes in taxes. At any given level of income, an increase in taxes means that people have less to spend, and this will cause people to consume less. Hence, the expenditure line shifts down when taxes rise. The reverse of this, a cut in taxes, causes the expenditure line to shift up. We will use the symbol *T* to refer to taxes. For example, if *T* = $1,500 billion, then people pay and the government receives $1,500 billion in taxes.

Determining Real GDP Through Spending Balance

Having derived the expenditure line and the 45-degree line, we can combine the two to find real GDP. Figure 23.8 shows the expenditure line and the 45-degree line combined in one diagram. Observe that the two lines intersect. They must intersect because they have different slopes. Real GDP is found at the point of intersection of these two lines. Why?

Income and spending are always equal, and the 45-degree line is drawn to represent this equality. Therefore, at any point on the 45-degree line, income equals spending. Moreover, income and spending must be on the expenditure line, because only at points on that line do people consume according to the consumption function.

If both relationships hold—that is, income and spending are the same (we are on the 45-degree line) and people's consumption is described by the consumption function (we are on the expenditure line)—then logically we must be at the intersection of these two lines. We call that point of intersection **spending balance.** The level of income determined by that point is just the right level to cause people to purchase an amount of consumption that—when added to investment, government purchases, and net exports—gives exactly the same level of income. We would not have spending balance at either a higher or a lower level of income. The diagram in Figure 23.8 showing that the 45-degree line and the expenditure line cross is sometimes called the "Keynesian Cross" after John Maynard Keynes.

Table 23.2 provides an alternative way to determine spending balance. It uses a numerical tabulation of the consumption function rather than graphs. Total expenditure is obtained by adding the four columns on the right of Table 23.2. Consumption is shown to depend on income according to the same consumption function as in Table 23.1. Observe that there is only one row where income equals total expenditure. That row is where spending balance occurs. The row is shaded and corresponds to the point of intersection of the 45-degree line and the expenditure line in Figure 23.8.

Because the point of spending balance is at the intersection of two lines, we can think of it as an equilibrium, much as the intersection of a demand curve and a supply curve for wheat is an equilibrium. Because real GDP is not necessarily equal to potential GDP at this intersection, however, there is a sense in which the equilibrium is temporary; eventually real GDP will move back to potential GDP, as we will show in later chapters.

spending balance: the level of income or real GDP at which the 45-degree line and the expenditure line cross; also called equilibrium income.

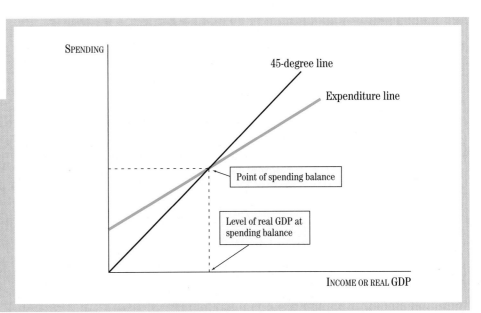

**Figure 23.8
Spending Balance**
Spending balance occurs when two relations are satisfied simultaneously: (1) income equals spending, and (2) spending equals consumption, which is a function of income, plus investment plus government purchases plus net exports. Only one level of income gives spending balance. That level of income is determined by the intersection of the 45-degree line and the expenditure line.

Table 23.2
A Numerical Example of Spending Balance (billions of dollars)

Income or Real GDP	Total Expenditure	Consumption	Investment	Government Purchases	Net Exports
6,000	8,000	5,000	1,500	2,000	−500
7,000	8,600	5,600	1,500	2,000	−500
8,000	9,200	6,200	1,500	2,000	−500
9,000	9,800	6,800	1,500	2,000	−500
10,000	10,400	7,400	1,500	2,000	−500
11,000	11,000	8,000	1,500	2,000	−500
12,000	11,600	8,600	1,500	2,000	−500
13,000	12,200	9,200	1,500	2,000	−500
14,000	12,800	9,800	1,500	2,000	−500

The point of spending balance is also an equilibrium in the sense that economic forces cause real GDP to be at that intersection. To see this, consider Table 23.2. As we noted, the shaded row corresponds to the intersection of the 45-degree line and the expenditure line: Income or real GDP equals expenditure. Suppose that income or real GDP were less than expenditure, as in one of the rows above the shaded row in Table 23.2. This would not be an equilibrium because firms would not be producing enough goods and services (real GDP) to satisfy people's expenditure on goods and services. Firms would increase their production, and real GDP would rise until it equaled expenditure. Similarly, if real GDP were greater than expenditure, as in one of the rows below the shaded row in Table 23.2, firms would be producing more than people would be buying. Hence, firms would reduce their production and real GDP would fall until it equaled expenditure.

A Better Forecast of Real GDP

Now let us return to forecasting real GDP using these new tools. Recall the example of making a forecast of real GDP for the year 2005 (from the vantage point of December 2004), conditional on a proposed decline in government purchases of $100 billion. Our new tools will enable us to take into account the effect of this decline on consumption, which we ignored in the simple forecast.

Figure 23.9 shows two expenditure lines. The top expenditure line is without the change in government purchases. In this case, G = $2,000 billion, C = $8,000 billion, I = $1,500 billion, and X = −$500 billion, yielding income, or real GDP, of $11,000 billion. For the conditional forecast, we assume that G is cut by $100 billion, to $1,900 billion. In Figure 23.9, that causes the expenditure line to shift down to the "new" line. Observe that the expenditure line shifts down by $100 billion—a parallel shift. This new expenditure line cuts the 45-degree line at a lower point.

Logic tells us that the economy will now operate at a different point of spending balance, where the expenditure line and the 45-degree line now intersect. Thus we move from one intersection to a new intersection as a result of the decline in the expenditure line. The new point of spending balance is at a lower level of GDP.

We now have a prediction that real GDP will fall if government spending declines. Observe in Figure 23.9 that the decline in real GDP is larger than the $100 billion decline in government purchases and, therefore, larger than the $100 billion decline in real GDP in the simple forecast. The reason is that in addition to the decrease in

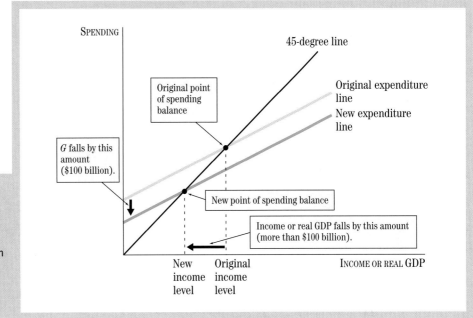

Figure 23.9
From One Point of Spending Balance to Another
The expenditure line shifts down because of a decline in government purchases. This shifts down the forecast for real GDP. A forecast of real GDP conditional on the decline in government purchases would therefore be lower.

government purchases, consumption has fallen because income has declined. The initial $100 billion is *multiplied* to create a larger than $100 billion change in real GDP because of the induced change in consumption. This multiplier phenomenon, which makes the change in real GDP larger than the change in government purchases, is called the *Keynesian multiplier* and applies to increases as well as to decreases in government purchases. In Figure 23.9, the multiplier looks quite large; the horizontal arrow is at least twice as large as the vertical arrow. It is certainly large enough to influence the administration's decision to reduce government purchases. The example and the application illustrate that it is not just for fun that we have derived the expenditure line. It is an essential tool of the practicing macroeconomist.

REVIEW

- Spending balance occurs when the identity $Y = C + I + G + X$ and the consumption function relating C to Y hold simultaneously.

- Spending balance can be shown on a graph with the 45-degree line and the expenditure line. The intersection of the two lines determines a level of income, or real GDP, that gives spending balance.

- A shift in the expenditure line brings about a new level of spending balance.

Spending Balance and Departures of Real GDP from Potential GDP

We have shown how to compute a level of real GDP for the purpose of making short-term forecasts. This level of real GDP is determined by aggregate demand—consumption, investment, government purchases, and net exports. It is not necessarily

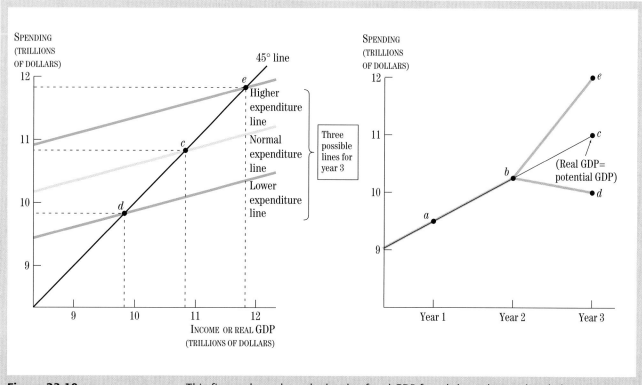

**Figure 23.10
Spending Balance and
Departures of Real GDP
from Potential GDP**

This figure shows how the levels of real GDP found through spending balance can explain the first steps of a recession or boom. The left panel shows spending balance for three expenditure curves; one (c) gives real GDP equal to potential GDP, a second (e) gives real GDP above potential GDP, and a third (d) gives real GDP below potential GDP. As shown in the right panel, two of these entail departures of real GDP from potential GDP.

equal to potential GDP, which depends on the supply of labor, capital, and technology. Thus, we can have real GDP departing from potential GDP, as it does in recessions and booms. Let's now show this graphically.

Stepping Away from Potential GDP

Figure 23.10 illustrates how the departures of real GDP from potential GDP can be explained by shifts in the expenditure line. The left panel of the figure shows three different expenditure lines. Each line corresponds to a different level of government purchases or a different level of net exports or investment. The right panel of Figure 23.10—which is much like Figure 23.2—shows real GDP and potential GDP during a three-year period. There is a close connection between the left and right panels of Figure 23.10. The vertical axes are identical, and the points c, d, and e represent the same level of spending in both panels.

Observe how the three expenditure lines intersect the 45-degree line at three different levels of real GDP. Let us suppose that the middle expenditure line intersects the 45-degree line at a level of real GDP that is the same as potential GDP in year 3. This is point c. The lower expenditure line represents a recession; real GDP at the intersection of this expenditure line and the 45-degree line (point d) is at a level below potential GDP and also below the level of real GDP in year 2. Thus, real GDP would decline from year

2 to year 3 with this expenditure line. On the other hand, the higher expenditure line corresponds to the case in which real GDP is above potential GDP in year 3.

By referring to these values of real GDP as the *first* steps, we are emphasizing that they are not the end of the story. We will see that there are forces in the economy that tend to bring real GDP back toward potential GDP. This calculation of real GDP gives only the short-run impact of changes in government spending, investment, net exports, or taxes.

REVIEW

- Shifts in the expenditure line can explain the departures of real GDP from potential GDP.

- When the expenditure line shifts down, real GDP declines, and, if it was previously equal to potential GDP, it will fall below potential GDP. Upward shifts in the expenditure line will bring real GDP above potential GDP.

- The expenditure line can shift for many reasons. Changes in taxes, government purchases, investment, and net exports will cause the expenditure line to shift.

Conclusion

With this chapter, we have begun to develop a theory of economic fluctuations. We have shown how economists explain departures of real GDP from potential GDP, using the idea that these fluctuations are due to changes in aggregate demand. A recession occurs when aggregate demand falls, bringing real GDP below potential GDP. We used this explanation to make short-term forecasts of real GDP. The expenditure line—showing how the demand for consumption, investment, and net exports depends on income—and the 45-degree line are key parts of the forecasting process. However, our analysis thus far has made several simplifying assumptions. For example, we assumed that the only thing people's consumption decisions respond to is a change in income.

In the next chapter, we show that consumption as well as investment and net exports responds to interest rates and inflation. The responses to interest rates and inflation will explain why real GDP returns to potential GDP in the long run.

KEY POINTS

1. Economic fluctuations are temporary deviations of real GDP from potential GDP.

2. Employment and unemployment fluctuate with real GDP. Unemployment increases in recessions and decreases in booms.

3. The fluctuations in real GDP and potential GDP are mainly due to fluctuations in aggregate demand.

4. The idea that fluctuations in real GDP are mainly due to aggregate demand is used to find real GDP when making a short-term forecast.

5. Real GDP can be predicted on the basis of forecasts of consumption, investment, net exports, and government purchases. But these items depend on income and, thus, on the forecast of real GDP itself.

6. The consumption function describes how consumption responds to income.

7. The expenditure line is built up from the consumption function.

8. The 45-degree line tells us that expenditures equal income.

9. Combining the expenditure line and the 45-degree line in a diagram enables us to determine the level of income, or real GDP.

10. The level of real GDP that gives spending balance changes when government spending changes. Real GDP will decline in the short run when government purchases are cut.

KEY TERMS

real business cycle theory
consumption function

marginal propensity to consume (MPC)

45-degree line
expenditure line

spending balance

QUESTIONS FOR REVIEW

1. Why do theories of economic fluctuations focus on aggregate demand rather than potential GDP as the main source of short-run economic fluctuations?

2. Why do theories of economic growth focus on potential GDP (with its three determinants) rather than aggregate demand as the main source of economic growth?

3. Why does the unemployment rate rise when real GDP falls below potential GDP?

4. What is the normal rate of capacity utilization in manufacturing firms? What is the significance of this normal rate for explaining economic fluctuations?

5. What is a forecast?

6. What accounting identity does the 45-degree line represent?

7. Why does the expenditure line have a slope less than 1?

8. Why do economic forecasters have to take into account the consumption function?

9. Why is real GDP given by the intersection of the 45-degree line and the expenditure line?

PROBLEMS

1. In the early part of 2001, the U.S. economy was hit by a sudden plunge in stock markets, accompanied by a slowdown in consumer and investor spending. Explain why these events would move real GDP below potential GDP.

2. Suppose the information in the following table describes the economic situation in the United States at the end of 2004.

Year	Real GDP (billions of 2004 dollars)	Potential GDP (billions of 2004 dollars)
2002	9,613	9,613
2003	9,854	9,854
2004	10,100	10,100
2005 (optimistic forecast)	10,600	10,353
2005 (pessimistic forecast)	9,900	10,353

a. Graph real GDP over time, placing the year on the horizontal axis. Calculate the growth rate of real GDP between 2003 and 2004.

b. The optimistic forecast for the year 2005 is based on the possibility that businesses are optimistic about the economy. What will the growth rate of real GDP be if the optimistic forecast turns out to be true?

c. The pessimistic forecast is based on the possibility that businesses will be pessimistic about the economy. What will the growth rate of real GDP be if this forecast is correct?

d. What is the deviation (in terms of dollars and as a percentage) of real GDP from potential GDP in 2005 if the optimistic forecast is correct? What is the deviation (in terms of dollars and as a percentage) from potential GDP in 2005 if the pessimistic forecast is correct?

3. The following table shows the relationship between income and consumption in an economy.

Income (Y) (in billions of dollars)	Consumption (C) (in billions of dollars)
0	5
10	11
20	17
30	23
40	29
50	35
60	41
70	47
80	53
90	59
100	65

Assume that investment (I) is $5 billion, government purchases (G) are $4 billion, and net exports (X) are $2 billion.

a. What is the numerical value of the marginal propensity to consume?

b. Construct a table that is analogous to text Table 23.2 for this economy. What is the level of income at the point of spending balance?

c. For this level of income, calculate national saving. Is national saving equal to investment plus net exports?

d. Sketch a diagram with a 45-degree line and an expenditure curve that describes the preceding relationships. Show graphically what happens to income when the government lowers taxes.

4. Describe what happens to the expenditure line in each of the following cases.
   a. Government spending on airport safety rises.
   b. The Koreans decide to spend $10 billion on aircraft built in the United States.
   c. Firms become very optimistic about the future.
   d. A law is enacted requiring that the government pay $10,000 to anyone who builds a new house.

5. Sketch a diagram with a 45-degree line and an expenditure line that describes macroeconomic spending balance. What factors determine how steep the expenditure line is? What macroeconomic relationship is described by the 45-degree line? Show on the diagram what will happen to the level of income if there is a rise in government purchases. Does U.S. income increase by more or by less than the upward shift in government purchases? Explain.

6. Suppose that business executives are very optimistic, and they raise their investment spending. What happens to the expenditure line? How will this affect real GDP? Sketch a diagram to demonstrate your answer.

7. Suppose that American goods suddenly become unpopular in Europe. What happens to net exports? How will this shift the expenditure line? What happens to real GDP? Demonstrate this in a diagram.

8. Suppose government purchases will increase by $100 billion, and a forecasting firm predicts that real GDP will rise in the short run by $100 billion as a result. Would you say that that forecast is accurate? Why? If you were running a business and you subscribed to that forecasting service, what questions would you ask about the forecast?

Deriving the Formula for the Keynesian Multiplier and the Forward-Looking Consumption Model

The Keynesian Multiplier

Here we derive a formula for the **Keynesian multiplier,** which gives the *short-run* impact on real GDP of things such as cuts in military purchases or a new federal program for construction of roads and bridges. We show how the multiplier depends on the marginal propensity to consume and on the marginal propensity to import.

A Graphical Review

Figure 23A.1 is a diagram like the one derived in Chapter 23, with income or real GDP on the horizontal axis and spending on the vertical axis. The 45-degree line equates spending and income. There are two expenditure lines in

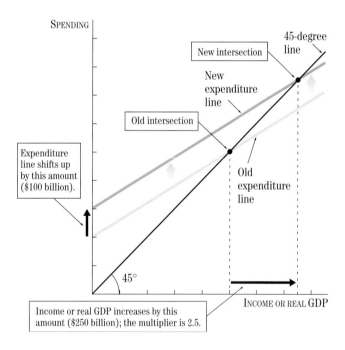

Figure 23A.1
Graphical Calculation of the Multiplier
An upward shift in the expenditure line raises real GDP in the short run by a multiple of the shift in the expenditure line. The multiplier can be found graphically. It is the ratio of the length of the black horizontal arrow to the length of the black vertical arrow.

Figure 23A.1. The "new" expenditure line is $100 billion higher than the "old" expenditure line, representing an upward shift due to an increase in government purchases, for example. Both expenditure lines show that expenditure in the economy—the sum of consumption plus investment plus government purchases plus net exports, or $C + I + G + X$—rises with income. We assume that the marginal propensity to consume (MPC) is equal to .6. Thus, the slope of both expenditure lines is .6.

Note that the "new" expenditure line intersects the 45-degree line at a different point from the "old" expenditure line. At this new intersection, the level of income, or real GDP, is higher than at the old intersection. On the horizontal axis, the black arrow pointing to the right shows this shift to a higher level of real GDP. Look carefully at the diagram to note the *size* of the change in real GDP along the horizontal axis and compare it with the change in the expenditure line. Observe that the horizontal change is *larger* than the vertical change. This is due to the multiplier. In fact, the term *multiplier* is used because the change in real GDP is a multiple of the shift in the aggregate expenditure line.

The multiplier is the ratio of the change in real GDP to the shift in the expenditure line, regardless of the reason for the shift in the expenditure line (whether it is due to a change in government purchases, a change in taxes, a change in investment, or a change in foreign demand). Thus, the multiplier is equal to the ratio of the length of the arrow along the horizontal axis to the length of the arrow along the vertical axis in Figure 23A.1. You can find the multiplier by measuring these lengths. If you do so, you will find that for the expenditure line with a slope of .6 in Figure 23A.1, the multiplier is 2.5.

The multiplier applies to anything that shifts the expenditure line. For example, an increase in government purchases of $100 billion would shift the expenditure line up by $100 billion. This would increase real GDP by $250 billion if the multiplier for government purchases is 2.5.

The Algebraic Derivation

We now want to derive a formula for the multiplier using algebra. Let us focus first on the case where the MPC is .6. To be specific, let us suppose that the particular reason for a change in the aggregate expenditure line is an increase in government purchases. Then the multiplier is the ratio of the change in real GDP to the change in government purchases.

The identity that income or real GDP (Y) equals consumption (C) plus investment (I) plus government purchases (G) plus net exports (X) can be written algebraically as

$$Y = C + I + G + X$$

To find the multiplier, we want to determine the impact of a *change* in government purchases on real GDP. That is, we want to find the change in Y that occurs when G changes. Any change in Y must come either directly from a change in G or indirectly from a change in C, I, or X, according to the preceding identity. Denote the change in any of these items by the Greek letter Δ. Then we can write the identity in terms of changes:

$$\Delta Y = \Delta C + \Delta I + \Delta G + \Delta X$$

That is, the *change* in real GDP is equal to the *change* in consumption plus the *change* in investment plus the *change* in government purchases plus the *change* in net exports. Now consider each of the four terms on the right.

The change in government purchases (ΔG) equals $100 billion. For convenience, to make things simple, we continue to assume that there is no change in investment or in net exports. In other words, we assume that neither responds to changes in income. Expressed in symbols, $\Delta I = 0$ and $\Delta X = 0$.

But we cannot assume that $\Delta C = 0$. The *consumption function* tells us that consumption changes when income changes. The consumption function we use for the algebraic calculation has an MPC of .6. Using algebra, we write $\Delta C = .6\Delta Y$. That is, the change in consumption equals .6 times the change in income; for example, if the change in income $\Delta Y = \$10$ billion, then the change in consumption $\Delta C = \$6$ billion if the MPC is .6.

Now let us take our ingredients:

1. $\Delta Y = \Delta C + \Delta I + \Delta G + \Delta X$.

2. The changes in investment and net exports are zero ($\Delta I = \Delta X = 0$).

3. The change in consumption is .6 times the change in income ($\Delta C = .6\Delta Y$).

Replacing ΔI with zero and ΔX with zero removes ΔI and ΔX from the right-hand side of the identity. Replacing ΔC with $.6\Delta Y$ in the same identity results in

$$\Delta Y = .6\Delta Y + \Delta G$$

Note that the term ΔY appears on both sides of this equation. Gathering terms in ΔY on the left-hand side of the equation gives

$$(1 - .6)\Delta Y = \Delta G$$

Dividing both sides by ΔG and by $(1 - .6)$ results in

$$\Delta Y / \Delta G = 1/(1 - .6)$$
$$= 1/.4$$
$$= 2.5$$

Thus, the change in income, or real GDP, that occurs when government purchases change, according to this calculation, is 2.5 times the change in government purchases. That is, $\Delta Y = 2.5\Delta G$. The number 2.5 is the multiplier. The algebraic calculation agrees with the graphical calculation.

You can perform this same calculation for *any value* of the marginal propensity to consume (MPC), not just .6. To see this, note that the change in consumption equals the MPC times the change in income, where the MPC is any number. Using the same approach as in the case of MPC = .6, we obtain a *formula for the multiplier*, which is

$$\frac{\Delta Y}{\Delta G} = \frac{1}{(1 - \text{MPC})}$$

The derivation of this formula is summarized in Table 23A.1.

Table 23A.1
Derivation of a Formula for the Keynesian Multiplier

Start with the identity

$$Y = C + I + G + X$$

and convert it to change form:

$$\Delta Y = \Delta C + \Delta I + \Delta G + \Delta X$$

Substitute $\Delta I = 0$, $\Delta X = 0$, and

$$\Delta C = \text{MPC} \times \Delta Y$$

into the change form of the identity to get

$$\Delta Y = \text{MPC} \times \Delta Y + \Delta G$$

Gather terms involving ΔY to get

$$(1 - \text{MPC}) \times \Delta Y = \Delta G$$

Divide both sides by ΔG and by $1 - \text{MPC}$ to get

$$\frac{\Delta Y}{\Delta G} = \frac{1}{1 - \text{MPC}}$$

Following the Multiplier Through the Economy

To get a more complete understanding of the formula for the multiplier, it is useful to examine what happens as a change in government purchases winds its way through the economy.

Assume that the government increases its military purchases, perhaps to build a new missile defense system. In this example, the government increases purchases of electronic and aerospace equipment at defense firms. The immediate impact of the change in government purchases is an increase in the production of this equipment. With an increase in demand, defense firms produce more, and real GDP rises. The initial increase in real GDP from an increase in government purchases of $100 billion is that same $100 billion. If the government is purchasing more equipment, the production of equipment increases. We call this initial increase in real GDP the *first-round* effect, which includes only the initial change in government purchases.

The first round is not the end of the story. A further increase in real GDP occurs when the workers employed in making the equipment start working more hours and new workers are hired. As a result, the workers' income rises, and the profits made by the manufacturers increase. With both wage income and profit income rising, income in the economy as a whole rises by $100 billion. According to the consumption function, people will consume more. How much more? The consumption function tells us that .6 times the change in income, or $60 billion, will be the additional increase in consumption by the workers and owners of the defense firms. Real GDP rises by $60 billion, the increased production of the goods the workers and owners consume. This $60 billion increase in real GDP is the *second-round* effect. It is hard for anyone to know what the workers in the defense industry or the owners of the defense firms will start purchasing; presumably it will be an array of goods: clothes, VCRs, movies, and restaurant meals. But with an MPC of .6, we do know that they will purchase $60 billion more of these goods. The increase in production spreads throughout the economy. After this second round, real GDP has increased by $160 billion, the sum of $100 billion on the first round and $60 billion on the second round. This is shown in the first and second rows of Table 23A.2.

The story continues. The workers who make the clothes, VCRs, and other goods and services for which there is $60 billion more in spending also have an increase in their income. Either they are no longer unemployed or they work more hours. Similarly, the profits of the owners of those firms increase. As a result, they consume more. How much more? According to the consumption function, .6 times the increase in their income.

Table 23A.2
A Numerical Illustration of the Multiplier at Work
(billions of dollars)

Round	Change in Real GDP	Cumulative Change in Real GDP
First round	100.000	100.000
Second round	60.000	160.000
Third round	36.000	196.000
Fourth round	21.600	217.600
Fifth round	12.960	230.560
.	.	.
.	.	.
.	.	.
After an infinite number of rounds	0.000	250.000

The increase in income outside of defense production was $60 billion, so the increase in consumption must now be .6 times that, or a $36 billion increase. This increase is the *third-round* effect. As the increase permeates the economy, it is impossible to say what particular goods will increase in production, but we know that total production continues to increase. After three rounds, real GDP has increased by $196 billion, as shown in the third row of Table 23A.2.

The increase does not stop there. Another $36 billion more in consumption means that there is $36 billion more in income for people somewhere in the economy. This increases consumption further, by .6 times the $36 billion, or $21.6 billion. According to the column on the right of Table 23A.2, the cumulative effect on real GDP is now up to $217.6 billion after four rounds. Observe that each new entry in the first column is added to the previous total to get the cumulative effect on real GDP.

The story is now getting repetitive. We multiply .6 times $21.6 billion to get $12.96 billion. The total effect on real GDP is now $230.56 billion at the fifth round. In fact, we are already almost at $250 billion. If we kept on going for more and more rounds, we would get closer and closer to the $250 billion amount obtained from the graphs and the formula for the multiplier.

What if Net Exports Depend on Income?

Thus far, we have made the simplifying assumption that net exports do not respond to income. When net exports do respond to income, the formula for the multiplier is a bit different. We now incorporate this response into our analysis.

We first need to consider how net exports respond to income. Recall that net exports are exports minus imports. To examine the effect of income on net exports, we look first at exports and then at imports.

Exports are goods and services that we sell to other countries—aircraft, pharmaceuticals, telephones. Do U.S. exports depend on income in the United States? No, not much. If Americans earn a little more or a little less, the demand for U.S. exports is not going to increase or decrease. What is likely to make the demand for U.S. exports increase or decrease is a change in income abroad—changes in income in Japan, Europe, or Latin America will affect demand for U.S. exports. U.S. exports will not be affected even if the United States has a recession. Of course, if Japan or Europe has a recession, that is another story. In any case, we conclude that U.S. exports are unresponsive to the changes in U.S. income.

Imports are goods and services that people in the United States purchase from abroad—automobiles, sweaters, vacations. Does the amount purchased of these goods and services change when our incomes change? Yes, because imports are part of consumption. Just as we argued that consumption responds to income, so must imports respond to income. Higher income will lead to higher consumption of both goods purchased in the United States and goods purchased abroad. That reasoning leads us to hypothesize that imports are positively related to income. The hypothesis turns out to be accurate when we look at observations on income and imports.

The **marginal propensity to import (MPI)** is the amount that imports change when income changes. Suppose the MPI is .2. The MPI is smaller than the MPC because most of the goods we consume when income rises are not imported.

If exports are unrelated to income and imports are positively related to income, then net exports—exports less imports—must be negatively related to income. Algebraically, we have

$$\Delta X = -\text{MPI} \times \Delta Y$$

Using this expression for ΔX, we can now follow the same algebraic steps we followed earlier to derive a formula for the multiplier. The multiplier now depends on the MPI along with the MPC. The derivation is summarized in Table 23A.3. The formula for the multiplier is

$$\frac{\Delta Y}{\Delta G} = \frac{1}{1 - \text{MPC} + \text{MPI}}$$

For example, if MPC = .6 and MPI = .2, the multiplier is 1.7.

Table 23A.3
Derivation of a Formula for the Keynesian Multiplier with Both the MPC and the MPI

Start with

$$\Delta Y = \Delta C + \Delta I + \Delta G + \Delta X$$

Assume that

$$\Delta I = 0$$

and that

$$\Delta C = \text{MPC} \times \Delta Y$$

and that

$$\Delta X = -\text{MPI} \times \Delta Y$$

Putting the above expressions together, we get

$$\Delta Y = (\text{MPC} \times \Delta Y) + \Delta G - (\text{MPI} \times \Delta Y)$$

and solving for the change in Y, we get

$$\frac{\Delta Y}{\Delta G} = \frac{1}{1 - \text{MPC} + \text{MPI}}$$

The Forward-Looking Consumption Model

Although the consumption function introduced in Chapter 23 gives a good prediction of people's behavior in many situations, it sometimes works very poorly. For example, the marginal propensity to consume (MPC) turned out to be very small when taxes were cut in 1975; people saved almost the entire increase in disposable income that resulted from the tax cut. However, the MPC turned out to be very large for the tax cuts in 1982, only seven years later; people saved very little of the increase in disposable income in that case. The forward-looking consumption model was designed to explain such changes in the MPC.

The **forward-looking consumption model** assumes that people anticipate their future income when making consumption decisions. The forward-looking consumption model was developed independently and in different ways by two Nobel Prize–winning economists, Milton Friedman and Franco Modigliani. Friedman's version is called the **permanent income model,** and Modigliani's version is called the **life-cycle model.** Both models improved on the idea that consumption depends only on current income.

Forward-Looking People

The forward-looking model starts with the idea that people attempt to look ahead to the future. They do not simply consider their current income. For example, if a young medical doctor decides to take a year off from a high-paying suburban medical practice to do community service at little or no pay, that doctor's income will fall below the poverty line for a year. But the doctor is unlikely to cut consumption to a fraction of the poverty level of income. Even if the doctor were young enough to have little savings, borrowing would be a way to keep consumption high and even buy an occasional luxury item. The doctor is basing consumption decisions on expected income for several years in the future—making an assessment of a more permanent income, or a life-cycle income—not just for one year.

There are many other examples. Farmers in poor rural areas of Asia try to save something in good years so that they will be able to maintain their consumption in bad years. They try not to consume a fixed fraction of their income. In many cases, the saving is in storable farm goods like rice.

As these examples indicate, instead of allowing their consumption to vary with their income, which may be quite erratic, most people engage in **consumption smoothing** from year to year. Once people estimate their future income prospects, they try to maintain their consumption around the same level from year to year. If their income temporarily falls, they do not cut their consumption by much; *the marginal propensity to consume (MPC) is very small—maybe about .05—in the case of a temporary change in income.* But if they find out that their income will increase permanently, they will increase their consumption a lot; *the MPC is very large—maybe .95—in the case of a permanent change in income.* For example, if a new fertilizer doubles the rice yield of a rice farmer's land permanently, we can expect that the farmer's consumption of other goods will about double because of higher permanent income.

The difference between the forward-looking consumption model and the simple consumption function where consumption depends only on current income is illustrated in Figure 23A.2. In the right panel of Figure 23A.2, income is expected to follow a typical life-cycle pattern: lower when young, higher when middle-aged, and very low when retired. However, consumption does not follow these ups and downs; it is flat. The left panel shows the opposite extreme: the standard consumption function with a fixed MPC. In this case, people consume a lot when they are middle-aged but consume very little when they are young or old.

Occasionally, some people are prevented from completely smoothing their income because they have a **liquidity constraint;** that is, they cannot get a loan, and so they cannot consume more than their income. Such liquidity constraints do not appear to be important enough

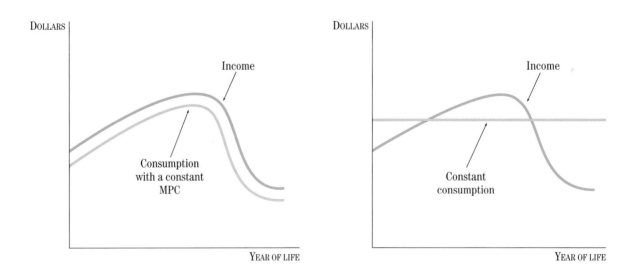

Figure 23A.2
Two Extreme Forms of Consumption Behavior
The right panel shows the future outlook of a young person or family described by the forward-looking model of consumption. The left panel shows the outlook of a young family with a constant MPC. The path of income is the same in both cases.

in the economy as a whole to negate the forward-looking model completely. Of course, not all people try to smooth their income; some people like to go on binges, spending everything, even if the binge is followed by a long lull.

Tests and Applications of the Forward-Looking Model

Observations on consumption and income for the economy as a whole indicate that the forward-looking model significantly improves our understanding of observed changes in the MPC. For example, economists have demonstrated that the measured MPC for the economy as a whole is lower for the temporary changes in income that occur during recessions and booms than for the more permanent increases in income that occur as potential GDP grows over time. Studies of thousands of individual families over time show that the individual MPC for temporary changes in income is about one-third of the MPC for permanent changes in income.

Permanent versus Temporary Tax Cuts   The forward-looking model is also the most promising explanation for the low MPC during the tax cut of 1975. That tax cut was explicitly temporary—a one-time tax rebate, good for only one year. In contrast, the tax cut in the early 1980s was explicitly permanent and was expected to apply for many years into the future. The MPC was large in this case.

With a permanent tax cut, the MPC is high, so there is a big impact on real GDP. For a temporary tax cut, the MPC is low, so there is only a small impact on GDP. In estimating the effects of various tax proposals on the economy, economic forecasters try to take these changes in the MPC into account.

Anticipating Future Tax Cuts or Increases   The forward-looking model changes our estimate of the impact of changes in taxes that are expected to occur in the future. For example, if people are certain of tax cuts in the future, they may begin to increase their consumption right away, before the tax decreases. In this case, the MPC is technically huge, because consumption increases with little or no observed change in current income. Conversely, people may reduce their consumption in anticipation of a tax increase.

It is difficult to know how large these effects are because we do not observe people's expectations of the future. Estimates based on the assumption that people forecast the future no better and no worse than economic forecasters—this is the *rational expectations assumption*—suggest that the effects are large and significant.

In situations where the expectations effects are obvious, we do see an impact. For example, in December 1992, after the 1992 presidential election, when a tax increase became more likely, there was evidence that many people who could do so shifted their reported income for tax purposes from 1993 to 1992. But whether people held back their consumption in anticipation of future tax increases is difficult to say. In any case, because people's behavior is affected by their expectations of the future, attempts to estimate the impact of a policy proposal like a change in taxes need to take these expectations into account.

Key Points

1. The multiplier can be found with graphs and with algebra. The algebraic approach results in a convenient formula.

2. The formula for the multiplier is $1/(1 - \text{MPC})$ when net exports do not depend on income.

3. If net exports are negatively related to income, then the formula for the multiplier is $1/(1 - \text{MPC} + \text{MPI})$.

4. The forward-looking consumption model explains why the MPC is low in some cases and high in others. It helps economists deal with the uncertainty in the multiplier.

5. The forward-looking consumption model also implies that anticipated changes in taxes affect consumption and are a further reason for uncertainty about the MPC. Although such effects have been observed, it is difficult to estimate their size in advance.

6. The rational expectations assumption, which suggests that people forecast the future no better and no worse than economic forecasters, is one basis for making such estimates. With this assumption, the effects of anticipated tax changes on consumption are quite high.

Key Terms and Definitions

Keynesian multiplier: the ratio of the change in real GDP to the shift in the expenditure line; the formula is $1/(1 - \text{MPC})$, where MPC is the marginal propensity to consume.

marginal propensity to import (MPI): the change in imports because of a given change in income.

forward-looking consumption model: a model that explains consumer behavior by assuming that people anticipate future income when deciding on consumption spending today.

permanent income model: a type of forward-looking consumption model that assumes that people distinguish between temporary changes in their income and permanent changes in their income; the permanent changes have a larger effect on consumption.

life-cycle model: a type of forward-looking consumption model that assumes that people base their consumption decisions on their expected lifetime income rather than on their current income.

consumption smoothing: the idea that although their incomes fluctuate, people try to stabilize consumption spending from year to year.

liquidity constraint: the situation in which people cannot borrow to smooth their consumption spending when their income is low.

Questions for Review

1. Why is the size of the multiplier positively related to the MPC?

2. Why is the size of the multiplier negatively related to the marginal propensity to import?

3. Why do imports but not exports depend on income?

4. How does the forward-looking consumption model differ from the consumption function with a fixed MPC?

5. Why is the MPC for a temporary tax cut less than the MPC for a permanent tax cut? Are there examples that prove the point?

6. What is consumption smoothing?

7. Why do changes in future taxes that are anticipated in advance affect consumption?

Problems

1. Are the following statements true or false? Show using algebra.
   a. The multiplier is greater than 1 and rises if the marginal propensity to consume rises.
   b. The multiplier for an economy in which net exports respond to income is smaller than the multiplier for an economy in which net exports do not respond to income.

2. Suppose that the marginal propensity to consume in a closed economy (with no net exports) is estimated to be .6, but there is a 10 percent margin of error on either side. In other words, the MPC could be anywhere between .54 and .66. In what range will the multiplier lie? Quantify the range of impacts on real GDP of a $100 million increase in G. Do the same when the margin of error is 20 percent on either side of .6.

3. The following table shows real GDP and imports (in billions of dollars) for an economy.

Real GDP or Income	Imports
2,000	400
3,000	500
4,000	600
5,000	700
6,000	800
7,000	900

Suppose that exports are equal to $700 billion.
   a. Construct a graph showing how imports depend on income.
   b. Construct a graph showing how net exports depend on income.
   c. If the level of real GDP that occurs at spending balance is $6,000 billion, will there be a trade surplus or a trade deficit? What type of policy regarding government purchases would bring the trade deficit or trade surplus closer to zero?
   d. If the marginal propensity to consume is .6, what is the size of the multiplier?

4. The following numerical example shows how an economy's consumption and net exports depend on income.

Real GDP or Income	Consumption	Net Exports
100	80	30
200	160	20
300	240	10
400	320	0
500	400	−10
600	480	−20
700	560	−30

   a. Find the marginal propensity to consume, the marginal propensity to import, and the multiplier.
   b. Suppose that $I = 60$ and $G = 50$, and taxes are zero. Find the total expenditure for each level of income listed in the table. What is the level of real GDP, consumption, and net exports at which spending balance occurs?
   c. Suppose that government purchases rise by 10. What happens to real GDP?

5. a. Suppose Joe spends every additional dollar of income that he receives. What is Joe's marginal propensity to consume? What does his consumption function look like?
   b. Suppose that Jane spends half of each additional dollar of income that she receives. What is the slope of Jane's consumption function?
   c. What differences in Joe's and Jane's incomes or jobs might explain the differences in their MPCs?

6. Each month, a certain fraction of employees' pay is withheld and sent to the government as part of what is owed for personal income taxes. If the taxes owed for the year are less than the amount withheld, then a refund is sent early in the following year. Otherwise, additional taxes must be paid by April 15. In 1992, the amount of income tax *withheld* was lowered by about $10 billion to increase consumption and real GDP and thereby speed recovery from the 1990–1991 recession. However, the amount of taxes owed was not changed. Discuss why the impact of this 1992 change would be smaller than that of a cut in taxes of $10 billion during 1992.

CHAPTER 24

The Economic Fluctuations Model

The president of the United States is undeniably a very powerful person. But how much power does the president have to help the U.S. economy if it goes into a recession? Will a cut in taxes or an increase in spending end the recession earlier or speed up the recovery? Do such fiscal actions have to be well timed to be successful? Could a long delay in getting the needed legislation through Congress actually hurt the economy? What if the president simply stood by, watching while the Fed cut interest rates and underlying economic forces halted the decline in real GDP? How long would such a process take—one year? Five years?

To answer these important questions, we need a model of economic fluctuations—a simplified description of how the economy adjusts over time when it moves away from potential GDP, as in a recession.

The purpose of this chapter is to present, in graphical form, an economic fluctuations model. Economic fluctuations models are used to make decisions about monetary policy at the Fed and at other central banks all over the world. Private business analysts use the ideas to track the economy and predict central bank decisions.

This model is much newer than the supply and demand model, which has been around for over 100 years. It combines Keynes's idea, developed 50 years ago, that aggregate demand causes the departure of real GDP from potential GDP with newer ideas, developed in the 1980s and 1990s, about how expectations and inflation adjust over time.

Though newer, the economic fluctuations model is analogous to the supply and demand model (Chapter 3). Just as we presented the supply and demand model in a graph consisting of three elements:

- A *demand curve*
- A *supply curve*
- An *equilibrium* at the intersection of the two curves

we present the economic fluctuations model in a graph consisting of three elements:

- An *aggregate demand* (AD) *curve*
- An *inflation adjustment* (IA) *line*
- An *equilibrium* at the intersection of the curve and the line

We use the economic fluctuations model to explain fluctuations in real GDP and inflation in much the same way that we used supply and demand curves to explain quantity and price in the peanut or other microeconomic markets. In the microeconomic supply and demand model, the intersection of the *demand curve* and the *supply curve* gives us a prediction of price and quantity. In the economic fluctuations model, the intersection of the *aggregate demand (AD) curve* and the *inflation adjustment (IA) line* gives us a prediction of real GDP and inflation.

We will start our construction of the economic fluctuations model by deriving the aggregate demand curve and then the inflation adjustment line. We will then show how their intersection determines real GDP and inflation.

The Aggregate Demand Curve

aggregate demand (*AD*) curve: a line showing a negative relationship between inflation and the aggregate quantity of goods and services demanded at that inflation rate.

The **aggregate demand (*AD*) curve** is a relationship between two economic variables: real GDP and the inflation rate. Real GDP is usually measured as the percentage deviation from potential GDP, and the inflation rate is usually measured as the annual percentage change in the overall price level from year to year. Figure 24.1 shows an aggregate demand curve for the United States. Observe that inflation is measured on the vertical axis, that real GDP is measured on the horizontal axis, and that we have drawn a vertical dashed line to mark the point where real GDP equals potential GDP. The aggregate demand curve shows different combinations of real GDP and inflation. It is downward-sloping from left to right because real GDP is negatively related to inflation along the curve. The term *aggregate demand* is used because we interpret the movements of real GDP away from potential GDP as being due to fluctuations in the sum (aggregate) of the demand for consumption, investment, net exports, and government purchases.

Why does the aggregate demand curve slope downward? We will answer this question and derive the curve in three stages. First, we show that there is a negative

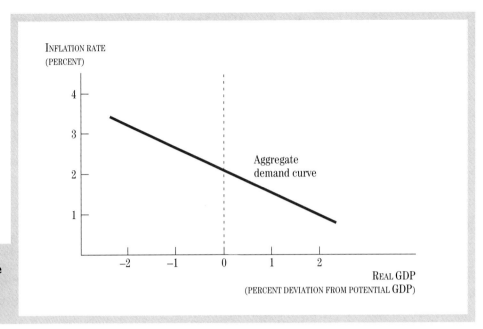

Figure 24.1
The Aggregate Demand Curve
The aggregate demand curve shows that higher inflation and real GDP are negatively related.

relationship between the real interest rate and real GDP. Second, we show that there is a positive relationship between inflation and the real interest rate. Third, we show that these two relationships imply that there is a negative relationship between real GDP and inflation, and that that relationship is the aggregate demand curve. The following schematic chart shows how the three stages fit together.

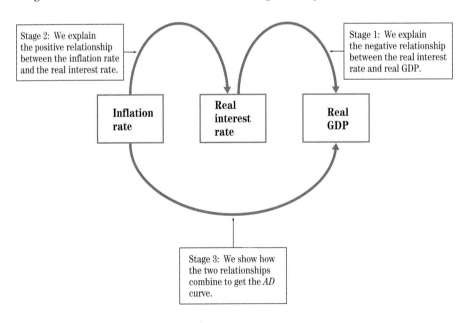

Interest Rates and Real GDP

Consumption, investment, and net exports are each negatively related to the interest rate. Combining these components helps provide an explanation of the negative relationship between real GDP and the interest rate. Keep in mind that the real interest rate is a better measure of the effects of interest rates on investment, consumption, and net exports because it corrects for inflation. Recall from Chapter 17 that the real interest rate equals the stated, or nominal, interest rate minus the inflation rate. The negative effect of the real interest rate on consumption, investment, and net exports is no different from that discussed in Chapter 19. If you have already studied that chapter, the next few pages will serve as review.

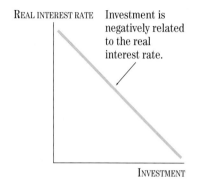

REAL INTEREST RATE   Investment is negatively related to the real interest rate.

INVESTMENT

■ **Investment.**   Investment is the component of expenditure that is probably most sensitive to the real interest rate. Recall that part of investment is the purchase of new equipment or a new factory by a business firm. Many firms must borrow funds to pay for such investments. Higher real interest rates make such borrowing more costly. The additional profits the firm might expect to earn from purchasing a photocopier or a truck are more likely to be lower than the interest costs on the loan if the real interest rate is high. Hence, businesses that are thinking about buying a new machine and need to borrow funds will be less inclined to purchase such an investment good if real interest rates are higher, and so higher real interest rates reduce investment spending by businesses. Also, remember that part of investment is the purchase of new houses. Most people need to take out a mortgage in order to buy a house. Like any loan, the mortgage has an interest rate, and higher interest rates make mortgages more costly. Hence, with higher real interest rates, fewer people take out mortgages and buy new houses. Spending for new housing declines.

The same reasoning works to show why lower real interest rates will increase investment spending: Lower real interest rates reduce the cost of borrowing and make investment more attractive to firms and households.

To summarize, both business investment and housing investment decline when the real interest rate rises, and they increase when the real interest rate falls. At any time there are some firms or households deciding whether to buy a new machine or a new house, and they are going to be less inclined to buy such things when the interest rate is higher.

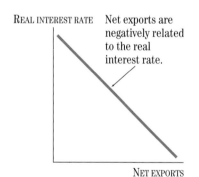

REAL INTEREST RATE   Net exports are negatively related to the real interest rate.

NET EXPORTS

■ **Net Exports.**   The negative relationship between net exports and the real interest rate requires a somewhat more involved explanation than the relationship between the real interest rate and investment. The relationship exists because higher real interest rates in the United States tend to lead to a higher dollar exchange rate and, in turn, a higher exchange rate reduces net exports.

A higher real interest rate in the United States compared with other countries increases the demand for U.S. dollar bank accounts and other assets that pay interest. That increased demand bids up the price of dollars; hence, the exchange rate—the price of dollars—rises. Now, with a higher exchange rate, net exports will be lower because U.S.-produced exports become more expensive to foreigners, who must pay a higher price for dollars, and imported foreign goods become cheaper for Americans, who can get more foreign goods for higher-priced dollars. With exports falling and imports rising, net exports—exports less imports—must fall. In sum, higher real interest rates reduce net exports.

The same reasoning works for lower real interest rates as well. If the real interest rate falls in the United States, then U.S. dollar bank accounts are less attractive compared with bank accounts in other currencies, such as those of Germany or Japan. This bids down the price of dollars, and the exchange rate falls. Now, with a lower exchange rate, net exports will be higher because U.S.-produced exports are less expensive to foreigners and imported foreign goods are more expensive for Americans. With exports rising and imports falling, net exports must rise. Thus, lower real interest rates increase net exports.

To summarize, there is a negative relationship between the interest rate and the net exports that works through the exchange rate, as shown on the next page.

Interest Rate		Value of the Domestic Currency		Net Exports
up	→	up	→	down
down	→	down	→	up

If the interest rate goes up, then the value of the domestic currency goes up, causing net exports to go down. If the interest rate goes down, then the value of the domestic currency goes down, causing net exports to go up.

■ **Consumption.** We have shown that two of the components of expenditure—investment and net exports—are sensitive to the real interest rate. What about consumption?

Although consumption is probably less sensitive to the real interest rate than the other components, there is some evidence that higher real interest rates encourage people to save a larger fraction of their income. Higher real interest rates encourage people to save because they earn more on their savings. Because more saving means less consumption, this implies that consumption is negatively related to the interest rate. However, most economists feel that the effect of interest rates on consumption is much less than on investment and net exports.

■ **The Overall Effect.** To summarize the discussion thus far, investment, net exports, and consumption are all negatively related to the real interest rate. The overall effect of a change in real interest rates on real GDP can now be assessed.

Figure 24.2 shows the 45-degree line and two different expenditure lines corresponding to two different interest rates. Higher interest rates shift the expenditure line down because a higher interest rate lowers investment, net exports, and consumption, which are all part of expenditure.

Figure 24.2
The Interest Rate, Spending Balance, and Real GDP
A higher real interest rate shifts the expenditure line down because consumption, investment, and net exports depend negatively on the real interest rate. Thus, real GDP declines with a higher real interest rate. Conversely, a lower real interest rate raises real GDP.

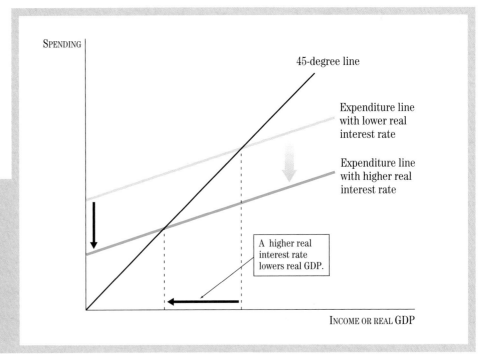

Finished with Stage 1: Real GDP is negatively related to the real interest rate.

Why?

- Consumption (*C*) is negatively related to the *real interest rate.*
- Investment (*I*) is negatively related to the *real interest rate.*
- Net exports (*X*) are negatively related to the *real interest rate.*

Observe how the downward shift of the expenditure line leads to a new point of spending balance. The intersection of the expenditure line with the 45-degree line occurs at a lower level of real GDP. Note that real GDP is lower not only because the higher real interest rate lowers investment, net exports, and consumption, but also because a decline in income will lower consumption further. Real GDP declines by the amount shown on the horizontal axis, which is larger than the downward shift in the expenditure line. *Thus, an increase in the real interest rate lowers real GDP.*

What about a decline in the real interest rate? A lower real interest rate will raise the expenditure line. In that case, when the expenditure line shifts up, the point of spending balance at the intersection with the 45-degree line will be at a higher level of real GDP. *Thus, a decrease in the real interest rate raises real GDP.*

In sum, we have shown that there is a negative relationship between the real interest rate and real GDP.

Interest Rates and Inflation

Now that we have seen why interest rates affect real GDP, let us proceed to the second stage in our analysis. We want to show why a rise in inflation will increase the real interest rate and thereby lower real GDP, or why a decline in inflation will decrease the real interest rate and thereby raise real GDP.

■ **Central Bank Interest Rate Policy.**   The easiest way to see why the real interest rate rises when the inflation rate increases is to examine the behavior of the Fed. The Fed and central banks in other countries typically follow policies in which they respond to an increase in the inflation rate by raising the nominal interest rate. By far the most widely followed and analyzed decision by the Fed is its nominal interest rate decision.

Why do central banks raise the nominal interest rate when they think the inflation rate is rising? The inflation rate is ultimately the responsibility of the Fed, and the goal of controlling inflation requires that the central bank raise the nominal interest rate so that the real interest rate rises when the inflation rate rises. If the central bank raises the real interest rate successfully, then the higher real interest rate will reduce investment, consumption, and net exports. The reduced demand will then reduce inflationary pressures and bring inflation back down again.

The goal of controlling inflation also requires that the central bank lower the real interest rate when inflation falls. Suppose that the inflation rate starts to fall. If the central bank lowers the nominal interest rate so that the real interest rate falls, then the lower real interest rate will increase investment, consumption, and net exports. The increase in demand will put upward pressure on inflation.

Table 24.1 illustrates these actions of the Fed using a hypothetical example. For each inflation rate, a nominal interest rate decision by the Fed is shown. For example, when inflation is 2 percent, the nominal interest rate decision is 4 percent. When inflation rises to 4 percent, the nominal interest rate decision by the Fed is 7 percent. Thus, when inflation rises, the central bank raises the nominal interest rate, and when inflation falls, the central bank lowers the nominal interest rate.

Note that the nominal interest rate rises more than inflation rises in Table 24.1. The reason is that for an increase in the nominal interest rate to reduce demand, the real interest rate must rise because investment, consumption, and net exports depend negatively on the real interest rate, as described in the previous section. The nominal interest rate has to rise by more than the inflation rate in order for the real interest rate to rise and demand to decline. If, instead, the nominal interest rate rose by less than the increase in the inflation rate, then the real interest rate would not rise; rather, it would fall. The behavior of the central bank illustrated in the third column of Table 24.1 is called a **monetary policy rule** because it describes the systematic response of the real interest rate to inflation as decided by the central bank.

monetary policy rule: a description of how much the interest rate or other instruments of monetary policy respond to inflation or other measures of the state of the economy.

■ **How the Fed Changes the Interest Rate.** Keep in mind that the central bank does not set interest rates by decree or by direct control. Governments sometimes do control the price of goods; for example, some city governments control the rents on apartments. The central bank does not apply such controls to the interest rate. Rather, it enters the market in which short-term interest rates are determined by the usual forces of supply and demand. In the United States, the short-term interest rate

Table 24.1
A Numerical Example of Central Bank Interest Rate Policy

(a) Inflation Rate	(b) Nominal Interest Rate Decision (made by the central bank)	Resulting Real Interest Rate (b) − (a)
0.0	1.0	1.0
1.0	2.5	1.5
2.0	4.0	2.0
3.0	5.5	2.5
4.0	7.0	3.0
5.0	8.5	3.5
6.0	10.0	4.0
7.0	11.5	4.5
8.0	13.0	5.0

federal funds rate: the interest rate on overnight loans between banks that the Federal Reserve influences by changing the supply of funds (bank reserves) in the market.

> **Actions the Fed takes:** To reduce the federal funds rate, the Fed increases the supply of reserves by buying bonds. To raise the federal funds rate, the Fed decreases the supply of reserves by selling bonds. The buying and selling of bonds are called *open market operations.*

target inflation rate: the central bank's goal for the average rate of inflation over the long run.

the Fed focuses on is the interest rate on overnight loans between banks. This is called the **federal funds rate,** and the overnight loan market is called the federal funds market because reserves at the Fed are what are loaned or borrowed in this market. When the Fed wants to lower this interest rate, it supplies more reserves to this market. When it wants to raise the interest rate, it reduces reserves. Recall from Chapter 22 that the Fed can change the amount of reserves in the banking system through *open market operations*—that is, by buying and selling government bonds. If the Fed wants to increase reserves and thereby lower the federal funds rate, it buys government bonds. If the Fed wants to decrease reserves and thereby increase the federal funds rate, it sells government bonds.

■ **A Graph of the Response of the Interest Rate to Inflation.** Figure 24.3 represents the monetary policy rule graphically, using the information in Table 24.1. When the inflation rate rises, the nominal interest rate rises along the green upward-sloping line. When the inflation rate declines, the nominal interest rate declines. The nominal interest rate must rise by more than the inflation rate if the *real* interest rate is to rise when inflation rises; this requires that the slope of the monetary policy rule in Figure 24.3 be greater than 1. For example, if the slope is 1.5, then when the inflation rate increases by 1 percentage point, the interest rate rises by 1.5 percentage points, as in Table 24.1. In other words, the nominal interest rate rises by .5 percentage point *more* than the inflation rate rises, causing the *real* interest rate to rise by .5 percentage point. The resulting real interest rate decision of the Fed is indicated by the purple line: The real interest rate changes by .5 percentage point when the inflation rate changes by 1 percentage point. The real interest rate policy rule is shown in Figure 24.4.

Most central banks have a **target inflation rate,** the inflation rate that the central bank tries to maintain on average over the long run. Because of various shocks to the economy, the central bank cannot control the inflation rate perfectly; sometimes the inflation rate will rise above the target inflation rate, and sometimes the inflation rate will fall below the target inflation rate. By reacting to these movements in inflation according to a monetary policy rule—that is, by increasing the interest rate when

Figure 24.3
A Monetary Policy Rule
The monetary policy rule shows that the Fed raises the real interest rate when inflation rises and lowers the real interest rate when inflation falls. In order to accomplish this, the Fed has to move the nominal interest rate by more than 1 percentage point when there is a 1 percentage point change in the rate of inflation.

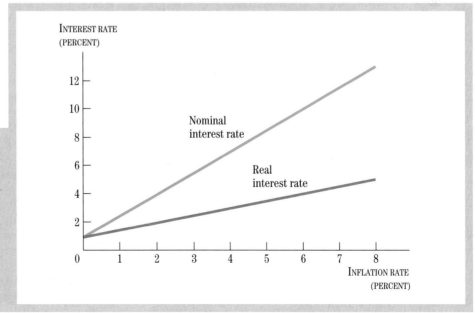

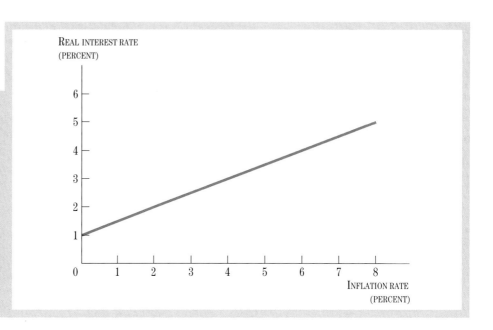

Figure 24.4
The Real Interest Rate Positively Related to Inflation
From now on, the monetary policy rule of the Fed will be presented as a relationship between the inflation rate and the real interest rate. When inflation rises, the Fed raises the real interest rate (through a more than proportional increase in the nominal interest rate), whereas when inflation falls, the Fed lowers the real interest rate (by decreasing the nominal rate in a more than proportional manner).

Finished with Stage 2: The interest rate is positively related to inflation.

The Fed and other central banks tend to

- Raise the real interest rate when inflation rises.
- Lower the real interest rate when inflation falls.

This is the *behavioral description* of the people at the Fed, much as a demand curve is a behavioral description of consumers.

This response is called a *monetary policy rule.*

inflation rises and cutting the interest rate when inflation falls—the central bank will cause the actual inflation rate to move back toward the target inflation rate over time. Some central banks, such as the Bank of England and the Reserve Bank of New Zealand, have explicit inflation targets. Other central banks, like the Fed, have implicit inflation targets that are not explicitly announced, but that can be assessed by observing central bank decisions over time. The target inflation rate for many central banks is about 2 percent. For the economy described in Figure 24.4, at the target inflation rate of 2 percent, the central bank sets real interest rates at 2 percent by choosing a nominal rate of 4 percent.

■ **A Good Simplifying Assumption.** The behavior of the central bank described in this section provides the easiest explanation of the response of interest rates to inflation, but it is not the only possible explanation. Economists have found that the general upward-sloping relationship in Figure 24.3, which we call the monetary policy rule, is common to many different types of monetary policies, including policies in which the central bank focuses on money growth. Although the position and shape of the monetary policy rule will differ for these different types of policies, the overall response of interest rates to inflation will be similar. Our reason for using this particular derivation is that it is the easiest to explain and describes the actual behavior of the Fed and other central banks.

Derivation of the Aggregate Demand Curve

Thus far, we have shown that the level of real GDP is negatively related to the real interest rate and that the real interest rate is positively related to the inflation rate through the central bank's policy rule. We now combine these two concepts to derive the aggregate demand curve—the inverse relationship between the inflation rate and real GDP.

The chain of reasoning that brings about the aggregate demand curve can be explained by considering what would happen if the inflation rate rose. First, the interest rate would rise because the Fed would raise the real interest rate in response to the higher inflation rate. Next, the higher real interest rate would mean less

The following is a press release issued by the Federal Reserve on February 2, 2005, explaining its decision to raise the federal funds rate from 2.25 percent to 2.5 percent. This press release contains information that subsequently appeared in many newspapers around the world.

Notice that the Fed is raising interest rates even though the rate of inflation is "expected to be relatively low." If this seems unusual, keep in mind that during the recession of 2001, when inflation was falling, the Fed lowered interest rates dramatically. As the economy recovers and inflation rises from its prior low levels, the Fed will typically raise interest rates, as it is doing here. The model says that the Fed will raise rates when the rate of inflation rises, even if the rate of inflation is low.

Note also that the Fed is careful to refer to its decision as raising its "target for the federal funds rate." This reflects the fact that the Fed has no direct control over interest rates, even though it will influence rates toward a targeted value using open market operations.

For immediate release

Summary of the policy decision

The Federal Open Market Committee decided today to raise its target for the federal funds rate by 25 basis points to 2½ percent.

The Committee believes that, even after this action, the stance of monetary policy remains accommodative and, coupled with robust underlying growth in productivity, is providing

The Fed also comments on its outlook for the economy and future policy.

ongoing support to economic activity. Output appears to be growing at a moderate pace despite the rise in energy prices, and labor market conditions continue to improve gradually. Inflation and longer-term inflation expectations remain well contained. The Committee perceives the upside and downside risks to the attainment of both sustainable growth and price stability for the next few

quarters to be roughly equal. With underlying inflation expected to be relatively low, the Committee believes that policy accommodation can be removed at a pace that is likely to be measured. Nonetheless, the Committee will respond to changes in economic prospects as needed to fulfill its obligation to maintain price stability.

Finished with Stage 3: Real GDP is negatively related to inflation.

Suppose that *inflation increases:*

- The Fed will raise the real interest rate.
- The higher real interest rate will *decrease real GDP.*

Suppose that *inflation decreases:*

- The Fed will lower the real interest rate.
- The lower real interest rate will *increase real GDP.*

This negative relationship is the *AD* curve.

investment spending, a decline in net exports, and a decline in consumption. Lower investment spending would occur because investment would be made more costly by the high real interest rate. American goods would become more expensive, and foreign goods would become cheaper. Thus, net exports—exports minus imports—would decline.

The opposite chain of events would occur if there were a fall in inflation. First, the Fed would lower the real interest rate according to the monetary policy rule. The lower real interest rate, in turn, would cause investment, net exports, and consumption to rise. Hence, real GDP would rise.

In sum, we see that when the inflation rate rises, real GDP decreases, and when the inflation rate falls, real GDP increases. In other words, there is a negative relationship between inflation and real GDP. When we graph this relationship in a diagram with real GDP on the horizontal axis and inflation on the vertical axis, we get a downward-sloping curve like the one shown in Figure 24.1; this curve is the aggregate demand curve, which we have thus derived.

If you would like to go over the derivation again, seeing all the paragraphs together on the same page, a self-guided graphical overview is provided in Figure 24.5. If you read the explanatory boxes in numerical order, you will trace through the chain of events following an increase in inflation, including the Fed's real interest rate increase according to its policy rule and the decline in real GDP.

■ **Movements Along the Aggregate Demand Curve.** Thus far, we have explained why the aggregate demand curve has a negative slope—that is, why higher inflation means a lower real GDP. A *change in real GDP* due to a *change in inflation* is

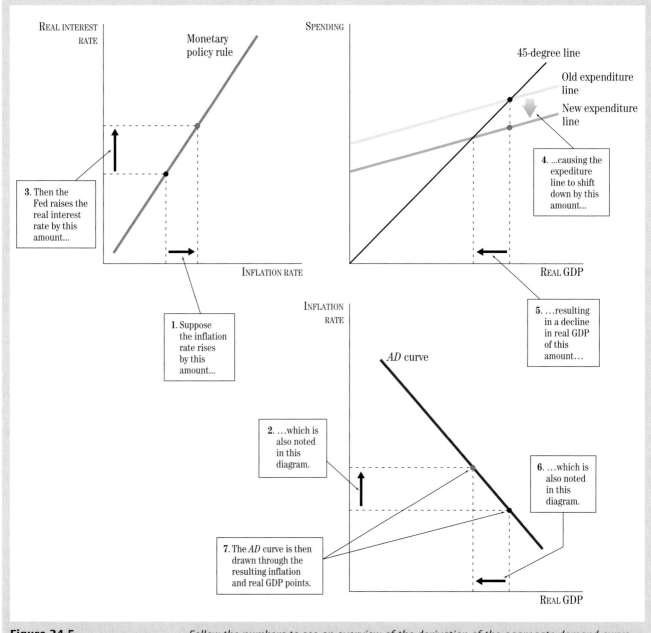

Figure 24.5
A Self-Guided Graphical
Overview

Follow the numbers to see an overview of the derivation of the aggregate demand curve. The black dots represent the situation *before* we increase the inflation rate. The orange dots represent the situation *after* we increase the inflation rate. When inflation rises, the central bank raises the real interest rate, and this lowers real GDP. Hence, we have the aggregate demand curve.

thus a *movement along* the aggregate demand curve. Recall that in microeconomics, a similar movement along the demand curve occurs when a *change in the price* leads to a *change in quantity demanded*. When inflation rises, causing the Fed to raise the interest rate, and real GDP declines, there is a movement up and to the left along the aggregate demand curve. When inflation declines and the Fed lowers the interest rate, causing GDP to rise, there is a movement down and to the right along the aggregate demand curve.

■ **Shifts of the Aggregate Demand Curve.** Now, the inflation rate is not the only thing that affects aggregate demand. Changes in government purchases, shifts in monetary policy, shifts in foreign demand for U.S. exports, changes in taxes, and changes in consumer confidence, among other things, affect aggregate demand. When any of these factors changes aggregate demand, we say there is a *shift* in the aggregate demand curve. Let us briefly consider some of those sources of shifts in the aggregate demand curve.

Government Purchases   Imagine that government purchases rise. We know from our analysis of spending balance in Chapter 23 that an increase in government purchases will increase real GDP in the short run. This increase in real GDP occurs at any inflation rate: at 2 percent, at 4 percent, or at any other level. Now, if real GDP increases at a given inflation rate, the aggregate demand curve will shift to the right. This is shown in Figure 24.6. The new aggregate demand curve will be parallel to the original aggregate demand curve because no matter what the inflation rate is in the economy, the shift in government purchases is going to have the same effect on real GDP. The same reasoning implies that a decline in government spending shifts the aggregate demand curve to the left.

Changes in the Target Inflation Rate   Suppose the Fed has an inflation target of 2 percent. Consider what happens when the Fed shifts its policy objectives. Suppose, for instance, that a new Fed chair becomes convinced that inflation should be higher, say, 3 percent. In order to get inflation to rise, the Fed will immediately try to increase spending by lowering the real interest rate: The *AD* curve will shift to the right, as shown in Figure 24.7. In contrast, suppose that the new Fed chair wants to lower inflation, say, to 1 percent. In order to get inflation to fall, the Fed will immediately try to lower spending by raising the real interest rate: The *AD* curve will shift to the left.

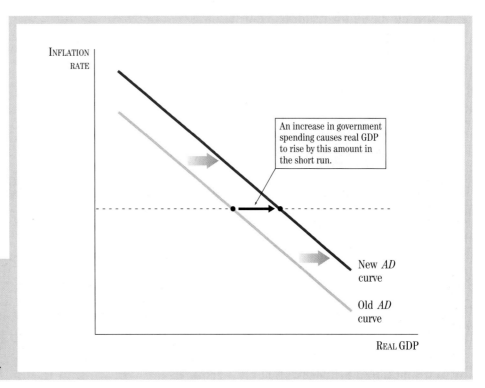

Figure 24.6
How Government Purchases Shift the Aggregate Demand Curve
An increase in government purchases shifts the *AD* curve to the right. Real GDP rises by the same amount at every level of inflation.

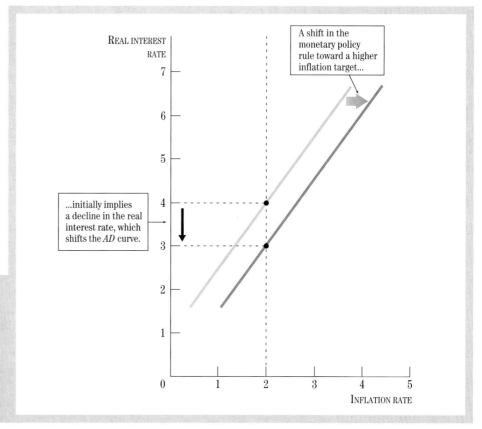

Figure 24.7
A Shift in the Monetary Policy Rule
A shift in the policy rule to higher inflation implies a decline in the real interest rate. The lower real interest rate increases real GDP in the short run. As a result, at a given inflation rate, the *AD* curve shifts to the right.

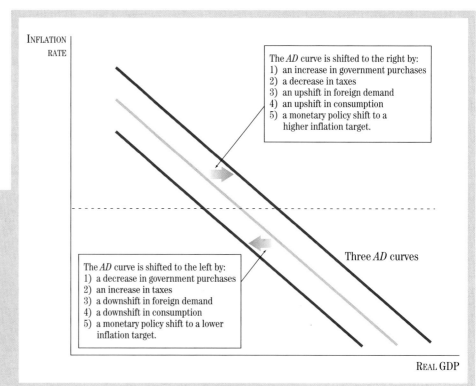

Figure 24.8
A List of Possible Shifts in the Aggregate Demand Curve
Many things shift the *AD* curve. An increase in government purchases shifts the *AD* curve to the right. A change in the monetary policy rule toward a higher inflation target shifts the *AD* curve to the right. A decline in government purchases and a change in the monetary policy rule toward a lower inflation target shift the curve to the left.

Other Changes   Many other changes in the economy (other than a change in the inflation rate, which is a movement along the *AD* curve) will shift the *AD* curve. We considered many such possibilities in Chapter 23; their effects on the aggregate demand curve are listed in Figure 24.8. For example, an increase in the foreign demand for U.S. products will increase net exports, raise real GDP, and shift the aggregate demand curve to the right. A drop in consumer confidence that reduces the amount of consumption at every level of income will shift the aggregate demand curve to the left. Finally, an increase in taxes shifts the aggregate demand curve to the left, while a decrease in taxes shifts the aggregate demand curve to the right.

REVIEW
- The aggregate demand curve is an inverse relationship between inflation and real GDP.

- Investment, net exports, and consumption are negatively related to the real interest rate. Hence, real GDP falls when the real interest rate rises, and vice versa.

- When inflation increases, the central bank raises the real interest rate, and this lowers real GDP. Conversely, when inflation falls, the central bank lowers the real interest rate, and this raises real GDP. It does so by moving nominal interest rates by more than 1 percentage point when inflation changes by 1 percentage point. These are movements along the aggregate demand curve.

- The aggregate demand curve shifts to the right when the central bank changes its monetary policy rule toward more inflation and shifts to the left when the central bank changes its policy rule toward less inflation.

- Higher government purchases shift the aggregate demand curve to the right. Lower government purchases shift the aggregate demand curve to the left.

The Inflation Adjustment Line

inflation adjustment (*IA*) line: a flat line showing the level of inflation in the economy at a given point in time. It shifts up when real GDP is greater than potential GDP, and it shifts down when real GDP is less than potential GDP; it also shifts when expectations of inflation or raw materials prices change.

Having derived the aggregate demand curve and studied its properties, let us now look at the inflation adjustment line, the second element of the economic fluctuations model. The **inflation adjustment (*IA*) line** is a flat line showing the level of inflation in the economy at any point in time. Figure 24.9 shows an example of the inflation adjustment line in a diagram with inflation on the vertical axis and real GDP on the horizontal axis. For example, if the line touches 4 percent on the vertical axis, it tells us that inflation is 4 percent.

The inflation adjustment line describes the economic behavior of firms and workers setting prices and wages in the economy. There are several important features about the slope and position of the inflation adjustment line.

The Inflation Adjustment Line Is Flat

That the inflation adjustment line is flat indicates that firms and workers adjust their prices and wages in such a way that the inflation rate remains steady in the short run

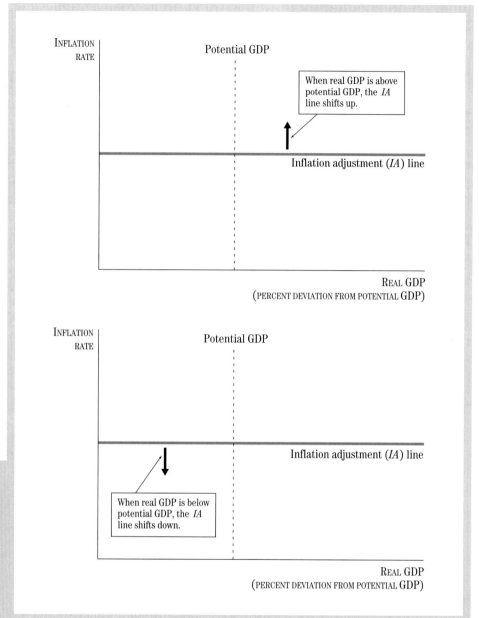

Figure 24.9
Inflation Adjustment and Changes in Inflation
In the top panel, real GDP is above potential GDP and inflation is rising; the inflation adjustment line shifts up. In the bottom panel, real GDP is below potential GDP and inflation is falling; thus, the inflation adjustment line shifts down.

as real GDP changes. Only over time does inflation change significantly and the line move. In the short run, inflation stays at 4 percent, or wherever the line happens to be when real GDP changes.

In interpreting the inflation adjustment line, it is helpful to remember that it is part of a *model* of the overall economy and is thus an approximation of reality. In fact, inflation does not remain *perfectly* steady, and the inflation adjustment line can have a small upward slope. But it is a good approximation to assume that the inflation adjustment line is flat.

There are two reasons why inflation does not change very much in the short run even if real GDP and the demand for firms' products changes: (1) expectations of continuing inflation and (2) staggered wage and price setting at different firms throughout the economy.

■ **Expectations of Continuing Inflation.** Expectations about the price and wage decisions of other firms throughout the economy influence a firm's price and wage decisions. For example, if the overall inflation rate in the economy has been hovering around 4 percent year after year, then a firm can expect that its competitors' prices will probably increase by about 4 percent per year, unless circumstances change. To keep prices near those of the competition, this firm will need to increase its price by about 4 percent each year. Thus, the inflation rate stays steady at 4 percent per year.

Wage adjustments are also influenced by expectations. If firms and workers expect that workers at other firms will be getting large wage increases, then meeting the competition will require similar large wage increases. A smaller wage increase would reduce the wage of the firm's workers relative to that received by other workers. Many firms base their wage decisions on the wages paid by other firms. If they see the wages at other firms rising, they will be more willing to increase wages.

Firms and workers also look to expectations of inflation when deciding on wage increases. In an economy with 4 percent inflation, wages will have to increase by 4 percent for workers just to keep up with the cost of living. Lower wage increases would result in a decline in workers' real wages.

■ **Staggered Price and Wage Setting.** Not all wages and prices are changed at the same time throughout the economy. Rather, price setting and wage setting are staggered over months and even years. For example, autoworkers might negotiate three-year wage contracts in 1996, 1999, 2002, and so on. Dockworkers might negotiate three-year contracts in 1997, 2000, 2003, and so on. Bus companies and train companies do not adjust their prices at the same time, even though they may compete for the same riders. On any given day, we can be sure that there is a wage or price adjustment somewhere in the economy, but the vast majority of wages and prices do not change.

Staggered price and wage setting slows down the adjustment of prices in the economy. When considering what wage increases are likely in the next year, firms and workers know about the most recent wage increases. For example, an agreement made by another firm to increase wages by 4 percent per year for three years into the future will affect the expectations of wages paid to competing workers in the future. This wage agreement will not change unless the firm is on the edge of bankruptcy, and perhaps not even then. Hence, workers and firms deciding on wage increases will tend to match the wage increases recently made at other firms. Thus, price and wage decisions made today are directly influenced by price and wage decisions made yesterday.

As with many things in life, when today's decisions are influenced by yesterday's decisions, inertia sets in. The staggering of the decisions makes it difficult to break the inertia. Unless there is a reason to make a change—such as a persistent decline in demand or a change in expectations of inflation—the price increases or wage increases continue from year to year. The flat inflation adjustment line describes this inertia.

The Inflation Adjustment Line Shifts Gradually When Real GDP Departs from Potential GDP

The inflation adjustment line does not always stay put; rather, it may shift up or down from year to year. If real GDP stays above potential GDP, then inflation starts to

The following is a shorthand summary of inflation adjustment in the economy as a whole:

If real GDP = potential GDP, then the inflation rate does not change (*IA* line does not shift).

If real GDP > potential GDP, then the inflation rate increases (*IA* line shifts up).

If real GDP < potential GDP, then the inflation rate decreases (*IA* line shifts down).

rise. Firms see that the demand for their products is remaining high, and they begin adjusting their prices. If the inflation rate is 4 percent, then the firms will have to raise their prices by more than 4 percent if they want their relative prices to increase. Hence, inflation starts to rise. The inflation adjustment line is shifted upward to illustrate this rise in inflation; it will keep shifting upward as long as real GDP is above potential GDP.

However, if real GDP is below potential GDP, then firms will see that the demand for their products is falling off, and they will adjust their prices. If inflation is 4 percent, the firms will raise their prices by less than 4 percent—perhaps by 2 percent—if they want the relative price of their goods to fall. Hence, inflation will fall. The inflation adjustment line is shifted down to illustrate this fall in inflation. Figure 24.9 shows the direction of these shifts.

If real GDP stays at potential GDP, neither to the left nor to the right of the vertical potential GDP line in Figure 24.9, then inflation remains unchanged. This steady inflation is represented by an unmoving inflation adjustment line year after year.

Changes in Expectations or Commodity Prices Shift the Inflation Adjustment Line

Even if real GDP is at potential GDP, some special events in the economy can cause the inflation adjustment line to shift up or down. One important example is *shifts in expectations* of inflation. If firms and workers expect inflation to rise, they are likely to raise wages and prices by a large amount to keep pace with the expected inflation. Thus, an increase in expectations of inflation will cause the inflation adjustment line to shift up to a higher inflation rate. And a decrease in expectations of inflation will cause the inflation adjustment line to shift down.

Another example is a change in commodity prices that affects firms' costs of production. For example, we will examine the effects on inflation of an oil price increase in Chapter 25. By raising firms' costs, such an oil price increase would lead firms to charge higher prices, and the inflation adjustment line would rise, at least temporarily.

Does the Inflation Adjustment Line Fit the Facts?

Are these assumptions about the inflation adjustment line accurate? Does inflation rise when real GDP is above potential GDP and fall when real GDP is below potential GDP? Figure 24.10 provides the relevant evidence. The points in the figure indicate the level of inflation and the percent deviation of real GDP from potential GDP for years when real GDP was more than 2 percent above or below potential GDP. (We use only deviations that are greater than 2 percent because it is difficult to measure the deviations with much better than 2 percent accuracy.) Up arrows indicate that inflation increased from the year before the labeled year. Down arrows indicate that inflation decreased. The length of the arrow is the size of the change.

Inflation usually declines when real GDP is less than—to the left of—potential GDP in Figure 24.10. The biggest decline in inflation occurred in 1982, when real GDP was far below potential GDP. When real GDP is greater than—to the right of—potential GDP, inflation is rising in the majority of cases. Figure 24.10 indicates that the theory of the inflation adjustment line shown in Figure 24.9 fits the facts very well. From 1993 to 1997, real GDP was very close to potential GDP, so inflation did not change much, and thus these years are not on the graph. In 1998 and 1999, real GDP rose above potential GDP, but inflation did not immediately start to rise. This led some commentators to think that the inflation adjustment relationship was changing, but by late 1999 and 2000, inflation rose as predicted by the theory.

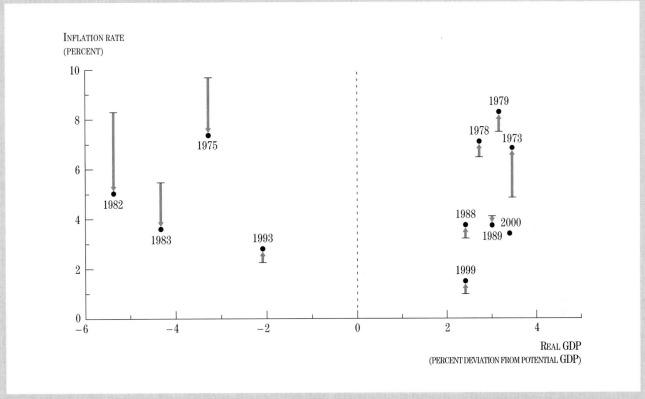

Figure 24.10
Declines and Increases in Inflation

The data show that inflation falls when real GDP is below potential GDP, and inflation rises when real GDP is above potential GDP.

REVIEW

- The inflation adjustment (*IA*) line, the second element of the economic fluctuations model, is a flat line showing the level of inflation in the economy at any point in time. The inflation adjustment line describes the economic behavior of firms and workers setting prices and wages in the economy.

- Firms do not change their prices instantaneously when the demand for their product changes. Thus, when aggregate demand changes and real GDP departs from potential GDP, the inflation rate does not immediately change; the inflation adjustment line does not shift in response to such changes in the short run.

- Staggered wage and price setting tends to slow down the adjustment of inflation in the economy as a whole.

- Over time, inflation does respond to departures of real GDP from potential GDP. This response can be described by upward and downward shifts in the inflation adjustment line over time.

Combining the Aggregate Demand Curve and the Inflation Adjustment Line

We have now derived two relationships—the aggregate demand curve and the inflation adjustment line—that describe real GDP and inflation in the economy as a whole. The two relationships can be combined to make predictions about real GDP and inflation.

Along the aggregate demand curve in Figure 24.1, real GDP and inflation are negatively related. This curve describes the behavior of firms and consumers as they respond to a higher real interest rate caused by the Fed's response to higher inflation. They respond by lowering consumption, investment, and net exports. This line presents a range of possible values of real GDP and inflation.

The inflation adjustment line in Figure 24.9, on the other hand, tells us what the inflation rate is at any point in time. Thus, we can use the inflation adjustment line to determine exactly what inflation rate applies to the aggregate demand curve. For example, if the inflation adjustment line tells us that the inflation rate for 2004 is 5 percent, then we can go right to the aggregate demand curve to determine what the level of real GDP will be at that 5 percent inflation rate. If the aggregate demand curve says that real GDP is 2 percent below potential GDP when inflation is 5 percent, then we predict that real GDP is 2 percent below potential GDP. The inflation adjustment line tells us the current location of inflation—and therefore real GDP—on the aggregate demand curve.

Figure 24.11 illustrates the determination of real GDP and inflation graphically. It combines the aggregate demand curve from Figure 24.1 with the inflation adjustment line from Figure 24.9. At any point in time, the inflation adjustment line is given, as shown in Figure 24.11. The inflation adjustment line intersects the aggregate demand curve at a single point. It is at this point of intersection that inflation and real GDP are determined. The intersection gives an *equilibrium* level of real GDP and inflation. At that point, we can look down to the horizontal axis of the diagram to determine the level of real GDP corresponding to that level of inflation. For example, the point of intersection in the left panel of Figure 24.11 might be when inflation is 5 percent and real GDP is 2 percent below potential GDP. The point of intersection in the right panel is at a lower inflation rate when real GDP is above potential GDP. The point of intersection in the middle panel of Figure 24.11 has real GDP equal to potential GDP.

As Figure 24.11 makes clear, the intersection of the inflation adjustment line and the aggregate demand curve may give values of real GDP that are either above or below potential GDP. But if real GDP is not equal to potential GDP, then the economy has not fully recovered from a recession, as on the left of Figure 24.11, or returned to potential GDP after being above it, as on the right. To describe dynamic movements of inflation and real GDP, we must consider how the inflation adjustment line and the aggregate demand curve shift over time. That is the subject of Chapter 25.

REVIEW

- In any year, the inflation adjustment line tells what the inflation rate is. Using the aggregate demand curve, we can then make a prediction about what real GDP is.

- The intersection of the aggregate demand curve and the inflation adjustment line gives a pair of observations on real GDP and inflation at any point in time.

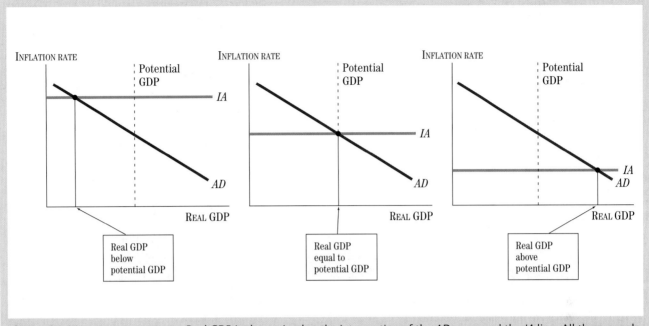

**Figure 24.11
Determining Real GDP and
Inflation**

Real GDP is determined at the intersection of the *AD* curve and the *IA* line. All three panels have the same *AD* curve and the same vertical line marking potential GDP. Three different levels of the *IA* line give three different levels of real GDP: less than, equal to, and greater than potential GDP.

Conclusion

With the essential elements of the economic fluctuations model—the aggregate demand curve, the inflation adjustment line, and their intersection—put together, we are now ready to use the model to explain the fluctuations of real GDP and inflation. In reviewing the model, it is useful to consider the scissors analogy mentioned in our discussion of the supply and demand model in Chapter 3.

The aggregate demand curve is like one blade of the scissors. The inflation adjustment line is the other blade. Either blade alone is insufficient to explain economic fluctuations. Either blade alone is an incomplete story. But when the two blades of the scissors are put together to form a pair of scissors, they become a practical tool to explain the ups and downs in the economy. And compared to the complexity and vastness of the whole economy with millions of firms and consumers, this particular pair of scissors is amazingly simple.

KEY POINTS

1. Along the aggregate demand curve, real GDP is negatively related to inflation.

2. Investment, net exports, and consumption depend negatively on the real interest rate. Hence, real GDP, which includes investment, net exports, and consumption, depends negatively on the real interest rate.

3. Central banks' actions to adjust the nominal interest rate to maintain low inflation result in a relationship between the real interest rate and inflation. When inflation rises, the real interest rate rises. When inflation falls, the real interest rate falls.

4. The combined behavior of (1) the real interest rate response to inflation and (2) the private sector adjusting spending in response to the interest rate generates an

inverse relationship between real GDP and inflation—the aggregate demand curve.

5. Movements along the aggregate demand curve occur when inflation rises, causing the real interest rate to rise and real GDP to fall. Such movements along the curve also occur when inflation falls, the interest rate declines, and real GDP rises.

6. The aggregate demand curve shifts for many reasons, including a change in government purchases and a change in monetary policy toward a higher inflation target.

7. When adjusting prices, firms respond slowly to changes in demand and take into account expectations of inflation. So do workers when wages are being adjusted. As a result, inflation tends to increase when real GDP is above potential GDP and tends to decrease when real GDP is below potential GDP.

8. The staggering of price and wage decisions tends to slow the adjustment of prices in the economy as a whole.

9. When combined with the aggregate demand curve, the inflation adjustment line provides us with a way to determine real GDP and inflation.

KEY TERMS

aggregate demand (*AD*) curve	monetary policy rule federal funds rate	target inflation rate	inflation adjustment (*IA*) line

QUESTIONS FOR REVIEW

1. Why are investment, net exports, and consumption inversely related to the real interest rate?

2. Why is real GDP inversely related to the real interest rate in the short run?

3. Why does the real interest rate rise when inflation begins to rise?

4. Why is real GDP inversely related to inflation in the short run? What is this relationship called?

5. What are examples of movements along the aggregate demand curve?

6. Why does a change in government purchases shift the aggregate demand curve to the right or left?

7. Why does a shift in monetary policy shift the aggregate demand curve to the right or left?

8. Why does inflation increase when real GDP is above potential GDP?

9. What is the significance of expectations of inflation for inflation adjustment?

10. Why does staggered price setting slow down price adjustment in the economy?

PROBLEMS

1. Compare and contrast the graphs used in the microeconomic supply and demand model with those used in the economic fluctuations model.

2. Which of the following statements are true, and which are false? Explain your answers in one or two sentences.
   a. An increase in the U.S. real interest rate will cause the dollar exchange rate to decline.
   b. The central bank typically raises the real interest rate when inflation rises.
   c. A higher real interest rate leads to greater net exports because the higher interest rate raises the value of the dollar.

3. Suppose that Japanese real interest rates are low relative to the rates in the United States, and the Fed decides to raise the real interest rate in order to counter an increase in the rate of inflation. What effect will this have on the dollar-yen exchange rate? Will U.S. net exports be higher or lower? Why?

4. Suppose the Fed is considering two different policy rules, shown in the following table. Graph the policy rules.

Inflation	Policy Rule 1 Interest Rate	Policy Rule 2 Interest Rate
0	1	3
2	3	5
4	5	7
6	7	9
8	9	11

If the Fed is currently following policy rule 1 and then shifts to policy rule 2, which way will the aggregate demand curve shift? What reasons might the Fed have for changing its policy? What effect will this have on real GDP in the short run?

5. Suppose you have the following information on the Fed's and the European Central Bank's (ECB) policy rules:

Fed real interest rate = 0.5(inflation rate − 2)

ECB real interest rate = 0.2(inflation rate − 2) + 1

   a. Graph these policy rules. If the inflation rate is 2 percent in both countries, what will be the real interest rate in each country?

b. Some argue that Europe has a much lower tolerance for inflation than the United States. Can you tell—either from the diagram or from the equations—whether this is true?

6. The table below gives a numerical example of an aggregate demand curve.
   a. Sketch the curve in a graph.
   b. What is the average rate of inflation in the long run?
   c. Suppose that the central bank shifts policy so that the average rate of inflation in the long run is 2 percentage points higher than in (b). Sketch a new aggregate demand curve corresponding to the higher inflation rate.

Real GDP (percent deviation from potential GDP)	Inflation (percent per year)
3.0	1.0
2.0	1.5
1.0	2.0
0.0	3.0
−1.0	4.0
−2.0	6.0
−3.0	9.0

7. Suppose Japan's economy stagnates and the demand for U.S. exports is reduced.
   a. Assuming that U.S. imports of Japanese goods are unaffected, which way will the expenditure line shift?
   b. Will this cause a shift in the aggregate demand curve? Sketch the effects of this change in a diagram.

8. State which of the following changes cause a shift in the aggregate demand curve and which ones are a movement along it.
   a. A cut in government purchases
   b. A crash in the U.S. stock market
   c. A shift to lower inflation in the monetary policy rule
   d. Being thrifty becoming fashionable
   e. An increase in the European interest rate

9. Suppose you could use either a change in government purchases or a shift in monetary policy to increase real GDP in the short run. How would each policy affect investment in the short run? Why?

10. The following table gives a numerical example of an inflation adjustment line in the year 2006.

Real GDP (percent deviation from potential GDP)	Inflation (percent per year)
3.0	2.0
2.0	2.0
1.0	2.0
0.0	2.0
−1.0	2.0
−2.0	2.0
−3.0	2.0

   a. Sketch the line in a graph.
   b. If real GDP is above potential GDP in the year 2006, will the inflation adjustment line shift up or down in the year 2006? Explain.
   c. In the same graph as part (a), sketch in the aggregate demand curve given in problem 6. Find the equilibrium level of real GDP and inflation in the year 2006.
   d. Show what happens to the inflation adjustment line if there is a sudden increase in inflation expectations.

CHAPTER 25

Using the Economic Fluctuations Model

The economic fluctuations model is one of the most powerful models in economics. Versions of this model are used in practice by business economists making forecasts for their clients, by regional economists in state capitals looking at the impact of changes in federal laws, by policy economists in Washington analyzing the effects of the president's economic policy proposals, and by international economists working at organizations like the International Monetary Fund trying to determine the effect of tax or spending changes in hundreds of countries around the world.

The purpose of this chapter is to show how to use this model. We use the model to determine the path the economy takes after a shift in aggregate demand, whether that shift is due to a big change in government purchases, a shift in monetary policy, or some other factor. We trace the path of real GDP from the time of its initial departure from potential GDP—as in a recession—to its recovery. We explain why a recovery occurs and how long it takes to occur. We then look at the effect of price shocks on the economy, and examine a case study that demonstrates how well the model works in practice in explaining the most recent recession experienced by the United States.

Keeping in mind that there is a similarity between *using* the supply and demand model and *using* the economic fluctuations model will help you learn the material in this chapter.

Changes in Government Purchases

We first use the economic fluctuations model to examine the forces leading to a return of real GDP to potential GDP. To do so, we focus on a particular example, a change in government purchases. In Chapter 23, we showed how a change in government purchases could push real GDP away from potential GDP in the short run. Now let's see the complete story.

Real GDP and Inflation over Time

Suppose the government cuts military purchases permanently. We want to examine the effects of this decrease in government purchases on the economy in the short run (about one year), the medium run (two to three years), and the long run (four to five years and beyond). The three lengths of time given in the parentheses are approximations; in reality, the times will not be exactly these lengths, but somewhat longer or shorter. We use the term *short run* to refer to the initial departure of real GDP from potential GDP, *medium run* to refer to the recovery period, and *long run* to refer to when real GDP is nearly back to potential GDP.

Figure 25.1 shows the aggregate demand curve and the inflation adjustment line on the same diagram. The intersection of the aggregate demand curve and the inflation adjustment line determines a level of inflation and real GDP. Let us assume

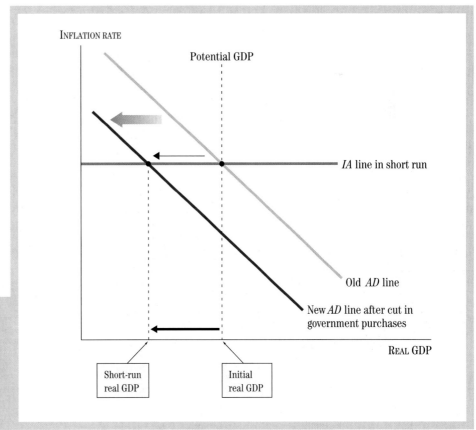

Figure 25.1
Short-Run Effects of a Reduction in Government Purchases
In the short run, the *IA* line does not move. Thus, in the short run, real GDP declines by the amount of the shift in the *AD* curve, as noted on the horizontal axis.

INFLATION RATE

Potential GDP

IA line in short run

Old *AD* line

New *AD* line after cut in government purchases

REAL GDP

Short-run real GDP

Initial real GDP

that we began with real GDP equal to potential GDP. Thus, the initial intersection of the aggregate demand curve and the inflation adjustment line occurs at a level of real GDP equal to potential GDP.

Now, recall from Chapter 24 that a change in government purchases shifts the aggregate demand curve; in particular, a decline in government purchases shifts the aggregate demand curve to the left. Because the inflation adjustment line is flat, and because it does not move in the short run, a change in government purchases—shown by the shift from the "old" to the "new" aggregate demand curve in Figure 25.1—leads to a change in real GDP of the same amount as the shift in the aggregate demand curve. This is the short-run effect. The decrease in government purchases initially moves the aggregate demand curve to the left, and real GDP falls to the point indicated by the intersection of the inflation adjustment line and the new aggregate demand curve. At the new intersection, real GDP is below potential GDP.

As real GDP falls below potential GDP, employment falls because the decline in demand forces firms to cut back on production and lay off workers. The model predicts that unemployment rises, just as it does during actual declines in real GDP.

Now consider what happens over time. The tendency for inflation to adjust over time is represented by upward or downward shifts of the inflation adjustment line. Only in the short run does the inflation adjustment line stay put. What is likely to happen over time when real GDP is below potential GDP? Inflation should begin to decline, because firms will increase their prices by smaller amounts. We represent a decline in inflation by shifting the inflation adjustment line down, as shown in Figure 25.2. The initial impact of the change in government spending took us to a point we label *SR*, for short run, in Figure 25.2. At that point, real GDP is lower than potential GDP. Hence, inflation will fall and the inflation adjustment line shifts down, as shown in the diagram. There is now a new point of intersection; we label that point *MR*, for medium run.

Note that real GDP has started to recover. At the point labeled *MR* in the diagram, real GDP is still below potential GDP, but it is higher than at the low (*SR*) point in the downturn. The reason real GDP starts to rise is that the lower inflation rate causes the central bank to lower the real interest rate. The lower real interest rate increases investment spending and causes net exports to rise. As a result, real GDP rises, and as it does, firms start to call back workers who were laid off. As more workers are employed, unemployment begins to fall.

Because real GDP is still below potential GDP, there is still a tendency for inflation to fall. Thus, the inflation adjustment line continues to shift downward until real GDP returns to potential GDP. Figure 25.2 shows a third intersection at the point marked *LR*, for long run, where production has increased all the way back to potential GDP. At this point, real GDP has reached long-run equilibrium in the sense that real GDP equals potential GDP. With real GDP equal to potential GDP, the inflation adjustment line stops shifting down. Inflation is at a new lower level than before the decline in government purchases, but at the final point of intersection in the diagram, it is no longer falling. Thus, real GDP remains equal to potential GDP.

Note how successive downward shifts of the inflation adjustment line with intersections along the aggregate demand curve trace out values for real GDP and inflation as the economy first goes into recession and then recovers. In the short run, a decline in production comes about because of the decrease in government spending; that decline is followed by successive years of reversal as the economy recovers and real GDP returns to potential GDP. This behavior is shown in the sketch in the lower part of Figure 25.2. Thus, we have achieved one of the major goals of this chapter: showing how real GDP returns to potential GDP after an initial departure due to a shift in aggregate demand. In the case where the shift in aggregate demand is large enough to cause real GDP to decline, as in a recession, we have shown how recessions end and recoveries take the economy back to normal.

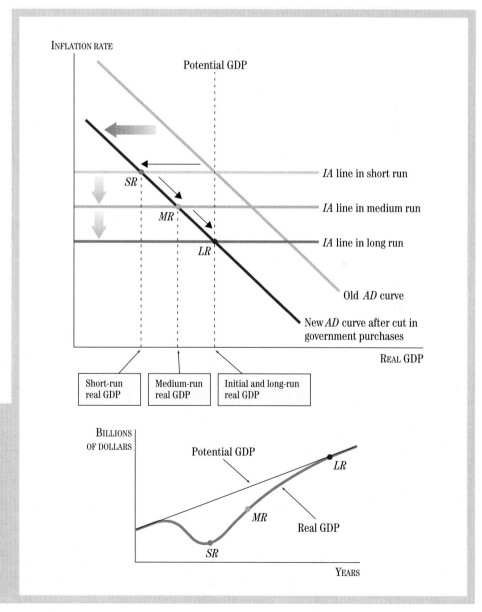

Figure 25.2
Dynamic Adjustment After a Reduction in Government Purchases
Initially, the reduction in government purchases shifts the *AD* curve to the left. This reduces real GDP to the point labeled *SR*, or the short run. Then the *IA* line begins to shift down because real GDP is less than potential GDP. The *IA* line keeps shifting down until real GDP is back to potential GDP.

Details on the Components of Spending

It is possible to give a more detailed report on what happens to consumption, net exports, and investment during this temporary departure from, and return to, potential GDP.

Let's focus first on the short run and then on the long run. Figure 25.3 summarizes how each component of real GDP changes in the short run and the long run. The arrows in the table indicate what happens compared with what would have happened in the absence of the change in government purchases. The path of the economy in the absence of the hypothetical change is called the *baseline*. The term *baseline* is commonly used in public policy discussions to refer to what would happen if a contemplated policy action were not taken; the arrows in the table tell whether a variable is up or down relative to the baseline. In this case, the baseline for real GDP is potential GDP. Thus, a downward-pointing arrow in the real GDP column means that real GDP is below potential GDP; the sideways arrows indicate that real GDP is equal to the baseline or potential GDP; an upward-pointing arrow would mean that real GDP is above potential GDP.

■ **Short Run.** The decline in government spending gets things started, lowering aggregate demand and the level of real GDP. With lower real GDP, income is down, and so people consume less, as explained by the consumption function in Chapter 23. In the short run, investment does not change because interest rates have not yet changed. However, net exports rise because the lower level of income in the United States means that people will import less from abroad. Recall that *net exports is defined as exports minus imports*. Thus, if imports fall, then net exports must rise.

These short-run effects are shown in the first row in the table. Real GDP and consumption are down *relative to the baseline*. Net exports are up *relative to the baseline*.

■ **Long Run.** Now consider the long run, approximately four to five years. By this time, real GDP has returned to potential GDP. Government spending is still lower than it was originally because we have assumed that this is a permanent decline in military spending. Because real GDP is equal to potential GDP, aggregate income in the economy—which equals real GDP—is back to normal. Because income is back to normal, the effects of income on consumption and net exports are just what they would have been in the absence of the change in government purchases.

What about interest rates and their effect on consumption, investment, and net exports? We know that real GDP is back to potential GDP, so the sum of consumption, investment, and net exports must be higher to make up for the decrease in government purchases. Thus, the real interest rate must remain lower, because investment, consumption, and net exports depend negatively on the real interest rate. With a lower real interest rate, more real GDP will go to investment, net exports, and consumption to make up for the decline in the amount of real GDP going to the government. The diagram in Figure 25.3 shows that consumption, investment, and net exports are higher in the long run. We would expect the consumption effects to be small, however, because consumption is not very sensitive to interest rates. Most of the long-run impact of the decline in government purchases is to raise investment and net exports.

To summarize, a decrease in government purchases has negative effects on the economy in the short run.

	Y	C	I	X	G
SR	↓	↓	↔	↑	↓
LR	↔	↑	↑	↑	↓

**Figure 25.3
More Detailed Analysis of a Reduction in Government Purchases**
The arrows in the diagram keep track of the changes in the major variables relative to the baseline.

Real GDP declines. Workers are laid off. Unemployment rises. In the long run, the economy is back to potential GDP, and consumption, investment, and net exports have gone up. Workers are called back, and unemployment declines to where it was before the recession. In the long run, the decrease in government purchases permits greater private investment and more net exports. The increase in investment benefits long-run economic growth, as we know from Chapter 19; hence, the path of potential GDP over time has risen, and now real GDP is growing more quickly, as shown in Figure 25.4.

Observe also that the rate of inflation is lower in the long run than it was before the temporary decline in real GDP. Inflation declined during the period when real GDP was lower than potential GDP, and it did not increase again. This lower inflation rate means that the Fed has implicitly allowed the *target* rate of inflation—the average level of inflation over the long run—to drift down. If the Fed had wanted to keep the target rate of inflation from falling, it would have had to lower interest rates before the inflation rate started to fall. This decline in the interest rate would have pushed the aggregate demand curve back to the right and thereby kept the inflation rate from falling. Such a cut in the interest rate by the Fed would be appropriate if it knew that the reduction in government spending was permanent and would therefore lower the real interest rate in the long run. For example, when government purchases were cut in the 1990s in an effort to reduce the federal budget deficit, economists in both the Bush and the Clinton administrations argued that the Fed should cut interest rates by an extra amount. They recognized that such action would cause the aggregate demand curve to shift to the right and prevent real GDP from declining in the short run while at the same time keeping the inflation rate from falling in the long run.

The Return to Potential GDP After a Boom

What if real GDP rises above potential GDP? Surprisingly, the adjustment of real GDP back to potential GDP can be explained using the same theory. For example, suppose an increase in real GDP above potential GDP is caused by an increase in government purchases for new highway construction. Starting from potential GDP, the aggregate demand curve would shift to the right. Real GDP would increase above potential GDP in the short run.

**Figure 25.4
Increase in the Long-Term Growth After a Recession Caused by a Decrease in Government Purchases**
The higher investment share of real GDP that results from the decline in government purchases leads to more capital and a higher growth of potential GDP. After the recession, real GDP will grow along, or fluctuate around, this higher growth path.

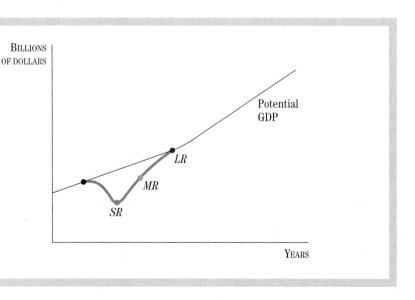

With real GDP above potential GDP, however, firms start to raise their prices more rapidly; inflation begins to rise. We would represent that as an upward shift in the inflation adjustment line. In the medium run, real GDP would still be above potential GDP, and inflation would continue to rise. Eventually, real GDP would go back to potential GDP and the boom would be over. Thus, we predict that real GDP goes back to potential GDP. However, in this case, because government purchases have risen, the new long-run equilibrium will have a higher interest rate, and the sum of consumption, investment, and net exports will be lower.

REVIEW

- Using the inflation adjustment line and the aggregate demand curve, we can now explain both the initial steps of real GDP away from potential GDP and the return to potential GDP.

- In the short run, a decline in government purchases shifts the aggregate demand curve to the left and causes real GDP to fall below potential GDP.

- In the medium run, when the interest rate starts to fall, real GDP begins to increase again. Investment and net exports start to rise and partly offset the decline in government purchases.

- In the long run, real GDP returns to potential GDP. Interest rates are lower, and consumption plus investment plus net exports have risen.

Changes in Monetary Policy

A large change in government spending is, of course, not the only thing that can temporarily push real GDP away from potential GDP. Changes in taxes, consumer confidence, or foreign demand can also cause recessions. But a particularly important factor is a change in monetary policy.

Consider, for example, a change in monetary policy that aims to lower the rate of inflation. Suppose that the inflation rate is 10 percent, as it was in the late 1970s, and a new head of the central bank is appointed who has the objective of reducing inflation. Suppose the aim is to reduce the inflation rate to 4 percent. In effect, the central bank changes the target inflation rate from 10 percent to 4 percent. A reduction in the inflation rate is called **disinflation. Deflation** means declining prices, or a negative inflation rate, which is different from a declining inflation rate. The aim of the policy in this example is disinflation, not deflation.

disinflation: a reduction in the inflation rate.

deflation: a decrease in the overall price level, or a negative inflation rate.

Figure 25.5 shows the short-run, medium-run, and long-run impact of such a shift in monetary policy. Recall from Chapter 24 (see Figures 24.7 and 24.8) that a change in monetary policy will shift the aggregate demand curve. A change in monetary policy toward higher inflation will shift the *AD* curve to the right, and a change in monetary policy toward lower inflation will shift the *AD* curve to the left. In this case, we are examining a change in monetary policy that aims to lower the inflation rate, so the change shifts the aggregate demand curve to the left. This occurs because the Fed raises interest rates to curtail demand and thereby lower inflationary pressures.

One effect of the increase in the interest rate is to lower investment. In addition, the higher interest rate causes the dollar to appreciate, and this tends to reduce net exports. Since inflation is slow to adjust, we do not move the inflation adjustment

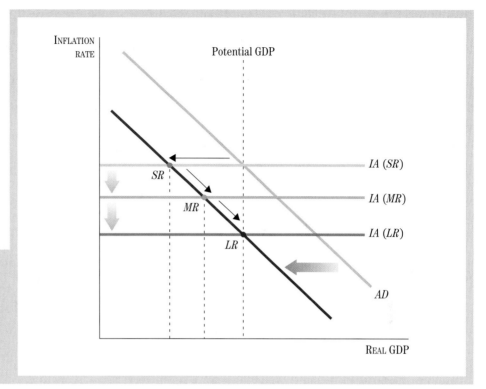

Figure 25.5
Disinflation: A Transition to Lower Inflation
The figure shows how a change in monetary policy to a lower target for inflation affects real GDP over time. In the end, inflation is lower and real GDP is back to potential GDP.

line yet. Thus, inflation remains at 10 percent in the short run. At this time, things seem very grim. The short-run effect of the change to a new monetary policy is to cause real GDP to fall below potential GDP. If the disinflation is large enough, this might mean a decline in real GDP, or a recession. If the disinflation is very small and gradual, then the decline in real GDP could result in a *temporary growth slowdown*. In a temporary growth slowdown, real GDP growth does not turn negative, as it does in a recession.

In any case, with real GDP below potential GDP, inflation will begin to decline. We show this in the diagram in Figure 25.5 by moving the inflation adjustment line down. The lower inflation adjustment line, labeled *MR* for medium run, intersects the aggregate demand curve at a higher level of real GDP. Thus, the economy has begun to recover. The recovery starts because as inflation comes down, the Fed begins to lower the interest rate. As the interest rate declines, investment and net exports begin to rise again, and we move back along the aggregate demand curve.

However, at this medium-run situation, real GDP is still below potential GDP, so the inflation rate continues to decline. We show this in the diagram by shifting the inflation adjustment line down again. To make a long story short, we show the inflation adjustment line shifting all the way down to where it intersects the aggregate demand curve at potential GDP. Thus, in the long-run equilibrium, the economy has fully recovered, and the inflation rate is at its new lower target. The long-run equilibrium has consumption, investment, and net exports back to normal.

The overall dynamic impacts of this change in monetary policy are very important. The initial impact of a monetary policy change is on real GDP. It is only later that the change shows up in inflation. Thus, there is a long lag in the effect of monetary policy on inflation.

Lower inflation is likely to make potential GDP grow faster, perhaps because there is less uncertainty and productivity rises faster. If this is so, the return of real GDP to potential GDP will mean that real GDP is higher, and the long-run benefits of the disinflation to people in the economy may be great over the years. But such changes in the growth of real GDP will appear small in the span of years during which a disinflation takes place and will not change the basic story that a reduction in the rate of inflation, unless it is very gradual, usually results in a recession.

The Volcker Disinflation

The scenario we just described is very similar to the disinflation in the United States in the early 1980s under Paul Volcker, the head of the Fed from 1979 to 1987. First, interest rates skyrocketed as the disinflation began. The federal funds rate went over 20 percent. By any measure, real GDP fell well below potential GDP in the early 1980s. Workers were laid off, the unemployment rate rose to 10.8 percent, investment declined, and net exports fell. Eventually, pricing decisions began to adjust and inflation began to come down. As inflation came down, the Fed began to lower the interest rate. The economy eventually recovered: In 1982, the recovery was under way, and by 1985, the economy had returned to near its potential. The good news was that inflation was down from over 10 percent to about 4 percent.

Reinflation

reinflation: an increase in the inflation rate caused by a change in monetary policy.

The opposite of disinflation might be called **reinflation,** an increase in the inflation rate caused by a shift in monetary policy. This could be analyzed with our theory simply by reversing the preceding process, starting with a change in monetary policy to a higher inflation rate target. This would cause the aggregate demand curve to shift right. Real GDP would rise above potential GDP, and unemployment would decline. But eventually inflation would rise and real GDP would return to potential.

Although it would be unusual for central bankers to explicitly admit they were raising the target inflation rate, there could be political pressures that would lead to less concern about inflation. In such a case, there would be an implicit rise in the target for inflation.

Reinflation is one way to interpret the increase in inflation in the United States and other countries in the 1970s. But there were other things going on at that time, including a quadrupling of oil prices as petroleum-exporting countries, many of which are located in the Middle East, banded together and formed a cartel. We consider oil price shocks in the next section.

REVIEW

- Disinflation is a reduction in inflation. It occurs when the central bank shifts monetary policy in the direction of a lower inflation target.

- According to the theory of economic fluctuations, disinflation has either a temporary slowing of real GDP growth or a recession as a by-product. A higher interest rate at the start of a disinflation lowers investment spending and net exports. This causes real GDP to fall below potential GDP. Eventually the economy recovers. Inflation comes down, and so does the interest rate.

- The large disinflation in the early 1980s in the United States was accompanied by a recession, as predicted by the theory.

Explaining the Recovery from the Great Depression

The Great Depression was the biggest economic downturn in American history. There is simply no parallel either before or since. As shown in the figure, from 1929 to 1933, real GDP declined 35 percent. Between 1933 and 1937, real GDP rose 33 percent; it then declined 5 percent in a recession in 1938. Real GDP increased by a spectacular 49 percent between 1938 and 1942. By 1942, real GDP had caught up with potential GDP, as estimated in the figure.

There is still much disagreement among economists about what caused the Great Depression—that is, what caused the initial departure of real GDP from potential GDP. In their monetary history of the United States, Milton Friedman and Anna Schwartz argue that it was caused by an error in monetary policy, which produced a massive leftward shift in the aggregate demand curve. Unfortunately, it took several years of continually declining real GDP, declining inflation, and even deflation before the errors in monetary policy were corrected.

Another explanation is that there was a downward shift in consumption and investment spending that lowered total expenditures. Peter Temin of MIT has argued that such a spending shift was a cause of the Great Depression.

But whatever the initial cause, there seems to be more consensus that monetary policy was eventually responsible for the recovery from the Great Depression. Interest rates (in real terms) fell precipitously in 1933 and remained low or negative throughout most of the second half of the 1930s. These low interest rates led to an increase in investment and net exports. Christina Romer of the University of California at Berkeley estimates that without the monetary response, "the U.S. economy in 1942 would have been 50 percent below its pre-Depression trend path, rather than back to its normal level." Could the recovery from the Great Depression have been associated with an increase in government purchases or a reduction in taxes? Evidently not. Romer shows that government purchases and tax policy were basically unchanged until 1941, when government spending increased sharply during World War II. By that time, the economy had already made up most of the Depression decline in real GDP relative to potential GDP.

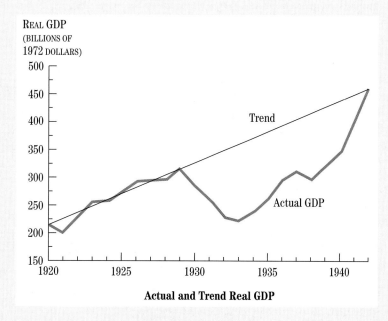

Actual and Trend Real GDP

Price Shocks

demand shock: a shift in one of the components of aggregate demand that leads to a shift in the aggregate demand curve.

Shifts in the aggregate demand curve are called **demand shocks.** The change in government purchases and the shift in monetary policy described in the previous two sections of this chapter are examples of demand shocks. However, shifts in the aggregate demand curve are not the only things that can push real GDP away from potential GDP. In particular, the inflation adjustment line can shift.

What Is a Price Shock?

price shock: a change in the price of a key commodity such as oil, usually because of a shortage, that causes a shift in the inflation adjustment line; also sometimes called a supply shock.

Shifts in the inflation adjustment line are called **price shocks.** A price shock usually occurs when a temporary shortage of a key commodity, or group of commodities, drives up prices by such a large amount that it has a noticeable effect on the rate of inflation. Oil price shocks have been common in the last 25 years. For example, oil prices rose sharply in 1974, in 1979, in 1990, in 2000, and again in 2005. After such shocks, there have usually been declines in real GDP and increases in unemployment. Hence, such shocks appear to move real GDP significantly, though temporarily, away from potential GDP.

Price shocks are sometimes called *supply shocks* in an attempt to distinguish them from demand shocks due to changes in government spending or monetary policy. However, a shift in potential GDP—rather than a shift in the inflation adjustment line—is more appropriately called a supply shock. Shifts in potential GDP—such as a sudden spurt in productivity growth due to new inventions—can, of course, cause real GDP to fluctuate. Recall that *real business cycle theory* places great emphasis on shifts in potential GDP. Although a price shock might be accompanied by a shift in potential GDP, it need not be. Here we are looking at departures of real GDP from potential GDP and thus focusing on price shocks.

real business cycle theory: a theory of macroeconomics that stresses that shifts in potential GDP are a primary cause of fluctuations in real GDP; the shifts in potential GDP are usually assumed to be caused by changes in technology. (Ch. 23)

The Effect of Price Shocks

How does our theory of economic fluctuations allow us to predict the effect of price shocks? The impact of a price shock can be illustrated graphically, as shown in Figure 25.6. In the case of a large increase in oil prices, for example, the inflation adjustment line will shift up to a higher level of inflation. Why? Because a large increase in oil prices will at first lead to an increase in the price of everything that uses oil in production: heating homes, gasoline, airplane fuel, airfares, plastic toys, and many other things. The overall inflation rate is affected. When the inflation rate rises, the inflation adjustment line must shift up.

The immediate impact of the shock is to lower real GDP, as the intersection of the inflation adjustment line with the aggregate demand curve moves to the left. The reason this occurs is that the higher inflation rate causes the central bank to raise interest rates, reducing investment spending and net exports.

With real GDP below potential GDP, however, the reduction in spending will put pressure on firms to adjust their prices. The lower price increases bring about a lower rate of inflation. Thus, in the period following the rise of inflation, we begin to see a reversal. Inflation starts to decline. As inflation falls, interest rates begin to decline, and the economy starts to recover again. The rate of inflation will return to where it was before the price shock.

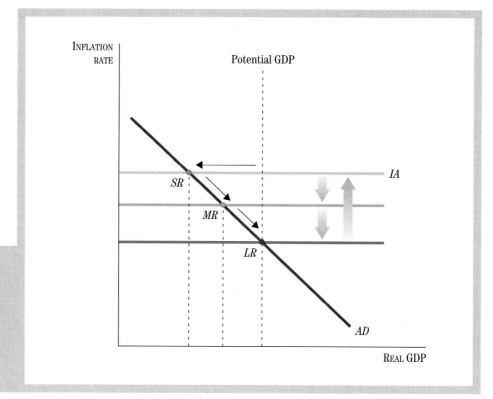

Figure 25.6
A Price Shock
Initially, inflation and the *IA* line rise because of a shock to oil or agricultural prices. This causes real GDP to fall. With real GDP below potential GDP, inflation begins to decline. As inflation declines, real GDP returns to potential GDP.

■ **Temporary Shifts in the Inflation Adjustment Line.**   In this analysis of the price shock, the central bank raises interest rates, and the resulting decline in real GDP exerts a countervailing force to reduce inflation. It is possible for some price shocks to have only a temporary effect on inflation. Such a temporary effect can be shown graphically as a rise followed by a quick fall in the inflation adjustment line. In such a situation—where the price shock would be expected to automatically reverse itself—it would be wise for the central bank to delay raising the interest rate. Then if the price shock has only a temporary effect on inflation, the decline in real GDP can be avoided. In reality, whenever there is a price shock, there is a great debate about whether it will have a temporary or a permanent effect on inflation. The debate is rarely settled until after the fact.

Price shocks can also occur when commodity prices fall. In this case there would be a *downward* shift in the inflation adjustment line—just the opposite of the case of an increase in commodity prices—and this would cause real GDP to rise as the Fed lowered interest rates. For example, in 1986 there was a decline in oil prices. This resulted in a temporary decrease in inflation and a rise in real GDP—exactly what would be predicted by the theory of economic fluctuations.

■ **Stagflation.**   An important difference between price shocks and demand shocks is that in the case of a price shock, output declines while inflation rises. With demand shocks, inflation and output are positively related over the period of recession and recovery. The situation in which inflation is up and real GDP is down is called **stagflation.** As we have shown, price shocks can lead to stagflation.

stagflation: the situation in which high inflation and high unemployment occur simultaneously.

> **REVIEW**
> - A price shock is a large change in the price of some key commodity like oil. Such shocks can push real GDP below potential GDP.
> - In the aftermath of a price shock, the interest rate rises. Eventually, with real GDP below potential GDP, inflation begins to come down, and the economy recovers.

The 2001 Recession

Let's see how the economic fluctuations model can explain actual fluctuations of the economy by studying the most recent slowdown of the U.S. economy in 2001, following 10 years of uninterrupted economic growth.

The Facts: Higher Inflation, Then Recession, Then Signs of a Recovery

The dating of U.S. recessions is formally done by a panel of economists at the National Bureau of Economic Research, who look at a wide variety of economic data. The panel has determined that the U.S. economy slid into recession most recently in March of 2001. It has also determined that the recession ended in November of 2001, making this recession one of the shortest on record. We will take a look at some important economic indicators in the period leading up to the recession, as well as in the aftermath of the recession.

This recession, like others, was preceded by a rise in real GDP above potential GDP, and by an increase in inflation. The behavior of real GDP in the late 1990s and the early 2000s is shown graphically in Figure 25.7. The graph of real GDP shows real GDP fluctuating around potential GDP. The lower graph shows inflation, measured as the percent change in the Consumer Price Index. Notice that in the years 1999 and 2000, when output was somewhat higher than potential output, inflation was showing signs of increasing. In 2001, in the aftermath of the recession, real GDP fell below potential GDP and inflation was much lower.

Also important to our analysis of this case is the rise in the interest rate as fears of inflation increased before the recession. Once the recession began, interest rates fell sharply. Finally, as in all recessions, the unemployment rate rose as the recession hit the economy. These two variables are shown in Figure 25.8.

To summarize, Figure 25.7 shows that the economic fluctuations during the years from 1995 to 2004 can be viewed as a combination of two distinct periods: (1) a period when real GDP was above potential GDP and inflation was rising, and (2) a period when real GDP was below potential GDP and inflation was falling. The two periods are linked together. In the first period, interest rates were rising, while in the second period, interest rates were falling.

How Does the Economic Fluctuations Model Explain the Facts?

The best explanation of these economic fluctuations is achieved by combining a rightward shift of the *AD* curve with a subsequent leftward shift of the *AD* curve.

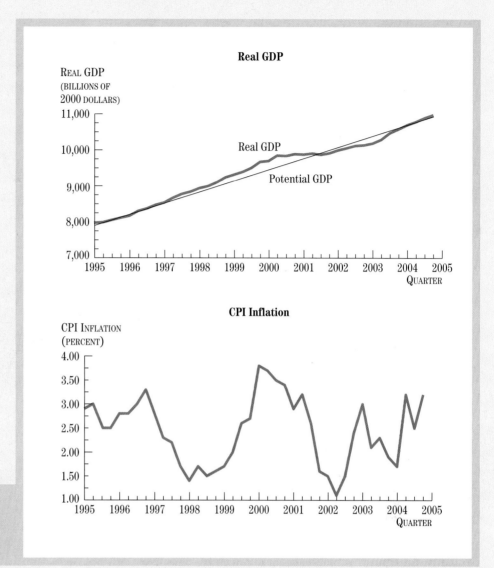

Figure 25.7
Real GDP and Inflation from 1995 to 2004
These economic fluctuations are the focus of this case study.

■ **Patching Together the Two Shifts.**   To see how this works, look at the *AD-IA* diagram in Figure 25.9. It shows a shift in the *AD* curve to the right (the shifting arrow is labeled "1"). This shift first causes real GDP to rise above potential GDP, and then leads to rising inflation as the *IA* line shifts up gradually. Three intersections of the *AD* curve and the *IA* curve, labeled SR_1, MR_1, and LR_1, show this movement.

Figure 25.9 then shows a shift in the *AD* curve to the left (the shifting arrow is labeled "2"). This shift causes a recession, with real GDP falling below potential GDP, and leads to a reduction in inflation as the *IA* line shifts down gradually over time. Three intersections of the *IA* line and the *AD* curve during this period are labeled SR_2, MR_2, and LR_2. In sum, the movements in real GDP and inflation are represented by patching together two shifts of the *AD* curve.

The time-series sketches in the lower part of Figure 25.9 show the movement in real GDP and inflation that is traced out by the combination of these shifts. On the left, real GDP first rises above potential GDP, which is assumed to be growing over

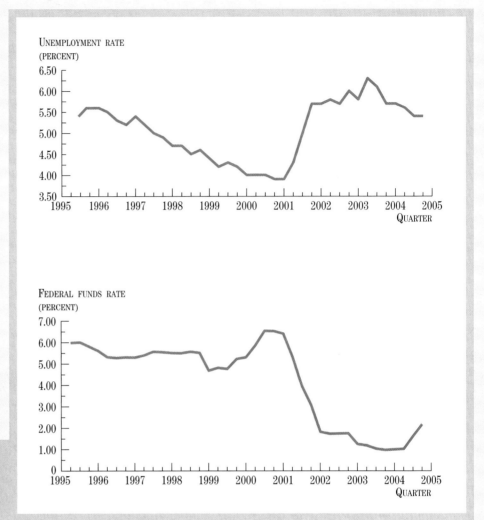

Figure 25.8
Unemployment and Interest Rates from 1995 to 2004
Unemployment rises and interest rates fall during a recession.

time, and then falls below potential GDP. If you compare these fluctuations in real GDP with what actually happened, shown in Figure 25.7, you will see a close resemblance. The model seems to explain the actual data very well. The same close fit is seen for inflation. The movements in inflation implied by the model—a rise and then a fall—are very close to the movements in the data as shown in Figure 25.7.

■ **Why Did the *AD* Curve Shift Out Before the Recession?**   Finding a single explanation for economic booms or recessions is almost always impossible. One potentially important explanatory variable for the boom in the latter part of the 1990s was the rapid rise in the stock market, particularly in technology stocks. The rising stock market led to both higher consumption, as stock-owning households spent some of their new-found wealth, and higher investment, as firms rushed to put out new products or to upgrade their technology infrastructure to take advantage of the Internet. These spending booms shifted the *AD* curve out and may even have pushed the economy above potential output. Note, however, that the new Internet technology could in fact increase potential output as well, as some of the "new economy" advocates were arguing. If, however, the increase in spending was substantial, or if the increase in potential output was not as substantial as some argued, the economy would see inflationary pressure starting to mount.

■ **Why Did the *AD* Curve Shift In During the Recession?** What brought about the end of the long boom? Once the euphoria over some of the technology stocks died down, investors started to have doubts about the profitability of high-profile Internet companies, and started selling off these stocks. The Federal Reserve, concerned about higher inflation down the road, made a preemptive strike by raising

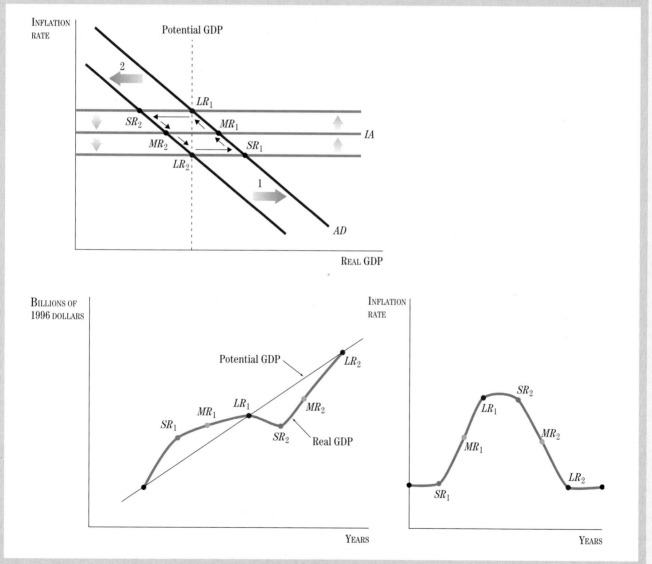

Figure 25.9
A Complete Boom-Bust Cycle

First, the *AD* curve shifts to the right, causing real GDP to rise above potential GDP. Inflation then rises. The central bank notices inflation rising and shifts the *AD* curve back, causing a recession. Eventually, real GDP is brought to potential GDP. The short-run, medium-run, and long-run points for the initial stimulus and the reversal are shown on both the upper and the lower panels.

From Boom to Bust
Webvan, the online grocer; went bankrupt in 2001, as did many other Internet startups. The assets of Webvan were sold at a large auction in October 2001, signaling the abrupt end of a company whose prospects had seemed so bright only a year or so earlier.

interest rates, leading to a further slowdown in technology investment by firms. Once the stock market started to fall, consumer confidence soon followed, and the effects were tragically compounded by the events of September 11. These cutbacks in spending moved the *AD* curve to the left and moved the economy into recession.

■ How Did the *AD* Curve Shift Out Again?

Finally, let's discuss the recovery. The fall in inflation resulted in the Fed's lowering interest rates and moving the economy back toward potential, just as the model predicted. In the year 2001, the Fed lowered interest rates on eleven separate occasions! The government also responded with tax cuts. Furthermore, the need for higher military expenditures in Iraq and Afghanistan provided a short-run boost to spending. These helped to move the *AD* curve to the right and to move GDP back toward potential GDP even faster.

A difference between macroeconomics and microeconomics is that in macroeconomics, identifying the reasons for the shifts of the curves is more difficult. Because macroeconomics is about the whole economy, the whole world economy, many different things can shift curves. Macroeconomics is therefore more controversial than microeconomics, and is likely to remain so.

REVIEW

- The economic fluctuations that occurred around the time of the 2001 recession included a period with real GDP above potential GDP followed by a period with real GDP below potential GDP. Inflation was rising in the first period and falling in the second period.

- These actual economic fluctuations can be explained by the model of economic fluctuations. Shifts in the *AD* curve cause real GDP to move away from potential GDP, followed by changes in inflation.

- The shifts in the *AD* curve could have been caused by lower consumer spending, by lower investment spending, or by the preemptive actions of the Fed.

Conclusion

Using a diagram with the aggregate demand curve and the inflation adjustment line, we can explain not only the first steps toward recessions but also the recovery of the economy. The model works well in explaining actual economic fluctuations and is thus useful for analyzing macroeconomic policy, as we do in Chapters 26 and 27.

That the model implies that real GDP returns toward potential GDP in the long run is an attractive feature of the model because, in reality, all recessions have ended. Real GDP appears to fluctuate around potential GDP rather than getting stuck forever in a recession. The tendency for real GDP to return toward potential GDP allows us to use the theory of long-run growth when discussing long-run trends in the economy. As the economy fluctuates, potential GDP gradually increases over time.

KEY POINTS

1. To use the economic fluctuations model, you shift the aggregate demand curve and the inflation adjustment line.

2. Using the model is much like using the supply and demand model of microeconomics.

3. An increase in government purchases temporarily causes real GDP to rise, but eventually real GDP returns to potential GDP.

4. A decline in government purchases temporarily reduces real GDP, but over time the economy recovers.

5. Shifts in monetary policy, including explicit attempts to disinflate or reinflate, cause real GDP to depart from potential GDP temporarily. But eventually real GDP returns to potential GDP and only the inflation rate is changed.

6. Price shocks can cause recessions. A price shock that raises the inflation rate will cause the interest rate to rise and real GDP to fall.

7. If the Fed sets interest rates according to a monetary policy rule, then it will raise interest rates following a rise in inflation, and eventually inflation will come back down.

8. If a price shock is clearly temporary, then the Fed should not change the interest rate.

9. Shifts of the aggregate demand curve and the inflation adjustment line trace out actual observations fairly closely. Thus, the economic fluctuations model works well, but, like most models in economics and elsewhere, it is not perfect.

KEY TERMS

disinflation	reinflation	price shock	stagflation
deflation	demand shock		

QUESTIONS FOR REVIEW

1. What causes the economy to recover after a recession?

2. What is the difference between the long-run and short-run effects of a change in government spending?

3. What is disinflation, and how does the central bank bring it about?

4. What is reinflation, and what impact does it have on real GDP in the short run and the long run?

5. What is a price shock, and why have price shocks frequently been followed by increases in unemployment?

6. What is the difference between a price shock and a supply shock?

7. Why do monetary policy errors lead to economic fluctuations?

8. In what way is the economic fluctuations model discussed in this chapter consistent with real-world observations?

PROBLEMS

1. Using the aggregate demand curve and the inflation adjustment line, describe what would happen to real GDP and inflation in the short run, in the medium run, and in the long run if there were a permanent increase in government spending on highway construction. Be sure to provide an economic explanation for your results.

2. Suppose there is a cut in government spending on defense. What would happen to consumption, investment, and net exports in the short run and in the long run? Explain your results, using a diagram with the aggregate demand curve and the inflation adjustment line.

3. Suppose the central bank wants to return to the original inflation rate before the increase in government spending in problem 1. How can it achieve its objective? Describe the proposed change in policy and its short-run, medium-run, and long-run effects on real GDP and inflation.

4. Using the aggregate demand curve and the inflation adjustment line, show what happens if the central bank reinflates the economy. Suppose the target inflation rate is changed from 2 percent to 5 percent. What is the impact on the major components of spending in the short run and in the long run?

5. Suppose potential GDP is $5,000 billion. Use the following data to graph the aggregate demand curve with the percentage deviation of real GDP from potential GDP on the horizontal axis.

Inflation (percent)	Real GDP (billions of dollars)
5	4,800
4	4,900
3	5,000
2	5,100
1	5,200

   a. Suppose the current inflation rate is 2 percent. Draw the inflation adjustment line. What is the current deviation of real GDP from potential GDP?
   b. In the long run, what will the inflation rate be if there is no change in economic policy? Explain how this adjustment takes place.

6. For the data in problem 5, suppose that after the long-run adjustment back to potential, the Fed changes its policy rule so that the relationship between real GDP and inflation becomes the following:

Inflation (percent)	Real GDP (billions of dollars)
5	4,700
4	4,800
3	4,900
2	5,000
1	5,100

   a. Draw the aggregate demand curve and compare it with the one in problem 5.
   b. If the current inflation rate is 2 percent, what is the short-run deviation from potential GDP?
   c. How will the inflation adjustment line adjust in the medium run and the long run? Explain how this adjustment takes place.

7. The economy begins at potential GDP with an inflation rate of 3 percent. Draw this situation with an aggregate demand curve and an inflation adjustment line. Suppose there is a price shock that pushes inflation up to 6 percent in the short run, but the effect on inflation is viewed as temporary by the Fed. It expects the inflation adjustment line to shift back down to 2 percent the next year, and in fact the inflation adjustment line does shift back down.
   a. If the Fed follows its usual policy rule, where will real GDP be in the short run? How does the economy adjust back to potential?
   b. Now suppose that since the Fed is sure that this inflationary shock is only temporary, it decides not to follow its typical policy rule, but instead maintains the interest rate at its previous level. What happens to real GDP? Why? What will the long-run adjustment be in this case? Do you agree with the Fed's handling of the situation?

8. Suppose that in 2004 the GDP deflator is 100, and in 2005 it is 105.
   a. Suppose that real GDP equals potential GDP in 2004 and 2005. What is the rate of inflation in 2005?
   b. Suppose instead that real GDP is below potential GDP in 2005. How is the adjustment back to potential made in this situation?

9. Suppose that there are two countries that are very similar except that one has a central bank with a higher target inflation rate. They have identical potential GDP and are both at their long-run equilibrium. Explain this situation by using two diagrams with an aggregate demand curve and an inflation adjustment line. Explain how these different equilibrium levels of inflation are possible. How do workers' and firms' expectations of inflation differ between the two countries?

10. Using the spending allocation model from Chapter 19, show the effect of a decrease in government spending as a share of GDP. Show that you get the same answer *in the long run* using the aggregate demand curve and the inflation adjustment line.

CHAPTER 26

Fiscal Policy

Over the last decade, the budgetary situation of the federal government has resembled a roller coaster ride, moving from deficit to surplus to deficit again. In 1997, the U.S. government ran a budget deficit for the *twenty-eighth* year in a row. Further deficits were projected for 1998, 1999, 2000, and beyond. The political debate at that time centered around the consequences of running sustained budget deficits, concerns about how much debt was being accumulated, and how to trim spending and raise revenue to lower the budget deficit.

Then, seemingly overnight, there was a radical change. Unexpectedly, a budget surplus appeared in 1998. More surpluses appeared in 1999, and by the presidential election of 2000, forecasts called for budget surpluses as far as the eye could see. The political debate changed accordingly, focusing on how to best distribute the surplus among domestic spending, tax cuts, and paying down the federal debt.

Just as the tax cuts were being passed by Congress, the budgetary situation took another turn, this time for the worse. The arrival of the U.S. recession in 2001 and the higher government expenditures associated with September 11 and the increased military buildup for the campaign in Afghanistan sent the budget projections into deficit mode again. Even though the economy has recovered, the deficits still linger. There is considerable uncertainty at this time about what the budget situation will be for the next few years.

An understanding of the U.S. budget, the factors that caused it to switch from deficit to surplus and back to deficit again, and the projections for future budget deficits is vital if we are to improve our understanding of fiscal policy—spending and taxation decisions taken by the government. In this section, we will show how countercyclical fiscal policies (tax cuts and spending increases in recessions, tax hikes and spending cuts in booms) can help move the economy to potential output and minimize economic fluctuations. Expansionary fiscal policy may have played a significant role in cushioning the economy during the most recent recession, and as such, fiscal policy remains a useful tool that policymakers have at their disposal.

We will begin this section by reviewing the U.S. budget and providing an explanation for the recent fluctuations. We will then move on to a discussion of the effectiveness and scope of fiscal policy in minimizing economic fluctuations.

The Government Budget

federal budget: a summary of the federal government's proposals for spending, taxes, and the deficit.

The **federal budget** is the major summary document describing fiscal policy in the United States. The budget includes not only the estimates of the surplus or deficit that get so much attention, but also proposals for taxes and spending. Let's look at how the federal budget in the United States is put together.

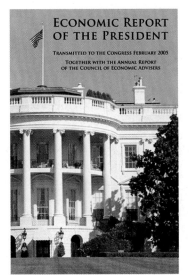

The CEA
The economic assumptions used for the federal budget are presented by the Council of Economic Advisers (CEA) in the Economic Report of the President.

Setting the Annual Budget

In the United States, the president submits a new budget to Congress each year for the following fiscal year. The fiscal year runs from October to October. For example, *The Budget of the United States: Fiscal Year 2005* applied to spending and taxes from October 1, 2004, through September 30, 2005. It was submitted to Congress by the president in early 2004. The president typically devotes part of the State of the Union address to describing the budget and fiscal policy. Also at the start of each year, the *Economic Report of the President* is released, providing the economic forecasts underlying the budget, prepared by the Council of Economic Advisers (CEA). The Congressional Budget Office (CBO) makes its own economic forecasts. During the budget battles between President Clinton and Congress in the 1990s, one of the main points of dispute was a discrepancy between the economic forecasts of the CEA and the CBO.

In putting together the federal budget, the president proposes many specific spending programs that fit into an overall philosophy of what government should be doing. However, in any one year, most of the spending in the budget is determined by ongoing programs, which the president usually can do little to change. For example, payments of social security benefits to retired people are a large item in the budget, but the amount of spending on social security depends on how many eligible people there are. As more people retire, spending automatically goes up unless the social security law changes. Thus, in reality, the president can change only a small part of the budget each year.

■ **A Balanced Budget versus a Deficit or Surplus.** Taxes to pay for the spending programs are also included in the budget. As part of the budget, the president may propose an increase or a decrease in taxes. *Tax revenues* are the total dollar amount

Note the difference between **tax rate** and **tax revenues.** For the income tax, if the average tax rate is 20 percent and income is $3,000 billion, then tax revenues are $600 billion.

balanced budget: a budget in which tax revenues equal spending.

budget surplus: the amount by which tax revenues exceed government spending.

budget deficit: the amount by which government spending exceeds tax revenues.

Budget Deficit	**Budget Balance**	**Budget Surplus**
Tax revenues < spending	Tax revenues = spending	Tax revenues > spending

the government receives from taxpayers each year. When tax revenues are exactly equal to spending, there is a **balanced budget.** When tax revenues are greater than spending, there is a **budget surplus.** When spending is greater than tax revenues, there is a **budget deficit,** and the government must borrow to pay the difference.

■ **The Proposed Budget versus the Actual Budget.** Keep in mind that the budget the president submits is only a *proposal.* The actual amounts of tax revenues and spending during the fiscal year are quite different from what is proposed. There are two main reasons for this difference.

First, Congress usually modifies the president's budget, adding some programs and deleting others. Congress deliberates on the specific items in the president's budget proposal for months before the fiscal year actually starts. After the president's budget has been debated and modified, it is passed by Congress. Only when the president signs the legislation is the budget enacted into law. Because of this congressional modification, the enacted budget is always different from the proposed budget.

Second, because of changes in the economy and other unanticipated events such as wars and natural disasters, the actual amounts of spending and taxes will be different from what is enacted. After the fiscal year has begun and the budget has been enacted, various *supplementals* are proposed and passed. A supplemental is a change in a spending program or a change in the tax law that affects the budget in the current fiscal year. In addition, recessions or booms always affect tax revenues and spending to some degree.

Figure 26.1 shows the difference between proposed tax revenues and expenditures for the fiscal year 2004 budget (submitted in February 2003) and the actual tax revenues and expenditures that occurred. Revenues were lower than forecast, and expenditures were higher than forecast. As a result, the deficit turned out to be much larger than anticipated.

Figure 26.2 shows how the fiscal year 2005 budget moved from a proposal in early 2004 to enactment in late 2004 to completion at the beginning of October 2005. The same *budget cycle* occurs every year. Because the whole cycle takes over two years, at any one time discussions about three budgets are taking place. For example, in September 2004, the budget for fiscal year 2004 was coming to a close, the budget for fiscal year 2005 was being considered by Congress, and the budget for fiscal year 2006 was being put together by the president's staff. The budget cycle does not always progress smoothly. In many years the president and Congress do not settle on a budget until well into the fiscal year.

A Look at the Federal Budget

Table 26.1 contains summary totals from the federal budget for fiscal year 2004. The full budget, which is over 2,000 pages long, provides much more detail.

■ **The Deficit.** Table 26.1 shows that expenditures were greater than tax revenues, so there was a deficit. Budget deficits were common in the United States for many years. For every year from 1970 to 1997, there was a deficit. From 1997 to 2001, there were four

Table 26.1

FY 2004 Federal Tax Revenues and Expenditures (billions of dollars)

Tax revenues	1,880	
Personal income		809
Corporate income		189
Payroll		734
Other		148
Expenditures	2,292	
Social security		496
Medicare		269
Defense		456
Interest		160
Other		911
Deficit	412	

Source: Economic Report of the President, 2005, Table B-80.

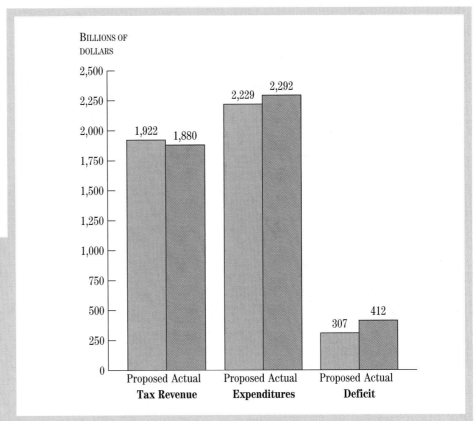

Figure 26.1
The Rising Deficit
When the fiscal year 2004 budget was submitted to Congress in early 2003, a large deficit of more than $300 billion was forecast. By the time the fiscal year was over—almost two years later—the deficit was almost $100 billion larger. Tax revenues were lower and spending was slightly higher than in the proposed budget.

consecutive years of surplus. This run of surpluses ended in 2002 with another string of deficits.

■ **Taxes and Spending.**   The tax revenues of $1,880 billion include *personal income taxes* paid by individuals on their total income, *corporate income taxes* paid by businesses on their profits, *sales taxes* paid on items such as gasoline and beer, and *payroll*

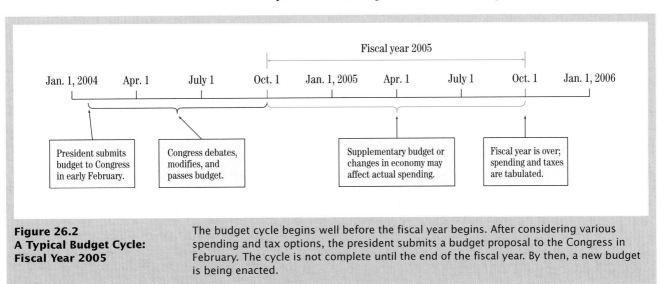

Figure 26.2
A Typical Budget Cycle:
Fiscal Year 2005

The budget cycle begins well before the fiscal year begins. After considering various spending and tax options, the president submits a budget proposal to the Congress in February. The cycle is not complete until the end of the fiscal year. By then, a new budget is being enacted.

ECONOMICS IN ACTION

Why Did All the Deficits Go Away in the Late 1990s?

During 1998, the Congressional Budget Office, the Council of Economic Advisers, and all private economic forecasters started to change their forecasts for the federal budget radically, from a long series of future deficits to a long series of future surpluses. And starting in 1998, the budget itself started moving from deficit to surplus. Why did the federal budget situation change so dramatically in 1998? Were tax rates suddenly increased? Did Congress eliminate the Department of Commerce and other government agencies, as some politicians had proposed as cost-saving measures?

No. Although spending growth was curtailed somewhat, the main reason that the deficits went away was that tax revenues grew faster than anyone had anticipated, especially in the period from 1995 to 1998. Tax revenue grew in this period not because tax rates were increased (tax rates were increased in 1993), but because people's incomes grew very rapidly as the economy expanded.

The income growth was particularly rapid for rich people with high tax rates. The table on the right shows the share of income earned and taxes paid by high-income people—those with incomes of more than $200,000. Although such people are a very small percentage of the population, they pay a very large percentage of income taxes. Observe that from 1994 to 1998, the percentage of these high-income taxpayers rose rapidly, from 1.1 percent to 1.6 percent. The percentage of all income in the United States earned by this group also increased, from 15 percent to 22 percent.

And—most important for the disappearance of the deficits—the share of taxes paid by this group rose from 30 percent to 40 percent. These data imply, of course, that there has been a rapid spreading apart of the income distribution, with the rich getting an increasing share of income. Since tax rates on the rich are higher than those on everyone else, tax revenues soared.

People with More Than $200,000 in Income

	1994	1995	1996	1997	1998	1999	2000
Percentage of taxpayers	1.1	1.2	1.4	1.5	1.6	1.9	2.1
Percentage of U.S. income	15	16	18	20	22	24	26
Percentage of taxes paid	30	32	35	38	40	43	45

Source: Congressional Budget Office.

Why was there such a huge increase in the income of the rich? The stock market boomed in the 1990s. The gains from selling such stock are treated as income on which taxes must be paid. In addition, income and bonuses to people in start-up firms and to partners in law firms and financial firms grew rapidly, too. Whatever the reasons, this spreading of the income distribution underlies the switch from deficits to surpluses.

taxes, a percentage of wages paid by workers and their employers that supports government programs such as social security. Sales taxes are the smallest of the four components of total revenue, and corporate tax revenues are only slightly larger. Payroll taxes provide a large amount of revenues, nearly as much as personal income tax revenues. Payroll taxes have grown rapidly as a share of federal government revenues in recent years, while the other types of taxes have fallen in relative importance.

On the expenditure side of the budget, one must distinguish between *purchases* of goods and services (such as defense), *transfer payments* (such as social security and Medicare), and *interest payments.* Only purchases are included in the symbol *G* that we have been using in the text. Purchases represent *new* production, whether of computers, federal courthouses, or food for military troops. A surprisingly small fraction of the budget—less than 40 percent—is for the purchase of goods and services.

Interest payments are what the federal government pays every year on its debt. The government pays interest on its borrowings just like anyone else. In fiscal year 2004, interest payments amounted to $160 billion. Total interest payments equal the interest rate multiplied by the amount of government debt outstanding. For example, the interest rate on federal government debt averaged 3.7 percent in 2004, and total outstanding debt held by the public was about $4,295 billion ($160 billion in interest payments is approximately .037 times $4,295 billion).

The Federal Debt

federal debt: the total amount of outstanding loans owed by the federal government.

The **federal debt** is the total amount of outstanding loans that the federal government owes. If the government runs a surplus, the debt comes down by the amount of the surplus. If there is a deficit, the debt goes up by the amount of the deficit.

Consider an example involving thousands of dollars rather than trillions of dollars. Think of a student, Sam, who graduates from college with a $14,000 outstanding loan. In other words, he has a debt of $14,000. Suppose that the first year he works, his income is $30,000, but he spends $35,000. Sam's deficit for that year is $5,000, and his debt rises to $19,000. Assume that in his second year of work, he has income of $35,000 and spends $38,000; his deficit is $3,000, and his debt rises to $22,000. Each year his debt rises by the amount of his deficit. In the third year, Sam earns $40,000 and spends $33,000; he has a surplus of $7,000. This would reduce his debt to $15,000.

The laws of accounting that we apply to Sam also apply to Uncle Sam. The federal government's deficit of $412 billion in 2004 meant that the outstanding government debt increased by $412 billion. Figure 26.3 shows the debt, deficit, and surpluses in the United States since 1955. Observe how the debt started to decline in 1998 when surpluses began, and started to increase again once the surpluses ended in 2002.

■ **The Debt to GDP Ratio.** When looking at the debt and the deficit over time, it is important to consider the size of the economy. For example, a $3 trillion debt may not be much of a problem for an economy with a GDP of $10 trillion but could be over-

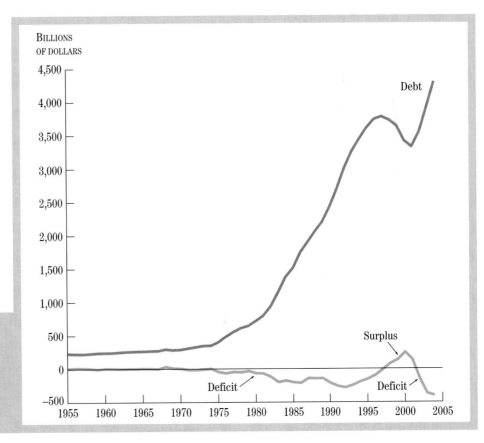

**Figure 26.3
The Rise and Fall of Government Debt**
When there is a deficit, the debt increases. When there is a surplus, the debt falls. The debt in 1950 was largely due to deficits during World War II.

debt to GDP ratio: the total amount of outstanding loans the federal government owes divided by nominal GDP.

whelming for an economy with a GDP of $1 trillion. An easy way to compare the debt to the size of the economy is to measure the debt as a percentage of GDP—the **debt to GDP ratio.** It is appropriate to consider the ratio of debt to nominal GDP rather than real GDP because the debt is stated in current dollars, just as nominal GDP is.

Figure 26.4 shows the behavior of the debt as a percentage of GDP in the United States since 1950. Note that the debt was a high percentage of GDP at the end of World War II because the U.S. government had borrowed large amounts to finance its military expenditures during the war. The debt to GDP ratio fell in the late 1990s, but it began to increase again when deficits returned. The debt to GDP ratio is a good overall gauge of how a government is doing in managing its fiscal affairs.

State and Local Government Budgets

Much of the government spending and taxation in the United States occurs outside of the federal government, in state and local governments. Although fiscal policy usually refers to the plans of the federal government, it is the combined action of federal, state, and local governments that has an impact on the overall economy. For example, in the 1990–1991 recession, many states cut back on spending and raised taxes; both actions would tend to reduce real GDP in the short run, just as reduced spending and higher taxes at the federal level would. Taken as a whole, state and local governments are a large force in the economy. In 2004 state and local government expenditures were about two-thirds of federal government expenditures.

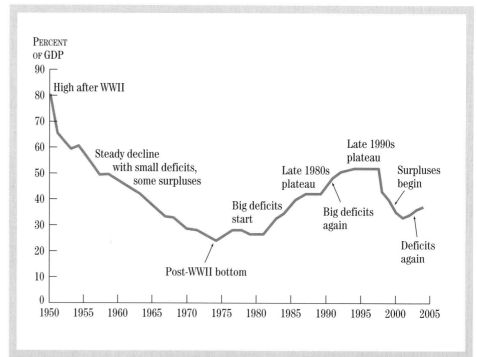

Figure 26.4
Debt as a Percentage of GDP
Relative to the size of GDP, the debt declined during the years after World War II. After rising for 20 years, the debt fell as a percentage of GDP in the late 1990s before rising again when deficits returned.

Most of the state and local government expenditures are for public schools, local police, fire services, and roads. Observe that state and local government *purchases* of goods and services are larger than federal government purchases, especially when national defense is excluded.

Like the federal government, the state and local governments have, on average, been running deficits after a few years of surpluses in the late 1990s.

REVIEW

- In the United States, the president submits a budget to Congress giving proposals for spending, for taxes, and for the deficit or surplus. The actual budget is different from the proposed budget because of congressional modifications and unforeseen events like unusually fast or slow economic growth.

- A budget surplus occurs when spending is less than tax revenues. Deficits occur when spending exceeds revenues.

- When a government or individual runs a deficit, the debt increases. Surpluses reduce the debt.

- It is appropriate to consider the debt in relation to the size of the economy by measuring it as a percentage of GDP.

- Federal government expenditures are larger than state or local government expenditures, but state and local government purchases are larger than federal government purchases.

Countercyclical Fiscal Policy

Government spending and taxes are called the *instruments* of fiscal policy. They are the variables that affect the economy. Now let's see how changes in the instruments of fiscal policy affect the size of economic fluctuations.

Impacts of the Instruments of Fiscal Policy

We first consider a change in government purchases and then go on to consider a change in taxes.

■ **Changes in Government Purchases.** We know that if there is a change in government purchases, real GDP will initially change. If real GDP equaled potential GDP at the time of the change in government purchases, then real GDP would move away from potential GDP. Hence, a first lesson about fiscal policy is "do no harm." Erratic changes in government purchases can lead to fluctuations of real GDP away from potential GDP.

But suppose real GDP was already away from potential GDP. Then the change in government purchases could move real GDP closer to potential GDP. This is shown in Figure 26.5. In the top panel, real GDP starts out below potential GDP. An increase in government purchases shifts the aggregate demand curve to the right and moves real GDP back toward potential GDP. In the bottom panel, real GDP is above potential GDP, and a decrease in government purchases shifts the aggregate demand curve to

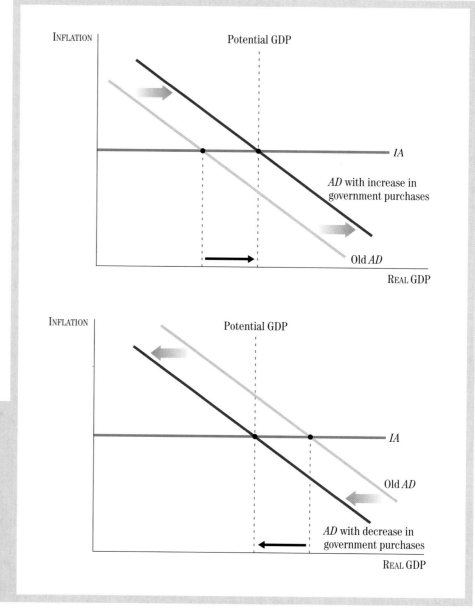

Figure 26.5
Effect of a Change in Government Purchases
If real GDP is below potential GDP, as in the top panel, an increase in government purchases, which shifts the *AD* curve to the right, will move real GDP toward potential GDP. If real GDP is above potential GDP, as in the bottom panel, a decrease in government purchases will move real GDP toward potential GDP. These are short-run effects.

the left, bringing real GDP back toward potential GDP. The important point is that a change in government purchases shifts the aggregate demand curve from wherever it happens to be at the time of the change.

Now, these effects of government purchases are short term. Eventually, prices will adjust; consumption, investment, and net exports will change; and real GDP will return to potential GDP, regardless of the change in government purchases. Nevertheless, as we will see, the short-run impacts of government purchases provide fiscal policy with the potential power to reduce the size of economic fluctuations.

A decrease in government purchases for defense is one example of a leftward shift in the aggregate demand curve. An increase in government purchases on roads and bridges works in the opposite direction. Because the changes in government

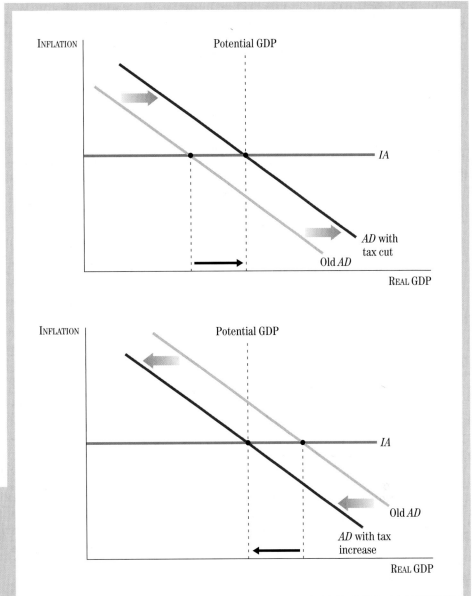

Figure 26.6
Effects of a Change in Taxes
A decrease in taxes shifts the *AD* curve to the right and can move real GDP toward potential GDP, as in the top panel. An increase in taxes moves real GDP toward potential in the lower panel.

spending affect investment, in the long run they may affect potential GDP. But for now, we focus on how they can move the economy closer to potential GDP.

■ **Changes in Taxes.** A change in taxes also affects real GDP in the short run. At any given level of real GDP, people will consume less if there is a tax increase because they have less income to spend after taxes. They will consume more if there is a tax cut. In either case, the aggregate demand curve will shift. The top panel of Figure 26.6 shows how a tax cut will shift the aggregate demand curve to the right and push real GDP closer to potential GDP if it is below potential GDP. The bottom panel shows a tax increase reducing real GDP from a position above potential GDP. Again, these are short-term effects. Eventually prices will adjust and real GDP will return to potential GDP.

Both increases and decreases in taxes can also affect potential GDP. For example, if an increase in tax rates causes some people to work less, then the labor supply will not be as large and potential GDP will be lower. But here our focus is on the departures of real GDP from potential GDP.

Countercyclical Fiscal Policy

counductercyclical policy: a policy designed to offset the fluctuations in the business cycle.

Because government spending and taxes affect real GDP in the short run, fiscal policy can, in principle, offset the impact of shocks that push real GDP away from potential GDP. Such use of fiscal policy is called **countercyclical policy,** because the cyclical movements in the economy are being "countered," or offset, by changes in government spending or taxes. Both booms and recessions can be countered, in principle. Recessions require cuts in taxes or increases in spending; booms require increases in taxes or cuts in spending.

Figure 26.7 shows what such a policy would ideally do. A possible recession in the year 2006 is shown, perhaps caused by a drop in foreign demand for U.S. products. Without any change in government purchases or taxes, the economy would eventually recover, as shown in the figure. But suppose that the government quickly cuts taxes or starts a road-building program. The hope is that this will raise real GDP, as shown in the figure, and hasten the return to potential GDP.

How would this work when prices are adjusting and the inflation rate is changing as well? Figure 26.8 provides the analysis. The recession is seen to be caused by the leftward shift in the aggregate demand curve. But the cut in taxes or increase in spending shifts the aggregate demand curve in the opposite direction. The aggregate demand curve shifts back to the right. If these countercyclical measures are timely enough and neither too small nor too large—both big ifs—then the recession may be small and short-lived. The example shows real GDP falling only slightly below potential GDP.

Figure 26.9 shows a less ideal case. Here government purchases are increased, but the response is too late. The increase occurs the year after the recession, during the recovery; it causes a boom, which could cause inflation to increase.

Figure 26.7
Effect of a Well-Timed Countercyclical Fiscal Policy
The figure shows a likely path of recovery from a recession caused by a decline in demand for U.S. products. A well-timed cut in taxes or increase in government purchases can reduce the size of the recession and bring real GDP back to potential GDP more quickly. The size of the economic fluctuation is smaller. The analysis is shown in Figure 26.8.

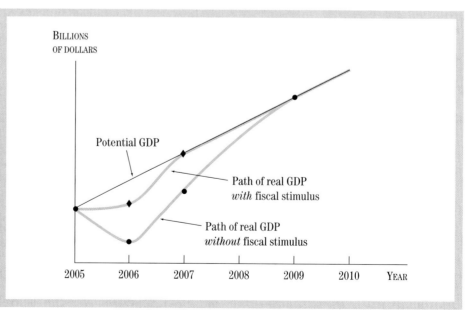

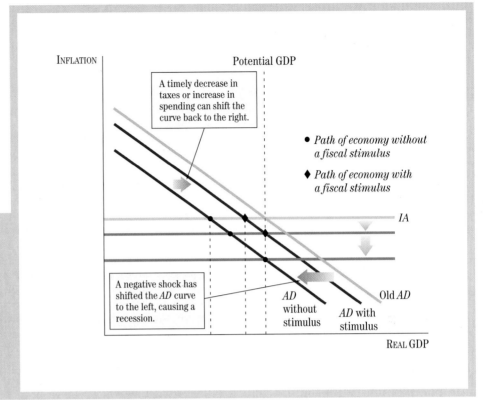

Figure 26.8
Analysis of a Well-Timed Countercyclical Fiscal Policy
A decline in demand—perhaps through a decrease in exports—shifts the *AD* curve to the left. Without a countercyclical fiscal policy, real GDP recovers back to potential GDP, but a timely cut in taxes or increase in government purchases can offset the drop in demand and bring real GDP back to potential GDP more quickly.

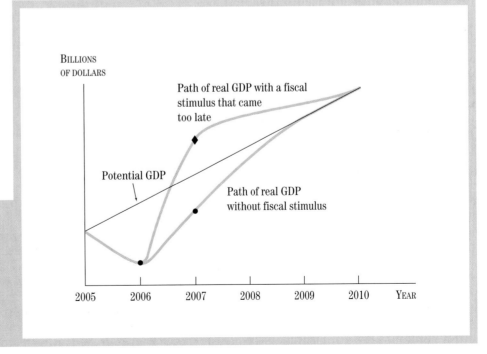

Figure 26.9
Effect of a Poorly Timed Fiscal Policy
Here, in contrast to Figure 26.7, the fiscal stimulus comes too late, when the economy is already recovering. A boom is caused that could lead to inflation and perhaps another recession in later years.

This article from the *New York Times* (January 26, 2005) discusses the continued rise in the budget deficit. The article discusses possible reasons why the deficit increased and also gives an insight into how politically charged a topic the budget deficit is in Washington. Finally, take note of how the article presents budget deficits as putting constraints on discretionary fiscal policymaking.

White House Says Budget Deficit Will Rise Again

By EDMUND L. ANDREWS

David E. Sanger and Eric Schmitt contributed reporting for this article.

WASHINGTON, Jan. 25—The White House announced on Tuesday that the federal budget deficit was expected to rise this year to $427 billion, a figure that includes a new request from President Bush to help pay for the war in Iraq. The White House's announcement makes it the fourth straight year in which the budget deficit was expected to grow; as recently as last July the administration had predicted that the deficit, which was $412 billion last year, would fall this year to $331 billion.

Some reasons for the rising deficit

The deficit figure announced by the White House, which includes part of an additional $80 billion that Mr. Bush requested mostly for Iraq, was higher than the $368 billion estimate announced earlier in the day by the nonpartisan Congressional Budget Office, though that figure did not include supplemental costs for the war. The deficit estimates are roughly consistent with each other with the inclusion of those costs, which cover bombs, bullets, armor for vehicles used in Iraq, and the replacement of tanks and Humvees blown up by insurgent forces. Neither estimate includes the cost of privatizing part of the Social Security program, the leading element of Mr. Bush's domestic agenda. Estimates of the cost of creating those accounts range from $1 trillion to $2 trillion over the next two decades.

The Congressional Budget Office noted that if Mr. Bush wins Congressional approval to make his tax cuts permanent, a top priority for the administration, the deficit would grow by $2 trillion over the next 10 years. If war costs in Iraq and Afghanistan taper off gradually, the agency estimated that price tag over the next 10 years could total nearly $600 billion. In a briefing for reporters on Tuesday, senior administration officials insisted they were still on track to fulfill Mr. Bush's campaign promise of reducing the federal budget deficit by half by 2009. But Mr. Bush is already well behind in reaching his goal. The deficit this year will amount to about 3.5 percent of the nation's gross domestic product, the broadest measure of the economy, a figure that is still below where the United States was in the late 1980's.

Beyond the war costs, administration officials did not spell out the precise reasons for the deficit increase. Tax receipts are expected to climb by about $200 billion in 2005, but mandatory spending for entitlement programs like Medicare and Medicaid is expected to rise significantly faster than the rate of inflation. Mr. Bush defended his $80 billion request for Iraq in a written statement on Tuesday—he had no public events where he could be questioned about it by reporters—saying "our troops will have whatever they need to protect themselves and complete their mission."

But on Capitol Hill, Democrats made clear that while the $80 billion was likely to be approved, they would use the debate on it to question Mr. Bush's war strategy, just as they have done with the confirmation hearings for Condoleezza Rice, the nominee for secretary of state. The White House made no estimate of the cost of the war beyond the next year, being careful not to tip its hand about how long Mr. Bush expects American troops to remain. But on Monday, Lt. Gen. James J. Lovelace, the director of Army operations, said that the Army was operating on the assumption that the number of American troops in Iraq would remain above 100,000 through 2006. One military expert who has been briefed by the Pentagon said on Tuesday that part of the $80 billion would be used to establish more permanent military bases in

Disagreements about the usefulness of fiscal policy boil down to an assessment of whether Figure 26.7 or Figure 26.9 is more likely. Let's first consider some examples.

discretionary fiscal policy: changes in tax or spending policy requiring legislative or administrative action by the president or Congress.

■ **Discretionary Changes in the Instruments of Fiscal Policy.** **Discretionary fiscal policy** refers to specific changes in laws or administrative procedures, such as a change in an existing program to speed up spending, the creation of a new program (such as a new welfare program), or a change in the tax system (such as lower tax rates). These changes in the law are discretionary changes because they require action on the part of the Congress or the president.

Iraq, assuming the new Iraqi government permits a long-term American military presence. The Congressional agency estimated that the war in Iraq and other military operations against terrorism could cost $285 billion over the next 5 years.

Democrats quickly seized on the administration's announcement and the new Congressional deficit report, accusing Mr. Bush of making a bad fiscal situation worse by pushing for permanent tax cuts at a time of war. "The administration remains in denial about these fiscal results," said Representative John M. Spratt Jr., Democrat of South Carolina and the ranking Democrat on the House Budget Committee.

Projections of future deficits

In contrast to the White House budget forecasts, which extend only 5 years, the Congressional projections look ahead 10 years and include many of Mr. Bush's most costly initiatives. For example, extending his tax cuts adds little to the deficits over 5 years but would add $1.8 trillion over 10 years. Preventing an expansion of the Alternative Minimum Tax, a parallel tax that was designed to prevent wealthy people from taking advantage of loopholes, would cost about $500 billion. Administration officials dispute the notion that creating private Social Security accounts would be as expensive as it first appears. They argue that the government would eventually save at least as much money as it spends by lowering the cost of future benefits to retirees. The government, however, might have to borrow as much as $100 billion a year over the next 20 years to pay full benefits to existing retirees, as even the administration has begun to acknowledge.

Even without any changes to current law, the Congressional agency predicted that annual interest costs on the federal debt would almost double from $160 billion last year to $314 billion in 2012. That would be about six times what the federal government spent last year on education.

White House officials provided few details about how they want to use the $80 billion in supplemental war costs that Mr. Bush plans to request. A senior administration official said on Tuesday that about $75 billion would go for military operations in Iraq and Afghanistan, and would come on top of $25 billion that Congress already appropriated for the first few months of this fiscal year, which began on Oct. 1. Much of the request, which is a big jump from last year, is to cover rapidly rising costs of repairing and replacing equipment. Many soldiers and their families have complained about a shortage of properly armored vehicles. But Pentagon officials have been struggling even more with the wear and tear on tanks and weapons that are being used constantly in grueling conditions. One official said on Tuesday that Bradley fighting vehicles were being driven about 4,000 miles a year in Iraq, six times their normal mileage.

The administration also intends to spend about $1 billion on technology and equipment to fend off "improvised explosive devices," the roadside bombs that have killed hundreds of American soldiers and many more Iraqis over the last year. About $5 billion of the $80 billion would be used on programs like financial aid to Palestinians as they try to build a democratic government and a heavily fortified embassy in Iraq for the State Department. Administration officials predicted they would spend about $35 billion of the emergency request this year, and the balance in 2006 and later.

Why reducing the deficit will be difficult

The biggest fiscal problem confronting Mr. Bush is that more than 80 percent of the $2.3 trillion federal budget is currently off-limits for cutting. More than two-thirds of the annual budget goes to mandatory entitlement programs, mainly Social Security, Medicaid and Medicare. More than $500 billion will go to the military and domestic security, not counting the extra money being spent in Iraq and Afghanistan. Administration officials want to increase financing for the military and domestic security above the rate of inflation for the foreseeable future. That leaves less than $500 billion for all the other discretionary domestic programs, like space exploration, education and tax collection. Administration officials hope to freeze that spending at current levels, which would lead to real cuts after adjusting for inflation. But that, according to the Congressional Budget Office, would save only about $9 billion a year.

One of the most significant post–World War II discretionary fiscal policy actions was the 1964 tax cut, proposed by President John F. Kennedy and enacted after his death when Lyndon Johnson was president. The early 1960s were a period when real GDP was below potential GDP, and this large discretionary tax cut was a factor in speeding the economic recovery. This cut in taxes also probably stimulated the growth of potential GDP and was therefore good for the long run.

Another example was the 1968 temporary income tax surcharge that raised tax rates by 10 percent. It was passed during the Vietnam War, when real GDP was above potential GDP, perhaps because the aim was to bring real GDP back toward potential GDP. However, in this case, the boom continued. The tax increase came long after the boom had started.

689

Another large discretionary fiscal policy action was the Reagan tax cut of the early 1980s, which lowered personal income tax rates by 25 percent. This tax cut helped the economy recover from the 1981–1982 recession. Like the Kennedy tax cut, this tax cut also probably raised the growth rate of potential GDP.

A more recent example of a discretionary fiscal policy was the Economic Growth and Tax Relief Reconciliation Act of 2001, enacted by Congress in June 2001. Among the sweeping changes in tax law introduced by this plan were lower income tax rates, more generous tax exemptions for married couples, and more generous tax exemptions for children. The first part of the plan was a $300 ($600 for couples) rebate check that the government mailed out to eligible taxpayers in the summer of 2001. The tax cut was helpful in raising spending during the recession, although the extent to which it helped is the source of some debate among economists, since many of the provisions were to be phased in over the next ten years instead of being effective immediately.

The impact of these examples of discretionary fiscal policy was neither as good as Figure 26.7 shows nor as bad as Figure 26.9 shows. In none of these cases was the change in taxes speedy enough to offset a recession or a boom. The tax cuts came after the recessions, and the tax increase came after the boom. At best, the tax cuts speeded up the recovery.

■ **Automatic Changes in the Instruments of Fiscal Policy.** Discretionary actions by the government are not the only way in which taxes and spending can be changed. In fact, many of the very large changes in taxes and spending are automatic. Income tax revenues expand when people are making more and fall when people are making less. Thus, tax revenues respond automatically to the economy. Tax payments rise when the economy is in a boom and more people are working. Tax revenues fall when the economy is in a slump and unemployment rises.

These changes in tax revenues are even larger with a progressive income tax. With a *progressive tax* system, individual tax payments *rise* as a proportion of income as income increases. With a progressive tax, a person earning $100,000 per year pays proportionately more in taxes than a person earning $20,000 per year: Because of this progressive tax system, as people earn more, they pay a higher tax rate, and when they earn less, they pay a lower tax rate.

Parts of government spending also change automatically. Unemployment compensation, through which the government makes payments to individuals who are unemployed, rises during a recession. When unemployment rises, so do payments to unemployed workers. Social security payments also increase in a recession because people may retire earlier if job prospects are bad. Welfare payments rise in a recession because people who are unemployed for a long period of time may qualify for welfare. As poverty rates rise in recessions, welfare payments increase.

automatic stabilizers:
automatic tax and spending changes that occur over the course of the business cycle that tend to stabilize the fluctuations in real GDP.

These automatic tax and spending changes are called **automatic stabilizers** because they tend to stabilize the fluctuations of real GDP. How significant are these automatic stabilizers? Consider the 2001 recession. Real GDP in 1999 and 2000 was above potential GDP. But by late 2001 and 2002, real GDP was dropping below potential GDP. As this happened, government spending went up and taxes went down.

The magnitude of these effects was quite large. The difference between proposed and actual taxes and spending in the 2002 budget provides an estimate of the effect of the recession on taxes and spending. Tax revenue was $336 billion less than had been proposed before the recession. Thus, taxes were automatically reduced by this amount. However, spending was $50 billion more than had been proposed before the recession. Thus, spending rose by $50 billion in response to the recession. The combined effect of a $336 billion reduction in taxes and a $50 billion increase in spending was vital in keeping the recovery going. Since tax receipts went down in the recession and transfer payments went up, people's consumption was at a higher level than it would otherwise have been. These automatic changes in tax revenues and government spending tended to stabilize the economy and probably made the recession less severe than it would otherwise have been. These changes did not completely offset other factors, however, because there still was a recession.

The Discretion versus Rules Debate for Fiscal Policy

For many years economists have debated the usefulness of discretionary and automatic fiscal policy. Automatic fiscal policy is an example of a fiscal policy rule describing how the instruments of fiscal policy respond to the state of the economy. Thus, the debate is sometimes called the "discretion versus rules" debate.

The case for discretionary fiscal policy was made by President Kennedy's Council of Economic Advisers, which included Walter Heller and Nobel Prize–winning economist James Tobin. Proponents of discretionary fiscal policy argue that the automatic stabilizers will not be large enough or well-timed enough to bring the economy out of a recession quickly. Critics of discretionary policy, such as Milton Friedman, another Nobel Prize winner, emphasize that the effect of policy is uncertain and that there are long lags in the impact of policy. By the time spending increases and taxes are cut, a recession could be over; if so, the policy would only lead to an inflationary boom. Three types of lags are particularly problematic for discretionary fiscal policy: a *recognition lag,* the time between the need for the policy and the recognition of the need; an *implementation lag,* the time between the recognition of the need for the policy and its implementation; and an *impact lag,* the time between the implementation of the policy and its impact on real GDP.

Although lags and uncertainty continue to contribute to the discretion versus rules debate, other issues have also become central. Many economists feel that policy rules are desirable because of their stability and reliability. A fiscal policy rule emphasizing the automatic stabilizers might make government plans to reduce the deficit more believable. Countercyclical fiscal policy raises the deficit or reduces the surplus during recessions. With discretionary policy, there is no guarantee that the surplus will return or increase after the recession. With an automatic policy rule, there is an expectation that the deficit will decline after the recession is over.

In the 1980s and 1990s, there were few discretionary fiscal policy actions to counter recessions or booms in the United States or Europe. One reason discretionary actions did not occur was the high budget deficits and public concerns about the governments that had caused these deficits in the first place. In recent times, the use of discretionary fiscal policy has increased in the United States. However, the tax cut enacted in June 2001 was facilitated by the large surpluses predicted for the economy, before the recession came along.

REVIEW
- Countercyclical fiscal policy is undertaken by governments to reduce economic fluctuations. The aim is to keep real GDP closer to potential GDP.

- Two types of countercyclical fiscal policy are (1) discretionary policy, such as the 1964 Kennedy-Johnson tax cut, the 1981 Reagan tax cut, and the 2003 Bush tax cuts, and (2) automatic stabilizers, such as changes in unemployment payments, social security payments, and tax revenues due to changes in people's incomes.

The Structural versus the Cyclical Surplus

structural surplus: the level of the government budget surplus under the scenario where real GDP is equal to potential GDP; also called the full-employment surplus.

We noted earlier that taxes and spending change automatically in recessions and booms. These automatic changes affect the budget, so in order to analyze the budget, it is important to try to separate out these automatic effects. The *structural,* or *full-employment, surplus* was designed for this purpose. The **structural surplus** is what the surplus would be if real GDP equaled potential GDP.

Figure 26.10 introduces a graph to help explain the structural surplus. On the horizontal axis is real GDP. On the vertical axis is the budget surplus: tax revenues less expenditures. The budget is balanced when the surplus is zero, which is marked by a horizontal line in the diagram. The region below zero represents a situation in which taxes are less than spending and the government has a deficit. The region above zero is a situation in which the government budget has a surplus. On the horizontal axis, *A, B,* and *C* represent three different levels of real GDP.

The upward-sloping line in Figure 26.10 indicates that as real GDP rises, the budget surplus gets larger. Why? The automatic stabilizers are the reason. When real GDP rises, tax revenues rise and spending on transfer programs falls. Because the surplus is the difference between tax revenues and spending, the surplus gets larger. Conversely, when real GDP falls, tax receipts decline and spending on transfer programs increases, so the surplus falls. The upward-sloping line in Figure 26.10 pertains to a particular set of government programs and tax laws. A change in these programs or laws would *shift* the line. For example, a decrease in tax rates would shift the line down.

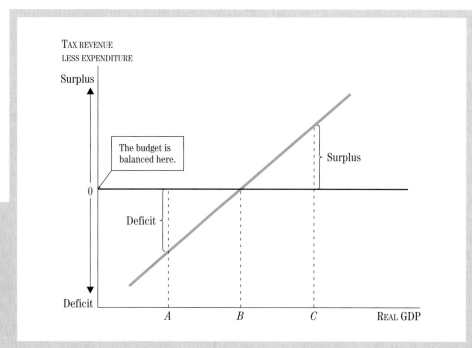

Figure 26.10
The Effect of Real GDP on the Budget
When real GDP falls, the budget moves toward deficit because spending rises and tax receipts fall. When real GDP is at point *A*, there is a deficit; at point *B*, the budget is balanced; and at point *C*, there is a budget surplus.

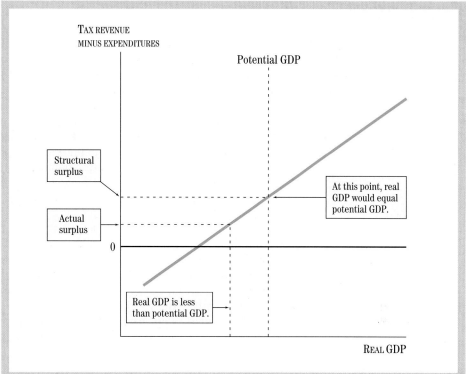

Figure 26.11
The Structural Surplus versus the Actual Surplus in a Recession Year
The surplus that would occur when real GDP is equal to potential GDP is called the structural surplus, as shown in the figure. The actual surplus falls below the structural surplus when real GDP falls below potential GDP. If there is a big recession, there could be an actual deficit even though there is a structural surplus.

Figure 26.11, a similar diagram, shows potential GDP and real GDP in a year when real GDP is below potential GDP. Imagine raising real GDP up to potential GDP. We would predict that the surplus would go up, because tax receipts would rise as the economy grew and transfer payments would go down since there would be fewer people unemployed, fewer people retiring, and fewer people on welfare. As we move to the right in the diagram, the surplus gets larger. The structural surplus occurs when real GDP equals potential GDP.

The structural surplus provides a way to separate out cyclical changes in the budget caused by cyclical changes in the economy.

REVIEW
- Because tax revenues and spending fluctuate as the economy fluctuates, the surplus, or deficit, is cyclical. Deficits frequently arise or get bigger in recessions.
- The structural surplus adjusts the actual surplus for these cyclical changes in the economy.

Conclusion

Because the government is such a large player in the economy, its fiscal actions (spending, taxing, and borrowing) exert a powerful influence on real GDP and employment. Such actions can cause real GDP to depart from potential GDP and can alter the long-term growth rate of potential GDP.

A first principle of fiscal policy, therefore, is that government not take actions that would harm the economy. Avoiding erratic changes in fiscal policy and making sure that taxes are not increased during recessions are part of this first principle.

A second principle is that fiscal policy can be used to help smooth the fluctuations in the economy. Tax cuts and spending increases during recessions can help offset the declines in demand that cause recessions. Conversely, tax increases and spending cuts during booms can help offset the forces leading to inflation in the economy.

There is debate among economists about whether the government is capable of taking discretionary actions that will have these effects. Policy lags and uncertainty make discretionary fiscal policy difficult. There is little disagreement, however, about the importance of automatic stabilizers, under which tax and spending actions occur automatically without legislation. Automatic stabilizers cause the deficit to rise in recessions and fall during booms.

Another part of government policy that has powerful effects on the economy is monetary policy. We take up monetary policy in Chapter 27.

KEY POINTS

1. Fiscal policy consists of the government's plans for spending and taxes.

2. The government's budget is the primary document of fiscal policy. It gives the priorities for spending and taxes. In the United States, the president must submit a budget proposal to Congress.

3. The United States had large federal budget deficits from 1970 to 1997, surpluses from 1998 to 2001, and deficits since then.

4. Because Congress modifies the proposals and because of unanticipated events, the actual budget differs considerably from the proposed budget.

5. Changes in spending and taxes can move real GDP away from potential GDP in the short run. But in the long run, real GDP returns to potential GDP.

6. Discretionary changes in taxes and spending can be used to keep real GDP near potential GDP.

7. Lags and uncertainty make discretionary fiscal policy difficult.

8. Automatic stabilizers are an important part of fiscal policy. Tax revenues automatically decline in recessions. Transfer payments move in the reverse direction.

KEY TERMS

federal budget	budget deficit	countercyclical policy	automatic stabilizers
balanced budget	federal debt	discretionary fiscal policy	structural surplus
budget surplus	debt to GDP ratio		

QUESTIONS FOR REVIEW

1. Why are actual expenditures and revenues always different from the president's proposals?

2. How is the government's debt affected by the government's budget surplus?

3. Why would a tax cut in a recession reduce the size of the recession?

4. Why might a proposal to cut taxes in a recession do little to mitigate the recession?

5. What is meant by the discretion versus rules debate?

6. What are automatic stabilizers, and how do they help mitigate economic fluctuations?

7. What is the difference between the structural surplus and the actual surplus?

8. What would happen to the actual surplus in a recession?

PROBLEMS

1. Suppose real GDP is less than potential GDP. Use a diagram with inflation on the vertical axis and real GDP on the horizontal axis to show the short-run, medium-run, and long-run effects of an increase in government purchases on the inflation rate and real GDP. Show how the aggregate demand curve and the inflation adjustment line shift over time.

2. Suppose you have the following data on projected and actual figures for the U.S. budget for 2005 (in billions of dollars).

	Projected Budget	Actual Budget
Taxes	2,200	2,100
Expenditures	2,100	2,200

   a. What was the projected budget surplus or deficit? What was the actual budget surplus or deficit? Why might this happen?
   b. If the government debt is $3,000 billion at the end of 2004, what is the debt at the end of 2005?
   c. If GDP is $11,000 billion in 2005, what is the debt to GDP ratio? How does this compare to the debt to GDP ratio around 1990?

3. The Thai economy went into a recession in 1997 and 1998. Some people recommended reducing government spending in this situation. Was that good advice? Explain with a diagram.

4. Suppose the economy is currently $100 billion above potential GDP, and the government wants to pursue discretionary fiscal policy to cool off the economy. Show this situation using the aggregate demand curve. Indicate the effect on government purchases.

5. The federal budget deficit for the United States rose from about 3 percent of GDP in 1990 to about 5 percent of GDP in 1991.
   a. Explain why at least part of this increase in the deficit was the result of the recession in 1991.
   b. Suppose real GDP was equal to potential GDP in 1990 and below potential GDP in 1991. Sketch a diagram that shows the responsiveness of the deficit to GDP and show the structural surplus. Is it positive or negative?
   c. Is it good or bad for the economy that the deficit increased as a result of the recession?

6. Examine the hypothetical budget data, shown below, for calendar years 2005–2008 (in billions of dollars).

Year	Budget Surplus	Government Debt as of January 1	GDP
2005	−150	1,000	4,000
2006	−100	1,150	4,200
2007	100		4,800
2008	200		5,400

   a. Fill in the missing values in the table.
   b. What is the percentage change in debt and GDP from 2005 to 2006?
   c. Calculate the debt to GDP ratio for each year. How does this ratio change over time? Why?

7. Suppose you get a summer job working in Congress and a recession begins while you are there. Write a memo to your boss, who is a member of Congress, on the pros and cons of a big highway-building program to combat the recession.

8. Suppose the government surplus is 3 percent of real GDP, but economists say that the structural surplus is 2 percent.
   a. Is real GDP currently above or below potential GDP? Why? Draw the diagram showing this situation.
   b. In your diagram, show the situation when real GDP falls.

9. Suppose that real GDP has just fallen below potential GDP in a recession and the Council of Economic Advisers is trying to forecast the recovery from the recession. They are uncertain about whether Congress will pass the president's proposed tax cut right away or will delay it a year. Trace out two possible scenarios with an *AD-IA* diagram that describes the uncertainty.

10. Suppose Congress is considering a balanced budget amendment to the Constitution that requires that the budget be balanced every fiscal year. Explain how this law could make the economy more unstable.

Monetary Policy

I t was February 2005, and Federal Reserve Chairman Alan Greenspan was testifying before Congress about the Fed's most recent *Monetary Policy Report to Congress*. Greenspan testified that "[i]n the seven months since I last testified before this Committee, the U.S. economic expansion has firmed, overall inflation has subsided, and core inflation has remained low. Over the first half of 2004, the available information increasingly suggested that the economic expansion was becoming less fragile and that the risk of an undesirable decline in inflation had greatly diminished." Greenspan reiterated his belief that the Fed had helped minimize the adverse impact of the 2001 recession by acting quickly to cut interest rates by "an extraordinary degree." However, in his outline of the stance of monetary policy, the chairman indicated that the recovery of the economy meant that interest rates would rise from their low levels in the months ahead. "The Federal Open Market Committee began to raise the federal funds rate at its June meeting, and the announcement following that meeting indicated the need for further, albeit gradual, withdrawal of monetary policy stimulus."

Notice, though, that Greenspan was not appearing before Congress to get permission to act; he was merely providing Congress with information about the policy decisions the Fed had made, and would be making in the future. What is the rationale for Congress giving Alan Greenspan and the Fed so much independence to set rates? After all, the Fed seemed to indicate that output had returned to potential output, thus making it more likely that the Fed would raise interest rates instead of lower them. How confident was the Fed that no more stimulus was needed? Should we give one individual (Alan Greenspan) or one group of people (the FOMC) the power to decide what is acceptable and what is not?

The purpose of this chapter is to answer these and other monetary policy–related questions. We will first explain why central banks that are independent may bring about better economic performance. We will then examine the complex decisions faced by the independent monetary policymaker, and also consider some policy tools that such policymakers have at their disposal. Finally, we will look at how governments can choose to restrict their monetary policymakers' freedom by choosing to tie the value of their currency to another country's currency.

Why Are Central Banks Independent?

The most important feature of a central bank, whether it is the Fed, the Bank of Japan, or the European Central Bank, is the degree of independence from the government that the law gives it.

Fed officials are appointed to long terms that may span several different presidents; the four-year term of the chair of the Fed does not necessarily coincide with the term of any president. For example, Paul Volcker served through most of the Reagan years, even though he was appointed by President Carter. Alan Greenspan, originally appointed by President Reagan, served throughout the eight years of the Clinton presidency. Therefore, like Supreme Court justices in the United States, Fed officials develop an independence from governmental influence.

William McChesney Martin
1951–1969

Arthur Burns
1969–1978

G. William Miller
1978–1979

Paul Volcker
1979–1987

Alan Greenspan
1987–2006

Fifty-five Years of Fed Chairs
There have been five chairs of the Federal Reserve Board during the past 55 years. Ben Bernanke is expected to take over as the next Fed Chairman when Alan Greenspan leaves his post at the end of January 2006.

central bank independence: a description of the legal authority of central banks to make decisions on monetary policy with little interference by the government in power.

What is the rationale for **central bank independence?** The main rationale, as explained below, is that an independent central bank can prevent the government in power from using monetary policy in ways that appear beneficial in the short run but that can harm the economy in the long run.

The "Gain Then Pain" Scenario

We showed in Chapter 25 that a shift in monetary policy toward a higher inflation target will temporarily raise real GDP above potential GDP, but that only inflation will be higher in the long run. Such a change in monetary policy would first entail a reduction in interest rates and would shift the aggregate demand (*AD*) curve to the right, as shown in Figure 27.1. Real GDP would rise along with investment, consumption, and net exports; unemployment would fall. In the short run, there would be no effect on inflation because of the slowness of firms to change their price decisions. The economic gain from the reduction in unemployment without an increase in inflation might help in a reelection campaign, or it might enable the government to push legislation for new programs through the political system. The economic pain—higher inflation in the long run, also shown in Figure 27.1—would not be seen until after the election or after the legislation is passed.

Thus, there is a natural tendency toward higher inflation in the political system. If the government in power had complete control over the decisions of the central bank, it could take actions to make the economy look good in the short run for political purposes and not worry that the economy might look bad in the long run. Removing the central bank from the direct control of the government reduces this politically induced bias toward higher inflation because it is then more difficult for the government to get the central bank to take such actions.

■ **The Phillips Curve.** Observe that during the period of time when the *IA* line is shifting up in the gain then pain scenario, real GDP is above potential GDP, and the inflation rate is higher than at the start of the scenario. For example, there is higher

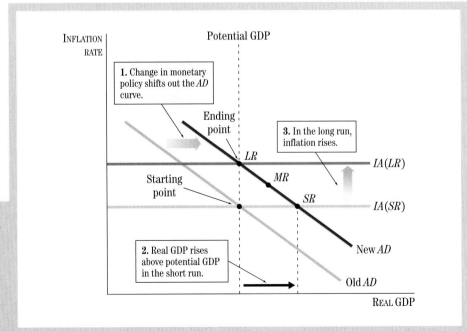

Figure 27.1
The "Gain Then Pain" Scenario
The Fed can temporarily stimulate the economy in the short run—real GDP rises above potential GDP. But soon inflation starts to rise. In the long run, the inflation rate is higher and real GDP is back to potential GDP.

inflation and higher real GDP at the point labeled *MR* in Figure 27.1 than at the starting point. And during this period, the unemployment rate is lower because the unemployment rate falls when real GDP rises. In sum, during the period of time between the initial shift of the *AD* curve and the end of the scenario, the unemployment rate is *down* and the inflation rate is *up*. Thus, there is a negative correlation between unemployment and inflation.

In fact, a negative correlation between unemployment and inflation has been observed for many years in the real world, because of such shifts in the *AD* curve. This negative correlation between inflation and unemployment is called the *Phillips curve*, after A. W. Phillips, the economist who first showed that such correlations existed in British data from 1861–1957. A replica of the original Phillips curve is shown in Figure 27.2.

The Phillips curve was used in the 1960s and 1970s to justify a monetary policy that included higher inflation. People argued that higher inflation would lead to lower unemployment. In other words, they argued that there was a long-run tradeoff between inflation and unemployment.

How did they use the Phillips curve to support this view? Look at the Phillips curve in Figure 27.2. You might think that a monetary policy that aimed for higher inflation could lead to a lower unemployment rate in the long run. That is what the curve seems to suggest. But the theory in the *AD-IA* diagram, and, in particular, the gain then pain scenario, shows that there is no such tradeoff in the long run. If monetary policy raised inflation, eventually real GDP would return to potential GDP, the unemployment rate would return to the natural rate, and we would be left with only higher inflation, not lower unemployment.

It has become a basic principle of modern macroeconomics—implied by the *AD-IA* diagram—that there is no long-run tradeoff between inflation and unemployment. The facts are consistent with the principle: In the 1950s and early 1960s, inflation was low; in the late 1960s and 1970s, inflation was high; and in the 1980s and 1990s, inflation was low again. But the average unemployment rate in all these periods was roughly the same, around 5 or 6 percent. Furthermore, the lower unemployment rate in the late 1990s did not result in much higher inflation. Any tendency for unemployment and inflation to be negatively correlated will disappear in the long

Check your thinking about the implications of the gain then pain scenario for the relationship between unemployment and inflation.

In the short run, between the start and end of the scenario:

Inflation ↑
Real GDP > potential GDP
Unemployment rate <
                 natural rate

So there is a negative correlation between inflation and unemployment, a Phillips curve.

In the long run:

Inflation ↑
Real GDP = potential GDP
Unemployment rate =
                 natural rate

So there is no long-run tradeoff between inflation and unemployment.

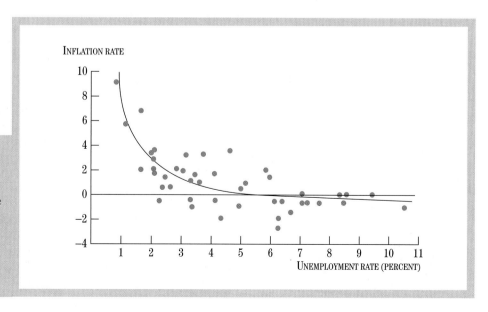

Figure 27.2
The Original Phillips Curve
A. W. Phillips first published this graph. Each point represents one year. The negatively sloped curve drawn through the scatter of points had enormous influence and led some to argue, mistakenly, that there was a long-run tradeoff between inflation and unemployment.

run. This does not mean that there will be no short-run gain from a higher-inflation monetary policy. It does mean that there will be long-run pain.

political business cycle: a business cycle caused by politicians' use of economic policy to overstimulate the economy just before an election.

■ **The Political Business Cycle.** The **political business cycle** is the tendency of governments to use economic policy to cause real GDP to rise and unemployment to fall just before an election and then let the economy slow down right after the election. Many economic and political studies have shown that an incumbent's chances of being reelected are increased greatly if the economy is doing well. After the election, inflation may rise and cause a bust, but that would be long before the next election.

Research in the 1970s by William Nordhaus of Yale University uncovered some evidence of a political business cycle in the United States. For example, the strong economy before the 1972 election may have been due to a monetary policy change that pushed real GDP above potential GDP. On the other hand, the U.S. economy was in a recession just before the 1980 and 1992 elections—the exact opposite of a political business cycle. Thus, the evidence of a political business cycle in the United States is no longer strong. In any case, political business cycles are harmful to the economy. Preventing political business cycles is another reason for having a central bank that has some independence from the politicians that are in power.

■ **Time Inconsistency.** The temptation to use monetary policy for short-run gain despite the long-run pain is difficult for governments to resist. Even governments whose sole aim is to improve the well-being of the average citizen will say that they want low inflation but then stimulate the economy in order to lower unemployment, even though they are fully aware of the inflationary consequences down the road.

time inconsistency: the situation in which policymakers have the incentive to announce one economic policy but then change that policy after citizens have acted on the initial, stated policy.

This situation is known as **time inconsistency** because governments say they want low inflation but are later inconsistent by following policies that lead to higher inflation. They act like a teacher who tells the class that there will be an exam to get the students to study, but then, on the day of the exam, announces that the exam is canceled. The students are happy to miss the exam, and the teacher does not have to grade it. Everyone appears better off in the short run.

However, just as the teacher who cancels the exam will lose credibility with future classes, a central bank that tries the inconsistent policy will lose credibility. People will assume that the central bank will actually raise inflation even if it says it is aiming for low inflation.

Potential Disadvantages of Central Bank Independence

Central bank independence is no guarantee against monetary policy mistakes, however, and it could even lead to more mistakes. In principle, an independent central bank could cause more inflation than a central bank under the control of the government. For example, those in charge of the central bank could—after they are appointed—succumb to arguments that high inflation is not so harmful after all. Or, at the other extreme, those in charge of the central bank could become so focused on inflation that they are blinded to the effects of monetary policy on real GDP and employment and could either cause a recession or make an existing recession deeper or longer. Thus, a disadvantage of central bank independence is that it can be taken too far.

Whether independent or not, central banks need to be held *accountable* for their actions. If those in charge of the central bank do not perform their job well, it is appropriate that they not be reappointed. When the central bank of New Zealand was given greater independence in the 1980s, its accountability was formalized very

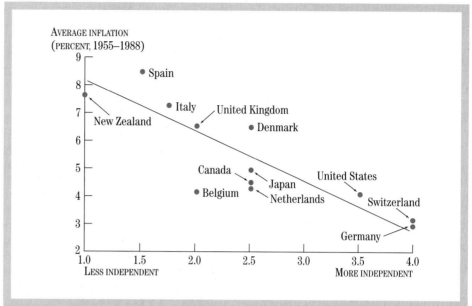

Figure 27.3
Central Bank Independence and Inflation
The scatter plot shows that the more independent a central bank is, the lower the average inflation rate. The independence of the central bank is calculated by studying the laws of each country, including the length of the term of office of the head of the central bank (a longer term means more independence) and restrictions on the central bank lending to the government.

explicitly: If the head of the central bank does not achieve low inflation goals agreed to in advance, the head is fired. But the central bank has independence in determining how to achieve these goals.

Is there any evidence that independence has led to better inflation performance without any increase in the severity or frequency of recessions? If you look at Figure 27.3, you will see that central banks that have more independence have had lower inflation. This lower inflation has not been associated with more or longer recessions. Note that the graph shows New Zealand *before* the central bank was given more independence; since then, it has moved down and to the right, toward lower inflation.

REVIEW

- The gain then pain scenario shows that a central bank can lower unemployment below the natural unemployment rate in the short run, but by doing so it will raise inflation in the long run.

- The Phillips curve is a negative correlation between inflation and unemployment. However, there is no long-run tradeoff between inflation and unemployment.

- Central bank independence insulates the central bank from short-run political pressures to overstimulate the economy, which would ultimately raise inflation.

- Countries with more independent central banks have tended to have lower inflation than countries with less independent central banks.

Trying to Bring the Aggregate Demand Curve into Line in 2000

The previous section showed the inflationary harm caused by a monetary policy that intentionally pushes the aggregate demand curve to the right and raises real GDP above potential GDP. But even independent central bankers who have no intention of pursuing such an inflationary policy must still worry about shocks or uninten-tional shifts in the aggregate demand curve that would push real GDP away from potential GDP.

In fact, when the inflation rate is at the target inflation rate, monetary policy is a constant struggle to manage aggregate demand so as to keep real GDP near potential GDP, and thereby prevent inflation from veering away from its target. In this section, we illustrate this struggle with a case study of monetary policy in the United States in early 2000. It then appeared to the Fed that aggregate demand was too high and needed to be reduced with higher interest rates.

Aggregate Demand: Just Right, Too Hot, or Too Cold?

First consider Figure 27.4, which illustrates the problem monetary policy faces in trying to keep real GDP near to potential GDP. There are three graphs in Figure 27.4, each illustrating a different situation.

■ **The Goldilocks Economy: Just Right.** In the middle graph, the aggregate demand curve intersects the inflation adjustment line at the point where real GDP equals potential GDP and the inflation rate is equal to the target inflation rate. Because real GDP is equal to potential GDP, there is no tendency for inflation to rise or to fall. Thus, this graph represents an ideal point: The inflation rate is equal to the target inflation rate, and real GDP is equal to potential GDP. The aggregate demand curve is in the correct place, because it intersects the inflation adjustment line at the point where real GDP equals potential GDP *and* where the inflation rate equals the target inflation rate. Financial market analysts refer to this situation as a "Goldilocks economy": not too hot, not too cold, just right.

■ **A Misalignment: Aggregate Demand Is Too High.** In contrast to the middle panel in Figure 27.4, the other two panels represent misalignments of real GDP and potential GDP. In the right-hand panel, aggregate demand has increased too much—perhaps because of an expansionary shift in consumption, investment, or net exports. At this position, there are inflationary forces in place that will soon cause the inflation adjustment line to rise. Unlike the short-run position in Figure 27.1 (the gain then pain scenario, where the central bank has intentionally shifted monetary policy), the situation in the right-hand panel of Figure 27.4 is unintentional. The task of monetary policy is to try to prevent such misalignments, and to correct such misalignments once they occur.

How would the central bank correct this type of misalignment? It would raise the real interest rate above the level it would choose in the middle graph. The higher real interest rate would reduce aggregate demand and bring the *AD* curve back to a point where it intersected the inflation adjustment line at potential GDP. Financial market analysts would say that the Fed was trying to "cool off the economy" by raising the interest rate in this way.

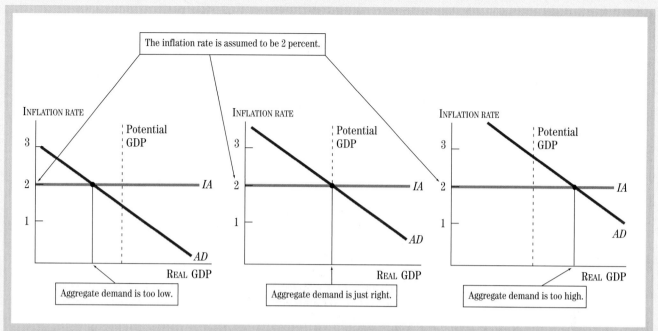

The inflation rate is assumed to be 2 percent.

Aggregate demand is too low.

Aggregate demand is just right.

Aggregate demand is too high.

Figure 27.4
Aligning the Aggregate
Demand Curve

The aggregate demand curve is lined up correctly when real GDP equals potential GDP and the inflation rate is on target, as in the graph in the middle. Otherwise, aggregate demand is too high, and the Fed must raise the interest rate; or aggregate demand is too low, and the Fed must lower the interest rate.

■ **Another Type of Misalignment: Aggregate Demand Is Too Low.**   The left panel of Figure 27.4 represents the opposite, but no less undesirable, type of misalignment of real GDP and potential GDP. In this case, aggregate demand has gotten too low—perhaps because of a contractionary shift in consumption, investment, or net exports. With real GDP less than potential GDP, the inflation adjustment line will soon fall below the target inflation rate. Moreover, with real GDP below potential GDP, unemployment has increased. Monetary policy should try to prevent or correct this type of misalignment, too.

To correct such a misalignment, the central bank would lower the real interest rate below the level it would choose in the top middle graph. The lower real interest rate would increase consumption, investment, and net exports and bring the *AD* curve back to the right.

Monetary Policy in Early 2000

For much of the economic expansion of the 1990s, the U.S. economy was much like the Goldilocks economy in the middle graph in Figure 27.4. The Fed had done a good job at estimating potential GDP and had managed to keep real GDP close to potential GDP during this period.

■ **"Rising Inflationary Pressure."**   However, by 1999, real GDP was clearly growing faster than potential GDP, and by early 2000, the Fed was convinced that real GDP was above potential GDP, a situation "that contains the seeds of rising inflationary and financial pressure," as the Fed put it in the February 2000 *Monetary Policy Report to Congress*.

The situation in early 2000 was exactly the one in the "Aggregate Demand Is Too High" graph of Figure 27.4. There had been no increase in inflation, but with real GDP above potential GDP, the Fed was concerned that inflation would rise. The Fed's analysis is the same as that contained in the *AD-IA* diagram, which is not surprising, since the type of model used by the economists at the Fed is essentially the same as the one in that diagram.

Why did the Fed think the aggregate demand curve had shifted? The main factor was the U.S. stock market. With stock prices having risen rapidly in 1998 and 1999, people were feeling wealthier, the Fed reasoned, and they would raise their consumption purchases, shifting up aggregate demand. Here is how Alan Greenspan put it in his congressional testimony: "Perhaps three to four cents out of every additional dollar of stock market wealth eventually is reflected in increased consumer purchases. The sharp rise in the amount of consumer outlays . . . has been consistent with this so-called wealth effect on household purchases."

Because of this shift in the aggregate demand curve, the Fed explained, "the level of interest rates needed to align demand with potential supply may have increased substantially." The Fed felt that it would have to raise the nominal interest rate to raise the real interest rate and rein in aggregate demand to bring real GDP back into equality with potential GDP. In the spring and summer of that year, the Fed did raise the federal funds rate to $6\frac{1}{2}$ percent from $5\frac{1}{2}$ percent. At its last summer meeting that year (August 22, 2000), the Federal Open Market committee decided that $6\frac{1}{2}$ percent was enough for the time being, and it issued a statement explaining its decision. Here is the statement, along with a hint of what the risks looked like:

> The Federal Open Market Committee at its meeting today decided to maintain the existing stance of monetary policy, keeping its target for the federal funds rate at $6\frac{1}{2}$ percent. Recent data have indicated that the expansion of aggregate demand is moderating. . . . Nonetheless, the Committee remains concerned about the risk of a continuing gap between the growth of demand and potential supply. . . . The Committee believes the risks continue to be weighted mainly toward conditions that may generate heightened inflation pressures in the foreseeable future.

Observe how the *AD-IA* diagram captures six key elements in the Fed's analysis in this case study:

1. Real GDP rose above potential GDP because aggregate demand had shifted.

2. Aggregate demand shifted as a result of a shift in consumption spending.

3. With real GDP above potential GDP, inflation was predicted to rise.

4. But inflation had not yet risen, because it adjusts slowly.

5. The Fed increased interest rates to bring real GDP back to potential GDP.

6. After increasing the interest rate, the Fed took a breather and reported that aggregate demand was moderating.

■ **The Inherent Uncertainty in Monetary Policy.** This case study also illustrates that, in practice, it is not easy for the Fed to keep real GDP near potential GDP by varying the interest rate. Although the Fed increased interest rates to rein in aggregate demand, there was concern that real GDP would not respond as quickly as in the past. At the time, it appeared that investment and consumption might be less responsive than the Fed thought they would be to the increase in the interest rate. That is why the Fed said it was "concerned about the risk" that aggregate demand might still grow too rapidly.

In general, there is a great deal of uncertainty about how long it takes for a change in the interest rate to affect aggregate demand. Other things affect aggregate demand too, and some of those things might work in the opposite direction to the change in interest rates.

Moreover, potential GDP is very difficult to estimate. Recall that potential GDP is determined by the underlying supply of labor, capital, and technological change. In many situations, central banks do not know for sure whether real GDP is or is not equal to potential GDP. Uncertainty about potential GDP is particularly high during periods when technology seems to be changing rapidly and the path of potential GDP is changing, as it was in 2000.

The Reaction to the Gap Between Real GDP and Potential GDP

Observe that in order to bring real GDP into alignment with potential GDP in this case study, the Fed reacted to the *gap,* or the *difference,* between real GDP and potential GDP. That is, it raised the real interest rate when real GDP rose above potential GDP. Similarly, if real GDP were to fall below potential GDP, as shown in the top left graph of Figure 27.4, the Fed would lower the real interest rate.

This type of interest rate reaction to the gap between real GDP and potential GDP is typical of the Fed and many other central banks. It represents a good policy response, because it tends to move the aggregate demand curve in a way that brings real GDP back into equality with potential GDP.

This interest rate reaction is similar to the reaction of central banks to changes in the inflation rate. Recall that such reactions of the real interest rate to inflation are described by the monetary policy rule introduced in Chapter 24. In fact, it is possible to combine both reactions—the reaction to inflation and the reaction to the gap—into one monetary policy rule, and thereby obtain a more accurate description of central bank behavior. Remember that a monetary policy rule is a description of a central bank's behavior in the same sense that a microeconomic demand curve is a description of a person's consumption behavior. Just as a person's purchase decisions may depend on two variables, (1) price and (2) income, so too the central bank's real interest rate decisions may depend on two variables, (1) the inflation rate and (2) the gap between real GDP and potential GDP.

Table 27.1 shows a numerical example of this type of policy rule. On the left is the inflation rate. On the top is the gap between real GDP and potential GDP. The entries

Table 27.1
Real Interest Rate Reaction to Inflation and to the Gap Between Real GDP and Potential GDP (Compare with Table 24.1 on page 640.)

		Percent Gap Between Real GDP and Potential GDP		
		−2	0	2
Inflation Rate (percent)	0	0	1	2
	2	1	2	3
	4	2	3	4
	6	3	4	5
	8	4	5	6

(The entries in the shaded area show the real interest rate for each inflation rate and gap between real GDP and potential GDP.)

in the shaded part of the table show the real interest rate. For example, the blue entry shows that when inflation is 2 percent and real GDP is equal to potential GDP (the percent gap between real GDP and potential GDP is zero), the real interest rate is 2 percent. When inflation rises to 4 percent, the real interest rate rises to 3 percent. Each column of Table 27.1 tells the same story: When inflation rises, the central bank raises the real interest rate. Note that in order to raise the real interest rate, the nominal interest rate has to rise by more than inflation rises.

Now observe in Table 27.1 that the central bank's response also depends on what happens to real GDP. When real GDP rises above potential GDP—and the gap increases—the central bank raises the real interest rate. And when real GDP falls below potential GDP, the central bank lowers the real interest rate.

The monetary policy rule in Table 27.1 is a more accurate description of monetary policy than the rule in Table 24.1 because central banks do react to the gap between real GDP and potential GDP, as the case study of the Fed makes clear. Hence, financial market analysts use monetary policy rules like this one to predict interest rate changes in many different countries.

> The **Taylor Rule,** a form of the monetary policy rule described by Table 27.1, is used by economists to describe the behavior of the Federal Reserve.

REVIEW

- Monetary policy is a constant struggle to keep aggregate demand from getting too high or too low. The Fed carries out this policy by trying to keep the aggregate demand curve in a position where real GDP is equal to potential GDP and the inflation rate is equal to the target inflation rate.

- The Fed and other central banks increase the real interest rate when real GDP grows above potential GDP and lower the real interest rate when real GDP falls below potential GDP.

- In early 2000, the Fed increased the real interest rate because it thought real GDP was greater than potential GDP.

- The response of the real interest rate to the gap between real GDP and potential GDP can be combined with the response to inflation in order to get a monetary policy rule that accurately describes central bank behavior.

Money and Other Instruments of Monetary Policy

> **Look back for a quick review:** Chapter 22, page 585, defines open market operations and shows how the Fed uses them to make changes in the supply of bank reserves. Chapter 24, page 641, shows how the Fed increases or decreases the federal funds rate through such changes in the supply of bank reserves.

So far, we have focused entirely on the Fed's decisions about the interest rate, and in particular about the overnight interest rate called the federal funds rate. Recall from Chapter 24 that the Fed changes the overnight interest rate by increasing or decreasing the supply of bank reserves in the overnight market where the federal funds rate is determined. Recall that the federal funds rate is the interest rate on overnight loans of reserves between banks. The Fed changes the supply of bank reserves by *open market operations*, which, as defined in Chapter 22, are purchases or sales of bonds by the Fed. Purchases of bonds increase the supply of bank reserves and thus lower the overnight interest rate. Sales of bonds decrease the supply of bank reserves and thus raise the overnight interest rate.

The overnight interest rate is now the main instrument of monetary policy at central banks around the world, but it is not the only instrument. The money supply, the discount rate, and reserve requirements are other potential instruments of policy. In this section we examine how the changes in the interest rate have important implications for the amount of money that the Fed supplies. We also define the discount rate and show how it and reserve requirements fit into monetary policy decisions.

Money Demand, the Interest Rate, and the Money Supply

The quantity of money in the economy is closely related to the interest rate decisions of the central bank. To show this, we first look at the demand for money and show that it depends on the nominal interest rate.

money demand: a relationship between the nominal interest rate and the quantity of money that people are willing to hold at any given nominal interest rate.

■ **Money Demand.**   **Money demand** is defined as a relationship between the interest rate and the quantity of money people are willing to hold at any given interest rate. As shown in Figure 27.5, the amount of money demanded is negatively related to the nominal interest rate. One reason people hold money is to carry out transactions: to buy and sell goods and services. People will hold less money if the nominal interest rate is high. That is, a higher interest rate reduces the amount of money people want to carry around in their wallets or hold in their checking accounts. Conversely, a lower nominal interest rate will increase the amount of money people want to hold. Why is money demand negatively related to the nominal interest rate?

Money (currency plus checking deposits) is only part of the wealth of most individuals. People also hold some of their wealth in financial assets that pay interest. For example, some people have time deposits at banks. Others hold securities, such as Treasury bills. If you bought Treasury bills in 2004, they paid 3.5 percent interest. Holding money is different from holding time deposits or Treasury bills because currency does not pay interest and checking deposits pay low, or no, interest. If you hold all your money in the form of cash in your wallet, clearly you do not earn any interest. Thus, an individual's decision to hold money is best viewed as an alternative to holding some other financial asset, such as a Treasury bill. If you hold money, you get little or no interest; if you hold one of the alternatives, you earn interest.

The interest rate on the vertical axis in Figure 27.5 is the average nominal interest rate on these other interest-bearing assets that people hold as alternatives to money. Now, if the interest rate on these alternatives rises, people want to put more funds in the alternatives and hold less as money. If they hold the funds as currency, they get no interest on the funds. If they hold the funds in a checking account, they may get a small amount of interest, but certainly less than they would get from other financial assets. There is a lower quantity of money demanded at higher interest rates because putting the funds in interest-bearing assets becomes more attractive compared to keeping the funds in a wallet.

The interest rate on the alternatives to holding money is the *opportunity cost* of holding money. When the opportunity cost increases, people hold less money. When the opportunity cost decreases, people hold more money.

Figure 27.5 represents money demand in the economy as a whole. The curve is obtained by adding up the money demanded by all the individuals in the economy at each interest rate. The money held by businesses—in cash registers or in checking accounts—should also be added in.

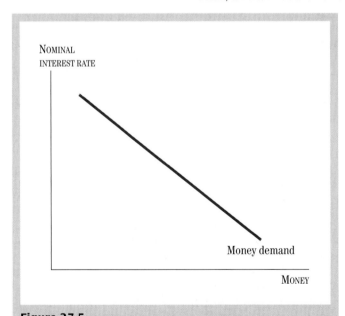

Figure 27.5
The Demand for Money
The interest rate is the opportunity cost of holding money. A higher interest rate on Treasury bills or other interest-bearing assets raises the opportunity cost of holding money and lowers the quantity of money demanded.

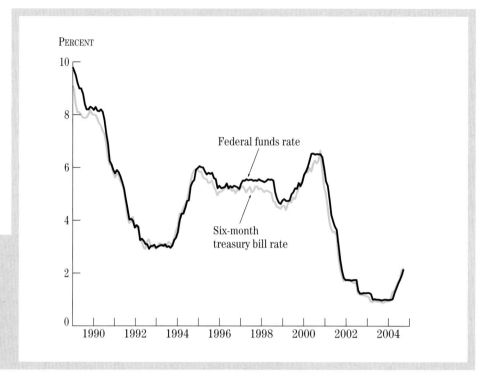

Figure 27.6
Short-Term Interest Rates
The federal funds rate is the interest rate the Fed focuses on when deliberating about policy. Other short-term interest rates, such as the 6-month Treasury bill rate, move up and down with the federal funds rate.

■ **The Interest Rate and the Quantity of Money.** Using the money demand curve, it is possible to find the quantity of money in the economy that will be associated with any given nominal interest rate decision by the Fed. First note that there is a very close correlation between the federal funds rate set by the Fed and interest rates on Treasury bills and other interest-bearing assets that people can hold as an alternative to holding money. This close correlation is shown in Figure 27.6. Thus, when the Fed changes the federal funds rate, other interest rates tend to change in the same direction.

Now, for any given interest rate, one can use the money demand curve to find the quantity of money in the economy. This is illustrated in Figure 27.7. If the Fed lowers the federal funds rate, then the lower interest rate increases the quantity of money demanded and, as shown in the left panel, the quantity of money in the economy rises. Or, if the Fed raises the interest rate, the quantity of money in the economy decreases, as shown in the graph on the right of Figure 27.7.

■ **What About Focusing on the Money Supply?** One question you might ask about Figure 27.7 is, "Where is the money supply?" Recall from Chapter 22 that the Fed controls the quantity of money supplied in the economy. Does the quantity of money supplied equal the quantity of money demanded? Yes, of course it does. The demand and supply of money is no different from any other demand and supply model. As monetary policy now works in the United States and most other countries, the central bank automatically adjusts the money supply so that it intersects the money demand curve at the nominal interest rate chosen by the central bank. For example, as the interest rate falls in the left graph of Figure 27.7, the money supply is automatically increased so that the intersection of money demand and money supply moves as shown. Figure 27.8 shows how the money supply shifts in both cases shown in Figure 27.7.

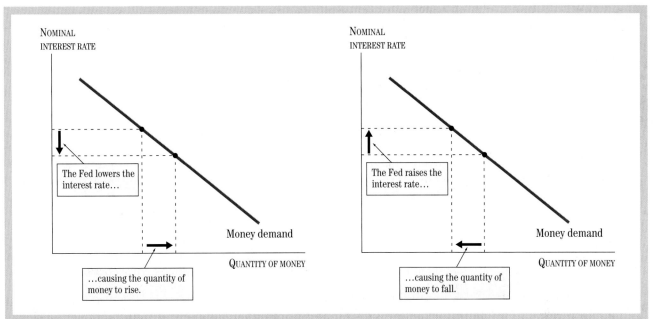

Figure 27.7
When the Fed Changes the Interest Rate, the Quantity of Money Changes

When the Fed lowers the interest rate, people want to hold more money. When the Fed raises the interest rate, people want to hold less money.

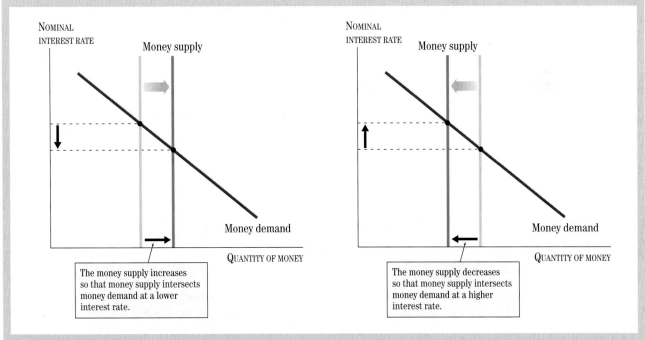

Figure 27.8
Money Supply Changes Implied by Interest Rate Changes

When the Fed decides to lower or raise the interest rate, the money supply must change.

Review: Recall the connection between reserves and the money supply:

Monetary base = currency + reserves

Money supply = $m \times$ (monetary base)

where m is the money multiplier. Thus, when reserves change, so does the monetary base and so does the money supply.

Such movements in the money supply occur as the Fed makes open market purchases or sales to change the interest rate. When the Fed decides to lower the interest rate, for example, it must increase reserves. And we know from Chapter 22 that when the Fed increases reserves, the money supply increases. Thus, the increase in the money supply in the left graph of Figure 27.8 is exactly what the analysis in Chapter 22 tells us will happen when the central bank increases reserves. Whether you focus on the interest rate or the money supply, the story is the same.

Then why doesn't the Fed simply focus on the money supply? Because the money demand curve tends to shift around a lot; if the Fed simply kept the money supply constant, there would be fluctuations in the interest rate as money demand shifted back and forth. These fluctuations in the interest rate would cause fluctuations in real GDP—perhaps large enough to cause a recession—and thus would not be good policy.

Some economists, such as Milton Friedman, have argued that the Fed should simply hold the growth of the money supply constant, a policy that is called a *constant money growth rule*. However, central banks now feel that money demand shifts around too much for a constant money growth rule to work well. Nevertheless, an inflationary monetary policy—such as the gain then pain scenario—would mean that there would be an increase in money growth. Money growth would increase as the Fed lowered the interest rate. As we saw in Chapter 22, throughout history higher money growth has been associated with higher inflation.

Those who object to the constant money growth rule do not object to keeping inflation low. They feel that a constant money growth rule will lead to more and larger fluctuations in real GDP and inflation than other policies would. That is why they recommend that the Fed and other central banks focus more on interest rates.

Two Other Instruments of Monetary Policy

In addition to the federal funds rate and the money supply, two other instruments are sometimes used in conducting monetary policy.

discount rate: the interest rate that the Fed charges commercial banks when they borrow from the Fed.

■ **The Discount Rate.** The **discount rate** is the rate the Fed charges commercial banks when they borrow from the Fed. To understand why commercial banks borrow from the Fed, we must consider another role of central banks: the role of *lender of last resort*. During recessions and depressions in the nineteenth and early twentieth centuries, there were frequently "runs" on banks, in which people scrambled to withdraw their deposits for fear that the bank was going under. Rumors caused runs even on sound banks. By agreeing to lend to banks if they experience a run, the Fed can bolster confidence in the bank. The mere existence of a central bank that is willing to lend reduces the chances of runs by raising confidence. That is why the Fed stands ready to make loans to banks.

However, if the discount rate fell much below the federal funds rate, then banks would save on interest costs by borrowing from the Fed rather than borrowing in the federal funds market. Thus, the Fed must make sure that the discount rate does not depart too much from the federal funds rate. When the Fed changes the federal funds rate, it frequently changes the discount rate as well so that the two rates stay near each other. The federal funds rate is the main focus of monetary decisions. The discount rate is usually adjusted when the federal funds rate changes.

■ **Reserve Requirements.** Another tool of monetary policy is the reserve requirement. If the Fed decreases the required reserve ratio—that is, decreases reserve requirements—then the banks will demand fewer reserves and the federal funds rate will fall.

In practice, however, the Fed very rarely changes reserve requirements, and when it does so, its aim is not to change the federal funds rate, because open market operations are sufficient to achieve any desired change in that rate. Sometimes the Fed changes reserve requirements in order to affect the profits of banks. For example, in 1990, the Fed lowered reserve requirements in order to raise banks' profits and thereby reduce the chance that some banks would become insolvent during the 1990–1991 recession. Banks do not receive interest on reserves; thus, lower reserve requirements mean that they can make more profits by making more interest-earning loans.

In 1990, when the Fed lowered reserve requirements, it used open market sales to reduce the supply of reserves. This action exactly offset the effect of the reserve requirement change on the interest rate.

REVIEW
- The Fed affects the short-term nominal interest rate by changing reserves through open market operations.
- Money demand depends negatively on the nominal interest rate.
- When the Fed changes the interest rate, the quantity of money changes.
- Changes in the quantity of money supplied automatically match these changes. Changes in reserves mean changes in the money supply.
- The Fed also has two other instruments: the discount rate and reserve requirements. But the main instrument of monetary policy is the federal funds rate.

The Exchange Rate and Monetary Policy

Quick review: The *exchange rate* is the rate at which one country's currency is exchanged for another country's currency. For example, one U.S. dollar could be exchanged for 11.15 Mexican pesos on December 31, 2004. An *appreciation* of the dollar—say, from 11.15 to 12.00 pesos—means that it can be exchanged for more pesos.

flexible exchange rate policy: a policy in which exchange rates are determined in foreign exchange markets and governments do not agree to fix them.

fixed exchange rate policy: a policy in which a country maintains a fixed value of its currency in terms of other currencies.

The exchange rate is another important economic variable that is influenced by monetary policy. When the Fed increases the interest rate, the dollar tends to appreciate in value. The reason is that the higher U.S. interest rate makes dollar assets more attractive, and this bids up the price of dollars. Conversely, when the Fed lowers the interest rate, the dollar depreciates.

These changes in the exchange rate affect net exports. For example, an appreciation of the dollar makes imported goods more attractive to Americans and makes U.S. exports less attractive to foreigners. Thus, imports rise and exports fall, causing net exports (exports minus imports) to decline. The decline in net exports in turn causes real GDP to decline. Such changes in exchange rates are an essential part of the impact of monetary policy in the economic fluctuations model explained in Chapters 24 and 25, because the United States follows a **flexible exchange rate policy,** allowing the exchange rate to fluctuate in this way.

But what if the Fed did not want the exchange rate to change? Or what if the U.S. government and another country, such as Japan, agreed to fix the exchange rate? Such a policy is called a **fixed exchange rate policy.** How would that affect monetary policy?

Such questions are not simply hypothetical. Throughout history, governments have decided from time to time to adopt fixed exchange rate policies. The United States and most developed countries were part of a fixed exchange rate system—called the Bretton Woods system—from the end of World War II until the early 1970s.

A Single European Currency and a Single Central Bank
The euro is the single currency used in the European Monetary Union. On January 1, 2002, euro notes and coins came into circulation in twelve European countries, replacing the national currencies of each of the countries, including Germany, where the European Central Bank (shown at right) is located. The seven banknote denominations have a common design in all the countries, while the eight coin denominations have different national designs on one side and a common European design on the other. Ten new member states joined the European Union in May, 2004, and they are expected to introduce the euro into their countries as soon as they have met the conditions set out by the Treaty on European Union.

Most recently, twelve countries in Europe have permanently fixed their exchange rates by forming a monetary union with a single currency, the euro. Until recently, Argentina fixed its exchange rate to the U.S. dollar. Other countries, like Ecuador, have adopted the U.S. dollar as their currency, and some people have suggested that the other countries in the Western hemisphere join in with the United States in a permanently fixed exchange rate system, with countries in Asia joining in a fixed exchange rate system with Japan. There would then be three large fixed exchange rate systems in the world—centered around the dollar, the euro, and the yen. Some have even imagined a whole world with fixed exchange rates—with the dollar, the yen, and the euro all fixed together. Thus, it is important to look at the implications of a fixed exchange rate for monetary policy, as we do in this section, not only to understand what is happening in different countries today, but also to understand proposals that would affect the United States and the whole world in the future.

The Effects of a Fixed Exchange Rate System on Monetary Policy

Suppose the United States decided to set up or join a fixed exchange rate system with Japan. Suppose also that after the United States joins the system, inflation starts to rise in the United States, and monetary policymakers want to raise the interest rate. Such an increase in the interest rate will tend to raise the value of the dollar relative to the Japanese currency. But if the dollar were fixed in value, as it would be with a fixed exchange rate policy, such a rise in the dollar would not be possible. Hence, if exchange rates were fixed, the Fed could not raise the interest rate in the United States relative to the interest rate in Japan. The fixed exchange rate would impose a serious restriction on U.S. monetary policy because interest rates in the United States could not be changed.

In general, if two countries have a fixed exchange rate and people are free to move funds back and forth between the two countries, then the interest rates in the two countries must move together. If, in the example of the United States and Japan, the Fed wanted to raise interest rates, then the Bank of Japan would have to raise interest rates by the same amount. But that might not be in the best interests of Japan, especially if the Japanese economy was in a recession. Like the two steering wheels of a driver's training car, which move in tandem, interest rates in any two countries with a fixed exchange rate must move together.

The connection between interest rates in different countries is very visible to people in smaller countries that fix their currencies to the dollar, as Argentina painfully found out in 2001 and 2002. In 1991, Argentina chose to fix the value of the peso to the dollar, thus forcing its central bank to give up an independent monetary policy. When interest rates in the United States fell in the mid-1990s, this was beneficial to Argentina, as its interest rates fell as well. However, when U.S. rates rose very rapidly in the year 2000 as the Fed battled inflation, Argentina was forced to raise its interest rates as well, pushing the weakened economy into a recession that lasted almost four years.

Ever since the twelve countries in the European Monetary Union permanently fixed their exchange rates with each other, there has effectively been only one overnight interest rate in Europe. The central banks of Germany, France, Italy, Spain, and other countries in the European Monetary Union have had to band together into a new European Central Bank. The overnight interest rates in France, Germany, Italy, and the other countries move together, so there is really only one interest rate to decide about. With the European Monetary Union, there cannot be separate monetary policies in Germany and in France. They have only one monetary policy. If real GDP fell below potential GDP in France and remained equal to potential GDP in all the other countries, then a reduction in the interest rate by the European Central Bank, which would be right for France, would be wrong for Europe as a whole, so it probably would not occur. In such a circumstance it might be necessary to use countercyclical *fiscal* policy in France—spending increases or tax cuts, as described in the previous chapter—because monetary policy would not be changed.

A real-life example of the effect of fixed exchange rates on monetary policy arose in Britain in 1992. At that time, interest rates were rising in Germany because the German inflation rate was rising. But policymakers in Britain, which was facing hard economic times, did not want British interest rates to rise. The British faced a decision: Either they could raise their interest rates to keep them near Germany's, or they could let their interest rates fall below Germany's. In the latter case, their exchange rate would depreciate. For much of 1991 and 1992, the British kept their exchange rate stable, and that required a rise in British interest rates. But by the end of 1992, increasingly poor economic conditions in Britain forced the British to give up the fixed exchange rate. Then interest rates in Britain could fall.

Interventions in the Exchange Market

exchange market intervention: purchases and sales of foreign currency by a government in exchange markets with the intention to affect the exchange rate.

Why wasn't it possible for the British government to go into the exchange market and buy and sell foreign exchange and thereby prevent these changes in the exchange rate? For example, if the British government purchases British pounds, this increases the demand for pounds and thereby raises the pound exchange rate. Thus, if the high interest rates in Germany were reducing the value of the British pound, why couldn't the British government buy pounds to offset these pressures? Such buying and selling of foreign currency by governments is called **exchange market intervention.** Such intervention does occur, and it can affect the exchange rate for short periods of time. However, the world currency

In December of 2001, Argentina abandoned the rigid fixed exchange rate system that had pegged the value of the Argentinean peso at a 1-to-1 rate with the U.S. dollar. This decision came in the face of a deepening recession that threatened to reverse years of economic progress made by Argentina in the 1990s. This article, taken from the *Economist* of December 20, 2001, describes the dire straits of the Argentinean economy.

When reading the article, you should think about how the increase in U.S. interest rates in 2000 would affect Argentina's economy. Without the fixed exchange rate, would Argentina have chosen to raise interest rates when the economy was contracting by 11 percent and unemployment was as high as 20 percent? Did the government make the right decision when it dismantled the currency board about a week later, and eventually let the peso's value fluctuate freely?

Patience Wears Thin

Dec 20th 2001 | BUENOS AIRES
From the *Economist* print edition

In 1989, Raul Alfonsin was forced to step down as Argentina's president when mobs began to loot supermarkets amid hyperinflationary chaos. That event is burnt into the country's political memory. So it looked like a grim augury for Fernando de la Rua, the current president who, like Mr Alfonsin, is a member of the Radical party, when looters attacked supermarkets in several cities recently to obtain food. A one-day general strike on December 13th attracted more support than had seven previous stoppages during Mr de la Rua's term. After 42 months of recession, the patience of some Argentines has snapped.

Since July, Argentina's economy has contracted at an annual rate of 11%, according to Miguel Angel Broda, a local economic consultant. The latest official survey says that in October unemployment exceeded 18% (it is now probably 20%). And that was before the government this month imposed limits on cash withdrawals from banks, which have hit retail sales and the informal economy hard.

The looting is still isolated. But it comes as Mr de la Rua and Domingo Cavallo, his economy minister, try to persuade Congress, dominated by the opposition Peronists, to approve a stern budget, aimed at restoring $2.7 billion in loans suspended by the IMF and other multilateral bodies. Those loans

Argentina's economic woes

are the government's last hope of avoiding a unilateral debt default and the collapse of the currency board which pegs the peso at par to the dollar.

Though much-delayed, the budget is still vague on details. It includes no estimate for economic growth, but does recognise that tax revenues will fall (by 3.8%). To reach the government's balanced-budget target, spending is to fall by $9.2 billion, or almost a fifth, compared with this year. Mr Cavallo claims that $5 billion will be saved in lower interest payments as a result of debt restructuring. Some $3 billion will be saved by maintaining for a full year the cuts in provincial finances and in public-sector salaries introduced in August.

The potential benefits of getting new loans and exercising fiscal restraint

markets are so huge and fast-moving that even governments do not have the funds to affect the exchange rate for long by buying and selling foreign exchange.

If there is a substantial interest rate advantage in favor of one currency, funds will flow into that currency, driving up its value; exchange market intervention by governments cannot do much about this. Empirical studies have shown that exchange market intervention—if it is not matched by a change in interest rates by the central bank—can have only small effects on the exchange rate.

Another possibility is to prevent funds from flowing between the countries. If there were a law restricting the flow of funds into and out of a country, then that country could have both a fixed exchange rate and a separate interest rate policy.

Such controls on the flow of capital were discussed intensely after the collapse of fixed exchange rates in Asia in 1997, and Malaysia did institute some restrictions on financial capital flows. However, such restrictions have disadvantages. They are difficult to enforce and can reduce the amount of foreign capital a country needs for development.

Why Fixed Exchange Rates?

If fixed exchange rates lead to the loss of a separate monetary policy, then why do countries form fixed exchange rate systems? One reason to adopt a fixed exchange rate is that exchange rate volatility can interfere with trade. This is certainly one of the reasons the European countries set up the European Monetary Union. Firms may not develop long-term relationships and contacts with other countries if they are worried about big changes in the exchange rate.

Another, perhaps more important, reason is that some countries have had a history of very poor monetary policies. For example, Italy had very high inflation before it decided to join with the other countries of Europe in a monetary union. And Argentina had many years of hyperinflation before it fixed its exchange rate with the United States and gave up having its own monetary policy.

The goal of fixing the exchange rate in these cases is to adopt the good monetary policy of a country whose central bank has a history of good policy: the Fed in the case of Argentina, and the central banks of Germany and France in the case of Italy. In these cases, the benefits of a fixed exchange rate system may outweigh the loss of a separate monetary policy. However, the evidence is mixed. In the case of Italy, the policy seems to have worked: Inflation has been in single digits for many years. However, in Argentina, where the policy seemed to work well initially in bringing inflation down, restricting the hand of monetary policymakers seemed to make it very tough for the country to recover from its recession of the late 1990s.

REVIEW
- Interest rates must move together in countries with fixed exchange rates and with a free flow of funds between the countries.

- With a fixed exchange rate, there can be no separate monetary policy for each country.

- By permanently fixing exchange rates, a country can adopt the monetary policy of another country.

Conclusion

Monetary policymaking is a powerful, but difficult, job. Central bankers like to say that the job is like driving a car by looking only through the rear-view mirror. They have to take actions that greatly affect the economy without knowing where the economy is going, only where it has been.

In this chapter, we have seen exactly why the job is difficult. It is difficult to resist political pressure to raise inflation for short-term benefits at the expense of long-term costs. And it is difficult to keep aggregate demand in line with potential GDP in a world where potential GDP is hard to estimate and policy effects on aggregate demand are uncertain.

We have also learned that while monetary policy has a powerful effect, it cannot do everything. It cannot lower unemployment permanently, and trying to do so will only raise inflation. And a country cannot have both a fixed exchange rate and the ability to adjust interest rates to control inflation and prevent recessions.

All these ideas are useful for understanding the frequent headlines and news stories about the Fed. And they help take some of the mystique out of what many people feel is the most mysterious institution in the world.

KEY POINTS

1. Central bank independence is a way to avoid political business cycles and the temptation to raise inflation for short-term gain.

2. The gain then pain scenario illustrates that a monetary policy shift to high inflation has short-run benefits but long-run costs.

3. An important task of monetary policy is to manage aggregate demand so that real GDP equals potential GDP.

4. In early 2000, the Fed raised the real interest rate to reduce aggregate demand. In 2001 and 2002, it lowered the real interest rate to increase aggregate demand in the midst of a recession.

5. A good monetary policy rule is responsive to real GDP as well as to inflation.

6. The demand for money is negatively related to the interest rate.

7. The Fed changes the quantity of money when it changes the interest rate.

8. Reserve requirements are rarely changed.

9. Fixed exchange rates restrict monetary policy.

KEY TERMS

central bank independence
political business cycle
time inconsistency

money demand
discount rate

flexible exchange rate policy
fixed exchange rate policy

exchange market
intervention

QUESTIONS FOR REVIEW

1. What are the advantages and disadvantages of central bank independence?

2. What is an example of a political business cycle?

3. Why would the Fed raise real interest rates if real GDP were above potential GDP?

4. Why is it important that real GDP be close to potential GDP?

5. What is the Phillips curve?

6. Why is the demand for money inversely related to the interest rate?

7. What is the opportunity cost of holding money?

8. Why is there a loss of monetary policy independence with fixed exchange rates?

9. Why would a country adopt a fixed exchange rate policy?

PROBLEMS

1. In recommending central banking reforms for Eastern European economies, the *Economic Report of the President, 1990*, p. 202, asserted, "It is widely agreed that the central bank should have a high degree of independence from the central government so that it can resist political pressures." Explain the reasoning behind this assertion. What are some counterarguments?

2. The original Federal Reserve Act of 1913 allowed the secretary of the Treasury to be a member of the Federal Reserve Board, but a later amendment prohibited this. How would allowing the secretary of the Treasury to be a member affect the conduct of monetary policy?

3. Suppose the Fed wants to raise the federal funds rate. Describe in detail how it accomplishes this policy. What happens to the quantity of money?

4. What is the discount rate? How does it differ from the federal funds rate? Describe how the Fed affects each of these interest rates.

5. Suppose there is an increase in money demand at every interest rate. Show this in a diagram. What effect will this have on the interest rate if the Fed does not increase the money supply?

6. Suppose there are two countries, identical except for the fact that the central bank of one country lets interest

rates rise sharply when real GDP rises above potential GDP and the other does not. Draw the aggregate demand curve for each country. What are the benefits and drawbacks of each country's policy?

7. During the early 1990s in Japan, there was deflation and real GDP was below potential GDP.
   a. Draw a diagram showing the situation in which there is deflation at potential GDP.
   b. Suppose the Japanese central bank decides that it must reinflate and sets a target inflation rate of 2 percent. How does it accomplish this? Show the short-, medium-, and long-run effects.
   c. Is it possible that the central bank can have a fully credible reinflation? What are the benefits of immediate increases in the inflation rate?

8. Using the aggregate demand curve and the inflation adjustment line, show what the Fed should do if real GDP is below potential GDP and inflation is equal to the target inflation rate.

9. Real GDP, consumption, and investment in the United States all declined from 1990 to 1991 and increased in 1992.
   a. Using an aggregate demand curve and an inflation adjustment line, show how a change in monetary policy in 1991 could explain these developments.
   b. Net exports increased from 1990 to 1991. Is the explanation in part (a) consistent with this development? If not, what other factors may have explained the behavior of net exports?

10. Sweden and the United Kingdom did not join the European Monetary Union (EMU) at the start. Explain why the central banks of these two countries would no longer be able to make separate interest rate decisions if they joined the EMU.

11. Explain why restricting flows of funds into or out of a country can give that country's central bank the ability to conduct monetary policy even with a fixed exchange rate. What are some of the disadvantages of such a restriction?

The Issue:
(How) Should Social Security Be Reformed?

In the first press conference that George W. Bush held after being reelected to office in November of 2004, the president outlined his agenda for the next four years. One of the key issues he mentioned was social security, saying, "We must show our leadership by strengthening Social Security for our children and our grandchildren. This is more than a problem to be solved; it is an opportunity to help millions of our fellow citizens find security and independence that comes from owning something, from ownership." This quote highlights the two most important issues in the current debate about the future of social security: the financial health of the social security system, and the possibility of changing social security from its current form to incorporate individually owned investment accounts.

A thorough description of the current social security system can be found at the Social Security Administration.[1] Several core features from that description are included here:

- An estimated 159 million workers, 96 percent of all workers, are covered under social security. More than 90 percent of individuals 65 years of age and above receive social security retirement benefits.
- Social security is a pay-as-you-go system; the payroll taxes paid by employers and employees are used to fund social security benefit payments to eligible retirees, disabled workers, survivors of deceased workers, and dependents of beneficiaries. Workers pay 6.2 percent of wage income in payroll taxes, with their employers contributing another 6.2 percent. Payroll taxes are assessed up to a certain income limit; in 2005 that limit was $90,000.
- Social security benefits are calculated using a benefits formula. In general, individuals who have 10 years of payroll tax contributions can start drawing benefits.
- Individuals can collect full retirement benefits when they are between 65 and 67 years of age, depending on their birth year. Social security retirement benefits represent 39 percent of the income of the elderly. The average benefit in 2005 was $955 per month for an individual and $1,574 per month for a couple.

Social security has been famously described as the "third rail of American politics." But since President Bush's November 2004 press conference, an extended

---

[1] A concise description of social security benefits can be found on the Social Security Administration web site at http://www.ssa.gov/pubs/10024.html.

---

public debate about it has taken place. Much of this debate has centered on the issues of solvency and individual investment accounts. However, by the time Congress adjourned for the summer in 2005, there was still no specific Social Security reform plan being discussed. A CNN/*USA Today*/Gallup poll on May 1, 2005, found that more than 81 percent of the respondents believed that substantial changes to social security were needed, but there seemed to be significant disagreement on what changes should be made. Only 35 percent approved of the president's approach to reforming social security, 27 percent said that a plan favored by most Republicans would be better, and 22 percent favored a plan supported by most Democrats. Almost half the respondents said that they would be better off if Congress did not come up with a plan. The third rail seemed to be live again!

As a student taking Principles of Economics, you are more than capable of following this debate. In the absence of a specific congressional plan, we turn to two of the leading social security reform plans proposed by economists. The plan by Martin Feldstein proposes substantial changes to the existing system, especially in the area of introducing individual investment accounts. The plan by Peter Diamond and Peter Orszag preserves many of the core features of the existing system and does not include individual investment accounts.

Individual Investment Accounts and Social Security Reform Are Synonymous

POINT

Martin Feldstein presents a social security reform plan that involves moving from a pure pay-as-you-go system to what he describes as a "mixed system," one that combines the defined benefits of the existing system with individual investment accounts. Feldstein argues that social security has offered an unsustainably high rate of return for previous generations of retirees, and as a result, current and future generations will receive very low rates of return. A person joining the labor force today can expect to earn a return of 2.5 percent or less per year on every dollar that he or she contributes to social security. This rate of return will only get worse as time passes because the solvency problems of the social security system will force the government to increase taxes further or cut benefits in the future. Therefore, Feldstein advocates a transition to a mixed system, in which a portion of individual payroll taxes will be diverted to investment accounts, while the remainder is used to fund the traditional social security system. At retirement, the worker will collect a traditional social security benefit, in addition to being able to draw income from the assets accumulated in the individual account. Using historical rates of return from stock and bond investments, Feldstein calculates a real rate of return of 6.9 percent, which is substantially higher than the implicit rate of return from social security. If this higher return is realized, individuals will enjoy benefits equal to well over 120 percent of current benefits.

Under Feldstein's plan, even though diverting payroll taxes to individual accounts will reduce government saving, it will raise private saving and hence will leave national saving unchanged.

COUNTERPOINT Social Security Needs Only Modest Reforms. There Is No Need for Individual Investment Accounts

Peter Diamond of MIT and Peter Orszag of the Brookings Institution have proposed a plan that tries to fix the long-term fiscal health of social security by making "modest adjustments" to the present system.[2] Diamond and Orszag agree that social security has a long-term financing deficit that needs to be closed. Eliminating this financing deficit will require either that guaranteed benefits be cut or that payroll taxes be raised, whether or not individual investment accounts are added. Diamond and Orszag point out, however, that this gap is equivalent to about 0.7 percent of GDP over the next 75 years, so they recommend only a combination of modest benefit reductions and tax increases to restore solvency. Key elements of their argument are summarized here:

• Since social security was first introduced, life expectancy at age 65 has increased by four years for men and five years for women. Longer lives mean more years of collecting social security benefits, which in turn adds to the long-term financial solvency pressures. Diamond and Orszag suggest obtaining an actuarial calculation of the cost to social security from the increased life expectancy, and then splitting that cost 50/50 in the form of lower benefits and higher taxes for workers younger than 60 years. This would eliminate almost a third of the existing 75-year deficit.

• Over the past two decades, the incomes of high earners have increased rapidly, resulting in more than 15 percent of all earnings being above the $90,000 limit on which social security taxes are assessed. Diamond and Orszag propose gradually raising this limit at a rate fast enough to leave only 13 percent of earnings untaxed by 2063. In other words, they would ask 6 percent of high-earning workers to pay payroll taxes on a greater percentage of their income.

• Past (and current) generations of social security recipients all received more than they paid in to the system, what Orszag and Diamond term the legacy debt.[3] The legacy debt needs to be paid off in order to make the system financially viable.

Diamond and Orszag lay out the implications of their plans for people in various age groups. Workers who are older than 55 will see no changes in benefits. Workers in younger cohorts will see larger changes, with the youngest workers seeing the largest fall in benefits (9 percent for a 25-year-old). The payroll tax will rise from 12.4 percent today to 13.2 percent in 2035 and 15.4 percent in 2078. Their plan does not allow for individual investment accounts. One of their major concerns here is that the success of individual investment accounts depends on the ability of individuals to make smart investment decisions, taking risk into account. Inexperienced investors may end up with nondiversified portfolios, incur high costs by switching into and out of various investments, and end up with far less money in their investment accounts than more experienced investors. Those inexperienced investors may be the ones who are most reliant on social security. The bottom line, according to Diamond and Orszag, is that individual investment accounts like IRAs and 401(k)s are a good idea when treated as a complement to social security. They do not belong within the social security system.

Using Your Economics

1. In what areas do you think the Feldstein plan is stronger or weaker than the Diamond/Orszag plan?

2. Diamond and Orszag are concerned about the risks associated with individual investment accounts, particularly if there is a crash in the financial markets. Under the Feldstein plan, should the government promise to help out individuals if such a crash should occur? Explain your answer.

2 Peter Diamond and Peter Orszag, *Saving Social Security,* The Brookings Institution, 2004. For a synopsis, see Peter Diamond and Peter Orszag, "Saving Social Security," *The Economists' Voice* 2(1), 2005. Available online at http://www.brookings.edu/views/papers/orszag/200504security.pdf.

3 This is primarily a result of the pay-as-you-go feature of social security and the demographics of the baby-boom generation, which led to there being more workers than retirees.

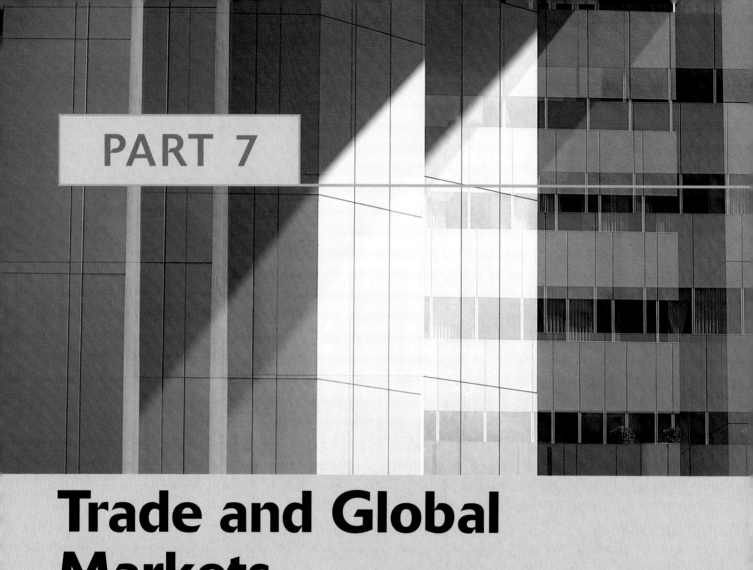

PART 7

Trade and Global Markets

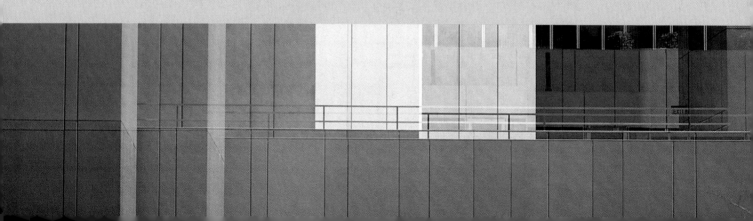

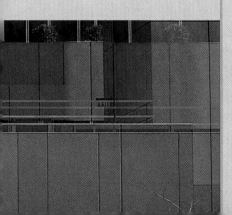

CHAPTER 28

Economic Growth Around the World

Half a million foreign students are now studying in colleges and universities in the United States. Maybe you know some of these students. Maybe you *are* one of these students. There are also about half a million foreign students studying in Germany, France, Japan, and other countries. Many of those foreign students are Americans. Studying abroad is one of the ways in which technical knowledge is spread around the world. Thanks to improvements in telecommunications, including the Internet, the ability to spread information is increasing rapidly.

This highly visible diffusion of information raises some fundamental questions about economic theory, especially about economic growth theory. While economic growth theory tells us how technology and capital have provided people with the means to raise their productivity, there is something disquieting about the theory when we look around the world. As we compare living standards, it is clear that people in some countries are much better off than people in other countries. Why has the theory applied so unevenly to different countries around the world, with some growing rapidly and some stuck in poverty, not growing at all? Why hasn't the spread of technological information allowed poor countries to grow faster?

In this chapter, we look for answers to these crucial questions about the uneven patterns of economic growth in different countries. We begin our quest for the answers by looking at economic growth performance in different parts of the world.

Catching Up or Not?

If technological advances can spread easily, as seems reasonable with modern communications, then poorer regions with low productivity and low income per capita will tend to catch up to richer regions by growing more rapidly. Why? If the spread of new technology is not difficult, then regions with lower productivity can adopt the more advanced technology of other regions to raise their productivity. Recall from the **growth accounting formula** that an increase in the growth of technology leads to an increase in productivity growth.

Investment in new capital would also tend to cause poor regions to catch up to the rich. Consider a relatively poor region in which both capital per worker and output per worker are low. Imagine several hundred workers constructing a road with only a little capital—perhaps only a few picks and shovels, not even a jackhammer. With such low levels of capital, the returns to increasing the amount of capital would be very high. The addition of a few trucks and some earthmoving equipment to the construction project would bring huge returns in higher output. Regions with relatively low levels of capital per worker would therefore attract a greater amount of investment, and capital would grow rapidly. The growth accounting formula tells us that productivity grows rapidly when capital per worker grows rapidly. Thus, productivity would grow rapidly in poorer regions where capital per worker is low.

A rich region where the capital per worker is high, however, would gain relatively little from additional capital. Such a region would attract little investment, and the growth rate of capital would be lower; therefore, the growth of productivity would also be lower.

In summary, economic growth theory predicts that regions with low productivity will grow relatively more rapidly than regions with high productivity. Regions with low productivity will tend to catch up to the more advanced regions by adopting existing technology and attracting capital.

Figure 28.1 illustrates this catch-up phenomenon. It shows the level of productivity on the horizontal axis and the growth rate of productivity on the vertical axis. The downward-sloping line is the **catch-up line.** A country or region on the upper left-hand part of the line is poor—with low productivity and, therefore, low income per capita—but growing rapidly. A country on the lower right-hand part of the line is rich—with high productivity and, therefore, high income per capita—but growth is relatively less rapid. That the catch-up line exists and is downward-sloping is a prediction of growth theory.

Catch-up Within the United States

Let us first see how the catch-up line works when the regions are the states within the United States. Figure 28.2 presents the data on real income per capita and the growth rate of real income per capita for each of the states. Because productivity and real income per capita move closely together, we can examine the accuracy of the catch-up line using the real income per capita data. (Again, the adjective *real* means that the income data are adjusted for inflation.) Real income per capita in 1880 is on the horizontal axis, and the growth rate of real income per capita from 1880 to 1980 is on the vertical axis. Each point on the scatter diagram represents a state, and a few of the states are labeled. If you pick a state (observe Nevada, for example, down and to the right), you can read its growth rate by looking over to the left scale, and you can read its 1880 income per capita level by looking down to the horizontal scale.

The diagram clearly shows a tendency for states with low real income per capita in 1880 to have had high growth rates since then. The state observations fall

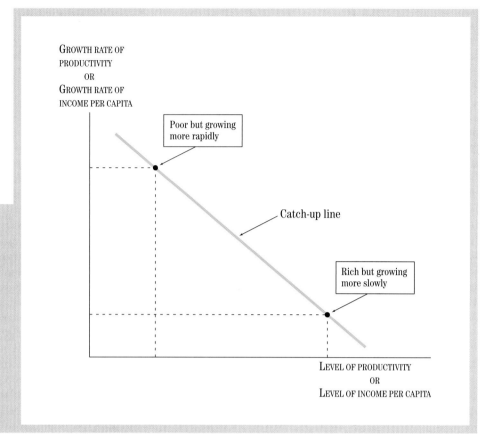

Figure 28.1
The Catch-up Line
Growth theory with spreading technology and diminishing returns to capital and labor predicts that regions with lower productivity will have higher growth rates of productivity. The catch-up line illustrates this prediction. Because productivity is so closely related to income per capita, the catch-up line can also describe a relationship between income per capita and the growth rate of income per capita.

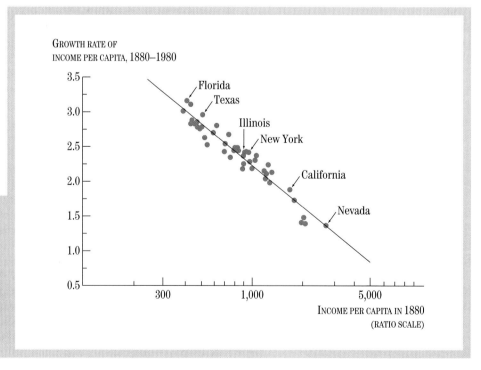

Figure 28.2
Evidence of Catch-up Within the United States
In the United States, those states that had low real income per capita in 1880 grew relatively rapidly compared to states that had high income per capita. The poor states tended to catch up to the richer states. A catch-up line is drawn through the dots.

remarkably near a catch-up line. Southern states like Florida and Texas are in the high-growth group. On the other hand, in states that had a relatively high income per capita in 1880, income per capita grew relatively slowly. This group includes California and Nevada.

Thus, the theory of growth works quite well in explaining the relative differences in growth rates in the states of the United States. There is a tendency for relatively poor regions to grow more rapidly than relatively rich regions.

Catch-up in the Advanced Countries

What if we apply the same thinking to different countries? After all, communication is now global. Figure 28.3 is another scatter diagram with growth rate and income per capita combinations. It is like Figure 28.2 except that it plots real GDP per capita in 1960 against growth in real GDP per capita from 1960 to 2000 for several advanced countries.

Observe in Figure 28.3 that the richer countries, such as Switzerland, grew less rapidly. In contrast, relatively less rich countries, such as Japan, Ireland, and Spain, grew more rapidly. Canada and France are somewhere in between. These countries tend to display the catch-up behavior predicted by the growth theory. Apparently, technological advances are spreading and capital-labor ratios are rising more rapidly in countries where they are low and returns to capital are high. So far, our look at the evidence confirms the predictions of growth theory.

Catch-up in the Whole World

However, so far we have not looked beyond the most advanced countries. Figure 28.4 shows a broader group of countries that includes not only the more advanced countries in Figure 28.3 but also countries that are still developing. It is apparent

Figure 28.3
Evidence of Catch-up in More Advanced Countries, 1960–2000
For the advanced countries shown in the diagram, GDP per capita growth has been more rapid for those that started from a lower level of GDP per capita. Thus, there has been catching up, as shown by the catch-up line drawn through the points.

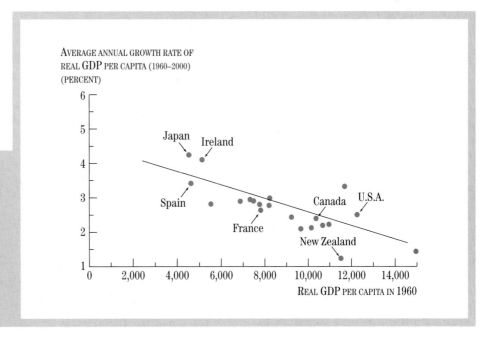

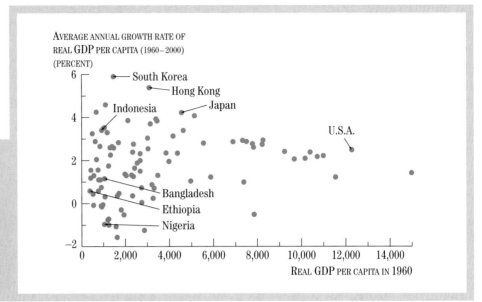

AVERAGE ANNUAL GROWTH RATE OF
REAL GDP PER CAPITA (1960–2000)
(PERCENT)

REAL GDP PER CAPITA IN 1960

Figure 28.4
Lack of Catch-up for Developing Countries, 1960–2000
Unlike the states in the United States or the advanced countries, there has been little tendency for poor countries to grow more rapidly than rich countries. The gap between rich and poor has not closed.

that there is little tendency for this larger group of countries to fall along a catch-up line.

The countries with very low growth rates, such as Bangladesh and Ethiopia, are also the countries with very low GDP per capita. On the other hand, many countries with higher growth rates had a much higher GDP per capita. Japan and Hong Kong had higher growth rates than Nigeria and Ethiopia even though their GDP per capita was above that of these countries.

Comparing countries like Indonesia and South Korea with countries like Bangladesh and Nigeria is striking. South Korea and Indonesia had about the same real GDP per capita as Nigeria and Bangladesh in 1960, but South Korea and Indonesia surged ahead with a more rapid growth rate over the next 30 years, leaving Bangladesh and Nigeria behind. And this is not the exception. Contrary to the predictions of the economic growth theory, which says that technological advances should spread and capital per hour of work should rise from low levels, Figure 28.4 shows little tendency for relatively poor countries to grow relatively rapidly. It appears that something has been preventing either the spread and the adoption of new technology or the increase in investment needed to raise capital-labor ratios. We examine possible explanations as this chapter proceeds.

REVIEW

- Economic growth theory predicts that poorer regions will tend to catch up to richer ones. The flow of technology around the world and investment in new capital will bring this about.

- Data for the states in the United States and for the more advanced countries show that such catch-up exists and is quite strong.

- However, there has been little evidence of catch-up in the world as a whole. Many of the poor countries have fallen even further behind the developed countries, while other poor countries, in particular those in East Asia, have grown very rapidly.

Economic Development

As well as raising questions about economic growth theory, the lack of catch-up evidenced in Figure 28.4 presents a disturbing situation. There are huge disparities in world income distribution, and billions of people in low-income countries lack the necessities that those in high-income countries frequently take for granted.

Billions Still in Poverty

The richest countries in the world, with more than $10,000 income per capita, account for about 850 million people. The United States, with 300 million people, is among the richest, along with Japan and most of Western Europe. Another 650 million people live in countries that have an income per capita between $5,000 and $10,000. But the vast majority of the world's people—about 70 percent—live in countries with an income per capita of less than $5,000 per year. This is below the poverty level in advanced countries. Income per capita in Argentina, Venezuela, and Malaysia is only about one-third that in the United States. In China and Peru, income per capita is only one-eighth that in the United States. Income per capita for Ethiopia is a mere 2 percent of that in the United States.

Low income per capita is a serious economic problem, but the implications go well beyond economics. Large differences in income per capita and vast amounts of poverty can lead to war, revolution, or regional conflicts. Will these differences persist? Or is the lack of catch-up that has left so many behind a thing of the past?

Geographical Patterns

Figure 28.5 shows the location of the relatively rich and the relatively poor countries around the world. Notice that the higher-income countries tend to be in the northern part of the world. An exception to this rule is the relatively high income per capita in Australia and New Zealand. Aside from these exceptions, income disparity appears to have a geographical pattern—the North is relatively rich and the South relatively poor. Often people use the term *North-South problem* to describe world income disparities.

But whether it is North versus South or not, there do appear to be large contiguous regions where many rich or many poor countries are located together. The original increase in economic growth that occurred at the time of the Industrial Revolution started in northwestern Europe—England, France, and Germany. It then spread to America, which industrialized rapidly in the nineteenth and twentieth centuries. It also spread to Japan during the late-nineteenth-century Meiji Restoration, one of the main purposes of which was to import Western technology into the Japanese economy.

Terminology of Economic Development

economic development: the process of growth by which countries raise incomes per capita and become industrialized; also refers to the branch of economics that studies this process.

developing country: a country that is poor by world standards in terms of real GDP per capita.

Economic development is the branch of economics that endeavors to explain why poor countries do not develop faster and to find policies to help them develop faster. Economists who specialize in economic development frequently are experts on the problems experienced by particular countries—such as a poor educational system, political repression, droughts, or poor distribution of food. The term **developing country** describes those countries that are relatively poor. In contrast, the term *industrialized country* or *advanced economy* describes relatively well-off countries.

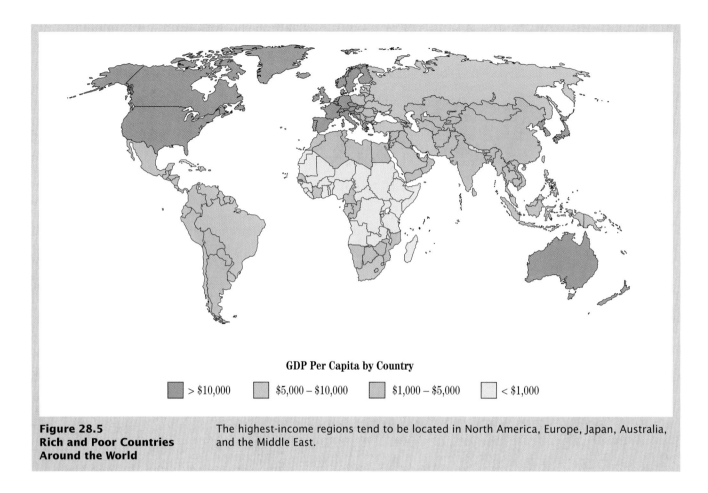

GDP Per Capita by Country

■ > $10,000	■ $5,000 – $10,000	■ $1,000 – $5,000	□ < $1,000

**Figure 28.5
Rich and Poor Countries
Around the World**

The highest-income regions tend to be located in North America, Europe, Japan, Australia, and the Middle East.

Sometimes the term *less-developed country (LDC)* is used rather than *developing country*. There are also terms to distinguish between different developing countries. *Newly industrialized countries* such as Chile and Malaysia are relatively poor countries that are growing rapidly. *Countries in transition* are relatively poor countries, such as Russia and Poland, that are moving from central planning to market economies.

Table 28.1 shows the shares of world GDP produced by advanced economies, developing countries, and countries in transition. Thus, this table looks at aggregate income (which equals GDP) rather than at income per capita. Over 50 percent of world GDP comes from industrialized countries.

Most striking is the nearly 24 percent share of world GDP in Asia outside of Japan. This large share is due to the newly industrialized countries and to China. China's GDP is already almost twice as large as Japan's. Although income per capita is less, China is a major force in the world economy.

Economic development economists working at universities, the World Bank, the International Monetary Fund, the United Nations, and of course in the developing countries themselves focus their research on reasons why poor countries have grown so slowly. We now proceed to examine these reasons; in doing so, we will touch on some of the central issues of economic development. Our examination will consider the two key determinants of increasing productivity—improvements in technology and higher capital per worker. We consider technology in the next section and then go on to consider capital in the following section.

Table 28.1
Shares of World GDP Produced by Different Countries

	Number of Countries	Percent of World GDP
Advanced Economies	**29**	**55.5**
Major industrialized countries	7	43.9
United States		21.1
Japan		7.0
Germany		4.5
France		3.2
Italy		3.0
United Kingdom		3.2
Canada		1.9
Other advanced economies	22	11.6
Developing Countries	**125**	**37.5**
By region		
Africa	51	3.2
Asia	25	23.9
Middle East and Europe	16	2.8
Western Hemisphere	33	7.6
Countries in Transition	**28**	**7.0**
Central and Eastern Europe	16	3.3
Russia	1	2.6
Transcaucas and Central Asia	11	1.1

Source: From *World Economic Outlook*, September 2004, p. 197. Reprinted by permission of International Monetary Fund.

REVIEW

- The slow productivity growth in poor countries has resulted in extreme income inequality around the world. The growth miracle has spread to parts of the world, but productivity in many developing countries of the world has remained low.

- With a few exceptions, most of the rich countries are in the northern regions of the globe and most of the poor countries are in the southern regions, thus giving rise to the term *North-South problem*.

- About 70 percent of the world's population lives in countries with less than $5,000 income per capita.

Spreading and Using Technology

There are two important facts to remember about economic growth. First, a large and persistent increase in economic growth began during the Industrial Revolution about 200 years ago, and this increase in economic growth raised income per capita in some countries to levels experienced only by royalty throughout most of human history. Second, economic growth did not spread throughout much of the world, leaving people in many countries hardly better off than their ancestors. Could these two facts be linked? Could they have the same explanation? A number of ideas have been put forth to explain the increase in economic growth in the late 1700s, and some of these may help explain why growth has not accelerated in many developing countries.

Empowering Entrepreneurs

Some economists and historians have pointed to developments in science as the explanation of the rapid increase in economic growth in Europe in the 1700s. But if that is the explanation, why did the Industrial Revolution not begin in China or in the Islamic nations, where scientific knowledge was far more advanced than in Europe? Others note the importance of natural resources, but these were available in many other countries where there was no Industrial Revolution; also, growth in Japan has been high since the mid-nineteenth century, yet Japan has almost no natural resources. Still others have focused on exploitation, slavery, colonialism, and imperialism, but these evils existed long before the Industrial Revolution.

What, then, is the reason for this increase in economic growth that we associate with the Industrial Revolution? Historians of capitalist development from Karl Marx onward have stressed that in the 1700s, for the first time in human history, entrepreneurs were gaining the freedom to start business enterprises. Economic historian Angus Maddison shows in an influential book, *Phases of Capitalist Development*, that the Dutch were the first to lead in productivity, with the British and then the United States soon catching up. He also shows that in the 1700s, many Dutch farmers owned their land, the feudal nobility was small and weak, and the potential power was in the hands of entrepreneurs. Hence there was greater freedom to produce and sell manufactured and agricultural products. By the late 1700s and early 1800s, similar conditions existed in the United Kingdom and the United States. Firms could ship their products to market and hire workers without political restrictions.

Moreover, these firms were able to earn as much as they could by selling whatever they wanted at whatever price the market determined. They began to invent and develop products that were most beneficial to individuals. The business enterprises could keep the profits. Profits were no longer confiscated by nobles or kings. Individual property rights—including the right to earn and keep profits—were being established and recognized in the courts.

Karl Marx—although known more for his critique of capitalism—saw earlier than others that the unleashing of business enterprises and entrepreneurs was the key to economic growth. He credited the business and entrepreneurial class—what he called the bourgeois class—with the creation of more wealth than had previously been created in all of history.

In sum, the sudden increase in technology and productivity may have occurred when it did because of the increased freedom that entrepreneurs had to start businesses, to invent and apply new ideas, and to develop products for the mass of humanity where the large markets existed.

This knitting cooperative in Ecuador opens up a market for women who traditionally knitted at home for their families. The freedom to start businesses and to produce and sell manufactured products without restriction is a critical piece of the economic growth puzzle for many developing countries.

Remaining Problems in Developing Countries

If true, the idea that the economic growth surge in the late 1700s and 1800s was caused by the removal of restrictions on business enterprises may have lessons for economic development. In many developing countries, there are restrictions on entrepreneurial activity and weak enforcement of individual property rights.

▧ Regulation and Legal Rights.   Good examples of these restrictions have been documented in the research of economist Hernando de Soto on the economy of Peru. De Soto showed that there is a tremendous amount of regulation in the developing countries. This regulation has been so costly that a huge informal economy has emerged. The **informal economy** consists of large numbers of illegal businesses that can avoid the regulations. Remarkably, de Soto found that 61 percent of employment in Peru was in the informal, unregulated, illegal sector of the economy. In the city of Lima, around 33 percent of the houses were built by this informal sector. About 71,000 illegal vendors dominated retail trade, and 93 percent of urban transportation was in the informal sector.

informal economy: the portion of an economy characterized by illegal, unregulated businesses.

This large informal sector exists because the costs of setting up a legal business are high. It takes 32 months—filling out forms, waiting for approval, getting permission from several agencies—for a person to start a retail business. It takes 6 years and 11 months to start a housing construction firm. Hence, it is essentially impossible for someone to try to start a small business in the legal sector. Therefore, the informal sector grows.

Why does it matter if the informal sector is large? How does this impede development? Precisely because the sector is informal, it lacks basic legal rights such as the enforcement of the laws of property rights and contracts. These laws cannot be enforced in a sector that is outside the law. Bringing new inventions to market requires the security of private property so that the inventor can capture the benefits from taking the risks. Without this, the earnings from the innovation might be taken away by the government or by firms that copy the idea illegally. For example, if a business in the informal sector finds that another firm has reneged on a contract to deliver a product, that firm has no right to use the courts to enforce the contract because the business itself is illegal.

Some economists feel that weak enforcement of individual property rights is at the heart of the poor economic performance of Russia. The explanation given earlier for why the Industrial Revolution occurred in Western countries seems to point to this as a reason. In Europe in the 1700s, a new freedom for businesses to operate in the emerging market economy led to new products and technology. Laws to prevent theft or fraud gave people more certainty about reaping the returns from their entrepreneurship.

▧ Lack of Human Capital.   In order for existing technology to be adopted—whether in the form of innovative organizational structures of firms or as new products—it is necessary to have well-trained and highly skilled workers. For example, it is hard to make use of sophisticated computers to increase productivity when there are few skilled computer programmers.

Recall that human capital refers to the education and training of workers. Low investment in human capital is a serious obstacle to increasing productivity because it hampers the ability of countries that are behind to use new technology.

In fact, economists have found that differences in human capital in different countries can explain why some countries have been more successful at catching up than others. The developing countries that have been catching up most rapidly—in particular the newly industrialized countries like South Korea, Hong Kong, Taiwan, and Singapore—have strong educational systems in grade school and high school. This demonstrates the enormous importance of human capital for raising productivity.

REVIEW
- The removal of restrictions on private enterprise and enforcement of individual property rights may have been the key factors unleashing the growth of productivity at the time of the Industrial Revolution. Similar restrictions in developing countries may have tended to stifle development in recent years.

- An educated work force is needed to adopt technology. Better-educated and more highly skilled workers—those with human capital—can also use available capital more efficiently.

Increasing Capital per Worker

In addition to obstacles to the spread and adoption of new technology, there are obstacles to the increase in capital per worker that can prevent poor countries from catching up.

Population Growth

In order for the capital-to-labor ratio to increase, it is necessary to invest in new capital. However, the amount of investment in new capital must be larger than the increase in labor, or capital will increase by less than labor, and the ratio of capital to labor—the factor influencing productivity—will fall. Thus, high population growth raises the amount of investment needed in order to increase, or even maintain, the level of capital per worker. High population growth rates can, therefore, slow down the increase in capital per worker.

Population growth rates have declined substantially in countries where income per capita has risen to high levels, such as Europe, Japan, and the United States. Economic analysis of the determinants of population indicates that the high income per capita and resulting greater life expectancy may be the reason for the decline in population growth. When countries reach a level of income per capita where people can survive into their old age without the support of many children, or where there is a greater chance of children reaching working age, people choose to have fewer children. Hence, higher income per capita in developing countries would probably reduce population growth in these countries.

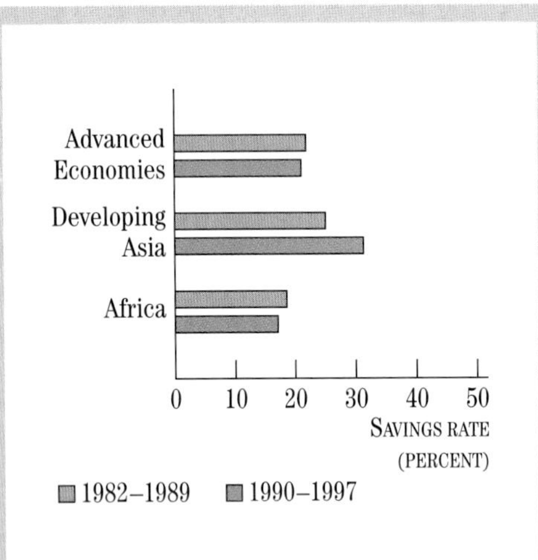

Figure 28.6
The Highest- and Lowest-Saving Countries
Very low national saving rates in poor countries impede capital accumulation and growth.
Source: From *World Economic Outlook*, September 2004, pp. 270–271. Reprinted by permission of International Monetary Fund.

National Saving

Capital accumulation requires investment, which requires saving. From our national income accounting equation, $Y = C + I + G + X$, we get the equation $Y - C - G = I + X$, which states that national saving is equal to the sum of investment plus net exports. Recall that national saving is the sum of private saving and government saving. In some developing countries where income per capita is barely above subsistence levels, the level of private saving—people's income less their consumption—is low. Government saving—tax receipts less expenditures—is also often low, perhaps because there is little income to tax and because governments have trouble controlling expenditures. Figure 28.6 shows the very low saving rates in Africa compared with the higher saving rates in advanced economies and in Asia.

For a poor country, it is natural for national saving to be less than investment and thus for imports to be greater than exports (net exports less than zero). In other words, a poor country naturally looks to investment from abroad as a source of capital formation for economic growth.

National saving =
investment + net exports
$$S = I + X$$

Foreign Investment from the Advanced Economies

Investment from abroad can come in the form of **foreign direct investment,** such as when the U.S. firm Gap Inc. opens a store in Mexico. Technically, when a foreign firm invests in more than 10 percent of the ownership of a business in another country, that investment is defined as direct investment.

Foreign investment also occurs when foreigners buy smaller percentages (less than 10 percent) of firms in developing economies. For example, foreign investment in Mexico takes place when a German buys newly offered common stock in a Mexican firm. In that case, the foreign investment from abroad is defined as **portfolio investment,** that is, less than 10 percent of ownership in a company.

Another way investment can flow in from abroad is through borrowing. Firms in developing economies or their governments can borrow from commercial banks, such as the Bank of America, Dai-Ichi Kangyo, or Crédit Lyonnais. Sometimes the governments of developing economies obtain loans directly from the governments of industrialized economies. Borrowing from government-sponsored international financial institutions, such as the International Monetary Fund (IMF) and the World Bank, can also occur.

■ **The Role of International Financial Institutions.** The **World Bank** and the **International Monetary Fund (IMF)** were established after World War II as part of a major reform of the international monetary system. Both institutions make loans to the developing countries. They serve as intermediaries, channeling funds from the industrialized countries to the developing countries.

foreign direct investment: investment by a foreign entity of at least a 10 percent direct ownership share in a firm.

portfolio investment: investment by a foreign entity of less than a 10 percent ownership share in a firm.

World Bank: an international agency, established after World War II, designed to promote the economic development of poorer countries through lending channeled from industrialized countries.

International Monetary Fund (IMF): an international agency, established after World War II, designed to help countries with balance of payments problems and to ensure the smooth functioning of the international monetary system.

Anti-Globalization Protests
In recent years, the annual meetings of the World Bank and the IMF have attracted thousands of demonstrators protesting the poverty and pollution they associate with the drive for globalization. Many demonstrators have called for the reduction of the debt that poor countries owe to rich ones.

ECONOMICS IN ACTION

Is There a Global Savings Glut?

In March 2005, (then) Federal Reserve Governor Ben Bernanke, at the Sandridge Lecture of the Virginia Association of Economics, remarked that "over the past decade a combination of diverse forces has created a significant increase in the global supply of saving—a global saving glut," and that this increase in saving helped to explain "the relatively low level of long-term real interest rates in the world today." However, a recent article in the *Economist* magazine showed that world saving rates had in fact decreased slightly, from about 23 percent of world GDP in the 1990s to about 22 percent of world GDP in 2004. If world saving had decreased, why was Bernanke talking about a "saving glut," and why had world interest rates fallen over the last decade?

We can utilize the saving-investment diagram introduced in Chapter 19, and shown here, to illustrate the mechanism that Bernanke was discussing in his lecture. The world interest rate is measured on the vertical axis, and world saving or investment as a share of world GDP is shown on the horizontal axis. Recall that along the saving curve, the saving rate rises as the interest rate rises because a higher interest rate gives people a greater incentive to save. Recall also that along the investment curve, the investment rate declines as the interest rate rises because a higher interest rate discourages businesses from investing in plants and equipment. (We can conveniently ignore net exports in the analysis because for the whole world, net exports must be zero.) The world investment rate must equal the world saving rate; hence, the equilibrium interest rate is found at the intersection of the two curves.

The interest rate/saving rate observations are shown in the diagram. It turns out that even though the world saving curve shifted left, the world investment curve must have shifted left even further. This causes the equilibrium real interest rate to decline

even though saving was declining. So Bernanke's discussion of a "saving glut" was simply a statement that the countries of the world were saving more than they wanted to invest, not necessarily that they were saving more than they had been doing before. In order to restore equilibrium between world saving and world investment, the world interest rate fell, driving investment higher and reducing saving until the two became equal again.

Why was global investment so low? The *Economist* suggests that a series of events in the late 1990s and early 2000s, including the financial crisis in East Asia and the collapse of the dot-com bubble in the United States in 2000, may have reduced the desire to invest in virtually all economies other than China and India. Similarly, increases in saving in countries like Japan and Germany may have led to the imbalance between saving and investment that resulted in world interest rates falling to restore equilibrium.

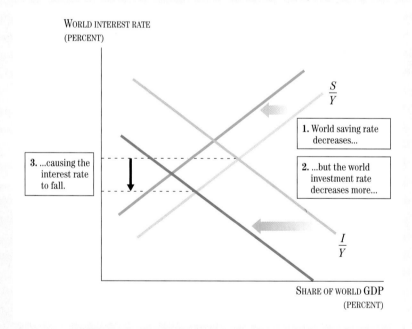

WORLD INTEREST RATE (PERCENT)

$\frac{S}{Y}$

1. World saving rate decreases...

2. ...but the world investment rate decreases more...

3. ...causing the interest rate to fall.

$\frac{I}{Y}$

SHARE OF WORLD GDP (PERCENT)

Many of the World Bank's loans are for specific projects—such as building a $100 million dam for irrigation in Brazil and a $153 million highway in Poland. Although these project loans have been helpful, they are much smaller in total than private investment in these countries.

In recent years, the IMF has tried to use its loans to encourage countries to implement difficult economic reforms. Frequently, it tries to induce countries to make these reforms by making the loans conditional on the reforms; this is the idea of *conditionality*. Under conditionality, the IMF gives loans to countries only if the countries undertake economic reform—such as eliminating price controls or privatizing firms. This conditionality is viewed as a way to encourage reforms that are difficult to put into effect because of the various vested interests in each country.

However, the IMF has been heavily criticized in recent years for going too far with its conditions and actually giving bad economic advice to developing countries. For example, during the financial crisis in East Asia in 1997 and 1998, the IMF insisted that the countries in crisis implement politically controversial reforms before it would agree to make loans to deal with the crisis.

The United States has more recently developed some programs which avoid attaching heavy conditions to grants and loans. The concept of the Millennium Challenge Account, proposed by President Bush in 2002 and established and funded by Congress in January 2004, was designed to fund initiatives to improve the economies and standards of living in qualified developing countries. Millennium Challenge Corporation grants are earmarked for programs that focus on improving health and education, helping businesses find new markets for their products, developing new ways to grow more food, and fighting AIDS. Assistance is offered to poor countries that adopt sound economic policies and root out government corruption. MCC grants have been made, for instance, to support water management and agriculture support services, such as drip irrigation in Cape Verde, which could result in the production of higher value crops, and a recent compact was signed with Georgia to address poverty and stimulate economic growth in the regions outside of Georgia's capital, Tbilisi, where more than 50 percent of rural households live below the poverty line.

■ **Are the Advanced Countries Saving Enough?** Despite the existence of these channels by which capital can flow to developing economies, there is a serious question as to whether the advanced economies are saving enough to provide the increased capital to developing countries. When an individual country saves more than it invests at home, it makes foreign investment abroad. A country can invest more than it saves by borrowing from abroad. In the whole world economy, saving must equal investment, because (as of this writing) there seems to be no one in outer space to borrow from.

REVIEW
- High rates of population growth and low national saving rates are two of the obstacles to raising capital per worker in developing economies.

- The International Monetary Fund makes loans to developing countries. The loans are frequently conditional on an economic reform program, a practice that came under heavy criticism in the Asian financial crisis of the 1990s.

- The World Bank makes loans mainly for specific projects.

Conclusion

In this chapter, we have shown how productivity has increased in many countries because of higher capital per worker and technological change. In some cases there has been a convergence of productivity, with the poorer countries moving closer to the richer countries. However, for many developing countries, productivity has not been catching up, and income per capita remains very low. The many countries in Africa are still in extreme poverty.

Among the possible explanations for the lack of catch-up are obstacles to the spread of technology, such as government restrictions on entrepreneurs and a shortage of human capital, and obstacles to higher capital per worker, such as low saving rates and low foreign investment. The removal of similar obstacles in Western Europe in the eighteenth century may have been the cause of the Industrial Revolution. Their removal today may result in another great growth wave in the developing economies.

In fact, there are already signs of the removal of such obstacles to economic growth. Hence, in the absence of retrenchments or setbacks from ethnic and military conflicts, we may see higher productivity growth in the poorer countries in the future than we have seen in the past. If so, the economic landscape of the world will be transformed.

Suppose, for example, that real GDP in the industrialized countries grows at a 2.5 percent pace for the next 50 years. Suppose that real GDP in all the other countries of the world grows at 5 percent per year. With these growth rates, the countries we now classify as developing or in transition would produce 75 percent of world GDP in the year 2050, and the countries we now classify as industrialized would produce 25 percent—a complete about-face from the current situation. This, of course, is an example, not a forecast, but it hints at some of the amazing possibilities for the future.

KEY POINTS

1. Economic growth theory pinpoints capital accumulation and technological change as the two key ingredients of productivity growth. In a world without obstacles to the spread of technology or to investment in new capital, growth theory predicts that poor regions will catch up to rich regions.

2. Catch-up has occurred in the states of the United States and among the industrialized countries but is distressingly absent from developing countries.

3. Low incomes and poverty have persisted for the vast majority of the world's population while other countries have become richer.

4. Insufficient capital accumulation in the poor countries, due to high population growth, low saving rates, or insufficient capital flows from the advanced countries, is part of the problem.

5. Higher population growth means that more investment is required in order to raise capital per worker.

6. Some countries may have poor growth performance because of restrictions on markets and a lack of property rights. The lifting of those restrictions in Europe in the 1700s was a cause of the economic growth associated with the Industrial Revolution.

7. The removal of such restrictions may be a key to increased productivity and economic development.

8. Low investment in human capital is another reason for low productivity growth.

9. In many countries today, especially in Latin America and China, there is a great potential for higher economic growth, as the market system is being encouraged and restrictions on entrepreneurs are being removed.

10. Another great growth wave would change the economic landscape of the whole world.

KEY TERMS

catch-up line	informal economy	portfolio investment	International Monetary
economic development	foreign direct investment	World Bank	Fund (IMF)
developing country			

QUESTIONS FOR REVIEW

1. Why does economic growth theory predict that productivity and real income per capita will grow relatively more rapidly in poor countries?

2. In what way does the catch-up line describe more rapid growth in poor countries?

3. Why is catch-up observed among the industrialized economies but not for the whole world?

4. Why is the identity that investment plus net exports equals saving important for understanding the flow of capital around the world?

5. What is the difference between foreign direct investment and portfolio investment?

6. Why is human capital important for the spread of technology?

7. What is the significance of conditionality for IMF loans?

8. What do government restrictions on entrepreneurs have to do with economic growth?

9. What harm does an informal economy cause?

PROBLEMS

1. Plot on a scatter diagram the data for the Asian countries that appear below. Does there appear to be a catch-up line in the scatter diagram?

Country	Per Capita Real GDP in 1960 (2000 U.S. dollars)	Average Annual Rate of Growth from 1960 to 2000 (%)
Thailand	1,051	4.6
Pakistan	526	2.9
Philippines	1,581	1.3
China	746	4.3
Malaysia	1,918	3.9
Indonesia	403	3.4

2. In 1997 and 1998, there was a financial crisis in some of the countries listed in problem 1 that caused recessions, apparently temporary deviations of real GDP from potential GDP. How do you think the crisis will affect the catch-up phenomenon in the future?

3. The states of the United States have moved toward one another in real income per capita over the past 100 years, but the countries of the world have not. What differences are there between state borders and country borders that might explain this problem?

4. Suppose a developing country does not allow foreign investment to flow into the country and, at the same time, has a very low saving rate. Use the fact that saving equals investment plus net exports and the growth accounting formula to explain why this country will have difficulty catching up with the industrialized countries. What can the country do to improve its productivity if it does not allow capital in from outside the country?

5. Which of the following will increase the likelihood of poor countries catching up to rich countries, and which will decrease the likelihood? Explain.
   a. Industrial countries do not allow their technology to be bought or leased by firms in developing countries.
   b. Worldwide saving rates shift up.
   c. The legal system in developing countries is improved to protect property rights.
   d. Governments in developing countries make use of their international aid to buy armaments from developed countries.
   e. Investment in human capital increases in the developing countries.

6. Most developing countries have low saving rates and governments that run budget deficits. What will be required for such countries to have large increases in their capital stocks? What will happen if industrialized countries' saving rates decline as well? How does this affect the developing countries' prospects for catching up?

7. What would be the effect of a decrease in the Japanese saving rate on the growth rate of developing countries? Why?

8. The rule of 72 gives the approximate doubling time of a variable if you know its rate of growth. For example, if the population of a country is 200 million and the rate of growth of the population is 2 percent per year, then it will take approximately 35 years for the country's population to reach 400 million. Suppose real income per capita does not grow at all in the United States in the future, and suppose that the per capita growth rate in China is 4 percent per year. About how long will it take for China to catch up with the United States? What is likely to happen to the growth rates before this period of time passes? Assume that per capita income is now $32,000 in the United States and $3,400 in China.

CHAPTER 29

The Gains from International Trade

Bangalore, an Indian city of about 6 million people, has undergone a remarkable economic transformation in recent times. Bangalore is now one of the leading cities in the production of computer software; according to India's National Association of Software and Service Companies, the value of software produced in Bangalore has increased 750-fold in the last 15 years! The rapid increase in jobs in the software and information technology industry has brought prosperity to an increasing number of workers in Bangalore. An article that appeared in *USA Today* on March 22, 2004, describes the transformation of the lives of Bangalore's software workers, who earn a salary doing work outsourced by U.S. companies and then spend their earnings on IBM computers, Hyundai cars, Domino's Pizza, and Stairmasters (to work off the pizza!).

Similar stories can be told about U.S. trade with many countries in the world. Every day, people in countries like China, Germany, Korea, Japan, and Sri Lanka buy American products: Caterpillar tractors, Motorola cellular phones, Microsoft software, Boeing 747s, and Merck pharmaceuticals. At the same time, Americans drive cars made in Germany and Japan, listen to CDs and MP3s on electronic equipment made in China and Malaysia, play tennis wearing Nike shoes made in Korea, or go swimming in Ocean Pacific swimsuits made in Sri Lanka.

These stories about firms selling their products around the world and people consuming goods made in other countries illustrate reasons why people benefit from international trade. First, international trade allows firms such as Merck access to a very large world market, enabling them to invest heavily in research and reduce costs by concentrating production. Second, international trade allows different countries to specialize in what they are relatively efficient at producing, such as pharmaceuticals in the United States or electronic equipment in Malaysia.

gains from trade: improvements in income, production, or satisfaction owing to the exchange of goods or services. (Ch. 1)

This chapter explores the reasons for these *gains from trade* and develops two models that can be used to measure the actual size of these gains. We begin, however, with a brief look at recent trends in international trade.

Recent Trends in International Trade

international trade: the exchange of goods and services between people or firms in different nations. (Ch. 1)

International trade is trade between people or firms in different countries. Trade between people in Detroit and Ottowa, Canada, is international trade, whereas trade between Detroit and Chicago is trade within a country. Thus, international trade is just another kind of economic interaction; it is subject to the same basic economic principles as trade between people in the same country.

International trade differs from trade in domestic markets, however, because national governments frequently place restrictions, such as **tariffs** or **quotas,** on trade between countries that they do not place on trade within countries. For example, the Texas legislature cannot limit or put a tariff on the import of Florida oranges into Texas. The **commerce clause** of the U.S. Constitution forbids such restraint of trade between states. But the United States can restrict the import of oranges from Brazil. Similarly, Japan can restrict the import of rice from the United States, and Australia can restrict the import of Japanese automobiles.

International trade has grown much faster than trade within countries in recent years. Figure 29.1 shows the trade in goods and services between countries for all countries in the world as a percentage of the world GDP. International trade has

tariff: a tax on imports.

quota: a governmental limit on the quantity of a good that may be imported or sold.

commerce clause: the clause in the U.S. Constitution that prohibits restraint of trade between states.

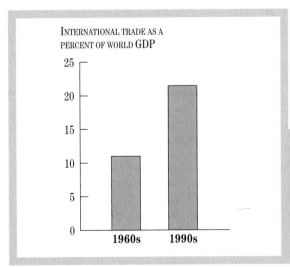

INTERNATIONAL TRADE AS A PERCENT OF WORLD GDP

**Figure 29.1
Rapidly Expanding
International Trade**
International trade has increased faster than GDP as trade restrictions and the cost of transportation have gone down. By 2002, international trade accounted for a 24 percent share of GDP.

doubled as a proportion of the world GDP during the last 30 or so years. Why has international trade grown so rapidly?

One reason is that the cost of transportation and communication has been reduced dramatically. The cost of air travel fell to 9.5 cents per mile in 2000 from 87 cents per mile in 1930, while the cost of a three-minute phone call from New York to London fell to $0.24 in 2002 from $315 in 1930 (adjusting the 1930 prices for general inflation). E-mail and the Internet, unheard of in 1930, reduce costs even further.

However, the most important reason that trade has expanded so rapidly is that government restrictions on trade between countries have come down. Western European countries are integrating into a single market. Canada, Mexico, and the United States have agreed to integrate their economies into a free trade area, where the term *free* indicates the elimination of restrictions on trade. Previously closed economies have opened themselves to world trade through major political and economic reforms. The formerly closed economies in Eastern Europe, Russia, and especially, China, have joined the world trading system. Export-oriented countries in Asia are growing rapidly, and governments in South America such as Argentina and Chile are opening their economies to competition and foreign trade.

These countries are making these changes in an effort to help people. But how do people gain from international trade? Let's now consider that question.

REVIEW

- The basic principles of economics apply to international trade between people in different countries.

- There is a greater tendency for governments to interfere with trade between countries than with trade within their own country.

- International trade has grown rapidly in recent years because of reduced transportation and communication costs and, especially, lower government barriers to trade.

Comparative Advantage

comparative advantage: a situation in which a person or country can produce one good at a lower opportunity cost than another person or country. (Ch. 1)

According to the theory of *comparative advantage*, a country can improve the income of its citizens by allowing them to trade with people in other countries, even if the people of the country are less efficient at producing all items.

Getting a Gut Feeling for Comparative Advantage

First, consider a parable that conveys the essence of comparative advantage. Rose is a highly skilled computer programmer who writes computer-assisted drawing programs. Rose owns a small firm that sells her programs to architects. She has hired an experienced salesman, Sam, to contact the architects and sell her software. Thus, Rose specializes in programming, and Sam specializes in sales.

absolute advantage: a situation in which a person or country is more efficient at producing a good in comparison with another person or country.

You need to know a little more about Rose. Rose is a friendly, outgoing person, and because she knows her product better than Sam does, she is better at sales than Sam. We say that Rose has an **absolute advantage** over Sam in both programming and sales because she is better at both jobs. But it still makes sense for Rose to hire Sam because her efficiency at programming compared to Sam's is greater than her efficiency at sales compared to Sam's. We say that Rose has a *comparative advantage* over Sam in programming rather than in sales. If Rose sold her programs, then she would have to sacrifice her programming time, and her profits would fall. Thus, even though Rose is better at both programming and sales, she hires Sam to do the selling so that she can program full time.

All this seems sensible. However, there is one additional part of the terminology that may at first seem confusing but is important. We said that Rose has the comparative advantage in programming, not in sales. But who does have the comparative advantage in sales? Sam does. Even though Sam is less efficient at both sales and programming, we say he has a comparative advantage in sales because, compared with Rose, he does relatively better at sales than he does at programming. A person cannot have a comparative advantage in both of only two activities.

opportunity cost: the value of the next-best forgone alternative that was not chosen because something else was chosen. (Ch. 1)

■ **Opportunity Cost, Relative Efficiency, and Comparative Advantage.** The idea of comparative advantage can also be explained in terms of *opportunity cost*. The opportunity cost of Rose or Sam spending more time selling is that she or he can produce fewer programs. Similarly, the opportunity cost of Rose or Sam spending more time writing programs is that she or he can make fewer sales.

Observe that, in the example, Sam has a lower opportunity cost of spending his time selling than Rose does; thus, it makes sense for Sam to do the selling rather than Rose. In contrast, Rose has a lower opportunity cost of spending her time writing computer programs than Sam does; thus, it makes sense for Rose to write computer programs rather than Sam.

Opportunity costs give us a way to define comparative advantage: A person with a lower opportunity cost of producing a good than another person has a comparative advantage in that good. Thus, Rose has a comparative advantage in computer programming, and Sam has a comparative advantage in sales.

Comparative advantage can also be explained in terms of relative efficiency: A person who is relatively more efficient at producing good X than good Y compared to another person has a comparative advantage in good X. Thus, again, we see that Rose has a comparative advantage in computer programming because she is relatively more efficient at producing computer programs than at making sales compared to Sam.

■ **From People to Countries.** Why is this story about Rose and Sam a parable? Because we can think of Rose and Sam as two countries that differ in efficiency at producing one product versus another. In the parable, Rose has a comparative advantage over Sam in programming, and Sam has a comparative advantage over Rose in sales. In general, *country A has a comparative advantage over country B in the production of a good if the opportunity cost of producing the good in country A is less than in country B*, or, alternatively but equivalently stated, *if country A can produce the good relatively more efficiently than other goods compared to country B*. Thus, if you understand the Rose and Sam story, you should have no problem understanding comparative advantage in two countries, which we now examine in more detail.

Productivity in Two Countries

Consider the following two goods: (1) vaccines and (2) TV sets. Different skills are required for the production of vaccines and TV sets. Vaccine production requires knowledge of chemistry and biology, and the marketing of products where doctors make most of the choices. Producing TV sets requires knowledge of electrical engineering and microcircuitry, and the marketing of goods where consumers make most of the choices.

Perhaps no trend in international trade has attracted as much recent attention as the increase in global outsourcing, whereby a U.S.-based company uses a foreign company to perform a portion of the work involved in producing a good or a service. The following article, which appeared in *The New York Times* on June 19, 2005, discusses why some of the fears associated with outsourcing may be a little misplaced.

True or False: Outsourcing Is a Crisis

By EDUARDO PORTER

June 19, 2005, Late Edition Final—

If you read only the headlines, the future of globalization may seem scary, indeed. American jobs have already been heading abroad. And as telecommunications and more powerful computers enable companies to take even more jobs overseas, the service sector, which accounts for about 85 percent of the United States work force, will be increasingly vulnerable to competition from the cheap labor pools of the developing world.

[*Describes what outsourcing is*]

So the question looms: Is America on the verge of losing oodles of white-collar jobs? Probably not. The threat of global outsourcing is easily overstated. The debate over the global competition for jobs is awash in dire projections. All those legal assistants in New York and Washington, for example, could be replaced with smart young graduates from Hyderabad. Office support occupations—jobs like data entry assistant, file clerk and the entire payroll department—could also be carried out in remote locations. "We are really at the beginning stages of this, and it is accelerating rapidly," said Ron Hira, assistant professor of public policy at the Rochester Institute of Technology.

[*Identifies occupations most likely to be affected*]

In a study published this year, two economists at the Organization for Economic Cooperation and Development in Brussels estimated that 20 percent of the developed world's employment could be "potentially affected" by global outsourcing. That could include all American librarians, statisticians, chemical engineers and air traffic controllers, the study said. What does "potentially affected" mean? Even if offshoring didn't drain away all these jobs, global competition for employment—including workers in developing countries who earn so little by comparison—could severely dent the livelihoods of American workers. "It isn't going to hurt in terms of jobs," said William J. Baumol, an economics professor at New York University who has studied the costs of globalization. "It is going to hurt in terms of wages."

But even if millions of tasks can be done by cheaper labor on the other side of the planet, businesses won't rush to move every job they can to wherever the cost is lowest. The labor market isn't quite that global, and it's unlikely to be anytime soon. In a new set of reports, the McKinsey Global Institute, a research group known for its unabashedly favorable view of globalization, argued that 160 million service jobs—about 10 percent of total worldwide employment—could be moved to remote sites because these job functions don't require customer contact, local knowledge or complex interactions with the rest of a business.

Yet after surveying dozens of companies in eight sectors, from pharmaceutical companies to insurers, it concluded that only a small fraction of these jobs would actually be sent away. The report estimates that by 2008, multinational companies in the entire developed world will have located only 4.1 million service jobs in low-wage countries, up from about 1.5 million in 2003. The figure is equivalent to only 1 percent of the total number of service jobs in developed countries.

Some sectors, like retail and health care, are likely to put very few jobs in poor countries. McKinsey estimated that less than 0.07 percent of health care jobs in 2008 would be outsourced to low-wage countries. But even designers of packaged software, whose work can easily be done abroad, will outsource only 18 percent of their jobs, the report said.

Moving tasks to faraway sites isn't simple. According to McKinsey's study, many business processes are difficult to separate into discrete chunks that can be sent away. Many insurance companies use information technology systems that have been cobbled together over time and would be difficult to manage remotely. Managers can be unwilling or unprepared to work overseas. And sometimes the tasks that can be sent offshore are too small to make the move worthwhile.

[*Limitations on outsourcing*]

To top it off, there aren't that many suitable cheap workers available. Human-resources managers interviewed for the McKinsey study said that for reasons ranging from poor language skills to second-rate education systems, only about 13 percent of the young, college-educated professionals in the big developing countries are suitable to work for multinationals. And competition from local companies reduces this pool.

[*Potential number of jobs affected*]

Sure, there are a billion Indians, but only a tiny percentage of the Indian work force have the appropriate qualifications. "Only a fraction have English as a medium of instruction, and only a fraction of those speak English that you or I can understand," said Jagdish N. Bhagwati, a professor of economics at Columbia University.

[*The number of jobs that may actually be outsourced*]

Of course, many of these obstacles can be overcome with time. The pool of adequate workers in poorer countries will grow, and companies will eventually iron out many of the logistical complications.

But that is likely to take a while. "The rate at which companies are willing and able is much slower than you would realize," said Diana Farrell, director of the McKinsey Global Institute. "We see this as being evolutionary, continuous but measured change."

Electronics versus Pharmaceuticals
In the example used in this chapter, Korea has a comparative advantage in an electronic good
(TV sets), and the United States has a comparative advantage in a pharmaceutical (vaccines).
Thus, with trade, the electronic good will be produced in Korea, as shown in the left-hand
photo, and the pharmaceutical good will be produced in the United States, as shown in the
right-hand photo.

Table 29.1 provides an example of productivity differences in the production of
vaccines and TV sets in two different countries, the United States and Korea.
Productivity is measured by the amount of each good that can be produced by a
worker per day of work. To be specific, let us suppose that the vaccines are measured
in vials, that the TVs are measured in numbers of TV sets, and that labor is the only
factor of production in making vaccines and TV sets. The theory of comparative
advantage does not depend on any of these assumptions, but they make the exposition much easier.

According to Table 29.1, in the United States it takes a worker one day of work to
produce 6 vials of vaccine or 3 TV sets. In Korea, one worker can produce 1 vial of vaccine or 2 TV sets. Thus, the United States is more productive than Korea in producing
both vaccines and TV sets. We say that a country has an *absolute advantage* over
another country in the production of a good if it is more efficient at producing that
good. In this example, the United States has an absolute advantage in both vaccine
and TV set production.

However, the United States has a comparative advantage over Korea in the
production of vaccines rather than TV sets. To see this, note that a worker in the

Table 29.1
Example of Productivity in the United States and Korea

	Output per Day of Work	
	Vials of Vaccine	*Number of TV Sets*
United States	6	3
Korea	1	2

United States can produce 6 times as many vials of vaccine as a worker in Korea but only 1.5 times as many TV sets. In other words, the United States is relatively more efficient in vaccines than in TV sets compared with Korea. Korea, being able to produce TV sets relatively more efficiently than vaccines compared to the United States, has a comparative advantage in TV sets.

Observe also how opportunity costs determine who has the comparative advantage. To produce 3 more TV sets, the United States must sacrifice 6 vials of vaccine; in other words, *in the United States, the opportunity cost of 1 more TV set is 2 vials of vaccine.* In Korea, to produce 2 more TV sets, the Koreans must sacrifice 1 vial of vaccine; in other words, *in Korea, the opportunity cost of 1 more TV set is only ½ vial of vaccine.* Thus, we see that the opportunity cost of producing TV sets in Korea is lower than in the United States. By examining opportunity costs, we again see that Korea has a comparative advantage in TV sets.

■ **An American Worker's View.** Because labor productivity in both goods is higher in the United States than in Korea, wages are higher in the United States than in Korea in the example. Now think about the situation from the point of view of American workers who are paid more than Korean workers. They might wonder how they can compete with Korea. The Korean workers' wages seem very low compared to theirs. It doesn't seem fair. But as we will see, comparative advantage implies that American workers can gain from trade with the Koreans.

■ **A Korean Worker's View.** It is useful to think about Table 29.1 from the perspective of a Korean worker as well as that of a U.S. worker. From the Korean perspective, it might be noted that Korean workers are less productive in both goods. Korean workers might wonder how they can ever compete with the United States, which looks like a productive powerhouse. Again, it doesn't seem fair. As we will see, however, the Koreans can also gain from trade with the Americans.

Finding the Relative Price

> **Another example of relative prices may be helpful:**
> Price of U2 concert = $45
> Price of U2 T-shirt = $15
> Relative price = 3 T-shirts per concert

To measure how much the Koreans and Americans can gain from trade, we need to consider the *relative price* of vaccines and TVs in Korea and the United States. The relative price determines how much vaccine can be traded for TVs and, therefore, how much each country can gain from trade. For example, suppose the price of a TV set is $200 and the price of a vial of vaccine is $100. Then 2 vials of vaccine cost the same as 1 TV set; we say the relative price is 2 vials of vaccine per TV set. The next few paragraphs show how to determine the relative price from data on the costs of production.

■ **Relative Price Without Trade.** First, let us find the relative price with no trade between the countries. The relative price of two goods should depend on the relative costs of production. A good for which the cost of producing an additional quantity is relatively low will have a relatively low price.

Consider the United States. In this example, a day of work can produce either 6 vials of vaccine or 3 TV sets. With labor as the only factor of production, 6 vials of vaccine cost the same to produce as 3 TV sets; that is, 2 vials of vaccine cost the same to produce as 1 TV set. Therefore, the relative price should be 2 vials of vaccine per TV set.

Now consider Korea. Electronic goods should have a relatively low price in Korea because they are relatively cheap to produce. A day of work can produce either 1 vial of vaccine or 2 TV sets; thus 1 vial of vaccine costs the same to produce as 2 TV sets in Korea. Therefore, the relative price is ½ vial of vaccine per TV set.

■ **Relative Price with Trade.** Now consider what happens when the two countries trade without government restrictions. If transportation costs are negligible and markets are competitive, then the price of a good must be the same in the United States and Korea. Why? Because any difference in price would quickly be eliminated by trade; if the price of TV sets is much less in Korea than in the United States, then traders will buy TV sets in Korea and sell them in the United States and make a profit; by doing so, however, they reduce the supply of TV sets in Korea and increase the supply in the United States. This will drive up the price in Korea and drive down the price in the United States until the price of TV sets in the two countries is the same. Thus, with trade, the price of vaccines and the price of TV sets will converge to the same levels in both countries. The relative price will therefore converge to the same value in both countries.

If the relative price is going to be the same in both countries, then we know the price must be somewhere between the prices in the two countries before trade. That is, the price must be between 2 vials of vaccine per TV set (the U.S. relative price) and $1/2$ vial of vaccine per TV set (the Korean relative price). We do not know exactly where the price will fall between $1/2$ and 2. It depends on the *demand* for vaccines and TV sets in Korea and the United States. *Let us assume that the relative price is 1 vial of vaccine per TV set after trade,* which is between $1/2$ and 2 and is a nice, easy number for making computations. The calculation of the price with trade is summarized in Table 29.2.

Measuring the Gains from Trade

How large are the *gains from trade* due to comparative advantage? First, consider some examples.

■ **One Country's Gain.** Suppose that 10 American workers move out of electronics production and begin producing pharmaceuticals. We know from Table 29.1 that these 10 American workers can produce 60 vials of vaccine per day. Formerly, the 10 American workers were producing 30 TV sets per day. But their 60 vials of vaccine can be traded for TV sets produced in Korea. With the relative price of 1 vial per TV set, Americans will be able to exchange these 60 vials of vaccine for 60 TV sets. Thus, Americans gain 30 more TV sets by moving 10 more workers into vaccine production. This gain from trade is summarized in Table 29.3.

■ **The Other Country's Gain.** The same thing can happen in Korea. A Korean manufacturer can now hire 30 workers who were formerly working in vaccine

---

Table 29.2
The Relative Price (The relative price—vials of vaccine per TV set—must be the same in both countries with trade)

	United States	Korea
Relative price before trade:	2 vials of vaccine per TV set	$1/2$ vial of vaccine per TV set
Relative price range after trade:	Between $1/2$ and 2	Between $1/2$ and 2
Relative price assumption:	1	1

Table 29.3
Changing Production and Gaining from Trade in the United States and Korea

	United States (10 workers)		
	Change in Production	*Amount Traded*	*Net Gain from Trade*
Vaccines	Up 60 vials	Export 60 vials	0
TV sets	Down 30 sets	Import 60 sets	30 sets

	Korea (30 workers)		
	Change in Production	*Amount Traded*	*Net Gain from Trade*
Vaccines	Down 30 vials	Import 60 vials	30 vials
TV sets	Up 60 sets	Export 60 sets	0

production to produce TV sets. Vaccine production declines by 30 vials, but TV production increases by 60 TV sets. These 60 TV sets can be traded with Americans for 60 vials of vaccine. The reduction in the production of vaccine of 30 vials results in an import of vaccine of 60 vials; thus, the gain from trade is 30 vials of vaccine. The Koreans, by moving workers out of vaccine production and into TV set production, are getting more vaccine. This gain from trade for Korea is summarized in Table 29.3. Observe that the exports of TV sets from Korea equal the imports of TV sets to the United States.

■ **Just Like a New Discovery.**   International trade is like the discovery of a new idea or technique that makes workers more productive. It is as if workers in the United States figured out how to produce more TV sets with the same amount of effort. Their trick is that they actually produce vaccines, which are then traded for the TV sets. Like any other new technique, international trade improves the well-being of Americans. International trade also improves the well-being of the Koreans; it is as if they discovered a new technique, too.

A Graphical Measure of the Gains from Trade

The gains from trade due to comparative advantage can also be found graphically with production possibilities curves, as shown in Figure 29.2. There are two graphs in the figure—one for the United States and the other for Korea. In both graphs, the horizontal axis has the number of TV sets and the vertical axis has the number of vials of vaccine produced.

■ **Production Possibilities Curves Without Trade.**   The solid lines in the two graphs show the production possibilities curves for vaccines and TV sets in the United States and in Korea before trade. To derive them, we assume, for illustrative purposes, that there are 10,000 workers in the United States and 30,000 workers in Korea who can make either vaccines or TV sets.

If all the available workers in the United States produce vaccines, then total production will be 60,000 vials of vaccine ($6 \times 10,000$) and zero TV sets. Alternatively,

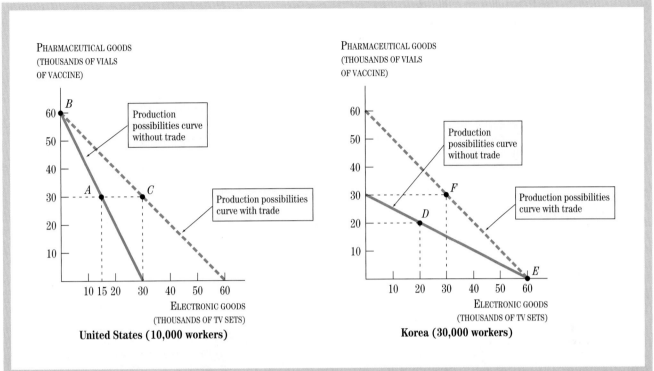

**Figure 29.2
Comparative Advantage**

On the left, Americans are better off with trade because the production possibilities curve shifts out with trade; thus, with trade, Americans reach a point like C rather than A. The gains from trade due to comparative advantage are equal to the distance between the two production possibilities curves—one with trade and the other without trade. On the right, Koreans are also better off because their production possibilities curve also shifts out; thus, Koreans can reach point F, which is better than point D. To reach this outcome, Americans specialize in producing at point B and Koreans specialize in producing at point E.

if 5,000 workers produce vaccines in the United States and 5,000 workers produce TV sets, then total production will be 30,000 vials of vaccine (6 × 5,000) and 15,000 TV sets (3 × 5,000). The solid line in the graph on the left of Figure 29.2 shows these possibilities and all other possibilities for producing vaccines and TV sets. It is the production possibilities curve without trade.

Korea's production possibilities curve without trade is shown by the solid line in the graph on the right of Figure 29.2. For example, if all 30,000 Korean workers produce TV sets, a total of 60,000 TV sets can be produced (2 × 30,000). This and other possibilities are on the curve.

The slopes of the two production possibilities curves without trade in Figure 29.2 show how many vials of vaccine can be transformed into TV sets in Korea and the United States. The production possibilities curve for the United States is steeper than that for Korea because an increase in production of 1 TV set reduces vaccine production by 2 vials in the United States but by only ½ vial in Korea. The slope of the production possibilities curve is the opportunity cost; the opportunity cost of producing TV sets in the United States is higher than it is in Korea.

■ **Production Possibilities Curves with Trade.** The dashed lines in the two graphs in Figure 29.2 show the different combinations of vaccine and TV sets avail-

ECONOMICS IN ACTION

Doing Politics and Economics

David Ricardo was a man of action. He went to work as a stockbroker at age 14 and eventually accumulated a vast fortune, including a beautiful country estate. He then became one of the most influential economists of all time. He also ran for and won a seat in the British Parliament from which to argue his economic position.

As an economist, Ricardo continued the tradition of Adam Smith. In fact, he got interested in economics after reading Smith's *Wealth of Nations* during a vacation. But Ricardo greatly extended and improved on Smith's theories and made them more precise. Along with Smith and Thomas Robert Malthus—who was Ricardo's close friend but frequent intellectual opponent—Ricardo is considered by historians to be in the classical school, which argued for laissez-faire, free trade, and competitive markets in eighteenth- and nineteenth-century Britain.

Ricardo grappled with three of the most important policy issues in economics: inflation, taxes, and international trade. But Ricardo's most famous contribution is to international trade—in particular, his theory of comparative advantage. Ricardo used this theory when he was in Parliament to argue for repeal of the restrictions on agricultural imports known as the corn laws.

Ricardo's theory of comparative advantage is a good example of how he improved on the work of Adam Smith.

Smith used commonsense analogies to illustrate the gains from trade; one of his examples was "The tailor does not attempt to make his own shoes, but buys them from the shoemaker." As with this tailor and shoemaker example, Smith focused on cases in which one person had an absolute advantage in one good and the other person had an absolute advantage in the other good. But Ricardo showed how there were gains from trade even if one person was better at producing both goods. Here is how Ricardo put it way back in 1817:

Two men can both make shoes and hats, and one is superior to the other in both employments; but in making hats, he can only exceed his competitor by one-fifth or 20 per cent., and in making shoes he can excel him by one-third or 33 per cent.;—will it not be for the interest of both that the superior man should employ himself exclusively in making shoes, and the inferior man in making hats?

DAVID RICARDO, 1772–1823

Born: London, 1772

Education: Never attended college

Jobs:
Stockbroker, 1786–1815
Member of Parliament, 1819–1823

Major Publications:
The High Price of Bullion, 1810;
On the Principles of Political Economy and Taxation, 1817;
A Plan for a National Bank, 1824

able in Korea and the United States when there is trade between the two countries at a relative price of 1 vial of vaccine for 1 TV set. These dashed lines are labeled "production possibilities curve with trade" to contrast them with the "production possibilities curve without trade" label on the solid line. The diagram shows that the production possibilities curves with trade are shifted out compared with the curves without trade.

To see how the production possibilities curve with trade is derived, consider how the United States could move from point *A* to point *C* in Figure 29.2. At point *A*, without trade, Americans produce and consume 15,000 TV sets and 30,000 vials of vaccine by having 5,000 workers in each industry. Now suppose all U.S. workers move out of TV set production into vaccine production, shifting U.S. production to zero TV sets and 60,000 vials of vaccine, as shown by point B. Then by trading some of the vaccine, Americans can obtain TV sets. As they trade more vaccine away, they move down the production possibilities curve with trade: 1 less vial of vaccine means 1 more TV set along the curve. If they move to point C in the diagram, they have traded 30,000 vials of vaccine for 30,000 TV sets. Americans now have 30,000 TV sets and are left with 30,000 vials of vaccine. By producing more vaccine, the Americans get to purchase more TV sets. The distance from point A (before trade) to point C (after trade) in Figure 29.2 is the gain from trade: 15,000 more TV sets.

It would be possible, of course, to choose any other point on the production possibilities curve with trade. If Americans prefer more TV sets and fewer vials of vaccine, they can move down along that dashed line, trading more of their vaccine for more TV sets. In general, the production possibilities curve *with* trade is further out than the production possibilities curve *without* trade, indicating the gain from trade.

Observe that the slope of the production possibilities curve with trade is given by the relative price: the number of vials of vaccine that can be obtained for a TV set. When the relative price is 1 vial per TV set, the slope is −1 because 1 less vial gives 1 more TV set. If the relative price were ½ vial per TV set, then the production possibilities curve with trade would be flatter.

The gains to Korea from trade are illustrated in the right-hand graph of Figure 29.2. For example, at point D, without trade, Koreans produce 20,000 TV sets with 10,000 workers and, with the remaining 20,000 workers, produce 20,000 vials of vaccine. With trade, they shift all production into TV sets, as at point E on the right graph. Then they trade the TV sets for vaccine. Such trade allows more consumption of vaccine in Korea. At point F in the right diagram, the Koreans could consume 30,000 vials of vaccine and 30,000 TV sets, which is 10,000 more of each than before trade at point D. As in the case of the United States, the production possibilities curve shifts out with trade, and the size of the shift represents the gain from trade.

This example of Americans and Koreans consuming more than they were before trade illustrates the *principle of comparative advantage: By specializing in producing products in which they have a comparative advantage, countries can increase the amount of goods available for consumption.* Trade increases the amount of production in the world; it shifts out the production possibilities curves.

■ **Increasing Opportunity Costs: Incomplete Specialization.** One of the special assumptions in the example we have used in Table 29.2 and Figure 29.2 to illustrate the theory of comparative advantage is that opportunity costs are constant rather than increasing. It is because of this assumption that the production possibilities curves without trade in Figure 29.2 are straight lines rather than the bowed-out lines that we studied in Chapter 1. With increasing opportunity costs, the curves would be bowed out.

The straight-line production possibilities curves are the reason for *complete* specialization, with Korea producing no vaccines and the United States producing no TV sets. If there were increasing opportunity costs, as in the more typical example of the production possibilities curve, then complete specialization would not occur. Why? With increasing opportunity costs, as more and more workers are moved into the production of vaccine in the United States, the opportunity cost of producing more vaccine will rise. And as workers are moved out of vaccine production in Korea, the opportunity cost of vaccine production in Korea will fall. At some point, the U.S. opportunity cost of vaccine production may rise to equal Korea's, at which point further specialization in vaccine production would cease in the United States. Thus, with increasing opportunity costs and bowed-out production possibilities curves, there will most likely be incomplete specialization. But the principle of comparative advantage is not changed by increasing opportunity costs. By specializing to some degree in the goods they have a comparative advantage in, countries can increase world production. There are still substantial gains from trade, whether between Rose and Sam or between America and Korea.

REVIEW

- Comparative advantage shows that a country can gain from trade even if it is more efficient at producing every product than another country. A country has a comparative advantage in a product if it is relatively more efficient at producing that product than the other country.

- The theory of comparative advantage predicts that there are gains from trade from increasing production of the good a country has a comparative advantage in and reducing production of the other good. By exporting the good it has a comparative advantage in, a country can increase consumption of both goods.

- Comparative advantage is like a new technology in which the country effectively produces more by having some goods produced in another country.

Reasons for Comparative Advantage

What determines a country's comparative advantage? There are some obvious answers. For example, Central America has a comparative advantage over North America in producing tropical fruit because of weather conditions: Bananas will not grow in Kansas or Nebraska outside of greenhouses.

In most cases, however, comparative advantage does not result from differences in climate and natural resources. More frequently, comparative advantage is due to decisions by individuals, by firms, or by the government in a given country. For example, a comparative advantage of the United States in pharmaceuticals might be due to investment in research and in physical and human capital in the areas of chemistry and biology. An enormous amount of research goes into developing technological know-how to produce pharmaceutical products.

In Korea, on the other hand, there may be less capital available for such huge expenditures on research in the pharmaceutical area. A Korean comparative advantage in electronic goods might be due to a large, well-trained work force that is well suited to electronics and small-scale assembly. For example, the excellent math and technical training in Korean high schools may provide a large labor force for the electronics industry.

Comparative advantages can change over time. In fact, the United States did have a comparative advantage in TV sets in the 1950s and early 1960s, before the countries of East Asia developed skills and knowledge in these areas. A country may have a comparative advantage in a good it has recently developed, but then the technology spreads to other countries, which develop a comparative advantage, and the first country goes on to something else.

Perhaps the United States's comparative advantage in pharmaceuticals will go to other countries in the future, and the United States will develop a comparative advantage in other, yet unforeseen areas. The term *dynamic* comparative advantage describes changes in comparative advantage over time because of investment in physical and human capital and in technology.

Labor versus Capital Resources

To illustrate the importance of capital for comparative advantage, imagine a world in which all comparative advantage can be explained through differences between countries in the amount of physical capital that workers have to work with. It is such a world that is described by the Heckscher-Ohlin model, named after the two Swedish economists, Eli Heckscher and Bertil Ohlin, who developed it. Ohlin won a Nobel Prize for his work in international economics. The Heckscher-Ohlin model provides a particular explanation for comparative advantage.

capital abundant: a higher level of capital per worker in one country relative to another.

labor abundant: a lower level of capital per worker in one country relative to another.

capital intensive: production that uses a relatively high level of capital per worker.

labor intensive: production that uses a relatively low level of capital per worker.

Here is how comparative advantage develops in such a model. Suppose America has a higher level of capital per worker than Korea. In other words, America is **capital abundant** compared to Korea, and—what amounts to the same thing—Korea is **labor abundant** compared to America. We noted that pharmaceutical production uses more capital per worker than electronics production; in other words, pharmaceutical production is relatively **capital intensive,** while electronics production is relatively **labor intensive.** Hence, it makes sense that the United States has a comparative advantage in pharmaceuticals: The United States is relatively capital abundant, and pharmaceuticals are relatively capital intensive. On the other hand, Korea has a comparative advantage in electronics because Korea is relatively labor abundant, and electronics are relatively labor intensive. Thus, the Heckscher-Ohlin model predicts that if a country has a relative abundance of a factor (labor or capital), it will have a comparative advantage in those goods that require a greater amount of that factor.

The Effect of Trade on Wages

An important implication of the Heckscher-Ohlin model is that trade will tend to bring factor prices (the price of labor and the price of capital) into equality in different countries. In other words, if the comparative advantage between Korea and the United States was due only to differences in relative capital and labor abundance, then trade would tend to increase real wages in Korea and lower real wages in the United States.

factor-price equalization: the equalization of the price of labor and the price of capital across countries when they are engaging in free trade.

More generally, trade tends to increase demand for the factor that is relatively abundant in a country and decrease demand for the factor that is relatively scarce. This raises the price of the relatively abundant factor and lowers the price of the relatively scarce factor. Suppose the United States is more capital abundant than Korea and has a comparative advantage in pharmaceuticals, which are more capital intensive than electronics. Then with trade, the price of capital will rise relative to the price of labor in the United States. The intuition behind this prediction—which is called **factor-price equalization**—is that demand for labor (the relatively scarce factor) shifts down with trade as the United States increases production of pharmaceuticals and reduces its production of electronic goods. On the other hand, the demand for capital (the relatively abundant factor) shifts up with trade. Although there is no immigration, it is as if foreign workers competed with workers in the labor-scarce country and bid down the wage.

Because technology also influences wages and productivity, it has been hard to detect such movements in wages due to factor-price equalization. Wages of workers in the developed world with high productivity due to high levels of technology remain well above wages of workers in the less-developed world with low productivity due to low levels of technology.

In other words, changes in technology can offset the effects of factor-price equalization on wages. If trade raises technological know-how sufficiently, then no one has to suffer from greater trade. In our example of comparative advantage, American workers are paid more than Korean workers both before and after trade; that is because their overall level of productivity is higher. Workers with higher productivity will be paid more than workers with lower productivity even in countries that trade.

Factor-price equalization can explain another phenomenon: growing wage disparity in the United States during the past 25 years, in which the wages of high-skilled workers have risen relative to the wages of less-skilled workers. The United States is relatively abundant in high-skilled workers, and developing countries are relatively abundant in low-skilled workers. Thus, high-skilled workers' wages should rise and low-skilled workers' wages should fall in the United States, according to factor-price equalization. In this application of factor-price equalization, the two factors are high-skilled workers and low-skilled workers.

In the next section, we show that there are gains in efficiency and lower cost from trade that can benefit all workers.

REVIEW
- Comparative advantage changes over time and depends on the actions of individuals in a country. Thus, comparative advantage is a dynamic concept.

- International trade will tend to equalize wages in different countries. Technological differences, however, can keep wages high in high-productivity countries.

Gains from Expanded Markets

In the introduction to this chapter, we mentioned the gains from trade that come from larger-sized markets. Having discussed the principle of comparative advantage, we now examine this other source of the gains from trade.

An Example of Gains from Trade Through Expanded Markets

Let us start with a simple example. Consider two countries that are similar in resources, capital, and skilled labor, such as the United States and Germany. Suppose there is a market in Germany and the United States for two medical diagnostic products—magnetic resonance imaging (MRI) machines and ultrasound scanners. Suppose the technology for producing each type of diagnostic device is the same in each country. We assume that the technology is identical because we want to show that trade will take place without differences between the countries.

Figure 29.3 illustrates the situation. Without trade, Germany and the United States each produce 1,000 MRIs and 1,000 ultrasound scanners. This amount of production meets the demand in the two separate markets. The cost per unit of producing each MRI machine is $300,000, while the cost per unit of producing each ultrasound scanner is $200,000. Again, these costs are the same in each country.

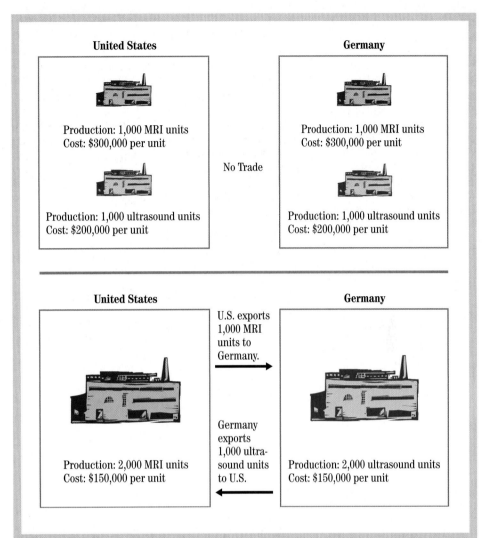

Figure 29.3
Gains from Global Markets
In this example, the technology of producing magnetic resonance imaging (MRI) machines and ultrasound scanners is assumed to be the same in the United States and Germany. In the top panel, with no trade between the United States and Germany, the quantity produced in each country is low and the cost per unit is high. With trade, the U.S. firm increases its production of MRIs and exports to Germany; the German firm increases its production of ultrasound scanners and exports to the United States. As a result, cost per unit comes down significantly.

■ **Effects of a Larger Market.**   Now suppose that the two countries trade. Observe in Figure 29.3—and this is very important—that the *cost per unit* of producing MRIs and ultrasound scanners *declines as more are produced*. Trade increases the size of the market for each product. In this example, the market is twice as large with trade as without it: 2,000 MRIs rather than 1,000 and 2,000 ultrasound scanners rather than 1,000. The production of MRIs in the United States can expand, and the production of ultrasound scanners in the United States can contract. Similarly,

ECONOMICS IN ACTION

Writing "Talking Points" for the President

To promote trade and reduce trade barriers, the president of the United States and other executive branch officers must make speeches and hold meetings with members of Congress and other interested groups. Many of their "talking points"—short phrases that people can easily remember and repeat—are developed by their economic advisers and give examples of the gains from trade through larger markets. Here are some examples of the actual talking points used to promote the North American Free Trade Agreement that reduced trade barriers between the United States and Mexico and Canada in the 1990s. This agreement was a high priority in the administrations of both President George H. W. Bush and President Bill Clinton.

Observe how these talking points are related to the model illustrated in Figure 29.4, which shows the gains from trade through expanded markets. The term *economies of scale* refers to the decline in cost per unit. *Product rationalization* refers to locating production in fewer factories in order to reduce cost per unit. *Internal distortions* means that trade barriers had caused factories to be too small.

Talking Points on Gains from Trade

- The further integration of North American manufacturing facilities and the resulting product rationalizations would increase trade and the competitiveness of U.S. producers.

- U.S. companies operating in both Mexico and the United States will be able to reduce costs through product rationalization. They will no longer have to make the same vehicles, or the same parts for those vehicles, in two countries.

- Removal of internal distortions and economies of scale would enhance the international competitiveness of the North American automotive industry.

the production of ultrasound scanners in Germany can expand, and the production of MRIs in Germany can contract. With the United States specializing in production of MRIs, the cost per unit of MRIs declines to $150,000. Similarly, the cost per unit of ultrasound scanners declines to $150,000. The United States exports MRIs to Germany so that the number of MRIs in Germany can be the same as without trade, and Germany exports ultrasound scanners to the United States. The gain from trade is the reduction in cost per unit. This gain from trade has occurred without any differences in the efficiency of production between the two countries.

Note that we could have set up the example differently. We could have had Germany specializing in MRIs and the United States specializing in ultrasound scanner production. Then the United States would have exported ultrasound scanners, and Germany would have exported MRIs. But the gains from trade would have been exactly the same. Unlike the comparative advantage motive for trade, the expanded markets motive alone cannot predict what the direction of trade will be.

intraindustry trade: trade between countries in goods from the same or similar industries. (Ch. 11)

interindustry trade: trade between countries in goods from different industries. (Ch. 11)

■ **Intraindustry Trade versus Interindustry Trade.** MRIs and ultrasound scanners are similar products; they are considered to be in the same industry, the medical diagnostic equipment industry. Thus, the trade between Germany and the United States in MRIs and ultrasound scanners is called *intraindustry trade*, which means trade in goods in the same industry.

In contrast, the trade that took place in the example of comparative advantage was *interindustry trade*, because vaccines and TV sets are in different industries. In that example, exports of vaccines from the United States greatly exceed imports of vaccines, producing a U.S. industry trade surplus in vaccines. Imports of TV sets into the United States are much greater than exports of TV sets, producing a U.S. industry trade deficit in TV sets.

These examples convey an important message about international trade. Trade due to comparative advantage tends to be interindustry, and trade due to expanded markets tends to be intraindustry. In reality, a huge amount of international trade is intraindustry trade. This indicates that creating larger markets is an important motive for trade.

Measuring the Gains from Expanded Markets

The medical equipment example illustrates how larger markets can reduce costs. To fully describe the gains from trade resulting from larger markets, we need to consider a model.

■ **A Relationship Between Cost per Unit and the Number of Firms.**   Let us examine the idea that *as the number of firms in a market of a given size increases, the cost per unit at each firm increases*. The two graphs in Figure 29.4 are useful for this purpose. In each graph the downward-sloping line shows how cost per unit (or average total cost) at a firm decreases as the quantity produced at that firm increases. Cost per unit measured in dollars is on the vertical axis, and the quantity produced and sold is on the horizontal axis. Observe that cost per unit declines through the whole range shown in the graph. Cost per unit declines because the larger quantity of production allows a firm to achieve a greater division of labor and more specialization.

Focus first on the graph on the left. The total size of the market (determined by the number of customers in the market) is shown by the bracket on the horizontal axis. We assume that the firms in the market have equal shares of the market. For example, if there are 4 firms in the market, then each firm will produce 1/4 of the market. Suppose that there are 4 firms; then, according to Figure 29.4, the cost per unit at each firm will be $30. This is the cost per unit for the quantity labeled by the box "1 of 4," which means that this is the quantity produced by each 1 of the 4 firms.

Now, suppose that there are 3 firms in the market and each firm produces 1/3 of the market. The cost per unit at each firm will be $25, as shown by the box labeled

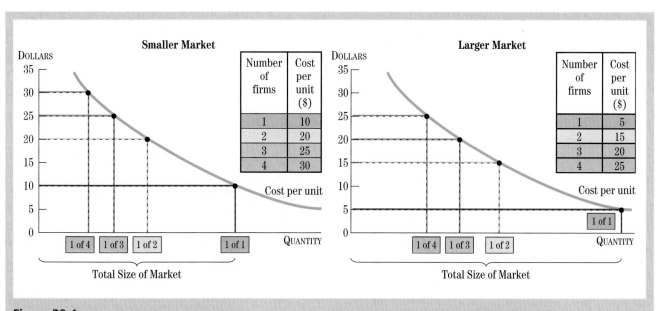

Figure 29.4
Cost per Unit: The Number of Firms and Market Size
(1) The market on the right is larger than the market on the left. Hence, cost per unit is lower on the right with the larger market. (2) Regardless of the size of the market, cost per unit declines as the number of firms declines.

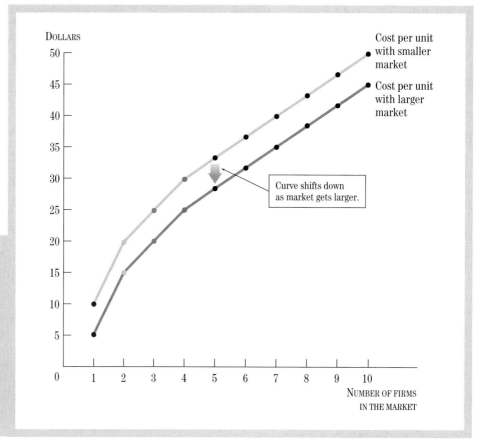

Figure 29.5
The Relationship Between Cost per Unit and the Number of Firms
The first four points on each curve are plotted from the two tables in Figure 29.4 for 1 to 4 firms; the other points can be similarly obtained. Each curve shows how cost per unit at each firm rises as the number of firms increases in a market of a given size. The curve shifts down when the size of the market increases.

"1 of 3" in Figure 29.4. Cost per unit at each firm is lower with 3 firms than with 4 firms in the market because each firm is producing more: That is, 1/3 of the market is more than 1/4 of the market. Continuing in this way, we see that with 2 firms in the market, the cost per unit is $20. And with 1 firm in the market, the cost per unit is $10. In sum, as we decreased the number of firms in the market, each firm produced more and cost per unit decreased. If the number of firms in the market increased, then cost per unit at each firm would increase.

■ **The Effect of the Size of the Market.** Now compare the graph on the left with the graph on the right of Figure 29.4. The important difference is that the graph on the right represents a larger market than the graph on the left. The bracket in the right-hand graph is bigger to show the larger market.

By comparing the graph on the left in Figure 29.4 (smaller market) with that on the right (larger market), we see that an increase in the size of the market reduces cost per unit at each firm, holding the number of firms in the industry constant. For example, when there is one firm in the market, cost per unit is $5 for the larger market compared with $10 for the smaller market. Or with four firms, cost per unit is $25 for the larger market compared with $30 for the smaller market. Compare the little tables in Figure 29.4. As the market increases in size, each firm produces at a lower cost per unit.

Figure 29.5 summarizes the information in Figure 29.4. It shows the positive relationship between the number of firms in the market, shown on the horizontal axis, and the cost per unit at each firm. As the figure indicates, more firms mean a higher cost per unit at each firm. (Be careful to note that the horizontal axis in Figure 29.5 is the *number* of firms in a given *market*, not the quantity produced by a given firm.) When the size of the market increases, the relationship between the number of firms in the market and the cost per unit shifts down, as shown in Figure 29.5. In other words, as the market increases in size, cost per unit declines at each firm if the number of firms does not change.

■ **A Relationship Between the Price and the Number of Firms.** A general feature of most markets is that as the number of firms in the market increases, the price at each firm declines. More firms make the market more competitive. Thus, there is a relationship between the price and the number of firms, as shown in Figure 29.6. As in Figure 29.5, the number of firms is on the horizontal axis. The curve in Figure 29.6 is downward-sloping because a greater number of firms means a lower price.

■ **Equilibrium Price and Number of Firms.** In the long run, as firms either enter or exit an industry, price will tend to equal cost per unit. If the price for each unit were greater than the cost per unit, then there would be a profit opportunity for new firms, and the number of firms in the industry would rise. If the price were less than the cost per unit, then firms would exit the industry. Only when price equals cost per unit is there a long-run equilibrium. Because price equals cost per unit, the curves in Figure 29.5 and 29.6 can be combined to determine the price and the number of firms in long-run equilibrium. As shown in Figure 29.7, there is a long-run equilibrium in the industry when the downward-sloping line for Figure 29.6 intersects the upward-sloping line (for the smaller market) from Figure 29.5. At this point, price equals cost per unit.

Corresponding to this long-run equilibrium is an equilibrium number of firms. More firms would lower the price below cost per unit, causing firms to leave the industry; fewer firms would raise the price above cost per unit, attracting new firms to the industry. Figure 29.7 shows how the possibility of entry and exit results in a long-run equilibrium with price equal to cost per unit.

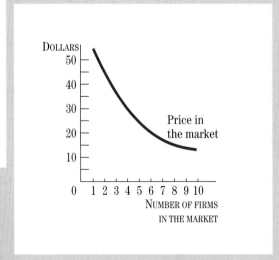

Figure 29.6
The Relationship Between the Price and the Number of Firms
As the number of firms increases, the market price declines. This curve summarizes this relationship.

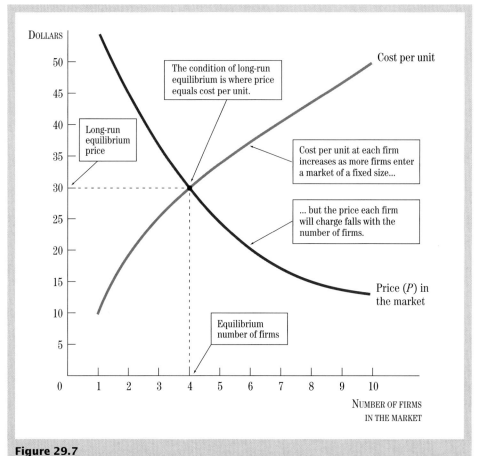

Figure 29.7
Long-Run Equilibrium Number of Firms and Cost per Unit
A condition for long-run equilibrium is that price equals cost per unit. In this diagram, this condition is shown at the intersection of the two curves.

■ **Increasing the Size of the Market.** Now let us see how the industry equilibrium changes when the size of the market increases due to international trade. In Figure 29.8, we show how an increase in the size of the market, due perhaps to the creation of a free trade area, reduces the price and increases the number of firms. The curve showing the cost per unit of each firm shifts down and out as the market expands; that is, for each number of firms, the cost per unit declines for each firm. This brings about a new intersection and a long-run equilibrium at a lower price. Moreover, the increase in the number of firms suggests that there will be more product variety, which is another part of the gains from trade.

■ **The North American Automobile Market.** The gains from trade due to larger markets arise in many real-world examples. Trade in cars between Canada and the United States now occurs even though neither country has an obvious comparative advantage. Before 1964, trade in cars between Canada and the United States was restricted. Canadian factories thus had to limit their production to the Canadian market. This kept cost per unit high. When free trade in cars was permitted, the production in Canadian factories increased, and the Canadian factories began to export cars to the United States. With more cars produced, cost per unit declined.

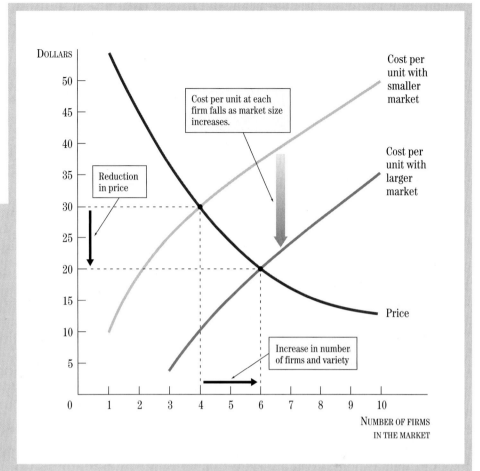

**Figure 29.8
Gains from Trade Due to
Larger Markets**
When trade occurs, the market
increases from the size of the
market in one country to the
combined size of the market in
two or more countries. This
larger market shifts the upward-
sloping line down because cost
per unit for each firm is lower
when the market is bigger. In the
long-run equilibrium at the intersection of the two new curves,
the price is lower and there are
more firms. With more firms,
there is more variety. Lower price
and more variety are the gains
from trade.

REVIEW
- Lowering cost per unit through the division of labor requires large markets. International trade creates large markets.

- A graphical model can be used to explain the gains from international trade; the model shows that a larger market reduces prices.

Conclusion

In this chapter, we have focused on the economic gains to the citizens of a country from international trade. We have mentioned two reasons for such gains: comparative advantage and larger markets that reduce cost per unit. Both reasons apply to trade within a country as well as to international trade. Most of the chapter was spent showing how to measure the gains due to comparative advantage and larger markets.

In concluding this chapter, it is important to point out that the benefits of international trade go well beyond economic gains.

International trade sometimes puts competitive pressure on governments to deliver better policies. Within the United States, competition between states can make regulatory and tax policies more efficient. Similarly, competition can make regulatory policies in countries more efficient.

International trade can also improve international relations. Trade enables Americans to learn more about Southeast Asians or Europeans or Latin Americans. This improves understanding and reduces the possibilities for international conflict. Developing international trade with Russia and the other countries of the former Soviet Union might even reduce the possibility of another cold war or new international conflict in the future. If many people have an economic stake in a relationship, they will not like a military action that threatens that relationship.

KEY POINTS

1. The principles of economics can be used to analyze international trade just as they can be used to analyze trade within a country.

2. International trade is different from within-country trade because national governments can place restrictions on the trade of goods and services between countries and on immigration.

3. According to the principle of comparative advantage, countries that specialize in producing goods that they have a comparative advantage in can increase world production and raise consumption in their own country.

4. The gains from trade due to comparative advantage can be shown graphically by shifting out the production possibilities curve.

5. The relative price of two goods with trade is between the relative prices in the two countries without trade.

6. Comparative advantage is a dynamic concept. If people in one country improve their skills or develop low-cost production methods through research, they will alter the comparative advantage.

7. If differences in the relative abundance of capital and labor are the reason for differences in comparative advantage, then international trade will tend to equalize real wages.

8. Lower cost per unit in larger markets is another key reason for gains in trade.

9. When the size of the market increases, the price declines, there are more firms, and there is greater variety of products.

KEY TERMS

tariff	absolute advantage	labor abundant	labor intensive
quota	capital abundant	capital intensive	factor-price equalization
commerce clause			

QUESTIONS FOR REVIEW

1. Why has international trade grown so rapidly in recent years?

2. What is the difference between absolute advantage and comparative advantage?

3. If the relative price of two goods is 4 in one country and 6 in another country before trade, in what range will the relative price be after trade?

4. What is the difference between the production possibilities curve before trade and after trade?

5. In what sense is comparative advantage a dynamic concept?

6. Why does trade take place even if one country does not have an absolute advantage over another?

7. What is the difference between capital abundant and capital intensive?

8. Why might costs per unit decline when the market increases in size?

9. What is the difference between interindustry trade and intraindustry trade?

PROBLEMS

1. Suppose the production of wheat and strawberries per unit of labor in the United States and Mexico is as follows:

	Wheat	Strawberries
Mexico	1 bushel	3 pints
United States	2 bushels	3 pints

   a. Which country has a comparative advantage in wheat production? Why?
   b. With free trade between the United States and Mexico, is it possible that 1 bushel of wheat will trade for 1 pint of strawberries? Why or why not?
   c. Suppose the free trade price is 1 bushel of wheat for 2 pints of strawberries. Draw a diagram indicating the production possibilities curve with and without trade if the United States has 200 million units of labor. What is the maximum amount of wheat the United States can produce?

2. What is the shape of the production possibilities curves in problem 1? What does this shape imply about the nature of the tradeoff between wheat and strawberries? Is this a realistic assumption? Explain.

3. Suppose there are two goods, wheat and clothing, and two countries, the United States and Brazil, in the world. The production of wheat and clothing requires only labor. In the United States, it takes 1 unit of labor to produce 4 bushels of wheat and 1 unit of labor to produce 2 items of clothing. In Brazil, it takes 1 unit of labor to produce 1 bushel of wheat and 1 unit of labor to produce 1 item of clothing.
   a. Suppose the United States has 100 units of labor and Brazil has 120. Draw the production possibilities curve for each country without trade. Which country has the absolute advantage in each good? Indicate each country's comparative advantage.
   b. In what range would the world trading price ratio lie when these countries open up to free trade? Will both countries be better off? Why? Show this on your diagram.

4. Suppose France has 250 units of labor and Belgium has 100 units of labor. In France, 1 unit of labor can produce 1 shirt or 3 bottles of wine. In Belgium, 2 units of labor can produce 1 shirt or 3 bottles of wine. Draw the production possibilities curve for each country. If these countries open up to trade, what will happen? Why?

5. Suppose an economics professor can type 15 pages in an hour or write half an economics lecture in an hour. Will she ever have a reason to hire an assistant who can type 10 pages per hour? Use the idea of comparative advantage to explain.

6. "Developing countries should exploit their own comparative advantage and quit trying to invest in physical and human capital to develop high-tech industries." Comment.

7. How does the relative abundance of factors of production affect comparative advantage? Suppose you found that imports to the United States from China were mainly goods, such as airplanes, that require much capital compared to labor, and that exports from the United States to China were mainly goods, such as toys, that require much labor compared to capital. Would your finding constitute evidence against the theory of comparative advantage?

8. Comparative advantage explains interindustry trade in different goods between countries. How do economists explain intraindustry trade, that is, trade in the same industry between countries? Why might people in the United States want to buy German cars, and Germans want to buy cars from the United States?

9. Suppose that each firm in an industry has the total costs shown below.

Quantity of Output	Total Costs (dollars)
1	50
2	54
3	60
4	68
5	80
6	90
7	105
8	112

   a. Suppose that the quantity demanded in the market is fixed at 4. Calculate the average total cost for each firm when there are 1, 2, and 4 firms in the industry. Draw a diagram indicating the relationship between average total cost and number of firms.
   b. Suppose the quantity demanded in the market expands because of an opening of trade and is now fixed at 8. Draw a diagram similar to the one in part (a) indicating the relationship between average total cost and the number of firms. Why does this opening of trade cause this shift in the curve?

10. The following relationship between price, cost per unit, and the number of firms describes an industry in a single country.

Number of Firms	Cost per Unit ($)	Price ($)
1	10	90
2	20	80
3	30	70
4	40	60
5	50	50
6	60	46
7	70	43
8	80	40
9	90	38
10	100	36

a. Graph (1) the relationship between cost per unit and number of firms, and (2) the relationship between price and number of firms. Why does one slope up and the other slope down?

b. Find the long-run equilibrium price and number of firms.

c. Now suppose the country opens its borders to trade with other countries; as a result, the relationship between cost per unit and the number of firms becomes as follows:

Number of Firms	Cost per Unit ($)
1	5
2	10
3	15
4	20
5	25
6	30
7	35
8	40
9	45
10	50

Find the long-run equilibrium price and number of firms.

d. What are the gains from expanding the market through the reduction in trade barriers?

11. Compare and contrast the following: international trade versus trade within a country, absolute advantage versus comparative advantage, tariff versus quota, labor abundant versus labor intensive, intraindustry trade versus interindustry trade.

CHAPTER 30

International Trade Policy

The violent riots in Seattle in December 1999 made newspaper headlines all over the world and were shown on TV news hour after hour. The riots grew out of what was expected to be a peaceful protest of a big meeting of the World Trade Organization (WTO), an organization that includes most countries in the world. The WTO was founded in 1993. Its purpose is to develop policies to reduce the many barriers to international trade that still exist and to keep countries from enacting new barriers. The WTO's specific goal for the Seattle meeting was to negotiate a new plan to reduce trade barriers. This goal is in keeping with the economic findings of Chapter 29 that people gain from international trade.

The protesters objected to many things about the WTO. Some objected to reducing trade barriers because they thought this would reduce jobs in certain industries. Others objected to a lack of concern for the environment on the part of the members of the WTO. Still others felt that the WTO was not doing enough to promote higher labor standards in poor countries. Many were suspicious of the WTO, believing that it had too much power; they said that the WTO was run by international bureaucrats who did not have to answer to anyone.

It is not clear how and why the riots got started, but they were brutal; stores were looted, the police used tear gas, and delegates to the WTO could not leave their hotel rooms. The riots were a reminder that the reduction of trade barriers is still strongly opposed by some people for many different reasons. As the twenty-first century began, many worried that a powerful political movement demanding higher trade barriers could arise.

This chapter considers both the economics and the politics of international trade policy. It examines the economic impact of the trade barriers that currently exist, reviews the political history of past trade barriers in the United States, and considers the political-economic arguments given in favor of trade barriers, including some of the arguments made by the protesters in Seattle. It then goes on to evaluate alternative international trade policies in terms of their effectiveness in reducing trade barriers.

Tariffs, Quotas, and VRAs

Governments use many methods to restrict international trade. Policies that restrict trade are called *protectionist policies* because the restrictions usually protect industries from foreign imports.

Examining the economic impact of trade restrictions helps you understand why some industries lobby for protectionist policies. As you delve into the economic analysis, think about whether a protectionist policy would help or hurt you. If the United States restricts trade for clothing, how would this restriction impact U.S. clothing producers, foreign clothing producers, U.S. retailers that sell clothing, and U.S. consumers who buy clothing? How would the restriction affect U.S. employment in clothing production and the price of clothing? We'll see that there are winners and losers as a result of trade restrictions, but that the gains for the winners

Seattle, 1999
The goal of the WTO is to reduce trade barriers. But not everyone agrees with the goal, as the protest against the WTO meeting in Seattle reminds us.

will be smaller than the losses of the losers. That is, the losses from trade restrictions outweigh the gains, creating deadweight loss.

As you learn the impact of a new trade restriction, check your understanding by considering the removal of an existing trade restriction. Again, there will be winners and losers as a result of removing trade restrictions, but the gains for the winners will be larger than the losses of the losers. Removing trade restrictions therefore eliminates deadweight loss.

Tariffs

ad valorem tariff: a tax on imports evaluated as a percentage of the value of the import.

specific tariff: a tax on imports that is proportional to the number of units or items imported.

The oldest and most common method by which a government restricts trade is the *tariff*, a tax on goods imported into a country. The higher the tariff, the more trade is restricted. An **ad valorem tariff** is a tax equal to a certain percentage of the value of the good. For example, a 15 percent tariff on the value of goods imported is an ad valorem tariff. If $100,000 worth of goods are imported, the tariff revenue is $15,000. A **specific tariff** is a tax on the quantity sold, such as 50 cents for each kilogram of zinc.

The economic effects of a tariff are illustrated in Figure 30.1. We consider a particular good—automobiles, for example—that is exported from one country (Japan, for example) and imported by another country (the United States, for example). An *import demand curve* and an *export supply curve* are shown in Figure 30.1. The *import demand curve* gives the quantity of imported goods that will be demanded at each price. It shows that a higher price for imported goods will reduce the quantity of the goods demanded. A higher price for Nissans and Toyotas, for example, will lead to a smaller quantity of Nissans and Toyotas demanded by Americans. Like the standard demand curve, the import demand curve is downward-sloping.

The *export supply curve* gives the quantity of exports that foreign firms are willing to sell at each price. In the case of Nissans and Toyotas, the export supply curve gives the quantity of Toyotas and Nissans that Japanese producers are willing to sell in

Figure 30.1
The Effects of a Tariff
A tariff shifts the export supply curve up by the amount of the tariff. Thus, the price paid for imports by consumers rises and the quantity imported declines. The price increase (upward-pointing black arrow) is less than the tariff (upward-pointing blue arrow). The revenue to the government is shown by the shaded area; it is the tariff times the amount imported.

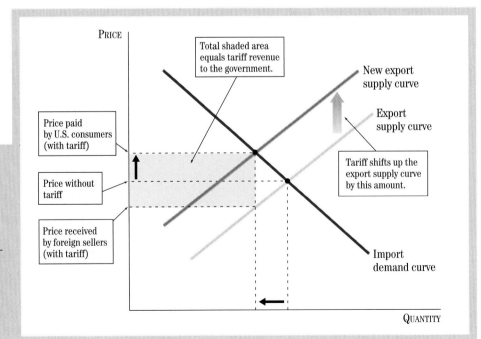

the United States. The supply curve is upward-sloping, just like any other supply curve, because foreign producers are willing to supply more cars when the price is higher.

In equilibrium, for any single type of good, the quantity of exports supplied must equal the quantity of imports demanded. Thus, the intersection of the export supply curve and the import demand curve gives the amount imported into the country and the price.

When the government imposes a tariff, the supply curve shifts up, as shown in Figure 30.1. The tariff increases the marginal cost of supplying cars to the United States. The amount of the tariff in dollars is the amount by which the supply curve shifts up; it is given by the length of the blue arrow in Figure 30.1.

The tariff changes the intersection of the export supply curve and the import demand curve. At the new equilibrium, a lower quantity is imported at a higher price. The price paid for cars by consumers rises, but the increase in the price is less than the tariff. In Figure 30.1, the upward-pointing black arrow shows the price increase. The blue arrow, which shows the tariff increase, is longer than the black arrow along the vertical axis. The size of the price increase depends on the slopes of the demand curve and the supply curve.

The price received by suppliers equals the price paid by consumers less the tariff that must be paid to the government. Observe that the price received by the sellers declines as a result of the tariff.

The amount of revenue that the government collects is given by the quantity imported times the tariff, which is indicated by the shaded rectangle in Figure 30.1. For example, if the tariff is $1,000 per car and 1 million cars are imported, the revenue is $1 billion. Tariff revenues are called *duties* and are collected by customs.

The tariff also has an effect on U.S. car producers. Because the tariff reduces imports from abroad and raises their price, the demand for cars produced by import-competing companies in the United States—General Motors or Ford—increases. This increase in demand will raise the price of U.S. cars. Thus, consumers pay more for both imported cars and domestically produced cars.

The Impact of a Tariff on Two Different Industries

In the following two cases, consider the case for and the impact of a tariff to protect the domestic industry. In 2002, an increasing amount of steel in the United States was imported and steel prices were low. Many U.S. steel-producing companies were in debt and in the past five years, 30 steelmakers had sought bankruptcy protection. To avoid additional bankruptcies and loss of jobs, the steel industry lobbied for protection from imported steel. In March 2002, President Bush imposed tariffs on steel imports. The tariffs were as high as 30% and were to last three years.

We would predict that a tariff on steel would increase the price of steel in the United States, increasing the profits of steelmakers and hurting steel consumers. As predicted, steel prices increased, steelmakers profited, and the steel-consuming industry was hurt by the higher prices. Some manufacturers claimed the tariffs jeopardized more jobs in the steel-consuming industry than they saved in the steel-producing industry. Steelmakers in the rest of the world filed complaints with the World Trade Organization. The WTO ruled that the U.S. tariffs on steel were illegal. In December 2003, President Bush reversed this protectionist policy, removing the tariffs on steel. If you were determining trade policy, how would you view the tradeoff between U.S. steel jobs and the effects of the higher price of steel on the U.S. manu-facturing industry?

Between 2000 and 2004, shrimp imports in the United States increased 70%. This increase in the supply of shrimp caused the price of shrimp to tumble. U.S. shrimp fishermen lobbied for tariffs on imported shrimp, claiming foreign shrimp was being dumped on the U.S. market at prices below production costs. In July 2004, the United States proposed tariffs on shrimp imported from some countries.

U.S. consumers benefit from the increase in shrimp imports and the tumble in shrimp prices. Foreign shrimp producers profit from their sale of shrimp in the United States. U.S. shrimp producers are requesting protection from these low shrimp prices. With tariffs, we would expect profits to increase for U.S. shrimp producers, imports to fall, the price of shrimp to increase, and foreign producers' profits to fall. If you were determining trade policy, how would you view this tradeoff between the health of the U.S. shrimp producing industry and the price of shrimp for U.S. consumers? Does your answer to this question about tradeoffs depend on whether the protected industry is steel or shrimp?

Quotas

Another method of government restriction of international trade is the *quota*. A quota sets a limit, a maximum, on the amount of a given good that can be imported. The United States has quotas on the import of ice cream, sugar, cotton, peanuts, and other commodities. Foreigners can supply only a limited amount to the United States.

The economic effect of a quota is illustrated in Figure 30.2. The export supply curve and the import demand curve are identical to those in Figure 30.1. The quota, the maximum that foreign firms can export to the United States, is indicated in Figure 30.2 by the solid purple vertical line labeled "quota." Exporters cannot supply more cars than the quota, and, therefore, American consumers cannot buy more than this amount. We have chosen the quota amount to equal the quantity imported with the tariff in Figure 30.1. This shows that if it wants to, the government can achieve the same effects on the quantity imported using a quota or a tariff. Moreover, the price increase in Figure 30.2, represented by the black arrow along the vertical axis, is the same as the price increase in Figure 30.1. Viewed from the domestic market, therefore, a quota and a tariff are equivalent: If the quota is set to allow in the same quantity of imports as the tariff, then the price increase will be the same. Consumers will pay more for imports in both cases, and the demand for domestically produced goods that are substitutes for imports will increase. The price of domestically produced cars will also increase if there is a quota on foreign cars.

Then what is the difference in the effects of a tariff and a quota? Unlike the situation with a tariff, no revenue goes to the government with a quota. The difference between the price that the foreign suppliers get and the higher price that the consumers pay goes to the holders of the quota—the ones who are allowed to import into the country. Frequently foreign countries hold the quotas. The revenue the quota holders get is indicated by the shaded rectangle in Figure 30.2. It is equal to the quantity imported times the difference between the price paid by the consumers and the price received by the producers. The size of that rectangle is identical to the size of the rectangle showing the revenue paid to the government in the case of the tariff in Figure 30.1.

On January 1, 2005, the 1973 Multi-fiber Agreement, a set of quotas on textiles and apparel, expired. This system of global quotas restricting imports added an estimated 20% to the cost of clothing, while benefiting companies in places like Hong Kong that specialized in supplying clothing under this quota system. The lifting of the quotas created widespread fears among U.S. and European Union clothing manufacturers about the flood of cheap Chinese apparel into these markets. A coalition of U.S. producers claimed that 650,000 jobs were at risk. Since then, the European Union and the United States have both struggled to find a solution that will work for China and for domestic manufacturers, retailers, and consumers.

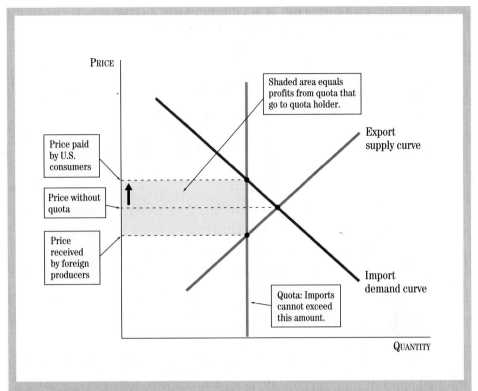

Figure 30.2
The Effects of a Quota
A quota can be set to allow the same quantity of imports as a tariff. The quota in this figure and the tariff in Figure 30.1 allow the same quantity of imports into the country. The price increase is the same for the quota and the tariff. But, in the case of a quota, the revenue goes to quota holders, not to the U.S. government.

We would predict that the expiration of the global quotas will cause U.S. clothing prices to fall and imports of clothing to rise. This will benefit foreign producers who import more to the United States, benefit U.S. consumers, benefit U.S. clothing retailers, hurt the Hong Kong companies supplying clothing, and hurt U.S. clothing producers. You can understand why U.S. clothing producers are lobbying for new quotas while U.S. clothing retailers are opposed to them. If you were determining trade policy, how would you view this tradeoff between U.S. clothing prices and U.S. clothing production?

Voluntary Restraint Agreements (VRAs)

voluntary restraint agreement (VRA): a country's self-imposed government restriction on exports to a particular country.

Another alternative to tariffs and quotas is the **voluntary restraint agreement (VRA).** Such a restraint is similar to a quota except that one country, such as the United States, asks another country to "volunteer" to restrict its firms' exports to the United States. Although a tariff or a quota must be passed by Congress, VRAs can be negotiated by the president without Congress approving.

The United States negotiated VRAs with Japan for automobiles in the early 1980s. The Japanese government agreed to limit the number of automobiles Japanese firms exported to the United States to 2.8 million. There are also VRAs on machine tools and textiles exported to the United States. These voluntary agreements usually occur because of pressure that one country, such as the United States, exerts on the other country. Hence, they are not actually voluntary. For example, a foreign government might agree to a VRA because the other country was about to impose steep tariffs. Or there may be diplomatic pressures unrelated to economics that one country can use to pressure another country into these so-called voluntary actions.

What is the economic effect of a VRA? Figure 30.3 examines the impact. The supply and demand curves are identical to those in Figures 30.1 and 30.2. The amount of the VRA chosen for illustration is the same as the quota in Figure 30.2 and the quantity resulting from the tariff in Figure 30.1. This shows that the effect of the VRA on price and quantity can be made identical to that of the quota and the tariff. Consumers pay more under tariffs, quotas, or VRAs. The difference between VRAs and quotas is the recipient of the equivalent of the tariff revenue. In the case of the VRA, these revenues go to the foreign firms. As firms reduce their production, the price rises, and their profits rise. Thus, what would have been tariff revenue to the U.S. government in the case of a U.S. tariff becomes increased profits for foreign firms in the case of a VRA.

Studies show that the VRAs used in the United States in the 1980s for automobiles did lead to a higher price and additional revenue to the Japanese automobile producers. The price of Japanese cars sold in the United States rose by about $1,000, and the increase in demand for U.S. cars led to their price increasing by about $1,400 for the average car.

The Costs of Trade Restrictions

Trade barriers such as tariffs, quotas, and VRAs distort prices and reduce the quantity consumed, benefiting domestic producers at the expense of domestic consumers and foreign producers. For example, the United States imposes quotas on

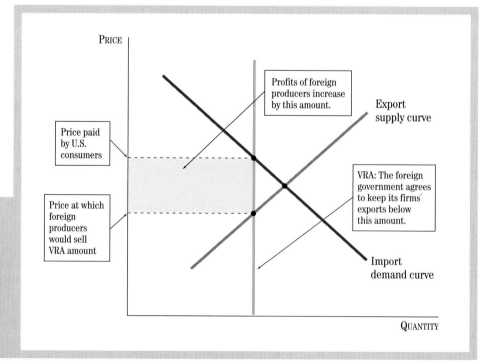

Figure 30.3
The Effects of a Voluntary Restraint Agreement (VRA)
The effects are just like those of the quota in Figure 30.2 except that the revenue goes to foreign firms rather than quota holders. Because of the VRA, the foreign firms act as if they are in a cartel to restrict output and raise prices.

The following news story from the Associated Press discusses the economic impact of the termination of the Multi-Fiber Agreement on the economy of Sri Lanka. In this particular case, the cost to Sri Lanka is the loss of the quota rents that they had earned under the Multi-Fiber agreement. The winners will be the lower cost producers in countries like Mexico, who will no longer be shut out of the U.S. market, as well as consumers in the U.S. market.

Sri Lanka's revenue from garment exports to America set to drop 20 percent as trade agreement expires

> Benefits to U.S. consumers

November 15, 2004

From the *Associated Press*

COLOMBO, Sri Lanka

Sri Lanka's revenue from garment and textile exports to the United States, its biggest customer, is expected to fall about 20 percent next year following the expiration of a preferential trade agreement, an industry official said Monday. The United States has purchased an annual average of about US$2.5 billion (€1.9 billion) garments and textiles from Sri Lanka since the two countries signed the Multi-Fiber Agreement in 1974. But the agreement is set to expire next month.

> The expiration of the MFA by the end of 2004

Tuli Cooray, who heads a committee of Sri Lankan business and government officials advising the industry, said American buyers will probably switch to lower cost manufacturers in China, Mexico and elsewhere in South Asia. As a result, he said Sri Lanka's shipments of garments and textiles to the United States will likely fall about 20 percent to about US$2 billion (€1.5 billion), in 2005.

Cooray said most small and medium garment manufacturers may need to downsize to stay in business, but added that the industry will bounce back by focussing on markets closer to home, such as India and Japan. "We don't envisage any serious shocks," Cooray told Dow Jones Newswires. "We have already initiated talks with Indian partners amid efforts to obtain a piece of that market," he said.

Overseas shipments of textiles and garments comprise 50 percent of Sri Lanka's total export earnings, and the United States has been the largest buyer of garments from Sri Lanka.

> Impact on Sri Lanka

sugar to increase the price of domestic sugar beets and sugar cane. Producers receive $1 billion a year in additional surplus as a result of higher prices, but U.S. consumers lose $1.9 billion, for a net loss of welfare of $.9 billion to the United States.

Another trade restriction with big implications for U.S. consumers is the Multi-Fiber Agreement, a set of quotas on textiles and apparel that resulted in an estimated reduction of consumer surplus of $24.4 billion in 1990, and that generates over $10 billion a year in deadweight loss for the United States. Most of this loss comes from transferring the quota rents—the shaded area in Figure 30.2—to foreign producers. Using tariffs instead of quotas would have reduced the cost to the United States to about $2.5 billion a year. The Multi-Fiber Agreement ended in December 2004.

REVIEW

- The most common ways for government to restrict foreign trade are tariffs, quotas, and voluntary restraint agreements. Each has the same effect on price and quantity.

- With a tariff, the revenue from the tariff goes to the government. With a quota, that revenue goes to quota holders. With a VRA, that revenue goes to foreign producers.

- Trade restrictions alter the allocation of resources in the economy and are significant sources of deadweight loss.

The History of Trade Restrictions

revenue tariff: an import tax whose main purpose is to provide revenue to the government.

As stated earlier, tariffs are the oldest form of trade restriction. Throughout history, governments have used tariffs to raise revenue. **Revenue tariffs,** whose main purpose is raising revenue, were by far the most significant source of federal revenue in the United States before the income tax was made constitutional by the 16th amendment to the U.S. Constitution in 1913 (see Figure 30.4). Revenue tariffs are still common in less-developed countries because they are easy for the government to collect as the goods come through a port or one of a few checkpoints.

U.S. Tariffs

Tariffs are a big part of U.S. history. Even before the United States was a country, a tariff on tea imported into the colonies led to the Boston Tea Party. One of the first acts of the U.S. Congress placed tariffs on imports. Figure 30.5 summarizes the history of tariffs in the United States since the early 1800s.

■ **From the Tariff of Abominations to Smoot-Hawley.**   Tariffs were high throughout much of U.S. history, rarely getting below 20 percent in the nineteenth century. In addition to raising revenue, these tariffs had the purpose of reducing imports of manufactured goods. The tariffs offered protection to manufacturers in the North but raised prices for consumers. Since the South was mainly agricultural and a consumer of manufactured goods, there was a constant dispute between the North and the South over these tariffs.

The highest of these tariffs was nicknamed the "tariff of abominations." This tariff, passed in 1828, brought the average tariff level in the United States to over 60 percent. The tariff made purchases of farm equipment much more expensive in the southern states. It almost led to a civil war before the actual Civil War, as the southern states threatened to secede. However, because the tariff was so high, it was soon repealed, and for the next 10 years tariffs were relatively low by nineteenth-century standards.

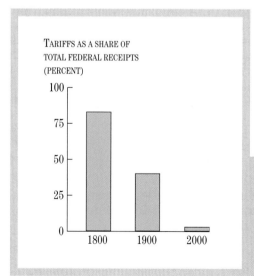

Figure 30.4
Tariffs as a Share of Total Federal Revenue
The first tariff, passed in 1789, represented nearly all of the federal government's revenue; 200 years later, tariff revenues were only about 1 percent of the total.

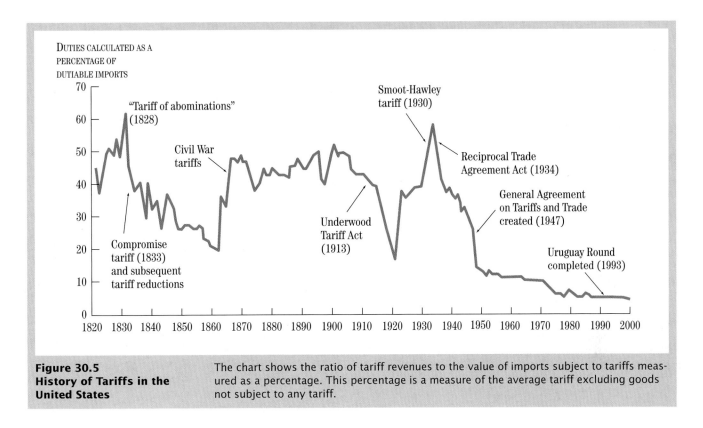

DUTIES CALCULATED AS A
PERCENTAGE OF
DUTIABLE IMPORTS

**Figure 30.5
History of Tariffs in the
United States**

The chart shows the ratio of tariff revenues to the value of imports subject to tariffs measured as a percentage. This percentage is a measure of the average tariff excluding goods not subject to any tariff.

Smoot-Hawley tariff: a set of tariffs imposed in 1930 that raised the average tariff level to 59 percent by 1932.

trade war: a conflict among nations over trade policies caused by imposition of protectionist policies on the part of one country and subsequent retaliatory actions by other countries.

The most devastating increase in tariffs in U.S. history occurred during the Great Depression. The **Smoot-Hawley tariff** of 1930 raised average tariffs to 59 percent. Congress and President Hoover apparently hoped that raising tariffs would help stimulate U.S. production and offset the Great Depression. But the increase had precisely the opposite effect. Other countries retaliated by raising their tariffs on U.S. goods. Each country tried to beat the others with higher tariffs, a phenomenon known as a **trade war.** The Smoot-Hawley tariff had terrible consequences. Figure 30.6 is a dramatic illustration of the decline in trade that occurred at the time of these tariff increases during the Great Depression. The Smoot-Hawley tariff made the Great Depression worse than it would have otherwise been.

■ **From the Reciprocal Trade Agreement Act to the WTO.** The only good thing about the Smoot-Hawley tariff was that it demonstrated to the whole world how harmful tariffs can be. In order to achieve lower tariffs, the Congress passed and President Roosevelt signed the *Reciprocal Trade Agreement Act* in 1934. This act was probably the most significant event in the history of U.S. trade policy. It authorized the president to cut U.S. tariffs by up to 50 percent if other countries would cut their tariffs on a reciprocating basis. The reciprocal trade agreements resulted in a remarkable reduction in tariffs. By the end of World War II, the average tariff level was down from a peak of 59 percent under Smoot-Hawley to 25 percent. The successful approach to tariff reduction under the Reciprocal Trade Agreement Act was made permanent in 1947 with the creation of a new international organization, the *General Agreement on Tariffs and Trade (GATT)*. GATT was set up to continue the process of tariff reduction. During

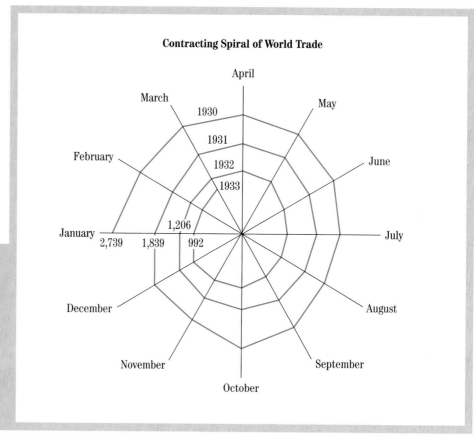

Figure 30.6
Decline in World Trade During the Great Depression
This circular graph, used by Charles Kindleberger of MIT, illustrates how world trade collapsed after tariffs increased during the Great Depression. The distance from the middle of the graph to the point on each spoke is the amount of trade (in millions of dollars) during each month.

World Trade Organization (WTO): an international organization that can mediate trade disputes.

the half century since the end of World War II, tariffs have continued to decline on a reciprocating basis. By 1992, the average U.S. tariff level was down to 5.2 percent.

In 1993, GATT was transformed into the **World Trade Organization (WTO),** which will continue to promote reciprocal reductions in tariffs and other trade barriers. But the WTO also has authority to resolve trade disputes between countries. For example, if the United States complains that Europe is violating a trade agreement by restricting U.S. beef imports in some way, then the WTO will determine whether the complaint has merit and what sanctions should be imposed on Europe. This dispute resolution authority has led to complaints, such as those made by the protesters in Seattle in 1999, that the WTO represents a loss of sovereignty for individual countries. On the other side of the argument, by resolving disputes, the WTO can avoid misunderstandings that otherwise can lead to trade wars between countries when trade disputes occur.

antidumping duty: a tariff imposed on a country as a penalty for dumping goods.

■ **Antidumping Duties.** No history of U.S. tariffs would be complete without a discussion of antidumping duties. **Antidumping duties** are tariffs put on foreign firms as a penalty for dumping. When a firm sells products in another country at prices below average cost or below the price in the home country, it is called *dumping.* Dumping can occur for many reasons. For example, the firm might want to sell at a lower price in the foreign market than in the home market because the demand in the foreign market is more elastic. If so, consumers in the foreign market benefit. But some people argue that dumping is a way for foreign firms to drive domestic firms out of business and thereby gain market share and market power. In any case, in the United States and other countries, dumping is illegal; the penalty is a high tariff—the antidumping duty—on the good that is being dumped. Steel is one of the industries protected with antidumping duties in the United States, at a cost to consumers of as much as $732,000 per job protected, about 10 times what a steelworker earns. President Bush's increase in steel tariffs in 2002 provoked retaliation by the European Union and Japan, adding to the deadweight loss caused by trade barriers.

Many economists are concerned that antidumping duties, or even the threat of such duties, are serious restrictions on trade. They reduce imports and raise consumer prices. Moreover, they are frequently used for protectionist purposes. Firms in industries that desire additional protection can file dumping charges and request that tariffs be raised. Frequently, they are successful. Thus, an important issue for the future is how to reduce the use of antidumping duties for restricting trade.

■ **The Rise of Nontariff Barriers.**   As tariffs were being reduced in the post–World War II period, a conflicting trend began to emerge. Some of the other methods of restricting trade—called **nontariff barriers** to trade—grew in popularity. Nontariff barriers include anything from quotas to quality standards aimed at reducing the import of foreign products. Nontariff barriers may have arisen as a replacement for tariffs in response to political pressure for protection of certain industries.

nontariff barrier: any government action other than a tariff that reduces imports, such as a quota or a standard.

Quality and performance standards are sometimes nothing more than barriers to trade. Some standards may have a good purpose, such as safety or compatibility with other products, but others do not. Consider the Canadian plywood standards for building construction, which keep out U.S. plywood. The Canadians argue that the standards are needed to satisfy building requirements in Canada, but Americans argue that plywood that does not meet the Canadian standards works just as well. A safety restriction against American-made baseball bats in Japan during the 1980s is another example. Most Americans viewed the bats as perfectly safe and viewed the Japanese safety standard as a restriction on trade.

Quality and performance standards, therefore, are a tricky problem because governments can argue that they are for the purpose of improving economic conditions in their own country. The U.S. Food and Drug Administration does not allow untested drugs into the United States even though foreign governments deem them safe. The FDA argues that the restriction is necessary to protect consumers, but foreign governments view it as a trade restriction. Such a standard does seem like a trade barrier, but in reality it is a matter of dispute.

REVIEW
- Tariffs were used by governments to raise revenue long before income taxes were invented.

- Tariffs have also been used for protectionist purposes in several important instances in U.S. history. Manufacturing firms in the North were protected by tariffs at the expense of consumers of manufactured goods, many of whom were in the South.

- The Smoot-Hawley tariff of the 1930s was one of the most harmful in U.S. history. It led to a trade war in which other countries raised tariffs in retaliation.

- Tariffs have come down since the 1930s. However, in recent years, nontariff barriers to trade have gone up.

Arguments for Trade Barriers

Are there any good economic arguments for trade barriers? Let's examine some of the arguments that are typically made.

High Transition Costs

When an industry shrinks as a result of the removal of restrictions on trade, the cost of adjustment in the short run may be quite large, even if other industries grow. Those who lose their jobs in the protected industry, even temporarily, suffer. In the short run, it is difficult to retrain workers. Workers who are laid off as the industry shrinks cannot move easily to another industry. Many have to retire early. Retraining is possible, but it takes time and is difficult for older workers.

■ **Phaseout of Trade Restrictions.**   Some people argue that these costs are so high that we should not reduce trade barriers. But there is a better approach. These costs of adjustment are a reason for a slow phaseout of trade barriers. *Phaseout* means that trade barriers are reduced a little bit each year. A slow phaseout of trade barriers was part of the North American Free Trade Agreement between Canada, Mexico, and the United States. This agreement called for a phaseout period of 10 to 15 years, depending on the product. For example, some tariffs were scheduled to be cut by 25 percent in the first year, 50 percent after 5 years, and 100 percent after 10 years. The purpose of the slow phaseout was to allow production to shift from one industry to another slowly. The intention was to adjust the work force through attrition as workers normally retired.

■ **Trade Adjustment Assistance.**   Another approach is to use *trade adjustment assistance*, which refers to transfer payments to workers who happen to be hurt because of a move to free trade. Unemployment insurance and other existing transfer programs may go a long way toward providing such assistance. However, because society as a whole benefits from free trade, some increased resources can be used to help the workers who bear the brunt of the adjustment. In other words, the extra income that can be obtained by trade may be used to ease the adjustment.

Transition costs are not a reason to avoid free trade. They are a reason to phase out the restrictions on trade gradually and to provide trade adjustment assistance to workers as needed.

The Infant Industry Argument

infant industry argument: the view that a new industry may be helped by protectionist policies.

One of the earliest statements of the **infant industry argument** in favor of trade restrictions was put forth by Alexander Hamilton in 1791 in his *Report on Manufactures*. Hamilton argued that manufacturing firms in the newly created United States should be protected from imports. Once the industries were established, they could compete with foreign imports. But as they got started, they needed protection until they reached a certain scale.

A danger with the infant industry argument is that the protection may last long after it was initially justified. In Latin America, for example, infant industry arguments were used to justify import protection in the 1950s. However, these barriers to trade lasted long after any kind of reasonable infant industry argument could be made.

The National Security Argument

A nation's security is another argument for trade restrictions. The national security argument is that there are certain goods, such as special metals, computers, ships, or aircraft, that the country needs to be able to produce in time of war. If it does not have an industry that produces them, it could be at a severe disadvantage.

However, national security arguments can be used by firms seeking protection from foreign imports. Japanese rice farmers, for example, made national security arguments for protection from rice imports. In fact, the rice restriction has little to do with national security because rice can be imported from many different countries. In the United States, the textile industry has argued on national security grounds that it needs protection because it provides military uniforms made from U.S. textiles.

It is important to examine whether there are alternatives to trade restrictions before applying the national security argument and restricting trade. For example, rather than restricting rice imports, the Japanese could store a large amount of rice in case of a war emergency. Or the United States could store millions of extra uniforms rather than restrict textile imports if it was really thought that uniforms were a national security issue. In fact, the United States does have stockpiles of many rare minerals and metals needed for national defense production.

The Retaliation Argument

Threatening other countries or retaliating against them when they have trade restrictions is another possible reason to deviate from free trade. If the United States threatens the Japanese by saying it will close U.S. markets, this may encourage Japan to open its markets to the United States. Thus, by retaliating or threatening, there is a possibility of increasing international trade around the world.

However, the retaliation argument can also be used by those seeking protection. Those in the United States who are most vocal about retaliation against other countries are frequently those who want to protect an industry. Many economists worry about threats of retaliation because they fear that other countries will respond with further retaliation, and a trade war will occur.

The Foreign Subsidies Argument

If foreign governments subsidize their firms' exports, does this justify U.S. government subsidies to U.S. firms to help them compete against the foreign firms?

Foreign subsidies to foreign producers are a particularly difficult issue. If foreign subsidies lower the price of U.S. imports, then U.S. consumers benefit. If Europe wants to use taxpayer funds to subsidize aircraft manufacturers, then why not enjoy the lower-cost aircraft? However, foreign subsidies enable industries to thrive more for political reasons than for economic ones. From a global perspective, such government intervention should be avoided, since it hurts consumers.

Environment and Labor Standards Arguments

During the 1990s a new type of argument against reducing trade barriers emerged: that tariffs or quotas should not be removed against countries with weak or poorly enforced environmental protection laws and labor standards, such as child labor laws and workplace safety laws. Because such laws and standards are generally weaker in developing countries than in developed countries, this argument frequently opposes reducing trade barriers to the imports of goods from relatively poor countries. For example, this argument is made by people who are against reducing tariffs on imports of Brazilian oranges into the United States.

Environmental and labor standard arguments are of two main types. First, some argue that holding back on the reduction of trade barriers until countries change their environmental and labor policies is a good way to persuade these countries to change. However, there is an important counterargument: Low trade barriers themselves lead to improvements in environmental and working conditions. History has shown that as their income grows, people become more concerned with the environment and their working conditions; people in deep poverty do not have the time or resources to deal with such issues. Thus, by raising income per capita, lower trade barriers can improve the environment and the workplace. Moreover, more effective and cheaper technologies to improve the environment or increase safety become available through trade.

A second type of argument is that it is difficult for workers and firms in the advanced countries to compete with those in less-developed countries who do not have to pay the costs of complying with environmental protection laws. However, by keeping trade barriers high, income growth may not be sufficient to address the environmental problems in developing countries, so the differences in the law will persist.

The Political Economy of Protection

Firms seek protection from foreign competition simply because the protection raises their profits. But the firms may use any of the above arguments to justify their case. In a famous satire of firms seeking protection from foreign competitors, a French economist, Frédéric Bastiat, wrote more than 150 years ago about candlemakers complaining about a foreign rival—the sun! The candlemakers in Bastiat's satire petitioned French legislators to pass a law requiring the closing of all shutters, curtains, and blinds during the day to protect them from this competition. The behavior Bastiat described seems to apply to many modern producers who seek protection from competition.

One reason that firms seeking protection are frequently successful is that they spend a lot more time and money lobbying the Congress than do the people who would be hurt by the protection. Even though consumers *as a whole* benefit more from reducing trade barriers than firms in the protected industry are harmed, each consumer benefits relatively little, so spending a lot of time and money lobbying is not worthwhile. It is difficult to get enough votes to remove trade barriers when a few firms each have a lot to lose, even though millions of consumers have something to gain.

REVIEW

- Transition costs, environmental and labor standards, national security, infant industry, and retaliation are some of the arguments in favor of trade restrictions. Each has the possibility of being used by protectionists.

- Although many arguments in favor of trade barriers have been put forth over the years, in each case there are better ways to deal with the problems raised. The case for free trade holds up well in the debates when the economic rationale for the gains from trade is applied correctly and understood.

How to Reduce Trade Barriers

Viewed in their entirety, the economic arguments against trade restrictions seem to overwhelm the economic arguments in favor of trade restrictions. The economic arguments in favor of free trade have been in existence for over 200 years. The recommendation of early economists such as Adam Smith and David Ricardo was simple: Reduce trade barriers.

However, it was not until many years after Smith and Ricardo wrote that their recommendations were translated into a practical trade policy. Then, as now, political pressures favoring protection made the repeal of trade barriers difficult. Hence, a carefully formulated trade policy is needed in order to reduce trade barriers. There are a variety of approaches.

Unilateral Disarmament

One approach to removing trade barriers in a country is simply to remove them unilaterally. Making an analogy with the arms race, we call this policy *unilateral disarmament.* When a country unilaterally reduces its arms, it does so without getting anything in arms reduction from other countries. With unilateral disarmament in trade policy, a country reduces its trade barriers without other countries also reducing their trade barriers. Unilateral disarmament is what Smith and Ricardo recommended for England.

The problem with unilateral disarmament is that some individuals are hurt, if only temporarily, and it is hard to compensate them. Of those who gain, each gains only a little. Of those who lose, each loses a lot. The political pressures they exert are significant. As a result, unilateral disarmament is rarely successful in the developed countries today as a means of reducing trade barriers.

Multilateral Negotiations

multilateral negotiations: simultaneous tariff reductions on the part of many countries.

An alternative to unilateral disarmament is **multilateral negotiations,** which involves simultaneous tariff reductions by many countries. With multilateral negotiations, opposing political interests can cancel each other out. For example, import-competing domestic industries that will be hurt by the reduction of trade barriers, such as textiles in the United States or agriculture in Europe and Japan, can be countered by export interests that will gain from the reduction in trade barriers. Since consumers will gain, they are also a potential counter to protectionism, but they are too diffuse to make a difference, as we just discussed. With multilateral negotiations, interested exporters who gain from the reduction in barriers will push the political process to get the reductions.

Multilateral negotiations also balance international interests. For example, to get less-developed countries to remove their barriers to imports of financial and telecommunications services, the United States had to agree to remove agricultural trade barriers in the United States.

Uruguay Round: the most recent round of multilateral negotiations, completed in 1993.

■ **The Uruguay Round.** Multilateral trade negotiations have taken place in a series of negotiating rounds, each of which has lasted several years. During each round, the countries try to come to agreement on a list of tariff reductions and the removal of other trade restrictions. There have been eight rounds of negotiations since 1947. The most recent was the **Uruguay Round,** named after the country where the first negotiations occurred in 1986. The Uruguay Round negotiations ended in 1993.

The reduction in tariffs through multilateral negotiations under GATT has been dramatic. Tariffs are expected to go below 3 percent on average in the United States with the implementation of the Uruguay Round agreement. Recall that this compares with nearly 60 percent in the mid-1930s.

■ **Most-Favored Nation Policy.** Multilateral negotiations are almost always conducted on a *most-favored nation (MFN)* basis. MFN means that when the United States or any other country reduces its tariffs as part of a multilateral trade agreement, it reduces them for everyone. Since the late 1990s, the term *normal trade relations (NTR)* has frequently been used in place of MFN because it is a more accurate description of the policy. Today, if a country is not granted MFN or NTR status, the United States imposes very high tariffs on the country. For example, concern about human rights in China has led some to argue that the United States should not grant MFN or NTR status to China. Without MFN/NTR, tariffs on Chinese imports to the United States would be about 60 percent.

Regional Trading Areas

Creating regional trading areas is an increasingly popular approach to reducing trade barriers. For example, the free trade agreement between the United States, Canada, and Mexico removes all trade restrictions among those countries. An even wider free trade area covering the whole Western Hemisphere has been proposed.

Regional trading areas have some advantages over multilateral approaches. First, fewer countries are involved, so the negotiations are easier. Second, regional political factors can help offset protectionist pressures. For example, the political goal of European unity helped establish grassroots support to reduce trade barriers among the countries of Europe.

trade diversion: the shifting of trade away from the low-cost producer toward a higher-cost producer because of a reduction in trade barriers with the country of the higher-cost producer.

trade creation: the increase in trade due to a decrease in trade barriers.

■ **Trade Diversion versus Trade Creation.** But there are disadvantages to regional trading areas in comparison with multilateral reductions in trade barriers under GATT. **Trade diversion** is one disadvantage. Trade is diverted when low-cost firms from countries outside the trading area are replaced by high-cost firms within the trading area. For example, as a result of NAFTA, producers of electronic equipment in Southeast Asia have to pay a U.S. tariff, while producers of the same equipment in Mexico do not have to pay the tariff. As a result, some production will shift from Southeast Asia to Mexico; that is viewed as trade diversion from what might otherwise be a low-cost producer. The hope is that **trade creation**—the increase in trade due to the lower tariffs between the countries—will outweigh trade diversion.

free trade area (FTA): an area that has no trade barriers between the countries in the area.

customs union: a free trade area with a common external tariff.

■ **Free Trade Areas versus Customs Unions.** There is an important difference between two types of regional trading areas: **free trade areas (FTAs)** and **customs unions.** In both, barriers to trade between countries in the area or the union are removed. But external tariffs are treated differently: Under a customs union, such as the European Union (EU), external tariffs are the same for all countries. For example, semiconductor tariffs are exactly the same in France, Germany, and the other members of the EU. Under a free trade area, external tariffs can differ for the different countries in the free trade area. For example, the United States's external tariffs on textiles are higher than Mexico's. These differences in external tariffs under an FTA cause complications because a good can be shipped into the country with the low tariff and then moved within the FTA to the country with the high tariff. To prevent such external tariff avoidance, *domestic content restrictions* must be incorporated into the agreement. These restrictions say that in order for a product to qualify for the zero tariffs between the countries, a certain fraction of the product must be made

Ending the Corn Laws

Corn laws, recorded as far back as the twelfth century, restricted imports of grains, including wheat, rye, and barley, into England. Adam Smith devoted an entire chapter of his 1776 *Wealth of Nations* to the corn laws, arguing that "the praises which have been bestowed upon the law . . . are altogether unmerited."* But legislation introduced in 1791 raised the grain import tariff even further. The corn laws were unpopular with everyone except landowners and farmers.

The Anti-Corn League, founded in 1839 by Richard Cobden, was the most significant pressure group in nineteenth-century England. The Anti-Corn League used the economic arguments of Smith and Ricardo that the corn laws were an economic disaster and a moral tragedy: The laws impoverished and even starved the working class, constrained the growth of manufacturing, and provided government support to the wealthy. The catalyst was the Irish potato famine of 1845, which raised agricultural prices even further.

Robert Peel was the Tory prime minister from 1841 to 1846. Until 1845, he was against repeal of the corn laws, primarily because of strong support for them from landowners in the Tory party. But under pressure from Cobden and the Anti-Corn League, he changed his position after the potato famine and argued for the repeal of the corn laws.

In February 1846, Peel introduced a package of measures abolishing duties on imported corn over a three-year period. Only a minority of his party supported him, but the package passed. The split in the Tory party ended Peel's career, and the party did not win another election until 1868.

Thus, Peel paid a high political price for his policy of reducing trade protection, a policy that many feel helped make the British economy strong for the rest of the nineteenth century. How do you think he would have fared had he used one of the other methods (such as multilateral negotiations) to reduce protection rather than "unilaterally disarming"?

*Adam Smith, *Wealth of Nations* (New York: Modern Library, 1994), p. 560.

within the FTA. For example, under NAFTA, the majority of parts in television sets and automobiles must be manufactured in Canada, Mexico, or the United States in order for the television or car to qualify for a zero tariff.

REVIEW

- There are many different approaches to removing restrictions on international trade, including unilateral disarmament, multilateral negotiations, and regional trading areas—FTAs and customs unions.

- Of all these approaches, unilateral disarmament is the most difficult politically. Multilateral and regional approaches are both more common and more successful in lowering trade barriers and keeping them low.

Conclusion

Very few economists disagree with the proposition that tariffs, quotas, and other trade barriers reduce the economic well-being of a society. In fact, polls of economists show that they disagree less on this proposition than on virtually any other in economics. This unanimity among economists was reflected in the debate over the North American Free Trade Agreement in the United States. Every living Nobel Prize–winning economist endorsed the agreement to eliminate tariffs and quotas among Canada, Mexico, and the United States.

This chapter has shown that despite this unanimity, many restrictions on international trade still exist. There is continued political pressure to erect new trade barriers or prevent the existing ones from being removed.

Thus, the need for good trade policies to reduce trade barriers is likely to increase rather than decrease in the future. The challenge is to develop a means for conducting international trade policy in a world with many sovereign governments, each of which is free to formulate its own policy.

KEY POINTS

1. Despite the economic arguments put forth in support of free trade, there are still plenty of restrictions on trade in the world.

2. Tariffs and quotas are the two main forms of restricting international trade. They are equivalent in their effects on prices and imports.

3. Tariffs were originally a major source of government revenue but are relatively insignificant sources of revenue today.

4. Quotas do not generate any revenue for the government. The quota holders get all the revenue.

5. Voluntary export restraints are much like quotas except that they can be negotiated without an act of Congress, and the revenue usually goes to the foreign producer in the form of increased profits.

6. National security and infant industry are two arguments frequently put forth in support of trade barriers. In most cases, they are overwhelmed by the arguments in favor of reduced trade barriers.

7. Eliminating restrictions on trade unilaterally is difficult because of the harm done to those who are protected by the restrictions.

8. Regional trading areas and multilateral tariff reductions endeavor to reduce trade barriers by balancing export interests against import-competing interests.

9. Free trade areas and customs unions both create trade and divert trade.

KEY TERMS

ad valorem tariff	Smoot-Hawley tariff	nontariff barrier	trade creation
specific tariff	trade war	infant industry argument	free trade area (FTA)
voluntary restraint agreement (VRA)	World Trade Organization (WTO)	multilateral negotiation	customs union
revenue tariff	antidumping duty	Uruguay Round	
		trade diversion	

QUESTIONS FOR REVIEW

1. In what sense are a tariff and a quota equivalent?

2. Why might a tariff raise the price of the imported product by less than the amount of the tariff?

3. How does a voluntary restraint agreement encourage the restriction of supply in the foreign country?

4. What are some examples of quality standards being used as trade barriers?

5. Why is unilateral disarmament a difficult way to reduce trade barriers?

6. How do multilateral negotiations or regional trading areas make the reduction of trade barriers easier politically?

7. Why might a free trade area cause trade diversion?

8. What is the infant industry argument in favor of trade protection?

9. What are the disadvantages of using retaliation in trade policy?

PROBLEMS

1. India has a 70 percent tariff on imported chocolate.
   a. Sketch a diagram to show the impact of this tariff on the price of imported chocolate in India.
   b. Suppose India cuts the tariff to zero but imposes a quota that results in the same price for imported chocolate. Show this in a diagram. What happens to the government's tariff revenue?

2. Use a supply and demand diagram to show what happens to the price and quantity of sugar in the United States when the quotas on sugar are removed.

3. Estimates show that the voluntary export restraints through which the government of Japan restricted automobile exports to the United States in the mid-1980s raised the price of Japanese cars in the United States by about $1,000. Sketch a diagram to show how this occurred and briefly explain the price increase.

4. Suppose French wine suddenly becomes popular in the United States. How does this affect the price and quantity of imports of French wine? Suppose the U.S. wine industry lobbies for protection. If the government imposes a tariff in order to restore the original quantity of imports, what will happen to the price of French wine in the United States? Show how much tariff revenue the government will collect.

5. Suppose that in order to encourage tourism, a Caribbean country subsidizes hotel construction. Draw an export supply and demand curve to show what will happen. Is the United States better off? Might the hotel owners in Florida ask the U.S. government to complain about this?

6. Suppose the U.S. government has decided that for national security reasons, it must protect the machine tools industry. Name two ways in which the government can accomplish this goal. Which policy would you recommend? Why?

7. Suppose the North American Free Trade Agreement (NAFTA) causes the United States to import lumber from Canada instead of Finland, even though Finland is a lower-cost producer than Canada. Identify and explain this phenomenon.

8. Suppose the United States decides to withdraw most-favored-nation treatment from China. What will happen to the price and quantity of U.S. imports from China? Use a diagram to explain your answer.

9. Suppose the president of a nation proposes a switch from a system of import quotas to a system of tariffs, with the idea that the switch would not affect the quantity of goods imported. Who will be in favor of the switch? Who will oppose it? Would you expect the proponents and the opponents to have the same political influence on the president?

10. Assume that several hundred independent farmers in Argentina are the only producers of a rare plant used for medicinal purposes around the world.
    a. Graphically show the world demand and supply for this plant when there are no trade restrictions. Show the equilibrium quantity and price.
    b. Imagine you are an economic adviser to the Argentine government. The president asks you to find a way to capture some of the economic rents from the production of this rare plant, so that more profits stay in Argentina. Your job is to design a trade policy that accomplishes the president's goal. Explain verbally and graphically what your trade policy would be, how it would affect quantity and price in the market, and how it would affect the profits and surpluses of all the players in this market. Make sure your policy is designed in such a way that it will have support from the Argentine voters. Include any potential drawbacks of this policy in your analysis.

CHAPTER 31

Transition Economies

One of the most significant economic changes in the last decade of the twentieth century was the transition of China and the countries of the former Soviet Union from centrally planned or *command economies* to *market economies*. In a command economy, the government sets prices and decides what, how, and for whom goods will be produced. In a market economy, most decisions about what, how, and for whom goods will be produced are made and prices are set by individual buyers and sellers.

Many of these transition economies, especially those of countries from the former Soviet Union like Georgia, Belarus, Moldova, and Kazakhstan, suffered in the early years of the transition. The financial crisis that hit Russia in 1998 was a sobering reminder of how slow the transition from communism to a market economy was in much of Eastern Europe. Despite the slow start, however, many of these countries have seen improved economic performance over the last decade, aided by high oil prices, which are beneficial to oil exporters. Russia has rebounded well, growing on average by 3.9 percent a year over the last decade, while the countries that made up the former Soviet Union grew at 4.1 percent a year over the last decade, according to the International Monetary Fund. Other countries made the transition much more successfully. China has been one of the most remarkable success stories of recent times, growing on average by 8.3 percent a year over the last decade. Hungary, Poland, Estonia, Latvia, and Lithuania all did much better than the countries that were part of the former Soviet Union.

Rising Star
A man looks at a billboard depicting development along East Chang'An Avenue in Beijing, China. China's economy grew even faster than expected in the first half of 2005, expanding 9.5 percent.

socialism: an economic system in which the government owns and controls all the capital and makes decisions about prices and quantities as part of a central plan.

capitalism: an economic system based on a market economy in which capital is individually owned, and production and employment decisions are decentralized.

communism: an economic system in which all capital is collectively owned.

In this chapter, we take a special look at economies that are making the transition from central planning. We first look back at what life was like under central planning, and how central planning grew out of communist revolutions induced by Marxist criticism of market economies. We then examine the alternative approaches chosen by economies that made the transition.

What Were Centrally Planned Economies Like?

With a few exceptions, such as North Korea and Cuba, centrally planned economies no longer exist. But it is important to remember essential economic lessons from the experience of countries that tried central planning during the twentieth century. A well-known expert on communism and socialism, Robert Heilbroner, summarizes the lessons this way: "The Soviet Union, China and Eastern Europe have given us the clearest possible proof that capitalism organizes the material affairs of humankind more satisfactorily than socialism."[1]

Under **socialism** the government owns the capital—factories, stores, farms, and equipment—and decisions about production and employment are made by those who run the government as part of a central plan for the economy. In contrast, in a market economy, also called **capitalism,** individuals own the capital, and decisions about production and employment are decentralized and made by many individuals buying and selling goods in markets. The term **communism** refers to a theoretical situation in which all the people of a country *collectively* own the capital and the land without direct government ownership. Those who advocated communism viewed collective ownership by the people as a long-term goal: A socialist economy would evolve into communism, with the government gradually withering away. However, today most economists and historians use the word *communism* to mean the same thing as *socialism*, as that term is defined here.

Not all socialist economies are the same; there are different degrees of government ownership and centralization. For example, in some socialist economies, farmers could sell a portion of their agricultural output and use the proceeds to buy farm equipment or even consumer goods. Similarly, not all market economies are the same; in most market economies, the government owns the public infrastructure capital, such as roads and bridges, and is involved in the production of education, health services, and other goods. The degree of government involvement differs from market economy to market economy. For example, a much larger fraction of medical care is produced by the government in the United Kingdom than is produced by the government in the United States.

However, in reality, the differences between socialist economies as a group and market economies as a group are much larger than the differences among the economies within each group. In other words, there is a "night-and-day" distinction

---

1. See Robert Heilbroner, "The Triumph of Capitalism," *The New Yorker*, January 1993, pp. 98–109.

between centrally planned economies with government ownership of firms that do not have to compete and market economies with private ownership of firms that do have to compete. To understand this distinction, we need to examine how centrally planned economies worked.

Central Planning in the Soviet Union

V. I. Lenin and the Bolshevik party (also known as the Communist party) gained control of the government of Russia in the October Revolution of 1917. At this time, the Russian economy was much less developed than most of Western Europe. GDP per capita in Russia was less than one-third that in the United Kingdom or the United States. The economy was mostly agricultural. Although large-scale manufacturing industries were growing, they were still much smaller than those in Germany, the United Kingdom, or the United States. For more than 1,000 years before the communists gained control, Russia had been ruled by tsars, who held enormous power and resisted economic and political change.

For those reasons, the Russian people were dissatisfied with both their economy and their political system. Lenin and the Bolsheviks seized the opportunity, forcing through a completely new economic system. Most significantly, Lenin decreed that private firms would be taken over by the government, a process called **nationalization.** The Bolsheviks immediately nationalized the banking system, and by mid-1918, a massive nationalization of large- and small-scale industry was under way. Although the alleged reason for the Bolshevik takeover was to give the workers control of the economy, Lenin soon rejected worker control. He argued that people like himself were needed to run the economy on behalf of the workers. He began controlling production from the center, appointing administrators to run each industry from offices in Moscow. In doing so, he laid the foundation of a command economy, in which government *diktats*, or commands, rather than prices and decentralized markets, would determine what was produced. In 1921, **Gosplan,** the state planning commission, was established. In 1922, the Communist party established the Soviet Union, incorporating Ukraine and other countries along with Russia into one large command economy.

At the very start, the experiment in central planning was unsuccessful. Production fell and inflation rose dramatically. Much of the blame for the early lack of success could be placed on the civil war between the communists (the Reds) and the anticommunists (the Whites). Moreover, Lenin had little guidance on how to set up a socialist economy. Karl Marx, whose analysis of capitalism provided the intellectual support for the communist revolution, wrote virtually nothing about how a socialist economy or central planning would work (see the box "Starting a Revolution"). In any case, the early 1920s saw a retreat from central planning and a partial reinstatement of the market economy under Lenin's New Economic Policy. But with Lenin's death in 1924 and Joseph Stalin's becoming leader of the Communist party in 1928, central planning was reinstated with even more force than previously.

■ **The Five-Year Plans.** The goal of catching up with Western Europe and the United States quickly came to dominate Stalin's thinking about the economy. Catching up required raising the level of investment in factories and industrial equipment, increasing labor hours, and shifting workers out of agriculture into industry. Stalin wanted to do this rapidly and on a massive scale. To do so, he needed to raise investment in heavy industry and reduce consumption. He saw a command economy as the only way to accomplish his goal.

Stalin, therefore, gave Gosplan much more authority to run the economy from the center. In 1928, Gosplan issued a **five-year plan** stipulating production goals for the entire economy. This turned out to be the first of a succession of many more

nationalization: the taking over of private firms by the government.

Gosplan: the planning agency of the Soviet Union.

five-year plan: a document that stated production goals for the entire Soviet economy for the succeeding five years.

Starting a Revolution

What led to the rejection of markets and the acceptance of socialism in Russia, China, and Eastern Europe in the twentieth century? The economic writings of Karl Marx in the nineteenth century played a key role.

Karl Marx was an economist and social philosopher. He was an outspoken critic of the existing economic and political system in Europe. He spent much of his adult life in London, studying and writing in the archives of the British Museum. Marx eked out a modest living—his wife and children struggled at the brink of poverty—through his journalistic writings and through financial assistance from his long-time friend and collaborator, Friedrich Engels.

Marx's polemical writings were influential. The widely read and often-quoted *Communist Manifesto* was a short pamphlet written in 1848 by Marx and Engels. It was a stirring call for a revolution:

> A specter is haunting Europe—the specter of communism. . . . Let the ruling classes tremble at a Communist revolution. The proletarians have nothing to lose but their chains. They have a world to win. Working men of all countries, unite!

Surprisingly, Marx and Engels found much to admire in capitalism. They wrote that the bourgeoisie—the class that owned or ran the business firms—

> has accomplished wonders far surpassing the Egyptian pyramids, Roman aqueducts, and Gothic cathedrals. . . . [D]uring its rule of scarcely one hundred years, [it] has created more massive and more colossal productive forces than have all preceding generations together.

It is in Marx's economic writings—longer and more ponderous—that his detailed criticism of capitalism is found. In particular, his treatise *Das Kapital* aimed to show why Adam Smith and David Ricardo were wrong in their praise of the market economy. Referring to Smith's idea that workers would benefit from the increased labor productivity resulting from the division of labor or more machinery, Marx wrote in *Das Kapital*:

> Adam Smith, by a fundamentally perverted analysis, arrives at [this] absurd conclusion. . . .

In truth, Adam Smith breaks his investigation off, just where its difficulties begin.

Marx argued instead that increases in labor productivity would not benefit workers; capitalists, trying to maintain their profits, would keep workers' wages from rising. But history shows that wages have increased by huge amounts in the 150 years since Marx wrote.

Although socialism may have originally seemed like an attractive alternative to the market system, socialism's own severe problems eventually became obvious. Surprisingly, however, Marx wrote almost nothing about how a socialist economy would work. His writings focused entirely on capitalism.

KARL MARX, 1818–1883

Born: Trier, Germany, 1818

Education:
University of Bonn, 1835; University of Berlin, 1836–1841; University of Jena, doctorate in philosophy, 1841

Jobs:
Editor, freelance journalist, Cologne, Paris, Brussels, 1842–1848; independent study, freelance journalist, London, 1849–1883

Major Publications:
Communist Manifesto (with Friedrich Engels), 1848; *Das Kapital*, 1867 (Vol. I); Russian translation, 1868; English translation, 1886

---

state enterprise: an organization, analogous to a firm in a market economy, that is owned and controlled by the government.

five-year plans, and the methods of central planning that would last for 60 years were put in place. Gosplan, under the command of the Communist party leaders, controlled production not only for Russia but for the entire Soviet Union, which was spread over eleven time zones and covered one-sixth of the world's land area.

Production of most goods took place at **state enterprises**—organizations similar in function to business firms in market economies but owned and controlled by the

collectivized farm: a farm in a planned economy that is in theory collectively owned by peasants, but is controlled by the government.

production target: a goal set for the production of a good or service in a planned economy.

government. Stalin also virtually abolished private property in agriculture in the Soviet Union. He created **collectivized farms,** through which the government took ownership of most farmland, farm equipment, and livestock.

By setting **production targets** for millions of products throughout the Soviet Union, Gosplan tried to control what and how much should be produced at each state enterprise and collectivized farm. Through this method, Stalin was successful in raising the level of investment and reducing people's consumption, thereby rapidly expanding the number of machines and factories devoted to manufacturing. In order to make sure that the labor force was sufficient for this rapid industrialization, the communist government also placed restrictions on workers. For example, new graduates were assigned jobs in different parts of the country, and restrictions on moving to and living in certain areas made it difficult for workers to change jobs if they wanted to.

■ **Centrally Controlled Prices.**   Prices for individual goods were also set at the center, but Gosplan rarely set these prices at levels that would equate the quantity supplied with the quantity demanded. Shortages were typical. Food prices were set very low, resulting in food shortages. The managers of state enterprises frequently found themselves having to wait for parts or inputs to production. At other times they produced an excess supply that no one could use. To be sure, when shortages got very severe, markets would develop: Enterprise managers who were in desperate need of materials would offer side payments, or bribes, to other managers or workers in order to get the materials. These markets operated outside of the normal central planning process and were called *gray* or *black markets*. Some economists feel that by reducing crucial shortages, these markets enabled central planning to function.

Recall from Chapter 1 that prices have three roles: They transmit information, coordinate actions by providing incentives, and affect the distribution of income. In a market economy, a change in demand or supply causes a change in the price, which transmits information throughout the economy. Such changes in prices were thwarted by central planning. Central planners simply did not have enough information to know how to change the prices. Thus, the information transmission role of prices did not exist.

The coordination role of prices was de-emphasized, although the central planners recognized that prices affected incentives. The managers of the state enterprises were given rewards for hitting production targets, but the rewards were not designed in a way that encouraged efficient management practices. To poke fun at Gosplan, a famous cartoon showed a picture of a nail factory producing *one* large but useless 500-ton nail in order to meet the factory's production target of 500 tons of nails. There were also few rewards for inventing new products or even for finding more efficient ways to produce the existing products. State enterprises thus became very inefficient. Competition between enterprises was discouraged, and production became highly concentrated in a few firms in each industry.

Gosplan did not ignore the role of prices in affecting the distribution of income. Prices were held low on most staple items and high on the few consumer durable items that were produced. By setting prices this way, Gosplan tried to make the distribution of goods and services more equal. But income distribution was by no means egalitarian under central planning. Communist party officials and enterprise managers were given extra payments in the form of better housing, transportation, and the opportunity to shop in stores that contained consumer goods unavailable to ordinary consumers. Because virtually all prices were set by the government, there was no measured inflation, although because prices for many products were set too low, the economy was frequently in a condition of shortage. The central bank (Gosbank) was the only bank in the country. It provided loans to state enterprises and collectivized farms in the amounts Gosplan instructed. Gosbank also issued currency (rubles) and accepted deposits from consumers.

Gosplan did not have to worry much about taxes because it could set the price of everything. For example, to finance the production of military goods, the central planners could set the price of inputs to defense production low and the price of defense goods high. They could also simply order increased production of military goods and reduced production of some other goods.

Trade Between the Soviet Union and Eastern Europe

After World War II, when communist governments were installed in Poland, Hungary, Czechoslovakia, East Germany, Romania, and Bulgaria, Soviet-style central planning was extended to each of these countries. How did international trade take place between the Soviet Union and its close neighbors in the Soviet bloc?

Trade among these countries and the Soviet Union took place through a trading organization called the *Council for Mutual Economic Assistance*. The trade did not take place at world market prices. For example, the Soviet Union, which was rich in energy resources such as oil and natural gas, would supply energy to the Eastern European countries at prices well below the market prices prevailing throughout the world. The prices were established through political negotiations between the governments, which undoubtedly involved noneconomic considerations such as the placement of military troops and weapons. In exchange for the low-priced energy, the Eastern European countries would provide manufactured goods, although those were lower in quality than similar goods produced in the West. Prices for trade between the countries of Eastern Europe were similarly negotiated. Thus, neither domestic trade nor international trade between the centrally planned economies was market-based.

Technological Change and the Quality of Goods

By most accounts, Stalin's forced investment and forced labor strategy did increase economic growth in the 1930s in the Soviet Union. In the years after World War II, both the Soviet Union and Eastern Europe grew rapidly. However, it eventually became apparent that the great inefficiencies associated with central planning were starting to offset the high levels of investment and labor force participation. The growth of technology began to slow down. Investment rates and labor force participation rates had reached their limits, and technology growth was lagging seriously. Environmental pollution was severe in cities such as Warsaw and Bucharest.

State-owned retail shops had few consumer goods, and those that they had were of very poor quality. Long lines were evident at stores, especially those selling anything special, such as candy bars or gasoline. The availability of goods was also poor.

One of the apparent puzzles about central planning was its success in certain areas. The space exploration achievements of the Soviet Union, for example, were outstanding enough for the United States to get involved in the space race. They were the source of President Kennedy's goal of a manned flight to the moon.

One explanation for this success was that an enormous amount of resources was put into defense production. Just as East German athletes dominated the Olympics because of all the resources that went into their training, a centrally planned economy could excel at certain things. Students with talents useful for defense production—mathematics, science, and engineering—were given excellent training in the Soviet Union. Even inefficiency can be offset by enough resources. Moreover, as mentioned previously, economists have found that managers in defense production had ways to go outside the central planning system, essentially using gray markets to obtain parts or equipment that was in short supply. Such markets were tolerated more frequently in the defense industry than in consumer goods industries.

From Perestroika to the End of the Soviet Union

Pressures to reform the central planning system began in the 1960s and 1970s and gained momentum in the 1980s. In 1985, Mikhail Gorbachev became the leader of the Communist party. To deal with the problems of inefficiency, poor quality, and slow technology growth, he tried to change central planning through a process called **perestroika,** which translates as "restructuring." Perestroika changes were put into the twelfth five-year plan, formulated in 1985. For example, enterprise managers were to be made more accountable for their actions through worker and public criticism. By 1989, however, it was clear that perestroika was doing little to increase economic growth. Economists complained that perestroika was piecemeal because it continued to rely on the central planning process to set prices. An alternative plan, called the Shatalin Plan, after one of Gorbachev's advisers, would have used the market much more. However, it was rejected by Gorbachev because it would have initiated a transition to a market economy and thereby done away with central planning.

perestroika: the restructuring of the Soviet economy by reforming the central planning process.

But perestroika started a process that could not easily be stopped. The open criticism of the central planning process made it acceptable to criticize the political authorities. Soon people in Eastern Europe were criticizing their own governments and their close ties with the Soviet Union. Gorbachev decided to "let go" of the Eastern European countries in 1989, and by 1990 the republics of the Soviet Union also wanted their freedom. Gradually the Russian Republic began to take over the responsibility for the Soviet Union. After an aborted military coup in 1991, Gorbachev resigned and the Soviet Union ceased to exist. Boris Yeltsin, the president of Russia, disbanded central planning and began to follow a more radical series of reforms aimed at creating a market economy. Many of Yeltsin's reforms were opposed by the Russian parliament, and the reforms that were put in place were not sufficient to avoid serious problems for the Russian economy, evidenced by the financial crisis in 1998. In 2000 Vladimir Putin became president of Russia, marking the first democratic transition between leaders in Russian history.

Soviet-Style Central Planning in China

The Chinese communists under Mao Zedong gained control of China in 1949. Mao's goals were similar to those of the Soviet Union—to rapidly industrialize. In fact, Mao originally viewed the Soviet Union as an economic model. He imported Soviet-style central planning to China. Under Mao and the Communist party, most economic production was controlled by the central government, just as in the Soviet Union. In the 1950s, growth was rapid due to heavy investment.

Starting in 1958, Mao began the "Great Leap Forward," which briefly raised economic growth by promoting a warlike work effort throughout the country and calling for a massive expansion of production. But the Great Leap Forward could raise economic growth for only a short period. The communist spirit was not enough to make people work hard year after year. The Great Leap Forward ended in a huge decline in production.

A misguided attempt to revive the spirit of the communist revolution took place in the late 1960s with the Cultural Revolution. But the Cultural Revolution ended up severely hurting the Chinese economy. Productive managers and technicians were forced to leave their jobs and do manual labor. Universities were closed. By the late 1970s, it was clear that economic reform was necessary in China.

Market-based reforms began earlier in China than in Russia. The first reforms were in the agriculture sector. By the late 1970s, the Chinese government was leasing land back to individual farmers in order to give them more incentive to produce. The reform resulted in a huge increase in the growth rate of farm output. Agricultural production grew by 3 percent per year from 1952 to 1978; from 1978 (when the reforms began) to 1981, the growth rate was about 6 percent per year. Moreover, the increased efficiency in agriculture increased the supply of labor in the industrial sector.

By the mid-1980s, about the same time as perestroika was starting in the Soviet Union, economic reforms were already spreading beyond the farm sector. Individual state enterprises were first given more discretion to experiment with new products and to use the profits generated from those products. As in the case of agriculture, industrial enterprises were leased to the managers, who could then keep part of the profits. As a result of these reforms, real GDP growth increased rapidly. Economic growth averaged a remarkably rapid 9.6 percent per year from 1987 to 1994. Real GDP growth in China remained strong throughout the 1990s and has been the highest in the world in the 2000s.

China also reduced restrictions on foreign trade. In fact, much of China's growth has come from producing goods for foreign trade. Exports grew even more rapidly than real GDP.

REVIEW

- Central control of the economy began in Russia soon after the Bolsheviks rose to power. Central planning grew and dominated the Soviet economy under Stalin in the 1920s and 1930s and spread to Eastern Europe and China after World War II.

- Although the high investment and high labor force participation led to strong growth initially, central planning eventually broke down. Inefficiency, poor-quality goods, and slow growth of technology were the most obvious problems.

- China started its market-based reforms in the late 1970s by selling off a large amount of land to the farmers. Controls on state enterprises have been lifted more gradually.

Economic Transition

The Elements of Reform

How does a country change from central planning to a market economy? There is general agreement that in any successful transition from central planning to a market economy, a legal system specifying property rights and enforcing the law must be set up, and a system of tax collection must be put in place. And, of course, the government must stop controlling prices, and let prices be determined in decentralized markets. Enforcing competition among firms—including the former state enterprises—is also important. Finally, if there is a large government budget deficit, it must be substantially reduced so that the government is not forced to print money in order to finance the deficit, causing inflation.

As is true of many areas of economics, however, there is disagreement about how to achieve these goals of a transition.

Shock Therapy or Gradualism?

A major question about the transition to a market economy is how fast it should be. The two basic alternatives are **shock therapy** and **gradualism.** Under shock therapy, or the *big bang* approach, all the elements of the market economy are put in place at once. Under gradualism, the reforms are phased in slowly.

One of the most remarkable aspects of the transition from central planning in the countries of Eastern Europe was the strong commitment to the move to market economies on the part of government policymakers and the general public at the start of the reforms in 1989 and 1990. Most officials went out of their way to emphasize that they were not looking for a third way and to recognize the need to move to a Western-style market-based economic system in order to raise living standards.

Such positive attitudes toward reform were part of the motivation behind shock therapy. Those in favor of a shock-therapy approach argue that such positive attitudes are probably temporary, creating a brief window of opportunity for reform. The enthusiasm for reform may diminish if, as is likely, the reforms do not bring noticeable improvements quickly. Thus, rather than see the reform movement aborted in midstream, it is better to sweep through the reforms quickly. This was one of the arguments for the shock-therapy approach that was used in Poland.

Another argument in favor of shock therapy is that all the elements of reform are interrelated. Making state enterprises private without enforcing competition, for example, could make things worse by creating monopolies.

The arguments against shock therapy are that people require time to adjust to new circumstances. Even though the production of low-quality black and white television sets in Warsaw is inefficient compared with importing televisions from Malaysia, it might be better to move gradually to free trade. This would give firms time to move into some other business and workers time to find other jobs.

shock therapy: the abrupt introduction of free markets in a formerly centrally planned economy.

gradualism: the slow phasing in of free market reforms.

Economic Transition in Practice

Poland was the first country in Eastern Europe to start a transition to a market economy. The Polish program has typified the shock-therapy approach.

The Polish stabilization program made use of several policy initiatives. Government expenditures and the budget deficit were reduced sharply, largely through a reduction in government subsidies to state enterprises and a halting of public infrastructure investment. Most prices were deregulated at once and were left to be determined by state enterprises or private firms. Coal prices increased significantly, but internal transportation prices and rents remained low. Wage growth was controlled by government guidelines.

The result of these policies was a substantial decline in demand. There was also a reduction in shortages—the lines of people waiting to be served in butcher shops disappeared, for example. This reduction was brought about partly by the decline in demand, but also because free prices began to bring the quantity supplied into equality with the quantity demanded. Goods started appearing on the shelves, and firms could get intermediate inputs without long delays. Imported consumer goods, most noticeably fruits and vegetables, were more available. The trade account went into surplus in 1990, with exports increasing rapidly and imports declining rapidly.

At the start of the reform program, employment declined surprisingly little despite the large declines in production. The unemployment rate increased only to about 2 percent of the work force in the first few months of the program, but then unemployment increased sharply. Many workers were laid off because the state enterprises needed to reduce wage costs in order to avoid losses as the demand for their products dropped.

privatization: the process of converting a government enterprise into a privately owned enterprise.

In order for a market economy to take root, it is necessary that existing state enterprises become privately owned, a process called **privatization,** and that new private firms be able to start up. Moreover, private investment from abroad provides technological know-how. Privatization helps provide managers with the incentive to allocate resources efficiently and increase productivity.

Four months after the reform program was put in place in Poland, there were many visible signs of its effects, including a decline in inflation and a reduction of shortages. Inflation, which averaged 420 percent in 1989 and 1990, had fallen to 25 percent by 1992, but the adjustment costs, as evidenced by large declines in production and employment, were painful. Real GDP declined by 12 percent in 1990 and another 7 percent in 1991. However, by 1992 real GDP had stopped falling and showed a small increase. By 1994 economic growth was 6 percent, and it has generally remained strong since, although there was a minor slowdown in 2001–2002.

REVIEW

- The goals of a transition to a market economy are much easier to state than to achieve; the goals can be defined in terms of the key ingredients of a market economy.

- Shock therapy and gradualism are two different paths to a market-based economy.

- Poland took the lead in major economic reform in Eastern Europe. Its reform program is the prototype of shock therapy.

- The transition has been hard on the Polish economy. However, real GDP growth started increasing in 1992 and was strong in most of the 1990s. Institutions have been put in place that will help foster the market economy in the future.

Conclusion

It was the economic failure of central planning and strict state control that led to socialism's demise. The failure of the centrally planned economy in East Germany in comparison with the success of the market economy in West Germany was as close as the real world ever gets to a controlled experiment.

The transition from the failed centrally planned economies to market economies did not go smoothly for many countries, especially Russia and other countries that belonged to the former Soviet Union. However, in recent times, many of these countries have seen higher rates of economic growth and reason for optimism about the future. Other centrally planned economies, like Poland, Hungary, and especially China, have made more successful transitions and made great progress in raising living standards over the past decade.

KEY POINTS

1. China and the countries of the former Soviet Union are making the transition from central planning to a market economy.

2. Central planning and state control grew out of the communist revolutions under Lenin in Russia in 1917 and under Mao in China in 1949. Central planning was extended to Eastern Europe after World War II. At communism's height, over one-third of the world's population lived in centrally planned economies.

3. By mounting an intellectual criticism of the classical economists' model, Marx spearheaded the communist revolutions that eventually led to central planning.

4. Most centrally planned economies grew rapidly in their early stages because of heavy investment, but eventually productivity growth slowed down sharply and even declined.

5. The transition from central planning to a free market economy is much more difficult than the reverse transition. The road from socialism to free markets will be long, with the gains perhaps not noticeable for many years in some cases.

6. There are two different approaches to transition: shock therapy and gradualism.

KEY TERMS

socialism	Gosplan
capitalism	five-year plan
communism	state enterprise
nationalization	

collectivized farm	shock therapy
production target	gradualism
perestroika	privatization

QUESTIONS FOR REVIEW

1. When did central planning begin, and why?

2. What led to dissatisfaction with central planning and the end of socialism in Russia?

3. What comparison of countries is most useful for demonstrating the inefficiencies of central planning?

4. What are the elements of an economic reform program?

5. What is the difference between shock therapy and gradualism in the transition to a market economy?

6. What political argument favors shock therapy?

PROBLEMS

1. In 1960, Mao Zedong wrote, "The whole Socialist camp headed by the Soviet Union . . . now accounts for nearly 40 percent of the world's . . . gross industrial output . . . and it will not be long before it surpasses the gross industrial output of all the capitalist countries put together." Explain why such a statement was believable at the time, and why the prediction turned out to be so inaccurate.

2. Why was central planning successful in increasing real GDP growth for a while? Why did real GDP growth eventually falter under central planning?

3. Explain why it may be easier to move from a market economy with private property to a command-and-control economy without private property than the other way around. Give a real-world example to prove your point.

4. Describe Gosplan's role during the period of central planning in the Soviet Union.

5. Could state-owned firms be made to operate as if they were private firms? For example, suppose that the managers of state enterprises were instructed to maximize profits with prices and wages set by the central planners. According to the Hungarian economist Janos Kornai, the answer to this question is no. In *The Road to a Free Economy*, he writes, "It is futile to expect a state-owned unit to behave as if it were privately owned." Provide an argument supporting Kornai's view. Be sure to mention the role of prices as well as the role of private property and incentives.

6. Compare and contrast how the three key questions—*how, what,* and *for whom* goods and services should be produced—are dealt with in a centrally planned economy and in a market economy.

7. Comment on the validity of the following statement in the *New York Times Book Review* on March 30, 1997. Support your answer with historical examples and economic reasoning: "Capitalism was and is a destructive and revolutionary phenomenon. It leveled European feudalism and aristocracy, then proceeded, in this century, to destroy statism, both fascist and communist. It has created a dynamic, materialistic, and dominating global culture with an aspiring middle class at its helm."

The Issue:
Should We Applaud the Signing of CAFTA?

Late in the evening of July 27, 2005, the House of Representatives prepared to vote on the Central American Free Trade Agreement (CAFTA), an agreement that would eliminate most tariff barriers to trade between the United States and six countries: Costa Rica, the Dominican Republic, El Salvador, Guatemala, Honduras, and Nicaragua. The vote was expected to be extremely close, and the lobbying of undecided members of Congress by supporters and opponents alike was intense. After a vote that dragged on past midnight, the measure passed by the narrowest of margins: 217 votes for to 215 votes against.

The core features of CAFTA, as summarized by the United States Trade Representative's Office,[1] are as follows:

- About 80 percent of U.S. exports of consumer and industrial goods will become duty-free in the six CAFTA countries immediately, and the remaining tariffs will be phased out over 10 years.
- More than 50 percent of U.S. farm exports will become tariff-free immediately, with the remaining tariffs being phased out over the next 15 to 20 years.
- About 98 percent of the types of goods exported by the CAFTA countries will be allowed to enter the United States free of tariffs. However, barriers to increased imports will remain high for two key exports: sugar and textiles. Clothing made in Central America will be free of tariffs if it uses U.S. fabric and yarn. Increased access to the U.S. sugar market is a minuscule 1 percent.
- There is increased support of measures to improve the monitoring of labor standards in the six countries, as well as initiatives to increase transparency and reduce official corruption.

Supporters of CAFTA hailed the vote as a triumph for free trade over protectionism. They argued that lowering trade barriers would result in increased exports from the United States to the six nations, while at the same time affording products from those countries access to the lucrative U.S. market free of tariffs. Opponents of CAFTA took a much less rosy view. They claimed that CAFTA would do little to benefit the lives of the poor in these countries because it maintained tariffs on some key products; that CAFTA gave priority to protecting the intel-

lectual property rights of pharmaceutical companies over the protection of poor patients who needed access to cheap drugs; and that CAFTA would weaken workers' rights. How does a policy that seems to have so many positive features end up being opposed by 215 members of Congress? How does a policy that seems to be so flawed end up being supported by 217 members of Congress? Examine both sides of this issue and answer these questions for yourself.

CAFTA Is Good for the Economies of All the Signatory Countries **POINT**

The Cato Institute has been strongly in favor of CAFTA. A study by Daniel Griswold and Daniel Ikenson at the Cato Institute's Center for Trade Policy Studies argues that CAFTA is important not just because it is good economic policy, but also because it is good foreign policy.[2] Griswold and Ikenson emphasize these points about CAFTA:

- The primary purpose of a free-trade agreement is to enhance cross-border trade and investment flows. With two glaring exceptions—sugar and textiles—CAFTA will accomplish these objectives. Griswold and Ikenson would clearly prefer a truly "free" trade agreement that does not create complicated exceptions, but they still believe that CAFTA is an improvement over the status quo.
- CAFTA expands U.S. export opportunities, especially in the agricultural sector. Trade groups for beef, chicken, and other producers praised the enhanced access that they expect to enjoy. The six CAFTA countries combined represent a market of almost 50 million people and rank collectively as the 13th-largest trading partner of the United States.
- Investors in the United States will benefit greatly from CAFTA's liberalization of services in areas such as telecommunications, financial services, e-commerce, insurance, and computers. Previously, U.S. firms had to form permanent partnerships with local firms, but CAFTA removes many of those provisions and gives more rights to foreign investors to invest their money on their terms.

1 United States Trade Representative's Office, "CAFTA Briefing Book." Available at http://www.ustr.gov/Trade_Agreements/Bilateral/CAFTA/Briefing_Book/Section_Index.html.

2 Daniel Griswold and Daniel Ikenson, "The Case for CAFTA: Consolidating Central America's Freedom Revolution," Center for Trade Policy Studies Briefing Paper, Sept. 21, 2004. Available online at http://www.freetrade.org/pubs/briefs/tbp-021es.html.

Selected Prophecies of
NOSTRADAMUS